W9-CAH-259

Organizational Behavior and The Practice of Management

DAVID R. HAMPTON
School of Business Administration
San Diego State College

CHARLES E. SUMMER
Graduate School of Business Administration
Columbia University

ROSS A. WEBBER
Wharton School of Finance and Commerce
University of Pennsylvania

SCOTT, FORESMAN AND COMPANY

To Dorothy, Carol, and Mary Lou

Library of Congress Catalog No.: 68-19606

Glenview, Illinois 60025

Printed in the United States of America
Regional Offices of Scott, Foresman and Company are located in Atlanta, Dallas, Glenview, Palo Alto, and Oakland, N.J.

Preface

As that well-known modern philosopher of song, Bob Dylan, tells us: "The Times, They are a Changing." And so it is with education—especially education for management. One youthful undergraduate explained it to an older alumnus as follows: "You fellows used to memorize numbers and lists and stuff like that. Now we have to learn 'cepts'—and know how to use them."

"Cepts" are, of course, concepts, and the study of management is in the process of moving from memorization of rules and principles to the understanding and utilization of concepts to aid more rigorous analysis and prediction. We hope that this volume will help the students, educators, and practitioners who desire to participate in this more challenging endeavor.

Many concepts from the behavioral sciences are relevant to practical problems in administration and can be used as powerful tools in managerial thinking. The manager works with individuals, face-to-face groups, and the technical aspects of organizations. All of these affect one another, and they affect the manager. The manager of course affects them. Our understanding of all of these elements of organizational behavior and their dynamic interplay has been enriched by both theory and research in the behavioral sciences. The now familiar approach to planning, organizing, staffing, and other topics of a similar nature had the advantage of pointing directly to pragmatic problems of running an organization, but it did not make use of new and deep insights into the nature of organizations, the nature of people, and the nature of human behavior in organizations. In the past, management education has tended to rely heavily on art or skill and make comparatively little use of growing scientific knowledge.

Virtually all applied disciplines, including management, engineering, and medicine, share the same dilemma as they become more firmly rooted in science. Harvey Brooks, dean of engineering and applied physics at Harvard, has described the problem:

> . . . in both medicine and engineering the importance of the underlying sciences has become so great that medical and engineering faculties are increasingly populated with basic scientists who do research or teaching in sciences which are relevant to but by no means identical with the practice of medicine or engineering. The old form of teaching primarily by practicing physicians or engineers was found wanting because practical knowledge was too rapidly being made obsolete by new scientific developments which could not be fully absorbed or appreciated by the mature practitioner.

The Citizens Commission on Graduate Medical Education, after quoting Dean Brooks, went on to say:

> The problem is not that . . . [the research] aspects of medicine have grown too rapidly. The problem is to add a new dimension to the practice of medicine that will help to utilize this growth and to bring the practice of medicine up to its high potential.*

Management's kindred educational problem is to create channels through which knowledge from the behavioral sciences can be incorporated in skillful managerial practice.

The problem has two critical components: selection and arrangement—selecting powerful and relevant ideas from research, and arranging them in ways that will help the management student learn to use them. The issue no longer is whether to accept or reject the use of behavioral science in management, but how to bring into being those new channels which will actually link science, analysis, and practice. Facile yet illusory solutions are possible. To attach importance indiscriminately to ideas because they come labeled as "concepts from the behavioral sciences" is to make the mistake that the label provides an unimpeachable character reference. To require management students to read behavioral science research findings on a grand scale is to presume that the material will be relevant to the manager's job. Accordingly, our emphasis in this book is not to "cover" the behavioral sciences, but to *uncover* the deeper structure of human behavior in organizations and to utilize the knowledge gained in designing, managing, and leading organizations.

Since Chapters 1 and 2 explain how this book is designed, we will not repeat the explanation here. In the field of management, courses in organizational behavior, organization theory, human behavior in organizations, and related titles are now commonplace. This book is designed for courses, whatever their titles, which undertake to utilize behavioral science concepts as working tools in the study of management.

We should like to express our gratitude to all those who have helped us to prepare the book.

We appreciate the careful reading of the manuscript by Professor Kenneth E. Knight of Stanford University.

As with most authors, our barely legible manuscripts had to be deciphered and typed by patient secretaries. We are grateful to Regan McNair and Loretta Hentz. We are also indebted to the many authors and publishers who have permitted us to reprint selections of their work in this volume. We hope that our use of their works will draw deserved attention to the whole books or articles from which we have borrowed parts.

Finally, we all owe something to the doctoral program of the Graduate School of Business Administration, Columbia University, for bringing us together and providing the stimulus for our work.

David R. Hampton
Charles E. Summer
Ross A. Webber

---

* "The Report of the Citizens Commission on Graduate Medical Education," *Saturday Review,* L, No. 1 (January 7, 1967), p. 124.

Contents

READINGS

READINGS

READINGS

I

Behavioral Science and Management

Chapter One

The Manager and Behavioral Science

Disaster stalks the plush executive offices of World Wide Wicket Corporation. Management's new television show has been a fiasco, the public and competitors are laughing at its ineptitude, and the potential loss of millions of dollars looms. In the final scene of this tale, which has enlivened theater stages and movie screens as "How to Succeed in Business Without Really Trying," Wally Wumper, the self-educated, self-made chairman of the board, criticizes the stereotyped "Old Ivy" grad who is the company president. Voicing the time-honored American feeling of the self-educated toward the school-educated, of the practical man toward the theoretician, Wally exclaims: "I should have expected this from a college man!"

Recently, one of the authors of this book encountered a somewhat similar attitude at a college reunion. The alumni all exchanged the normal remarks on increasing girth, exploding families, and career achievements. One of his classmates, an amazingly successful entrepreneur with no exposure to formal academic study of business or economics, asked what he did. He explained that he taught management at a business school, what was involved, and so on. The classmate's incredulous response: "You teach that from books?"

The suggestion by Abe Burrows' fictional character and our real financial genius of 32 is that business success depends upon innate ability, common sense, and work experience—not book knowledge, theory, and classroom discussion. We do not argue with the order of importance suggested—at least with the order up to now. What we do take exception to is the mutual exclusivity implied. Intuition and practical experience need not be divorced from knowledge and analytical exercise. Each can inform the other. It is our firm premise that the management knowledge derived from behavioral science is growing in scope, reliability, and validity—and that this knowledge, coupled with personal ability and experience, will lead to more effective management.

Behavioral science consists mainly of the development and testing of theory. A criticism of the academic study of management that is often advanced is that it is too theoretical for practical people—and certainly most of the people reading this book are practical people. But the greatest and the worst practitioners are theorists. Behind every action lies a theory; behind every management decision regarding people there lies some philosophy or theory of human nature. Managers act from thought, from theories, from ideas, from concepts, from assumptions. Whatever their validity, the manager's theories always impinge on his actions—especially his dealings with people. There are no options about this. As Douglas McGregor [6] put it, "It is possible to have more or less adequate theoretical assumptions; it is not possible to reach a managerial action uninfluenced by assumptions, whether adequate or not" (p. 7).

We might better be aware of our theories so that our actions are valid and consistent. John Maynard Keynes' observation [4] is relevant: "Practical men, who believe themselves to be quite exempt from any intellectual influence, are usually the slaves of some defunct economist. Madmen in authority, who hear voices in the air, are distilling their frenzy from some academic scribbler [of] a few years back" (p. 383). Inasmuch as the practice of management is interwoven with the application of concepts, anything which improves the validity and usefulness of the concepts employed is a clear-cut gain, even for the most practical of men.

Theory and Practice

But which comes first? Intuition or theory, experience or knowledge? This is like the proverbial chicken-egg question, for the pendulum of influence and progress swings back and forth. Technology and physical science provide an example. The late Harvard physiologist L. J. Henderson was reportedly fond of remarking that before 1850 the steam engine did more for science than science did for the steam engine. His point was that practical accomplishments often run ahead of science and provide it with empirical examples or cases whose properties and dynamics science understands systematically only at some later date. Charles Walker [9] makes the same point:

> For any historical study of modern technology, there is no more crucial theme than the relation between technology and science. Most historians and many scientists are agreed that in important respects, the relation is today reciprocal, advances in "pure" science are rapidly reflected in new technological revolutions. The phrase "science-based corporation" is a popular acknowledgment of this fact.
>
> The mounting debt of science to technology is not always as fully realized. Without the telescope, a technological invention, the science of modern astronomy would have been impossible. Without the microscope, the modern sciences of zoology, biology, and bacteriology would not have been developed. But the cases are endless and to be found in nearly every department of modern science and modern technology. One of the latest and most striking debts of science to technology lies in the fields of mathematics and physics. Progress in both is now dependent in part on the high speed, automatic computer. The computer in turn owes its development to information theory, and the researches of the mathematician (p. 14).

So technology and science are interdependent. Nonetheless, the recent trend has been for science to become the dominant factor influencing technology; in short, for theory to precede practice. As Charles Singer [8] writes:

> In our own time, technology has become almost synonymous with the application of scientific knowledge to practical ends. To us it seems that science is the source, the parent of technology. Up to about 1500, and perhaps much later, it would be more accurate to say that technology was the parental science. But from the rather indeterminate period usually called the Renaissance, natural phenomena came to be more and more systematically observed. . . . The use of experiment and the recession of empiricism from technology will become increasingly evident . . . (p. 274).

Management practice and behavioral science are perhaps in the relationship of technology and physical science in the Renaissance era: to date, the management of organizations has done more for behavioral science than science has done for management. Actual organizational behavior has provided a great laboratory of behavior for systematic study. But even now, progress in behavioral science is revising the terms of this relationship and is beginning to give significant knowledge to management practice.

Do not be misled, however, by our parallel between technology-physical science and managerial practice-behavioral science. Emphatically, behavioral science is not at the stage of physical science in guiding practice—and indeed it may never be. There are three stages in the development of a science, according to George Homans [3], and behavioral science has passed through only two of these:

> First comes the painstaking observation and description of situations; second, the recognition and naming of what I shall call factors, of kinds of things that seem to recur in situations and be important; and third, the statement of recurring relations among the factors (p. 105).

Though physical science may promise and, indeed, produce marvels at the third stage, behavioral science has reached only the first two and still is working toward the third.

Yet management education can draw upon the behavioral sciences now, without waiting for attainments at the third stage. Management courses can be infused with the work of careful observation and description of organizational behavior. In addition, in working with cases or specific situations, stress can be put upon the recognition of recurrent factors. The recognition of recurrent factors and the defining of them informs subsequent observation and description of new cases. We must then reach for a comprehension of recurring relations among the factors, though we may find we have to make only tentative statements and predictions at this ambitious level.

What Homans [3] says about sociology's contribution to management education in the following remarks holds true for the contribution of other behavioral sciences as well:

> Mere exposure to realistic descriptions of industrial behavior will do much for the young manager. But this is not all that sociology can give him. The second stage in the development of a science is that of recognizing and giving names to recurrent factors in the situations observed and described. Indeed the observation itself will grow in detail with the recog-

nition of the kinds of things to be looked for. As he describes industrial situations, the sociologist will begin to point out to his students the factors that often make their presence felt. And I argue that the possession of such a simple set of concepts—of things to be looked for—is of the greatest use to the young manager.

Let me illustrate. Suppose two departments are to be merged—I speak of a situation I was once familiar with—and the first consists in large part of fairly senior men, the second of junior women. The first group formerly worked in the main office of the company downtown, and the second in a somewhat outlying building, which will be the location of the merged departments. The head of the department will be the former head of the second group and will keep the title of assistant superintendent, though the other department heads are superintendents. No doubt an experienced manager in this situation will foresee trouble: in the relations between the two groups, in their different attitudes toward the "boss" and the company, in the effectiveness with which the joint job is carried on, and not the least in the manager's own feelings.

I am not interested in him, but in speeding up the learning process of an inexperienced manager caught in such a squeeze. If he has been exposed to realistic descriptions of industrial behavior, and if his teacher has gone just a little further, set apart certain kinds of observations, called them observations of *status,* and illustrated them with a range of problems called status problems, he will be in a better position to expect trouble, recognize its nature, and avoid the blind reactions of bewilderment and anger. Mind you, the ordinary sensible man, without training, may expect trouble, too—if he stops to think.

The whole point about training is that it may make the inexperienced manager just a little more apt to stop and think. The sociologist will give him little to help him predict just what form the trouble will take or just what he is to do about it, for the sociologist, while recognizing some of the factors, has not much to say about their relations: he has not reached the third stage of science. But I hold it an advantage to know that something is apt to swing around and hit you in the back of the neck, even if you do not know just how (pp. 108–109).

Behavioral Science and Human Relations

Recently one of the authors of this book proposed a management development program to a major American corporation. Human behavior in organizations was to be the subject of the first week, new decision-making tools the second, and business and society relationships the third. The latter two weeks were accepted, the first rejected rather strongly—with an oath about having had enough human relations! Of course, this may reflect one chief executive's opinion, but it does seem symptomatic of the suspicion and perhaps cynicism that characterizes management's view on the subject of human relations. "Not useful," "too fuzzy," "theoretical," "soft," "not operational" are all responses we have received to pleas for consideration of behavior.

Such skepticism has some validity. The early writers in human relations often did confuse their intentions, observations, and conclusions. Rather than offering the manager information on tools, they seemed to limit his ability to control his organization in the name of "fairness," "supportiveness," "democracy," or "cooperativeness." Worse, the human relations tradition encouraged some managers to use their insights to manipulate subordinates or treat them as irrational, immature children. "Although man has reached a remarkable degree of mastery of nature," wrote Eric Fromm [2], "society is not in control of the very forces it has created. The rationality of the system of production, in its technical aspects, is accompanied by the irrationality of our system of production in its social aspects" (p. 117).

Fromm was passing a judgment on the quality of human life in twentieth-century organizations. Simply put, he said that it was bad and therefore irrational. Many of the researchers in organizational behavior have implicitly shared this opinion and it has colored their research.

However well grounded management's skepticism about the study of human behavior in organizations may be, it is unfortunate, for we are in danger of "throwing out the baby with the bath water." There is much that is essential in the subject of human relations. After all, a business organization, or any organization, is a complex of formal and informal human behavior. Every organization is a dynamic composite of people communicating, functioning, and bargaining—in short, behaving, in the richest sense of the term.

In designing and constructing an engine, the engineer must understand the material with which he works, the principles of the particular kind of engine to be designed, and the dynamic kinetic relationships between parts. Managers have long recognized the need to understand the first two parallel needs in their organization—(1) the nature of the materials, i.e., people and technology, and (2) the principles of management and organization. Yet the operating manager must go beyond these static concepts to the dynamic—just as the engineer does. In short, we believe the manager's effectiveness will be increased if he understands the dynamics of human relationships and behavioral patterns in his organization.

Efficiency, effectiveness, and innovative flexibility should be the results of management's understanding of organizational dynamics. This knowledge may make people happy or sad, just as every other bit of human knowledge has been used for good or evil. However, we are not here concerned as to whether human relationships at work are themselves satisfying or dissatisfying. Our concern *is* whether or not the social system is rational or irrational. In other words, are the dynamic patterns of human relationships in the organization *rationally* understood and *rationally* designed by the manager?

Behavioral Science and the Manager

Amateur, casual, and personal mental habits for ordering our experience are something we all possess. All thinking notes only certain features of specific things or situations and then relates those features to an abstracted "type" or concept. If we begin to compare jobs we have held, books we have read, or people we have known, we will see that we begin to reason in the dimensions of our own private concepts which represent features of jobs, books, and people. Our idiosyncratic thought processes may be more or less serviceable to us, but they are very much our own, grown out of our intuition.

Getting beyond intuitive mental habits and acquiring professional ones is another matter. This task poses a major intellectual and emotional challenge, for it requires the conscious, disciplined buildup of ways of thinking and acting. The hallmark of a professional is his possession of systematic intellectual resources and the disciplined ability to relate his knowledge to specific cases. What distinguishes him from the intuitive practitioner is his ability to use "skillfully, a well-stocked kit of well-designed tools to handle problems that are comprehensible in their deep structure but unfamiliar in their detail [7, p. 40]."

The manager's tools are the concepts with which he thinks about organizational behavior. These tools of behavioral science should be just as much a part of the manager's repertoire as production techniques or administrative principles. Through bettering his understanding of the concepts he uses and through using better, clearer, and more powerful ones, the manager takes some important preparatory steps toward coping knowledgeably and effectually with organizational behavior. As he comes to see more of the resemblances and connections between events in organizational behavior, he understands more of the options and constraints with which he works. Hopefully, he becomes less of a blind responder to emergencies and more of an initiator of organizational development.

This is where science comes in. Behavioral science research into management practice provides a rich resource of conceptualized experience which can be channeled into management awareness. We can now take back the cases managerial practice has given to behavioral science and convert their conceptual and empirical content into education for management. We can take apart the components and dynamics of organizational processes in ways that resemble the mechanical engineering class' systematic analysis of the features and operations of a jet engine. The advantage of these science-practice cases is in their explicit linking of experience with communicable intellectual recognition and understanding. What was intuitively based organizational behavior is transformed into an especially instructive kind of case after it has been carefully observed and conceptualized with the analytical perspectives of the behavioral sciences.

The development of management theories and research findings is extremely helpful for the education of practitioners. The inarticulate, intuitive knowledge built out of the practitioner's trials and errors does not lend itself to serving society's interest in producing a supply of good practitioners. Articulate, intellectual knowledge can be more readily taught, and such teaching is more efficient, because the learner doesn't need to keep discovering the same old ground over and over again intuitively; his intuition is free to do what it is uniquely capable of, to go ahead of understanding and explore new territory.

For example, we can read about how a manager, newly assigned to a plant with a deteriorating performance record and atmosphere, set out to strengthen the organization: how he assured employees there would be no "house cleaning," sought out the views of subordinate managers, met often with them and helped implement their ideas. He acted on his judgment and practical knowledge and built within a few years a markedly improved climate and performance record. When the sociologist Robert H. Guest analyzed this case study of leadership, he carefully observed and measured changes in three key variables: interaction, performance, and sentiment. He wrote the case, which is excerpted in Chapter 9, furnishing explicit recognition and understanding of these critical elements. He abstracted them from the intuitive behavior of a thoroughly effective manager. In so doing, Guest made it possible for students to share the plant manager's experience, to make a start toward recognizing the same elements in otherwise different cases, and so intellectually to get beyond the limits of their own experience.

The Rationale of the Book

We have developed this book to help students and managers build professional managerial skills. This task centers on a core of behavioral science concepts which shed light on organizational behavior. Our strategy is to make these conceptual foundations explicit *before* using them and exemplifying them in specific studies of organizational behavior. The objective is to help build analytic skill. The idea of concepts first, cases second, derives from the needs of the professional to comprehend events in their deeper structure. The student needs to see the family resemblances, the patterns, in superficially dissimilar matters. The meaning in experience or symptomatic evidence is not apparent to everyone; the "facts" are only comprehensible to the mind intellectually prepared to recognize and understand them.

We consider the theories and examples in this volume as means, not ends. The ideal result of reading these materials is not a manager with a knowledge of theories, but a manager who can use theories to analyze, diagnose, predict, and control human behavior in organizations. The objective of the analytical materials is, in the words of Alexander Leighton [5]:

> . . . first . . . to understand any item as part of a larger whole, as the product of multiple, interacting forces, rather than the result of a single cause that can be ferreted out like a detective uncovering a murderer. . . .
>
> . . . second [in order that] the forces are regarded as natural rather than good or bad. One's own hopes, fears, and ideas of what *should be* are set aside in favor of discovering what *is* (p. 157).

The book is structured to help the student equip himself with a "well-stocked kit of well-designed tools" for analysis and action. It is not a book designed merely to "get across" some information about organizational behavior and management. To paraphrase Jerome Bruner's observation on the appropriate purpose of a course of study, the book offers an opportunity to the student to master himself, discipline his taste, and deepen his view of the world [1, p. 73].

The Plan of the Book

We are in this book concerned with the theories of human behavior as individuals or in small and large groups; the application of these theories to analyze ongoing organizations; and, most important, some preliminary consideration of the practicing manager's use of theory and analysis. This is the organization of the book. In Part I we make a survey of some conceptual and theoretical schema for thinking about organizations—what we call the manager's analytical tools. In Part II, using these concepts, we analyze the behavior of individuals, small groups, and organizations.

Finally, in Part III, the focus shifts from the illumination and explanation of organizational behavior patterns to the making of them, from the scientific analysis of such patterns to the engineering of them. The original and selected contributions here will concentrate on management action—not theory. The authors in Part III are seeking primarily to contribute not to behavioral science theory but to management practice. Thus we move from theory to analysis to practice in a sequence which suggests the importance of studying how organizations operate before studying how to operate organizations.

The overall plan of the book may be easily visualized with the aid of Table 1-1, which shows the grand design. We will explore its details, the contents of each part, in Chapter 2, "Conceptual Foundations of Organizational Behavior."

TABLE 1-1

Part I		Part II		Part III
Surveys key behavioral science concepts for the manager	⟶	Uses behavioral science concepts as tools to understand organizational behavior	⟶	Uses behavioral science concepts as tools—as applied technology—to manage and change organizations

References

1. Bruner, J. S. *Toward a Theory of Instruction.* Harvard University Press, 1966.
2. Fromm, E. *Escape from Freedom.* Holt, Rinehart & Winston, 1941.
3. Homans, G. C. *Sentiments and Activities: Essays in Social Science.* The Free Press, 1962.
4. Keynes, J. M. *The General Theory of Employment, Interest and Money.* Harcourt, Brace & World, 1936.
5. Leighton, A. H. *Human Relations in a Changing World.* Dutton, 1949.
6. McGregor, D. *The Human Side of Enterprise.* McGraw-Hill, 1960.
7. Simon, H. A. *The New Science of Management Decision.* Harper & Row, 1960.
8. Singer, C., *et al. A History of Technology.* Oxford University Press, 1956.
9. Walker, C. R. *Modern Technology and Civilization.* McGraw-Hill, 1962.

Chapter Two

Conceptual Foundations of Organizational Behavior

The history of a society can be viewed from many perspectives. It can be seen in terms of the rise of democracy, the fall of aristocracy, the advance of technology, or the recession of religion. It can be conceived, with Toqueville, as a work of equality; as Acton considered it, the work of freedom; or, in Bertrand Russell's terms, the story of power. Each mode of consideration is, as Alfred North Whitehead [31] reminded us, "a sort of searchlight elucidating some of the facts and retreating the remainder into an omitted background" (p. 44). We are going to probe organizational behavior with such searchlights. Our searchlights are theories about behavior in organizations.

"Perspectives on organization" is perhaps a better phrase, because none of the theories or conceptual tools for analysis to be considered purports to explain the totality of organizational life. Rather, approaches have been suggested which highlight different features of organizational dynamics. These approaches stem from the somewhat artificial specialization of the basic behavioral sciences. Although the lines which divide their interests are more apparent than real, psychology concentrates on individual behavior, sociology on groups, and anthropology and political science on larger social units, such as organized societies. Hence the research and the developing knowledge of these sciences are organized in terms of the individual, the group, the organization, and the interplay among them. These are the categories we will use in studying organizational behavior.

Behavioral Concepts in Organizational Analysis and Management

Behavioral scientists have specialized not only their interests but also the corollary ways of thinking with which they pursue them. Over the years they have abstracted key features of individuals, groups, organizations, and their interrelations, and transformed these into conceptual tools for understanding new facts about these categories. The fundamental innovation for management education embodied in this text is the conversion of powerful and broadly useful analytical tools into integral, structural parts of the study of organizational behavior and management.

This approach reflects the widely held desires of contemporary management educators to incorporate the observational and conceptual rigors of the behavioral sciences into management study. The aversion felt by many teachers for less analytical texts was sharply phrased by one British reviewer [17]:

> Books on management are of two sorts. One sort is firmly based on the careful examination of actual cases; is cautious, scholarly, and verifiable; and advances knowledge. . . . The other sort gives little description except of the most sketchy or general kind, and no facts that are not known already; concentrates on the enunciation of "general principles" that turn out to be either tautologous or elementary common sense, or limited to quite particular circumstances or mere expressions of prejudice; distils, in short, what is often considerable experience into an orgy of avuncular pontification (p. 278).

The appeal for more analytical approaches suited to building professional managerial thought patterns was well expressed by George L. Bach [3]:

> Given the certainty of change and the uncertainty as to its direction and outcome, it seems clear that we must place central importance in our university training—for business as elsewhere—on students' thought processes and not on particularized subject matter. In such a world, surely anything we can do to develop flexibility of mind, openness and receptivity to new and changing ideas, habitual skills in learning for oneself, and other such mental characteristics must promise more use to the individual and to society over the quarter century of change ahead, than would comparable attention to descriptive information about today's institutions and today's best business practice. It suggests equally that insofar as we build in analytical tools, we must continually reach for those of broad and general applicability, with emphasis on how to use them effectively in widely varying situations, rather than on detailed particular skills and techniques (p. 352).

Two sets of educational values are fused in the structure of this book: the commitment to developing students' thought processes and analytical abilities described by Bach, and a commitment to broad coverage of the major issues and problems of organizational behavior which face the manager. By systematically applying selected perspectives of behavioral science to the real world of the manager, we will be able to see issues and problems in lights not ordinarily available to the layman. Thus deepened and disciplined, the study of organizational behavior and management will help build both the students' analytical skill and his knowledge of management issues and problems. The purpose of this chapter is to introduce the student to a selection of these tools or core concepts and explain the way this book integrates them in the study of organizational behavior and management.

We will present five sets of tools for analysis in a sequence which tends to parallel the progressive complexity of the subcategories of organizational behavior from individuals to large organizations:

- A Theory of Individual Motivation
- The Concept of Social Exchange
- Interaction Theory
- Functional Analysis
- Political Concepts for Organizational Analysis

The first set of concepts is most useful in the study of individual behavior; the next two deal with groups; the last two deal with whole organizations. All of the concepts relate to the interplay of individuals, groups, and organizations.

After presenting five sets of conceptual foundations or analytical tools for the manager in this chapter, we will use them throughout the chapters of Parts II and III. We will elaborate on these tools and add new tools for analysis as well as new substantive knowledge about key areas of management as we move through Parts II and III, but the five conceptual contributions of this chapter play especially prominent roles throughout the book. The links from the conceptual foundations of this chapter to the organizational analysis of Part II and the management practice or technology of Part III will be consistently visible. In this way the selective relevance and applicability of behavioral concepts to organizational realities can be communicated and learned.

To illustrate: because the theory of individual motivation to be summarized in this chapter is a powerful concept for understanding individual behavior, we develop it further in the *analysis* of Chapter 3, "The Individual in the Organization: Psychological Factors in Organizational Behavior." The same theory is *applied* in Chapter 8, "Managing and Changing Organizations by Direct Influence." Here the theory is used not to *explain* or *analyze* organizational behavior, but deliberately to *manage* it. These are the chapters in which this particular analytical tool is primarily useful. It also contributes secondarily to other chapters in which ideas about groups and large organizations are more prominent and central.

Formal organization, informal organization, conflict, and structural change are the subjects of Chapter 4, "The Impact of Formal Organization: Structural Factors in Organizational Behavior," Chapter 5, "The Impact of Informal Organization: Social Factors in Organizational Behavior," Chapter 6, "Conflict in the Organization: Interpersonal and Intergroup Factors in Organizational Behavior," and Chapter 10, "Managing and Changing Organizations by Modifying Structure," respectively. In various combinations, the concept of social exchange, interaction theory, and functional analysis produce deepened understanding of these aspects of organizational behavior. Accordingly, these are the behavioral concepts which will be most prominent in focusing our study of those chapters.

Finally, what we designate as political concepts—a central one being authority systems—are the tools which inform the organizational analysis of Chapter 7, "Political Behavior in Organizations," and the management techniques of Chapter 9, "Influencing Behavior Through Political Action."

One point deserves added emphasis: the manager is foremost a man who must take action. Analytical ability to use science to explain reality is not all that the practical, professional man needs. Parkinson's caricature of the British physician [23] pictures a practitioner who leaves something to be desired:

> Once a disease has been identified, named, described, and accounted for, the British are usually quite satisfied and ready to investigate the next problem that presents itself. If asked about treatment, they look surprised and suggest the use of penicillin preceded or followed by the extraction of all of the patient's teeth. It becomes clear at once that this is not an aspect of the subject that interests them (p. 86).

In management, as in medicine or engineering, the commitment and the worldly obligation is to action. For the skilled professional in these applied fields, the commitment is also to a "knowing" or "understanding" line of action—one rooted in articulate, intellectual comprehension of the general properties of specific cases.

Our strategy is to foster scientifically based, analytically informed management practice. Accordingly, we have not paired a traditional exposition of administrative theory with topically related but analytically unrelated readings in behavioral science. Rather, we have used analytical concepts of Parts I and II in the action-oriented techniques of Part III.

Though it is not intended as anything approaching a full and detailed description of the usage of behavioral science concepts in management study, the schema shown in Table 2-1 depicts some of the main avenues through which the ideas to be developed in this chapter contribute to the remainder of the book.

TABLE 2-1

Chapter 2 Conceptual Foundations	Part II Understanding Organizational Behavior	Part III Applying Management Practices or Technologies
A theory of individual motivation	Individual behavior (Ch. 3)	Influencing individual behavior (Ch. 8)
Functional analysis	The impact of formal organization (Ch. 4)	
Social exchange	The impact of informal organization (Ch. 5)	Political action (Ch. 9)
Interaction theory	Organizational conflict (Ch. 6)	
Political concepts	Political behavior (Ch. 7)	Modifying structure (Ch. 10)

In this section we have offered only a preliminary overview of the structural integration of behavioral concepts, organizational analysis, and management. In the next section we will briefly introduce the concepts—each is presented more completely in a selected reading—and preview some of the perspectives they afford in studying the subject matter of subsequent chapters.

Perspectives on Organizational Behavior

A Theory of Individual Motivation

In exploring why people do what they do, psychologists have formed a theory of motivation which concentrates on need satisfaction as the central explanation. Though there is more to contemporary motivation theory than this, the idea that man reduces tension by satisfying needs occupies a central place in the study of individual behavior. In the study of individual behavior in organizations, A. H. Maslow's scheme of man's hierarchy of needs has stimulated and influenced much contemporary thought. Maslow's theory has laid a foundation which is utilized in many studies of behavioral processes such as perception, the effects of organization on personality and vice versa, and the basic orientations people have toward others. These ideas are so pervasive that Warren Bennis [6] has commented that "most contemporary organizational theory, when it does deal with personality, bases its view of man on Maslow's hierarchy-of-needs theory" (p. 196). The first reading following this chapter, "A Theory of Human Motivation," is an abridgment of the original presentation of Maslow's theory.

Maslow depicts man's needs as arranged over a hierarchy, from physiological at the base, through safety, love, and esteem, to self-actualization at the top. The only needs which motivate behavior, according to the theory, are those which are unsatisfied. Motivation must appeal to unmet, operative needs. Offering the opportunity to satisfy already fulfilled needs has no impact on behavior.

We have not gone into the full complexities of the theory here, but even this simplified version suggests some of its applications in management. For example, visualize the situation of a low-ranking but well-paid staff assistant to an engineering manager in an aerospace firm. The assistant holds a B.S. degree in electronic engineering and an M.B.A. degree. With these qualifications, he could easily find a host of good jobs. Assume that his lower level needs, the more physical and social ones, are relatively well satisfied. This means, theoretically, that his higher level, egoistic needs are what he wants to satisfy. Suppose his superior tends to delegate to him only those assignments which pose very little challenge—and to supervise his performance closely. These jobs do not demand the exercise of his professional skills. He complains that his job is a bore and that his boss is always looking over his shoulder; the boss complains that he has now had this assistant for eighteen months and the fellow is less productive than when he started—why isn't he more productive?

If we examine this simplified situation in terms of the hierarchy-of-needs motivation theory, the analysis would be as follows: The staff assistant's work is not keyed to his egoistic needs—for achievement, for competence, for recognition. The activities in his job are *intrinsically* unrewarding; the job must somehow be changed so that it meets these higher level needs which are operative. The less the job challenges the assistant's appetite for mastery, importance, and so on, the less it will motivate him. Improving peripheral working conditions, granting a modest pay increase, or offering verbal encouragement would not go to the heart of the matter. These responses would probably have more to do with needs that are already satisfied. The under-utilized source of motivation here is probably the work itself.

Some of the writers who have applied this perspective suggest that managers often seem to expect to stimulate human productivity by offering rewards more relevant to comparatively well-satisfied needs than to unmet ones. While offering good wages and fringe benefits, these managers design highly organized and regulated work environments which, despite their technological and economic benefits, create motivational problems.

We will see that Maslow's ideas are the basis for the thinking of several authors about the "discontents of work" and the classic conflict between man and organization. McGregor, Argyris, and Leavitt, for example—and, from a critical standpoint, Strauss—all make use of this approach. The theory informs the ways some of these authors would rebuild organization structures, controls, and leadership practices to be more congruent with human needs. Ideas such as decentralization, job enlargement, management by self-control, and participative leadership, as well as many others, have roots in the psychology of human motivation. These practices organize work in ways more responsive to egoistic needs and accordingly are of greater motivational value.

The Concept of Social Exchange

When interpersonal or group behavior is the category of organizational behavior under study, the tools of analysis provided by the concept of social exchange become particularly useful. The essence of social exchange, as Homans explains in a selected reading following this chapter, is that "interaction between persons is an exchange of goods material and non-material." This means that interpersonal relations can be looked upon as a matter of exchanging both behavior and sentiment as well as things and money. Not all aspects of the bargain one makes with an organization when one works in it are stipulated and discharged in economic terms. Many matters are worked out in social terms: vaguely specified obligations grow which are not neatly dischargeable in economic terms, inducements and rewards for special informal contributions evolve, and so on.

If you are on good working terms with the company's electronics laboratory, you might get your TV set repaired free. Someone who is on good terms with the purchasing staff might get tires for his own car at a discount. The examples are endless, but every organization seems to have an unofficial rewards system. The reading by Dalton, "The Interlocking of Official and Unofficial Rewards," in Chapter 5 portrays an amazing variety of exchange patterns involving material goods and services.

In non-material terms, an equally wide array of exchanges of behavior and sentiment are involved in daily life in organizations. Positively, one might give help and receive gratitude. Negatively, one might give punishment and receive resentment. One might give help and get help, give punishment and get punishment, and so on. Social exchanges are more or less costly, more or less rewarding, and on balance more or less profitable to the parties involved.

To illustrate, let's go back to the relations between the engineering manager and his subordinate staff assistant, which we earlier looked at in terms of motivation. Utilizing the perspective of social exchange, one would deal with the same facts in an alternative way. The superior assigns routine work and supervises it closely. In short, he gives the subordinate uninteresting activities and no autonomy or independence in performing them. The subordinate complains and performs poorly. That is, the subordinate gives the supervisor a worsening behavior pattern. In this case the costs for each party are high, the rewards are low, and the resultant profit for each is little.

With a little imagination, the case could be rewritten to illustrate a situation in which the exchange is a more profitable one. The subordinate could be doing challenging work with relatively great autonomy. He could be turning in an impressive performance. The supervisor could be giving general assignments and receiving a highly valued contribution. Whatever the facts of the case, each party's behavior and sentiments are reciprocal parts of the exchange pattern.

According to the social exchange perspective, the manager is a kind of bargainer, and management is a kind of brokerage of activity and sentiment. The manager's problem is to make the best exchanges or bargains he can. If the work of a manager is conceived in these terms, the formula for human relations is "to give the other man behavior that is more valuable to him than it is costly to you and to get from him behavior that is more valuable to you than it is costly to him" [12, p. 62]. The manager faces the challenge of learning how costly or how valuable different behavior patterns are to all concerned—to himself, to other individuals, and to groups of several persons as well. Different standards of value are involved, as are different degrees of bargaining power. So formulated, the manager's lot is not an easy one, but one in which he can build his skill by focusing on the analysis and management of his exchange patterns.

So far our explanation of social exchange suggests a rational or at least intentional give-and-take—"an eye for an eye" so to speak. Some researchers have seen the process of exchange of attitude and behavior as a non-rational or reflex action. Reflex indicates that the behavior and its interpersonal intentions are not necessarily planned or executed. For example, Leary [15] has suggested a scheme for classifying interpersonal behavior along two axes: dominance-submission and affection-hostility (see Figure 2-1). He developed sixteen categories of behavior which fit into this scheme. Point 1 on the figure illustrates a strong affection but dominance toward the other person—"smotherly love"; point 2 describes hateful submissiveness, and so on.

Figure 2-1

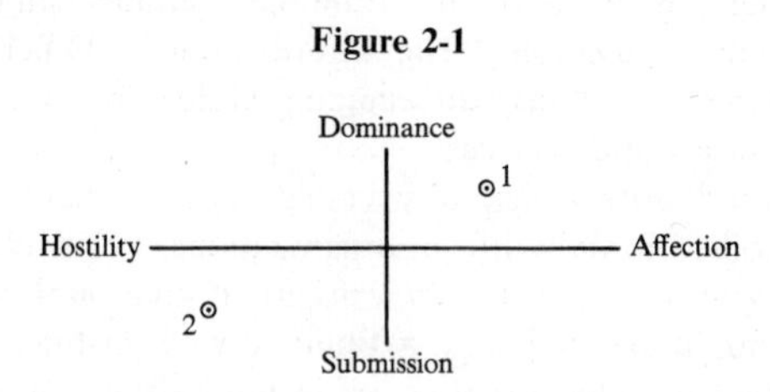

What has been suggested is that to each behavioral act of one person toward another, the latter responds with a complementary act and attitude. Along the vertical axis—dominance/submission—acts of one kind tend to evoke opposites: submissive behavior evokes domination; domination evokes obedience. Along the horizontal axis—affection/hostility—acts of one kind tend to evoke the same kind of act: seeking friendship evokes affection, acting hostile evokes hostility.

In short, one person's interpersonal mechanisms tend to "pull" a complementary reflex from the other. Of course, the process is not as simple or mechanical as we have described it, for the behavior of a particular person will not only be automatic but will also reflect the time and place—and his needs. Thus, the individual's definition of the situation or his own personality will influence his response to a domineering act by another. That is, he may be more likely to give a passive or submissive response (be well out on the submission axis) if the domineering other is his father or his boss. In contrast, he will probably give a competitive response (probably just above zero on the dominance axis) to a domineering friend or peer.

Even this short description of the interpersonal reflex process should give some indication of the dynamic movement in the social relationship of two people. There are always forces operating to modify the terms of exchange of behavior and attitudes. This has important implications for the willingness of two persons to work together cooperatively. Such cooperation demands some harmony in their perceptions of the work situation, and such concurrence is influenced by the exchange of attitudes and behavior.

Figure 2-2. A's Attitudes toward B and X, and B's Attitudes toward A and X.

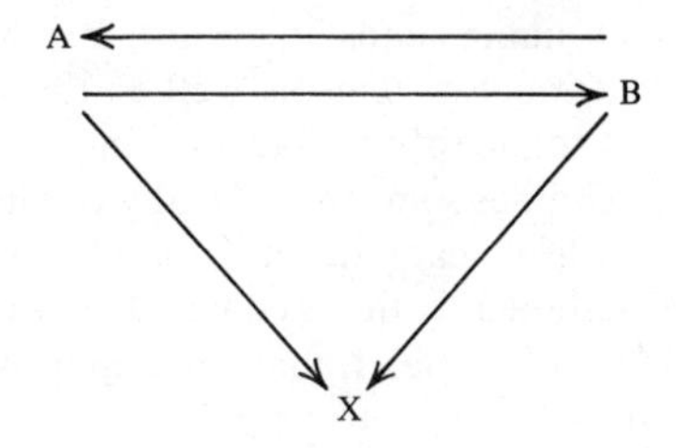

For example, Newcomb [22] has pointed out that we tend to agree with those we like and like those with whom we agree. We also tend to disagree with those we dislike and dislike those with whom we disagree. Newcomb has formalized these ideas into a theoretical model that summarizes many of the concepts in this area (see Figure 2-2). Two persons (A and B) are engaged in interaction about one or more objects (X's), which can be ideas, machines, or people. The set of attitudes which A and B have about each other and about the X's constitutes a system of interrelated parts. This set of attitudes is a system because the parts are interdependent; when one part changes, other parts are likely to show compensatory changes. In fact, there may be movement toward certain patterns of attitudes that are balanced or in equilibrium. These balanced states would be:

1. Mutual attraction between A and B, along with agreement about X's.
2. Mutual rejection between A and B, along with disagreement about X's.

All other states are unstable states and will tend toward one or another of the equilibrium patterns. For example, if A and B like each other and have good relations, disagreement about X will tend to be resolved into some compromise on which they can agree. They move toward the first balanced state above.

In contrast, if A and B dislike each other but agree about X, there may be some pressure to move toward either of the equilibrium states—and it is difficult to predict which.

At a more general level, we are suggesting that in the social relationships between persons, interpersonal attitudes, perceptions, and attitudes toward work or other people are all interdependent with one another, tend to be compatible, and tend to change together as a system.

George Homans has formulated this social exchange perspective on interpersonal relations in the second selected article, "Social Behavior as Exchange." The social exchange perspective contributes to the analytical chapters of Part II in several places. In Chapter 5, "The Impact of Informal Organization: Social Factors in Organizational Behavior," we use the concept of social exchange to analyze the relations that emerge unofficially among individuals and groups in organizations. The informal group gives its members opportunities to satisfy social needs, emotional support in an impersonal formal system, and assistance in performing tasks and meeting goals. These benefits are traded in some proportion to the individual's contribution to the group, in terms of some evolved concept of distributive justice. Discipline and control are similarly worked out in terms of the values members attach to one another and to membership in the group and in the organization.

Whether he likes or understands it or not, the manager's behavior is implicated in a web of informal systems as well as the formal one, and he is engaged in a continuous round of transactions in those systems. When he promotes, transfers, or disciplines someone officially or alters someone's job, the manager rearranges the terms of bargains in an unofficial status system. His act may or may not be well attuned to that system. If it is not, the manager may find, as Homans suggested in Chapter 1, that something swings around and hits him in the back of the neck.

Interaction Theory

In 1940 two anthropologists, Eliot Chapple and Conrad Arensberg [8], set forth a method for applying some of the more rigorous measurement standards of the natural sciences to the study of human relations. They felt that progress would be made if behavioral scientists based their description and interpretation of social relations primarily on objective, measurable phenomena, not on words, symbols, attitudes, or other secondary evidence of behavior. The core concept in their thinking was interaction, which they defined as follows:

> As a matter of everyday observation, we see individuals coming together, and from the evidence of what we see and hear we unconsciously make certain judgments about their behavior. Such judgments are that one individual started to talk, and that the second individual to whom he was talking replied, and that both accompanied their speech with facial or bodily gestures. Even if three or four or a hundred individuals come together and we observe more complex variations on this pattern, we are still able to resolve what we see into words and gestures which have this character—that the actions of one individual are followed in some fashion by the actions of another. When we observe such events taking place, we have recognized what we may call interaction (pp. 21–22).

About the same time, one of the classic management writers, Chester Barnard [4], was saying:

> When the individual has become associated with a cooperative enterprise [organization] he has accepted a position of contact with others similarly associated. From this contact there must arise interactions between these persons individually, and these interactions are social. . . . They . . . *cannot be avoided*. . . . such interactions are consequences of cooperation, and constitute one set of social factors involved in cooperation.
>
> These factors operate on the individuals affected; and, in conjunction with other factors, become incorporated in their mental and emotional characters (pp. 40–41).

Work in organizations, particularly managerial work, involves interaction—indeed, this may be most of the manager's job. Recent studies [27] report that managers spend a very high proportion of their time interacting. The way employees, managerial and operative, are positioned by their jobs in the flow of work, in the hierarchy, and in patterns of staff-line relations determines to a large extent what their interaction networks will be. And what these networks are like, as Barnard anticipated, will influence how they think and how they feel.

Let us return to our engineering manager and his subordinate staff assistant to show how the tools for analysis of interaction theory would be used to look at a specific case. We said that the manager supervised the subordinate closely. This suggests that the manager frequently initiated communication with the subordinate, and that communication tended to be unidirectional—with little of it flowing upward.

When we revised the facts of the case in the last section, we gave the staff assistant new activities and more challenging work. We also reported that the boss allowed the staff assistant to work with increased autonomy. This would suggest that, along with the new pattern of activity, there was less frequent interaction between the two and perhaps greater balance in the flow up and down. We reported that, with these changes, the staff assistant's feelings, or sentiments, about his work became more positive. All of these patterns can be pictured as linked in a systemic relationship. Instead of conceiving of the manager as principally engaged in bargaining, we can conceive of his work in terms of designing, building, modifying, and maintaining systems of interaction, activity, and sentiment.

Interaction theory deals with the study of interaction networks and their relation to two other variables with which they are linked: sentiment and activity. The things people do, the way they feel, and their communication patterns are all interrelated and interdependent, according to this approach. The state of interdependence means that if a change is introduced into one variable, the others will be affected in some way. Applied to the study of organizational behavior and management, interaction theory pictures the relations of individuals and groups as social systems made up of interaction, activity, and sentiment patterns in dynamic interdependence.

The selected reading, "An Interaction Approach to the Theory of Organization," by William F. Whyte presents a model of organizational behavior in these terms. This new set of tools for analysis helps the student develop an ability to see, and intellectually to control, a very important set of "social facts" in organizational behavior.

We will use the concepts of interaction theory in several chapters. In particular, Chapter 6, "Conflict in the Organization: Interpersonal and Intergroup Factors in Organizational Behavior," traces the roots of many types of organizational stress to organizationally prescribed interaction patterns. As Barnard indicated and as we will observe, the "role prescriptions" in organization charts, job descriptions, authority allocations, work flow sequences, and other elements of official "structure" largely determine who sees whom, who initiates, who stabilizes, and who disrupts; consequently, they largely determine typical and predictable stress patterns. It won't take much experience in, say, a modern, complex aerospace organization for the recent graduate to see or to feel that there is conflict between inspection and production, designers and checkers, procurement or purchasing and engineering, and between everybody and the auditors. The intuitive manager often dismisses these problems as "personality clashes"—even when the conflicts persist after new personalities fill the same roles. Interaction theory helps illuminate the general, recurrent, structural elements embedded in seemingly dissimilar cases.

Chapter 10, "Managing and Changing Organizations by Modifying Structure," also makes especially concentrated use of interaction theory. In this instance, as with the other chapters (8 and 9) of Part III, the focus is primarily on use of the managerial technology or practical application of the same concepts. Here they are tools for action. Having explained the structural sources of some types of organizational stress in Chapter 6, we study techniques for containing and altering the determinants of conflict and problems of organizational ineffectiveness in Chapter 10.

Functional Analysis

As defined by the sociologist Robert K. Merton [19], "*Functions* are those observed consequences which make for the adaptation or adjustment of a given system; and *dysfunctions,* those observed consequences which lessen the adaptation or adjustment of the system" (p. 51). Those consequences which are intended by the participants in the system are referred to by the behavioral scientist as *manifest;* those consequences which are unintended would be called *latent.* If, for example, we look at our engineering manager-staff assistant situation once more, we can illustrate these terms concretely. In the first place, the manager supervised closely because, we assume, he intended this to assure good performance. The consequences were the opposite. In terms of the productivity values of the organization, the consequence of deteriorating productivity was dysfunctional. At the same time, the manager may have intended by this same practice to serve another organizational value, keeping well informed about operations under his responsibility. In terms of achieving this value, the results might be functional. The consequence of diminished productivity was unintended, or latent. That of keeping informed was intended, or manifest. Perhaps the most basic lesson of functional analysis for management is that consequences of policy actions are separate from the purposes or motives behind them. We can illustrate what this means by citing a few cases.

A plant superintendent undertakes to measure—for the purpose of gathering information and for no other—some aspect of the performance of a department. As he obtains his data, several unanticipated results may occur. Men are compromising other aspects of performance to excel in the one being measured. Quality is slighted, maintenance is neglected, and up goes output—for the time being. Unwittingly, the superintendent's information gathering has affected organizational behavior, somewhat like a mini-skirted secretary walking through a crowded company cafeteria. The superintendent does not see the goal displacement he produces; the secretary does not see the collisions she precipitates; but in both cases the effects have nonetheless occurred. They have generated what functional analysis would view as latent dysfunctions. The securing of data, which was naïvely intended as measurement with no impact on current behavior, may be the least significant result of the process of collecting information.

In another case, a supervisor in a state employment agency introduced a series of statistical measures of the performance of interviewers [7, pp. 82–99]. The new records showed such items as the number of interviews held, the number of clients (unemployed) referred to a job, the number of referred clients hired, and the proportion of referrals resulting in placement. Although the statistical measures were not designed to stimulate the placement of Negro clients, they had this effect. The Negro clients were relatively more willing to accept the low-paying jobs the interviewers sought to fill. The more the interviewers concentrated on improving their measured productivity, the less were the Negroes subject to the operation of conscious or unconscious prejudice against them. This consequence, impartial treatment, was a latent function of the overriding emphasis on productivity. It was functional because impartial treatment was also a goal; it was latent because the statistics were not intended to have any relationship to that goal.

Visualizing the organization as a dynamic system is perhaps difficult enough; anticipating all of the repercussions throughout the system from a change in one of its elements is impossible. Completely reliable prediction presupposes more advanced knowledge than behavioral science has attained. Recall that while the behavioral sciences can teach us much about careful observation and description, and about recognizing and conceptualizing important recurrent elements or factors, they can't go very far in expressing the nature of the relations between the elements. Appropriately, Charles Lindblom [16] has remarked: "Neither social scientists . . . nor . . . administrators yet know enough about the social world to avoid repeated error in predicting the consequences of policy moves. A wise policy maker consequently expects that his policies will achieve only part of what he hopes and at the same time will produce unanticipated consequences which he would have preferred to avoid" (p. 86). As the last example shows, the policy might also produce unintended but desired results.

Because of the modest state of organizational knowledge, the manager needs some ways of identifying and assessing the consequences of his policies in terms of their effects throughout various elements of the organizational system. The concepts of functional analysis are especially useful tools for the study of consequences of behavior patterns. Peter Blau's selection, "The Empirical Study of Bureaucratic Structure and Function," explains the ideas of function, dysfunction, manifest, and latent much more completely than has this introductory treatment. Blau explains the relevance of functional analysis to bureaucracy, or what we more often speak of as formal organization or simply organization. We have excerpted his explanation of the tools of functional analysis from his book, *The Dynamics of Bureaucracy,* which reports his own research in two government organizations.

In Chapter 4, "The Impact of Formal Organization: Structural Factors in Organizational Behavior," we discuss the functions and dysfunctions, both manifest and latent, of key structural properties of organizations: hierarchy, standing plans, and controls. All of these are necessary components of organization. They facilitate goal setting, communicating, decision making, and maintaining direction. But structure is not an unmixed blessing. Structure can frustrate organizational effectiveness, it can produce fearful overconformity, superficial compliance, and displacement of goals. Hierarchy, standing plans, and control can conflict with the needs of people for autonomy and the exercise of their higher-level abilities. Alternatively, structure can facilitate personal achievement and self-expression. We will understand the particular effects of structure on behavior not by morally judging them as good or bad but by patiently sorting out the consequences in cases we investigate. The Chapter 4 readings by March and Simon and by Strauss provide a view of some of the positive contributions of structural factors. Cases reported by Schlesinger, Thompson, Jasinski, and Ridgway show a wide range of dysfunctional consequences of bureaucratic structures, controls, and measurement systems.

Political Perspectives in Organizational Analysis

In the final selected reading for this chapter, "The Body Politic of the Corporation," Earl Latham cites five characteristics which political systems exhibit. These are:

1. An authoritative allocation of principal functions.
2. A symbolic system for the ratification of collective decisions.
3. An operating system of command.
4. A system of rewards and punishment.
5. Institutions for the enforcement of common rules.

Latham demonstrates that, however unaccustomed we may be to conceiving of corporate organizations in these terms, these five elements are as evident in corporations as they are in states. As we have indicated earlier, Chapters 7 and 9 will demonstrate the power of such political concepts as authority, power, delegation, and responsibility in organizational analysis and management technology.

Chapter 7, "Political Behavior in Organizations," points out that the very functions of managers, if explained in terms of planning (decision making and rule making), organizing (writing job descriptions and authority specifications), direction (issuing instructions or orders), and control (examining results, making new decisions for corrective action if results do not correspond to plans), all add up to the building of a political system. When we look at organizational behavior from a political perspective, we highlight features heretofore relegated to the background. Now we will stress that organizations govern themselves internally: they formulate their own rules (laws) and administer them; they superimpose this political system of authority on the technical system of work and on the human organization. Policy making is a kind of legislating, and managing, in this view, is like the work of governing. Beardsley Ruml [24] suggested: "A business is a *government* because within the law it is authorized to make rules for the conduct of its affairs. It is a *private* government because the rules it makes within law are final and not reviewable by any public body" (p. vi).

A business organization can be viewed as a balanced interlocking system of work to be done, a technological system. With a little imagination, we can think of the organization not yet enlivened by people, as a purely technical, unhuman system. Some management writers have recommended that organization planning start out this way, with what they call a "drawing-office approach." In such an approach we could lay out the physical equipment and the departmental responsibilities, prescribe the sequence of operations, specify the structure, and determine all the positions to be staffed.

When the organization is animated with people carrying out the prescribed activities and interactions, a social system, or what some authors call a sociotechnical system, comes into being. The problem of management can be conceived as one of coordinating the elements of the system, of making sure the organization moves in the desired direction and is not an anarchy.

Management needs to assure that the behavior of the individuals and groups in the organization conforms to the demands of the technological system. This requires the creation of some system of authority whereby organizational behavior conforms to the technological and human necessities of the enterprise. Chapter 9, "Influencing Behavior Through Political Action," describes and demonstrates how such management techniques as delegation (Newman, Summer, and Warren), decentralization (Cordiner), functional authority (Koontz and O'Donnell), standing plans (Newman), and appeals procedures (Brown) contribute to this objective.

Some of the most insightful management writers make especially productive use of political concepts. For example, an early and extremely perceptive author, Mary Parker Follett [20], directly addressed the issue of how authoritative political systems should be formulated in business organizations. Her thesis was that the imperatives of the technical work system contained the "law of the situation."

To illustrate this thesis, let us assume that two members of the same department disagree on a particular procedure. These two may be a "superior" and a "subordinate," a line supervisor and a staff coordinator, or "equals." Such *conflicts,* a concept of central importance in political science, are natural in a business organization because people tend to view matters in different ways. In this respect, Miss Follett was posing the same argument for the internal workings of a business organization that political philosophers such as Locke and Hobbes posed for the workings of society.

Miss Follett's next argument is that *constructive conflict* is necessary to discover "the *law* of the situation." This process involves a frank and open discussion of the area of disagreement in an attempt to develop a solution which satisfies all parties. In this second argument, Miss Follett is again applying the concept of *pluralism in the corporation*—another argument put forth by political scientists when they view society as an organization.

Miss Follett's third and final argument is that if people engage in constructive conflict, the corporation will arrive at *legitimate* decisions and policies (the laws of the situation) which are accepted and obeyed by all concerned.

In Chapters 7 and 9, consideration is given to why people obey, and why they believe (if they do) in the legitimacy of company decisions and rules. In the writings of such men as Chester Barnard and Wilfred Brown, we shall see how some successful executives have tried to engineer the application of pluralism, constructive conflict, and legitimate authority to business organizations.

Whether one regards individuals as likely to cooperate and respond to the law of the situation has a lot to do with the kind of controls, rules, leadership styles, and organization structures one will regard as suitable for the government or management of an organization. The political scientist Herbert Kaufman [13] relates how political theory and organizational theory, respectively, have sought the best means of coordinating organizations:

> Political theorists who believe men are inclined to take advantage of one another tend to stress central direction as the best means of coordinating [men]. Without an overriding central figure, according to them, any system breaks down in disorder, confusion, and internal warfare. Hobbes, of course, presented this argument in its purest, most logical form [25]. On the other side, philosophers who assume [that] the interests and tendencies of men are harmonious emphasize the possibility and desirability of coordination through reciprocity, and regard central direction as an exploitative or disturbing factor in what would otherwise be a highly coordinated system, distributing maximum satisfaction to all its members. The anarchists, both Marxist and non-Marxist, pushed this reasoning to its logical extreme [9]. It matters little for this discussion whether the extremists on both sides meant their doctrines to be taken literally, or as analogies for the sake of clarity and vigor of statement. They bracketed the range of possibilities. In the history of political thought, not only the extremes but virtually all conceivable intermediate positions have at some time or other been advanced or defended.
>
> During most of the short history of organization[al] theory, few theorists seriously questioned the premise that central direction (expressed structurally as a hierarchy of authority because of the need of leaders to delegate formal powers and because of the assumed inability of men to supervise directly more than a small number of colleagues) is the primary method of achieving coordination; indeed, hierarchy and organization were sometimes treated as almost synonymous. [Fn: "The scalar principle is the same form in organization that is sometimes called hierarchical. . . . The common impression regards this scale or chain merely as 'type' of organization, characteristic only of the vaster institutions of government, army, church, and industry. This impression is erroneous. It is likewise misleading, for it seems to imply that the scalar chain in organization lacks universality. These great organizations differ from others only in that the chain is longer. The truth is that wherever we find an organization even of two people, related as superior and subordinate, we have the scalar principle. This chain constitutes the universal process of coordination, through which the supreme coordinating authority becomes effective throughout the entire structure" (21, pp. 14–15). "The transition from individuality to division of labor and the acceptance of hierarchy in the form of a leadership structure . . . represents the point at which an 'organization' can be said

> to exist" (30, p. 150).] Yet very early some questioning voices were heard, particularly after experimental studies in the sociology of industry drew attention to the responsiveness of workers to cues and signals emanating from sources other than (and sometimes hostile to) the designated managers of the firms examined. Mary Parker Follett [20], a political scientist of Pluralist persuasion, became well known to students of organization for her advocacy of "power with rather than power over" and for her criticism of "the illusion of final responsibility." Later on, Argyris [2] and Thompson [29] and others [5, 10, 11] would search explicitly for a pattern of organization that is non-hierarchical. An electronics firm on the West Coast recently reorganized itself on what are alleged to be non-hierarchical lines [14]. It would be grossly inaccurate to equate these organizational analyses with the anarchists, but there can be no question that organization[al] theory has begun to display an awareness of a range of positions on the central-reciprocal scale that political philosophers have explored extensively for centuries (pp. 7–8).

Despite their promise, political thought and particularly the concept of authority systems have been relatively little used in organizational behavior analysis. We believe that our addition of political science concepts will help the student acquire a set of tools for analysis which are especially well adapted to understanding the organization itself and the interplay between it and subsidiary groups and individuals.

Summary

The readings which follow in this chapter provide the basic statement of the core concepts: the hierarchy of needs, social exchange, interaction theory, functional analysis of bureaucracy, and a view of organizations as political systems. These conceptual foundations provide the tools for analysis with which, in the second part of the book, we will take apart organizational behavior to understand its components and dynamics. Both the original materials and the selected readings in Part II will demonstrate the intellectual power of these ideas in examining such management processes as organizing, leading, measuring and controlling, and participating in lateral organizational relations. Part II illuminates the deeper structure of the real world of the manager by systematically conceptualizing its events and recurrent patterns, making use of the ideas of Part I. As the student progresses, he will gain facility in knowing which ideas underpin each selection and in recognizing key ideas at work even when they are not identified by the author. Ultimately, the student must convert the tools for analysis into his own professional analytic skills.

References

1. Argyris, C. "Human Problems with Budgets." *Harvard Business Review,* Vol. 31, No. 1 (1953).
2. ———. *Personality and Organization.* Harper & Row, 1957.
3. Bach, G. L. "Some Observations on the Business School of Tomorrow." *Management Science,* Vol. 4, No. 4 (July 1958).
4. Barnard, C. I. *The Functions of the Executive.* Harvard University Press, 1938.

5. Bass, B. M. "Industrial Organization for the Space Age." Unpublished paper, Graduate School of Business, University of Pittsburgh, 1963.

6. Bennis, W. *Changing Organizations.* McGraw-Hill, 1966.

7. Blau, P. M. *The Dynamics of Bureaucracy* (rev. ed.). University of Chicago Press, 1963.

8. Chapple, E. D., and C. M. Arensberg. "Measuring Human Relations: An Introduction to the Study of the Interaction of Individuals." Genetic Psychology Monograph No. 22, The Journal Press, 1940.

9. Coker, F. W. *Recent Political Thought.* 1934.

10. Evan, W. M. "Indices of the Hierarchical Structure of Industrial Organizations." *Management Science,* Vol. 9, (1963).

11. Fisch, G. G. "Line-Staff is Obsolete." *Harvard Business Review,* Vol. 39 (1961).

12. Homans, G. C. *Social Behavior: Its Elementary Forms.* Harcourt, Brace & World, 1961.

13. Kaufman, H. "Organizational Theory and Political Theory." The American Political Science Review, Vol. 58, No. 1 (March 1964).

14. Kuriloff, A. H. "Management by Integration and Self-Control." *Proc. Industrial Engineering Institute* (Feb. 1963).

15. Leary, T. *Interpersonal Diagnosis of Personality.* Ronald, 1957.

16. Lindblom, C. E. "The Science of 'Muddling Through'." *Public Administration Review,* Vol. 19, No. 2 (1959).

17. McClelland, W. G. [Review of *Management Principles,* by Walter Puckey.] In *British Journal of Industrial Relations,* Vol. 1, No. 2 (June 1963).

18. McGregor, D. *The Human Side of Enterprise.* McGraw-Hill, 1960.

19. Merton, R. K. *Social Theory and Social Structure.* The Free Press, 1957.

20. Metcalf, H. C., and L. Urwick (eds.). *Dynamic Administration: The Collected Papers of Mary Parker Follett.* Harper & Row, 1941.

21. Mooney, J. O. *The Principles of Organization.* Harper & Row, 1947.

22. Newcomb, T. M. "An Approach to the Study of Communicative Acts." *Psychological Review,* Vol. 4 (1953).

23. Parkinson, C. N. *Parkinson's Law.* Houghton-Mifflin, 1957.

24. Ruml, B. *Tomorrow's Business,* as quoted in *The Government of Corporations,* by R. Eells. The Free Press, 1962.

25. Sabine, G. H. *A History of Political Theory* (3rd ed.). Holt, Rinehart & Winston, 1961.

26. Sayles, L. R. "Discussion." *Human Organization,* Vol. 21, No. 2 (1962).

27. ———. *Managerial Behavior.* McGraw-Hill, 1964.

28. Stinchcombe, A. L. "Social Structure and Organizations." In *Handbook of Organizations,* ed. J. G. March. Rand-McNally, 1965.

29. Thompson, V. A. *Modern Organizations.* Knopf, 1961.

30. Weiner, M. G. "Observations on the Growth of Information-Processing Centers." In *Some Theories of Organization,* ed. A. H. Rubenstein and C. J. Haberstroh. Irwin, 1960.

31. Whitehead, A. N. *Adventures of Ideas.* Macmillan, 1933.

Readings

A Theory of Human Motivation: The Basic Needs

A. H. MASLOW

The "Physiological" Needs

The needs that are usually taken as the starting point for motivation theory are the so-called physiological drives. Two recent lines of research make it necessary to revise our customary notions about these needs: first, the development of the concept of homeostasis, and, second, the finding that appetites (preferential choices among foods) are a fairly efficient indication of actual needs or lacks in the body.

Homeostasis refers to the body's automatic efforts to maintain a constant, normal state of the blood stream. Cannon[1] has described this process for (1) the water content of the blood, (2) salt content, (3) sugar content, (4) protein content, (5) fat content, (6) calcium content, (7) oxygen content, (8) constant hydrogen-ion level (acid-base balance) and (9) constant temperature of the blood. Obviously this list can be extended to include other minerals, the hormones, vitamins, etc.

Young in a recent article[2] has summarized the work on appetite in its relation to body needs. If the body lacks some chemical, the individual will tend to develop a specific appetite or partial hunger for that food element.

Thus it seems impossible as well as useless to make any list of fundamental physiological needs for they can come to almost any number one might wish, depending on the degree of specificity of description. We cannot identify all physiological needs as homeostatic. That sexual desire, sleepiness, sheer activity, and maternal behavior in animals are homeostatic, has not yet been demonstrated. Furthermore, this list would not include the various sensory pleasures (tastes, smells, tickling, stroking) which are probably physiological and which may become the goals of motivated behavior.

Abridged from "A Theory of Human Motivation," *Psychological Review,* Vol. 50 (1943), pp. 370–396. Abridgement originally published in *Readings in Managerial Psychology,* ed. H. Leavitt and L. Pondy. The University of Chicago Press, 1964.

[1] W. B. Cannon, *Wisdom of the Body* (New York: Norton, 1932).

[2] P. T. Young, "The Experimental Analysis of Appetite," *Psychological Bulletin,* XXXVIII (1941), 129–64.

In a previous paper[3] it has been pointed out that these physiological drives or needs are to be considered unusual rather than typical because they are isolable and because they are localizable somatically. That is to say, they are relatively independent of each other, of other motivations and of the organism as a whole, and, in many cases, it is possible to demonstrate a localized, underlying somatic base for the drive. This is true less generally than has been thought (exceptions are fatigue, sleepiness, maternal responses), but it is still true in the classic instances of hunger, sex, and thirst.

It should be pointed out again that any of the physiological needs and the consummatory behavior involved with them serve as channels for all sorts of other needs as well. The person who thinks he is hungry may actually be seeking more for comfort or dependence than for vitamins or proteins. Conversely, it is possible to satisfy the hunger need in part by other activities such as drinking water or smoking cigarettes. In other words, these physiological needs are only relatively isolable.

Undoubtedly these physiological needs are the most prepotent of all needs. What this means specifically is that, in the human being who is missing everything in life in an extreme fashion, it is most likely that the major motivation would be the physiological needs rather than any others. A person who is lacking food, safety, love, and esteem would most probably hunger for food more strongly than for anything else.

If all the needs are unsatisfied, and the organism is then dominated by the physiological needs, all other needs may become simply non-existent or be pushed into the background. It is then fair to characterize the whole organism by saying simply that it is hungry, for consciousness is almost completely pre-empted by hunger. All capacities are put into the service of hunger-satisfaction, and the organization of these capacities is almost entirely determined by the one purpose of satisfying hunger. The receptors and effectors, the intelligence, memory, habits, all may now be defined simply as hunger-gratifying tools. Capacities that are not useful for this purpose lie dormant or are pushed into the background. The urge to write poetry, the desire to acquire an automobile, the interest in American history, the desire for a new pair of shoes are, in the extreme case, forgotten or become of secondary importance. For the man who is extremely and dangerously hungry, no other interests exist but food. He dreams food, he remembers food, he thinks about food, he emotes only about food, he perceives only food, and he wants only food. The more subtle determinants that ordinarily fuse with the physiological drives in organizing even feeding, drinking, or sexual behavior, may now be so completely overwhelmed as to allow us to speak at this time (but *only* at this time) of pure hunger drive and behavior, with the one unqualified aim of relief.

Another peculiar characteristic of the human organism when it is dominated by a certain need is that the whole philosophy of the future tends also to change. For our chronically and extremely hungry man, utopia can be defined very simply as a place where there is plenty of food. He tends to think that, if only he is guaranteed food for the rest of his life, he will be perfectly happy and will never want anything more. Life itself tends to be defined in terms of eating. Anything else will be defined as unimportant. Freedom, love, community

[3] A. H. Maslow, "A Preface to Motivation Theory," *Psychosomatic Medicine,* (1943), 85–92.

feeling, respect, philosophy, may all be waved aside as fripperies which are useless, since they fail to fill the stomach. Such a man may fairly be said to live by bread alone.

It cannot possibly be denied that such things are true, but their *generality* can be denied. Emergency conditions are, almost by definition, rare in the normally functioning peaceful society. That this truism can be forgotten is due mainly to two reasons. First, rats have few motivations other than physiological ones, and since so much of the research upon motivation has been made with these animals, it is easy to carry the rat-picture over to the human being. Second, it is too often not realized that culture itself is an adaptive tool, one of whose main functions is to make the physiological emergencies come less and less often. In most of the known societies, chronic extreme hunger of the emergency type is rare rather than common. In any case, this is still true in the United States. The average American citizen is experiencing appetite rather than hunger when he says, "I am hungry." He is apt to experience sheer life-and-death hunger only by accident and then only a few times through his entire life.

Obviously a good way to obscure the "higher" motivations, and to get a lopsided view of human capacities and human nature, is to make the organism extremely and chronically hungry or thirsty. Anyone who attempts to make an emergency picture into a typical one and who will measure all of man's goals and desires by his behavior during extreme physiological deprivation is certainly being blind to many things. It is quite true that man lives by bread alone—when there is no bread. But what happens to man's desires when there *is* plenty of bread and when his belly is chronically filled?

At once other (and "higher") needs emerge and these, rather than physiological hungers, dominate the organism. And when these in turn are satisfied, again new (and still "higher") needs emerge and so on. This is what we mean by saying that the basic human needs are organized into a hierarchy of relative prepotency.

One main implication of this phrasing is that gratification becomes as important a concept as deprivation in motivation theory, for it releases the organism from the domination of a relatively more physiological need, permitting thereby the emergence of other more social goals. The physiological needs, along with their partial goals, when chronically gratified cease to exist as active determinants or organizers of behavior. They now exist only in a potential fashion in the sense that they may emerge again to dominate the organism if they are thwarted. But a want that is satisfied is no longer a want. The organism is dominated and its behavior organized only by unsatisfied needs. If hunger is satisfied, it becomes unimportant in the current dynamics of the individual.

This statement is somewhat qualified by a hypothesis to be discussed more fully later, namely, that it is precisely those individuals in whom a certain need has always been satisfied who are best equipped to tolerate deprivation of that need in the future; furthermore, those who have been deprived in the past will react to current satisfactions differently from the one who has never been deprived.

The Safety Needs

If the physiological needs are relatively well gratified, there then emerges a new set of needs, which we may categorize roughly as the safety needs. All that has been said of the physiological needs is equally true, although in lesser degree, of these desires. The organism may equally well be wholly dominated by them. They may serve as the almost exclusive organizers of behavior, recruiting all the capacities of the organism in their service, and we may then fairly describe the whole organism as a safety-seeking mechanism. Again we may say of the receptors, the effectors, of the intellect and the other capacities that they are primarily safety-seeking tools. Again, as in the hungry man, we find that the dominating goal is a strong determinant not only of his current world-outlook and philosophy but also of his philosophy of the future. Practically everything looks less important than safety (even sometimes the physiological needs which being satisfied, are now underestimated). A man, in this state, if it is extreme enough and chronic enough, may be characterized as living almost for safety alone.

Although in this paper we are interested primarily in the needs of the adult, we can approach an understanding of his safety needs perhaps more efficiently by observation of infants and children, in whom these needs are much more simple and obvious. One reason for the clearer appearance of the threat or danger reaction in infants is that they do not inhibit this reaction at all, whereas adults in our society have been taught to inhibit it at all costs. Thus even when adults do feel their safety to be threatened, we may not be able to see this on the surface. Infants will react in a total fashion and as if they were endangered, if they are disturbed or dropped suddenly, startled by loud noises, flashing light, or other unusual sensory stimulation, by rough handling, by general loss of support in the mother's arms, or by inadequate support.[4]

In infants we can also see a much more direct reaction to bodily illnesses of various kinds. Sometimes these illnesses seem to be immediately and per se threatening and seem to make the child feel unsafe. For instance, vomiting, colic, or other sharp pains seem to make the child look at the whole world in a different way. At such a moment of pain, it may be postulated that, for the child, the appearance of the whole world suddenly changes from sunniness to darkness, so to speak, and becomes a place in which anything at all might happen, in which previously stable things have suddenly become unstable. Thus a child who because of some bad food is taken ill may, for a day or two, develop fear, nightmares, and a need for protection and reassurance never seen in him before his illness.

Another indication of the child's need for safety is his preference for some kind of undisrupted routine or rhythm. He seems to want a predictable, orderly world. For instance, injustice, unfairness, or inconsistency in the parents seems to make a child feel anxious and unsafe. This attitude may be not so much because of the injustice per se or any particular pains involved, but rather because this treatment threatens to make the world look unreliable or unsafe or unpredictable. Young children seem to thrive better under a system which has at least a skeletal outline of rigidity, in which there is a schedule of a kind, some sort of routine, something that can be counted upon, not only for the present, but also far into the future. Perhaps one could express this more accu-

[4] As the child grows up, sheer knowledge and familiarity as well as better motor development make these "dangers" less and less dangerous and more and more manageable. Throughout life it may be said that one of the main conative functions of education is this neutralizing of apparent dangers through knowledge, e.g., I am not afraid of thunder because I know something about it.

rately by saying that the child needs an organized world rather than an unorganized or unstructured one.

The central role of the parents and the normal family setup are indisputable. Quarreling, physical assault, separation, divorce, or death within the family may be particularly terrifying. Also parental outbursts of rage or threats of punishment directed to the child, calling him names, speaking to him harshly, shaking him, handling him roughly, or actual physical punishment sometimes elicit such total panic and terror in the child that we must assume more is involved than the physical pain alone. While it is true that in some children this terror may represent also a fear of loss of parental love, it can also occur in completely rejected children, who seem to cling to the hating parents more for sheer safety and protection than because of hope of love.

Confronting the average child with new, unfamiliar, strange, unmanageable stimuli or situations will too frequently elicit the danger or terror reaction, as, for example, getting lost or even being separated from the parents for a short time, being confronted with new faces, new situations, or new tasks, the sight of strange, unfamiliar or uncontrollable objects, illness, or death. Particularly at such times, the child's frantic clinging to his parents is eloquent testimony to their role as protectors (quite apart from their roles as food-givers and love-givers).

From these and similar observations, we may generalize and say that the average child in our society usually prefers a safe, orderly, predictable, organized world which he can count on and in which unexpected, unmanageable, or other dangerous things do not happen and in which, in any case, he has all-powerful parents who protect and shield him from harm.

That these reactions may so easily be observed in children is in a way a proof of the fact that children in our society feel too unsafe (or, in a word, are badly brought up). Children who are reared in an unthreatening, loving family do *not* ordinarily react as we have described above.[5] In such children the danger reactions are apt to come mostly to objects or situations that adults too would consider dangerous.[6]

The healthy, normal, fortunate adult in our culture is largely satisfied in his safety needs. The peaceful, smoothly running, "good" society ordinarily makes its members feel safe enough from wild animals, extremes of temperature, criminals, assault and murder, tyranny, etc. Therefore, in a very real sense, they no longer have any safety needs as active motivators. Just as a sated man no longer feels hungry, a safe man no longer feels endangered. If we wish to see these needs directly and clearly we must turn to neurotic or near-neurotic individuals, and to the economic and social underdogs. In between these extremes, we can perceive the expressions of safety needs only in such phenomena as, for instance, the common preference for a job with tenure and protection, the desire for a savings account, and for insurance of various kinds (medical, dental, unemployment, disability, old age).

---

[5] M. Shirley, "Children's Adjustments to a Strange Situation," *Journal of Abnormal and Social Psychology,* XXXVII (1942), 201–17.

[6] A "test battery" for safety might be confronting the child with a small exploding firecracker or with a bewhiskered face, having the mother leave the room, putting him upon a high ladder, giving him a hypodermic injection, having a mouse crawl up to him, etc. Of course I cannot seriously recommend the deliberate use of such "tests," for they might very well harm the child being tested. But these and similar situations come up by the score in the child's ordinary day-to-day living and may be observed. There is no reason why these stimuli should not be used with, for example, young chimpanzees.

Other broader aspects of the attempt to seek safety and stability in the world are seen in the very common preference for familiar rather than unfamiliar things, or for the known rather than the unknown. The tendency to have some religion or world-philosophy that organizes the universe and the men in it into some sort of satisfactorily coherent, meaningful whole is also in part motivated by safety-seeking. Here too we may list science and philosophy in general as partially motivated by the safety needs (we shall see later that there are also other motivations to scientific, philosophical, or religious endeavor).

Otherwise the need for safety is seen as an active and dominant mobilizer of the organism's resources only in emergencies, e.g., war, disease, natural catastrophes, crime waves, societal disorganization, neurosis, brain injury, chronically bad situation.

Some neurotic adults in our society are, in many ways, like the unsafe child in their desire for safety, although in the former it takes on a somewhat special appearance. Their reaction is often to unknown, psychological dangers in a world that is perceived to be hostile, overwhelming and threatening. Such a person behaves as if a great catastrophe were almost always impending, i.e., he is usually responding as if to an emergency. His safety needs often find specific expression in a search for a protector, or a stronger person on whom he may depend, or perhaps a *Führer.*

The neurotic individual may be described in a slightly different way with some usefulness as a grown-up person who retains his childish attitudes toward the world. That is to say, a neurotic adult may be said to behave "as if" he were actually afraid of a spanking or of his mother's disapproval or of being abandoned by his parents or of having his food taken away from him. It is as if his childish attitudes of fear and threat reaction to a dangerous world had gone underground and, untouched by the growing up and learning processes, were now ready to be called out by any stimulus that would make a child feel endangered and threatened.[7]

The neurosis in which the search for safety takes its clearest form is in the compulsive-obsessive neurosis. Compulsive-obsessives try frantically to order and stabilize the world so that no unmanageable, unexpected, or unfamiliar dangers will ever appear.[8] They hedge themselves about with all sorts of ceremonials, rules, and formulas so that every possible contingency may be provided for and so that no new contingencies may appear. They are much like the brain-injured cases, described by Goldstein,[9] who manage to maintain their equilibrium by avoiding everything unfamiliar and strange and by ordering their restricted world in such a neat, disciplined, orderly fashion that everything in the world can be counted upon. They try to arrange the world so that anything unexpected (dangers) cannot possibly occur. If, through no fault of their own, something unexpected does occur, they go into a panic reaction as if this unexpected occurrence constituted a grave danger. What we can see only as a none-too strong preference in the healthy person, e.g., preference for the familiar, becomes a life-and-death necessity in abnormal cases.

---

[7] Not all neurotic individuals feel unsafe. Neurosis may have at its core a thwarting of the affection and esteem needs in a person who is generally safe.

[8] A. H. Maslow and B. Mittelmann, *Principles of Abnormal Psychology* (New York: Harper & Bros., 1941).

[9] K. Goldstein, *The Organism* (New York: American Book Co., 1939).

The Love Needs

If both the physiological and the safety needs are fairly well gratified, then there will emerge the love and affection and belongingness needs, and the whole cycle already described will repeat itself with this new center. Now the person will feel keenly, as never before, the absence of friends or a sweetheart or a wife or children. He will hunger for affectionate relations with people in general, namely, for a place in his group, and he will strive with great intensity to achieve this goal. He will want to attain such a place more than anything else in the world and may even forget that once, when he was hungry, he sneered at love.

In our society the thwarting of these needs is the most commonly found core in cases of maladjustment and more severe psychopathology. Love and affection, as well as their possible expression in sexuality, are generally looked upon with ambivalence and are customarily hedged about with many restrictions and inhibitions. Practically all theorists of psychopathology have stressed thwarting of the love needs as basic in the picture of maladjustment. Many clinical studies have therefore been made of this need and we know more about it perhaps than any of the other needs except the physiological ones.[10]

One thing that must be stressed at this point is that love is not synonymous with sex. Sex may be studied as a purely physiological need. Ordinarily sexual behavior is multi-determined, that is to say, determined not only by sexual but also by other needs, chief among which are the love and affection needs. Also not to be overlooked is the fact that the love needs involve both giving *and* receiving love.[11]

The Esteem Needs

All people in our society (with a few pathological exceptions) have a need or desire for a stable, firmly based, (usually) high evaluation of themselves, for self-respect, or self-esteem, and for the esteem of others. By firmly based self-esteem, we mean that which is soundly based upon real capacity, achievement, and respect from others. These needs may be classified into two subsidiary sets. These are, first, the desire for strength, for achievement, for adequacy, for confidence in the face of the world, and for independence and freedom.[12] Second, we have what we may call the desire for reputation or prestige (defining it as respect or esteem from other people), recognition, attention, importance, or appreciation.[13] These needs have been relatively stressed by Alfred Adler and his followers, and have been relatively neglected by Freud and the psycho-

---

[10] Maslow and Mittelmann, *op. cit.*

[11] For further details see A. H. Maslow, "The Dynamics of Psychological Security-Insecurity," *Character and Personality,* X (1942), 331–44, and J. Plant, *Personality and the Cultural Pattern* (New York: Commonwealth Fund, 1937), chap. v.

[12] Whether or not this particular desire is universal we do not know. The crucial question, especially important today, is, "Will men who are enslaved and dominated inevitably feel dissatisfied and rebellious?" We may assume on the basis of commonly known clinical data that a man who has known true freedom (not paid for by giving up safety and security but rather built on the basis of adequate safety and security) will not willingly or easily allow his freedom to be taken away from him. But we do not know that this is true for the person born into slavery. The events of the next decade should give us our answer. See discussion of this problem in E. Fromm, *Escape from Freedom* (New York: Farrar & Rinehart, 1941), chap. v.

[13] Perhaps the desire for prestige and respect from others is subsidiary to the desire for self-esteem or confidence in one's self. Observation of children seems to indicate that this is so, but clinical data give no clear support of such a conclusion.

analysts. More and more today, however, there is appearing widespread appreciation of their central importance.

Satisfaction of the self-esteem need leads to feelings of self-confidence, worth, strength, capability, and adequacy, of being useful and necessary in the world. But thwarting of these needs produces feelings of inferiority, of weakness, and of helplessness. These feelings in turn give rise to either basic discouragement or else compensatory or neurotic trends. An appreciation of the necessity of basic self-confidence and an understanding of how helpless people are without it, can be easily gained from a study of severe traumatic neurosis.[14]

The Need for Self-Actualization

Even if all these needs are satisfied, we may still often (if not always) expect that a new discontent and restlessness will soon develop, unless the individual is doing what he is fitted for. A musician must make music, an artist must paint, a poet must write, if he is to be ultimately happy. What a man *can* be, he *must* be. This need we may call self-actualization.

This term, first coined by Kurt Goldstein, is being used in this paper in a much more specific and limited fashion. It refers to the desire for self-fulfillment, namely, to the tendency for one to become actualized in what one is potentially. This tendency might be phrased as the desire to become more and more what one is, to become everything that one is capable of becoming.

The specific form that these needs take will of course vary greatly from person to person. In one individual it may be expressed maternally, as the desire to be an ideal mother, in another athletically, in still another aesthetically, in the painting of pictures, and in another inventively in the creation of new contrivances. It is not necessarily a creative urge although in people who have any capabilities for creation it will take this form.

The clear emergence of these needs rests upon prior satisfaction of the physiological, safety, love and esteem needs. We shall call people who are satisfied in these needs, basically satisfied people, and it is from these that we may expect the fullest (and healthiest) creativeness.[15] Since, in our society, basically satisfied people are the exception, we do not know much about self-actualization, either experimentally or clinically. It remains a challenging problem for research.

The Preconditions for the Basic Need Satisfactions

There are certain conditions which are immediate prerequisites for the basic need satisfactions. Danger to these is reacted to almost as if it were a direct danger to the basic needs themselves. Such conditions as freedom to speak, freedom to do what one wishes so long as no harm is done to others, freedom to express one's self, freedom to investigate and seek for information, freedom

[14] A. Kardiner, *The Traumatic Neuroses of War* (New York: Hoeber, 1941). For more extensive discussion of normal self-esteem, as well as for reports of various researches, see A. H. Maslow, "Dominance, Personality, and Social Behavior in Women," *Journal of Social Psychology,* X (1939), 3–39.

[15] Clearly creative behavior, like painting, is like any other behavior in having multiple determinants. It may be seen in "innately creative" people whether they are satisfied or not, happy or unhappy, hungry or sated. Also, it is clear that creative activity may be compensatory, ameliorative, or purely economic. It is my impression (as yet unconfirmed) that it is possible to distinguish the artistic and intellectual products of basically satisfied people from those of basically unsatisfied people by inspection alone. In any case, here too we must distinguish, in a dynamic fashion, the overt behavior itself from its various motivations or purposes.

to defend one's self, justice, fairness, honesty, orderliness in the group are examples of such preconditions for basic need satisfactions. Thwarting in these freedoms will be reacted to with a threat or emergency response. These conditions are not ends in themselves but they are *almost* so, since they are so closely related to the basic needs, which are apparently the only ends in themselves. These conditions are defended because without them the basic satisfactions are quite impossible, or at least, very severely endangered.

If we remember that the cognitive capacities (perceptual, intellectual, learning) are a set of adjustive tools, which have, among other functions, that of satisfaction of our basic needs, then it is clear that any danger to them, any deprivation or blocking of their free use, must also be indirectly threatening to the basic needs themselves. Such a statement is a partial solution of the general problems of curiosity, the search for knowledge, truth, and wisdom, and the ever persistent urge to solve the cosmic mysteries.

We must therefore introduce another hypothesis and speak of degrees of closeness to the basic needs, for we have already pointed out that *any* conscious desires (partial goals) are more or less important as they are more or less close to the basic needs. The same statement may be made for various behavior acts. An act is psychologically important if it contributes directly to satisfaction of basic needs. The less directly it so contributes, or the weaker this contribution is, the less important this act must be conceived to be from the point of view of dynamic psychology. A similar statement may be made for the various defense or coping mechanisms. Some are very directly related to the protection or attainment of the basic needs, others are only weakly and distantly related. Indeed, if we wished, we could speak of more basic and less basic defense mechanisms and then affirm that danger to the more basic defenses is more threatening than danger to less basic defenses (always remembering that this is so only because of their relationship to the basic needs).

The Desires to Know and to Understand

So far, we have mentioned the cognitive needs only in passing. Acquiring knowledge and systematizing the universe have been considered as, in part, techniques for the achievement of basic safety in the world, or, for the intelligent man, expressions of self-actualization. Also freedom of inquiry and expression have been discussed as preconditions of satisfactions of the basic needs. True though these formulations may be, they do not constitute definitive answers to the question as to the motivation role of curiosity, learning, philosophizing, experimenting, etc. They are, at best, no more than partial answers.

This question is especially difficult because we know so little about the facts. Curiosity, exploration, desire for the facts, desire to know may certainly be observed easily enough. The fact that they often are pursued even at great cost to the individual's safety is an earnest of the partial character of our previous discussion. In addition, the writer must admit that, though he has sufficient clinical evidence to postulate the desire to know as a very strong drive in intelligent people, no data are available for unintelligent people. It may then be largely a function of relatively high intelligence. Rather tentatively, then, and largely in the hope of stimulating discussion and research, we shall postulate a basic desire to know, to be aware of reality, to get the facts, to satisfy curiosity, or as Wertheimer phrases it, to see rather than to be blind.

This postulation, however, is not enough. Even after we know, we are impelled to know more and more minutely and microscopically, on the one hand, and, on the other, more and more extensively in the direction of a world philosophy, religion, etc. The facts that we acquire, if they are isolated or atomistic, inevitably get theorized about, and either analyzed or organized or both. This process has been phrased by some as the search for "meaning." We shall then postulate a desire to understand, to systematize, to organize, to analyze, to look for relations and meanings.

Once these desires are accepted for discussion, we see that they too form themselves into a small hierarchy in which the desire to know is prepotent over the desire to understand. All the characteristics of a hierarchy of prepotency that we have described above, seem to hold for this one as well.

We must guard ourselves against the too easy tendency to separate these desires from the basic needs we have discussed above, i.e., to make a sharp dichotomy between "cognitive" and "conative" needs. The desire to know and to understand are themselves conative, i.e., have a striving character, and are as much personality needs as the "basic needs" we have already discussed.[16]

The Degree of Fixity of the Hierarchy of Basic Needs

We have spoken so far as if this hierarchy were a fixed order but actually it is not nearly as rigid as we may have implied. It is true that most of the people with whom we have worked have seemed to have these basic needs in about the order that has been indicated. However, there have been a number of exceptions.

1. There are some people in whom, for instance, self-esteem seems to be more important than love. This most common reversal in the hierarchy is usually due to the development of the notion that the person who is most likely to be loved is a strong or powerful person, one who inspires respect or fear and who is self-confident or aggressive. Therefore, such people who lack love and seek it, may try hard to put on a front of aggressive, confident behavior. But essentially they seek high self-esteem and its behavior expressions more as a means-to-an-end than for its own sake; they seek self-assertion for the sake of love rather than for self-esteem itself.
2. There are other, apparently innately creative people in whom the drive to creativeness seems to be more important than any other counterdeterminant. Their creativeness might appear as self-actualization released not by basic satisfaction but in spite of lack of basic satisfaction.
3. In certain people the level of aspiration may be permanently deadened or lowered. That is to say, the less prepotent goals may simply be lost and may disappear forever, so that the person who has experienced life at a very low level, i.e., chronic unemployment, may continue to be satisfied for the rest of his life if only he can get enough food.
4. The so-called "psychopathic personality" is another example of permanent loss of the love needs. These are people who, according to the best data available,[17] have been starved for love in the earliest months of their lives

[16] M. Wertheimer, unpublished lectures at the New School for Social Research.
[17] D. M. Levy, "Primary Affect Hunger," *American Journal of Psychiatry*, XCIV (1937), 643–52.

and have simply lost forever the desire and the ability to give and to receive affection (as animals lose sucking or pecking reflexes that are not exercised soon enough after birth).

5. Another cause of reversal of the hierarchy is that when a need has been satisfied for a long time, this need may be underevaluated. People who have never experienced chronic hunger are apt to underestimate its effects and to look upon food as a rather unimportant thing. If they are dominated by a higher need, this higher need will seem to be the most important of all. It then becomes possible, and indeed does actually happen, that they may, for the sake of this higher need, put themselves into the position of being deprived in a more basic need. We may expect that after a long-time deprivation of the more basic need there will be a tendency to re-evaluate both needs so that the more prepotent need will actually become consciously prepotent for the individual who may have given it up very lightly. Thus, a man who has given up his job rather than lose his self-respect, and who then starves for six months or so, may be willing to take his job back even at the price of losing his self-respect.
6. Another partial explanation of *apparent* reversals is seen in the fact that we have been talking about the hierarchy of prepotency in terms of consciously felt wants or desires rather than of behavior. Looking at behavior itself may give us the wrong impression. What we have claimed is that the person will *want* the more basic of two needs when deprived in both. There is no necessary implication here that he will act upon his desires. Let us say again that there are many determinants of behavior other than needs and desires.
7. Perhaps more important than all these exceptions are the ones that involve ideals, high social standards, high values, and the like. With such values people become martyrs; they will give up everything for the sake of a particular ideal, or value. These people may be understood, at least in part, by reference to one basic concept (or hypothesis) which may be called "increased frustration-tolerance through early gratification." People who have been satisfied in their basic needs throughout their lives, particularly in their earlier years, seem to develop exceptional power to withstand present or future thwarting of these needs simply because they have strong, healthy character structure as a result of basic satisfaction. They are the "strong" people who can easily weather disagreement or opposition, who can swim against the stream of public opinion, and who can stand up for the truth at great personal cost. It is just the ones who have loved and been well loved and who have had many deep friendships who can hold out against hatred, rejection or persecution.

I say all this in spite of the fact that there is a certain amount of sheer habituation which is also involved in any full discussion of frustration tolerance. For instance, it is likely that those persons who have been accustomed to relative starvation for a long time are partially enabled thereby to withstand food deprivation. What sort of balance must be made between these two tendencies, of habituation on the one hand, and of past satisfaction breeding present frustration tolerance on the other hand, remains to be worked out by further research. Meanwhile we may assume that they are both operative, side by side, since they do not contradict each other. In respect to this phenomenon of increased frustration tolerance, it seems probable that the most important gratifications come in the first two years of life. That is to say, people who have been made secure and strong in the earliest years tend to remain secure and strong thereafter in the face of whatever threatens.

Degrees of Relative Satisfaction

So far, our theoretical discussion may have given the impression that these five sets of needs are somehow in a stepwise, all-or-none relationship to one another. We have spoken in such terms as the following: "If one need is satisfied, then another emerges." This statement might give the false impression that a need must be satisfied 100 per cent before the next need emerges. In actual fact, most members of our society who are normal are partially satisfied in all their basic needs and partially unsatisfied in all their basic needs at the same time. A more realistic description of the hierarchy would be in terms of decreasing percentages of satisfaction as we go up the hierarchy of prepotency. For instance, if I may assign arbitrary figures for the sake of illustration, it is as if the average citizen is satisfied perhaps 85 per cent in his physiological needs, 70 per cent in his safety needs, 50 per cent in his love needs, 40 per cent in his self-esteem needs, and 10 per cent in his self-actualization needs.

As for the concept of emergence of a new need after satisfaction of the prepotent need, this emergence is not a sudden, saltatory phenomenon but rather a gradual emergence by slow degrees from nothingness. For instance, if prepotent need A is satisfied only 10 per cent then need B may not be visible at all. However, as this need A becomes satisfied 25 per cent, need B may emerge 5 per cent; as need A becomes satisfied 75 per cent, need B may emerge 90 per cent; and so on.

Unconscious Character of Needs

These needs are neither necessarily conscious nor unconscious. On the whole, however, in the average person, they are more often unconscious. It is not necessary at this point to overhaul the tremendous mass of evidence which indicates the crucial importance of unconscious motivation. It would by now be expected, on a priori grounds alone, that unconscious motivations would on the whole be rather more important than the conscious motivations. What we have called the basic needs are very often largely unconscious although they may, with suitable techniques and with sophisticated people, become conscious.

The Role of Gratified Needs

It has been pointed out above several times that our higher needs usually emerge only when more prepotent needs have been gratified. Thus gratification has an important role in motivation theory. Apart from this, however, needs cease to play an active determining or organizing role as soon as they are gratified.

What this means, for example, is that a basically satisfied person no longer has the needs for esteem, love, safety, etc. The only sense in which he might be said to have them is in the almost metaphysical sense that a sated man has hunger or a filled bottle has emptiness. If we are interested in what *actually* motivates us and not in what has, will, or might motivate us, then a satisfied need is not a motivator. It must be considered for all practical purposes simply not to exist, to have disappeared. This point should be emphasized because it has been either overlooked or contradicted in every theory of motivation I know.[18] The perfectly healthy, normal, fortunate man has no sex needs or hunger needs, or needs for safety or for love or for prestige or for self-esteem, except in stray moments of quickly passing threat. If we were to say otherwise, we should also have to aver that every man had all the pathological reflexes, e.g., Babinski, etc., because if his nervous system were damaged, these would appear.

It is such considerations as these that suggest the bold postulation that a man who is thwarted in any of his basic needs may fairly be envisaged simply as a sick man. This is a fair parallel to our designation as "sick" of the man who lacks vitamins or minerals. Who is to say that a lack of love is less important than a lack of vitamins? Since we know the pathogenic effects of love starvation, who is to say that we are invoking value-questions in an unscientific or illegitimate way, any more than the physician does who diagnoses and treats pellagra or scurvy? If I were permitted this usage, I should then say simply that a healthy man is primarily motivated by his needs to develop and actualize his fullest potentialities and capacities. If a man has any other basic needs in any active, chronic sense, then he is simply an unhealthy man. He is as surely sick as if he had suddenly developed a strong salt-hunger or calcium hunger.[19]

If this statement seems unusual or paradoxical the reader may be assured that this is only one among many such paradoxes that will appear as we revise our ways of looking at man's deeper motivations. When we ask what man wants of life, we deal with his very essence.

Summary

1. There are at least five sets of goals which we may call basic needs. These are briefly physiological, safety, love, esteem, and self-actualization. In addition, we are motivated by the desire to achieve or maintain the various conditions upon which these basic satisfactions rest and by certain more intellectual desires.
2. These basic goals are related to one another, being arranged in a hierarchy of prepotency. This means that the most prepotent goal will monopolize consciousness and will tend of itself to organize the recruitment of the various capacities of the organism. The less prepotent needs are minimized, even forgotten or denied. But when a need is fairly well satisfied, the next prepotent ("higher") need emerges, in turn to dominate the conscious life and to serve as the center of organization of behavior, since gratified needs are not active motivators.

   Thus man is a perpetually wanting animal. Ordinarily the satisfaction of these wants is not altogether mutually exclusive but only tends to be. The average member of our society is most often partially satisfied and partially unsatisfied in all of his wants. The hierarchy principle is usually empirically observed in terms of increasing percentages of non-satisfaction as we go up the hierarchy. Reversals of the average order of the hierarchy are sometimes

[18] Note that acceptance of this theory necessitates basic revision of the Freudian theory.

[19] If we were to use the "sick" in this way, we should then also have to face squarely the relations of man to his society. One clear implication of our definition would be that (1) since a man is to be called sick who is basically thwarted, and (2) since such basic thwarting is made possible ultimately only by forces outside the individual, then (3) sickness in the individual must come ultimately from a sickness in the society. The "good" or healthy society would then be defined as one that permitted man's highest purposes to emerge by satisfying all his prepotent basic needs.

observed. Also it has been observed that an individual may permanently lose the higher wants in the hierarchy under special conditions. There are not only ordinarily multiple motivations for usual behavior but, in addition, many determinants other than motives.

3. Any thwarting or possibility of thwarting of these basic human goals, or danger to the defenses which protect them or to the conditions upon which they rest, is considered to be a psychological threat. With a few exceptions, all psychopathology may be partially traced to such threats. A basically thwarted man may actually be defined as a "sick" man.
4. It is such basic threats which bring about the general emergency reactions.
5. Certain other basic problems have not been dealt with because of limitations of space. Among these are (*a*) the problem of values in any definitive motivation theory, (*b*) the relation between appetites, desires, needs and what is "good" for the organism, (*c*) the etiology of the basic needs and their possible derivation in early childhood, (*d*) redefinition of motivational concepts, i.e., drive, desire, wish, need, goal, (*e*) implication of our theory for hedonistic theory, (*f*) the nature of the uncompleted act, of success and failure, and of aspiration-level, (*g*) the role of association, habit, and conditioning, (*h*) relation to the theory of interpersonal relations, (*i*) implications for psychotherapy, (*j*) implication for theory of society, (*k*) the theory of selfishness, (*l*) the relation between needs and cultural patterns, (*m*) the relation between this theory and Allport's theory of functional autonomy. These as well as certain other less important questions must be considered as motivation theory attempts to become definitive.

Social Behavior as Exchange

GEORGE C. HOMANS

The Problems of Small-Group Research

As I survey small-group research today, I feel that, apart from just keeping on with it, three sorts of things need to be done. The first is to show the relation between the results of experimental work done under laboratory conditions and the results of *quasi-* anthropological field research on what those of us who do it are pleased to call "real-life" groups in industry and elsewhere. If the experimental work has anything to do with real life—and I am persuaded that it has everything to do—its propositions cannot be inconsistent with those discovered through the field work. But the consistency has not yet been demonstrated in any systematic way.

The second job is to pull together in some set of general propositions the actual results, from the laboratory and from the field, of work on small

Reprinted from *American Journal of Sociology,* Vol. 62 (May 1958), pp. 597–606, by permission of groups—propositions that at least sum up, to an approximation, what happens in elementary social behavior, even though we may not be able to explain why the propositions should take the form they do. A great amount of work has been done, and more appears every day, but what it all amounts to in the shape of a set of propositions from which, under specified conditions, many of the observational results might be derived, is not at all clear—and yet to state such a set is the first aim of science.

The third job is to begin to show how the propositions that empirically hold good in small groups may be derived from some set of still more general propositions. "Still more general" means only that empirical propositions other than ours may also be derived from the set. This derivation would constitute the explanatory stage in the science of elementary social behavior, for explanation *is* derivation.[1] (I myself suspect that the more general set will turn out to contain the propositions of behavioral psychology. I hold myself to be an "ultimate psychological reductionist," but I cannot know that I am right so long as the reduction has not been carried out.)

I have come to think that all three of these jobs would be furthered by our adopting the view that interaction between persons is an exchange of goods, material and non-material. This is one of the oldest theories of social behavior, and one that we still use every day to interpret our own behavior, as when we say, "I found so-and-so rewarding"; or "I got a great deal out of him"; or, even, "Talking with him took a great deal out of me." But, perhaps just because it is so obvious, this view has been much neglected by social scientists. So far as I know, the only theoretical work that makes explicit use of it is Marcel Mauss's *Essai sur le don,* published in 1925, which is ancient as social science goes.[2] It may be that the tradition of neglect is now changing and that, for instance, the psychologists who interpret behavior in terms of transactions may be coming back to something of the sort I have in mind.[3]

An incidental advantage of an exchange theory is that it might bring sociology closer to economics—that science of man most advanced, most capable of application, and, intellectually, most isolated. Economics studies exchange carried out under special circumstances and with a most useful built-in numerical measure of value. What are the laws of the general phenomenon of which economic behavior is one class?

In what follows I shall suggest some reasons for the usefulness of a theory of social behavior as exchange and suggest the nature of the propositions such a theory might contain.

An Exchange Paradigm

I start with the link to behavioral psychology and the kind of statement it makes about the behavior of an experimental animal such as the pigeon.[4] As a pigeon explores its cage in the laboratory, it happens to peck a target, whereupon the psychologist feeds it corn. The evidence is that it will peck the target

[1] See R. B. Braithwaite, *Scientific Explanation* (Cambridge: Cambridge University Press, 1953).
[2] Translated by I. Cunnison as *The Gift* (Glencoe, Ill.: Free Press, 1954).
[3] In social anthropology D. L. Oliver is working along these lines, and I owe much to him. See also T. M. Newcomb, "The Prediction of Interpersonal Attraction," *American Psychologist,* XI (1956), 575–86.
[4] B. F. Skinner, *Science and Human Behavior* (New York: Macmillan Co., 1953).

again; it has learned the behavior, or, as my friend Skinner says, the behavior has been reinforced, and the pigeon has undergone *operant conditioning.* This kind of psychologist is not interested in how the behavior was learned: "learning theory" is a poor name for his field. Instead, he is interested in what determines changes in the rate of emission of learned behavior, whether pecks at a target or something else.

The more hungry the pigeon, the less corn or other food it has gotten in the recent past, the more often it will peck. By the same token, if the behavior is often reinforced, if the pigeon is given much corn every time it pecks, the rate of emission will fall off as the pigeon gets *satiated.* If, on the other hand, the behavior is not reinforced at all, then, too, its rate of emission will tend to fall off, though a long time may pass before it stops altogether, before it is *extinguished.* In the emission of many kinds of behavior the pigeon incurs *aversive stimulation,* or what I shall call "cost" for short, and this, too, will lead in time to a decrease in the emission rate. Fatigue is an example of a "cost." Extinction, satiation, and cost, by decreasing the rate of emission of a particular kind of behavior, render more probable the emission of some other kind of behavior, including doing nothing. I shall only add that even a hard-boiled psychologist puts "emotional" behavior, as well as such things as pecking, among the unconditioned responses that may be reinforced in operant conditioning. As a statement of the propositions of behavioral psychology, the foregoing is, of course, inadequate for any purpose except my present one.

We may look on the pigeon as engaged in an exchange—pecks for corn—with the psychologist, but let us not dwell upon that, for the behavior of the pigeon hardly determines the behavior of the psychologist at all. Let us turn to a situation where the exchange is real, that is, where the determination is mutual. Suppose we are dealing with two men. Each is emitting behavior reinforced to some degree by the behavior of the other. How it was in the past that each learned the behavior he emits and how he learned to find the other's behavior reinforcing we are not concerned with. It is enough that each does find the other's behavior reinforcing, and I shall call the reinforcers—the equivalent of the pigeon's corn—*values,* for this, I think, is what we mean by this term. As he emits behavior, each man may incur costs, and each man has more than one course of behavior open to him.

This seems to me the paradigm of elementary social behavior, and the problem of the elementary sociologist is to state propositions relating the variations in the values and costs of each man to his frequency distribution of behavior among alternatives, where the values (in the mathematical sense) taken by these variable for one man determine in part their values for the other.[5]

I see no reason to believe that the propositions of behavioral psychology do not apply to this situation, though the complexity of their implications in the concrete case may be great indeed. In particular, we must suppose that, with men as with pigeons, an increase in extinction, satiation, or aversive stimulation of any one kind of behavior will increase the probability of emission of some other kind. The problem is not, as it is often stated, merely, what a man's values

[5] *Ibid.,* pp. 297–329. The discussion of "double contingency" by T. Parsons and E. A. Shils could easily lead to a similar paradigm (see *Toward a General Theory of Action* [Cambridge, Mass.: Harvard University Press, 1951], pp. 14–16).

are, what he has learned in the past to find reinforcing, but how much of any one value his behavior is getting him now. The more he gets, the less valuable any further unit of that value is to him, and the less often he will emit behavior reinforced by it.

The Influence Process

We do not, I think, possess the kind of studies of two-person interaction that would either bear out these propositions or fail to do so. But we do have studies of larger numbers of persons that suggest that they may apply, notably the studies by Festinger, Schachter, Back, and their associates on the dynamics of influence. One of the variables they work with they call *cohesiveness,* defined as anything that attracts people to take part in a group. Cohesiveness is a value variable; it refers to the degree of reinforcement people find in the activities of the group. Festinger and his colleagues consider two kinds of reinforcing activity: the symbolic behavior we call "social approval" (sentiment) and activity valuable in other ways, such as doing something interesting.

The other variable they work with they call *communication* and others call *interaction.* This is a frequency variable; it is a measure of the frequency of emission of valuable and costly verbal behavior. We must bear in mind that, in general, the one kind of variable is a function of the other.

Festinger and his co-workers show that the more cohesive a group is, that is, the more valuable the sentiment or activity the members exchange with one another, the greater the average frequency of interaction of the members.[6] With men, as with pigeons, the greater the reinforcement, the more often is the reinforced behavior emitted. The more cohesive a group, too, the greater the change that members can produce in the behavior of other members in the direction of rendering these activities more valuable.[7] That is, the more valuable the activities that members get, the more valuable those that they must give. For if a person is emitting behavior of a certain kind, and other people do not find it particularly rewarding, these others will suffer their own production of sentiment and activity, in time, to fall off. But perhaps the first person has found their sentiment and activity rewarding, and, if he is to keep on getting them, he must make his own behavior more valuable to the others. In short, the propositions of behavioral psychology imply a tendency toward a certain proportionality between the value to others of the behavior a man gives them and the value to him of the behavior they give him.[8]

Schachter also studied the behavior of members of a group toward two kinds of other members, "conformers" and "deviates."[9] I assume that conformers are people whose activity the other members find valuable. For conformity is behavior that coincides to a degree with some group standard or norm, and the only meaning I can assign to *norm* is "a verbal description of behavior that many members find it valuable for the actual behavior of themselves and others to

---

[6] K. W. Back, "The Exertion of Influence through Social Communication," in L. Festinger, K. Back, S. Schachter, H. H. Kelley, and J. Thibaut (eds.), *Theory and Experiment in Social Communication* (Ann Arbor: Research Center for Dynamics, University of Michigan, 1950), pp. 21–36.

[7] S. Schachter, N. Ellertson, D. McBride, and D. Gregory, "An Experimental Study of Cohesiveness and Productivity," *Human Relations,* IV (1951), 229–38.

[8] Skinner, *op. cit.,* p. 100.

[9] S. Schachter, "Deviation, Rejection, and Communication," *Journal of Abnormal and Social Psychology,* XLVI (1951), 190–207.

conform to." By the same token, a deviate is a member whose behavior is not particularly valuable. Now Schachter shows that, as the members of a group come to see another member as a deviate, their interaction with him—communication addressed to getting him to change his behavior—goes up, the faster the more cohesive the group. The members need not talk to the other conformers so much; they are relatively satiated by the conformers' behavior: they have gotten what they want out of them. But if the deviate, by failing to change his behavior, fails to reinforce the members, they start to withhold social approval from him: the deviate gets low sociometric choice at the end of the experiment. And in the most cohesive groups—those Schachter calls "high cohesive-relevant"—interaction with the deviate also falls off in the end and is lowest among those members that rejected him most strongly, as if they had given him up as a bad job. But how plonking can we get? These findings are utterly in line with everyday experience.

Practical Equilibrium

At the beginning of this paper I suggested that one of the tasks of small-group research was to show the relation between the results of experimental work done under laboratory conditions and the results of field research on real-life small groups. Now the latter often appear to be in practical equilibrium, and by this I mean nothing fancy. I do not mean that all real-life groups are in equilibrium. I certainly do not mean that all groups must tend to equilibrium. I do not mean that groups have built-in antidotes to change: there is no homeostasis here. I do not mean that we assume equilibrium. I mean only that we sometimes *observe* it, that for the time we are with a group—and it is often short—there is no great change in the values of the variables we choose to measure. If, for instance, person A is interacting with B more than with C both at the beginning and at the end of the study, then at least by this crude measure the group is in equilibrium.

Many of the Festinger-Schachter studies are experimental, and their propositions about the process of influence seem to me to imply the kind of proposition that empirically holds good of real-life groups in practical equilibrium. For instance, Festinger *et al.* find that, the more cohesive a group is, the greater the change that members can produce in the behavior of other members. If the influence is exerted in the direction of conformity to group norms, then, when the process of influence has accomplished all the change of which it is capable, the proposition should hold good that, the more cohesive a group is, the larger the number of members that conform to its norms. And it does hold good.[10]

Again, Schachter found, in the experiment I summarized above, that in the most cohesive groups and at the end, when the effort to influence the deviate had failed, members interacted little with the deviate and gave him little in the way of sociometric choice. Now two of the propositions that hold good most often of real-life groups in practical equilibrium are precisely that the more closely a member's activity conforms to the norms the more interaction he receives from

[10] L. Festinger, S. Schachter, and K. Back, *Social Pressures in Informal Groups* (New York: Harper & Bros., 1950), pp. 72–100.

other members and the more liking choices he gets from them too. From these main propositions a number of others may be derived that also hold good.[11]

Yet we must ever remember that the truth of the proposition linking conformity to liking may on occasion be masked by the truth of other propositions. If, for instance, the man that conforms to the norms most closely also exerts some authority over the group, this may render liking for him somewhat less than it might otherwise have been.[12]

Be that as it may, I suggest that the laboratory experiments on influence imply propositions about the behavior of members of small groups, when the process of influence has worked itself out, that are identical with propositions that hold good of real-life groups in equilibrium. This is hardly surprising if all we mean by equilibrium is that all the change of which the system is, under present conditions, capable has been effected, so that no further change occurs. Nor would this be the first time that statics has turned out to be a special case of dynamics.

Profit and Social Control

Though I have treated equilibrium as an observed fact, it is a fact that cries for explanation. I shall not, as structural-functional sociologists do, use an assumed equilibrium as a means of explaining, or trying to explain, why the other features of a social system should be what they are. Rather, I shall take practical equilibrium as something that is itself to be explained by the other features of the system.

If every member of a group emits at the end of, and during, a period of time much the same kinds of behavior and in much the same frequencies as he did at the beginning, the group is for that period in equilibrium. Let us then ask why any one member's behavior should persist. Suppose he is emitting behavior of value A_1. Why does he not let his behavior get worse (less valuable or reinforcing to the others) until it stands at $A_1 - \Delta A$? True, the sentiments expressed by others toward him are apt to decline in value (become less reinforcing to him), so that what he gets from them may be S_1-ΔS. But it is conceivable that, since most activity carries cost, a decline in the value of what he emits will mean a reduction in cost to him that more than offsets his losses in sentiment. Where, then, does he stabilize his behavior? This is the problem of social control.[13]

Mankind has always assumed that a person stabilizes his behavior, at least in the short run, at the point where he is doing the best he can for himself under the circumstances, though his best may not be a "rational" best, and what he can do may not be at all easy to specify, except that he is not apt to think like one of the theoretical antagonists in the *Theory of Games.* Before a sociologist rejects this answer out of hand for its horrid profit-seeking implications, he will do well to ask himself if he can offer any other answer to the question posed.

[11] For propositions holding good of groups in practical equilibrium see G. C. Homans, *The Human Group* (New York: Harcourt, Brace & Co., 1950), and H. W. Riecken and G. C. Homans, "Psychological Aspects of Social Structure," in G. Lindzey (ed.), *Handbook of Social Psychology* (Cambridge, Mass.: Addison-Wesley Publishing Co., 1954), II, 786–832.

[12] See Homans, *op. cit.,* pp. 244–48, and R. F. Bales, "The Equilibrium Problem in Small Groups," in A. P. Hare, E. F. Borgatta, and R. F. Bales (eds.), *Small Groups* (New York: A. A. Knopf, 1953), pp. 450–56.

[13] Homans, *op. cit.,* pp. 281–301.

I think he will find that he cannot. Yet experiments designed to test the truth of the answer are extraordinarily rare.

I shall review one that seems to me to provide a little support for the theory, though it was not meant to do so. The experiment is reported by H. B. Gerard, a member of the Festinger-Schachter team, under the title "The Anchorage of Opinions in Face-to-Face Groups."[14] The experimenter formed artificial groups whose members met to discuss a case in industrial relations and to express their opinions about its probable outcome. The groups were of two kinds: high-attraction groups, whose members were told that they would like one another very much, and low-attraction groups, whose members were told that they would not find one another particularly likable.

At a later time the experimenter called the members in separately, asked them again to express their opinions on the outcome of the case, and counted the number that had changed their opinions to bring them into accord with those of other members of their groups. At the same time, a paid participant entered into a further discussion of the case with each member, always taking, on the probable outcome of the case, a position opposed to that taken by the bulk of the other members of the group to which the person belonged. The experimenter counted the number of persons shifting toward the opinion of the paid participant.

The experiment had many interesting results, from which I choose only those summed up in Tables 1 and 2. The three different agreement classes are made up of people who, at the original sessions, expressed different degrees of agreement with the opinions of other members of their groups. And the figure 44, for instance, means that, of all members of high-attraction groups whose initial opinions were strongly in disagreement with those of other members, 44 per cent shifted their opinion later toward that of others.

TABLE 1. Percentage of Subjects Changing Toward Someone in the Group

	Agreement	Mild Disagreement	Strong Disagreement
High attraction	0	12	44
Low attraction	0	15	9

TABLE 2. Percentage of Subjects Changing Toward the Paid Participant

	Agreement	Mild Disagreement	Strong Disagreement
High attraction	7	13	25
Low attraction	20	38	8

In these results the experimenter seems to have been interested only in the differences in the sums of the rows, which show that there is more shifting toward the group, and less shifting toward the paid participant, in the high-attraction than in the low-attraction condition. This is in line with a proposition

[14] *Human Relations,* VII (1954), 313–25.

suggested earlier. If you think that the members of a group can give you much—in this case, liking—you are apt to give them much—in this case, a change to an opinion in accordance with their views—or you will not get the liking. And, by the same token, if the group can give you little of value, you will not be ready to give it much of value. Indeed, you may change your opinion so as to depart from agreement even further, to move, that is, toward the view held by the paid participant.

So far so good, but, when I first scanned these tables, I was less struck by the difference between them than by their similarity. The same classes of people in both tables showed much the same relative propensities to change their opinions, no matter whether the change was toward the group or toward the paid participant. We see, for instance, that those who change least are the high-attraction, agreement people and the low-attraction, strong-disagreement ones. And those who change most are the high-attraction, strong-disagreement people and the low-attraction, mild-disagreement ones.

How am I to interpret these particular results? Since the experimenter did not discuss them, I am free to offer my own explanation. The behavior emitted by the subjects is opinion and changes in opinion. For this behavior they have learned to expect two possible kinds of reinforcement. Agreement with the group gets the subject favorable sentiment (acceptance) from it, and the experiment was designed to give this reinforcement a higher value in the high-attraction condition than in the low-attraction one. The second kind of possible reinforcement is what I shall call the "maintenance of one's personal integrity," which a subject gets by sticking to his own opinion in the face of disagreement with the group. The experimenter does not mention this reward, but I cannot make sense of the results without something much like it. In different degrees for different subjects, depending on their initial positions, these rewards are in competition with one another: they are alternatives. They are not absolutely scarce goods, but some persons cannot get both at once.

Since the rewards are alternatives, let me introduce a familiar assumption from economics—that the cost of a particular course of action is the equivalent of the foregone value of an alternative[15]—and then add the definition: Profit = Reward − Cost.

Now consider the persons in the corresponding cells of the two tables. The behavior of the high-attraction, agreement people gets them much in the way of acceptance by the group, and for it they must give up little in the way of personal integrity, for their views are from the start in accord with those of the group. Their profit is high, and they are not prone to change their behavior. The low-attraction, strong-disagreement people are getting much in integrity, and they are not giving up for it much in valuable acceptance, for they are members of low-attraction groups. Reward less cost is high for them, too, and they change little. The high-attraction, strong-disagreement people are getting much in the way of integrity, but their costs in doing so are high, too, for they are in high-attraction groups and thus foregoing much valuable acceptance by the group. Their profit is low, and they are very apt to change, either toward the group or toward the paid participant, from whom they think, perhaps, they will get some acceptance while maintaining some integrity. The low-attraction,

[15] G. J. Stigler, *The Theory of Price* (rev. ed.; New York: Macmillan Co., 1952), p. 99.

mild-disagreement people do not get much in the way of integrity, for they are only in mild disagreement with the group, but neither are they giving up much in acceptance, for they are members of low-attraction groups. Their rewards are low; their costs are low too, and their profit—the difference between the two—is also low. In their low profit they resemble the high-attraction, strong-disagreement people, and, like them, they are prone to change their opinions, in this case, more toward the paid participant. The subjects in the other two cells, who have medium profits, display medium propensities to change.

If we define profit as reward less cost, and if cost is value foregone, I suggest that we have here some evidence for the proposition that change in behavior is greatest when perceived profit is least. This constitutes no direct demonstration that change in behavior is least when profit is greatest, but if, whenever a man's behavior brought him a balance of reward and cost, he changed his behavior away from what got him, under the circumstances, the less profit, there might well come a time when his behavior would not change further. That is, his behavior would be stabilized, at least for the time being. And, so far as this were true for every member of a group, the group would have a social organization in equilibrium.

I do not say that a member would stabilize his behavior at the point of greatest conceivable profit to himself, because his profit is partly at the mercy of the behavior of others. It is a commonplace that the short-run pursuit of profit by several persons often lands them in positions where all are worse off than they might conceivably be. I do not say that the paths of behavioral change in which a member pursues his profit under the condition that others are pursuing theirs too are easy to describe or predict; and we can readily conceive that in jockeying for position they might never arrive at any equilibrium at all.

Distributive Justice

Yet practical equilibrium is often observed, and thus some further condition may make its attainment, under some circumstance, more probable than would the individual pursuit of profit left to itself. I can offer evidence for this further condition only in the behavior of subgroups and not in that of individuals. Suppose that there are two subgroups, working close together in a factory, the job of one being somewhat different from that of the other. And suppose that the members of the first complain and say: "We are getting the same pay as they are. We ought to get just a couple of dollars a week more to show that our work is more responsible." When you ask them what they mean by "more responsible," they say that, if they do their work wrong, more damage can result, and so they are under more pressure to take care.[16] Something like this is a common feature of industrial behavior. It is at the heart of disputes not over absolute wages but over wage differentials—indeed, at the heart of disputes over rewards other than wages.

In what kind of proposition may we express observations like these? We may say that wages and responsibility give status in the group, in the sense that a man who takes high responsibility and gets high wages is admired, other things equal. Then, if the members of one group score higher on responsibility than do the members of another, there is a felt need on the part of the first to score

[16] G. C. Homans, "Status among Clerical Workers," *Human Organization,* XII (1953), 5–10.

higher on pay too. There is a pressure, which shows itself in complaints, to bring the *status factors,* as I have called them, into line with one another. If they are in line, a condition of *status congruence* is said to exist. In this condition the workers may find their jobs dull or irksome, but they will not complain about the relative position of groups.

But there may be a more illuminating way of looking at the matter. In my example I have considered only responsibility and pay, but these may be enough, for they represent the two kinds of thing that come into the problem. Pay is clearly a reward; responsibility may be looked on, less clearly, as a cost. It means constraint and worry—or peace of mind foregone. Then the proposition about status congruence becomes this: If the costs of the members of one group are higher than those of another, distributive justice requires that their rewards should be higher too. But the thing works both ways: If the rewards are higher, the costs should be higher too. This last is the theory of *noblesse oblige,* which we all subscribe to, though we all laugh at it, perhaps because the *noblesse* often fails to *oblige.* To put the matter in terms of profit: though the rewards and costs of two persons or the members of two groups may be different, yet the profits of the two—the excess of reward over cost—should tend to equality. And more than "should." The less-advantaged group will at least try to attain greater equality, as, in the example I have used, the first group tried to increase its profit by increasing its pay.

I have talked of distributive justice. Clearly, this is not the only condition determining the actual distribution of rewards and costs. At the same time, never tell me that notions of justice are not a strong influence on behavior, though we sociologists often neglect them. Distributive justice may be one of the conditions of group equilibrium.

Exchange and Social Structure

I shall end by reviewing almost the only study I am aware of that begins to show in detail how a stable and differentiated social structure in a real-life group might arise out of a process of exchange between members. This is Peter Blau's description of the behavior of sixteen agents in a federal law-enforcement agency.[17]

The agents had the duty of investigating firms and preparing reports on the firms' compliance with the law. Since the reports might lead to legal action against the firms, the agents had to prepare them carefully, in the proper form, and take strict account of the many regulations that might apply. The agents were often in doubt what they should do, and then they were supposed to take the question to their supervisor. This they were reluctant to do, for they naturally believed that thus confessing to him their inability to solve a problem would reflect on their competence, affect the official ratings he made of their work, and so hurt their chances for promotion. So agents often asked other agents for help and advice, and, though this was nominally forbidden, the supervisor usually let it pass.

Blau ascertained the ratings the supervisor made of the agents, and he also asked the agents to rate one another. The two opinions agreed closely. Fewer agents were regarded as highly competent than were regarded as of middle or

[17] Peter M. Blau, *The Dynamics of Bureaucracy* (Chicago: University of Chicago Press, 1955), 99–116.

low competence; competence, or the ability to solve technical problems, was a fairly scarce good. One or two of the more competent agents would not give help and advice when asked, and so received few interactions and little liking. A man that will not exchange, that will not give you what he has when you need it, will not get from you the only thing you are, in this case, able to give him in return, your regard.

But most of the more competent agents were willing to give help, and of them Blau says:

> A consultation can be considered an exchange of values: both participants gain something, and both have to pay a price. The questioning agent is enabled to perform better than he could otherwise have done, without exposing his difficulties to his supervisor. By asking for advice, he implicitly pays his respect to the superior proficiency of his colleague. This acknowledgment of inferiority is the cost of receiving assistance. The consultant gains prestige, in return for which he is willing to devote some time to the consultation and permit it to disrupt his own work. The following remark of an agent illustrates this: "I like giving advice. It's flattering, I suppose, if you feel that others come to you for advice."[18]

Blau goes on to say: "All agents liked being consulted, but the value of any one of very many consultations became deflated for experts, and the price they paid in frequent interruptions became inflated."[19] This implies that, the more prestige an agent received, the less was the increment of value of that prestige; the more advice an agent gave, the greater was the increment of cost of that advice, the cost lying precisely in the foregone value of time to do his own work. Blau suggests that something of the same sort was true of an agent who went to a more competent colleague for advice: the more often he went, the more costly to him, in feelings of inferiority, became any further request. "The repeated admission of his inability to solve his own problems . . . undermined the self-confidence of the worker and his standing in the group."[20]

The result was that the less competent agents went to the more competent ones for help less often than they might have done if the costs of repeated admissions of inferiority had been less high and that, while many agents sought out the few highly competent ones, no single agent sought out the latter much. Had they done so (to look at the exchange from the other side), the costs to the highly competent in interruptions to their own work would have become exorbitant. Yet the need of the less competent for help was still not fully satisfied. Under these circumstances they tended to turn for help to agents more nearly like themselves in competence. Though the help they got was not the most valuable, it was of a kind they could themselves return on occasion. With such agents they could exchange help and liking, without the exchange becoming on either side too great a confession of inferiority.

The highly competent agents tended to enter into exchanges, that is, to interact with many others. But, in the more equal exchanges I have just spoken of, less competent agents tended to pair off as partners. That is, they interacted with a smaller number of people, but interacted often with these few. I think

[18] *Ibid.*, p. 108.
[19] *Ibid.*, p. 108.
[20] *Ibid.*, p. 109.

I could show why pair relations in these more equal exchanges would be more economical for an agent than a wider distribution of favors. But perhaps I have gone far enough. The final pattern of this social structure was one in which a small number of highly competent agents exchanged advice for prestige with a large number of others less competent and in which the less competent agents exchanged, in pairs and in trios, both help and liking on more nearly equal terms.

Blau shows, then, that a social structure in equilibrium might be the result of a process of exchanging behavior rewarding and costly in different degrees, in which the increment of reward and cost varied with the frequency of the behavior, that is, with the frequency of interaction. Note that the behavior of the agents seems also to have satisfied my second condition of equilibrium: the more competent agents took more responsibility for the work, either their own or others', than did the less competent ones, but they also got more for it in the way of prestige. I suspect that the same kind of explanation could be given for the structure of many "informal" groups.

Summary

The current job of theory in small-group research is to make the connection between experimental and real-life studies, to consolidate the propositions that empirically hold good in the two fields, and to show how these propositions might be derived from a still more general set. One way of doing this job would be to revive and make more rigorous the oldest of theories of social behavior—social behavior as exchange.

Some of the statements of such a theory might be the following. Social behavior is an exchange of goods, material goods but also non-material ones, such as the symbols of approval or prestige. Persons that give much to others try to get much from them, and persons that get much from others are under pressure to give much to them. This process of influence tends to work out at equilibrium to a balance in the exchanges. For a person engaged in exchange, what he gives may be a cost to him, just as what he gets may be a reward, and his behavior changes less as profit, that is, reward less cost, tends to a maximum. Not only does he seek a maximum for himself, but he tries to see to it that no one in his group makes more profit than he does. The cost and the value of what he gives and of what he gets vary with the quantity of what he gives and gets. It is surprising how familiar these propositions are; it is surprising, too, how propositions about the dynamics of exchange can begin to generate the static thing we call "group structure" and, in so doing, generate also some of the propositions about group structure that students of real-life groups have stated.

In our unguarded moments we sociologists find words like "reward" and "cost" slipping into what we say. Human nature will break in upon even our most elaborate theories. But we seldom let it have its way with us and follow up systematically what these words imply.[21] Of all our many "approaches" to social behavior, the one that sees it as an economy is the most neglected, and yet it is the one we use every moment of our lives—except when we write sociology.

[21] *The White-Collar Job* (Ann Arbor: Survey Research Center, University of Michigan, 1953), pp. 115–27.

An Interaction Approach to The Theory of Organization

WILLIAM FOOTE WHYTE

My purpose in this article is (1) to present a general model for the analysis of human relations in organizations, and (2) to examine some specific applications of this model. At this point, I am not attempting to prove anything. The cases will simply be illustrative of what seem to me the possibilities of the model. The model itself is crude at this stage. I hope to be able to refine it in later writings.[1]

The Model

The theoretical model is shown in Figure 1. I shall begin with three concepts: interaction, activities, and sentiments, which I take to be mutually dependent, each upon the other two, and any one of which may be modified by forces in the environment. I shall deal with these aspects of the environment: social and cultural, technical and physical, legal, and economic.

The three social system concepts I define in this way: *Interaction* refers to interpersonal contacts. We can observe and even measure how often *A* interacts with *B* and how long each interaction lasts. We can also note whether *A* or *B* initiated the interaction and, for a given time period, what proportion of the interactions between them were initiated by *A* and what proportion by *B*. We can do this for pair events (involving just two individuals) or, to use the terminology of Chapple and Arensberg (1940), set events involving three or more individuals. We can also seek to determine whether, in their interaction, *A* has initiated a change in activity for *B*, although here we run into some methodological and theoretical problems that I shall discuss later.

By *activities,* I mean the things that people do, i.e., the physical acts they perform. Activities can be observed and, in some cases, we can find indices for their measurement. For example, the work that employees in a factory perform is one type of activity, and the indices in this case are the production figures of the individual or the group in question.

By *sentiments,* I refer to the way individuals feel about the world around them. Sentiments have three elements.[2]

1. An idea about something or somebody, i.e., a cognitive element.
2. Emotional content or affect.
3. A tendency to recur, upon presentation of the same symbols that have been associated with the sentiment in the past.

Abridged from "An Interaction Approach to the Theory of Organization," in *Modern Organization Theory,* ed. Mason Haire. John Wiley & Sons, Inc. (1959), pp. 155–183. Reprinted by permission of the author.

[1] Many of these ideas presented here are developed more fully in my *Man and Organization: Three Problems in Human Relations in Industry* (1959).

[2] For this definition, I am indebted to Alexander H. Leighton.

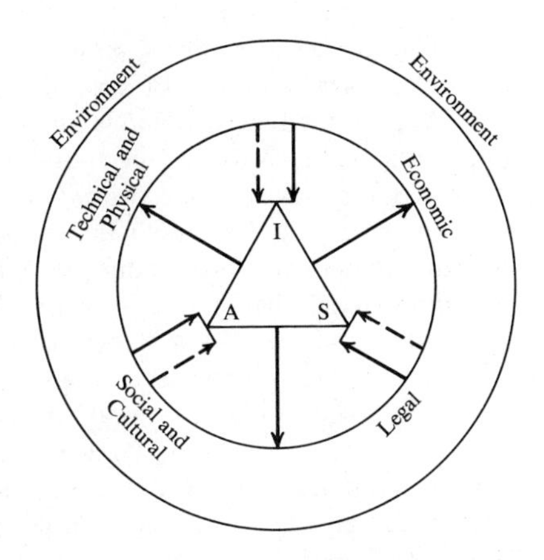

Figure 1. The diagram represents *I* (Interaction), *A* (Activity), *S* (Sentiments) in mutual dependence with each other and in relation to the forces of the environment. Environmental forces may have an impact upon the social system of any of the three points. The impact may come directly (solid line) or symbolically (dotted line). The outwardly pointing arrows indicate that the social system has impact upon the environment.

As the definition suggests, I am not concerned with momentary or fleeting reactions. Probably we shall only be able to deal systematically with those personal reactions which manifest some stability.

By mutual dependence, I mean that a change can be introduced into the interaction-activity-sentiment system at any of the three points, and such a change will effect changes in the other two. I assume that in an organization interactions are not a random matter, but that they tend to develop a regular pattern. A change in this pattern of interaction can be expected to lead to changes in activities and sentiments. Similarly, activities in an organization tend to take a patterned form, and changes introduced into this pattern tend to be accompanied by changes in interactions and in sentiments. As the sentiments individuals have toward each other, toward the organization, and toward their work undergo changes, we can expect to see changes in interactions and activities.

This is not a self-contained system. For a work group whose behavior we are trying to analyze, changes can be introduced through the forces affecting this group in the environment. The impact can come directly or symbolically. For example, changes in the technical and physical environment, such as new machines and a new organization of the work-flow, will have a direct effect upon the activities and interactions of the workers involved. On the other hand, the establishment of a new incentive rate for this work group or for a neighboring group will not have a direct physical impact upon the group but will have its impact through symbolic channels, as will be discussed later. . . .

The Impact of the Environment

I shall illustrate here the impact of technical and physical forces upon the social system. Examples of the impact of economic and legal forces will appear later in the discussion of *Patterns of Sentiments.* Examples illustrating the impact of social and cultural forces have been described in some detail elsewhere.[3]

I take the technical and physical forces to include the formal organization structure,[4] the technology, the work-flow, the layout of machines or processes, the allocation of tasks, and the physical conditions and requirements of work.

[3] *Man and Organization.* See Acknowledgment, footnote 1.
[4] For illustrations of this impact, see *Man and Organization.*

The impact of some of these forces of the environment upon the social system can best be shown by several examples.

As examined by Charles Walker, Robert Guest, and Arthur Turner (Walker and Guest, 1952; Walker, Guest, and Turner, 1956), the automotive assembly line has some clear-cut and drastic effects upon the social system. In the first place, it restricts and channels interaction among the men. While he is on the line, the individual can only interact with the man immediately above and the man immediately below him in the work-flow, plus sometimes the man on the other side of the line. The activities of the worker are, of course, controlled within very narrow limits by the technology and the work-flow.

The technical and physical forces also have a marked effect upon the foreman's interaction with the men. Observation shows him to be moving constantly up and down the line, interacting with a large number of men but for exceedingly short periods of time—forty-five seconds, on the average, for line subordinates. It was observed also that interaction was initiated more often from workers to foreman than *vice versa,* as Peter Blau (1957) has suggested. The explanation of this ratio of interactions seemed to be that the control of the men was provided by the technical and physical forces, with little intervention from the foreman, while frequent minor technical difficulties which occurred on the line moved the workers to call on the foreman for action.

Systematic interaction measures have not been made for foreman-worker relations in other types of organizations. However, even casual observation of that relationship in, for example, a department of skilled maintenance men indicates that there the interactions are much less frequent but of a much longer duration.

Most human beings seem to find the assembly-line environment an exceedingly severe one. Usually the work is physically taxing and workers resent the routine nature of the job, the restraints upon physical freedom, and the lack of opportunities for interaction. This leads to negative sentiments toward the job, and this, in turn, seems to affect worker sentiments toward higher management and the company in general. The foreman, for whom they initiate more than he does for them, is not necessarily caught in this web of negative sentiments. He may be viewed as a good guy who is caught in the machine just as they are.

The impact of the technical and physical environment can be observed at any level of the organization. Consider this example of work-flow problems (Chapple and Sayles, 1958):

> In another manufacturing company, the general sales manager and the credit manager, who reported to the treasurer, were constantly at loggerheads. The sales manager complained to the general manager that the credit department was constantly interfering in the sales effort—refusing credit to old customers, writing letters at cross-purposes, and upsetting sales in general. The credit manager retorted that management had given him the responsibility for sound credit policies and that the sales department was violating them by trying to get orders passed through on poor risks. The battle became so intense that the general manager had just about decided to let at least one of the men go.
>
> After it was found that there were no major personality problems or temperamental reasons for the incompatibility, an analysis of the work-flow

situation tends to facilitate the formation of a cohesive work group which acts in a unified fashion in relation to management and the union. On the other hand, when the department in question is highly differentiated as to jobs, pay, and working conditions faced, the individual worker tends to find little resonance for expression of his sentiments on his problem, and the members of the department have difficulty in acting in concert.

This suggests one of the reasons why in the past we have had such difficulty in predicting behavior on the basis of a study of attitudes or sentiments.

We have known that what the individual will do depends upon what his associates feel and want to do, but we have had no systematic way of dealing with this phenomenon. For organizational studies, Sayles is pointing out how we may look at behavior in terms of a structure of sentiments as well as the structure of interactions and activities.

Patterns of Interaction

As is to be expected, theorists who have built their scheme of analysis around the concept of interaction have given primary attention to the impact of interaction upon sentiments and activities. We have been concerned with two general questions: (1) What pattern of interaction tends to be associated with what pattern of sentiments and activities? (2) How can we effect changes in sentiments and activities by introducing changes in interaction?

In seeking to answer these questions, we have not been concerned solely with the frequency, duration, and initiation of interpersonal contacts. Within these interpersonal contacts, we have also been seeking to develop rough measures of the frequencies of attempts, through interaction, to introduce changes in the activities of other people. We have given our attention here to two fields of study: relations up and down the hierarchy of the organization; and relations between management and the union.

It is one of the best-substantiated propositions in supervisor-subordinate relations that the sentiments between the two depend in an important part upon the ratio of initiations of activity-change from one to the other. This does not mean that favorable sentiments from subordinates to superior depend upon an approximate balance in the initiations between them. What the appropriate ratios are must depend, to some extent, upon the impact of environmental forces, as we have seen in the assembly-line case. Clearly, our formulations here are exceedingly crude. However, we seem to be able to make valid discriminations as we look at extreme cases. Whenever we see a high frequency of initiation down the line and little or no initiation upward, we always find workers expressing dissatisfaction with their superiors—and generally with other aspects of the work situation also. If we find, on the contrary, the subordinates are initiating upward for a significant portion of the time, then we tend to find quite different sentiments expressed toward the supervisor.

We need to look at initiation in both directions. We might at first be inclined to assume that subordinates do not express favorable sentiments towards superiors unless they initiate to them fairly frequently. In the study reported in this book, Chris Argyris describes a situation in which workers rarely initiated upward and yet expressed favorable sentiments toward their foremen. However, he also points out that initiations from foremen to workers were also exceedingly rare. The workers seem to be saying, in effect, "they don't bother us, and we don't

> through the two departments was made. This revealed that orders v first processed in the sales department and then sent to the credit dep ment for the customer's credit rating to be checked. As a result, a custo might receive an acknowledgment from the sales department leaving l with the impression that his order was being attended to, and a day so later another letter from the credit department to the effect that order could not be shipped because of his poor credit rating. Changi the work-flow so that all orders went first to the credit department, th to the order editor to check whether the order could be filled, and fina to the sales department, eliminated the conflict which management h attributed to incompatible personalities.

The importance of the work environment is strikingly demonstrated in tw significant books which have been recently published on the subject.

Zaleznik, Christenson, and Roethlisberger—with the collaboration o Homans (1958)—have shown that it is possible, with an impressive degree o success, to predict the structure of informal group organization of workers and of group leadership in a department, when one knows the technology, the layout of the department, the placement of workers at work stations, and the pay system of the department, plus such objectively identifiable factors that the workers bring into the system as their age, sex, education, and ethnic identifications. They have not been nearly so successful in their attempts to predict satisfaction and productivity from the same data. However, even here they have developed some interesting theoretical statements that may yet prove of great value.

Leonard Sayles (1958) has been impressed by the apparent similarities in behavior of groups doing the same type of work in the same technological environment in different plants and companies. Kerr and Siegel (in Kornhauser, Dubin, and Ross, 1954) earlier made the same type of observation in their paper "On the Inter-Industry Propensity to Strike." Sayles argues that these environmental factors tend to condition the behavior of work groups: the technology, the organization of the work (individual jobs, a team of men all doing the same thing, a hierarchically organized team, an assembly line, and so on), the level of skill, and the range of pay within the work group. On the basis of accounts he has received regarding the behavior of more than two hundred work groups, Sayles has developed his four-fold classification of apathetic, erratic, strategic, and conservative groups.

It seems to me highly unlikely that this type of classification will stand without modification from further research. However, I am convinced that the factors Sayles is considering are of tremendous importance in molding work-group behavior, and that he has pushed us ahead in a highly fruitful direction.

Whatever the ultimate fate of the scheme of classification, some of the ideas underlying it are bound to be of significance. For example, I have found the concept of "resonance" highly useful. The idea is simply that when the work group is relatively undifferentiated as to tasks performed, pay received, and working conditions faced by individual members, it is highly likely that the problems faced by any one individual will be perceived as similar to the problems faced by other members of the work group. In this situation, as one individual gives voice to his sentiments, he is likely to find other individuals echoing the same sentiments and thus reinforcing his own. The factor of resonance in this bother them." In this situation, Argyris found expressions of liking—if not of respect—for the foremen. This suggests that while the ratio of initiations in the two directions is certainly of importance, we may be able to make further discriminations in sentiments as we examine the absolute frequencies of initiation.

This also suggests that a supervisor who has been initiating with a high frequency toward subordinates and allowing them little initiation in return can improve their sentiments toward him by decreasing his initiations for them and/or encouraging them to increase their initiations to him. The extent to which an individual can change his interactional behavior is another problem for study. Certainly we see changes of this nature much more frequently when one supervisor is substituted for another than when a given supervisor changes his interactional behavior. However, a recent study by Paul Lawrence (1958) provides us both with evidence of quantitative interactional changes for the same individuals over time, and with valuable methods for measuring these quantities.

What patterns of interaction fit with union-management cooperation? What with conflict? One of the obvious effects of the entry of a union into a plant is the rechanneling of interactions. Workers, being unable to initiate activity-changes up the regular line of authority, organize themselves into a union, which provides them with channels for initiating at the level of a foreman, superintendent, plant manager, and so on. If management people do not respond sufficiently to these initiations, the union brings about activity-changes at the work level, such as slowdowns and stoppages.

How does management respond to these union initiations? This is naturally a difficult adjustment to make. Some management people respond by taking up a defensive stance and trying to limit so far as possible the area of union initiation. When management responds in this way, we find sentiments of hostility and mutual distrust between management people and union officers.

Where the sentiments are different, we find a different pattern of interaction. More specifically, let us assume that we find expressions of mutual trust, liking, and respect between management people and union officers. They do not tell us that they have no disagreements. In fact, they tell us that they often disagree and argue their differing points of view most vigorously. However, they take pride in being able to arrive at mutually acceptable solutions to their problems. Where we find such a pattern of sentiments, we *always* find that management people are not only responding to union initiation, but are also initiating for their opposite numbers in the union structure. In other words, they are calling upon the union officers to help them work out problems in the organization of work activity in the plant.

It may seem presumptuous in this field to say that any *X* is always associated with *Y*. However, the ideas underlying these generalizations were first stated in systematic form a decade ago (*Human Organization,* 1949), and no exception has as yet come to my attention.

Patterns of Sentiments

We now come to the most slippery term in the present conceptual model. In fact, the concept is so slippery that some have advocated discarding it altogether—as we shall see.

First, we must recognize that people have sentiments about a wide variety of things. If we are going to say that the sentiments of an individual change, we must specify what sentiments, and this leads us to some sort of categorization.

The sentiments with which I have been dealing seem to fall into four categories. I make no claim that this is an exclusive scheme of classification. It simply covers sentiments that I have so far found most important in organizational life.

1. *Evaluation of behavior.* We constantly hear people saying that a certain action is good or bad, appropriate or inappropriate. We note this at the level of the individual. The individual's sentiments may be peculiar to him alone, but we often find members of a group expressing a high degree of consensus as to what is good or bad behavior, and rewarding individual members or punishing them according to their conformity to these collective judgments. When we observe this sort of consensus, supported by sanctions, we refer to *norms* of behavior, as do Homans and many others. (Note here a linking of sentiments and norms, which, Homans insists, must be kept separate.)
2. *Identification.* Here we are concerned with the way the individual identifies himself with other individuals, groups, or with the organization in which he works. How does he answer these questions: Who are my friends? Who are my enemies? To what group do I belong? And how much does that group mean to me? How do I feel about the organization itself?
3. *Ranking.* We might say that there are two dimensions to interpersonal relations. Under identification, we are covering such questions as, "Do I like or dislike Joe?" Under ranking, we are concerned with evaluations of relative prestige: "Does Joe have more or less prestige than Al?" People are expressing this type of judgment, explicitly or implicitly, all the time. Furthermore, we find that there is a high degree of agreement among judges in these evaluations (Warner, Meeker, and Eels, 1949). Apparently we are dealing with something that is both significant and tends to show a high degree of stability.

   Prestige evaluations are not limited to people. Workers are also concerned with prestige evaluations of the various jobs in the plant. Here again we find a high degree of consensus in rankings.
4. *Goals.* People also have ideas as to what they want to achieve. Research has shown that perceived progress or lack of progress toward these goals has an important impact upon behavior. We are here dealing with what sociologists call the individual's "level of aspiration" and with the effects of success or failure in reaching this level.

Let us turn to the controversy regarding sentiments. The charge against sentiments consists of two points: (1) They cannot be directly observed; (2) If they have any standing at all, they are simply dependent variables, changing in response to interactional changes.

Regarding the observability point, there are two answers. In the first place, the charge is not completely true, because often we observe people behaving toward each other in ways which provide us with clear inferences of the sentiments they feel toward each other. Even when this is not so, we find innumerable instances in the other sciences where concepts have proven useful even though there are no direct means of observing and measuring the phenomena to which they point.

On the second point, let us consider the argument posed by Eliot Chapple in a *Human Organization* editorial comment on the article by Arthur M. Turner, "Interaction and Sentiment in Foreman-Worker Relationship."

The editorial is entitled "Sentiment *vs.* Interaction: A Query" (*Human Organization,* 1955)—although the point of view expressed hardly represents a query. Chapple makes his point this way:

> In describing his two opposed variables, Dr. Turner brings sharply into focus the nature of the definitions that are used to make the dichotomy and provide him with the data for his analysis. He asks each worker to tell him how frequently he interacts with his foreman; he then asks how well the worker thinks the foreman gets along with his men. The first question defines interaction as the number of times interaction takes place; the second derives sentiment or attitude from the description by the worker of what he means by "getting along."
>
> But when we look at his cited examples of how the foreman "gets along," we find the workers describing how he behaves in the interaction that takes place. "You tell him something, he just walks away"; "an experienced foreman will listen to you"; "he's authority crazy; he wants you to bow down to him"; "this one blows up at everything." All of these are behavioral descriptions of the pattern of interaction within the contact, ordinarily amplified by statements of the attitude or sentiment or feeling accompanying them. From our view, then, what has been done is to correlate the frequency of events or contacts between worker and foreman with the patterns of interaction within the contact. Where there are deviations in the general uniformity—that the more frequent the interaction, the more favorable the sentiment—the author shows that they result from personalities who require little interaction, or who avoid being exposed to a pattern to which they find it difficult to adjust.
>
> . . . one can ask whether observation of the interaction of these workers and their foremen would not lead one to conclude that sentiment is the resultant of the interaction pattern, and has no useful existence as an explanatory concept.

Chapple assumes that a change in interactions necessarily involves a change in interpersonal sentiments. By his logic, however, changes in interpersonal sentiments do not precede and give rise to changes in interactions. I do not believe such a generalization stands the test of experience or research.

Consider the situation in which a number of people found themselves at the height of the McCarthy Communist hunt. Let us say that John Smith has a pattern involving several interactions a week with a number of his friends and neighbors in his community. Then one day newspaper headlines announce that he has been charged with being a Communist. All of a sudden, Smith finds that he is not interacting with the people that he was before. While I have not investigated such cases myself, there have been several newspaper reports which make it quite clear that the interactional changes followed publication of the Communist charge. The ordinary person would be inclined to conclude that the reading of the newspaper report changed the sentiments or attitudes of certain individuals toward Smith and that the interactional changes followed. In somewhat more technical terms, a change in the social and cultural environment produces symbols that change sentiments, and, the sentiment-changes produce interaction-changes.

Let us look at the concept in terms of a more familiar research problem: worker-response to financial incentives in industry. Research has certainly shown that worker-reactions to incentives are strongly influenced by the interaction pattern among workers, management people, and union officers (Whyte, 1955). However, their response can also be examined by giving attention first to sentiments. Workers seem to have certain well-defined sentiments regarding how much a particular job and a particular level of effort and skill should be worth. Furthermore, these sentiments do not arise entirely out of the interactions within the plant. Workers compare their lot with that of others doing similar work elsewhere, so that worker-sentiments regarding what is a "fair" income for their work can change, quite independently of what is going on within the plant.

Now, if the incentive payoff is markedly below what the sentiments indicate, then it is not always possible to get the workers to change their sentiments on the adequacy of rewards through changing the interaction pattern. Sometimes management has to make a change in the incentive rate to bring it in line with worker-sentiments, and only when this is done will the workers begin to modify their sentiments regarding the incentive system, management, and so on. In this context, then, sentiments do not seem to be mere passive accompaniments of interactions.

To explore further how changes may be introduced into the social system through sentiments, let us consider two cases in more detail. The first involves a sentiment-change that led to the establishment of new interactional relations: the recognition of a union. The second involves the impact of sentiment-changes within a given social system.

Mr. Buchsbaum Recognizes the Union

Herbert J. Buchsbaum, president of a small Chicago company manufacturing jewelry and plastics, recognized the union in 1941, after a five-day strike (Whiteford, Whyte, and Gardner, 1946). Up until this strike, Mr. Buchsbaum had been a bitter opponent of unions. When his employees went out on strike in 1935, he hired a labor spy to furnish him daily reports from the enemy camp and, by means of bringing in strike breakers, was able to eliminate the union.

He speaks this way about the period between the two strikes. (I have italicized in this and later quotations what seem to me the key symbols.)

> Nothing happened between 1935 and 1940 to change the way I felt about unions. I had a few friends who could see some good in unions, but I was arguing with them just as strongly in 1940 as I had in 1935. I thought they were crazy.
>
> My mother has always been on the side of the workers. She used to say, "The poor people. They work so hard, and what do they get to show for it?" In the middle of the 1935 strike, she came into my office and pleaded with me to settle and take the people back. I certainly didn't want to listen to her then, because I knew that I was breaking the strike. I said to her, "Mama, you've got the wrong idea. This whole thing was stirred up by a few *troublemakers*—just a *bunch of reds*. When we get rid of them,

> everything will be all right." That didn't satisfy her, but still she wasn't able to make me change—then or later.
>
> But while I stayed the same, the world around me changed. By the time of the strike in January 1941, the Wagner Act had been declared constitutional by the Supreme Court, and we were getting used to the idea. I didn't want to violate the law, and it wasn't just because of the penalty involved. *Capital must believe in law and order because if you don't have law and order what protection is there for your capital?*

By 1941, the legal situation regarding unions and public opinion in these matters had changed so that Mr. Buchsbaum felt somewhat more limited in his freedom of action than he had in 1935. However, he went into the strike determined to break it. Furthermore, he faced no economic pressures forcing him toward a settlement. The strike came in early January, just after the Christmas rush, and in what was normally a slack season for the company. From Buchsbaum's standpoint, the strike could not have come at a better time. Why then did he settle so quickly?

Let us examine the answers provided us by some of the key participants in the case. First a statement by Sidney Garfield, union business agent:

> I think something that made him (Mr. Buchsbaum) trust me was rather interesting. During the strike, things were pretty rough for a while and we had a number of clashes when people tried to get into the plant. One time one of the men came flying down the street about sixty miles an hour in a car and ran right up on the sidewalk to the doors of the plant and tried to let people in that way. He might easily have run over some of our boys standing around, but they got between him and the door of the plant and had him trapped there. The strikers were all for taking care of him quickly right then and there and turning the car over in the street, but I knew enough to realize that that would be a bad move because of *the great American tradition of respect for property* so I made them leave the car alone. I don't mean that I was easy. There was one fellow who was trying to sneak in, and I pulled him out of his car and just kicked him down the street.
>
> When this incident came up, the chief company detective was standing right inside the door with a gun in his hand, but he was afraid to use it, and I found out later that he was impressed by what had happened and had gone up and told Herb Buchsbaum about my respect for property which apparently made some impression on Herb, too. It's the little things which make the difference.

Let us see how this situation looked to Mr. Buchsbaum.

> While I made my plans to break the strike, I couldn't help noticing that it was different from our 1935 struggle. There were nearly all *our own people* on the picket line. I thought I knew [them] pretty well, even though they had turned against me. It was zero weather, and it was pretty cold out on that picket line. I stopped and talked to the boys, and I told them to come in the vestibule and picket. That's the kind of strike it was.
>
> There was quite a bit of *violence and sabotage in our 1935 strike.* Expen-

> sive equipment was smashed, sand was thrown in bearings, materials were destroyed, and there were some bricks thrown through the windows.
>
> The 1941 strike was quite different. A few people got beaten up, but *the company suffered no property damage.* The union had good discipline on that point. There was one time when some of our people were trying to get through the picket line into the plant. They drove up in a car onto the sidewalk and right in front of the plant entrance to get the people in. That car endangered the lives of some of the picketers, and they rushed up and wanted to turn it over. Garfield stepped in then and wouldn't let them do anything to the car. That made an impression on me when I was told about it. I felt that these were *responsible people.* I didn't agree with them, but I could see that they were going out of their way not to harm the company.

Mr. Buchsbaum now continues with the story of the events leading up to union recognition:

> As soon as the strike started, Sam Laderman (Union general manager), asked me to meet with him and a committee of the strikers. I didn't want to do it, and I called my lawyer three times to try to find some way out of it. Each time he told me I had to accept the invitation because it would have been a *violation of the law* not to meet with them.
>
> On the second day of the strike I had lunch with Laderman and with a business acquaintance of mine who had a contract with his union. Up to that time I thought *all union people were a bunch of racketeers.* My friend reassured me on this point. He said that you could count on Sam Laderman *keeping his word.* He told me that Sam was a real human being. He *liked opera.* He *disliked fights.* There would be nothing he would like better than being friends with the employer if it were possible. He assured me that the union was always willing to discuss things from a reasonable point of view. And Laderman assured me that our contract would contain the standard clause that it would be no less advantageous to the employer than contracts the same union made with any other firm.
>
> That made an impression on me. I still had no idea of settling the strike but I agreed to meet with Laderman and a committee of the employees on the third day.
>
> Well, we sat around the table and began talking. I knew all the men there. We were just a small firm at the time.
>
> The first question one of the men asked me was this: "Mr. Buchsbaum, why are you against unions?" Now that was a good question and I welcomed it. I thought that gave me a chance to win them over to my line of reasoning. I stated: "I'm against unions because they *limit production.* They put production down to the level of the slowest employee and at the same time force impossible wage increases, driving the company out of business."
>
> They started talking all at once. *They didn't want to limit production, but increase it.* They wanted to see the company go ahead.
>
> I asked: "How can you increase production?"
>
> I got answers fast. Each one had a sound suggestion for his department.

> First spoke one of the polishers. He told of the large door behind the polishing department used for in and out shipments—how in zero weather this door was opened many times daily, obliging the perspiring men to leave their wheels and go to the washroom to save themselves from catching cold. How a simple protecting partition would save about an hour and a half per man per day. Other suggestions equally good came from everyone in the circle. I took notes that I could see would save the company thousands of dollars annually.
>
> In that first meeting they really sold me a bill of goods. There was one thing that convinced me. When the workers began talking I saw that they had my interests at heart—as well as their own. I realized I had done them a great injustice in thinking that they had turned traitor to the company.

At this point Herbert Buchsbaum announced his decision to recognize the union and furthermore stated that he was prepared to do everything possible to establish a cooperative relationship.

I shall return to an analysis of this case after I take up the "Watchman Case," to be described below.

The Watchman Case

In the spring of 1943, the Oil Workers International Union (CIO) was undertaking to organize the workers in the Hi-Test plant and related plants of Blank Oil Company in "Oil City." After making some initial gains, the organization drive seemed to have stalled.

The workers had a number of grievances, which are discussed in detail elsewhere (*Human Organization,* 1956), but about a year before the event to be described, management had made some strategic changes in personnel in the local area. The new works' manager, superintendent, and foreman were all proving to be quite popular with the workers. Many of the workers continued to distrust the main office, but the smoothing-out of relations locally caused some workers to wonder whether they could not solve their problems with these new and reasonable men, without recourse to the union.

At this time, representatives of the company union were carrying on some discussions with main office management. Few if any of the workers had faith in the company union. They looked upon the company union as a helpless organization, that could only give them whatever management was prepared to give in the first place. In fact, the existing contract between the company union and management was a most unusual document, in that it contained no references to wages. These were determined solely by the company—although management people expressed a willingness to listen to company-union representatives on the question of pay rates.

Management's willingness to listen to the company union seemed to be greatly increased at this time when the CIO organizing drive was going on. So the company-union representatives met with higher-management negotiators to discuss a number of problems, including wages.

While the workers themselves had little hope of gaining any advantage from these discussions, they naturally followed them with interest. A symbolic bombshell exploded when the company-union representatives were seeking to make a case that the number one operators in the Hi-Test plant should receive a pay increase. They sought to back up this claim by emphasizing the high degree of skill of these men and the great responsibility they carried. The management people were not agreeing to any increase, but the formal discussion ended without any bitterness. After the meeting, the chief company negotiator expressed his views informally—and graphically. The Hi-Test company-union representative reported the incident in this way to his fellow workers:

> Did you hear what Masters said about us? He told us that we were only watchmen. He said, "Down there in that plant you have got automatic controls and charts. If anything goes wrong with the meters, you just call a meter man. If anything goes wrong with the engines, you call a repairman. If anything goes wrong with operations, you call an engineer, and he tells you what to do. There is no skill in that work. You just have to watch the charts."

This statement had a sudden and dramatic effect on the social system. For the workers who had been trying to organize for the CIO, an uphill struggle had suddenly become downhill. One man reported that in the week following the watchman statement, he had signed fifty workers to union pledge cards. He added that many of these were men who previously would not even listen to his union argument. A number of men put the case to me in these or similar words: "I used to think the company had respect for its men. If this is what they really feel about us, then we sure need the protection of a union."

The statement also had an impact upon human relations in the local area. The plant engineer had always gotten along with the Hi-Test workers reasonably well, but now, for a period of several days, he found them complaining against him on matters that had previously been passed over without a comment.

On the day after the watchman statement, the chief engineer for the division dropped in on the Hi-Test plant and noted that the number four fractionating column was giving the workers some difficulty. He asked what the trouble was. The number one operator on the shift replied: "You're the engineer. You're supposed to tell us." The chief engineer had had no previous difficulties in communicating with these men.

The Role of Symbols

So far, I have been undertaking to demonstrate how changes in sentiments can effect changes in interactions and activities. Now let us examine further the process whereby sentiments change. At this point, I shall have to deal explicitly with the concept of "symbols" which has been implicit in the discussion all along.

In earlier writings, I have recognized the importance of symbols, but I have not been clear as to their relations to the other parts of the social system. For example, in *Pattern for Industrial Peace* (Whyte, 1951), I announced that my "theory" was based upon four terms: interaction, symbols, activities, and sentiments. I did not state what relationship symbols bore to the other three concepts because I was not clear on this point at the time. Now I would put it this way: symbols are the link between the individual's sentiments and his social and physical world.

Before we go farther, a definition: symbols are words, physical objects, or acts that *stand for* relations between man and man, and between man and his physical environment.

The individual, in the course of his experience, endows words, objects, and acts with symbolic significance. The symbols furthermore take on a positive or negative value for the individual, according to the character of the experiences he has had in previous association with a given symbol. The sentiment in question arises out of a response to a given symbol in this positive or negative aspect.

Generally speaking, we find a fairly stable pattern of sentiments and also of symbols. The symbols presented to us fit so well with our existing sentiments that we are not aware of the impact of the symbols. They simply reinforce our view of the world.

It is only when the symbols depart sharply from the sentiment-pattern that we are able to see the impact of symbols on sentiments, and, through sentiments, on interactions and activities. It is for that reason that I discuss at length these two cases of striking sentiment-changes.

To deal with them more systematically, let us introduce at this point Osgood's Semantic Differential (Osgood, Suci, and Tannenbaum, 1957), adapted for present purposes. The problem is to determine the sentiments that are important to the individual in the social context we are studying. We can then get him to evaluate other people along the dimensions of his sentiment pattern. We can do this by arranging the positive and negative aspects of each sentiment on opposite sides of a piece of paper with seven short lines in between, giving the individual an opportunity to locate any other individual at any of seven points along this dimension (see Table 1).

TABLE 1. Dimensions of Sentiments of Herbert J. Buchsbaum

Bad								Good
no respect for private property	—	—	—	—	—	—	—	respect for private property
racketeers	—	—	—	—	—	—	—	dependable, honest people
combative	—	—	—	—	—	—	—	peace loving
crude	—	—	—	—	—	—	—	cultured
limiting production	—	—	—	—	—	—	—	production minded
outside agitators	—	—	—	—	—	—	—	our own people
illegal	—	—	—	—	—	—	—	legal

For example, in the Buchsbaum Case, it is evident that respect for private property is an important value. The opposite of this would be no respect for private property. As in the chart, we can pick out five other dimensions of Buchsbaum's sentiments, inferred from his own account of his clash with the union. These are shown in Table 1.

Let us assume that we had been able to make a study of Buchsbaum's sentiments before the crisis arose and had established these seven dimensions for him. We might then have asked him to check where he would place a union leader on each dimension. We can assume that he would have placed the union leader at the extreme negative end of each dimension, with two possible exceptions. Perhaps he might have recognized at least a slight distinction between union leaders and men whose only occupation is in the rackets: And the Supreme Court's decision, even then, would have made it difficult for him to place a union leader as "illegal."

Now suppose we had given him the same instrument and asked him to score it for a particular union leader, Garfield or Laderman, immediately following the strike settlement. If we follow his own account, we can assume that he would have made his check marks in this instance much farther over to the good end of the dimension. Since this is a hypothetical example, we cannot demonstrate where exactly he would have placed the particular union leader on these dimensions, but the exact location is not important. I am simply trying to demonstrate a method, whereby the connection between symbols and sentiment can be shown.

Here, Garfield's dramatic intervention in preventing the men from turning over the automobile seemed to demonstrate a high degree of respect for private property. Changes in the next three dimensions do seem indeed to be related to interactions—in this case interaction with a trusted business friend who spoke of the dependability, and of the peace-loving and cultured aspects of Sam Laderman. Incidentally, in this connection, it is interesting to note that Mr. Buchsbaum himself had no liking for opera. However, he did recognize opera as a symbol of advanced culture. Hearing that the union leader was a devotee of opera seemed to establish him for Buchsbaum as a cultured individual. The shift from limiting production to production-mindedness seemed to occur particularly in the meeting Buchsbaum held with his own workers, but which included also the union leaders. Finally, we see that it is important for Buchsbaum to look upon workers as "our own people" and, as the union leaders undertake to reassure him on this point, he can accept even them as part of the new social system in which he is going to interact.

It is important to note that while important shifts in sentiments took place, they all took place along an established dimension. If the union leaders or Mr. Buchsbaum's business friend had appealed to him for the union in behalf of social justice, the rights of man, or some other concepts that had no place in Buchsbaum's pattern of sentiments, we can assume that no change would have taken place in this respect. It was only after some period of experience in dealing with the union that new sentiments such as these gained a place in Mr. Buchsbaum's sentiment pattern.

I shall not undertake to analyze the Watchman Case in such detail. However, here there is obviously at least one important dimension involved. We might establish the dimension as "respect for the men" and "no respect for the men." A number of the men told me they had assumed that higher management had some respect for the men, and that the watchman statement convinced them that management had no such respect.

Following this scheme, we can assume that as individuals and the organizations they represent shift in the subject's sentiment-dimensions toward the favorable end, he will show an increased willingness to interact with these individuals, and he will evince a greater sentiment of loyalty to the other individuals in the organizations they represent. On the other hand, as the symbolic shift takes place toward the negative direction, we can expect individuals to withdraw from interaction in the sphere represented and to increase their interactions with individuals and organizations considered to be in conflict with those symbolized.

Shifts seem to occur when the individual is presented with symbols which fit into an established dimension of sentiments but in a markedly different position on this dimension. No doubt there are many times when the individual is able to overlook or rationalize away these symbolic discrepancies, while there are critical occasions (such as the two cases just analyzed) where the symbol changes have dramatic impact upon sentiments. We need to know much more than we now do regarding the conditions under which symbol changes will or will not affect sentiment changes.

Interaction and the Leadership Problem

Before concluding this theoretical statement, it is important to point to some of the confusions that are to be found in the literature regarding one of its key concepts: interaction. I feel particularly obligated to do this, because I have contributed my share to the confusion.

Since interaction is a concept around which some of us have erected our theoretical scheme, you have a right to expect that at least this concept would be clearly defined and consistently used. Such is not the case.

First we need to make a distinction between what we might call micro-interaction and macro-interaction: micro-, dealing with fine measures of interpersonal adjustment within a given contact, and macro-, dealing with broader interpersonal patterns and influences.

Working with the interaction chronograph,[5] which he invented and developed, Eliot Chapple is dealing with micro-interaction. The chronograph is a machine designed to measure the interaction between two individuals: the length of time each talks or gestures, who continues talking following interruption, who starts acting again following a pause and so on.

The interaction chronograph and the methodology that goes with it may prove to be the most important social science invention of a generation, but nevertheless I shall not discuss it further here. The chronograph has been used primarily to study personalities in relation to organizational position and performance. In this paper, I am concerned with other problems.

If we pass over the micro-analysis of interpersonal adjustment within a given contact, we find that certain aspects of macro-interaction are easy to specify and observe, whereas others present very complex problems. We can observe who makes the contact, what individuals are involved in the interaction, and how long a time they spend together. We can measure the frequency and duration of interaction between Jones and Smith. We can also determine what proportion of the time Jones made the contact as against the proportion of the time in which Smith makes the contact.

To complicate our problem, let us consider two hypothetical cases:

1. Smith comes up to Jones and says, "Go get me a cup of coffee." Jones replies, "Sure, right away." Jones then walks away and returns in five minutes to give a cup of coffee to Smith.

---

[5] See E. D. Chapple, "The Standard Experimental (Stress) Interview as Used in Interaction Chronograph Investigations," *Human Organization,* **12,** No. 2 (1953). Also E. D. and Martha F. Chapple, and Judith Rapp, "Behavioral Definitions of Personality and Temperament Characteristics," *Human Organization,* **13,** No. 4 (1953). For a useful summary, see Joseph D. Matarazzo, George Saslow, and Ruth G. Matarazzo, "The Interaction Chronograph as an Instrument for Objective Measurement of Interaction Patterns During Interviews," *The Journal of Psychology,* **41,** 347–367 (1956). See also George Saslow, Joseph D. Matarazzo, and Samuel B. Guze, "The Stability of Interaction Chronograph Patterns in Psychiatric Interviews," and "Stability of Interaction Patterns During Interviews: A Replication," *Journal of Consulting Psychology,* **19,** No. 6 (1955), and **20,** No. 4 (1956).

2. Smith comes up to Jones and says, "Go get me a cup of coffee." Jones replies, "Go jump in the lake." Jones then walks away. He returns five minutes later to speak to Smith—but without the coffee.

The two cases are identical, in so far as we are simply concerned with the origination of interaction. In both cases, Smith originated interaction for Jones and then, five minutes later, Jones originated interaction for Smith. However, if we are concerned with questions of personal influence or leadership, there is obviously a marked difference between them.

It is this concern of some of us for studies of leadership that [has] led us beyond the simple counting of originations of interaction and frequencies and duration of interaction. I am not saying that such observations and measurements are not significant. I am saying simply that they do not tell us some of the important things we want to know.

In my own work, I have spoken of origination of action (or activity) in the sense of Smith getting Jones to do something Smith wishes done. See, for example, my article, "Patterns of Interaction in Union-Management Relations" (*Human Organization,* 1949). However, this article was not based upon observational data. In interviews, people seem to have little difficulty in reporting not only who made the contact, how often they got together, but whether or not Smith got Jones to act. I have found this sort of approach useful in providing a general framework for the understanding of union-management relations, and yet it conceals a methodological problem which becomes apparent as we try to observe the origination of action or activity.

It is relatively easy to observe whether Smith or Jones makes the contact in their meeting. It is not so easy to observe whether Smith gets Jones to do what Smith wants him to do, and, in fact, we cannot get at this on a strictly observational basis. Some inferences must be made.

Some years ago, Chris Argyris and I spent several months in developing and trying out a system of coding observed interactions, in the hope that we could not only get who contacted whom but also who got action out of whom. Applying our scheme to a factory department, we bogged down in the face of certain methodological and coding problems and abandoned our efforts.

We seemed to face two major difficulties. If Smith asks Jones to act, Jones may respond in ways that cannot be classified simply as positive or negative. He may agree to act and then not act—but this could only be determined by some follow-up interviewing or observation. He may agree to act and indeed act but at a time much later than what Smith had in mind. He may indeed act in response to Smith's initiative and yet do something quite different from what Smith proposed. Finally, Jones may do part of what Smith indicated but leave another part undone. All of these cases may look the same to the observer at the moment, and yet they would seem to have quite different consequences, if we were able to follow up on each origination.

We were also not clear as to how we should handle the very frequent situation where Smith asks Jones a question and Jones gives him the answer, and only a simple provision of information seems to be involved.

As I review our records, I am not inclined to believe that we bogged down because we were facing an insoluble problem. I think now that our major difficulty was that our effort was purely a methodological one. In many of the instances where we had disagreement among coders, it now seems quite possible to establish a convention dictating how the type of incident should be scored. However, how the scoring should be done will depend in part upon what kinds of research questions we are trying to answer. If we do not know what we are trying to find out, we have no standards for determining whether, when Smith asks Jones a question and Jones answers, (*a*) Smith has originated for Jones, (*b*) Jones has originated for Smith, or (*c*) neither has originated.

Probably we can solve the methodological problems if we are seeking the answer to some significant theoretical question. At least, those of us who want to continue to talk about origination of activity would seem to be under an obligation to develop a defensible methodology for handling the concept on an observational basis.

In a study of work groups in the Steuben Division of Corning Glass Works, Frank Miller (1958) ran into another problem which has involved a disagreement in observation and coding among interactionists. This was an observational study in a situation where six to eight men worked together as a team, and there was a high frequency of interactions among them. However, Miller early noted that there seemed to be one class of interactions that could not readily be coded in terms of origination by Jones or by Smith. There were no methodological problems involved when Miller could see an action by Jones following words spoken or gestures given by Smith. However, there were recurring interactions among the men in which it was impossible to say that either Smith or Jones originated for the other—because no word was spoken nor was any gesture made. The men came together and performed certain actions together because they were at the point in the production of the glass object where the process required such interaction. In other words, they were responding to the point that had been reached in the work-flow.

This type of observational problem might exist in many work groups. It has been noted in studies of hospital operating rooms. One whose knowledge of the operating room is limited to what he sees in the movies may have the impression that every move made by the nurse is in response to a command or gesture from a surgeon. In any smoothly functioning operating room, this is hardly the case. The skillful nurse knows, on the basis of training and experience, what stages the operation will go through and what actions and tools are required by the surgeon at each stage. Through her observation of the surgeon and more particularly of the patient, she often provides the surgeon with the tool he will need next without his making any overt sign to her.

Miller decided to call these interactions "situational" and coded them separately from interactions in which Smith originated for Jones through word or gesture.

It is not my aim to resolve here the methodological problems that arise in field studies of interaction. I include this section to indicate that theories based on the interaction concept are quite firm at some points and on somewhat shaky ground at others.

Conclusions

Having just pointed to some of the weaknesses involved in the theory presented here, let me conclude with pointing to some of the strengths.

In much of the work done on organizations today, and particularly in studies using the questionnaire as the major research instrument, the focus of attention has been on attitudes (or sentiments, to use my terminology). There have been important technical advances in methods of measuring sentiments with a questionnaire, and this work can be used in the present conceptual scheme as well as in others. However, if we can demonstrate that sentiments are changed by changes in interactions and activities and that all three are subject to influence from forces in the environment, then it follows that any methodology or any theory which focuses exclusive or primary attention upon sentiments is seriously deficient.

I am not implying that those who use the questionnaire as their primary research instrument are not interested in anything except sentiments. They are concerned not only with how the worker feels about his foreman but with what happens in the foreman-worker relationship. However, the questionnaire can only tell us how the worker and the foreman *perceive* the relationship. The perceptions of people are important to know, but it is certainly at least equally important to know what is actually going on. For getting at what is going on, the questionnaire is an exceedingly blunt instrument. At Cornell, we once tried to use it in this way in a study of a local union. As Lois Dean has reported (1958), we used a questionnaire containing some questions about attendance at union meetings, and we also had an observer, George Strauss, to report to us which employees were actually present in union meetings during the year. Comparison of data from the two methods indicated that twenty-nine percent of those who reported attendance at union meetings had actually not been present.

The theory presented here is, of course, crude, and yet I hope that it opens the way for advances in the understanding and control of organizations. At the present time, it is little more than the presentation of a pattern of leading ideas. However, in a large measure the behavior underlying each of these ideas is subject to observation and measurement. As we proceed with such observation and measurement, we should be able to develop a much tighter and more systematic scheme in which we show in much more detail the relations among the various concepts. We may even hope to reach the point where we can show what quantities of interactional changes will be associated with what type of sentiment changes and so on. At the present time, we can do this as we deal with extreme cases. The hope is that improvements in methodology and theory will enable us to make finer discriminations.

The theoretical scheme presented here also has some important implication for human relations training. Much of the human relations training carried on today seems to be based on the assumption that there is *the* foreman and *the* executive and that therefore we should develop a foreman-training program and an undifferentiated executive-development program.

If we take seriously the statements presented here regarding the impact of the environment upon the social system and also the impact of different types of activities upon interactions and sentiments, then we must recognize that there is no such thing as the good foreman and the good executive.

I am not saying that each foreman's job and each executive's job is unique. This is true only in the sense that we cannot find two jobs that are exactly identical in all respects. However, of course we can find important similarities between jobs. We need to look for these similarities and undertake, then, to train people in terms of the common problems they face.

This means that we are not going to get very far with foreman training or executive development in human relations until we observe and analyze the activity and interactions involved in the jobs in question and build training programs to fit jobs and not to fit such empty and relatively meaningless titles as foreman and executive.

References

Blau, P. M. 1957. Formal organization: dimensions of analysis. *Amer. J. of Sociol.* **LXIV,** No. 1 (July).

Chapple, E. D., and C. M. Arensberg. 1940. *Measuring human relations: an introduction to the study of the interaction of individuals.* Genetic Psychology Monograph, 22.

Chapple, E. D. 1953. The standard experimental (stress) interview as used in interaction chronograph investigations. *Human Organization.* **12,** No. 2.

Chapple, E. D., M. F. Chapple, and J. Rapp. 1953. Behavioral definitions of personality and temperament characteristics. *Human Organization.* **13,** No. 4.

Chapple, E. D., and L. R. Sayles. 1958. The man, the job, and the organization. *Personnel,* March–April.

Dean, L. R. 1958. Interaction, reported and observed: the case of one local union. *Human Organization.* **17,** No. 3 (Fall).

Homans, G. C. 1950. *The human group.* Harcourt, Brace, New York.

Human Organization. 1949. **8,** No. 4 (Fall).

Human Organization. 1955. **14,** No. 1 (Spring).

Human Organization. 1956. **14,** No. 4 (Winter).

Kornhauser, A., R. Dubin, and A. M. Ross (eds.). 1954. *Industrial conflict.* McGraw-Hill, New York.

Lawrence, P. 1958. *The changing of organizational behavioral patterns.* Harvard Graduate School of Business Administration, Harvard University, Boston.

Matarazzo, J. D., G. Saslow, and R. G. Matarazzo. 1956. The interaction chronograph as an instrument for objective measurement of interaction patterns during interviews. *The J. of Psychol.* **41,** 347–367.

Miller, F. 1958. "Situational" interactions—a worthwhile concept? *Human Organization.* **17,** No. 3 (Fall).

Osgood, C. E., G. J. Suci, and P. H. Tannenbaum. 1957. *The measurement of meaning.* University of Illinois Press, Urbana.

Saslow, G., J. D. Matarazzo, and S. B. Guze. 1955. The stability of interaction chronograph patterns in psychiatric interviews. *J. of Consulting Psychol.* **19,** No. 6.

———. 1956. Stability of interaction patterns during interviews: a replication. *J. of Consulting Psychol.* **20,** No. 4.

Sayles, L. 1958. *The behavior of industrial work groups.* Wiley, New York.

Walker, C., and H. Guest. 1952. *The man on the assembly line.* Harvard University Press, Cambridge, Mass.

Walker, C., H. Guest, and A. N. Turner. 1956. *The foreman on the assembly line.* Harvard University Press, Cambridge, Mass.

Warner, W. L., M. Meeker, and K. Eels. 1949. *Social class in America.* Science Research Associates, Chicago.

Whiteford, A. H., W. F. Whyte, and B. B. Gardner. 1946. From conflict to cooperation. *Appl. Anthrop.* **5,** No. 4 (Fall).

Whyte, W. F. 1951. *Pattern for industrial peace.* Harper's, New York.

———. 1955. *Money and motivation.* Harper's, New York.

———. 1959. *Man and organization: three problems in human relations in industry.* Richard Irwin, Homewood, Ill.

Zaleznik, A., C. R. Christenson, and F. Roethlisberger. 1958. *The motivation, productivity, and satisfaction of workers: a prediction study.* Harvard Graduate School of Business Administration, Boston.

The Empirical Study of Bureaucratic Structure and Function

PETER M. BLAU

> The fully developed bureaucratic mechanism compares with other organizations exactly as does the machine with the non-mechanical modes of production. Precision, speed, unambiguity, knowledge of the files, continuity, discretion, unity, strict subordination, reduction of friction and of material and personal costs—these are raised to the optimum point in the strictly bureaucratic administration.
>
> Its specific nature . . . develops the more perfectly the more the bureaucracy is "dehumanized," the more completely it succeeds in eliminating from official business, love, hatred, and all purely personal, irrational, and emotional elements which escape calculation.

In these words Max Weber characterized the bureaucratic form of organization.[1] It is designed to induce an impersonal and rational orientation toward tasks which is conducive to efficient administration. Weber specified the following requirements that an organization must meet to be considered a bureaucracy:

1. "The regular activities required for the purposes of the bureaucratically governed structure are distributed in a fixed way as official duties."[2]
2. "A specified sphere of competence . . . has been marked off as part of a systematic division of labor. . . ."

Reprinted from *The Dynamics of Bureaucracy* by Peter M. Blau, rev. ed., pp. 1–14, by permission of the University of Chicago Press.

[1]The two quotations are taken from Max Weber, *Essays in Sociology,* trans. H. H. Gerth and C. W. Mills (New York: Oxford University Press, 1946), pp. 214 and 215–16. The term "bureaucracy" is used in this study for a certain type of administrative organization and without the negative connotations it has colloquially assumed.

[2]*Ibid.,* p. 196.

3. The official "is subject to strict and systematic discipline and control in the conduct of his office."
4. All operations are governed by "a consistent system of abstract rules . . . [and] consist in the application of these rules to particular cases."
5. "The organization of offices follows the principle of hierarchy; that is, each lower office is under the control and supervision of a higher one."
6. Officials are "subject to authority only with respect to their impersonal official obligations."
7. "Candidates [for bureaucratic positions] are selected on the basis of technical qualifications. In the most rational case, this is tested by examinations, or guaranteed by diplomas certifying technical training, or both. They are *appointed,* not elected."
8. Being a bureaucratic official "constitutes a career. There is a system of 'promotions' according to seniority or to achievement, or both."[3]

In his analysis of bureaucratic structure, Weber focused on official regulations and requirements and their significance for administrative efficiency. Of course, he knew that the behavior of the members of an organization does not precisely correspond to its blueprint. But he was not concerned with this problem and did not investigate systematically the way in which operations actually are carried out. Consequently, his analysis ignored the fact that, in the course of operations, new elements arise in the structure that influence subsequent operations. Recent students of organization have emphasized the importance of these emergent factors, such as informal relations or unofficial norms. Chester I. Barnard, for instance, showed that "personal contacts and interactions" always develop within formal organizations and called them "informal organizations." He concluded that "informal organizations are necessary to the operations of formal organizations as a means of communication, of cohesion, and of protecting the integrity of the individual."[4]

This concept has greatly influenced recent research in factories[5] and other organizations, but its crucial insight has hardly been exploited. Most discussions on the subject contrast informal relations and practices with the formal blueprint of the organization. This emphasizes the least interesting aspect of the concept of "informal organization," namely, that behavior and relationships often fail to conform exactly to formal prescriptions, which is certainly not a novel discovery. Much more significant is the insight that such activities and interactions are not simply idiosyncratic deviations but form consistent patterns that are new elements of the organization. In other words, Barnard's concept calls attention to the fact that organizations do not statically remain as they had been conceived but always develop into new forms of organization.

The objective of this study is to analyze these processes of organizational development on the basis of an examination of the daily operations and the interpersonal relations of government officials. Two segmental structures are

---

[3]The last seven quotations are taken from Max Weber, *The Theory of Social and Economic Organization,* trans. A. M. Henderson and T. Parsons (New York: Oxford University Press, 1947), pp. 330–34 (italics in original).

[4]Chester I. Barnard, *The Functions of the Executive* (Cambridge, Mass.: Harvard University Press, 1938), pp. 115 and 123.

[5]The classical example is found in F. J. Roethlisberger and William J. Dickson, *Management and the Worker* (Cambridge, Mass.: Harvard University Press, 1939).

analyzed in detail: a departmental group of two dozen individuals in a state employment agency and a slightly smaller department in a federal agency of law enforcement. It will be essential to note which practices correspond to official procedure and which do not and to determine how formally institutionalized patterns differ from others. But, whether recurrent activities and interactions exactly follow official rules or directly violate them, they are part of the bureaucratic organization. It is hoped that this book will contribute to an understanding of the dynamic character of this type of organization.

The Case-Study Method

This is an empirical study based on the direct observation of the behavior of officials in two government agencies. The field work was conducted in the second half of 1948 in the federal agency and in the first half of 1949 in the state agency. At first, in each case, administrative officials explained the organization and its procedures to the observer, and he familiarized himself with official regulations and other written documents pertaining to operations. After this period of orientation, a department was selected for intensive study.

In both agencies the observer was introduced to the staff as a sociologist by a senior official at a departmental meeting, and he was given an opportunity briefly to explain that he was interested in studying the interpersonal relations of civil servants. However, the fact that top administrators permitted the presence of the observer—a prerequisite for doing this study—made officials suspicious. Many believed that he was a member of a government commission (in the federal agency, it was the "Hoover Commission") and not a social scientist, as he claimed. But after some time his role as a researcher was accepted as genuine by most officials, if not all. This shift in role perception originated primarily in the course of informal social intercourse, in which the observer could not help revealing his ignorance of civil service and government agencies and some knowledge of academic and scientific matters.

The activities in each departmental office were observed daily for over three months. The observer also accompanied officials on their field visits to clients and participated in their informal get-togethers, notably at lunch. Small "side-studies" of related departments were subsequently made. The examination of operational records provided additional data. Throughout, the observer attempted to collect systematic information. For example, to determine the pattern of interaction in the department, all social contacts of its members were tallied during one week; to compare the productivity of officials, a quantitative index was derived from performance records.

All members of these two departments were interviewed in their homes immediately after the observation period in each case. Interviews were not designed to obtain attitude frequencies but to clarify the social relations and operating practices in the two departments. Most questions elicited the respondent's opinions and feelings about his work, his career, and his clients. A few direct questions concerning attitudes to colleagues provided the basis for sociometric indices. For comparative purposes, a similar interview was administered to three other groups, clerks in the federal agency and members of two other departments in the state agency. Not counting brief interviews at the office, sixty-nine operating and sixteen supervisory officials were interviewed.

For the most part, then, this is a case study of two bureaucratic departments.

The limitations of this approach must be recognized at the outset. Of course, the findings of such a study are not representative. How typical the processes investigated are of American bureaucracies cannot be ascertained by this method. Moreover, the focus on a small segment within each bureaucratic structure makes it impossible to determine *systematically* the functional significance of all observed practices *for the larger organization.* To minimize this limitation, the implications of the processes examined for the agency as a whole are explored whenever possible.

On the other hand, case studies of small groups have the major advantage of lending themselves to interlocking various research procedures. Direct observation, documents, and interviews can be used to obtain a variety of systematic empirical data on any particular problem. An impressionistic study of bureaucracy may show that informal relations between officials influence their work, but it cannot determine the exact network of informal relations in a group or the extent to which the competence of an official affects his informal relations or the processes through which his position in the group influences his performance. This requires precise information about very different phenomena, available only if several systematic research techniques can be used. In this respect, the case study is also superior to the interview survey, which is confined to those data that can be obtained from responses to questions.

Social processes can be examined directly in a case study, and explanatory hypotheses can be tested immediately. For example, the observer's impression that competitive practices in the state agency interfered with productivity was confirmed through the analysis of records. The more competitive a group was, the lower was its productivity. A plausible explanation of this relationship is that competition reduced social cohesion, the condition most conducive to effective performance. Observation and interviews provided data to test these inferences. An index of social cohesion that was independent of competitive practices could be obtained, which showed that the less competitive group actually was more cohesive. Moreover, the processes responsible for this relationship could be determined, that is, how competitive tendencies created tensions and conflicts and how the resulting strained relations interfered with efficient performance.

Access to different research techniques improves the accuracy of the data collected as well as their range. The most pertinent technique to ascertain a given fact can be used. If the concern is with the extent of contact between officials at work, it is not necessary to rely on procedure manuals stating how many contacts officials *should* have or on their own statements of how many contacts they *remember,* but the frequency and duration of interactions can be determined by direct observation. This is especially important when a bias distorts the information obtainable with a particular research tool. Thus the concealment of illegitimate competitive practices made it impossible to determine the extent of competition either by direct observation or from interview responses. Analysis of the case files, however, yielded an unbiased index of competitive practices.

The case-study method also provides an opportunity for comparing the reliability of different research techniques. For example, the extent of association between officials during their free time at noon was determined by asking in the interview which colleagues an official had never joined for lunch, by observing which ones went to lunch together, and from a record of his luncheon partners each member of the department kept for two weeks. Interview responses proved to be unreliable indices of social interaction in this and in similar comparisons. This does not mean, of course, that people's actions always provide more accurate data than their statements do. Systematic questioning rather than making inferences from overt behavior reveals most clearly certain types of information, such as the relative esteem each individual enjoys among the other members of the group. However, the recurrent interactions that constitute the most direct expression of social relationships are not fully within the awareness of participants and thus cannot be reported accurately by them. Most officials in these groups did not know whether they talked more often to the colleague who sat on their left or to their neighbor on the right, or whether they or he usually started their conversations. They even forgot that they had occasionally spent a lunch period with a particular colleague. These patterns must, therefore, be determined largely by observation. The examination of interpersonal relations in this study will be based on observational indices of interaction and on indices of mutual attitudes derived from interview responses.

The Functional Approach

Data do not speak for themselves but only answer questions the investigator puts to them. Conceptions of functional analysis are used to organize the data of this study, taking as a starting point the conceptual scheme developed by Robert K. Merton.[6] The basic tenet of this theoretical framework is that the social consequences of phenomena, not merely their origins, must be taken into account in sociological inquiry. Specifically, their contribution to and interference with adjustment or functioning in the social structure must be examined. This approach helps clarify the relationships between seemingly disparate observations and the processes of structural change.

The first concept, that of function, directs the researcher to ascertain the consequences of a given phenomenon and to evaluate their significance for the structure. For example, statistical records provided superior officials with accurate information about the operations of their subordinates in both agencies studied. They supplied a rational basis for supervision, which was intended to improve operations. Did they actually fulfil this function?

It is possible to answer questions like this one empirically because the main organizational objectives in these agencies were clearly defined. This is a peculiar advantage of the analysis of bureaucratic structures, not shared by investigations of institutions that have not been deliberately established, where it is

---

[6]Robert K. Merton, *Social Theory and Social Structure* (rev. ed.; Glencoe, Ill.: Free Press, 1957), pp. 19–84. Émile Durkheim, in 1895, was the first to set forth principles of functional analysis in the social sciences. See *Rules of Sociological Method* (Chicago: University of Chicago Press, 1938), pp. 89–124. Although Weber explicitly rejected this approach (*op. cit.,* pp. 102–7), his discussion of bureaucracy is implicitly a functional analysis. For further formulations of this theory, parts of which are antithetical to that followed here, see Bronislaw Malinowski, "Culture," in *Encyclopaedia of the Social Sciences,* IV (1931), 621–45, and "The Group and the Individual in Functional Analysis," *American Journal of Sociology,* XLIV (1939), 939–64; A. R. Radcliffe-Brown, "On the Concept of Function in Social Science," *American Anthropologist,* XXXVII (1935), 349–402, and "On Social Structure," *Journal of the Royal Anthropological Institute of Great Britain and Ireland,* LXX (1940), 1–12; Clyde Kluckhohn, *Navaho Witchcraft,* in Papers of the Peabody Museum of American Archeology and Ethnology, Harvard University, Vol. XXII, No. 2 (Cambridge, Mass.: Peabody Museum, 1944); Talcott Parsons, *Essays in Sociological Theory* (Glencoe, Ill.: Free Press, 1949), pp. 3–41; and Marion J. Levy, Jr., *The Structure of Society* (Princeton, N.J.: Princeton University Press, 1952).

often impossible to find unequivocal standards for deciding whether a given consequence enhances structural adjustment. But in the employment agency an exact criterion for determining the function of statistical records existed, since its major objective was officially specified as locating jobs for clients. The finding that the introduction of statistical records increased the proportion of clients placed in jobs therefore indicates that these records served the function of improving operations.

The second functional consideration is: What are the mechanisms or processes through which a contribution is effected? Originally, it may have seemed that statistical records promoted efficiency because the better-informed superior can correct deficiencies more easily by giving the appropriate directives to his subordinates. Actually, however, more complex processes were involved. It suffices to state here that the official's knowledge that statistical records provided his superior with accurate information on his operations induced him to improve his performance *without* direct intervention of the superior.

Third, latent functions are the unanticipated consequences of social behavior that contribute to structural adjustment. The discussion of mechanisms assumes new significance for the analyst sensitized by this concept. The existence of statistical records, since it constrained officials to improve their performance on their own initiative, enabled supervisors to criticize subordinates less often than their responsibility for operations would otherwise require. One of them put it aptly by saying, "I let the figures speak for themselves." With fewer criticisms, more cordial relations between supervisor and subordinates could develop, a latent function of performance records.

The tracing of unanticipated consequences is especially important for the understanding of unofficial practices that appear, at first, irrational and irrelevant to operations. Why did officials, though rushed for time, voluntarily perform tasks for which they were not responsible? Why did some white officials, no less prejudiced than others, treat Negro clients more impartially? Why did many officials ridicule clients when among themselves? Why did the very officials least familiar with regulations most strongly object to their being replaced by new regulations? The examination of latent functions provides answers to such questions.

The distinction between manifest and latent function raises the problem of the significance of awareness. What difference does it make whether a contribution is effected by deliberate effort or unintentionally? At several points in this study two different practices will be examined that had virtually the same function, but in one case participants were aware of this consequence of their behavior, and in the other they were not. These comparisons will indicate how recognition influences the way in which, and the extent to which, a given function is served.

Fourth, since behavior patterns have not only beneficial results, attention must also be paid to "*dysfunctions,* those observed consequences which lessen the adaptation or adjustment of the system."[7] The introduction of statistical records in the employment agency, for instance, generated competition among officials and made them reluctant to part with the job openings needed for serving clients. A group of specialists had no job openings of their own but were expected

[7] Merton, *op. cit.,* p. 50 (italics in original).

to serve their clients by obtaining openings from their colleagues. Competitive officials, however, tended to refuse such co-operation. This made it most difficult for the specialists to discharge their duties. Record-keeping was dysfunctional for the adjustment among officials and for providing employment service to the clients of the specialists.

The study of dysfunctions is of particular interest because they frequently are indicators of potential modifications of the structure. The distribution of specialized tasks in bureaucratic organizations makes each official responsible for the accomplishment of explicitly specified objectives.[8] In this context, a dysfunction that interferes with operations is experienced as a disturbance by certain members of the organization. The specialists, in the illustration cited, had to cope with the problem posed by the lack of co-operation of their colleagues in order to fulfil their responsibilities. A practice developed that seemed to be unrelated to this difficulty. Specialists voluntarily accepted the cases of the most unpopular clients of other officials. This put these officials under obligation to the specialists, constraining them, despite their competitive tendencies, to co-operate with specialists who looked for job openings. As a result, specialists were able to discharge their duty of providing employment service to their clients.

Dysfunctions often give rise to structural change. The disruption of operations consequent to the use of statistical records evoked new practices and interpersonal relations, in effect, a modification of the departmental structure. Similarly, performance records had been originally instituted in this department in response to practices that interfered with employment service. The very innovation introduced to cope with one disturbance may in due course have consequences that create new problems and lead to new adjustments.

The central thesis of this study is that bureaucratic structures continually create conditions that modify these structures. In the study of larger social systems, it is now generally acknowledged that processes of social development must be taken into account, but bureaucracy is still too often regarded as a rigid equilibrium exempt from these processes. It, as well as other social structures, however, contains the seeds, not necessarily of its own destruction, but of its own transformation. The analysis of bureaucracies as organizations in flux is facilitated by the conceptions of functionalism.

Functional Analysis of Processes of Social Change

Functionalism was conceived by anthropologists as an alternative to the evolutionary approach. It was intended to substitute explanations of cultural phenomena on the basis of empirical evidence for interpretations in terms of speculations about historical origins and evolutionary progress.[9] This was an advance in scientific method. However, the limitations of the specific research situation—namely, that historical developments cannot be empirically traced in illiterate societies—were elevated into a scientific principle: past conditions are irrelevant for investigations of social systems. This ahistorical orientation and

---

[8] See on this point Herbert A. Simon, *Administrative Behavior* (New York: Macmillan Co., 1945), p. 172 and *passim.*

[9] See A. R. Radcliffe-Brown, "The Methods of Ethnology and Social Anthropology," *South African Journal of Science,* 1923, pp. 124–47, and "On the Concept . . . ," *op. cit.*

the parallel assumption of social equilibrium, which prevented systematic treatment of historical trends and social change, were serious deficiencies of functionalism.

Merton's paradigm constitutes a fundamental departure, which directs functional thinking toward problems of disequilibrium and social change. Empirical research benefits from these conceptions and simultaneously provides a testing ground for them. The concrete problems that arose in the analysis of the data of this study indicated some limitations of Merton's theoretical framework. There are insights that he does not make explicit and issues that he fails to consider, and these offer a challenge to extend his conceptual scheme.

By defining "function" as a type of *consequence* of a social pattern, Merton implicitly calls attention to the fact that social phenomena must be examined in the time sequence in which they occur. This requires the transformation of functional analysis from a synchronic into a diachronic approach, which is primarily concerned with the effects of patterns of social behavior on subsequent patterns. When specialists did favors for other interviewers, for example, this influenced the subsequent interaction between these two groups; the others became more co-operative. Of course, the expectation of the recurrence of favors was a main determinant of this co-operative behavior, but the doing of favors had preceded the emergence of these expectations as well as the co-operative practices. The recurrence of socially standardized acts obscures the time differential between antecedent and consequence, but it becomes apparent and can be empirically tested when the development of new patterns is examined.

Merton proposes to distinguish between functions and dysfunctions on the basis of whether consequences enhance or lessen "the adaptation or adjustment of the system."[10] This definition does not furnish precise criteria for making the distinction in empirical investigations. Whether a certain condition constitutes adjustment or maladjustment is by no means self-evident. The absence, or reduction, of social conflict is not a sufficient criterion of adjustment, as is apparent in cultures in which some types of competitive conflict are defined as socially desirable. It would be absurd to consider monopolistic practices as functional for a free-enterprise system, although they eliminate competitive conflicts. Indeed, the same social condition may be experienced as adjustment or as maladjustment, depending on the value-orientation of participants. Ultimately, therefore, the distinction between functions and dysfunctions rests on value judgments.

Of course, scientists should not introject their own values into scientific analysis. Quite the contrary, they must guard against the intrusion of their personal prejudices by recognizing that functional analysis involves value judgments and specifying the value criteria employed. Arbitrary standards are preferable to none, but they are not satisfactory. Consequences of social patterns are experienced by people in terms of their value orientations, and not neutrally. Functional analysis takes this crucial aspect of social life into account by determining not merely the objective consequences of patterns but also their evaluative significance for participants. This necessitates that the values that prevail in the social system under consideration be ascertained and that they be used as criteria for defining function and dysfunction. The greater the precision with which value

[10] Merton, *op. cit.*, p. 51.

standards specify objectives, the greater their utility for scientific research. The explicit objectives of bureaucratic organizations, therefore, facilitate functional analysis.

Functions, then, can be defined as observed consequences of social patterns that change existing conditions in the direction of socially valued objectives or, more briefly, as consequences that contribute to the attainment of valued objectives. Dysfunctions, conversely, are those observed consequences of social patterns that change existing conditions in the direction opposite to socially valued objectives or consequences that interfere with the attainment of valued objectives.

Both functions and dysfunctions modify social conditions, but in opposite ways. The conditions *produced* by a dysfunctional pattern are identical, in one important respect, with those *relieved* by a functional pattern; both are experienced, in terms of prevailing values, as necessitating some improvement. Such conditions can be defined as social needs. Functions meet existing needs, whereas dysfunctions generate new needs.[11]

What happens if new social needs arise? There are three possibilities. First, the need may persist without being met. Many problems in bureaucratic organizations as well as in societies continue to require solutions for long periods of time. To be sure, if social needs were defined as prerequisites for survival, as they often are, it would be impossible to speak of needs that have not been met in an enduring social system. The advantage of the more limited concept adopted here is that it permits the empirical testing of functional hypotheses even when no information about extinct social systems is available.

To test the hypothesis that a pattern of behavior has a given function, it must be demonstrated that a condition necessitating improvement persists in structures in which this pattern does not occur, but does not exist in those in which it prevails. An alternative method is to show that the emergence of the pattern in a social structure eliminates this condition. Correspondingly, the test of a dysfunction of a social pattern requires evidence that a condition in need of improvement develops only in the presence of this pattern and not in its absence. In the study of prerequisites for survival, such comparisons have to be made between extinct social structures and enduring ones. Since this is rarely possible in the social sciences, functional imputations have often remained unproved assumptions. In the study of needs for the achievement of valued objectives, on the other hand, the comparison required is one between different surviving social structures which have attained a specific objective with varying degrees of success. Reliable data of this nature are much more readily accessible, which greatly increases the chances of being able to test functional hypotheses systematically.

A second possibility is that social needs disappear as a result of changes in value orientations. This involves more than becoming resigned to living under troublesome conditions, which indicates merely an adaptation to persisting needs. It means that situations that were once experienced as objectionable are now felt to be satisfactory because a new orientation has emerged. Learning is one of the processes through which such changes are brought about. As officials in the federal agency, for instance, learned to cope with the difficult problems of

[11]Often functions only reduce, and dysfunctions only intensify, social needs.

their work, their attitudes toward these problems changed, transforming them from disruptive threats into stimulating challenges.[12]

Finally, social needs may give rise to new social patterns that serve to meet them. Since this is only one of three alternatives, the existence of a need for improvement is not a sufficient condition for the development of such improvements. To explain their emergence, the conditions in social structures under which the need persisted and those under which it was met in a certain way must be contrasted. This analysis of structural constraints entails the comparison of historical developments in different structures, since past social experiences do, of course, influence present behavior.

A further specification of social needs and functions is important for this purpose, namely, an indication of the substructures particularly affected.[13] Which groups in a differentiated structure suffer from the existence of a given need, and which ones are relatively immune to it? Which groups benefit from the specific way a need is met, and which ones are not advantaged or are even disadvantaged? It is not possible to account for the persistence of needs, for practices that have serious dysfunctions, or for the fact that one pattern rather than another serves a given function, without inquiring into their differential effect on groups variously located in the power structure.

When a social pattern has a series of consequences, its dysfunctions may be looked upon as the social cost of its contributions. Presumably, once the cost outweighs the functions, the pattern will be abandoned. Often, however, social action is more constructive and less patient. People attack troublesome conditions, even if they cannot, or will not, eliminate the factors that produced them, and without waiting for a negative net balance of their consequences. We try to reduce highway accidents by means other than junking all cars and before their toll becomes so great that it would be preferable to give up motor transportation. Many emergent needs, in the two agencies studied, gave rise to social innovations that met the need without disturbing the pattern that had created it or the positive contributions of this pattern. The new practices, in turn, sometimes had dysfunctions as well as functions. Since the same social pattern that meets some needs frequently also generates others and since problems often lead to new solutions rather than to the elimination of their source, social structures continuously develop into different social structures.

---

[12] Conversely, changes in value orientations also produce new needs; conditions that were once considered satisfactory are defined by new objectives as necessitating improvement. Changes in value orientations in the two organizations studied are discussed in chap. xii.

[13] See Merton, *op. cit.*, p. 52.

The Body Politic of The Corporation

EARL LATHAM

One of America's most important political problems is a long-needed and now urgent redefinition of the relation between giant corporations and the commonwealth, for the growth of the corporation has produced a tension of power in which giant enterprises have at points come to rival the sovereignty of the state itself. The great corporations are political systems in which their market, social, and political influence goes far beyond their functional efficiency in the economy. Indeed, in the very culture of the American people, the influence of the larger principalities overflows the banks of their corporate jurisdiction or economic reason. In the name of free enterprise, corporate collectivism has made deep inroads upon the celebrated individualism of the economy, and corporate welfarism has gone an equal distance toward tranquilizing the historic initiative of the individual in a smother of narcotic "togetherness."

It is the purpose of this paper to discuss these corporations as systems of private government.

The Concept of the Corporation

Although the political influence of the corporation on public affairs is widely appreciated, its political nature as a system of private government is not. It is easy to see it as an economic institution, as a complex of legal rights and duties and even as a social system. But the economic and political natures of the corporation do not dwell apart in a Nestorian separation. To go back no further than Hobbes, we find a clear statement that the elements of the corporate nature are welded in a single body; and that the dominant characteristic is the political. In speaking of the infirmities of the commonwealth, of the diseases from which governments might suffer or perish, Hobbes spoke of "the great number of corporations; which are as it were many lesser commonwealths in the bowels of a greater, like worms in the entrails of a man."[1]* Although the physiology may be distracting, the political figure is unexceptionable, for, indeed, corporations were "lesser commonwealths," distinguished from Leviathan, according to Hobbes, only in that they are normally less absolute in their dominion than the state. The identity they share with the state, he said, is their characteristic as *systems,* public systems, and like all public systems they are known as a "body politic." Or, as Arthur Bentley put it twenty-five decades later, "A corporation is government through and through." To be sure, "certain technical methods which political government uses, as, for instance, hanging, are not used by corporations, generally speaking, but that is a detail."[2]

Reprinted by permission of the publisher from *The Corporation in Modern Society,* ed. Edward S. Mason. Harvard University Press, pp. 218–236.

*Superior numbers in text indicate references on pages 94–97.

Although the economic aspects of the corporation have received widest notice, the concept of the corporation as a political system is by no means unknown. The work of Walton Hamilton makes free use of the Hobbesian concept that the corporation is a lesser commonwealth, and indeed in some cases not the lesser but the greater.[3] Merriam has spoken of business enterprise as a form of private government and has concluded that sectors of it at times have controlled the public government.[4] C. Wright Mills refers to the corporation as a political institution.[5] A. A. Berle, Jr., also talks of the corporation as a political institution, and thinks that it should be studied as such because this "is the stuff of pure political theory," which stuff is, however, otherwise unidentified.[6] In another flash of fateful precocity, Berle found politics in all manner of organized enterprises besides the corporation, a view he shares with Aristotle and Walton Hamilton.[7]

In the literature on corporations, there are even corporate equivalents of bad German theories of the state. Thus the citizen of the corporate state—the individual stockholder—is made to disappear in the mystic organic unity of the corporate totality in the statement, "It might even be said without much exaggeration that the corporation is really socially and politically a priori whereas the shareholder's position is derivative and exists only in contemplation of law."[8] This is a little like Gierke's belief in the fundamental reality of the Group-person from which so much misfortune has flowed, from concentration camps to the euphoric groupism of the "organization man."[9]

Besides modest recognition of the political concept of the corporation, some small attention has been given to certain institutional aspects of the corporation as a political system. More should be done in this field, since the corporation surrenders a rich yield of political experience and confirmation. Dimock, for example, has said of business firms that they, like governmental organizations, "are inescapably involved in the distribution of power and influence in the society,"[10] and his earlier work in the Temporary National Economic Committee did much to demonstrate the essential identity of the problem of bureaucracy in both business enterprises and the public government.[11] A recent work on business leadership in large corporations carries inquiry into the bureaucratic characteristics of the corporation well beyond the point to which the authors of the Temporary National Economic Committee monograph were able to or perhaps cared to carry the analysis.[12]

But the literature lacks full-scale examination of the corporation as a political system, as a lesser commonwealth (to return to Hobbes), and some of the writing that does exist makes faulty analyses.[13] A mature political conception of the corporation must view it as a rationalized system for the accumulation, control, and administration of power. Speculative theories of the corporation, like speculative theories of the state, whether metaphysical or juristic, yield less understanding than do more empirical approaches. The corporation is a body politic which exhibits describable characteristics common to all bodies politic. In a functional view of all such political systems it can be said that there are five essential elements: (1) an authoritative allocation of principal functions; (2) a symbolic system for the ratification of collective decisions; (3) an operating system of command; (4) a system of rewards and punishments; and (5) institutions for the enforcement of the common rules. A system of organized human behavior which contains these elements is a political system, whether one calls it the state or the corporation. And state and corporation are mature political systems to the degree in which they exhibit all the essential characteristics.

The Authoritative Allocation of Functions

In the state, the constituent power makes an authoritative allocation of governmental powers and functions through a constitution, whether written or unwritten. In the lesser commonwealth of the corporation, this allocation is made through the corporate charter. The earliest corporations were groups of private adventurers, created as bodies politic in order to fulfill some public purpose. The charters of the early corporations were not only instruments to organize the internal government of the corporation. They created what were, in effect, branches of the public government. The companies of the mercantilist period, for example, were "charged with responsibility for commercial regulations and fiscal administration in particular spheres of foreign trade, and were equipped even with military forces and their own courts."[14]

The use of corporations to fulfill political ends and the exercise by corporations of the functions of the public government are illustrated by the colonial charters in America. The first charter of Virginia in 1606 vested in certain "loving and well-disposed Subjects," Knights, and Gentlemen not only the right to take up part of the royal domain in America for a colony but to exercise in it some of the powers of the Crown, including the creation and management of military forces and the coinage of money.[15] In the Second Charter of Virginia, granted in 1609, the company was given "full and absolute Power and Authority to correct, punish, pardon, govern, and rule" all "such Subjects of Us" as might journey to Virginia and come under the jurisdiction of the local company.[16] At the northern end of the Atlantic seaboard, the First Charter of Massachusetts in 1628 created "one body corporate and politique in fact and name" and gave to the "Governor and Company of the Mattachusetts Bay in Newe England" the authority to exercise powers of the public government.[17]

It is clear that these corporations were created for public purposes, indeed, more specifically, to exercise for the state certain functions of the Crown, such as the regulation of the economy and the spread of empire. This is not to say that there were no more narrowly commercial companies than those that established the colonies, for there were such. But of the thirty-four joint stock companies incorporated in England and Scotland before 1700, fourteen were established to perform some peculiarly public function, and of the rest, the principal aim was to introduce some new line or process of manufacture.[18]

In the nineteenth century, the management of the economy passed largely from the state into the hands of private enterprisers. The charters of the seventeenth century were instruments by which private persons served public purposes; the nineteenth-century charters became instruments by which private groups used the state in the enrichment of private interest.[19] Or rather, it may be said that this was the consequence at the end of the century of a process that started rather slowly. In the early years, "it was not considered justifiable to create corporations for any purpose not clearly public in nature; each application was considered by itself, and if favorably was followed by an act of incorporation."[20] The great change in the basic relation of the state and private interest in the control of the economy came with the abandonment of the special act of incorporation and the adoption of general incorporation laws for special classes of corporations.

The climax was reached in some states when permission was accorded in advance for incorporation "for any lawful purpose."[21] At the same time the competition of the states with each other for the privilege of giving away privileges to the corporations produced a great relaxation of the safeguards by which the rights and interests of the public were preserved and protected in the earlier limitations.[22] For example, directors were given the authority to reshape the capital structure of the corporation at will, and only a few states enforce the principle of accountability to the state for the manner in which the corporation exercises its franchise.[23]

This trend made it possible for incorporators, not the state, to define the values both of the corporation and the state, and to fix the allocation of fundamental functions in the corporation. The corporation thus acquired the constituent power from the state, and came to share the sovereignty. For constituent power is the power to make the constitution which fixes the basic distribution of powers, rights, and functions in the society. Those who share the constituent power share the sovereignty.[24] The corporations have acquired the power to make their own constitutions.

The formal view is that the corporation is a dependency of the state, owing its existence to the state, and receiving only those rights and privileges which the state chooses to grant, but this overlooks the politics of the relation between the corporation and its legal creator. Can one suppose that the great Dupont empire is a dependent of the state of Delaware, and forced, without influence, to accept the mandate of state functionaries? Or that the political power and influence represented by control of the international oil market, which is in the hands of seven integrated companies, is of equal weight with and may be countervailed by bucolic legislators in provincial states?[25]

Having the constituent power which they pre-empted from the state, the corporations have designed the basic functions and distributed power within the corporation in a standard structure which violates the prevailing values of the American democracy. Corporation charters permit the disenfranchisement of the qualified through manipulation of the voting rights of owners of various classes of stock, they institutionalize minority rule through the diffusion of stock ownership and the separation of ownership and control, and they deny the principles of due process in the adjudication, within the corporation, of relative rights, such, for example, as those of dealers, minority stockholders, workers, and consumers. More will be said below of the elements of due process in corporate adjudication. As William Graham Sumner said fifty years or more ago, "Industry may be republican; it can never be democratic." In the exercise of their constituent power, the corporations have fashioned massive clusters of antidemocratic force and influence. As another writer has put it, management has "substantially absolute power," and the "only real control which guides or limits their economic and social action is the real, though undefined and tacit, philosophy of the men who compose them."[26]

Symbols and Ratifications

Every political system, whether the state or the corporation, has an apparatus for ratifying and making legitimate the basic choices of the collectivity. It has a ritual for approval of the choices of policy, of the fundamental decisions, of the selections among broad alternatives of action—in short, a legislative system. The corporation has its legislature, and, moreover, it has parties and publics which attempt, respectively, to win the legislative power and to influence its course.

Let us first consider the legislative power. The legal constituency of the corporation is the multitude of owners; it is they who are the citizens of the corporate state. They are the lawful electorate. This electorate, like that of the public at large, holds the franchise which chooses the corporate legislature—the board of directors—and gives it legal authority to legislate. But it is only a mockery of the representative principle to say that the owner-constituency of the corporation elects its representatives in the board of directors who then meet to enact legislation that the president and his officialdom carry out. The constituency is either apathetic, or otherwise normally incapable of exercising its franchise. Over a million stockholders of American Telephone and Telegraph cannot possibly get together to wield the formal authority of the ballot on issues they don't understand for candidates they know nothing about. The managerial class of the corporation has come to diminish the role of the owner-constituent-stockholder-citizen who is usually interested only in a pecuniary result. His normal recourse is to withdraw from the corporate state, if he isn't satisfied, and to take up citizenship in another.

The election of the legislature in the corporate political system is practiced every year, however, with farcical solemnity. The annual stockholders' meeting is held, the managers are bright and brisk with the agenda, the newspapers get the usual laugh out of the usual crank who wants to protest, the business of the meeting is conducted with slick efficiency, and the winning slate wins as predictably as it does in a rigged election in a gangster-ridden union.

The meetings of this legislature, once elected and re-elected, are as rigidly ritualized as those of a conclave, a Zuñi ceremony, or a fraternity meeting. Board meetings have a pomp and circumstance appropriate to the occasion and the class. The walnut-paneled rooms, the grey flannel suits, the boned-and-polished shoes, the good cigars, the deep rugs, murmurous acolytes and courtiers—these are some of the appurtenances that legitimize decisions about big money. Crap games have their rituals also, and a special vocabulary, but this is generally a lower-class pursuit favored by soldiers, and the stakes are trifling compared with corporate standards. Imperial decisions are ratified in this regal atmosphere—decisions to divide up the United States, develop Venezuela, support an Arab oligarchy, lengthen cars so that they fit nobody's garage, approve treaties with other satrapies of economic power and influence—in short, *govern* in the name of free enterprise.

This oligarchic regimen is occasionally moderated by the appearance of party factions.[27] In the public government, the party system exists as a regular method by which the government can be changed. It is one of the more important functions of the party that it enables the electorate to line itself up—for and against. Thus the element of party affords the voters the voice that would, unorganized, be a meaningless babble, or mute. But corporation governments can be changed only rarely by the owner-constituencies they presumably represent, because there is no continuous party system to organize their grievances or to test periodically the confidence of the electorate in the corporation government. However, corporate parties do appear often enough to take them out of the statistical limbo of remote contingency. The operation of the party system in the corporate state, as a device for challenging the government of the corporation, is best seen when there is a contest over control of the corporation. In the make-believe democracy of the corporate commonwealth, the stockholders vote by casting ballots, or by giving their proxies to others to cast. This is a refinement of machine politics that no public party organization would dare propose.

Famous fights for control were the successful raid by Robert Young against the management of the New York Central Railroad, and the battles between A. P. Giannini and the Bank of America, Louis Wolfson and Montgomery Ward, and Charles Green and Spyros Skouras in the struggle over 20th Century–Fox. Although the rituals of a democratic contest are practiced and the symbols of democracy are brandished, these struggles are usually contests between adversary political machines. All of the rhetoric of a national campaign is employed—the apostrophes to reason and good sense, the celebration of virtues like honesty and loyalty, the promises to reform, the campaign literature in which party leaders are portrayed in flattering hyperbole by their partisans, while the opposition is seared, crimped, and shrunken by caustic reductives. In the meantime, behind the scenes, professional organizations hired for the purpose solicit the proxies of the sovereign owner-electors, much as a city machine quietly organizes the vote while the candidates fill the air and the press with outrageous declamation.

Then the sovereign owner-elector comes into his brief own. The showdown in the New York Central fight took place in the Tenth Regiment Armory in Albany. Public-relations men, company employees, and some owner-electors wore buttons for the president of the road, bearing the legend "We Want White"; while the insurgent partisans wore buttons with the caption "Young At Heart." Rival slates of candidates were read off, they made speeches, the balloting took place, and Young was declared the winner by 1,067,273 shares, of which 800,000 were contributed by two members of his alliance from Texas.[28] Although these fights are expensive, there are certain opportunities for the winner to recoup. At the annual meeting of the stockholders of the New York Central in 1954, it was voted to reimburse the Allegheny Corporation, of which Mr. Young was again chairman, in the amount of $1,308,737.71, this for the necessary expenses of the campaign by which Mr. Young secured control of the road.

The two-party system in the corporate commonwealth, however, is not a permanent institution. The corporate state normally is a one-party state, in the hands of the managers. But no oligarchy works in a political vacuum, however much it may be dominated by the management. In the making of the broad choices which represent policy, in the decision-making process, both the symbolic and the operative agencies of choice find their autonomy inhibited by various "publics" with which they must contend. These publics may operate as a moderating influence upon the otherwise unchecked power of the managers, even although stockholders may not be able to supply much restraint through the exercise of their franchise.

In the important field of labor relations, for example, the unions have managed to acquire a share of the former autonomous power of the managers to legislate wages, hours, and other working conditions. Here the existence of strong unions constitutes a two-house structure for the making of decisons that affect workers, and legislation is enacted only by the consent of both houses. The bargaining table is the corporate equivalent of Capitol Hill.

Other publics of the corporations also have from time to time limited the power of managers to legislate the rules that affect those publics. The significance of the mass of regulatory legislation that began to grow in the 1880's is that each Act represents a compromise that corporations had to make with disaffected publics—farmers, shippers, customers, competitors, and so on—who were strong enough to influence the public legislatures to establish protective agencies.[29] The weakness of these compromises is that sometimes they do not continue to be operated in favor of the publics that forced them, because these publics do not represent themselves and are not represented within the management structure of the corporation, but are outside it.

Some of the publics with which corporate legislatures have to deal—like the financiers—have come to represent their own interests very skillfully, occupying inside entries of access, and some—like consumers—have rarely learned to represent themselves at all, and don't do it very well when permitted.[30] As to the financiers, when large corporations depended almost exclusively on the market for their capital requirements, the financiers cut themselves in for important slices of control to protect their investments, and to expand their power. Increasingly, however, corporations have been able to free themselves in considerable part from reliance on the market for capital requirements, and this freedom has removed one form of control from the decisional autonomy they have recovered.

The consumer interest, however, has never been satisfactorily structured nor continuously organized to serve as an internal check to the power of corporation governments. Widespread consumer resistance to the vulgarities of automobile design that the manufacturers said the consumer insisted upon having is thought to have had something to do with the recession of 1958. And the commuters on the New Haven Railroad were able to force the resignation of a president when highhanded inefficiency threatened to collapse the service on the line. But these are peasants' revolts; they do not, and did not, achieve anything like a share in the enactment of corporate legislation. Their historical prototype is Wat Tyler, not the barons at Runnymede. *Piers Plowman,* not Magna Carta, is their text.

Although occasionally moderated by parties and publics, the power to legislate, like the constituent power, is almost absolute in the corporate oligarchy. The growth of virtually unchecked corporate power has drawn some speculation about the course of the future, with many answers of varying kinds. The inner circle of the legislative power of the corporation may be a family, a dynasty, a managerial group, or, as C. Wright Mills has lately suggested, in an elite with some class characteristics, but however animated, the power is formidable. Control of this power by a supposed automatic countervailance in the economy is unlikely, for the countervailance is, for the most part, leverage on the seller's side of the market; and it doesn't work in times of inflation, which has been most of the time in the last two decades. It has been suggested that corporations—anthropomorphic corporations, endowed with intelligence, will, personality, and other human attributes—will develop that final testimonial to St. Augustine and Freud, a conscience, the operation of which will curb and control the excesses of corporate power and establish a benevolent regimen: the new "City of God," no less. But one of the lessons of politics is that it is power that checks and controls power and that this is not done automatically and without human hands. The unions show the way, and the consumers are the example of ineptitude. If the legislative power of the corporation is to be curbed and controlled, the checks will have to be built into the structure of corporate enterprise, and not just merely laid on from without, nor entrusted to the subjective bias of the hierarchs within.

The Corporate Bureaucracy

The third requirement for a political system is an operating structure of command. In the classic definition of bureaucracy, supplied by Max Weber, there must also be added a structure of functions, and methodical provision for the recruitment and replacement of qualified personnel.[31] When these three elements are in conjunction, the resultant organization of the wit and muscle of numbers of people is a bureaucracy; and corporations have bureaucracies, just as does every large rationalized organization, like the Pentagon, the Roman Catholic Church, and United States Steel. Indeed it is hardly necessary to point out that bureaucracy, in this technical meaning,[32] has existed in the business world since long before Frederick Taylor discovered the one best way to do everything; and it was two General Motors executives who wrote books to establish the proposition that the principles of large-scale organization are universal social laws.[33]

There are critics who say that the term "bureaucrat" as applied to the top levels of the business world is as anachronistic, or at least as misleading, as the word "entrepreneur," not because corporations do not exhibit most of the characteristics of large organizations, but because corporate practice violates the third of Weber's qualifications for bureaucracy. C. Wright Mills has said that the "bureaucratic" career in corporations means not only a climb through a hierarchy of offices but "more importantly, it means the setting up of strict and unilateral qualifications for each office occupied." Usually these qualifications involve both specified formal training and qualifying examinations. The bureaucratic career also means that men work for salaried advancement without any expectation of coming to own even a part of the enterprise. But the advancement of corporation executives to the higher levels is "definitely mixed up in a 'political' world of corporate cliques."[34] Choice is in the hands of superiors, "and there are no strict impersonal rules of qualifications or seniority known to all concerned in this process."[35]

Support for this view is provided from an unintended source, the former president of the New Jersey Bell Telephone System, who formulated the functions of the executive in the corporation as three in number: maintaining communications; securing services; and formulating purpose.[36] These were for the most part an arrangement of familiar principles of administration, including the third. But his discussion of informal executive organization, at the time, was fresh. The general method of maintaining an informal executive organization, he wrote, "is so to operate and to select and promote executives that a general condition of compatibility of personnel is maintained."[37] Those are chosen who "fit," and fitness includes "education, experience, sex [it is not clear whether this is compulsory], personal distinctions, prestige, race, nationality, faith, politics, sectional antecedents," and "manners, speech, personal appearance, etc."[38] This informal executive organization is based upon few if any rules, and represents, according to Barnard, the "political aspects of personal relationship in formal organization."

Bureaucracies are systems for the making of decisions; and central to the success of decision-making is leadership. Few will now disagree that the leadership function in corporations has been transferred from owners to salaried managers.[39] And this transfer is properly thought to raise important questions concerning the "distribution of powers within the corporation"[40] and the functioning of the free enterprise economy itself. In the discussion of symbols and ratifications, attention was centered on the gulf that stretches between the owners and the management, and the problem was treated *ex hypothesi* as though the board of directors were the effective legislature of the corporate commonwealth. Attention here is centered on the decline of this legislature (just as the legislature in the public government has tended to decline in the importance it once had) as an "active and independent decision-making body."[41] The legislature in the public government—the Congress, at least—has developed compensatory institutions for the control of the executive. In this respect, as in other aspects of governance, the corporation is behind the public government.

A great deal of the initiative in the making of corporate decisions comes from the lower ranks, as Gordon has demonstrated and as Barnard earlier stated. The small size of the stockholdings of professional managers frees them from the impulses that generate decisions oriented toward the maximization of profits, impulses that presumably worked for the owner-entrepreneur. Although profits may not be disregarded, since the directors and the stockholders regard the corporation as a revenue-producing agency, the professional managers are free to respond to such considerations as prestige, power, and social welfare. They become private planners.

The hearings of the Senate Subcommittee on Antitrust and Monopoly of the Senate Judiciary Committee gave evidence that much of the administration of General Motors is done through committees, one of which, the price review committee, receives price recommendations from the divisions, and then makes recommendations to the operations policy committee, which usually ratifies the recommendation. In view of the profit of over a billion a year, after taxes, that General Motors has recently been making, interest was expressed in the method by which prices are reached. The theory of pricing requires a standard, which has not changed in twenty years, under which the planned yield is 15 to 20 per cent on the net capital employed. That is to say, the leaders of General Motors plan their pricing as though the corporation were a public utility; and although the return to General Motors from 1948 to 1955 far exceeded the standard, prices were not lowered because, it was said, the volume at some time in the future might decline.[42] In these determinations, which are largely free of market considerations, the General Motors managers closely resemble the top functionaries of the public bureaucracies, and are almost exactly like the managers of socialist enterprises, the difference being that between the public collectivism of the socialist state and the private collectivism of the corporate state.[43] Price rigidity is not the result of factors external to the firm but is in part the result of factors internal to the firm.[44]

Rewards and Punishments

The fourth requirement in a political system, whether that of the corporation or the state, is a system of rewards and punishments. The system is internal—to the ranks under the command of the corporation—and external—to various publics that threaten the security of the corporation. The growth of corporate welfarism and the bureaucratization of benevolence are recent trends in the development of complex reward systems. The execution of sanctions against threatening publics external to the corporation has a range from the violence of a Memorial Day massacre to the Byzantine subtleties of legal sabotage against the antitrust laws.

The bureaucratization of benevolence is a function of the depersonalization of work. Pats on the back by the entrepreneur-owner and an extra day off around the time of the accouchement of the worker's wife were the equivalents of the fringe benefits that are now written with scrupulous and mechanical generosity into union contracts. Bureaucratized benevolence for the lower classes of corporate society is paralleled by the development of corporate welfarism for the middle classes of that society. Millions are bound in a system of tribal dependence through paternalistic personnel policies, conformitarian training programs, tax-deductible expense accounts, an ever-ringing celebration of corporate interest through advertising propaganda, and the growth of the new company towns in suburbia and exurbia. The new middle class of suburban split-level Babbitts, riding the 8:05 into the city and the 5:05 out of it, wearing the status badges that mark their level in the corporate world, more anxious than yearning, looks for solace and safety in the "togetherness" of the corporate collective. For the upper classes of corporate society, bonuses play an important part in the reward system, as do the numerous opportunities for beating the tax laws; and the risk of loss of status is a powerful incentive to conform when the juniors are being looked at closely to see whether they will "fit." For all classes the threat of deprivation of these social sweets is a strong sanction that makes the cruder forms of discipline less necessary.

In the relations between the corporation and its various publics, the political function of crime and punishment is somewhat more difficult to administer because the corporation is unable to control as many of the variables as it does in its internal affairs. An example, however, of the rather full range of sanctions against threatening publics was provided by the Cement Institute, which the Supreme Court held to be in violation of the antitrust laws in 1948.[45] The Institute was a security system for cement producers in which truckers, dealers, customers, domestic rivals, foreign importers, and Federal and state agencies were subjected to discipline. Punitive taxes, for example, were laid in the form of differential charges on customers who wanted delivery to trucks and not to railroads. When this penalty pricing did not work, members of the combination in many instances refused by flat prohibition to allow delivery by truck. Penalties and prohibitions were also used to prevent dealers from competing in the manufacturers' products at prices lower than those that the manufacturer was charging the customer. Efforts of customers to beat the basing-point system by diversion of traffic were met by the use of no-diversion bills of lading, which the railroads were invited to honor. The companies influenced government procurement officers to buy from dealers at a higher price than the companies could have got from the manufacturers direct. When the TVA threatened to make its own cement to avoid the squeeze of noncompetitive prices, the companies complained about coercion, arbitrary government, and ruthless declarations. The appearance of imported cement in the American market brought upon the dealers who handled it attacks that included espionage, encirclement, systematic price undercutting, boycotts, and reprisals.[46]

The courts themselves may become a form of harassment of rivals. Early in 1953, the organized truckers of Pennsylvania sued the eastern railroads in a United States District Court for $250,000,000 in treble damages. The Pennsylvania Motor Truck Association and thirty-seven trucking firms sought damages because, counsel for this combination said, the railroads had used dishonorable means to restrain commerce illegally. Thirty railroads and the Eastern Railroad Presidents Conference filed a countersuit for $120,000,000 in treble damages. The total damages of $370,000,000 claimed by both sides represented the symbolic stakes in a rivalry that had nothing to do with the damages claimed. The railroad attorney charged that the truckers had filed their suit after the president of the Pennsylvania Railroad had refused to withdraw his objections to the removal of certain truck limitations on the highways. The suit was pressure on the roads, if not reprisal, and the countersuit of the railroads was counter-reprisal.[47]

Although the state has a theoretical monopoly of violence, the corporation has command of forces that commit violence when this ultimate resort seems necessary. The history of labor relations in the steel industry through the 1930's provides many examples of naked warfare and death on both sides. Not unusual are company-maintained detective services, constabularies of guards and security forces, police forces in company towns, and access to the state soldiery through the intervention of compliant public officials. These add up to a body of militia of considerable strength. Bentley's remarks about hanging seem particularly apt at this place.

The Judicial Function

The fifth requirement for a political system is a set of institutions for the enforcement of the common rules. We have already seen in the discussion of the previous two sections that corporations have an administrative apparatus and a system of rewards and punishments, and these are part of the machinery for the enforcement of the common rules. But the most mature political systems also provide an objective agency for making judgments about the application of the common rules to individual cases—a judiciary of some kind—and although the judicial function is not as fully developed in the corporation as in the state, it nevertheless exists.

In the hearings on General Motors held in 1956 by the Senate Judiciary Committee Subcommittee on Antitrust and Monopoly, there was evidence that dealers were bound to the company by agreements which gave the company practically unrestricted rights to renew or to cancel.[48] GM lawyers, in the few cases in which dealers sought to enforce their agreements in the courts, argued successfully that the "contracts" were not enforceable. Unenforceable though they were in the public courts, these contracts were nevertheless litigated in a private judiciary maintained by the company. Provision was made for the appeals of dealers from decisions of nonrenewal or termination by division heads, to a court of last resort established in 1939, and staffed with "judges" who were company men. In this corporation court of last resort, over a period of eighteen years, few cases were decided in favor of dealers. The proceedings in this private judiciary lacked the basic elements of due process of law, for only dealers and members of their organizations, without benefit of counsel, were permitted to appeal and appear.[49]

The quality of the justice that was strained through this private judiciary appears in the testimony of a dealer in Lake Orion, Michigan, who had strongly irritated the company officials by provocatively criticizing the company policy that granted to GM employees and executives in his territory the right to buy cars from the manufacturer at the same price he had to pay. The company was competing with one of its dealers. For his protests against the company policy of selling cars at the factory discount in his territory, the dealer was given notice that his franchise would not be renewed. At his hearing before the final court of corporate appeal he was called a "Red" and sneered at by the president of GM, who asked him what Art Summerfield (Postmaster General and a former automobile dealer) was "going to do for [him] now."[50] The dealer was not allowed to take counsel with him, nor was he given a transcript or other record of the proceedings made by General Motors.

Corporations in certain industries like the garment trades made regular use of arbitrators, who comprise a lay court, and the American Arbitration Association is a serviceable private judiciary, from which "judges" may be assigned for specific commercial and labor cases as they arise. Arbitration by private "lay" judges has been a well-known procedure for years in certain areas of labor relation. The procedures used by firms working on government contracts for the discharge of persons thought to be security risks may be scrutinized by the United States courts for compliance with the minimum requirements of due process. It is possible that the public courts may require the private judiciaries within the corporations to conform to the standards of the public judiciary in such cases.

Commonwealths: Greater and Lesser

Hobbes might think that today's corporations were not "lesser commonwealths" embodied in a greater but, in fact, rivals to the formal sovereign both in size and power. The Temporary National Economic Committee reported with awe the existence of billion-dollar corporations. In less than two decades after the TNEC, General Motors produced a billion-dollar profit after taxes. Through the General Motors Acceptance Corporation, GM controls the financing of approximately 50 per cent of total car sales. Although the GMAC and GM were found guilty of violating the antitrust laws in 1939, "nothing was done to separate them so as to deprive General Motors of this competitive advantage."[51] They did pay a fine of $20,000. The yearly budget for advertising in GM is around $100,000,000. Although this corporate prodigy is outstanding, it is by no means unique.

The literature of law and economics has tended to discuss corporations and the concentrates into which many have clustered in terms of the legal rules, like the antitrust laws and courts decisions, optimum size, economic efficiency, and welfare considerations that touch upon the condition of small business. New concepts of function and control must be devised, and these formulations cannot neglect the basically political character of the corporation.

References

1. Thomas Hobbes, *Leviathan* (1651) (New York, 1924), p. 218.

2. Arthur Bentley, *The Process of Government* (Bloomington, Ind., 1935), p. 268.

3. Walton Hamilton, *The Politics of Industry* (New York, 1957). He says, "There has arisen, quite apart from the ordinary operations of state, a government of industry which in its own distinctive way has its constitution and its statutes, its administrative and judicial processes, and its own manner of dealing with those who do not abide by the law of the industry" (p. 7).

4. Charles E. Merriam, *Public and Private Government* (New Haven, 1944), pp. 7–8.

5. C. Wright Mills, *The Power Elite* (New York, 1956), p. 165.

6. A. A. Berle, Jr., *The Twentieth Century Capitalist Revolution* (New York, 1954), p. 22.

7. A. A. Berle, Jr., *Natural Selection of Political Forces* (Lawrence, Kan., 1950), p. 24. Hamilton in speaking of politics said that "the word is used in the Aristotelian sense as an over-all term for the usages and traditions, for the arrangements and policies through which men are governed and through which men—usurping the function of the gods—attempt to shape destiny" (*The Politics of Industry,* p. 6). Some considerable time before either of the cited works of Berle and Hamilton, N. R. Danielian, using materials provided by the Federal Communications Commission investigation of the telephone industry, did a study of the American Telephone and Telegraph Company that was "Aristotelian" in its concept of politics. See *A. T. and T.* (New York, 1939).

8. Peter F. Drucker, *Concept of the Corporation* (New York, 1946), p. 21.

9. Otto Gierke, *Natural Law and the Theory of Society, 1500 to 1800* (Boston, 1957), p. lxvi. The reference is to the introduction by the translator, Ernest Barker, who examines various theories of the nature of the personality of the corporation and says that when we seek to discover what lies behind the legal Group-person, and constitutes its inner core, "We must not talk of 'fictions' which hover in a shadowy and unreal existence above a number of real individuals; we must not talk of 'collections' or 'brackets' or contractual nets, flung over so many individuals to bind them one to another in the bonds of an impersonal nexus." We must, in short, be prepared to accept an anthropomorphic superperson whose reality is as real as that of human beings. For a criticism of similar views stated by others, see Earl Latham, "Anthropomorphic Corporations, Elites, and Monopoly Power," *American Economic Review,* 57: 303–310 (May 1957).

10. Marshall E. Dimock, *Business and Government* (New York, 1949), p. 47.

11. Marshall E. Dimock and Howard K. Hyde, *Bureaucracy and Trusteeship in Large Corporations,* United States Temporary National Economic Committee, Monograph no. 11 (Washington, D. C., 1940).

12. Robert Aaron Gordon, *Business Leadership in the Large Corporation* (Washington, D.C., 1945). The text of this useful work uses the vocabulary of politics throughout much of the discussion of such concepts as hierarchy, leadership, power, coordination, and the like.

13. See, for example, Andrew Hacker, *Politics and the Corporation* (New York, n.d.), where the whole concept of corporate citizenship is confused with corporate employment, which is quite a different thing and is covered fully by William H. Whyte, Jr.

14. Leverett S. Lyons, Myron W. Watkins, and Victor Abramson, *Government and Economic Life* (Washington, D. C., 1939), I, 51–52.

15. William McDonald, ed., *Documentary Source Book of American History, 1606–1926* (New York, 1928), pp. 1ff.

16. *Ibid.,* p. 13. The jurisdiction of the "Treasurer and Company of Adventurers and Planters of the city of London for the first Colony in Virginia" was extended to Bermuda and other islands in 1612, but was soon revoked (*ibid.,* p. 15). The Virginia Company in its ordinance of 1621 established the pattern for the government of Virginia that was to be followed by the later English colonies (*ibid.,* p. 20). Thus the basic form of the public government in America derived from the provenance of a commercial corporation. The corporation created the government.

17. *Ibid.,* p. 22.

18. Lyons, Watkins, and Abramson, *Government and Economic Life,* I, 52.

19. At the end of a two-volume study of old corporations, John P. Davis in a chapter on modern corporations said: "Modern corporations seem to be substantially new bodies, modern not only in time but also in the nature of their activity." Second thought convinced him that the change was not fundamental, for "when a group of associated individuals is confirmed in its character as a group for the accomplishment of a public purpose through the pursuit by the group of private interest, the group is as much a corporation under the new definitions as it would have been under older ones." John P. Davis, *Corporations, Their Origin and Development* (New York, 1905), II, 248–249. Of the growth of corporations in the nineteenth century, Davis further said, ". . . the growth of corporations in western Europe and the United States signifies nothing less than a social revolution" (*ibid.,* p. 261).

20. *Ibid.,* p. 269. Lyons, Watkins, and Abramson point out that even as late as the ninth decade, the corporation had not entirely taken hold as the master form of business enterprise. Only half of the fourteen enterprises originally combined in the Standard Oil Trust Agreement of 1882 were incorporated (*Government and Economic Life,* I, 46).

21. Davis, *Corporations,* II, 269.

22. While safeguards for the public were being relaxed, protections for the corporation were being increased. Two key cases in the Supreme Court of the United States were decisive in the development of constitutionally vested interest. In Dartmouth College v. Woodward, 4 Wheaton 518 (1819), a corporate charter was held to be a contract under the protection of that clause of the Constitution that forbids a state to impair the obligations of a contract. And when the contract clause of the Constitution became eroded through state-favoring decisions under the police power doctrine, the Supreme Court held that corporations were persons under the protection of the due process clauses of the Fifth and Fourteenth Amendments. See San Mateo County v. S.P.R.R., 116 U.S. 138 (1885); Santa Clara County v. S.P.R.R., 118 U.S. 394 (1886). Justices Black and Douglas later argued that these cases should be overruled. See Connecticut Life Insurance Company v. Johnson, 303 U.S. 77 (1938) and Wheeling Steel Corporation v. Glander, 337 U.S. 562 (1949).

23. Lyons, Watkins, and Abramson, *Government and Economic Life,* I, 57.

24. See Carl J. Friedrich, *Constitutional Government and Democracy* (Boston, 1941), p. 128, for a discussion of the constituent power and the right of revolution.

25. U.S. Senate, Select Committee on Small Business, Subcommittee on Monopoly, *The International Petroleum Cartel,* Committee Print No. 6, 82 Cong., 2 Sess.; see summary of organization of the seven companies, pp. 32–33.

26. Berle, *Twentieth Century Capitalist Revolution,* p. 180.

27. The self-perpetuation of oligarchic control is aided by the membership in boards of directors of large numbers of operating officials. But even where "the active board is likely to be dominated by officer-directors who constitute a large minority or indeed even a majority of the board, the conclusion that the board does not typically serve to any marked extent as *an active and independent* participant in the leadership function holds with even greater force." Gordon, *Business Leadership in Large Corporations,* p. 134.
28. David Karr, *Fight for Control* (New York, 1956), p. 38.
29. The ICC, for example, by concerning itself with accounting procedure, the extension and withdrawal of facilities, rate-fixing, reorganizations, and other changes in the capital structure of the roads, "has much to do with the management of the railroads." Dimock and Hyde, "Bureaucracy and Trusteeship in Large Corporations," p. 36.
30. See Gordon, *Business Leadership in the Large Corporation,* pp. 189ff., for a discussion of the influence and leadership of active financial groups.
31. H. H. Gerth and C. Wright Mills, eds., *From Max Weber: Essays in Sociology* (New York, 1946), p. 196.
32. Bureaucracy, of course, is also a word of disparagement, suggesting ineptitude, insolence, extravagance, waste, nepotism, and other ills to which the institutional flesh is inclined. See the complaint of a distinguished economist who tried to get space on the "New England States," operated by the New York Central, and was told that the railroad was not interested in the business. Sumner Slichter, Letter to the Editor, *Boston Herald,* January 4, 1957.
33. James D. Mooney and Alan C. Reiley, *Onward Industry* (New York, 1931) and *The Principles of Organization* (New York, 1939).
34. Mills, *The Power Elite,* p. 133.
35. *Ibid.,* p. 134.
36. Chester I. Barnard, *The Functions of the Executive* (Cambridge, Mass., 1947), pp. 215ff.
37. *Ibid.,* p. 224.
38. *Ibid.*
39. Gordon, *Business Leadership in the Large Corporation,* p. 319.
40. *Ibid.*
41. *Ibid.*
42. United States Senate, Committee on the Judiciary, *Hearings* before the Subcommittee on Antitrust and Monopoly Pursuant to S. Res. 61, 84 Cong., 1 Sess., VII, 3609.
43. Joseph A. Schumpeter, *Capitalism, Socialism, and Democracy* (New York, 1947), thought that the trend represented by General Motors, if widespread, might lead to the overthrow of capitalism by the managers, not in any revolutionary spirit, nor by any aggressive action, but by ousting the entrepreneur and by robbing the bourgeoisie of its function. Gordon, *Business Leadership in the Large Corporation,* notes the Schumpeter thesis, p. 319 n.
44. See Gordon, *Business Leadership in the Large Corporation,* p. 85.
45. Federal Trade Commission v. Cement Institute, 333 U.S. 683 (1948), by certiorari from the Seventh Circuit Court of Appeals, Cement Institute v. FTC, 175 F. (2d) 533.
46. Earl Latham, *The Group Basis of Politics, A Study in Basing-Point Legislation* (Ithaca, 1952), pp. 78ff.

47. *Boston Herald,* October 2, 1956.

48. United States Senate, Committee on the Judiciary, *Report of the Committee on the Judiciary Containing the Staff Report of the Subcommittee on Antitrust and Monopoly,* Senate Report 1879, 84 Cong., 1 Sess.

49. It was the final Board of Appeals in which dealers lost so drastically. Of 80 cases appealed to this Board between 1938 and 1952, 44 were settled without hearing by the Board, and of these in 34 cases the car division withdrew its decision not to renew, and granted the dealer a new selling agreement for a period of less than one year. But of a total of 53 cases heard by the final Board from 1938 to 1955, dealers won only 6. See Senate Subcommittee on Antitrust and Monopoly, *Hearings,* VIII, 4382 and 4383.

50. *Ibid.,* pp. 3332–3336.

51. Senate Report 1879, p. 11. Previous litigation against Ford and Chrysler had resulted in separation of their financial affiliates. *Ibid.,* p. 69.

Questions for Discussion

1. Using appropriate tools for analysis, discuss the underlying structure of the management problems in the following three situations, reported, respectively, by Professors Arthur L. Stinchcombe [28], Chris Argyris [1], and Leonard R. Sayles [26]*:
   (a) ". . . under existing rules, the keeper of the tool bin is implicitly rewarded for keeping the tools out of the hands of workers" (p. 149).
   (b) ". . . success for budget supervisors means failure for factory supervisors. . . . In other words, the success of the finance man derives from finding errors, weaknesses, and faults that exist in the plant" (p. 103).
   (c) ". . . many times the staff group or the consultant or someone else in the organization has a reward system whereby he gets paid off for changes (regardless of their necessity) but those in key positions are not in any way rewarded for change and therefore resist it" (p. 85).

2. As a manager, what changes would you make to deal with the problems stated above? What problems would you expect to *create* by your remedial actions?

3. In some studies of the social structure of restaurants, William F. Whyte documented several problems in human relations. For example, there was tension and conflict between cooks and supplymen and between countermen and waitresses. In each case, lower-status employees were giving orders regularly to higher-status persons. It might be suggested that these cases involved inconsistencies between the authority system and the technological or work-flow system. Discuss this idea, using facts from other kinds of organizations as well as restaurants to illustrate your points.

4. A manufacturing manager who had installed a wage incentive system reported six months later that the system was a success because production was up and unit costs were down. A quality control manager in the same company said, however, that the percentage of rejects had increased markedly and that this was creating a backlog of rework requirements. An industrial engineering manager said that the expenditures for industrial engineering studies in that manufacturing department were up by 50 per cent. An industrial relations manager said arbitration fees resulting from incentive grievances had tripled. Discuss this case, using the tools for analysis which you judge appropriate.

5. Prepare a brief report in which you analyze an organizational behavior case, possibly a work experience in which you were a participant or observer, using explicitly the tools of interaction theory.

---

*See References following Chapter 2, pages 25–26.

6. Prepare a brief report in which you analyze an organizational behavior case, possibly a work experience in which you were a participant or observer, using explicitly the tools of functional analysis.

7. Discuss the following observation by Douglas McGregor [18]:

> The typical industrial organization offers only limited opportunities for the satisfaction of egoistic needs to people at lower levels in the hierarchy. The conventional methods of organizing work, particularly in mass production industries, give little heed to these aspects of human motivation (p. 38).

II

The Analysis of Organizational Behavior

Chapter Three

The Individual in the Organization: Psychological Factors in Organizational Behavior

Ever since the United States rejected Thomas Jefferson's attractive but simplistic vision of a nation of independent yeomen, and chose Alexander Hamilton's dream of a wealthy, complex and interdependent society, work has meant for most of us a job in an organization. And working in an organization means we must relate to other people in patterns of interdependence. In this chapter we will examine the nature of work, review Maslow's hierarchy of human needs, and then look at two aspects of a job: the relation of the job to the hierarchy of needs, and our orientations toward other people encountered on the job. Both influence the behavior of managers and subordinates.

The Meaning of Work

In examining the relationship of work to human nature, there is no more appropriate place to start than with the Bible. At the very beginning of the Old Testament, dealing with the origins of life and man, the issue of work and its meaning is considered. Whether the Book of Genesis is literal, allegorical, metaphorical, or pure myth, it does deal with the fundamental issue of work—and its viewpoint has been pervasive.

In the garden of Eden all the necessities of life were supplied, the physical wants were met without effort or anxiety. It was Paradise. But we are told that Adam and Eve disobeyed certain divine laws, and God was angered. The Lord said to Adam:

> Because thou has harkened to the voice of thy wife—and hast eaten of the tree wherefore I commanded thee that thou shouldst not eat, cursed is the earth with thy work; with labor and toil shalt thou eat thereof all the days of thy life.
>
> In the sweat of thy face shalt thou eat bread till thou return to the earth out of which thou wast taken, for dust thou art and unto dust thou shalt return [9].

What is the meaning of work in this passage? Clearly it implies that work is a punishment. It suggests further that work will be dirty, demeaning, and generally unpleasant—befitting the punishment that it is. And the reason for this work? To provide the physical necessities of life. The very meaning of the expulsion from Paradise is man's confrontation with his animal nature, his physical needs—and his mortality.

In addition to indicating that work is an unpleasant punishment, but necessary for physical survival, the Biblical passage implies that much of man's life will be consumed trying to satisfy his most basic needs. Most of man's life is to be a brutal struggle for survival. It was a good prediction! Certainly for most of mankind in most societies throughout most of history, much of life has consisted of working to satisfy the lowest levels of man's needs.

Many people have wondered if man's life should not come to something more than economic effort. Amateur metaphysicians over the years have speculated upon what Adam and Eve did in the Garden before the fall. They didn't have to work to meet the necessities of life; these were provided *gratis.* Genesis contains only one phrase discussing what they did before the expulsion: they cultivated the garden. Supposedly, then, they exerted physical effort, but clearly this was not to satisfy physical needs. It must have been related to some higher pursuits. Hannah Arendt [4] maintains that, as a result of the Biblical sin, man encountered the necessity to "labor"—that is, provide food, clothing, and shelter for himself. But from the beginning, according to Arendt, man always had the ability and need to "work" as a central expression of his humanity. Hence labor and work are separate conceptions—the former relating to necessities, the latter to aspirations.

The early Athenian Greeks anticipated this dichotomy between work and labor by their rigid distinction between economic and noneconomic activities. The Athenian conception of man's highest pursuit was something other than economic. Slaves performed the labor necessary to supply necessities for the Athenians who were in a position to have slaves. It was not only the dirty, mundane, and unpleasant physical labor that slaves handled, however. They were also in charge of economic activity—including the intellectual tasks associated with managing a business. A slave could even rise to some wealth and independence within Athenian society because of his management activities. The free Athenian, however, was not concerned with efforts to satisfy the lower needs. To be free (and obviously only a small proportion were ever really free) meant that one devoted himself to the pursuit of higher level satisfactions. In Greek society this consisted of teaching, the arts, athletics, or philosophic speculation. Most valued, however, was the pursuit of political justice. Yet any economic activity would interfere with a man's capacity for such political and philosophic action. The two realms—labor for economic purposes and work for higher purposes—were thus completely divorced, and no man faced with the problem of making a living was sufficiently free to be active in political affairs.

Athenians denigrated labor not only because it was mundane and physically hard. It made no intellectual demands. For the philosopher kings there were more complex and interesting political, ethical, and philosophical problems that required greater ingenuity. This is a point of great significance to managers in considering the problem of effectively motivating employees.

Let us consider the place of work in the modern world. Surely most of us today cannot make such an easy distinction between labor and work. No one has slaves anymore (and only a few can afford servants). We must find jobs. What is the relation of this job to the need hierarchy?

The Hierarchy of Human Needs

In the early 1800s, a band of pioneers led by a man named Donner crossed the western plains with ox-drawn covered wagons, and climbed into the Rocky Mountains. For most of the party, the trip ended there. Marooned by enormous snow drifts and slowly freezing on the wind-swept slopes, they were unable to move forward or go back. As they exhausted their supply of food, the party gradually deteriorated.

Some years ago, a diary kept by a member of the party was published [7], in which the writer described his compatriots at the beginning of the journey as "salt of the earth"—God-fearing and individualistic, but cooperative and concerned for each other's welfare. During their protracted ordeal in the mountains, they withdrew upon themselves; concern shifted from the larger group to the immediate family; then to the individual; finally, as in McKinley Kantor's description of a Civil War prison camp [16], the strong began to prey on the weak for personal survival, and the ultimate horror emerged—cannibalism.

The tragedy of the Donner party is an unpleasant illustration of Abraham Maslow's hierarchy of human needs in action. To the party, food eventually came to be all important and all motivating. If one is without food long enough, he becomes a sort of human piranha—thinking, dreaming, and hunting food without any other concern.[1] Such a food-seeking monster is not interested in building monuments, wearing fine clothes, or worshipping God. The satisfaction of the physiological drives is essential to the maintenance of life; thus Maslow described them as prepotent for the motivation of behavior.

Happily, the hierarchical model suggests that, as physical needs are met (at least at a minimum level), new needs emerge to motivate behavior. We have seen that man is a "wanting creature," striving to satisfy many different needs. Maslow described these needs and their order of potency as follows: (1) physiological, (2) safety, (3) love, (4) esteem, and (5) self-actualization.

Even the church has implicitly recognized the need hierarchy [15]. In recent years there has been a redirection of missionary work toward the lower end of the need structure. Much time, effort, and money today is directed toward developing the work skills that will enable people to meet their lower level physical and security needs. There are also substantial efforts to develop stronger and more stable families, which help satisfy affiliation needs. Spiritual needs may also exist, but the modern church recognizes that the higher needs are less motivating and less important to the individual if lower level needs are unsatisfied. The Bible tells us that "man does not live by bread alone," but as Maslow suggested, "man may live by bread alone . . . when there is no bread."

In discussing the hierarchy of needs, we are not merely presenting a mechanical device for fitting every individual we encounter into a simple category. To some extent, most people have all these drives. But their motivation for behavior differs with time and situation. The deprived ghetto youth apparently striving only for safety or sexual conquest is probably not really truncated in his need hierarchy. He may simply be unaware of the possibilities for fulfilling higher needs through legitimate means. Consequently, his drives for esteem, power, and achievement are expressed in anti-social activities.

The list of needs may not seem inclusive. After all, where is sex? Where

[1] For a classic literary example of this kind of behavior, see Ref. 12.

is altruism? It must be pointed out that specific behavior may reflect multiple motivations. Such complex motivation undoubtedly characterizes both sex and altruism. As any *Playboy* reader should be aware, sex in our society is a complex vehicle for need satisfaction, ranging from simple physiological drives to aspirations for affiliation, status, and power. Altruism may be an ego drive, reflecting needs for affection and achievement. We do not mean to imply that altruism and sex are always Machiavellian or necessarily selfish. Both express love and affiliation needs, but self-interest is intimately involved. This is not to be cynical; it is merely an observation on human nature.[2]

Do all individuals have the same needs? Obviously not. Although need structures in a particular sub-culture and culture tend to be similar, they still vary with individuals—because we each have a unique personality.

Entire schools of psychology have grown up around each of several perspectives on personality. Each definition reflects a central psychological commitment. A behaviorist's definition of personality will differ from a psychoanalyst's. The former will emphasize a pattern of behavior; the latter, underlying configurational or integrative psychological forces. Unfortunately, many theories of personality have been considered inclusive, when, actually, an understanding of personality development requires a study of the interrelationships of influences.

It is beyond the purpose of this volume to describe the different perspectives on personality. Nonetheless, we can still develop a usable concept of individual personality. According to Adorno and his associates [2], personality is

> a more or less enduring organization of forces within the individual. These persisting forces of personality help to determine response in various situations, and it is thus largely to them that consistency of behavior—whether verbal or physical—is attributable. But behavior, however consistent, is not the same thing as personality; personality lies behind behavior and within the individual. The forces of personality are not responsive, but [are a] readiness for response.

Thus, an individual personality may be viewed as the particular order and strength of each need in the hierarchical model. The hermit treasures autonomy above all except physiological necessities; the need for autonomy for this individual would have to be placed *low* on his hierarchy. The artist—at least as found in novels—may place creativity low on his hierarchy; that is, this need must be satisfied before he thinks of affiliation, status, or power.

Obviously, there can be argument over the order of needs. However, even with all its limitations, the concept of the need hierarchy is useful for the manager. As lower-level needs are relatively satisfied, they become less directly motivating for behavior. One is motivated mainly by the next level of unsatisfied need. Thus gratified needs, in a sense, disappear. They are not motivating. Since any manager attempts to influence human behavior, he must consider what needs are relatively unsatisfied, and hence can serve as levers for motivation. (In Part III of this volume we shall elaborate on this process.)

---

[2] In T. S. Eliot's play, *Murder in the Cathedral,* Part I, the character Thomas Becket says, "The last temptation is the greatest treason: to do the right deed for the wrong reasons."

Work and the Basic Needs

Certainly a job is directly related to obtaining physiological necessities and satisfying safety and security needs. We must work to earn the money to pay for the goods necessary to meet the lowest level of needs. In the United States, there is not enough arable land to allow every man to be an independent "yeoman," making his living without working for someone else. As Eric Hoffer, the philosopher-longshoreman of San Francisco, put it during a television interview: Thoreau is dead . . . and so are the possibilities for the Walden-Pond type of independent existence. We work on a job to get the money to buy necessities. We would also like the job to be steady, so that we can feel reasonably secure about our future.

But this situation is a fairly recent development in history. For many a man, even having a job has been no guarantee that he could really live. The history of the Industrial Revolution is replete with examples of concerted efforts by workers to elevate the rewards of industrial employment to the point where they would satisfy the basic necessities of life. Even subsistence as a reward for work was at times in doubt. Thomas Carlyle [5], discussing the demands of industrial workers engaged in an insurrection in Manchester in 1819, wrote:

> . . . these poor Manchester manual workers mean only, by day's-wages for day's work, certain coins of money adequate to keep them living;—in return for their work, such modicum of food, clothes and fuel as will enable them to continue their work itself! They as yet clamour for no more; the rest, still inarticulate, cannot yet shape itself into a demand at all, and only lies in them as a dumb wish; perhaps only, still more inarticulate, as a dumb, altogether unconscious want.

But what of the next levels, the needs above physiology and security on the hierarchy? What is the relationship of the job to the social needs for affiliation, membership, affection, or love?

Work and Affiliation

Historically, the primary source of satisfaction for the affiliation need has been the family. But American families in the 20th century have changed. We have fewer children than our grandparents did (although recently this trend has reversed itself). More fundamentally, the consanguine family unit has become a nuclear family unit. Infrequently do grandparents, children, uncles, aunts, cousins, and grandchildren live together, as they used to. Often the separate generations do not even live in the same neighborhood, city, or state. This means that the family unit is smaller.

Inside this smaller unit, encouraged by the availability of bicycles, motor scooters, motorcycles, and "personal" cars, family members tend to turn to outside associates for recreation, and satisfaction of the needs for membership, affection, affiliation, etc. Moreover, in our modern society, maintaining a family to supply affiliation requires a job and at least a modicum of economic stability. Thus the job has come to serve as the primary source of social satisfaction. But must the need for affiliation on the job be recognized by managers?

Employers of the 19th and early 20th century saw no need for social satisfaction on the job. In office and shop their posted policies frequently included dictums forbidding "socializing", "idle gossip" or "conspiratorial meetings." When Frederick Taylor and scientific management came along, managers were advised to treat people strictly as individuals and to offer individual piece-rate incentive pay which would encourage each employee to produce to his maximum ability. Managers in the 1920s were aware, and in the famous Hawthorne plant studies at Western Electric academic researchers corroborated, that many workers (if not most) limited their personal effort in order to maintain their membership in an informal social structure [14, 22]. At some point, for virtually everyone except the individualistic "rate-busters," the desire for communication, support, and friendship with associates on the job and during work hours became more important than the little bit of extra money that might be earned.

The relationship between work and affiliation varies, of course. For young, unmarried female clerical workers in an office, physical conditions and management policy must be adjusted to recognize the affiliation need. For ambitious young salesmen working on a commission, on-the-job social satisfaction is less relevant.

In addition to the two ways that the job aids in the satisfaction of the affiliation need (that is, maintenance of a family and social relations with fellow workers) Freud [8] suggested a third social contribution of the job. For him, a job forces a person to set aside his own concerns and confront the world. A job imposes discipline. It requires interpersonal communication that assists the individual to learn about the norms of society around him—and to maintain a sense of reality, identity, and stability by continually testing his own views against societal norms. Not that these norms are always right, but the job and the contact with the world that the job requires enables a man to live more easily in that world and to find desired social satisfactions.

Research on the mental health and attitudes of long-term unemployed males support Freud's suggestions [10]. These studies indicate very directly the relevance of the job to a man's sense of membership in society. Even though welfare and a variety of governmental programs remove the fears and anxieties about the satisfaction of physiological and security needs, the men feel out of place. They are not members; they are not fulfilling the requirements of the head of a household. In many cases they become withdrawn and depressed, unable even to take satisfaction in their families. They are simply not confronting the world in ways that our culture values.

Work and Social Esteem

In reply to the question "What do you do?" Americans generally respond with "I'm associated with IBM," or "I'm with General Electric." Fifty years ago, the replies would have been "I'm a machinist," or "I'm an accountant." The earlier responses were a legacy of the traditional societies of Europe, where a man's craft has always been a major determinant of his social esteem, status, or prestige. However, craft in these societies is generally determined by birth or family, which are the true determinants of status or prestige in these societies. The United States has always been a much less rigid society in terms of social class; for example, attitudes toward status distinctions vary with geography and socio-economic background—the criteria for social esteem in the Northeast or among the middle class is quite different from those in the Southwest or among the working class. But a man's association with a particular company of wide repute is a reliable source of status. Thus, in the United States, the corporation as a source of social prestige has begun to obliterate the older tradition of status differentiation on the basis of vocation or craft.

Within the corporation, elaborated hierarchies of positions and their attendant status symbols and perquisites also reflect the desire for status differentiation. Management ignores the necessity to correlate pay, title, authority, and symbols of status at its peril. A large regional insurance office is a case in point. The two or three huge rooms stretch out like an airplane hanger, aisle after aisle. With clerks, secretaries, representatives, claims men, supervisors, and department heads all seated at seemingly identical desks row after row, the scene resembles a Franz Kafka novel in its mechanistic oppressiveness. Not surprisingly, the management has difficulty with superior-subordinate relations, and particularly with supervisory morale. Giving out important-sounding job titles—or even more money—would be inadequate to satisfy the desire for status on the job. One of the principal causes of dissatisfaction is the lack of physical manifestation of status differences, including individual offices to give quiet and privacy.

The Higher Needs

In the years since the hierarchical model was advanced, substantial research has been conducted on the nature and impact of these needs on human behavior. Of special concern has been the upper levels of the hierarchy—the so-called "higher needs." Philosophers and psychologists alike have felt that the term "self-actualization" is too ambiguous to provide much help in understanding man. Thus three higher needs have been identified: competence, power, and achievement. Although they are undoubtedly not entirely distinct from one another—or from self-actualization—we shall describe each separately.

Competence

As many novelists have suggested, social esteem is for most people necessary but not sufficient.[3] In the long run, we are told, it is more important what we think of ourselves. So emerges the need for self-esteem, competence, and the feeling that one is capable of meeting challenge. We are dealing now with a complex drive, and perhaps we shall end up by lumping disparate needs into one package. But the thrust of the set of needs referred to as self-esteem or competence is clear. The individual is more than just a vehicle for instincts; he is also an active observer and shaper of his environment. As Robert White [27] suggests, one of the mainsprings of human motivation is an interest in getting to know what the world is like and in learning to get what one wants from it. He calls this a competence motive. The teacher hopes that this drive exists in his students as a desire to master an academic discipline, and in general expand themselves intellectually. Obviously, the competence motive may also take other directions. Self-esteem may be derived from competence in a wide variety of vocational and avocational activities.

This competence motive can be seen as active even in very young infants, in the fun of random fingering of objects, poking around, and touching whatever is in reach. Later, it is exploring, tinkering, taking things apart, putting them

---

[3] In the business field, the best-known novels making this point are *Point of No Return,* by J. P. Marquand; *Executive Suite,* by Cameron Hawley; and *The Man in the Grey Flannel Suit,* by Sloan Wilson.

together, and the like. Whether an adult's sense of competence is strong or weak depends on the balance of successes and failures he has experienced in his various encounters with the world.

Implicit in this need for self-esteem—and related to the need for social esteem—is a further desire: Most men want to feel that they are doing something important, that their activities have social purpose. We want to feel that we are contributing members of society. There is ego satisfaction in an awareness of the dependence and gratitude of others. Nonetheless, the drive for competence is mainly internal. In order to satisfy ourselves, we strive to understand, explore, and, as the mountain climber declares, to conquer a peak "because it is there." David Reisman [21] gave us the terms to describe an old American view: The "other-directed" man is driven by desires for recognition and status from others; the more mature and independent "inner-directed" individual, however, strives to satisfy only himself. Of course, the distinction is a simplification. Most men are both types. The need hierarchy suggests that as we obtain *some* social esteem, we shift from being other-directed and become inner-directed, in an effort to satisfy ourselves. The selected reading by Saul Gellerman following this chapter further elaborates on White's work and the competence motive.

Notice that we lose some people as we move up the hierarchy of needs. Not everyone advances to new needs for competence, power, or achievement as the lower needs are relatively satisfied. Also, as we move up the hierarchy, the order becomes less clear-cut. The relative importance of higher level needs and the distinctions among them are ambiguous. This is especially true with the power and achievement needs. Both are powerful drives to exceptional performance.

Power

Virtually everybody has Freud's pleasure-seeking and life-sustaining drives—needs much lower on the hierarchy. However, Freud's contemporary, Alfred Adler [3], maintained that power is the best explanation for the behavior of exceptional people. By power we mean the ability to influence others to behave in ways that suit our purposes. David McClelland [17] explains that it is measured by the degree of an individual's desire to control the means of influencing other people. This desire may be inferred from his emotional reaction to a dominance situation. For example: his pleasure in winning or anger at losing an argument; a concern with avoiding weakness; disputing a position; trying to put a point across; giving a command; etc.

As with social esteem, most of us have mixed feelings about the drive for power. Adler pointed out that the process of influencing and controlling other people is intrinsically enjoyable. "Power and glory," wrote Bertrand Russell [23], "are chief among the infinite desires of man." Friedrich Nietzsche [20] declared: "All [that] life desires above all [else] is to express its power. Life is itself will to power. The impulse of survival is only an indirect consequence of this will." But for Lord Acton [1], power corrupts. And in the views of the Protestant theologian Reinhold Niebuhr [19], the desire for power may reflect man's inherent weakness or basic sinfulness. To him, power emphasizes the "I" at the expense of the "Thou." Adler felt (and most of us would agree) that the drive for power would be healthier if it were a desire to control environment rather than human beings.

The inverse of power over others is freedom *from* the power of others. Freedom from arbitrary and unilateral authority, even that exercised by a benevolent ruler, is a persistent theme in history. Indeed, Adler suggested that the power drive had its roots in childhood, when the child is dependent upon and controlled by adults. The child wants to gain power over these superiors. With maturity, he attempts to gain autonomy through developing his abilities. The drive for autonomy reflects both a fear of dependence on others for the satisfaction of physiological needs, and a desire for freedom to pursue higher needs. The selected reading by Saul Gellerman following this chapter examines the power drive and its implications for management.

Achievement

Achievement may be considered the apex of human needs. At the top of the need hierarchy, drives for achievement, creativity, or self-actualization emerge. Again, as with the competence need, we are perhaps inappropriately combining separate motives, but they all point in the same direction. What a man can be, he must be; he should create and achieve everything he is capable of. Overcoming challenge, solving difficult and novel problems, creating new institutions and objects, developing attributes and capabilities—all these are sources of satisfaction for this need. Such drives characterize healthy and mature individuals, those who have moved beyond the lower level needs.

The achievement need, as McClelland and his associates [18] show, is manifest in efforts to meet standards of excellence: that is, the high achiever commits himself emotionally to tasks which he considers worth while and difficult. What we are talking about is a basic attitude toward life—when challenged, the individual with a high achievement need tries harder and demands more of himself. Consequently, he accomplishes more.

The most fascinating aspect of the achievement motive is that it seems to make accomplishment an end in itself. If anything, it is the person with little achievement motivation who expects a tangible reward for greater effort. Although the achievement-motivated person does not spurn tangible rewards, he does not regard them as essential. He takes a special joy in winning, or in competing successfully against a difficult standard; this means more to him than money or a pat on the back. He is not an altruist: he simply finds enough delight in doing difficult things that he does not need to be bribed to do them.

In general, people with a high degree of achievement motivation are more consistent, realistic, and action-minded than people with other kinds of motivational patterns. But this does not necessarily make them more productive; that seems to depend on whether the task requires some degree of personal initiative or inventiveness. If it does, the achievement-motivated person is very likely to leave his competitors far behind. But if it doesn't, he is likely to turn in an uninspired performance.

The achievement drive is especially relevant to managers in business organizations. Indeed, in a selected reading following this chapter, David McClelland maintains that the need for achievement is the most important factor in managerial success.

Work and the Higher Needs

The job is a source of satisfaction for physical demands, safety and security, affiliation, and social esteem. What about the more elusive concepts of competence, power, and achievement? Undoubtedly a major contribution to self-esteem can come from competent performance of one's job. Indeed, Thorsten Veblen many years ago described what we would call the drive for self-esteem and competence as the "instinct for good workmanship," which he said was a universal human characteristic untapped by most employers [26]. For some men, the job can be a major satisfier of the drives for self-actualization. Nonetheless, the jobs of many men (and probably most) do not provide this kind of satisfaction—and it may be unreasonable to expect that they ever will. As we relate jobs to the human need structure, it becomes clear that for some of us there is a unity (or at least substantial overlap) between labor and work—between activity to satisfy the lower needs and activity to satisfy higher needs. For most men, however, there is something of the ancient Greek divorce between work and labor.

As Ely Chinoy has clearly shown [6], the automobile worker's job is only a means to satisfy his basic needs. His other needs—for affiliation, status, self-esteem, and so on—must be fulfilled elsewhere if at all. Certainly the growth of hobbies among blue and white collar employees demonstrates the common desire to satisfy the competence drive, and perhaps even the achievement motive, through avocational activities. Sebastian de Grazia [11] has observed that today's father actually spends more time working than his 1890 great-grandfather—and this even though the work-week has been reduced by over twenty hours. When he came home from work, the 1890 father simply rested, and that was it. The contemporary father paints the house, mows the lawn, works on the car, and does a variety of other odd jobs around the house. His total working time is greater than his grandfather's and his avocational activity may be a major satisfier of his needs for competence and achievement.

In contrast, there is a greater unity to life for many managers and professionals. The labor which a man performs to gain the physiological necessities of life may also be the work he does to express his higher level drives. The idealistic M.D. cures the sick, obtains the necessary victuals, pays for his Cadillac, and expresses his creativity—all with the same activity. This perhaps accounts for the long hours that professionals and executives work, and their oft-quoted statements that they find recreation and fun in work, that their work is their life, etc. This view of the centrality of work as an expression of a man's higher nature is illustrated by the somewhat romantic phrases of Henry Van Dyke in a little grammar school pamphlet he wrote: "This is my work; my blessing, not my doom; of all who live, I am the one by whom this work can best be done in the right way." Such sentiment seems out of date now, but it resembles Frederick W. Taylor's 1911 statement [25] that work could be engineered so that everyone could be perfectly suited to his job—an optimistic if not realistic conclusion.

It is a moot point whether a sense of self-esteem and competence can be derived from work when there is no achievement. Van Dyke and Taylor suggest that doing a good job is a reward unto itself. On the other hand, the celebrated Russian novelist, Feodor Dostoevski, has told us in *Letters from the Underworld* that, no matter how good one is at a task, if the work has no intrinsic meaning or makes no contribution to anyone, it is torture. To work in the salt mines of Siberia was the worst of punishments—not because one couldn't do it well, but because it was meaningless. Former enlisted men in the Army remember the futility of being ordered to dig holes and later fill them, just to be kept busy.

Three Concepts of Work and Their Implications for Management

From the foregoing discussion, three major perspectives on work emerge:

1. A job may be viewed as a punishment, necessary to satisfy physiological and security requirements. Higher drives are to be pursued elsewhere—if at all.
2. A job is seen as good in itself. "Work is noble," states the Talmud, "because it honors the workman." In the United States, this has become the secularized Protestant ethic of Benjamin Franklin and Henry Van Dyke.
3. Work is good only insofar as it is a means to at least partial satisfaction of a wider range of needs—for physical necessities, for social satisfaction and esteem, and, more importantly, for competence and achievement. In other words, work must have a purpose known to the worker.

In a selected reading following this chapter, the late Douglas MacGregor points out that management has too often assumed that employes view work as punishment (Theory X). If this assumption was ever correct, it is no longer. According to MacGregor, management should shift its policies to recognize and appeal to higher needs (Theory Y). Frederick Herzberg [13] has also distinguished between different needs and their motivation at work. He reports, in a study of accountants and engineers, that both groups mention different factors in their jobs when they talk about what satisfies them and what dissatisfies them. They tend to cite factors inherent in performing work as satisfying, and factors surrounding work as dissatisfying. Achievement, recognition, and work itself are satisfiers. Interpersonal relations, company policy and administration, and working conditions are dissatisfiers. Herzberg reports that improved performance on the job is associated with increases in the satisfiers. He calls the satisfiers, for this reason, "motivators." He calls the environmental dissatisfiers "hygiene factors," in a suggested analogy with the way the term is used in preventive medicine.

Because satisfaction and dissatisfaction, or motivation and hygiene, are two different dimensions (not different parts of one dimension), less dissatisfaction does not equal more motivation. The fundamental implications for management of Herzberg's work are that making jobs "hygienic" through good conditions, good policies, and good interpersonal relations only avoids dissatisfaction; making jobs motivating requires designing them to yield intrinsic higher level need satisfactions. Herzberg suggests that a good share of managerial effort to motivate employees is misconceived and misdirected out of a failure to see the relationship between the factors in and around work and needs at different levels. While it may indeed be wise to stave off dissatisfactions, the policy which does so effectively probably cannot be expected to motivate.

It is obvious that a manager cannot assume what work means to his subordinates, nor that they all agree on its meaning—at least not above the necessity to obtain funds to satisfy the basic needs. Depending upon the overlay of the incumbent's expectations and the job's realities, we get a number of possibilities. A convenient—if over-simplified—outline of these possibilities follows:

1. A person with a truncated need structure (one who is influenced *only* by lower level needs) will be motivated to obtain only money or social satis-

faction through his job. Whether the job or the manager offers opportunities for competence, power, or achievement, is irrelevant. (Indeed, the employee may become confused and upset if the job contains these opportunities and the manager attempts to appeal to these higher needs.) The manager's effectiveness will depend upon how well he exercises his authority over the means to satisfy the lowest needs—e.g., pay, working conditions, hours, etc.

2. A person with developed higher needs who has been taught or believes that a job is an unpleasant necessity and work a punishment will be motivated to obtain only money and social satisfaction on the job. Money may be used to satisfy higher needs off the job. Whether the job or the manager offers opportunities for competence, power, or achievement is irrelevant. The manager's effectiveness will depend upon how well he exercises his authority over the means to satisfy the lowest needs.
3. A person with developed higher needs who believes that a job is a legitimate outlet for these needs will be motivated to achieve competence, power, and achievement on the job. (*a*) If the job or the manager provides no opportunity to fulfill these needs, the employee will probably respond with behavior detrimental both to himself and to the organization. (*b*) If the job or the manager provides opportunities for the fulfillment of such needs, the employee will respond with behavior constructive to himself and the organization.

The Chris Argyris selection following this chapter elaborates on the response patterns of people in various organizational situations—particularly 3(*a*) and (*b*) above. Argyris describes retaliatory and defensive efforts to cope with the frustration and conflict characteristic of many jobs.

Orientations Toward Other People on the Job

Each of us must relate to other people on a job. This process of interaction and the predispositions we bring to the job influence our behavior in the organization. More fundamentally, we must perceive the world around us. That a person notices, sees, and interprets everything through his own "rose or violet-colored glasses" is a well-known cliché. In his selected reading following this chapter, Harold Leavitt helps us understand what goes on in the human mind in its efforts to make sense of the complex world outside. Important in Leavitt's explanation are how the mind operates in perceiving things, how it may have a deep, general outlook of good and bad, and how it works in perceiving the self. Another reading on perception, by Dearborn and Simon, gives an important example of how an individual's private experience in an organization influences what he will see in the operations of a business corporation.

Perceptions are sharply influenced by the individual's needs and attitudes—for example, his attitudes toward authority figures, toward work, toward personal ambition, etc. The human mind interprets people and events in relation to these beliefs. It is beyond the scope of this book to present a comprehensive description of the formation of attitudes. Certain of them, however, are of special importance in organizations. These are deep, relatively unchanging beliefs or orientations, formed by past experience as a person comes in contact with different people. If the dynamic chain of events described in the two readings by Argyris and Bennis and Shepard are studied carefully, some very helpful insights can be derived about the nature of attitudinal orientations and how they are learned. Some of these orientations are accurate in that the belief represents what is "out there"—others are wrong in that they are distortions of what is "out there." In the latter case, they are perpetuations of past maladaptive defense mechanisms, as if the person were learning the wrong lesson over and over again.

Be this as it may, all of the attitudinal orientations are true and accurate in one sense: if a person holds a certain orientation in his mind, and acts upon it, this is a fact of organizational life. Our purpose is to understand what is happening with individuals in an organization. If Joe Jones has a certain orientation, his superior will be more effective if he identifies Jones' orientation as reality. The executive who is less effective may blame Jones for something over which poor Joe has no control—his whole past life.

These perceptual distortions and pervasive attitudes are illustrated by the cartoon that shows a cigar-smoking, well-fed executive sitting in the office of a psychologist and staring at an amorphous ink blot. In reply to a question about what he sees, our successful stereotype exclaims: "I see creeping socialism, welfare chiselers, long-haired hippies, and Communist threats to our American way of life!" Beauty is truly in the eye of the beholder.

In order to study the orientations that people bring to interpersonal relations, a number of researchers have used so-called T groups or sensitivity training techniques. Behavior in an unstructured small group can suggest much about the question "What are people like when they interact with other people?" Bennis and Shepard present a picture of man derived from observations during such T group training experiences. Developed first by the National Training Laboratories, sensitivity training is being used quite extensively in business, church, hospital, and governmental organizations. In Chapter 8, we will see how this training works in a business firm. But before studying its practical applications, we need to know what group dynamics has taught us about the nature of man.

Attitudes Toward Authority

According to Bennis and Shepard, man faces two big problems when he comes into contact with others. The first is the problem of authority relationships—commonly referred to as the problem of the pecking order. Based on their authority orientations, there are apparently three kinds of human beings:

1. People who have a pronounced feeling of comfort in having others be leaders, or in having rules and procedures, are called "dependents."
2. People with pronounced feelings of discomfort toward other people in authority, or toward rules and regulations, are called "counterdependents."
3. People with lesser feelings on both dimensions, who have an ability to watch real people without stereotyping them, are called "independents."

If a person falls in one of the first two groups—either accepting or rejecting *all* authority systems—he begins to develop certain other deeper views of man. For example, the man who trusts all bosses as being helpful on the surface may cling to this comforting view, but since the world is not really like this, he may also develop an underlying distrust of authority systems. He will vacillate between the extremes of submissiveness and rebelliousness. The same is true of the compulsive[4] counterdependent. Believing that all authority figures and systems are bad in spite of the fact there are some good leaders and organizations, he too may vacillate between wanting more direction (submissiveness) and hating all direction (rebelliousness).

Attitudes Toward Intimacy

An additional problem which all men face is that of intimacy. Again we have three classes, with differing views of man. The first cannot rest until he has stabilized a relatively high degree of intimacy with others (personals). The second man tends to avoid any intimacy with others and to be uncomfortable at any show of feelings, whether it be hostility or affection (counter-personals). Third, there is the man who has a realistic view of other men—he is independent. As in relation to authority, those people who have strong tendencies to be either personal or counter-personal are frequently destructively competitive, exploit relations with other people, and are deeply distrustful.

Implications for Behavior

When a person joins an organization, he may reveal himself to be crippled in his ability to work with others and solve problems because he has one of four stereotyped notions about authority and intimacy: dependent, counter-dependent, personal, or counter-personal. These are his fixed orientations about how he should treat others and how they will treat him. We can also propose what this man *ought* to be like (and hopefully can be helped to be like through T-group training). He ought to be more capable of looking at himself, other people, and relationships for what they *are.* He should not be so prone to engage in rebellion, submission, destructive competition, or exploitation of others. In addition to causing unhappy stress, such behavior may interfere with work and hinder the ability of an organization to move toward its goal.

Summary

In this chapter we have sketched a model of the human resources that both lead and follow in an organization. We have considered a flexible hierarchy of human needs, ranging from physiological imperatives to creative desirables. What are the implications of our discussion of human needs and the meaning of work? In many ways, response to this question is the major subject of this book, but we can anticipate by keeping several points in mind:

1. Gratified needs disappear as motivators of behavior. Since we shall maintain in Part III that the most pervasive task of the manager is influencing human behavior, this implies that the manager must be aware of the next relevant levels of unsatisfied needs among his subordinates, because these must be his primary motivational focus.
2. The manager cannot ignore the basic needs. These must continue to be satisfied or they will emerge as motivators of behavior. Indeed, at times

[4]"Compulsive" here simply means one who has a particular orientation and holds to it, even if the facts "out there" do not always correspond to that orientation.

the manager may want to move down the ladder, to lead by appealing to a fear for the basic needs (e.g., by threatening to fire a recalcitrant individual).

3. The manager must understand the orientations toward work (e.g., as punishment, as good, as a means of high-level satisfaction) that characterize the culture in which he lives, the subculture from which he hires, and the people whom he wishes to manage.
4. A good manager endeavors to understand his own basic orientations toward other people as well as the views on authority and intimacy characterizing his key subordinates. None of us can be completely unbiased, but we may be able to compensate and more closely approximate reality.

In the selected readings following this chapter, we shall find psychologists and sociologists describing people engaged in endless conflict, games, and defensive behavior to protect themselves or strike out against others—all in a somewhat futile attempt to satisfy needs ranging from basic desires to independence and achievement. In Chapter 7, "Political Behavior in Organizations," we shall see a quite different view of man—the reasonable man who wants law and order, with rules and authority in moderation, and wise leaders who direct and allow freedom within reason. How do these fit together? The only answer is that we are dealing with one of the oldest questions to plague man. How can we achieve freedom and self-actualization on the one hand, and law and order on the other—both at the same time? This book cannot answer this question. But it can acknowledge the existence of the problem and examine some of its analytic components and selected attempts at solution.

In Part III, where we consider the process of management, we shall return to the needs and work attitudes developed in this chapter to show how individual and organizational behavior may be influenced.

A moving illustration of the multiple need satisfaction which a job may provide is shown by the case of a Harlem sign painter who was retired at 93. After a lifetime of work and two days of retirement, William Washington Brooks went to the State Unemployment Office—not to apply for unemployment compensation or social security, but to find a new job. When asked why, he responded: "A man, if he is a man, has got to work. A man with no work has part of his manhood taken away from him, and also his pride" [24].

References

1. Acton, Baron (John E. Dalberg). *Essays on Freedom and Power.* Noonday Press, 1948.
2. Adorno, T. W., *et al. The Authoritarian Personality.* Harper & Row, 1950.
3. Ansbacher, H. L., and R. R. Ansbacher (eds.). *The Individual Psychology of Alfred Adler.* Basic Books, 1956.
4. Arendt, H. *The Human Condition.* University of Chicago Press, 1958.
5. Carlyle, T. *Past and Present.* Macmillan, 1927.
6. Chinoy, E. *The Automobile Worker and the American Dream.* Doubleday, 1955.
7. Croy, H. *Wheels West.* Hastings House, 1955.

8. Freud, S. *Civilization and its Discontents,* tr. J. Riviere. Doubleday-Anchor (no date).
9. *Genesis,* Chapter 3, Verses 17–20.
10. Ginzberg, E., *et al. The Unemployed.* Harper & Row, 1943.
11. Grazia, S. de. *Of Time, Work and Leisure.* 20th Century Fund, 1962.
12. Hamsun, K. *Hunger* (1899). Farrar, Straus & Giroux, 1967.
13. Herzberg, F. *Work and the Nature of Man.* World, 1966.
14. Homans, G. *The Human Group.* Harcourt, Brace & World, 1950.
15. Horan, H. "A Missionary's Predicament: To Be Who? To Become What?" *America* (Aug. 26, 1967).
16. Kantor, McK. *Andersonville.* World, 1955.
17. McClelland, D. C. *The Achieving Society.* Van Nostrand, 1961.
18. ———, *et al. The Achievement Motive.* Appleton-Century-Crofts, 1953.
19. Niebuhr, R. *The Nature and Destiny of Man.* Scribners, 1949.
20. Nietzsche, F. *The Will to Power,* tr. A. M. Ludovici. Macmillan, 1929.
21. Reisman, D., *et al. The Lonely Crowd.* Yale University Press, 1961.
22. Roethlisberger, F. J., and W. J. Dickson. *Management and the Worker.* Harvard University Press, 1939.
23. Russell, B. R. *Power, A New Social Analysis.* Norton, 1938.
24. Talese, G. "A Sign Hanger, 93, Asks State to Help Him Start New Career." *The New York Times* (June 17, 1963).
25. Taylor, F. W. *The Principles of Scientific Management.* Harper & Row, 1911.
26. Veblen, T. "The Instinct of Workmanship." *The Portable Veblen,* ed. Max Lerner. Viking, 1961.
27. White, R. W. "Motivation Reconsidered: The Concept of Competence." *Psychological Review,* Vol. 66 (1959).

Readings

The Competence and Power Motives

SAUL W. GELLERMAN

The Competence Motive: Robert W. White

A great many people have been diagnosed and treated psychologically since Freud and Adler did their pioneering work in the early part of the century. Out of this vast body of observation and experience have come a number of modifications of the original theories. While the main outlines of the classical theories have stood the test of time fairly well—which is, of course, a tribute to the genius of Freud and Adler—modern psychologists have found it necessary to extend or reinterpret certain aspects of these theories in order to make them fit the facts more closely.

A recent reinterpretation of this type which has considerable significance for our understanding of work motivation has been advanced by Robert W. White of Harvard University. White notes that the original Freudian theory, for all its complexity, is still a little too simple to account for all the facets of human behavior. Specifically, the individual is more than just a vehicle for a set of instincts; he is also an active observer and shaper of his environment. For White, one of the mainsprings of human motivation is an interest in getting to know what the world is like and in learning to get what one wants from it. Whereas Freud stressed the life-preserving and comfort-seeking instincts and Adler, going a step further, stressed the drive for power over others, White notes that people also want to understand and manipulate their physical environment (and, later on, their social environment too). In the broadest sense, they like to be able to make things happen—to create events rather than merely to await them passively.

White calls this desire for mastery "the competence motive." It can be seen even in very young infants, he believes, in the form of random fingering of objects, poking around, and feeling whatever is in reach. Later on it takes the form of exploring, tinkering, taking things apart, putting them together, and the like. As a result of years of learning his way around his own small world, learning what its possibilities are and how to exploit them, the young boy develops a

From *Motivation and Productivity,* by Saul W. Gellerman. The American Management Association, Inc. (1963), pp. 109–114. Reprinted by permission.

certain assurance that he can handle himself equally well in the larger world he will enter as an adult. Whether his sense of competence is strong or weak depends on the balance of successes and failures the boy has experienced in his pint-sized forays into the world around him. If successes have predominated, he will probably come to regard life as a fairly promising venture where a little common sense and persistence can take him a long way. On the other hand, if the failures have outweighed the successes, the boy may regard life as a hazardous game at best, one in which running risks is likely to lead to nothing but another fiasco, so that it makes more sense simply to wait for circumstances to come along and have their will with him than to try to influence them.

Because the individual can hardly avoid some kind of transactions with his environment every day, the ledger of successes and failures is altered constantly. Consequently, one's fate is never entirely sealed. There is always the possibility that a particularly fortunate set of experiences will come along to bolster a timid ego, or contrariwise an unfortunate set may knock the props out from under an overly confident one. While the emerging personality may be pretty well jelled in a number of important respects by age five, this is not true of the sense of competence: It can get off to a bad start and still develop strongly as the result of later successes.

But there is, alas, a limit to this. After a time the sense of competence is also likely to reach a sort of plateau from which it may vary somewhat but not (ordinarily) a great deal. This is because after a while the sense of competence begins to affect the likelihood of a given experience's turning into a success or a failure. The more venturesome spirits will be out trying to win things or change things, and by brushing aside obstacles and persisting toward their goals they tip the scales of chance in their favor. Meeker individuals will venture less and therefore gain less and will perhaps shrink a little too readily from obstacles. Thus the sense of competence gradually becomes a sort of self-fulfilling prophecy: The individual seldom achieves more than he expects because he does not try to achieve more than he thinks he can.

Whereas the Freudians feel that the crucially determining years are from birth to five or so, White considers the years from about six to nine to be especially important in the development of the competence motive. These are the awkward in-between years when the child is no longer entirely under the family wing but by no means altogether out from under it. He is developing his contacts with other boys outside the family—contacts which in a few more years will blossom into a far more congenial and attractive society for the boy than his family. Out of the pre-teen pal and club relationships comes the full-blown microcosm of adolescence, with its own codes of conduct and its raucous, sometimes rebellious, experimentation with being grown-up. The seeds of this independence are just beginning to sprout in the six-to-nine period, which is why it is so important as far as competence is concerned. This is where a shy child can be brought out of his shell by contacts with people who, being his own age, had nothing to do with his retiring into a shell in the first place. It is where the spoiled, willful, or self-important child can get his much-needed comeuppance at the hands of his contemporaries. It is where the adventurous child can try his wings for the first time outside the protecting sphere of his family. It is, in a word, the first significant test to which the emerging sense of competence is put.

Although the results of the test do not conclusively determine just how strong a sense of competence the boy will have thereafter, they have a lot to do with it. The pattern set in these years will repeat itself later because of the competence—behavior cycle which soon starts to operate. The seemingly radical changes in outlook that sometimes occur in the twenties or even later may be more apparent than real: Somewhere along the line the beginnings of a sense of competence—of a constructive attitude toward opportunities—have probably been tucked away. At the right moment and in the right atmosphere, this latent optimism about oneself can burst forth.

In adults the competence motive is very likely to express itself as a desire for job mastery and professional growth. It may therefore have a great deal to do with Herzberg's finding that the most lasting satisfactions of accountants and engineers are derived from solving difficult technical problems. The need for a suitable outlet for this motive, in a civilized society that has had most of the elemental challenges engineered out of it, may even underlie the growing tendency for people to identify themselves with their professions rather than with a particular employer or the region or group in which they were born and raised.

The job can be one of the few remaining arenas in which a man can match his skills against the environment in a contest that is neither absurdly easy nor prohibitively difficult. Where such a contest is possible, the competence motive may be exercised and considerable rewards may be enjoyed. But, where it is impossible, as in most routinized or oversupervised jobs, a strong competence motive leads only to frustration, while a weak one merely encourages resignation and dependency.

Further, the sense of competence probably plays a key role in effecting job success, especially in those jobs where initiative or innovation is essential. A man who trusts his own ability to influence his environment will actually try to influence it more often and more boldly than someone who is inclined to let the environment influence him. Can it be, then, that the games and horseplay of seven- and eight-year-olds have something to do with events in the executive suite thirty years later? White's theory suggests that they may.

The Power Motive: Alfred Adler

Alfred Adler, a one-time collaborator of Freud's who later broke with him to establish his own school of thought, has also had an important influence on our understanding or work motivation. Adler is not as well known as Freud, even among professionals; in fact, many of his ideas have become accepted today without having his name attached to them. Unlike Freud, who stressed the pleasure-seeking and life-sustaining motives, Adler placed a great deal of emphasis on the power motive. By "power" he meant the ability to require others to behave in ways that suited one's purposes. An infant actually has a great deal of power over others. As any parent can testify, a baby can cause a considerable commotion among all the adults within earshot with the merest yelp.

According to Adler, this ability to manipulate other people is inherently pleasurable. Not only does the child have a hard time unlearning it, but he may also spend a good deal of his adult life trying to recapture that blissful condition of having other people do as he wills. However, Adler did not consider the child to be merely a miniature dictator. He recognized, first of all, that power was not sought for its own sake so much as it was a refuge from the utter helplessness of childhood. Adults are the child's lifeline, and it is a life-and-death matter to the child that the adults in his world be reliable; therefore, the power motive acquires an urgency which it never quite loses even though it eventually becomes unnecessary. It is especially strong in an older child or in an adult who feels handicapped in some way in his ability to win the respect and attention of others. Such people may go to considerable lengths to command attention, thereby overcoming whatever real or imagined weakness it was that had disturbed them in the first place. In describing this process, Adler introduced two well-known terms to psychology: *inferiority complex* (underlying fears of inadequacy or handicap which need not necessarily have a basis in fact) and *compensation* (the tendency to exert extreme efforts to achieve the goals which the "inferiority" would ordinarily deny).

Second, Adler recognized that power was not the only way to solve the problem of helplessness. In time the growing child realizes that cooperativeness wins a more permanent assurance to safety for him than power ever could, and at considerably less cost in terms of watchfulness and fear of retaliation. If the child's development proceeds normally and does not encounter too much tension, the power motive gradually transforms itself into a desire to perfect his relationships with others—that is, to make these relationships more confident, open, and helpful. Thus the mature adult would be able to move among others freely, without fear or suspicion. On the other hand, if the process were stunted somewhere along the line, perhaps by too many disappointing contacts with untrustworthy adults, the power motive would not only persist but would actually become stronger. The adult who had grown up in this way would be on guard, rarely willing to reveal very much of his plans or feelings and continually on the lookout for an advantage that would secure his position in what seemed a treacherous world.

Adler, like Freud, held that the basic life style of an individual was determined quite early by the quality of the child's experiences with the adults in his little world. By age five or thereabouts the child would either have developed a flexible confidence in others, a guarded determination not be hurt by them, or, as is more likely, some kind of in-between variation including both trust and power strivings to some degree.

Both Freud and Adler were primarily concerned with understanding psychological disorders in order to treat them more effectively. Therefore, their ideas dwell more on the making of a neurosis than on how people get to be normal. Only recently have modern psychologists begun to extend the thinking of these great classical theorists to the understanding of normal psychological development and, more specifically, to the adjustment of the adult to his career.

The Achievement Motive

DAVID C. McCLELLAND

What accounts for the rise in civilization? Not external resources (i.e., markets, minerals, trade routes, or factories), but the entrepreneurial spirit which exploits those resources—a spirit found most often among businessmen.

Who is ultimately responsible for the pace of economic growth in poor countries today? Not the economic planners or the politicians, but the executives whose drive (or lack of it) will determine whether the goals of the planners are fulfilled.

Why is Russia developing so rapidly that—if it continues its present rate of growth—it will catch up economically with the most advanced country in the world, the United States, in 25 or 30 years? Not, as the U.S.S.R. claims, because of the superiority of its Communist system, but because—by hook or by crook—it has managed to develop a stronger spirit of entrepreneurship among executives than we have today in the U.S.

How can foreign aid be most efficiently used to help poor countries develop rapidly? Not by simply handing money over to their politicians or budget makers, but by using it in ways that will select, encourage, and develop those of their business executives who have a vigorous entrepreneurial spirit or a strong drive for achievement. In other words: *invest in a man, not just in a plan.*

What may be astonishing about some of these remarks is that they come from a college professor, and not from the National Association of Manufacturers. They are not the defensive drum rattlings of an embattled capitalist, but are my conclusions, based on nearly 15 years of research, as a strictly academic psychologist, into the human motive that appears to be largely responsible for economic growth—research which has recently been summarized in my book, entitled *The Achieving Society.*[1]

Since I am an egghead from way back, nothing surprises me more than finding myself rescuing the businessman from the academic trash heap, dusting him off, and trying to give him the intellectual respectability that he has had a hard time maintaining for the last 50 years or so. For the fact is that the businessman has taken a beating, not just from the Marxists, who pictured him as a greedy capitalist, and the social critics, who held him responsible for the Great Depression of the 1930's, but even from himself, deep in his heart.

One of the queerest ironies of history, as John Kenneth Galbraith points out in *The Affluent Society,*[2] is that in a sense Marx won his case with his sworn enemies, the capitalists. Marx loudly asserted that they were selfish and interested only in profits. In the end many agreed. They accepted the Marxist materialistic view of history. The modern businessman, says Galbraith, "suspects that the

From "Business Drive and National Achievement," *Harvard Business Review* (July–August 1962), pp. 99–112.

[1] Princeton, D. Van Nostrand Co., Inc., 1961.
[2] Boston, Houghton Mifflin Company, 1958.

moral crusade of reformers, do-gooders, liberal politicians, and public servants, all their noble protestations notwithstanding, are based ultimately on self-interest. 'What,' he inquires, 'is their gimmick?' "[3]

If not only the Marxists, but Western economists, and even businessmen themselves, end up assuming that their main motive is self-interest and a quest for profit, it is small wonder that they have had a hard time holding their heads high in recent years.

But now the research I have done has come to the businessman's rescue by showing that everyone has been wrong, that it is *not* profit per se that makes the businessman tick but a strong desire for achievement, for doing a good job. Profit is simply one measure among several of how well the job has been done, but it is not necessarily the goal itself.

The Achievement Goal

But what exactly does the psychologist mean by the "desire for achievement"? How does he measure it in individuals or in nations? How does he know that it is so important for economic growth? Is it more important for businessmen to have this desire than it is for politicians, bishops, or generals? These are the kinds of questions which are answered at great length and with as much scientific precision as possible in my book. Here we must be content with the general outline of the argument, and develop it particularly as it applies to businessmen.

To begin with, psychologists try to find out what a man spends his time thinking and daydreaming about when he is not under pressure to think about anything in particular. What do his thoughts turn to when he is by himself or not engaged in a special job? Does he think about his family and friends, about relaxing and watching TV, about getting his superior off his back? Or does he spend his time thinking and planning how he can "sell" a particular customer, cut production costs, or invent a better steam trap or toothpaste tube?

If a man spends his time thinking about doing things better, the psychologist says he has a concern for achievement. In other words, he cares about achievement or he would not spend so much time thinking about it. If he spends his time thinking about family and friends, he has a concern for affiliation; if he speculates about who is boss, he has a concern for power, and so on. What differs in my approach from the one used by many psychologists is that my colleagues and I have not found it too helpful simply to *ask* a person about his motives, interests, and attitudes. Often he himself does not know very clearly what his basic concerns are—even more often he may be ashamed and cover some of them up. So what we do is to try and get a sample of his normal waking thoughts by asking him just to tell a few stories about some pictures.

Stories Within Stories

Let us take a look at some typical stories written by U.S. business executives. These men were asked to look briefly at a picture—in this case, a man at a worktable with a small family photograph as one side—and to spend about five minutes writing out a story suggested by the picture. Here is a very characteristic story:

---

[3] *Ibid.,* p. 71.

> "The engineer is at work on Saturday when it is quiet and he has taken time to do a little daydreaming. He is the father of the two children in the picture—the husband of the woman shown. He has a happy home life and is dreaming about some pleasant outing they have had. He is also looking forward to a repeat of the incident which is now giving him pleasure to think about. He plans on the following day, Sunday, to use the afternoon to take his family for a short trip."

Obviously, no achievement-related thoughts have come to the author's mind as he thinks about the scene in the picture. Instead, it suggests spending time pleasantly with his family. His thoughts run along *affiliative* lines. He thinks readily about interpersonal relationships and having fun with other people. This, as a matter of fact, is the most characteristic reaction to this particular picture. But now consider another story:

> "A successful industrial designer is at his 'work bench' toying with a new idea. He is 'talking it out' with his family in the picture. Someone in the family dropped a comment about a shortcoming in a household gadget, and the designer has just 'seen' a commercial use of the idea. He has picked up ideas from his family before—he is 'telling' his family what a good idea it is, and 'confidentially' he is going to take them on a big vacation because 'their' idea was so good. The idea will be successful, and family pride and mutual admiration will be strengthened."

The author of this story maintains a strong interest in the family and in affiliative relationships, but has added an achievement theme. The family actually has helped him innovate—get a new idea that will be successful and obviously help him get ahead. Stories which contain references to good new ideas, such as a new product, an invention, or a unique accomplishment of any sort, are scored as reflecting a concern for achievement in the person who writes them. In sum, this man's mind tends to run most easily along the lines of accomplishing something or other. Finally, consider a third story:

> "The man is an engineer at a drafting board. The picture is of his family. He has a problem and is concentrating on it. It is merely an everyday occurrence—a problem which requires thought. How can he get that bridge to take the stress of possible high winds? He wants to arrive at a good solution of the problem by himself. He will discuss the problem with a few other engineers and make a decision which will be a correct one—he has the earmarks of competence."

The man who wrote this story—an assistant to a vice president, as a matter of fact—notices the family photograph, but that is all. His thoughts tend to focus on the problem that the engineer has to solve. In the scant five minutes allowed, he even thinks of a precise problem—how to build a bridge that will take the stress of possible high winds. He notes that the engineer wants to find a good solution by himself, that he goes and gets help from other experts and finally makes a correct decision. These all represent different aspects of a complete achievement sequence—defining the problem, wanting to solve it, thinking of means of solving it, thinking of difficulties that get in the way of solving it (either in one's self or in the environment), thinking of people who might help in solving it, and anticipating what would happen if one succeeded or failed.

Each of these different ideas about achievement gets a score of +1 in our scoring system so that the man in the last incident gets a score of +4 on the scale of concern or need for achievement (conventionally abbreviated to *n* Achievement). Similarly, the first man gets a score of −1 for his story since it is completely unrelated to achievement, and the second man a score of +2 because there are two ideas in it which are scorable as related to achievement.

Each man usually writes six such stories and gets a score for the whole test. The coding of the stories for "achievement imagery" is so objective that two expert scorers working independently rarely disagree. In fact, it has recently been programed for a high-speed computer that does the scoring rapidly, with complete objectivity, and fairly high accuracy. What the score for an individual represents is the frequency with which he tends to think spontaneously in achievement terms when that is not clearly expected of him (since the instructions for the test urge him to relax and to think freely and rapidly).

Thinking Makes It So

What are people good for who think like this all the time? It doesn't take much imagination to guess that they might make particularly good business executives. People who spend a lot of their time thinking about getting ahead, inventing new gadgets, defining problems that need to be solved, considering alternative means of solving them, and calling in experts for help should also be people who in real life *do* a lot of these things or at the very best are readier to do them when the occasion arises.

I recognize, of course, that this is an assumption that requires proof. But, as matters turned out, our research produced strong factual support. . . . In three countries representing different levels and types of economic development, managers or executives scored considerably higher on the average in achievement thinking than did professionals or specialists of comparable education and background. Take the two democratic countries [considered here]:

In the United States the comparison was between matched pairs of unit managers and specialists of the same position level, age, educational background, and length of service in the General Electric Company. The managers spent more of their time in the test writing about achievement than the specialists did.

The same was true of middle-level executives from various companies in Italy when contrasted with students of law, medicine, and theology who were roughly of the same intelligence level and social background.

In other words it takes a concern for achievement to be a manager in a foreign country like Italy, for instance, just as it does in the United States. It is worth noting in passing, however, that the level of achievement thinking among Italian managers is significantly lower than it is among American managers—which, . . . quite probably has something to do with the lower level and rate of economic development in Italy.

What about a Communist country? The figures for Poland are interesting, because (1) the level of concern for achievement is about what it is in the United States, and (2) even in businesses owned and operated by the state, as in Poland, managers tend to have a higher concern for achievement than do other professionals.

Another even more striking result . . . is the fact that there is *no real difference* between the average *n* Achievement score of managers working for the U.S. government (9.3) and those in U.S. private business generally (8.90). Apparently, a manager working for the Bureau of Ships in the Department of the Navy spends as much time thinking about achievement as his counterpart in Ford or Sears, Roebuck; government service does not weaken his entrepreneurial spirit. Whether he is able to be as effective as he might be in private business is another matter, not touched on here.

Careful quantitative studies of the prevalence of achievement concern among various types of executives also yield results in line with what one would expect. Thus, sales managers score higher than other types of managers do.

In general, more successful managers tend to score higher than do less successful managers (except in government service where promotion depends more on seniority). The picture is clear in small companies, where the president tends to score higher than his associates. In large companies, the picture is a little more complicated. Men in the lowest salary brackets (earning less than $20,000 a year) definitely have the lowest average *n* Achievement scores, while those in the next bracket up ($20,000 to $25,000 a year) have the highest average *n* Achievement level. Apparently an achievement concern helps one get out of the ranks of the lowest paid into a higher income bracket. But from there on, the trend fades. Men in the highest income brackets have a somewhat lower average concern for achievement, and apparently turn their thoughts to less achievement-oriented concerns. Possibly these men are doing well enough to relax a little.

Businessmen and Achievement

Businessmen usually raise either one of two questions at this point:

1. "Where can I get this test for *n* Achievement? It sounds like a good way of picking young executives!"
2. "Why is this concern for achievement specific to being a success as a business manager? What about other types of achievement? Why isn't the entrepreneurial spirit necessary for success as an opera star, a preacher, a great teacher, or a great scientist?"

The answer to the first question, unfortunately, is simple: no practicable, marketable test for assessing achievement concern exists as yet. The method of measurement we have been using is too sensitive, too easily influenced by the social atmosphere surrounding the people who take the test, to give reliable individual results. Under carefully controlled conditions it works adequately to distinguish large groups of people like managers versus professionals, but it is not yet useful for individual selection. What we have here is a theoretical, scientific "breakthrough," not a practicable working device.

The second question is harder to answer but it takes us further in the direction of understanding exactly what kind of a person it is who spends a lot of his time thinking about achievement. To begin with, the facts are clear: many important types of professionals (doctors, lawyers, priests, or research scientists) fail to score on the average as high as business executives, yet clearly their work is in every sense as much of an achievement as the businessman's. How come?

Let us consider a particular case for a moment—that of the research scientist. Certainly his work represents an important achievement, for he is the one who often makes the breakthrough on which new technological and economic advances depend. Shouldn't he be thinking about defining a problem, doing a good job of solving it, getting help from experts, etc.?

Yet, when we tested a number of such scientists—including several outstanding Nobel prize winners—we found, somewhat to our surprise, that they were not unusually high in *n* Achievement but rather tended to be average. Then it occurred to us that having a very high concern for achievement might make a person unsuitable for being a research scientist. Why? Simply because in research a man must often work for what may become very long periods of time without any knowledge of how well he is doing. He may not even know if he is on the right track for as much as five or ten years. But a man with a high need for achievement likes to know quickly whether he is accomplishing anything and quite possibly would become frustrated by the lack of feedback in basic science as to whether he is getting anywhere. He would then more likely move into an area such as management where results are more tangible. On the other hand, the research scientist obviously needs *some* achievement concern, or he is not likely to want to engage in his occupation at all.

Characteristics of Achievers

Considerations like these focus attention on what there is about the job of being a business entrepreneur or executive that should make such a job peculiarly appropriate for a man with a high concern for achievement. Or, to put it the other way around, a person with high *n* Achievement has certain characteristics which enable him to work best in certain types of situations that are to his liking. An entrepreneurial job simply provides him with more opportunities for making use of his talents than do other jobs. Through careful empirical research we know a great deal by now about the man with high *n* Achievement, and his characteristics do seem to fit him unusually well for being a business executive. Specifically:

1. *To begin with, he likes situations in which he takes personal responsibility for finding solutions to problems.*

The reason is obvious. Otherwise, he could get little personal achievement satisfaction from the successful outcome. No gambler, he does not relish situations where the outcome depends not on his abilities and efforts but on chance or other factors beyond his control.

For example, some business school students in one study played a game in which they had to choose between two options, in each of which they had only one chance in three of succeeding. For one option they rolled a die and if it came up, say, a 1 or a 3 (out of six possibilities), they won. For the other option they had to work on a difficult business problem which they knew only one out of three people had been able to solve in the time allotted.

Under these conditions, the men with high *n* Achievement regularly chose to work on the business problem, even though they knew the odds of success were statistically the same as for rolling the dice.

To men strong in achievement concern, the idea of winning by chance simply does not produce the same achievement satisfaction as winning by their own personal efforts. Obviously, such a concern for taking personal responsibility is useful in a business executive. He may not be faced very often with the alternative of rolling dice to determine the outcome of a decision, but there are many other ways open to avoid personal responsibility, such as passing the buck, or trying to get someone else (or a committee) to take the responsibility for getting something done.

The famed self-confidence of a good executive (which actually is related to high achievement motivation) is also involved here. He thinks it can be done if *he* takes responsibility, and very often he is right because he has spent so much time thinking about how to do it that he does it better.

2. *Another characteristic of a man with a strong achievement concern is his tendency to set moderate achievement goals and to take "calculated risks."*

Again his strategy is well suited to his needs, for only by taking on moderately difficult tasks is he likely to get the achievement satisfaction he wants. If he takes on an easy or routine problem, he will succeed but get very little satisfaction out of his success. If he takes on an extremely difficult problem, he is unlikely to get any satisfaction because he will not succeed. In between these two extremes, he stands the best chance of maximizing his sense of personal achievement.

The point can be made with the children's game of ring toss, some variant of which we have tried out at all ages to see how a person with high *n* Achievement approaches it.

To illustrate, the child is told that he scores when he succeeds in throwing a ring over a peg on the floor, but that he can stand anywhere he pleases. Obviously, if he stands next to the peg, he can score a ringer every time; but if he stands a long distance away, he will hardly ever get a ringer.

The curious fact is that the children with high concern for achievement quite consistently stand at moderate distances from the peg where they are most apt to get achievement satisfaction (or, to be more precise, where the decreasing probability-of-success curve crosses the increasing satisfaction-from-success curve). The ones with low *n* Achievement, on the other hand, distribute their choices of where to stand quite randomly over the entire distance. In other words, people with high *n* Achievement prefer a situation where there is a challenge, where there is some real risk of not succeeding, but not so great a risk that they might not overcome it by their own efforts.

Again, such a characteristic would seem to suit men unusually well for the role of business entrepreneur. The businessman is always in a position of taking calculated risks, of deciding how difficult a given decision will be to carry out. If he is too safe and conservative, and refuses to innovate, to invest enough in research or product development or advertising, he is likely to lose out to a more aggressive competitor. On the other hand, if he invests too much or overextends himself, he is also likely to lose out. Clearly, then, the business executive should be a man with a high concern for achievement who is used to setting moderate goals for himself and calculating carefully how much he can do successfully.

Therefore, we waste our time feeling sorry for the entrepreneur whose constant complaints are that he is overworking, that he has more problems than he knows how to deal with, that he is doomed to ulcers because of overwork, and so on. The bald truth is that if he has high *n* Achievement, he loves all those challenges he complains about. In fact, a careful study might well show that he creates most of them for himself. He may talk about quitting business and living on his investments, but if he did, he might then *really* get ulcers. The state of mind of being a little overextended is precisely the one he seeks, since overcoming difficulties gives him achievement satisfaction. His real problem is that of keeping the difficulties from getting *too* big for him, which explains in part why he talks so much about them because it is a nagging problem for him to keep them at a level he can handle.

3. *The man who has a strong concern for achievement also wants concrete feedback as to how well he is doing.*

Otherwise how could he get any satisfaction out of what he had done? And business is almost unique in the amount of feedback it provides in the form of sales, cost, production, and profit figures. It is really no accident that the symbol of the businessman in popular cartoons is a wall chart with a line on it going up or down. The businessman sooner or later knows how well he is doing; salesmen will often know their success from day to day. Furthermore, there is a concreteness in the knowledge of results which is missing from the kind of feedback professionals get.

Take, for example, the teacher as a representative professional. His job is to transmit certain attitudes and certain kinds of information to his students. He does get some degree of feedback as to how well he has done his job, but results are fairly imprecise and hardly concrete. His students, colleagues, and even his college's administration may indicate that they like his teaching, but he still has no real evidence that his students have *learned* anything from him. Many of his students do well on examinations, but he knows from past experience that they will forget most of that in a year or two. If he has high *n* Achievement and is really concerned about whether he has done his job well, he must be satisfied with sketchy, occasional evidence that his former pupils did absorb some of his ideas and attitudes. More likely, however, he is not a person with high *n* Achievement and is quite satisfied with the affection and recognition that he gets for his work which gratify other needs that he has.

The case of the true entrepreneur is different. Suppose he is a book publisher. He gets a manuscript and together with his editors decides that it is worth publication. At time of issuance, everyone is satisfied that he is launching a worthwhile product. But then something devastatingly concrete happens—something far more definite than ever happens to a teacher—namely, those monthly sales figures.

Obviously not everyone likes to work in situations where the feedback is so concrete. It can prove him right, but it also can prove him wrong. Oddly enough, the person with high *n* Achievement has a compelling interest to know whether he was right or wrong. He thrives and is happier in this type of situation than he is in the professional situation.

Two further examples from our research may make the point clearer. Boys with high *n* Achievement tend to be good with their hands, to like working in a shop or with mechanical or electrical gadgets. What characterizes such play again is the concrete feedback it provides as to how well a person is doing. If he wires up an electric circuit and then throws the switch, the light either goes on or it does not. Knowledge of results is direct, immediate, and concrete. Boys with high *n* Achievement like this kind of situation, and while some may go on to become engineers, others often go into business where they can continue getting this kind of concrete feedback.

What Money Means

In business, this feedback comes in the form of money, in costs and profits that are regularly reported. It is from this simple fact that the confusion between the so-called profit motive and the achievement motive has arisen in the minds of both Marxist and classical economists. For, in the typical case, a concern for profit in a capitalist economy does *not* mean that the businessman is primarily interested in money for its own sake. Rather, this concern is merely the *symptom* of a strong achievement concern, since profitability in a capitalist economy provides the best and simplest measure of success. It provides the same sort of concrete knowledge of achievement that a person with high *n* Achievement seeks all the time. Research findings clearly support this analysis. If you simply offer a person with high *n* Achievement a larger money reward for doing a certain task, he doesn't do any better than he did without the prize. In fact, he tends to do a little worse because the money makes him nervous. Not so the person with low *n* Achievement; he works harder when he has a chance of taking some money away from a situation. The money in and of itself means more to him than it does to the person with high *n* Achievement.

Of course, it follows that concrete measures of achievement other than money could be devised by other types of economic systems to satisfy the entrepreneurial spirit. Something like this has apparently happened in Communist states like Poland and Russia, where plant managers work under a fairly rigid quota system which demands that they make their quotas—or else! In the free enterprise system a businessman must make his profit—or else. The psychological effects, so far as the achievement motive is concerned, are apparently pretty much the same. In both systems the manager gets feedback in concrete terms as to how well he is doing. If he has high *n* Achievement, he is more likely to live and survive under such a challenge.

While these three characteristics of people with a strong concern for achievement—the desire for personal responsibility, the tendency to set moderate achievement goals, and the need for concrete feedback of results—are the most important, there are some other minor characteristics possessed by these people which tend to suit them for an entrepreneurial job. They like to travel, they are willing to give up one bird in the hand to get two in the bush, and they prefer experts to friends as working partners. . . .

Sources of Achievement

Where does strong achievement motivation come from? Values, beliefs, ideology—these are the really important sources of a strong concern for achievement in a country. Studies of the family have shown, for instance, that for a boy three factors are important in producing high *n* Achievement—parents' high standards of achievement, warmth and encouragement, and a father who is not dominating and authoritarian. Here is a typical study that reveals this fact:

A group of boys were blindfolded and asked to stack irregularly shaped blocks on top of each other with their left hands, at home in front of their parents.

Separately, the mothers and fathers were asked how high they thought their sons could stack the blocks. Both parents of a boy with high *n* Achievement estimated that their boys should do better; they expected more of him than did the parents of a boy with low *n* Achievement. They also encouraged him more and gave him more affection and reward while he was actually doing the task. Finally, the fathers of boys with high *n* Achievement directed the behavior of their sons much less when they were actually stacking the blocks; that is, they told them less often to move their hands this way or that, to try harder, to stop jiggling the table, and so forth, than did the fathers of boys with low *n* Achievement.

Other studies have shown that fathers must be respected by their sons; but after the boy is capable of achieving something for himself, his father must stop directing every step he takes if the boy is to develop a strong concern for achievement.

In a sense, however, these family studies only push the question further back. Where did the parents get their standards? Why do some emphasize achievement and affectionately reward self-reliance? Because, very simply, they themselves believe in achievement for their family or for their political, social, or religious group. For one reason or another they are caught up in some great wave of achievement ideology.

One of the paradoxes of history is that often the achievement concern was not itself initially directed toward business or economics. For instance, two great waves of achievement concern in the history of England were each associated with waves of Protestant reform or revival, whose explicit aims were not secular but strictly religious. The Methodists, for example, in the second wave of the English Protestant revival, stressed religious perfection in this life; yet even John Wesley recognized with some puzzlement that devout Methodists tended to get rich, a fact which he considered a handicap in attaining religious perfection.

But now we can understand what happened. The strong concern for Christian perfection in this world tended to produce an achievement orientation in Methodist parents and their sons that turned the boys toward business because, as we have shown above, an achievement concern is most easily satisfied in business. In our day, it is the secular religions of nationalism and communism that have placed the highest emphasis on achievement and tended to create higher levels of *n* Achievement in underdeveloped and Communist countries. Communism lays the same claims to superiority as a means of salvation that Christianity once did. However wrong we may feel it to be, we must recognize that it tends to create a strong atmosphere of achievement that has important consequences for economic growth. . . .

If there is one thing that all this research has taught me, it is that men can shape their own destiny, that external difficulties and pressures are not nearly so important in shaping history as some people have argued. It is how people respond to those challenges that matters, and how they respond depends on how strong their concern for achievement is. So the question of what happens to our civilization or to our business community depends quite literally on how much time tens of thousands or even millions of us spend thinking about achievement, about setting moderate achievable goals, taking calculated risks, assuming personal responsibility, and finding out how well we have done our job. The answer is up to us.

Theory X and Theory Y

DOUGLAS McGREGOR

Theory X: The Traditional View of Direction and Control

Behind every managerial decision or action are assumptions about human nature and human behavior. A few of these are remarkably pervasive. They are implicit in most of the literature of organization and in much current managerial policy and practice:

1. *The average human being has an inherent dislike of work and will avoid it if he can.*

This assumption has deep roots. The punishment of Adam and Eve for eating the fruit of the Tree of Knowledge was to be banished from Eden into a world where they had to work for a living. The stress that management places on productivity, on the concept of "a fair day's work," on the evils of featherbedding and restriction of output, on rewards for performance—while it has a logic in terms of the objectives of enterprise—reflects an underlying belief that management must counteract an inherent human tendency to avoid work. The evidence for the correctness of this assumption would seem to most managers to be incontrovertible.

2. *Because of this human characteristic of dislike of work, most people must be coerced, controlled, directed, threatened with punishment to get them to put forth adequate effort toward the achievement of organizational objectives.*

The dislike of work is so strong that even the promise of rewards is not generally enough to overcome it. People will accept the rewards and demand continually higher ones, but these alone will not produce the necessary effort. Only the threat of punishment will do the trick.

The current wave of criticism of "human relations," the derogatory comments about "permissiveness" and "democracy" in industry, the trends in some companies toward recentralization after the postwar wave of decentralization—all these are assertions of the underlying assumption that people will only work under external coercion and control. The recession of 1957–1958 ended a decade of experimentation with the "soft" managerial approach, and this assumption (which never really was abandoned) is being openly espoused once more.

3. *The average human being prefers to be directed, wishes to avoid responsibility, has relatively little ambition, wants security above all.*

This assumption of the "mediocrity of the masses" is rarely expressed so bluntly. In fact, a good deal of lip service is given to the ideal of the worth of the average human being. Our political and social values demand such public expressions. Nevertheless, a great many managers will give private support to this assumption, and it is easy to see it reflected in policy and practice. Paternalism has become a nasty word, but it is by no means a defunct managerial philosophy.

I have suggested elsewhere the name Theory X for this set of assumptions. . . .

Theory X provides an explanation of some human behavior in industry. These assumptions would not have persisted if there were not a considerable body of evidence to support them. Nevertheless, there are many readily observable phenomena in industry and elsewhere which are not consistent with this view of human nature.

Such a state of affairs is not uncommon. The history of science provides many examples of theoretical explanations which persist over long periods despite the fact that they are only partially adequate. Newton's laws of motion are a case in point. It was not until the development of the theory of relativity during the present century that important inconsistencies and inadequacies in Newtonian theory could be understood and corrected.

The growth of knowledge in the social sciences during the past quarter century has made it possible to reformulate some assumptions about human nature and human behavior in the organizational setting which resolve certain of the inconsistencies inherent in Theory X. While this reformulation is, of course, tentative, it provides an improved basis for prediction and control of human behavior in industry.

Some Assumptions about Motivation

At the core of any theory of the management of human resources are assumptions about human motivation. This has been a confusing subject because there have been so many conflicting points of view even among social scientists. In recent years, however, there has been a convergence of research findings and a growing acceptance of a few rather basic ideas about motivation. These ideas appear to have considerable power. They help to explain the inadequacies of Theory X as well as the limited sense in which it is correct. In addition, they provide the basis for an entirely different theory of management. . . .

Man is a wanting animal—as soon as one of his needs is satisfied, another appears in its place. This process is unending. It continues from birth to death. Man continuously puts forth effort—works, if you please—to satisfy his needs.

Human needs are organized in a series of levels—a hierarchy of importance. At the lowest level, but preeminent in importance when they are thwarted, are the physiological needs. Man lives by bread alone, when there is no bread. Unless the circumstances are unusual, his needs for love, for status, for recognition are inoperative when his stomach has been empty for a while. But when he eats regularly and adequately, hunger ceases to be an important need. The sated man has hunger only in the sense that a full bottle has emptiness. The same is true of the other physiological needs of man—for rest, exercise, shelter, protection from the elements.

A satisfied need is not a motivator of behavior! This is a fact of profound significance. It is a fact which is unrecognized in Theory X and is, therefore, ignored in the conventional approach to the management of people. I shall return to it later. For the moment, an example will make the point. Consider your own need for air. Except as you are deprived of it, it has no appreciable motivating effect upon your behavior.

When the physiological needs are reasonably satisfied, needs at the next higher level begin to dominate man's behavior—to motivate him. These are the safety needs, for protection against danger, threat, deprivation. Some people mistakenly refer to these as needs for security. However, unless man is in a dependent relationship where he fears arbitrary deprivation, he does not demand security. The need is for the "fairest possible break." When he is confident of this, he is more than willing to take risks. But when he feels threatened or dependent, his greatest need is for protection, for security.

The fact needs little emphasis that since every industrial employee is in at least a partially dependent relationship, safety needs may assume considerable importance. Arbitrary management actions, behavior which arouses uncertainty with respect to continued employment or which reflects favoritism or discrimination, unpredictable administration of policy—these can be powerful motivators of the safety needs in the employment relationship at every level from worker to vice president. In addition, the safety needs of managers are often aroused by their dependence downward or laterally. This is a major reason for emphasis on management prerogatives and clear assignments of authority.

When man's physiological needs are satisfied and he is no longer fearful about his physical welfare, his social needs become important motivators of his behavior. These are such needs as those for belonging, for association, for acceptance by one's fellows, for giving and receiving friendship and love.

Management knows today of the existence of these needs, but it is often assumed quite wrongly that they represent a threat to the organization. Many studies have demonstrated that the tightly knit, cohesive work group may, under proper conditions, be far more effective than an equal number of separate individuals in achieving organizational goals. Yet management, fearing group hostility to its own objectives, often goes to considerable lengths to control and direct human efforts in ways that are inimical to the natural "groupiness" of human beings. When man's social needs—and perhaps his safety needs, too—are thus thwarted, he behaves in ways which tend to defeat organizational objectives. He becomes resistant, antagonistic, uncooperative. But this behavior is a consequence, not a cause.

Above the social needs—in the sense that they do not usually become motivators until lower needs are reasonably satisfied—are the needs of greatest significance to management and to man himself. They are the egoistic needs, and they are of two kinds:

1. Those that relate to one's self-esteem: needs for self-respect and self-confidence, for autonomy, for achievement, for competence, for knowledge
2. Those that relate to one's reputation: needs for status, for recognition, for appreciation, for the deserved respect of one's fellows

Unlike the lower needs, these are rarely satisfied; man seeks indefinitely for more satisfaction of these needs once they have become important to him. However, they do not usually appear in any significant way until physiological, safety, and social needs are reasonably satisfied. Exceptions to this generalization are to be observed, particularly under circumstances where, in addition to severe deprivation of physiological needs, human dignity is trampled upon. Political revolutions often grow out of thwarted social and ego, as well as physiological, needs.

The typical industrial organization offers only limited opportunities for the satisfaction of egoistic needs to people at lower levels in the hierarchy. The conventional methods of organizing work, particularly in mass production industries, give little heed to these aspects of human motivation. If the practices of "scientific management" were deliberately calculated to thwart these needs—which, of course, they are not—they could hardly accomplish this purpose better than they do.

Finally—a capstone, as it were, on the hierarchy—there are the needs for self-fulfillment. These are the needs for realizing one's own potentialities, for continued self-development, for being creative in the broadest sense of that term.

The conditions of modern industrial life give only limited opportunity for these relatively dormant human needs to find expression. The deprivation most people experience with respect to other lower-level needs diverts their energies into the struggle to satisfy *those* needs, and the needs for self-fulfillment remain below the level of consciousness.

Now, briefly, a few general comments about motivation:

We recognize readily enough that a man suffering from a severe dietary deficiency is sick. The deprivation of physiological needs has behavioral consequences. The same is true, although less well recognized, of the deprivation of higher-level needs. The man whose needs for safety, association, independence, or status are thwarted is sick, just as surely as is he who has rickets. And his sickness will have behavioral consequences. We will be mistaken if we attribute his resultant passivity, or his hostility, or his refusal to accept responsibility to his inherent "human nature." These forms of behavior are *symptoms* of illness—of deprivation of his social and egoistic needs. . . .

The "carrot and stick" theory of motivation which goes along with Theory X works reasonably well under certain circumstances. The *means* for satisfying man's physiological and (within limits) safety needs can be provided or withheld by management. Employment itself is such a means, and so are wages, working conditions, and benefits. By these means the individual can be controlled so long as he is struggling for subsistence. Man tends to live for bread alone when there is little bread.

But the "carrot and stick" theory does not work at all once man has reached an adequate subsistence level and is motivated primarily by higher needs. Management cannot provide a man with self-respect, or with the respect of his fellows, or with the satisfaction of needs for self-fulfillment. We can create conditions such that he is encouraged and enabled to seek such satisfactions for himself, or we can thwart him by failing to create those conditions. . . .

Theory Y: The Integration of Individual and Organizational Goals

To some, the preceding analysis will appear unduly harsh. Have we not made major modifications in the management of the human resources of industry during the past quarter century? Have we not recognized the importance of people and made vitally significant changes in managerial strategy as a consequence? Do the developments since the twenties in personnel administration and labor relations add up to nothing?

There is no question that important progress has been made in the past two or three decades. During this period the human side of enterprise has become a major preoccupation of management. A tremendous number of policies, programs, and practices which were virtually unknown thirty years ago have become commonplace. The lot of the industrial employee—be he worker, professional, or executive—has improved to a degree which could hardly have been imagined by his counterpart of the nineteen twenties. Management has adopted generally a far more humanitarian set of values; it has successfully striven to give more equitable and more generous treatment to its employees. It has significantly reduced economic hardships, eliminated the more extreme forms of industrial warfare, provided a generally safe and pleasant working environment, *but it has done all these things without changing its fundamental theory of management.* There are exceptions here and there, and they are important; nevertheless, the assumptions of Theory X remain predominant throughout our economy.

Management was subjected to severe pressures during the Great Depression of the thirties. The wave of public antagonism, the open warfare accompanying the unionization of the mass production industries, the general reaction against authoritarianism, the legislation of the New Deal produced a wide "pendulum swing." However, the changes in policy and practice which took place during that and the next decade were primarily adjustments to the increased power of organized labor and to the pressures of public opinion.

Some of the movement was away from "hard" and toward "soft" management, but it was short-lived, and for good reasons. It has become clear that many of the initial strategic interpretations accompanying the "human relations approach" were as naïve as those which characterized the early stages of progressive education. We have now discovered that there is no answer in the simple removal of control—that abdication is not a workable alternative to authoritarianism. We have learned that there is no direct correlation between employee satisfaction and productivity. We recognize today that "industrial democracy" cannot consist in permitting everyone to decide everything, that industrial health does not flow automatically from the elimination of dissatisfaction, disagreement, or even open conflict. Peace is not synonymous with organizational health; socially responsible management is not coextensive with permissive management.

Now that management has regained its earlier prestige and power, it has become obvious that the trend toward "soft" management was a temporary and relatively superficial reaction rather than a general modification of fundamental assumptions or basic strategy. Moreover, while the progress we have made in the past quarter century is substantial, it has reached the point of diminishing returns. The tactical possibilities within conventional managerial strategies have been pretty completely exploited, and significant new developments will be unlikely without major modifications in theory.

The Assumptions of Theory Y

There have been few dramatic break-throughs in social science theory like those which have occurred in the physical sciences during the past half century. Nevertheless, the accumulation of knowledge about human behavior in many specialized fields has made possible the formulation of a number of generalizations which provide a modest beginning for new theory with respect to the management of human resources. Some of these assumptions were outlined in the discussion of motivation in [the section on Theory X]. Some others, which will hereafter be referred to as Theory Y, are as follows:

1. *The expenditure of physical and mental effort in work is as natural as play or rest.* The average human being does not inherently dislike work. Depending upon controllable conditions, work may be a source of satisfaction (and will be voluntarily performed) or a source of punishment (and will be avoided if possible).
2. *External control and the threat of punishment are not the only means for bringing about effort toward organizational objectives. Man will exercise self-direction and self-control in the service of objectives to which he is committed.*
3. *Commitment to objectives is a function of the rewards associated with their achievement.* The most significant of such rewards, e.g., the satisfaction of ego and self-actualization needs, can be direct products of effort directed toward organizational objectives.
4. *The average human being learns, under proper conditions, not only to accept but to seek responsibility.* Avoidance of responsibility, lack of ambition, and emphasis on security are generally consequences of experience, not inherent human characteristics.
5. *The capacity to exercise a relatively high degree of imagination, ingenuity, and creativity in the solution of organizational problems is widely, not narrowly, distributed in the population.*
6. *Under the conditions of modern industrial life, the intellectual potentialities of the average human being are only partially utilized.*

These assumptions involve sharply different implications for managerial strategy than do those of Theory X. They are dynamic rather than static: They indicate the possibility of human growth and development; they stress the necessity for selective adaptation rather than for a single absolute form of control. They are not framed in terms of the least common denominator of the factory hand, but in terms of a resource which has substantial potentialities.

Above all, the assumptions of Theory Y point up the fact that the limits on human collaboration in the organizational setting are not limits of human nature but of management's ingenuity in discovering how to realize the potential represented by its human resources. Theory X offers management an easy rationalization for ineffective organizational performance: It is due to the nature of the human resources with which we must work. Theory Y, on the other hand, places the problems squarely in the lap of management. If employees are lazy, indifferent, unwilling to take responsibility, intransigent, uncreative, uncooperative, Theory Y implies that the causes lie in management's methods of organization and control.

Personality and Organization

CHRIS ARGYRIS

The Source of Psychological Energy

The energy that most researchers postulate is pictured as being located in the need systems of the personality.

People behave. They love, hate, eat, cry, fight, work, strike, study, shop, go to the movies, play bridge, bring up children, go to church. The psychological energy to behave in all these ways comes from the need systems that exist in our personalities. . . .

The energy in every need system is always ready to release itself, to bubble over. But so long as the boundary of the need system is strong enough, the energy will not release itself. When the energy bubbles over, the need system is in action. Need systems that are quiet and not in action are inert needs or potential active needs. This is similar to the pressure in a boiler. So long as the pressure does not become too great, the boiler will not burst. . . .

Let us ask, "So what?"

What is the advantage of saying that people have needs in tension in relation to goals? Why go all through this fuss? To answer the question let us imagine that there are two foremen. Mr. A. is hard-working, does an exceptional job, and is up for promotion. Mr. B., on the other hand, is slow, is lax on the job, has many problems which he does not seem to care about, and is being considered for a demotion.

Common sense answers to why these two foremen behave the way they do usually go like this:

"Well, that's human nature."

"I guess Mr. B. just doesn't give a damn."

"Mr. A. is really loyal to our company. Looks like Mr. B. isn't."

"Mr. A.'s attitudes are better; that's why he works harder."

"Maybe B. has been having some 'off days.'"

Tackling the same question by using the scheme above, we would have to say:

"Mr. A. has a need in tension which is directed at certain goals. He needs to be hard-working."

"Mr. B. had a need in tension which is also directed at a certain goal. He needs to be slow."

Examining both sets of answers, we note that the practical set jumps immediately to such vague, high-sounding conclusions as "human nature," "doesn't give a damn," "loyalty." None of these conclusions provides a jumping-off point for constructive action. Every one of them immediately implies there is something wrong with Mr. B.

The second list, on the other hand, jumps to questions. It forces the person to find out more facts. For example, "What need is in tension?" "At what goal is it directed?" "Why does Mr. A. have a certain need and why does Mr. B. have a different need in action?" The second list points out one of the most important rules in trying to understand human behavior. The real causes of human behavior are rarely found in the observable behavior. It is important to ask, "What is behind this behavior that we see?"

The second list does not immediately classify someone as "bad" and someone as "good." . . . Therefore, the second list is more useful, in that it does not automatically condemn Mr. B., or praise Mr. A. . . . Probably one of the greatest weaknesses in trying to understand others is the immediate attempt at labeling them "good" or "bad." Once this is done, it is impossible to think objectively about a person. . . .

Personality and Abilities

Bordering the needs, and in most cases evolving from them, are the abilities. Abilities are the tools, so to speak, with which a person expresses and fulfills his needs. Abilities are the communications systems for the needs to express themselves. Once the energy bubbles over from the needs, it goes "through" the appropriate ability designed to express the need. . . .

Interests are usually a product of a fusion of several needs. This fusion usually comes about at an early age and is unconscious. Interests, therefore, are indicators of the kinds of needs people have. For example, a person with a strong need to be independent, to achieve, and to know things, might make a good scientist.

The skills that are given to us by inheritance are such skills as finger dexterity and other manual and manipulative skills. Few abilities are inherited. The majority of the more important abilities are learned and developed in interaction with others. This is especially true for such abilities as leadership. There are no born leaders. The personality of a leader is developed, probably during early home life and by the situations in which this personality finds appropriate expression.

Abilities, in summary, function between needs and the environment, thus providing the line of communication for needs. . . .

The Organization of Personality

It has been found convenient to label the unique personality whole created by the specific inter-relationships of the parts, the self. To put it another way, the basic parts of the personality are the same (needs and abilities). However, the way these parts are organized may differ for each individual and even within the same individual as he develops. The self is a concept used by the scientists to focus on the unique integration of the parts of the personality for any given individual.

To introduce this concept, let us consider the growing infant. As soon as he discovers his physical body (his hands, feet, face), he turns to the task of discovering who he is, i.e., his self. He becomes aware that there is a "me" that exists. From the day this awareness begins, the child will throughout his life be discovering and rediscovering, changing, and adding new parts to the picture he has of himself. This marks the beginning of awareness of the self.

The self is more than just the physical body. It includes the child's unique organization, conscious and unconscious, of his needs, goals, abilities, and the resulting feelings, values, and prejudices. It includes how he evaluates his abilities (e.g., the confidence he has in them). Finally, it includes his sensitivity for understanding himself and others. This sensitivity is called "empathy." A person who has empathy usually has a lot of insight (understanding) into people's feelings.

The self is seldom built up by the person by merely reflecting about himself. It is built through his social contacts (interaction) with others. We cannot become "whole" by ourselves. We need contact with others.

Once the picture of the self is formed, it serves as a frame-work or a guide with which to make sense out of experience. All future experiences are either (1) accepted and integrated with the picture one already has of the self, (2) ignored because the experiences do not make sense to the person in terms of his self concept, and (3) denied or distorted because the experience is inconsistent with the picture of the self. Those ways of behaving are adopted that are consistent with, or in agreement with, the self picture. Because individuals tend to see only that which agrees with their concept of self, it is difficult to be a truly objective observer. There is in fact no objective world for the individual; rather, it is always his picture of the objective world. It is always his "private world."

Maintaining the Self Against Threat

Generally speaking, there are at least two ways to reduce feelings of threat. One is to change the self so that it becomes congruent with whatever is causing the difficulty. This involves "accepting" the fact that one is "wrong." It involves admitting the limitations associated with the difficulty will not arise again. The second approach is to defend the self by somehow denying or destroying (consciously or unconsciously) what is threatening and clinging to the present self concept. This behavior is called a defense reaction. A defense reaction, therefore, is any sequence of behavior in response to a threat whose goal is to maintain the present state of the self against threat.

A defensive reaction may create difficulty if it happens that the individual instead of the situation in the environment, is "wrong." A defense reaction reduces the awareness of threat but never affects that which is causing the threat. For example, let us say that supervisor A is threatened because he "knows" his boss does not think that he (supervisor A) is doing a good job. Let us assume that he defends his self by placing the blame on the boss. This will not in any way stop the boss from feeling the way he does about supervisor A. Soon the supervisor will have to justify his defensive reactions to himself. He may do this by saying that the boss is "out to get him." Each of these defenses is a distortion which in turn will require further justification and further defense. After some time supervisor A has built up deep layers of defense, all of which will have to be uncovered if he is to understand the cause. . . .

Defense mechanisms are therefore developed to be used any time that the self feels threatened. All individuals have a set of defenses. This set of defenses is not to be viewed as necessarily being "bad" or "good." It is best to view them as simply the individual's way of defending himself from threat. The four most frequently threatening experiences are anxiety, conflict, frustration, and failure.

Since defense mechanisms are primarily related to experiences of anxiety, conflict, frustration, and failure, it may be wise to define these experiences before the defense mechanisms are listed.

Anxiety

Anxiety is an emotional state that resembles fear and anger in that it is aroused by something that is threatening to the individual. Anxiety is a response to nothing particular in the environment, while fear is always a response to a genuine threat, which clearly requires some sort of escape or attack. When we are in a state of fear, we have something before us that we can see, that we can try to remove, or that we can run away from. We can point to it and say, "This is what makes me fearful." Anxiety, on the other hand, "attacks from behind." We experience it but we cannot figure out where it is coming from or what causes it. Thus, we do not know whether to run or to attack.

Some specific symptoms of anxiety are: . . . sleeplessness, stage fright, headaches, stubbornness, stomach upsets, and prejudice. Anxiety usually appears as a symptom, that is to say, it makes itself as some specific form of behavior, using that word in its broadest sense; but in its "pure" form it usually appears as a vague sort of uneasiness; a feeling of panic, discomfort, or helplessness; or an awareness of tension with no identifiable cause. . . .

Conflict

Conflict, generally speaking, refers to the event which occurs when a person is not able to act in a specific situation. All conflict involves opposite needs being in action (tension) at the same time. The conflict may be due to indecision over doing something, or it may be due to wanting to do two things simultaneously which cannot be done simultaneously.

Behavioral scientists have analyzed four types of conflict.

Conflict will tend to exist when the person desires to do two things which he likes equally well but it is possible to do only one. A child tries to decide whether to buy a vanilla cone or a candy bar, both of which he likes equally well.

Conflict will tend to exist when a person has the choice of doing two things, each of which he dislikes equally. It is being, so to speak, "between the devil and the deep blue sea." For example, there is the person who hates his job but has not found another one and therefore risks unemployment if he quits.

Conflict will tend to exist when the person has the choice of doing something he likes, but runs the risk of punishment or loss. For some people, gambling provides this conflict.

Conflict will tend to exist when the person has the alternative choices of doing something he likes but running the risk of some loss or punishment. For example, there is the investor who has before him three or four equally good investment possibilities, each with an equal possibility of failure.

Many people have been brought up to think that conflict is bad. This is not necessarily so. True, conflict can be uncomfortable, but it is even more true that conflict harms a person's personality when the personality uses incorrect ways of dealing with the conflict. Conflict dealt with correctly, is an experience of growth for the personality. In fact, without conflict (psychologists suggest) there would be little need for us to develop new ways of behaving. The old ways would merely be sharpened up a bit, but there would be little reason to try something new. Odd but true, conflict can be used to help build the personality as well as to distort and even destroy it.

Frustration

Coupled with, and perhaps a special case of, conflict is the problem of not being able to overcome some barrier in order to arrive at a goal. If the goal is not reached, the person will become emotional, uneasy, antagonistic—he will show signs of being frustrated. The person under frustration does release emotions, whether he shows these emotions in his observable behavior or not. These emotions act like a sleeping pill, so to speak, on the person's whole personality (especially his abilities) and reduce his efficiency.

For example, if prior to frustration the person's efficiency is said to equal ten, under frustration it is usually reduced (e.g., to five) without the person's realizing it (i.e., unconsciously). The person therefore cannot figure out what is wrong with himself. "Why can't I overcome these barriers? I was certain I could. What's wrong with me?" All these are typical questions. This worry only increases the emotional imbalance, which increases the action of the emotions on the efficiency of the personality, and down goes the efficiency some more. It is like quicksand; the more he struggles the deeper he sinks. The thing that makes frustration most destructive is that a person may not know why he is less efficient.

The reduction of psychological efficiency is called regression. Regression means that the personality has returned to a more primitive, childlike state, where efficiency is much lower. The important property of regression is that while the person becomes more like a child, he is not a child; he is still an adult.

Every person has developed his own tolerance against frustration. Some people have little tolerance and become easily frustrated. Others have developed a high resistance and therefore it takes quite a bit to frustrate them. The individual's ability to withstand frustration is known as frustration tolerance. The higher the frustration tolerance, up to a point, the more adaptive life will be. We emphasize "up to a point" because a person who never becomes frustrated, no matter how difficult the situation, is not necessarily a healthy personality.

Failure

Perhaps the easiest way to explain psychological failure is to define what is not failure. Psychological success, the opposite of failure, occurs when the individual is able to direct his energy toward a goal that he defines, whose achievement will fulfill his inner needs, and which cannot be reached without overcoming a barrier strong enough to make him "put up a fight" but just weak enough to be overcome. (In other words, the individual has a realistic level of aspiration.)

Failure occurs when an individual lives in a world in which he is not able to define his own goals in relation to his inner needs and whose barriers are either too great to overcome or so small that no success is derived in overcoming them.

Defense Mechanisms

Aggression. One of the common results of regression is aggression. Aggression means trying to injure or hurt the person, group, object that is acting as the barrier or as the cause of conflict. By the words "injure" and "hurt" we include all types of injuries, including social and psychological injury, such as name-calling insults, and cheating.

Guilt. If the "block" is due to the limitations of one's own personality, (e.g., the individual who desires to become a supervisor but does not have a good enough record), then the aggression can be turned toward the self. The person usually feels guilt, criticizes himself, or may even go so far as to hurt himself. Guilt is, therefore, aggression from ourselves to ourselves.

Continuation. Sometimes the conflict is not resolved but the person continues to live by making another choice which is "second best." For example, a student who becomes a businessman but still wishes he could have gone to medical school is in a sense continuing his conflict.

Discriminatory Decision. At times, a conflict is resolved by sitting down and writing the reasons for and the reasons against doing something. We try to make a list of the reasons and then pick out (discriminate) the best one. This mechanism almost always occurs on a conscious level. In general, it may be used when the personality is healthy and the conflict is not strong. For example, an executive, in order to choose between foreman A and foreman B for a new promotion, may sit down, list the "goods" and "bads" of each foreman, and then pick (discriminate) one.

Denial. An easy course to follow when threatened is simply to remain unaware of the facts which could create one side of a conflict. An example that is particularly annoying to supervisors occurs when employees apparently do not seem to hear instructions concerning a new regulation or a forthcoming change. Although the supervisor may speak clearly and concisely, the employees will insist "they didn't quite hear what he said" or "they had difficulty in understanding what he said." Actually, what happens under denial is that the employees do not allow what has just been said to penetrate into their consciousness. (Denial, it should be pointed out, is a different thing from deliberate pretense, in which the individual knows something but decides to make believe that he does not.)

Repression. When the threat is due to factors active within ourselves, we often forbid ourselves to recognize them. Repression is thus forcing down into the unconscious that part of a threat which we do not like. Repression almost always occurs unconsciously. It is usually a response to an inner threat. For example, a patient once complained of a great fear of running water. She could not go near a drinking fountain. A careful analysis brought out the fact that as a young child she fell in a lake near a waterfall and nearly drowned. The incident had been repressed, all except the noise of running water. Once the patient was able to recognize and accept the fact, progress could be made in therapy.

Suppression. Suppression is somewhat like repression. Whereas in repression we push things into the unconscious without realizing it, in suppression we push things into the unconscious and generally know it. Suppression is hardly ever permanent, while repression is usually permanent.

Inhibition. Inhibition is like repression but it most often occurs on a conscious level. In inhibition the person purposely and knowingly refrains from doing something. For instance, an inhibited person would be one who never speaks up in a conference because he fears he may say something wrong or he fears what he has to say is not important.

Conversion. Conversion occurs when a person fears he will not be capable of meeting an unusual situation and converts this fear into some bodily trouble. An example would be the child who because he fears to take an examination in school, suddenly develops some kind of illness. Or the newly elected foreman feeling inadequate, becomes "run down" after the first week in his new job. Finally, the foreman, who is afraid to see the boss in the boss's office suddenly becomes ill (e.g., gets a splitting headache) and has the meeting postponed. He may actually be converting his difficulty into a physical problem (i.e., headache).

Overcompensation. Sometimes a person resolves his fear of not being able to do something by working so hard that he accomplishes his goal and usually goes way beyond it. The person who thinks that he is incapable of doing something tries to make up for his limitations and in fact makes up too much or overcompensates for these limitations. A typical example is the hard-working executive who accomplishes his goal, does better than expected, but never seems to relax once the goal is achieved.

Rationalization. Rationalization occurs when we knowingly invent some acceptable excuse (acceptable to our own personality) to cover up a failure or to cover up an inability to accept something. Rationalization occurs when an alibi is created for otherwise untenable behavior. For example, a person might walk to the drug store to buy some cigarettes. On arriving at the drug store, he finds it is closed and remarks, "Oh well, I did not want to smoke anyway." Or the employee who, upon finding out he did not become a foreman (although he was hoping he would be) remarks, "Who wants all that responsibility anyway?" Rationalization can also occur unconsciously, for example, some multimillionaires who feel guilty about their wealth try to cover up these feelings by giving away huge fortunes to charity.

Identification. Identification refers to the desire to be like someone else or to identify with other people's experiences. We have identified with someone when we act in a situation as we feel that person would act. Top management men usually have some subordinates who tend to identify with them.

Projection. The concept of projection has two meanings. Colloquially, it is usually used to mean any attempt we make to avoid blame for, or to ascribe to others, ways of behaving, feeling and thinking which we really have ourselves. Some employees, for example, continually "get into trouble" and, despite all evidence to the contrary, really believe the other fellow is always to blame.

In the true psychological sense, projection is a mechanism whereby we "see" in other people a quality which would embarrass us greatly if we were to admit it is our own. For example, a person might be watching someone go up to a stage to make a speech and remark, "I bet he (the speaker) is scared." Actually, it is the person watching the potential speaker who is frightened. Another example is the well-behaved employee who continually "squeals" on the other employees who break the rules. The employee is actually pointing to something happening outside of him (e.g., the other employees breaking the rules) as a way of denying his own desire to break the rules. The employee who does this is usually sincere and does not feel he is a hypocrite.

Vacillation. At one time people in conflict may decide in favor of solution A, then a minute later reject it and accept solution B. This constant rejection and acceptance and never coming to a conclusion is called vacillation.

Ambivalence. People attempt to resolve some conflict situations by hating and liking the same person who is the focus of the threat. For example, a foreman working for an autocratic boss once said, "The s.o.b. I hate his guts, but you know, I really admire him. He's a pretty good egg." This contradictory statement is hardly ever seen as contradictory by the person who makes it. In this case, the ambivalence is probably due to the fact that an autocrat never permits real freedom, but is always quick to do personal favors to keep the subordinates happy, and thereby keep them dependent on him. . . .

One resultant of defense mechanisms is that they make it difficult to differentiate between an individual's underlying motivations and the skin-surface ones. We observe Mr. A. and Mr. B. while we interview them for a job. Mr. A. talks so much that we cannot speak. Mr. B. hardly says a word. These two bits of behavior at the immediately observed "manifest" level seem to be different. But on the "latent" or deeper level—the level to which we must learn to go—both people may really have the same self-concept and, as a result, may feel insecure and fear unknown situations. But they make up for their fear in different ways. Mr. B. adapts by doing little talking. Mr. A. adapts by talking so much that no one else is able to say a word.

Or it may be that the personalities of supervisor A., who "works himself to death," and supervisor B. who "hardly lifts a finger," are basically similar. Both may feel they are not competent. One works hard and overcompensates for limitations he senses in himself. The other does very little for fear of doing something wrong.

The practical implications are that a clear distinction between "manifest" and "latent" must be made if we want to predict how individual supervisors, for example, will react to frustration, conflict, and anxiety. The same is true if changes are to be made.

If the changes made satisfy only manifest behavior, then the underlying latent reasons will not be satisfied. We can predict that the complaining will continue but probably shift to another area. It is similar to taking an aspirin to relieve migraine headaches. The headache will be relieved but not cured.

Ball parks, athletic teams, company picnics, and company lectures are programs that fulfill the skin-surface or manifest needs of the workers. Company newspapers, slogan schemes, and pep talks are also in the same category. If so, increased benefit and communications programs will not tend to decrease the company's human problems. Moreover, since these programs tend to focus on skin-surface needs, they tend to leave the employees' important needs unfilled (e.g., the need to be led by effective leaders). The employees, not truly satisfied and therefore still requiring need fulfillment, ask for more. Soon management begins to feel that the quality of the employees is going down. "All the employees want is more. How much do they expect us to give them?" According to this analysis, the management trains the workers to focus on material satisfactions (e.g., ball teams, pictures in the newspaper, and so on), and then complains when the workers want more. . . .

Personality Growth

Most personality theories are in agreement that as the individual matures, he not only acquires more parts (i.e., more needs, abilities), but he also deepens many of them. As these parts are acquired, they are also integrated with the already existing parts of the personality. Every part which is added must be added so that the balance (organization) is not upset. Simultaneously with the personality growth of the individual is the expansion of the individual's private world or environment. Every time a new part is created "in" his personality, a new part is also experienced in his own private world. The world of experience is called "private" because it can never include the total objective world. It is impossible for the individual to experience everything, no matter how long he lives. . . .

Most personality theories state that the personality becomes complete, organized, and integrated only when it interacts with other people, ideas, and social organizations. Growth cannot occur if the person exists alone. He must interact with others in order to understand himself and thereby develop. Thus, we cannot understand ourselves unless we understand others, and we cannot understand others unless we understand ourselves.

To summarize, man in his need-fulfilling, goal directed behavior is to some extent "like all other men, like some other men, like no other men."

He is like all other men because some of his personality is derived from common biological roots. He is like all other men because he always lives in a culture and must adjust to the traditionally defined expectations of the culture. He is like all other men because he has to use other men to develop. Finally, he is like all other men in that he experiences both gratification and deprivations. These experiences accumulate and become a storehouse of learning which, in turn, he uses to adapt to the continual occurrence of new problems and situations.

Man is like some other men in that he shares common experiences with his own work group, social class, sporting club, or other cultural organization. . . .

Basic Development Trends of Personality

Since the human personality is a developing organism, one way to become more precise is to define the basic growth or development trends "inherent" in it (so long as it remains in the same culture). One can then logically assume that, at any given moment in time, the human personality is a developing organism, one will be predisposed to find expression for these developmental trends. Such an assumption implies another, namely, that there are basic development trends characteristic of a relatively large majority of the population being considered. . . .

It is assumed that human beings in our culture:

1. Tend to develop from a state of passivity as infants to a state of increasing activity as adults. . . .
2. Tend to develop from a state of dependence upon others as infants to a state of relative independence as adults. Relative independence is the ability to

"stand on one's own two feet" and simultaneously to acknowledge healthy dependencies. . . .

3. Tend to develop from being capable of behaving only in a few ways as an infant to being capable of behaving in many different ways as an adult.
4. Tend to develop from having erratic, casual, shallow, quickly-dropped interests as an infant to having deeper interests as an adult. The mature state is characterized by an endless series of challenges, where the reward comes from doing something for its own sake. The tendency is to analyze and study phenomena in their full-blown wholeness, complexity, and depth.
5. Tend to develop from having a short time perspective (i.e., the present largely determines behavior) as an infant to a much longer time perspective as an adult (i.e., where the behavior is more affected by the past and the future). . . .
6. Tend to develop from being in a subordinate position in the family and society as an infant to aspiring to occupy an equal and/or superordinate position relative to their peers.
7. Tend to develop from a lack of awareness of self as an infant to an awareness of and control over self as an adult. The adult who tends to experience adequate and successful control over his own behavior tends to develop a sense of integrity (Erikson) and feelings of self-worth. Bakke shows that one of the most important needs of workers is to enlarge those areas of their lives in which their own decisions determine the outcome of their efforts. . . .

Formal Organization vs. Personality

Bringing together the evidence regarding the impact of the formal organizational principles upon the individual, it is concluded that there are some basic *incongruencies between the growth trends of a healthy personality and the requirements of the formal organization.* If the principles of formal organization are used as ideally defined, employees will tend to work in an environment where (1) they are provided minimal control over their workaday world, (2) they are expected to be passive, dependent, and subordinate, (3) they are expected to have a short time perspective, (4) they are induced to perfect and value the frequent use of a few skin-surface shallow abilities and, (5) they are expected to produce under conditions leading to psychological failure.

All these characteristics are incongruent to the ones human beings are postulated to desire. They are much more congruent with the needs of infants in our culture. *In effect, therefore, organizations are willing to pay high wages and provide adequate seniority if mature adults will, for eight hours a day, behave in a less than mature manner!*

If the analysis is correct, this inevitable incongruency increases as (1) the employees are of increasing maturity, (2) as the formal structure (based upon the above principles) is made more clear-cut and logically tight for maximum formal organizational effectiveness, (3) as one goes down the line of command, and (4) as the jobs become more and more mechanized (i.e., take on assembly line characteristics). . . .

It is not difficult to see why some students of organization suggest that immature and even mentally retarded individuals would probably make excellent employees. . . .

Individual Adaptation

If the formal organization is defined by the use of such "organization" principles as task specialization, unity of direction, chain of command, and span of control, and if these principles are used correctly, the employees will work in situations in which they tend to be dependent, subordinate, and passive toward the leader. They will tend to use few of their abilities (probably none of which are important ones for the individual anyway). The degree of passivity, dependence, and submissiveness tends to increase for those employees as one goes down the line of command and as the work takes on more of the mass production characteristics. As a result, it is hypothesized that the formal organization creates in a healthy individual feelings of failure and frustration, short time perspective, and conflict. . . .

An employee experiencing frustration, failure, conflict and short time perspective may behave in any one or a combination of the following ways:

1. He may leave the organization. (But where else can he go? Most other companies are organized in the same way.)
2. He may work hard to climb the ladder and become the president. (But how many can become presidents?)
3. He may defend his self-concept and adapt through the use of defense mechanisms.
4. He may "pressure" himself to stay and, in spite of the conflict simultaneously adapt as much as possible by lowering his work standards and becoming apathetic and uninterested.
5. Apathy and disinterest may lead him to place more value on material rewards and to depreciate the value of human or nonmaterial rewards.
6. Although not directly inferable from the above, the employee may teach his children not to expect satisfaction on the job: to expect rather to earn good wages and "live" outside the plant (the same lesson the formal organizational experts are teaching him). This hypothesis is based on the known property of human beings of evaluating life in terms of their own self-concept . . . If the employee's self-concept includes as "good" activities, goldbricking, learning the ropes, and quota restricting, then these will tend to be passed on to his children through the process of acculturation. . . .

*The Use of Defense Mechanisms.*The third mode of adaptation, the use of defense mechanisms, is perhaps the least explored. As we have seen . . . in a defense reaction the individual distorts or denies the "facts" in order that he may live in some sort of equilibrium with himself and his environment. Systematic research is so meager in this area that our illustrations are mostly abstracted anecdotal accounts obtained from field research. We present a few:

1. To rationalize the fact that they are not accomplishing what they know the company requires. For example (one operator to another) "Take it easy—don't work too hard; this outfit has plenty of dough. They don't need whatever you give them by breaking your ass." Or, "I know the company doesn't want me to work too fast; I can get all worn out." (typist-secretary). Or (piece rate employee), "Well, they don't need those extra pieces until Monday anyway. Why should I knock myself out?"

2. To project their feelings upon others. They may blame them and ignore their own part in the problem.

For example (foreman), "it's those goddamned budgets. If I didn't have those on my neck, I'd have no problem—absolutely none." Or (an order department clerk), "Have you ever tried to keep the sales orders straight with the selfcentered thickheads we have for salesmen? All they think of is themselves." Or (a production manager), "The basic problem we have is that everything we produce is custom-made. We ain't got no long runs like most other plants. We have to be careful of every order." Or (a piece-rate worker), "To hell with it," he said, "let the day man run 'em. He likes 'em. He turned in nine dollars today."

"You've got time to make another dollar yourself," I said. "To hell with that job!" Gus exclaimed. "I'm not going to bust my neck any more on it. Let the day man run it."

Another example is found in a recent study of a hospital which reports that the nurses partially adapt to their own inability to be what they believe is an effective administrator by projecting their limitations upon the administrative staff of the hospital. As one nurse describes it: "If you ask me, administration doesn't even know we exist. If they did, they would get busy and solve the many annoying administrative difficulties we have. Just take scheduling. They haven't been able to solve that at O.R. (Operating room) or X-ray or the chemical laboratories. If you want to help us nurses, please go upstairs and make administrators out of them."

Finally workers may defend their resistance to increased mechanization or to the way management is handling the change by blaming increased technology for unemployment. Centers find that blaming technology for unemployment increases as one goes toward the lower levels of the organization.

3. To be ambivalent. "I cannot make up my mind. I like the job—yet I don't. I like the company—yet I'd leave. I don't know what it is, except I know it ain't the boss or the pay" (a clerk-typist). "I run hot and cold about this outfit."

"I can't seem to make up my mind if I should stay or ask for a transfer" (tool and die maker).

Researcher: "What kinds of things do you like and dislike about the company?" Worker: "I like the pay; I like the management—I think they're trying to be fair. But I don't like not being my own boss. I want to be my own boss, I guess. Here you got to be on a schedule. You're always working under pressure for someone else."

4. To escape from reality. An increasingly used defense against nonsatisfying work is for the individual to detach himself from his work. For example, a group of adolescent girls learned to use certain semi-automatic bookkeeping equipment. "Without advance notice," as one girl put it, "you suddenly realize you can work and at the same time think of a million other things. You know what I mean, daydream. You feel free."

5. To develop psychosomatic illnesses. Another type of defensive mechanism which has hardly been studied is the one by which the individual transforms a psychological problem into a physiological one. On the top management level, ulcers is a well-known psychosomatic disease. On the employee level, there is increasing evidence that employees are developing dubious backaches, headaches, and run-down feelings, to adapt to anxieties they tend to experience on the job.

Individual Apathy and Noninvolvement. Apathy, lack of interest, and noninvolvement are types of defense mechanisms that may be becoming so popular that they require special emphasis. The basis of these defenses, we have pointed out, is the continuous frustration, conflict and failure an employee experiences.

Let us picture an employee whom we may call Dick. He works on an assembly line and finds that he cannot obtain minimal personality expression on his job. He is frustrated. From the studies of frustration it is hypothesized that Dick will tend to regress to a more childlike state. He will not be as "mature" as he was before he was frustrated. This "primitivation" (regression) of his personality may cause him (1) to leave the situation, (2) to try to change the work situation constructively or destructively, (3) to accept (internalize) the tension and "hand on," i.e., keep working.

If Dick accepts the third possible course, he places himself in a difficult situation. On the one hand, his predisposition for health and maturity puts pressure on him to leave.

He feels his own pressure to leave. On the other hand, if he decides to stay, he must create new self-pressures to overcome the ones caused by his own desire to leave and to remain healthy. Dick is surrounded by his own pressures. He may blame management for creating the assembly line world but he also knows they are not forcing him to stay. He is forcing himself to stay. If he blames anyone for being where he is, he blames himself. The tension that builds up tends to increase his human ineffectiveness. Recent research suggests quite clearly that such tension leads to a decrease in self-confidence, and increase in aggression and regression.

One way for Dick to defend himself is to reduce the psychological importance of the work situation. He may say (unconsciously) in effect, "To hell with it: I am not going to permit myself to become involved. Why should I pressure myself to leave and to stay? Why should all this mean so much to me? I'll do just enough to get by. I'll block up my need for self-actualization until I get out of work. Then I will live!"

Group Adaptation

The individual adapts to the impact of the organization by any one or some combination of: (1) leaving the organization, (2) climbing the organizational ladder, (3) using defensive mechanisms, and (4) becoming apathetic and disinterested. These are all adaptive mechanisms and therefore need fulfilling. People will want to maintain these adaptive behaviors.

In order to guarantee their existence, the individual seeks group sanctions. The informal work groups are "organized" to perpetuate these adaptive processes (to reward those employees who follow the informal codes and to penalize those who do not). The individual adaptive acts now become sanctioned by the group, and therefore feed back to reinforce the continuance of the individual need-fulfilling adaptive behavior. . . .

Formal Groups (Trade Unions)

Up to now we note that the individual adapts on the psychological level and on the small informal group level. The latter are initially created to sanction and therefore perpetuate those activities that the work group on any level of the organization finds need-fulfilling.

However, if the company decides to disband the informal activities, in the final analysis they could be defended by the employees only by threatening to do harm to the productive process (e.g., strike, slow down). Such measures are not easily used and the psychological and financial costs on both sides are high.

Management's formal power is basically derived by making the employees dependent on management for their rewards, directions, positions, and so forth. It follows logically from the above that one way for the employees to reduce their dependence is to take away some of the management's formal authority and place it within their own control. According to Coleman this is an important basis for the rise of trade unions. As McGregor states, "And to the extent to which unions have attempted to place restrictions upon management's authority reflects not only a desire for power, but a conscious attempt to reduce the dependence of the workers upon their bosses." . . .

In order to create trade unions, the employees must reach outside the organization into the political world, where their power and managements (due to our political system) is, man for man, equal. Once trade unions come to existence, the employees can sanction many of their informal activities through the formal power residing in the union as an organization.

The employees now live between two sets of dependencies. They depend upon both management and the trade union leaders. Theoretically, the critical difference is that the former dependence is mandatory while the latter is voluntary. In actual practice, however, it is common knowledge that trade unions are becoming increasingly formalized and routinized. Many have already reached the stage where a primary objective is to maintain themselves internally and adapt to their external environment.

In order to do this, the unions tend to organize themselves by creating a formal organization whose structure is based upon the principles of chain of command, unity of direction, task specialization and span of control. The moment this occurs, they become, in administrative make-up (not necessarily in philosophy) similar to other industrial organizations. The members become dependent, passive, and subordinate to their trade union officers. . . .

Management Reaction

We have been primarily concerned with the employees' adaptation to the formal organizational structure, such as decreases in production and identification with the organization; increases in waste, errors, absenteeism, sickness, apathy, disinterest in work, and increase in importance of material (financial) aspects of work. These are all understandable and predictable ways for relatively healthy employees to adapt to the conflict, frustration, and failure they experience as a result of the formal organization. . . .

The top administrators, however, tend to diagnose the problems in another way. They observe their employees while at work and they conclude: (1) The employees are lazy. (2) The employees are uninterested and apathetic. (3) The employees are money crazy. (4) The employees create errors and waste.

Management blames the employees and "sees" the disloyalty, disinterest, and goldbricking as being "in" and caused by the employees. It follows logically for management, that if any changes are to occur the employees must be changed. Thus management initiates programs to "change peoples' attitudes," to "sell them free enterprise," to "make people more interested in the company."

The basic action policy that management tends to define to solve the above "problems" actually stems from the logics of the formal organization and formal leadership already discussed . . .

For example, the logics of the formal organization tend to influence management to assume that: (1) The only relations that matter between people in organizations are those defined by organization charts and manuals. (2) The behavior of people in organizations is governed by explicit logical thinking. (3) The subordinates will do what the purpose and circumstances of the organization require only under logical incentives and clear communications. (4) The administrator is responsible to solve the problem. He knows best what should be done. (5) The way to get things done is through authority of the leader's position. He can apply persuasion and compulsion if necessary. (6) The employees at the bottom would behave differently if they understood the economic problems of the business.

There are three fundamental policy decisions running through these six policy assumptions. The first is the importance of strong, "dynamic," loyal leadership. Second, is the importance of a logical and systematic control over the employees' behavior. Finally, is the importance of communicating to the employees management's thinking related to their organization and its economic problems. Let us examine each of these to see what action management takes to implement these policy decisions and then to analyze the impact of management's actions on the employees and the organization.

Directive Leadership

An important pillar of most management policy is to develop competent executives who among other things: (1) are able to "needle," "drive," "sell," "push," "pressure," "persuade," "urge," "coerce," "win" employees to increase productivity, loyalty, and interest for the organization and for their job; (2) are able to get all the facts, weigh them correctly, and make effective decisions; (3) know clearly management's objectives, policies, and practices; (4) communicate these policies and practices clearly to the employees; and (5) evaluate the performance of the employee strictly and honestly according to these policies and practices.

There is ample evidence to illustrate management's use of pressure-oriented leadership.

Summarizing the characteristics found in most of the research, one may conclude that the autocratic, directive leader places the followers in a situation where they tend to be (1) passive, dependent, subordinate, and submissive; (2) centered toward the organization's and the leader's needs rather than the needs of all the followers; (3) competing with each other for the leader's favor; (4) confronted with a short time perspective; and (5) experiencing psychological failure.

We must conclude that the *impact of directive leadership upon the subordinates is similar to that which the formal* organization *has upon the subordinate. Pressure-oriented directive* leadership *"compounds the felony" that the formal organization* commits every *minute every hour of the day and every day of the year.* Authoritarian leadership *reinforces and perpetuates* the "damage" created *by the organizational structure.* The adaptive activities . . . are also caused by directive leadership. Directive leadership helps to reinforce, in the employees' minds, the necessity for the same adaptive activities that this leadership is originally designed to decrease.

Management Controls

The second policy decision made by many managers to combat reduced productivity is careful definition, inspection, and evaluation of the quality and quantity of every employee's performance. This leads us to the field of management controls.

Management controls are becoming increasingly important in the eyes of top management. Management control is seen as a fundamental process in all organization. . . .

Management controls are not only necessary and inevitable if the traditional formal organizational structure is to be maintained, but they also become increasingly important as the formal organization becomes larger and more decentralized. Management decision making would suffer if management controls were abandoned. . . .

As a result of the pressure, tension, and general mistrust of management controls, employees tend to unite against management.

Psychological research shows that people can stand only a certain amount of pressure and tension, after which it becomes intolerable. One method people use to reduce the effect of the pressure (assuming that the employees cannot reduce the pressure itself) is to join groups, which help absorb much of the pressure and thus relieve the individual personally. Gradually, therefore, the individuals become a group because in so doing they are able to satisfy their need to (1) reduce the pressure on each individual; (2) get rid of tension; (3) feel more secure by belonging to a group which can counteract the pressure. In short, new cohesive groups developed to *combat* management pressure. In a sense, the people had learned that they could be happier if they combined against it. This result is predicted . . . [above] as a "natural" consequence of the employees' adapting to the dependence and submissiveness that they experience.

To summarize up to this point, management controls like budgets tend to make the employees feel dependent, passive, and subordinate to management. As a result of budgets, they experience pressure, interdepartmental strife, psychological failure, lack of control over their work environment, barriers to communication between the budget people and the line people, pressure to be department-centered rather than organization centered.

The impact of management controls is similar to that which the formal organization and directive leadership have upon the subordinates. Management controls feed back upon and give support to directive leadership as both "compound the felony" committed by the formal organization every hour of the day and every day of the year. . . .

Human Relations

The third response by management to the problems of inadequate productivity and employee apathy is the let's-be-human approach. If directive leadership and tight management controls do not succeed, perhaps helping the workers to identify with their jobs and the company might succeed.

How did the human relations fad begin? The growth of trade unionism brought to light much of the discontent the employees had been feeling for years, and placed much of the blame on poor management. A second important stimulus was the research by Mayo, Roethlisberger and Dickson, who presented concrete evidence showing that productivity and human relations were intimately tied up. Poor human relations, wrote the authors, creates low production (e.g., rate-setting and goldbricking) which leads to worse human relations which in turn leads to lower production. A key to the solution, Mayo suggests, is to help the employees feel that they belong to a small primary work group. If people could be helped to feel they belong, he suggested, human relations would be better. Both of these events had a strong impact upon management, many of whom still did not fully accept trade unionism. Third, many executives were beginning to develop a sense of social responsibility.

A difficulty with Mayo and other [human relations theorists] is that they observed employees goldbricking, rate-setting, expressing low feelings of identification, apathy, and disinterest and they conclude, like management, that this is "bad." It may be bad from management's point of view, but as our analysis suggests, it may also be adaptive as long as relatively mature workers are working in a difficult work situation.

Management picked up the message and for the next fifteen to twenty years there existed a great interest in human relations. . . .

To summarize, research shows that under democratic conditions people do tend to feel that they are part of a team and respected. However, this does not mean this will tend to be the case if a supervisor tries to be pseudo democratic or democratic under autocratic conditions. We must not forget that the formal structure of most organizations and the management controls are fundamentally autocratic. The small groups experiments from which the use of "democratic leadership" seems to have arisen never coped with these two factors. . . .

Communications programs, benefits, suggestion programs, better working conditions, cafeterias, clean locker rooms, uniforms become part of "good" human relations. In an analysis of thirty communication programs, for example, management "communicates" frequently the following topics: (1) "Make the worker feel he's part of the company." (2) "Tell him how important his job is to the whole picture." (3) "Show him that management is truly interested in the employees." (4) "Keep him informed of costs, errors, and the financial progress of the company." (5) "Sell him on the importance of free enterprise system." (6) "Emphasize the possibilities of opportunity for advancement."

With the possible exception of aspects of 4 and 6, topics like these represent management's worries more than they do employees' needs. Communication programs have become an excellent medium for management to express and try to do something about its own worries.

Research suggests that telling a worker he is an important part of the company, when through actual experience he sees he is a very minor part (thanks to task specialization) with little responsibility (thanks to chain of command, directive leadership, and management controls) may only increase the employees' dissatisfaction with management. As one worker concluded, "Who are they kidding, us or themselves?" To emphasize to an assembly line worker that he sould feel proud of the four bolts that he puts into the right rear end of a car may be viewed as an insult by the worker who is a "whole" human being (although it allays management's anxieties about employee apathy). As one employee remarked, "It's ironic—damn. It hurts to know that four bolts are important. What a hell of a life." . . .

These "fads" assume it is possible to make human relations better, not by attacking the causes (formal organization, directive leadership, and management controls) but in effect by making the activities outside the actual work situation more pleasant for the worker (e.g., new toilets, new cafeterias, sports, picnics, newspapers), or by sugar-coating the work situation. In the case of the former, management is in effect paying the worker to live in the tension-producing life of the plant. Thus employees find their predisposition for more materialistic things reinforced by management's own behavior. In the case of the latter, they are simply ignoring the problem and maybe teaching the employees, by their behavior, that it is acceptable to sugar-coat problems. . . .

Perception: From The Inside Looking Out

HAROLD LEAVITT

In this article the issue is the person's influence on the world. The major questions are these: How and why do people see things differently? How objective can people be? Do people see only what they want to see? or don't want to see? What part do people's personal views of the world play in the supervisory process?

The Perceptual World

Most of us recognize that the world-as-we-see-it is not necessarily the same as the world-as-it-"really"-is. Our answer depends on what we heard, not on what was really said. The housewife buys what she likes best, not what is best. Whether we feel hot or cold depends on us, not on the thermometer. The same job may look like a good job to one of us and a sloppy job to another.

To specify the problem, consider the line drawing in Figure 1 (p. 156). This is a picture of a woman. Here are some questions about it: (1) How old is the woman at the time of the picture? (2) Does she have any outstanding physical characteristics? (3) Is she "reasonably attractive" or "downright ugly"?

Show the picture to ten other people. Do they all see the same thing? If some think she looks between twenty and thirty, does anyone think she's over fifty? If some think she's over fifty, does anyone think she's between twenty and thirty? How does one account for the conflicts? Are the differences simply

---

differences in taste? Or in standards of beauty? Or is each person distorting the "real" world in a different way?

This old psychology-textbook picture is intentionally ambiguous. It can be seen either as an ugly old hag with a long and crooked nose and toothless mouth or as a reasonably attractive young girl with head turned away so that one can barely see one eyelash and part of a nose. More importantly, the picture will be based on the "facts" as they are seen by the viewer, which may be different from the "facts" seen by another viewer.

Figure 1. Wife or Mother-in-Law?

Incidentally, if the reader still sees only one of the two figures, he is getting a good feeling of what a "need" is. The tension or discomfort that one feels when he thinks he is missing something others can see or when he feels he hasn't quite closed a gap in his knowledge—that is a need. And it will probably be difficult to concentrate on reading further until he satisfies that unsatisfied need by finding the second face in the picture.

The Influence of Our Needs on Our Perceptions

The hag picture is another demonstration of a commonplace observation, i.e., that people see things differently, that the world is what we make it, that everyone wears his own rose-colored glasses. But consider some additional questions: Whence the rose-colored glasses? Are the glasses always rose-colored? That is, does one always see what he wants to see, or does he see what he is afraid he will see, or both?

These questions are important because the primary issue of "human relations" is to consider ways in which individuals can affect the behavior of other individuals. If it is true that people behave on the basis of the perceived world, then changing behavior in a predetermined direction can be made easier by understanding the individual's present perception of the world. For if there is any common human-relations mistake made by industrial superiors in their relations with subordinates, it is the mistake of assuming that the "real" world is all that counts, that everyone works for the same goals, that the facts speak for themselves.

But if people do act on their perceptions, different people perceive things differently. How, then, is the manager, for example, to know what to expect? What determines how particular people will perceive particular things?

The answer has already been given in the preceding chapters. People's perceptions are determined by their needs. Like the mirrors at amusement parks, we distort the world in relation to our own tensions. Children from poorer homes, when asked to draw a quarter, draw a bigger than actual one. Industrial employees, when asked to describe the people they work with, talk more about their bosses (the people more important to their needs) than about their peers or subordinates, and so on.

But the problem is more complicated than that. People may perceive what is important to their needs, but does this mean people see what they want to see, or what they are afraid to see? Both wishes and fears are important to one's needs. The answer seems to be that we perceive both, but according to certain rules. We magnify a compliment from higher up in the organization but we also magnify a word of disapproval. We dream of blondes, but we also have nightmares. And sometimes we just don't pay attention at all to things that are quite relevant. We forget dentist's appointments; we oversleep when we have examinations coming up; we manage to forget to clean the basement or to call on this particular customer.

Selective Perception

What, then, are the rules of selective perception? The best answer we can give is this one: If one re-examines his memories of the past, he may find that his recall of positive, satisfying things is better than his recall of negative, unpleasant things. He may find it easier to wake early to go fishing than to get to a dentist's appointment. He may look forward, in fact, to doing pleasant, satisfying jobs but may evade mildly disturbing and unpleasant jobs. One senior executive recently commented to the author that the biggest problem he encounters with young management people is their tendency to avoid the little unpleasant decisions—like disciplining people or digging through boring and repetitive records or writing unpleasant letters. This executive felt that his younger men would be far more effective if they could learn to deal as promptly with these uncomfortable little decisions as they did with the big ones.

But we can see some sense in this selective remembering if we look for it. There are some advantages to a person in being blind to unpleasantness, even if such blindness cuts down his working effectiveness. Ignoring the unpleasant may represent more than "laziness." It may be a sensible defensive device, psychologically speaking. Thus, most people are able to ignore soft background conversation while working. In effect they are psychologically deaf to a potentially distracting part of the real world. And this defense helps them to concentrate on their work. Similarly, most people manage to ignore the threat of the hydrogen bomb and to go on eating and sleeping as though this dangerous part of the real world were not here. It can even be shown experimentally that words with unpleasant connotations tend to be recognized more slowly when exposed for very brief intervals than words with pleasant connotations.

The strange part of this defensive process, however, is that in order *not* to hear the distracting music or *not* to see the unpleasant words one must first hear and see them. One has to see the word, recognize that it is unpleasant, and reject it almost simultaneously, so that one can say, "No. I didn't see what that word was." Hence the label "defense" attached to this phenomenon—defense against the entry of preselected things mildly disturbing to one's equilibrium. So two of our rules of selective perception become: (1) see what promises to help satisfy needs, and (2) ignore mildly disturbing things.

Suppose, though, that while one is successfully ignoring background talk someone back there starts to shout; or, while one is successfully ignoring the H-bomb, an H-bomb falls on London. At those points, when the unpleasantness becomes intense and dangerous, people stop defending and begin attacking. They stop ignoring the irritation and start directing all their attention to it. This reversal seems to happen suddenly, at some specific threshold. The distant irritation increases to a point at which it becomes so real, so imminent, and so threatening that we reverse our course, discard the blindfold, and preoccupy ourselves completely with the thing previously ignored.

This is the third rule: Pay attention to things that are really dangerous. The whole picture now begins to look like this: *People perceive what they think will help satisfy needs; ignore what is disturbing; and again perceive disturbances that persist and increase. . . .*

This process may not seem entirely logical to an outside observer, but it is quite reasonable psychologically. For this kind of self-imposed psychological blindness helps the person to maintain his equilibrium while moving toward his objectives. An organism lacking this ability to fend off minor threats might well find itself torn apart in its attempt to deal simultaneously with all of them. Or, at least, an individual unable to ignore unpleasant realities might spend so much of his energy dealing with them that he would make little progress toward his major goals. For once a person has learned to perceive a multitude of threats and dangers in his world he needs a system of defense against them. One should add, however, that some individuals may see relatively few things as dangerous and therefore have little need for defense, while for others the world holds dangers at every turn.

. . . A person who has encountered a relatively helpful world is likely to perceive more of his environment as potentially helpful. If, however, the world has been mostly frustrating, then more of it, and especially new things in it, will be seen as potentially dangerous. Being dangerous, they must be fended off. But, paradoxically, to be fended off they must first be seen. So to protect himself from more insecurity, the insecure person must first see the things that will provoke insecurity and then manage to deny to himself that he has seen them.

Projections of the Perceived World

The basic point of this chapter, the point that the world as it is perceived is the world that is behaviorally important, underlies the development of the now generally familiar projective tests. Originally projectives were designed for the diagnosis of aberrations in personality, but the chapter on assessment will show how they are being used industrially. The same idea also underlies what market researchers now call "motivation research" into consumer attitudes, techniques for discovering people's personal views of the "facts" of advertising and product design. Consumer research in general can be thought of as an attempt to make a diagnosis of the relevant parts of the consumer's view of the world so that products can be designed to be seen as aids rather than obstacles.

For managerial purposes, the importance of the perceptual world is clear. If one's concern as a supervisor or counselor or committee member is to try to effect some change in the behavior of other people, and if in turn people's present behavior is determined largely by their perceptions of their environments, then it is critical that one seek to understand their perceptions if one is to understand the circumstances under which their behavior might change.

For example, managers assume almost universally that subordinates want promotions. And yet more than one subordinate has been driven into panic and disappointment because he felt psychologically forced to accept a promotion that no one (sometimes even himself) bothered to find out he did not want.

Often assumptions about the perceptions of others are wrong because they are incomplete. One may assume correctly that employees want more money, but he may fail to understand that more money is acceptable only within a certain framework of independence. This is the paternalism problem.

Sometimes the problem is simple lack of sensitivity for other people. Thus a foreman once complained to the writer about how odd people seemed. He said one of his employees had gotten terribly upset "for no reason at all." The foreman had said, "Hey, boy, go over there and pick that up!" The employee got angry. He had said, "Don't call me 'boy'; I have a name!" The foreman couldn't understand why the employee, a Negro, should get angry about a "perfectly reasonable" request like that.

Or again many parents argue for the importance of heredity over environment because their own children seem to be so different from one another. "Our second child," they will say, "was just a completely different person from the first, though we treated them both *exactly* alike." Parents may be truthful in feeling that they treated two children alike, but it is unwise to assume that the children were therefore treated alike. The first child's world did not include the second child; but the second's did include the first. Moreover, for the infant whose slate is relatively blank, the minor marks made by parents may be major marks for the child. Thus many parents pass lightly over the differences between feeding an infant now or ten minutes from now. But the child is not likely to pass over the same thing nearly so lightly. The manager is likely to pay little attention to his criticism of a subordinate's work. But for the subordinate it is a week's food for worry.

One more example. Sales managers often complain of the difficulties they encounter in getting salesmen to make cold calls. The salesman says he was too busy, or there were better prospects, or he had to catch up on some reports. Is he lazy? Or just defending himself—perhaps unconsciously—against a perceived threat? If it is a defensive process, there are two general ways in which the manager can try to shake the salesman loose. He can teach him to feel comfortable about cold calls, or he can change the mild threat to a major one so that it can no longer safely be ignored. But if he chooses the latter course he had better consider the by-products.

Perceiving Oneself

So far we have talked about perceptions of things and other people. But one of the people each of us perceives is himself, as he is, and also as he would like other people to see him. Each of us struts his own act before the world, as it were, in an effort to have other people see us as the kind of person we value.

Quite early in life, we begin to learn what kinds of groups we want to join, what kinds of social classes to aspire to, what kinds of status to achieve. Two of us may have equally intense needs for status and prestige, but if we have grown up in different environments, one of us may seek that status by acting masculine and powerful, or by affecting the long haircut and the leather jacket. Another may seek to fulfil the same needs by costuming himself as an aesthetic or an Ivy League conservative, or by donning the gray flannel uniform of the executive.

Teenagers are often painfully awkward as they strive to perfect their own private acts. They seem to feel it terribly important to appear to be what they doubt they really are. Later they become more skilful, either because their acts are better or because their acts are not very far from what the actors really are.

Note that our acts are functional for us. They are performed by both teenagers and adults for good reasons. An act is a way of filling a role. It is also a way of protecting the vulnerable parts of ourselves from real or fancied attack. But our act is effective in performing its functions only if other people accept it. And other people usually accept acts when the gap between our acting selves and their estimate of our "real" selves is small. Other people tend to be reasonably accurate judges, too. So acting problems arise as the distance between act and reality increases.

It is also true that acts are often uncomfortable for the actor. The girl friend happily abandons the courting dance as soon as the wedding is over. But until she has the man tied down and delivered, she must play her version of the coquette, no matter how much worry and fret it requires. Similarly the company executive must act decisively, though privately he may yearn for a chance to weep on someone's shoulder.

But though our acts are functional, they contribute to a social world full of distorted signals. You are trying to tell me that you are strong, worldly, and decisive (and you may be—or you may not), and I am just as busily trying to communicate to you that I am the sagacious, understanding, intellectually stimulating character I would like to be (and may actually be—or may not). We have both been practicing our acts for a long time. So we have both developed clever ways of being convincing, ways that the poor inept adolescent has not even dreamed of. But we have also developed clever ways of spotting the other guy's act.

Our relationship becomes even further confounded by the fact that we read one another's cover stories through our own need-distorted glasses. While you stand there trying to radiate strength and decisiveness, I see you as brash and immature. And you, wanting action and recognition, see my efforts at quiet pipe-smoking wisdom as dullness and lack of imagination. Looked at this way the wonder is not that we find it so difficult to understand one another, but that we are able to understand one another at all.

The first big problem then is the problem of accuracy, of somehow gaining more accurate information about other people—estimating the discrepancy between the actor and the "real" person. The second problem is to estimate how well our act is working. For surely we are in considerable trouble if the self we want to present to the world is presented so badly, so weakly, so transparently that everyone else is discounting it. We are in a bad way if the people around us are saying: "There is a man who is trying to act decisive and sure of himself, while in fact it is as plain as the nose on your face that he is really unsure of himself, indecisive, anxious."

To the best of this writer's knowledge there is only one general mechanism by which such distortions in relationships can be reduced, and that is the mechanism of *feedback.* If somehow we can develop better ways by which we can learn from other people how our act is getting across, then we can either modify it so that it gets across more fully or we can try to reduce the discrepancy between the act and ourselves, so that it is an easier act to play convincingly. The first course leads to a world of intrigue and gamesmanship; the second, to a simpler, less distorted world.

By this reasoning, other people, if we can get them to provide us with appropriate feedback, can do us considerable service in helping us to bring what we wish to be closer to what we are, and to reduce our uncertainty and anxiety in the process. . . .

In Summary

People see things differently. Even "facts" may be seen quite differently by different people. Relevance to one's needs is the most important determinant of one's personal view of the world. Things that seem to be aids to satisfying one's needs are seen quickly. But things that look like obstacles, if they are not critically threatening, may also be seen quickly, only then to be denied so that they appear not to have been seen at all. By denying obstacles, people "protect" themselves temporarily from them. If they really become dangerous, however, people drop the blinders and face the obstacles.

One of the things we perceive is ourselves and other people. To protect and enhance ourselves, we try to manipulate the picture other people have of us by putting up a front that will make them think we are what we want to be. The problem of our act, and getting it across successfully, depends mostly on our ability to pick up audience reactions accurately. And accurate audience reactions are hard to come by because the audience is acting too.

To ignore differences in perception is to ignore a major determinant of behavior. Yet it is easy to assume unwarrantedly that everyone views the world from the same perspective as the viewer. Time spent trying to reach a common view is not wasted time.

Selective Perception

DE WITT C. DEARBORN
HERBERT A. SIMON

An important proposition in organization theory asserts that each executive will perceive those aspects of the situation that relate specifically to the activities and goals of his department[1]. The proposition is frequently supported by anecdotes of executives and observers in organizations, but little evidence of a systematic kind is available to test it. It is the purpose of this note to supply some such evidence.

The proposition we are considering is not peculiarly organizational. It is simply an application to organizational phenomena of a generalization that is central to any explanation of selective perception: Presented with a complex stimulus, the subject perceives in it what he is "ready" to perceive; the more complex or ambiguous the stimulus, the more the perception is determined by what is already "in" the subject and the less by what is in the stimulus[2].

Cognitive and motivational mechanisms mingle in the selective process, and it may be of some use to assess their relative contributions. We might suppose either: (1) selective attention to a part of a stimulus reflects a deliberate ignoring of the remainder as irrelevant to the subject's goals and motives, or (2) selective attention is a learned response stemming from some past history of reinforcement. In the latter case we might still be at some pains to determine the nature of the reinforcement, but by creating a situation from which any immediate motivation for selectivity is removed, we should be able to separate the second mechanism from the first. The situation in which we obtained our data meets this condition, and hence our data provide evidence for internalization of the selective processes.

Method of the Study

A group of 23 executives, all employed by a single large manufacturing concern and enrolled in a company sponsored executive training program, was asked to read a standard case that is widely used in instruction in business policy in business schools. The case, Castengo Steel Company, described the organization and activities of a company of moderate size specializing in the manufacture of seamless steel tubes, as of the end of World War II. The case, which is about 10,000 words in length, contains a wealth of descriptive material about the company and its industry and the recent history of both (up to 1945), but little evaluation. It is deliberately written to hold closely to concrete facts and to leave as much as possible of the burden of interpretation to the reader.

Abridged from "Selective Perception: A Note on the Departmental Identifications of Executives," *Sociometry,* Vol. 21 (1958), 140–144. Reprinted by permission of the authors and the American Sociological Association. Abridgement originally published in *Psychology in Administration,* Timothy W. Costello and Sheldon S. Zalkind, © 1963 by Prentice-Hall, Inc. Used by permission.

[1] Simon, H. A., *Administrative Behavior,* New York: Macmillan, 1947, Chs. 5 and 10.
[2] Bruner, J. S., "On Perceptual Readiness," *Psychological Review,* 1957, 64, 123–152.

When the executives appeared at a class session to discuss the case, but before they had discussed it, they were asked by the instructor to write a brief statement of what they considered to be the most important problem facing the Castengo Steel Company—the problem a new company president should deal with first. Prior to this session, the group had discussed other cases, being reminded from time to time by the instructor that they were to assume the role of the top executive of the company in considering its problems.

The executives were a relatively homogeneous group in terms of status, being drawn from perhaps three levels of the company organization. They were in the range usually called "middle management," representing such positions as superintendent of a department in a large factory, product manager responsible for profitability of one of the ten product groups manufactured by the company, and works physician for a large factory. In terms of departmental affiliation, they fell in four groups:

Sales (6): Five product managers or assistant product managers, and one field sales supervisor.

Production (5): Three department superintendents, one assistant factory manager, and one construction engineer.

Accounting (4): An assistant chief accountant, and three accounting supervisors—for a budget division and two factory departments.

Miscellaneous (8): Two members of the legal department, two in research and development, and one each from public relations, industrial relations, medical and purchasing.

The Data

. . . We tested our hypothesis by determining whether there was a significant relation between the "most important problem" mentioned and the departmental affiliation of the mentioner. In the cases of executives who mentioned more than one problem, we counted all those they mentioned. We compared (1) the executives who mentioned "sales," "marketing," or "distribution" with those who did not; (2) the executives who mentioned "clarifying the organization" or some equivalent with those who did not; (3) the executives who mentioned "human relations," "employee relations" or "teamwork" with those who did not. The findings are summarized in Table 1.

The difference between the percentages of sales executives (83%) and other executives (29%) who mentioned sales as the most important problem is significant at the 5 per cent level. Three of the five nonsales executives, moreover, who mentioned sales were in the accounting department, and all of these were in positions that involved analysis of product profitability. This accounting

TABLE 1

		Number Who Mentioned		
Department	*Total Number of Executives*	*Sales*	*"Clarify Organization"*	*Human Relations*
Sales	6	5	1	0
Production	5	1	4	0
Accounting	4	3	0	0
Miscellaneous	8	1	3	3
Totals	23	10	8	3

activity was, in fact, receiving considerable emphasis in the company at the time of the case discussion and the accounting executives had frequent and close contacts with the product managers in the sales department. If we combine sales and accounting executives, we find that 8 out of 10 of these mentioned sales as the most important problem; while only 2 of the remaining 13 executives did.

Organization problems (other than marketing organization) were mentioned by four out of five production executives, the two executives in research and development, and the factory physician, but by only one sales executive and no accounting executives. The difference between the percentage for production executives (80%) and other executives (22%) is also significant at the 5 per cent level. Examination of the Castengo case shows that the main issue discussed in the case that relates to manufacturing is the problem of poorly defined relations among the factory manager, the metallurgist, and the company president. The presence of the metallurgist in the situation may help to explain the sensitivity of the two research and development executives (both of whom were concerned with metallurgy) to this particular problem area. It is easy to conjecture why the public relations, industrial relations, and medical executives should all have mentioned some aspect of human relations, and why one of the two legal department executives should have mentioned the board of directors.

Conclusion

We have presented data on the selective perceptions of industrial executives exposed to case material that support the hypothesis that each executive will perceive those aspects of a situation that relate specifically to the activities and goals of his department. Since the situation is one in which the executives were motivated to look at the problem from a company-wide rather than a departmental viewpoint, the data indicate further that the criteria of selection have become internalized. Finally, the method for obtaining data that we have used holds considerable promise as a projective device for eliciting the attitudes and perceptions of executives.

A Theory of Group Development

WARREN G. BENNIS
HERBERT A. SHEPARD

If attention is focused on the organic properties of groups, criteria can be established by which phenomena of development, learning, or movement toward maturity can be identified. From this point of view, maturity for the group means something analogous to maturity for the person: a mature group knows very well what it is doing. The group can resolve its internal conflicts, mobilize its resources, and take intelligent action only if it has means for consensually

Abridged from "A Theory of Group Development," *Human Relations,* Vol. 9, No. 4 (1965), pp. 415–457. Used by permission of Plenum Publishing Company, Ltd.

validating its experience. The person can resolve his internal conflicts, mobilize his resources, and take intelligent action only if anxiety does not interfere with his ability to profit from his experience, to analyse, discriminate, and foresee. Anxiety prevents the person's internal communication system from functioning appropriately, and improvements in his ability to profit from experience hinge upon overcoming anxiety as a source of distortion. Similarly, group development involves the overcoming of obstacles to valid communication among the members, or the development of methods for achieving and testing consensus. Extrapolating from Sullivan's definition of personal maturity we can say a group has reached a state of valid communication when its members are armed with

> ". . . referential tools for analyzing interpersonal experience, so that its significant differences from, as well as its resemblances to, past experience, are discriminable, and the foresight of relatively near future events will be adequate and appropriate to maintaining one's security and securing one's satisfactions without useless or ultimately troublesome disturbance of self-esteem" (19, p. 111).

Relatively few investigations of the phenomena of group development have been undertaken. This paper outlines a theory of development in groups that have as their explicit goal improvement of their internal communication systems.

A group of strangers, meeting for the first time, has within it many obstacles to valid communication. The more heterogeneous the membership, the more accurately does the group become, for each member, a microcosm of the rest of his interpersonal experience. The problems of understanding, the relationships, that develop in any given group are from one aspect a unique product of the particular constellation of personalities assembled. But to construct a broadly useful theory of group development, it is necessary to identify major areas of internal uncertainty, or obstacles to valid communication, which are common to and important in all groups meeting under a given set of environmental conditions. These areas must be strategic in the sense that until the group has developed methods for reducing uncertainty in them, it cannot reduce uncertainty in other areas, and in its external relations.

The Two Major Areas of Internal Uncertainty: Dependence (Authority Relations) and Interdependence (Personal Relations)

Two major areas of uncertainty can be identified by induction from common experience, at least within our own culture. The first of these is the area of group members' orientations toward authority, or more generally toward the handling and distribution of power in the group. The second is the area of members' orientations toward one another. These areas are not independent of each other: a particular set of inter-member orientations will be associated with a particular authority structure. But the two sets of orientations are as distinct from each other as are the concepts of power and love. A number of authorities have used them as a starting-point for the analysis of group behavior.

---

[1]This theory is based for the most part on observations made over a 5-year period of teaching graduate students "group dynamics". The main function of the seminar as it was set forth by the instructors was to improve the internal communication system of the group, hence, a self-study group.

In his *Group Psychology and the Analysis of the Ego,* Freud noted that "each member is bound by libidinal ties on the one hand to the leader . . . and on the other hand to the other members of the group" (6, p. 45). Although he described both ties as libidinal, he was uncertain "how these two ties are related to each other, whether they are of the same kind and the same value, and how they are to be described psychologically." Without resolving this question, he noted that (for the Church and the Army) "one of these, the tie with the leader, seems . . . to be more of a ruling factor than the other, which holds between members of the group" (6, p. 52).

More recently, Schutz (17) has made these two dimensions central to his theory of group compatibility. For him, the strategic determinant of compatibility is the particular blend of orientations toward authority and orientations toward personal intimacy. Bion (1, 2) conceptualizes the major dimensions of the group somewhat differently. His "dependency" and "pairing" modalities correspond to our "dependence" and "interdependence" areas; to them he adds a "fight-flight" modality. For him these modalities are simply alternative modes of behavior; for us, the fight-flight categorization has been useful for characterizing the means used by the group for maintaining a stereotyped orientation during a given subphase.

The core of the theory of group development is that the principal obstacles to the development of valid communication are to be found in the orientations toward authority and intimacy that members bring to the group. Rebelliousness, submissiveness, or withdrawal as the characteristic response to authority figures; destructive competitiveness, emotional exploitiveness, or withdrawal as the characteristic response to peers prevent consensual validation of experience. The behaviors determined by these orientations are directed toward enslavement of the other in the service of the self, enslavement of the self in the service of the other, or disintegration of the situation. Hence, they prevent the setting, clarification of, and movement toward group-shared goals.

In accord with Freud's observation, the orientations toward authority are regarded as being prior to, or partially determining of, orientations toward other members. In its development, the group moves from preoccupation with authority relations to preoccupation with personal relations. This movement defines the two major phases of group development. Within each phase are three subphases, determined by the ambivalence of orientations in each area. That is, during the authority ("dependence") phase, the group moves from preoccupation with submission to preoccupation with rebellion, to resolution of the dependence problem. Within the personal (or "interdependence") phase the group moves from a preoccupation with intermember identification to a preoccupation with individual identity to a resolution of the interdependence problem.

The Relevant Aspects of Personality in Group Development

The aspects of member personality most heavily involved in group development are called, following Schutz, the dependence and personal aspects.

The dependence aspect is comprised by the member's characteristic patterns related to a leader or to a structure of rules. Members who find comfort in rules of procedure, an agenda, an expert, etc. are called "dependent." Members who are discomfited by authoritative structures are called "counterdependent."

The personal aspect is comprised by the member's characteristic patterns with respect to interpersonal intimacy. Members who cannot rest until they have stabilized a relatively high degree of intimacy with all the others are called "overpersonal." Members who tend to avoid intimacy with any of the others are called "counterpersonal."

Psychodynamically, members who evidence some compulsiveness in the adoption of highly dependent, highly counterdependent, highly personal, or highly counterpersonal roles are regarded as "conflicted." Thus, the person who persists in being dependent upon any and all authorities thereby provides himself with ample evidence that authorities should not be so trustingly relied upon; yet he cannot profit from this experience in governing his future action. Hence, a deep, but unrecognized, distrust is likely to accompany the manifestly submissive behavior, and the highly dependent or highly counterdependent person is thus a person in conflict. The existence of the conflict accounts for the sometimes dramatic movement from extreme dependence to extreme rebelliousness. In this way counterdependence and dependence, while logically the extremes of a scale, are psychologically very close together.

The "unconflicted" person or "independent," who is better able to profit from his experience and assess the present situation more adequately, may of course act at times in rebellious or submissive ways. Psychodynamically, the difference between him and the conflicted is easy to understand. In terms of observable behavior, he lacks the compulsiveness and, significantly, does not create the communicative confusion so characteristic of, say, the conflicted dependent, who manifests submission in that part of his communication of which he is aware, and distrust or rebellion in that part of his communication of which he is unaware.

Persons who are unconflicted with respect to the dependence or personal aspect are considered to be responsible for the major movements of the group toward valid communication. That is, the actions of members unconflicted with respect to the problems of a given phase of group development move the group to the next phase. Such actions are called barometric events, and the initiators are called catalysts. This part of the theory of group development is based on Redl's thesis concerning the "infectiousness of the unconflicted on the conflicted personality constellation." The catalysts (Redl calls them "central persons") are the persons capable of reducing the uncertainty characterizing a given phase. "Leadership" from the standpoint of group development can be defined in terms of catalysts responsible for group movement from one phase to the next. This consideration provides a basis for determining what membership roles are needed for group development. For example, it is expected that a group will have great difficulty in resolving problems of power and authority if it lacks members who are unconflicted with respect to dependence.

Phase Movements

The foregoing summary has introduced the major propositions in the theory of group development. While it is not possible to reproduce the concrete group experience from which the theory is drawn, we can take a step in this direction by discussing in more detail what seem to us to be the dominant features of each phase. The description given below is highly interpretive, and we emphasize what seem to us to be the major themes of each phase, even though many minor themes are present. In the process of abstracting, stereotyping, and interpreting, certain obvious facts about group process are lost. For example, each group meeting is to some extent a recapitulation of its past and a forecast of its future. This means that behavior that is "regressive" or "advanced" often appears.

Phase I: Dependence

Subphase 1: Dependence-flight. The first days of group life are filled with behavior whose remote, as well as immediate, aim is to ward off anxiety. Much of the discussion content consists of fruitless searching for a common goal. Some of the security-seeking behavior is group-shared—for example, members may reassure one another by providing interesting and harmless facts about themselves. Some is idiosyncratic—for example, doodling, yawning, intellectualizing.

The search for a common goal is aimed at reducing the cause of anxiety, thus going beyond the satisfaction of immediate security needs. But just as evidencing boredom in this situation is a method of warding off anxiety by denying its proximity, so group goal-seeking is not quite what it is claimed to be. It can best be understood as a dependence plea. The trainer, not the lack of a goal, is the cause of insecurity. This interpretation is likely to be vigorously contested by the group, but it is probably valid. The characteristic expectations of group members are that the trainer will establish rules of the game and distribute rewards. He is presumed to know what the goals are or ought to be. Hence his behavior is regarded as a "technique"; he is merely playing hard to get. The pretense of a fruitless search for goals is a plea for him to tell the group what to do, by simultaneously demonstrating its helplessness without him, and its willingness to work under his direction for his approval and protection.

We are here talking about the dominant theme in group life. Many minor themes are present, and even in connection with the major theme there are differences among members. For some, testing the power of the trainer to affect their futures is the major concern. In others, anxiety may be aroused through a sense of helplessness in a situation made threatening by the protector's desertion. These alternatives can be seen as the beginnings of the counterdependent and dependent adaptations. Those with a dependent orientation look vainly for cues from the trainer for procedure and direction, sometimes paradoxically they infer that the leader must want it that way. Those with a counterdependent orientation strive to detect in the trainer's action elements that would offer ground for rebellion, and may even paradoxically demand rules and leadership from him because he is failing to provide them.

The ambiguity of the situation at this stage quickly becomes intolerable for some, and a variety of ultimately unserviceable resolutions may be invented, many of them idiosyncratic. Alarm at the prospect of future meetings is likely to be group-shared, and at least a gesture may be made in the direction of formulating an agenda for subsequent meetings.

This phase is characterized by behavior that has gained approval from authorities in the past. Since the meetings are to be concerned with groups or with human relations, members offer information on these topics, to satisfy the presumed expectations of the trainer and to indicate expertise, interest, or achievement in these topics (ex-officers from the armed services, from fraternities, etc. have the floor). Topics such as business or political leadership, discrimination and desegregation, are likely to be discussed. During this phase the contributions made by members are designed to gain approval from the trainer, whose reaction to each comment is surreptitiously watched. If the trainer comments that this seems to be the case, or if he notes that the subject under discussion (say, discrimination) may be related to some concerns about membership in this group, he fails again to satisfy the needs of members. Not that the validity of this interpretation is held in much doubt. No one is misled by the "flight" behavior involved in discussing problems external to the group, least of all the group members. Discussion of these matters is filled with perilous uncertainties, however, and so the trainer's observation is politely ignored, as one would ignore a *faux-pas* at a tea-party. The attempts to gain approval based on implicit hypotheses about the potential power of the trainer for good and evil are continued until the active members have run through the repertoire of behaviors that have gained them favor in the past.

Subphase 2: Counterdependence-flight. As the trainer continues to fail miserably in satisfying the needs of the group, discussion takes on a different tone, and counterdependent expressions begin to replace overt dependency phase. In many ways this subphase is the most stressful and unpleasant in the life of the group. It is marked by a paradoxical development of the trainer's role into one of omnipotence and powerlessness, and by division of the group into two warring subgroups. In subphase 1, feelings of hostility were strongly defended; if a slip were made that suggested hostility, particularly toward the trainer, the group members were embarrassed. Now expressions of hostility are more frequent, and are more likely to be supported by other members, or to be met with equally hostile responses. Power is much more overtly the concern of group members in this subphase. A topic such as leadership may again be discussed, but the undertones of the discussion are no longer dependence pleas. Discussion of leadership in subphase 2 is in part a vehicle for making explicit the trainer's failure as a leader. In part it is perceived by other members as a bid for leadership on the part of any member who participates in it.

The major themes of this subphase are as follows:

1. Two opposed subgroups emerge, together incorporating most of the group members. Characteristically, the subgroups are in disagreement about the group's need for leadership or "structure." One subgroup attempts to elect a chairman, nominate working committees, establish agenda, or otherwise "structure" the meetings; the other subgroup opposes all such efforts. At first this appears to be merely an intellectual disagreement concerning the future organization of group activity. But soon it becomes the basis for destroying any semblance of group unity. Fragmentation is expressed and brought about in many ways: voting is a favorite way of dramatizing the schism; suggestions that the group is too large and should be divided into subgroups for the meetings are frequent; a chairman may be elected and then ignored as a demonstration of the group's ineffectualness. Although control mechanisms are sorely needed and desired, no one is willing to relinquish the rights of leadership and control to anyone else. The trainer's abdication has created a power gap, but no one is allowed to fill it.
2. Disenthrallment with the trainer proceeds rapidly. Group members see him as at best ineffectual, at worst damaging, to group progress. He is ignored and bullied almost simultaneously. His interventions are perceived by the counterdependents as an attempt to interrupt group progress; by the dependents,

as weak and incorrect statements. His silences are regarded by the dependents as desertion; by the counterdependents as manipulation. Much of the group activity is to be understood as punishment of the trainer, for his failure to meet needs and expectations, for getting the group into an unpleasant situation, for being the worst kind of authority figure—a weak and incompetent one, or a manipulative, insincere one. Misunderstanding or ignoring his comments, implying that his observations are paranoid fantasies, demonstrations that the group is cracking up, references to him in the past tense as though he were no longer present—these are the punishments for his failure.

As, in the first subphase, the trainer's wisdom, power, and competence were overtly unquestioned, but secretly suspected; so, in the second subphase, the conviction that he is incompetent and helpless is clearly dramatized, but secretly doubted. Out of this secret doubt arises the belief in the trainer's omnipotence. None of the punishments meted out to the trainer are recognized as such by the group members; in fact, if the trainer suggests that the members feel a need to punish him, they are most likely to respond in injured tones or in tones of contempt that what is going on has nothing to do with him and that he had best stay out of it. The trainer is still too imposing and threatening to challenge directly. There is a secret hope that the chaos in the group is in fact part of the master plan, that he is really leading them in the direction they should be going. That he may really be helpless as they imply, or that the failure may be theirs rather than his, are frightening possibilities. For this reason subphase 2 differs very little in its fundamental dynamics from subphase 1. There is still the secret wish that the trainer will stop all the bedlam which has replaced polite uncertainty, by taking his proper role (so that dependent members can cooperate with him and counterdependent can rebel in the usual ways).

Subphase 2 thus brings the group to the brink of catastrophe. The trainer has consistently failed to meet the group's needs. Not daring to turn directly on him, the group members engage in mutually destructive behavior: in fact, the group threatens suicide as the most extreme expression of dependence. The need to punish the trainer is so strong, however, that his act of salvation would have to be magical indeed.

Subphase 3: Resolution-Catharsis. No such magic is available to the trainer. Resolution of the group's difficulties at this point depends upon the presence in the group of other forces, which have until this time been inoperative, or ineffective. Only the degenerative aspects of the chain of events in subphases 1 and 2 have been presented up to this point and they are in fact the salient ones. But there has been a simultaneous, though less obvious, mobilization of constructive forces. First, within each of the warring subgroups bonds of mutual support have grown. The group member no longer feels helpless and isolated. Second, the trainer's role, seen as weak or manipulative in the dependence orientation, can also be perceived as permissive. Third, his interpretations, though openly ignored, have been secretly attended to. And, as the second and third points imply, some members of the group are less the prisoners of the dependence-counterdependence dilemma than others. These members, called the independents, have been relatively ineffective in the group for two reasons. First, they have not developed firm bonds with other members in either of the warring subgroups, because they have not identified with either cause. Typically, they have devoted their energies to an unsuccessful search for a compromise settlement of the disagreements in the group. Since their attitudes toward authority are less ambivalent than those of other members, they have accepted the alleged reason for disagreement in the group—for example, whether a chairman should be elected—at face value, and tried to mediate. Similarly, they have tended to accept the trainer's role and interpretations more nearly at face value. However, his interpretations have seemed inaccurate to them, since in fact the interpretations have applied much less to them than to the rest of the group.

Subphase 3 is the most crucial and fragile in group life up to this point. What occurs is a sudden shift in the whole basis of group action. It is truly a bridging phase; if it occurs at all, it is so rapid and mercurial that the end of subphase 2 appears to give way directly to the first subphase of Phase II. If it does not occur thus rapidly and dramatically, a halting and arduous process of vacillation between Phases I and II is likely to persist for a long period, the total group movement being very gradual.

To summarize the state of affairs at the beginning of subphase 3: 1. The group is polarized into two competing groups, each unable to gain or relinquish power. 2. Those group members who are uncommitted to either subgroup are ineffective in their attempts to resolve the conflict. 3. The trainer's contributions only serve to deepen the cleavage in the group.

As the group enters subphase 3, it is moving rapidly toward extinction: that is, splintering into two or three subgroups. The independents, who have until now been passive or ineffectual, become the only hope for survival, since they have thus far avoided polarization and stereotypic behavior. The imminence of dissolution forces them to recognize the fruitlessness of their attempts at mediation. For this reason, the trainer's hypothesis that fighting one another is off-target behavior is likely to be acted upon at this point. A group member may openly express the opinion that the trainer's presence and comments are holding the group back, suggest that "as an experiment" the trainer leaves the group "to see how things go without him". When the trainer is thus directly challenged, the whole atmosphere of the meeting changes. There is a sudden increase in alertness and tension. Previously, there had been much acting out of the wish that the trainer were absent, but at the same time a conviction that he was the *raison d'être* of the group's existence—that it would fall apart without him. Previously, absence of the trainer would have constituted desertion, or defeat, fulfilment of the members' worst fears as to their own inadequacy or the trainer's. But now leaving the group can have a different meaning. General agreement that the trainer should leave is rarely achieved. However, after a little further discussion it becomes clear that he is at liberty to leave, with the understanding that he wishes to be a member of the group, and will return if and when the group is willing to accept him.

The principal function of the symbolic removal of the trainer is in its effect of freeing the group to bring into awareness the hitherto carefully ignored feelings toward him as an authority figure, and toward the group activity as an off-target dramatization of the ambivalence toward authority. The leadership provided by the independents (whom the group sees as having no vested interest in power) leads to a new orientation toward membership in the group. In the discussion that follows the exit of the trainer, the dependents' assertion that the trainer deserted and the counterdependents' assertion that he was kicked out are soon replaced by consideration of whether his behavior was "responsible" or "irresponsible." The power problem is resolved by being defined in terms of member responsibilities, and the terms of the trainer's return to the group are settled by the requirement that he behave as "just another member of the group". This phrase is then explained as meaning that he should take neither more nor less responsibility for what happens in the group than any other member.

The above description of the process does not do justice to the excitement and involvement characteristic of this period. How much transferable insight ambivalent members acquire from it is difficult to assess. At least within the life of the group, later activity is rarely perceived in terms of submission and rebellion.

An interesting parallel, which throws light on the order of events in group development, is given in Freud's discussion of the myth of the primal horde. In his version:

> "These many individuals eventually banded themselves together, killed [the father], and cut him in pieces. . . . They then formed the totemistic community of brothers all with equal rights and united by the totem prohibitions which were to preserve and to expiate the memory of the murder" (6, p. 112).

The horde's act, according to Freud, was soon distorted into an heroic myth: instead of murder by the group, the myth held that the father had been overthrown single-handed by one person, usually the youngest son. In this attribution of the group act to one individual (the hero) Freud saw the "emergence of the individual from group psychology." His definition of a hero is ". . . a man who stands up manfully against his father and in the end victoriously overthrows him" (8, p. 9). (The heroic myth of Freud thus shares much in common with Sullivan's "delusion of unique individuality.")

In the training group, the member who initiates the events leading to the trainer's exit is sometimes referred to as a "hero" by the other members. Responsibility for the act is felt to be shared by the group, however, and out of their experience comes the first strong sense of group solidarity and involvement—a reversal of the original version, where the individual emerges from the group. This turn of events clarifies Freud's remark concerning the libidinal ties to the leader and to the other group members. Libidinal ties toward the other group members cannot be adequately developed until there is a resolution of the ties with the leader. In our terms, those components of group life having to do with intimacy and interdependence cannot be dealt with until those components having to do with authority and dependence have been resolved.

Other aspects of subphase 3 may be understood by investigating the dramatic significance of the revolt. The event is always marked in group history as "a turning-point", "the time we became a group", "when I first got involved", etc. The mounting tension, followed by sometimes uproarious euphoria, cannot be entirely explained by the surface events. It may be that the revolt represents a realization of important fantasies individuals hold in all organizations, that the emotions involved are undercurrents wherever rebellious and submissive tendencies toward existing authorities must be controlled. These are the themes of some of our great dramas—*Antigone, Billy Budd, Hamlet,* and our most recent folk-tale, *The Caine Mutiny.* But the event is more than the presentation of a drama, or an acting-out of fantasies. For it can be argued that the moments of stress and catharsis, when emotions are labile and intense, are the times in the group life when there is readiness for change. Leighton's analysis of a minor revolution at a Japanese relocation camp is worth quoting in full on this point:

> "While this [cathartic] situation is fraught with danger because of trends which may make the stress become worse before it gets better, there is also an opportunity for administrative action that is not likely to be found in more secure times. It is fairly well recognized in psychology that at periods of great emotional stir the individual human being can undergo far-reaching and permanent changes in his personality. It is as if the bone structure of his systems of belief and of his habitual patterns of behavior becomes soft, is fused into new shapes and hardens there when the period of tension is over. . . . Possibly the same can be true of whole groups of people, and there are historical examples of social changes and movements occurring when there was widespread emotional tension, usually some form of anxiety. The Crusades, parts of the Reformation, the French Revolution, the change in Zulu life in the reign of Chaca, the Meiji Restoration, the Mormon movement, the Russian Revolution, the rise of Fascism, and alterations in the social sentiments of the United States going on at present are all to some extent examples" (12, p. 360).

Observers of industrial relations have made similar observations. When strikes result from hostile labor-management relations (as contrasted to straight wage demands), there is a fluidity of relationships and a wide repertoire of structural changes during this period not available before the strike act.[2]

So it is, we believe, with the training group. But what are the new values and behavior patterns that emerge out of the emotional experience of Phase I? Principally, they are acceptance by each member of his full share of responsibility for what happens in the group. The outcome is autonomy for the group. After the events of subphase 3, there is no more attribution of magical powers to the trainer—either the dependent fantasy that he sees farther, knows better, is mysteriously guiding the group and protecting it from evil, or the very similar counterdependent fantasy that he is manipulating the group, exploiting it in his own interests, that the experience is one of "brain-washing." The criterion for evaluating a contribution is no longer who said it, but what is said. Thereafter, such power fantasies as the trainer himself may have present no different problem from the power fantasies of any other group member. At the same time, the illusion that there is a struggle for power in the group is suddenly dissipated, and the contributions of other members are evaluated in terms of their relevance to shared group goals.

Summary of Phase I. The very word development implies not only movement through time, but also a definite order of progression. The group must traverse subphase 1 to reach subphase 2, and subphase 3 before it can move

[2] See A. Gouldner (10), W. F. Whyte, Jr. (22). Robert E. Park, writing in 1928, had considerable insight on some functions of revolution and change. See (14).

into Phase II. At the same time, lower levels of development coexist with more advanced levels. Blocking and regression occur frequently, and the group may be "stuck" at a certain phase of development. It would, of course, be difficult to imagine a group remaining long in subphase 3—the situation is too tense to be permanent. But the group may founder for some time in subphase 2 with little movement. In short, groups do not inevitably develop through the resolution of the dependence phase to Phase II. This movement may be retarded indefinitely. Obviously much depends upon the trainer's role. In fact, the whole dependence modality may be submerged by certain styles of trainer behavior. The trainer has a certain range of choice as to whether dependency as a source of communication distortion is to be highlighted and made the subject of special experiential and conceptual consideration. The personality and training philosophy of the trainer determine his interest in introducing or avoiding explicit consideration of dependency.

There are other important forces in the group besides the trainer, and these may serve to facilitate or block the development that has been described as typical of Phase I. Occasionally there may be no strong independents capable of bringing about the barometric events that precipitate movement. Or the leaders of opposing subgroups may be the most assertive members of the group. In such cases the group may founder permanently in subphase 2. If a group has the misfortune to experience a "traumatic" event early in its existence—exceedingly schizoid behavior by some member during the first few meetings, for example—anxieties of other members may be aroused to such an extent that all culturally suspect behavior, particularly open expression of feelings, is strongly inhibited in subsequent meetings.

Table I summarizes the major events of Phase I, as it typically proceeds. This phase has dealt primarily with the resolution of dependence needs. It ends with acceptance of mutual responsibility for the fate of the group and a sense of solidarity, but the implications of shared responsibility have yet to be explored. This exploration is reserved for Phase II, which we have chosen to call the Interdependence Phase.

Phase II: Interdependence

The resolution of dependence problems marks the transfer of group attention (and inattention) to the problems of shared responsibility.

Sullivan's description of the change from childhood to the juvenile era seems pertinent here:

> "The juvenile era is marked off from childhood by the appearance of an urgent need for compeers with whom to have one's existence. By 'compeers' I mean people who are on our level, and have generically similar attitudes toward authoritative figures, activities and the like. This marks the beginning of the juvenile era, the great developments in which are the talents for cooperation, competition and compromise" (20, pp. 17–18).

The remaining barriers to valid communication are those associated with orientations toward interdependence: i.e. intimacy, friendship, identification. While the distribution of power was the cardinal issue during Phase I, the distribution of affection occupies the group during Phase II.

TABLE I. Phase I. Dependence—Power Relations*

	Subphase 1 Dependence-Submission	Subphase 2 Counterdependence	Subphase 3 Resolution
1. Emotional Modality	Dependence—Flight	Counterdependence—Fight. Off-target fighting among members. Distrust of staff member. Ambivalence.	Pairing. Intense involvement in group task.
2. Content Themes	Discussion of interpersonal problems external to training groups.	Discussion of group organization; i.e. what degree of structuring devices is needed for "effective" group behavior?	Discussion and definition of trainer role.
3. Dominant Roles (Central Persons)	Assertive, aggressive members with rich previous organizational or social science experience.	Most assertive counterdependent and dependent members. Withdrawal of *less* assertive independents and dependents.	Assertive independents.
4. Group Structure	Organized mainly into multi-subgroups based on members' past experiences.	Two tight subcliques consisting of leaders and members, of counterdependents and dependents.	Group unifies in pursuit of goal and develops internal authority system.
5. Group Activity	Self-oriented behavior reminiscent of most new social gatherings.	Search for consensus mechanism: Voting, setting up chairmen, search for "valid" content subjects.	Group members take over leadership roles formerly perceived as held by trainer.
6. Group movement facilitated by:	Staff member abnegation of traditional role of structuring situation, setting up rules of fair play, regulation of participation.	Disenthrallment with staff member coupled with absorption of uncertainty by most assertive counterdependent and dependent individuals. Subgroups form to ward off anxiety.	Revolt by assertive independents (catalysts) who fuse subgroups into unity by initiating and engineering trainer exit (barometric event).
7. Main Defenses	Projection Denigration of authority		Group moves into Phase II

*Course terminates at the end of 17 weeks. It is not uncommon for groups to remain throughout the course in this phase.

Subphase 4: Enchantment-Flight. At the outset of subphase 4, the group is happy, cohesive, relaxed. The atmosphere is one of "sweetness and light". Any slight increase in tension is instantly dissipated by joking and laughter. The fighting of Phase I is still fresh in the memory of the group, and the group's efforts are devoted to patching up differences, healing wounds, and maintaining a harmonious atmosphere. Typically, this is a time of merrymaking and group minstrelsy. Coffee and cake may be served at the meetings. Hours may be passed in organizing a group party. Poetry or songs commemorating the important events and persons in the group's history may be composed by individuals or, more commonly, as a group project. All decisions must be unanimous during this period, since everyone must be happy, but the issues on which decisions are made are mostly ones about which group members have no strong feelings. At first the cathartic, healing function of these activities is clear; there is much spontaneity, playfulness, and pleasure. Soon the pleasures begin to wear thin.

The myth of mutual acceptance and universal harmony must eventually be recognized for what it is. From the beginning of this phase there are frequent evidences of underlying hostilities, unresolved issues in the group. But they are quickly, nervously smoothed over by laughter or misinterpretation. Subphase 4 begins with catharsis, but that is followed by the development of a rigid norm to which all members are forced to conform: "Nothing must be allowed to disturb our harmony in the future; we must avoid the mistakes of the painful past." Not that members have forgotten that the painful past was a necessary preliminary to the autonomous and (it is said) delightful present, though that fact is carefully overlooked. Rather, there is a dim realization that all members must have an experience somewhat analogous to the trainer's in subphase 3, before a mutually understood, accepted, and realistic definition of their own roles in the group can be arrived at.

Resistance of members to the requirement that harmony be maintained at all costs appears in subtle ways. In open group discussion the requirement is imperative: either the member does not dare to endanger harmony with the group or to disturb the *status quo* by denying that all problems have been solved. Much as members may dislike the tedious work of maintaining the appearance of harmony, the alternative is worse. The house of cards would come tumbling down, and the painful and exacting work of building something more substantial would have to begin. The flight from these problems takes a number of forms. Group members may say, "We've had our fighting and are now a group. Thus, further self-study is unnecessary." Very commonly, the possibility of any change may be prevented by not coming together as a total group at all. Thus the members may subgroup through an entire meeting. Those who would disturb the friendly subgroups are accused of "rocking the boat."

The solidarity and harmony become more and more illusory, but the group still clings to the illusion. This perseveration is in a way a consequence of the deprivation that members have experienced in maintaining the atmosphere of harmony. Maintaining it forces members to behave in ways alien to their own feelings; to go still further in group involvement would mean a complete loss of self. The group is therefore torn by a new ambivalence, which might be verbalized as follows: 1. "We all love one another and therefore we must maintain the solidarity of the group and give up whatever is necessary of our selfish desires." 2. "The group demands that I sacrifice my identity as a person;

but the group is an evil mechanism which satisfies no dominant needs." As this subphase comes to a close, the happiness that marked its beginning is maintained only as a mask. The "innocent" splitting of the group into subgroups has gone so far that members will even walk around the meeting table to join in the conversation of a subgroup rather than speak across the table at the risk of bringing the whole group together. There is a certain uneasiness about the group; there is a feeling that "we should work together but cannot." There may be a tendency to regress to the orientation of subphase 1: group members would like the trainer to take over.

To recapitulate: subphase 4 begins with a happy sense of group belongingness. Individual identity is eclipsed by a "the group is bigger than all of us" sentiment. But this integration is short lived: it soon becomes perceived as a fake attempt to resolve interpersonal problems by denying their reality. In the later stages of this subphase, enchantment with the total group is replaced by enchantment with one's subgroup, and out of this breakdown of the group emerges a new organization based on the anxieties aroused out of this first, suffocating, involvement.

Subphase 5: Disenchantment-Fight. This subphase is marked by a division into two subgroups—paralleling the experience of subphase 2—but this time based upon orientations toward the degree of intimacy required by group membership. Membership in the two subgroups is not necessarily the same as in subphase 2: for now the fragmentation occurs as a result of opposite and extreme attitudes toward the degree of intimacy desired in interpersonal relations. The counterpersonal members band together to resist further involvement. The overpersonal members band together in a demand for unconditional love. While these subgroups appear as divergent as possible, a common theme underlies them. For the one group, the only means seen for maintaining self-esteem is to avoid any real commitment to others; for the other group, the only way to maintain self-esteem is to obtain a commitment from others to forgive everything. The subgroups share in common the fear that intimacy breeds contempt.

This anxiety is reflected in many ways during subphase 5. For the first time openly disparaging remarks are made about the group. Invidious comparisons are made between it and other groups. Similarly, psychology and social science may be attacked. The inadequacy of the group as a basis for self-esteem is dramatized in many ways—from stating "I don't care what you think," to boredom, to absenteeism. The overpersonals insist that they are happy and comfortable, while the counterpersonals complain about the lack of group morale. Intellectualization by the overpersonals frequently takes on religious overtones concerning Christian love, consideration for others, etc. In explanations of member behavior, the counterpersonal members account for all in terms of motives having nothing to do with the present group; the overpersonals explain all in terms of acceptance and rejection in the present group.

Subphase 5 belongs to the counterpersonals as subphase 4 belonged to the overpersonals. Subphase 4 might be caricatured as hiding in the womb of the group; subphase 5 as hiding out of sight of the group. It seems probable that both of these modalities serve to ward off anxieties associated with intimate interpersonal relations. A theme that links them together can be verbalized as follows: "If others really knew me, they would reject me." The overpersonal's formula for avoiding this rejection seems to be accepting all others so as to be protected by the others' guilt; the counterpersonal's way is by rejecting all others before they have a chance to reject him. Another way of characterizing the counterpersonal orientation is in the phrase, "I would lose my identity as a member of the group." The corresponding overpersonal orientation reads, "I have nothing to lose by identifying with the group." We can now look back on the past two subphases as countermeasures against loss of self-esteem; what Sullivan once referred to as the greatest inhibition to the understanding of what is distinctly human, "the overwhelming conviction of self-hood—this amounts to a delusion of unique individuality". The sharp swings and fluctuations that occurred between the enchantment and euphoria of subphase 4 and the disenchantment of subphase 5 can be seen as a struggle between the "institutionalization of complacency" on the one hand and anxiety associated with fantasy speculations about intimacy and involvement on the other. This dissociative behavior serves a purpose of its own: a generalized denial of the group and its meaning for individuals. For if the group is important and valid then it has to be taken seriously. If it can wallow in the enchantment of subphase 4, it is safe; if it can continually vilify the goals and objectives of the group, it is also safe. The disenchantment theme in subphase 5 is perhaps a less skilful and more desperate security provision with its elaborate wall of defenses than the "group mind" theme of subphase 4. What should be stressed is that both subphase defenses were created almost entirely on fantastic expectations about the consequences of group involvement. These defenses are homologous to anxiety as it is experienced by the individual; i.e. the state of "anxiety arises as a response to a situation of danger and which will be reproduced thenceforward whenever such a situation recurs" (7, p. 72). In sum, the past two subphases were marked by a conviction that further group involvement would be injurious to members' self-esteem.

Subphase 6: Consensual Validation. In the groups of which we write, two forces combine to press the group toward a resolution of the interdependency problem. These are the approaching end of the training course, and the need to establish a method of evaluation (including course grades).

There are, of course, ways of denying or avoiding these realities. The group can agree to continue to meet after the course ends. It can extricate itself from evaluation activities by asking the trainer to perform the task, or by awarding a blanket grade. But turning this job over to the trainer is a regression to dependence; and refusal to discriminate and reward is a failure to resolve the problems of interdependence. If the group has developed in general as we have described, the reality of termination and evaluation cannot be denied, and these regressive modes of adaptation cannot be tolerated.

The characteristic defenses of the two subgroups at first fuse to prevent any movement toward the accomplishment of the evaluation and grading task. The counterpersonals resist evaluation as an invasion of privacy: they foresee catastrophe if members begin to say what they think of one another. The overpersonals resist grading since it involves discrimination among the group members. At the same time, all members have a stake in the outcome of evaluation and grading. In avoiding the task, members of each subgroup are perceived by members of the other as "rationalizing," and the group becomes involved in a vicious circle of mutual disparagement. In this process, the fear of loss of self-esteem through group involvement is near to being realized. As in subphase

3, it is the independents—in this case those whose self-esteem is not threatened by the prospect of intimacy—who restore members' confidence in the group. Sometimes all that is required to reverse the vicious circle quite dramatically is a request by an independent for assessment of his own role. Or it may be an expression of confidence in the group's ability to accomplish the task.

The activity that follows group commitment to the evaluation task does not conform to the expectations of the overpersonal or counterpersonal members. Its chief characteristic is the willingness and ability of group members to validate their self-concepts with other members. The fear of rejection fades when tested against reality. The tensions that developed as a result of these fears diminish in the light of actual discussion of member roles. At the same time, there is revulsion against "capsule evaluations" and "curbstone psychoanalysis." Instead, what ensues is a serious attempt by each group member to verbalize his private conceptual scheme for understanding human behavior—his own and that of others. Bringing these assumptions into explicit communication is the main work of subphase 6. This activity demands a high level of work and of communicative skill. Some of the values that appear to underlie the group's work during this subphase are as follows: (1) Members can accept one another's differences without associating "good" and "bad" with the differences. (2) Conflict exists but is over substantive issues rather than emotional issues. (3) Consensus is reached as a result of rational discussion rather than through a compulsive attempt at unanimity. (4) Members are aware of their own involvement, and of other aspects of group process, without being overwhelmed or alarmed. (5) Through the evaluation process, members take on greater personal meaning to each other. This facilitates communication and creates a deeper understanding of how the other person thinks, feels, behaves; it creates a series of personal expectations, as distinguished from the previous, more stereotyped, role expectations.

The above values, and some concomitant values, are of course very close to the authors' conception of a "good group." In actuality they are not always achieved by the end of the group life. The prospect of the death of the group, after much procrastination in the secret hope that it will be over before anything can be done, is likely to force the group into strenuous last-minute efforts to overcome the obstacles that have blocked its progress. As a result, the sixth subphase is too often hurried and incomplete. If the hurdles are not overcome in time, grading is likely to be an exercise that confirms members' worst suspicions about the group. And if role evaluation is attempted, either the initial evaluations contain so much hostile material as to block further efforts, or evaluations are so flowery and vacuous that no one, least of all the recipient, believes them.

In the resolution of interdependence problems, member-personalities count for even more than they do in the resolution of dependence problems. The trainer's behavior is crucial in determining the group's ability to resolve the dependence issue, but in the interdependence issue the group is, so to speak, only as stong as its weakest link. The exceedingly dependent group member can ride through Phase I with a fixed belief in the existence of a private relationship between himself and the trainer; but the person whose anxieties are intense under the threats associated with intimacy can immobilize the group. (*Table II* summarizes the major events of Phase II.)

TABLE II. Phase II. Interdependence—Personal Relations

	Subphase 4—Enchantment	Subphase 5—Disenchantment	Subphase 6—Consensual Validation
Emotional Modality	Pairing-Flight. Group becomes a respected icon beyond further analysis.	Fight-Flight. Anxiety reactions. Distrust and suspicion of various group members.	Pairing, understanding, acceptance.
Content Themes	Discussion of "group history", and generally salutary aspects of course, group, and membership.	Revival of content themes used in Subphase 1: What is a group? What are we doing here? What are the goals of the group? What do I have to give up—personally—to belong to this group? (How much intimacy and affection is required?) Invasion of privacy vs. "group giving". Setting up proper codes of social behavior.	Course grading system. Discussion and assessment of member roles.
Dominant Roles (Central Persons)	General distribution of participation for first time. Overpersonals have salience.	Most assertive counterpersonal and overpersonal individuals, with counterpersonals especially salient.	Assertive independents.
Group Structure	Solidarity, fusion. High degree of camaraderie and suggestibility. Le Bon's description of "group mind" would apply here.	Restructuring of membership into two competing predominant subgroups made up of individuals who share similar attitudes concerning degree of intimacy required in social interaction, i.e. the counterpersonal and overpersonal groups. The personal individuals remain uncommitted but act according to needs of situation.	Diminishing of ties based on personal orientation. Group structure now presumably appropriate to needs of situation based on predominantly substantive rather than emotional orientations. Consensus significantly easier on important issues.
Group Activity	Laughter, joking, humor. Planning out-of-class activities such as parties. The institutionalization of happiness to be accomplished by "fun" activities. High rate of interaction and participation.	Disparagement of group in a variety of ways: high rate of absenteeism, tardiness, balkiness in initiating total group interaction, frequent statements concerning worthlessness of group, denial of importance of group. Occasional member asking for individual help finally rejected by the group.	Communication to others of self-system of interpersonal relations; i.e. making conscious to self, and others aware of, conceptual system one uses to predict consequences of personal behavior. Acceptance of group on reality terms.
Group movement facilitated by:	Independence and achievement attained by trainer-rejection and its concomitant, deriving consensually some effective means for authority and control. (Subphase 3 rebellion bridges gap between Subphases 2 and 4.)	Disenchantment of group as a result of *fantasied expectations of group life.* The perceived threat to self-esteem that further group involvment signifies creates schism of group according to amount of affection and intimacy desired. The counterpersonal and overpersonal assertive individuals alleviate source of anxiety by disparaging or abnegating further group involvement. Subgroups form to ward off anxiety.	The external realities, group termination and the prescribed need for a course grading system, comprise the barometric event. Led by the personal individuals, the group tests reality and reduces autistic convictions concerning group involvement.
Main Defences	Denial, isolation, intellectualization, and alienation.		

Conclusions

Dependence and interdependence—power and love, authority and intimacy—are regarded as the central problems of group life. In most organizations and societies, the rules governing the distribution of authority and the degree of intimacy among members are prescribed. In the human relations training group, they are major areas of uncertainty. While the choice of these matters as the focus of group attention and experience rests to some extent with the trainer, his choice is predicated on the belief that they are the core of interpersonal experience. As such, the principal obstacles to valid interpersonal communication lie in rigidities of interpretation and response carried over from the anxious experiences with particular love or power figures into new situations in which they are inappropriate. The existence of such autisms complicates all discussion unduly and in some instances makes an exchange of meanings impossible.

Stating the training goal as the establishment of valid communication means that the relevance of the autistic response to authority and intimacy on the part of any member can be explicitly examined, and at least a provisional alternative formulated by him. Whether this makes a lasting change in the member's flexibility, or whether he will return to his more restricted formula when confronted with a new situation, we do not know, but we expect that it varies with the success of his group experience—particularly his success in understanding it.

We have attempted to portray what we believe to be the typical pattern of group development, and to show the relationship of member orientations and changes in member orientations to the major movements of the group. In this connection, we have emphasized the catalytic role of persons unconflicted with respect to one or the other of the dependence and interdependence areas. This power to move the group lies mainly in his freedom from anxiety-based reactions to problems of authority (or intimacy): he has the freedom to be creative in searching for a way to reduce tension.

We have also emphasized the "barometric event" or event capable of moving the group from one phase to the next. The major events of this kind are the removal of the trainer as part of the resolution of the dependence problem; and the evaluation-grading requirements at the termination of the course. Both these barometric events require a catalytic agent in the group to bring them about. That is to say, the trainer-exit can take place only at the moment when it is capable of symbolizing the attainment of group autonomy, and it requires a catalytic agent in the group to give it this meaning. And the grading assignment can move the group forward only if the catalytic agent can reverse the vicious circle of disparagement that precedes it.

Whether the incorporation of these barometric events into the training design merely makes our picture of group development a self-fulfilling prophecy, or whether, as we wish to believe, these elements make dramatically clear the major forward movements of the group, and open the gate for a flood of new understanding and communication, can only be decided on the basis of more, and more varied, experience.

The evolution from Phase I to Phase II represents not only a change in emphasis from power to affection, but also from role to personality. Phase I activity generally centers on broad role distinctions such as class, ethnic background, professional interests, etc.; Phase II activity involves a deeper concern with personality modalities, such as reaction to failure, warmth, retaliation, anxiety, etc. This development presents an interesting paradox. For the group in Phase I emerged out of a heterogeneous collectivity of individuals; the individual in Phase II emerged out of the group. This suggests that group therapy, where attention is focused on individual movement, begins at the least enabling time. It is possible that, before group members are able to help each other, the barriers to communication must be partially understood.

References

1. Bion, W. R. "Experiences in Groups: I." *Hum. Relat.,* Vol. I, No. 3, pp. 314–320, 1948.

2. Bion, W. R. "Experiences in Groups: II." *Hum. Relat.,* Vol. I, No. 4, pp. 487–496, 1948.

5. Frenkel-Brunswik, E. "Intolerance of Ambiguity as an Emotional and Perceptual Personality Variable." In Bruner, J. S., and Krech, D. (eds.), *Perception and Personality.* Durham, N. C.: Duke Univ. Press, 1949 and 1950, p. 115.

6. Freud, Sigmund. *Group Psychology and the Analysis of the Ego.* Translated by J. Strachey. London: International Psycho-Analytical Press, 1922; New York: Liveright, 1949.

7. Freud, Sigmund. *The Problem of Anxiety.* Translated by H. A. Bunker. New York: Psychoanalytic Quarterly Press and W. W. Norton, 1936.

8. Freud, Sigmund. *Moses and Monotheism.* London: Hogarth Press, 1939; New York: Vintage Books, 1955.

10. Gouldner, Alvin. *Wildcat Strike.* Yellow Springs, Ohio: Antioch Press, 1954; London: Routledge & Kegan Paul, 1955.

12. Leighton, A. H. *The Governing of Men.* Princeton: Princeton Univ. Press, 1946.

14. Park, Robert E. "The Strike." *Society.* New York: Free Press of Glencoe, 1955.

16. Schutz, W. C. "Group Behavior Studies, I–III." Cambridge, Mass.: Harvard Univ., 1954 (mimeo).

17. Schutz, W. C. "What Makes Groups Productive?" *Hum. Relat.,* Vol. VIII, No. 4, p. 429, 1955.

19. Sullivan, H. S. "Tensions, Interpersonal and International." In Cantril, Hadley (ed.), *Tensions that Cause Wars.* Urbana, Ill.: Univ. of Illinois Press, 1950.

20. Sullivan, H. S. *Conceptions of Modern Psychiatry.* Washington, D.C.: William Alanson White Psychiatric Foundation, 1940, 1945; London: Tavistock Publications, 1955.

22. Whyte, W. F., Jr. *Patterns for Industrial Peace.* New York: Harper, 1951.

Questions for Discussion

1. How would you fit religion into the hierarchical model of human needs? How would Karl Marx, or an atheist, or a believer?

2. A few years ago a meeting of psychologists, psychiatrists, philosophers, and artists was held in New York. The topic was: Is the sacrificing single-interest artist sane or insane? Views were expressed on both sides. Discuss this with reference to the hierarchy of needs.

3. In much of West Africa, managers have had great difficulty in attracting and holding natives in factory work. They work a few weeks, collect their money, and go back to their villages. Why?

4. The graduated personal Federal income tax (rising above 90 per cent at upper levels) severely limits the executive's ability to increase his take-home pay by salary increases at the top organizational levels. Recently, the Internal Revenue Service has been attempting to tax stock dividends and bonuses at the same income tax rate. Do you think that such taxes adversely affect business management? In particular, do you think such taxes limit the business world's ability to attract and motivate ambitious and hard-working men?

5. In the light of the preceding two questions, discuss the meaning of money as an incentive in the United States.

6. "Many a man is entirely incapable of assuming responsibility. He is a success as the led, but not as the leader. He lacks the courage of willingness to assume responsibility and the ability of handling others. He was born for a salaried man, and a salaried man he had better remain." This is a statement by N. C. Fowler entitled, *The Boy, How to Help Him Succeed,* published in 1902. The position taken by this author was common in the 19th and early 20th centuries. The only avenue for the really successful man was entrepreneurship—the ownership and management of his own business. Working for others was simply for those less qualified. Discuss this statement: (*a*) with relevance to 1902; (*b*) with relevance to the present.

7. As a freshman Senator, Charles Percy was talked of as a candidate for President of the United States. He was formerly president of Bell and Howell, a position he reached at the age of 29 without benefit of family influence or personal wealth. Over a period of 13 years, he drove Bell and Howell to a strong economic position and an important market

share in competition with Eastman Kodak. Although he never owned a substantial portion of the company, he worked long hours, sacrificed time with his family (although he found time to father five children), and created quite a mystique about himself as a business leader. What might be some of the reasons for this individual effort?

8. In spite of repeated efforts to organize them, most engineers have refused to join unions. Many might even agree that strong collective action would help them as a body, but they don't want to join. Why?

9. A recent study in one of the largest U.S. corporations indicates that the two criteria of rank in class and quality of college attended are apparently the best predictors of future success as a manager. If you were a recruiter for a large company, would you use these criteria? Why or why not?

10. In *The Practice of Management,* Peter Drucker wrote: "Management by objectives and self-control makes the commonwealth the aim of every manager. It substitutes for control from the outside the stricter, more exacting and more effective control from the inside. It motivates the manager to action not because somebody tells him to do something or talks him into doing it, but because the objective needs of the task demand it. He acts, not because somebody wants him to, but because he himself decides that he has to—he acts, in other words, as a free man." In their international study of management, *Management in the Industrial World,* Harbison and Myers observed that "management by objectives and self-control" exists in few countries outside the United States and the United Kingdom (and is probably rare in the U.K.). Why?

Chapter Four

The Impact of Formal Organization: Structural Factors In Organizational Behavior

Hierarchy may be essential and inevitable. "Empirically," writes Herbert Simon [22], "a large proportion of the complex systems we observe in nature exhibit hierarchical structure. On theoretical grounds we would expect complex systems to be hierarchies in a world in which complexity had to evolve from simplicity. . . . Hierarchy is one of the central structural schemes that the architect of complexity uses." The basic form is found in atoms and galaxies, in inanimate computers and living organisms. In short, complexity and hierarchy are close companions—and this is especially so in human organizations, because hierarchy reflects the basic functions of organizational management. Although class, influence, and personality frequently determine who is at the top, organizational structure (looking something like a pyramid) would be necessary even if people were identical and even if we lived in a communist utopia without private property or class distinction.

Essential and inevitable as they are, however, hierarchy and organization create problems. People do not behave as they should—not because they are perverse but because life in organizations will always be aggravating and confining. By definition, organization prescribes and limits behavior. Few men are so submissive and authority-oriented that they won't feel frustrated from time to time. Most of us will experience frequent conflict with organizational structure as we attempt to respond to demands, to influence behavior, and to accomplish objectives. Nonetheless, this inevitable conflict between individual and organization is not a tragedy—however much Ayn Rand [20] may pine for a simpler existence. A critical question is how we take it. Do we demonstrate courage and patience, accepting the inevitable restrictions of organization but never easing pressure on those aspects which can be changed? Or do we lose spontaneity and direction by lapsing into a kind of organizational sleepwalking? A paraphrase of the well-known prayer of Alcoholics Anonymous is appropriate: "Give me the patience to accept what cannot be changed in the organization, the courage to change what can be changed, and the wisdom to know the difference."

But why bother? Why not repudiate confining organization and choose smaller and simpler bodies less restrictive and frustrating? The choice is only theoretical. As mentioned in Chapter 3, when we rejected Thomas Jefferson's vision of a semirural America of independent, property-owning farmers and craftsmen, we chose Alexander Hamilton's view of a complex, interdependent, and organized society [13]. The clock cannot be turned back and the choice reversed. Nor would most of us want to. Organization has brought satisfaction and opportunity nonexistent in the simpler era. As Dwight Waldo [24] puts it:

> To most of our essayists, critics, philosophers—the intelligentsia as an establishment: organization is evil. As the literary men, they suffer with K and refresh their souls at Walden Pond; but they live by choice in Manhattan, Princeton, or Connecticut. Of course, organization is an evil—gray, brutal, obscene as charged. It thwarts, deforms, destroys human beings. It is also good: it sends royalty checks and honoraria to its critics, provides them with food, clothing, shelter, transportation, education, recreation, protects them against many forms of loss and violence, care in sickness, and on request, sacraments and solace (p. 4).

It is well to keep these points in mind as we consider the problems growing out of organizational structure and hierarchy. Our purpose is not to slay the dragon of organization. Rather, it is to describe and analyze the impact of formal organization structure, hierarchy, and management controls on people and their performance. Specifically, we shall consider three problems: (1) the loss of direction when means become ends, (2) the adverse response of people to managerial standards and controls, and (3) individual and organizational stress.

Before discussing the impact of formal organization, however, let us consider the reasons why hierarchy is essential. This will give us a picture of the fundamental functions of managers and the differentiated roles which exist in any formal organization.

The Necessity for Hierarchy

From before Adam Smith, organizational hierarchy has been explained and justified by ownership. All of the power and authority in a business organization was concentrated in the owner. Since the business was his property, and since Judeo-Christian tradition has recognized property as an extension of the owner's person, it was natural that he issued orders unilaterally about the use of his property. Adam Smith and the later classical economists recognized that workers' jobs were dictated by technology and division of labor. But the manager was still the owner, and authority flowed from property.

However valid and valuable may be the institution of private property, it is not a good explanation of the necessity for hierarchy. As corporations grew in America, the ranks of owners swelled, and as ownership became divorced from direct management, hierarchy became even more essential. In fact, managerial hierarchy is essential even without private property; the critical functions of management still exist.

Even older than private property as explanation for hierarchy are human differences. Prestige, caste, and class suggest that people are different. Supposedly, some are born to lead, others to follow, and the prudent man is satisfied with his lot. In the business organization, as well as society, inferiors should obey their betters. This view of a divinely or naturally ordained social structure (including business) was especially strong in 19th century Europe. Even in Henri

Fayol's trailblazing analysis [10] of the rational aspects of management, the manager's leadership style rests heavily upon class structure and built-in obedience by the working class to their upper-class leaders. In the United States, the more popular explanation of class differences, leadership, and followship was Social Darwinism. Some people were born to be more vigorous, competitive, and able. These people supposedly became owners and managers by virtue of their personal characteristics—the winners in life's race.

Modern psychology has indeed demonstrated that there are differences between men—although most are caused by environment rather than determined by genes. For example, greater achievement drives may well explain why some people become managers. Nonetheless, like property, personality is not a sufficient explanation for hierarchy. Even in that propertyless communist utopia, with all people the same in class, ambition, intelligence, and energy, we would still need a management structure.

Short-Range Objectives

One hundred years ago, anarchists all over the world were engaged in bombings, knifings, and shootings designed to destroy the institutions of class and private property. From the aberrant Russian prince, Peter Kropotkin, to the 19th century French hippie, Ravachol, these dedicated anarchists saw themselves as great individualists and libertarians. They hoped to free man from oppression by destroying class and property—the twin buttresses to social structure and hierarchy. Princes, presidents, and captains of industry were shot—but the structure did not fall. Anarchism faded away. The movement never consisted of much more than a rabble of dedicated and semi-crazed individuals operating independently. Their effectiveness was limited sharply because they never really recognized the need for hierarchy and management.

Vladimir Ulyanov saw this need. As Nikolai Lenin, he was the leading power in the development of the Russian Communist party. His goals were essentially the same as the anarchists', the overthrow of property and privilege, and he never thought much about the future after the revolution. It was not long-range goals, therefore, that were the leader's special concern in the Communist party. Rather, it was short and intermediate range objectives. There was just as much personal commitment among the anarchists as among the Bolsheviks; many died in the pursuit of their long-range goals. The difference is that Bolshevik leaders developed and imposed short-range, operational objectives. Hierarchy and control were vital: "We need iron discipline," stated Lenin [15, p. 287].

Strong operational objectives formulated by management created the Communist organization. The anarchists, in contrast, were never more than isolated activists, for they refused to allow any central direction. They believed that the creation of hierarchy would simply reproduce the autocratic evil that they were attempting to overthrow. Short-range objectives were left completely to the individual. Without a coordinated plan, the anarchists were annoying, even terrifying, but impotent. With coordinated planning and operational objectives, the Bolsheviks shook the world. The recognition of the essential need for hierarchy and management created an organization that could accomplish far more than the sum of the members working as individuals. As Lenin himself put it in 1913:

> The Party is the vanguard of the working class. The force of this vanguard is ten or a hundred more times greater than its number. Is that possible? Can a strength of a hundred people be greater than that of one thousand people? It can and is, *when the one hundred are organized.* Organization multiplies one's strength ten-fold . . . [5, p. 18].

So the development and imposition of short-range objectives is an essential reason for hierarchy and management—even without property or individual differences.

Decision Making

In addition to the violent anarchists and Bolsheviks, more gentle men dreamed of easing the worker's burden by abolishing property. The pleas of Fourier, St. Simon, and John Stuart Mill for business cooperatives pre-date Marx and Engel's call for a communist society. Nonetheless, even in a business cooperative, management functions must be performed. M. Touzot, a student from France, provided one of the authors with an interesting example of the development of management structure in such a cooperative.

After the chaos of World War II, some French companies were reconstituted on the basis of cooperative ownership. In one of these firms, the workers, as owners, were to receive equal pay and shares of profit. In addition, all would participate in important decisions. Finally, all were to work at all jobs. In Marx's relatively rare speculation[1] about future communist society, he suggested that eventually each man will be able to decide for himself what he will work at each day. A social commitment by the individual should insure that all necessary duties are performed. This French cooperative attempted to give such choice; each worker could choose his job for each day. So, the free, equal, worker-owners began to labor in their business without hierarchy. But utopia was not to be.

Jobs were not the same. Some were dirty or boring or hard; others were clean or interesting or easy. After a period of voluntary selection of the former, men began to choose the latter. Free choice did not work; the necessary jobs were not filled. In order to correct the imbalance in job selection, an assignment system was needed. Therefore, a worker of integrity and popularity was chosen by his fellows to set up and run such a system. It was to be a fair method for rotating people equally through all positions. Our honored worker was to labor at the regular jobs as well as make the necessary assignments. He was to continue to receive the same equal share of profits.

Pierre was honest and trustworthy, but there were problems. First, what was fair? Should he assign weak, sickly Andre to arduous duties just as often as he assigned the strong, healthy Jacques? Should he make this decision himself, or should he raise the question with the entire work force? Even more difficult, although he was scrupulously honest in seeing that everyone worked at desirable and undesirable jobs equally, Andre and Jacques did not perceive themselves as putting in equal time. Exaggerating their assignments to difficult positions, some workers accused Pierre of bias. He began to feel lonely—alienated from his friends and distrusted by his associates. In short, his election turned out to be no privilege.

---

[1]See the discussion in Ref. 5: "Marx's Conception of the Worker," pp. 7–13; "Control," pp. 73–80; "Work Time and Leisure Time," pp. 93–97; and "The Promised Land," pp. 237–243.

After some time and much unhappiness, unlucky Pierre went to his fellow workers with an ultimatum: either he gave up his unpleasant duties, or he received a greater reward. In the cooperative described, he eventually received a reduction of duties and an increase in pay. *Voila!*: managerial hierarchy—complete with differentiated power, prestige, and pay.

This evolution of a managerial structure rests on two needs. Allocation of people and jobs is the first. Given strong social conscience, freedom of choice may work for a while. Buttressed with lengthy consultation, exhortation, and social pressure, it may work for a longer period. Eventually, however, greater direction and central control become necessary. One would be naive to think otherwise. When differentiating between strong Jacques and weak Andre, Pierre was making certain allocational and structural decisions. Long ago, Frederick W. Taylor [23] understood that organizational effectiveness does not come from all people performing all tasks equally. Effectiveness depends upon people doing those jobs for which they are best suited. This requires both assignment of people and restructuring of jobs.

More important (and the moral of this tale of the French cooperative), managers must make unpopular decisions. In all cooperative endeavors there will be unpleasant duties to be performed and displeasing decisions to be made. Many people, perhaps most, will be upset and not agree. Nonetheless, some mechanism for making these decisions must be provided—and one mechanism is organizational hierarchy. No matter how equal or dispersed the ownership of property, no matter how equal and reasonable the people, unpopular decisions must be made. The people who make these decisions need to be differentiated from the organization in position and reward. The differential reward may be in power, prestige, or psychic satisfaction rather than money, but it still must be there.

Communication Networks

Many years ago, on the basis of his analysis of the German Socialist party, Roberto Michels [18] formulated his famous "Iron Law of Oligarchy." Part of his argument was that hierarchies become strong and organizations autocratic because of different personal abilities and ambitions among members. In addition, however, there was another theme in his argument. Simply put, this was that it is impossible to keep everyone informed, no matter how much the members may desire democracy. Only a few can monitor the necessary information flow and know enough about what is going on to participate in organizational decisions. These few who occupy critical communication points emerge as leaders who make decisions that affect others.

Dramatic corroboration of Michels' observation is reported by behavioral research [12] on communication networks. A number of researchers investigated how the structure of an organization affected speed and accuracy in solving problems. Two findings suggest the inevitable and essential nature of management. In a group structured like a wheel, as illustrated in Figure 1*a* (p. 190), the man at the hub was able to communicate with all of the men at the spokes. The latter, however, could communicate only with the hub. Regardless of personality, whether he is forceful or indecisive, the man at the hub emerges after repeated problems as the decision-maker or leader. A "natural leader" at one of the spoke positions may attempt to lead, but among all groups tested, the spoke men came to recognize that the hub man must be the decision maker. Why? Because the man at the hub can get all the necessary information more easily than anyone else. In a simple problem, that of identifying the one common color among agate marbles held by the participants, the hub man collected information about the colors from the others, compared, decided, and simply informed the others of the answer. Since he occupied a critical communication link, he became a manager.

Figure 4-1. Communication Networks. (a) Wheel. (b) All-Channel.

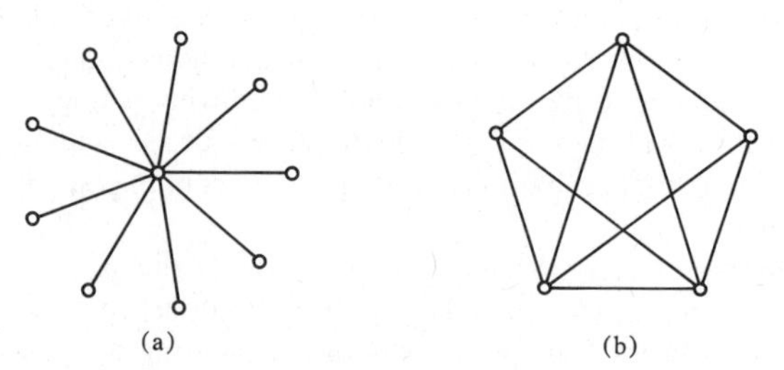

In another network (Figure 1*b*), the participants were arranged in an "all-channel" group. Everyone could communicate with everyone else. Yet, in a series of trials, most of the all-channel men found it utterly impractical to operate on this basis and transformed the arrangement into a wheel network. Voluntarily, they restricted their communication links. In most groups some individual emerges as the occupant of the critical communication point at the hub. The others communicate only with him. The process is facilitated if one individual is clearly a leader in terms of personality and presence. Nonetheless, even where the members of the group are balanced as to personality and prestige, the all-channel network tends to convert itself to the wheel. In short, management emerges because of the difficulty and inefficiency of transmitting all information to every member of the organization.

The degree of centralization depends upon the nature of the task, however. For example, if mottled-color agate marbles (such as those we all treasured as boys) are substituted for the single-color marbles in the problem mentioned above, the group runs into trouble. In this case, both wheel and all-channel nets have great difficulty in finding the common color. The hub man in the wheel is overwhelmed. He collects all the marble descriptions—but no two are alike! The perception and communication problems are just too great. The all-channel net also has difficulty, but it is able to find a solution because of the advantages of this type of net. Everyone can listen in, so a freer exchange of perceptions is possible—"You remember that color, Mike, it's what Sam was telling you about last time!" and so on. Faucheux and Mackenzie [9] conducted an experiment in which all-channel groups first worked eight simple, routine problems, and then a series of four very difficult problems involving the need for inference. Most of the groups centralized (formed wheel networks) for the easier problems; speed increased, errors decreased, and the groups showed more satisfaction. When the more difficult problems were given to the same groups, however, the heavy pressure on the central position led to quick decentralization (return to the all-channel net) by every group.

The Advantages of Hierarchy

We have presented some practical examples of reasons for hierarchical structure and managerial roles in organizations, involving short-range objectives, unpopular decisions, and critical communication links. The *raison d'etre* underlying these managerial functions, however, is the fact of limited resource. Be they material, financial, temporal, or human, limited resources impose restraints on organizational action, requiring decisions, decision rules, and data communication. If every participant in organizational activity had every resource needed to meet his own goals, there would be no organizations and no hierarchies. Kenneth Mackenzie [16], a mathematically oriented organizational theorist, explains the development of hierarchical structures and its advantages in dealing with conflict about limited resources:

> "The major structural characteristic of a hierarchy is that it is a concatenation of wheel structure subgroups. Interactions will usually occur on channels other than those to the chief executive, but those communications involving the resolution of conflict and the exercise of authority flow along the channels between the chief executive and his subordinates. The first level subordinates in turn are centers of wheels with second level subordinates, etc. Of course not all subordinates on one level have assistants on the next because some are staff and secretarial personnel. The answer why hierarchies form must be explained by why wheel structures occur.
>
> "There are two main features of a wheel structure. First, a wheel has the minimum number of channels necessary to connect a group. However, the chain structure (like a bucket brigade) also has this property. Second, the wheel is the most centralized primary group. Let us examine the implications of these two features.
>
> "Let us assume that in order to minimize conflict and to have the benefits of a division of labor each participant in a group has nearly autonomous roles and each is necessary for survival. Assume further that resources are scarce and that each participant has the goal of maximizing his share. Then any intersection among the participants set up conditions for conflict among the participants due to attempts to extend his control into the realm of another. In such a situation the network which has the minimum number of intersections (connections) would tend to reduce the potential for conflict. Since the wheel and the chain share the property, it is not sufficient to explain why wheels form. If, as assumed, resources are scarce and each participant wishes to maximize his share, it is clear that some form of procedure for allocating the resources is necessary. In the chain structure the participants in the middle have the potential of gaining control of so much of the resources that the ones on the ends do not get enough to continue functioning. If this occurs, a vital role is no longer performed and hence the organizations may fail. In a wheel structure, by virtue of one center with intersections with all the others, there is less possibility of the subordinate positions engaging in uncontrolled competition for resources. The center acts as the allocator of resources by resolving conflicts

and balancing the costs and benefits of each post. He must give a sufficient amount to survive in pursuit of his own self interests. Of course, if one of the roles is no longer necessary for survival and continues to consume more resources than it brings into the organization, it will be dropped or disconnected from the group. The more centralized a group is, the greater the control of the center. Hence a wheel structure is preferable in the described situation over all others because it is the most centralized.

"Stability of structure tends to reduce interaction time and to allow increased span of control of the center. But if the group continues to grow, there comes a point when the capacity of the center is exceeded. The group is faced with an emergency because the center can no longer control the allocation of resources. Linkages begin to form among some of the subordinate positions in order to obtain the necessary resources or to get more than required. This endangers the others. Conflict again arises between and within the new coalition or subgroups. The process of wheel formation begins again. But who is to control the subwheel from disruptive competition? The solution is to form a hierarchy with two levels of wheels. The center of the original wheel (if he kept his position during the reorganization period) or his successor (if he did not) forms a wheel with the subgroup leaders as his subordinates. They in turn have their wheel subgroups made up of members of the coalition. Thus a hierarchy is born. As the group continues to grow more layers are added. The need for control of resources becomes even more necessary because of the increased dependence of the subgroups. Roles tend to become fixed" (pp. 24–26).

The selected reading by March and Simon following this chapter describes the basis of formal organizational structure in terms of resources and decisions.

Development of Standing Plans and Controls

We have suggested that formulating operational goals, structuring duties, assigning people, and making unpopular decisions are primary functions requiring a formal organizational hierarchy. There are others, but all imply the need for a sense of direction in any organization. Therefore, the loss of awareness of purpose and direction is a major problem as an organization matures and its hierarchy stabilizes. In its early days, a business may be quite successful by depending almost entirely on objectives, with few policies, procedures, or controls. Eventually, however, controls are necessary and they develop—and when they develop, there is danger of inverting means and ends. The Xerox Company [6] offers an example.

For more than a decade Xerox has been one of the most impressive organizations in American business. Between 1954 and 1964 the old family-dominated Haloid Company, manufacturing specialized photographic products, transformed itself into the modern Xerox Company—and jumped from 30 to over 300 million dollars a year in sales. In 1959 the company was chaotic. Offices were located all over Rochester, N.Y.—over delicatessens and in abandoned schools. Job descriptions were few, policies broad, procedures ignored, and controls weak. Yet the company was successful. And it was successful because of top management's ability to point out direction. Chairman Sol Linowitz and President Joseph Wilson saw their roles as the laying down of objectives—long, intermediate, and short range. Wilson spent much of his time selling the Xerox Company to his own managers, describing the revolutionary and beneficial impact of its information technology on society—and also pointing out how each manager's own interest would be served if the company advanced. Given the fantastic expansion, he was aware that it would be impossible to control the entire company from the president's office. In order to take advantage of a divergent market and to exploit their technologically superior product, it was essential that managers at all levels be committed to manufacturing the product and getting it out to the market as quickly as possible. Premature policies, procedures, and controls would have interfered with the spontaneous cooperation and initiative demonstrated by Xerox management.

Nonetheless, standing plans and controls did emerge in the Xerox Company—and for good reason. First of all, why go on reinventing the wheel? Why must a company handle every problem as unique? Sam Jones wonders how Gil Smith has handled the problem of quality control on his gears. He asks about it. Gil's answer seems reasonable, and rather than search for new alternatives, Sam adopts Gil's procedure. Or Mike Stratton has had great success in handling rush orders within his production area. How does he do it? Some questioning will disclose his methods. Why not let everyone know about it? So an information memo is drafted and distributed. The basis for standing plans and procedures, then, rests upon an awareness of the usefulness of past experience. There is no reason why one should repeat the same mistakes over and over again without taking advantage of the accumulated knowledge of people in the organization. The famous words, in another context, of Oliver Wendell Holmes apply: "Three generations of idiots are enough!" The company decides to make some rules that trade upon experience and give guidance to people facing similar problems for the first time.

So in the beginning these procedures and policies are developed from the organization's own experience. After a while, however, management may feel that they should take advantage of other people's experience instead of restricting themselves to their own company. Experts can provide this knowledge, and so specialists, advisers, auditors, and controllers are hired. Once they are hired, there is a natural tendency for management to see that they are used by giving them some authority to impose their experience on the rest of the organization.

At Xerox, the expansion of staff activities in the development of job descriptions, policies, and procedures was given impetus when management became concerned about internal efficiency. When their product is clearly superior and the market is fertile, management's main concern is getting the product made and out the door. Internal costs and efficiencies are of minor importance when production cost is a relatively small percentage of the selling or rental price. Xerox's main problem in the late fifties and early sixties was to get the jump on the competition and to put its machines into offices all over the world. Competition has developed, however, and although the price factor is apparently not critical yet, there has been increased concern within Xerox about manufacturing costs. Such concern inevitably means rationalization of production operations: rationalization means finding out what the best methods are, applying them throughout the organization, and seeing that people adhere to them—just as F. W. Taylor suggested many years ago.

A Xerox research and development engineer has indicated how such elaboration of procedures affected him. When he had an idea that required funds in 1959, he would walk into the office of the vice-president with a scratch pad and pencil, sit down, and sketch out the idea. A decision would be made quickly, and the researcher would go to work. In 1967, however, the same researcher must complete, in multiple copies, a prescribed project form indicating potential equipment cost, material requirements, potential return, cash flow, etc. This is not simply red tape; multiple forms are not required just to complicate the lives of people in the organization. The decisions that have to be made about fund allocation are much more complex than they were in a simpler day. More and different projects are involved; they must be compared with one another on some consistent basis; and priority decisions have to be made about organizational objectives. Specific procedures for allocating capital funds facilitate comparison, prediction, and control—essential functions of management in any organization.

This development of job descriptions, policies, and procedures aids efficiency by promoting coordination and predictability. However fine the initiative of Xerox managers had been in the expansion stage, it was stressful and unstable. For awhile, people will put up with instability, but order, regularity, and predictability become essential in the long run—especially if the rate of growth and promotional opportunities start to decline. Nor do managers necessarily dislike the development of standing plans and controls. Order will be brought out of chaos and predictability out of instability, and simple relief from making the same mistakes over and over again will be achieved. Indeed, many managers perceive the development of some control procedures as progress.

The Loss of Direction

However inevitable and necessary the development of standing plans and controls, equally inevitable is the development of problems with those plans and controls. One of the so-called management principles of long repute has been the rule that delegated duties should be explicit and specific—with no gaps or overlaps. If this is true, and if standing plans are inclusive, and if controlled measurements are feasible, theoretically each manager need only follow directions. No initiative is required.

Of course, we have described an impossible condition. Such perfect delegation, planning, and controlling is impossible. Therefore, spontaneity is essential. To a greater or lesser degree, every manager must fill in the gaps, work out the conflicts resulting from overlaps, and exercise discretion in following standing plans. If standing plans are followed blindly, the organization loses direction. There is an inversion of means and ends. To some people, rules, plans, and controls become ends to be followed without thought as to whether or not they contribute to the organization's objectives. Indeed, in the eyes of many, such inversion of means and ends is almost synonymous with bureaucracy in an organization. Most frequently, we assume such distortion to characterize governments and other public, non-profit institutions. The comments of John Knowles, former Director of Massachusetts General Hospital, are illustrative: "In the teaching hospital, it has become set that the patient exists for the teaching programs, and not that the hospital exists for the patient" [8, p. 113]. In his Pulitzer Prize-winning study of the Kennedy presidency, *A Thousand Days,* Arthur Schlesinger provides several, almost caricatured, examples of the loss of direction in governmental groups. Among our selected readings is a chapter from

Schlesinger's book, describing the organizational paralysis stemming from tradition and conservatism in the U.S. Department of State.

Such inversion of means and ends, however, also occurs in business. An advertisement in a prominent management journal once showed a hand holding a fancy notebook entitled "Policy Manual" over a wire-basket incinerator in which several similar notebooks were burning. Who was the advertiser? A management consulting firm. Its message? That one shouldn't allow standing plans, policies, procedures, and controls to exist unchanged for too long because they get out of date and hinder the organization instead of helping—better to burn them (and call in a consultant to write a new set!).

Once established and accepted, standing plans and controls tend to limit flexibility and initiative. In the beginning at least, standing plans are usually good, and an organization gains in coordination and predictability what it may lose in initiative. Nonetheless, it is difficult to keep policies, procedures, and controls up to date: policies no longer apply to new conditions; controls measure irrelevant factors; and those rational plans and controls which were developed to promote effectiveness begin to interfere with the accomplishment of objectives. If managers blindly follow these rules, spontaneity is lost. A selected reading from Victor Thompson's *Modern Organization* vividly analyzes and describes the problems of bureaucracy and bureaupathology that endanger all organizations.

Response to Managerial Controls

Spontaneity may be maintained but direction still lost if control standards are misplaced or overly tight. In this case, managers develop elaborate devices for adapting to controls by meeting the standards on paper but not necessarily in ways that contribute to organizational effectiveness. Therefore, overly restrictive control systems are one of the gravest threats to organizational initiative. People will try to meet the numbers they are measured by. If they cannot meet these numbers by accepted and desirable behavioral patterns, undesirable patterns will be attempted.

In a pioneering study, Chris Argyris [2] examined the impact of budget controls on those being controlled. He gave repeated examples of short-run compliance with control standards that in either the short run or the long run had adverse cost consequences to the organization. He reported instances of people who worked under fixed quotas of output with some opportunity to select items to be worked on, choosing easy, rapidly completed jobs as fillers toward the end of a period in order to meet the quota. Peter Blau [4] reports similar behavior among law enforcement officials who maintain an established case load and who pick easy or fast cases towards the end of each month if they anticipate falling short of their quotas.

In a selected reading following this chapter, Frank Jasinski describes a similar adaptation by foremen of "bleeding the line" in assembly line production by stuffing all work in progress through the measuring point (using augmented crews) in order to meet a quota but losing efficiency in the succeeding period until the line is refilled with work in progress.

An even more seriously distorting adaptive response to controls is reported by Blau [4] in his analysis of a state employment service. The interviewers are appraised on the basis of the number of interviews completed. As a result they maximize the number of interviews but do not spend enough time determining the capabilities of their clients to fit them with available jobs—the obvious purpose of the interviews in the first place.

Deliberate evasion is also a response. Jasinski describes "making out with the pencil" as a means of giving the appearance on paper of meeting expected standards without actually doing so. Melville Dalton [7] reports a comparable instance of evasion where local plant officials through blandishment of, and subsequent conspiracy with, the central office representative were able to evade cost control checks imposed by the central office.

Such managerial adaptation to controls is not culture bound. David Granick [11] points out that monetary rewards and glory attend the Soviet plant manager who sets a new production record. There is pressure to set a record at the expense of operating repairs and preventive maintenance. The result is lower output in the subsequent period while the delayed maintenance is attended to—or its effects are felt in breakdowns, but the manager has received his payoff for the over-quota output of the earlier period. In addition, Berliner [3] and Richman [21] note the practice in Soviet industry of "storming" production to meet output standards toward the end of a quota period, again at the expense of maintenance and balanced output.

Obviously there exists a strong tendency to meet formal performance criteria, even if high but hidden costs are generated in so doing. It also seems highly probable that the severity of penalties incurred for failure to meet control standards generates a proportional adaptive effort to make a showing of compliance, regardless of the other costs involved to the organization.

In all these examples, managers exercise spontaneous initiative to overcome control systems imposed on them. Perhaps even more dangerous for the organization is the disappearance of spontaneity. After a while under restrictive control systems, some managers don't care if mistakes are avoided. If they feel that punishment awaits an unsuccessful departure from procedure, they may do what the book requires—and that's all. No spontaneity will be demonstrated, and apathy will prevail. Two selections, by Frank Jasinski and V. F. Ridgway, consider in greater detail the adverse impact of managerial controls.

Individual and Organizational Stress

In every organization there is continual tension between change and stability. Change is exciting, and much literature is devoted to the manager's responsibility for initiating change. But stability is even more important. Much of the time, most managers are trying to establish and maintain equilibrium and workflow in human relations—not because they fear change but because individuals and systems can absorb only a limited amount of innovation. For effective relations and efficient production, there should be relative stability most of the time. Without such stability, the advantages of specialized division of labor are not realized, cooperative human relationships are hindered, and organizational control is handicapped. In any organization, jobs are interdependent; people must be able to predict the behavior of people in interacting positions. Coordinated work flow, whether in the engine-block casting and machining operations at Ford or in the policy production unit at Metropolitan Life Insurance Company, will collapse into confused individual effort unless behavior is highly predictable.

In short, conformity to job demands, predictable behavior, repetition, and stability are essential in any organization. To state that organizations require conformity is merely to pronounce the obvious: no interdependent network of relationships can exist without conformity.

Nonetheless, organizations should not demand blind conformity to formal job descriptions or organizational rules. As we have seen, spontaneity is also essential—and its loss is one of the greatest problems for management. Especially within the management hierarchy, the meaning of predictability is not that associates will do exactly what they are told, but that you can be sure, if organizational rules are insufficient, that they will spontaneously attempt to behave in ways to promote organizational effectiveness. Sam Jones will be more willing to take some action not covered by organizational procedures if he knows that Bill Smith and Gil Mack are willing to respond with flexibility and initiative. But if Sam knows that Bill and Gil will be afraid to depart from the ordinary, his own initiative will be curbed.

To some people, following stable and inflexible rules can be reassuring and satisfying. As Eric Fromm tells us in *Escape from Freedom,* such dependent people are frightened by ambiguity and freedom. Need for guidance, protection, and comfort may also account for the inversion of means and ends. Yet such fear of autonomy does not characterize the mature and healthy individual. As Chapter 3 indicated, normal people should have drives for autonomy and self-actualization. And as David McClelland [17] has shown us, managers, especially, have high needs for achievement. Some people in an organization at least desire challenging positions with variety, and opportunity to make meaningful decisions that help move the organization towards its goals. Chris Argyris [1], among others, suggests that the need for hierarchy, standing plans, and control inevitably conflicts with the higher needs of people. Frustration, apathy, or aggression are the result of such incompatibility. More polemical observers such as William H. Whyte [25], Alex Harrington [14], and C. Wright Mills [19] observe that many managers don't want high-achieving and aspiring subordinates. Rather, conforming "yes" men are courted and rewarded.

Others suggest that the conflict between personality and organization and the demand for conformity are exaggerated. Leonard Sayles points out in his book, *Individualism and Big Business,* that the complaint that top management wants only conformers may be a convenient rationalization for lack of personal success. On a more positive note, a number of articles in Sayles' book suggest that organizations are not so structured and monolithic as critics maintain. In fact, business organizations offer major opportunities, perhaps *the* major opportunities in our society, for the sort of power, achievement, and self-expression that ambitious people desire. From this perspective, George Strauss considers the organization-individual conflict in his selection following this chapter.

Summary

Hierarchy, control, and predictability are essential for organizational effectiveness. Managers must structure organizations, allocate people to jobs, fill communication links, and determine short-range goals. Standing plans, policies, procedures, and performance standards are means of reaching these goals. In short, formal organization and structure are necessary to maintain a sense of direction and momentum for the achievement of organizational goals.

Yet hierarchy and formal organization create problems. They may be incompatible with the needs of individuals—although the conflict is possibly exaggerated. More detrimental to organizational effectiveness, standing plans and control standards get out of touch with the real needs of the organization. People may conform to rules without thought to their contribution to goals, and the organization loses direction. Rules usually work; that is, they influence behavior. People will try to follow prescribed rules in order to meet the numbers they are measured by. However, because of the expense and effort involved in continuous revision, these rules or numbers become obsolete. With time, all organizations face the problem of employees following rules without thought to their purpose. Personnel may sleepwalk through their jobs, responding blindly to policies without seeing the unplanned task that should be handled.

Every organization, with time and success, is in danger from the inversion of means and ends. Standing plans and controls are management's major tools for giving direction to organizational activities. They are imposed in order to promote goals. Yet, to the unspontaneous personnel, standing plans and controls become ends in themselves—to be followed without question. Narrow bureaucrats follow rules when all around them organizational effectiveness is being destroyed. Such a development is not uncommon. Such destructive stagnation is perhaps the businessman's primary vision of government organization. But business is not exempt—as the selected readings following this chapter illustrate.

No organization can fully plan the behavior of its members because not every necessary activity can be anticipated. Spontaneity, therefore, is essential. With good faith and ingenuity, managers must fill in the gaps. They must develop informal work practices that compensate for inadequate job descriptions and ambiguous organizational definition.

References

1. Argyris, C. *Personality and Organization.* Harper & Row, 1957.
2. ———. *The Impact of Budgets on People.* Controllership Institute, 1952.
3. Berliner, J. S. "A Problem in Soviet Business Management." *Administrative Science Quarterly,* Vol. 1 (June 1956), 87–101.
4. Blau, P. *The Dynamics of Bureaucracy.* University of Chicago Press, 1955.
5. Broderson, A. *The Soviet Worker.* Random House, 1966.
6. "Copy Machine Boom—And Xerox Boom." *Newsweek,* Vol. 66 (Nov. 8, 1965), 84–90.
7. Dalton, M. "Managing the Managers." *Human Organization,* Vol. 14 (Fall 1955), 4–10.
8. De Hartog, J. "What Money Cannot Buy." *Atlantic Monthly,* Vol. 218 (July 1966), 113.
9. Faucheux, C., and K. D. Mackenzie. "Task Dependency of Organizational Centrality: Its Behavioral Consequences." *Journal of Experimental Sociology and Psychology,* Vol. 2 (1966), 361–375.
10. Fayol, H. *General and Industrial Management* (1916). London: Pitman, 1949.
11. Granick, D. *The Red Executive.* Doubleday, 1960.
12. Guetzkow H., and H. R. Simon. "The Impact of Certain Communication Nets upon Organization and Performance in Task-Oriented Groups." *Management Science,* Vol. 1, No. 3 and No. 4 (April-July 1955).
13. Hacker, L. *The Triumph of American Capitalism.* Columbia University Press, 1947.

14. Harrington, A. *Life in the Crystal Palace.* Knopf, 1959.

15. Leites, N. *A Study of Bolshevism.* University of Chicago Press, 1953.

16. Mackenzie, K. D. "Some Thoughts on the Span of Control Problem." Working Paper No. 66, Department of Industry, Wharton School of Finance and Commerce, University of Pennsylvania, Sept. 1967.

17. McClelland, D. C. *The Achieving Society.* Van Nostrand, 1961.

18. Michels, R. *Political Parties* (1915). Dover, 1959.

19. Mills, C. W. *White Collar.* Oxford University Press, 1951.

20. Rand, A. *For the New Intellectual: The Philosophy of Ayn Rand.* Random House, 1961.

21. Richman, B. M. *Soviet Management.* Prentice-Hall, 1965.

22. Simon, H. A. "The Architecture of Complexity." *Proc. American Philosophical Society,* Vol. 6 (1962).

23. Taylor, F. W. *The Principles of Scientific Management.* Harper & Row, 1911.

24. *The Wharton Account,* Vol. 5, No. 2 (Dec. 1965).

25. Whyte, W. H. *The Organization Man.* Simon & Schuster, 1956.

Readings

Organizations

JAMES G. MARCH
HERBERT A. SIMON

Theories of Departmentalization

Although an explicit theory of departmentalization can be traced back to Aristotle (*Politics,* Book IV, Chap. 15), we will consider the theory here in its contemporary form in the well-known essay by Luther Gulick (Gulick and Urwick, 1937). To have a short name for this line of development, we label it the "administrative management theory." Among the prominent exponents of the theory, in addition to Gulick, have been Haldane (1923), Fayol (1930), Mooney and Reiley (1939), and Urwick (1943).

Although there was considerable communication and overlap between the students of organization we have assigned to "scientific management" or "physiological organization theory" and those we are now labelling "administrative management theorists," the two bodies of doctrine are conceptually rather distinct. They share, particularly in their more formal versions, a preoccupation with the simpler neuro-physiological properties of humans and the simpler kinds of tasks that are handled in organizations. As we shall see, however, the administrative management theorists tended to carry their analysis, at least at the level of wisdom and insight, beyond the boundaries set by their formal models.

Since the formal body of theory is somewhat more limited in scope than the area considered in a less formal way, we will begin our analysis with the formal structure, and later supplement it with comments on the broader ramifications.

The general problem to which the formal theory addresses itself is the following: Given a general purpose for an organization, we can identify the unit tasks necessary to achieve that purpose. These tasks will normally include basic productive activities, service activities, coordinative activities, supervisory activities, etc. The problem is to group these tasks into individual jobs, to group the jobs into administrative units, to group the units into larger units, and finally to establish the top level departments—and to make these groupings in such a way as to minimize the total cost of carrying out all the activities. In the organizing process each department is viewed as a definite collection of tasks

Taken from James G. March and Herbert A. Simon, *Organizations.* John Wiley & Sons, Inc. (1958), pp. 22–26, 29–32, 141–150, 158–161. Reprinted by permission.

to be allocated among, and performed by, the employees of the department. To understand the formal theory, it is important to recognize that the total set of tasks is regarded as given in advance.

Departmentalization as an Assignment Problem

The problem of allocating a given set of activities efficiently among a number of persons has received some attention from mathematicians and game theorists, who refer to it as the optimal assignment problem. The form of the problem that has usually been considered is a little different from that treated here. The usual statement (Kuhn and Tucker, 1953, p. 5) is:

> Given n persons and n jobs, and a set of real numbers a_{ij}, each representing the value of the ith person on the jth job, what assignments of persons to jobs will yield the maximum total value?

A brute-force solution to the assignment problem involves testing all possible permutations of persons among jobs. Since the number of possible arrangements is $n!$, this becomes obviously infeasible if n is more than a very small number. Several efforts have been made to reduce the computational task to manageable dimensions, with some measure of success (Kuhn, 1955). What has emerged has not been general propositions about optimal assignment, but computational routines that, when combined with the power of modern digital computers, give promise of providing numerical solutions for the problem in individual cases.

The form of the assignment problem that is particularly relevant to the theory of departmentalization is somewhat different from that described above, and has received little attention in the literature. With any possible set, S, of activities, we associate a number, $t(S)$, that measures the time required for a person to perform this set of activities. By $(S_1 + S_2)$ we mean the set of activities obtained by adding the activities S_1 to the activities S_2. In general, the time required to perform the sum of the two sets of activities will not be equal to the sum of the times required for each set alone: $t(S_1 + S_2) \neq t(S_1) + t(S_2)$.

A set of activities, S, is a *task* if it can be performed by a person in a certain specified time, T (say 8 hours): $t(S) \geq T$. To determine the total number of persons required to perform the whole set of activities, we partition it into subsets, each of which is a task. There are many such partitionings, and the number of tasks will vary from one partitioning to another. We define an *efficient* partitioning as one that minimizes the number of tasks—and consequently, the number of persons and number of man-hours.

The complication in finding an efficient partitioning lies in the nonadditivity in times required to perform sets of activities. The rationale of this, as applied to first-level jobs, is that most activities involve initial "setup" costs of various kinds, and that these costs often can be economized by combining activities that have them in common. There are short-run costs of this kind associated with changeover from one activity to another; there are longer-run costs associated with various kinds of training and information-gathering. Because there are numerous and important complementarities of these kinds, there are great differences in the economy of performance of tasks with different groupings (Simon, Smithburg, and Thompson, 1950, pp. 137–145). . . .

In an organization that has the usual pyramidal structure, a single task must include only activities related to a single department; the department to which the employee performing that task is assigned. Further, if for reasons of economy in the use of personnel, a single task must be limited to a range of activities requiring only a restricted number of skills and processes (e.g., clerical skills and processes), then the task partitioning must be a subpartitioning of *both* the departmental and process partitionings. It may well happen that the most efficient task partitioning that satisfies these two constraints is not by any means the most efficient of all possible task partitionings. That is to say, it might be more efficient, if it were only feasible, to combine stenographic activities from one department with those from another into a single task; or it might be efficient to define a task requiring skill in both medicine and legal analysis. The constraints forbid combinations of these sorts.

The constraints on combining activities into tasks are likely to be most significant when the total number of activities is small relative to the range of different purposes and processes, for then it will be impossible to group activities into full-time tasks preserving similarity of both purpose and process. Hence, in small organizations, purpose departmentalization, by interfering with process specialization, can lead to serious inefficiencies; while in large organizations it may be possible to introduce process specializations as subdivisions of the purpose departmentalization, and hence to preserve the important complementarities.

These propositions have been made in common-sense terms by Gulick (Gulick & Urwick, 1937) and others:

> First [organization by major process] . . . by bringing together in a single office a large amount of each kind of work (technologically measured), makes it possible in each case to make use of the most effective divisions of work and specialization.
>
> Second, it makes possible also the economies of the maximum use of labor saving machinery and mass production. These economies arise not from the total mass of the work to be performed, not from the fact that the work performed serves the same general purpose but from the fact that the work is performed with the same machine, with the same technique, with the same motions. (p. 23)
>
> . . . there is danger that an organization erected on the basis of purpose will fail to make use of the most up-to-date technical devices and specialists because . . . there may not be enough work of a given technical sort to permit efficient subdivision. (p. 22)
>
> Is there any advantage in placing specialized services like private secretaries or filing in [process departments]? In a very small organization, yes; in a large organization, no. In a small organization, where there is not a full-time job on some days for each secretary, it is better to have a central secretarial pool than to have a private secretary for each man. In a large organization, the reverse is true. (p. 20)

A study of the mathematical structure of the assignment problem suggests that there is little to be hoped for in the way of global generalizations beyond the propositions, just stated, that are already to be found in the nonmathematical literature on the subject. Task allocations will be efficient to the extent that they are based upon similarities in activities that are recognized as yielding important complementarities in task performance. These are what we generally mean by "process" similarities.

A serious limitation of the theory is that there is apparently no way of recognizing process similarities in general, except through the complementarities associated with them. Hence, propositions like "with low work volume, organization by process is efficient" are largely tautological. At best, they instruct us to search for possible complementarities of activities as a basis for grouping.

Beyond this point, solution of the assignment problem requires specific empirical knowledge of the specific empirical complementarities that exist—e.g., the structure of human skills and machine capacities—an obvious point that is not always made clear in the discussion of recommendations for organizational structure.

Generalization: Coordination Problems

One peculiar characteristic of the assignment problem, and of all the formalizations of the departmentalization problem in classical organization theory, is that, if taken literally, problems of coordination are eliminated. Since the whole set of activities to be performed is specified in advance, once these are allocated to organization units and individuals the organization problem posed by these formal theories is solved.

Of course, writers on organization theory are aware that coordination is a highly significant problem. Our point is simply that this problem is absent from the formal models, and hence that the formal models depart widely from what is asserted in a common-sense way about organizations. As is often the case, common sense appears to be more relevant to the real-world phenomena than do the models. . . .

The problem of departmentalization that emerges out of this section and the previous one centers on two variables: self-containment (or, alternatively, coordination requirements), and skill specialization. Its central proposition is that the forms of departmentalization that are advantageous in terms of one of these outcomes are often costly in terms of the other: Process departmentalization generally takes greater advantage of the potentialities for economy through specialization than does purpose departmentalization; purpose departmentalization leads to greater self-containment and lower coordination costs than does process departmentalization. As size of organization increases, the marginal advantages accruing to process organization from the first source become smaller, while the coordination costs become larger. Hence, the balance of net efficiency shifts from process to purpose organization as the size of organization increases.

Operational and Empirical Problems of Classical Administrative Science

Thus far, our primary focus has been on the mode of problem formulation in the classical school. Some comments are also necessary regarding the meaningfulness and validity of the major propositions that have been proposed. In an earlier work, Simon (1947, Chap. 2) has discussed in some detail a number of the problems connected with making the propositions in organization theory operational. Consequently, we will limit our present attention to a pair of examples that seem to us to illustrate the range of problems involved.

Principles of Organization

We consider first the so-called "principles of organization" listed by James D. Mooney in his essay in the Gulick-Urwick volume of 1937. Mooney specifies five "principles": (1) perpendicular coordination, (2) horizontal coordination, (3) leadership, (4) delegation, and (5) authority. What is distinctly unclear from his presentation, however, is precisely what a "principle" is. Among other things, it is "fundamental," "essential," "inevitable," and "universal." Literally, in his exposition, each principle is essentially a word or at most a word with one qualifier, the distinctive feature of which is that it is italicized in print.

Mooney never makes clear whether his "principles" are action recommendations or definitions. Perhaps the most charitable interpretation is that a principle is a phenomenon or state of affairs that is (empirically) observed to be present whenever an organization is observed. From Mooney's point of view, however, it then becomes necessary to define some independent specifications of what is meant by an "organization" so that the principles do not become simply a part of the definition of an organization. Since this is not done with any consistency, the Mooney essay and other similar essays tend to become empirically vacuous.

Theory of Departmentalization

Our second example is less transparent and, consequently, raises more interesting problems. In Gulick's theory of departmentalization, the independent variable is the mode of grouping work in the organization. Gulick (Gulick and Urwick, 1937) proposes the following values for this variable, i.e., the following alternative ways of grouping work: (*a*) by purpose, (*b*) by process, (*c*) by clientele, (*d*) by place, (*e*) by time. In most classifications in writings on business administration the same values are used, but with the substitution of (*a*) product for (*a*) purpose.

The observational problem posed by Gulick's theory is this: How do we determine which of these bases of departmentalization characterizes a particular organization? To consider the problem in its simplest form we take into account only the formal organizational hierarchy and we assume that there is formal unity of command, so that any one employee can belong to only one department.

Under one set of assumptions, the problem is not difficult. Suppose that we are given (*a*) a complete list of the tasks performed in the organization; and (*b*) a map of the means-ends relations of the individual tasks to the organizational purpose. Then, we will call the organization a "purpose" organization if the separate departments correspond to separate subgraphs of the means-ends graph. To distinguish among "process," "clientele," "place," and "time" departmentalization we must define what we mean by similarity with respect to these variables. Place and time are relatively simple; perhaps clientele is also. Similarity of process appears to mean similarity with respect to skills employed, knowledge employed, information employed, and equipment employed. Hence, to classify activities by process, we need a whole series of propositions with respect to what kinds of "similarities" are relevant.

The problem of determining what is in fact the basis of departmentalization becomes more difficult if we are not given in advance a map of the means-ends hierarchy. In this case, we first have to construct this map before we can distinguish purpose from process specialization. Moreover, unless the map thus constructed is unique, or substantially so, the form of departmentalization will be ambiguous. In what sense does a unique means-ends map of a set of tasks exist?

Logical Sense. It might be possible to show that there is only one logically consistent way of analyzing the means-ends connections of a set of activities. Unfortunately, this is almost certainly not the case. In general, means are sufficient, but not necessary, sets of activities for achieving goals. Hence, a priori logical analysis is inadequate for discovering a unique means-ends map.

Physical Sense. The world may be so constructed that there are in fact (not by logical necessity) only a few ways of reaching any particular objective. This seems to be true of some, but not all, objectives; but we have at least the small consolation that the world appears to be so constructed that the means-ends relations are not nearly as complicated and intertwined as they might be.

Psychosociological Sense. Even if the objective task environment does not impose a unique means-ends ordering on activities, limits on human inventive abilities in a particular social environment may accomplish approximately that result. That is, members of a particular culture, faced with the task of skinning a cat, may think of only one of all the possible ways: the particular way that is current in that culture. If ready-made means exist in a culture—so that most tasks are accomplished simply by combining numbers of these—then those cultural givens could be discovered as a starting point for constructing the means-ends map. Discovering the cognitive means-ends maps would perhaps require nothing more sophisticated than questions like: "Why do you . . . ?" or "How do you . . . ?" or possibly observations of behavior.

Our point is not merely that it is no trivial matter to determine what the means-ends map is in a particular situation. What is more important is that none of the classical literature even raises this problem or regards its solution as essential to the empirical testing of its propositions. It is not surprising that, as a consequence, the propositions have received very little testing indeed.

Empirical Tests of Theory

Perhaps the most critical failure of classical administrative science is that it does not confront theory with evidence. In part, this is a consequence of the difficulties of operationalism mentioned above. The theories tend to dissolve when put into testable form. This, however, does not account completely for the neglect of empirical work. As workers in the same general area, we must share the onus of blame for the paucity of empirical evidence that we observe surrounding the "practical" recommendations of administrative theorists. . . .

Performance Programs in Organizations

At the limit, an environmental stimulus may evoke immediately from the organization a highly complex and organized set of responses. Such a set of responses we call a *performance program,* or simply a *program.* For example, the sounding of the alarm gong in a fire station initiates such a program. So does the appearance of a relief applicant at a social worker's desk. So does the appearance of an automobile chassis in front of the work station of a worker on the assembly line.

Situations in which a relatively simple stimulus sets off an elaborate program of activity without any apparent interval of search, problem-solving, or choice are not rare. They account for a very large part of the behavior of all persons, and for almost all of the behavior of persons in relatively routine positions. Most behavior, and particularly most behavior in organizations, is governed by performance programs.

The term "program" is not intended to connote complete rigidity. The content of the program may be adaptive to a large number of characteristics of the stimulus that initiates it. Even in the simple case of the fire gong, the response depends on the location of the alarm, as indicated by the number of strokes. The program may also be conditional on data that are independent of the initiating stimuli. It is then more properly called a *performance strategy.* For example, when inventory records show that the quantity on hand of a commodity has decreased to the point where it should be reordered, the decision rule that governs the behavior of the purchasing agent may call upon him to determine the amount to be ordered on the basis of a formula into which he inserts the quantity that has been sold over the past 12 months. In this case, search has been eliminated from the problem, but choice—of a very routinized kind, to be sure—remains.

We will regard a set of activities as routinized, then, to the degree that choice has been simplified by the development of a fixed response to defined stimuli. If search has been eliminated, but a choice remains in the form of a clearly defined and systematic computing routine, we will still say that the activities are routinized. We will regard activities as unroutinized to the extent that they have to be preceded by program-developing activities of a problem-solving kind.

There are several ways to determine what programs a particular organization uses:

1. Observing the behavior of organization members. In relatively routine positions, where the same situations recur repetitively and are handled in terms of fairly definite programs, it is easy to infer the program from behavior. This is a common method for inducting new members of an organization into its procedures.
2. Interviewing members of the organization. Most programs are stored in the minds of the employees who carry them out, or in the minds of their superiors, subordinates, or associates. For many purposes, the simplest and most accurate way to discover what a person does is to ask him.
3. Examining documents that describe standard operating procedures. Programs may be written down, more or less completely and more or less accurately. The relation of a written operating procedure to the actual program that is carried out is complex, for the program may have been written down: (*a*) as an instruction to initiate a new program and communicate it to those who will carry it out; (*b*) as a description of an existing program to instruct new organization members; or (*c*) as an exposition (with or without amendments) of an existing program to legitimize or "formalize" it. There are other possibilities besides these three. In any event, when a document is used as a source of information about a program, the purposes for which it was prepared are relevant to its interpretation.

A person who has been trained in the observation of organizations can extract by these and other techniques a large part of the program that governs routine behavior. This is such a common-sense fact that its importance has been overlooked: Knowledge of the program of an organization permits one to predict in considerable detail the behavior of members of the organization. And the greater the *programming* of individual activities in the organization, the greater the *predictability* of those activities.

To be sure, prediction of behavior from the knowledge of a program has none of the element of "surprise" that we commonly associate with scientific prediction—any more than prediction of the lines that will be uttered by a Hamlet on the stage. It is no less important for its common-sense obviousness.

In general, we would anticipate that programs will be generated by past experience and in expectation of future experience in a given situation. Thus, the greater the *repetitiveness* of individual activities, the greater the programming. From this one would predict that programming will be most complete for clerical and factory jobs, particularly when the work is organized largely by process.

The prediction of behavior from a program when tasks are relatively simple and routine is illustrated by findings of Guetzkow and Simon (1955) using five-man experimental groups in the Bavelas network. Employing methods-analysis techniques, they were able to predict average trial times of groups to within 10% from a knowledge of the methods the groups were using to perform the task.

If the program determines in some detail the behavior of individuals and groups performing relatively routine tasks, then we can predict behavior to the extent that we can answer the following questions: (1) What motivates members of the organization to accept a program as a determinant of their behavior? What processes, other than motivation, are involved in implementation of programs? This question has already been examined in earlier chapters. (2) What determines the content of a program? To what extent can the program be predicted uniquely from the requirements of the task? How are programs invented and developed, and what are the determinants of this process? (3) What are the consequences of programs, as developed and executed, for the goal and subgoal structure of the organization? (4) What are the predictors of behavior in areas that are not routinized and are unprogrammed? This question will be taken up in the next chapter.

We turn now to the second and third of these questions.

Program Content

The extent to which many human activities, both manual and clerical, can be programmed is shown by the continuing spread of automation to encompass a wider and wider range of tasks. In order to substitute automatic processes for human operatives, it is necessary to describe the task in minute detail, and to provide for the performance of each step in it. The decomposition of tasks into their elementary program steps is most spectacularly illustrated in modern computing machines which may carry out programs involving thousands of such steps. The capabilities of computers have now been extended to many tasks that until recently have been thought to be relatively complex, involving problem-solving activities of a fairly high order. Some examples are several existing computer programs for the automatic design of small electric motors and transformers, a program that enables a computer to discover proofs for certain kinds of mathematical theorems, and a program for translating languages.

Even on routine jobs, *program content* varies. We have already mentioned the extreme case: the detailed specification of output, methods, and pace in a man-paced assembly operation. But not all programs are of this type. They may not contain detailed time specifications (e.g., in typical machine-paced operations). In fact, programs usually specify the content of an activity more closely than its timing. They may specify the properties of the product (e.g., in blueprints, tolerances, etc.) rather than the detail of the methods to be used. We need propositions that will explain variations in program content along these dimensions: (*a*) The extent to which pacing rules are built into the program. (*b*) The extent to which work activities are detailed in the program. (*c*) The extent to which product specifications are detailed in the program.

Since performance programs are important aspects of the organizational system, their content will presumably tend to be related to the functions they perform. We can identify two major functions that such programs fulfill, or at least are intended to fulfill. First, they are a part of the control system in the organization. Organizations attempt to control employees by specifying a standard operating procedure and attaching organizational rewards and penalties to it. Second, performance programs are important parts of the coordination system in the organization. They help fulfill the needs for interdepartmental predictability (Blau, 1955).

Insofar as they are to function as controls, the programs must be linked to variables that are observable and measurable. We would expect program content to be a function of the *ease of observing job activities,* the *ease of observing job output,* and the *ease of relating activities to output.* Thus, we would predict that programs will contain activity specifications in preference to product specifications to the extent that: (*a*) the activity pattern is easily observed and supervised; (*b*) the quantity and quality of output are not easily observed and supervised; (*c*) the relations between activity pattern and output are highly technical, and are matters of scientific and engineering knowledge, better known to specialists in the organization than to the operatives (Ridley and Simon, 1938).

Conversely, programs will contain specifications of quality and quantity of output to the extent that: (*a*) the activity pattern is difficult to observe and supervise; (*b*) the quantity and quality of output are easily observed and supervised; (*c*) the relations between activity pattern and output are matters of common sense, are matters of skill in the specific occupation for which the operatives are trained, or are highly variable, depending upon circumstances of the individual situation that are better known to the operatives than to supervisors and specialists.

For performance programs to serve as coordinative devices, they must be linked to the coordination needs that are felt by the organization. Consequently, we would hypothesize that program content will be a function of the *need for activity coordination* and the *need for output coordination.* The more minutely other members of the organization need to synchronize or coordinate their activities with the activities of a particular member, the more completely will the program specify the activity pattern and/or the pacing of those activities. But to the extent that the activities of the former depend on the characteristics of the output of the latter, rather than on his activities, the program will specify product characteristics.

These propositions about program content are derived from the assumption that the program will be rationally adapted to the organization's objectives. To the extent that this assumption actually determines program, program content becomes a technological question in exactly the same way as the form of the production function is a technological question. In the experiment with the Bavelas network, mentioned previously, determining the most efficient program for performing the task is an exercise in methods study resting upon knowledge of human physiological constants—the times required to perform certain simple acts. If we assume that over some period of time an organization will actually arrive at an efficient program, we can predict its long-run behavior from our technical analysis.

Suppose, however, that we substitute for the maximizing assumption implicit in this method of prediction the assumption that behavior is rational in the more limited sense described earlier: that programs are sought that will operate "satisfactorily," and that the "best" program is not necessarily sought or found. In this case, predicting the program becomes more difficult. Which of the (presumably numerous) satisfactory potential programs the organization will adopt depends, under these circumstances, upon the procedures it employs to construct new programs and to improve existing ones. These procedures will provide the principal subject matter for the next chapter.

The Structure of Programs

To illustrate further the structure of programs for handling recurrent events, we will describe some formal procedures often used by business concerns for controlling inventory. We will analyze first the common "two bin" system of inventory control, then a more elaborate system.

In the two-bin system of inventory control, two quantities are established for each item kept in stock: (1) the order quantity (the amount to be purchased on a single order), (2) the buffer stock (the amount that should be on hand when a new order is placed). The program is very simple:

1. When material is drawn from stock, note whether the quantity that remains equals or exceeds the buffer stock. If not:
2. Write a purchase order for the specified order quantity.

Let us call the first step the "program-evoking" step, and the second step the "program-execution" step. The bifurcation is characteristic of programs—a program includes a specification of the circumstances under which the program is to be evoked. In the example just cited, the program specifies certain observations, which are to be made (whether the buffer stock is intact) whenever a certain event occurs (withdrawal of material from stock). A decision to act or not to act (to apply or not to apply the program) is based on the result of the observation.

The program-evoking step may involve only observation auxiliary to some other activity (as in this example), or it may invoke systematic scanning of some part of the environment (e.g., the activity of a quality inspector). Further, a program-execution step by one member of an organization may serve as a program-evoking step for another member. In the example above, the receipt of a purchase order from the inventory clerk is a program-evoking step for the purchasing department.

In our very simple example, the program-execution step requires neither discretion nor problem-solving. In more complicated situations, the program will be a strategy; i.e., action will be contingent on various characteristics of the situation. For example, in a more elaborate inventory control scheme, the purchase quantity may depend on a forecast of sales. Then the program might look like this:

1. When material is drawn from stock, note whether the quantity that remains equals or exceeds the buffer stock. If not:
2. Determine from the sales forecast provided by the sales department the sales expected in the next k months.
3. Insert this quantity in the "order quantity formula," and write a purchase order for the quantity thus determined.

This program, although it is contingent on certain changing facts (the sales forecast), does not allow discretion to the person who executes it—at least in ordinary meanings of the word "discretion." If, however, the organization does not provide the inventory clerk with an official sales forecast, or does not establish a specific order quantity, we would say that the clerk's activity was, to that extent, discretionary. We might discover by observation and interview that the clerk was in fact following a very definite and invariable program, but one stored in his own memory and not recorded in official instructions.

The Nature of Discretion

The amounts and kinds of *discretion* available to the organizational participant are a function of his performance program and in particular the extent to which the program specifies activities (means) and the extent to which it specifies product or outcome (ends). The further the program goes in the latter direction, the more discretion it allows for the person implementing the program to supply the means-end connections. Compare the programs cited earlier with the following alternative program:

1. It is the duty of the inventory clerk to determine when each item should be recorded and in what quantity, and to place orders with the purchasing department. He should perform this function with attention to the costs of holding inventories, the costs of shortages, and the economies associated with bulk orders.

If we interpret the last sentence as enjoining the clerk to minimize the sum of specified costs, we see that this program specifies a goal, but leaves the means undetermined. To construct a "rational" program starting from these premises requires the following steps: (1) defining the total cost function in specific terms; (2) estimating the coefficients that appear in the cost function; (3) deriving a formula or "strategy" that specifies the ordering rules as functions of: (*a*) the coefficients that appear in the cost function, (*b*) the sales forecasts (i.e., finding the policy that minimizes step 1), and (4) inserting in the formula the coefficients estimated in step 2, and the sales forecasts.

It is difficult to find a place for discretion within the framework of traditional theories of rational behavior. In the present theory, however, a whole host of phenomena fall under this heading.

First, when a program involves search activities, the actual course of action depends on what is found. We may regard the choice of a course of action after search as discretionary.

Second, when a program describes a strategy, application of the strategy to specific circumstances requires forecasts or other estimates of data. We may regard the application of the strategy to select a course of action as discretionary.

Third, a program may exist in the memory of the individual who is to apply it, having arrived there either as a result of extraorganizational training (e.g., professional training or apprenticeship), or as a product of learning from experience rather than as a result of formal instructions. Under these circumstances we often regard him as behaving in a discretionary fashion.

In all of the cases listed above, the decision process may in fact be highly routinized—the term "discretionary" referring in these instances to the form of the performance program or the source from which it was acquired. These cases need to be distinguished from a fourth meaning of "discretionary": A program may specify only general goals, and leave unspecified the exact activities to be used in reaching them. Moreover, knowledge of the means-ends connections may be sufficiently incomplete and inexact that these cannot be very well specified in advance. Then "discretion" refers to the development and modification of the performance program through problem-solving and learning processes. Although it is difficult to draw a perfectly sharp line between changing a program and changing a datum in applying a strategy, we have already argued that there is an important difference of degree here. With these several meanings of the term "discretionary" in mind, we do not need separate propositions about the amount of discretion, for these will be subsumed under the propositions already noted that specify the form, content, and completeness of programs.

Interrelation of Programs

A program, whether simple or complex, is initiated when it is evoked by some stimulus. The whole pattern of programmed activity in an organization is a complicated mosaic of program executions, each initiated by its appropriate program-evoking step.

Insofar as the stimuli that evoke programs come from outside the organization, the individual pieces of this mosaic are related to each other only in making claims on the same time and resources, and hence in posing an allocation problem. Nevertheless, if the goal of optimizing is taken seriously, this allocation problem will usually complicate the problem-solving process greatly, for it requires the marginal return from activity in response to any particular stimulus to be equated with the marginal return from activities in response to all other stimuli. Hence, all programs must be determined simultaneously.

When the goal is to respond to stimuli in a satisfactory, but not necessarily optimal, fashion, choice is much simpler; for the standards may be set at levels that permit a satisfying response to each stimulus without concern for the others. The organization, under these circumstances, normally has some slack that reduces the interdependence among its several performance programs.

Apart from resource-sharing, there may be other and more integral connections among programs. Program A may be a *higher-level* program, i.e., a problem-solving activity whose goal is to revise other programs, either by constructing new ones, reconstructing existing ones, or simply modifying individual premises in existing programs. In this case, the *content* of the lower-level programs that are related to A will depend on A. Or, program A may be a program one of whose execution steps serves as an initiating stimulus for program B.

The inventory example illustrates both possibilities. As to the first, program

A may be a forecasting program, or a program for periodic revision of the coefficients in the cost function. As to the second possibility, the order that goes from the inventory clerk to the purchasing department serves to initiate one of the purchasing programs of the latter.

Program and Organization Structure

In organizations there generally is a considerable degree of parallelism between the hierarchical relations among members of the organization and the hierarchical relations among program elements. That is to say, the programs of members of higher levels of the organization have as their main output the modification or initiation of programs for individuals at lower levels.

Any organization possesses a repertory of programs that, collectively, can deal in a goal-oriented way with a range of situations. As new situations arise, the construction of an entirely new program from detailed elements is rarely contemplated. In most cases, adaptation takes place through a recombination of lower-level programs that are already in existence. An important objective of standardization is to widen as far as possible the range of situations that can be handled by combination and recombination of a relatively small number of elementary programs.

Limitation of high-level action to the recombination of programs, rather than the detailed construction of new programs out of small elements, is extremely important from a cognitive standpoint. Our treatment of rational behavior rests on the proposition that the "real" situation is almost always far too complex to be handled in detail. As we move upwards in the supervisory and executive hierarchy, the range of interrelated matters over which an individual has purview becomes larger and larger, more and more complex. The growing complexity of the problem can only be matched against the finite powers of the individual if the problem is dealt with in grosser and more aggregative form. One way in which this is accomplished is by limiting the alternatives of action that are considered to the recombination of a repertory of programs (Simon, 1953).

We may again illustrate this point with the inventory example. Top management decides upon the total dollar inventories without controlling the distribution of inventories among individual items. Specific inventory control programs are found at lower levels of the organization. . . .

The Division of Work

Insofar as tasks are highly programmed, the division of work is a problem of efficient allocation of activities among individuals and among organizational units—a version of the assignment problem already discussed. However, we need to make two distinctions that tend to be overlooked in the classical theory: First, there is a problem of specialization among individual employees, and a problem of specialization among organizational units. There is no reason to suppose that both sets of problems have the same answers or that the same general principles apply to both. Second, the division of work that is most effective for the performance of relatively programmed tasks need not be the same as that which is most effective for the performance of relatively unprogrammed tasks. In the present discussion, we shall be concerned primarily with programmed tasks.

The economies of individual specialization arise principally from opportunities for using programs repetitively. To develop in a person the capacity to carry out a particular program requires an investment in training. In automatic operations, there is an analogous capital investment in machinery capable of carrying out the program. In the case of a computing machine, a substantial part of this investment actually consists of the cost of programming the machine for the particular operations in question. In all of these cases there are economies to be derived, *ceteris paribus,* from assigning the work so as to minimize this investment cost per unit of program execution.

Programs that are built into machines or acquired by humans usually take the form of generalized means—skills or processing capacities that can be used in executing a wide variety of tasks. Typing skill, for example, is a skill of transforming any manuscript into typewritten form, and typing occurs as a subprogram in a wide range of programs. Similarly, a drill press is a bundle of capacities for drilling holes; the program can be called into play whenever the fabrication of some product requires holes to be drilled.

This rather obvious point underlies the central problem in specializing highly programmed activities. Consider an organization that performs a large number of tasks, each consisting of the fabrication of a product. If we analyze the fabrication process into subprograms, we find that it becomes economical to arrange the work so that there will be specialized means (machines and trained employees) for performing some of these subprograms. But since a number of these specialties will be required for the manufacture of each product, we create in this way considerable interdependence and need for coordination among them. The greater the *specialization by subprograms* (process specialization), the greater the *interdependencies among organizational subunits.*

Interdependence does not by itself cause difficulty if the pattern of interdependence is stable and fixed. For in this case, each subprogram can be designed to take account of all the other subprograms with which it interacts. Difficulties arise only if program execution rests on contingencies that cannot be predicted perfectly in advance. In this case, coordinating activity is required to secure agreement about the estimates that will be used as the basis for action, or to provide information to each subprogram unit about the relevant activities of the others. Hence, we arrive at the proposition that the more repetitive and predictable the situation, the greater the *tolerance for interdependence.* Conversely, the greater the elements of variability and contingency, the greater is the burden of coordinating activities that are specialized by process (MacMahon, Millet, and Ogden, 1941).

Thus, we predict that process specialization will be carried furthest in stable environments, and that under rapidly changing circumstances specialization will be sacrificed to secure greater self-containment of separate programs. A second prediction is that organizations, in order to permit a greater degree of process specialization, will devise means for increasing stability and predictability of the environment.

Three important devices come under this heading. All of these devices may be regarded as instances of the more general practice of standardization—of reducing the infinite number of things in the world, potential and actual—to a moderate number of well-defined varieties. The greater the *standardization of the situation,* the greater the tolerance for subunit interdependencies.

The first step in almost all major manufacturing sequences that lead from natural raw materials to finished goods is refining. In steel manufacture, a complex of natural materials—ores, coke, and flux—is reduced to a relatively homogeneous, standard material—pig iron. In the natural textile industries, fibers are transformed into threads of uniform size, strength, and elasticity by carding and spinning processes. In all such cases, the complexity of subsequent manufacturing processes and their contingency on raw materials is reduced by transforming highly variable natural materials into much more homogeneous semimanufactured products. After homogeneity has been attained, subsequent steps in the manufacturing process may again produce great variety in the product—alloy steels in the first example, dyed fabrics in the second. But it is often difficult and expensive to program this subsequent elaboration unless the processing begins with a simple, homogeneous material of known properties.

A second important device for dealing with the interdependencies created by specialization is the use of interchangeable parts. When the fit of two parts is assured by setting minimum and maximum size limits, the interdependency between the units that make them is decreased and the burden of coordination partly removed.

Third, the need for coordinated timing between successive process steps is reduced by holding buffer inventories. If process A precedes process B in the manufacture of some item, then the effect of variations in the rate of process A upon process B can be largely removed by maintaining an inventory of products on which process A has been completed.

Even with such devices, the need for coordination typically remains. The most common device for securing coordination among subprograms where there is a high degree of process specialization is scheduling. A schedule is simply a plan, established in advance, that determines what tasks will be handled and when. It may have greater or less detail, greater or less precision. The *type of coordination* used in the organization is a function of the extent to which the situation is standardized. To the extent that contingencies arise, not anticipated in the schedule, coordination requires communication to give notice of deviations from planned or predicted conditions, or to give instructions for changes in activity to adjust to these deviations. We may label coordination based on pre-established schedules *coordination by plan,* and coordination that involves transmission of new information *coordination by feedback.* The more stable and predictable the situation, the greater the reliance on coordination by plan; the more variable and unpredictable the situation, the greater the reliance on coordination by feedback.

Insofar as coordination is programmed and the range of situations sufficiently circumscribed, we would not expect any particularly close relation between the coordinative mechanisms and the formal organizational hierarchy. That is to say, scheduling information and feedback information required for coordination are not usually communicated through hierarchical channels. Hierarchy may be important in establishing and legitimizing programs, but the communication involved in the execution of highly programmed activities does not generally follow the "lines of command" (Bakke, 1950).

In addition, from the standpoint of any particular organization, specialization and the structure of subprograms is as much sociological as it is technological. The organization depends to a great extent upon the training that employees bring to it—training acquired by apprenticeship or in schools. Hence the boundaries of specialization of individual jobs tend to be determined by the structure of trades and professions in the broader social environment.

References

Bakke, E. W. *Bonds of Organization,* 1950.

Blau, P. M. *The Dynamics of Bureaucracy,* 1955.

Fayol, H. *Industrial and General Administration,* 1930.

Guetzkow, H., and H. A. Simon. "The Impact of Certain Communication Nets upon Organization and Performance in Task-Oriented Groups." *Management Science,* Vol. 1 (1955), 233–250.

Gulick, L. H., and L. Urwick, eds. *Papers on the Science of Administration,* 1937.

Haldane, R. B. H. *Report of the Machinery of Government Committee,* 1918.

Kuhn, H. W. "The Hungarian Method for the Assignment Problem." *Naval Research Logistics Quarterly.* Vol. 1 (1955), 83–97.

———, and A. W. Tucker, eds. *Contributions to the Theory of Games,* Vol. 2, 1953.

MacMahon, A. W., J. D. Millett, and G. Ogden. *The Administration of Federal Work Relief,* 1941.

Mooney, J. D., and A. C. Reiley. *The Principles of Organization,* 1939.

Ridley, C. E., and H. A. Simon. *Measuring Municipal Activities,* 1938.

Simon, H. A. *Administrative Behavior,* 1947.

———. "Birth of an Organization: the Economic Cooperation Administration." *Public Administration Review,* Vol. 13 (1953), 227–236.

Simon, H. A., D. W. Smithburg, and V. A. Thompson. *Public Administration.* 1950.

Urwick, L. *The Elements of Administration.* 1943.

The United States Department of State

ARTHUR M. SCHLESINGER, Jr.

The frustrations of the summer [of 1961] over Berlin brought the President's discontent with his Department of State to a climax. One muddle after another—the Department's acquiescence in the Bay of Pigs, the fecklessness of its recommendations after the disaster, the ordeal of trying to change its attitude toward Laos, the maddening delay over the answer to Khrushchev's *aide-mémoire* and the banality of the result, the apparent impossibility of developing a negotiating position for Berlin—left Kennedy with little doubt that the State Department

Abridged from *A Thousand Days,* by Arthur M. Schlesinger, Jr. Houghton-Mifflin, 1965. Used by permission of Houghton-Mifflin Company and Andre Deutsch, Ltd.

was not yet an instrumentality fully and promptly responsive to presidential purpose.

He well understood the difficulty of converting a tradition-ridden bureaucracy into a mechanism for swift information and decision. But resistance was no less great in Defense, where McNamara was plainly making progress in annexing the Pentagon to the United States government. Other departments provided quick answers to presidential questions and quick action on presidential orders. It was a constant puzzle to Kennedy that the State Department remained so formless and impenetrable. He would say, "Damn it, Bundy and I get more done in one day in the White House than they do in six months in the State Department." Giving State an instruction, he remarked, snapping his fingers with impatience, is like dropping it in the dead-letter box. "They never have any ideas over there," he complained, "never come up with anything new." "The State Department is a bowl of jelly," he told Hugh Sidey of *Time* in the summer of 1961. "It's got all those people over there who are constantly smiling. I think we need to smile less and be tougher."

The Institutionalization of Foreign Policy

Kennedy had come to the Presidency determined to make the Department of State the central point, below the Presidency itself, in the conduct of foreign affairs. As Dean Rusk told the Department's policy-making officers a few weeks after the inauguration, there was not "a passive reliance but an active expectation on his part that this Department will in fact take charge of foreign policy." McGeorge Bundy emphasized to the Jackson Subcommittee, which had long been casting a critical eye on the organization of national security policy, that the President wanted no question to arise concerning "the clear authority and responsibility of the Secretary of State, not only in his own Department, and not only in such large-scale related areas as foreign aid and information policy, but also as the *agent of coordination* in all our major policies toward other nations."[1]

In embarking on this course, Kennedy was influenced not only by a desire to clarify and concentrate the making of foreign policy but also, I believe, by a basic respect for the skills of the Foreign Service. No doubt his attitude toward professional diplomats was mixed. He probably recalled his father's complaints as ambassador to England (Harold Ickes noted in his diary in 1938 that Joe Kennedy "inveighed eloquently against 'the career boys' . . . insisted that the State Department did not know what was going on . . . that nothing got to the President straight unless he sent it to the President direct"). And his visit to Southeast Asia as a young Congressman in 1951 had left him, as he said on his return, with an impression that Foreign Service officers often knew all too little about the nations to which they were accredited, were indifferent to their language and customs, did not represent contemporary America and spent too much time at tennis and cocktails.[2] Nevertheless there were always the Charles Bohlens, Llewellyn Thompsons and Edmund Gullions; and Kennedy's disappointment about the State Department as President sprang in part, I think, from a special sympathy for the diplomatic enterprise. He expected generals and

---

[1] My italics.
[2] Meet the Press, December 2, 1951.

admirals to be refractory and obtuse, but he was not inclined, like Franklin Roosevelt, to write off professional diplomats as inherently stuffy and wrong. In other circumstances he would have liked to be an ambassador himself. He knew that many of 'the career boys' had resented the Dulles regime, and he had looked forward to fruitful collaboration with the Foreign Service and the Department.

The Foreign Service, after all, was the elite unit of the American government. It was in great measure a self-administered body, selecting, assessing and promoting from within. It had deep pride in its *esprit de corps.* "Foreign Service work," as George Kennan wrote, "breeds its own morale, outwardly undemonstrative, often not externally visible, but inwardly far tougher and more devoted than is generally realized." The typical career officer, Kennan continued, was able and patriotic, anxious to learn, to grow in his work and to serve the nation, only too anxious to give loyalty where loyalty was given in return. The process of 'lateral transfer'—the admission to the upper levels of the Service of men trained in other parts of the government—had somewhat diluted the mandarin character of the Service during and after the war; and it entered the postwar world with new accessions of skill and spirit. Anyone who had seen the Service in action well knew the intelligence, decency and selflessness of this group of exceptionally devoted men and women. The White House could always win any battle it chose over the Service; but the prestige and proficiency of the Service limited the number of battles any White House would find it profitable to fight.

Still, as his pre-election task forces reminded Kennedy, the Service had its professional deformations. Moreover, both its vast increase in size and the trauma of the Dulles-McCarthy period had had a disturbing impact on its thought and operation. Thus Adlai Stevenson in his foreign policy report mentioned the "tremendous institutional inertial force" in the Department of State "which, unless manipulated forcefully from the outset, will overwhelm and dictate to the new regime. A similar institutional force in the Defense Department has systematically absorbed a series of Secretaries of Defense." With such comments in mind, Kennedy set up after the election a task force on "State Department Operations Overseas and in Washington." "Even such a distinguished career group as the Foreign Service," the new group soon reported, "has failed to keep pace with the novel and expanding demands of a changing world." The Department had to recognize that "the prototype diplomatic officer of the past, the so-called 'generalist' whose experience was largely 'political,' cannot be the apogee of the Service." Reform, the report conceded, would provoke the cry that the morale of the Service was in danger; but "that raises the question of whose morale? The morale of real concern to the country is that of the young, imaginative, all too frequently circumscribed officer." The task force pointed out that, if Kennedy himself had entered the Foreign Service instead of politics, he could at this point barely qualify for appointment to Class II under existing Foreign Service regulations and would have to wait for seven more years before he could even hope to become a Career Minister.

These strictures emerged from the experience of the years since the Second World War. The role of American diplomacy in prewar days had been largely spectatorial and ceremonial. But in the postwar world our diplomats could no longer be merely observers. They were operators in more than a hundred countries around the planet, and they needed regional knowledge and technical skill as well as personal initiative to make their interventions effective. But in many cases the older career men deplored the new tendencies toward specialization, whether functional or (except for the Russia and China services) regional. They continued to see themselves as gentlemen, not players; the political officer remained the Service's beau ideal. Economic, scientific, cultural, commercial and agricultural attachés made up a rather grubby supporting cast. As for regional expertise, the State Department efficiency report as late as 1963 did not even include the heading "Knowledge of Country and Area," long standard in USIA forms; of seventeen items under "Qualities" not one pertained to area specialization. Younger officers feared that, the better their qualifications for a particular country, the lower rating they would get under "General Usefulness."

Nearly every problem inherent in the Foreign Service process had been compounded by its prodigious growth. In 1930 the Department of State had a budget of about $15 million, the total membership of the Foreign Service was about 1700, and the telegraphic traffic for the whole year amounted to little more than two million words. By the 1960s State had a budget rising toward $300 million, there were over 9000 in the Foreign Service, and every two months the telegraphic traffic was greater than in all 1930. The Department itself had moved from its pleasant and leisured home beside the White House, with its high ceilings, great fireplaces and swinging doors, to a vast, unlovely building in Foggy Bottom, correctly described by August Heckscher, the President's Special Consultant on the Arts, as a "monument to false functionalism and false grandeur."

As it grew in size, the Department diminished in usefulness. This was in part the consequence of bureaucratization. 'Layering'—the bureaucrat's term for the imposition of one level of administrative responsibility on top of another—created a system of 'concurrences,' which required every proposal to run a hopelessly intricate obstacle course before it could become policy. Obviously clearance was necessary to avoid anarchy, but it often became an excuse for doing as little as possible. The mounting unwieldiness of the procedures drove Kennan to the gloomy conclusion that, in really delicate and urgent situations, "American statesmen will have to take refuge in a bypassing of the regular machinery and in the creation of ad hoc devices—kitchen cabinets, personal envoys, foreign offices within foreign offices, and personal diplomacy—to assure the intimacy of association, the speed, the privacy, and the expression of personal style essential to any effective diplomacy." . . .

The Service was not so much an instrument of action as a way of life. And it was a way of life which not seldom divested career officers of strong views of their own. The way to success lay in the faithful support of established policy. The lack of continuity in assignment—Iceland one year, Tanganyika the next—made it difficult to develop an intense interest in new policies. It was no coincidence that the Russia and China services, where the necessity of learning a difficult language compelled continuity, were precisely the services where the professionals were most outspoken on policy matters—and were in consequence most punished in the Dulles-McCarthy years. By the time, moreover, that career officers received independent responsibility, they were often, as Kennan said, too old "to grow in the exercise of it." At times it almost looked as if the Service inducted a collection of spirited young Americans at the age of twenty-five and transmuted them in twenty years into bland and homologous denizens of a conservative men's club. "I have seen, over the decades," Kennan said, "an unduly high percentage of older men in this Service who prematurely lost physical and intellectual tone, who became, at best, empty bundles of good manners and, at worst, rousing stuffed shirts."

Foggy Bottom in 1961

This was the situation which confronted Kennedy in his attempt to make the Department the agent of coordination.

The new administration almost immediately bogged down in the bureaucratic tangle. Men like Harriman and Kennan, who had known the Department as late as the Truman administration, were startled by the transformation of a decade. When a foreign ambassador made a courtesy call on Harriman early in 1961, a junior officer mysteriously appeared to record the conversation. Harriman ascertained that he planned to write an *aide-mémoire,* submit it to Harriman for correction and send copies to all interested bureaus and embassies, where presumably it would have to be read, pondered and filed. Shuddering at the proliferation of paper and the expenditure of energy, Harriman said that, if by chance anything of consequence were said, he would inform somebody and told the officer to go away.

The machinery was becoming an end in itself. Dean Rusk remarked to the Jackson National Security Subcommittee that he often read in the morning telegrams specific questions to which he knew the specific answer, but each telegram would nonetheless have to go "on its appointed course into the Bureau, and through the office and down to the desk. If it doesn't go down there, somebody feels that he is being deprived of his participation in a matter of his responsibility. Then it goes from the action officer back up through the Department to me a week or ten days later, and if it isn't the answer that I knew had to be the answer, then I [have to] change it." (We experienced the results with some exasperation at the other end of the White House line. The Department had the habit of sending cables over at the end of the day and demanding immediate presidential clearance in the most urgent terms, when we knew that the document had probably taken three weeks to move from the country desk into and out of the top offices on the seventh floor.) And all this involved more than just the waste of time. "The heart of the bureaucratic problem," Rusk once observed, "is the inclination to avoid responsibility." The President used to divert himself with the dream of establishing a secret office of thirty people or so to run foreign policy while maintaining the State Department as a facade in which people might contentedly carry papers from bureau to bureau.

Nor did the Department respond to the President's own emphasis on the values of specialization. A friend of Kennedy's on a trip to Morocco came upon a young officer who loved the country and had learned the Berber languages but was about to be transferred to the Caribbean. When this was reported to the President, he said wearily that he had sent the Department a memorandum six months ago saying that it was better to let officers build up expertise than to rotate them mechanically every two years. An acquaintance of mine in the Service had sixteen years of Japanese language competence; he never was assigned to a State Department post in Japan. An officer who spoke and wrote Korean, served seven years in Korea and published articles in American and Korean scholarly journals, came to the conclusion that specialization in countries of small size constituted a dead end in the Service. In his letter of resignation, he wrote, "We have been willing to leave 30,000 men on the battlefields of Korea, but we have seemed unwilling to support with consistency and hope of ultimate success a single career dedicated to American relations with Korea. . . . The tacit assumption that countries of medium size can absorb American blood and treasure, but are somehow unworthy of the sustained interest of an intelligent mind or an ambitious career is, in these areas, unhelpful to our interests and repute."

Worst of all, bureaucratization and McCarthyism had strengthened the most defensive and conservative impulses within the Foreign Service. I remember sitting in our Georgetown garden on an August night in 1961 when Harriman came back to Washington during a break in the interminable Geneva conference on Laos. The Foreign Service, he said, had been so thoroughly brainwashed by Dulles that it almost required what the Chinese called "thought correction" in order to adjust to the New Frontier. The Service, he added sadly, had declined greatly in purpose, clarity and liberalism since he had last known it. One's own experience documented this resistance to the spirit of the new administration. When José Figueres came to Washington in the spring of 1961, our embassy in San José cabled that it viewed the prospect of his seeing President Kennedy "with consternation"; it feared that a meeting with the former president of Costa Rica would upset the present Costa Rican regime. Naturally Kennedy wanted to talk to a leader of Latin American democracy who had been among the first to endorse the Alliance for Progress and whose knowledge and influence went far beyond the borders of his own small country. The Department in Washington, more sensitive to the new mood, interposed no obstacle, the meeting took place, and the Costa Rican regime survived. But it was a constant struggle.

One almost concluded that the definition of a Foreign Service officer was a man for whom the risks always outweighed the opportunities. Career officers had always tended to believe that the foreign policy of the United States was their institutional, if not their personal, property, to be solicitously protected against interference from the White House and other misguided amateurs; and by 1961 those favored in the Dulles years added to this proprietary instinct an immovable devotion to the attitudes of the past, whether good or bad. The hardest thing of all was to change anything—attitudes, programs, clichés. No one was more annoyed by this fidelity to the past, or more poignant in expressing his annoyance, than Galbraith. "You have no idea," he wrote me from New Delhi in 1961, "how difficult it is to control one's reaction over the smug pursuit of what experience has already shown to be disastrous policies." The situation led Galbraith's more philosophical associate, the social analyst Mark Epernay, to point out that, for the sophisticated man, the wisdom of policy naturally mattered far less than its stability. "Few things more clearly mark the amateur in diplomacy than his inability to see that even the change from the wrong policy to the right policy involves the admission of previous error and hence is damaging to national prestige." This insight stimulated Epernay to design a "fully automated foreign policy" guaranteed to produce the proper response to every crisis. So, if Khrushchev threatened to sign a peace treaty with East Germany, the electronic computer could immediately type out the appropriate reply: "We stand willing to negotiate but we cannot act under threat or pressure and we must not make concessions. The reunification of Germany is essential but we do not thereby concede the existence of East Germany. We support the brave people of West Berlin."[3]

At times, it almost seemed that we had achieved the fully automated foreign policy. Thus I spent three years in the White House in a plaintive and unavailing effort to beg the State Department to stop using the phrase 'Sino-Soviet bloc.' This was a typical Foreign Service expression—barbarous in form (the parallelism would be 'Russo-Chinese' or, if absolutely necessary, 'Sino-Russian') and obsolescent in content. In a memorandum to the State Department Secretariat in January 1963, I wrote:

> Whatever substance [the phrase] might once have had as referring to a unified Russo-Chinese operation has surely been trickling away rather fast in recent months. Today the phrase is in most instances simply absurd. It suggests that those who use it don't know what is going on in the world. I assume that this is not the case.

Again in July, when the feud between Moscow and Peking seemed beyond all possibility of denial:

> In view of what is going on currently in Moscow, could not the Department bring itself to abolish the usage 'Sino-Soviet bloc'? The relationship of that phrase to reality grows more tenuous all the time.[4]

This dedication to the past found its ultimate sanction in what seemed the Service's unshakable determination to protect those who, if wrong, were wrong in the right way and to penalize those who, though right, were right out of channels or out of cadence. The Foreign Service operated as a sort of benevolent society, taking care of its worst as well as—sometimes better than—its best. The promotion system was in effect a conspiracy of the conventional against the unconventional. J. Graham Parsons, having drastically misconceived the situation in Laos, was made ambassador to Sweden. His successor as Assistant Secretary for Far Eastern Affairs, a blameless but unimaginative career officer, having displayed no initiative in Washington, was sent as ambassador to a pivotal Asian state.

On the other hand, zeal for good, but new, policies at the expense of bad, but established, ones was likely to gain an officer the reputation for causing trouble and —under the system where the challenged officer wrote the 'efficiency reports'—a place at the bottom of his Foreign Service class. When Kennedy ended the unrelenting American opposition to the center-left coalition in Italy, the Deputy Chief of Mission in Rome, who had been single-handedly responsible for the prolongation of that policy long after it had become obsolete, became ambassador to Czechoslovakia; while an intelligent junior officer who had fought prematurely for the new policy in the Rome Embassy was marked down for insubordination, his offense having been that of carrying the case past the D.C.M.

[3] Mark Epernay, *The McLandress Dimension* (Boston, 1963), 61, 67.

[4] It was a losing fight. As I write—on May 9, 1965—I note Thomas C. Mann, Under Secretary of State for Economic Affairs, running on in an interview with the *New York Times* about "instruments of Sino-Soviet military power" and "orders from the Sino-Soviet military bloc."

to the ambassador. This man was saved only by White House intervention from being 'selected out' (a phrase apparently adapted from Samuel Goldwyn) of the Service. Another young officer had served in an Iron Curtain capital. Visiting his country some years before, I had been impressed not only by his insight into the country but by his skill in the language and his exceptional range of acquaintances among writers, journalists and scholars. I ran into him again in 1962 and noted: "His is the all too familiar story. His independence and originality of mind brought him into conflict with his superior. . . . They denounced him as insubordinate; he was rated in the bottom five per cent of his class by the selection board; and is now slated for a consulship in [an Asian country]—obviously a punitive assignment." As Harriman told the Jackson Subcommittee in 1963, "I have noted that men because they haven't gotten along with one individual have been given very low ratings, when others have given them high ratings. . . . Men with a spark and independence of expression are at times held down, whereas caution is rewarded."

Caution even smothered the Department's relations with its own envoys abroad. In Western Europe after the Bay of Pigs one ambassador after another asked me in varying tones of perplexity and anguish what in hell had happened. On my return I called for the cable files and found that Washington had confined itself to sending around bland official 'explanations' couched in language suitable for public release. For what had really happened American diplomats overseas did better to rely on *Newsweek* and *Time.* Even though the Attorney General interested himself in the problem, we were never able to persuade State to level with its own embassies on this matter. This sort of thing was all too common. Galbraith, after receiving a similarly useless 'explanation' of policy, sent a crisp cable to the Department suggesting that in the future the confidential communications of the State Department not be used for purposes of "internal bemusement." The suggestion was unavailing.

A Note on Language

The intellectual exhaustion of the Foreign Service expressed itself in the poverty of the official rhetoric. In meetings the men from State would talk in a bureaucratic patois borrowed in large part from the Department of Defense. We would be exhorted to 'zero in' on 'the purpose of the drill' (or of the 'exercise' or 'operation'), to 'crank in' this and 'phase out' that and 'gin up' something else, to 'pinpoint' a 'viable' policy and, behind it, a 'fall-back position,' to ignore the 'flak' from competing government bureaus or from the communists, to refrain from 'nit-picking' and never to be 'counterproductive.' Once we were 'seized of the problem,' preferably in as 'hard-nosed' a manner as possible, we would review 'options,' discuss 'over-all' objectives, seek 'breakthroughs,' consider 'crash programs,' 'staff out' policies—doing all these things preferably 'meaningfully' and 'in depth' until we were ready to 'finalize' our deliberations, 'sign on to' or 'sign off on' a conclusion (I never could discover the distinction, if any, between these two locutions) and 'implement' a decision. This was not just shorthand; part of the conference-table vocabulary involved a studied multiplication of words. Thus one never talked about a 'paper' but always a 'piece of paper,' never said 'at this point' but always 'at this point in time.'

Graceless as this patois was, it did have a certain, if sometimes spurious, air of briskness and efficiency. The result was far worse when the Department stopped talking and started writing. Whether drafting memoranda, cables or even letters or statements for the President, the Department fell into full, ripe, dreariness of utterance with hideous ease. The recipe was evidently to take a handful of clichés (saying something in a fresh way might create unforeseen troubles), repeat at five-minute intervals (lest the argument become clear or interesting), stir in the dough of the passive voice (the active voice assigns responsibility and was therefore hazardous) and garnish with self-serving rhetoric (Congress would be unhappy unless we constantly proclaimed the rectitude of American motives).

After the Bay of Pigs, the State Department sent over a document entitled "The Communist Totalitarian Government of Cuba as a Source of International Tension in the Americas," which it had approved for distribution to NATO, CENTO, SEATO, the OAS and the free governments of Latin America and eventually for public release. In addition to the usual defects of Foggy Bottom prose, the paper was filled with bad spelling and grammar. Moreover, the narrative, which mysteriously stopped at the beginning of April 1961, contained a self-righteous condemnation of Castro's interventionist activities in the Caribbean that an unfriendly critic, alas! could have applied, without changing a word, to more recent actions by the United States. I responded on behalf of the White House:

> It is our feeling here that the paper should not be disseminated in its present form. . . .
>
> Presumably the document is designed to impress, not an audience which is already passionately anti-Castro, but an audience which has not yet finally made up its mind on the gravity of the problem. Such an audience is going to be persuaded, not by rhetoric, but by evidence. Every effort to heighten the evidence by rhetoric only impairs the persuasive power of the document. Observe the title: 'The Communist Totalitarian Government of Cuba . . .' This title presupposes the conclusion which the paper seeks to establish. Why not call it 'The Castro Regime in Cuba' and let the reader draw his own conclusions from the evidence? And why call it both 'Communist' and 'totalitarian'? All Communist governments are totalitarian. The paper, in our view, should be understated rather than overstated; it should eschew cold war jargon; the argument should be carried by facts, not exhortations. The writing is below the level we would hope for in papers for dissemination to other countries. The writing of lucid and forceful English is not too arcane an art.

The President himself, with his sensitive ear for style, led the fight for literacy in the Department; and he had the vigorous support of some State Department officials, notably George Ball, Harriman and William R. Tyler. But the effort to liberate the State Department from automatic writing had little success. As late as 1963, the Department could submit as a draft of a presidential message on the National Academy of Foreign Affairs a text which provoked this resigned White House comment:

> This is only the latest and worst of a long number of drafts sent here for Presidential signature. Most of the time it does not matter, I suppose, if the prose is tired, the thought banal and the syntax bureaucratic; and,

> occasionally when it does matter, State's drafts are very good. But sometimes, as in this case, they are not.
>
> A message to Congress is a fairly important form of Presidential communication. The President does not send so many—nor of those he does send, does State draft so many—that each one cannot receive due care and attention. My own old-fashioned belief is that every Presidential message should be a model of grace, lucidity and taste in expression. At the very least, each message should be (a) in English, (b) clear and trenchant in its style, (c) logical in its structure and (d) devoid of gobbledygook. The State Department draft on the Academy failed each one of these tests (including, in my view, the first).
>
> Would it not be possible for someone in the Department with at least minimal sensibility to take a look at pieces of paper designed for Presidential signature before they are sent to the White House?

It was a vain fight; the plague of gobbledygook was hard to shake off. . . .

Theodore H. White summed it all up in a letter he sent me from the Far East in the summer of 1961—a dispatch the President read with great interest. "The State Department and its competitive instruments," White wrote, "have in the years since I worked with them become so tangled as to be almost unfit for any policy-making purpose or decision. . . . Somewhere there exists in the State Department a zone, or a climate, or inertia, which prevents it from thinking in terms of a new kind of politics, new departures in technique, an inertia which binds it rigidly to the fossil routine of conferences, negotiations, frozen positions. . . ."

Bureaucracy and Bureaupathology

VICTOR A. THOMPSON

Some Characteristics of Modern Organizations

Modern organization has evolved from earlier forms by incorporating advancing specialization. In an earlier period organizations could depend much more on the "line of command." The superior could tell others what to do because he could master the knowledge and techniques necessary to do so intelligently. As science and technology developed, the superior lost to experts the *ability* to command in one field after another, but he retained the *right* as part of his role.

A great structure of specialized competencies has grown up around the chain of command. Organizations have grown in size because they must be able fully to employ the new specialists and the specialized equipment associated with them if the organizations are to meet their competition. As more specialists appear and the organization continues to grow in size, it becomes necessary to group employees into units, and the units into larger units. Some of the larger of these units in government have been called "bureaus," and so the kind of organization resulting from this process has been called "bureaucracy." (These units were called "bureaus" from the French word for writing table or desk.)

The impact of specialization upon modern organization accounts for many of the latter's characteristic features. Because the modern organization evolves in response to modern science and technology, it reflects the guiding spirit of science and technology. This is the spirit of *rationalism.*[1] No longer are traditional or religious standards to be the guardians of knowledge. The quest for truth is to be limited and guided only by reason and empirical verification. Within the modern bureaucratic organization this rationalism expresses itself in constant self-scrutiny. The pragmatic test grows in importance. "How does it promote the organizational goal?" is the question most often heard. Although other evaluative criteria can be observed in modern bureaucracy, the pragmatic test seems to have become institutionalized. By this we mean that people seem to feel that they ought to apply that test to all arrangements.

The growing dominance of the spirit of rationalism in modern bureaucracy simply reflects the growing influence of scientific and technical specialists upon organizational decisions. The bureaucratic organization is the arena where science and technology are applied. With a few rapidly disappearing exceptions, such as medicine, we can say that the application and development of science and technology depend upon bureaucratic organization. As a consequence of the dominance of this spirit of rationalism and the influence of specialists on decisions, modern bureaucratic organization is the most productive arrangement of human effort that man has thus far contrived. Its ability to accomplish objective organizational goals has produced the highest standard of living yet achieved by man, while allowing populations to expand enormously at the same time. Not only has the poverty of the industrial worker been eliminated, but, as we shall see later, the industrial laborer is becoming a technically trained specialist.

Dependence upon highly trained specialists requires *appointment by merit* rather than election or political appointment. It requires *a system of assured careers;* otherwise, the individual would not invest the time needed to acquire specialized skill. It requires that the organization have a definite and reasonably assured division of work into defined jobs or offices. The trained specialist would not usually allow himself to be used as a jack-of-all-trades. In fact, the division of work in organizations for the most part simply follows the existing specializations in society at large.

As Weber said, charismatic forms of organization give way to bureaucracy because the former are inadequate for daily, regularized activity. Charisma functions in new situations and is not compatible with highly defined situations. Charismatic organization is dependent upon the reputed genius of individuals and is, therefore, unstable and precarious. To secure stability, continuity, and predictability of product, the activities of the organization are reduced to procedures or routines. *Routinization of organizational activity* is implicit in the process

[1]We are using the term "rationalism" and its various derivatives according to common usage—not in its philosophically technical sense as an antiempirical theory of knowledge.

of specialization and is a characteristic of bureaucracy. Specialization requires a stable environment and a guarantee of continuity of function. Within the organization, the specialist must practice his specialty—a group of related routines.[2] Although managerial ideology still strongly contains the charismatic image, bureaucratic organizations seek to avoid dependence upon individuals by reducing relevant information to classes, and organizational activity to routines which are activated when the appropriate class of information is perceived.[3] It would seem, therefore, that the advance of specialization requires routinization, one of the central characteristics of bureaucratic organization.

Organizations as problem-solving mechanisms depend upon a *factoring of the general goal into subgoals* and these into sub-subgoals, and so on, until concrete routines are reached. These subgoals are allocated to organizational units and become the goals of those units. Individuals in the units are not given the impossible task, therefore, of evaluating their every action in terms of the general goal of the organization, but only in terms of the particular subgoal allocated to their unit. The definition of the situation is sufficiently simplified to bring it within the rational capacity of the human mind. If the factoring is accurate, rationality in terms of each unit will be rationality in terms of the organization as a whole. In this way, bureaucratic organizations achieve rationality far beyond the capacity of any individual.

In addition to accurate factoring, rationality in terms of the whole organization requires that individuals in the subunits accept their assigned subgoal as the end or objective of their activities. It must be the principal given value. Normally, individuals accept the assignment, since they accept the authority of the organization. Various forces, in addition, reinforce this identification with subgoals, particularly the fact that communication within the unit, and between it and the rest of the organization is heavily concerned with the subgoal. Looked at from our point of view, factoring of the organizational goal is simply differentiation of function—namely, specialization. People are to be concerned with a certain area of activities, not with all activities. Thus, specialization results in strong attachment to subgoals.

From a point of view outside a particular unit, the unit's goal is seen not as a goal, but as a means to a larger goal. From this external vantage point, therefore, the members of a unit seem to be attached to means rather than ends. One of the characteristics of bureaucratic organization based on specialization, consequently, is an *apparent inversion of ends and means.* For example, people outside a budget office frequently accuse budget officers of believing the organization exists for the purpose of operating budget procedures. From the point of view of a client interested in the general organizational goal, members of all subunits appear to have inverted means into ends. Such "inversion" may be a problem of factoring, of dividing up the work; and any necessary corrections

[2] Reinhard Bendix defines bureaucratization as routinization. See his *Work and Authority in Industry* (New York: John Wiley & Sons, Inc.; 1956), ch. iv.

[3] See March and Simon: [*Organizations*]. Alfred Krupp, the German industrialist, remarked: "What I shall attempt to bring about is that nothing shall be dependent upon the life or existence of any particular person; that nothing of any importance shall happen or be caused to happen without the foreknowledge and approval of the management; that the past and determinate future of the establishment can be learned in the files of the management without asking a question of any mortal." See Frederick J. Nussbaum: *A History of the Economic Institutions of Modern Europe* (New York: F. S. Crofts & Co., Inc.; 1933), p. 379. Quoted in Gouldner: [*Studies in Leadership: Leadership and Democratic Action*], pp. 179–80.

may not be in the direction of reducing subgoal identification but, rather, of reorganization.

A *formalistic impersonality* is a readily discernible characteristic of modern organization. In interpersonal relationships, total involvement probably never occurs. Each person is concerned with somewhat less than all of the actual or potential needs of the other. In specialist relationships, involvement is limited to the needs for which the specialized function is relevant. The relationship is partial, and functional; it is "secondary" rather than "primary." The specialist performs his function for many, and so he must limit his participation in the relationship to the area of his specialty. The resulting "impersonal" relationship need not be cold or painful. When both sides recognize their mutual interdependence—the client's dependence on the specialist for the fulfillment of some need, and the specialist's dependence on the client for the opportunity to work at his calling—the relationship is not necessarily without human warmth and mutual appreciation. Pleasant though impersonal relationships of mutual interdependence abound in everyday life—the motorist and the mechanic, the doctor and the patient, the householder and the postman. Impersonality is inevitably associated with bureaucratic organization, resting as it does on specialization.

An organization based on specialization must allow specialists to practice their specialties, to carry out the routines of which their specialties are composed. Specialists do not improvise for each unique event. Improvisation is charismatic, "dilettantish." Although there are unique aspects to all events, it is only to the repeated aspects that the routines of the specialty can be applied. Consequently, specialization requires that the raw data of reality be organized into classes or categories that often recur. Furthermore, enormous amounts of information needed in a specialized world can be summarized and communicated quickly by *categorization of data,* thereby greatly facilitating the solution of problems. Therefore, although an individual is to himself a total, complete person, in some ways unique, to the specialist he is a carrier of a class of data relevant to the practice of the specialty in question. He is a speeder, an income-tax evader, a disciplinary case, an applicant for a job, a coronary, etc. The reality of the specialist is created by his classes and categories. We are all specialists in some sense, so that the realities we perceive vary from person to person. In fact, language itself is a system of categories by which we organize the raw sensory data of experience. There would appear to be no basis, therefore, for criticizing bureaucratic organizations merely because they interpret reality through specialist categories and classes. What may be important, however, is to ensure through organization that differing conceptions of reality have ample opportunity to be heard and are not simply buried under an official reality.

Bureaucratic *classification of persons* for differential treatment is reinforced by the confusion in our culture between the norm of "evenhanded" justice, on the one hand, and on the other, the ideal conception of justice as giving to each man his due. People want equality before the law in general, but individualized treatment in particular. The grouping of individuals into classes is an attempt to come closer to ideal justice without losing equality before the law. Clientele behavior enforces classification. If one individual is treated out of class, many persons who feel similarly situated will insist on equal treatment. If they are denied, it is called "discrimination." This reaction shows that these classes do exist subjectively in the particular society. Frequently this process results in the creation of new classes. Elaboration of the system of client classification approaches the ideal of individual justice. Whether one's function is regulation or service, he disregards this social process of classification at his peril.[4]

A final aspect of bureaucratic organizations, and one which often comes under criticism, is their *seeming slowness to act or to change.* In discussing this topic we must concede at the outset that bureaucratic organizations, in the face of emergencies, do often act with tremendous speed. A serious note is received from Russia, let us say, in the morning, and a reply with warlike implications is dispatched in the afternoon. A rush order is received, and all regular procedures are tacitly suspended, protocol is forgotten, and a busy, happy, problem-solving atmosphere pervades the organization until the order is out. Later in this book we shall consider this aspect of bureaucratic behavior. Here we shall point out merely that crisis situations, since they are by definition ones for which routines are not available, evoke a nonroutinized approach—a charismatic rather than a bureaucratic approach.

Under more normal conditions, organizations based upon specialization and its routines cannot be expected to react immediately to each stimulus. Great amounts of information must be accumulated if knowledge is to be substituted for impulse, thus assuring greater effectiveness of action and greater chance of success. Since action involves many interdependent specialists, co-ordination time must be expended. In order that all necessary parts of the organization act in co-ordinated fashion, clearances must be obtained, meetings held, many copies of proposals and information memoranda prepared and properly routed. In short, if the organization could act with the speed of an individual, the organization would not be needed.

With regard to *resistance to change,* it should be noted that this phenomenon is not uniquely related to bureaucratic organizations but is a characteristic of all institutions—hence the term "cultural lag." In the case of the bureaucratic organization, however, there is special need for caution with regard to change. As we have said before, specialization requires some guarantee of stability. Specialties must not soon go out of date, or people would not invest the time needed to acquire them.

Furthermore, the members of an organization become socially specialized. They become specialized in working with one another. It takes time to convert a number of abstract, related positions into a flesh-and-blood working organization. Consequently, any suggestion for change must be measured against its effect on the co-operative system as a whole. Bureaucratic organizations must plan and control changes. Although the persons urging change may feel that the resistances they encounter represent "bureaucratic" stubbornness, the desirability of any particular change, all things considered, is usually an open question.

Internally, the bureaucratic organization is a complex structure of technical interdependence superimposed upon a strict hierarchy of authority. The entire structure is characterized by a *preoccupation with the monistic ideal.* The hierarchical institution is monocratic. It is a system of superior and subordinate

---

[4]For an extended discussion of the problems and processes of client classification, see Victor A. Thompson: *The Regulatory Process in OPA Rationing* (New York: King's Crown Press; 1950), pp. 122–30.

role-relationships in which the superior is the *only* source of legitimate influence upon the subordinate. Everyone in the organization finds himself in such a relationship. Since this was the original organizational relationship, it has dominated organizational theory and practice and still does so. This exclusive emphasis on hierarchy has produced our prevailing organizational theory and informed management practice. We shall refer to this theory as the monistic or monocratic conception of organization. Although conditions are undoubtedly changing, it is our prevailing organizational ideal. It is well illustrated by the following quotations from the first Hoover Commission report:

> The line of command and supervision from the President down through his department heads to every employee, and the line of responsibility from each employee . . . up to the President has been weakened, or actually broken, in many places and in many ways. . . . On some occasions the responsibility of an official to his superior is obscured by laws which require him, before acting, to clear his proposals with others. This breaks the line of responsibility. . . .
>
> Under the President, the heads of departments must hold full responsibility for the conduct of their departments. There must be a clear line of authority reaching down through every step of the organization and no subordinate should have authority independent from that of his superior.[5]

Under the influence of the primitive monistic ideal, modern organizations are modeled more on the parent-child relationship than on the adult relationships of specialist equals and colleagues. Attempts to maintain the legitimacy of the ideal lead to a great deal of hypocrisy and pretense and to the creation of myths, such as "the ignorance of the masses," "the indispensability of leadership," and "the magical power of fear."[6] Since a monocratic institution cannot admit the legitimacy of conflicts, the legitimacy of divergent goals and interests, much effort is spent securing the appearance of consensus and agreement—securing a "smooth-running organization." The modern organization wants converts as much as it wants workers. It is concerned with the thoughts of its members as well as their actions, and with the thoughts of its public about the thoughts and actions of its members. Consequently, it is concerned with its members' total lives, with what they think and do away from work as well as at work.

Preoccupation with hierarchy governs the distribution of rewards by modern organizations. Ranks of deference correspond to ranks of authority, and deference is manifested by the bestowal of good things. Success within our society means, for the most part, progression up an organizational hierarchy. Modern organizations, consequently, face a growing problem of rewarding specialists. To be socially regarded as successful, specialists must give up their technical fields and enter a hierarchy. Many do, leaving us with growing shortages of many kinds of technically trained people. A few entrepreneurial specialists, such as medical

---

[5] Commission on Organization of the Executive Branch of the Government: *General Management of the Executive Branch* (Washington, D.C.: Government Printing Office; 1949), pp. 3–4, 34.
[6] Peter Blau: *The Dynamics of Bureaucracy* (Chicago: University of Chicago Press; 1955), p. 219.

doctors, have been able to avoid this dilemma, but the advance of specialization will force them all into organizations eventually—in the case of medical doctors because specialized equipment will be too costly for an individual to own, and because the health of the patient will require the co-ordinated services of many specialists.

Bureaupathic Behavior

Dependence upon specialization imparts to modern organizations certain qualities. Among these are routinization, strong attachment to subgoals, impersonality, categorization, resistance to change, etc. The individual must adjust to these qualities because they cannot be eliminated from bureaucratic organization. In our society there are many people who have been unable to make this adjustment and who therefore find modern organization a constant source of frustration. They suffer from the social disease of "bureausis." In the last part of this article we shall try to diagnose this disease.

Personal behavior patterns are frequently encountered which exaggerate the characteristic qualities of bureaucratic organization. Within bureaucracy we often find excessive aloofness, ritualistic attachment to routines and procedures, and resistance to change; and associated with these behavior patterns is a petty insistence upon rights of authority and status. From the standpoint of organizational goal accomplishment, these personal behavior patterns are pathological because they do not advance organizational goals. They reflect the personal needs of individuals. To the extent that criticism of modern bureaucracy is not "bureautic," it is directed at these self-serving personal behavior patterns. Responsible criticism of bureaucratic pathology does not constitute a nostalgic longing to go back to a simpler era, but is an attempt to find the causes of pathological behavior with the hope of eliminating it. When people use the term "bureaucratic" in a critical sense, they are frequently referring to these personally oriented behavior patterns. Because the term is also used in a descriptive, noncritical sense, as Weber used it and as it has been used throughout this book, we shall avoid this critical use of the term and use in its stead a word which clearly denotes the pathological. We shall call these behaviors "bureaupathic."

The appropriation of major aspects of bureaucratic organization as means for the satisfaction of personal needs is pathological. It is a form of behavior which is functional for less than the system as a whole, including in this connection the clientele as part of the system. It involves a shifting in the costs[7] of the system by those with more authority to those with less, be they subordinates or clientele. It is a kind of behavior possible to those in the organization who have the best opportunity to use the organization to satisfy personal needs, namely, those in authority positions. It can only be exercised "downward." It cannot be exercised by clientele over authoritative officials, and it cannot be

[7]The obligation to accept another's decision may have a number of negative aspects, or *costs.* First is the dislike of subordination itself. Furthermore, the decision may not accord with one's moral beliefs, or it may conflict with one's self-interest. It may not appeal to one's reason and is likely in any case to require some change in habits. Therefore, the possible costs involved in being a subordinate or a regulated client are subordination costs, moral costs, self-interest costs, rationality costs, and inertial costs. See Herbert A. Simon, Donald W. Smithburg, and Victor A. Thompson: *Public Administration* (New York: Alfred A. Knopf; 1959), ch. xxi.

exercised by subordinates over superiors. It is, in short, a phenomenon of the system of authority, both hierarchical and nonhierarchical.[8]

Insecurity and the Need to Control

This pathological behavior starts with a need on the part of the person in an authority position to control those subordinate to himself. To "control" means to have subordinate behavior correspond as closely as possible with one set of preconceived standards. While the need to control arises in large part from personal insecurity in the superior, it has conceptual sources as well, which we shall briefly state.

In the United States, we have still the ghost of the absolute king in the guise of the theory of sovereignty. Sovereignty theory supports the monistic conception of bureaucratic organization, with its associated institution of hierarchy. The superior has the right, by delegation ultimately from the absolute sovereign, to obtain a unique outcome; and he has the duty, or the responsibility to his superior, to obtain it. In profit organizations, it is held that there is only one outcome which will satisfy profit maximization under the specific conditions of the market. It is also held that the duty to seek this outcome is an overriding one because only in this way can the welfare of all be best promoted, even though in individual instances it may not seem so. In the monocratic society of Russia, only one outcome can be tolerated because only one is consistent with the laws of history; only one is possible. (Why it is necessary to seek bureaucratic control in the face of this historical determinism has never been satisfactorily explained so far as we know.)

Although these conceptual sources for the need to control exist, they are hardly compelling. Much more important in explaining the authoritative need to control is personal insecurity.[9] Here we may well recap these sources of personal insecurity and anxiety in modern bureaucratic organization.

Hierarchical structure with its monopoly of "success" is a potent source of anxiety. The person in a superordinate position has a near final control over the satisfaction of subordinates' needs, their personal goals.[10] While at the bottom of the hierarchy the standards which must be met are frequently made explicit and objectively measurable, managerial personnel have generally resisted a like invasion of their own superordinate rights.[11] As we have said before, the objec-

[8] Writers on bureaucracy like Merton, Selznick, Gouldner and others use essentially the same concept of "bureaucratic," although, except by Gouldner, the distinction between the descriptive and critical sense of the term is never made clear. In general, they start with a need of some authority figure for control, followed by behavior which creates conditions exaggerating the need for control, etc., in a vicious circle. On this point see James G. March and Herbert A. Simon: *Organizations* (New York: John Wiley & Sons, Inc.; 1958), pp. 36–46; and Chris Argyris: "The Individual and Organization: Some Problems of Mutual Adjustment," *Admin. Sci. Q.*, Vol. II (1957), pp. 1–22, and "Understanding Human Behavior in Organizations: One Viewpoint," in Mason Haire, ed.: *Modern Organization Theory* (New York: John Wiley & Sons, Inc.; 1959).

[9] Although the conceptual basis for the need to control is more thoroughly worked out in Russia, it has been observed that the attempt by Russian top management to concentrate power and control in its own hands results from insecurity generated by pressure from above. See Reinhard Bendix: *Work and Authority in Industry* (New York: John Wiley & Sons, Inc.; 1956), ch. vi.

[10] For a theory of individual accomodation to the organization based on hierarchically generated anxiety, see Robert V. Presthus: "Toward a Theory of Organizational Behavior," *Admin. Sci. Q.*, Vol. III, No. I (June 1958), pp. 48 ff. See also Peter Blau: *The Dynamics of Bureaucracy* (Chicago: University of Chicago Press; 1955), p. 173.

[11] This resistance was apparently the basis of the managerial opposition to Taylorism and Scientific Management generally. See Bendix: op. cit. pp. 274–81.

tivity of performance standards decreases as one mounts the hierarchy until at some point they become largely subjective. At the same time, we would expect an increasing concentration of success-hungry people in the upper reaches of the hierarchy. Strong status needs and strong doubts as to what will please the person who can satisfy those needs can only result in anxiety and, for many, in "automaton conformity"[12] to the wishes of the boss. Hierarchical anxiety is much like Calvinism in that it generates painful doubt as to who is chosen. Like Calvinism, these doubts can be reduced, not only by automaton conformity but by excessive activity and the appearance of extreme busyness.[13]

Anxiety is also associated with insecurity of function. To occupy a position not fully accepted by significant others in the organization tends to make one isolated, a minority in a hostile world. This kind of insecurity may result from a new specialty not yet fully accredited and accepted; or it may result from the authoritative assignment of jurisdiction (the delegation of nonhierarchical authority) in defiance of the needs of specialization.

Finally, the source of insecurity which is becoming the most significant in modern organizations is the growing gap between the rights of authority (to review, to veto, to affirm) and the specialized ability or skill required to solve most organizational problems. The intellectual, problem-solving, content of executive positions is being increasingly diverted to specialists, leaving hierarchical rights (and duties) as the principal components of executive posts.[14] Persons in hierarchical positions are therefore increasingly dependent upon subordinate and nonsubordinate specialists for the achievement of organizational (or unit) goals. The superior tends to be caught between the two horns of a dilemma. He must satisfy the nonexplicit and nonoperational demands of a superior through the agency of specialized subordinates and nonsubordinates whose skills he only dimly understands.[15] And yet, to be counted a success he must accept this dilemma and live with its increasing viciousness throughout his life. He must live with increasing insecurity and anxiety.[16] Although a particular person may have great maturity and general psychological security, an insecure superior at any point in the hierarchy above him can, and probably will, generate

---

[12] See Erich Fromm: *Escape From Freedom* (New York: Holt, Rinehart and Winston, Inc.; 1941), p. 185. See also Clara Thompson: *Psychoanalysis: Evolution and Development* (New York: Thomas Nelson & Sons; 1950), p. 208. See also Fromm: *Man for Himself: An Inquiry into the Psychology of Ethics* (New York: Holt, Rinehart and Winston, Inc.; 1947), p. 72. Of 75 middle-management people questioned by Harold Leavitt, most thought that conformance to the wishes of the boss was the principal criterion for evaluating subordinates. Harold J. Leavitt: *Managerial Psychology* (Chicago: University of Chicago Press; 1958), p. 288.

[13] See Rollo May: *The Meaning of Anxiety* (New York: The Ronald Press Company; 1950), p. 172.

[14] For a discussion of this process in industrial management, see Bendix: op. cit., pp. 226 ff. His discussion is based on a work by Ernest Dale: *Planning and Developing the Company Organization Structure* (New York: American Management Association, Inc.; 1952), Research Report No. 20. Advancing specialization in the problem-solving aspect of organizations is further reflected in these figures from Bendix: op. cit., pp. 211 ff. Between 1899 and 1947 the proportion of administrative to production workers in American industry increased from 7.7 per cent to 21.6 per cent. From 1910 to 1940 the work force in America increased by 49 per cent. Entrepreneurs increased by 17 per cent; manual workers, by 49 per cent; and salaried employees, by 127 per cent. Bendix sees bureaucratization in industry as the continuing subdivision of the functions of the early owner-manager.

[15] Of course, the extent of the dilemma varies with position in the hierarchy and with the extent to which complex specialties are required by the particular organization. The ongoing process of specialization will move the dilemma down the hierarchy and to more and more organizations.

[16] Middle-management executives interviewed by William H. Whyte referred to their lives as "treadmills" or "rat races," thereby expressing the tensions generated by this dilemma. *The Organization Man* (Garden City, New York: Doubleday & Company, Inc.; 1953), p. 176.

pressures which must inevitably be passed down the line, creating insecurity and tensions all the way to the bottom.[17] Given a person's hierarchical relationship with his superior, he is always subject to blame for outcomes which he could control only remotely, if at all.

The Bureaupathic Reaction

Insecurity gives rise to personal (nonorganizational) needs which may be generalized in the need for control. This need often results in behavior which appears irrational from the standpoint of the organization's goals because it does not advance them; it advances only personal goals and satisfies only personal needs. In so doing, it creates conditions which do not eliminate the need for control but rather enhance it.[18]

Alvin W. Gouldner studied the succession to the position of plant manager by a man from outside the plant.[19] This man was obligated to upper management and felt dutybound to realize its efficiency and production values. He started out, therefore, with heavy pressure from above. Coming from outside, he did not understand the informal system prevailing in the plant and was unable to use it. As his insecurity and anxiety mounted, he turned more and more to the formal system of rules, defined competencies, impersonality, and close supervision. He met resistance and felt his position between the horns of the dilemma, between those above and those below, increasingly insecure. He reacted with increased aloofness and formality. He exaggerated the characteristics of bureaucratic organization. He became bureaupathic.

The example illustrates the circularity in the bureaupathic reaction. Since the manager's behavior was so strongly influenced by his personal needs to reduce his own anxiety, the employees' responses deviated more and more from organizational needs, thereby increasing the manager's anxiety and completing the circle. The mechanisms underlying this process are not difficult to understand. Control standards encourage minimal participation.[20] They encourage employees to meet the standards and no more. Furthermore, meeting the control devices tends to become the aim of the subordinates because that is how they manage their own insecurities and avoid sanctions. For example, if agents are rated on

---

[17] William Caudill has shown that tensions starting at the very top of a mental hospital were easily communicated all the way down to the patients, creating symptoms in them that were generated entirely within the hospital. *The Psychiatric Hospital as a Small Society* (Cambridge: Harvard University Press; 1958).

[18] March and Simon (op. cit.) criticize some of the sociological treatments of bureaupathic behavior because they feel that these theories do not explain why functional learning on the part of authority figures does not take place. It will be recalled that these theories posit a need for control, followed by behaviors which create conditions which exaggerate the need for control. If this behavior is conceived as organization problem solving, there is indeed a problem of functional learning involved. However, bureaupathic behavior is functional in personal rather than organizational terms. It must be admitted that most of these sociological treatments do not clearly distinguish between personal and organizational goals—between bureaupathic and bureaucratic behavior. The "dysfunctional learning" involved is failure to learn that employees cannot very effectively be treated according to the machine model. However, this learning can be considered dysfunctional only by applying the machine model to management. If management operated like a rational machine, it would learn that employees are not machines. The basic methodological flaw of the "management" approach is that it assumes that persons described by the term "management" behave according to sociopsychological laws different from those governing the behavior of others—that the manager is an independent variable in the organization.

[19] The following discussion of succession is taken from his *Patterns of Industrial Bureaucracy* (Glencoe, Illinois: The Free Press; 1954), Part Two.

[20] Ibid., pp. 174–6.

the number of violations they uncover, cases of compliance are not likely to give them great joy.[21] Strict control from above encourages employees to "go by the book," to avoid innovations and chances of errors which put black marks on the record. It encourages the accumulation of records to prove compliance, resulting in *paperasserie,* as the French call it.[22] It encourages decision by precedent, and unwillingness to exercise initiative or take a chance. It encourages employees to wait for orders and do only what they are told. It is not hard to understand, therefore, why the superior may come to feel that he must apply more control. If he is also subject to strict bureaupathic control from above, this situation is likely to contribute to ulcers, if not, indeed, to complete breakdown.

The Drift to Quantitative Compliance

An exaggerated dependence upon regulations and quantitative standards is likely to stem from a supervisor's personal insecurity in the parentlike role of the boss. It has been observed that women supervisors are more likely to insist upon strict compliance with all organizational rules and regulations than are men. The bureaupathic tendency of women has been attributed to their greater insecurity in the superordinate role because the general role of women in our society is somewhat subordinate.[23] A battery of regulations makes it unnecessary for the superior to give the detailed face-to-face order very often. Everybody, including the supervisor, is simply carrying out instructions imposed from above. If they are unpleasant instructions, it is not the supervisor's fault. For much the same reason, an insecure superior will probably appreciate a large number of quantitative control standards because his ratings of his subordinates then appear to be inevitable results of the performances of the subordinates, not merely the personal judgments of the superior. The anger and aggressions of the subordinates can then be displaced to the impersonal "system," and the superior can continue to get their indispensable co-operation upon which his own "success" depends.[24] Furthermore, disparities of power are hidden by the rules, and if punishment is meted out, it comes from the rules, not from the superior. In all of these ways, the rules and regulations make the parentlike role less uncomfortable for insecure people.[25]

Only the observable and measurable aspects of behavior can be controlled. These aspects are often the most trivial and unimportant from the standpoint of the long-range success of the organization. Where the need to control exists, therefore, it often manifests itself in procedures, reports, and clearances governing trivia, while at the same time very important matters are left to discretion because controlling them is not feasible. The need to control is sufficiently widespread to have given sometimes a petty and ludicrous quality to modern organization.

---

[21] See Blau: op. cit., p. 192

[22] Walter Rice Sharp: *The French Civil Service: Bureaucracy in Transition* (New York: The Macmillan Co.; 1931), pp. 446–50.

[23] See Arnold W. Green and Eleanor Melnick: "What Has Happened to the Feminist Movement," Alvin W. Gouldner, ed.: *Studies in Leadership: Leadership and Democratic Action* (New York: Harper & Brothers; 1950), pp. 277–302.

[24] See Blau: op. cit., pp. 175–6

[25] Gouldner: *Patterns of Industrial Bureaucracy,* ch. ix. On the relationship between ritualistic compliance with regulations and personal insecurity, see Rose Laub Coser: "Authority and Decision Making in a Hospital: A Comparative Analysis," *Am. Sociol. Rev.* (February 1958). See also Reinhard Bendix: *Higher Civil Servants in American Society* (Boulder, Colorado: University of Colorado Press; 1949), pp. 14–19, 112–22.

We venture to predict that if one looks hard enough in any modern organization, he will find instructions just as ridiculous as those of the military on how to wash a dog, pick a flower, or use a fork.[26] Since the controls can successfully be applied only to the observable and measurable aspects of a job, and since the employee must concentrate on satisfying the control standards in order to reduce his own personal insecurities, his emphasis shifts from the more important, qualitative aspects of the job to the less important, quantitative aspects. In an employment office, for example, the goal shifted from good placement, in the beginning, to the highest possible number of people put to work. Interviewers felt constrained to use whatever sanctions they have to induce a client to take a job, whether he wanted it and was suited to it or not.[27]

Exaggerated Aloofness

Organizational relationships are by nature less warm and personal than the relations of friendship. It is only when this impersonality is exaggerated to cold aloofness and apparent disinterest that we can with any fairness call it pathological. As with other kinds of bureaupathic behavior, exaggerated aloofness can usually be attributed to personal insecurity.

A cold aloofness protects an insecure superior from commitments to his subordinates which he fears will be inconsistent with demands upon him from above. It makes it easier for him to mete out punishment or to perform other aspects of his hierarchical role, such as rating his subordinates. It protects him from the aggressions of his subordinates of maintaining a psychic distance between him and them. In extreme cases it can come close to a complete breakdown of communication between the superior and his subordinates.

The same considerations apply to relations between officials and clients. A certain impersonality is necessary both to protect the goals of the organization and to secure objective and therefore effective service to the client. This impersonality may be exaggerated into a cold disinterest by an insecure official. When officials are caught between demands or "rights" of clients and tight administrative controls from above, dissociation from the clients and disinterest in their problems may seem to be the only way out of the dilemma. Client hostility, generated by what appears to be official emphasis on the wrong goals, creates tension. Inconsiderate treatment of the clients may become a device for reducing tensions and maintaining the cohesion of the officials. Blau has shown how such a situation leads to backstage demeaning of clients which, by putting psychic distance between the officials and the clients, protects the officials. Officials then tend to seek satisfactions from the abstract values of the enterprise rather than from the concrete values of personal service to a client.[28]

Within the organization, technically unnecessary interdependence creates insecurity of function. As we have seen in previous chapters, authority is some-

---

[26] There is another source of extreme, detailed controls in modern organizations, one which can be dealt with rationally. Units are frequently established whose goals are defined *entirely* in terms of writing instructions. Since they have nothing assigned to them except to write instructions, in time they can be expected to "cover" everything—even as a monkey, if given enough time on the typewriter, would eventually type out the complete works of Shakespeare. Involved in this situation is goal factoring, not bureaupathic behavior.

[27] Blau: op. cit., p. 96.

[28] Ibid., pp. 91–5. See also Erving Goffman: *The Presentation of Self in Everyday Life* (Garden City, New York: Doubleday & Company, Inc.; 1959), p. 177.

times delegated for political rather than technical reasons, to meet personal rather than organizational needs. Because the resulting relationship is not accepted and is constantly under attack, the person with the delegated authority lives in insecurity. Here, also, patterns of cold and imperious aloofness are often observed, and abstract values rather than personal service become goals. Officials exercising such disputed, delegated authority frequently demean their clients as narrow-minded, if not stupid. Procedures to govern the relationship are elaborated and, because they stabilize the relationship, such procedures acquire an exaggerated value for these officials.

Resistance to Change

Bureaucratic organizations have to administer change carefully. Perhaps most people resist change just for the sake of change. The burden of proof is on the side of those advocating change. However, resistance to change may also be exaggerated by insecure officials; it may become bureaupathic. In an organizational context dominated by the need to control, innovation is dangerous because, by definition, it is not controlled behavior. It creates risks of errors and therefore of sanctions. To encourage innovation, an insecure superior would have to extend the initiative to subordinates and thereby lose control. Furthermore, in an insecure, competitive group situation, innovation threatens the security of all members of the group and for this reason tends to be suppressed by informal group action, as well as by the insecure superior. Innovation is facilitated by a secure, noncompetitive group administrative effort dominated by a professional outlook. Since this kind of situation is thought to be rare in modern bureaucracy, some people might regard excessive resistance to change as an inherent feature of bureaucratic organization, rather than as a form of bureaupathology. We feel, however, that excessive bureaucratic inertia is much less widespread than is supposed.[29] In an era of ever more rapid change, it seems unlikely that man has evolved a kind of organization which is particularly resistive to innovation. The traditionalistic organization was the kind most resistive, and in many places it had to be blasted off the scene by revolutionary action. The bureaucratic form replaced it, partly because it was able to accommodate to a changing world.

There is another source of resistance to change which is not bureaupathic and which is therefore subject to rational corrective procedures. The communication pattern determines who gets feed-back information. A particular official may never get intimate knowledge of the results of his own actions. Consequently, he may feel no need for a change which others who do have this knowledge think should be made. Bringing the "offending" official into direct communication with respondents might cure in a hurry this particular case of resistance to change.

[29] In a state employment office and a federal enforcement agency, Blau found little evidence of resistance to change. The cases he did find were based upon the fear of a superior and fear of the loss of security in relations with subordinates or clients. (Op. cit., pp. 184–9.) He found that new employees and less competent employees were more resistive to change than others. (Ibid., p. 197.) He found also that ritualistic compliance with rules and regulations stemmed from personal insecurity in important relationships at work. (Ibid., p. 188.) Secure officials welcomed change because it made their work interesting by providing new challenges.

Insistence on the Rights of Office

The bureaupathic official usually exaggerates the official, non-technical aspects of relationships and suppresses the technical and the informal. He stresses rights, not abilities. Since his behavior stems from insecurity, he may be expected to insist on petty rights and prerogatives, on protocol, on procedure—in short, on those things least likely to affect directly the goal accomplishment of the organization. For example, a rather functionless reviewing officer will often insist violently on his right of review and scream like an injured animal if he is by-passed. He will often insist on petty changes, such as minor changes in the wording of a document. If he has a counterpart at a higher organizational level, he will probably insist on exclusive contact with that higher clearance point. By controlling this particular communication channel he protects his authority and influence, even perhaps enhancing them somewhat by being the sole interpreter of the higher-clearance-point's requirements.[30] In like fashion and for the same reasons, an insecure superior can be expected to exert his right to the monopoly of outgoing and incoming communication. Everything must go through "formal channels." In this way he can hide his weakness and suppress information which might reveal his insecurity. He also hopes to maintain his influence and authority by suppressing the influence of external specialists, the "staff." One of the great difficulties of modern organization arises from the inescapable fact that specialist communication must break through such blockades.

Insistence upon the full rights of the superordinate role is what is meant by "close supervision." It seems to be related to doubts about the loyalty or ability of subordinates, combined with pressure from above.[31] Close supervision can be regarded as bureaupathic under conditions where the right to act and the ability to do so have become separated because of the advance of specialization. However, where the position has a great deal of technical content so that subordinates are technically dependent upon their supervisor, as in a railroad maintenance section, close supervision may be tolerated and even demanded by subordinates. It may be a necessary means to the organization's goal. The right to supervise closely gets further legitimation from the technical ability to do so.[32]

Bureaupathology and Organization Structure

Institutions are staffed by persons, and so personality is always an element in institutional behavior. It will account for differences of degree and minor variations in form. For the major outlines of institutional behavior, however, we must seek the causes in the institutions themselves. Bureaupathic behavior is caused by the structures and conditions within our bureaucratic organizations. To say this is not to deny the reinforcing impact of personality. Some people

---

[30] See Victor A. Thompson: *The Regulatory Process in OPA Rationing* (New York: King's Crown Press; 1950), pp. 298–303.

[31] In addition to other references cited throughout this chapter, see Walter L. Dorn: "The Prussian Bureaucracy in the 18th Century," *Polit. Sci. Rev.,* Vol. XLVI (September 1931). See also Alexander Barmine: *One Who Survived* (New York: G. P. Putnam's Sons; 1945); and "The Stewardship of Sewell Avery," *Fortune,* Vol. XXXIII (May 1946).

[32] See D. Katy, N. Maccoby, G. Gurin, and L. G. Floor: *Productivity, Supervision and Morale among Railroad Workers* (Ann Arbor: Survey Research Center, University of Michigan; 1951). See also A. W. Halpin: "The Leadership Behavior and Combat Performance of Airplane Commanders," *J. Abnorm. and Soc. Psychol.,* Vol. XLIX (1954), pp. 19–22.

are undoubtedly more inclined than others to be aloof, to get enmeshed in details, to be officious, to be excessively cautious, to be insensitive to others, to be insecure. What we do deny is that there is a bureaupathic personality type, or that observed cases of bureaupathic behavior will always, or even usually, be associated with one type of person.[33] Any person, regardless of personality type, may behave in some or all of the ways we have just described under the appropriate conditions, and these conditions occur very frequently in the modern bureaucratic organization.

It has been argued that a kind of rigidity grows out of prolonged role enactment, and that bureaucrats, over a period of time, become insensitive to the needs of clients.[34] We have shown that a certain impersonal treatment is inherent in bureaucratic structure. The charge of insensitivity may therefore be a bureautic reaction. One must not forget that clients are notoriously insensitive to the needs of bureaucrats. The question is, when does bureaucratic insensitivity become pathological? In many bureaucratic organizations, relations with clients are warm and cordial, as for example, between the postman and the householder.

Although prolonged role enactment undoubtedly has a profound effect on a person,[35] what is the "bureaucratic role?" People move around quite freely in bureaucracies. They perform various roles. We do not think it makes sense to speak of the "bureaucratic role." We have emphasized specialist roles and hierarchical roles. In the hierarchy, people go from position to position as they advance. Specialists often move from organization to organization. The truly prolonged role is the entrepreneurial professional role, such as the physician. It seems doubtful that physicians, as a group, are "insensitive to the needs of clients."

Although there is no "bureaucratic role," there is bureaucratic structure. It is obvious that some people are able to achieve personal goals within this structure more easily and comfortably than others. These people have been called bureaucratic types; but they are not necessarily bureaupathic. In fact, it may be that the person who moves most easily within the bureaucratic structure is the one who can hide his insecurity, his "inner rumblings," as Whyte puts it. His insecurity may express itself internally as ulcers but not externally as bureaupathic behavior.

---

[33] For example, attempts have been made to show that "compulsive neurotics" predominate in bureaucracy. See Otto Sperling: "Psychoanalytic Aspects of Bureaucracy," *Psychoan. Q.*, Vol. XIX (1950), pp. 88–100.

[34] Theodore R. Sarbin: "Role Theory," in Gardner Lindzey, ed.: *Handbook of Social Psychology* (Reading, Massachusetts: Addison-Wesley Publishing Company, Inc.; 1954), Vol. I, pp. 223–58. Sarbin points out that this proposition is only an hypothesis, and one would have to find these qualities of rigidity and impersonality in non-occupational behavior as well in order to demonstrate it. We might point out that one would also have to show that these qualities were not present at the beginning of the period of "prolonged role enactment." Sarbin relies somewhat on Robert K. Merton's well-known essay, "Bureaucratic Structure and Personality," in *Social Theory and Social Structure*, rev. ed. (Glencoe, Illinois: The Free Press; 1957). However, Merton does not seem to be talking about the interaction of self and role. Generally, he is explaining "bureaucratic" behavior by reference to bureaucratic structure (graded careers, seniority, *esprit de corps*, the appropriateness of secondary, i.e., impersonal, relations, etc.). He also suggests that the ideal patterns of bureaucratic behavior become exaggerated by being affectively backed, as we have argued. However, he does not explain the origin of this affect ("sentiments") to our satisfaction. We have argued that it comes from personal insecurity in an authority position. Merton does not distinguish between the descriptive and critical uses of the term "bureaucratic."

[35] See Willard Waller: *The Sociology of Teaching* (New York: John Wiley & Sons, Inc.; 1932).

Bureaupathic behavior is one result of the growing insecurity of authority in modern organizations. This insecurity exists because nonhierarchical authority is so frequently delegated without regard to the ability to exercise it; such is the practice of politics.[36] More important, however, is the fact that the culturally defined institution of hierarchy, with its rather extreme claim of rights, is increasingly uncomfortable with advancing specialization. Hierarchical rights change slowly; specialization, the result of technology, changes with increasing speed. The situation is unstable. The legitimacy of organizational authority is in danger. Bureaupathic behavior is one result of this situation.

Bureaupathology and Routinization

The bureaupathic response to insecurity is facilitated by the routinization of organizational problem solving. When the development of appropriate routines is the dominant imperative, when technical problems must be solved, the emphasis must be on abilities rather than rights.[37] Charismatic patterns predominate. These facts are illustrated by wartime experience.

When World War II broke out, a large regulatory structure had to be quickly created. People with many types of skill, from many walks of life, and with many different statuses were quickly assembled in Washington. A whole host of brand new problems was given to them. In those early days, emphasis was on technical problem solving. Anyone who could come up with an idea on how to proceed "got ahead." Bureaupathic patterns were almost nonexistent. The emphasis was on what one could do, not on rights and prerogatives. People became quite scrambled up, with permanently low-status people temporarily elevated to high-status positions. Very young people found themselves in high positions.

Gradually technical problems were mastered and reduced to procedures and programs. Bureaupathic patterns became more pronounced. There were constant reorganizations, a growing volume of reports, increasing insistence upon clearance protocol, authority impressed for its own sake, not as a problem-solving device. Hierarchical dominance was pressed through a great variety of rituals—"control" boards, frequent staff meetings, calls to the "front office," progress reports, increasing insistence upon formal channels, etc.[38] These manifestations of authority were ritualistic because they were not related to winning the war, but to the "need for control." The organization product was not affected by them, because it was secured through an elaborate routine, of which no one comprehended more than a small part. Bureaupathic behavior occupied much more

---

[36] In organizational terms, politics means those activities concerned with the delegation of authority on bases other than a generally recognized ability to exercise it. It involves some kind of exchange between the person desiring the authority and the authority figure who has it to give. It is made possible by the fact that authority may be delegated. Since the specialist content of executive positions is increasingly attenuated as one mounts the hierarchy, so that ability criteria become less and less relevant, placement in these positions becomes more and more a political phenomenon, a matter of "office politics"; the incumbents are "political types." See Harold Lasswell: *Politics: Who Gets What, When, How* (New York: McGraw-Hill Book Co.; 1936).

[37] Studies of decision-making groups in business and government show that the groups prefer strict and formal performances by the conference leader when the subject matter is trivial but not when the subject is important. L. Berkowitz: "Sharing Leadership in Small, Decision-Making Groups," *J. Abnorm. and Soc. Psychol.,* Vol. XLVIII (1953), pp. 231–8.

[38] See Victor A. Thompson: op. cit., Part Two.

of the time of officials. They became kings' messengers after the kings were gone.[39]

Bureaucratic Behavior

The bureaucratic culture makes certain demands upon clients as well as upon organization employees. There are many people in our society who have not been able to adjust to these demands. To them bureaucracy is a curse. They see no good in it whatsoever, but view the demands of modern organization as "red tape." This kind of behavior is external to the organization, and is not simply a reaction to bureaupathology. Its source will be found within the critic himself, not within the organization. It is, in fact, a kind of social disease which we propose to call "bureausis."

Whereas the basic ingredient of bureaupathology is personal insecurity in authority positions, the basic ingredient of bureausis is immaturity, the dysfunctional persistence of childish behavior patterns. Before describing and analyzing the symptoms of bureauticism, let us briefly list those childish patterns which we believe to underlie this disease.

The child feels powerless and constantly fears abandonment by his parents. He does not feel that he can do anything by himself, but must depend upon others over whom he has no assured control. The child does not abstract well and so personalizes the world to make it comprehensible. He sees human agency in most events and imputes human motives to events, motives like his own. Thus, he projects himself into his environment.

The child cannot bind time; he cannot invest or cathect energy in future goals. The image of the object and the investment of energy occur together. He must have the object immediately; tomorrow he will have forgotten. The child has little skill in taking on the roles of others, in putting himself in someone else's place. He experiences himself directly and immediately and expects others to experience him in the same way. Consequently, to have to explain himself, especially to a parent, frequently makes him furious. If the parent were not so dense he would know the child as the child knows himself. On the other hand, the child never imagines a consciousness different from his own and so never really knows anybody but himself.

When the child is very small, he grows accustomed to receiving love without a price. Most very small children today are loved by their parents simply because they are there, not for what they do. Most parents gradually wean the child from this absolute security by making their love somewhat contingent upon performance and by withdrawing love for poor performance. In this way the child is gradually socialized and acquires a conscience. Many children, however, never have to pay much for their parents' love; they become "spoiled." They carry into adulthood the habit of receiving gratifications without a corresponding return or effort on their part.

---

[39]The technical problem military organizations must solve is winning a war. In peacetime, with no technical problem to solve, bureaupathic patterns are more pronounced. Arthur K. Davis says they live and survive in peacetime on ritual. "Bureaucratic Patterns in the Navy Officer Corps," *Social Forces,* Vol. XXVII (1948), pp. 143–53. He hypothesizes that "the effectiveness of military leaders tends to vary inversely with their exposure to a conventionally routinized military career." This study is reproduced in Merton, *et al.,* eds.: *Reader in Bureaucracy* (Glencoe, Illinois: The Free Press; 1952), pp. 380 ff.

In our discussion of the actual symptoms of bureausis, we will depend heavily upon Alvin Gouldner's short but suggestive study of the "red-tape" reaction.[40] Gouldner began his study with the very commonsensical, but nevertheless unusual assumption that when a person criticizes an organizational action or requirement as red tape, we should investigate the person so reacting as well as the organization.

As would be expected, Gouldner's respondents discussed their feelings about red tape in the language of efficiency, referring to things which were "unnecessary." However, efficiency, like its synonym, rationality, is a term which, though universal in form, is relative in content. The efficient or rational action is the one that gives the actor the most favorable ratio between accomplishments and costs, between its positively valued consequences and its negatively valued consequences. The efficient action, therefore, always promotes a system or ordering of values, never a single goal or end-in-view. People order their values differently, so that even if two people sought the same goal they might not agree as to which means for achieving it was most efficient or rational. Terms like efficient, rational, wasteful, or unnecessary, therefore, seem to refer to universal qualities of actions but actually hide personal preferences under these universalistic façades. Gouldner found a great differentiation of values behind the concept of "unnecessary." What was "unnecessary" to one person was not so to another.

The fact that someone feels requirements are unnecessary is certainly no reason to punish him by calling him "sick." People are entitled to their values and beliefs. If, however, a person's values and beliefs make it difficult for him to adjust to the kind of world he must live in, we are at least entitled to label them "dysfunctional." On the other hand, the innovator is also a person who is not completely adjusted to things as they are. Here, then, as in our discussion of bureaupathology, we are dealing with questions of degree. We wish to use our disease metaphor only for rather extreme cases of resistance to bureaucracy. There is a striking similarity between the reaction patterns of bureautics and certain behavior patterns of children, and so we have concluded that the bureautic syndrome is essentially a failure of maturation. It is important to remember, however, that immaturity, like insecurity, is a matter of degree.

From Gouldner's material, and from common observation, we can see that the bureautic resists interrogation and investigation as "unnecessary." They invade his privacy. Other people have no right to know these things about him—for example, his father's occupation (about which he may or may not be proud). Furthermore, they should not have to check up on *him.* He knows he is honest and his claim is valid, why don't they? The processing of his case shows he is dependent upon outside powers and processes beyond his control. It challenges his security and impugns his worth. He, as a person, is being weighed in the balance. Security patterns of childhood are being frustrated; a price is being charged for his satisfactions. The bureaucracy does not respond to him simply because he is *he.* Consequently, all the processing is unnecessary. "It's just a lot of red tape."

The bureautic has low powers of abstraction. He personalizes his world to make it comprehensible. Gouldner found that his critics of bureaucracy

---

[40] Alvin W. Gouldner: "Red Tape as a Social Problem," in Robert K. Merton, *et. al.,* eds.: *op. cit.,* pp. 410 ff.

frequently preferred situations where "cash talked," or where relationships were personalized. The corner grocery store was a model; there was no red tape there. They could not understand complex, impersonal procedures and regarded them all as being "befuddled," "confused," and meaningless. This desire for simpler, more personalized relationships is often verbalized as a preference for "the good old days," but the only "good old days" which modern bureautics ever knew were the good old days of childhood.

By virtue of his need to personalize the world, the bureautic can rarely enter successfully into an impersonal, functional, or *bureaucratic,* relationship. The world is peopled only with friends and enemies; it does not have impartial, impersonal functionaries. The doctor, the postman, the service-station attendant, all must be taken into the bosom of the family. Only first names will do.

Bureautics fear the world beyond, the nonpersonalized world, and they fear bureaucracy because they cannot personalize it. They feel powerless in relation to it, on the "outside;" they feel alienated from the larger part of society. There are many things they are entitled to, but cannot get because this monstrous impersonal world does not respond to their desires. They crave the response to their needs that they used to get in childhood, an immediate and tender response from everyone. The bureautic is not satisfied with the limited number of situations in which he does have power, but wants to be the center of attraction *everywhere.* When this is denied, as it must be, he feels powerless and alienated.[41]

Because the bureautic cannot abstract and therefore personalizes the world, his frustrations must be the work of enemies. He tends to be suspicious of everything. The "unnecessary" requirements are a deliberate attempt to frustrate him or to deprive him of his rights. He is likely to believe that special privilege exempts others from these requirements and assures *their* satisfactions. "You have to have pull." He suspects that everyone in power has "pull," and that is how they got there. There is no point in working hard or being otherwise virtuous because "they" never reward merit. He projects his personal failings onto the "system," and his personal motives onto every one else. Since he rewards his friends and punishes his enemies, he suspects that the whole world operates on this principle. Consequently, he is likely to believe that the only successful approach to bureaucracy is through the personalized route of special favors and bribes or threats to "get them." He has no confidence in securing justice through an impersonal, abstract system of norms and routines, and he interprets justice as getting what is his by right. For him, "what is his by right" and what he wants are easily confused. Suspicion of others not only is a projection of his own motives, but it also builds up his ego. It is hard for him to believe that other people are so little concerned with him, so involved in their own problems, that they have neither the time nor the inclination to fabricate plots against him.

The bureautic is not skillful in taking on the roles of others. This lack of skill is part of the more general inability to abstract. He puts himself in another's

---

[41]Gouldner (op. cit.) suggests that an ideological group, the ultraconservatives, is composed largely of such alienated people. The "good old days" of special privilege are passing. Bureaucracy is hostile to "amicism"—the pursuit of interests by means of personal contacts with strategically situated high-status social peers. This group has been important in developing the epithet "red tape." However, as we said above, as time goes by, the "good old days" must be interpreted as the "good old days" of childhood.

place and therefore imputes malicious motives to other people, but he cannot put *another* in *his* place and therefore cannot imagine how others really feel. Because he cannot take on the role of the generalized other, he regards any checking of his claims as an unnecessary invasion of his privacy. He knows his claim is justified, his information honest and correct, and so of course he would not check himself. Therefore, why does the "other" check him? It is either unnecessary or malicious meddling. Of course, when others make claims on him, he will check them out carefully because they are "trying to put something over" on him. The fact that others require what is "unnecessary" can only be attributed to stupidity or maliciousness; in either case it is red tape. The bureautic's inability to abstract or generalize makes it impossible for him to understand why an exception cannot be made in his case. How could this one little exception possibly hurt anything? Refusal to grant the exception is bureaucratic officiousness, inconsiderateness, or disinterest. It is the ritualistic application of rules and regulations "whether they make sense or not."

The bureautic person probably has an underdeveloped power of investing energy in future objects. Gouldner's data suggest this. Waiting for gratification is therefore unusually painful and provokes the red-tape reaction. Of course, the dislike of waiting is particularly a matter of degree. No one likes it, but normally a person's ability to wait grows stronger as he matures. If this ability is underdeveloped in an adult, experiences with bureaucracy will be especially frustrating because, as we have shown, the large complex organization must normally move with a certain deliberateness. Perhaps the impact of the inability to defer gratifications must be assessed in connection with the other bureautic characteristics discussed above. If the waiting is "necessary," it is tolerable. If it is "unnecessary," it is intolerable; it is red tape. The question again becomes, what is "unnecessary"? The inability to defer gratifications provides emotional reinforcement for all of the frustrations of the bureautic in a bureaucratized world.

We have been discussing the bureautic as a client, but bureautics also become employees of bureaucratic organizations. Alternatives to this kind of employment are becoming fewer and fewer. Within the organization, the bureautic manifests the same suspiciousness of the motives of others. People are "out to get him." He feels that only those with "pull" get ahead. He cannot understand the reasons for many regulations and procedures, does not bother to familiarize himself with them, and constantly violates them. He will frequently refuse to keep required records or make required reports, often thereby creating vast confusion and enormous amounts of additional work for others. He insists on personalizing all relationships. To him the organization is a great battleground between his friends and him, on the one side, and "the rest," his enemies, on the other. In this battle, personal loyalties are all that count. He tends to lose sight of the organization as an instrument for accomplishing goals, as a structure of instrumental functions and relationships.

The bureautic employee is not likely to get into the hierarchy, and so may come to be regarded as a failure. Because of his inability to enter intelligently into abstract, complex, co-operative relationships, he tends to be pushed to one side, unless he has some unusual skill that the organization badly needs. He is often regarded as "queer." All of these facts add to his bitterness and increase his suspiciousness. He projects his failures onto the organization and the impersonal "others" who are his enemies. He feels he is surrounded by stupidity and maliciousness. He feels powerless and alienated from the organization.

In the preceding pages we have suggested that some adverse reactions to modern organizations stem from inadequacies in the reacting person rather than from inadequacies in these organizations. We realize that this subject is a delicate one and that people may honestly differ as to where the inadequacy resides in specific cases. Nevertheless, the fact remains that some people are uncomfortable with almost all aspects of modern organizations, while others work with them quite effectively. The former we have called bureautics, suggesting some failure in their maturation. We are aware that some people will argue that anyone who *can* adapt to modern bureaucracy should be called bureautic, and in one way it does not matter which group gets the name. However, there is the distinction of maturity and immaturity which will survive any semantic switching of names.

Of course, a well man shares many behaviors with a sick one. Who has not felt powerless before the large organization? It is true that, with a request, one is likely to be shunted from person to person; that he can find many who can say "no" but has difficulty finding the one who can say "yes." The reason for this fact, as we explained in a previous chapter, is that hierarchical institutions overstress the veto. A veto is final, but an approval frequently must go to a higher source, where it is again subject to a veto.

It is also undoubtedly true that modern organizations have many routines and requirements that really are unnecessary. Frequently people react to requirements as red tape simply because they do not know the reasons for them. The organization can remove this reaction by explaining the reasons for the requirements. In attempting to explain these reasons, officials sometimes find that there are no very good ones, and the requirements are changed. This sort of self-scrutiny to remove traditional deposits is part of the ethos of bureaucracy. It reflects the dominance of a spirit of rationalism brought into organizations by science and technology.

We have distinguished three kinds of behavior patterns which have often been conceptually confused. First are patterns characteristic of large, complex organizations based upon advanced specialization. These are *bureaucratic* patterns of behavior; *specialization* determines their nature.

A second kind consists essentially of exaggerations of bureaucratic behavior by insecure persons in hierarchical and nonhierarchical authority positions. These behaviors are oriented to personal needs rather than to organizational goals. They interfere with goal accomplishment and are, therefore, pathological from the standpoint of the organization. Consequently, we have called them *bureaupathic* behaviors; they arise from personal *insecurity*.

Finally, we have described a pattern of behavior which is a *reaction* to modern organizations by people (including both employees and clients) who are unable to adjust to the complexity, impersonality, and impartiality of these organizations. We have argued that the basis of this nonadjustive reaction is personal immaturity. We have called this pattern of behavior *bureautic*. Bureaucratic behavior is associated with specialization, bureaupathic behavior with personal insecurity, and bureautic behavior with personal immaturity.

Use and Misuse of Efficiency Controls

FRANK J. JASINSKI

To improve plant management, businessmen demand accounting controls that are current, easy to interpret, and readily applied. In response, accountants have devised a variety of "efficiency" reports which can be highly useful if regarded as red flags, but highly dangerous if not supplemented by other sources of information.

The Danger

Overreliance on efficiency controls can lead to an impressive roster of problems, such as:

- Waste of executive time.
- Increased production and maintenance costs.
- Low morale.
- Impaired quality and irregular or inadequate output.
- Labor recruitment problems.
- Cynicism or dishonesty on the part of workers and supervisory personnel.
- Interdepartmental friction.

The list of counts in this indictment is a long and lurid one, but every one of these charges can be substantiated by specific case histories that are not, unfortunately, as untypical as they ought to be.

Output and Time

While, as will be seen, it is dangerous for management to rely on any one single index of efficiency, the controls that cause most of the trouble are those based on or derived from the concept that the efficiency of an operator or department can be determined by measuring the time actually spent to complete an item against a predetermined or "standard" time. This concept of course dates back to the 1920's and 1930's, when it came into great vogue as a formal system in industry. Any system that equates efficiency with quantity of output and compares output records for set, short-run time periods ends up with much the same effect.

As might be supposed, in recent years many companies have found addi-

From "Use and Misuse of Efficiency Controls," *Harvard Business Review,* Vol. 34, No. 4 (July-August, 1956), pp. 105–112.

tional and often better ways to compute efficiency. For example, among the factors now widely considered are quality, tool costs, inventory levels, and production schedules. However, the development of newer and more sensitive controls does not mean that the old approach has been abandoned. More important in terms of practical consequence is the fact that most operating people still feel that production time provides the best and most decisive way to measure efficiency. This holds true of the worker on the bench, of the foreman, of the second-line supervisor, and apparently of many an executive even higher up in the production department.

In one way or another, then, the behavior of people on the job is conditioned by their almost single-minded observance of just two variables—pieces produced and man-hours expended. But in seeking to make efficiency, measured this way, *look* good, many workers and managers act in a manner that serves to impair *real* efficiency.

Defensive Behavior

How can controls boomerang in this way?

The answer must be found by watching the behavior of people whose efficiency is judged—or misjudged—on the basis of these quick, simple indexes that never were designed to tell the whole story or reveal the whole picture. People who must pass these rigid tests quickly acquire a pattern of behavior that has but one objective—to make their scores look better, even though this may mean the sacrifice of other less tangible advantages and of longer run gains for the business as a whole.

The failure of management to see and rectify its mistakes more quickly can probably be traced to the veneration which most businessmen have for figures. In the words of the old saw, "Figures don't lie." Maybe they don't lie, but that does not mean they are capable of dictating action without the aid of judgment or careful weighing of information gleaned from varied sources.

Case Histories

Each of the following case histories exemplifies one or more of the dangers ascribable to misuse of efficiency controls. The illustrations presented here may strike the more sophisticated reader as examples of extremely backward practice, but actually they are drawn from several of the largest corporations in the country. Most of the firms involved have excellent earnings records and enjoy deserved reputations for being generally progressive. Therefore, let no top executive sit back and complacently reassure himself by saying, "This couldn't happen in my company."

Let us first look at a large company that measured efficiency daily and monthly for each department by the following in the plant rule-of-thumb calculations:

> In each department, a daily efficiency rating was computed, based on the "time value" of completed units transferred to finished stores compared with the number of hours spent "on production" during the day of transfer. Efficiency was reported daily and accumulated to the end of the month. Thus each department earned 12 efficiency ratings each year.
>
> In this company, the plant manager accepted the monthly efficiency

figures as indicative of every department's accomplishments or progress. He placed a high value on this figure and called his subordinates to task whenever the monthly efficiency figure was low, or whenever it fell significantly under the figure of the preceding month.

Wasted Time

When efficiency as measured by this index dropped, top supervisory personnel rushed to find out why, and lower supervisory personnel employed their wits in preparing iron-clad excuses. For example, the company's production superintendent found it necessary to compile figures to "prove" that departments with low ratings were not as inefficient as they appeared:

> "No doubt I'll be hearing from my boss in a couple of days about the four or five departments which are low in efficiency. I'm ready for him, though. I've got a report on all parts undergoing inspection on the last day of the month for each department. If you add the time those parts represent, the low departments won't be as low as they're reported."

Even where subordinate supervisors could offer what appeared to be legitimate reasons for precipitous declines in their efficiency, company "brass" devoted much time to looking for additional explanations. For example, one foreman described the following experience:

> "Once we ran out of forgings for one of the two parts I make, and so we ran the other part. Then we got the late forgings in, and they wanted them done in a hurry. I had to put the parts I had been working on aside and set up the new job. By the time we got the machines changed over and got the first piece through, the end of the month came. My efficiency dropped 20 points.
>
> "*Boy, you should have seen the brass pile in here—men four and five levels above me in management.* They spent almost the whole month in my department. If a man stopped to talk to someone, they stepped right up and told him to go back to work. The thing was, I had had the original parts which I had been working on lying on the floor—partly done. I could have finished them easily by the end of the month and got a 90%–92% efficiency. But with the changeover, I had to leave them unfinished."

Needless to say, the managerial energy and time used up in this seemingly fruitless exploration of a problem already sufficiently explained had to be subtracted from the sum of energy and time available for working on other, perhaps more pressing, issues.

That the company had plenty of more serious problems will be seen as soon as we look a little further into the behavior of lower management in this situation. Production jams, high costs, low morale, and some dishonesty were present, all traceable in part to the emphasis placed on efficiency ratings.

Production Jams

Because management in this company paid so much attention to the end-of-month efficiency ratings, department supervisors left no stone unturned to get as many units into finished stores as possible. They even resorted to such expensive and disruptive processes as "bleeding the line"—that is, stopping operations near the start of the cycle and shifting labor to final operations in order to complete more units by the deadline. This process is summarized by what another foreman said:

> "For the last two weeks of the month we're driving hell out of the men. We have to get pieces out, and we're always jammed up at the end of the month. . . . What actually happens is that in the beginning of the month I have to put all of my men at the beginning of the line to get pieces going for the month's production. This is because we cleaned out the department in the previous month. Then, during the last two weeks I have to put all of the men at the end of the line to finish up the pieces.
>
> "What we should be doing is to have each man work on his machine. At the end of the month we should have a piece in each machine—not cleaned out the way we are. That way we could keep a steady flow all month and not have the rush at the end of the month."

The irregular work flow resulting from this process of bleeding the line in one department generated still more scheduling jams in departments to which the work piece went later. A foreman whose department was near the end of the fabricating process and another who handled parts after machining, both reported on the month-end snarls as follows:

> "Material flow from previous departments is very irregular, especially at the end of the month when you have a terrific rush. And the type of men we have as employees just can't handle the rush when it does come at the end of the month."

> "My main trouble is with material flow. I look around the department and either it's empty or I'm overloaded. Most of the rush comes from the 15th to the end of the month. Toward the end of the month the departments send me one or two parts at a time and ask me to rush them through. I guess they want credit for the piece in the month's production report."

Higher Maintenance Costs

Just as anxiety to earn a high efficiency rating led foremen to "bleed the line" and "drive hell out of the men," so it prompted them to "run a machine right to the ground at the end of the month, trying to get pieces out." As, again, one foreman put it:

> "We really can't stop to have our machines repaired. In fact, one of our machines is off right now, but we'll have to gimmick something immediately and keep the machine going because at the end of the month, as it is now, we simply can't have a machine down. We've got to get those pieces out. Many times we run a machine right to the ground at the end of the month trying to get pieces out, and we have to spend extra time at the beginning of the month trying to repair the machine."

"Fudging" Figures

A more subtle but not less deleterious result of the quest for steady, high efficiency ratings was figure fudging by the top supervisors. Some of these men, anxious to equalize efficiencies among departments in their charge, did so by transferring personnel "on paper" from departments with relatively low efficiencies to those with relatively high ratings. This move had a leveling result when the ratio of "man-hours" to "time value per piece in finished stores" was computed.

If this practice tended to protect the weak, it also tended to penalize the more successful foremen by forcing them to "carry" their less efficient peers.

Some foremen also suffered a sense of moral affront at what they regarded as less than complete honesty. As one of them put it:

> "They even want you to lie about production here so as to make the record look better than it is. I won't do that. O.K. if *they* want to, but I won't."

Low Morale

This combination of falsehood and impaired morale is also found in another case history, where it was perhaps the outstanding problem caused by a system of efficiency ratings.

This case involved a plant where machine repair, processing, tooling, and service from the cribs was not fully adequate. Management, however, tended to disregard these factors and pressed for high efficiencies regardless. One foreman stated:

> "Top management just won't take any excuses at all when it comes to efficiency. They just want you to keep up your efficiency, and they don't want any alibis."

A few workers, who were confronted with time losses which management refused to acknowledge, falsified their time tickets. Many other workers simply became resigned to the situation and turned in low efficiencies. Foremen, recognizing the factors leading to low output, did not care to press operators for higher production.

Management became convinced that most operators were falsifying their records and, more important, that foremen were too lax with their employees. It fired a few foremen and middle supervisors and made a few drastic organizational changes. Morale among hourly employees and supervisors was low because of management's pressure, on the one hand, for increased efficiency, and management's failure, on the other hand, to recognize and to act on inadequate service from supporting departments. As another foreman said:

> "It does seem in this shop as if too much is put on the foreman without giving him the help he needs. Take in my case: I have to push for everything I get. I keep pushing the inspector to get the pieces out so that we can meet the schedule. I chase up tools and materials personally, and I am the one who has to keep pushing maintenance, tool repair, and the equipment. It seems to me that in a well-run shop all of these other

departments should be made just as responsible for getting production out as the production people themselves. . . . It shouldn't have to be the way it is."

Impaired Recruitment

Still another case history illustrates how worker recruitment can be impaired by the unwise application of efficiency ratings ill-adapted to meet unusual requirements.

In this company, top management became aware that the number of production workers was inadequate to meet current output schedules. Because experienced operators were difficult to find, new untrained laborers were hired. These were to be carried for a certain length of time at no charge to production; only when the period of training was over would the new employees become a full charge on their departments.

To meet the shortage of manpower on production, management shortened training time considerably and transferred the trainees to the production rolls. This manipulation brought the paper figure of manpower available closer to that required for scheduled production and removed potential criticism of the managers who knew they would be held responsible if there were too apparent a discrepancy between the two.

Unfortunately, when this plan was evolved, the duration of the training time needed for the work was not given full recognition, and the trainees were unable to produce enough to translate this paper improvement into reality.

As a result, foremen who were faced with a full charge for half-trained employees reacted by keeping only the exceptional men, firing the rest even though they were badly needed. As a foreman explained it:

> "These jobs take months of experience to get even a fair operator. I can't do it in 40 working days. I keep the trainees until the 40 days are up and let all the fellows go except the unusual one who can give me production. I usually net about one or two out of ten. What else can I do? I can't keep my efficiency up with trainees who give me 20%–30% efficiency."

The labor recruitment problem is this company was further aggravated by the fact that many trainees, pushed for efficiency, left even before the training period was over. Indeed, of all trainees who left the company in a seven-month period, 53% left before the second month had elapsed. Once news of the situation at the plant had leaked through the community, it became difficult for the personnel department to recruit replacements.

Management Friction

As might be expected, the above situation provoked ill feeling between people in production and personnel. A member of the personnel department was bitterly critical of the treatment of trainees, especially in the light of the tight labor market. He complained:

> "I don't know what production supervision is trying to do. Most of the trainees who left were good kids. They wanted to learn and most of them really tried. But most of them never saw the inside of a machine shop

before. How can they be expected to produce at 100% efficiency in a month or even two? Their treatment doesn't help us getting new employees either."

The problem of friction is illustrated by still another case history. In this situation the trouble started when the accounting department prepared a graph showing that in-process inventory was steadily increasing in relation to sales. Acting on this information, the plant manager's assistant decided to reduce work-in-process by not replacing employees lost through attrition. Since fewer workers would produce fewer pieces and thus reduce inventory, the action would bring the "in-process to sales" graph into balance.

This action, designed to improve an accountant's graph, overlooked the fact that plant sales were growing and orders on the books were piling up unfilled. The gradual decrease of the work force in the face of rising backlogs provoked one superintendent to the following outburst against the middle manager responsible for the "no-replacement" order:

> "What the hell is going on around here? Turning down a request for one man. What the hell do these schoolboys think they're doing? They come around with their figures and think they can run a shop by the book."

Higher Unit Costs

In addition to slowing up deliveries and aggravating friction, the actions in the case just described raised the per-unit costs on output. As production fell further and further behind schedule, angry customers had to be appeased by pushing through particular orders. Split lots became the rule rather than the exception, and costs were boosted by the extra setup time. People at the lower supervisory levels could see that expenses must be rising and why. One of them reported:

> "We have to break a job down because some other job is a rush job, and we have to reset the job afterward. But time standards only allow us a certain percentage of time for one setup based on the job as a whole. As a result we lose time and can't make our efficiency—especially when we make as little as five pieces at a time. . . . This business of 50 pieces here, and 50 pieces there, break up a machine, set it up, break it up—you lose a lot of efficiency.
>
> "You've got to have stuff on the floor. It's like working capital—and you've got to have working capital. If you cut down on inventory, you increase your costs—every part becomes a special job, and you pay premiums on special treatment."

Lowered Quality

Finally, it is possible to show that poor quality and high costs often go hand in hand, both together being caused by the efforts of production personnel to make their efficiency ratings look better.

These problems in conjunction were observed in a manufacturing division where plant efficiency was measured by the number of work pieces passing a certain point on the production line. Plant managers in the division pressed for getting pieces past this critical point, even if they were defective and would have to be reworked later on. Indeed, the division manager was seriously considering a plan whereby certain operations would purposely be left undone until after the "payoff" point, so that his plant efficiencies would "look good."

As a result of these production methods, costs per item were higher, and products were patched up. Hourly operators could not feel they had done a job well, so their morale was low. All employees were affected by the knowledge that management had adopted the doubtful expedient of trying to put quality back into a product where it was originally lacking.

In another corporation, where plant efficiency was measured by low costs, a plant manager spoke of the danger to quality in the following manner:

> "Suppose we get rolling along fairly well. All of a sudden, one day, one manager jumps ten points ahead of the rest in the division. We get a delegation from the main office wanting to know why we're so far behind. What they should find out is why *he* is ten points ahead—and what it will mean for the future. But, of course, we don't want to be behind so we fall back on the rules of the game—you have to follow the rules to stay in the game. We start cutting corners to bring our percentage up—but at a sacrifice that nobody considers.
>
> "Not only do we pay premium time to the people in the repair area, but the workers in the shop learn "let-it-go" habits. We're putting out patched-up products—products which never can be fixed up right. This patched-up quality is going to hurt in five or six years."

Corrective Action

It should be emphasized that the problems diagnosed in the above case histories do not arise because efficiency ratings are used, but because they are misused by some managements. The fault does not lie with the figures or with the accountants who compute them. It lies rather with the managers who fail to recognize the limitations of these very helpful but hardly all-sufficing tools.

If the problem were an isolated one, the quick replacement of an occasional manager might be the best solution. Remember, however, that the case examples are drawn from various industries and from several of the largest corporations in the country. The problem does not stem from the idiosyncrasies of a few individuals, but from the fact that it has become such an ingrained tradition to appraise the worth of a production worker or department by the length of time it takes to produce an item. After all, this is the evaluation method by means of which many present-day supervisors became members of management.

Even where top management has tried to deemphasize the importance of the short-run efficiency figure and to introduce new programs which would improve long-run costs, resistance occurs. One foreman who was participating in a plan to increase flexibility had this to say of his superintendent:

> "I'll tell you now that we have a long way to go on this program. I have serious doubts whether it's going to work or not. You see the foremen are all for it and it helps them, and I think that most of the general foremen

are for it. It's the superintendents that we're not sure about. They are always worried about efficiency. They just can't stand seeing any more men on the line than are absolutely necessary.

"The way it works is this. . . . A day when there are no absentees, why, this has the effect of having temporary excess in manpower and the superintendent will start to yell. He can't see anything beyond the day's efficiency and doesn't seem to want to understand that we must maintain this program even if efficiency suffers slightly.

"That's the understanding we have about this thing and it comes all the way from the top, but it has not sunk in with the superintendents yet. . . . When the chips are down, it is a battle on the floor. . . . It's that old efficiency figure again staring the superintendent in the face."

Corrective action seems to lie in re-evaluation and re-education. Once the proper perspective for efficiency reports has been established, it is important to transmit that perspective to all members of management. How this job can be accomplished is too large a subject to discuss in detail, but a three-point program may be briefly suggested:

1. Make an inventory of existing accounting reports; then take a critical look at them to determine exactly what they do and do not reveal.
2. Determine what information is required to make certain decisions, and what portion of this information can be supplied by existing or additional accounting reports.
3. Develop nonaccounting sources and channels for information required for decisions.

A Critical Inventory

If existing controls are inventoried and the things they can and cannot do are considered, managers will quickly become aware that the figures they collect may fail to measure important aspects of reality. For example, as we have seen, it was possible to increase *reported* efficiency by practices which raised costs, cut quality, jammed production schedules, piled up overdue orders, and left a growing plant undermanned! Most efficiency reports simply show relationships between two variables. These relationships can continue to "look good" while the company is actually "going to the dogs." Indeed, as has been shown, it is sometimes possible to make reported efficiency look better by actions that actually aggravate major business problems!

Some so-called efficiency controls can hardly be said to measure efficiency in even the most limited sense. For example, a daily plant efficiency based on parts transferred into finished stores and on the number of productive hours expended on the day of transfer does not represent the departmental efficiency for that day. After all, it might have taken three months to fabricate the parts, and a lot of employees might have been absent on the day of transfer. Further, such an efficiency measurement does *not* include tool and other operating costs. Nor does it mean a department is maintaining its schedule. In one plant, a department's efficiency doubled, from 53% to 106%, in a month's time, but so did the number of parts behind schedule!

Better Reports

Once an inventory has been made of existing reports, the kinds of information that these reports yield can be compared with the information needed. Some reports can perhaps be eliminated, others improved.

Another possibility, no less real because it is too complex for us even to scratch the surface at this point, is to broaden the base of reality from which the accounting department derives its figures.* With the increasing use of electronic accounting equipment this may become more feasible.

The fact remains that accounting reports, regardless of scope and equipment used, will probably yield only part of the data required for executive decision.

Other Sources

The development of nonaccounting sources and channels of information is perhaps the most vital step in any remedial program. It is essential that executives place less reliance on what they read in figures and more on what they learn from talking with people, especially from talking with their own subordinates.

The people affected by executive decisions are a valuable source of information, experience, and advice. As such they should be tapped; they should be accorded freedom of expression and a chance to make their opinions known topside. If evidence for this statement is needed, it is surely available in the case histories reviewed in the earlier portions of this article. Low-ranking executives, supervisors, even foremen, had they been consulted, could have pointed up the problem of misused controls. They knew where improvements were needed and why. To consult subordinates is not to abdicate in their favor; it is merely a way of utilizing a rich and too often neglected human resource.

In spite of its importance, this suggestion is the one most likely to encounter strong resistance. One reason for this lies in the fact, already referred to, that businessmen believe "figures don't lie." The unspoken corollary is that "people do." We have tried to cast some doubt on this comforting conviction by pointing out that though figures may not lie, they do not always tell the whole truth; further, that even this partial truth may be and frequently is manipulated and modified.

Another reason for resisting the advice to talk more with more people lies in the fact that it is far easier and much faster to obtain summaries from forms and figures than it is from other humans. Yet most successful managers have developed the skill of eliciting necessary information from their subordinates in a reasonable amount of time.

Finally, some managers will resist this advice because it calls for a fundamental change in their relationships with subordinates. Too long and too often managers have gone to the people below them, not for additional information, but for "explanations" of some shortcoming that the managers have "caught" through consulting the accountants' reports. Subordinates are regarded more or less with suspicion; what they say is called an alibi or an excuse. With this kind of attitude managers can hear, but they can hardly listen and learn.

---

*For a description of a new kind of index based on many variables reflecting long-run production efficiency, which General Electric has developed, see Willard B. Merrihue and Raymond A. Katzell, "ERI—Yardstick of Employee Relations," HBR November-December 1955, p. 91.

Managers by Default

The practical effect of this high-handed behavior, oddly enough, is not to make top management the boss. Rather, the accountant, with his rows of figures, becomes a dominant voice in the company. He becomes a manager by default, as it were, because knowledge is power, and the knowledge on which action is based is what the accountant puts into his reports.

The fact is that the day accountants can devise a balance sheet or graph which encompasses total reality, we can do away with executives—but not until then. The accountants themselves know that day will never come. Most of them are conscious of the limitations of their figures and are aghast when they realize the full extent and consequences of misuse. And the best of them are constantly trying to build real usefulness into their services (rather than any illusion of one-hundred-per-cent accuracy or to-the-last-digit preciseness).

Recently I spoke on this subject to some 90 members of the National Machine Accountants Association. In the discussion that followed, the accountants concurred that management tended to ask for reports which were too narrow in scope and to place an inordinate amount of emphasis on them. They also felt that their capacity to broaden the scope of the reports or to minimize the emphasis put on the figures was limited by their status in management.

Perhaps, then, one of the most basic steps for top management is to call on the accountants themselves for guidance out of this dilemma—to treat them as the helpful counselors that they could be rather than as the final figures that they never have been.

Dysfunctional Consequences of Performance Measurements

V. F. RIDGWAY

There is today a strong tendency to state numerically as many as possible of the variables with which management must deal. The mounting interest in and application of tools such as operations research, linear programming, and statistical decision making, all of which require quantifiable variables, foster the idea that if progress toward goals can be measured, efforts and resources can be more rationally managed. This has led to the development of quantitative performance measurements for all levels within organizations, up to and including measurements of the performance of a division manager with profit responsibility in a decentralized company. Measurements at lower levels in the organization may be in terms of amount of work, quality of work, time required, and so on.

From "Dysfunctional Consequences of Performance Measurements," *Administrative Science Quarterly*, Vol. 1, No. 2 (September 1956), pp. 240–247. Reprinted by permission.

Quantitative measures of performance are tools, and are undoubtedly useful. But research indicates that indiscriminate use and undue confidence and reliance in them result from insufficient knowledge of the full effects and consequences. Judicious use of a tool requires awareness of possible side effects and reactions. Otherwise, indiscriminate use may result in side effects and reactions outweighing the benefits, as was the case when penicillin was first hailed as a wonder drug. The cure is sometimes worse than the disease.

It seems worthwhile to review the current scattered knowledge of the dysfunctional consequences resulting from the imposition of a system of performance measurements. For the purpose of analyzing the impact of performance measurements upon job performance, we can consider separately single, multiple, and composite criteria. Single criteria occur when only one quantity is measured and observed, such as total output or profit. Multiple criteria occur when several quantities are measured simultaneously, such as output, quality, cost, safety, waste, and so forth. Composite criteria occur when the separate quantities are weighted in some fashion and then added or averaged.

Single Criteria

A single criterion of performance was in use in a public employment agency studied by Peter M. Blau.[1] The agency's responsibility was "to serve workers seeking employment and employers seeking workers." Employment interviewers were appraised by the number of interviews they conducted. Thus the interviewer was motivated to complete as many interviews as he could, but not to spend adequate time in locating jobs for the clients. The organization's goal of placing clients in jobs was not given primary consideration because the measurement device applied to only one aspect of the activity.

Blau reports another case in a federal law enforcement agency which investigated business establishments. Here he found that work schedules were distorted by the imposition of a quota of eight cases per month for each investigator. Toward the end of the month an investigator who found himself short of the eight cases would pick easy, fast cases to finish that month and save the lengthier cases till the following month. Priority of the cases for investigation was based on length of the case rather than urgency, as standards of impartiality would require. This is one of many instances in which the existence of an "accounting period" adversely affects the over-all goal accomplishment of the organization.

Chris Argyris also reports this tendency to use easy jobs as fillers toward the end of a period in order to meet a quota.[2] In this case, a factory supervisor reported that they "feed the machines all the easy orders" toward the end of the month, rather than finish them in the sequence in which they were received. Such a practice may lead to undue delay of the delivery of some customers' orders, perhaps the most profitable orders.

David Granick's study of Soviet management reveals how the attention and glory that accrues to a plant manager when he can set a new monthly production record in one month leads to the neglect of repairs and maintenance, so that in ensuing months there will be a distinct drop in production.[3] Similarly,

---

[1]Peter M. Blau, *The Dynamics of Bureaucracy* (Chicago, Ill., 1955).
[2]Chris Argyris, *The Impact of Budgets on People* (New York, 1952).
[3]David Granick, *Management of the Industrial Firm in the U.S.S.R.* (New York, 1954).

the output of an entire plant may be allowed to fall off in order to create conditions under which one worker can make a production record, when the importance of such a record is considered greater than over-all plant production.

Joseph S. Berliner's report on Soviet business administration points out sharply how the accounting period has an adverse effect upon management decisions.[4] The use of monthly production quotas causes "storming" at the end of the month to reach the quota. Repairs and maintenance are postponed until the following month, so that production lags in the early part of the month, and storming must again be resorted to in the following month. This has impact upon the rate of production for suppliers and customers who are forced into a fluctuating rate of operations with its attendant losses and wastes.

Standard costs as a criterion of performance is a frequent source of dissatisfaction in manufacturing plants.[5] The "lumpiness" of indirect charges that are allocated to the plants or divisions (indirect charges being unequal from month to month), variations in quality and cost of raw materials, or other factors beyond the control of the operating manager, coupled with inaccuracies and errors in the apportionment of indirect charges, causes distrust of the standards. A typical reaction of operating executives in such cases seems to be to seek explanations and justifications. Consequently, considerable time and energy is expended in discussion and debate about the correctness of charges. Only "wooden money" savings accrue when charges are shifted to other accounts and there is no increase in company profits. It should be pointed out, however, that having charges applied to the proper departments may have the advantage of more correctly directing attention to problem areas.

Granick discusses two measures of the success of the Soviet firm which have been considered and rejected as over-all measures by Soviet industrial leaders and economists.[6] The first, cost-reduction per unit of product, is considered inadequate because it does not provide a basis for evaluating new products. Further, variations in amount of production affect the cost-reduction index because of the finer division of overhead costs, quality changes, and assortment. The second over-all measure of a firm's performance, profitability, has been rejected as the basic criterion on the grounds that it is affected in the short run by factors outside the control of management, such as shortages of supplies. Profitability as a measure of success led to a reduction in experimental work and de-emphasized the importance of production quantity, quality, and assortment. Neither cost-reduction nor profitability was acceptable alone; each was only a partial index. The Soviets had concluded by 1940 that no single measure of success of a firm is adequate in itself and that there is no substitute for genuine analysis of all the elements entering into a firm's work.

Difficulties with single criteria have been observed in operations research, where one of the principal sources of difficulty is considered to be the choice of proper criteria for performance measurement.[7] The difficulty of translating

---

[4]Joseph S. Berliner, A Problem in Soviet Business Management, *Administrative Science Quarterly,* I (1956), 86–101.

[5]H. A. Simon, H. Guetzkow, G. Kozmetsky, G. Tyndall, *Centralization vs. Decentralization in Organizing the Controller's Department* (New York, 1954).

[6]Granick, *op. cit.*

[7]Charles Hitch and Roland McKean, "Suboptimization in Operations Problems" J. F. McCloskey and Flora F. Trefethen, eds., *Operations Research for Management* (Baltimore, Md., 1954).

the several alternatives into their full effect upon the organization's goal forces the operations researcher to settle for a criterion more manageable than profit maximization, but less appropriate. The efficiency of a subgroup of the organization may be improved in terms of some plausible test, yet the organization's efficiency in terms of its major goal may be decreased.

In all the studies mentioned above, the inadequacy of a single measure of performance is evident. Whether this is a measure of an employee at the working level, or a measure of management, attention is directed away from the over-all goal. The existence of a measure of performance motivates individuals to effort, but the effort may be wasted, as in seeking "wooden money" savings, or may be detrimental to the organization's goal, as in rushing through interviews, delaying repairs, and rejecting profitable opportunities.

Multiple Measurements

Recognition of the inadequacies of a single measure of success or performance leads organizations to develop several criteria. It is felt then that all aspects of the job will receive adequate attention and emphasis so that efforts of individuals will not be distorted.

A realization in the employment office studied by Blau that job referrals and placements were also important led eventually to their inclusion in measuring the performance of the interviewers.[8] Merely counting the number of referrals and placements had led to wholesale indiscriminate referrals, which did not accomplish the employment agency's screening function. Therefore, to stress the qualitative aspects of the interviewer's job, several ratios (of referrals to interviews, placements to interviews, and placements to referrals) were devised. Altogether there were eight quantities that were counted or calculated for each interviewer. This increase in quantity and complexity of performance measurements was felt necessary to give emphasis to all aspects of the interviewer's job.

Granick relates that no single criterion was universally adopted in appraising Soviet management.[9] Some managers were acclaimed for satisfying production quotas while violating labor laws. Others were removed from office for violating quality and assortment plans while fulfilling production quotas. Apparently there is a ranking of importance of these multiple criteria. In a typical interfirm competition the judges were provided with a long list of indexes. These included production of finished goods in the planned assortment, an even flow of production as between different ten-day periods and as between months, planned mastery of new types of products, improvement in product quality and reduction in waste, economy of materials through improved design and changing of technological processes, fulfillment of labor productivity tasks and lowering of unit cost, keeping within the established wage fund, and increase in the number of worker suggestions for improvements in work methods and conditions and their adoption into operation. But no indication of how these indexes should be weighted was given. The pre-eminence of such indexes as quantity, quality, assortment of production, and remaining within the firm's allotment of materials and fuels brought some order into the otherwise chaotic picture. The presence of "campaigns" and "priorities" stressing one or more factors also has aided

---

[8]Blau, *op. cit.*
[9]Granick, *op. cit.*

Soviet management in deciding which elements of its work are at the moment most important.

Without a single over-all composite measure of success, however, there is no way of determining whether the temporarily increased effort on the "campaign" criteria of the month represents new effort or merely effort shifted from other criteria. And the intangibility of some of these indexes makes it impossible to judge whether there has been decreased effort on other aspects. Hence even in a campaign period the relative emphases may become so unbalanced as to mitigate or defeat the purpose of the campaign.

The Soviet manager is working then under several measurements, and the relative influence or emphasis attached to any one measurement varies from firm to firm and from month to month. Profits and production are used, among other measurements, and these two may lead to contradictory managerial decisions. Granick hypothesizes that some managers have refused complicated orders that were difficult to produce because it would mean failure to produce the planned quantities. Acceptance of these orders would have been very profitable, but of the two criteria, production quantity took precedence.

Numerous American writers in the field of management have stressed the importance of multiple criteria in evaluating performance of management. Peter Drucker, for example, lists market standing, innovation, productivity, physical and financial resources, profitability, manager performance and development, worker performance and attitude, and public responsibility.[10] This list includes many of the same items as the list used by Soviet management.

The consensus at a round-table discussion of business and professional men[11] was that although return on investment is important, additional criteria are essential for an adequate appraisal of operating departments. These other criteria are fairly well summed up in Drucker's list above.

Thus we see that the need for multiple criteria is recognized and that they are employed at different levels of the organization—lower levels as in the employment agency, higher levels as considered by Granick and Drucker. At all levels these multiple measurements or criteria are intended to focus attention on the many facets of a particular job.

The use of multiple criteria assumes that the individual will commit his or the organization's efforts, attention, and resources in greater measure to those activities which promise to contribute the greatest improvement to over-all performance. There must then exist a theoretical condition under which an additional unit of effort or resources would yield equally desirable results in over-all performance, whether applied to production, quality, research, safety, public relations, or any of the other suggested areas. This would be the condition of "balanced stress on objectives" to which Drucker refers.

Without a single over-all composite measure of performance, the individual is forced to rely upon his judgment as to whether increased effort on one criterion improves over-all performance, or whether there may be a reduction in performance on some other criterion which will outweigh the increase in the first. This is quite possible, for in any immediate situation many of these objectives may be contradictory to each other.

---

[10]Peter M. Drucker, *The Practice of Management* (New York, 1954).
[11]William H. Newman and James P. Logan, *Management of Expanding Enterprises* (New York, 1955).

Composites

To adequately balance the stress on the contradictory objectives or criteria by which performance of a particular individual or organization is appraised, there must be an implied or explicit weighting of these criteria. When such a weighting system is available, it is an easy task to combine the measures of the various subgoals into a composite score for over-all performance.

Such a composite is used by the American Institute of Management in evaluating and ranking the managements of corporations, hospitals, and other organizations.[12] These ratings are accomplished by attaching a numerical grade to each of several criteria, such as economic function, corporate structure, production efficiency, and the like. Each criterion has an optimum rating, and the score on each for any particular organization is added to obtain a total score. Although there may be disagreement on the validity of the weighting system employed, the rating given on any particular category, the categories themselves, or the methods of estimating scores in the A.I.M. management audit, this system is an example of the type of over-all performance measurement which might be developed. Were such a system of ratings employed by an organization and found acceptable by management, it presumably would serve as a guide to obtaining a balanced stress on objectives.

A composite measure of performance was employed in Air Force wings as reported by K. C. Wagner.[13] A complex rating scheme covering a wide range of activities was used. When the organizations were put under pressure to raise their composite score without proportionate increases in the organization's means of achieving them, there were observable unanticipated consequences in the squadrons. Under a system of multiple criteria, pressure to increase performance on one criterion might be relieved by a slackening of effort toward other criteria. But with a composite criterion this does not seem as likely to occur. In Wagner's report individuals were subjected to tension, role and value conflicts, and reduced morale; air crews suffered from intercrew antagonism, apathy, and reduced morale; organization and power structures underwent changes; communications distortions and blockages occurred; integration decreased; culture patterns changed; and norms were violated. Some of these consequences may be desirable, some undesirable. The net result, however, might easily be less effective over-all performance.

These consequences were observable in a situation where goals were increased without a corresponding increase in means, which seems to be a common situation. Berliner refers to the "ratchet principle" wherein an increase in performance becomes the new standard, and the standard is thus continually raised. Recognition of the operation of the "ratchet principle" by workers was documented by F. J. Roethlisberger and William J. Dickson.[14] There was a tacit agreement among the workers not to exceed the quota, for fear that the job would then be rerated. Deliberate restrictions of output is not an uncommon occurrence.

Although the experiences reported with the use of composite measures of

---

[12]*Manual of Excellent Managements* (New York, 1955).

[13]Kenneth C. Wagner, Latent Functions of an Executive Control: A Sociological Analysis of a Social System under Stress, *Research Previews,* vol. 2 (Chapel Hill: Institute for Research in Social Science, March 1954), mimeo.

[14]F. J. Roethlisberger and William J. Dickson, *Management and the Worker* (Cambridge, Mass., 1939).

performance are rather skimpy, there is still a clear indication that their use may have adverse consequences for the over-all performance of the organization.

Conclusion

Quantitative performance measurements—whether single, multiple, or composite—are seen to have undesirable consequences for over-all organizational performance. The complexity of large organizations requires better knowledge of organizational behavior for managers to make best use of the personnel available to them. Even where performance measures are instituted purely for purposes of information, they are probably interpreted as definitions of the important aspects of that job or activity and hence have important implications for the motivation of behavior. The motivational and behavioral consequences of performance measurements are inadequately understood. Further research in this area is necessary for a better understanding of how behavior may be oriented toward optimum accomplishment of the organization's goals.

The Personality vs. Organization Theory

GEORGE STRAUSS

Over the years, out of the contributions of individuals such as Argyris, Herzberg, Maier, Maslow, and McGregor, has come a consistent view of human motivation in industry.[1] With due credit to Chris Argyris, I should like to call it the "personality-versus-organization hypothesis." I shall state this hypothesis briefly first and then criticize it.

The Hypothesis

1. Human behavior in regard to work is motivated by a hierarchy of needs, in ascending order: physical well-being, safety, social satisfaction, egoistic gratification, and self-actualization. By hierarchy is meant that a higher, less basic need does not provide motivation unless all lower, more basic needs are satisfied, and that once a basic need is satisfied, it no longer motivates.

   Physical needs are the most fundamental; but once a reasonable level of

[1] See, for example, Chris Argyris, *Personality and Organization,* Harper & Row, Publishers, Incorporated, New York, 1957; Frederick Herzberg, Bernard Mausner, and Barbara Snyderman, *The Motivation to Work,* John Wiley & Sons, Inc., New York, 1960; Norman R. F. Maier, *Psychology in Industry,* 2d ed., Houghton Mifflin Company, Boston, 1955; A. H. Maslow, *Motivation and Personality,* Harper & Row, Publishers, Incorporated, New York, 1954; Douglas McGregor, *The Human Side of Enterprise,* McGraw-Hill Book Company, Inc., New York, 1960. For an excellent summary of this hypothesis and its application, see James V. Clark, "Motivation and Work Groups: A Tentative View," *Human Organization,* vol. 19, no. 4, pp. 199–208, Winter, 1960–1961. Somewhat the same position is taken by Robert K. Merton in *Social Theory and Social Structure,* rev. ed., The Free Press of Glencoe, New York, 1957, and by Philip Selznick in *TVA and the Grassroots,* University of California Press, Berkeley, Calif., 1949; both suggest that organizational attempts to obtain conformity lead to unanticipated consequences, such as lack of innovation and even rebellion.

physical-need satisfaction is obtained (largely through pay), individuals become relatively more concerned with other needs. First they seek to satisfy their security needs (e.g., through seniority and fringe benefits). When these, too, are reasonably satisfied, social needs (e.g., friendship and group support) take first priority. And so forth. Thus, for example, hungry men have little interest in whether or not they belong to strong social groups; relatively well-off individuals are more anxious for good human relations.

Only when most of the less pressing needs are satisfied will individuals turn to the ultimate form of satisfaction, self-actualization, which is described by Maslow as "the desire to become more and more what one is, to become everything that one is capable of becoming. . . . A musician must make music, an artist must paint, a poet must write, if he is to be ultimately happy. What a man *can* be, he *must* be."[2]

2. Healthy individuals desire to mature, to satisfy increasingly higher levels of needs; in practice they want more and more opportunity to form strong social groups, to be independent and creative, to exercise autonomy and discretion, and to develop and express their unique personalities with freedom.
3. The organization, on the other hand, seeks to program individual behavior and reduce discretion. It demands conformity, obedience, dependence, and immature behavior. The assembly-line worker, the engineer, and the executive are all subject to strong pressures to behave in a programmed, conformist fashion.[3] As a consequence, many individuals feel alienated from their work.
4. Subordinates react to these pressures in a number of ways, most of which are dysfunctional to the organization. Individuals may fight back through union activity, sabotage, output restriction, and other forms of rational or irrational (aggressive) behavior. Or they may withdraw and engage in regression, sublimation, childish behavior, failure to contribute creative ideas, or to produce more than a minimum amount of work. In any case, employes struggle not to conform (at least at first). To keep these employes in line, management must impose still more restrictions and force still more immature behavior. Thus a vicious cycle begins.
5. Management pressures often lead to excessive competition and splintering of work groups and the consequent loss of cooperation and social satisfaction. Or work groups may become even stronger, but their norms may now be anti-management, those of protecting individuals against pressures from above.
6. A subtle management, which provides high wages, liberal employee benefits, "hygienic," "decent" supervision, and not too much pressure to work, may well induce employees to think they are happy and not *dissatisfied.*[4] But they

---

[2] A. H. Maslow, "A Theory of Human Motivation," *Psychological Review,* vol. 40, p. 372, 1943.

[3] These three groups are discussed in Charles R. Walker and Robert H. Guest, *The Man on the Assembly Line,* Harvard University Press, Cambridge, Mass., 1952; Herbert Shepard, "Nine Dilemmas in Industrial Research," *Administrative Science Quarterly,* vol. 1, no. 3, pp. 245–259, Fall, 1960; and William H. Whyte, Jr., *The Organization Man,* Simon and Schuster, Inc., New York, 1956.

[4] Herzberg, Mausner, and Snyderman distinguish between *dissatisfiers* (basically, the absence of "hygienic" factors such as good "supervision, interpersonal relations, physical working conditions, salary, company policies, and administrative practices, benefits, and job security," *op. cit.,* p. 113) and *motivators* (basically, challenge, autonomy, interesting work). Similar conclusions are reached by Gerald Guerin, Joseph Veroff, and Sheila Feld, *Americans View Their Mental Health,* Basic Books, Inc., Publishers, New York, 1960. The Herzberg, Mausner, and Snyderman analysis is criticized by Victor Vroom and Norman R. F. Maier in "Industrial Social Psychology," Paul Farnsworth (ed.), *Annual Review of Psychology, Annual Reviews,* vol. 12, Palo Alto, Calif., 1960.

are not (or should not be) truly *satisfied;* they are apathetic and have settled for a low level of aspiration. They do as little work as they can get away with and still hold their jobs. This unhealthy situation is wasteful both to the individual and to the organization.

7. Some differences in emphasis are found among authorities as to whether the behavior of the typical subordinate under these circumstances will be rational (reality-oriented) or irrational (frustration-oriented). In any case, organizational pressures, particularly the subjection to programmed work, may lead to serious personality disturbances and mental illness.[5] Traditional organizational techniques thus not only prevent the organization from operating at maximum efficiency, but in terms of their impact on individual adjustment, are also very expensive to the society as a whole.
8. The only healthy solution is for management to adopt policies which promote intrinsic job satisfaction, individual development, and creativity, according to which people will willingly and voluntarily work toward organizational objectives because they enjoy their work and feel that it is important to do a good job.[6] More specifically, management should promote job enlargement, general supervision, strong, cohesive work groups, and decentralization. In a nutshell, management should adopt what Harold Leavitt calls "power-equalization techniques."

Criticism

The view expressed above is, in a sense, a hypothesis as to human behavior in organizations. But it is more than a coldly objective hypothesis: It is a prescription for management behavior, and implicit in it are strong value judgments.[7] With its strong emphasis on individual dignity, creative freedom, and self-development, this hypothesis bears all the earmarks of its academic origin.

Professors place high value on autonomy, inner direction, and the quest for maximum self-development. As much as any other group in society, their existence is work-oriented; for them, creative achievement is an end in itself and requires no further justification. Most professors are strongly convinced of the righteousness of their Protestant ethic of hard work and see little incongruity in imposing it upon the less fortunate.

And yet there are many misguided individuals (perhaps the bulk of the population) who do not share the professors' values and would not be happy in a professor's job. Further, the technical requirements of many lines of work are very different from those of academia. Academie work is best accomplished

[5] Recent evidence suggests that unskilled workers are significantly more likely to suffer from personality disturbances and psychosomatic illnesses than are skilled workers, and that these differences become manifest only after the individuals take up their work. (In other words, once individuals land in unskilled jobs, they tend to become more maladjusted.) Arthur Kornhauser, "Mental Health of Factory Workers: A Detroit Study," *Human Organization,* vol. 21, no. 1, pp. 43–46, Spring, 1962; John R. P. French, Jr., Robert L. Kahn, and Floyd C. Mann (eds.), "Work, Health and Satisfaction," *The Journal of Social Issues,* vol. 18, no. 3, July, 1962.

[6] Perhaps the most general statement of this position is McGregor's Theory Y. See McGregor, *op. cit.*

[7] There seems to be a certain amount of confusion as to whether prescriptions for power equalization are written from the point of view of organizational efficiency or mental health (and possibly the degree of confusion has increased since the primary source of research funds in this area has shifted from the military to the National Institute of Mental Health). There are those who claim that what is good for the individual will, in the long run, be good for the organization and vice versa. Nevertheless, it is useful to keep one's criteria explicit.

by those who adhere to academic values, but it is questionable whether these values are equally functional in other lines of work, where creativity is not required to get the job done, but only the ability to follow orders.

In the pages which follow, I shall seek to reevaluate the personality-versus-organization hypothesis. I shall suggest, first, that it contains many debatable value judgments and, second, that it ignores what Harold Leavitt has called "organizational economics." I shall conclude that a broad range of people do not seek self-actualization on the job—and that this may be a fortunate thing, because it might be prohibitively expensive to redesign some jobs to permit self-actualization.

Value Judgments

It seems to me that the hypothesis, as often stated, overemphasizes (1) the uniqueness of the personality-organization conflict to large-scale industry, (2) the universality of the desire to achieve self-actualization, and (3) the importance of the job (as opposed to the community or the home) as a source of need satisfaction. Too little attention is given to economic motivation.[8]

The Uniqueness of the Problem

At least some authors seem to overdramatize the personality-organization conflict as something unique to large-scale organization (particularly to mass-production industry). But this conflict is merely one aspect of what has been variously characterized as the conflict between individual and society, individual and environment, desire and reality, id and super ego. "Thus the formal organization . . . is not truly the real villain; rather any kind of organized activity, from the most democratic to the most authoritarian, contains within itself the necessary conditions for conflict."[9]

Similarly the impact of the industrial revolution on work satisfaction can be overemphasized. Much is made of "alienation" (dictionary meaning: *turning away*) from work. Comparisons are constantly made between the old-time craftsman who did the entire job and the mass-production worker of today. But I doubt whether the medieval serf or the Egyptian slave enjoyed much sense of autonomy or creativity (though, one might perhaps argue that he had more of a sense of identification and less of a feeling of anomie than does his better-fed modern counterpart). Perhaps there is less job satisfaction today than there was 100 years ago. Obviously no objective ways can be devised to measure this change, but my surmise is that the turning away has been less dramatic than some have suggested. Boring, programmed jobs have existed throughout history.

Others are as skeptical as I am of the theory of increased alienation. In his conclusion to a survey of job-satisfaction studies, Robert Blauner questions

> . . . the prevailing thesis that most workers in modern society are alienated and estranged. There is a remarkable consistency in the findings that the

---

[8]I must confess that many of these criticisms apply to my own writing. See George Strauss and Leonard R. Sayles, *Personnel: The Human Problems of Management,* Prentice-Hall, Inc., Englewood Cliffs, N.J., 1960, especially chaps. 4–8 and 12, chapters for which I was responsible. See the review by Arthur Brayfield, "Treating Faint Workers," *Contemporary Psychology,* vol. 2, no. 3, pp. 92–93, March, 1962.

[9]Warren G. Bennis, "Leadership Theory and Administrative Behavior," *Administrative Science Quarterly,* vol. 4, no. 3, p. 281, December, 1959. Ironically, some of those most concerned with the tyranny of the organization would substitute for it the tyranny of the participative group.

vast majority of workers, in virtually all occupations and industries, are moderately or highly satisfied, rather than dissatisfied with their jobs. . . . The real character of the [pre-mass production] craftsman's work has been romanticized by the prevalent tendency to idealize the past. . . .[10]

And J. A. C. Brown asserts that "in modern society there is far greater scope of skill and craftsmanship than in any previous society."[11]

The Universality of the Desire for Self-Actualization

The basic hypothesis implies a strong moral judgment that people should want freedom and self-actualization,[12] that it is somehow morally wrong for people to be lazy, unproductive, and uncreative. It seems to me that the hypothesis overemphasizes individuals' desires for freedom and underemphasizes their desire for security. It can even be argued that some of the personality-versus-organization writing has a fairly antisocial, even nihilistic flavor; it seems to emphasize individual freedom and self-development as the all-important value. Yet mature behavior does not mean freedom from all restrictions; it means successful adjustment to them.

As Erich Fromm has suggested, most people don't want complete freedom. They want to know the limits within which they can act (and this is true both on and off the job). To put it another way: Most people are willing to tolerate and may even be anxious for a few areas of their lives to be unpredictable and exciting, but they insist that in a majority of areas events should occur as expected. The research scientist, for example, may relish the novelty and uncertainty of laboratory work, but he insists that his secretary always be on call, that his technician give predictable responses, and that his car start with complete regularity.

True, some people seek much less confining limits than do others, and some are not too upset if the limits are fuzzy. Many, however, feel most comfortable if they work in a highly defined situation. For them freedom is a burden; they want firm, secure leadership. And many more, if not fully happy with programmed work, accommodate to it rather easily.

Argyris, for example, might reply that such individuals are immature personalities who have adjusted to organization restrictions by becoming apathetic and dependent; were the organization environment healthy, these individuals would react differently. But in many cases the restrictions which conditioned these people occurred in childhood or are present in the culture. Such individuals may be too far gone in dependence to react well to power equalization, and their attitude is not likely to be changed short of intensive psychotherapy. Indeed many people may have internalized and made part of their self-concept a low level of aspiration regarding their on-the-job responsibilities and their ability to handle them. What psychologists call the "theory of dissonance" suggests that sudden attempts to increase their sense of autonomy and self-determination might be quite disturbing.

---

[10] "Work Satisfaction and Industrial Trends in Modern Society," in Walter Galenson and Seymour Martin Lipset, *Labor and Trade Unionism,* John Wiley & Sons, Inc., New York, 1960, pp. 352–353.

[11] J. A. C. Brown, *The Social Psychology of Industry,* Penguin Books, Inc., Baltimore, 1954, p. 207.

[12] Though the concept of self-actualization seems penetrating, I tend to agree with Bennis that it "is at best, an ill-defined concept . . . [and that] self-actualized man seems to be more myth than reality," *op. cit.,* p. 279.

Impressive evidence of the need for self-actualization is provided by the preliminary results of the mental-health studies which suggest that poor mental health is correlated with holding low-skilled jobs. And yet the evidence is still not complete. Apparently not everyone suffers equally from unskilled work, and some adjust more easily than others. (Perhaps these studies will help us to improve the prediction process, so that we can do a better job of selecting and even training people for this kind of work.)

Further, it is far from clear whether this lower mental health is caused primarily by the intrinsic nature of unskilled work, or by the fact that such work pays poorly and has low status both off and on the job.[13] In so far as mental disturbances are caused by economic and social pressures at home, higher wages may be a better solution than improved human relations on the job or a rearrangement of work assignments.

A hasty glance at the research in this field, as summarized in two reviews,[14] makes it abundantly clear that unskilled workers are not the only ones who suffer from poor mental health. Depending on which study one looks at or what mental-health index is used, one can conclude that executives, clerical personnel, salespeople, and lower-level supervisors all suffer from below-average mental health. The evidence makes one sympathize with the old Quaker, "All the world is queer save me and thee; and sometimes I think even thee is a little queer."

The Job as the Primary Source of Satisfaction

There is an additional value judgment in the basic hypothesis that the *job* should be a primary form of need satisfaction for everyone (as it is for professors). But the central focus of many people's lives is not the job (which is merely a way of getting a living), but the home or the community. Many people find a full measure of challenge, creativity, and autonomy in raising a family, pursuing a hobby, or taking part in community affairs. As Robert Dubin puts it:

> Work, for probably a majority of workers, and even extending into the ranks of management, may represent an institutional setting that is not the central life interest of the participants. The consequence of this is that while participating in work a general attitude of apathy and indifference prevails. . . . Thus, the industrial worker does not feel imposed upon by the tyranny of organizations, company, or union.[15]

In my own interviewing experience in factories, I often ran across women who repeated variants of, "I like this job because it gets me away from all the kids and pressures at home." One girl even told me, "The job is good because

---

[13] Both the Wayne State and the Michigan studies emphasize that no single factor explains the relationship. Kornhauser concludes (*op. cit.*, p. 46): "Both on rational grounds and from empirical evidence, I see no reason to think that it is useful to single out one or a few of the job-related characteristics as distinctly important. . . . If we are to understand why mental health is poorer in less-skilled, more routine factory jobs, we must look at the entire pattern of work and life conditions of people in these occupations—not just at single variables."

[14] Stanislav V. Kasl and John R. P. French, Jr., "The Effects of Occupational Status on Physical and Mental Health," *Journal of Social Issues,* vol. 18, no. 3, pp. 67–89, July, 1962; Vroom and Maier, *op. cit.* See also Guerin, Veroff, and Feld, *op. cit.,* p. 162.

[15] "Industrial Research and the Discipline of Sociology," *Proceedings of the 11th Annual Meeting, Industrial Relations Research Association,* Madison, Wis., 1959, p. 161.

it gives me a chance to think about God." Such individuals may feel little need for power equalization.

In any case, as Kerr, Harbison, Dunlop, and Myers predict, work, in the future, will doubtless be increasingly programmed and will provide fewer and fewer opportunities for creativity and discretion on the job.[16] On the other hand, the hours will grow shorter, and there will be a "new bohemianism" off the job. All this suggests the irreverent notion that *perhaps* the best use of our resources is to accelerate automation, shorten the workweek just as fast as possible, forget about on-the-job satisfactions, and concentrate our energies on making leisure more meaningful.

Underemphasis on Economic Rewards

At the same time that the hypothesis overemphasizes the job as a source of need satisfaction, it also underemphasizes the role of money as a means of motivation. The hypothesis says that once employees obtain a satisfying level of economic reward they go on to other needs and, presumably, are less concerned with money. However, the level of reward which is *satisfying* can rise rapidly over time. Further, money is a means of satisfying higher needs, too—ego, safety, and, for some, even self-actualization, e.g., the individual who (perhaps misguidedly) seeks to live his life off the job engaging in "creative" consumption. True, employees expect much better physical, psychological, and social conditions on the job today than they did fifty years ago. But they also expect more money. There is little evidence that money has ceased to be a prime motivator.

Organizational Economics

Perhaps the most fundamental criticisms of the personality-organization hypothesis is that it ignores (or at least misapplies) "organizational economics," that is, it fails to balance carefully the costs and gains of power equalization. To be sure, most power-equalization advocates point out the hidden costs of autocracy: apathetic and resentful employees, turnover, absenteeism, sabotage, resistance to change, and all the rest. Traditional forms of supervision may be expensive in terms of the lost motivation and energy which might have been turned to organizational ends; they are even more expensive in terms of mental health. Yet some writers, in their moments of wilder enthusiasm, tend to overestimate the gains from what they propose and underestimate the costs.

The Gains From Power Equalization

It is argued that traditional organizational methods lead either to dissatisfaction, anxiety, and aggression or to dependency, conformity, and doing only a minimum of work—and that these problems would be reduced by power equalization.

Carried to excess, anxiety and aggression are undoubtedly harmful both to the organization and the individual. But many psychological studies suggest that dissatisfaction and anxiety (and even aggression, depending on how it is defined)

---

[16] Clark Kerr, John T. Dunlop, Fredrick H. Harbison, and Charles A. Myers, *Industrialism and Industrial Man: The Problems of Labor and Management in Economic Growth,* Harvard University Press, Cambridge, Mass., 1960.

spur individuals to work harder. Autocratic, work-oriented bosses very often get out high production; on occasion, their subordinates even develop high morale and cohesive work groups.[17]

Still, beyond certain limits, dissatisfaction, anxiety, and aggression are not in the organization's interests. There is much more doubt about apathy and conformity. It is often argued that an apathetic worker who is subject to "hygienic" supervision will work only enough to avoid getting fired, that he will never exercise creativity or imagination or execute an outstanding performance. On many jobs, however, management has no use for outstanding performance. What is outstanding performance on the part of an assembly-line worker? That he works faster than the line? That he shows creativity and imagination on the job? Management wants none of these. *Adequate* performance is all that can be used on the assembly line and probably on a growing number (I know no figures) of other jobs in our society. Here the conformable, dependent worker may well be the best.[18] As Leavitt and Whisler put it, "The issue of morale versus productivity that now worries us may pale as programming moves in. The morale of programmed personnel may be of less central concern because less (or at least a different sort of) productivity will be demanded of them."[19]

Even at the management level, there may be an increasing need for conforming, unimaginative types of "organization men," if the future verifies Leavitt's and Whisler's prediction that "jobs at today's middle-management levels will become highly structured. Much more of the work will be programmed, i.e., covered by sets of operating rules governing the day-to-day decisions that are made."[20] Despite *The Organization Man* it might be argued that nonconformity will be useful to the organization only in increasingly limited doses.

The Costs of Power Equalization

On the other hand, power equalization can be quite costly to the organization. To make general supervision or participative management work, many of the old-line autocratic supervisors must be retrained or replaced; this is a costly process, which may result in the demoralization or elimination of the organization's most technically competent individuals. It is extremely difficult to develop internalized motivation on many routine jobs; once the traditional, external sanctions (for example, monetary rewards and fear of discharge) are removed, *net* motivation may fall on balance. And it is fairly meaningless to talk of delegation of authority to assembly-line workers or girls on a punch-card operation; the very nature of the technology requires that all essential decisions be made centrally.

"But if the nature of the job makes power-equalization techniques imprac-

---

[17]For a list of the conditions under which "authoritarian leadership might be as effective as its alternatives," see Harold L. Wilensky, "Human Relations in the Workplace," Arensberg and others (eds.), *Research in Industrial Human Relations,* Harper & Row, Publishers, Incorporated, New York, 1957, pp. 25–50. Interestingly, the personality-organization hypothesis is strongly influenced by Freud. Yet Freud postulated that "productive work is partially a function of the expression of hostility to the leader" (Bennis, *op. cit.,* p. 292).

[18]For an outstanding example see William J. Goode and Irving Fowler, "Incentive Factors in a Low Morale Plant," *American Sociological Review,* vol. 14, no. 5, pp. 619–624, October, 1949.

[19]Harold Leavitt and Thomas Whisler, "Management in the 1980s" *Harvard Business Review,* vol. 36, no. 6, p. 46, November, 1958.

[20]Ibid., p. 41.

tical," some may argue, "change the nature of the job." Rensis Likert puts this well:

> To be highly motivated, each member of the organization must feel that the organization's objectives are of significance and that his own particular task contributes in an indispensable manner to the organization's achievement of its objectives. He should see his role as difficult, important, and meaningful. This is necessary if the individual is to achieve and maintain a sense of personal worth and importance. *When jobs do not meet this specification they should be reorganized so that they do.*[21]

True, there are many opportunities to redesign jobs and work flows so as to increase various forms of job satisfaction such as autonomy and achievement.[22] But whether such changes should be made is a matter for organization economics.

These changes, when accompanied by appropriate forms of supervision and proper selection of personnel, may sometimes result in substantial increases of productivity. (Purely technological losses in efficiency may be more than offset by increased motivation, less work-flow friction, and the like.) Obviously, in such instances organizational economics would dictate that the changes should be introduced.

But in other areas technological changes can be made only at a substantial cost in terms of productivity—and the impact of automation and information technology seems to be increasing the number of jobs where change would prove costly. Should we scrap the advances of technology in these areas in order to foster good human relations? Or should we say "Thank God for the number of people who have made an apparent adjustment to routine jobs. Would that there were more!"? Perhaps—as has been suggested earlier—it would be best to devote our resources to shortening the workweek continuously and helping people to enjoy their leisure more fully.

Considerable evidence leads to the conclusion that a relatively stable situation can exist, in which workers perform relatively routine, programmed jobs under hygienic supervision.[23] Though these workers may not be satisfied (in the Herzberg sense) and may be immature, apathetic, and dependent (in the Argyris sense), they are not actively dissatisfied; they do not feel a need for additional responsibility; and they seek meaning in life from their home and community rather than from their job. To be sure, these individuals are maximizing neither their productive efforts nor their possible job satisfaction. But both management and employees find the situation suffices their needs. Barring sudden change, it is stable. It may well be the best we are likely to get in many situations without costly changes in such important matters as technology and child upbringing.

---

[21] Rensis Likert, *New Patterns of Management,* New York, McGraw-Hill Book Company, Inc., 1960, p. 103. (The italics are my own.)

[22] See, for example, Louis E. Davis and Richard Werling, "Job Design Factors," *Occupational Psychology,* vol. 34, no. 2, pp. 109–132, April, 1960, Georges Friedmann, *Industrial Society,* The Free Press of Glencoe, New York, 1955; Eliot D. Chapple and Leonard R. Sayles, *The Measure of Management,* The Macmillan Company, New York, 1961; Strauss and Sayles, *op. cit.,* chaps. 2 and 16.

[23] For example, Chris Argyris, *Understanding Human Behavior,* Richard D. Irwin, Inc., Homewood, Ill., 1960, Chap. 5.

Summary

My concern has been with the personality-versus-organization hypothesis. I have tried to demonstrate:

1. Though many individuals find relatively little satisfaction in their work, the absence of gratification may not be so great a deprivation as the hypothesis would suggest, since many of these same individuals center their lives off the job and find most of their satisfaction in the community and the home. For these individuals power equalization may not liberate much energy.
2. Individuals are not motivated solely to obtain autonomy or self-actualization. With various degrees of emphasis, individuals also want security and the knowledge of what is expected of them. Power equalization may certainly stir up a good deal of anxiety among those who are not prepared for it, and at least some individuals may be reluctant to assume the responsibility it throws upon them.
3. Power-equalization techniques have little meaning when management needs no more than an adequate level of production, as is often the case when work is highly programmed. Under such circumstances the costs entailed by modification in job design and supervisory techniques may be greater than the gains obtained from increased motivation to work.

All of the above does not mean either that the personality-versus-organization hypothesis is meaningless or that power-equalization techniques are not useful. Quite the contrary. What it does mean is that many individuals can accommodate themselves to the demands of the organization without too much psychological loss, and that for them the personality-organization conflict is not particularly frustrating. Similarly, in many circumstances the gains to the organization from power equalization may be moderate and more than offset by its costs.

For other individuals (for example, scientists working in large companies) the personality-organization conflict may be felt quite acutely. For the most part they are the very individuals whose work cannot be programmed and from whom management wants more than merely adequate production.

Our summary reemphasizes the often-made point that no single style of leadership can be universally appropriate. The techniques which work on the assembly line will almost certainly fail with research scientists. Indeed it is fair to predict that, over time, the differences among supervisory styles may increase. Perhaps in the future we shall have at one extreme research scientists and others doing creative work, who will be putting in a forty-hour or longer workweek under conditions of relative power equalization. At the other extreme may be those who submit to close supervision on highly programmed jobs, but for only twenty hours or so. Shades of Brave New World: the alphas and gammas!

Questions for Discussion

1. Why does hierarchy characterize virtually all human organizations?

2. A theologian once observed that man is the only creature who has the ability to plan. How is this reflected in organizations?

3. What is the danger in specifying *any* policies, procedures, or performance standards?

4. Thomas Jefferson once described the Presidency of the United States as "a splendid misery." To a lesser extent, this might be said of any executive position. Why?

5. One observer of modern business has written: "The so-called private business corporation owned by many individual stockholders is in effect a private government with officials who are only loosely responsible to the owners. They are even less responsible to the citizens of the government—the employes. In spite of management's appeal to rational decision making and scientific organization, its fundamental internal administration is authoritarian. The business organization especially implies more of Genghis Khan than Thomas Jefferson. This centralized authority is not justified and must be replaced by a more democratic system whereby employes at all levels have guarantees about due process and representation." How would you agree or disagree with this position?

6. Recently, students at a number of large universities have organized "free universities" with small, specialized courses on contemporary and esoteric subjects offered gratis by volunteer instructors. The founders' intentions were to offer a wider choice of courses, more flexibility, and greater individual attention than was available in the regular universities with their red tape and bureaucracy. The student founder of the largest of these free universities later resigned with a bitter comment on the growth of bureaucratic structure and inhibiting rules even within the new institution. Discuss.

7. "Publish or perish" is a phrase describing one aspect of academic practice. Discuss why publication has apparently come to carry such weight in the promotion and tenure of professors. What are the pros and cons of such criteria?

8. In a large eastern state, high-school teachers were once evaluated and rewarded by school administrators on the basis of their students' scores on statewide Regents' examinations. Discuss the advantages and disadvantages of such a measure.

9. You have seen that a number of writers feel that there is conflict between human needs and organization requirements. The needs of the mature individual (for autonomy, satisfying social relationships, and self-actualization) seem to conflict with the organization's needs for hierarchy, subordination, control, and predictability. Why might management want to alleviate the conflict? How might management (or anyone) do this? Do you expect management to make more or fewer such efforts in the future?

10. A 1960 study by Sergio Talacchi reported that employe morale and job satisfaction tend to be lower in larger organizations than in smaller ones. As corporations grow larger, he reports, there is a significant decrease in satisfaction with the company, supervision, fellow employes, and the job. Other studies report higher rates of absenteeism and turnover in larger organizations. On the other hand, a 1963 study by Lyman Porter indicates that management positions in larger organizations are seen as more rewarding and satisfying than those in smaller organizations. In addition, Porter reports that managers in larger organizations say that they have more freedom and autonomy and less need for conformity than in smaller companies. How would you explain these findings?

Chapter Five

The Impact of Informal Organization: Social Factors in Organizational Behavior

In thermodynamics we learn that nature abhors vacuum, instability, and chaos. Void is replaced by activity, instability by stability, and disorder by order. Similarly, man abhors ambiguity and formlessness. In his human relationships, he tends to create structure and impose order. Since man is a social animal, as the saying goes, the informal construction and elaboration of organization is common human practice. Informal organization is most evident in the development of small groups. "What is distinctly human," stated Berelson and Steiner [3], "comes from the primary fact that man lives his life in groups with other people (p. 325)." Behavioral scientists, therefore, have given a great deal of attention to groups—from families to military squads to work groups.

Informal Organization and the Individual

In a fascinating study, Edgar Schein [16] suggests the essential purposes of informal organization and groups. During and after the Korean War in the early 1950's, widespread concern was voiced about the behavior of U.S. Army prisoners of war in North Korea. Since there were few escapes, many deaths from disease, and numerous instances of apparent collaboration, many Americans in this country were distressed. POW behavior was interpreted to indicate that America's youth were decadent, soft, ignorant of their mission, and unpatriotic [13]. The implication: Unless our moral fiber stiffens, all will be lost to Communism.

It is probably true that the men fighting in Korea were not as clear about the issues involved as were the soldiers in World War II. Schein, nonetheless, suggests other reasons for the problems of death, escape and collaboration in the Korean camps.

First-hand observers were impressed by the different attitudes characterizing newly liberated American prisoners in Korea as compared with American prisoners freed in Germany. Cheering, jubilation, and happiness characterized the latter; quiet, sullenness, and anxiety the former. Subsequent investigation indicated differences in the conditions, treatment, and organization of the prisoners in Nazi Germany and Communist Korea:

- In the Nazi camps sharp disparities existed between the conditions of prisoners and guards. The prisoners received worse food, clothing, and shelter.
- The Nazis dealt with the prisoners through a military structure by recognizing rank, requiring American officers to police and maintain the internal organization.
- When interrogating, prisoners were brought in individually, questioned, and returned to the unit. If any torture had been applied, the theory was that the unfortunate sufferer would serve as an example to frighten the others and induce them to talk when they were brought in.
- Under these conditions, there was a relatively low death rate from illness, almost no instances of collaboration, and many escapes.

Conditions in Korea were very different:

- Many of the prisoners were taken after the Chinese attacked across the Yalu River and the Americans retreated in one of the few routs in U.S. Army history. Disorganized, separated from their units, wandering in a strange land, the soldiers were captured by the Chinese and marched to prison camps. On the march the Chinese continually reminded them that they were the Americans' friends and that the prisoners were lucky to have been captured by the Chinese. If they had been taken by the North Koreans, the Chinese maintained, the Americans would have been killed because as capitalist imperialists they had attacked the homeland of the North Koreans.
- During the march there were few contrasts between conditions for the prisoners and for their guards. The Chinese captors shared their limited food and medicine and, by and large, had things about as bad as the prisoners.
- At the prison camps, officers were separated from enlisted men. In some instances lower ranking men were intentionally placed in charge of noncommissioned officers—a situation that many privates might enjoy.
- Groups were systematically broken up and people transferred between barracks in order to forestall the development of a military or informal organization.
- With some notorious exceptions, the Chinese used relatively little physical torture, and even their so-called brain washing techniques were relatively simple. After a man was interrogated, however, he was not sent back to his old unit. He would reappear elsewhere in the camp, perhaps with new clothes. This meant that the prisoners in the barracks did not know what kind of experience they were facing or what kind of questions they were going to be asked. It was difficult for them to prepare themselves psychologically for the experience. Finally, there was some suspicion over how their former buddy had behaved.
- Under these conditions, there was low morale, much illness and a high death rate, few escapes, and compromising answers in the interviews.

The major problems in the Communist prisoner of war camps resulted from inadequate military or social structure; neither support nor discipline was given to the individual. In the German camps, on the other hand, there was a structure which enabled a prisoner to prepare himself and to gain some strength from his buddies prior to interrogation. He also had to come back to his friends, which would be difficult and dangerous if he compromised himself to the Nazis. In the Chinese camps the prisoner did not have adequate preparation for the interviews, and he did not have to go back to face his barracks mates. Consequently, when asked questions that sounded rather unimportant and innocuous, or when told that his friend had provided information, the soldier tended to respond more than he should.

Escapes were rare in Korea, according to Schein, because escape is a group activity; trust is essential. The men simply could not get organized. Because of frequent transfers, they did not have time to develop the cooperative efforts necessary for escape. In addition, of course, they were Occidentals in an Oriental world, and this made escape much more difficult than it had been for American prisoners in Germany. So, in the Communist prisoner of war camps, morale was low, the will to survive declined, and the death rate was greater than physical differences between the Chinese and Nazi camps would explain. Friends can help a man to fight even germs.

What the Group Offers the Individual

The foregoing narrative indicates that the group serves three functions for the individual: (1) the satisfaction of complex social needs, (2) emotional support in identifying oneself and dealing with the world, and (3) assistance in meeting goals. The Korean memoirs of General William Dean [6] well describe some of these functions. General Dean won the Congressional Medal of Honor for his heroism in Korea. Nonetheless, he points out that he talked to his captors more than he should have. After prolonged solitary confinement and existence on poor rations slipped under a door, Dean had an overwhelming compulsion to talk when taken to the Chinese interrogator. He responded positively to his interrogator even though he knew the man was his enemy.

Satisfaction of Social Needs

Most fundamentally, men join groups because of a need for affiliation. The basis of affiliation ranges from simple enjoyment of other human beings to more complex desires for group affirmation of an individual's self-conception. Thus, affiliation can either be a means to an end or an end in itself. For General Dean, desires for companionship flowed automatically from the human relationship—even between the prisoner and his keeper. Similarly, veteran soldiers comment on the tendency of new recruits to stick together for friendship and support when under stress—even though they know it increases rather than decreases the danger.

Research indicates that employees who have no opportunity for social contact find their work unsatisfying. This lack of satisfaction may reflect itself in low production, high turnover, and absenteeism. In the earliest of his classic research efforts, Elton Mayo [14] observed that employees in a textile plant who worked in isolated jobs were highly dissatisfied and consistently failed to meet production standards. When the company permitted these workers to take rest periods as a group, production and satisfaction increased. Similarly, other observers have suggested that maids in hospitals feel uncomfortable when they work only in the company of doctors and nurses. Some hospitals have discovered that, when three or four maids are grouped together as a team, turnover is reduced and a more effective job is done [5]. Donald Roy's selected article following this chapter offers a vivid picture of the enjoyment and assistance derived from informal games, banter, and horseplay on the job.

Identification and Emotional Support

Our prisoner examples do not mean that compromise and collaboration are inevitable just because man craves affection; the process is more subtle. As General Dean points out, he just wasn't sure what was right and what was wrong. Isolated from human companionship and communication, he lost touch with the essential basis and support for ethical behavior—social corroboration of individual conscience. Even the development of that conscience is heavily influenced by social contact, because self-identification is greatly affected by others. This is clear in the teenager, for example. He tries to be everything his friends say he should be. Unintelligible songs, mini-skirts, and Neanderthal haircuts all reflect the teenager's efforts to define himself in terms of his companions. Self-image derives from social image. The painful search for self-identity has, of course, been the subject of moving literature from James Joyce to J. D. Salinger.

In a prisoner of war situation, a strong group can assist the individual to define the basis of ethical behavior. So also in the shop and office, the group can guide the individual in knowing what is desirable and undesirable behavior. How much time should he take for a coffee break? Is it all right to talk to fellow employees while the boss is in the room? Must all copy be shown to the advertising manager? Even where there are established rules, a question remains: Is everyone expected to live by the letter of the law? Most employees don't want to violate the generally accepted rules of the game; at the same time, they don't want to conform to restrictive rules that everyone else ignores. They want to know the right thing to do. The group fills an important function by providing its members with a kind of guide to correct behavior—not correctness in terms of written policies but in terms of what is actually acceptable.

Not only does the group influence the individual's conception of intangible values. Social pressure may also affect perception of physical events. In a famous study, Solomon Asch [2] demonstrated that a single individual has difficulty in holding out against the weight of an otherwise unanimous group judgment even on matters in which the group is clearly in error. A selected article following this chapter by Dorwin Cartwright and Ronald Lippitt describes this process.

Research in military units indicates that the group can give support, perhaps even courage, to the individual in a dangerous situation. Young Joe Marm, a second lieutenant on duty in South Vietnam in the autumn of 1965, grabbed up two side arms and a pile of grenades, ran up a hill alone, and attacked and destroyed a machine gun nest, killing eight Viet Cong. Upon being recommended for the Congressional Medal of Honor, Marm was asked why he made the attack. His reply was simple: "What would the fellows have thought of me if I had been afraid to do it?" (*New York Times,* 17:2, Nov. 17, 1966). Similarly, in studies of soldiers in World War II, there is evidence that those men closely tied to cohesive groups were more responsible in carrying out their duties, more confident of being able to perform well as soldiers, less fearful in battle, and less likely to capitulate or surrender under stress [17]. These studies also indicated that the soldier's willingness to show bravery and make sacrifices was correlated not with loyalty to country or understanding of the war issues but with loyalty to the immediate group. In other words, men who performed heroic acts were motivated largely by the desire not to let their buddies down. The case of Lieutenant Joe Marm would seem to indicate that things have not changed.

Of course, some people have stronger self-identification and conscience than others. They could stand against a group or initiate action on their own. Nonetheless, the group can assist most individuals, if not all, in being true to themselves. Support of the group in maintaining morale and identity was critical in the Korean prisoner of war situation; its absence helped to explain why there was so much distrust, sickness, and death among the prisoners. As the poet John Donne said, "No man is an island entire of itself."

Life in the business organization is not so dangerous. Nonetheless, group support can be just as necessary to the individual—especially to the low-skilled worker who, as one person, is relatively unimportant to management. In a selected article following this chapter, Fred E. Katz describes how informal work groups at low levels serve as a vehicle for expressing independence from management and help bind blue-collar workers to the formal organization: "This produces continuity between the workman's outside life and his participation in the work setting—a setting to which he [may have] very limited allegiance."

Assistance in Meeting Objectives

Groups do more than just satisfy social, psychological, and metaphysical needs. The group can assist in solving very specific problems and protect the individual from his mistakes. A new sales clerk may not be sure about how to handle a complicated problem of returning merchandise. A lab technician may be hesitant about asking his boss to repeat instructions yet be afraid he may ruin the experiment unless he receives additional information. In each case the employee turns to his fellow workers for assistance; most prefer this source of help. Peter Blau has illustrated how federal agents consistently prefer getting assistance from fellow employees as opposed to going to their manager [4]. Indeed, this ability to provide assistance is a source of substantial prestige for the giver.

So far, we have emphasized what the group can do for the individual; in addition, a group as a collectivity develops goals. The behavior of groups in pursuit of these goals is of primary concern to the manager. We shall analyze the strategy and tactics of goal-oriented actions in the next chapter. Before we consider this, however, let us investigate the development of informal organization on the job.

The Development of Informal Organization

When we speak of informal organization, we usually mean small groups:

> By small groups is meant an aggregate of people, from two up to an unspecified but not too large a number, who associate together in face-to-face relations over an extended period of time, who differentiate themselves in some regard from others around them, and who are mutually aware of their membership in the group [3, p. 325].

Such informal work groups develop out of formal organizations. When management brings people together in the office or in the plant where it expects them to communicate and work together, inevitable elaboration occurs. Interaction theory provides one of the best perspectives for describing the emergence of informal organization and groups. As we have seen, interaction theory views an organization of individuals as a system of communications, activities, and sentiment—a social system. These elements are in mutual dependency; that is, a change in any one affects the others. However, the logical place to start is with formal activities. A manager assigns certain duties to individuals as part of their jobs. In carrying out these activities, they customarily interact or communicate with others. Theoretically, this is all the manager need be concerned about—whether they perform the activities effectively and efficiently, communicating as necessary. Nonetheless, it does not stop here. Unplanned sentiments inevitably emerge. People dislike or like (and rarely are neutral about) the people with whom they work. In turn, these sentiments encourage them to elaborate their communications and activities with others in a variety of unplanned and informal patterns. Sayles and Strauss [15] describe this development:

> Employees form friendship groups based on their contact and common interest—and these groups arise out of the life of the organization. Once these groups have been established, however, they develop a life of their own that is almost completely separate from the work process from which it arose. This is a dynamic, self-generating process. Brought together by the formal organization, employees interact with one another. Increasing interaction builds favorable sentiments toward fellow group members. In turn, these sentiments become the foundation for an increased variety of activities, many not specified by the job description: special lunch arrangements, trading of job duties, fights with those outside the group, gambling on paycheck numbers. And these increased opportunities for interaction build stronger bonds of identification. Then the group becomes something more than a mere collection of people. It develops a customary way of doing things—a set of stable characteristics that are hard to change. It becomes an organization in itself (p. 89).

Membership in a group thus is related to technology and work flow. There has to be some physical proximity and communication opportunity in order for people to form mutually interacting groups. People who communicate are more likely to develop mutual sentiments and hence become attached to each other in some informal structure. Research in this area has attempted to explain the technical conditions facilitating or hindering group development and strength. Personality, ethnicity, race, religion, and various socioeconomic factors all seem to influence the membership of informal groups. Two short selections by Charles Walker, following this chapter, illustrate the conditions aiding and hindering the development of strong groups.

Informal Status Systems

Most men have need for affiliation and membership. Yet once they have established mutual relationships, many individuals want to be better than their companions. Everyone wants to be equal, but as George Orwell put it in *Animal*

Farm, "Some want to be more equal than others." With affiliation, a new need emerges—desire for social esteem, prestige or status—that is, some differentiation of social position from associates and peers.

Prestige or status are frequently defined as a set of unwritten rules about the kind of conduct that people are expected to show in one's presence: what degree of respect or disrespect, familiarity or unfamiliarity, reserve or frankness. Notwithstanding the barbs of contemporary social critics, prestige seeking is not solely a 20th century American phenomenon. Mankind has apparently always created social structure, differentiating the power and glory of his fellows. "Like it or not," Saul Gellerman [10] tells us, "people have evidently been sorting themselves out into chiefs and Indians, nobles and peasants, executives and hourly workers from time immemorial, and they show no signs of stopping (p. 151)." The classless society is yet to appear, and as the Yugoslav, Milovan Diljias [7], courageously showed us, the Communist states also develop class distinctions.

Even within the small informal group, subtle status differences begin to emerge. The type of membership and status within a work group that a person enjoys depend upon factors that he brings to the organization, and factors derived from his job.

External Factors

What a man brings to the workplace influences what his status will be on the job. This pertains to who and what a man is, not what he does. When one of the authors worked in a large chemical manufacturing company, a fellow engineer was the second largest stockholder in this large company. Stock ownership was widely dispersed and his inherited ownership was less than 1%, but it still constituted a large fortune. In the formal organization, however, he was only an engineer with no real indication that his stock ownership was going to help him directly in his hierarchical career. Nonetheless, he obviously had status in the plant regardless of what he did—especially since he prominently displayed on his desk Christmas cards received from the chairman-of-the-board!

Among the off-the-job qualities that confer status are education, age, seniority, sex, and ethnic background. Typically, in business, women are ranked below men. In our society, Negroes are usually accorded low status. Other ethnic groups are also arranged according to a status hierarchy, with Anglo-Saxons usually at the top, and people of southern European background near the bottom. The relative positions on this status ladder may vary from one community to another. For example, to be a "regular" at one plant requires Irish extraction, regardless of other personal characteristics [20]. At other plants, one might find it helpful to be Polish, and so on.

Personality also plays a role, although research findings in this area are not clear. Among informal student groups there is evidence that higher status is associated with physical size, appearance and dress, self-confidence and self-assurance, sociability or friendliness, and intelligence—although the leaders must not exceed their followers by a very large margin in any of these characteristics [18]. The importance of these factors in determining status change from time to time and with cultures. We have asked many classes of American students for factors determining informal group status. Age is seldom mentioned and, if it is, only as the last item. In most of history and in most societies, age has been the major determinant of formal and informal status—as witness Japanese industry, even today [19].

Internal Factors

The job also influences the status system. In fact, when management creates an organization, it consciously creates a status system, based primarily on pay and authority. Titles, job descriptions, evaluation programs, pay systems, and work-measurement practices all influence the informal social structure.

- *Job title*—Obviously a superintendent is more important than a general foreman, and a general foreman outranks a foreman. Engineers outrank technicians; secretaries are above stenographers. In almost every organization, although organizations are certainly not consistent on this, job titles are subtly graded according to levels of status, and the status of each individual depends in part on the job he holds.

- *Pay*—This is one of the most important determinants of status. Higher pay means higher status, and even a difference of a few cents per hour may have a significant effect on a job's status. How one is paid also helps to determine status. Being a salaried man on a monthly payroll may be less convenient, but it carries much more prestige than getting a weekly or daily wage.

- *Work schedules*—The freedom to choose one's hours, or being excused from punching the time clock, is a mark of distinction. Working a day schedule is usually thought of as a higher-status job than a shift schedule.

- *Mobility*—Generally, a job which allows a man to move around freely, interacting and communicating with many different people, is thought of as having higher prestige than a position that allows no autonomy or discretion over one's movements. This mobility is also related to autonomy or freedom from close management supervision. Again, this is a status factor generally giving higher prestige in the informal social structure.

- *Symbols of office*—There is a vast range of physical factors which are desirable in themselves but which also serve as symbols for higher status. These include such things as in which company lunchroom you can eat. Can you leave the building for morning coffee? Do you have a reserved parking space? What kind of clothing do you wear in the office? Also the type of office—what kind of furnishings do you have? Telephone? Desk? Carpeting? and so on.

What we are suggesting is that people on the job structure themselves in various relationships, integrating on-job and off-job status factors. An informal social structure will be created; employees will look up to certain people and consider certain jobs attractive; they may even plan their careers around movement through these positions. The highest status positions will tend to be occupied especially by people high in both external and internal status factors. This informal status system may approximate the formal structure of the company, but it will probably deviate in a number of ways, as we shall illustrate in the last part of this chapter.

Attitude and Behavior Expectations

In describing the development of groups, we emphasized what social organizations provide for the individual—affiliation, self-identification, and assistance. Once a social structure develops, however, it takes on a life of its own. A group pursues objectives which may contribute to individual goals—but which may also limit the individual.

At several universities, undergraduate students voted against adoption of academic honor systems which would have abolished faculty proctoring of examinations. Considering the widespread and well-publicized activities in support of greater student participation in university administration, these rejections seem contradictory. The explanation lies with the proposals voted upon. They placed individual responsibility on the student not to cheat but also required him to take some action if he observed someone else cheating. At one Ivy League university the required action was a report either to a faculty committee or to a student group. The students rejected this proposal because it conflicted with an underlying student norm—one should not "fink" on classmates. Indeed, in recent Air Force Academy cheating scandals, the parents of several cadets suspended for not reporting code infractions were vociferous in support of this norm as applying to American society as a whole [8]: one should not be punished for not reporting a crime if one didn't commit it.

After the first defeat at the Ivy League university referred to above, the honor system was amended to make optional the report to the faculty and to require only that the student tell the cheater that he has been observed. He did not have to take any further action, although he did have the option. Again, the proposal was defeated. The undergraduates are apparently not willing to approve any system that requires them to exercise any control over their peers. It contradicts the student conception of proper behavior.

On a more positive note, among junior faculty members at many universities, there is an informal social expectation that one will read and comment on a colleague's rough draft articles. The colleague unwilling to conform to this expectation is not well regarded.

Informal groups, then, develop attitudinal norms and standards of behavior. That is, people in groups tend to think and act alike; continuous association leads to shared values and norms. The shared values include those associated with education, age, class, or ethnicity; beyond that, they reflect such matters as attitudes, tastes, beliefs, and behavioral norms. As Homans [11] puts this general point:

> Interaction between persons leads to sentiments of liking, which express themselves in new activities, and these in turn mean further interaction. . . . The more frequently persons interact with one another, the stronger their sentiments of friendship for one another are apt to be. . . . The more frequently persons interact with one another, the more alike in some respects both their activities and sentiments tend to become (pp. 119, 120, 133).

To a greater or lesser extent, all informal groups are characterized by such attitudinal norms and behavioral expectations. Of special importance are attitudes toward assistance and work effort. As mentioned, one of the reasons for the development of informal groups is mutual assistance. Accordingly, most groups value and expect cooperation and helpfulness among regular members of the group—hints on how to machine parts, assistance on difficult jobs, warning against management inspection, assistance in camouflaging mistakes, and a whole host of informal practices. In order to maintain standing in a group and receive its benefits, this aid must be given. In his selected article, referred to earlier, Donald Roy describes some of its values.

If the basic attitude of the group towards the company is positive, informal expectations can greatly assist management. If the group is fundamentally interested in getting the job done, the workers will fill in the gaps and work out the ambiguities in management assignments. They will be willing to shift with the varying demands of the job in order to assist hard-pressed colleagues without specific management direction. Even under the best conditions, however, a strong informal group will oppose some of management's desires. And when the basic attitudes towards management are adverse, the group's behavioral expectations may be directed against management's desires in a variety of amazing ways. Melville Dalton, in his selected article following this chapter, colorfully describes the informal reward practice (often bordering on theft) that managers and workers develop to compensate for inadequacies in the formal system of rewards.

Output and Effort Standards

Limitation of output has long been a prominent anti-management behavior pattern. A wide variety of studies, starting with the Hawthorne research of the late 1920's, has demonstrated how informal groups limit their output. Indeed, much earlier, Frederick W. Taylor devoted much of his life to attempting to stamp out the widespread "soldiering," which he thought endangered the very existence of the United States.

The term "soldiering" connoted anti-management motivation, but this need not be the case. Any group of individuals tends to develop some conception of a "fair day's work." In the absence of piece rates, in particular, a group tends to develop agreement on how much should be done. To be sure, not everyone concurs, but among both students and crate handlers, there is a tendency to define what should be done so that there is relative equality of effort. The definition of output is not always harmful to management; the level of effort decided upon by the group may be higher than some individuals might demonstrate. In addition, the group's standard of performance may facilitate management's prediction of output, thus simplifying scheduling and costing.

Spectacular tests of will may result, however, when group output norms are below management expectations. Such disagreements can lead to protracted ill feeling. The authors well remember a ten-month controversy when a closely knit group of women film splicers disagreed with management about how many rolls of 8-millimeter film they should be able to process. The girls simply thought that management's output desires on a new product were unreasonable. No fear of unemployment and no union were involved. Employer-employee relations were outstanding—but both sides had to re-define proper output. This was not done, however, until many rolls of amateur 8-millimeter film were "accidentally" dropped, to roll around the floor and become entangled in serpentine knots.

Group Discipline

Like all societies, informal groups at work develop common values and behavioral expectations—management is dangerous, don't fink on your buddies, don't goof off but don't work too hard. . . . Whether the members of the group act or don't act upon these norms and standards depends upon whether the individual wants to be a member of the group and whether the group can enforce its desires. The more eager an individual is to be a member of a group, the more he will conform to its norms of behavior, and the easier it will be to enforce group rules. As Leon Festinger [9] put it: "If a person wants to stay in a group, he will be susceptible to influences coming from the group, and he will be willing to conform to the rules which the group sets up (p. 91)."

Withdrawal of the group's contribution to the individual is the primary method of enforcement. The group strongly influences the behavior of its members by providing them with support, reinforcement, security, encouragement, protection, rationale, rationalization, etc., for their "proper" behavior, and by punishing them for deviations through the use of ridicule, hostility, threat of expulsion, etc. When an individual is genuinely attached to a group and in close and continuous contact with it, his group behaviors and beliefs are extremely resistant to change. In such circumstances the group can exercise firm control over him.

In addition, among some informal social groups there is indication that popularity is associated with respect for the group's norms. One study [1] concludes, "Deviates are rejected while conformers become popular (p. 155)." The closer an individual conforms to the accepted norms of the group, the better liked he will be; the better liked he is, the closer he conforms; the less he conforms, the more disliked he will be. To the extent that these judgments based upon observations of teenage groups are general, people like to be liked, so they tend to engage in actions that will maintain or increase the esteem received from those around them. This means that there is always a tendency to go along with a group—a tendency that is realized unless there are strong countervailing influences.

If an independent soul refuses to abide by group values and standards, initial group reaction may simply be gentle ribbing or good-natured sarcasm. If these fail to alter the individual's behavior, more serious reasoning, discussion, and persuasion result, followed by more heated arguments. At the same time some of the social benefits derived from group membership, such as assistance and socializing, may be reduced. The member's status in the group is thereby reduced. If he still does not conform, overt coercion or complete ostracism may be used, depending upon the importance of the issue and the moral standards of the group. To quote George Homans [12] once again:

> Men give social approval, as a generalized reinforcement, to others that have given them activity they value, and so make it more likely that the others will go on giving the activity. One of the kinds of activity some men find valuable is that their own behavior and that of others they are associated with in a group should be similar in conforming to a norm. . . .
>
> People that find conformity valuable reward conformers with social

> approval, but they withhold approval from those that will not conform, or even express positive dislike for nonconformists as having denied them a reward they had a right to expect.
>
> Some members of a group conform for the norm's sake, . . . and some for the approval's sake, but both will come to say that they do it for the norm. The more a member values an activity incompatible with conformity . . . and the more valuable are his sources of social approval other than the conformers in his group, the less likely he is to conform (p. 129).

If the errant individual doesn't derive satisfaction or benefits from the group, if he has alternative sources of satisfaction, or if he just doesn't give a damn, the group's ability to enforce its norms and standards is weakened.

Implications for the Manager

We shall elaborate on the manager's influencing of groups in Part III. But we must at least point out here that, like it or not, every manager will have to deal with informal groups, because they will emerge from the formal organization. A manager cannot treat people only as individuals. Particularly important is understanding of the relationship between formal and informal status systems and the impact of technology on informal social systems.

Sometimes there is inconsistency or incongruity between internal and external status factors—that is, between the attributes a man brings to the job and the kind of position he fills. George Homans explains this by his theory of distributive justice:* First, there are the personal attributes that a man brings to his job—the external status factors such as age, seniority, sex, ethnicity, responsibility, and education. Homans calls these investments. Second, there are the status factors the worker expects to get out of his job—internal status factors such as pay, the intrinsic nature of the job, organizational status, the prestige accorded him by his fellows, special privileges, etc. According to Homans, when the investments of one individual member are higher than those of another, distributive justice requires that the rewards should be higher too. When distributive justice does not prevail—when investment is not equal to rewards—Homans predicts that there will be trouble.

The Negro and Distributive Justice

Given the efforts of Negroes to climb to higher positions, distributive justice is a problem in American society. Most people still assign low external status to the Negro. Historically, this has been consistent with the job he has filled—low skilled, low paying, dirty, and monotonous. There was consistency between off-job and on-job status factors. At present, however, one of the most in-demand persons in American society is the Negro M.B.A. graduate. How far he will climb in business is still undetermined, but the Negro college graduate's movement into positions of relative importance, high on internal status (in such factors as pay, skill, authority, office furnishings, etc.), brings status incongruity—in the opinion of some white men. Because the white man thinks he brings higher external status factors to the job, he may be upset when he has lower job status.

---

*In addition to the Homans books mentioned, the best description of "distributive justice" is found in Ref. 20, pp. 53–56.

As Homans puts it, the person who brings high status factors to the organization expects equal job status in return.

The solution to the Negro status problem is the elimination of race (and sex, according to the 1964 Civil Rights Act) as a source of external status—at least at work. The tobacco companies in the Carolinas apparently have had some success in putting Negro supervisors over white workers at relatively low levels. To be a Negro implies low external status, but the Negroes appointed are brighter, harder working, and better educated than the Caucasians working under them.

A manager's ability to hire, transfer, and promote people is hindered to the extent that people are upset by incongruent status comparisons. Of course, we are not implying that management should limit its activity because of fear of status incongruity and the resulting stresses. What we do say is that the manager should be aware of possible causes and consequences of such status comparisons when he takes actions that affect the informal status system within the organization.

When Formal and Informal Norms Conflict

Difficulty is created for management when formal organizational structure conflicts with an informal status system—that is, when management evaluation of jobs and positions does not correspond to group evaluation. For example, in one chemical manufacturing company, the formal hierarchy of jobs was as indicated in Table 1.

TABLE 1. Formal and Informal Job Status

Formal Status System *Before* Change		Formal Status System *After* Change		Informal Status System *Before* and *After* Change
Head operator of continuous processing . . .	$2.75/hr	Tank room operator	$3.00/hr	Head operator of continuous processing
↑		↑		↑
Tank room operator	$2.50/hr	Head operator of continuous processing . . .	$2.75/hr	Tank room operator
↑		↑		↑
Handler	$2.00/hr	Handler	$2.00/hr	Handler

The job of handler required a semi-skilled, manual operator to sort raw and finished materials. Working conditions were good, the area was clean and well lighted, but the job required relatively little training and skill. The pay rate was $2.00 per hour. The next higher position, tank room operator, was responsible for a batch chemical process, using eight large tanks in another room in the same building. He had to add chemicals, control flows, and make various tests. The job was a promotion from handler: it paid $2.50 an hour and required greater skill and experience, including some fairly sophisticated knowledge of chemical tests. In addition, the tank room operator had greater autonomy and responsibility. However, his working conditions were atrocious. Since various digestive processes using organic enzymes were percolating in open vats, the area was like the inside of a stomach. The smell, heat, and humidity all detracted from the desirability of the job.

The most desirable job in the department was as head operator of continuous processing equipment. A precursor of the "white coverall" worker of the future, the head operator received $2.75 an hour for manipulating a console and making some important decisions regarding chemical flows, times, temperatures, and so forth. He performed very little manual work. His work area was clean, well lighted, and much cooler than the tank room.

For years, the informal social structure and the formal organizational hierarchy were similar. Management and the men agreed on which jobs were more desirable. The wage rates reflected both management and group judgments of job status. Each worker saw his career as progressing up through these positions—from handler to tank room operator to head operator. In general, the more senior people were head operators, the next in seniority were tank room operators, and the newer people were handlers.

One day the harmony ended. Because of technological developments in another department, it was necessary to redesign some of the operations in the tank room, increasing the responsibilities of the tank room operator and the skill and technical sophistication necessary. Even greater decision-making discretion and autonomy were given to the tank room operator. The wage and salary administrator re-evaluated the job and pay was increased to $3.00 an hour—$.25 an hour more than the head operator received. However, working conditions were not improved. The tank room was still as dirty, smelly, and unpleasant. The formal status structure now went from handler to head operator to tank room operator. Unfortunately, the work group refused to modify their own status hierarchy. The pay increase for the tank room operator was not enough to give that job higher status than the head operator's position. The men could not see the high point of their careers as moving to the tank room. They still wanted to progress from handler to tank room operator to head operator—and were willing to take a cut in pay to move to the last job.

An additional problem was created. The junior men in the tank room were now making more money than the senior head operators—thus creating status incongruity. Eventually, the only way management was able to solve this problem was to make extensive physical modifications in the tank room to improve working conditions. These changes made the working conditions in the tank room roughly similar to the head operator's, which in turn raised the informal status of the tank room operator's job. In other words, management was able to solve the problem only by modifying the status factors to make informal and formal status systems congruent.

We are not saying that a manager must always accommodate informal groups and shift his formal organization, policy, and procedures to satisfy them. The manager may consider it necessary to change the norms of the informal group. To do this successfully requires understanding of informal group dynamics. This chapter and its selected readings are designed to help provide such understanding. In Part III we shall consider how the manager can apply this knowledge to influence the informal organization.

References

1. Argyle, M. *The Scientific Study of Social Behavior.* Methuen, 1957.
2. Asch, S. E. "Opinion and Social Pressure." *Scientific American,* Vol. 193, No. 5 (Nov. 1955), 31–34.
3. Berelson, B., and G. Steiner. *Human Behavior—An Inventory of Scientific Findings.* Harcourt, Brace & World, 1964.
4. Blau, P. *The Dynamics of Bureaucracy.* Univ. Chicago Press, 1955.
5. Burling, T., E. Lentz, and R. Wilson. *The Give and Take in Hospitals.* Putnam, 1956.
6. Dean, W. F. *General Dean's Story* (as told to W. L. Worden). Viking Press, 1954.
7. Diljias, M. *The New Class,* Praeger, 1957.
8. "Fall from Honor: Exam Cheating Scandal." *Newsweek,* 65:46 (Feb. 1, 1965). "Scandal in Colorado Springs." *Time,* 89:66 (March 3, 1967).
9. Festinger, L., S. Schachter, and K. Back. *Social Pressures in Informal Groups.* Harper & Row, 1950.
10. Gellerman, S. *Motivation and Productivity.* American Management Association, 1963.
11. Homans, G. C. *The Human Group.* Harcourt, Brace & World, 1950.
12. ———. *Social Behavior: Its Elementary Forms.* Harcourt, Brace & World, 1961.
13. Kinkead, E. *In Every War But One.* Norton, 1959.
14. Mayo, E. *The Human Problems of an Industrial Civilization.* Graduate School of Business Administration, Harvard University, 1946.
15. Sayles, L. R., and G. Strauss. *Human Behavior In Organizations.* Prentice-Hall, 1966.
16. Schein, E. "The Chinese Indoctrination Program for Prisoners of War." *Psychiatry,* Vol. 19 (1956), 149–172.
17. Shils, E. A. "Primary Groups In the American Army." In *Continuities in Social Research: Studies in the Scope and Method of the American Soldier,* ed. R. K. Merton and P. F. Lazarfeld (The Free Press, 1950), 16–39.
18. Stogdill, R. "Personal Factors Associated with Leadership: A Survey of the Literature." *Journal of Psychology,* Vol. 25 (1948), 35–71.
19. Takezawa, S. "Socio-Cultural Aspects of Management in Japan." *International Labour Review,* Vol. 94, No. 2 (August 1966).
20. Zalesnik, A., C. R. Christensen, and F. J. Roethlisberger. *The Motivation, Productivity and Satisfaction of Workers: A Prediction Study.* Graduate School of Business Administration, Harvard University, 1965.

Readings

Banana Time—Job Satisfaction and Informal Interaction

DONALD F. ROY

This paper undertakes description and exploratory analysis of the social interaction which took place within a small work group of factory machine operatives during a two-month period of participant observation. The factual and ideational materials which it presents lie at an intersection of two lines of research interest and should, in their dual bearing, contribute to both. Since the operatives were engaged in work which involved the repetition of very simple operations over an extra-long workday, six days a week, they were faced with the problem of dealing with a formidable "beast of monotony." Revelation of how the group utilized its resources to combat the "beast" should merit the attention of those who are seeking solution to the practical problem of job satisfaction, or employee morale. It should also provide insights for those who are trying to penetrate the mysteries of the small group.

Convergence of these two lines of interest is, of course, no new thing. Among the host of writers and researchers who have suggested connections between "group" and "joy in work" are Walker and Guest, observers of social interaction on the automobile assembly line.[1] They quote assembly-line workers as saying, "We have a lot of fun and talk all the time,"[2] and, "If it weren't for the talking and fooling, you'd go nuts."[3]

My account of how one group of machine operators kept from "going nuts" in a situation of monotonous work activity attempts to lay bare the tissues of interaction which made up the content of their adjustment. The talking, fun, and fooling which provided solution to the elemental problem of "psychological survival" will be described according to their embodiment in intra-group relations. In addition, an unusual opportunity for close observation of behavior involved in the maintenance of group equilibrium was afforded by the fortuitous introduction of a "natural experiment." My unwitting injection of explosive

From *Human Organization,* Vol. 18 (1960), pp. 158–168. Reprinted by permission of the author and The Society for Applied Anthropology.

[1]Charles R. Walker and Robert H. Guest, *The Man on the Assembly Line,* Harvard University Press, Cambridge, 1952.

[2]*Ibid.,* p. 77.

[3]*Ibid.,* p. 68.

materials into the stream of interaction resulted in sudden, but temporary, loss of group interaction.

My fellow operatives and I spent our long days of simple repetitive work in relative isolation from other employees of the factory. Our line of machines was sealed off from other work areas of the plant by the four walls of the clicking room. The one door of this room was usually closed. Even when it was kept open, during periods of hot weather, the consequences were not social; it opened on an uninhabited storage room of the shipping department. Not even the sound of work activity going on elsewhere in the factory carried to this isolated work place. There were occasional contacts with "outside" employees, usually on matters connected with the work; but, with the exception of the daily calls of one fellow who came to pick up finished materials for the next step in processing, such visits were sporadic and infrequent.

Moreover, face-to-face contact with members of the managerial hierarchy were few and far between. No one bearing the title of foreman ever came around. The only company official who showed himself more than once during the two month observation period was the plant superintendent. Evidently overloaded with supervisory duties and production problems which kept him busy elsewhere, he managed to pay his respects every week or two. His visits were in the nature of short, businesslike, but friendly exchanges. Otherwise he confined his observable communications with the group to occasional utilization of a public address system. During the two-month period, the company president and the chief chemist paid one friendly call apiece. One man, who may or may not have been of managerial status, was seen on various occasions lurking about in a manner which excited suspicion. Although no observable consequences accrued from the peculiar visitations of this silent fellow, it was assumed that he was some sort of efficiency expert, and he was referred to as "The Snooper."

As far as our work group was concerned, this was truly a situation of laissez-faire management. There was no interference from staff experts, no hounding by time-study engineers or personnel men hot on the scent of efficiency or good human relations. Nor were there any signs of industrial democracy in the form of safety, recreational, or production committees. There was an international union, and there was a highly publicized union-management cooperation program; but actual interactional processes of cooperation were carried on somewhere beyond my range of observation and without participation of members of my work group. Furthermore, these union-management get-togethers had no determinable connection with the problem of "toughing out" a twelve-hour day at monotonous work.

Our work group was thus not only abandoned to its own resources for creating job satisfaction, but left without that basic reservoir of ill-will toward management which can sometimes be counted on to stimulate the development of interesting activities to occupy hand and brain. Lacking was the challenge of intergroup conflict, that perennial source of creative experience to fill the otherwise empty hours of meaningless work routine.[4]

The clicking machines were housed in a room approximately thirty by twenty-four feet. They were four in number, set in a row, and so arranged along

---

[4] Donald F. Roy, "Work Satisfaction and Social Reward in Quota Achievement: An Analysis of Piecework Incentive," *American Sociological Review,* XVIII (October, 1953), 507–514.

one wall that the busy operator could, merely by raising his head from his work, freshen his reveries with a glance through one of three large barred windows. To the rear of one of the end machines sat a long cutting table; here the operators cut up rolls of plastic materials into small sheets manageable for further processing at the clickers. Behind the machine at the opposite end of the line sat another table which was intermittently the work station of a female employee who performed sundry scissors operations of a more intricate nature on raincoat parts. Boxed in on all sides by shelves and stocks of materials, this latter locus of work appeared a cell within a cell.

The clickers were of the genus punching machines; of mechanical construction similar to that of the better-known punch presses, their leading features were hammer and block. The hammer, or punching head, was approximately eight inches by twelve inches at its flat striking surface. The descent upon the block was initially forced by the operator, who exerted pressure on a handle attached to the side of the hammer head. A few inches of travel downward established electrical connection for a sharp, power-driven blow. The hammer also traveled, by manual guidance, in a horizontal plane to and from, and in an arc around, the central column of the machine. Thus the operator, up to the point of establishing electrical connections for the sudden and irrevocable downward thrust, had flexibility in maneuvering his instrument over the larger surface of the block. The latter, approximately twenty-four inches wide, eighteen inches deep, and ten inches thick, was made, like a butcher's block, of inlaid hardwood; it was set in the machine at a convenient waist height. On it the operator placed his materials, one sheet at a time if leather, stacks of sheets if plastic, to be cut with steel dies of assorted sizes and shapes. The particular die in use would be moved, by hand, from spot to spot over the materials each time a cut was made; less frequently, materials would be shifted on the block as the operator saw need for such adjustment.

Introduction to the new job, with its relatively simple machine skills and work routines, was accomplished with what proved to be, in my experience, an all-time minimum of job training. The clicking machine assigned to me was situated at one end of the row. Here the superintendent and one of the operators gave a few brief demonstrations, accompanied by bits of advice which included a warning to keep hands clear of the descending hammer. After a short practice period, at the end of which the superintendent expressed satisfaction with progress and potentialities, I was left to develop my learning curve with no other supervision than that afforded by members of the work group. Further advise and assistance did come, from time to time, from my fellow operatives, sometimes upon request, sometimes unsolicited.

The Work Group

Absorbed at first in three related goals of improving my clicking skill, increasing my rate of output, and keeping my left hand unclicked, I paid little attention to my fellow operatives save to observe that they were friendly, middle-aged, foreign-born, full of advice, and very talkative. Their names, according to the way they addressed each other, were George, Ike, and Sammy.[5] George, a stocky fellow in his late fifties, operated the machine at the opposite end of

[5]All names used are fictitious.

the line; he, I later discovered, had emigrated in early youth from a country in Southeastern Europe. Ike, stationed at George's left, was tall, slender, in his early fifties, and Jewish; he had come from Eastern Europe in his youth. Sammy, number three man in the line, and my neighbor, was heavy set, in his late fifties, and Jewish; he had escaped from a country in Eastern Europe just before Hitler's legions had moved in. All three men had been downwardly mobile as to occupation in recent years. George and Sammy had been proprietors of small businesses; the former had been "wiped out" when his uninsured establishment burned down; the latter had been entrepreneuring on a small scale before he left all behind him to flee the Germans. According to his account, Ike had left a highly skilled trade which he had practiced for years in Chicago.

I discovered also that the clicker line represented a ranking system in descending order from George to myself. George not only had top seniority for the group, but functioned as a sort of leadman. His superior status was marked in the fact that he received five cents more per hour than the other clickermen, put in the longest workday, made daily contact, outside the workroom, with the superintendent on work matters which concerned the entire line, and communicated to the rest of us the directives which he received. The narrow margin of superordination was seen in the fact that directives were always relayed in the superintendent's name; they were on the order of, "You'd better let that go now, and get on the green. Joe says they're running low on the fifth floor," or, "Joe says he wants two boxes of the 3-die today." The narrow margin was also seen in the fact that the superintendent would communicate directly with his operatives over the public address system; and, on occasion, Ike or Sammy would leave the workroom to confer with him for decisions or advice in regard to work orders.

Ike was next to George in seniority, then Sammy. I was, of course, low man on the totem pole. Other indices to status differentiation lay in informal interaction, to be described later.

With one exception, job status tended to be matched by length of workday. George worked a thirteen-hour day, from 7 A.M. to 8:30 P.M. Ike worked eleven hours, from 7 A.M. to 6:30 P.M.; occasionally he worked until 7 or 7:30 for an eleven and a half- or a twelve-hour day. Sammy put in a nine-hour day, from 8 A.M. to 5:30 P.M. My twelve hours spanned from 8 A.M. to 8:30 P.M. We had a half hour for lunch, from 12 to 12:30.

The female who worked at the secluded table behind George's machine put in a regular plant-wide eight-hour shift from 8 to 4:30. Two women held this job during the period of my employment; Mable was succeeded by Baby. Both were Negroes, and in their late twenties.

A fifth clicker operator, an Arabian *emigré* called Boo, worked a night shift by himself. He usually arrived about 7 P.M. to take over Ike's machine.

The Work

It was evident to me, before my first workday drew to a weary close, that my clicking career was going to be a grim process of fighting the clock, the particular timepiece in this situation being an old-fashioned alarm clock which ticked away on a shelf near George's machine. I had struggled through many dreary rounds with the minutes and hours during the various phases of my industrial experience, but never had I been confronted with such a dismal combination of working conditions as the extra-long workday, the infinitesimal cerebral excitation, and the extreme limitation of physical movement. The contrast with a recent stint in the California oil fields was striking. This was no eight-hour day of racing hither and yon over desert and foothills with a rollicking crew of "roustabouts" on a variety of repair missions at oil wells, pipe lines, and storage tanks. Here there were no afternoon dallyings to search the sands for horned toads, tarantulas, and rattlesnakes, or to climb old wooden derricks for raven's nests, with an eye out, of course, for the tell-tale streak of dust in the distance which gave ample warning of the approach of the boss. This was standing all day in one spot beside three old codgers in a dingy room looking out through barred windows at the bare walls of a brick warehouse, leg movements largely restricted to the shifting of body weight from one foot to the other, hand and arm movements confined, for the most part, to a simple repetitive sequence of place the die, ——— punch the clicker, ——— place the die, ——— punch the clicker, and intellectual activity reduced to computing the hours to quitting time. It is true that from time to time a fresh stack of sheets would have to be substituted for the clicked-out old one; but the stack would have been prepared by someone else, and the exchange would be only a minute or two in the making. Now and then a box of finished work would have to be moved back out of the way, and an empty box brought up; but the moving back and the bringing up involved only a step or two. And there was the half hour for lunch, and occasional trips to the lavatory or the drinking fountain to break up the day into digestible parts. But after each momentary respite, hammer and die were moving again: click, ——— move die, ——— click, ——— move die.

Before the end of the first day, Monotony was joined by his twin brother, Fatigue. I got tired. My legs ached, and my feet hurt. Early in the afternoon I discovered a tall stool and moved it up to my machine to "take the load off my feet." But the superintendent dropped in to see how I was "doing" and promptly informed me that "we don't sit down on this job." My reverie toyed with the idea of quitting the job and looking for other work.

The next day was the same: the monotony of the work, the tired legs and sore feet and thoughts of quitting.

The Game of Work

In discussing the factory operative's struggle to "cling to the remnants of joy in work," Henri de Man makes the general observations that "it is psychologically impossible to deprive any kind of work of all its positive emotional elements," that the worker will find *some* meaning in any activity assigned to him, a "certain scope for initiative which can satisfy after a fashion the instinct for play and the creative impulse," that "even in the Taylor system there is found luxury of self-determination."[6] De Man cites the case of one worker who wrapped 13,000 incandescent bulbs a day; she found her outlet for creative impulse, her self-determination, her meaning in work by varying her wrapping movements a little from time to time.[7]

So did I search for *some* meaning in my continuous mincing of plastic sheets into small ovals, fingers, and trapezoids. The richness of possibility for creative

[6]Henri de Man, *The Psychology of Socialism,* Henry Holt and Company, New York, 1927, pp. 80–81.
[7]*Ibid.*, p. 81.

expression previously discovered in my experience with the "Taylor system"[8] did not reveal itself here. There was no piecework, so no piecework game. There was no conflict with management, so no war game. But, like the light bulb wrapper, I did find a "certain scope for initiative," and out of this slight freedom to vary activity, I developed a game of work.

The game developed was quite simple, so elementary in fact, that its playing was reminiscent of rainy-day preoccupations in childhood, when attention could be centered by the hour on colored bits of things of assorted sizes and shapes. But this adult activity was not mere pottering and piddling, what it lacked in the earlier imaginative content, it made up for in clean-cut structure. Fundamentally involved were: a) variation in color of the materials cut, b) variation in shape of the dies used, and c) a process called "scraping the block." The basic procedure which ordered the particular combination of components employed could be stated in the form: "As soon as I do so many of these, I'll get to do those." If, for example, production scheduled for the day featured small, rectangular strips in three colors, the game might go: "As soon as I finish a thousand of the green ones, I'll click some brown ones." And, with success in attaining the objective of working with brown materials, a new goal of "I'll get to do the white ones" might be set. Or the new goal might involve switching dies.

Scraping the block made the game more interesting by adding to the number of possible variations in its playing; and, what was perhaps more important, provided the only substantial reward, save for going to the lavatory or getting a drink of water, on days when work with one die and one color of material was scheduled. As a physical operation, scraping the block was fairly simple; it involved application of a coarse file to the upper surface of the block to remove roughness and unevenness resulting from the wear and tear of die penetration. But, as part of the intellectual and emotional content of the game of work, it could be in itself a source of variation in activity. The upper left-hand corner of the block could be chewed up in the clicking of 1,000 white trapezoid pieces, then scraped. Next, the upper right-hand corner, and so on until the entire block had been worked over. Then, on the next round of scraping by quadrants, there was the possibility of a change of color or die to green trapezoid or white oval pieces.

Thus the game of work might be described as a continuous sequence of short-range production goals with achievement rewards in the form of activity change. The superiority of this relatively complex and self-determined system over the technically simple and outside-controlled job satisfaction injections experienced by Milner at the beginner's table in a shop of the feather industry should be immediately apparent:

> Twice a day our work was completely changed to break the monotony. First Jennie would give us feathers of a brilliant green, then bright orange or a light blue or black. The "ohs" and "ahs" that came from the girls at each change was proof enough that this was an effective way of breaking the monotony of the tedious work.[9]

---

[8]Roy, *op. cit.*
[9]Lucille Milner, *Education of An American Liberal,* Horizon Press, New York, 1954, p. 97.

But a hasty conclusion that I was having lots of fun playing my clicking game should be avoided. These games were not as interesting in the experiencing as they might seem to be from the telling. Emotional tone of the activity was low, and intellectual currents weak. Such rewards as scraping the block or "getting to do the blue ones" were not very exciting, and the stretches of repetitive movement involved in achieving them were long enough to permit lapses into obsessive reverie. Henri de Man speaks of "clinging to the remnants of joy in work," and this situation represented just that. How tenacious the clinging was, how long I could have "stuck it out" with my remnants, was never determined. Before the first week was out this adjustment to the work situation was complicated by other developments. The game of work continued, but in a different context. Its influence became decidedly subordinated to, if not completely overshadowed by, another source of job satisfaction.

Informal Social Activity of the Work Group: Times and Themes

The change came about when I began to take serious note of the social activity going on around me; my attentiveness to this activity came with growing involvement in it. What I heard at first, before I started to listen, was a stream of disconnected bits of communication which did not make much sense. Foreign accents were strong and referents were not joined to coherent contexts of meaning. It was just "jabbering." What I saw at first, before I began to observe, was occasional flurries of horseplay so simple and unvarying in pattern and so childish in quality that they made no strong bid for attention. For example, Ike would regularly switch off the power at Sammy's machine whenever Sammy made a trip to the lavatory or the drinking fountain. Correlatively, Sammy invariably fell victim to the plot by making an attempt to operate his clicking hammer after returning to the shop. And, as the simple pattern went, this blind stumbling into the trap was always followed by indignation and reproach from Sammy, smirking satisfaction from Ike, and mild paternal scolding from George. My interest in this procedure was at first confined to wondering when Ike would weary of his tedious joke or when Sammy would learn to check his power switch before trying the hammer.

But, as I began to pay closer attention, as I began to develop familiarity with the communication system, the disconnected became connected, the nonsense made sense, the obscure became clear, and the silly actually funny. And, as the content of the interaction took on more and more meaning, the interaction began to reveal structure. There were "times" and "themes," and roles to serve their enaction. The interaction had subtleties, and I began to savor and appreciate them. I started to record what hitherto had seemed unimportant.

Times

This emerging awareness of structure and meaning included recognition that the long day's grind was broken by interruptions of a kind other than the formally instituted or idiosyncratically developed disjunctions in work routine previously described. These additional interruptions appeared in daily repetition in an ordered series of informal interactions. They were, in part, but only in part and in very rough comparison; similar to those common fractures of the production process known as the coffee break, the coke break, and the cigarette break. Their distinction lay in frequency of occurrence and in brevity. As phases of the daily series, they occurred almost hourly, and so short were they in duration that they disrupted work activity only slightly. Their significance lay not so much in their function as rest pauses, although it cannot be denied that physical refreshment was involved. Nor did their chief importance lie in the accentuation of progress points in the passage of time, although they could perform that function far more strikingly than the hour hand on the dull face of George's alarm clock. If the daily series of interruptions be likened to a clock, then the comparison might best be made with a special kind of cuckoo clock, one with a cuckoo which can provide variation in its announcements and can create such an interest in them that the intervening minutes become filled with intellectual content. The major significance of the interactional interruptions lay in such a carryover of interest. The physical interplay which momentarily halted work activity would initiate verbal exchanges and thought processes to occupy group members until the next interruption. The group interactions thus not only marked off the time; they gave it content and hurried it along.

Most of the breaks in the daily series were designated as "times" in the parlance of the clicker operators, and they featured the consumption of food or drink of one sort or another. There was coffee time, peach time, banana time, fish time, coke time, and, of course, lunch time. Other interruptions, which formed part of the series but were not verbally recognized as times, were window time, pickup time, and the staggered quitting times of Sammy and Ike. These latter unnamed times did not involve the partaking of refreshments.

My attention was first drawn to this times business during my first week of employment when I was encouraged to join in the sharing of two peaches. It was Sammy who provided the peaches; he drew them from his lunch box after making the announcement, "Peach time!" On this first occasion I refused the proffered fruit, but thereafter regularly consumed my half peach. Sammy continued to provide the peaches and to make the "Peach time!" announcement, although there were days when Ike would remind him that it was peach time, urging him to hurry up with the mid-morning snack. Ike invariably complained about the quality of the fruit, and his complaints fed the fires of continued banter between peach donor and critical recipient. I did find the fruit a bit on the scrubby side but felt, before I achieved insight into the function of peach time, that Ike was showing poor manners by looking a gift horse in the mouth. I wondered why Sammy continued to share his peaches with such an ingrate.

Banana time followed peach time by approximately an hour. Sammy again provided the refreshments, namely, one banana. There was, however, no four-way sharing of Sammy's banana. Ike would gulp it down by himself after surreptitiously extracting it from Sammy's lunch box, kept on a shelf behind Sammy's work station. Each morning, after making the snatch, Ike would call out, "Banana time!" and proceed to down his prize while Sammy made futile protests and denunciations. George would join in with mild remonstrances, sometimes scolding Sammy for making so much fuss. The banana was one which Sammy brought for his own consumption at lunch time; he never did get to eat his banana, but kept bringing one for his lunch. At first this daily theft startled and amazed me. Then I grew to look forward to the daily seizure and the verbal interaction which followed.

Window time came next. It followed banana time as a regular consequence of Ike's castigation by the indignant Sammy. After "taking" repeated references to himself as a person badly lacking in morality and character, Ike would "finally" retaliate by opening the window which faced Sammy's machine, to let the "cold air" blow in on Sammy. The slandering which would, in its echolalic repetition, wear down Ike's patience and forbearance usually took the form of the invidious comparison: "George is a good daddy! Ike is a bad man! A very bad man!" Opening the window would take a little time to accomplish and would involve a great deal of verbal interplay between Ike and Sammy, both before and after the event. Ike would threaten, make feints toward the window, then finally open it. Sammy would protest, argue, and make claims that the air blowing in on him would give him a cold; he would eventually have to leave his machine to close the window. Sometimes the weather was slightly chilly, and the draft from the window unpleasant; but cool or hot, windy or still, window time arrived each day. (I assume that it was originally a cold season development.) George's part in this interplay, in spite of the "good daddy" laudations, was to encourage Ike in his window work. He would stress the tonic values of fresh air and chide Sammy for his unappreciativeness.

Following window time came lunch time, a formally designated half-hour for the midday repast and rest break. At this time, informal interaction would feature exchanges between Ike and George. The former would start eating his lunch a few minutes before noon, and the latter, in his role as straw boss, would censure him for malobservance of the rules. Ike's off-beat luncheon usually involved a previous tampering with George's alarm clock. Ike would set the clock ahead a few minutes in order to maintain his eating schedule without detection, and George would discover these small daylight saving changes.

The first "time" interruption of the day I did not share. It occurred soon after I arrived on the job, at eight o'clock. George and Ike would share a small pot of coffee brewed on George's hot plate.

Pickup time, fish time, and coke time came in the afternoon. I name it pickup time to represent the official visit of the man who made daily calls to cart away boxes of clicked materials. The arrival of the pickup man, a Negro, was always a noisy one, like the arrival of a daily passenger train in an isolated small town. Interaction attained a quick peak of intensity to crowd into a few minutes all communications, necessary and otherwise. Exchanges invariably included loud depreciations by the pickup man of the amount of work accomplished in the clicking department during the preceding twenty-four hours. Such scoffing would be on the order of "Is that all you've got done? What do you boys do all day?" These devaluations would be countered with allusions to the "soft job" enjoyed by the pickup man. During the course of the exchanges news items would be dropped, some of serious import, such as reports of accomplished or impending layoffs in the various plants of the company, or of gains or losses in orders for company products. Most of the news items, however, involved bits of information on plant employees told in a light vein. Information relayed by the clicker operators was usually told about each other, mainly in the form of summaries of the most recent kidding sequences. Some of this material was repetitive, carried over from day to day. Sammy would be the butt of most of this newscasting, although he would make occasional counter-reports on Ike and George. An invariable part of the interactional content of pickup time was Ike's introduction of the pickup man to George. "Meet Mr. Papeatis!" Ike would say in mock solemnity and dignity. Each day the pickup man "met" Mr. Papeatis, to the obvious irritation of the latter. Another pickup time invariably would bring Baby (or Mable) into the interaction. George would always issue the loud warning to the pickup man: "Now I want you to stay away from Baby! She's Henry's girl!" Henry was a burly Negro with a booming bass voice who made infrequent trips to the clicking room with lift-truck loads of materials. He was reputedly quite a ladies' man among the colored population of the factory. George's warning to "Stay away from Baby!" was issued to every Negro who entered the shop. Baby's only part in this was to laugh at the horseplay.

About mid-afternoon came fish time. George and Ike would stop work for a few minutes to consume some sort of pickled fish which Ike provided. Neither Sammy nor I partook of this nourishment, nor were we invited. For this omission I was grateful; the fish, brought in a newspaper and with head and tail intact, produced a reverse effect on my appetite. George and Ike seemed to share a great liking for fish. Each Friday night, as a regular ritual, they would enjoy a fish dinner together at a nearby restaurant. On these nights Ike would work until 8:30 and leave the plant with George.

Coke time came late in the afternoon, and was an occasion for total participation. The four of us took turns in buying the drinks and in making the trip for them to a fourth floor vending machine. Through George's manipulation of the situation, it eventually became my daily chore to go after the cokes; the straw boss had noted that I made a much faster trip to the fourth floor and back than Sammy or Ike.

Sammy left the plant at 5:30, and Ike ordinarily retired from the scene an hour and a half later. These quitting times were not marked by any distinctive interaction save the one regular exchange between Sammy and George over the former's "early washup." Sammy's tendency was to crowd his washing up toward five o'clock, and it was George's concern to keep it from further creeping advance. After Ike's departure came Boo's arrival. Boo's was a striking personality productive of a change in topics of conversation to fill in the last hour of the long workday.

Themes

To put flesh, so to speak, on this interactional frame of "times," my work group had developed various "themes" of verbal interplay which had become standardized in their repetition. These topics of conversation ranged in quality from an extreme of nonsensical chatter to another extreme of serious discourse. Unlike the times, these themes flowed one into the other in no particular sequence of predictability. Serious conversation could suddenly melt into horseplay, and vice versa. In the middle of a serious discussion on the high cost of living, Ike might drop a weight behind the easily startled Sammy, who hit him over the head with a dusty paper sack. Interaction would immediately drop to a low comedy exchange of slaps, threats, guffaws, and disapprobations which would invariably include a ten-minute echolalia of "Ike is a bad man, a very bad man! George is a good daddy, a very fine man!" Or, on the other hand, a stream of such invidious comparisons as followed a surreptitious switching-off of Sammy's machine by the playful Ike might merge suddenly into a discussion of the pros and cons of saving for one's funeral.

"Kidding themes" were usually started by George or Ike, and Sammy was usually the butt of the joke. Sometimes Ike would have to "take it," seldom

George. One favorite kidding theme involved Sammy's alleged receipt of $100 a month from his son. The points stressed were that Sammy did not have to work long hours, or did not have to work at all, because he had a son to support him. George would always point out that he sent money to his daughter; she did not send money to him. Sammy received occasional calls from his wife, and his claim that these calls were requests to shop for groceries on the way home were greeted with feigned disbelief. Sammy was ribbed for being closely watched, bossed, and henpecked by his wife, and the expression "Are you man or mouse?" became an echolalic utterance, used both in and out of the original context.

Ike, who shared his machine and the work scheduled for it with Boo, the night operator, came in for constant invidious comparison on the subject of output. The socially isolated Boo, who chose work rather than sleep on his lonely night shift, kept up a high level of performance, and George never tired of pointing this out to Ike. It so happened that Boo, an Arabian Moslem from Palestine, had no use for Jews in general; and Ike, who was Jewish, had no use for Boo in particular. Whenever George would extol Boo's previous night's production, Ike would try to turn the conversation into a general discussion on the need for educating the Arabs. George, never permitting the development of serious discussion on this topic, would repeat a smirking warning, "You watch out for Boo! He's got a long knife!"

The "poom poom" theme was one that caused no sting. It would come up several times a day to be enjoyed as unbarbed fun by the three older clicker operators. Ike was usually the one to raise the question, "How many times you go poom poom last night?" The person questioned usually replied with claims of being "too old for poom poom." If this theme did develop a goat, it was I. When it was pointed out that I was a younger man, this provided further grist for the poom poom mill. I soon grew weary of this poom poom business, so dear to the hearts of the three old satyrs, and, knowing where the conversation would inevitably lead, winced whenever Ike brought up the subject. . . .

Serious themes included the relating of major misfortunes suffered in the past by group members. George referred again and again to the loss, by fire, of his business establishment. Ike's chief complaints centered around a chronically ill wife who had undergone various operations and periods of hospital care. Ike spoke with discouragement of the expenses attendant upon hiring a housekeeper for himself and his children; he referred with disappointment and disgust to a teen-age son, an inept lad who "couldn't even fix his own lunch. He couldn't even make himself a sandwich!" Sammy's reminiscences centered on the loss of a flourishing business when he had to flee Europe ahead of Nazi invasion.

But all serious topics were not tales of woe. One favorite serious theme which was optimistic in tone could be called either "Danelly's future" or "getting Danelly a better job." It was known that I had been attending "college," the magic door to opportunity, although my specific course of study remained somewhat obscure. Suggestions poured forth on good lines of work to get into, and these suggestions were backed with accounts of friends, and friends of friends, who had made good via the academic route. My answer to the expected question, "Why are you working here?" always stressed the "lots of overtime" feature, and this explanation seemed to suffice for short-range goals.

There was one theme of especially solemn import, the "professor theme."

This theme might also be termed "George's daughter's marriage theme"; for the recent marriage of George's only child was inextricably bound up with George's connection with higher learning. The daughter had married the son of a professor who instructed in one of the local colleges. This professor theme was not in the strictest sense a conversation piece; when the subject came up, George did all the talking. The two Jewish operatives remained silent as they listened with deep respect, if not actual awe, to George's accounts of the Big Wedding which, including the wedding pictures, entailed an expense of $1,000. It was monologue, but there was listening, there was communication, the sacred communication of a temple, when George told of going for Sunday afternoon walks on the Midway with the professor, or of joining the professor for a Sunday dinner. Whenever he spoke of the professor, his daughter, the wedding, or even of the new son-in-law, who remained for the most part in the background, a sort of incidental like the wedding cake, George was complete master of the interaction. His manner, in speaking to the rank-and-file of clicker operators, was indeed that of master deigning to notice his underlings. I came to the conclusion that it was the professor connection, not the straw-boss-ship or the extra nickel an hour, which provided the fount of George's superior status in the group.

If the professor theme may be regarded as the cream of verbal interaction, the "chatter themes" should be classed as the dregs. The chatter themes were hardly themes at all; perhaps they should be labelled "verbal states," or "oral autisms." Some were of doubtful status as communication; they were like the howl or cry of an animal responding to its own physiological state. They were exclamations, ejaculations, snatches of song or doggerel, talkings-to-oneself, mutterings. Their classification as themes would rest on their repetitive character. They were echolalic utterances, repeated over and over. An already mentioned example would be Sammy's repetition of "George is a good daddy, a very fine man! Ike is a bad man, a very bad man!" Also, Sammy's repetition of "Don't bother me! Can't you see I'm busy? I'm a very busy man!" for ten minutes after Ike had dropped a weight behind him would fit the classification. Ike would shout "Mamariba!" at intervals between repetition of bits of verse, such as:

Mama on the bed,
Papa on the floor,
Baby in the crib
Says giver some more!

Sometimes the three operators would pick up one of these simple chatterings in a sort of chorus. "Are you man or mouse? I ask you, are you man or mouse?" was a favorite of this type.

So initial discouragement with the meagerness of social interaction I now recognized as due to lack of observation. The interaction was there, in constant flow. It captured attention and held interest to make the long day pass. The twelve hours of "click, _____ move die, _____ click, _____ move die" became as easy to endure as eight hours of varied activity in the oil fields or eight hours of playing the piece-work game in a machine shop. The "beast of boredom" was gentled to the harmlessness of a kitten.

Black Friday: Disintegration of the Group

But all this was before "Black Friday." Events of that dark day shattered the edifice of interaction, its framework of times and mosaic of themes, and reduced the work situation to a state of social atomization and machine-tending drudgery. The explosive element was introduced deliberately, but without prevision of its consequences.

On Black Friday, Sammy was not present; he was on vacation. There was no peach time that morning, of course, and no banana time. But George and Ike held their coffee time, as usual, and a steady flow of themes was filling the morning quite adequately. It seemed like a normal day in the making, at least one which was going to meet the somewhat reduced expectations created by Sammy's absence.

Suddenly I was possessed of an inspiration for modification of the professor theme. When the idea struck, I was working at Sammy's machine, clicking out leather parts for billfolds. It was not difficult to get the attention of close neighbor Ike to suggest *sotto voce,* "Why don't you tell him you saw the professor teaching in a barber college on Madison Street? . . . Make it near Halsted Street."

Ike thought this one over for a few minutes, and caught the vision of its possibilities. After an interval of steady application to his clicking, he informed the unsuspecting George of his near West Side discovery; he had seen the professor busy at his instructing in a barber college in the lower reaches of Hobohemia.

George reacted to this announcement with stony silence. The burden of questioning Ike for further details on his discovery fell upon me. Ike had not elaborated his story very much before we realized that the show was not going over. George kept getting redder in the face, and more tight-lipped; he slammed into his clicking with increased vigor. I made one last weak attempt to keep the play on the road by remarking that barber colleges paid pretty well. George turned to hiss at me, "You'll have to go to Kankakee with Ike!" I dropped the subject. Ike whispered to me, "George is sore!"

George was indeed sore. He didn't say another word the rest of the morning. There was no conversation at lunchtime, nor was there any after lunch. A pall of silence had fallen over the clicker room. Fish time fell a casualty. George did not touch the coke I brought for him. A very long, very dreary afternoon dragged on. Finally, after Ike left for home, George broke the silence to reveal his feelings to me:

> Ike acts like a five-year-old, not a man! He doesn't even have the respect of the niggers. But he's got to act like a man around here! He's always fooling around! I'm going to stop that! I'm going to show him his place! . . . Jews will ruin you, if you let them. I don't care if he sings, but the first time he mentions my name, I'm going to shut him up! It's always "Meet Mr. Papeatis! George is a good daddy!" And all that. He's paid to work! If he doesn't work, I'm going to tell Joe! [The superintendent.]

Then came a succession of dismal workdays devoid of times and barren of themes. Ike did not sing, nor did he recite bawdy verse. The shop songbird was caught in the grip of icy winter. What meager communication there was took a sequence of patterns which proved interesting only in retrospect.

For three days, George would not speak to Ike. Ike made several weak attempts to break the wall of silence which George had put between them, but George did not respond; it was as if he did not hear. George would speak to me, on infrequent occasions, and so would Ike. They did not speak to each other.

On the third day George advised me of his new communication policy, designed for dealing with Ike, and for Sammy, too, when the latter returned to work. Interaction was now on a "strictly business" basis, with emphasis to be placed on raising the level of shop output. The effect of this new policy on production remained indeterminate. Before the fourth day had ended, George got carried away by his narrowed interests to the point of making sarcastic remarks about the poor work performances of the absent Sammy. Although addressed to me, these caustic depreciations were obviously for the benefit of Ike. Later in the day Ike spoke to me, for George's benefit, of Sammy's outstanding ability to turn out billfold parts. For the next four days, the prevailing silence of the shop was occasionally broken by either harsh criticism or fulsome praise of Sammy's outstanding workmanship. I did not risk replying to either impeachment or panegyric for fear of involvement in further situational deteriorations.

Twelve-hour days were creeping again at snail's pace. The strictly business communications were of no help, and the sporadic bursts of distaste or enthusiasm for Sammy's clicking ability helped very little. With the return of boredom, came a return of fatigue. My legs tired as the afternoons dragged on, and I became engaged in conscious efforts to rest one by shifting my weight to the other. I would pause in my work to stare through the barred windows at the grimy brick wall across the alley; and, turning my head, I would notice that Ike was staring at the wall too. George would do very little work after Ike left the shop at night. He would sit in a chair and complain of weariness and sore feet.

In desperation, I fell back on my game of work, my blues and greens and whites, my ovals and trapezoids, and my scraping the block. I came to surpass Boo, the energetic night worker, in volume of output. George referred to me as a "day Boo" (day-shift Boo) and suggested that I "keep" Sammy's machine. I managed to avoid this promotion, and consequent estrangement with Sammy, by pleading attachment to my own machine.

When Sammy returned to work, discovery of the cleavage between George and Ike left him stunned. "They were the best of friends!" he said to me in bewilderment.

George now offered Sammy direct, savage criticisms of his work. For several days the good-natured Sammy endured these verbal aggressions without losing his temper; but when George shouted at him "You work like a preacher!" Sammy became very angry, indeed. I had a few anxious moments when I thought that the two old friends were going to come to blows.

Then, thirteen days after Black Friday, came an abrupt change in the pattern of interaction. George and Ike spoke to each other again, in friendly conversation:

> I noticed Ike talking to George after lunch. The two had newspapers of fish at George's cabinet. Ike was excited; he said, "I'll pull up a chair!"

> The two ate for ten minutes. . . . It seems that they went up to the 22nd Street Exchange together during lunch period to cash pay checks.

That afternoon Ike and Sammy started to play again, and Ike burst once more into song. Old themes reappeared as suddenly as the desert flowers in spring. At first, George managed to maintain some show of the dignity of superordination. When Ike started to sing snatches of "You Are My Sunshine," George suggested that he get "more production." Then Ike backed up George in pressuring Sammy for more production. Sammy turned this exhortation into low comedy by calling Ike a "slave driver" and by shouting over and over again, "Don't bother me! I'm a busy man!" On one occasion, as if almost overcome with joy and excitement, Sammy cried out, "Don't bother me! I'll tell Rothman! [the company president] I'll tell the union! Don't mention my name! I hate you!"

I knew that George was definitely back into the spirit of the thing when he called to Sammy, "Are you man or mouse?" He kept up the "man or mouse" chatter for some time.

George was for a time reluctant to accept fruit when it was offered to him, and he did not make a final capitulation to coke time until five days after renewal of the fun and fooling. Strictly speaking, there never was a return to banana time, peach time, or window time. However, the sharing and snitching of fruit did go on once more, and the window in front of Sammy's machine played a more prominent part than ever in the renaissance of horseplay in the clicker room. In fact, the "rush to the window" became an integral part of increasingly complex themes and repeated sequences of interaction. This window rushing became especially bound up with new developments which featured what may be termed the "anal gesture."[10] Introduced by Ike, and given backing by an enthusiastic, very playful George, the anal gesture became a key component of fun and fooling during the remaining weeks of my stay in the shop:

> Ike broke wind, and put his head in his hand on the block as Sammy grabbed a rod and made a mock rush to open the window. He beat Ike on the head, and George threw some water on him, playfully. In came the Negro head of the Leather Department; he remarked jokingly that we should take out the machines and make a playroom out of the shop.

Of course, George's demand for greater production was metamorphized into horseplay. His shout of "Production please!" became a chatter theme to accompany the varied antics of Ike and Sammy.

The professor theme was dropped completely. George never again mentioned his Sunday walks on the Midway with the professor.

Conclusions

Speculative assessment of the possible significance of my observations on information interaction in the clicking room may be set forth in a series of general statements.

---

[10] I have been puzzled to note widespread appreciation of this gesture in the "consumatory" communication of the working men of this nation. For the present I leave it to clinical psychologists to account for the nature and pervasiveness of this social bond.

Practical Application

First, in regard to possible practical application to problems of industrial management, these observations seem to support the generally accepted notion that one key source of job satisfaction lies in the informal interaction shared by members of a work group. In the clicking-room situation the spontaneous development of a patterned combination of horseplay, serious conversation, and frequent sharing of food and drink reduced the monotony of simple, repetitive operations to the point where a regular schedule of long work days became livable. This kind of group interplay may be termed "consumatory" in the sense indicated by Dewey, when he makes a basic distinction between "instrumental" and "consumatory" communication.[11] The enjoyment of communication "for its own sake" as "mere sociabilities," as "free, aimless social intercourse," brings job satisfaction, at least job endurance, to work situations largely bereft of creative experience.

In regard to another managerial concern, employee productivity, any appraisal of the influence of group interaction upon clicking-room output could be no more than roughly impressionistic. I obtained no evidence to warrant a claim that banana time, or any of its accompaniments in consumatory interaction, boosted production. To the contrary, my diary recordings express an occasional perplexity in the form of "How does this company manage to stay in business?" However, I did not obtain sufficient evidence to indicate that, under the prevailing conditions of laissez-faire management, the output of our group would have been more impressive if the playful cavorting of three middle-aged gentlemen about the barred windows had never been. As far as achievement of managerial goals is concerned, the most that could be suggested is that leavening the deadly boredom of individualized work routines with a concurrent flow of group festivities had a negative effect on turnover. I left the group, with sad reluctance, under the pressure of strong urgings to accept a research fellowship which would involve no factory toil. My fellow clickers stayed with their machines to carry on their labors in the spirit of banana time.

Theoretical Considerations

Secondly, possible contribution to ongoing sociological inquiry into the behavior of small groups, in general, and factory work groups, in particular, may lie in one or more of the following ideational products of my clicking-room experience:

1. In their day-long confinement together in a small room spatially and socially isolated from other work areas of the factory the Clicking Department employees found themselves ecologically situated for development of a "natural" group. Such a development did take place; from worker intercommunications did emerge the full-blown sociocultural system of consumatory interactions which I came to share, observe, and record in the process of my socialization.
2. These interactions had a content which could be abstracted from the total existential flow of observable doings and sayings for labelling and objective consideration. That is, they represented a distinctive sub-culture, with its

[11] John Dewey, *Experience and Nature,* Open Court Publishing Co., Chicago, 1925, pp. 202–206.

recurring patterns of reciprocal influencings which I have described as times and themes.

3. From these interactions may also be abstracted a social structure of statuses and roles. This structure may be discerned in the carrying out of the various informal activities which provide the content of the sub-culture of the group. The times and themes were performed with a system of roles which formed a sort of pecking hierarchy. Horseplay had its initiators and its victims, its amplifiers and its chorus; kidding had its attackers and attacked, its least attacked and its most attacked, its ready acceptors of attack and its strong resistors to attack. The fun went on with the participation of all, but within the controlling frame of status, a matter of who can say or do what to whom and get away with it.
4. In both the cultural content and the social structure of clicker group interaction could be seen the permeation of influences which flowed from the various multiple group memberships of the participants. Past and present "other-group" experiences or anticipated "outside" social connections provided significant materials for the building of themes and for the establishment and maintenance of status and role relationships. The impact of reference group affiliations on clicking-room interaction was notably revealed in the sacred, status-conferring expression of the professor theme. This impact was brought into very sharp focus in developments which followed my attempt to degrade the topic, and correlatively, to demote George.
5. Stability of the clicking-room social system was never threatened by immediate outside pressures. Ours was not an instrumental group, subject to disintegration in a losing struggle against environmental obstacles or oppositions. It was not striving for corporate goals; nor was it faced with the enmity of other groups. It was strictly a consumatory group, devoted to the maintenance of patterns of self-entertainment. Under existing conditions, disruption of unity could come only from within.

   Potentials for breakdown were endemic in the interpersonal interactions involved in conducting the group's activities. Patterns of fun and fooling had developed within a matrix of frustration. Tensions born of long hours of relatively meaningless work were released in the mock aggressions of horseplay. In the recurrent attack, defense, and counterattack there continually lurked the possibility that words or gestures harmless in conscious intent might cross the subtle boundary of accepted, playful aggression to be perceived as real assault. While such an occurrence might incur displeasure no more lasting than necessary for the quick clarification or creation of kidding norms, it might also spark a charge of hostility sufficient to disorganize the group.

   A contributory potential for breakdown from within lay in the dissimilar "other group" experiences of the operators. These other-group affiliations and identifications could provide differences in tastes and sensitivities, including appreciation of humor, differences which could make maintenance of consensus in regard to kidding norms a hazardous process of trial and error adjustments.
6. The risk involved in this trial and error determination of consensus on fun and fooling in a touchy situation of frustration—mock aggression—was made evident when I attempted to introduce alterations in the professor theme.

The group disintegrated, *instanter.* That is, there was an abrupt cessation of the interactions which constituted our groupness. Although both George and I were solidly linked in other-group affiliations with the higher learning, there was not enough agreement in our attitudes toward university professors to prevent the interactional development which shattered our factory play group. George perceived my offered alterations as a real attack, and he responded with strong hostility directed against Ike, the perceived assailant, and Sammy, a fellow traveler.

My innovations, if accepted, would have lowered the tone of the sacred professor theme, if not to "Stay Away From Baby" ribaldry, then at least to the verbal slapstick level of "finding Danelly an apartment." Such a downgrading of George's reference group would, in turn, have downgraded George. His status in the shop group hinged largely upon his claimed relations with the professor.

7. Integration of our group was fully restored after a series of changes in the patterning and quality of clicking-room interaction. It might be said that reintegration took place *in* these changes, that the series was a progressive one of step-by-step improvement in relations, that re-equilibration was in process during the three weeks that passed between initial communication collapse and complete return to "normal" interaction.

   The cycle of loss and recovery of equilibrium may be crudely charted according to the following sequence of phases: a) the stony silence of "not speaking"; b) the confining of communication to formal matters connected with work routines; c) the return of informal give-and-take in the form of harshly sarcastic kidding, mainly on the subject of work performance, addressed to a neutral go-between for the "benefit" of the object of aggression; d) highly emotional direct attack, and counter-attack, in the form of criticism and defense of work performance; e) a sudden rapprochement expressed in serious, dignified, but friendly conversation; f) return to informal interaction in the form of mutually enjoyed mock aggression; g) return to informal interaction in the form of regular patterns of sharing food and drink.

   The group had disintegrated when George withdrew from participation; and, since the rest of us were at all times ready for rapprochement, reintegration was dependent upon his "return." Therefore, each change of phase in interaction on the road to recovery could be said to represent an increment of return on George's part. Or, conversely, each phase could represent an increment of reacceptance of punished deviants. Perhaps more generally applicable to description of a variety of reunion situations would be conceptualization of the phase changes as increments of reassociation without an atomistic differentiation of the "movements" of individuals.

8. To point out that George played a key role in this particular case of re-equilibration is not to suggest that the homeostatic controls of a social system may be located in a type of role or in a patterning of role relationships. Such controls could be but partially described in terms of human interaction; they would be functional to the total configuration of conditions within the field of influence. The automatic controls of a mechanical system operate as such only under certain achieved and controlled conditions. The human body recovers from disease when conditions for such homeostasis are "right." The clicking-room group regained equilibrium under certain undetermined con-

ditions. One of a number of other possible outcomes could have developed had conditions not been favorable for recovery.

For purposes of illustration, and from reflection on the case, I would consider the following as possibly necessary conditions for reintegration of our group: a) Continued monotony of work operations; b) Continued lack of a comparatively adequate substitute for the fun and fooling release from work tensions; c) Inability of the operatives to escape from the work situation or from each other, within the work situation. George could not fire Ike or Sammy to remove them from his presence, and it would have been difficult for the three middle-aged men to find other jobs if they were to quit the shop. Shop space was small, and the machines close together. Like a submarine crew, they had to "live together"; d) Lack of conflicting definitions of the situation after Ike's perception of George's reaction to the "barber college" attack. George's anger and his punishment of the offenders was perceived as justified; e) Lack of introduction of new issues or causes which might have carried justification for new attacks and counter-attacks, thus leading interaction into a spiral of conflict and crystallization of conflict norms. For instance, had George reported his offenders to the superintendent for their poor work performance; had he, in his anger, committed some offense which would have led to reporting of a grievance to local union officials; had he made his anti-Semitic remarks in the presence of Ike or Sammy, or had I relayed these remarks to them; had I tried to "take over" Sammy's machine, as George had urged; then the interactional outcome might have been permanent disintegration of the group.

9. Whether or not the particular patterning of interactional change previously noted is somehow typical of a "re-equilibration process" is not a major question here. My purpose in discriminating the seven changes is primarily to suggest that re-equilibration, when it does occur, may be described in observable phases and that the emergence of each succeeding phase should be dependent upon the configuration of conditions of the preceding one. Alternative eventual outcomes may change in their probabilities, as the phases succeed each other, just as prognosis for recovery in sickness may change as the disease situation changes.
10. Finally, discrimination of phase changes in social process may have practical as well as scientific value. Trained and skillful administrators might follow the practice in medicine of introducing aids to re-equilibration when diagnosis shows that they are needed.

Group Dynamics and the Individual

DORWIN CARTWRIGHT
RONALD LIPPITT

How should we think of the relation between individuals and groups? Few questions have stirred up so many issues of metaphysics, epistemology, and ethics. Do groups have the same reality as individuals? If so, what are the properties of groups? Can groups learn, have goals, be frustrated, develop, regress, begin and end? Or are these characteristics strictly attributable only to individuals? If groups exist, are they good or bad? How *should* an individual behave with respect to groups? How *should* groups treat their individual members? Such questions have puzzled man from the earliest days of recorded history.

In our present era of "behavioral science" we like to think that we can be "scientific" and proceed to study human behavior without having to take sides on these problems of speculative philosophy. Invariably, however, we are guided by certain assumptions, stated explicitly or not, about the reality or irreality of groups, about their observability, and about their good or bad value.

Usually these preconceptions are integral parts of one's personal and scientific philosophy, and it is often hard to tell how much they derive from emotionally toned personal experiences with other people and how much from coldly rational and "scientific" considerations. In view of the fervor with which they are usually defended, one might suspect that most have a small basis at least in personally significant experiences. These preconceptions, moreover, have a tendency to assume a homogeneous polarization—either positive or negative.

Consider first the completely negative view. It consists of two major assertions: first, groups don't really exist. They are a product of distorted thought processes (often called "abstractions"). In fact, social prejudice consists precisely in acting as if groups, rather than individuals, were real. Second, groups are bad. They demand blind loyalty, they make individuals regress, they reduce man to the lowest common denominator, and they produce what *Fortune* magazine has immortalized as "group-think."

In contrast to this completely negative conception of groups, there is the completely positive one. This syndrome, too, consists of two major assertions: first, groups really do exist. Their reality is demonstrated by the difference it makes to an individual whether he is accepted or rejected by a group and whether he is part of a healthy or sick group. Second, groups are good. They satisfy deep-seated needs of individuals for affiliation, affection, recognition, and self-esteem; they stimulate individuals to moral heights of altruism, loyalty, and self-sacrifice; they provide a means, through cooperative interaction, by which man can accomplish things unattainable through individual enterprise.

From *International Journal of Group Psychotherapy,* Vol. 7 (January 1957), pp. 86–102. Reprinted by permission of the authors and International Universities Press.

This completely positive preconception is the one attributed most commonly, it seems, to the so-called "group dynamics movement." Group dynamicists, it is said, have not only *reified* the group but also *idealized* it. They believe that everything should be done by and in groups—individual responsibility is bad, man-to-man supervision is bad, individual problem-solving is bad, and even individual therapy is bad. The only good things are committee meetings, group decisions, group problem-solving, and group therapy. "If you don't hold the group in such high affection," we were once asked,"why do you call your research organization the Research Center FOR Group Dynamics? And, if you are *for* groups and group dynamics, mustn't you therefore be *against* individuality, individual responsibility, and self-determination?"

Five Propositions About Groups

This assumption that individuals and groups must necessarily have incompatible interests is made so frequently in one guise or another that it requires closer examination. Toward this end we propose five related assertions about individuals, groups, and group dynamics, which are intended to challenge the belief that individuals and groups must necessarily have incompatible, or for that matter, compatible interests.

1. Groups do exist; they must be dealt with by any man of practical affairs, or indeed by any child, and they must enter into any adequate account of human behavior. Most infants are born into a specific group. Little Johnny may be a welcome or unwelcome addition to the group. His presence may produce profound changes in the structure of the group and consequently in the feelings, attitudes, and behavior of various group members. He may create a triangle where none existed before or he may break up one which has existed. His development and adjustment for years to come may be deeply influenced by the nature of the group he enters and by his particular position in it—whether, for example, he is a first or second child (a personal property which has no meaning apart from its reference to a specific group).

   There is a wealth of research whose findings can be satisfactorily interpreted only by assuming the reality of groups. Recall the experiment of Lewin, Lippitt, and White [15] in which the level of aggression of an individual was shown to depend upon the social atmosphere and structure of the group he is in and not merely upon such personal traits as aggressiveness. By now there can be little question about the kinds of results reported from the Western Electric study [18] which make it clear that groups develop norms for the behavior of their members with the result that "good" group members adopt these norms as their *personal* values. Nor can one ignore the dramatic evidence of Lewin, Bavelas, and others [14] which shows that group decisions may produce changes in individual behavior much larger than those customarily found to result from attempts to modify the behavior of individuals *as* isolated individuals.

2. Groups are inevitable and ubiquitous. The biological nature of man, his capacity to use language, and the nature of his environment which has been built into its present form over thousands of years require that man exist in groups. This is not to say that groups must maintain the properties they now display, but we cannot conceive of a collection of human beings living in geographical proximity under conditions where it would be correct to assert

that no groups exist and that there is no such thing as group membership.

3. Groups mobilize powerful forces which produce effects of the utmost importance to individuals. Consider two examples from rather different research settings. Seashore [22] has recently published an analysis of data from 5,871 employees of a large manufacturing company. An index of group cohesiveness, developed for each of 228 work groups, permitted a comparison of members working in high and in low cohesive groups. Here is one of his major findings: "Members of high cohesive groups exhibit less anxiety than members of low cohesive groups, using as measures of anxiety: (a) feeling 'jumpy' or 'nervous,' (b) feeling under pressure to achieve higher productivity (with actual productivity held constant), and (c) feeling a lack of support from the company" (p. 98). Seashore suggests two reasons for the relation between group cohesiveness and individual anxiety: "(1) that the cohesive group provides effective support for the individual in his encounters with anxiety-provoking aspects of his environment, thus allaying anxiety, and (2) that group membership offers direct satisfaction, and this satisfaction in membership has a generalized effect of anxiety-reduction" (p. 13).

   Perhaps a more dramatic account of the powerful forces generated in groups can be derived from the publication by Stanton and Schwartz [24] of their studies of a mental hospital. They report, for example, how a patient may be thrown into an extreme state of excitement by disagreements between two staff members over the patient's care. Thus, two doctors may disagree about whether a female patient should be moved to another ward. As the disagreement progresses, the doctors may stop communicating relevant information to one another and start lining up allies in the medical and nursing staff. The patient, meanwhile, becomes increasingly restless until, at the height of the doctors' disagreement, she is in an acute state of excitement and must be secluded, put under sedation, and given special supervision. Presumably, successful efforts to improve the interpersonal relations and communications among members of the staff would improve the mental condition of such a patient.

   In general, it is clear that events occurring in a group may have repercussions on members who are not directly involved in these events. A person's position in a group, moreover, may affect the way others behave toward him and such personal qualities as his levels of aspiration and self-esteem. Group membership itself may be a prized possession or an oppressive burden; tragedies of major proportions have resulted from the exclusion of individuals from groups, and equally profound consequences have stemmed from enforced membership in groups.

4. Groups may produce both good and bad consequences. The view that groups are completely good and the view that they are completely bad are both based on convincing evidence. *The only fault with either is its one-sidedness.* Research motivated by one or the other is likely to focus on different phenomena. As an antidote to such one-sidedness it is a good practice to ask research questions in pairs, one stressing positive aspects and one negative: What are the factors producing conformity? *and* what are the factors producing nonconformity? What brings about a breakdown in communication? *and* what stimulates or maintains effective communication? An exclusive focus on pathologies or upon positive criteria leads to a seriously incomplete picture.

5. A correct understanding of group dynamics permits the possibility that desirable consequences from groups can be deliberately enhanced. Through a knowledge of group dynamics, groups can be made to serve better ends, for knowledge gives power to modify human beings and human behavior. At the same time, recognition of this fact produces some of the deepest conflicts within the behavioral scientist, for it raises the whole problem of social manipulation. Society must not close its eyes to Orwell's horrible picture of life in 1984, but it cannot accept the alternative that in ignorance there is safety.

To recapitulate our argument: groups exist; they are inevitable and ubiquitous; they mobilize powerful forces having profound effects upon individuals; these effects may be good or bad; and through a knowledge of group dynamics there lies the possibility of maximizing their good value.

A Dilemma

Many thoughtful people today are alarmed over one feature of groups: the pressure toward conformity experienced by group members. Indeed, this single "bad" aspect is often taken as evidence that groups are bad in general. Let us examine the specific problem of conformity, then, in order to attain a better understanding of the general issue. Although contemporary concern is great, it is not new. More than one hundred years ago Alexis de Tocqueville wrote: "I know of no country in which there is so little independence of mind and real freedom of discussion as in America. . . . In America the majority raises formidable barriers around the liberty of opinion. . . . The master (majority) no longer says: 'You shall think as I do or you shall die'; but he says: 'You are free to think differently from me and to retain your life, your property, and all that you possess, but they will be useless to you, for you will never be chosen by your fellow citizens if you solicit their votes; and they will affect to scorn you if you ask for their esteem. You will remain among men, but you will be deprived of the rights of mankind. Your fellow creatures will shun you like an impure being; and even those who believe in your innocence will abandon you, lest they should be shunned in their turn'" [25, pp. 273–275].

Before too readily accepting such a view of groups as the whole story, let us invoke our dictum that research questions should be asked in pairs. Nearly everyone is convinced that individuals should not be blind conformers to group norms, that each group member should not be a carbon copy of every other member, but what is the other side of the coin? In considering why members of groups conform, perhaps we should also think of the consequences of the removal of individuals from group membership or the plight of the person who really does not belong to any group with clear-cut norms and values. The state of anomie, described by Durkheim, is also common today. It seems as if people who have no effective participation in groups with clear and strong value systems either crack up (as in alcoholism or suicide) or they seek out groups which will demand conformity. In discussing this process, Talcott Parsons writes: "In such a situation it is not surprising that large numbers of people should . . . be attracted to movements which can offer them membership in a group with a vigorous esprit de corps with submission to some strong authority and rigid system of belief, the individual thus finding a measure of escape from painful perplexities or from a situation of anomie" [17, pp. 128–129].

The British anthropologist, Adam Curle, has stressed the same problem when he suggested that in our society we need not four, but five freedoms, the fifth being freedom from that neurotic anxiety which springs from a man's isolation from his fellows, and which, in turn, isolates him still further from them.

We seem, then, to face a dilemma: the individual needs social support for his values and social beliefs; he needs to be accepted as a valued member of some group which *he* values; failure to maintain such group membership produces anxiety and personal disorganization. But, on the other hand, group membership and group participation tend to cost the individual his individuality. If he is to receive support from others and, in turn, give support to others, he and they must hold in common some values and beliefs. Deviation from these undermines are possibility of group support and acceptance.

Is there an avenue of escape from this dilemma? Certainly, the issue is not as simple as we have described it. The need for social support for some values does not require conformity with respect to all values, beliefs, and behavior. Any individual is a member of several groups, and he may be a successful deviate in one while conforming to another (think of the visitor in a foreign country or of the psychologist at a convention of psychiatrists). Nor should the time dimension be ignored; a person may sustain his deviancy through a conviction that his fate is only temporary. These refinements of the issue are important and should be examined in great detail, but before we turn our attention to them, we must assert that we do *not* believe that the basic dilemma can be escaped. To avoid complete personal disorganization man must conform to at least a minimal set of values required for participation in the groups to which he belongs.

Pressures to Uniformity

Some better light may be cast on this problem if we refer to the findings of research on conformity. What do we know about the way it operates?

Cognitive Processes

Modern psychological research on conformity reflects the many different currents of contemporary psychology, but the major direction has been largely determined by the classic experiment of Sherif [23] on the development of social norms in perceiving autokinetic movement and by the more recent study of Asch [1] of pressures to conformity in perceiving unambiguous visual stimuli.

What does this line of investigation tell us about conformity? What has it revealed, for instance, about the conditions that set up pressures to conformity? Answers to this question have taken several forms, but nearly all point out that social interaction would be impossible if some beliefs and perceptions were not commonly shared by the participants. Speaking of the origin of such cognitive pressures to uniformity among group members, Asch says: "The individual comes to experience a world that he shares with others. He perceives that the surroundings include him, as well as others, and that he is in the same relation to the surroundings as others. He notes that he, as well as others, is converging upon the same object and responding to its identical properties. Joint action and mutual understanding require this relation of intelligibility and structural simplicity. In these terms the 'pull' toward the group becomes understandable" (1, p. 484).

Consistent with this interpretation of the origin of pressures to uniformity in a perceptual or judgmental situation are the findings that the major variables influencing tendencies to uniformity are (a) the quality of the social evidence (particularly the degree of unanimity of announced perceptions and the subject's evaluation of the trustworthiness of the other's judgments), (b) the quality of the direct perceptual evidence (particularly the clarity or ambiguity of the stimuli), (c) the magnitude of the discrepancy between the social and the perceptual evidence, and (d) the individual's self-confidence in the situation (as indicated either by experimental manipulations designed to affect self-confidence or by personality measurements).

The research in this tradition has been productive, but it has emphasized the individual and his cognitive problems and has considered the individual apart from any concrete and meaningful group membership. Presumably any trustworthy people adequately equipped with eyes and ears could serve to generate pressures to conformity in the subject, regardless of his specific relations to them. The result of this emphasis has been to ignore certain essential aspects of the conformity problem. Let us document this assertion with two examples.

First, the origin of pressures to uniformity has been made to reside in the person whose conformity is being studied. Through eliminating experimentally any possibility that pressures might be exerted by others, it has been possible to study the conformity of people as if they existed in a world where they can see or hear others but not be reacted to by others. It is significant, indeed, that conformity does arise in the absence of direct attempts to bring it about. But this approach does not raise certain questions about the conditions which lead to *social* pressures to conformity. What makes some people try to get others to conform? What conditions lead to what forms of pressure on others to get them to conform? The concentration of attention on the conformer has diverted attention away from the others in the situation who may insist on conformity and make vigorous efforts to bring it about or who may not exert any pressures at all on deviates.

A second consequence of this emphasis has been to ignore the broader social meaning of conformity. Is the individual's personal need for a social validation of his beliefs the only reason for conforming? What does deviation do to a person's acceptance by others? What does it do to his ability to influence others? Or, from the group's point of view, are there reasons to insist on certain common values, beliefs, and behavior? These questions are not asked nor answered by an approach which limits itself to the cognitive problems of the individual.

Group Processes

The group dynamics orientation toward conformity emphasizes a broader range of determinants. Not denying the importance of the cognitive situation, we want to look more closely at the nature of the individual's relation to particular groups with particular properties. In formulating hypotheses about the origin of pressures to uniformity, two basic sources have been stressed. These have been stated most clearly by Festinger and his co-workers [5], who propose that when differences of opinion arise within a group, pressures to uniformity will arise (a) if the validity or "reality" of the opinion depends upon agreement with the group (essentially the same point as Asch's), or (b) if locomotion toward a group goal will be facilitated by uniformity within the group.

This emphasis upon the group, rather than simply upon the individual, leads one to expect a broader set of consequences from pressures to uniformity. Pressures to uniformity are seen as establishing: (a) a tendency on the part of each group member to change his own opinion to conform to that of the other group members, (b) a tendency to try to change the opinions of others, and (c) a tendency to redefine the boundaries of the group so as to exclude those holding deviate opinions. The relative magnitudes of these tendencies will depend on other conditions which need to be specified.

This general conception of the nature of the processes that produce conformity emerged from two early field studies conducted at the Research Center for Group Dynamics. It was also influenced to a considerable extent by the previous work of Newcomb [16] in which he studied the formation and change of social attitudes in a college community. The first field study, reported by Festinger, Schachter, and Back [7], traced the formation of social groups in a new student housing project. As each group developed, it displayed its own standards for its members. The extent of conformity to the standards of a particular group was found to be related directly to the degree of cohesiveness of that group as measured by sociometric choices. Moreover, those individuals who deviated from their own group's norms received fewer sociometric choices than those who conformed. A process of rejection for nonconformity had apparently set in. The second field study, reported by Coch and French [3], observed similar processes. This study was conducted in a textile factory and was concerned with conformity to production standards set by groups of workers. Here an individual worker's reaction to new work methods was found to depend upon the standards of his group and, here too, rejection for deviation was observed.

The next phase of this research consisted of a series of experiments with groups created in the laboratory. It was hoped thereby to be able to disentangle the complexity of variables that might exist in any field setting in order to understand better the operation of each. These experiments have been reported in various publications by Festinger, Back, Gerard, Hymovitch, Kelley, Raven, Schachter, and Thibaut [2, 6, 8, 9, 11, 20]. We shall not attempt to describe these studies in detail, but draw upon them and other research in an effort to summarize the major conclusions.

First, a great deal of evidence has been accumulated to support the hypothesis that pressures to uniformity will be greater the more members want to remain in the group. In more attractive or cohesive groups, members attempt more to influence others and are more willing to accept influence from others. Note that here pressures to conformity are high in the very conditions where satisfaction from group membership is also high.

Second, there is a close relation between attempts to change the deviate and tendencies to reject him. If persistent attempts to change the deviate fail to produce conformity, then communication appears to cease between the majority and the deviate, and rejection of the deviate sets in. These two processes, moreover, are more intense the more cohesive the group. One of the early studies which documented the process of rejection was conducted by Schachter [20] on college students. It has recently been replicated by Emerson [4] on high school students, who found essentially the same process at work, but he discovered that among his high school students efforts to influence others continued longer, there was a greater readiness on the part of the majority to change, and there was a lower level of rejection within a limited period of time. Yet another study, conducted in Holland, Sweden, France, Norway, Belgium, Germany, and England, found the same tendency to reject deviates in all of these countries. This study, reported by Schachter, et al. [21], is a landmark in cross-cultural research.

Third, there is the question of what determines whether or not pressures to uniformity will arise with respect to any particular opinion, attitude, and behavior. In most groups there are no pressures to uniformity concerning the color of necktie worn by the members. Differences of opinion about the age of the earth probably would not lead to rejection in a poker club, but they might do so in certain fundamentalist church groups. The concept of *relevance* seems to be required to account for such variations in pressures to uniformity. And, if we ask, "relevance for what?" we are forced again to look at the group and especially at the goals of the group.

Schachter [20] has demonstrated, for example, that deviation on a given issue will result much more readily in rejection when that issue is relevant to the group's goals than when it is irrelevant. And the principle of relevance seems to be necessary to account for the findings of a field study reported by Ross [19]. Here attitudes of fraternity men toward restrictive admission policies were studied. Despite the fact that there was a consistent policy of exclusion in these fraternities, there was, surprisingly, little evidence for the existence of pressures toward uniformity of attitudes. When, however, a field experiment was conducted in which the distribution of actual opinions for each fraternity house was reported to a meeting of house members together with a discussion of the relevance of these opinions for fraternity policy, attitudes then tended to change to conform to the particular modal position of each house. Presumably the experimental treatment made uniformity of attitude instrumental to group locomotion where it had not been so before.

Sources of Heterogeneity

We have seen that pressures to uniformity are stronger the more cohesive the group. Shall we conclude from this that strong, need-satisfying, cohesive groups must always produce uniformity on matters that are important to the group? We believe not. We cannot, however, cite much convincing evidence since research has focused to date primarily upon the sources of pressures to uniformity and has ignored the conditions which produce heterogeneity. Without suggesting, then, that we can give final answers, let us indicate some of the possible sources of heterogeneity.

Group Standards about Uniformity

It is important, first, to make a distinction between conformity and uniformity. A group might have a value that everyone should be as different from everyone else as possible. Conformity to this value, then, would result not in uniformity of behavior but in nonuniformity. Such a situation often arises in therapy groups or training groups where it is possible to establish norms which place a high value upon "being different" and upon tolerating deviant behavior. Conformity to this value is presumably greater the more cohesive the group and the more it is seen as relevant to the group's objectives. Unfortunately, very little is known about the origin and operation of group standards about conformity itself. We doubt that the pressure to uniformity which arises from the need for "social reality" and for group locomotion can simply be obliterated by invoking a group standard of tolerance, but a closer look at such processes as those of group decision-making will be required before a deep understanding of this problem can be achieved.

Freedom to Deviate

A rather different source of heterogeneity has been suggested by Kelley and Shapiro [12]. They reason that the more an individual feels accepted by the other members of the group, the more ready he should be to deviate from the beliefs of the majority under conditions where objectively correct deviation would be in the group's best interest. They designed an experiment to test this hypothesis. The results, while not entirely clear because acceptance led to greater cohesiveness, tend to support this line of reasoning.

It has been suggested by some that those in positions of leadership are freer to deviate from group standards than are those of lesser status. Just the opposite conclusion has been drawn by others. Clearly, further research into group properties which generate freedom to deviate from majority pressures is needed.

Subgroup Formation

Festinger and Thibaut [8] have shown that lower group-wide pressures to uniformity of opinion result when members of a group perceive that the group is composed of persons differing in interest and knowledge. Under these conditions subgroups may easily develop with a resulting heterogeneity within the group as a whole though with uniformity within each subgroup. This conclusion is consistent with Asch's [1] finding that the presence of a partner for a deviate greatly stengthens his tendency to be independent. One might suspect that such processes, though achieving temporarily a greater heterogeneity, would result in a schismatic subgroup conflict.

Positions and Roles

A more integrative achievement of heterogeneity seems to arise through the process of role differentiation. Established groups are usually differentiated according to "positions" with special functions attached to each. The occupant of the position has certain behaviors prescribed for him by the others in the group. These role prescriptions differ, moreover, from one position to another, with the result that conformity to them produces heterogeneity within the group. A group function, which might otherwise be suppressed by pressures to uniformity, may be preserved by the establishment of a position whose responsibility is to perform the function.

Hall [10] has recently shown that social roles can be profitably conceived in the context of conformity to group pressures. He reasoned that pressures to uniformity of prescriptions concerning the behavior of the occupant of a position and pressures on the occupant to conform to these prescriptions should be greater the more cohesive the group. A study of the role of aircraft commander in bomber crews lends strong support to this conception.

In summary, it should be noted that in all but one of these suggested sources of heterogeneity we have assumed the process of conformity—to the norms of a subgroup, to a role, or to a group standard favoring heterogeneity. Even if the price of membership in a strong group be conformity, it need not follow that strong groups will suppress differences.

More Than One Group

Thus far our analysis has proceeded as though the individual were a member of only one group. Actually we recognize that he is, and has been, a member of many groups. In one of our current research projects we are finding that older adolescents can name from twenty to forty "important groups and persons that influence my opinions and behavior in decision situations." Indeed, some personality theorists hold that personality should be viewed as an "internal society" made up of representations of the diverse group relationships which the individual now has and has had. According to this view, each individual has a unique internal society and makes his own personal synthesis of the values and behavior preferences generated by these affiliations.

The various memberships of an individual may relate to one another in various ways and produce various consequences for the individual. A past group may exert internal pressures toward conformity which are in conflict with a present group. Two contemporaneous groups may have expectations for the person which are incompatible. Or an individual may hold a temporary membership (the situation of a foreign student, for example) and be faced with current conformity pressures which if accepted will make it difficult to readjust when returning to his more permanent memberships.

This constant source of influence from other memberships toward deviancy of every member of every group requires that each group take measures to preserve its integrity. It should be noted, however, that particular deviancy pressures associated with a given member may be creative or destructive when evaluated in terms of the integrity and productivity of the group, and conformity pressures from the group may be supportive or disruptive of the integrity of the individual.

Unfortunately there has been little systematic research on these aspects of multiple group membership. We can only indicate two sets of observations concerning (a) the intrapersonal processes resulting from multiple membership demands, and (b) the effects on group processes of the deviancy pressures which arise from the multiple membership status of individual members.

Marginal Membership

Lewin [13], in his discussion of adolescence and of minority group membership, has analyzed some of the psychological effects on the person of being "between two groups" without a firm anchorage in either one. He says: "The transition from childhood to adulthood may be a rather sudden shift (for instance, in some of the primitive societies), or it may occur gradually in a setting where children and adults are not sharply separated groups. In the case of the so-called 'adolescent difficulties,' however, a third state of affairs is often prevalent: children and adults constitute two clearly defined groups; the adolescent does not wish any longer to belong to the children's group and, at the same time, knows that he is not really accepted in the adult group. He has a position similar to what is called in sociology the 'marginal man' . . . a person who stands on the boundary between two groups. He does not belong to either of them, or at least he is not sure of his belongingness in either of them" (p. 143). Lewin goes on to point out that there are characteristic maladjustive behavior patterns resulting from this unstable membership situation: high tension, shifts between extremes of behavior, high sensitivity, and rejection of low status members of both groups. This situation, rather than fostering strong individuality, makes belonging to closely knit, loyalty-demanding groups very attractive. Dependency and acceptance are a welcome relief. Probably most therapy groups have a number of members who are seeking relief from marginality.

Overlapping Membership

There is quite a different type of situation where the person does have a firm anchorage in two or more groups but where the group standards are not fully compatible. Usually the actual conflict arises when the person is physically present in one group but realizes that he also belongs to other groups to which he will return in the near or distant future. In this sense, the child moves between his family group and his school group every day. The member of a therapy group has some sort of time perspective of "going back" to a variety of other groups between each meeting of the therapy group.

In their study of the adjustment of foreign students both in this country and after returning home, Watson and Lippitt [26] observed four different ways in which individuals cope with this problem of overlapping membership.

1. Some students solved the problem by "living in the present" at all times. When they were in the American culture all of their energy and attention was directed to being an acceptable member of this group. They avoided conflict within themselves by minimizing thought about and contact with the other group "back home." When they returned to the other group they used the same type of solution, quickly shifting behavior and ideas to fit back into the new present group. Their behavior appeared quite inconsistent, but it was a consistent approach to solving their problem of multiple membership.
2. Other individuals chose to keep their other membership the dominant one while in this country. They were defensive and rejective every time the present group seemed to promote values and to expect behavior which they felt might not be acceptable to the other group "back home." The strain of maintaining this orientation was relieved by turning every situation into a "black and white" comparison and adopting a consistently rejective posture toward the present, inferior group. This way of adjusting required a considerable amount of distorting of present and past realities, but the return to the other group was relatively easy.
3. Others reacted in a sharply contrasting way by identifying wholeheartedly with the present group and by rejecting the standards of the other group as incorrect or inferior at the points of conflict. They were, of course, accepted by the present group, but when they returned home they met rejection or felt alienated from the standards of the group (even when they felt accepted).
4. Some few individuals seemed to achieve a more difficult but also more creative solution. They attempted to regard membership in both groups as desirable. In order to succeed in this effort, they had to be more realistic about perceiving the inconsistencies between the group expectations and to struggle to make balanced judgments about the strong and weak points of each group. Besides taking this more objective approach to evaluation, these persons worked on problems of how the strengths of one group might be interpreted and utilized

by the other group. They were taking roles of creative deviancy in both groups, but attempting to make their contributions in such a way as to be accepted as loyal and productive members. They found ways of using each group membership as a resource for contributing to the welfare of the other group. Some members of each group were of course threatened by this readiness and ability to question the present modal ways of doing things in the group.

Thus it seems that the existence of multiple group memberships creates difficult problems both for the person and for the group. But there are also potentialities and supports for the development of creative individuality in this situation, and there are potentialities for group growth and achievement in the fact that the members of any group are also members of other groups with different standards.

Some Conclusions

Let us return now to the question raised at the beginning of this paper. How should we think of the relation between individuals and groups? If we accept the assumption that individuals and groups are both important social realities, we can then ask a pair of important questions. What kinds of effects do groups have on the emotional security and creative productivity of the individual? What kinds of effects do individuals have on the morale and creative productivity of the group? In answering these questions it is important to be alerted to both good and bad effects. Although the systematic evidence from research does not begin to provide full answers to these questions, we have found evidence which tends to support the following general statements.

Strong groups do exert strong influences on members toward conformity. These conformity pressures, however, may be directed toward uniformity of thinking and behavior, or they may foster heterogeneity.

Acceptance of these conformity pressures, toward uniformity or heterogeneity, may satisfy the emotional needs of some members and frustrate others. Similarly, it may support the potential creativity of some members and inhibit that of others.

From their experiences of multiple membership and their personal synthesis of these experiences, individuals do have opportunities to achieve significant bases of individuality.

Because each group is made up of members who are loyal members of other groups and who have unique individual interests, each group must continuously cope with deviancy tendencies of the members. These tendencies may represent a source of creative improvement in the life of the group or a source of destructive disruption.

The resolution of these conflicting interests does not seem to be the strengthening of individuals and the weakening of groups, or the strengthening of groups and the weakening of individuals, but rather a strengthening of both by qualitative improvements in the nature of interdependence between integrated individuals and cohesive groups.

References

1. Asch, S. E.: *Social Psychology.* New York: Prentice Hall, 1952.
2. Back, K. W.: Influence Through Social Communication. *J. Abn. & Soc. Psychol., 46*:9–23, 1951.

3. Coch, L. and French, J. R. P.: Overcoming Resistance to Change. *Hum. Relat., 1*:512–32, 1948.

4. Emerson, R. M.: Deviation and Rejection: An Experimental Replication. *Am. Sociol. Rev., 19*:688–93, 1954.

5. Festinger, L.: Informal Social Communication. *Psychol. Rev., 57*:271–292, 1950.

6. Festinger, L., Gerard, H. B., Hymovitch, B., Kelly, H. H., and Raven, B.: The Influence Process in the Presence of Extreme Deviates. *Hum. Relat., 5*:327–346, 1952.

7. Festinger, L., Schachter, S., and Back, K.: *Social Pressures in Informal Groups.* New York: Harper, 1950.

8. Festinger, L. and Thibaut, J.: Interpersonal Communication in Small Groups. *J. Abn. & Soc. Psychol., 46*:92–99, 1951.

9. Gerard, H. B.: The Effect of Different Dimensions of Disagreement on the Communication Process in Small Groups. *Hum. Relat., 6*:249–271, 1953.

10. Hall, R. L.: Social Influence on the Aircraft Commander's Role. *Am. Sociol. Rev., 20*:292–99, 1955.

11. Kelley, H. H.: Communication in Experimentally Created Hierarchies. *Hum. Relat., 4*:39–56, 1951.

12. Kelley, H. H. and Shapiro, M. M.: An Experiment on Conformity to Group Norms Where Conformity is Detrimental to Group Achievement. *Am. Sociol. Rev., 19*:667–677, 1954.

13. Lewin, K.: *Field Theory in Social Science.* New York: Harper, 1951.

14. Lewin, K.: Studies in Group Decision. In: *Group Dynamics: Research and Theory,* ed. D. Cartwright and A. Zander. Evanston: Row, Peterson, 1953.

15. Lewin, K., Lippitt, R., and White, R.: Patterns of Aggressive Behavior in Experimentally Created "Social Climates." *J. Soc. Psychol., 10*:271–99, 1939.

16. Newcomb, T. M.: *Personality and Social Change.* New York: Dryden, 1943.

17. Parsons, T.: *Essays in Sociological Theory:* (Rev. ed.) Glencoe: Free Press, 1954.

18. Roethlisberger, F. J. and Dickson, W. J.: *Management and the Worker.* Cambridge: Harvard University Press, 1939.

19. Ross, I.: Group Standards Concerning the Admission of Jews. *Soc. Prob., 2*:133–140, 1955.

20. Schachter, S.: Deviation, Rejection, and Communication. *J. Abn. & Soc. Psychol., 46*:190–207, 1951.

21. Schachter, S., *et al.:* Cross-cultural Experiments on Threat and Rejection. *Hum. Relat.,* 7:403–39, 1954.

22. Seashore, S. E.: *Group Cohesiveness in the Industrial Group.* Ann Arbor: Institute for Social Research, 1954.

23. Sherif, M.: *The Psychology of Social Norms.* New York: Harper, 1936.

24. Stanton, A. H. and Schwartz, M. S.: *The Mental Hospital.* New York: Basic Books, 1954.

25. Tocqueville, A.: *Democracy in America,* Vol. 1. New York: Alfred A. Knopf, 1945 (original publication, 1835).

26. Watson, J. and Lippitt, R.: *Learning Across Cultures.* Ann Arbor: Institute for Social Research, 1955.

Explaining Informal Work Groups in Complex Organizations: The Case for Autonomy in Structure

FRED E. KATZ

A generation after the Hawthorne studies, no one questions the existence of informal groups in complex organizations. Numerous studies have documented their existence, especially among employees in the lowest ranks. But the task remains of developing an adequate *conceptual* explanation of how persons in the lowest ranks, with their limited career prospects in their work and slight opportunity for advancement, are incorporated into work organizations on a relatively permanent basis. Stated differently, how can one account for the integration of organizations that include a large number of persons who are largely disenfranchised from the organization's reward system? How can one account for the apparent collaboration, if not loyalty, of persons who, since the time of Marx, have been described as being alienated from their work?[1] A brief, though oversimplified answer is that workers need work and factories need workers. One can hardly argue with this statement. Yet, the economic interdependence of workers and factories does not clarify the nature of the structural arrangement under which the interdependence is worked out.

The proposed answer to the question of how workers are incorporated into complex organizations has two aspects: (1) Workers have considerable autonomy within the confines of the organization. Even when their work is prescribed in exact detail, the work role tends to be defined narrowly. This leaves a considerable portion of the worker's life within the work organization *undefined.* (2) Workers tend to use this autonomy to bring their working-class culture into the organization, even though this is alien to the bureaucratic ethos of the higher echelons of the organization. This produces continuity between the workman's outside life and his participation in the work setting—a setting to which he has very limited allegiance.[2] This continuity in turn, promotes workers' integration into work organizations. After a general presentation of this perspective, it is illustrated

Fred E. Katz, "Explaining Informal Groups in Complex Organizations: The Case for Autonomy in Structure," *Administrative Science Quarterly,* Vol. 10, No. 2 (September 1965), pp. 204–221. Reprinted by permission of the author and the *Administrative Science Quarterly.*

[1] For a survey and research application of the theme of worker alienation, see Robert Blauner, *Alienation and Freedom: The Factory Worker and His Industry* (Chicago: University of Chicago, 1964).

[2] For a summary of the literature on the limited commitment of workers to the complex organizations in which they work, as well as to work itself, see Chris Argyris, *Integrating the Individual and the Organization* (New York: John Wiley, 1964). In Pt. IV the author provides a summary of the debate as to whether the worker is alienated. Argyris' book is addressed to the same general issue as the present paper, but his approach differs in that it focuses on the issue—a very important one—of developing organizational patterns so that there is congruence between the psychological needs of members and the administrative requirements of the organization. The present paper, in contrast, attempts to remain entirely on the level of social structure. See, also, R. Dubin, "Industrial Workers' World: A Study of the 'Central Life Interests' of Industrial Workers," in Erwin O. Smige (ed.), *Work and Leisure* (New Haven; College and University Press, 1963), pp. 53–72.

through a detailed review of one of Donald Roy's case studies of factory workers. No attempt will be made to assess the degree of fit of this perspective to particular types of industries.

The guiding perspective is that the culture of informal work groups is a manifestation of autonomy within the confines of the organization, and that autonomy is an aspect of organizational structure that needs systematic study. Autonomy is defined as independence from external control. Here, it means that the activities of workers within the organization are not fully controlled by the organization. This leaves room for development of informal patterns of various sorts—those that lessen boredom of workers, those that help get work done, as well as those that are alienative to the organization. I shall attempt to view autonomy as an aspect of the very structure of organizations, as spheres of independence which are delegated by the organization. Direct and indirect delegation of autonomy suggest themselves. The first refers to specific rules that delimit an area of autonomy. For example, a rule specifying that the foreman can decide who will work the night shift indicates a sphere in which the foreman has autonomy, one in which he exercises discretion. By contrast indirect delegation of autonomy results from the absence of rules; in a sphere where no clear rules exist, autonomy exists by default. Both direct and indirect delegation of autonomy promotes spheres of activity that are not closely controlled by the organization. The present thesis is that the resulting autonomous behavior needs to be considered as an aspect of organizational structure, not merely as deviance. This paper will mainly examine autonomy based on indirect delegation, since this seems to characterize informal patterns among workers.

Worker autonomy can be regarded as part of the barter arrangement between workers and the organization, where limited affiliation with the organization is exchanged for a degree of autonomy. The arrangement has important adaptive functions for both parties. For the organization it is a way of promoting the affiliation of some of its employees with the organization, while at the same time excluding them from certain vital spheres of organizational activity. For workers it permits continuation of the working-class style of life and provides ties of sociability in a context that in many ways is alien to the workman's culture. In short, the autonomy appears to have adaptive and pattern-maintenance functions for the workers, and adaptive and goal-attainment functions for the organization. It must be noted that worker autonomy, although enacted *in* the work organization is essentially *external* to his work role. This contrasts with the autonomy pattern for white collar workers, that is, all those who—from the lowliest clerk to the president—make up the administrative hierarchy. They have greater autonomy *within* their work role, but their role is more broadly defined than that of the worker.[3] In a sense the white-collar worker takes his work role *outside* the organization; the blue-collar worker brings his nonwork role *into* the organization. . . .

The definition of formal organization focuses on a planned system, and the definition of informal organization on actual behavior. This is a weak distinction, theoretically. Actual behavior is undoubtedly relevant to planned systems; and system characteristics, even planned ones, are relevant to actual

---

[3] This viewpoint is more fully developed in Fred E. Katz, "The School As a Complex Organization," *Harvard Educational Review,* 34 (Summer, 1964).

behavior. The distinction seems to need refocusing to enable orderly analysis of structure and ongoing behavior. I would suggest the following perspective: Organizational structure includes relatively controlled and relatively autonomous spheres. The controlled sphere is based on direct specification of behavior; the autonomous sphere is based on both direct and indirect specification of behavior. Direct specification of behavior approximates the formal organization concept; but it allows spheres of autonomy as well as spheres of controlled activity. The indirect specification of behavior approximates the traditional informal organization, but under comparable conceptual footing with the planned formal system.

The writings of Chester Barnard illustrate that autonomous and controlled behavior coexist within organizations and that the executive must fuse them together.[4] He notes that autonomy among personnel is not necessarily a disaster to executive control but may, in fact, be an asset to administrative processes. He suggests that the executive must rely on the "willingness to serve"[5] of those under his command; he must recognize that there is a "zone of indifference"[6] in which persons are prepared to accept orders, and beyond which they are prone to oppose orders. Informal patterns, in Barnard's view of the executive, are not divisive forces, but instead, are "expansion of the means of communication with reduction in the necessity for formal decisions, the minimizing of undesirable influences, and the promotion of desirable influences concordant with the scheme of formal responsibilities."[7] From Barnard's perspective both formal and informal patterns can be harnessed in the service of a "co-operating system." But it seems that the real point is not the blending of formally and informally organized behavior, but the blending of controlled and autonomous behaviors that exist within organizations. Barnard's model of the organization is suffused with autonomy patterns that can serve the whole organization; some of these patterns proceed from direct official specification of behavior and some come from indirect specification.

The Worker's Place in the Organization

Workers are here viewed as being permitted to develop relatively autonomous subcultures and subsystems of social interaction in their day-to-day routines. The autonomous patterns diverge from the officially prescribed patterns, but are very much in line with the workman's style of life and culture outside the organization. The culture of the working-class man is in many ways alien to the decorum and demeanor expected of white-collar members of the organization. In the routinized work of the white-collar worker there is no room for the sudden display of anger of the working-class male; in the face-the-public white-collar worker there is little scope for the pervasive sexual allusions of the working-class male. Yet within the working clique inside the organization the workman can enact the culture patterns of his life outside the organization. He can, for example, indulge freely in what is perhaps the workman's major form of creative mental activity: verbal play, imaginative exploits, and the romanticism

[4] Chester I. Barnard, *The Functions of the Executive* (Cambridge: Harvard University, 1938).
[5] *Ibid.*, 83 ff.
[6] *Ibid.*, 167 ff.
[7] *Ibid.*, p. 227.

on the theme of sex.[8] Indeed, the workman has a large sphere of verbal freedom, since much of what he says "doesn't count," so far as his work is concerned. Unlike the white-collar worker, whose work consists of a world of words, written and spoken, the worker is basically measured by the contributions of his hands. Therefore, his verbal jostlings, such as the razzing of the lowest person on the prestige totem pole, are not considered part of his job. There is every indication (as is shown in the review of the study by Donald Roy), that the content of the verbal banter contains reference to the workman's niche in the social order and the conditions of his social existence.[9] These are also reflected in patterns of practical jokes and prankish physical contact, which are characteristic of the workman's culture, but taboo in the culture of the white-collar worker.[10]

By contrast, the white-collar workers, whether senior executive or junior administrators, have a broad affinity for the organizational style of behavior. They are likely to be members of the middle or upper class, where they have learned the demeanor and proprieties of manner they will be expected to exercise in their position in the organization.[11] There is little abrupt discontinuity, for instance, between the style of dress and speech of their social class and that associated with the bureaucratic style of behavior. Stated differently, they can carry over elements of their external life into the organization and apply them to their job without having to make fundamental adjustments in their general style of behavior; although this does not mean that they have nothing to learn in their work. The organization-man thesis makes the same point in converse terms: The work habits and interests of the white-collar worker spill over into his family and community life. For the white-collar worker, the organization is less clearly differentiated from the culture of his private world than it is from the private world of the worker; the organization is not the enemy camp. The blue-collar worker, on the other hand, is eager to leave his work behind him as he leaves the gates of the factory.[12]

How does autonomy in the role of white-collar worker differ from that of the blue-collar worker? Briefly stated, white-collar workers have greater autonomy *in their task-related activities* than does the blue-collar worker; the time clock; the regimentation involved in feeding a machine and gearing one's work to the pace of a machine, of doing one's work exclusively at the location of a particular machine—these apply to the blue-collar worker to a far larger extent than to the white-collar worker. For the latter, work is defined more broadly than it is for the blue-collar worker, requiring a more diffuse commitment. This means that for the white-collar worker a broad range of activities and personal attributes

[8] I am not suggesting that middle and upper class males do not engage in this form of mental sport, but I do suggest that for the working-class male it is a *major* creative outlet, and much less so for the middle and upper classes.

[9] S. M. Miller and Frank Riessman suggest that the "factory 'horseplay,' the ritualistic kidding" are partly an expression of the working-class theme of person centeredness; see their "The Working-Class Subculture," in A. B. Shostak and W. Gomberg (eds.), *Blue Collar World* (Englewood Cliffs, N. J.: Prentice-Hall, 1964), pp. 24–35.

[10] Participating in physical contact—be it fighting, prankish shoving, or contact sports—are chiefly characteristic of male preadult culture. Presumably it is only at the low socioeconomic levels that this pattern continues into adulthood. It is not clear whether similar continuities exist between *preadult* and adult female culture among working-class women.

[11] It makes little difference whether they are members of the middle or upper class or use these classes as a reference group to guide their behavior.

[12] Robert Blauner "Occupational Differences in Work Satisfaction," in R. L. Simpson and I. H. Simpson (eds.), *Social Organization and Behavior* (New York: John Wiley, 1964), pp. 287–292.

are defined as relevant to work, from personal grooming to getting along with others. Organizing a Little League baseball team, the fate of the local community chest drive, and participation in college alumni affairs—a good organization man's allegiance to the organization and his style of work include taking part in these activities after working hours and communicating these interests to his work peers. It is difficult to assess which activities are regarded as clearly *external* to his work role. On the other hand, the worker's tasks are defined more narrowly, leaving scope for activity that is defined as *external* to his work, but enacted while he is at his place of work.

The limited bases for the worker's *allegiance* to the work organization are given tacit recognition not only in the worker being excluded from administrative decision making, but also in his being allowed to bring into the work setting working-class culture patterns and to fashion them into relatively autonomous subcultures. In short, the worker's external affiliations; i.e., with the working-class style of life, are permitted to intrude into the organization that employs him. This can be viewed as part of the exchange (in addition to monetary pay) for limited forms of reward and participation that the worker is allowed by the employing organization. In view of the differentiation between worker subculture and bureaucratic culture, the worker's immersion in working-class patterns may serve to perpetuate his disenfranchisement from the administrative sphere, resulting in a vicious cycle. . . .

The empirical study of workers in factories has been a favorite of sociologists and social psychologists. The focus of many of these studies is on what actually goes on in work settings. Among the most eloquently descriptive studies of the culture and interaction patterns of workers are those by Donald F. Roy. . . . Roy's article ["Banana Time—Job Satisfaction and Informal Interaction"] is perhaps a culmination in a series of research findings that, since the days of the Hawthorne studies, have pointed to the demise of the economic man without, however, completing the task of making social organization the focus of analysis. The early studies, in their opposition to the economic-man thesis, pointed out that the individual was not guided only by his own monetary self-interest. Indeed, he could be guided against his own self-interest by his worker peer group; the individual worker might actually lose income by following the output control patterns of his peers. It was emphasized that there was a "group factor" in work situations; but an individualistic, social psychological focus was retained for this group factor. In the Hawthorne studies there was much concern with changes in attitude toward work; the meaning of work was considered a basic factor in individuals' performance; and work groups were considered in molding the meaning and attitudes for members of the group.[13] Roy's interpretation of his findings is similarly social psychological. It is that the informal patterns serve primarily to provide job satisfaction by relieving *boredom.* Along with many students of industrial relations in the last thirty years, he notes the existence of relatively distinct subgroups that have relatively distinct culture and interaction patterns, and that are separate from the formal structure in the factory. Yet, the basic interpretation is in individualistic, psychological terminology: it relieves boredom. Even if one accepts the psychological perspective, one must

[13]Fritz J. Roethlisberger and William J. Dickson, *op. cit.*, and Edward Gross, *Work and Society* (New York: Thomas Crowell, 1958), ch. xiv.

question whether routine, repetitive work is necessarily conducive to boredom. For example, Chinoy's study of automobile assembly-line workers suggests that workers' response to routine, repetitive work is perhaps better characterized by irritation over lack of control over one's work than by boredom.[14] To realize that routine, repetitive activity does not necessarily lead to boredom, one should allow for the influence of culture. The researcher may be exaggerating the activistic theme of Western societies. The Jicarilla Apache, for example, "have an infinite capacity for not being bored. They can sit for hours on end and apparently do nothing; they certainly don't intellectualize about doing nothing."[15]

The focus of the present paper suggests attention to what seems to be a basic feature in the social organization of the work situation, the autonomy enjoyed by the work group.[16] It does this on Roy's evidence that *considerable structuring of the work situation is done by the workers themselves.* What, then, is the content of the autonomous group culture? As Roy describes it, the work situation includes a great variety of behaviors that are not directly connected with *work.* Many of these fit Simmel's description of play forms of social reality.[17] Subjects that are of serious concern, such as economic security, sexual virility, health and death, submission to the authority of other men, family loyalty, and status aspirations, are examined in a context where they are stripped of their serious content. But the manner in which attention is paid to these subjects is particularly important. Flitting from one topic to another—from the deeply serious to the comic, from the immediately practical to the remotely romantic—indicates the decided irrelevance of the practical, concrete reality in which each of the subjects is embedded. Perhaps it is because members are simultaneously engaged in serious work that they feel free to treat other concerns so detachedly. Roy's group appears to be a veritable haven for the enactment of play forms. Elements of life that are largely beyond the control of the individual are exposed and, in a fashion, are dealt with. All this is most clearly evident in the verbal themes. In addition to play forms, it may well be that the various social interaction patterns—the "razzing" of Sammy, the paternalism of George—are reiterations of serious realities in the larger social context in which the men find themselves. It is noteworthy that it is Sammy, the newest immigrant (all three men are immigrants) who is the scapegoat; it is George, the only Gentile, who quietly occupies the superior status; it is the Negro handyman who is the object of stereotypical banter about uncontrolled sexuality.

These elements, whether they are fairly explicit reiterations or play forms of the workman's life outside the factory, are continuities between life outside the factory and life inside the factory and therefore are important for understanding the nature of the bond between the worker and the organization in which he is employed. Work peers participate in a common culture, which relies heavily on their common fate both within and *outside* the organization. In their commonality they retain a fundamental alienation from the white-collar ranks

[14] Ely Chinoy, *Automobile Workers and the American Dream* (Garden City, N.Y.: Doubleday, 1955).
[15] Personal communication from H. Clyde Wilson.
[16] Focus on autonomy structure does not altogether avoid the pitfall of potentially overemphasizing one set of structures and one set of functions, just as social-psychological studies have done. But it should serve to broaden the existing basis of analysis.
[17] K. H. Wolff (ed. and transl.), *The Sociology of George Simmel* (New York: Free Press, 1950).

in the organization. This appears to be demonstrated in Chinoy's findings of workers' widespread lack of interest in becoming foremen or white-collar workers.[18] It is also supported by Walker and Guest's study of assembly-line workers. They found largely favorable reaction by workers to their immediate job, but intense dissatisfaction with the factory as a whole.[19] Although there is a lack of affiliation with the white-collar ranks of the organization, the worker *does* form bonds within the organization—with his own work peers.[20] For the organization, this dual relationship provides an uneasy truce without lessening the fundamental internal antithesis, and manifests itself in problems of morale and communications. At the same time the structure of the situation—the existence of two cultures—assures the continuity of the basic antithesis.

Roy points out that the group had developed a "full-blown socio-cultural system." The group was to a considerable extent a separate and distinct system, one in which the members had active, at times even creative, participation—in sharp contrast to their minimal participation in the larger organization. But it does not seem that *work* was at all a major focus of this sociocultural system! If one accepts this point, one gains a tool for reconciling the dilemma as to whether factory workers are strongly alienated from their work.[21] It appears that work is *one of a variety* of topics around which Roy's group had developed behavioral patterns, but work was by no means the central point of attention of this "full-blown sociocultural system."

The contention that work is not a central feature of Roy's work group differs considerably from traditional explanations of informal groups. Although no claim is made about the representativeness of the Roy group, it must be understood that the sort of data he presented has traditionally been interpreted largely in terms of its relevance to *work.* Statements to the effect that informal activities give meaning to dull, routine factory work[22] and that "work output is a function of the degree of work satisfaction, which in turn depends upon the informal social patterns of the work group"[23] are typical examples. These statements provide a social-psychological explanation of the group's mediating effect between the individual and his work, but they are hardly adequate in providing a structural explanation of the place of informal groups in a complex organization.

In addition to the social-psychological interpretations, there are well-docu-

---

[18] Ely Chinoy, *op. cit.;* see especially, ch. v. See also, E. W. Bakke, *The Unemployed Worker* (New Haven: Yale University, 1940); and poll conducted by *Fortune* (May, 1947), both cited by Chinoy. Chinoy's explanation of the lack of desire for promotion is that workers have become so discouraged in the course of their work careers that they have given up. He notes that workers are reacting to "the limited opportunities available, to the uncertainties stemming from the informal procedures by which foremen were chosen, and to the nature of the foreman's job itself . . ." (p. 49). This explanation is not irreconcilable with the one offered here. The young factory worker, who does have visions of advancement, is presumably not sufficiently knowledgeable about the culture wall between himself and the administrative bureaucrat.

[19] Charles R. Walker and Robert H. Guest, *The Man on the Assembly Line* (Cambridge, Mass.: Harvard University, 1952); see, for example, pp. 139–140.

[20] Dubin's studies suggest, however, that workers' friendship bonds with work peers are less important than bonds with peers outside the work setting; see Robert Dubin, *op. cit.*

[21] Argyris, *op. cit.,* believes that workers are strongly alienated; Walker and Guest, *op. cit.,* note that workers they studied were relatively contented doing simple, repetitive work.

[22] Edward Gross, *op. cit.,* p. 526.

[23] Reinhard Bendix and Lloyd H. Fisher, "The Perspectives of Elton Mayo," in Amitai Etzioni, (ed.), *Complex Organizations: A Sociological Reader* (New York: Holt, Rinehart, and Winston, 1961), p. 119.

mented studies—by Roy and others—which show production control and worker collusion against management by informal groups of workers.[24] Here there can be no doubt that informal patterns are relevant to work. But it is not certain, even here, that informal groups exist primarily for the worker's control over work or whether the explanation should not be reversed: that control over work exists because of the presence of informal groups which, in turn, exist because of the worker's relative autonomy.

In summary, it is suggested that Roy's work group exhibits a rich sociocultural system that is made possible by substantial worker autonomy. The autonomy exists by default; worker's roles are narrowly defined, leaving a considerable sphere of undefined action within the confines of the organization. The content of worker's sociocultural system is made up of a variety of elements from the culture and social context of workers outside the factory. These elements manifest themselves as direct reiterations as well as play forms of the reality. They provide continuity between the workman's life outside the factory and his participation within the factory.

In using the Roy study to illustrate autonomy patterns among informal groups, certain cautionary statements must be made. The group Roy studied may be atypical in the small amount of managerial supervision and in the degree of isolation from the rest of the factory, which might allow a disproportionately high degree of autonomy, as compared with other work groups. One can only answer that this requires investigation; it has not been demonstrated at this time. Also, worker autonomy structure is evident in other studies, as implied, for example, in Gouldner's conception of the managerial "indulgency pattern" toward workers,[25] and Bensman and Gerver's study of "deviancy in maintaining the social system" in a factory.[26] In addition, autonomy patterns among employees who are operating on higher echelons than laborers have been explored by Chester Barnard[27] and in the various writings of Peter Blau;[28] but these are outside the scope of the present paper.[29]

Note on the Theory of Integration of Complex Organizations

Complex organizations must have ways of procuring and integrating the services of a variety of participants. On a common-sense level one can see the process of procurement and integration accomplished most readily in organizations that have coercive means at their disposal. Prisons can force inmates to peel potatoes. But organizations that do not have coercion at their disposal provide a problem for the analyst. There can be little doubt that most complex organizations do, in fact, solve the problem. How is it accomplished?

The concern of this paper has been the integration of a particular segment of the membership of complex organizations, namely blue-collar workers in

[24] See, Donald Roy "Efficiency and 'The Fix': Informal Intergroup Relations in a Piecework Machine Shop," in S. M. Lipset and N. J. Smelser (ed.), *Sociology: The Progress of a Decade* (Englewood Cliffs, N.J.: Prentice-Hall, 1961), pp. 378–390; also his "Quota Restriction and Goldbricking in a Machine Shop," *American Journal of Sociology,* 57 (March, 1952), 427–442.

[25] Alvin W. Gouldner, *Wildcat Strike* (Yellow Springs, Ohio: Antioch Press, 1954).

[26] Joseph Bensman and Israel Gerver, "Crime and Punishment in the Factory: The Function of Deviancy in Maintaining the Social System," *American Sociological Review,* 28 (August, 1963), 588–598.

[27] Chester Barnard, *op. cit.*

[28] Peter M. Blau, "Structural Effects," *op. cit.,* and *The Dynamics of Bureaucracy, op. cit.*

[29] A broader formulation of autonomy structure has been attempted in Fred E. Katz, *op. cit.*

factories. The particular issue, here, is how these persons are recruited and integrated into the organization, which offers them few of the rewards that it can bestow. The answer is that a federalistic type of solution exists: Workers are permitted ample separation from the total organization and, to a considerable extent, their integration into the larger system is left to them. Informal work group cultures are the concrete structures that make up the solution.

The separation of workers from the employing organization provides workers with flexibility and options as to the degree of alienation from the whole organization. At the same time, the separation gives the organization freedom to adopt means and goals that are disparate, if not alien, to those of the workers. The federalistic balance of autonomy for the blue-collar workers as against the white-collar staff allows flexibility to both sides; but it is also a potential source of divergence and conflict, which finds nurture in the separate subcultures.

In contrast to the form of integration suggested here, other writings have shown much concern with models of organization that dwell on lessening internal differentiation. Workers and the white-collar staff are seen as diverging in interest and this divergence can *and needs to be* lessened if the organization is to operate effectively.[30] These writings differ from the present essay both in theoretical and practical focus. On the theoretical side, the present exposition is based strongly on the view that autonomy can be viewed as a structural principle of organizations, which can have positive or negative consequences for the operation of organizations. Structured autonomy manifests itself in internal divergencies, but these are not necessarily disruptive and maladaptive for the whole organization or any part of it. As to practical goals, many writers, notably Whyte and Argyris,[31] are concerned with the problem of improving human relations in industrial concerns. The practical focus here is not on improving social relationships in complex organizations; it is on the problem of improving the analytic theory of complex organizations. I do not claim that this is a more worthy or pressing problem than that of improving human relationships in complex organizations, merely that it *is* a problem. . . .

[30] Argyris, *op. cit.,* and other writings by the same author. See also the writings of W. F. Whyte; for example, *Patterns of Industrial Peace* (New York: Harper and Row, 1951) and *Money and Motivation* (New York: Harper and Row, 1955).
[31] *Ibid.*

Work Groups on the Assembly Line

CHARLES R. WALKER
ROBERT H. GUEST
ARTHUR N. TURNER

Nature and Importance of Groups on the Assembly Line

The technology of the assembly-line environment [is such as] to suggest that the workers under any given foreman are not the same as the close-knit groups or crews and teams common to many industries, where all members have separate but strictly interdependent functions, and tend to think of themselves as a "baseball nine" or a "football eleven." On the assembly line, men do work that is rarely related, team-wise or in a strict functional sense, to what other members of the group do. For this reason in our early study of assembly lines, our first impression was that technology had eliminated the work group altogether, leaving merely a tenuous relationship between individuals and the foremen.

But this is not true, whatever the logic of engineering. Every segment of the line under a foreman is an actual or potential work group or team.

Social scientists, in discussing groups, use the term cohesiveness rather than strength. This, as commonly understood, means a measure of the durability of the group. We are interested in the durability of a group, but more precisely we are interested in the resultant power of its members to think and act as a single unit and to fulfill their common objectives by so doing.

Before examining why groups vary in cohesiveness, we need to state two assumptions which should be kept in mind throughout this discussion:

The first is that there tends to be a positive correlation between the amount of interaction among members and the cohesiveness or strength of the group. In other words, the more frequently people in a group talk with one another—or otherwise interact—the stronger the group.[1]

A second assumption is that a strong and cohesive group with the foreman as its leading member is desirable. Personal satisfactions of its members are increased. Frictions are reduced. A sense of purpose develops which can lead to improved efficiency and quality. These assumptions can be justified, we believe, not only by our own observations and research at Plant X and elsewhere, but also by reference to the large volume of recent social-science research into the nature and functions of groups in industry and elsewhere.

---

[1] There are obvious exceptions to this statement and yet it remains a useful generalization. One exception is this: If the members markedly disagree on the group's goals, increasing interaction may increase their disagreement and so reduce the group's cohesiveness. For a discussion of this and related points, see W. F. Whyte, "Leadership and Group Participation," New York State School of Industrial and Labor Relations, Bulletin 24, Ithaca, N.Y., May, 1953, pp. 28–30. See G. G. Homans, *The Human Group,* Harcourt, Brace & World, Inc., New York, 1950, pp. 110–117, 243, 444. See also the "Note" by Paula Brown and Robert Brown, and Homans' reply, in *American Sociological Review,* vol. 20, no. 1, pp. 83–86, Feb., 1955.

One fundamental reason that a feeling of belonging to a cohesive group of men at work increases the average worker's satisfaction with his job and with the company may well be that without a group to identify with, there is in most large organizations a feeling of anonymity which most people dislike. Certainly this has been true for the automobile assembly workers interviewed in our studies. In both plants surveyed, considerable bitterness was expressed against what appeared to the workers as "impersonal treatment" by the company. A surprising number felt that "the company isn't interested in people," or "you're just a number as far as they're concerned."[2] This feeling of anonymity, caused at least in part by the relatively impersonal nature of the work itself on most assembly-line jobs, can create or accentuate problems of morale, absenteeism, turnover, and quality.

Our evidence is that the successful foreman at Plant X intuitively recognized the importance for the average worker of belonging to a group, and purposely related himself not only to each individual but to his group of men as a whole. This constituted one method, and an important one, by which the foreman counteracted the pressure and impersonality of the work environment.

We are now ready to look at the factors which weaken, and those which strengthen, work groups on the assembly line.

Factors That Tend to Weaken Groups

These factors are important because it is only by counteracting them that a foreman derives the advantages of a cohesive work team, and significantly, nearly all of them appear as barriers to interaction between men on the assembly line.

The first and most obvious barrier is noise. In many of the sections along the line, *verbal* interaction, at least, is difficult or impossible. Even where noise does not inhibit interaction, the average worker has to pay close attention to the line, which is always moving in front of him, if he isn't to "go into the hole." He can seldom or never stop even for a moment to chat with his neighbor. And unlike some assembly jobs in other industries, the work on an automobile assembly line often requires a degree of "surface mental attention"[3] which makes it difficult or impossible to work and talk at the same time, except for the occasional exchange of a few words—for example, when there is a gap in the line. Also, except when he takes personal relief, the average worker must remain at his station throughout the work day, which sharply limits the number of men with whom interaction is possible.

A more important and basic limiting factor is that the technical nature of the work of an assembly line neither suggests nor compels interaction. Interaction connected with the work, such as interchange of tools, signals, reciprocal or team activity, is not usually necessary. In other words, there are fewer absolute *functional* requirements for interaction between men in an assembly plant than in many other industries.

Group cohesiveness is also limited by the fact, characteristic as far as we know only of assembly lines, that every group under a foreman is, so to speak, blurred at both ends so far as interaction goes. To illustrate: imagine a moving

[2]See C. R. Walker and R. H. Guest, *The Man on the Assembly Line,* Harvard University Press, Cambridge, Mass., 1952, pp. 135–140. These attitudes were still more strongly expressed by the longer-service men in the second assembly plant studied.
[3]See *The Man on the Assembly Line,* pp. 12–13.

line, let us say, a hundred and fifty feet long with three groups of workers each occupying fifty feet of the line. The men are on each side of the line, and let us say each group of twenty men has ten on one side and ten on the other. Because of the noise and close attention to work, interactions can only occur with men who are near each other. Thus, an individual worker is likely to interact, in the course of a day or a month, with only a fraction of his own work group, and then only briefly and infrequently. And the workers at either end of the section interact as frequently, because of proximity, with members of the next group as they do with their own. Because of this interaction pattern, the boundaries between groups are blurred, and all the individuals in the group with which a worker tends to interact do not necessarily come under the same foreman.

Not only is the cohesiveness of the men in a foreman's section limited by this overlapping at the edges; equally important are changes in the composition of work groups caused by fluctuations in production, turnover, and absenteeism. Even when interaction among members of a potential group is frequent, it takes time for cohesiveness to develop. Whenever schedules fluctuate sharply up or down, the composition and size of the groups change, and often individual members report to different foremen. In the same way turnover and absenteeism disrupt the composition of a group, and make it more difficult for foremen to develop that feeling of belonging and loyalty which comes from stability of membership.

Characteristics of Strong Groups

In spite of these inhibiting factors, some foremen *were* able to build with and between their men a strong sense of belonging to a group. Under the foreman's leadership, members of that group helped each other out in performing what they thought were their common objectives in getting the work done. How was this possible? How did these foremen manage to overcome the various handicaps to group formation discussed above?

The evidence suggests that in those sections in which the foremen had been able to develop a sense of group or team spirit:

1. Interactions were more frequently reciprocal than unilateral between foreman and workers;
2. Key operators served as channels of communications;
3. Interactions between operators were functional or problem-solving. Some self-determination and informal job rotation was practiced.

When there were more reciprocal than unilateral interactions between the foreman and his men, that meant as a rule that when the foreman talked with a worker he was asking a question and listening to a response, rather than merely making a demand or transmitting an order. It was natural for such a foreman to delegate a certain amount of informal responsibility to his utility men or other key operators, so that there was more frequent interaction between the foreman and his other men. Thus, the group structure in such instances did not simply comprise two levels of communication, the level of the formal leader (the foreman), and the level of all his subordinates. There was in addition a third, informal level, consisting of one or more utility or other key men.

A foreman who believed that his section operated more effectively when greater responsibility was distributed to his key operators practiced the same philosophy when he also allowed and encouraged his regular operators to take some of the responsibility for ensuring that good work was done in the section. Thus this meant that there was more interaction between operators concerning the work than in other sections. Without waiting for the foreman or inspectors to point out trouble, the operators themselves kept each other posted about actual or potential trouble encountered in the section, and, furthermore, advised one another as to steps which should be taken to correct the difficulty.

This kind of interaction among the men also reflected a certain amount of group self-determination allowed by some of the foremen. Though they maintained full responsibility for the end results, some foremen allowed the operators to determine how the work load was to be distributed among the group. At times the group, with the foreman's guidance, established informal systems of job rotation, and so, over a period of time, the average man in the group came to interact with most, if not all, of the members of the section. He was not tied to one location or limited in his interactions to those immediately adjacent to his work station. Our previous studies indicated that informal job rotation among hourly workers increased their satisfaction.[4]

Conclusions

It is obvious that the more successful foremen, in whose sections these patterns of interaction were observed, had particular ways of perceiving their role. Most important were their willingness and ability to think of themselves as the leaders (and therefore members) of a group of men, and to delegate to them a greater amount of initiative and responsibility than was strictly called for in the formal organizational structure. A successful foreman not only pays attention to his relations with his men *as individuals,* but also *as a group,* with a certain group attitude and structure. He bases his approach to them upon the assumption that they are willing and able to help each other and himself out by doing the work well. Perhaps the most important characteristic of a good foreman, especially in helping him to strengthen group cohesiveness and loyalty among his men, is this readiness to think well of his men, to make a partial identification with the men's feelings and viewpoints—an identification not as a rule shared by upper management.

In conclusion, two further suggestions for increasing group strength and cohesiveness may be emphasized. The first is through periodic meetings held by the foremen with their men. Such meetings, either weekly or once a month, tend to develop effective group relations and are becoming increasingly prevalent in American industry. Their special importance on the assembly line is accentuated by the limits to interaction imposed by technology. The foreman who regularly meets with his men increases quality-consciousness, gains valuable production suggestions, and increases group morale.

A more fundamental requirement for realizing the potential benefits of greater group cohesiveness would be a basic re-design of assembly jobs themselves with a view toward satisfying and tapping more fully the plant's human resources. When engineers take fully into account individual and group dynamics in the design of jobs and processes, more enthusiasm and initiative will be released at work than is possible within the present limits of mass-production technology.

---

[4]See *The Man on the Assembly Line,* pp. 148–151.

Work Groups in a Semi-Automatic Steel Mill

CHARLES R. WALKER

After World War II a large American steel corporation decided to install one or more automatic seamless pipe mills "to make a better product more cheaply" and to solve the typical manufacturing problem of "sharper competition in an era of rising costs." They solved the problem—and in the process created, almost without knowing it, a wholly new working world for the men and supervisors affected. What happened in this mill is a story that, in many respects, may be happening over and over again in American industry.

The work environment of this new mill is quite unlike the old, where physical labor and manual control of tool and product prevailed. The complex system of conveyers and moving tables which now take the product through its complete work-flow cycle is wholly automatic, characterized by electric eyes, timing devices, limit switches, rotary controls, and so forth. The top operators are partly technicians, partly coordinators of operations. The furnace discharger has a mixed job, half of it consisting of watching truly automatic equipment, the other half of manually operating levers and buttons. Jobs like the bar inserter's and the stripper's are wholly automatic, performed by machinery without the operator's lifting a hand; but they must watch and, if anything goes wrong, intervene with manual correction.

In the long road toward the wholly automatic factory there will be many jobs like these. Our first vivid impression in talking to the participants in the technological revolution which had produced this automatic mill was that workers and management had not simply gone from one pipe mill to another, but had left one epoch in industrial time and entered a new one. The novelties of their experiences in a new factory world impressed them and impressed us, the researchers. Here are typical comments from hourly workers:

> I'd rather have to work hard for eight hours than to do nothing physical but have to be tense for eight hours, the way I do now.
>
> On my old job . . . my muscles got tired. I went home and rested a bit and my muscles were no longer tired. On this new automatic mill, your muscles don't get tired, but you keep on thinking, even when you go home.

The fact that technology is replacing muscular fatigue with increased tension or mental effort is one of the most striking parts of the story—but only one part. In many other ways the unique demands on the human personality

---

Abridged from Charles R. Walker, "Life in the Automatic Factory," *Harvard Business Review* (Jan.–Feb. 1958), pp. 111–119.

imposed by automation are affecting the working lives of both manager and worker in the modern factory.

But what about the impact of technology on the range of *human relationships?* Individuals function not just as individuals but as members of social groups. Does automation tend to destroy or create a more cohesive work community within the mill with a sense of common interest between its members?

Persons unfamiliar with mills and factories—farmers or professors, for example—often remark upon visiting them that they seem like another world. This is particularly true if, as in the steel industry, both tradition and technology have strongly and uniquely molded the ways men think and act when at work. The newly hired employee, the "green hand," is gradually initiated into what amounts to a miniature society. There he finds himself in a strange environment that assaults his senses with unusual sounds and smells and often with different "weather conditions" such as sudden drafts of heat, cold, or humidity. He discovers that the society of which he only gradually becomes a part has of course a formal government of its own—the rules which management and the union have laid down—but that it also differs from or parallels the world outside in social classes, folklore, ritual, and traditions.

Under the process in the old mills a very real "miniature society" had grown up, and in important ways the technological revolution described in this case history shattered it. But a new society or work community was born immediately, though for a long time it developed slowly. As the old society was strongly molded by the *discontinuous* process of making pipe, so was the new one molded by the *continouous* process and strongly influenced by the characteristics of new high-speed automatic equipment.

Group Cohesiveness

It was clear from our study that the advent of automatic equipment neither destroyed nor weakened primary work groups as represented by the three hot mill crews. Their internal structure was transformed, but as social units within a larger mill society they remained cohesive and strong. Most members of the mill crews had made or were likely in the future to make work careers out of pipe making. This was a life investment, in other words, and as they put it: "We actually spend more time together than with our own family." In fact, the crew members spent more time with the automatic machines than with any living or nonliving object in their lives (including their automobiles)!

In the seamless pipe mill the forces for social and functional unity were clearly triumphing toward the end of the period of our study. By that time, for example, all or nearly all production and nonproduction workers were sharing in an incentive based on the output of the entire mill. This condition corresponded to the men's wishes and to the nature of the productive process. Finally, although there were many ups and downs in the quantity and quality of worker-supervisor relations, the potential for functional—and friendly—relationships was being realized toward the end of our study.

Joint Problem Solving

The most striking evidence of the desire on the part of the workers to become integrated into a bona fide work community was their continuing eagerness to share in the solution of production problems.

For instance, we asked: "If you were boss, what would you do to make this a better mill?" The two most important answers as measured by frequency and emotion were (a) "better relations with supervision" and (b) "the chance to help solve mill problems." It was obvious that the two ideas were connected in the men's thinking. Moreover, they were talking about something much more intimate, meaningful, and continuous than a "suggestion box." In effect they were saying:

> Each one of us knows more about his own job than anyone else—including management. Besides being individuals, we are members of a closely knit work team, which also tells us important things about this mill and its product. We work at making seamless pipe eight hours a day and expect to do so the rest of our working lives. For these reasons the mill as a work community is as much our mill as management's. Why shouldn't we be asked, then, to contribute our brains and our imagination—as well as our muscle—to the solution of mill problems?

As the widespread success of suggestion systems and (at a more advanced stage of participation) of the Scanlon plans testifies, desire to participate in solving production problems and improving work processes is not confined to automated manufacturing plants. But it is especially strong here, for three reasons:

1. The ambition clearly accords with the real and practical needs of the plant, especially during the break-in period.
2. It springs from deep psychological needs.
3. The men's desire to join actively in applying their brains to technical and production problems clearly fits in with the technology.

In short, automation accents the *interdependence* of all the elements in a plant—men, machinery, maintenance, and management—in achieving uninterrupted production: and interdependence implies *participation.*

The Interlocking of Official and Unofficial Reward

MELVILLE DALTON

This is a study of how business and industrial managers[1] manage. There is of course endless literature on personnel problems in industry, and a flood of guidebooks for overriding obstacles to the goals of management. This literature has an important place, but according to one high authority[2] many of those who are being advised are unable to keep abreast of these encyclopedias of procedure. And a distinguished administrator has recently declared, "We do not need proof or provable theses so much as we need questions and hypotheses which will stimulate insights among practitioners."[3] Here we shall seek both to raise questions and hypotheses, and to give some supporting evidence for them.

As a study of how managers manage, this is not an effort at muckraking, or an apology, or a guidebook in disguise, or an attempt to belittle bureaucratic operations. Rather the aim is to get as close as possible to the world of managers and to interpret this world and its problems from the inside, as they are seen and felt at various points and levels. Such a project requires attention also to the counter influences between managers and firm, and the consequences for each and for the individual from what occurs in the process. Where relevance and data allow, we want to relate this world to the surrounding community. Finally we wish to describe both unique and typical experiences and events as bases for theory that is developed and related to other studies.

The case materials of the study were drawn chiefly from four firms located in or adjacent to Magnesia,[4] a city of Mobile Acres, a heavily industrialized region of Central United States. Three of the companies are factories: the Milo Fractionating Center, the Fruhling Works, and the Attica Assembly Company; the fourth, Rambeau Mart, is a department store. All are units of corporations with home offices located outside Mobile Acres. The Fruhling firm has a total work force fluctuating around 20,000; Milo, around 8000; Attica, 2600; and Rambeau upwards of 400. Other firms inside and outside Mobile Acres will be referred to in various contexts. I had considerable first-hand experience in two of these firms both before and concurrently with part of the inquiry. The period

From Melville Dalton, *Men Who Manage* (New York: John Wiley & Sons, Inc., 1959), pp. 1-2, 194-215. Reprinted by permission.

[1]This term is used loosely for all members of management—executives and foremen, staff specialists and supervisors.
[2]Lyndall F. Urwick, *The Pattern of Management* (Minneapolis: Univ. of Minnesota, 1956), p. 14.
[3]Gordon R. Clapp, "The Social Scientist and the Administrative Art," in L. D. White (ed.) *The State of the Social Sciences* (Chicago: Univ. of Chicago, 1956) p. 396.
[4]My indebtedness for trust and aid from dozens of industrial officials—management and union—requires compliance with their wish for anonymity of place, firm, and person. This is regrettable for scientific purposes but the case materials show why it must be. Those executives in other firms of Mobile Acres, and on the West Coast, who initially welcomed my research efforts and then blocked me as I approached the confidential areas reported here, will surely understand my obligation.

of employment, the direct field work, and follow-up visits continued for over a decade. . . .

As a participant at Milo and Fruhling, I was repeatedly puzzled by the gap between official and unofficial ways of doing things, and by the emotional splits and name-calling among associates devoted to one general approach or the other. This experience raised questions that I formulated as a guide for seeking answers. Returns from queries followed at Milo and Fruhling led me to utilize excellent contacts at Rambeau and Attica to look for similar problems there. In some cases I was able to see allied problems more closely, or I found conditions in one plant that stimulated further inquiry in the others.

Problems of Language and Definition

At Milo and Fruhling, I repeatedly saw cases of unofficial favor-bartering and of one-sided rewarding. Like the ongoing action, and buried in it, these rewards are fitful and expedient. They accompany the informal phases of many settlements to smooth the way for action, to bind cliques, to cement larger groups, and to heal ruptures. We saw in the preceding chapter how official compensation in the form of salaries admits of irregular variation in the firm's effort to reward uncommon merit.[5] Nevertheless the obstacle of formal controls, and limits to the proportion of organizational resources that can go into salaries, often forces unofficial use of company materials and services as supplementary rewards for variable contributions from people on the same level, and from the same person at different times.

Use of materials and services for personal ends, individual or group, is, of course, officially forbidden, for in both plant theory and popular usage this is *theft*. But our concern to pinpoint the informal phases of administration where possible requires scrutiny of this generally known but taboo subject.

Such practices are as delicate to discuss as they are to apply. For as long as rivalries can generate "reasons" there will be double talk around the concept of "reward," especially in organizations that stress "fair-dealing," "job evaluation," "merit-rated salaries," etc. The dynamics of individual and group action do not require that one agree fully with those who say that no word[6] ever has the same meaning twice, but they do demand that one recognize the difficulties of assigning absolute meanings to terms describing the kinds of situations we are dealing with. What in some sense is theft, may, in the context of preserving the group and solving present problems, lose much or all of its odious overtones. We only need note the gradations of terms referring to theft to suspect this. As theft requires more ingenuity, becomes larger in amount, and is committed by more distinguished persons (whose power is often related to their importance in the operation of society), its character is correspondingly softened by such velvety terms as *misappropriation, embezzlement,* and *peculation,* which often require special libraries to define. To spare the living[7] and some of the recent dead, and

---

[5] Drucker recognizes the internal pressures for more elastic rewards in noting that "the salary system should never be so rigid as to exclude special rewards for 'performance over and above the call of duty.'" See *The Practice of Management,* Harper and Brothers, New York, 1954, p. 152.

[6] S. I. Hayakawa, *Language and Thought in Action,* Harcourt, Brace and Co., New York, 1949, pp. 60–62.

[7] See Edwin H. Sutherland, *White Collar Crime,* The Dryden Press, New York, 1949; *The Autobiography of Lincoln Steffens,* Harcourt, Brace and Co., New York, 1931; John T. Flynn, *Graft in Business,* The Vanguard Press, New York, 1931, pp. 103–106.

to ignore differences in time and place, we can point to Cellini—and remember Pope Paul III's judgment of him that "men like Benvenuto, unique in their profession, are not bound by the laws"—Aretino, Casanova, and even Voltaire. These men were all scoundrels of a kind who, nevertheless, were esteemed for their commendable contributions to society.

Always there are genuine transitional nuances, with debatable margins, between covert internal theft and tacit inducement or reward. Immemorially the esteemed personality who also performs unique services can move closer to "theft" than others without censure.

Managerial Motivation

To talk of rewarding is to talk of motivation, and students declare, and show by their disagreement, that little is known of managerial motivation.[8] Distinguished executives and specialized students admit that the whole subject of reward is so dynamic that attempts either rigidly to define motivation,[9] or specifically to reward managers[10] are both likely to go amiss.

Our data have shown that what is a reward for one man is not for another; [11] that the rank a manager craves at one time, he rejects at another; that the same inducements cannot be given to all on a given level because of differences in ability and demand for reward (Hardy); uses of the office of assistant-to, etc.; [12] that the organization's contact with the community may demand greater reward for some managers than for others; that "power struggles" are forbidden but do occur and must be disguised; [13] and that more than financial reward is necessary.[14] We know that some managers are more venturesome and more inclined to "play the game" than others are.[15] This may mean unexpected errors, losses, and gains for the organization. In any case such managers must have greater resources and rewards than rigid planning will allow.[16] It was discovered that Milo managers were concerned to maintain social as well as productive

---

[8] Sumner Slichter, "Report on Current Research: Economics," *Saturday Review,* 36: 24, April 4, 1953; Arthur H. Cole, "An Approach to the Study of Entrepreneurship," *Journal of Economic History* 6, Supplement 1-15 (1946); Robert A. Gordon, *Business Leadership in the Large Organization,* Brookings Institution, Washington, D.C., 1945; Clare E. Griffin, *Enterprise in a Free Society,* R. D. Irwin, Chicago, 1949, chap. 5; John K. Galbraith, *American Capitalism,* Houghton Mifflin, Boston, 1952; Albert Lauterbach, *Man, Motives and Money,* Cornell University Press, Ithaca, New York, 1954; George Katona, *Psychological Analysis of Economic Behavior,* McGraw-Hill Book Co., New York, 1951; *Business Week,* "A Tempo Shapes a Type," April 25, 1953, pp. 56, 58, 60; C. C. Abbott, J. D. Forbes, L. A. Thompson, *The Executive Function and Its Compensation,* Graduate School of Business Administration, The University of Virginia, Charlottesville, 1957.

[9] C. I. Barnard, *Functions of the Executive,* Harvard University Press, Cambridge, 1938, pp. 138-160.

[10] P. F. Drucker, *The Practice of Management,* Harper and Brothers, New York, 1954, p. 152; Abbott, Forbes, and Thompson, *op. cit.,* pp. 46-55.

[11] See also Morris S. Viteles, *Motivation and Morale in Industry,* Norton, New York, 1953; Kornhauser, in Kornhauser, Dubin, and Ross, *op. cit.,* pp. 59-85; W. F. Whyte et al., *Money and Motivation,* Harper and Brothers, New York, 1955.

[12] Also see C. I. Barnard, "Functions and Pathology of Status Systems in Formal Organizations" in W. F. Whyte, ed., *Industry and Society,* McGraw-Hill Book Co., New York, 1946, pp. 207-243.

[13] The various struggles of Milo and Fruhling with their Offices. Also see Galbraith, *American Capitalism,* Houghton Mifflin, Boston, 1952, p. 28.

[14] Barnard, *op. cit.,* pp. 139-160.

[15] Griffin, *op. cit.,* chap. 5; Gordon, *op. cit.,* pp. 305-312. Geiger's "freewheeling" bent is suggested by his remark that "The engineers aren't practical. They want everything to be exact. They can't see that in operation you've got to lie and steal and cheat a little." See also W. H. Knowles, *Personnel Management: A Human Relations Approach,* American Book Co., New York, 1955, p. 130; Robert B. Fetter and Donald C. Johnson, *Compensation and Incentives for Industrial Executives,* Indiana University, Bloomington, 1952, p. 57.

[16] Abbott, Forbes, and Thompson, *op. cit.,* p. 41.

mechanisms, and that, in addition to the use of materials and services for this purpose, they juggled accounts to (*a*) allow full and part-time employment of the friends and relatives of plant and community associates, to (*b*) justify plush offices stemming from their rivalries, and to (*c*) keep a margin, or kind of "slush fund," in the naval sense, for emergencies—social and mechanical.

Although these practices may vary among cultures and inside a given culture,[17] and with the size, age and financial state of a firm,[18] as well as by industry,[19] they nevertheless occur widely and point to further problems for the manager who deals with other firms or other plants of his own corporation; we have but to recall Geiger's problems from having his unit compared with that of the Colloid plant.

As a result of these gaps between the inherent limitations of formal reward and the obscure complex of activities that must be rewarded, an organization's services and materials, designed for its official functioning, are repeatedly drawn on to fill the breach. Used injudiciously, this may lead to plunder.

Theft: Real and Questionable

Before we present cases, let us admit the probably universal existence of internal theft, individual and organized, that is more damaging than helpful to the firm and that would strain the term to be called reward for specific contributions. Various informants report almost incredible cases of empire-building with minimum functions or contributions for many members; of favors and perquisites granted to some for no obvious important service in return; organized pilfering rights—including regular paid frolics for some of the company's members as "representatives" or "spokesmen" at some "event", and the purely personal use of plant resources under the guise of "community relations," and sometimes not honored with a pretext. This is reported as common in some of the large firms doing contracted work for various governmental bodies where the pressure for economy is less.

There is, of course, widespread individual theft in which tools, clerical supplies, home fixtures, etc., are taken for personal use without the knowledge of superiors or concern for one's group or the organization, and which could not be justified in case of detection. Similar internal theft by subgroups and cliques, with lifting-license tied so closely to rank that stealing beyond one's station is punished by death, can occur even in sacred organizations.[20] Civic bodies of antiquity were similarly tapped by members.[21]

Theft may also be enforced in the group and occur systematically over a long period. For example, in a small cabinet factory in the Mobile Acres region, the employees of one department, on piece-rate pay, regularly turned in more pieces than they actually completed, and coerced newcomers to do the same to protect old hands.

Between theft and informal reward is the gray-green practice of expense-accounting, which is also related to rank. "Theft" is softened to "abuse of privilege," but the feeling of some companies is clear in their demands for

[17] Lauterbach, *op. cit.,* chap. 1.
[18] Katona, *op. cit.,* chap. 9.
[19] *Business Week,* April 25, 1953, pp. 56, 58, 60.
[20] Will Durant, *The Renaissance,* Simon and Schuster, New York, 1953, p. 401.
[21] Article "Aqueducts," *Encyclopaedia Britannica,* Vol. 2, 14th edition, 1932, p. 161.

explanations. Others, however, including those sensitive to the tax factor, see large accounts as "part of the man's compensation," or as necessary to "attract and hold top men," or as a practice comparable to the "employee medical program."[22]

One organization reflects this attitude in its contract with a well-known top executive. After defining his duties and authority, the company says that:

> During the continuance of the employment of [the executive] hereunder he shall be paid a weekly salary of Twenty-five Hundred ($2500) Dollars, and in addition a weekly general expense allowance of Five Hundred ($500) Dollars which shall not include travelling expenses or other items generally related thereto, which shall also be paid by the Company. There shall be no abatement or diminution of the compensation or expense allowance of [the executive] during such time, if any, as he may fail to perform the services required to be performed by him hereunder solely because of illness or physical incapacity even though such illness or incapacity may prevent the performance by him of any duties whatsoever for a period up to six consecutive months. . . . [If the executive shall be required to change headquarters around the Company operating areas he shall receive] such suitable office accommodations and such clerical and other assistance as shall, from time to time, be reasonably required by him, and of such type, character and extent as shall be consistent with the position of Chief Executive Officer of the Company. . . . [He] shall receive fair and reasonable vacations with pay, commensurate with the position and duties undertaken by him hereunder.[23]

Coercion in expense-accounting can function as in the cabinet factory cited above. An informant from an optical company reports that lower-ranking, and obviously less imaginative, employees who rarely used expense accounts were not permitted by higher-ranking members to list their costs exactly. Rather they were forced to inflate the report, sometimes very much, so as not to "show-up the fat accounts" of the habitual users. Internal coercion to protect one's own masquerade might at times be justified, but apparently was not in this case.

Though parallel cases only at times, feather-bedding by labor, and the various professional and managerial practices embracing pay-backs, split-fees and rebates,[24] also lie in this twilight area.

Unofficial Incentives

In crossing the middle ground between understood theft of materials and their controlled use as inducements and rewards, one must always fight the sheep-or-goat concept of truth. Responsible persons who succeed in this appar-

---

[22] *Newsweek,* "Those Big-Figure Expense Accounts," Vol. 41, No. 20, pp. 87, 90–92, May 20, 1957; Seymour Mintz, "Executive Expense Accounts and Fringe Benefits: A Problem in Management, Morality and Revenue," *Journal of Taxation,* 1: 2–9, June, 1954; Abbott, Forbes, and Thompson, *op. cit.,* p. 41.

[23] See various responses (public documents) to form 10-K of the Securities and Exchange Commission, Washington, D.C., for the Fiscal Year ended August 21, 1956.

[24] Fred H. Colvin, *The Industrial Triangle,* Columbia Graphs, Columbia, Connecticut, 1955, pp. 95–96; Benjamin Aaron, "Governmental Restraints on Featherbedding," *Stanford Law Review,* 5: 680–721, 1953.

ently broaden the system of rewards and are able to stimulate those not lured by standard appeals, or who also require other[25] incentives for greater effort.

Individual

Because of the tacit stress on flexibility and supplementation of the more common inducements, unofficial reward is naturally directed more toward specific contributions and situations than toward rank as such. But obviously if such reward is not confidential, or if it is known and not justified in the minds of others, it is likely to follow formal rank and become systematic theft of the kind we noted above.

Although informal reward ideally is given for effort and contribution beyond what is expected of a specific rank, it is also granted for many other purposes, often unexpected and formally taboo yet important for maintaining the organization and winning its ends. For example, it may be given (1) in lieu of a promotion or salary increase that could not be effected; (2) as a bonus for doing necessary but unpleasant or low-prestige things; (3) as an opiate to forget defeats in policy battles or status tiffs; (4) as a price for conciliating an irate colleague or making, in effect, a treaty with another department; (5) as a perquisite to key persons in clerical or staff groups to prevent slowdowns, and to bolster alertness against errors during critical periods; (6) as a frank supplement to a low but maximum salary; (7) for understanding and aid in the operation, and the defense, of the unofficial incentive system; (8) for great personal sacrifices. There are, of course, more subtle supports which may not be articulated but are intuitively recognized and rewarded where possible. These include: ability to maintain morale in the group or department; skill in picking and holding good subordinates; habitual tacit understanding of what superiors and colleagues expect but would not in some cases want to phrase, even unofficially; and expertness in saving the face of superiors and maintaining the dignity of the organization under adverse conditions. This last may be aptness in masking and supporting the fictions essential for regulation of error, and in perpetuating symbols considered necessary by the dominant group.[26]

These performances are not exhaustive and may overlap in the same person. There is no fixed tie either, of course, between services rendered and the kind of material reward or privilege granted. Though we are confining our discussion to positive rewards, there are also negative ones, such as exemptions from rules binding on others, which, . . . was but one in the first-line foreman's repertory of inducements for production workers.

Though his general contributions were great, the Milo foreman, Kustis, illustrates the privileges given for personal sacrifice. Kustis dropped his Catholicism, from choice but with suffering, to become a Mason and thus demonstrate his fealty and fitness. His freedom to "feed gravy jobs" to his brother was outlined [earlier]. But with the knowledge of his superiors, he built a machine shop in his home, largely from Milo materials. He equipped his drill press, shaper, and lathe with cutters and drills from Milo. He supplemented these with bench equipment, such as taps, reamers, dies, bolts and screws. Finally, piece by piece

[25] See the theory of Abbott, Forbes, and Thompson, *op. cit.,* pp. 34–38.

[26] See Havelock Ellis, *The Dance of Life,* The Modern Library, New York, 1923, pp. 89–98, and Robert Dubin, *Human Relations in Administration,* Prentice-Hall, New York, 1951, pp. 336–345.

and day by day he removed a retired grinder from his shop. Normally such tools were sent to another department or unit of the corporation.

Ted Berger, officially foreman of Milo's carpenter shop, was *sub rosa* a custodian and defender of the supplementary reward system. Loyal beyond question, he was allowed great freedom from formal duties and expected, at least through the level of department heads, to function as a clearinghouse for the system. His own reward was both social and material, but his handling of the system unintentionally produced a social glue that bound together people from various levels and departments. Not required to operate machines, Berger spent a minimum of six hours daily making such things as baby beds, storm windows, garage windows, doll buggies, rocking horses, tables, meat boards, and rolling pins. These objects were custom built for various managers. European-born[27] Berger was a craftsman and eager to display his skills. However, his American-born associates with their folklore of "one good turn deserves another," often gave him a "fee" for his work. Since everyone knew his thirst, these gifts[28] were usually wines, ranging from homemade "Dago Red" to choice imported varieties. But he also accepted dressed fowl, preferably duck and turkey. In some cases he made nothing, but used his influence to aid with a problem. In other cases he found a place in his department for the summer employment of someone's son, and again usually he received some unspoken favor. The transfer effect of these exchanges needs no elaboration.

Jim Speier, one of Peters' foremen, gave Peters great support in the latter's conflicts with Taylor. An understanding foreman and bulwark of the unofficial directorate, he made great use of both the structural and carpenter shops with Blanke's approval. He had a wood and steel archway for his rose garden prefabricated in the plant, and removed it piecemeal. Incentive-appliers estimated that exclusive of materials[29] the time spent on this object would have made its cost at least $400, in terms of the hourly charging rate. Also in Berger's shop, Speier had fourteen storm windows made, and a set of wooden lawn sprinklers cut in the form of dancing girls and brightly painted. For use on his farm, Speier had a stainless steel churn made that cost over a hundred and fifty dollars by the charging rate. In the same shop Speier had several cold-pack lifting pans made, also of stainless steel. According to self-styled experts on such matters, the design and workmanship of these pans was superior to anything obtainable on the market. Incentive-appliers declared that the welding, brazing, grinding, and polishing costs made the pans "worth their weight in gold."

Pete Merza, a general foreman in Springer's division, was given enough

---

[27] In a study of production workers on piece rate in a plant of Mobile Acres, I earlier indicated some of the differences in feeling for craftsmanship between European-apprenticed and American-born workers. See "Worker Response and Social Background," *Journal of Political Economy,* 55: 323–332, August, 1947.

[28] A colleague suggests that this "looks like bribery." It is hardly that. Rather these gifts were gestures of good will, and in some cases substitutes for favors due that could not be exchanged in the course of carrying out regular duties. One can argue that people were being persuaded to violate their official duties. With no more casuistry one can also argue that "bribes" of this kind contribute to the carrying out of official duties, and that, inside varying and debatable limits, they are a legitimate cost for the maintenance of solidarity. This is not to deny that bribery occurs in industry, as elsewhere (Flynn, *Graft in Business,* The Vanguard Press, New York, 1931, pp. 55–76), or that bestowal of gifts cannot be bribery. See "Should Companies Give?" *Newsweek,* December 24, 1956, pp. 59–60.

[29] No estimate was made of the cost of materials, since many of these came from the scrap pile and would have been discarded anyway.

freedom in the use of building materials that his reward was seen by some—ignorant of his unofficial contributions—as approaching theft. Like Kustis, he had withdrawn from the Church to become a Mason, but this was more a gesture than a personal sacrifice for him. An inimitably warm and helpful person acceptable to all factions, he was really rewarded as Milo's peacemaker in the clashes between Operation and Maintenance. Informants stated that he "carried out several hundred dollars worth" of bricks and cement and used Milo bricklayers on company time to build much, or most, of his house.

In another Milo case, reorganization dropped two general foremen to the first-line level. At that time, salary decreases followed automatically. Since the two men did not wish to continue at Milo as first-line foremen, they were put in charge of warehouses as positions there opened. They understood that discreet use of nails, paint, brushes, plumbing and electric fixtures, safety shoes, etc., was acceptable as long as inventories balanced.

Unofficial rewards are of course given for uncovering *pure* theft and misuse of materials. But this calls for internal espionage, which is a harrowing and impossible role for some people. This informal role of theft intelligencer is essential in many organizations. House detectives, various guards, and company police are the conventional guardians in business and industry. But this official role advertises itself. Everyone knows who to watch, and many resent the implications of being watched. Those who play the formal role of guard and investigator are not only likely to be compromised in various ways (see below), but they cannot function at the expected level of efficiency. For as they begin to accomplish official purposes they become the focus of informal attack and are made aware that they can be put in a bad light, as Bingham was from the outset. The theft intelligencer compensates for this defect. Simultaneously filling a formal role,[30] he must be one who has the tact and address to conceal his role of developing intimacies to discover misuse of materials.

At Milo, such investigations were usually carried on by selected persons in both staff and line. However as rule-makers and refiners who had to justify their existence, staff groups were especially eager to avoid blots on their professional escutcheons. Meeting this inherent perspective of the staff role limited the means of unofficially rewarding staff people. Materials and services would usually be inconsistent as a reward. Hence the staff agent who successfully carried out "intelligence" assignments was usually given his next promotion six months early, which admirably fitted *his* needs, and job logic.

Some inducements were both rewards and rights, but for different people. For example, what was at first a reward to some younger officer grew with his rank and seniority into a right which he in turn doled out judiciously as a reward to demanding subordinates.[31] Services and materials from the company garage, and long distance telephone calls were among the items spread along this axis

[30] In diplomacy, the old role of papal *legatus a latere* was similar in the sense that a formal role, usually that of cardinal, embraced a confidential unofficial function.

[31] Naturally, friendship was sometimes a consideration in meeting pressure from below. But where demands were made without significant contribution—and in the tone of "a right to share"—the "reward" given was sometimes a disguised penalty. At Attica one such aggressive person demanded a "share" of the house paint he knew others had received. He was given all the usual bulk-purchased and unmixed ingredients—except the drying fluid. Elated, he mixed and applied the paint. When it did not dry, the accumulations of dust and insects ruined his work. He became a laughing-stock without recourse.

of reward-rights. Line officers in good standing above the level of general foreman, and certain anointed staff figures including Rees at Milo and Reynolds at Attica, frequently, if not regularly, filled their gas tanks from company stock and received car servicing including washing and waxing. Rank was exercised, with the understanding for all that interference with garage personnel and use of materials culminating in defective operation or tie-up of company trucks and tractors, or accidents of any kind attributable to such interference, would threaten or even cut off reward-rights. As the balance of rewards and rights became too heavy with rights, inevitable crackdowns cut the rights and led higher executives to call on skilled machinists from the shops, instead of garage personnel, to give tune-ups, minor repairs, etc. Machinists in a sense shared these rewards and rights by (*a*) escape from repetitive work; (*b*) association with superiors whom they never met socially and seldom officially; (*c*) the privilege of taking Lincolns and Cadillacs out of the plant for "trial-spins" after tune-ups, and driving home "on company time" to take their wives shopping and "be seen." All time of machinists in such activity was of course charged to their regular jobs.

The axis of reward-right has another common phase: some executives ambiguously feel a "right" to use materials and services whether granted or not, and if questioned would defend their practice as a due reward. These are the managers who put in much overtime (emergencies, meetings, etc.) without extra compensation, and who resent the time-and-a-half overtime pay of hourly-paid workers, and who assist in compiling and circulating lists of these workers whose annual incomes exceed, say, six thousand dollars. Frequently these are also the officers who angrily agree that the organization owns them and in turn, quite within the range of normal madness, protest a counter ownership of its resources. These managers would say, sociologically, that unofficial demands call for unofficial rewards. Where people have been "oversold" by higher management's attempt to win their identification, they may of course expect greater reward than they receive and resort to supplementation.

Use of materials to supplement low salary is apparently rather common in some of the smaller firms that are less formalized and less able to pay incomes comparable to those of larger companies. In the Argo Transit Company, a firm of two hundred employees, several of the office force were variously rewarded to keep them from moving elsewhere. One individual who had reached the top pay bracket, was given an extra day off each week with pay. Another person, considered as an indispensable secretary, was each week given any half-day off she desired with pay. Since she sewed much for her family and was the only secretary in that office, she did most of her handwork there in connection with sewing. She also did all her letter writing on the job and used company materials and stamps. Use of stamps at Christmas time amounted to a bonus. As she was expected to conceal her unofficial pay and to guard the box from other employees, she evidently also received a certain psychic reward. As a practice this is of course not new. Saintly Charles Lamb, known to have hated his job at the East India Company, used his employer's time and materials and franked letters to his friends, whom he requested to write collect to him. This was probably understood and acceptable, and was not a positive reward as in the case above.

An X-ray technician—of unknown quality—in a general hospital reported that his salary was so low he was "expected to steal hams and canned food" from the hospital supplies to supplement it. Though not in the same hospital, this may be related to the Midwestern hospital thefts nationally reported in October, 1953. There many additional items were taken, but the thefts may have started as an internal reward system and then have grown to a pilfering right extending to outside persons. The typical internal use of materials is suggested by the defense of one of the hospital attendants who allegedly said she had "never seen a hospital where they didn't take things," and the hospital administrator's apparent knowledge of the thefts and reluctance to intervene.

Evidently leaks of information at the technician's hospital transformed the plan of salary supplementation into a problem of theft. For one person rewarded by the informal plan was also unofficially paid for his suggestion for keeping the system in bounds. Despite its obvious complications, his proposal that nurses leave the hospital by the rear exit was accepted. As they passed through this door their clothing and bundles were inspected. But professional indignation and the rights of rank ended the inspection when one nurse objected that she had worked there "twenty years only to be reduced to sharing the scrub woman's entrance!"

Unofficial Incentives for the Group

Berger's remarks above indicated the private use of work groups by some Milo managers. As one of those referred to, Hardy's worth to the firm was unquestioned. Presumably Stevens knew of his more overt use of materials and services, which included the necessary labor and supplies for building a fireplace in his home under construction. Through Milo offices he also ordered a plate glass for his picture window and removed the glass from Milo on Sunday. He may have paid part of the cost of the glass since one reward-right in many firms is to allow elect members to buy through the company at wholesale prices, and less.

A recently retired Milo executive, who was a bird lover, had an eleven unit aviary built in Milo shops and installed on his large rear lawn. Each spring he sent carpenters from the plant—and continues to receive this service possibly as a phase of his pension—to remove, recondition, renovate, and re-install the bird houses. This person, who started the emphasis on Masonry as an unannounced requirement, frequently used the same carpenters for redecorating his home. Lack of comparable maintenance skills apparently checked this practice at Attica, but it occurred at Fruhling though documentary support is inadequate for that plant. As with the use of materials alone, this double employment of facilities and stores obviously may become abused "rights" that blur the line between theft and reward. However, managers in both firms raised defenses that fluctuated between double talk and sound argument. My bantering of intimates raised certain questions. For example, when unavoidable emergencies, errors in planning, and market changes made work shortages, was it better to let "idle" men be seen by those who were busy, to reduce the work force, or to take the idle men out of the plant to do something else, something that was usually a lark for them? Management argued that unrest is promoted by "task inequities," and that men with nothing to do are pleased with a break in the monotony. Inquiries to Beemer, Brady, Spencer, and various maintenance workers usually elicited strong approval of this last alternative. For example, it was pointed out that "you get to sit down for twenty to forty minutes both ways" in traveling to and from an executive's home. Beemer saw this as equivalent to "several coffee breaks." Furthermore, the executive's wife "always gives us a lot of good eats." The president of the Milo union local supported the practice and held that it prevented layoffs. Management said essentially the same thing in noting that training costs and turnover were reduced, and at the same time there was no surplus of employees, for many of those "used on odd jobs" had to put in overtime at other periods. As with the machinists called on to service executive cars, those employees sporadically retained for out-plant work with some executive, derived both imponderable and concrete satisfactions. However, some first-line foremen and some workers saw the practice as "dirty," "unfair," and "taking advantage of your authority." And some people will call the practice high-level rationalization or collusion, but . . . it is more likely to be expediency periodically reclothed with new protective fictions.

Theft overlaps with reward-right where lower groups, foremen or workers, draw on plant resources, and higher management knows but dares not interfere, as in the hospital scandal. A European informant tells me of maintenance workers in railroad shops who drive their cars into the plant, rather than park outside as in our cases, and repair each other's cars on company time with company supplies. The cars are few and old and serve as busses as well as private vehicles. The practice is known to all, but since there is no fixed lunch hour, workers give the pretext if questioned that they work on the cars only during their lunch periods. Sometimes five to eight workers will be around one car for two or three hours at a stretch. With a short labor supply, and the practice apparently universal, management may officially protest, but usually looks the other way for fear the workers will seek jobs elsewhere.

The force of materials and services as unofficial incentives—internally for the company and externally for its ties with the community—was clearly visible in the activities of Magnesia's Yacht Club. . . . at least one hundred and fourteen members of Milo, and an unknown number from Fruhling, were active participants in the Club, at an individual annual fee of $50. Building additions to the Club and maintenance of its plant, as well as of privately owned boats, drew on the stores and services of Milo and Fruhling. Repair work was charged to various orders, which . . . was done with some regular work. Propeller shafts, bushings, fin keels, counterweights, pistons, hand railings, and the like, were made and/or repaired for boat owners among the managers as well as their friends in the community.

All of this was tied in with the prevailing practice here, and throughout industry, of doing "government jobs." These include original, as well as repair, work of many kinds usually done by maintenance forces—with plant materials and equipment on job time—as a "favor" for employees at all levels. At Milo, workers were singled out to aid the Club by doing miscellaneous government jobs. This was a compliment to their skills and a gesture of acceptance by higherups that appealed to the impulse to serve others, however weak this urge is according to cynics, or overpowering according to some theorists. Praise and minor perquisites were accepted as abundant rewards. And for some, inside and across all job divisions, old rifts born in the heat of past emergencies were often healed by shared work on these unofficial assignments. The opportunities offered by such work for exchange of obligations, for establishing warm understandings, and for blurring differences in official reward, needs no comment. Bureaucratic rationality is progressively, if unwittingly, reduced through these invasions by community recreational life. It can be argued that government jobs aid the survival of Maintenance, which is normally at conflict with Operation in their official functions.

We need more study on the ramifications of government jobs[32] and unofficial services, apart from understood rewards.

The Auditor's Dilemma

Together, theft and socially consumed materials cut into a firm's substance sufficiently to alarm auditors and staffs, committed as they are to compiling the statistics for detection, analysis, and control of all departures from the ideal, and to warrant their own pay.[33]

Above Milo's divisional level, concern was always shown when inventories turned up losses. The usual reaction was to state that non-supervisory employees were to blame, and to order plant police to be more vigilant in their inspection of lunch buckets, bags, and bulging coats of outgoing personnel at the four gates.

The volume of materials "lost" was not known exactly. But cost analysts totaled and classified all incoming materials, then removed from the compilations all items, about eighty-five per cent of the total, that "could not possibly" be taken from the plant by persons on foot without detection. According to one analyst:

> It's not right on the nose, but about $15,000 of every $100,000 worth of material that *could* be taken out disappears—and never can be accounted for. Books can be juggled on some things but not much on this. Besides it's too damn constant. There's no question that it's carried out. If it's not, where the hell does it go to?

Some of the Milo managers and police suspected each other of carrying out materials or of collusively working with others to that end. Voicing his suspicions, the police chief was notified that his distrust was unfounded and insulting. On its side, management pointed to "statistical evidence" of police laxity. In delivering materials and removing the product, outside truckers had somehow sandwiched in forty-seven of some six hundred motors stored in an empty bay before the theft was discovered by the police. Management suspected some of the guards of bribed collaboration. Hardy set up a plan for unsystematic rotation of police around the circuit of gates. He believed this would prevent collusion between them and outsiders. Rotations were made monthly, but instead of moving all the men from one gate to the next nearest gate, only one man moved at a time and not in any sequence of gates or period of the month. This theory was not based on what had happened, and it was faulty in assuming that the major "nonproductive" consumption of materials was pure theft and was confined to production workers. Both in underestimating the ingenuity of lower ranking employees and in not seeing the nature of human association, the scheme did not prevent production workers from carrying out materials.

First, the theft of motors was accomplished by collusion of a few laborers

---

[32] At least one large company outside this study sees government jobs as a problem unless limited to certain employees and done by specific people during given hours. In this case, only salaried people may take such work to a shop set up for that purpose which operates between 6 P.M. and 10 P.M., Monday through Friday.

[33] Probably all organizational groups demand the stimulus of extra reward whether it be more of what they are already receiving or a greater share of those things having prestige value. The perquisite of staffs is usually the less material one of late arrival, early departure, and more socializing on the job, though additionally they, too, may participate in small government jobs.

with the truckers, but was concealed to protect a night supervisor. The suspected laborers were officially laid off for other reasons. The police were not participants. Second, we have seen that the major unofficial consumption of materials was by management itself, and in many cases was not pure theft. Finally, the theory ignored both the backgrounds of the police and the significance of government jobs. The police were not overpaid, and as company watchdogs they were, of course, persons for production workers to stand in well with. But as exworkers, in most cases, the police also knew plant life and had need of government jobs for which they, too, were prepared to exchange favors. For example, when one of the gate guards knew that a friend wished to carry something from the plant, he told the friend which gate he was tending. At the gate, with a guard on each side, the friend making his exit approached his confidant who simulated an inspection and sent him through with a clap on the back.

In Department Stores

The use of internal materials and services as spurs and requitals of course is not confined to factories. Department stores, with their range of commodities, are a rich field for research in the use of implicit rewards.[34] The Rambeau Mart, member of a state chain, was one of the most flourishing department stores in the Mobile Acres area, and probably owed much of its solidarity to its flexible unofficial incentives.

Rambeau had a total of three hundred and seventy employees including the clerical force and three levels of management: the store chief and his assistants, the division heads, and the department heads. The store had the usual official structure—an auditing department with appropriate specialists, a quadruplicate reporting system, explicit rules against personal use of materials and services, and a budget allowance of ten per cent to cover shoplifting. Two store detectives supplemented the controls. They were gatetenders of a kind in seeing that only employees entered the store before opening time, and in checking the parcels of outgoing employees, at quitting time only, to see that they bore sales slips and the signature of a department head. Yet the managers of Rambeau tacitly adapted its resources to individual orientations, and in a showdown clearly approved the practice.

The unofficial incentive system took various forms. When conditions allowed, and within limits, some department heads privately altered the price of merchandise to fit the local market and to satisfy their own needs. Also, department heads aided each other, but in all cases they worked inside the dual requirement of having to show a profit and to pass the scrutiny of an annual audit. The latitude that ingenuity could establish inside these limitations showed that a brand of individual enterprise still exists and is rewarded in organizations that, at least unofficially, accent individual as well as group effort.

A common practice by department heads was to take items they wanted that were "shopworn" or "damaged" and mark them down "reasonably" for their own purchase. Some female heads regularly, but discreetly, gave certain items a "damaged" appearance. Division chiefs unofficially knew of this, and set no limit to the markdown that could be made, other things equal. However, those department heads who shrank from the ambiguities of exercising their

[34] For an intensive study of twenty salesgirls in the setting of a large department store, see George F. F. Lombard, *Behavior in a Selling Group,* Harvard University, Graduate School of Business Administration, Boston, 1955.

authority and asked a division manager the limit for a markdown were usually told "30 per cent."

Heads of the various men's departments usually clothed themselves from each other's stocks at little or no cost. This might be accomplished, for example, by selling a bargain stock of two thousand pairs of socks not at the agreed 59 cents per pair, but at 69 cents, which accumulated to a fund of $200 above profit requirements. A given head could draw from this to cover the suits, shoes, shirts, etc., essential for his proper grooming. The markup, like the kind and volume of stock, might vary.

Normally, merchandise control demanded that each item, even when the stock and price were uniform, have its individual stock number and price tag. But as in the case of the socks, some commodities might be thrown on a table, without their separate labels, under one posted price. This of course allowed inclusion of some lower-priced items of similar quality which, as with the socks, contributed to the private trading fund. Detailed records of what he removed for himself or others in the interdepartmental trading, and careful balancing of the dollar value of total merchandise withdrawn against the dollar value of unofficial markups enabled the department chief to meet the inventory. If emergencies prevented this, he reported his stock as larger than it was at the time of inventory; for instance, he might report thirty suits on hand, when he had only twenty-seven. Help from assistants in the inventory allowed this, but no help could postpone judgment day beyond the next inventory when this particular stock would be double-checked. To prevent abuse of this elastic incentive, there was always the threat that auditors from another unit would be present to assist at some inventory.

Department heads reciprocated in their markdown of items sold to each other. When the transaction had to be written up, the heads sometimes used a fictitious name, or the names of their new employees as customers. This utilized the fact that the employees themselves were as yet still naive, and their names were still strange in the auditing and shipping departments. Obviously intended in part to forestall such practices, the quadruplicate form requiring a name and address meant little in these cases until the employee became widely known. Where the women in these interchanges usually got only clothing, the men fully utilized the system. For example, Joe, in plumbing, wanted furniture, so he talked with Bill, head of furniture, to see what Bill wanted in plumbing of about the same value that could be exchanged. The total of their trades and adjusted records, however, did not prevent them from showing a profit in the annual audit. Where such persons work together for years this becomes simple and so unofficially acceptable that it seems natural.[35] Like the skeletons in every family closet, these practices are not for public consumption but serve to unify the firm, as the skeletons do the family.

---

[35] Favor-trading and adaptation of official procedures are likely to rise above any control. Even the outside organizations called in to assist in guaranteeing a certain conduct among given employees are similarly used by cliques to protect the group and to maintain the informal status of its individual members. For example, Rambeau subscribed to the service of "Willmark," an organization that checks on the selling behavior of clerks. This is done by confidentially sending representatives to make purchases from employees and then formally scoring and reporting each person's sales behavior to the store office. However, at Rambeau—and doubtless elsewhere—when the "shoppers" registered in the manager's office, an upper member of the grapevine heard of it and whispered the phrase "shoppers today" to an intimate on the selling floor who passed the word. But only insiders were alerted; they in effect commanded deference and aid from new and fringe members of the sales force by tacit threat of not notifying them.

However, two department heads were dropped from this unit of Rambeau because of their use of company resources. Officially, one was released because of theft; the other, L. Nevers, because he wanted to transfer to another unit of the firm. The first head flagrantly took money from the tills of his salesmen, so that the following morning their cash and sales tallies did not match. This person was fired outright before he had taken a hundred dollars. But in Nevers' case light is thrown on what the internal use of materials and services meant in the context of incentives.

Nevers followed the procedures we have sketched and added his own refinements. In his accounting he was aided by one of his saleswomen whom he regularly befriended by ringing his sales on her cash drawer. However, her friendly relations with a saleswoman in another department led her to report Nevers' accounting methods and use of merchandise to the store manager and to name it as theft and malfeasance. Nevers' saleswoman, a "rate-buster," had worked with the other woman for years at Rambeau and elsewhere. Her friend's husband, shortly to return from the armed forces, had been head of a Rambeau department before being drafted. However there was uncertainty about his getting his old position back. So his wife, seeing the interpretation that could be made of Nevers' bookkeeping, and the consequences, hoped to have him fired and have her husband succeed him. She persuaded Nevers' saleswoman to report him in as bad a light as possible. The officially ignorant general manager knew roughly of Nevers' techniques and regarded him as "too good a man for the organization to lose." Forced to defend procedural dignity, he simulated a release but gave Nevers his choice of workplace among the statewide units, vigorously recommended him, and aided him in the successful transfer.

Two common merchandising policies encourage the use of goods as a supplementary incentive. First, the department head, as in other organizations, is expected to interpret policy. Second, all items are age-coded and regarded as having an approximate life expectancy. Some items of women's clothing may be "old" in less than four months, whereas some merchandise in hardware has an indefinite life. The age-code, or purchase date of items, is recorded at inventory. If too old, this advertises both the department head's poor judgment in making the original purchase, and his failure to "move" the goods. Hence in part to escape discredit he marks down older items for disposal among employees. Of course, he simultaneously sets up counter claims. In the phraseology of Rambeau department heads these items were "odds and ends of merchandise lying around in the way that can't be sold anyhow." One of these heads declared that the "paper and handling costs" of storing or returning some items for disposal elsewhere exceeded the worth of the merchandise many times over and were, therefore, a drain on the firm.

The conditions attending demotion of a female department head support the existence of these policies. This person originally gained the post through her brother's office at state headquarters. She "worried the life out of" the division heads because only rarely could she "make decisions on her own." She, too, desired "shopworn" items, including jewelry with chipped stones, but she called on the merchandising chief for judgments on the markdown she should make and was repeatedly given the official "30 per cent." Knowing that others more than doubled this figure, she caused trouble by her gossip and insinuations. She was eventually demoted on the pretext that "store policy" demanded placement of a returning veteran—actually from another unit of Rambeau—and that hers was the logical post. Aware that the conditions of her original employment were contrary to Rambeau's merit system, she offered no resistance and was even "glad to get away from all that crazy paper work."

Thus inside the same unit, officially bureaucratic Rambeau could adjust its incentives to satisfy both its enterprising and its less ambitious managers. But in environments of this kind, the person who fits the ideal of believing that his pay matches or exceeds his worth to the firm becomes a potential isolate and requires special attention, though his contribution is valued and utilized. Higher managers naturally wish to reward this attitude, but since the employee may misinterpret any concrete informal reward as unacceptable "favoritism," the question is how? Rambeau had a female department head of this type. Of all the departments, her inventory came nearest to the expected dollar value. It would have been perfect except for the small surplus from single sales of three-for-a-price items. (The surplus also indicated departmental alertness against shoplifting.) Since she was a known devotee of bureaucratic procedure, her department in effect selected personnel like herself, and acquired a reputation for this. When new heads for the candy counter were required they were drawn from this woman's department because of the likelihood that they would not be "free-loaders," nor tolerant of such people among other employees. The only informal reward that Rambeau chiefs could give this person and her kind was deference, and praise before others.

Rambeau's rule-devotee had a counterpart in one unit of a drugstore chain near Mobile Acres. She managed the drugstore's soda fountain. A problem arose from her consistently having the highest percentage of profits among the chain's soda fountain managers. The matter was an issue among fountain heads in neighboring units of the chain, who were in personal rivalry with her. Her success was officially honored, for the situation was competitive and fountain supervisors received a percentage of profits above a given level. But a typical condition—which some students may mistakenly call "institutionalized theft"—existed among all the other units and worked to adversely interpret her achievement. Volume of business on the fountains was comparable in cities near the same size as was the seating capacity, facilities, and the margin of profits among all but the one fountain. The chief difference between practices in this fountain and the others—covertly charged by the woman and admitted by some of the store managers and pharmacists—was that the other fountain heads gave food and confections free to relatives and close friends, drinks to fountain employees, and variously bartered with nonfountain employees in much the manner of department heads at Rambeau. Unofficial reward, in the form of meals, to fountain employees was, of course, encouraged by the chain's wage rate which, while comparable to that of the local stores, was no higher than the minimum industrial rates. Most of the fountain heads covertly rewarded their "good workers" in this way to hold them.

The practices were engaged in up to the point of maintaining at least a narrow margin of profit for the store if not for the fountain heads. The latter were apparently guided more by concern to show a small profit for the fountain—which they did not share—than by a wish to achieve the higher departmental margin that would allow them a percentage of money profits from the fountain. Prices to the public, set by the chain's state-wide committee, were uniform throughout the system. Excepting the one, all fountain managers discreetly helped themselves to canned foods, dairy products, and meats from the departmental stock, with the knowledge of the store manager who received free meals, and coffee at any time. The one fountain chief allowed no gratis consumption to employees, friends, relatives, or herself. She kept the refrigerators locked and closely supervised the handling of stock. When emergencies prevented her from shopping for her family and she took a loaf of bread from the fountain stock, she deposited the price in the cash register. Married to a farmer-factory worker, she stressed loyalty to the store chief, customer service, and money profits for herself. Her superior could not condemn this, but he was disturbed by her boasting of her standing in the chain, and by the innuendoes from other store managers about her "pencil work." To minimize the woman's behavior, he backed his half-hearted praise of her with the logic that fountains are only a supplement to drug and cosmetic services, and that in total store profits his unit was sometimes second or lower in state rankings. But the resentment of other fountain managers—and of his own non-fountain employees against the woman's opposition to the perquisites usually allowed such personnel—forced him openly to check her records, to imply that she was making errors, and to withhold the praise she obviously craved. Higher chain officials also asked her to explain her unique performance and hinted that she could not be that much superior to other fountain managers. After two years of mounting resentments, she quit the firm. The store manager regarded her as a failure because she did not understand what he could not tell her—that her margin of profits was too high and that some social use of materials, not theft, was expected. In his mind, she was too little concerned with the system's internal harmony, and too devoted to formalities.

These practices at Rambeau and in the drugstore chain are doubtless common in many stores, but they are not made obvious to the students responsible for theory about organizational roles, job structure, resources, and pay. And they mean different things to the people involved.

Summary and Comment

The diversity and range of contributions required of an administrative or functional group cannot be exactly reflected in the official system of rewards. This is an inherent, not a diabolical, shortcoming. It springs largely from (1) the assumption that the total duties and essential skills for a given job are boxed in and paid for, and from (2) the impossibility of officially recognizing some of the extraordinary contributions made by various members—often out of role—during crises.

On the first point, not only must compensation be planned to maintain minimum harmony among personnel, but the limited resources of every firm require it. On the second point, open recognition of some essential contributions would advertise conditions that should not exist, promote rivalries,[36] hurt official

[36]We earlier noted Barnard's analysis of democratic rivalries, and the need in decision making to anticipate and avoid their consequences. In the 1830's an acute French visitor commented on the always smoldering envy among Americans. Here officially to study our prison system, he remarked that "the hatred which men bear to privileges increases in proportion as privileges become more scarce . . . so that democratic passions . . . seem to burn most fiercely . . . when they have least fuel." Americans, then as now, "dread all violent disturbance . . . and love public tranquillity." But in their mania for equality they attribute the success of an *equal* "mainly to some one of his defects" rather than "to his talents or virtues." For to do otherwise "is tacitly to acknowledge that they are themselves less virtuous and talented." See Alexis de Tocqueville, *Democracy in America* (trans. by Henry Reeve), 2 vols., The Cooperative Publication Society (The Colonial Press), New York, 1900, Vol. 1, p. 229; Vol. 2, pp. 307–308.

dignity, and encourage disrespect for regulations. Hence recourse is had to semiconfidential use of materials and services as a supplement. This can be both inducement and requital to those who must receive great recognition to do their best, and to those who would move elsewhere without the increment.

Supplementation may be accompanied by abuse to the extent (1) that the reward becomes habitual and is unrelated to contribution; (2) that it is shared by those who make no unusual contribution; or (3) that it expands and becomes coerced theft. The changing line between reward and abuse may be difficult to find and hold, but nothing can be done until the problem is faced. Evading it disposes nonparticipating personnel and the public to label all use of materials and services in this sense as theft. This cynicism cannot be eliminated by allocating ten to fifteen per cent of the budget to cover "shoplifting" by non-supervisory employees and the public. Such allocation may of course enable some managers and subordinates to hide their own theft up to this limit. But it fails to distinguish theft from essential maintenance of the social mechanism. The problem is pervaded by our tradition of political spoils,[37] and our logic that service to the organization must have a one-to-one relation to rank and explicit compensation. We must note that absence of this neat balance induces supplementation, and inflicts moral suffering among members inversely to their capacity for automatic hypocrisy.

It is unlikely that a universally applicable system of informal rewards can be set up, but it is certain that where abuse of the practice develops it will not be eliminated by moral exhortations, elaborate paper forms, or rigid policing. These restraints all help, but as we all know, those who make and apply controls may be like Cellini. If so, their close associates are likely to share their privileges[38] and echo the general lament of abuse by "others."

Admitting the potential disruptiveness of implicit rewards, can we assure the full commitment of all abler members without them? And since we dare not preach what we practice, how do we know that we would have less disturbance and as much or more contribution without supplementation and some abuse? Can we show that the cost of, say 15 per cent, to cover theft and unofficial reward is excessive in lieu of other inducements which also cost? This is not to say that what exists is good, but to say that we do not know how bad it is until we can see it more closely.

Abuse is indefensible, but for the sake of a sharper focus on the issue let us say that as varieties of supplementation and limited abuse sap one brand of company resources, they protect other assets. For example, do they not in many cases also reduce disruptive conflict, break the monotony of routine, allow more personal expression, ease the craving for spontaneity, and to some extent catch up all levels of personnel in a system of mutual claims so that aid can be requested and hardly denied?

However, even with revision of the sheep-or-goat outlook, the problem must mark time until serious students are able in many contexts to at least look

---

[37] Walter Lippmann, *A Preface to Politics,* The Macmillan Company, New York, 1913, chap. 1; Charles A. and Mary Beard, *The Rise of American Civilization,* 2 vols. in one, The Macmillan Co., New York, 1937, Vol. 1, pp. 547–557; V. O. Key, Jr., *Politics, Parties, and Pressure Groups,* 2nd edition, Thomas Y. Crowell Co., New York, 1947, pp. 316–339.

[38] Again speaking timelessly, but referring to earlier Americans, de Tocqueville declared that, "Whatever may be the general endeavor of a community to render its members equal and alike, the personal pride of individuals will always seek to rise above the line, and to form somewhere an inequality to their own advantage." *Op. cit.,* Vol. 2, p. 226.

at (1) the elusive nature of organization that requires unofficial performances; (2) the relation of reward to informal services given; and (3) the relation of all reward to organizational resources, material and social.

Those who regard this chapter as merely a series of episodes on theft have missed the point. Our study of unofficial rewards is not an attempt to justify internal plunder or to say that theft by membership is inevitable. Both "theft" and "reward" derive their meaning from the social context. To insist that this context is constant—so that we can preserve the admitted convenience of fixed definitions—is to pervert meaning, block the issue, and deny that there are ethics in reward.

To repeat, the aim has been to show that however well defined official tasks may be, and however neatly we think we have fitted our personnel to these roles, the inescapably fluid daily situation distorts expected working conditions. Circumstances require various out-of-role and unplanned actions. Regardless of formal rankings, which are often only nominally based on potential for such action, some personnel more aptly do what is essential than do others. Tacitly or not, both they and their rewarders are aware of who solves problems and sustains the organization. Through time they are compensated as resources and situations allow. The process may seem to overlap with theft, or it may escape control and become theft, but able executives both utilize and contain unofficial rewards.

Questions for Discussion

1. The naturalist Konrad Lorenz has observed that a chimpanzee alone is not a chimpanzee (he may simply die). Can anything similar be said about man?

2. "The formal organization could not effectively operate without the informal social groups which make up its infra structure." Respond to this thought by specifying (a) the functional contribution social groups may make to organization and (b) the dysfunctional effects social groups may have on the organization.

3. At a large chemical corporation, a new continuous-process installation plant was constructed to replace an old batch process. For three times the old output, the new plant required only seven men, compared to twenty-one for the old. The men were spread out over four floors in the main building and two smaller structures. These men sat and watched dials, maintained logs, and initiated corrective action when necessary. After beginning operations, management encountered substantial personnel difficulty. Discuss.

4. Contrary to popular belief, divorce, suicide, and rejection of family and society (and even sexual deviancy) tend to be correlated with lower socio-economic levels—not with the rich. Why? What role can money play in social satisfaction?

5. Make a list of the informal ethical codes or behavioral rules that exist in your college, fraternity, eating club, or dormitory. How are they enforced? Do the same for any job that you have held.

6. Critics of modern business (especially observers of banks, insurance companies, and Wall Street brokerage houses) have complained about management's purported irrational tendency to hire and promote junior executives on the basis of coming from the "right" social background, attending Ivy League colleges, and wearing "natural shoulder" suits. Discuss the advantages and disadvantages of such criteria.

7. Foremen in the printing trades occupy a very difficult position. They are members of management, promoted usually from the ranks. But most are still members of their printing unions. What problems do you think exist for such foremen? For higher management?

8. In a fine British movie, *Tunes of Glory,* Alec Guinness played an English army major who had enlisted as a foot soldier many years before. In World War II he had been given a battlefield commision and was now near retirement after being passed over for promotion to colonel. He expresses regret that he had not remained an enlisted man, for he never enjoyed nor was entirely successful being an officer. How would you explain his feelings?

Chapter Six

Conflict in the Organization: Interpersonal and Intergroup Factors in Organizational Behavior

"Life," as someone once observed, "is just one damned thing after another." For many people in organizations, a paraphrase is appropriate: Life is just one damned conflict after another! Conflict and stress are inevitable when such complex units as individuals and small groups are brought together in formal organizations.

The common thread in our discussion of the need for hierarchy, the development of formal organization, and the elaboration of informal organization can be summed up in one word—interdependence. When there is interdependence, the parties involved must work out their relations across boundaries—between individuals and among groups in organizations. The process is, in the words of Walton and McKersie [17], "the deliberate interaction of two or more complex social units which are attempting to define or redefine the terms of their interdependence (p. 3)." Such interaction is not infrequently accompanied by stress and conflict. Berelson and Steiner [2] define social conflict as "the pursuit of incompatible, or at least seemingly incompatible, goals, such that gains to one side come about at the expense of the other (p. 588)," although perhaps it is not necessary that one side "lose," in the absolute sense.

In this chapter we will analyze the most common sources and manifestations of explicit and implicit conflict and bargaining in organizations. First, we will consider the least important but most exaggerated—individual-to-individual conflict. Second, we will examine the stress growing out of certain structurally determined work patterns. Third, we will look at relations between staff and line executives, or, more properly, specialists and generalists. Fourth, and last, we will consider intergroup conflict, and bargaining.

The Universality of Conflict and Bargaining

The study of conflict and bargaining goes by many titles in the literature—conflict, social resolution, social negotiations, collective bargaining, and so on. Underlying all of these approaches, however, is a common set of assumptions:

> Many of the patterns and processes which characterize conflict in one area may also characterize it in others. Negotiation and mediation go on in

labor disputes as well as international relations. Price wars and domestic quarrels have much the pattern of an arms race. Frustration breeds aggression both in the individual and the state. The jurisdictional problems of labor unions and the territorial disputes of states are not dissimilar. It is not too much to claim that out of the contributions of many fields a general theory of conflict is emerging [5].

Conflict is usually accompanied by some form of bargaining, and the outcome depends upon the balance of power between the two parties. "Bargaining power," as Neil Chamberlain [3] tells us, "refers to another person's inducement to agree on your terms. Or, to put it in another way, your bargaining power is my cost of disagreeing on your terms relative to my cost of agreeing on your terms. This ratio measures the extent of my inducement to accept what you propose. Similarly, my bargaining power is your cost of disagreeing on my terms relative to your cost of agreeing on my terms (p. 227)." The power may have been bestowed by an external party—such as the power over working conditions given to the manager by his corporate directors, or the power to negotiate agreements delegated to elected union officers by the union membership. Or it may be power growing out of the relationship between the two parties—such as the power that management gives, perhaps inadvertently, to any workers (especially to skilled workers) when it hires them and becomes dependent upon them.

Bargaining can be explicit or implicit. In the explicit situation, the two parties are aware that each is trying to influence the other, and that agreement is a function of the power they bring to the situation and their skill as bargainers. Explicit bargaining is usually conducted by groups with power formally bestowed by outside authority—as is the case in union-management collective bargaining.

Where bargaining is implicit, at least one party does not consciously recognize the situation as one of bargaining. Harold Leavitt [10] describes this as a manipulative process: the manipulator attempts to develop a relationship of value to the other party, and then trade on that relationship by threatening to terminate or change it. Such bargaining is usually associated with individuals who have no formal power over one another, such as the production line foreman and the maintenance manager. Nonetheless, an individual may attempt to bargain implicitly with a large number of people. A paternalistic management who gives turkeys or bonuses at Christmas, or builds an employe recreation park, is often, consciously or unconsciously, attempting to manipulate subordinates into giving the firm greater loyalty.

The social patterns of stress, conflict, and bargaining are common phenomena in organizational life. Indeed, as Chester Barnard [1] suggested, such relations are inevitable, because they seem "inherent in the conception of free will in a changing environment (p. 36)."

Interpersonal Conflict and Stress

Managers often blame organizational upset on personality problems or individual incompetence. Sam just can't get along with Frank, or Bill has difficulty in cooperating with anyone. It is true that some people generate stress and conflict by their very nature and mannerisms.

The traditional psychological explanation for interpersonal conflict is frustration. When an external barrier stands between a motivated person and his goals, he normally tries to circumvent, remove, or otherwise master it. But when the barrier is not overcome or the motivation increases in intensity, the resulting frustration of goal-directed behavior produces a number of other responses. The barrier itself may be attacked physically (common in boys, infrequent among politicians, almost unheard of among managers), symbolically (such as sticking pins in a voodoo doll or throwing darts at a picture of the boss), or organizationally (by "forgetting," spreading rumors, and—in extremis—sabotage). The classical frustration-aggression hypothesis in psychology asserts that the occurrence of aggressive behavior presupposes the existence of frustration, and the existence of frustration leads to some form of aggression. The reading by Harold Leavitt following this chapter elaborates on the relationship between frustration and aggression.

To say that frustration will lead to some form of aggression does not imply that all aggression is caused by frustration; aggression may be a pleasurable experience in itself, as suggested by Konrad Lorenz [11]. Our earlier reading by Saul Gellerman describing Alfred Adler's analysis of man's power motives implies a certain love for conflict. On a more popular level, we have included a selected reading from Eric Berne's best-seller, *Games People Play,* in which he describes several interpersonal games, including one entitled "Now I've Got You, You Son of a Bitch." In Berne's analysis, interpersonal conflict becomes satisfying in itself, not just a response to the inability to satisfy other needs.

Work Flow as Cause of Stress and Conflict

Interpersonal conflict in organizations is widespread. Although people are sometimes the source, we contend that organizational weaknesses, in the form of certain structurally determined communication flows, are more often the cause.

Organizational structure, as we indicated in Chapter IV, is the formal design of work flow, including the organization chart, authority allocation, policy and procedure manuals, job descriptions, and flow of materials. More fundamentally, structure determines the flow of interactions in the organization—who sees whom, who initiates and who responds, how often they do so, and so on. These structurally determined interaction patterns produce stress when they conflict with characteristic personality patterns.

Everyone has a fundamental pattern of interaction suitable to his personality. Such patterns of interaction at work are initially structured by our attempts to adapt or reconcile the work process to our own personalities, and then become stable through habit. Elliot Chapple and Leonard Sayles [4] tell us that this basic activity pattern represents an equilibrium which may be disturbed when the individual encounters modifications in the work flow or the behavior of others, thus creating a stressful situation.

When stress does occur, we change our behavior to minimize the stress. For example, if a manager is transferred, his new job may require a different distribution of his time and contacts; if he continues to spend an accustomed amount of time consulting with and advising subordinates, his responsibilities for meeting with fellow department heads may be neglected. The first signs of trouble will be pressures coming from these other department heads. As the new pressures build up, our manager may modify his interactional patterns to reduce tension and dissatisfaction.

Not all stress should be eliminated from organizational life, nor should the manager's role be to preside over an environment free of all threats and upsets. On the contrary, a crucial aspect of any manager's job is the intentional creation of stress as a dynamic, motivating force. But this stress should be calculated and controlled. If not, organizational life will deteriorate into a welter of long-run conflicts and short-run upsets. Three interaction patterns among organizational participants can be singled out as causing dysfunctional stress: (1) uni-directional, (2) unpredictable or changing, and (3) intermittent and inadequate.

One-Way Patterns

Almost to a man, employes apparently resent always receiving communications, and responding to others (whether superiors, associates, or subordinates) with no opportunity to initiate. There is an adverse reaction to one-way initiation even if there is no other basis for bad feeling, but it is aggravated if the one-way flow is supplemented with criticism. A student who worked during the summer as a laborer suggests an example:

> On Friday, the general foreman again criticized our foreman for his poor work. Mike then began to berate the laborers for their slowness and incompetence.... Under a constant barrage of criticism all day, the workers began to criticize each other's work. The frayed tempers of the laborers caused a further lowering of output.

In Robert Guest's [7] study of an automobile plant, uni-directional interaction characterized inefficient operations. Supervisors at middle and lower levels reported an overwhelming number of contacts initiated by superiors, mostly short directives, and communication taking place only in response to immediate technical and organizational emergencies.

Continual response to lower-status individuals or groups is especially disliked. A student's description of a summer spent working in a resort hotel restaurant demonstrates the adverse effects of uni-directional initiation, combined with ambiguous status differences:

> . . . it was the policy of the management to employ college students wherever possible. . . . A great amount of antagonism was generated between the older kitchen staff and the waiters . . . The reason for this friction probably was the upward initiation inherent in the work flow. The waiters, most of whom were new at the job, initiated activity for people who had been in the business for thirty years. The situation was trying for both groups, for both saw themselves superior to the other. The waiters, thinking themselves more intelligent, resented ridicule from such stupid cooks. The kitchen workers, thinking of themselves as masters of the trade, resented initiation from snotty kids. The cooks attempted to maintain their pride by humbling the waiters at every opportunity.

Work flow and environment were the sources of conflict in this case. Amid noise and confusion, the waiters initiated demands upon the chefs. To facilitate the cooks' understanding, orders had to be stated in a prescribed manner, but the waiters were never certain that they were heard. The lack of adequate response was disquieting. In addition, if the chef was slow or incorrect, it was the waiter who bore the customer's anger.

The pattern of initiation and response was also unpleasant for the chef. There is a general expectation that high-status people should initiate for lower (i.e., order them around). In this case, however, the veteran, highly paid chefs had to respond to youthful college students. This conflicts with the normal work expectations that older people, with seniority and higher pay, have higher status than temporary and inexperienced youngsters.

Unpredictable Patterns

Most people do not like adjusting to unexpected and uncontrollable changes in initiation and response patterns. An airline employee provides a rather terrifying illustration:

> Suppose that on a busy Sunday in July, I am working in reservations and, inadvertently, I oversell the 8:00 P.M. flight by five seats. The effects of such a blunder could easily reverberate throughout the entire system. At 7:30 the ticket counter agent will encounter 76 happy faces and five tigers, holding a total of 81 valid tickets for a plane which seats 76. His job is made that much more difficult, and the ensuing series of unpleasantries delays departure well past 8:00. This puts operations on the spot; a new clearance must now be obtained, necessitating further delay. Finally, the plane is airborne at 8:35.
>
> But this would only be the beginning of events that could be traced to my error. Because of greater traffic than would have been encountered with an on-time 55-minute flight, the trip requires 85 minutes in all, arriving in New York at 10:00 P.M. Over an hour late, fourteen passengers have missed connecting flights, and the ticket counter at Kennedy is inundated with angry fliers. Kennedy operations also has a problem; the same equipment was scheduled for the New York–Miami flight at 10:30, and the inbound delay will cause a similar delay outbound of one hour. This, in turn, will anger the 76 Miami-bound passengers and countless others waiting for them at Miami airport, and will wreak further havoc on those poor souls handling the ticket counter.
>
> To complicate matters, there was no way to pass off this feeling of pressure save for kicking the water cooler. We were instructed that a loss of temper in front of a passenger could result in dismissal. Many times I was forced to withstand such searing invective and abuse as would have bowled over a less hearty soul. Little wonder that one of the agents suffered a nervous breakdown while working the ticket counter.

In the foregoing example, unpredictable work flow results from dependence on people with whom there is little face-to-face contact, and on environmental conditions over which there is no control.

Unpredictability can also be caused by changes in personnel. We become familiar with the patterns of certain individuals; when new individuals move in, these expectations are upset. A period of learning and adaptation is necessary, during which initiation and response may be unpredictable. The turnover of brand managers in a marketing branch of a large household-products company illustrates how frequent personnel transfers generate unpredictability and stress:

> One of the most unsettling conditions was the frequent relocation of employees and the shifting of jobs. This was especially true of the brand men, although other jobs were also changed frequently. . . . As a consequence of this flux of personnel, the work flow was disturbed. The disruptions became most apparent in the relationships between agency account executives and brand men. Once a 'smooth working relationship' had been established, both men knew what projects were planned for the brand and what was the current status of copy, art work, research and development. Both had become familiar with each other's working habits—how long it took on the average for each to come up with a solution to problems, how punctual they were, the type of suggestions each would automatically accept or reject, etc. The transfer of people upset these relationships, necessitating the building up of a new relationship between different men from scratch.

Changes in technology, organizational structure, and policy also modify interactional patterns. Especially when they are unexpected, changes can be stressful. Such was the case in a large electrical manufacturing company when a procedural change seriously damaged inter-group cooperation:

> The manager of an engineering department was concerned about the low productivity of an engineering section. . . . The engineers themselves complained about the time they had to spend with marketing personnel solving routine quotation problems. . . . Marketing relied on the engineers for sales engineering assistance. Individual marketing men consulted the engineers whenever they felt it necessary. These contacts included person-to-person discussion, written inquiries, and phone calls.
>
> The engineering manager issued a ruling that all marketing men should log in and out of the engineering section by signing a register. The stated purpose of the log was to measure the amount of time that marketing employees spent in the engineering section.
>
> When the first marketing man entered the engineering department after the order, he was advised by the engineering secretary to sign the log. The advice was ignored and the individual went to contact an engineer in the accustomed manner. The engineer refused to talk with the marketing man unless the register was signed. Higher-ups were brought in, an argument ensued, but the marketing man refused to sign and stomped away.
>
> In the next few days some of the marketing people signed the register but many refused. The engineering manager went to the marketing manager and demanded that all men sign the register, since the new policy would not work without complete cooperation. Each of the holdouts consented to sign when ordered to do so by their superior, but actually they ceased consulting the engineers.
>
> Relations between the two departments were further strained when individual engineers placed signs on their desks advising marketing men to sign the register. A previously healthy communication flow between

> the departments came to a screeching halt. Engineers sometimes contacted marketing men for specialized information, but the marketing department rebelled against the engineers by becoming very uncooperative. . . . Engineering, in reaction to hostile marketing actions, would not advise salesmen when special customers were delayed because of errors in ordering instructions. Several of the marketing men refused to request information from engineering. Naturally, company objectives suffered when salesmen advised their customers that they would not quote on products requiring engineering assistance. Refusal to quote enabled marketing men to avoid the engineering section but orders were lost in the process. . . .
>
> In talking to a sales manager who refused to sign the register, I discovered that he objected to the principle of the new arrangement. 'Why should I sign? Why can't the engineering secretary log marketing personnel in and out if it is so important? She doesn't do a day's work anyhow! If the manager of engineering had come to the marketing department and talked it over—O.K., I would have cooperated. Not now.'

Apparently, stress is aggravated if (1) change implies a status relationship different from that previously accepted, (2) change is unilaterally imposed without consultation, or (3) the parties see no functional or technological reason for the change.

Inadequate Interaction

Closely related to uni-directional and unpredictable patterns is the situation in which individuals are expected to cooperate from time to time, even though the total interactional flow between them—both social and work-oriented—is fragmented and infrequent. This is especially relevant to relations between line and staff groups. An engineer in the atomic-power-equipment department of an electrical manufacturer comments:

> Essentially I was in a staff position, aiding the salesmen in their work and transmitting their needs to the production groups. . . . Through intimacy and frequency of contact, both social and job, and the use of technical skills, I could gain acceptance by many of the line personnel I worked with. . . . But even my friendliness and technical background didn't facilitate harmonious and efficient relations with the development engineers. I was never able to become friendly because I was always working with different groups of engineers. Maybe one, two, or three people in the group would be familiar, but new faces would be always appearing. In addition, we apparently had different aspirations. They looked upon me as an engineer bucking for a sales job. 'Why isn't he creative like one of us?' seemed to be an unspoken question. One or two of the new engineers in the group would be antagonistic to me, resulting in letters indicating distrust of my ability to meet the deadline, for one reason or another.

In addition, change in work flow is especially resented when it originates with people with whom there has been little habitual interaction:

> A project manager who I'd never worked with before dumped two huge brochures on my desk. After sending the work on through graphics, I learned he had changed a few pages. He wasn't the most organized fellow. I began stockpiling his text waiting for changes. After receiving two complaining memos, I told him in no uncertain terms he was disturbing me—my main allegiance was to the sales staff, not to him.

In our own experience, we have seen that it is possible to overcome adverse feelings originating in erratic and infrequent work interaction by developing vigorous social relationships. However, a great deal of time is required for such activity, and this may have an adverse effect on normal work flow. Moreover, stressful conditions can be aggravated by excessive social intercourse—often caused by crowded working conditions and the group's resultant expectation of friendliness. A laboratory research associate comments on the heightening of stress as a result of crowded physical conditions and the basic cohesiveness of the group:

> Eight of us worked in an area more suitable for four. The result was that a disturbance for one became a disturbance for all. The interaction equilibrium level was high, requiring a large part of each individual's energy for gabbing and joking at the expense of work.

Although excessive social intercourse can be too demanding, there is widespread agreement that adequate social interaction is essential. Limitations on social interaction are experienced as stressful. In the reorganization of a food market chain to shift to customer self-service, the older employees were particularly upset; they all found out within a short time that it would be much more difficult to socialize with customers and even among themselves.

Not only is lack of social interaction stressful; scarcity of work communication is also disturbing. A worker comments adversely on the isolated aspects of his former job and tells how he went out of his way to initiate interaction; sometimes, this created extra work for other groups.

> I was a braider operator in a thread processing plant. I worked the 3 to 11 P.M. shift, so generally no one was around my end of the plant except the foreman, who came to see how I was doing two or three times a shift. He didn't talk to me but just waved from the end of the row of machines, because the noise was deafening. The 75 machines made braided string and my job was to keep them all going. A machine would automatically stop if one of the 16 threads broke or if a spool ran out. . . .
>
> The fact that I worked alone made the job uninteresting and dissatisfying. In order to get a chance to wander through the plant and talk with people, I tried to get all my machines working simultaneously—then I felt I could leave without being reproached. . . . This was difficult to do and occurred infrequently, because while I reloaded spools on stopped machines, others would stop at the other end of the row. Because I was isolated from other workers, I was reluctant to repair breakdowns that appeared to be serious. Since some machines were always broken, there

> were generally less than 75 of them running. The greater the number of machines shut down, the easier it was to keep the remaining ones running and the more I could wander through the plant. Actually, I could easily fix some breakdowns, but instead I would attach a red tag indicating that the mechanics should fix it the next day. I would have worked on them if there had been someone else around to talk to. I guess I was creating extra work for the mechanics.

We have seen that certain structurally and technologically determined interaction patterns are experienced as stressful. These upsetting patterns include (1) uni-directional communication flow, (2) unpredictable or changing relationships, and (3) intermittent and infrequent interactions. Now let us examine the behavioral manifestations or indications of such stressful conditions.

Symptoms of Stress

Under stress, people depart from their characteristic patterns of action. Their interactions become erratic, indicating the presence of stress by changes in volume, direction, and content.

Stress is often indicated by a stepping up of vertical and lateral communication. A disturbed manager will increase the frequency of interaction initiation with subordinates and associates, but they will be of shorter duration. "Whenever the Operations Officer became upset," comments a former naval officer, "he would soar to a high level of activity. Talking and moving about a great deal, he would go from one compartment to another, giving orders, shuffling papers, and griping." Stress may also be indicated by progressive withdrawal from interaction. Avoidance of contact with a specific individual is described by the same officer: "The Executive Officer's job was to check on my performance. I never liked having to respond to him. . . . I soon decided that to maintain my equilibrium I should avoid interaction with him if at all possible."

In a food market chain, under the stress of dissatisfaction among older employees, a new manager cut down on his direct relations with them. He required them to contact him "through the proper channels." Similarly, F. L. W. Richardson [14] describes an electronics production supervisor who withdrew from all contact. Under technologically created stress, he tried to isolate himself in order to avoid interpersonal stress, and tried to find time to repair defective parts himself. This ineffective supervisor spent 50% less time communicating than did a successful manager.

Emphasis on vertical relations is an indication of stress and a common result of both increased interaction and withdrawal. As is implicit in the supermarket manager's order to stick to formal channels, this creates poor lateral and diagonal communication. Every job should include contacts outside the chain of command as a part of the normal work flow. In addition, a manager who confines his relations to vertical interaction is also likely to limit his attention to short-run, emergency problems. He will ignore more basic technological and structural issues. Richardson's poor supervisor had virtually no contacts with staff or other production groups. Similarly, Robert Guest's ineffective supervisors in the automobile assembly plant constantly initiated interaction with subordinates, and resented any interaction with service groups because of the pressures of technological emergencies.

Stress is often accompanied by changed content in communication—what is said and how. Old-fashioned griping is indicative of stress in some cases (although it may also be a release mechanism that helps maintain relatively healthy relationships).

Change in the proportion of work and social content in interaction also characterizes stress situations. However, the direction of change is ambiguous. In a large chemical company, conflict between staff engineers and line supervision was characterized by reduced social contact. In contrast, in the same concern, conflict between staff engineers in different divisions was accompanied by increased social intercourse. Apparently, the engineers tried to avoid talking about technical matters but still wished to maintain contact. These observations imply that, under stress, vertical relations become more work related, while lateral relations become more superficial and unrelated to the job.

Under stress, verbal intercourse may grow more circumspect. In the engineering division just referred to, the inauguration of a budget charging system altered the content of interaction between engineering and production supervisors. Formerly, all engineering projects had been charged to general plant overhead. The new budget system was designed to allocate these hours to specific production departments. One effect was evasive relations between engineers and production supervisors. The engineers were uncertain whether they should publicize the value of their efforts, thereby raising fears about how much their service would cost, or whether they should minimize what they did and hope to not draw attention to their time charges. The results: selective bypassing in job requests, controlled distribution of final reports, avoidance of specific managers, and inadequate communication.

In his study of a food-store chain, Paul Lawrence [9] shows how stress is reflected in the changed proportions of interaction—more commands, and fewer questions and nondirective discussions. Similarly, when conditions were extremely chaotic and stressful in Guest's automobile plant, one-way or command interaction constituted virtually all communication. No one even had time to ask what was wrong.

The Propagation of Stress

In any cooperative system each person tries to develop a stable pattern of work and interaction. When these stable patterns are disturbed, individuals experience stress—an uncomfortable feeling of pressure or dissatisfaction. This stress is characterized by (1) increased interactions downward, (2) increased interactions laterally among subordinates, (3) avoidance of specific people, and (4) changed content of interaction—fewer social contacts, more complaining, etc. These breakdowns in relations create further problems as individuals struggle to restore equilibrium. The expected responses from other individuals in the work sequence prove inadequate, and new problems of coordination arise. Not only do these disturbed interaction patterns indicate stress stemming from structural and technological problems; they also produce further stress.

When the press of technological and personnel problems becomes great, systematic interaction patterns tend to deteriorate: their volume becomes too great, their frequency too high, and the duration of each communication too short. In our earlier restaurant example, saturation of the channels between waiters, waitresses, and chefs compounded and aggravated the bad interactional flow. Under stress, the tempo of contacts becomes so rapid, the number of interactions so frequent, that the interacting individuals fail to communicate sufficiently to solve problems.

Regularities of actions and interactions disappear when stress occurs; erratic variation takes over. People react emotionally, and because more than one individual is involved, stress is reinforced. This wave-like motion of stress is graphically illustrated in the full account of our former naval officer:

> Whenever the Operations Officer became upset, he would soar to a high level of activity. Talking and moving about a great deal, he would go from one compartment to another, giving orders, shuffling papers and griping. Of course, this reaction to stress was detrimental to the efficiency and morale of the department as a whole. Aside from interrupting any work which may have been going on, many of the orders he gave while working off this reaction would be contradictory to those he had given previously.
>
> The results of this could be observed all the way down the line—to the lowest rated man in the department. Because of this pressure from above, a man would react by modifying his usual activity level. Because of the new pattern, interaction with this person would be stressful. This upset person would react with someone else, and so on. As a result, the behavior of a great many men in the department was different than under normal conditions. Indeed, I could tell when the Operations Officer was upset simply by the behavior of my own men.

A vicious circle is established. Something happens in the work situation that causes the relationships of individuals to change or depart from the normal pattern. This creates stress, either opposition or non-response, which is aggravated by the reactions of higher level supervisors and staff specialists.

Conflict Between Specialists and Generalists

Whether in the serious work of Melman [12], or the satirical observations of Parkinson [13], numerous observations have been made on the growth of staff specialist positions. The expanding role of auxiliary staff is one of the salient features of modern organizational life which is expected to continue into the foreseeable future.

It is not easy, however, to fit specialists into an organization without problems. One of the examples of stress described above was unpredictable or intermittent interactions between staff and line. This is a particularly critical problem at present, because two of the most time-honored management "principles" are disappearing: "unity of command, or one should have only one boss" and "authority must equal responsibility." These long-time organizational postulates derive from common sense. A man can't be receiving conflicting orders from more than one superior. What would he do first? How would he assign priorities? Even the Bible tells us that no man can serve two masters. Similarly, how can a manager be held responsible for performance if he doesn't have the tools or managerial powers to direct others? If a manager is going to be held responsible for achievement of some objectives, he had better have enough authority to perform the necessary duties—or so the principle would suggest.

Nonetheless, the growth of specialization, sophistication, and complexity in modern organization has made it virtually impossible to respect these old principles. The aeronautical engineering group leader responsible for developing an airframe is dependent upon access to a wind tunnel controlled by a testing manager over whom he has no authority. It would be much too expensive for the group leader to have his own tunnel, nor does he have the necessary expertise to run it. Or a production manager is responsible for the productivity of his department, but he is dependent upon planning specialists, industrial and mechanical engineers, and industrial relations men, over whom he has no authority. Although he presumably receives no orders from these staff men, he does receive "suggestions," "schedules," and "procedures." As a result, conflict and implicit or explicit bargaining inevitably develop.

For the line manager, this proliferation of staff advisers and specialists means that he no longer has complete control over his own operation. In particular, he may lack the specialized knowledge necessary to innovate. There seems to be a growing gap between knowledge and authority, paralleling the gap between ownership and control which took managerial authority from the owners as they multiplied, and transferred it to professional management. It has been suggested that now the generalist manager is losing control to the specialist—and this generates stress, conflict, and anxiety. Victor Thompson [16] has described this development:

> Modern bureaucracy is an adaptation of older organizational forms, altered to meet the needs of specialization. Modern specialization is grafted on to it, but old traces of the past remain. Along with technological specialization we find survivals of Genghis Khan and aboriginal war chiefs. We find the latest in science and technology associated with the autocratic, monistic, hierarchical organization of a simpler time. We find, in short, specialization and hierarchy together. . . .
>
> We have said that modern bureaucracy attempts to fit specialization into the older hierarchical framework. The fitting is more and more difficult. There is a growing gap between the right to decide, which is authority, and the power to do, which is specialized ability. This gap is growing because technological change, with resulting increase in specialization, occurs at a faster rate than the change in cultural definitions of hierarchical roles. This situation produces tensions and strains the willingness to cooperate. Much bureaucratic behavior can be understood as a reaction to these tensions. In short, *the most symptomatic characteristic of modern bureaucracy is the growing imbalance between ability and authority*. . . .
>
> More and more, organizational interdependence involves personal specialization and with it the dependence of higher status persons upon lower status persons. In these conditions, the high status persons must accord face-to-face accommodations to lower status persons. This accommodation violates status expectations. . . . Whereas the boss-man relationship is *formally* unilateral with rights running in one direction from the boss to the man, the advance of personal specialization is converting the relationship *informally* into a unilateral one with ability running from the man to the boss. Authority is centralized, but ability is inherently decentralized because it comes from practice rather than from definition.

> Whereas the boss retains his full right to make all decisions, he has less and less ability to do so because of the advance of science and technology. For these reasons the man-boss relationship has become curiously distorted and unstable; formally unilateral boss to man, informally unilateral man to boss (pp. 5–6).

Three selected readings deal with the problems of specialist-generalist conflict in bargaining. Melville Dalton describes conflicts between staff and line managerial officers, George Strauss analyzes the problems of specialists attempting to influence people over whom they have no authority, and Ross Webber describes the stress in one kind of staff engineer's job.

Intergroup Conflict and Bargaining

The distinction between interpersonal and intergroup conflict is somewhat ambiguous. By "interpersonal" we mean the conflict and bargaining that takes place between two individuals (although they may represent categories, such as specialists and generalists). Intergroup conflict, in contrast, exists primarily between organizational interest groups, such as management, work groups, and employees (even though individuals, of course, may act for the group). In Chapter 5, we described the development of informal organization in small groups. We suggested that these groups do more than provide social satisfaction for members; they actively pursue group objectives. Such activity frequently results in conflict and bargaining, particularly with management.

The Behavior of Work Groups

Leonard Sayles [15] has described four kinds of groups, based on the nature of group relation to management authority—as he puts it: ". . . on the level of acceptance of and cooperation with management decisions, or, contrariwise, on the frequency and nature of the challenge issued by the group to management (p. 7)." The four kinds of groups are apathetic, erratic, strategic, and conservative.

Apathetic groups are least likely to exert concerted pressure on management. They manifest low cohesiveness and widely distributed leadership.

Erratic groups behave inconsistently towards management. There seems to be no relation between the seriousness of their grievances (from the point of view of the employes themselves) and the intensity of their protest. The kinds of activities they indulge in are apparently not contrived to solve their problems, but seem to be emotional reactions to frustration, which blinds them to their failure to deal effectively with reality. These groups tend to seek individual, autocratic leaders who are likely to be active in the organizing phase of union growth but shunted aside when more reasonable and stable union-management relations are required.

Strategic groups are shrewdly calculating pressure groups, who never tire of objecting to unfavorable management decisions, of seeking loopholes in existing policies and contract clauses that would redound to their benefit, of and comparing their benefits to those of other departments in the plant. They demand constant attention to their problems and can reinforce their demands by group action. Departments so classified seem to be highly cohesive. The leadership consists of a small core of highly active and influential group members, each of whom specializes in such functions as dealing with management, dealing with the union, maintaining internal unity, or taking the lead in voicing dissatisfaction.

Conservative groups are a secure, powerful elite, relatively independent of union activities. Their jobs usually involve critical skills. They are self-consciously assured, successful, and relatively stable in their external relations with management as well as in their internal affairs.

Sayles [15] lists the following factors as most influential on the overall behavior of groups towards management:

1. Relative position of the group on the formal status hierarchy.
2. Relative size and importance of the group.
3. Similarity of jobs and the degree of independence or interdependence within the group.
4. The degree to which the group's work is indispensable in the functioning of the plant and department.
5. The precision with which management can measure work load and pace for the group.

This typology of group behavior need not be restricted to blue-collar workers; it may extend to office employees and even professionals. For example, New York City school teachers can be described by the model:

> The grammar school teachers are an apathetic group. They have engaged in little active union organizing or agitation. Why? They tend to be women with a lesser stake in the job, perhaps seeing it merely as supplementary income or as a vehicle for expressing their desires to contribute to society. In either case, concrete steps to improve social-economic conditions are not seen as desirable. Nor, in fact, do these teachers probably have the power and the cohesion to successfully undertake such action.
>
> The junior-high-school teachers are an erratic group. This is the most difficult teaching level in the New York City system. Many of the delinquency problems such as truancy, lack of control, and violence occur among these pupils. By senior high school, many of the worst pupils have left or have been expelled. Some junior-high-school teachers have been the firebrands in the development of an independent labor union to improve the lot of teachers (and perhaps quality of education); many are just caretakers, rather apathetic about the situation.
>
> The high school teachers are a strategic group—especially in the competitive-admission high schools. Their power has given them certain privileges in pay and working conditions, so they have not been very active in the union movement, preferring to favor the professional association.
>
> The conservatives are the professors in the city university, whose importance and irreplacibility have insured them a preferential position. Their contracts are tied to high school pay, guaranteeing a certain spread, and college pay increases if lower echelon teachers are successful in union agitation.

Group Cohesion

The success of informal groups in bargaining with management depends to an important extent upon the internal strength or cohesion of the group.

Part of the difficulty in the Korean prisoner-of-war camps mentioned in Chapter 5 was inadequate group cohesion. That is, stable values and standards of behavior never developed; group members could not work together in mutual dependency. Cohesion is both cause and consequence: it aids the pursuit of group objectives, and, at the same time, it can be strengthened by the sharing of concerted effort. But the sources of cohesion are many and varied, as the following summary suggests.

Homogeneity. One of the most cohesive work groups we ever observed was composed entirely of an ethnic or national group called the "West of Englanders." All of the six to seven people in the group had come from the southwest—Land's End—section of England many years before, and they maintained their sense of identification—perhaps because they were very much an ethnic minority among Italians and Poles. The ethnic tie was so strong that this group was one of few we observed that contained both male and female members. (This combination usually destroys cohesion.) These production workers (including a foreman) held a stable set of values and assistance expectations; they controlled production (at a fairly high level) and were remarkably successful in getting management to respond to them.

In contrast, groups whose members have different interests and backgrounds are often less effective in promoting their interests. When, for example, people with sharp differences in rates of pay and job duties work near each other, the resulting group is seldom cohesive. The group may often be characterized by conflicting cliques, which hinder common action.

Even when doing similar work, competition among members of a group will often hinder cohesion—unless the group can agree to regulate the competition. At a large automobile dealer's, the bottom three of twenty-five salesmen are fired every month, regardless of their sales. Under these circumstances, the salesmen would hardly constitute a cohesive group. On the other hand, where expulsion depends upon absolute rather than relative performance, a basically homogeneous group with good cohesion will assist the poor performer in improving his output.

Stable membership contributes to higher cohesion. With time, the members come to know each other, they learn the values and expectations of the group, and they learn how to behave. This was one of the problems in the prisoner-of-war camps referred to earlier. Where the barracks groups were systematically broken up, no cohesive groups could develop. "A tightly knit group," Lasswell and Kaplan [8] maintain, "significantly means both a group difficult to enter and one whose members closely identify with one another. The less permeable the group, the more value attaches to membership and, in turn, the more intense the adherence to group perspective (p. 35)."

Communication. To be a group, people must be able to talk with one another. Only in this way can their similarities and common interests be developed, their values and standards established, and joint action initiated. Groups in which the members can communicate easily with one another are more likely to be cohesive. Internal group unity can be thwarted in such areas as noisy steel mills, long assembly lines, or even quiet offices, where "gossiping" is frowned upon, and there is no privacy for conversation.

Isolation. Physical isolation from other groups tends to build cohesiveness. Familiar to the student is the contrast between the school spirit of a college like Dartmouth, isolated in Hanover, New Hampshire, and the nonchalance characterizing students in large, urban universities in New York, Washington, D.C., or Philadelphia. Miners have demonstrated, in countless lengthy strikes, that isolated workers will stick together more stubbornly than workers who are socially integrated with the rest of the community.

Even simple physical boundaries on a group may be essential for cohesion. If a group can't identify its members and clearly differentiate itself, cohesion will be low. This is another of the problems in long assembly lines: it is difficult to distinguish logical groups. A large insurance company has a one-story office building which resembles nothing so much as an airplane hangar—or a setting from a Kafka novel. Several hundred clerical and supervisory personnel work together in one large area with no physical boundaries between people. It is difficult for cohesive groups to emerge.

Size. This insurance office also illustrates that too many people hinder development of cohesive groups. Larger groups hinder communication, lower homogeneity, and encourage breaking up into small cliques. Small departments, therefore, tend to be more closely knit than large ones. Loyalty, as in the military, is a product of frequent, face-to-face contacts. It is simply easier to have close relationships with all members of a small group than with all members of a large one.

Outside Pressure. We have already mentioned how members of groups tend to herd together under stress. Continuous outside pressure from management may produce high cohesion. We have mentioned that, under organizational stress, lateral and peer communications tend to increase while vertical communications decrease. Personal differences are minimized when threatened by a common danger—or a tough supervisor. And this closeness may remain after the threat is relieved. Perhaps the most closely knit army veterans of World War II are those of the 11th Armored Division, which was so badly mauled by the Germans in the Battle of the Bulge. They still publish a newsletter, meet frequently, hold annual conventions, and maintain high camaraderie, in spite of great differences among the members in economic and social achievement since the war.

A tough management policy towards personnel may well encourage them to form strong informal groups as a protective and retaliatory device. On the other hand, the more sophisticated and manipulative manager who, like the Korean War captors, systematically promotes internal competition, transfers people, and prevents communication will hinder the development of group cohesion.

Status of the Group. Our earlier discussion of individual needs suggests that people often prefer to identify with high-status groups. This means that people are more likely to feel loyalty toward a high-status group than toward a low status group. The factors conferring status upon a group as a whole are very much the same as those giving status to the individual within the informal organization. They include special skills, monopoly control over certain functions, responsibility and autonomy, opportunities for promotion out of the area, physical location and working conditions, influence of the supervisor in organization affairs, and so on.

Although it is true that high-status groups tend to have higher cohesion, it is not clear whether status *per se* is the cause of high cohesion—or whether the factors conferring status (such as seniority, ease in communication, autonomy, and freedom from close supervision) simply allow cohesion to develop.

Bargaining and Unions

Several of our selected readings look at the bargaining relationships between subordinate-superior and employe-manager. David Mechanic's article shows how implicit bargaining takes place in all organizations, because even the lowest subordinates have some power to influence management: management is dependent upon them to some extent, or they wouldn't have been hired.

The presence of a union is not essential for bargaining activities, although employees do tend to create formal structures for dealing with management. As Abraham Zalesnik and David Moment [18] tell us:

> Where this problem (conflict) occurs *within* an interacting group, some communication channels exist or are possible for increasing the mutual understanding of real differences in task requisites, as well as the amount and kind of social differences required for group maintenance. When this problem occurs *between* socially isolated groups, such as managers and workers, the tendency is to resort to institutionalized means for resolving intergroup conflict in lieu of primary systems of communication (p. 346).

Nonetheless, conflict and bargaining do take place between management and employe groups, whether formal unions are involved or not.

Implications for the Manager

We do not mean to add to the currently popular view of business as solely an arena of political infighting and polite back-stabbing. All organizational activity engenders some conflict—and business is no worse than any other area in this respect. Man is a political creature; this springs automatically from his social nature, his intelligence, and his ability to communicate. When competition and conflict appear, the manager must deal with them.

Chamberlain [3] extends this reasoning to suggest that virtually all organizational decisions are made on the basis of the relative bargaining powers of those whose views and interests clash. Because of the complexity of these internal bargaining processes and their potential danger to organizational effectiveness, management must guide and control them:

> Because of the number of individuals and groups involved, because of the number of issues concerned of which each has his preferences, because of the requirement that with respect to any issue only one resolution can be made, applying to all affected, and because of the further requirement that the decision on any issue must be consistent and compatible with the decisions on all other issues—because of all these conditions it is necessary that there be a coordinator of the bargaining (p. 228).

This task—the coordination of the bargains of all those who compose the organization—is a unique function of management. Only by understanding the process of bargaining and social exchange can the manager use conflict constructively, to "make conflict *do* something for us," as Mary Parker Follett [6] suggested.

References

1. Barnard, C. *The Functions of the Executive.* Harvard Univ. Press, 1950.
2. Berelson, B., and G. A. Steiner. *Human Behavior: An Inventory of Scientific Findings.* Harcourt, Brace & World, 1964.
3. Chamberlain, N. *A General Theory of Economic Process.* Harper & Row, 1955.
4. Chapple, E. D., and L. R. Sayles. *The Measure of Management.* Macmillan, 1961.
5. Editorial. *Journal of Conflict Resolution,* Vol. 1 (March 1957), 2.
6. Follet, M. P. *Dynamic Administration.* Harper & Row, 1940.
7. Guest, R. H. *Organizational Change—The Effect of Successful Leadership.* Irwin-Dorsey, 1962.
8. Lasswell, H. D., and A. Kaplan. *Power and Society: A Framework for Political Inquiry.* Yale Univ. Press, 1950.
9. Lawrence, P. R. *The Changing of Organizational Behavior Patterns.* Graduate School of Business Administration, Harvard University, 1958.
10. Leavitt, H. *Managerial Psychology* (2nd ed.). Univ. of Chicago Press, 1964.
11. Lorenz, K. *On Aggression.* Harcourt, Brace & World, 1966.
12. Melman, S. *Dynamic Factors in Industrial Productivity.* Oxford, England: Blackwell, 1956.
13. Parkinson, C. N. *Parkinson's Law.* London: John Murray, 1958.
14. Richardson, F. L. W. *Talk, Work, and Action.* Monograph No. 3, The Society for Applied Anthropology, 1961.
15. Sayles, L. *Behavior of Industrial Work Groups.* Wiley, 1958.
16. Thompson, V. *Modern Organization.* Knopf, 1963.
17. Walton, R. E., and R. B. McKersie. *A Behavioral Theory of Labor Negotiations—An Analysis of a Social Interaction System.* McGraw-Hill, 1963.
18. Zalesnik, A., and D. Moment. *The Dynamics of Interpersonal Behavior.* Wiley, 1964.

Readings

Frustration: The Roadblock

HAROLD LEAVITT

The hypothetical manager we have been talking about is now struggling continually to reach unattainable goals by a variety of means: first, by behaving in an attempt to satisfy his unsatisfied needs; second, by distorting his perceptions of the real world, i.e., by denying a multitude of minor obstacles in his environment that would push him into greater and greater disequilibrium and by spotlighting things that could be aids to the satisfaction of his needs; and, finally, by periodically stopping on his path toward some goals to deal with obstacles so significant he can no longer ignore them.

Another step is left in the development of this picture. It is the step of actually dealing with these serious obstacles between the person and his goals. The major questions are these: How do people behave under one special kind of pressure—the pressure created by a serious block between the person and what he wants? What kinds of people behave in what ways in the face of such blocks? Why do some people seem to run into more roadblocks than others? Why do some managers blow up so easily? Why don't some people seem to recognize what's good for them?

The Obstacle Course

Here is a hypothetical case that may illustrate some aspects of the problem:

Let's go back, if we can, to the days when we were eighteen or so. We have met a girl and taken her out once, and we like her. Now the junior prom is coming up and we decide to invite her. We extend our invitation, and Mary accepts.

This prom is important. It's the big event of the year. It will cost some money, and we don't have much, so we start saving our pennies. We take on extra odd jobs, washing cars, delivering groceries. We manage to borrow a car. We even work it so that a close friend and his girl will come with us and share the cost of the gas. We manage to scrounge up enough money so that by prom night we've rented a tux, gassed the car, and bought a corsage. Primped and combed and polished, we drive over to pick up our friend, and from there to Mary's house. We park at the gate and go up the walk with our corsage clutched in our little hot fist.

We've never met Mary's parents. When we ring the doorbell and a man appears, we correctly assume it is Mary's father.

We: "Is Mary home?"

Mary's Dad, gruffly, newspaper in one hand, pipe in the other: "Why no, Mary's gone out for the evening."

End of scene. Two questions for the reader: (1) How would you feel? (2) How would you act?

People's reactions to this situation may be grouped into three major classes:

First, there are those whose predominant reaction is *anger*—at Mary.

Second, many people do not feel nearly so angry as they feel *ashamed* and *disappointed* in themselves.

Third—and very rarely—essentially rational rather than emotional feelings occur, i.e., "I wonder which one of us forgot the right date?"

The actions that may follow these feelings can, of course, be direct expressions of the feelings. The man who feels angry may express himself in action—in door slamming, cussing, or in seeking out Mary for verbal or physical attack. But there is another possibility. He may suppress his feelings and act as though he felt calm. Similarly, the man who feels ashamed and inadequate may act accordingly—with weeping and wailing. On the other hand he may act in many other ways. He may, for example, *act* angry as a face-saving device—though he doesn't feel angry.

The rare third man may feel neither angry nor ashamed. He may simply view the situation as a not-very-important problem to be solved. He thus has an infinite variety of actions open to him—to double check, or find another date, or go alone, or spend his money elsewhere—all without major emotional upset.

Two Kinds of Aggression and Who Shows Them

The third man is a rarity. Most people would feel like one of the other two. These two have one thing in common: intense emotional feelings of aggression. In one case the aggression is directed toward some outside object—toward Mary or toward her parents or toward women in general. In the other case it is directed toward one's self, one's lack of ability in these realms, one's unattractiveness for women, one's stupidity in getting involved with a girl like Mary.

Probably there is some admixture of these feelings in almost everyone, much as in the dependency relationship of infancy. But the sets of feelings that would predominate can be guessed at fairly accurately if we know just a little about the person in the situation.

For example, suppose man A is the Beau Brummel of the high school. Every girl in town would love to go out with him. He is perfectly self-confident about his ability to handle women. This is his area of major success, though in many other areas he is less sure of himself. Now he gets stood up by Mary.

Contrast him with B, the low man on the high-school totem pole. This boy has acne. He knows he is not very successful in his social relationships. The girls tease him but pay little serious attention to him. He didn't want to go to the prom in the first place, but you, one of his friends, urged him to. You almost had to force him ("for his own good") to call Mary.

What differences would one expect in the way that these two personalities would handle this situation?

Secure, self-confident A, moving toward an important goal and encountering an entirely unexpected and apparently insurmountable obstacle will probably want to attack the obstacle directly. He will be angry. He will want to fight.

B, who is pessimistic about his abilities but who nevertheless would like very much to be successful, might behave quite differently. When he encounters the sudden, insurmountable obstacle, his anger and hostility will probably be directed toward himself—at this further proof of his own inadequacy, at his stupidity in even venturing into this danger area. He will be just that much harder to entice into boy-girl relations in the future.

Frustration Is a Feeling

This area begins to look like this: When people meet serious obstacles between themselves and their important goals, they get aggressive. If they are optimistic about their ability to reach their goal, they get aggressive outwardly—they attack the obstacle. If they are pessimistic about their own ability, they get aggressive inwardly—they attack themselves.

Clearly a *series* of frustrations can begin to turn the secure optimist into an insecure pessimist. The Beau Brummel may lose his confidence if, having been stood up once, he bounces back only to find himself stood up again—and again and again and again. A point may be reached in the process at which he can no longer feel certain that the world has gone wrong. At this point he will begin unhappily to worry about himself. Similarly, a series of successes may turn the shy boy into a Beau Brummel.

The rare third man is still worth thinking about. He is the one who feels no emotional upset—no anger at Mary or at himself. He treats the incident the way most of us might treat running out of ink in the middle of a letter—troublesome, but not worth getting into a stew about.

An explanation of the third man requires us to go back to the chapter on perception. Different people perceive the world in different ways. What kind of world can the third man be perceiving that permits him to toss off this obstacle so lightly? His world probably includes, for one thing, a wide range of alternative behaviors to fall back on when he meets a roadblock, so that no single roadblock seems insurmountable. His is a bigger world. It is probably also a world in which most of his other egoistic needs have been successfully satisfied, so that being stood up is not so important.

But what distinguishes an important goal from an unimportant one? The word "important" here means something like personal, or where-the-hair-is-short, or dear-to-one's-self-esteem-or-survival. For what is the goal that is blocked for our frustrated subject? He is not upset because he cannot get to the dance. He is upset because his personal egoistic needs for status and self-esteem are challenged. Most of us will agree that being stood up on an important date might have been a major frustration when we were adolescents. But as older adults whose social relationships have jelled, whose range of interests has expanded, we are likely in this situation to be more like the third man. Just the experience of a few years may make the problem look much less important or even emotionally minor. Adult security and self-assurance usually hang on firmer threads, not so readily ruptured by a single social setback.

Incidentally, we usually save the word "frustration" for incidents that cause emotional reactions. For the third man, and for most "minor" obstacles, we talk about "deprivation."

The Explosive Businessman

Some odd implications evolve out of these generalizations about who reacts to frustration in one way and who reacts in another. The position taken here, in effect, is that the confident, secure person will be less likely to encounter serious (for him) obstacles, but that he will be more likely to blow up at such obstacles when he does encounter them. Yet, although it is generally true that industry prefers secure, solid, optimistic people to shy, withdrawn, insecure people, it is also true that industry is likely to look askance at executives who have emotional outbursts. Emotional blowoff is seen as unbusinesslike behavior that earns the young executive only black marks on his boss's evaluation sheet. Hence we are likely to find in industry many cases of internal emotion and the external appearance of calm.

Thus it is possible for the secure optimist to avoid part of this problem—he can *feel* like blowing up but then stifle his corresponding actions so that what the boss sees is a controlled and rational façade. In fact, many executives in industry probably do just that, thereby perhaps contributing to the psychosomatic illnesses industrial executives are said to develop. For chronic failure to express intense emotion and through that expression to utilize the physiological products of emotion can lead to chronic physiological disturbance. Moreover, encountering an obstacle, then wanting to attack it, and then finding the avenue of attack is cut off by the disapproval of organizational superiors—such a series itself constitutes a secondary kind of frustration.

The occasional blowoff, therefore, ought to be viewed as an appropriate reaction by an imperfect but hard-working, highly motivated individual when he encounters, as he must at times, a difficult, unexpected, and apparently insurmountable obstacle.

It may be true that an executive would be an even better executive if he did not get frustrated to begin with; that is, if obstacles that were important for other people seemed minor to him, so that he did not even feel an emotional reaction. Most of us would consider it ideal if our model executive could be the rare third man, who would simply shrug his shoulders (both at himself and at the world) and start thinking about where to go from there. An ideal executive might then be one whose tolerance for things frustrating to other people would be so great, whose areas of personal security would be so broad, whose breadth of perception would be so wide, that only very, very few incidents in his lifetime would include insurmountable obstacles (because he would always have ways around them) or really important self-esteem needs (because his self-esteem would be so solid that few things could threaten it). His egoistic needs instead would be needs for accomplishment of organizational goals.

The problem is one of people's expectations about their ability to satisfy their needs; and expectations are, in turn, largely determined by past successes and failures. If through life one has come to expect failure, to feel unsure of his ability to satisfy his personal egoistic needs, then these needs loom larger in his perceptions than they do for the next man. The martini that is not dry enough stops being just a deprivation, i.e., *just* a martini that is not dry enough. It becomes instead a sign of disrespect from the bartender—a threat to one's self-esteem.

It follows that people whose self-esteem is easily threatened are less likely to be rational about their efforts to satisfy their needs. It follows, too, that if one can build up people's feelings of self-confidence, so that their expectations are optimistic, they will be able to deal with problems more rationally and objectively.

Frustration and Standards of Success

Perhaps the most important key to whether we encounter frequent frustration or not is our own individual standard of success. Two men may both want to make money, but "to make money" for one may mean $5,000 a year while for the other "to make money" means $50,000. If two such men are of about equal ability and have about equal opportunity, and if both actually achieve $15,000 a year, then one will be satisfied and the other frustrated. Both have achieved the same external level of success, but one may perceive himself a failure.

This problem has many facets: It is a question of the relationship between our aspirations and our ability to achieve our aspirations. If the two are close together, frustration is relatively unlikely. If our ability exceeds our level of aspiration—if we are much *better* than we need to be—then society probably suffers because we do not contribute as much as we can. If aspiration and ability are out of line in the other direction—if we want what we do not have the capacity to obtain—then we have a potential source of serious frustration.

It is useful to examine the ways in which people develop their individual ideas of how good is good and how high is high. Many of them seem to develop early in life. Even when quite young, some children seem always to need to win any game they play while others seem to want only to be "better than average." And occasionally we see still others who apparently can be perfectly happy as low man on the totem pole. Similarly, in industry some people seem consistently ready to accept the level at which they are working or only want to move ahead in small (but perhaps steady) steps. Others feel they are at the bottom unless they are at the top.

An illustration may show how such differences develop: Suppose someone puts a target on a wall and then leaves you alone with a set of darts and the target. Suppose you have never thrown darts before and have shown no particular interest in dart throwing. Do you set yourself a score to shoot for before you throw the darts for the first time? Probably not. But suppose you throw the five darts and score 75 out of a possible 250? Now what do you do? Before you throw the next dart do you set yourself a standard? Is the standard 250? Or is it anything better than 75? For most of us it would be the latter. In situations in which we are perfectly free to set our own standards, we are most likely to keep setting our goals just slightly ahead of our present abilities. Thereby, through learning and training and exercise, we can feel that we are continually moving ahead successfully.

Let us suppose, however, that instead of being alone in the room with the target and the darts, someone else is present—another man who has been a constant competitor of yours. The other man throws first and hits 100. Now what is your goal? And now how do you feel when you hit only 75?

Once other people enter into the goal-setting process the more or less "natural" tendency to set goals a little ahead of past achievement begins to give way. Goals may then, in fact, be set without any regard to ability. Thus one occasionally encounters a person who *must* become a great industrialist because his parents have hammered that notion into him since childhood. Failing to become a great industrialist constitutes failing to satisfy the people he wants most to satisfy and, hence, means frustration.

Take the case of a young engineer who was unhappy on his job. He had never wanted to be an engineer; he had always wanted to be a coach. But his father had been an engineer. His father, on his death bed, had extracted a promise from the student that he would become an engineer, and a good one. So the fellow was stuck first with a goal that had been imposed on him and, second, with abilities and interests that were not likely to allow him to reach that goal. He had no good solution to the problem except to continue through life jumping for the ring he would probably never reach—unless he could somehow change his attitude toward his now unreachable father.

It is a commonplace in industrial work situations to feel that one must set high standards for employees to "motivate" them. But may not standards beyond an individual's reach lead him into one of two other behaviors? They may lead him into a hopeless struggle to reach a goal that his abilities will not allow him to reach, and hence into a series of failures, and hence again into panic and insecurity. Or else overly high standards may lead a better-adjusted individual simply to remove himself physically or psychologically from the situation, to refuse to accept the standards that are set for him.

Perhaps one can argue that a person who is in a position to set standards for other people has a responsibility to set those standards neither so low as to provide inadequate opportunity for full expression nor so high as to guarantee feelings of failure.

In Summary

Frustration is a "feeling" rather than a "fact." It is a feeling that arises when one encounters certain kinds of blocks on paths to certain kinds of goals. These feelings arise when the block seems insurmountable and when failure to surmount it threatens one's personal well being—when the goal involves the self.

When people encounter such obstacles, they react with aggression; aggression mostly toward the obstacle when the person is sure of his own ability and aggression mostly toward one's self when the person is pessimistic about his ability, i.e., when he has had a history of failure.

Many obstacle situations are depriving rather than frustrating because the obstacles do not seem insurmountable or the goals are not central to the self. Some people may therefore meet fewer frustrations than others because they have more ways around more obstacles or because they are self-confident enough so that their self-esteem does not have to be proved again by every new problem they encounter.

Moreover, if a person's goals are in line with his abilities, then he may avoid another major source of frustration. If his objectives extend far beyond his abilities, he may consider himself a chronic failure because he cannot see that the carrot is really tied to his own nose.

Other people—parents, peers, managers—have a good deal to do with the development of self-confidence and hence with the ways people deal with obstacles. For self-confidence is tied to success, and success is in large part what other people may decide it is.

Games

ERIC BERNE

A game is an ongoing series of complementary ulterior transactions progressing to a well-defined, predictable outcome. Descriptively it is a recurring set of transactions, often repetitious, superficially plausible, with a concealed motivation; or, more colloquially, a series of moves with a snare, or "gimmick." Games are clearly differentiated from procedures, rituals, and pastimes by two chief characteristics: (1) their ulterior quality and (2) the payoff. Procedures may be successful, rituals effective, and pastimes profitable, but all of them are by definition candid; they may involve contest, but not conflict, and the ending may be sensational, but it is not dramatic. Every game, on the other hand, is basically dishonest, and the outcome has a dramatic, as distinct from merely exciting, quality.

It remains to distinguish games from the one remaining type of social action which so far has not been discussed. An *operation* is a simple transaction or set of transactions undertaken for a specific, stated purpose. If someone frankly asks for reassurance and gets it, that is an operation. If someone asks for reassurance, and after it is given turns it in some way to the disadvantage of the giver, that is a game. Superficially, then, a game looks like a set of operations, but after the payoff it becomes apparent that these "operations" were really *maneuvers;* not honest requests but moves in the game.

In the "insurance game," for example, no matter what the agent appears to be doing in conversation, if he is a hard player he is really looking for or working on a prospect. What he is after, if he is worth his salt, is to "make a killing." The same applies to "the real estate game," "the pajama game" and similar occupations. Hence at a social gathering, while a salesman is engaged in pastimes, particularly variants of "Balance Sheet," his congenial participation may conceal a series of skillful maneuvers designed to elicit the kind of informa-

From *Games People Play,* by Eric Berne. Reprinted by permission of Grove Press, Inc. and André Deutsch Limited, London.

tion he is professionally interested in. There are dozens of trade journals devoted to improving commercial maneuvers, and which give accounts of outstanding players and games (interesting operators who make unusually big deals). Transactionally speaking, these are merely variants of *Sports Illustrated, Chess World,* and other sports magazines.

As far as angular transactions are concerned—games which are consciously planned with professional precision under Adult control to yield the maximum gains—the big "con games" which flourished in the early 1900's are hard to surpass for detailed practical planning and psychological virtuosity.[1]

What we are concerned with here, however, are the unconscious games played by innocent people engaged in duplex transactions of which they are not fully aware, and which form the most important aspect of social life all over the world. Because of their dynamic qualities, games are easy to distinguish from mere static *attitudes,* which arise from taking a position.

The use of the word "game" should not be misleading. As explained in the introduction, it does not necessarily imply fun or even enjoyment. Many salesmen do not consider their work fun, as Arthur Miller made clear in his play, *The Death of a Salesman.* And there may be no lack of seriousness. . . .

All games have an important and probably decisive influence on the destinies of the players under ordinary social conditions; but some offer more opportunities than others for lifelong careers and are more likely to involve relatively innocent bystanders. This group may be conveniently called Life Games. It includes "Alcoholic," "Debtor," "Kick Me," "Now I've Got You, You Son of a Bitch," "See What You Made Me Do," and their principal variants. They merge on the one side with marital games, and on the other with those of the underworld. . . .

Now I've Got You, You Son of a Bitch

Thesis

This can be seen in classic form in poker games. White gets an unbeatable hand, such as four aces. At this point, if he is a NIGYSOB player, he is more interested in the fact that Black is completely at his mercy than he is in good poker or making money.

White needed some plumbing fixtures installed, and he reviewed the costs very carefully with the plumber before giving him a go-ahead. The price was set, and it was agreed that there would be no extras. When the plumber submitted his bill, he included a few dollars extra for an unexpected valve that had to be installed—about four dollars on a four-hundred-dollar job. White became infuriated, called the plumber on the phone and demanded an explanation. The plumber would not back down. White wrote him a long letter criticizing his integrity and ethics and refused to pay the bill until the extra charge was withdrawn. The plumber finally gave in.

It soon became obvious that both White and the plumber were playing games. In the course of their negotiations, they had recognized each other's potentials. The plumber made his provocative move when he submitted his bill. Since White had the plumber's word, the plumber was clearly in the wrong. White now felt justified in venting almost unlimited rage against him. Instead of merely negotiating in a dignified way that befit the Adult standards he set for himself, perhaps with a little innocent annoyance, White took the opportunity to make extensive criticisms of the plumber's whole way of living. On the surface their argument was Adult to Adult, a legitimate business dispute over a stated sum of money. At the psychological level it was Parent to Adult: White was exploiting his trivial but socially defensible objection (position) to vent the pent-up furies of many years on his cozening opponent, just as his mother might have done in a similar situation. He quickly recognized his underlying attitude (NIGYSOB) and realized how secretly delighted he had been at the plumber's provocation. He then recalled that ever since early childhood he had looked for similar injustices, received them with delight and exploited them with the same vigor. In many of the cases he recounted, he had forgotten the actual provocation, but remembered in great detail the course of the ensuing battle. The plumber, apparently, was playing some variation of "Why Does This Always Happen to Me?" (WAHM).

NIGYSOB is a two-handed game which must be distinguished from "Ain't It Awful?" (AIA). In AIA the agent seeks injustices in order to complain about them to a third party, making a three-handed game: Aggressor, Victim, Confidant. AIA is played under the slogan "Misery Loves Company." The confidant is usually someone who also plays AIA. WAHM is three-handed, too, but here the agent is trying to establish his pre-eminence in misfortune and resents competition from other unfortunates. NIGYSOB is commercialized in a three-handed professional form as the "badger game." It may also be played as a two-handed marital game in more or less subtle forms.

Antithesis

The best antithesis is correct behavior. The contractual structure of a relationship with a NIGYSOB player should be explicitly stated in detail at the first opportunity, and the rules strictly adhered to. In clinical practice, for example, the question of payment for missed appointments or cancellations must be settled clearly at once, and extra precautions must be taken to avoid mistakes in bookkeeping. If an unforeseen contretemps arises, the antithesis is to yield gracefully without dispute, until such time as the therapist is prepared to deal with the game. In everyday life, business dealings with NIGYSOB players are always calculated risks. The wife of such a person should be treated with polite correctness, and even the mildest flirtations, gallantries or slights should be avoided, especially if the husband himself seems to encourage them. . . .

Kick Me

Thesis

This is played by men whose social manner is equivalent to wearing a sign that reads "Please Don't Kick Me." The temptation is almost irresistible, and when the natural result follows, White cries piteously, "But the sign says '*don't* kick me.'" Then he adds incredulously, "Why does this always happen to me?" (WAHM.) Clinically, the WAHM may be introjected and disguised in the "Psychiatry" cliché: "Whenever I'm under stress, I get all shook up." One game element in WAHM comes from inverse pride: "My misfortunes are better than yours." This factor is often found in paranoids.

If the people in his environment are restrained from striking at him by kindheartedness, "I'm Only Trying to Help You," social convention or organizational rules, his behavior becomes more and more provocative until he transgresses the limits and forces them to oblige. These are men who are cast out, the jilted and the job losers.

The corresponding game among women is "Threadbare." Often genteel, they take pains to be shabby. They see to it that their earnings, for "good" reasons, never rise much above the subsistence level. If they have a windfall, there are always enterprising young men who will help them get rid of it, giving them in return shares in a worthless business promotion or something equivalent. Colloquially, such a woman is called "Mother's Friend," always ready to give judicious Parental advice and living vicariously on the experience of others. Their WAHM is a silent one, and only their demeanor of brave struggle suggests "Why does this always happen to me?"

An interesting form of WAHM occurs in well-adapted people who reap increasing rewards and successes, often beyond their own expectations. Here the WAHM may lead to serious and constructive thinking, and to personal growth in the best sense, if it takes the form "What did I really do to deserve this?"

See What You Made Me Do

Thesis

In its classical form this is a marital game, and in fact is a "three-star marriage buster," but it may also be played between parents and children and in working life.

1. *First-Degree SWYMD:* White, feeling unsociable, becomes engrossed in some activity which tends to insulate him against people. Perhaps all he wants at the moment is to be left alone. An intruder, such as his wife or one of his children, comes either for stroking or to ask him something like, "Where can I find the long-nosed pliers?" This interruption "causes" his chisel, paintbrush, typewriter or soldering iron to slip, whereupon he turns on the intruder in a rage and cries, "See what you made me do." As this is repeated through the years, his family tends more and more to leave him alone when he is engrossed. Of course it is not the intruder but his own irritation which "causes" the slip, and he is only too happy when it occurs, since it gives him a lever for ejecting the visitor. Unfortunately this is a game which is only too easily learned by young children, so that it is easily passed on from generation to generation. The underlying satisfactions and advantages are more clearly demonstrated when it is played more seductively.
2. *Second-Degree SWYMD:* If SWYMD is the basis for a way of life, rather than merely being used occasionally as a protective mechanism, White marries a woman who plays "I'm Only Trying to Help You" or one of its relatives. It is then easy for him to defer decisions to her. Often this may be done in the guise of considerateness or gallantry. He may deferentially and courteously let her decide where to go for dinner or which movie to see. If things turn out well, he can enjoy them. If not, he can blame her by saying or implying: "You Got Me Into This," a simple variation of SWYMD. Or he

may throw the burden of decisions regarding the children's upbringing on her, while he acts as executive officer; if the children get upset, he can play a straight game of SWYMD. This lays the groundwork through the years for blaming mother if the children turn out badly; then SWYMD is not an end in itself, but merely offers passing satisfaction on the way to "I Told You So" or "See What You've Done Now."

The professional player who pays his psychological way with SWYMD will use it also in his work. In occupational SWYMD the long-suffering look of resentment replaces words. The player "democratically" or as part of "good management" asks his assistants for suggestions. In this way he may attain an unassailable position for terrorizing his juniors. Any mistake he makes can be used against them by blaming them for it. Used against seniors (blaming them for one's mistakes), it becomes self-destructive and may lead to termination of employment or, in the army, to transfer to another unit. In that case it is a component of "Why Does This Always Happen To Me?" with resentful people, or of "There I Go Again" with depressives—(both of the "Kick Me" family).

3. *Third-Degree SWYMD:* In a hard form SWYMD may be played by paranoids against people incautious enough to give them advice (see "I'm Only Trying to Help You"). There it may be dangerous, and in rare cases even fatal. "See What You Made Me Do" (SWYMD) and "You Got Me into This" (UGMIT) complement each other nicely, so that the SWYMD-UGMIT combination is a classical basis for the covert game contract in many marriages. This contract is illustrated by the following sequence.

By mutual agreement Mrs. White did the family bookkeeping and paid the bills out of the joint checking account because Mr. White was "poor at figures." Every few months they would be notified of an overdraft, and Mr. White would have to square it with the bank. When they looked for the source of the difficulty, it would turn out that Mrs. White had made an expensive purchase without telling her husband. When this came to light, Mr. White would furiously play his UGMIT, and she would tearfully accept his rebuke and promise it would not happen again. Everything would go smoothly for a while, and then a creditor's agent would suddenly appear to demand payment for a long-overdue bill. Mr. White, not having heard of this bill, would question his wife about it. She would then play her SWYMD, saying that it was his fault. Since he had forbidden her to overdraw their account, the only way she could make ends meet was by leaving this large obligation unpaid and hiding the duns from him.

These games had been allowed to go on for ten years, on the basis that each occurrence would be the last, and that from then on it would be different—which it was, for a few months. In therapy Mr. White very cleverly analyzed this game without any assistance from the therapist, and also devised an effective remedy. By mutual agreement he and Mrs. White put all charge accounts and their bank account in his name. Mrs. White continued to do the bookkeeping and make out the checks, but Mr. White saw the bills first and controlled the outgoing payments. In this way neither duns nor overdrafts could get by him, and they now shared the budgetary labor. Deprived of the satisfactions and advantages of SWYMD-UGMIT, the Whites were at first at a loss, and were then driven to find more open and constructive types of gratification from each other.

Antithesis

The antithesis to First-Degree SWYMD is to leave the player alone, and to Second-Degree SWYMD to throw the decision back on White. The First-Degree player may react by feeling forlorn, but seldom angry; the Second-Degree player may become sulky if he is forced to take the initiative, so that systematic anti-SWYMD leads to disagreeable consequences. The antithesis to Third-Degree SWYMD should be put into competent professional hands.

Conflicts Between Staff and Line Managerial Officers

MELVILLE DALTON

In its concentration on union-management relations, industrial sociology has tended to neglect the study of processes inside the ranks of industrial management. Obviously the doors to this research area are more closely guarded than the entry to industrial processes through the avenue of production workers, but an industrial sociology worthy of the name must sooner or later extend its inquiries to include the activities of all industrial personnel.

The present paper is the result of an attempt to study processes among industrial managers. It is specifically a report on the functioning interaction between the two major vertical groupings of industrial management: (1) the *staff* organization, the functions of which are research and advisory; and (2) the *line* organization, which has exclusive authority over production processes.

Industrial staff organizations are relatively new. Their appearance is a response to many complex interrelated forces, such as economic competition, scientific advance, industrial expansion, growth of the labor movement, and so on. During the last four or five decades these rapid changes and resulting unstable conditions have caused top industrial officials more and more to call in "specialists" to aid them toward the goal of greater production and efficiency. These specialists are of many kinds including chemists, statisticians, public and industrial relations officers, personnel officers, accountants, and a great variety of engineers, such as mechanical, draughting, electrical, chemical, fuel, lubricating, and industrial engineers. In industry these individuals are usually known as "staff people." Their functions, again, for the most part are to increase and apply their specialized knowledge in problem areas, and to advise those officers who make up the "line" organization and have authority[1] over production processes.

This theoretically satisfying industrial structure of specialized experts advising busy administrators has in a number of significant cases failed to

From Melville Dalton, "Conflicts Between Staff and Line Managerial Officers," *American Sociological Review*, Vol. 15 (June 1950), pp. 342–351.

[1] *Inside* their particular staff organization, staff officers also may have authority over their subordinates, but not over production personnel.

function as expected. The assumptions that (a) the staff specialists would be reasonably content to function without a measure of formal authority[2] over production, and that (b) their suggestions regarding improvement of processes and techniques for control over personnel and production would be welcomed by line officers and be applied, require closer examination. In practice there is often much conflict between industrial staff and line organizations and in varying degrees the members of these organizations oppose each other.[3]

The aim of this paper is, therefore, to present and analyze data dealing with staff-line tensions.

Data were drawn from three industrial plants[4] in which the writer had been either a participating member of one or both of the groups or was intimate with reliable informants among the officers who were.

Approached sociologically, relations among members of management in the plants could be viewed as a general conflict system caused and perpetuated chiefly by (1) power struggles in the organization stemming in the main from competition among departments to maintain low operating costs; (2) drives by numerous members to increase their status in the hierarchy; (3) conflict between union and management; and (4) the staff-line friction which is the subject of this paper.[5] This milieu of tensions was not only unaccounted for by the blueprint organizations of the plants, but was often contradictory to, and even destructive of, the organizations' formal aims. All members of management, especially in the middle and lower ranks,[6] were caught up in this conflict system.

---

[2]To the extent that staff officers influence line policy they do, of course, have a certain *informal* authority.

[3]Some social scientists have noted the possibility of staff-line friction, and industrial executives themselves have expressed strong feelings on the matter. See Burleigh B. Gardner, *Human Relations in Industry* (Chicago: Richard D. Irwin, Inc., 1945) and H. E. Dimock, *The Executive in Action* (New York: Harper & Brothers, 1945). Dimock believes that we are too "staff-minded" and that we should become more "executive-minded" (p. 241). A high line officer in a large corporation denounced staff organizations to the writer on the ground of their "costing more than they're worth," and that "They stir up too much trouble and are too theoretical." He felt that their function (excepting that of accountants, chemists, and "a few mechanical engineers") could be better carried out by replacing them with "highly-select front-line foremen [the lowest placed line officers] who are really the backbone of management, and pay them ten or twelve thousand dollars a year."

[4]These plants were in related industries and ranged in size from 4,500 to 20,000 employees, with the managerial groups numbering from 200 to nearly 1,000. Details concerning the plants and their location are confidential. Methodological details concerning an intensive study embracing staff-line relations and several other areas of behavior in one of the plants are given in the writer's unpublished doctoral thesis, "A Study of Informal Organization Among the Managers of an Industrial Plant," (Department of Sociology, University of Chicago, 1949).

[5]Because these conflict areas were interrelated and continually shifting and reorganizing, discussion of any one of them separately—as in the case of staff-line relations—will, of course, be unrealistic to some extent.

[6]From bottom to top, the line hierarchy consisted of the following strata of officers: (1) first-line foremen, who were directly in charge of production workmen; (2) general foremen; (3) departmental superintendents; (4) divisional superintendents; (5) assistant plant manager; (6) plant manager. In the preceding strata there were often "assistants," such as "assistant general foreman," "assistant superintendent," etc., in which case the total strata of the line hierarchy could be almost double that indicated here.

In the staff organizations the order from bottom to top was: (1) supervisor (equivalent to the first-line foreman); (2) general supervisor (equivalent to the general foreman); (3) staff head—sometimes "superintendent" (equivalent to departmental superintendent in the line organization). Occasionally there were strata of assistant supervisors and assistant staff heads.

The term "upper line" will refer to all strata above the departmental superintendent. "Middle line" will include the departmental superintendent and assistants. "Lower line" will refer to general and first-line foremen and their assistants.

"Lower," "middle," and "upper" staff will refer respectively to the supervisor, general supervisor and staff head.

"Top management" will refer to the upper line and the few staff heads with whom upper line officers were especially intimate on matters of policy.

Even though they might wish to escape, the obligation of at least appearing to carry out formal functions compelled individuals to take sides in order to protect themselves against the aggressions of others. And the intensity of the conflict was aggravated by the fact that it was formally unacceptable and had to be hidden.

For analytical convenience, staff-line friction may be examined apart from the reciprocal effects of the general conflict system. Regarded in this way, the data indicated that three conditions were basic to staff-line struggles: (1) the conspicuous ambition and "individualistic" behavior among staff officers; (2) the complication arising from staff efforts to justify its existence and get acceptance of its contributions; and, related to point two, (3) the fact that incumbency of the higher staff offices was dependent on line approval. The significance of these conditions will be discussed in order.

The Mobile Behavior of Staff Personnel

As a group, staff personnel in the three plants were markedly ambitious, restless, and individualistic. There was much concern to win rapid promotion, to make the "right impressions," and to receive individual recognition. Data showed that the desire among staff members for personal distinctions often over-rode their sentiments of group consciousness and caused intra-staff tensions.[7]

The relatively high turnover of staff personnel[8] quite possibly reflected the dissatisfactions and frustrations of members over inability to achieve the distinction and status they hoped for. Several factors appeared to be of importance in this restlessness of staff personnel. Among these were age and social differences between line and staff officers, structural differences in the hierarchy of the two groups, and the staff group's lack of authority over production.

With respect to age, the staff officers were significantly younger than line officers.[9] This would account to some extent for their restlessness. Being presumably less well-established in life in terms of material accumulations, occupational status, and security, while having greater expectations (see below), and more energy, as well as more life ahead in which to make new starts elsewhere if

[7]In a typical case in one of the plants, a young staff officer developed a plan for increasing the life of certain equipment in the plant. He carried the plan directly to the superintendent of the department in which he hoped to introduce it, but was rebuffed by the superintendent who privately acknowledged the merit of the scheme but resented the staff officer's "trying to lord it over" him. The staff organization condemned the behavior of its member and felt that he should have allowed the plan to appear as a contribution of the staff group rather than as one of its members. The officer himself declared that "By G—it's my idea, and I want credit. There's not a damn one of you guys [the staff group] that wouldn't make the same squawk if you were in my place!"

[8]During the period between 1944 and 1950 turnover of staff personnel in these plants was between two and four times as great as that of line personnel. This grouping included all the non-managerial members of staff and line and all the hourly-paid (non-salaried) members of management (about 60 assistant first-line foremen). Turnover was determined by dividing the average number of employees for a given year (in line or staff) into the accessions or separations, whichever was the smaller.

[9]Complete age data were available in one of the larger plants. Here the 36 staff heads, staff specialists, and assistants had a mean age of 42.9 years. This value would have been less than 40 years, except for the inclusion of several older former line officers, but even a mean of 42.9 years was significantly less (C.R. 2.8) than that of the 35 line superintendents in the plant who had a mean age of 48.7 years. The age difference was even more significant when the staff heads were compared with the 61 general foremen who had a mean age of 50.0 years. And between the 93 salaried first-line foremen (mean age of 48.5 years) and the 270 salaried nonsupervisory staff personnel (mean age of 31.0 years) the difference was still greater.

necessary, the staff groups were understandably more dynamic and driving.[10]

Age-conflict[11] was also significant in staff-line antagonisms. The incident just noted of the young staff officer seeking to get direct acceptance by the line of his contribution failed in part—judging from the strong sentiments later expressed by the line superintendent—because of an age antipathy. The older line officers disliked receiving what they regarded as instruction from men so much younger than themselves, and staff personnel clearly were conscious of this attitude among line officers.[12] In staff-line meetings staff officers frequently had their ideas slighted or even treated with amusement by line incumbents. Whether such treatment was warranted or not, the effects were disillusioning to the younger, less experienced staff officers. Often selected by the organization because of their outstanding academic records, they had entered industry with the belief that they had much to contribute, and that their efforts would win early recognition and rapid advancement. Certainly they had no thought that their contributions would be in any degree unwelcome. This naiveté[13] was apparently due to lack of earlier first-hand experience in industry (or acquaintance with those who had such experience), and to omission of realistic instruction in the social sciences from their academic training. The unsophisticated staff officer's initial contacts with the shifting, covert, expedient arrangements between members of staff and line usually gave him a severe shock. He had entered industry prepared to engage in logical, well-formulated relations with members of the managerial hierarchy, and to carry out precise, methodical functions for which his training had equipped him. Now he learned that (1) his freedom to function was snared in a web of informal commitments; (2) his academic specialty (on which he leaned for support in his new position) was often not relevant[14] for carrying out his formal assignments; and that (3) the important thing to do was to learn who the informally powerful line officers were and what

---

[10]One might also hypothesize that the drive of staff officers was reflected in the fact that the staff heads and specialists gained their positions (those held when the data were collected) in less time than did members of the line groups. E.g., the 36 staff officers discussed above had spent a median of 10 years attaining their positions, as against a median of 11 years for the first-line foremen, 17 years for the general foremen, and 19 years for the superintendents. But one must consider that some of the staff groups were relatively new (13–15 years old) and had grown rapidly, which probably accelerated their rate of promotions as compared with that of the older line organization.

[11]E. A. Ross in *Principles of Sociology* (New York: D. Appleton-Century Co., 1938) pp. 238–48, has some pertinent comments on age conflict.

[12]Explaining the relatively few cases in which his staff had succeeded in "selling ideas" to the line, an assistant staff head remarked: "We're always in hot water with these old guys on the line. You can't tell them a damn thing. They're bull-headed as hell! Most of the time we offer a suggestion it's either laughed at or not considered at all. The same idea in the mouth of some old codger on the line'd get a round of applause. They treat us like kids."

Line officers in these plants often referred to staff personnel (especially members of the auditing, production planning, industrial engineering, and industrial relations staffs) as "college punks," "slide-rules," "crackpots," "pretty boys," and "chair-warmers."

[13]John Mills, a research engineer retired from the telephone industry, has noted the worldly naiveté of research engineers in that field in his *The Engineer in Society* (New York: D. Van Nostrand Co., 1946).

[14]Among the staff heads and assistants referred to earlier, only 50 per cent of those with college training (32 of the 36 officers) were occupied with duties related to their specialized training. E.g., the head of the industrial relations staff had a B.S. degree in aeronautical engineering; his assistant had a similar degree in chemical engineering. Considering that staff officers are assumed to be specialists trained to aid and advise management in a particular function, the condition presented here raises a question as to what the criteria of selection were. (As will be shown in a separate paper, the answer appeared to be that personal—as well as impersonal—criteria were used.) Among the college-trained of 190 line officers in the same plant, the gap between training and function was still greater, with 61 per cent in positions not related to the specialized part of their college work.

ideas they would welcome which at the same time would be acceptable to his superiors.

Usually the staff officer's reaction to these conditions is to look elsewhere for a job or make an accommodation in the direction of protecting himself and finding a niche where he can make his existence in the plant tolerable and safe. If he chooses the latter course, he is likely to be less concerned with creative effort for his employer than with attempts to develop reliable social relations that will aid his personal advancement. The staff officer's recourse to this behavior and his use of other status-increasing devices will be discussed below in another connection.

The formal structure, or hierarchy of statuses, of the two larger plants from which data were drawn, offered a frustration to the ambitious staff officer. That is, in these plants the strata, or levels of authority, in the staff organizations ranged from three to five as against from five to ten in the line organization. Consequently there were fewer possible positions for exercise of authority into which staff personnel could move. This condition may have been an irritant to expansion among the staff groups. Unable to move vertically to the degree possible in the line organization, the ambitious staff officer could enlarge his area of authority in a given position only by lateral expansion—by increasing his personnel. Whether or not aspiring staff incumbents revolted against the relatively low hierarchy through which they could move, the fact remains that (1) they appeared eager to increase the number of personnel under their authority,[15] (2) the personnel of staff groups *did* increase disproportionately to those of the line,[16] and (3) there was a trend of personnel movement from staff to line,[17] rather

[15]This was suggested by unnecessary references among some staff officers to "the number of men under me," and by their somewhat fanciful excuses for increase of personnel. These excuses included statements of needing more personnel to (1) carry on research, (2) control new processes, (3) keep records and reports up-to-date. These statements often did not square with (1) the excessive concern among staff people about their "privileges" (such as arriving on the job late, leaving early, leaving the plant for long periods during working hours, having a radio in the office during the World Series, etc.); (2) the great amount of time (relative to that of line officers) spent by lower staff personnel in social activities on the job, and (3) the constantly recurring (but not always provoked) claims among staff personnel of their functional importance for production. The duties of middle and lower staff personnel allowed them sufficient time to argue a great deal over their respective functions (as well as many irrelevant topics) and to challenge the relative merit of one another's contributions or "ideas." In some of the staffs these discussions could go on intermittently for hours and develop into highly theoretical jousts and wit battles. Where staff people regarded such behavior as a privilege of their status, line officers considered it as a threat to themselves. This lax control (in terms of line discipline) was in part a tacit reward from staff heads to their subordinates. The reward was expected because staff superiors (especially in the industrial relations, industrial engineering, and planning staffs) often overlooked and/or perverted the work of subordinates (which was resented) in response to pressures from the line. This behavior will be noted later.

[16]In one of the larger plants, where exact data were available, the total staff personnel had by 1945 exceeded that of the line. At that time the staff included 400 members as against 317 line personnel composed of managerial officers and their clerical workers, but not production workers. By 1948 the staff had increased to 517 as compared with 387 for the line (during this period *total* plant personnel declined over 400). The staff had grown from 20.8 per cent larger than the line in 1945 to 33.6 per cent larger in 1948, and had itself increased by 29.3 per cent during the three years as against a growth in the line of 22.1 per cent. Assuming the conditions essential for use of probability theory, the increase in staff personnel could have resulted from chance about 1.5 times in a hundred. Possibly post-war and other factors of social change were also at work but, if so, their force was not readily assessable.

[17]This movement from staff to line can disorganize the formal managerial structure, especially when (1) the transferring staff personnel have had little or no supervisory experience in the staff but have an academic background which causes them to regard human beings as mechanisms that will respond as expected; (2) older, experienced line officers have hoped—for years in some cases—to occupy the newly vacated (or created) positions.

than the reverse, presumably (reflecting the drive and ambition of staff members) because there were more positions of authority, as well as more authority to be exercised, more prestige, and usually more income in the line.

Behavior in the plants indicated that line and staff personnel belonged to different social status groups and that line and staff antipathies were at least in part related to these social distinctions. For example, with respect to the item of formal education, the staff group stood on a higher level than members of the line. In the plant from which the age data were taken, the 36 staff officers had a mean of 14.6 years of schooling as compared with 13.1 years for 35 line superintendents, 11.2 years for 60 general foremen, and 10.5 years for 93 first-line foremen. The difference between the mean education of the staff group and that of the highest line group (14.6–13.1) was statistically significant at better than the one per cent level. The 270 non-supervisory staff personnel had a mean of 13.1 years—the same as that of the line superintendents. Consciousness of this difference probably contributed to a feeling of superiority among staff members, while the sentiment of line officers toward staff personnel was reflected in the name-calling noted earlier.

Staff members were also much concerned about their dress, a daily shave, and a weekly hair-cut. On the other hand line officers, especially below the level of departmental superintendent, were relatively indifferent to such matters. Usually they were in such intimate contact with production processes that dirt and grime prevented the concern with meticulous dress shown by staff members. The latter also used better English in speaking and in writing reports, and were more suave and poised in social intercourse. These factors, and the recreational preferences of staff officers for night clubs and "hot parties," assisted in raising a barrier between them and most line officers.

The social antipathies of the two groups and the status concern of staff officers were indicated by the behavior of each toward the established practice of dining together in the cafeterias reserved for management in the two larger plants. Theoretically, all managerial officers upward from the level of general foremen in the line, and general supervisors in the staff, were eligible to eat in these cafeterias. However, in practice the mere taking of one of these offices did not automatically assure the incumbent the privilege of eating in the cafeteria. One had first to be invited to "join the association." Staff officers were very eager to "get in" and did considerable fantasying on the impressions, with respect to dress and behavior, that were believed essential for an invitation. One such staff officer, a cost supervisor, dropped the following remarks:

> There seems to be a committee that passes on you. I've had my application in for three years, but no soap. Harry [his superior] had his in for over three years before he made it. You have to have something, because if a man who's in moves up to another position the man who replaces him doesn't get it because of the position—and he might not get it at all. I think I'm about due.

Many line officers who were officially members of the association avoided the cafeteria, however, and had to be *ordered* by the assistant plant manager to attend. One of these officers made the following statement, which expressed more pointedly the many similar spontaneous utterances of resentment and dislike made by other line officers:

> There's a lot of good discussion in the cafeteria. I'd like to get in on more of it but I don't like to go there—sometimes I have to go. Most of the white collar people [staff officers] that eat there are stuck-up. I've been introduced three times to Svendsen [engineer], yet when I meet him he pretends to not even know me. When he meets me on the street he always manages to be looking someplace else. G—d— such people as that! They don't go in the cafeteria to eat and relax while they talk over their problems. They go in there to look around and see how somebody is dressed or to talk over the hot party they had last night. Well, that kind of damn stuff don't go with me. I haven't any time to put on airs and make out I'm something that I'm not.

The Complications of Staff Need to Prove Its Worth

To the thinking of many line officers, the staff functioned as an agent on trial rather than as a managerial division that might be of equal importance with the line organization in achieving production goals. Staff members were very conscious of this sentiment toward them and of their need to prove themselves. They strained to develop new techniques and to get them accepted by the line. But in doing this they frequently became impatient, and gave already suspicious line officers the impression of reaching for authority over production.

Since the line officer regards his authority over production as something sacred, and resents the implication that after many years in the line he needs the guidance of a newcomer who lacks such experience, an obstacle to staff-line cooperation develops the moment this sore spot is touched. On the other hand, the staff officer's ideology of his function leads him to precipitate a power struggle with the line organization. By and large he considers himself as an agent of top management. He feels bound to contribute something significant in the form of research or ideas helpful to management. By virtue of his greater education and intimacy with the latest theories of production, he regards himself as a managerial consultant and an expert, and feels that he must be, or appear to be, almost infallible once he has committed himself to top management on some point. With this orientation, he is usually disposed to approach middle and lower line with an attitude of condescension that often reveals itself in the heat of discussion. Consequently, many staff officers involve themselves in trouble and report their failures as due to "ignorance" and "bull-headedness" among these line officers.

On this point, relations between staff and line in all three of the plants were further irritated by a rift inside the line organization. First-line foremen were inclined to feel that top management had brought in the production planning, industrial relations, and industrial engineering staffs as clubs with which to control the lower line. Hence they frequently regarded the projects of staff personnel as manipulative devices, and reacted by cooperating with production workers and/or general foremen (whichever course was the more expedient) in order to defeat insistent and uncompromising members of the staff. Also, on occasion (see below), the lower line could cooperate evasively with lower staff personnel who were in trouble with staff superiors.

The Effect of Line Authority on Staff Promotion

The fact that entry to the higher staff offices in the three plants was dependent on approval of top line officers had a profound effect on the behavior of staff personnel. Every member of the staff knew that if he aspired to higher office he must make a record for himself, a good part of which would be a reputation among upper line officers of ability to "understand" their informal problems without being told. This knowledge worked in varying degrees to pervert the theory of staff-line relations. Ideally the two organizations cooperate to improve existing methods of output, to introduce new methods, to plan the work, and to solve problems of production and the scheduling of orders that might arise. But when the line offers resistance to the findings and recommendations of the staff, the latter is reduced to evasive practices of getting some degree of acceptance of its programs, and at the same time of convincing top management that "good relations" exist with officers down the line. This necessity becomes even more acute when the staff officer aspires (for some of the reasons given above) to move over to the line organization, for then he must convince powerful line officers that he is worthy. In building a convincing record, however, he may compromise with line demands and bring charges from his staff colleagues that he is "selling out," so that after moving into the line organization he will then have to live with enemies he made in the staff. In any case, the need among staff incumbents of pleasing line officers in order to perfect their careers called for accommodation in three major areas:[18] (1) the observance of staff rules, (2) the introduction of new techniques, and (3) the use of appropriations for staff research and experiment.

With respect to point one, staff personnel, particularly in the middle and lower levels, carried on expedient relations with the line that daily evaded formal rules. Even those officers most devoted to rules found that, in order not to arouse enmity in the line on a scale sufficient to be communicated *up* the line, compromising devices were frequently helpful and sometimes almost unavoidable both for organizational and career aims. The usual practice was to tolerate minor breaking of staff rules by line personnel, or even to cooperate with the line in evading rules,[19] and in exchange lay a claim on the line for cooperation on critical issues. In some cases line aid was enlisted to conceal lower staff blunders from the upper staff and the upper line.[20]

---

[18]The relative importance of one or more of these areas would vary with the function of a given staff.

[19]In a processing department in one of the plants the chemical solution in a series of vats was supposed to have a specific strength and temperature, and a fixed rate of inflow and outflow. Chemists (members of the chemical staff) twice daily checked these properties of the solution and submitted reports showing that all points met the laboratory ideal. Actually, the solution was usually nearly triple the standard strength, the temperature was about 10 degrees Centigrade higher than standard, and the rate of flow was in excess of double the standard. There are, of course, varying discrepancies between laboratory theory and plant practice, but the condition described here resulted from production pressures that forced line foremen into behavior upsetting the conditions expected by chemical theory. The chemists were sympathetic with the hard-pressed foremen, who compensated by (1) notifying the chemists (rather than their superior, the chief chemist) if anything "went wrong" for which the laboratory was responsible and thus sparing them criticism; and by (2) cooperating with the chemists to reduce the number of analyses which the chemists would ordinarily have to make.

[20]Failure of middle and lower staff personnel to "cooperate" with line officers might cause the latter to "stand pat" in observance of line rules at a time when the pressures of a dynamic situation would make the former eager to welcome line cooperation in rule-breaking. For example, a staff officer was confronted with the combined effect of (1) a delay in production on the line that was due to an indefensible staff error; (2) pressure on the line superintendent—with whom he was working—to hurry a special order; and (3) the presence in his force of new inexperienced staff personnel who were (a) irritating to line officers, and (b) by their inexperience constituted an invitation to line aggression. Without aid from the line superintendent (which could have been withheld by observance of formal rules) in covering up the staff error and in controlling line personnel, the staff officer might have put himself in permanent disfavor with all his superiors.

Concerning point two, while the staff organizations gave much time to developing new techniques, they were simultaneously thinking about how their plans would be received by the line. They knew from experience that middle and lower line officers could always give a "black eye" to staff contributions by deliberate mal-practices. Repeatedly top management had approved, and incorporated, staff proposals that had been verbally accepted down the line. Often the latter officers had privately opposed the changes, but had feared that saying so would incur the resentment of powerful superiors who could informally hurt them. Later they would seek to discredit the change by deliberate mal-practice and hope to bring a return to the former arrangement. For this reason there was a tendency for staff members to withhold improved production schemes or other plans when they knew that an attempt to introduce them might fail or even bring personal disrepute.

Line officers fear staff innovations for a number of reasons. In view of their longer experience, presumably intimate knowledge of the work, and their greater remuneration, they fear[21] being "shown up" before their line superiors for not having thought of the processual refinements themselves. They fear that changes in methods may bring personnel changes which will threaten the break-up of cliques and existing informal arrangements and quite possibly reduce their area of authority. Finally, changes in techniques may expose forbidden practices and departmental inefficiency. In some cases these fears have stimulated line officers to compromise staff men to the point where the latter will agree to postpone the initiation of new practices for specific periods.

In one such case an assistant staff head agreed with a line superintendent to delay the application of a bonus plan for nearly three months so that the superintendent could live up to the expedient agreement he had made earlier with his grievance committeeman to avoid a "wildcat" strike by a group of production workmen.[22] The lower engineers who had devised the plan were suspicious of the formal reasons given to them for withholding it, so the assistant staff head prevented them (by means of "busy work") from attending staff-line meetings lest they inadvertently reveal to top management that the plan was ready.

The third area of staff-line accommodations growing out of authority relations revolved around staff use of funds granted it by top management. Middle and lower line charged that staff research and experimentation was little more than "money wasted on blunders," and that various departments of the line could have "accomplished much more with less money." According to staff officers, those of their plans that failed usually did so because line personnel "sabotaged" them and refused to "cooperate." Specific costs of "crack-pot experimentation" in certain staff groups were pointed to by line officers. Whatever the truth of the charges and counter-charges, evidence indicated (confidants in both groups supported this) that pressures from the line organization (below the top level) forced some of the staff groups to "kick over" parts of the funds

[21]Though there was little evidence that top management expected line officers to refine production techniques, the fear of such an expectation existed nevertheless. As noted earlier, however, some of the top executives *were* thinking that development of a "higher type" of first-line foreman might enable most of the staff groups to be eliminated.

[22]This case indicates the over-lapping of conflict areas referred to earlier. A later paper will deal with the area of informal union-management relations.

appropriated for staff use[23] by top management. These compromises were of course hidden from top management, but the relations described were carried on to such an extent that by means of them—and line pressures for manipulation of accounts in the presumably impersonal auditing departments—certain line officers were able to show impressively low operating costs and thus win favor[24] with top management that would relieve pressures and be useful in personal advancement. In their turn the staff officers involved would receive more "co-operation" from the line and/or recommendation for transfer to the line. The data indicated that in a few such cases men from accounting and auditing staffs were given general foremanships (without previous line experience) as a reward for their understanding behavior.

Summary

Research in three industrial plants showed conflict between the managerial staff and line groups that hindered the attainment of organizational goals. Privately expressed attitudes among some of the higher line executives revealed their hope that greater control of staff groups could be achieved, or that the groups might be eliminated and their functions taken over in great part by carefully selected and highly remunerated lower-line officers. On their side, staff members wanted more recognition and a greater voice in control of the plants.

All of the various functioning groups of the plants were caught up in a general conflict system; but apart from the effects of involvement in this complex, the struggles between line and staff organizations were attributable mainly to (1) functional differences between the two groups; (2) differentials in the ages, formal education, potential occupational ceilings, and status group affiliations of members of the two groups (the staff officers being younger, having more education but lower occupational potential, and forming a prestige-oriented group with distinctive dress and recreational tastes); (3) need of the staff groups to justify their existence; (4) fear in the line that staff bodies by their expansion, and well-financed research activities, would undermine line authority; and (5) the fact that aspirants to higher staff offices could gain promotion only through approval of influential line executives.

If further research should prove that staff-line behavior of the character presented here is widespread in industry, and *if* top management should realize how such behavior affects its cost and production goals—and be concerned to improve the condition—then remedial measures could be considered. For example, a corrective approach might move in the direction of (1) creating a separate body[25] whose sole function would be the coordination of staff and line efforts; (2) increasing the gradations of awards and promotions in staff organizations (without increase of staff personnel); (3) granting of more nearly equal

[23]In two of the plants a somewhat similar relation, rising from different causes, existed *inside* the line organization with the *operating* branch of the line successfully applying pressures for a share in funds assigned to the *maintenance* division of the line.

[24]The reader must appreciate the fact that constant demands are made by top management to maintain low operating costs.

[25]This body, or "Board of Coordination," would be empowered to enforce its decisions. Membership would consist of staff and line men who had had wide experience in the plant over a period of years. The Board would (a) serve as an arbiter between staff and line; (b) review, screen, and approve individual recommendations submitted; and (c) evaluate contributions after a trial period. Such a body would incidentally be another high status goal for seasoned, capable, and ambitious officers who too often are trapped by the converging walls of the pyramidal hierarchy.

pay to staff officers, but with increased responsibility (without authority over line processes or personnel) for the practical working of their projects; (4) requiring that staff personnel have a minimum supervisory experience and have shared repeatedly in successful collaborative staff-line projects before transferring to the line; (5) steps by top management to remove the fear of veiled personal reprisal felt by officers in most levels of both staff and line hierarchies (this fear—rising from a disbelief in the possibility of bureaucratic impersonality—is probably the greatest obstacle to communication inside the ranks of management); (6) more emphasis in colleges and universities on realistic instruction in the social sciences for students preparing for industrial careers.

Tactics of Lateral Relationship: The Purchasing Agent

GEORGE STRAUSS

This is a study of the tactics used by one functional group in an organization—purchasing—to influence the behavior of other functional departments of relatively equal status. It deals in part with "office politics" and "bureaucratic gamesmanship."

Most studies of human relations in management have dealt with vertical relations between superiors and subordinates or between line and staff.[1] Yet the purchasing agent's internal relationships (as opposed to his external relationships with salesmen) are almost entirely *lateral;* they are with other functional departments of about the same rank in the organizational hierarchy—departments such as production scheduling, quality control, engineering, and the like. Most agents receive relatively little attention from their superiors; they must act on their own, with support being given by higher management only in exceptional cases. They are given broad freedom to define their own roles and are "controlled" chiefly by the client departments with which they deal.

Although purchasing is technically a staff department, its relations with other departments can best be analyzed in terms of work flow rather than according to the typical staff-line concept. At the beginning of the typical work flow the sales department receives an order; on the basis of this the engineering department prepares a blueprint; next the production scheduling department initiates a work order for manufacturing and a requisition for purchasing; with this requisition the purchasing department buys the needed parts.

From George Strauss, "Tactics of Lateral Relationships: The Purchasing Agent," *Administrative Science Quarterly,* Vol. 7, No. 2 (September 1962), pp. 161–186. Reprinted by permission.

[1]There have been many studies of lateral relations within or among primary work groups, but such studies have been concerned primarily with rank-and-file workers, not management. Three notable studies of horizontal relations within management are Melville Dalton, *Men Who Manage* (New York, 1959); Elliot R. Chapple and Leonard Sayles, *The Measure of Management* (New York, 1961); and Henry A. Landsberger, The Horizontal Dimension in a Bureaucracy, *Administrative Science Quarterly,* 6 (1961), 298–332.

But this process does not always work smoothly. Each department has its specialized point of view which it seeks to impose on others, and each department is struggling for greater authority and status. The purpose of this exploratory study is to illustrate the range of tactics available in the interdepartmental conflict which almost always results.

Research Method

The research methodology included a considerable number of informal contacts with agents, observation of them at work for periods of up to one week, twenty-five formal interviews, a written questionnaire, a review of purchasing journals, and an analysis of how agents, both individually and in groups, handled specially prepared case problems. In the selection of firms to be studied there was a strong bias in favor of those with large engineering staffs, since agents in these firms face the most complex problems.

The discussion which follows will be largely impressionistic and will deal with broad aspects of tactics used by purchasing agents, since their problems vary greatly and various means are used to solve them. It should also be noted that the examples illustrate extreme cases, which, being extreme, illustrate some of the basic dilemmas which most agents face, though often in an attenuated form. This study is primarily concerned with the agent himself, the man who heads the purchasing office. It does not directly concern the buyers and expediters under him or the added complications that occur when divisions or plant agents have a staff relationship with a corporation-wide purchasing office.

Causes of Friction

The agent originally had two primary functions: (1) to negotiate and place orders at the best possible terms—but only in accordance with specifications set by others—and (2) to expedite orders, that is, to check with suppliers to make sure that deliveries are made on time. This arrangement gave the agent broad power in dealing with salesmen but made him little more than an order clerk in terms of power or status within the company.

The ambitious agent feels that placing orders and expediting deliveries are but the bare bones of his responsibilities. He looks upon his most important function as that of keeping management posted about market developments: new materials, new sources of supply, price trends, and so forth. And to make this information more useful, he seeks to be consulted before the requisition is drawn up, while the product is still in the planning stage. He feels that his technical knowledge of the market should be accorded recognition equal to the technical knowledge of the engineer and accountant.

Specifically, the ambitious agent would like to suggest (1) alternative materials or parts to use, (2) changes in specifications or redesign of components which will save money or result in higher quality or quicker delivery, and (3) more economical lot sizes, and to influence (4) "make or buy" decisions. The agent calls these functions "value analysis."

One way of looking at the agent's desire to expand his influence is in terms of interaction. Normally orders flow in one direction only, from engineering through scheduling to purchasing. But the agent is dissatisfied with being at the end of the line and seeks to reverse the flow. Value analysis permits him to initiate for others. Such behavior may, however, result in ill feeling on the part of other departments, particularly engineering and production scheduling.

Conflicts with Engineering

Engineers write up the *specifications* for the products which the agents buy. If the specifications are too tight or, what is worse, if they call for one brand only, agents have little or no freedom to choose among suppliers, thus reducing their social status internally and their economic bargaining power externally. Yet engineers find it much easier to write down a well-known brand name than to draw up a lengthy functional specification which lists all the characteristics of the desired item. Disagreements also arise because, by training and job function, engineers look first for quality and reliability and thus, agents charge, are indifferent to low cost and quick delivery, qualities of primary interest to purchasing.

All these problems are aggravated by the "completion barrier." Usually the agent seeks to change specifications only after the engineer has already committed his plans to blueprints and feels he has completed his work—in fact, he may be starting another project; the agent's interference inevitably threatens the engineer's feeling of accomplishment and completion. In any case engineers are jealous of their professional status and often resent the efforts of the agent to suggest new techniques or materials. These are areas in which the engineer feels that he is uniquely competent. Finally, agents are particularly anxious to prevent "backdoor selling" which occurs when a salesman bypasses them and seeks to influence someone else in the organization (usually an engineer) to requisition the salesman's product by name or—more subtly—to list specifications which only this product can meet. Backdoor selling threatens the agent's status in two ways: (1) it encourages specification by brand and (2) it makes both salesmen and engineers less dependent on him.

Conflicts with Production Scheduling

The size of the order and the date on which it is to be delivered are typically determined by production scheduling. The agent's chief complaint against scheduling is that delivery is often requested on excessively short notice—that schedulers engage in sloppy planning or "cry wolf" by claiming they need orders earlier than they really do—and thus force the agent to choose from a limited number of suppliers, to pay premium prices, and to ask favors of salesmen (thus creating obligations which the agent must later repay). Schedulers, on the other hand, claim that "short lead times" are not their fault, but the fault of departments farther up the line, such as engineering (which delays its blueprints) or sales (which accepts rush orders). In addition agents claim that schedulers order in uneconomic lot sizes and fail to consider inventory costs or the savings from quantity discounts. In some instances, as we shall see, the purchasing agent seeks to solve these problems through combining production scheduling, inventory control, and purchasing into one "materials handling" department, which he hopes he will head.

Techniques for Dealing with Other Departments

Normally the agent attempts to fill requisitions as instructed. The majority of interdepartmental contacts are handled routinely and without friction in accordance with standard operating procedures. Yet many difficult problems cannot be easily programmed. Other departments are constantly placing pressures on the agent, who must take countermeasures, if only to preserve the *status quo.* And if the purchasing agent wishes to expand his power aggressively, as many do, he will inevitably run into conflict.

Understandably, then, successful agents have developed a variety of techniques for dealing with other departments, particularly when they wish to influence the terms of the requisitions received. These techniques will first be summarized briefly under five general headings and then discussed in greater detail.

1. *Rule-oriented tactics*
   a. Appeal to some common authority to direct that the requisition be revised or withdrawn.
   b. Refer to some rule (assuming one exists) which provides for longer lead times.
   c. Require the scheduling department to state in writing why quick delivery is required.
   d. Require the requisitioning department to consent to having its budget charged with the extra cost (such as air freight) required to get quick delivery.
2. *Rule-evading tactics*
   a. Go through the motions of complying with the request, but with no expectation of getting delivery on time.
   b. Exceed formal authority and ignore the requisitions altogether.
3. *Personal-political tactics*
   a. Rely on friendships to induce the scheduling department to modify the requisition.
   b. Rely on favors, past and future, to accomplish the same result.
   c. Work through political allies in other departments.
4. *Educational tactics*
   a. Use direct persuasion, that is, try to persuade scheduling that its requisition is unreasonable.
   b. Use what might be called indirect persuasion to help scheduling see the problem from the purchasing department's point of view (in this case it might ask the scheduler to sit in and observe the agent's difficulty in trying to get the vendor to agree to quick delivery).
5. *Organizational-interactional tactics*
   a. Seek to change the interaction pattern, for example, have the scheduling department check with the purchasing department as to the possibility of getting quick delivery *before* it makes a requisition.
   b. Seek to take over other departments, for example, to subordinate scheduling to purchasing in an integrated materials department.

Note that neither the over-all categories nor the tactics listed under them are all-exclusive and that there is a great deal of overlapping. They are proposed not as comprehensive tools of analysis, but merely as fairly common examples of bureaucratic gamesmanship.

Each agent interviewed in the study was evaluated in terms of his reported success (in terms of specific accomplishments) in getting other departments to accept a wider role for purchasing. Although this measure was crude and subjective,[2] there seemed to be quite clear differences between the tactics used by those

[2] *Reported* success obviously involves a fair amount of wishful thinking—aspiration rather than accomplishment—but for the general character of this study this limitation was not too serious. It should be emphasized, however, that whether an agent was a successful expansionist depended not only on his own personality and his choice of techniques but also on the institutional characteristics of the organization in which he worked.

who looked upon their job description as a defensive bastion and those who sought to expand their power beyond it. (Note that success is measured here in terms of expansion of power, rather than money saved for the company.)

Rule-Oriented Tactics

The tactics listed below are rule-oriented in the sense that the agent's approach is perfectly legitimate under the formal rules of the organization. Agents who emphasize these tactics seem to fit into Melville Dalton's category of "systematizers."

Appealing to the Boss

According to traditional organizational theory, whenever two executives on about the same level cannot agree, they should take the problem to their common superior for solution. Yet, most agents looked upon this as a drastic step, to be taken only when other means failed.

Only five of the agents interviewed mentioned appealing to their superior as a reasonably common means of dealing with interdepartmental problems. In three cases low status seemed to be largely responsible for their inability to handle problems on their own.

Two of these agents were new to the job. For example, one was a man in his early twenties, who had only a few months' experience and who commented that his chief problems were his age and his inability to understand what engineers were talking about. This man met daily to review his problems with his boss and commented that his boss ran interference for him, at least in big problems.

The purchasing agent of a large scientific laboratory was very successful in extending his authority. In dealing with research departments, however, he used the laboratory manager "as a buffer between me and the department heads." But in regard to equipment-maintenance departments, whose heads had much lower status than did the scientists, he commented that "if there were differences, I would discuss them with them. If we didn't agree the laboratory manager would have to arbitrate. But this has never happened here." Significantly, this agent did not have a college degree, while many of the scientists were Ph.D's.

The other two agents who frequently worked through their superiors came from branch plants of nation-wide firms, which placed strong emphasis on individual responsibility to live within rigid rules.

The more expansionist agents rarely relied on their superiors to help them in interdepartmental disputes (in part because they had little success in doing this). They often explained that they would take problems to a man's superior if necessary but that they rarely found it necessary. Many repeated versions of the following:

We have a policy against engineers having lunch with salesmen. Since the engineer is on my level I couldn't *tell* him to stop it. But in a nice way I could talk to him. If this didn't work, I'd see the plant manager.

Q: Have you ever done this [appealed to the boss]?

A: No.

The general feeling, particularly among stronger agents, was that too frequent reference to the superior would weaken their relations both with the superior and with their fellow employees. ("After all you've got to live with them.") To bring in top management too often would, in effect, be an admission that the agent could not handle his own problems. Moreover, there is a myth in many corporations of being "one great big happy family," and, as a consequence, it is difficult to bring conflicts out in the open. Furthermore, since the agent is usually the aggressor, in the sense that he is seeking to expand his power beyond its formal limits, he is unlikely to go to the boss unless his case is unusually good.

On the other hand, the threat of going to the boss loses its effectiveness as a weapon if the threat is *never* carried out. The following quotation summarizes a common position:

It depends on how much fuss you want to make. If it is really important, you can tell him you will discuss it with his boss. But, I don't want you to get the wrong impression. If you have to resort to this, you are probably falling down on the job. By and large, we have a good relationship with our engineers. However, there are times when you have to take a tough position. You aren't doing your job if you always go along with them in a wishy-washy fashion.

One agent explained how he "educated" engineers to accept substitute products instead of insisting on one brand.

We prepared our evidence and we were all set to take it to the top—and then, at the last minute, we backed down and told them it was too late in the game. But we indicated that in the future we would take similar issues to the top and they knew we would. So there has been much more understanding. . . . You have to risk making a few enemies once in a while.

Use of Rules

A second traditional bureaucratic means of dealing with other departments is to cite applicable rules or to rely on a formal statement of authority (such as a job description). For instance, an agent may circumvent pressure to place an order with a given company by referring to company rules requiring competitive bidding on all purchases in excess of $10,000. Most agents agreed, in theory, that rules of this sort are useful weapons, but they varied greatly in the extent to which they relied upon them in practice.

Some agents went very much "by the book," day in and day out. In general, these were men without college training, and they worked for larger, rule-oriented companies that were not changing rapidly. In answer to questions, these men often said, "This matter is governed by corporate policy" or made references to manuals and procedures. They also had a tendency to draw the lines of responsibility quite tightly, so that there were few areas of joint decision making; for example, "Engineering has the final word as far as specs are concerned. But we decide from whom to buy, provided they meet the specs." On the other hand, many agents operated very effectively without any formal written statement of their authority; their authority was understood by everybody in the organization and there was no need to put it in writing.

The evidence suggests that the most successful expansionists preferred to operate informally until there was an open conflict with another department. When this happened, they were very glad to refer to rules to bolster their position. Thus, paradoxically, we found strong agents who worked hard to introduce purchasing manuals and then paid relatively no attention to them in daily practice. In effect these agents take the position of "speak softly and carry a big stick." Indeed, the use of rules involves an implicit threat to appeal to higher management if the rules are not obeyed. ("When everyone in the organization knows what your responsibility is—and that you are backed up—then there is no need to mention it constantly.")

If flexibly used, procedure manuals provide the agent with an added bargaining weapon in dealing with other departments. Even though he may permit rules in the manual to be ignored most of the time, he can always do this as a favor in return for which he may ask favors. And the rules put a legal stamp on his efforts whenever he decides to ensnarl another department in a mass of red tape. But the expansionist agent must be careful not to become too rule-oriented. After all, his goal is to expand his influence beyond the areas over which the rules give him definite authority—not to retreat behind them.

Requiring Written Acceptance of Responsibility

Another bureaucratic technique used by many agents is to require others to justify their decisions in writing. For example, if a production scheduler orders a part for delivery with very short lead time, the agent can ask him to explain in writing why there is such a rush. He hopes the scheduler will be embarrassed unless he has a good excuse—and in any case, the effort will make him reluctant to make such last-minute requests in the future. Certainly this helps expose the scheduler who constantly cries "wolf."

Agents may ask for written explanations to clear themselves. Just as often, however, this is done to make others hesitate or to have evidence against them later. In insisting that such reports be written, the purchasing agent can refer to company rules or to possible audits. Thus in asking for such a statement, agents often say, "I need it to document my records."

Again, it is the weaker, noncollege agent who makes the most persistent use of such tactics. Many seem to feel that an approach of this sort is cowardly and defeatist. As one put it, "If you are trying to get a man to say 'yes,' I don't see any value in forcing him to put his 'no' in writing. Then he will never move." And another said, "I suppose you do punish an engineer by forcing him to give you a long written explanation, but that's hardly the way to win friends or advance your point of view." Furthermore, "You can always ask an engineer to give you a formal test result, but if he wishes he can always make the test fail."

Financial Charges

Cost-accounting procedures may also be used as a lever. A number of agents made comments like this:

Whenever I get a request for a rush delivery, I ask the department which wants it whether they are willing to authorize overtime[3] or air freight. Since this gets charged against their budget, they usually hesitate a bit. If they go along I know they really need it. And if they have too many extra charges the auditor starts asking questions.

This tactic resembles the one previously discussed, particularly when the agent enters a statement into his records that the product would have been cheaper had the requisition been received on time. (Some companies charge inbound freight to the budget of the purchasing or traffic department; in such cases purchasing's leverage is somewhat less effective.)

[3]That is, the vendor is authorized to make an extra charge for having his men work overtime.

Some companies have what is often called an efficiency (or profit) improvement plan. According to such a plan each department (and sometimes each executive) receives credit[4] for the cost savings which can be attributed to the department's activities. Agents in two companies reported that engineers showed little enthusiasm for value analysis because the purchasing department got all the credit, even though part of the work was done by the engineering department. The situation greatly improved in one of these companies when "primary" credit was transferred to engineering, with purchasing retaining "participating" credit.

Rule-Evading Tactics

Literal Compliance

In dealing with pressures from other departments the agent can always adopt a policy of passive resistance—that is, he can go through the motions in hopes of satisfying the demands. This tactic of feigned acceptance[5] is often used with production scheduling. For instance, after completing a lengthy phone call in which he half-heartedly tried to persuade a vendor to make a very quick delivery, an agent commented, "My buyer tried already and I knew that they just weren't going to be able to deliver that soon. Still production scheduling was screaming and they threatened to go to the plant manager. So I tried to handle it in such a way as not to hurt my relations with the vendor. They knew why I had to call."

This game of passive resistance can be skillfully played in such a way as to set a trap for the other department.

Example. One agent told how he dealt with an engineer who had placed a requisition for one company's products after having been lavishly entertained by its salesman. The agent wrote a long memo explaining why he felt this to be a poor choice and presented it to the engineer in a fashion which he knew the engineer would reject. The agent then placed the order. As he had predicted, the products arrived late and were totally inappropriate. The subsequent investigation led both to this engineer's transfer and demotion and to other engineers having greater respect for the agent's advice.[6]

It should be noted, however, that these tactics were reported by only a minority of agents. In almost every case the agent was "weak" (in terms of expansionism) or worked in large companies where there was considerable emphasis on following formal rule books. Instead of passively seeming to accept unreasonable requests, the stronger agents actively oppose them.

Exceeding Authority

Occasionally agents may revise the terms of requisitions on their own initiative, even though they have no formal authority to do so. For instance, an agent may extend a lead time if he knows the production scheduler has set the delivery date much earlier than is really required. Where a requisition calls for a given brand, he may purchase a substitute which he feels sure is an

---

[4] Though there is no direct pay-off, performance under the plan is often taken into account in determining bonuses or promotions.

[5] Dalton, *op. cit.,* p. 232.

[6] A tactic like this can always backfire. The agent himself may be blamed for the failure.

equivalent. Or, he may buy a larger quantity than requested in order to take advantage of quantity discounts.

When an agent revises requisitions in this manner, he may or may not tell the requisitioning department what he is doing. In either case he is exceeding his formal authority. In effect, he is daring the requisitioning department to make an issue of it. This requires considerable courage. No sensible agent will expose himself in this way unless (1) his over-all political position is secure and (2) he feels the terms of the original requisition were clearly so unreasonable that the requisitioning department will hesitate to raise the issue and expose its mistake.

Most agents were reluctant to use this tactic. Even if they could safely change orders in a given case, continual flouting of the requisitioning department's desires would create too much antagonism in the long run.

Personal-Political Tactics

Friendships and exchange of favors are used in almost every organization to get things done and to oil the wheels of formal bureaucracy. The agent is no exception to this rule; yet the author found to his surprise that informal relations played a less important role than he had expected. Agents, on the whole, seemed oriented to doing things "through channels."

None of the tactics which follow are contemplated by the company's formal scheme; all involve the use of personal relations. It would seem that Dalton's "adapters" would make greatest use of these tactics.

Friendships

Most agents prefer to deal with friends. Friendships help reduce the kinds of tensions to which agents are commonly subject. Even where friendship is not involved, it is easier to deal with people when you know their idiosyncrasies and special interests. Not surprisingly, comments like this were common: "[In handling problems] friendships count a lot. Many of the people here started when I did twenty-five years ago. We are all at about the same level and most of them are pretty good friends of mine. A lot is a matter of trust and confidence."

Agents seem to rely on friendship contacts as a means of communication and of getting quick acceptances of proposals that could be justified on their merits in any case. Rarely do agents rely on friendship alone. As one put it, "You can accomplish some things on the basis of friendship, but you can't do too much or you will strain your friendship."

Exchange of Favors

To some extent agents operate on the principle of "reward your friends, punish your enemies," and are involved in a network of exchange of favors—and sometimes even reprisals. Favors of various sorts may be given. Most agents are under pressure to make personal purchases, for example, to help someone in management buy a set of tires at wholesale rates. Since there are usually no formal rules as to such extracurricular purchasing, the agent has a strong incentive to help those who help him most. Similarly an agent is in a position to suggest to a salesman that it might be strategic to take a "co-operative" engineer to lunch. And there are always people in management who would like him to do a favor for a friend or relative who is a salesman or who owns a small business.

Other favors are more work-related. An agent may expedite delivery for a production scheduler who normally gives plenty of lead time for his orders but who now has a real emergency on his hands. Or he may rush parts for an engineer who is building a prototype model. "If a man is reasonable with me," one agent commented, "I'll kill myself to get him what he wants." The agent is less likely to exert himself for the man who has been uncooperative in the past. Yet, in general, agents seem to play down the exchange of favors, perhaps because they have relatively few favors to offer, other than trivial ones such as personal purchases or lunches for salesmen.[7]

The use of reprisals can be seen most clearly in dealing with salesmen. As one agent put it, "I play ball with those who play ball with me. If a salesman operates behind my back, he's going to have a hell of a time getting me to give him an order." Reprisals are more risky in dealing with management.

Example. One assistant agent, for example, told how he "delayed" getting catalogues for "uncooperative" engineers and gave "slow service" to engineers who habitually cried wolf. However, both this man's supervisor and his personnel director expressed concern over his poor human relations and his tendency to antagonize others.

The typical agent, however, seemed to feel that if he used such techniques he ran the risk of permanently impairing his relations with others. Furthermore, these techniques might always backfire; for example, if production were delayed because components were delivered late, he would be blamed.

Interdepartmental Politics

In addition to their personal relations with people, agents inevitably get involved in interdepartmental power struggles. Indeed, as the following quotation suggests, the agent is often a man in the middle, subject to conflicting pressures from all sides:

> Production scheduling wants quick delivery, engineering wants quality, manufacturing wants something easy-to-make, accounting wants to save money, quality control has their own interests. And then you've got to deal with the supplier—and present the supplier's position back to your own organization (sometimes you think you are wearing two hats, you represent both the supplier and the company). Everybody has his own point of view and only the agent sees the over-all picture.

Much of the agent's time is spent seeking informal resolution of such problems—and in these meetings[8] he often acts as a mediator. The following is a common situation:

Example. Production scheduling has been pushing hard to get early delivery of a particular component (perhaps because the sales department has been pressing for increased production). In response to this pressure the vendor puts new, inexperienced men on the job. But when the components are delivered, quality control declares the work is sloppy, rejects it *in toto,* and wants to

[7] Reciprocity in the broader sense, as suggested by Gouldner and others, is, of course, inherent in the entire framework of relations discussed here. Cf. Alvin W. Gouldner, The Norm of Reciprocity: A Preliminary Statement, *American Sociological Review,* 25 (1960), 161–177.

[8] Dalton (*op. cit.,* pp. 227–228) points out the function of meetings in short circuiting formal means of handling problems.

disqualify the vendor from doing further work for the company. Production scheduling and the vendor are naturally upset; the vendor insists that the defects are trivial and can be easily remedied; and purchasing is placed in the difficult position of trying to mediate the issue.

If the agent is not careful in situations like this, he may become a scapegoat; everyone may turn on him and blame him for the unhappy turn of events. On the other hand, the successful agent is able to play one pressure off against another and free himself— or he may enlist the support of a powerful department to back him. If he is shrewd, he can get both sides to appeal to him to make the final decision and thus gain prestige as well as bestow favors which he may later ask returned.

Like it or not, agents of necessity engage in power politics. In doing this, they necessarily develop allies and opponents. Each department presents a special problem.

1. *Engineering.* Unless the relationship with engineering is handled with great tact, engineering tends to become an opponent, since value analysis invades an area which engineers feel is exclusively their own. Purchasing is at a disadvantage here. Engineers have the prestige of being college-trained experts, and engineering is much more strongly represented than purchasing in the ranks of higher management.
2. *Manufacturing.* There is often a tug of war between purchasing and manufacturing over who should have the greatest influence with production scheduling. These struggles are particularly sharp where purchasing is trying to absorb either inventory control or all of production scheduling.
3. *Comptroller.* The comptroller is rarely involved in the day-to-day struggles over specifications or delivery dates. But when purchasing seeks to introduce an organizational change which will increase its power—for example, absorbing inventory control—then the comptroller can be a most effective ally. But the agent must present evidence that the proposed innovation will save money.
4. *Sales.* Sales normally has great political power, and purchasing is anxious to maintain good relations with it. Sales is interested above all in being able to make fast delivery and shows less concern with cost, quality, or manufacturing ease. In general, it supports or opposes purchasing in accordance with this criteria. But sales is also interested in reciprocity—in persuading purchasing "to buy from those firms which buy from us."
5. *Production scheduling.* Relations with production scheduling are often complex. Purchasing normally has closer relations with production scheduling than any other department, and conflicts are quite common. Yet these departments are jointly responsible for having parts available when needed and, in several companies at least, they presented a common front to the outside world. Unfortunately, however, production scheduling has little political influence, particularly when it reports relatively low down in the administrative hierarchy.

The shrewd agent knows how to use departmental interests for his own ends. Two quotations illustrate this:

> Engineering says we can't use these parts. But I've asked manufacturing to test a sample under actual operating conditions—they are easy to use.

> Even if engineering won't accept manufacturing's data, I can go to the boss with manufacturing backing me. On something like this, manufacturing is tremendously powerful.
>
> [To get acceptance of new products] I may use methods and standards. Or I might go to engineering first and then to methods and standards if engineering shows no interest. If I go to methods and standards I got to emphasize the cost-saving aspect [as contrasted to engineering's interest in quality].

Educational Tactics

Next we come to a set of tactics designed to persuade others to think in purchasing terms.

Direct Persuasion

Direct persuasion—the frank attempt to sell a point of view—is, of course, the agent's typical means of influencing others. Successful persuasion means "knowing your products backwards and forwards . . . building your case so that it can't be answered . . . knowing what you are talking about."

Most agents feel it essential that they have complete command of the facts, particularly if they are to bridge the status gap and meet engineers on equal terms. As one of them said, "The engineer thinks he is the expert; the only way you can impress him is to know more than he does." Thus many agents go to considerable lengths to acquire expertise; they spend a great deal of time learning production processes or reading technical journals.

Yet some of the stronger agents pointed out that too much expertise can be dangerous in that it threatens the other man's status. "Never put a man in a corner. Never prove that he is wrong. This is a fundamental in value analysis. It doesn't pay to be a know-it-all." Thus some agents look upon themselves primarily as catalysts who try to educate others to think in purchasing terms:

> Actually it is an asset not to be an engineer. Not having the [engineering] ability myself, I've had to work backwards. I can't tell them what to do but I can ask questions. They know that I'm not trying to design their instrument. . . . You have to give the engineer recognition. The less formal you are in dealing with them the better. It doesn't get their dander up.

Indirect Persuasion

Recognizing the danger of the frontal approach, agents often try forms of indirection—manipulation, if you like—which are designed to induce the other departments to arrive at conclusions similar to those of the agent but seemingly on their own. For example:

> We were paying $45.50 a unit, but I found a vendor who was producing a unit for $30 which I felt would meet our needs just as well. There was a lot of reluctance in engineering to accept it, but I knew the engineer in charge of the test was susceptible to flattery. So I wrote a letter for general distribution telling what a good job of investigating he was doing and how much money we'd save if his investigation was successful. . . .

That gave him the motivation to figure out how it *could* work rather than how it *could not* work.

Indirect persuasion often involves presenting the facts and then letting the other person draw his own conclusions. The agent may ask the engineer to run a test on a product or even simply attach a sample of the product to an interoffice buck slip, asking, "Can we use this?" Similarly, choosing which salesmen may see engineers, he can indirectly influence the specification process. (In fact, once an agent decides that a product should be introduced, he and the salesman will often co-ordinate their strategies closely in order to get it accepted by others in management.)

Most agents feel engineers should have no part in negotiating prices; they feel this would be encroaching on purchasing's jurisdiction. But one successful agent encourages engineers to help out in the bargaining because "that's the best way I know to make these engineers cost conscious." Another arranges to have foremen and production schedulers sit in while he negotiates delivery dates with salesmen. "In that way they will know what I'm up against when they give me lead times which are too short for normal delivery."

Organizational-Interactional Techniques

Organizational factors play an important part in determining (1) whether the agent's relations with other departments will be formal or informal (for example, whether most contacts will be face-to-face, by phone, or in writing), (2) whether it will be easy or hard for other departments to initiate for purchasing, and (3) whether purchasing can make its point of view felt while decisions are being considered—or can intervene only after other departments have already taken a position. All these involve interaction patterns. We shall consider here only two types of organizational changes: informal measures which make it easier for other departments to initiate change in the usual flow of orders and formal changes involving grants of additional authority.

Inducing Others to Initiate Action

In most of the examples discussed here, the agent seeks to initiate change in the behavior of other departments. He is the one who is trying to change the engineer's specifications, the production scheduler's delivery schedules, and so forth. The other departments are always at the receiving (or resisting) end of these initiations. As might be expected, hard feelings are likely to develop if the initiations move only one way.[9]

Recognizing this, many of the stronger agents seem to be trying to rearrange their relations with other departments so that others might initiate changes in the usual work flow more often for them. Specifically they hope to induce the other departments to turn instinctively to purchasing for help whenever they have a problem—and at the earliest possible stage. Thus one agent explained that his chief reason for attending production planning meetings, where new products were laid out, was to make it easier for others to ask him questions. He hoped

[9] Actually, of course, initiations do occur in both directions. The production schedulers initiate for the agent when they file requisitions and the engineers initiate when they determine specifications. This normal form of programmed, routine initiation is felt to be quite different from the agent's abnormal attempts to introduce innovation. This distinction is quite important.

to encourage engineers, for example, to inquire about available components before they drew up their blueprints. Another agent commented, "I try to get production scheduling to ask us what the lead times for the various products are. That's a lot easier than our telling them that their lead times are unreasonable after they have made commitments based on these."

Some purchasing departments send out what are, in effect, ambassadors to other departments. They may appoint purchase engineers, men with engineering background (perhaps from the company's own engineering group) who report administratively to purchasing but spend most of their time in the engineering department. Their job is to be instantly available to provide information to engineers whenever they need help in choosing components. They assist in writing specifications (thus making them more realistic and readable) and help expedite delivery of laboratory supplies and material for prototype models. Through making themselves useful, purchase engineers acquire influence and are able to introduce the purchasing point of view before the "completion barrier" makes this difficult. Similar approaches may be used for quality control.

Work assignments with purchasing are normally arranged so that each buyer can become an expert on one group of commodities bought. Under this arrangement the buyer deals with a relatively small number of salesmen, but with a relatively large number of "client" departments within the organization. A few agents have experimented with assigning men on the basis of the departments with which they work rather than on the basis of the products they buy. In one case work assignments in both purchasing and scheduling were so rearranged that each production scheduler had an exact counterpart in purchasing and dealt only with him. In this way closer personal relations developed than would have occurred if the scheduler had no specific individual in purchasing to contact.

Even the physical location of the agent's office makes a difference. It is much easier for the agent to have informal daily contacts with other departments if his office is conveniently located. Some companies place their agents away from the main office, to make it easier for salesmen to see them. Although this facilitates the agents' external communications, it makes their internal communications more difficult. Of course, those companies that have centralized purchasing offices and a widespread network of plants experience this problem in an exaggerated form. Centralized purchasing offers many economic advantages, but the agent must tour the plants if he is not to lose all contact with his client departments.

Value analysis techniques sharply highlight the agent's organizational philosophy. Some agents feel that value analysis should be handled as part of the buyer's everyday activities. If he comes across a new product which might be profitably substituted for one currently used, he should initiate engineering feasibility studies and promote the idea ("nag it" in one agent's words) until it is accepted. Presumably purchasing then gets the credit for the savings, but resistance from other departments may be high. Other agents, particularly those with college training, reject this approach as unnecessarily divisive; they prefer to operate through committees, usually consisting of engineers, purchasing men, and production men. Though committees are time consuming, communications are facilitated, more people are involved, more ideas are forthcoming—and, in addition, the purchasing department no longer has the sole responsibility for value analysis.

To the extent that he allows others to take the initiative, the agent himself must take a passive role. Not all agents are emotionally prepared to do this.[10] Some feel that it smacks too much of the "order clerk." A number commented, in effect, "I don't want to be everyone's door mat." Many asked questions like, "How far do you go in cost estimating, in getting quotes for hypothetical orders? . . . What do you do if a man throws a label at you and says get me some of this? After all, our time is limited."

Formal Organizational Change

The final approach is for the agent to seek to expand the formal grant of authority given his department (which might mean a larger budget too), as, for example, to place other functions such as traffic, stores, or even inventory control and production scheduling in one combined materials department. Agents who exert their energies in this direction generally reject the "human relations" or "participative" approach to management. They like to resolve problems through memoranda ("it helps keep emotions down") and are not particularly optimistic about the possibilities of converting other departments to think in purchasing terms ("after all every department has its own point of view—that's natural"). They spend considerable time developing statistical means of measuring their own efficiency and that of their subordinates, and they are more likely to be in companies that have similar philosophies. For example, one agent explained why value analysis in his organization was concentrated in the purchasing department, "[Our company] doesn't believe in joint assignments or committees. If a man isn't competent to do the job himself, then we find another man. We don't want weak sisters." And another argued, "The responsibility must be concentrated in one department or another. It can't fall between two stools."[11]

Choice of Techniques

The foregoing list of tactics are presented not as a formal typology but merely to illustrate the *range* of techniques available to the agent. Most agents use all of these techniques at one time or another, depending on the problem. A different technique might well be used in introducing a major policy change than in handling routine orders. In trying to promote changes, one agent observed:

> You have to choose your weapons. I vary them on purpose. . . . I ask myself, who has the final decision? How does the Chief Engineer operate? What does he delegate? What does he keep for himself? It all involves psychological warfare. Who are the people to be sold? Who will have the final say?

And even in dealing with one problem, a mixture of tactics will generally be used. Nevertheless, the over-all strategies used by various agents seem to vary greatly in terms of which tactics receive the greatest emphasis.

1. Some agents seek formal grants of power (for example, to get inventory placed

[10] After all, a certain type of active, initiating sort of personality is required if the agent is to bargain successfully with suppliers; it is hard for the same individual to adopt a passive role within the organization.

[11] Yet it could be argued that the committee system does not itself divide responsibility; it merely recognizes the fact that responsibility for value analysis is of necessity divided among departments.

under purchasing); others merely seek influence (for example, to persuade inventory control to order in more economic lot sizes).
2. Some agents want to influence decisions *before* they are made (for example, through encouraging engineers to turn instinctively to purchasing for help whenever they are even considering the use of a new component); others *after* (for example, through having their decisions upheld often enough for engineering to hesitate to make an issue of a request whenever purchasing questions a specification).
3. Some agents think in terms of their long-run position and thus seek to improve procedures; whereas others are interested chiefly in exerting their influence in each conflict as it comes along.

We have already noted a difference between successful expansionists and those content with their roles as they are. On the whole, expansionists seemed to be more likely to choose informal tactics such as indirect persuasion, inducing others to make changes in the work flow, and interdepartmental politics. They had long-run strategies and sought to influence decisions before they were made. Those who were successful in achieving more formal power were also well aware of the value of informal influence; those who merely *talked* about formal power seemed to be relatively unsuccessful even in informal influence. In fact, one of the most noticeable characteristics of successful expansionists was their flexibility. Most were equally adept at using both formal and informal tactics and were not averse to turning the formal organization against itself.

Differences in success in expansionism seem to be due to a number of factors:

1. *Technology.* Obviously the agent cannot expand very much in a service industry or one where only raw materials are bought. He has his greatest chance for power in companies which make goods to order and in which there is a great deal of subcontracting.
2. *Management philosophy.* Where lines of authority are sharply drawn, the agent has little chance to extend his influence—except through direct seizure of another department's power, which is not easy. Note the comments of one agent in a highly rule-oriented company:

   > We are a service department . . . We must see that parts are here at the proper time. . . . I usually let engineering pretty much make its own decisions. I may try to persuade an engineer to accept a new product. But if he says "no" all I can do is wait till he gets transferred and try to persuade his successor.

   Of the agents interviewed, the most successful was one in a company which had just introduced a new management and in which all relationships were in flux.
3. *Education.* Purchasing agents who were college graduates seemed to be more expansionist than those who were not. This may be due to their higher level of aspiration. Moreover, any company that appoints a college graduate may well expect to grant him greater influence. The college-trained man may feel more as an equal of the engineer and therefore more willing to come into conflict with him.

   Furthermore, the more educated men (and particularly those with a business school background) seemed more prone to rely on techniques that were informal and not rule-oriented. Specifically, they were less likely to rely on formal statements of authority, to require others to take formal responsibilities for decisions, or to insist that an agent should "yell loudly whenever his rights are violated"; and they were more willing to work through committees.[12]

Conclusion

Traditional organization theory emphasizes authority and responsibility; it deals largely with two types of relationships: (1) those between superiors and subordinates, which it conceives as being primarily authoritarian (though perhaps modifiable by participation, general supervision, and the like) and (2) those of staff and line, which are nonauthoritarian. Though the purchasing department is traditionally classified as a staff department, my own feeling is that the staff-line dichotomy in this case (as perhaps for most other purposes) tends to obscure more problems than it illuminates. As we have seen, the purchasing department's relations with other departments cannot be explained by any one simple phrase, such as "areas of responsibility," "exchange of favors," "advice," "control," or the like. Instead the skillful agent blends all these approaches and makes use of authoritarian and persuasive tactics as the situation requires. His effectiveness is largely dependent on the political power he is able to develop.

Recent authors have suggested that the study of organization should begin first with "the work to be done and resources and techniques available to do it."[13] The emphasis is on the technology of the job ("technology" being defined broadly to include marketing problems and the like as well as external environment) and the relationships between people which this technology demands. "Organizations should be constructed from the *bottom up,* rather than from the *top down.* In establishing work-group boundaries and supervisory units, management should start with the actual work to be performed, an awareness of who must co-ordinate his job with whom, when, and where."[14]

Some of us who are interested in this area are groping toward a concept of *work flow,* meaning the communications or interactions required by the job and including the flow of raw materials and products on the assembly line, the flow of paper work when a requisition moves through engineering, scheduling, and purchasing, as well as the flow of instruction, which may move down the chain of command from president to janitor.

This has been an exploratory study of the interrelationship between power struggles and lateral work flow. Of particular interest in this study, are: (1) the agent's strong desire for increased status, which upsets the stability of his relationship with other departments, (2) his attempts to raise his status

[12] These conclusions are consistent with the findings of the questionnaire sample (N = 142). The results are in the direction indicated for both degree of education and business school background (each taken separately) although only three out of eight relationships are significant at the .05 level. The questionnaire data are somewhat suspect, however, since the values which agents report are not always consistent with their observed behavior: in answering questionnaires many agents seem to place greater emphasis on formal techniques than they do in practice.

[13] Wilfred Brown, *Explorations in Management* (London, 1960), p. 18. See Chapple and Sayles, *op. cit.;* William F. Whyte, *Men at Work* (Homewood, Ill., 1961).

[14] George Strauss and Leonard R. Sayles, *Personnel: The Human Problems of Management* (Englewood Cliffs, N.J., 1960), p. 392. The sentence is Sayles's.

through influencing the terms of the requisitions he receives and thus make interactions flow both ways, (3) the relatively limited interference on the part of higher management, which makes the lateral relationship especially important for the agent, (4) the "completion barrier," which requires the agent to contact an engineer before a blueprint is finished if the agent is to be successful in influencing the terms of the requisition, and (5) the differing vested interests or terms of reference of the various departments, which make agreement more difficult.

Finer mapping and more intensive research into interdepartmental relations is required; interactions should be precisely counted[15] and work should be done with specialties other than purchasing.

---

[15] Albert H. Rubenstein of Northwestern University has completed an unpublished quantitative study of communications within a purchasing department.

Innovation and Conflict in Industrial Engineering

ROSS A. WEBBER

As Horatio Alger might have said: "You can't keep a good idea down." Alger reflected the American feeling that the individual is the key to business success—especially in innovation. Either the top man is the source of creative ideas, or they originate with some engineer or manager in the lower regions of the organization. In the latter case, these ideas supposedly rise through the hierarchy to be recognized by those who make decisions. Even if ideas really did flow upward like this, the actual movement would be interesting. It is known, of course, that ideas are not helium-filled balloons forced up by their very difference from surrounding environment. How many engineers have seen cherished ideas get nowhere? Most of them do not sit around in ivoried splendor just conjuring up new ideas. Their ideas grow out of their jobs; they are conceived within boundaries and constraints. They must proceed through staff and line hierarchies, and they must have some relation to what the business really needs. No matter how clever the thought, it means nothing if the company cannot use it.

What is being suggested here is that emphasis on the individual as the source of ideas may obscure other factors—organizational factors—of equal importance. An idea is not a goal but a means to more effective operations—and more profit. Acceptance of an idea is a function of time and company maturity. And it is related to social and economic forces operating on the firm through market preferences, technological advances, and political developments. Most important, the future of an idea depends upon organizational structure and the role that the innovator is able to play.

From Ross A. Webber, "Innovation and Conflict in Industrial Engineering." Reprinted from the May, 1967 issue of *The Journal of Industrial Engineering,* official Publication of the American Institute of Industrial Engineers, Inc., 345 East 47th Street, New York 10017.

The subject is not just of academic interest. As Thompson [13] has pointed out, innovation, authority, and capacity to act have become increasingly fragmented in modern complex organizations. To an increasing extent, because of technological specialization, innovation must be a staff function more than an executive one [8]. This specialization, however, heightens the universal tension between information suppliers and decision-makers—between thinkers and doers. Since the Industrial Engineer is one of the key information suppliers and innovators in modern industry, he experiences such tension.

It was once fashionable to refer to the first line foreman as "the man in the middle" [10]. With help, advice, and instruction coming from all sides, it is not surprising that a foreman can feel like the "monkey-in-the-middle" of the childhood game. But the foreman is not unique. Although one of the major sources of stress for the production foreman is the Industrial Engineer, the Industrial Engineer himself is buffeted by conflicting forces. He is caught between the demands of his staff supervisors and line clients—and also, caught between his ambitions as a professional engineer and his aspirations for production management. In this article, some of the stresses and strains in the Industrial Engineer's job will be examined and the impact they have on the engineer's contribution to organizational innovation will be indicated. As Schaffer [12, p. 1] points out:

> In all of this exhilarating expansion and forward movement [of Industrial Engineering techniques], relatively little attention has been paid to the strategy for maximizing the impact of those techniques on the real progress of the enterprise. As a whole, Industrial Engineering has concentrated on developing better weapons and providing its troops with the best equipment, but it has paid scant attention to how the war is to be won.

This war will be discussed in some detail. Specifically, three conflicts will be considered and the problems growing out of them:

1. Conflict between the objectives of Industrial Engineering and line departments.
2. Conflicts among the different functions that the Industrial Engineer must perform.
3. Conflicts in the career aspirations of the engineer.

It will be shown that all of these conflicts inhibit information flow and stifle creativity. This investigation may give some guidance concerning the proper location of innovators—centralized in insulated staff groups or decentralized in involved operational positions.

Conflicting Objectives

The author once set piece-rate standards on a group of middle-aged women—very middle-aged—and recalls this incident: "One day I brought a new standard rate card to the group's forelady. She glanced at it and told me that recently she had been purchasing meat at her butcher's when she looked into the refrigerator room. In chilling terms, she described how the great hanging carcasses were covered with ice and frozen blood. Because of the standards I had just set, she told me: 'Your heart must be just like that frozen meat!' I knew then that I was a successful Industrial Engineer."

As any other battered time and motion man will attest, conflict does exist between Industrial Engineers and various people in any business. No appeal to team spirit can eradicate the stress; what the Industrial Engineer tries to accomplish is often at odds with what other people want. Many of them attribute the conflict to personalities: "Bill just can't get along with anyone," or "Sam tries to block everything that we do." It is naive, however, to attribute this conflict solely to incompatible personalities. It is also an oversimplification to maintain that secret conspiracies are intentionally blocking Industrial Engineering from carrying out its job. No engineer can expect line personnel to be entirely happy with what he does; conflict is inherent in his relationships with operating people.

A new engineer has a rather naive belief in the traditional advisory concept of staff. He believes he will be called upon because of his superior training and knowledge. Most Industrial Engineering supervisors, however, envision the department not as a consultant or service group, but as a catalyst, a questioner of existing procedures, and a force in instituting new methods. Therefore, staff management tells the young engineer that he cannot sit around waiting for the phone to ring; it will not. He is encouraged to sell himself and his projects. Because the ambitious young man wants to impress his superiors and utilize his newly learned sophisticated techniques, he searches. He seeks a problem suited to his methods and then attempts to sell a project to production supervision.

This effort conflicts with the objectives of people with whom Industrial Engineers work. The typical foreman is interested in getting the work out—but without too much fuss. He wants to maintain stability among his personnel and equilibrium in his relationships. He is concerned only about problems that hinder him *now.* In contrast, the Industrial Engineer looks for problems that are not apparent to production people yet. To the foreman, the engineer seems to want to upset things—for no reason. It is easy to say that the foreman cannot see the forest for the trees, that he is shortsighted while the engineer looks ahead. But this is an oversimplified value judgment. Most foremen are rewarded for today's or this weeks' production, not next year's. His job is the here and now. He sees no real need for staff Industrial Engineering assistance in meeting his goal as rewarded by production management.

A production department head is also concerned with output, but this is supplemented by cost consciousness. His perspective is longer ranged than the foreman's, and he is interested in innovative change. Nonetheless, heaviest pressure is on relatively short-run costs. The average department head is not rewarded so much for long-term downtrends as for not exceeding weekly budgets. Industrial Engineering plays a major part in setting these budgets. Therefore, the department head's desire to have a loose budget clashes with the Industrial Engineer's desire to tighten the budget and show paper cost savings.

A higher level production supervisor usually has a greater interest in long-run costs and innovations, but frequently he is concerned with using mechanical, electrical, or chemical engineers whom he has on his own staff. He may maintain that this is cheaper, that he gets better work, and that he trains his future supervisory personnel at the same time.

Both Industrial Engineers and Industrial Engineering managers desire to broaden application of sophisticated techniques and to increase the power of the staff division to innovate. Selling Industrial Engineering services becomes essential. In many cases the engineer with his repertoire of techniques will simply try to find a problem to which he can apply his expertise. A Nobel physicist, Hans Bethe of Cornell, has commented that modern techniques have led to a tendency to think only about *how* to *solve* problems instead of *analyzing* the problems themselves. Among many Industrial Engineers, too much emphasis is placed on the techniques instead of the problems. Staff management aggravates this by overemphasizing Industrial Engineering as a professional discipline. Management may still proclaim loudly that Industrial Engineering is a "service" organization. Subtly, however, emphasis has shifted away from the often mundane problems of production departments. Rather, two objectives are pushed: first the development of a discipline; second, expansion in the power of Industrial Engineering to control and innovate.

If a man wants to sell something, naturally, he wraps up his product in the biggest and prettiest package. So it is with Industrial Engineering. In classic sales tradition, presentations are large and formal with aspirations of impressiveness. Emphasis is on completed staff work [9, p. 258], covering every alternative and requiring only management's signature for implementation. The results: assignments are overworked, overpolished, and diluted. Such effort is expended to impress line management with the caliber and completeness of Industrial Engineering work that embarrassing questions and radical viewpoints are minimized. Selling the solution rather than solving the problem is the objective. In addition, application of high-powered techniques to inappropriate and uneconomical situations leads to disappointing results—results which aggravate the difficulty of obtaining future jobs.

The primary fallacy of overemphasis on selling and image-making is that it bears little relevance to innovation or service. The staff tries to make decisions instead of determining and investigating alternatives. Of course, in any organization, selling is necessary to have legitimate alternatives considered. But, selling can be overdone. Salesmanship should not dominate the analysis and contemplation necessary for developing fresh ideas. In addition, it is not the function of a staff consulting department to formulate recommendations. Any staff group has a limited outlook; they are biased by their own skills and experience. Under ideal conditions, a decision-maker should receive studies of other staff groups. Each group should not recommend a solution. Rather, alternatives should be suggested that can be integrated into an overall plan of action. Industrial Engineering presentations frequently are designed to sell favored proposals to production supervision. In this way, the staff attempts to usurp decision-making responsibility at an inappropriate level and position.

Conflicting Functions

"Two-faced," "phonies," "actors," and "politicians," are epithets that production people have been heard to apply to Industrial Engineers. Their criticism is that Industrial Engineers sometimes are nice guys, other times are not. However appropriately these pejoratives may fit certain engineers, the real problem is not the personalities of engineers. It is the conflict built into the job.

Stress is produced because the Industrial Engineer's job is inconsistent; he must play different roles at different times. As advisory staff to a production department head, he answers questions about labor costs of various work methods. On another job, the same engineer serves as an auditor for a superior line superintendent by checking on the department head's reasons for using excess labor. On a third occasion, he exercises Industrial Engineering's authority over incentive plans by forcing through a maximum hour limit on a specific work crew. Finally, he is a salesman trying to convince manufacturing personnel to accept a new method of quality control. All of these relationships are made more difficult because the intervention of the engineer tends to be sporadic. As William F. Whyte has shown, production supervision reacts negatively to these unpredictable communications [14, p. 519].

In short, the Industrial Engineer often does not know where his job fits into the organization. Is he consultant to a production division superintendent, department head, or functionally responsible for installations of measured work plans? Is he adviser, auditor, controller, or innovator? In fact, he is all of these.

Most formal company procedures emphasize the Industrial Engineer's role as traditional advisory staff to a line authority. Staff management, however, points out that the engineer must sell himself and his projects. Selling requires frequent and vigorous initiation to production management. This is the reverse of the behavior required by an adviser—salesmen initiate, advisers respond. Moreover, in order to have something to sell, an engineer must have greater familiarity with departmental problems and possibilities than he would derive from passively waiting to be phoned. The growth of professionalism, the development of mathematical techniques, and the desires of new engineers all complement staff management's emphasis on salesmanship and innovation. This leads to search for problems, initiation from staff to line, and an innovative relationship not welcomed by production personnel.

In most companies Industrial Engineering once consisted mainly of work measurement. This legacy emphasizes the responsibility of IE for measured work plans everywhere in the company. There has developed a feeling that staff should control production departments to insure that line managers contribute to the company as a whole—and not work merely for their own departments. Staff management attempts to decide how production departments should contribute to corporate goals instead of what staff might do to help line supervisors best meet their own goals. As a result, many labor control plans require Industrial Engineering to act as inspector, controller, and auditor. In one company, for example, Industrial Engineering sets maximum hour limits for work crews. In order to pay his men, the production department head must request permission from an engineer. Because of varying production demands, it is not rare to exceed the allowed hours. The strain this puts on relations between the department head and Industrial Engineering is obvious: this interaction *must* be initiated by the department head to get Industrial Engineering action, and the authority relationship is just the reverse of that implied in the traditional advisory concept of staff.

Many Industrial Engineering supervisors also aggravate line-staff relations by their own behavior. They believe that production departments should be checked to see that they are contributing to company goals according to value criteria formulated by the Industrial Engineering division. Usually, there is no explicit justification for this attitude; it arises partly from the supervisor's experience and association with management people whose responsibilities do include such control, and partly as a result of insufficient job duties. Such a supervisor sits in his office checking budget figures and plant performance. Whenever he has a question, he notifies an engineer to call the production department and find out what happened. To answer his boss, the Industrial Engineer must call and question the production manager's activities. No manager likes to justify his performance to a staff man—much less to an inexperienced engineer who is younger and earns less money. The engineer may have worked hard to develop mutual trust and cooperation between himself and the production manager. Such checking can damage these relations.

The sensitive Industrial Engineer attempts to anticipate these questions from his supervisor so that he can answer without calling the production department. Because the staff supervisor influences advancement, the engineer wants to impress him with a ready answer. Also, he simply wants to avoid an unpleasant communication with the production department head. To have a ready answer requires a close relationship with the production department; otherwise, the engineer will not know what is going on.

It can be seen that the relationship between an Industrial Engineer and a production manager is characterized by confusion and inconsistency in communication patterns and organizational roles. Both the engineer and the production supervisor implicitly recognize that it is impossible to be a salesman, inspector, and consultant at the same time [14, p. 509]. The roles are incompatible. The engineer, therefore, is confused and anxious about his relations with the people he is supposed to serve.

So, armed with his arsenal of techniques, the engineer goes forth to find problems and "offer" his services to production supervision. He soon recognizes, however, that he cannot merely respond to staff management's call for selling. Selling stresses that the engineer is an outsider trying to get in. Geographic distance, social differences, and administrative centralization further emphasize the separation of Industrial Engineering from production. The engineer becomes aware that he must overcome this handicap of being a stranger to production people. To sell requires that the engineer have something of value. This should be an idea based upon observed conditions. Cultivation of these ideas is dependent upon search, and the search process requires an intimate knowledge of production activity. Besides, it is simply not possible to maintain a sufficient level of projects through search and selling only.

In short, the engineer realizes that he must cultivate requests from the production department for his services. He learns that he cannot be a remote Olympian oracle telling mere production mortals what to do. The engineer was taught to pursue change. To get things done, however, he needs to influence others to act. This requires a closer relationship than that of the expert.

To develop this closer relationship, the individual engineer attempts to camouflage his position as an outsider, minimize his selling, and increase his indispensability to production supervision. An example is the case of a junior Industrial Engineer who, without being requested, made a complete study of the future production trends, space requirements, and labor needs for a new product treatment area. A production department development engineer normally conducted such investigations but had not yet done so. The Industrial Engineer, at some risk, hid his hours in another assignment. When he presented the completed study to the production department head, the engineer became indispensable. He was consulted because he was a known information source. He also projected himself into consideration for a possible managerial post when and if the new product area expanded.

As Figure 1 illustrates, many Industrial Engineers desire a joint consultative-implementation relationship with production supervision: both would respond to the same department stimuli, 1, and either should be able to initiate consultation with the other, 2 and 3. Finally, engineers want to join in the implementation, 4.

Figure 1. The Industrial Engineer's Desired Work Pattern.

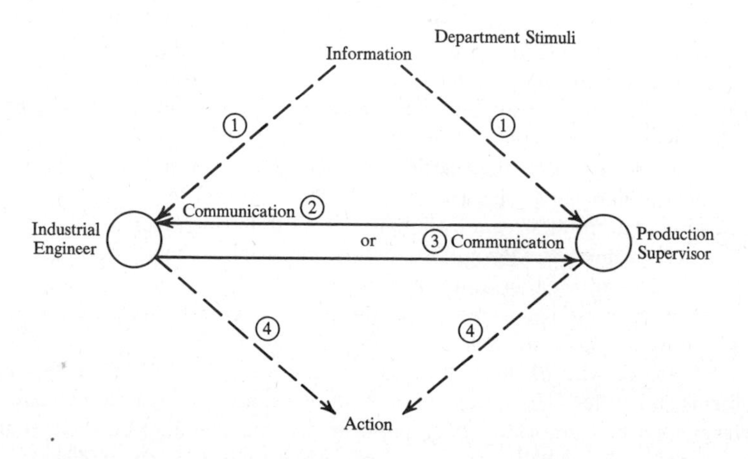

It is apparent, then, that a staff group oriented toward solving problems and seeing the future as resting on demonstration of sophisticated knowledge will develop every avenue for obtaining access to production departments. Formal procedures will be given mock observance, but various methods of search for problems and obtaining jobs will be explored. Inevitably, such activity creates stress and conflict.

Conflicting Career Aspirations

An additional source of stress for the Industrial Engineer is uncertainty about his career. Does he want management or engineering? Whom should he impress? Staff supervisors or production managers? This is a complex subject and extensive coverage is beyond the scope of this article. A few observations are pertinent, however. Unlike many professional employees (6), the Industrial Engineers who have been observed in large companies have been company and management rather than profession oriented. Many Industrial Engineering divisions historically have served as training areas for the whole company. Employment in Industrial Engineering has given promising people wide access to valuable contacts and experiences.

In one large chemical company, the normal period of service in the department was approximately three years after which the engineers generally moved into a production area—either as a manager or as a staff engineer directly assisting a production supervisor. The promotion path was definitely up the line hierarchy; few desired to stay in technical work. Such rapid turnover created problems for Industrial Engineering. In spite of high caliber young engineers, effective contribution was hindered by inexperience. In this company, as in many others, management decided to reduce promotions out of the department and emphasize careers in Industrial Engineering. By improving the performance of Industrial Engineering, they hoped that the engineers would be more effective in selling their ideas to production management. In addition, more engineers with advanced degrees in Industrial Engineering and Operations Research were recruited. In short, emphasis was placed on professional opportunity in Industrial Engineering.

Many companies have taken similar steps. Throughout Industrial Engineering there is a trend towards professionalism. Active research groups conduct courses in advanced mathematical techniques. Many engineers receive tuition refunds for graduate statistics, operations research, and industrial management programs. The natural desire of new graduates to use modern techniques is reinforced by the recognition given to those who demonstrate sophisticated applications. Invitations to give talks on their work to peers and supervisors, informal status, and formal staff promotions in recent years have tended to go to those who have had significant success in applying the more esoteric techniques.

Contemporary Industrial Engineers may be confused as to where their futures lie and whom they want to impress. The problem, however, may be resolved by the movement towards professionalism. The future Industrial Engineer may see his future in Industrial Engineering. He may not be frustrated by his inability to move out of the field. Accordingly, schizophrenia in the Industrial Engineer's aspirations may be eliminated. But such professionalism will aggravate the conflict between line and staff. The social and organizational gap will widen; the attempts of staff to control line will increase; and greater emphasis on professional development and sophisticated techniques will diminish the engineer's interest in assisting the production manager to solve the latter's mundane daily problems.

Inhibited Creativity

Creativity in problem-solving depends on memory, example, and analogy. Information plays a crucial role in all three aspects. The initial element of creativity is a search for problems and sources of information. When information is needed, most people start by asking someone else rather than searching through musty files and books. A man may turn around at his desk and ask the engineer sitting behind him in the cubicle. Or, he picks up the phone and calls some colleague. If pressed, he may rummage through his desk drawers to find some report or old copy of *Factory* magazine that has some information that he remembers vaguely. In order to locate information, however, he needs to know whom to ask and where to look. As March and Simon [6, p. 180] have observed:

> One important element of organizational structure is a set of understandings and expectations among the participants as to what bodies of information repose where in the structure. This set of expectations and understandings is a major determinant of the use of communication channels.

In addition, many observers comment that innovation requires emergence in the problem, long familiarity with all aspects, and extended thinking of possible alternatives, plus plain hard work [1]. Thomas Edison invented more by analogy and experimentation than imagination. He created by direct frontal assault—marshalling the widest array of facts and ideas and then carefully searching for previously unrecognized relationships between them. Similarly, Henry Eyring, drawing on his experience in various chemical laboratories, maintains that success is always related to and built upon the findings of others [3, p. 8]. Other observers define two more approaches to problem-solving:

1. Problem-solving is a cognitive process of learning and thinking.
2. Problem-solving is a manifestation of personality.

Essential for both approaches according to Ernest Hilgard [4, pp. 162–180] is a "mood" for the easy exchange of ideas.

These views emphasize the importance of free information flow among supervisors, subordinates, peers, and colleagues. Yet, Industrial Engineers experience extreme difficulty in obtaining information from production departments. The old "better communications" shibboleth is not being repeated here because it is not simply that two groups misunderstand each other. Engineers cannot search for and solve problems without free access to information. "But all you have to do is ask" is the reply of many production managers. In order to ask for information, however, the engineer has to know what he wants—and this is not possible in ambiguous situations, because what is valuable and pertinent is not known. To be innovative, an engineer must have access to all forms of departmental data: letters, production records, inspection reports, and engineering investigations. Engineers would prefer a running record of manufacturing department activities which they could peruse but it is difficult to obtain copies on a continuous basis. The department head "forgets" to tell his clerk to indicate Industrial Engineering as an information addressee, and the clerk "forgets" to send copies.

In addition, Industrial Engineers want to know what is going on in order to maintain and strengthen close relationships with the department. The desire to make oneself indispensable in order to increase requests initiated by production managers has already been described. The engineer can pursue this goal better if he is intimately familiar with production department activities.

Acquisition of this information frequently is hindered by the geographic and social isolation of the engineers. Industrial Engineers usually are located in one office separated from many of the production departments they serve. Distances are not great and do not seriously interfere with imperatives of the engineer's job, but they do influence the nature of communications with production supervisors. In many large companies, the distances discourage all but necessary business visits. Engineers do not often go out just to say hello or to have a cup of coffee. Thus, almost all visits and telephone calls initiated by Industrial Engineers are job-related. Indeed, Industrial Engineers are generally regarded as sticklers for work, both because of the "efficiency expert" connotation of their position and because of the job-oriented nature of their interactions.

Of course, some engineers have more energy than others, and these people do attempt to initiate informal relations. Social pressures, however, hinder them. Age, social, and educational differences between production supervisors and Industrial Engineers tend to minimize friendliness. On the one hand, young engineers tend to believe in respect for their elders—and most production supervisors are older. On the other hand, because Industrial Engineering requires college training, personnel and engineering managers seem to emphasize staff's higher status. There is even some pressure on engineers regarding dress; appearance is mentioned on some performance evaluation forms. In one company, production department supervisors wear ties and rough work jackets in the winter; in warm weather, they appear with no tie or jacket and sleeves rolled up. Engineers, in contrast, are expected to wear suits and keep jackets on at all times when in the plant. Completed with a felt hat, their appearance is less appropriate to a manufacturing department than it is to Madison Avenue.

These organizational, geographic, and social difficulties are not insurmountable obstacles to Industrial Engineers. They might be overcome by patience, sufficiently frequent trips to the production department, willingness to work in inadequate surroundings in making copies, and so forth. These factors, nonetheless, do reinforce the tendency to confine communications to specific job-related subjects. In addition, all these activities absorb energy and diminish the engineer's attention to problem-solving and innovation.

When the engineer has been given a specific problem that is of some concern to production management, he can overcome these information difficulties with energy and hard work. It is not so simple when the problems are not apparent and the staff group is searching for causes that will produce problems only in the future—if at all. Free movement of data and information is essential for such search [3, p. 12]. Some of this information flow should be without apparent relevance, without conscious request, and without specific purpose. It has been shown how various factors in Industrial Engineering relationships discourage such information flow and make it difficult to achieve the level of familiarity and commitment necessary for innovation. Valuable innovative effort depends on frequent discussion and information exchange between engineers and managers. By blocking information, the innovative process is hampered at its most critical stage—discovery of a problem.

Creativity, as with much human enterprise, prospers most in a friendly atmosphere of cooperation. This atmosphere frees individuals from pressure for uniformity and takes advantage of sympathetic "resonance" from contemporaries. A political scientist, Harold Laswell [5, p. 261], comments that the greatest boon to the innovator is an intellectual collaborator:

> In particular we are impressed by the peculiarly resonant relationships that successful innovators, at least, set up with individuals in their social environment. Similarly, although the means to which people resort in defeating themselves are devious and subtle, we suspect that potentially significant innovators are often stunted through lack of a friend to play the resonance role, and through dependence upon an environment only too willing to exert a dampening influence.

Resonance from production personnel available to Industrial Engineers in many organizations is very limited. In the initial stage of idea generation, the engineer's desire to maintain an air of knowledgeable superiority severely hampers discussion with production managers. Before they are talked about, the ideas of Industrial Engineers frequently freeze into proposals—proposals to be packaged and sold to dubious operating supervisors.

Alleviating the Conflicts

Three situations have been described that are of stress to the Industrial Engineer:

1. Conflict between his objectives and those of groups with whom he works.
2. Conflict among the functions he performs.
3. Conflict in his own career aspirations.

Finally, it has been shown how these conflicts inhibit communication flows and hamper creativity. With some oversimplification, two general methods of handling these problems are evident: first, centralization and increased authority for Industrial Engineering; second, decentralization and submission to stronger line control. The advantages and disadvantages of each in dealing with the problems raised will now be outlined.

The first problem—conflict between Industrial Engineering and other groups—is inevitable. In his innovating activities, the Industrial Engineer can always expect resistance from operating managers. Such conflict is inherent in organizations. "If I only had the power to . . ." often is the somewhat wistful refrain of the engineer. Perhaps vastly increased power to a centralized Industrial Engineering staff might enable them to persevere and force innovative changes. There are weaknesses in this approach, however. As many researchers have indicated [11], when power or authority is relied on exclusively to change behavior, the change is likely to be very superficial and half-hearted. No real effort will be exerted, ingenuity will be exercised *against* the change not *for* it, and compliance will be minimum. This tends to force the party with power to increase its observation, control, and power over the resistors. To concentrate such power in Industrial Engineering would probably be impossible, thankfully, because, if it were not, results would be disastrous. Complete breakdown in communication flow and cooperation would destroy the adviser-client relationship.

Unfortunately, the alternative of decentralization and submission to line authority also has its drawbacks. Frustration occurs daily in the engineer's life when his ideas are rejected arbitrarily without sufficient consideration—or so he thinks. A stagnant management may prevent innovative action long after a sensitive staff has recognized the need. So, the engineer must rely on persuasion to change behavior. If he is successful in convincing operating managers to make changes, the modifications are more likely to be made than if power were used. The use of persuasion, however, leads to the emphasis on salesmanship and other misdirected activities already described. No matter how aggravating IE's weakness may be, however, greater central power is not desirable.

When a person has multiple jobs or multiple roles to fill, one solution to conflicts between these roles is segregation or segmentation [2]. To eliminate the second problem of conflict among the Industrial Engineer's functions, the position might be broken up. For example, commercial bankers were once the largest stockbrokers and underwriters. In 1933, however, Congress and the Securities and Exchange Commission forced separation of the banking function from the underwriting activity. Similarly, there is current demand to separate the advisory functions of the present stockbrokers from their buying function. Such conflicts of interest lead to ethical problems. They were separated to resolve these conflicts.

Conflict of interests is not the problem for the Industrial Engineer as much as it is incompatibility between roles. As has been shown, the Industrial Engineer must be adviser, auditor, salesman, and innovator. Any of these roles are difficult to combine. Perhaps, a solution is to divide up the Industrial Engineer's functions among several positions.

Auditing or controlling interferes especially strongly with advising and innovating. As has been shown, the communication and authority relationships are directly contradictory; mutual trust and confidence are severely undermined. Therefore, control over incentive standards and payroll plans could be separated from the advisory and innovative roles. In a sense, this would be going back to the day when methods and measurement activities in Industrial Engineering were separate (a condition still existing in some companies). A problem here is that most engineers are not interested in careers in measurement because methods work is where the action is—where new analytical techniques are being applied and where big savings are possible. In addition, the distinction between the two types of Industrial Engineers interferes with communication and cooperation within Industrial Engineering. Proper methods are not installed before standards are set, methods men tend to get sloppy about labor costs, and so on. Neither the case for centralization nor decentralization is clearly stronger here.

Centralization, however, does offer some advantages for strengthening the Industrial Engineering profession and reducing career conflicts for the engineer. A centralized staff is usually associated with job variety, luxurious facilities, and organizational prominence. Of more importance, centralized Industrial Engineering encourages the development of a satisfying professional atmosphere. Formal training programs and informal bull sessions are facilitated; both promote technical performance. Such challenging and satisfying training experiences are extremely difficult when engineers are physically and administratively distributed among operating departments.

The last problem raised was the hindrance to creativity and innovation offered by communication barriers. The administrative, geographic, and social separation of Industrial Engineering from production supervision discourages the development of free communication flow essential for development of creative ideas. This is the most important question raised by consideration of the Industrial Engineer. Given the accelerated pace of innovation, the organizational location of innovative groups is of increasing importance. Just how closely should a staff group be involved in the operational problems of a production department?

The individual Industrial Engineer attempts to join in production department activities in order to make himself indispensable and to encourage line managers to initiate communication. Because of the technical and organizational familiarity and mastery essential for creativity, this closeness to production departments may facilitate innovation. Yet, there is a paradox. The more the innovative person becomes involved in handling operational problems, the greater the proclivity to accept the outlook of production people towards stability—just as long as no one is aware of any difficulty. Because an innovator must be dissatisfied when everyone else is satisfied, and because he must find problems before they are recognized as problems, such closeness to operations might stifle progress. In fact, it has been suggested that a requirement for innovation may be isolation of the innovator from operating pressures [3, p. 12].

Nonetheless, such isolation is not the answer. The innovator must be involved closely in the problems of the department or he will not become aware of possibilities. Innovation should not depend upon the efforts of centralized staff groups working in splendid isolation. These absent staff innovators cannot expect production personnel to respond amiably to their unpredictable appearances, cheerfully upsetting production because the engineer's proposals are rationally desirable. Rationality depends on whether one is getting or giving. At the same time, the harried production supervisor is not able to devote enough time to searching for problems that are not crucial and alternatives that are not apparent.

It is clear that neither centralization nor decentralization offers the perfect solution. There are advantages and disadvantages to both; neither extreme is justified; some balance is necessary. Detailed structural changes will not be proposed in this article, but one observation is pertinent. On the range from complete decentralization to complete centralization, it would appear that IE is too close to the centralized end. At least, the centralization of Industrial Engineering in a staff group should be reexamined. The biases, distortions, and overprofessionalism encouraged by such centralization may hinder organizational innovation. In short, consideration should be given to putting the Industrial Engineer closer—administratively, socially, and physically—to the people and technology he is trying to change.

References

1. Anderson, Harold (Editor), *Creativity and its Cultivation,* Harper & Row, New York, 1959.
2. Evan, William M., and Levin, Ezra G., "Status-set and Role-set Conflicts of the Stockbroker: A Problem in the Sociology of Law," *Social Forces,* Volume 45, No. 1, September, 1966, pp. 73–83.
3. Eyring, Henry, "Scientific Creativity," *Creativity and its Cultivation,* Harper & Row, New York, 1959.
4. Hilgard, Ernest R., "Creativity and Problem Solving," *Creativity and its Cultivation,* Harper & Row, New York, 1959.
5. Laswell, Harold, "The Social Settling of Creativity," *Creativity and its Cultivation,* Harper & Row, New York, 1959.
6. March, James, and Simon, Harold, *Organizations,* John Wiley & Sons, New York, 1958.
7. Moore, David G., and Renck, Richard, "The Professional Employee in Industry," *Journal of Business,* January, 1955, p. 60.
8. Moore, Wilbert, "The Use and Misuse of Creative People and Ideas," *Individualism and Big Business,* McGraw-Hill Book Company, New York, 1963, pp. 119–125.
9. Newman, William, and Summer, Charles R., *The Process of Management* Prentice-Hall, Englewood Cliffs, 1961.
10. Roethlisberger, Fritz J., "The Foreman: Master and Victim of Double Talk," *Harvard Business Review,* Volume 45, No. 5, September–October, 1965, p. 23ff.

11. Sayles, Leonard R., and Strauss, George, *Human Behavior in Organizations,* Prentice-Hall, Englewood Cliffs, 1966, pp. 184–209.

12. Schaffer, Robert H., *Maximizing the Impact of Industrial Engineering,* American Management Association, New York, Management Bulletin 82, 1966.

13. Thompson, Victor, *Modern Organizations,* Alfred A. Knopf, New York, 1963.

14. Whyte, William F., *Men at Work,* Irwin-Dorsey, Homewood, Illinois, 1961.

Sources of Power of Lower Participants in Complex Organizations

DAVID MECHANIC

It is not unusual for lower participants[1] in complex organizations to assume and wield considerable power and influence not associated with their formally defined positions within these organizations. In sociological terms they have considerable personal power but no authority. Such personal power is often attained, for example, by executive secretaries and accountants in business firms, by attendants in mental hospitals, and even by inmates in prisons. The personal power achieved by these lower participants does not necessarily result from unique personal characteristics, although these may be relevant, but results rather from particular aspects of their location within their organizations.

Informal Versus Formal Power

Within organizations the distribution of authority (institutionalized power) is closely if not perfectly correlated with the prestige of positions. Those who have argued for the independence of these variables[2] have taken their examples from diverse organizations and do not deal with situations where power is clearly comparable.[3] Thus when Bierstedt argues that Einstein had prestige but no power, and the policeman power but no prestige, it is apparent that he is comparing categories that are not comparable. Generally persons occupying high-ranking positions within organizations have more authority than those holding low-ranking positions.

One might ask what characterizes high-ranking positions within organizations. What is most evident, perhaps, is that lower participants recognize the right of higher-ranking participants to exercise power, and yield without difficulty to demands they regard as legitimate. Moreover, persons in high-ranking posi-

David Mechanic, "Sources of Power of Lower Participants in Complex Organizations," *Administrative Science Quarterly,* Vol. 7, No. 3 (December 1962), pp. 349–364. Reprinted by permission.

[1] The term "lower participants" comes from Amitai Etzioni, *A Comparative Analysis of Complex Organizations* (New York, 1961) and is used by him to designate persons in positions of lower rank: employees, rank-and-file, members, clients, customers, and inmates. We shall use the term in this paper in a relative sense denoting position vis-a-vis a higher ranking participant.

[2] Robert Bierstedt, An Analysis of Social Power, *American Sociological Review* 15 (1950), 730–738.

[3] Robert A. Dahl, The Concept of Power, *Behavioral Science,* 2 (1957), 201–213.

tions tend to have considerable access and control over information and persons both within and outside the organization, and to instrumentalities or resources. Although higher supervisory personnel may be isolated from the task activities of lower participants, they maintain access to them through formally established intermediary positions and exercise control through intermediary participants. There appears, therefore, to be a clear correlation between the prestige of positions within organizations and the extent to which they offer access to information, persons, and instrumentalities.

Since formal organizations tend to structure lines of access and communication, access should be a clue to institutional prestige. Yet access depends on variables other than those controlled by the formal structure of an organization, and this often makes the informal power structure that develops within organizations somewhat incongruent with the formally intended plan. It is these variables that allow work groups to limit production through norms that contravene the goals of the larger organization, that allow hospital attendants to thwart changes in the structure of a hospital, and that allow prison inmates to exercise some control over prison guards. Organizations, in a sense, are continuously at the mercy of their lower participants, and it is this fact that makes organizational power structure especially interesting to the sociologist and social psychologist.

Clarification of Definitions

The purpose of this paper is to present some hypotheses explaining why lower participants in organizations can often assume and wield considerable power which is not associated with their positions as formally defined within these organizations. For the purposes of this analysis the concepts "influence," "power," and "control" will be used synonymously. Moreover, we shall not be concerned with type of power, that is, whether the power is based on reward, punishment, identification, power to veto, or whatever.[4] Power will be defined as *any force that results in behavior that would not have occurred if the force had not been present.* We have defined power as a force rather than a relationship because it appears that much of what we mean by power is encompassed by the normative framework of an organization, and thus any analysis of power must take into consideration the power of norms as well as persons.

I shall also argue, following Thibaut, and Kelley,[5] that power is closely related to dependence. To the extent that a person is dependent on another, he is potentially subject to the other person's power. Within organizations one makes others dependent upon him by controlling access to information, persons, and instrumentalities which I shall define as follows:

Information includes knowledge of the organization, knowledge about persons, knowledge of the norms, procedures, techniques, and so forth.

Persons include anyone within the organization or anyone outside the organization upon whom the organization is in some way dependent.

---

[4] One might observe, for example, that the power of lower participants is based primarily on the ability to "veto" or punish. For a discussion of bases of power, see John R. P. French, Jr., and Bertram Raven, "The Bases of Social Power," in D. Cartwright and A. Zander, eds., *Group Dynamics* (Evanston, Ill., 1960), pp. 607–623.

[5] John Thibaut and Harold H. Kelley, *The Social Psychology of Groups* (New York: 1959). For a similar emphasis on dependence, see Richard M. Emerson, Inter-Dependence Relationships, *American Sociological Review,* 27 (1962), 31–41.

Instrumentalities include any aspect of the physical plant of the organization or its resources (equipment, machines, money, and so on).
Power is a function not only of the extent to which a person controls information, persons, and instrumentalities, but also of the importance of the various attributes he controls.[6]

Finally, following Dahl,[7] we shall agree that comparisons of power among persons should, as far as possible, utilize comparable units. Thus we shall strive for clarification by attempting to oversimplify organizational processes; the goal is to set up a number of hypothetical statements of the relationship between variables taken two at a time, "all other factors being assumed to remain constant.". . .

To state the hypothesis suggested, somewhat more formally:

H1 Other factors remaining constant, organizational power is related to access to persons, information, and instrumentalities.

H2 Other factors remaining constant, as a participant's length of time in an organization increases, he has increased access to persons, information, and instrumentalities.

While these hypotheses are obvious, they do suggest that a careful scrutiny of the organizational literature, especially that dealing with the power or counter-power of lower participants, might lead to further formalized statements, some considerably less obvious than the ones stated.

Sources of Power of Lower Participants

The most effective way for lower participants to achieve power is to obtain, maintain, and control access to persons, information, and instrumentalities. To the extent that this can be accomplished, lower participants make higher-ranking participants dependent upon them. Thus dependence together with the manipulation of the dependency relationship is the key to the power of lower participants.

A number of examples can be cited which illustrate the preceding point. Scheff, for example, reports on the failure of a state mental hospital to bring about intended reform because of the opposition of hospital attendants.[8] He noted that the power of hospital attendants was largely a result of the dependence of ward physicians on attendants. This dependence resulted from the physician's short tenure, his lack of interest in administration, and the large amount of administrative responsibility he had to assume. An implicit trading agreement developed between physicians and attendants, whereby attendants would take on some of the responsibilities and obligations of the ward physician in return for increased power in decision-making processes concerning patients. Failure of the ward physician to honor his part of the agreement resulted in information being withheld, disobedience, lack of co-operation, and unwillingness of the attendants to serve as a barrier between the physician and a ward full of patients demanding attention and recognition. When the attendant withheld co-operation, the physician had difficulty in making a graceful entrance and departure from

---

[6] Although this paper will not attempt to explain how access may be measured, the author feels confident that the hypotheses concerned with access are clearly testable.

[7] *Op. cit.*

[8] Thomas J. Scheff, Control over Policy by Attendants in a Mental Hospital, *Journal of Health and Human Behavior,* 2 (1961), 93–105.

the ward, in handling necessary paper work (officially his responsibility), and in obtaining information needed to deal adequately with daily treatment and behavior problems. When attendants opposed change, they could wield influence by refusing to assume responsibilities officially assigned to the physician.

Similarly, Sykes describes the dependence of prison guards on inmates and the power obtained by inmates over guards.[9] He suggests that although guards could report inmates for disobedience, frequent reports would give prison officials the impression that the guard was unable to command obedience. The guard, therefore, had some stake in ensuring the good behavior of prisoners without use of formal sanctions against them. The result was a trading agreement whereby the guard allowed violations of certain rules in return for co-operative behavior. A similar situation is found in respect to officers in the Armed Services or foremen in industry. To the extent that they require formal sanctions to bring about co-operation, they are usually perceived by their superiors as less valuable to the organization. For a good leader is expected to command obedience, at least, if not commitment.

Factors Affecting Power

Expertise

Increasing specialization and organizational growth has made the expert or staff person important. The expert maintains power because high-ranking persons in the organization are dependent upon him for his special skills and access to certain kinds of information. One possible reason for lawyers obtaining many high governmental offices is that they are likely to have access to rather specialized but highly important means to organizational goals.[10]

We can state these ideas in hypotheses, as follows:

H3 Other factors remaining constant, to the extent that a low-ranking participant has important expert knowledge not available to high-ranking participants, he is likely to have power over them.

Power stemming from expertise, however, is likely to be limited unless it is difficult to replace the expert. This leads to two further hypotheses:

H4 Other factors remaining constant, a person difficult to replace will have greater power than a person easily replaceable.

H5 Other factors remaining constant, experts will be more difficult to replace than nonexperts.

While persons having expertise are likely to be fairly high-ranking participants in an organization, the same hypotheses that explain the power of lower participants are relevant in explaining the comparative power positions of intermediate- and high-ranking persons. . . .

As a result of growing specialization, expertise is increasingly important in organizations. As the complexity of organizational tasks increases, and as organizations grow in size there is a limit to responsibility that can be efficiently

---

[9] Gresham M. Sykes, "The Corruption of Authority and Rehabilitation," in A. Etzioni, ed., *Complex Organizations* (New York, 1961), pp. 191–197.

[10] As an example, it appears that 6 members of the cabinet, 30 important subcabinet officials, 63 senators, and 230 congressmen are lawyers (*New Yorker,* April 14, 1962, p. 62). Although one can cite many reasons for lawyers holding political posts, an important one appears to be their legal expertise.

exercised by one person. Delegation of responsibility occurs, experts and specialists are brought in to provide information and research, and the higher participants become dependent upon them. Experts have tremendous potentialities for power by withholding information, providing incorrect information, and so on, and to the extent that experts are dissatisfied, the probability of organizational sabotage increases.

Effort and Interest

The extent to which lower participants may exercise power depends in part on their willingness to exert effort in areas where higher-ranking participants are often reluctant to participate. Effort exerted is directly related to the degree of interest one has in an area.

H6 Other factors remaining constant, there is a direct relationship between the amount of effort a person is willing to exert in an area and the power he can command.

For example, secretarial staffs in universities often have power to make decisions about the purchase and allocation of supplies, the allocation of their services, the scheduling of classes, and, at times, the disposition of student complaints. Such control may in some instances lead to sanctions against a professor by polite reluctance to furnish supplies, ignoring his preferences for the scheduling of classes, and giving others preference in the allocation of services. While the power to make such decisions may easily be removed from the jurisdiction of the lower participant, it can only be accomplished at a cost—the willingness to allocate time and effort to the decisions dealing with these matters. To the extent that responsibilities are delegated to lower participants, a certain degree of power is likely to accompany the responsibility. Also, should the lower participant see his perceived rights in jeopardy, he may sabotage the system in various ways.

Let us visualize a hypothetical situation where a department concludes that secretarial services are being allocated on a prejudicial basis as a result of complaints to the chairman of the department by several of the younger faculty. Let us also assume that, when the complaint is investigated, it is found to be substantially correct; that is, some of the younger faculty have difficulty obtaining secretarial services because of preferences among the secretarial staff. If in attempting to eliminate discretion by the secretarial staff, the chairman establishes a rule ordering the allocation of services on the basis of the order in which work appears, the rule can easily be made ineffective by complete conformity to it. Deadlines for papers, examinations, and the like will occur, and flexibility in the allocation of services is required if these deadlines are to be met. Thus the need for flexibility can be made to conflict with the rule by a staff usually not untalented in such operations.

When an organization gives discretion to lower participants, it is usually trading the power of discretion for needed flexibility. The cost of constant surveillance is too high, and the effort required too great; it is very often much easier for all concerned to allow the secretary discretion in return for co-operation and not too great an abuse of power.

H7 Other factors remaining constant, the less effort and interest higher-ranking participants are willing to devote to a task, the more likely are lower participants to obtain power relevant to this task.

Attractiveness

Another personal attribute associated with the power of low-ranking persons in an organization is attractiveness or what some call "personality." People who are viewed as attractive are more likely to obtain access to persons, and, once such access is gained, they may be more likely to succeed in promoting a cause. But once again dependence is the key to the power of attractiveness, for whether a person is dependent upon another for a service he provides, or for approval or affection, what is most relevant is the relational bond which is highly valued.

H8 Other factors remaining constant, the more attractive a person, the more likely he is to obtain access to persons and control over these persons.

Location and Position

In any organization the person's location in physical space and position in social space are important factors influencing access to persons, information, and instrumentalities.[11] Propinquity affects the opportunities for interaction, as well as one's position within a communication network. Although these are somewhat separate factors, we shall refer to their combined effect as centrality[12] within the organization.

H9 Other factors remaining constant, the more central a person is in an organization, the greater is his access to persons, information, and instrumentalities.

Some low participants may have great centrality within an organization. An executive's or university president's secretary not only has access, but often controls access in making appointments and scheduling events. Although she may have no great formal authority, she may have considerable power.

Coalitions

It should be clear that the variables we are considering are at different levels of analysis; some of them define attributes of persons, while others define attributes of communication and organization. Power processes within organizations are particularly interesting in that there are many channels of power and ways of achieving it.

In complex organizations different occupational groups attend to different functions, each group often maintaining its own power structure within the organization. Thus hospitals have administrators, medical personnel, nursing personnel, attendants, maintenance personnel, laboratory personnel, and so on. Universities, similarly, have teaching personnel, research personnel, administrative personnel, maintenance personnel, and so on. Each of these functional tasks within organizations often becomes the sphere of a particular group that controls activities relating to the task. While these tasks usually are co-ordinated at the

---

[11] There is considerable data showing the powerful effect of propinquity on communication. For summary, see Thibaut and Kelley, *op. cit.*, pp. 39–42.

[12] The concept of centrality is generally used in a more technical sense in the work of Bavelas, Shaw, Gilchrist, and others. For example, Bavelas defines the central region of a structure as the class of all cells with the smallest distance between one cell and any other cell in the structure, with distance measured in link units. Thus the most central position in a pattern is the position closest to all others, Cf. Harold Leavitt, "Some Effects of Certain Communication Patterns on Group Performance," in E. Maccoby, T. N. Newcomb, and E. L. Hartley, eds., *Readings in Social Psychology* (New York, 1958), p. 559.

highest levels of the organization, they often are not co-ordinated at intermediate and lower levels. It is not unusual, however, for coalitions to form among lower participants in these multiple structures. A secretary may know the man who manages the supply of stores, or the person assigning parking stickers. Such acquaintances may give her the ability to handle informally certain needs that would be more time-consuming and difficult to handle formally. Her ability to provide services informally makes higher-ranking participants in some degree dependent upon her, thereby giving her power, which increases her ability to bargain on issues important to her.

Rules

In organizations with complex power structures lower participants can use their knowledge of the norms of the organization to thwart attempted change. In discussing the various functions of bureaucratic rules, Gouldner maintains that such rules serve as excellent substitutes for surveillance, since surveillance in addition to being expensive in time and effort arouses considerable hostility and antagonism.[13] Moreover, he argues, rules are a functional equivalent for direct, personally given orders, since they specify the obligations of workers to do things in specific ways. Standardized rules, in addition, allow simple screening of violations, facilitate remote control, and to some extent legitimize punishment when the rule is violated. The worker who violates a bureaucratic rule has little recourse to the excuse that he did not know what was expected, as he might claim for a direct order. Finally, Gouldner argues that rules are "the 'chips' to which the company staked the supervisors and which they could use to play the game";[14] that is, rules established a punishment which could be withheld, and this facilitated the supervisors' bargaining power with lower participants.

While Gouldner emphasizes the functional characteristics of rules within an organization, it should be clear that full compliance to all the rules at all times will probably be dysfunctional for the organization. Complete and apathetic compliance may do everything but facilitate achievement of organizational goals. Lower participants who are familiar with an organization and its rules can often find rules to support their contention that they not do what they have been asked to do, and rules are also often a rationalization for inaction on their part. The following of rules becomes especially complex when associations and unions become involved, for there are then two sets of rules to which the participant can appeal.

What is suggested is that rules may be chips for everyone concerned in the game. Rules become the "chips" through which the bargaining process is maintained. Scheff, as noted earlier, observed that attendants in mental hospitals often took on responsibilities assigned legally to the ward physician, and when attendants refused to share these responsibilities the physician's position became extremely difficult.[15]

The ward physician is legally responsible for the care and treatment of each ward patient. This responsibility requires attention to a host of details. Medicine, seclusion, sedation and transfer orders, for example, require the

[13] Alvin W. Gouldner, *Patterns of Industrial Bureaucracy* (Glencoe, Ill., 1954).
[14] *Ibid,* p. 173.
[15] Scheff, *op. cit.*

doctor's signature. Tranquilizers are particularly troublesome in this regard since they require frequent adjustment of dosage in order to get the desired effects. The physician's order is required to each change in dosage. With 150 patients under his care on tranquilizers, and several changes of dosages a week desirable, the physician could spend a major portion of his ward time in dealing with this single detail.

Given the time-consuming formal chores of the physician, and his many other duties, he usually worked out an arrangement with the ward personnel, particularly the charge (supervisory attendant), to handle these duties. On several wards, the charge called specific problems to the doctor's attention, and the two of them, in effect, would have a consultation. The charge actually made most of the decisions concerning dosage change in the back wards. Since the doctor delegated portions of his formal responsibilities to the charge, he was dependent on her good will toward him. If she withheld her co-operation, the physician had absolutely no recourse but to do all the work himself.[16]

In a sense such delegation of responsibility involves a consideration of reward and cost, whereby the decision to be made involves a question of what is more valuable—to retain control over an area, or to delegate one's work to lower participants.

There are occasions, of course, when rules are regarded as illegitimate by lower participants, and they may disregard them. Gouldner observed that, in the mine, men felt they could resist authority in a situation involving danger to themselves.[17] They did not feel that they could legitimately be ordered to do anything that would endanger their lives. It is probably significant that in extremely dangerous situations organizations are more likely to rely on commitment to work than on authority. Even within nonvoluntary groups dangerous tasks are regarded usually as requiring task commitment, and it is likely that commitment is a much more powerful organizational force than coercive authority.

Summary

The preceding remarks are general ones, and they are assumed to be in part true of all types of organizations. But power relationships in organizations are likely to be molded by the type of organization being considered, the nature of organizational goals, the ideology of organizational decision making, the kind of commitment participants have to the organization, the formal structure of the organization, and so on. In short, we have attempted to discuss power processes within organizations in a manner somewhat divorced from other major organizational processes. We have emphasized variables affecting control of access to persons, information, and facilities within organizations. Normative definitions, perception of legitimacy, exchange, and coalitions have all been viewed in relation to power processes. Moreover, we have dealt with some attributes of persons related to power: commitment, effort, interest, willingness to use power, skills, attractiveness, and so on. And we have discussed some other variables: time, centrality, complexity of power structure, and replaceability of persons. It appears that these variables help to account in part for power exercised by lower participants in organizations.

---

[16] *Ibid.,* p. 97.
[17] Gouldner, *op. cit.*

Questions for Discussion

1. Why is conflict so common in human organizations?

2. Why do we tend to blame conflict on personality problems?

3. How can work flow and organizational structure cause conflict and stress?

4. In many business organizations, conflict exists between the credit manager and marketing managers. Regardless of personality similarities or differences, apparently people in these positions tend to conflict. Discuss.

5. A persistent problem in organizations is whether a staff in a local plant should be responsible to the plant manager, or the staff group at corporate headquarters. Discuss the advantages and disadvantages of each arrangement for (a) a plant personnel manager, (b) a plant comptroller, and (c) a plant industrial engineer.

6. The New York Telephone Company discourages careers in personnel and industrial relations. The industrial relations department is staffed mostly with operating managers who move in and out of staff positions as their careers progress. In contrast, the Radio Corporation of America recruits business-school personnel and industrial relations majors, and offers a professional career in that staff department. There is much less transfer between line management and the personnel staff. What might be some of the possible reasons for these two different philosophies?

7. In his book *Managerial Behavior,* Leonard R. Sayles describes how staff men attempt to change their relationship to line managers: for example, from service, to advisory, to auditing, to controlling. Why might staff men attempt to modify their work relationships in this way?

8. Concerned about the high incidence of mononucleosis, shingles, and Vincent's disease among shipboard Ensigns and Lieutenant j.g.'s in the Navy during the 1950's and 1960's, naval medical officers investigated and concluded that most of the cases were psychosomatic—caused by the stress in the junior officer's job. Discuss what might be the sources of such difficulties.

9. Several observers of union-management relations have commented on consistent patterns of behavior among employes in similar industries. For example, miners are characterized by strong collective action; they engage in slowdowns and strikes (and often violence) to wring concessions from management. On the other hand, migrant fruit pickers seldom demonstrate any form of group action—at least in opposition to management. It is exceedingly difficult even to organize them. Finally, tool-and-die machinists have strong unions but apparently seldom become agitated enough to initiate overt action against management. Explain the possible causes of the distinctive collective behavior patterns of these miners, pickers, and machinists.

Chapter Seven

Political Behavior in Organizations

We are attempting to understand behavior in organizations by examining ideas from the behavioral sciences—sociology, psychology, social psychology, and cultural anthropology. Although political science is not universally included among the behavioral sciences, we believe that no book on organizational behavior and management would be complete without an understanding of certain political phenomena—power, authority, delegation, and responsibility, for example.

There are two underlying reasons for this belief. First, human behavior in large organizations responds to political variables, particularly to *authority.* Thus, no concept of behavior in organizations is complete that fails to recognize the significance of these variables. Second, motivational analysis, as well as traditional political explanations, can be used to explain why systems of authority arise and why people continue to live in, and obey or disobey, such systems. It is the purpose of this chapter to present an overall view of authority systems, examine in detail the nature of authority systems in terms of what they are and how they work, and then consider why such systems arise and why the people in them act as they do.

The Political Nature of Organizations

If an investigator went into a business organization to find out what held it together—what coordinated it—he would see supervisors giving orders, he would see managers and their specialist staffs making rules, and he would hear references to policy. If he questioned an employee's action, he might be told, "Well, I did it this way because it's S.O.P." (*standard operating procedure*) or "I did it because *management has decided* to phase out this product line."

Continuing his tour through the company, he would hear statements like, "It is *part of my job* to answer customer complaints," "I have *authority* to make decisions regarding employee benefits," "It is his *responsibility* to supervise the salesmen," and "That part of the job has been delegated to the foreman." Or someone might say, "That particular activity comes within the *charter* of the electric motor division."

All of these statements are political in nature because they have to do with rules (laws) and authority (acceptance of rules, laws, or decisions as reasons for behavior). In fact, the very functions of managers, if explained in terms of planning (decision making and rule making), organizing (writing job descriptions and authority specifications), directing (issuing instructions or orders), and controlling (examining results and making new decisions for corrective action if results do not correspond to plans), all add up to building a political system.[1] In this system, a company board of directors is somewhat analogous to Congress, making (legislating) rules and policies (laws). The company management is the on-the-spot decision-making group, analogous to a President and his Cabinet, communicating decisions to subordinate personnel and expecting them to behave accordingly. Management is also somewhat analogous to the judiciary. Particularly in the control function, it is management's job to detect variance from overall plans and policies, determine why, determine who is responsible, and take corrective action.

What Is "Authority"?

In reading the selections, you will find that the authors attach varying meanings to the terms "authority," "power," and "influence." In order to establish a meaningful context for our purposes, it is necessary to formulate an overall idea of what an *authority system* is. Such a system has five attributes:

1. It is caused by, or necessary because of, certain deep-seated forces at work in the organization and in society. These forces are the ones that bring political systems into existence.
2. It is a system in which relatively few (line managers and their specialist staffs) make decisions for relatively many (lower managers, employees).
3. The decisions made are of two types: (a) standing decisions, to be carried out over a period of time by diverse people while they are in effect. In society these are called *laws,* and in the corporation they are called *policies, procedures, programs,* or *methods.* Sometimes, they are called *job descriptions.* Sociologists often lump all of these together and call them "rules" or "work rules." (b) *ad hoc* decisions, which are made by executives either to *interpret* standing decisions or to make certain decisions which are not covered by standing decisions.
4. Decisions, either standing or *ad hoc,* are communicated from managers to subordinates—from relatively few at any level in the organization to relatively many.
5. Certain human motivations tend to cause subordinates to obey or carry out the decisions of management communicated to them. As shown elsewhere in this book, there may also be motives to *disobey,* but in this chapter we are concerned with the motives to obey.

Having defined an authority system, we need also a more fundamental view, or microview, of authority—the authority event. The various authors of readings following this chapter all have differing definitions of authority events; indeed, the reader may find more than one of them useful. Our own definition, because it seems explicit and fundamental, is similar to that offered by Simon, Smithburg, and Thompson: An *authority event* is an observable phenomenon which exists

[1]The founder of this school of thought, the French industrialist Henri Fayol [2], was well versed in political philosophy, even though he was an engineer by profession and president of a large mining company.

when a person, B, carries out the decision of another person, A, without thinking through that decision himself, or, having thought it through, disagrees with A's conclusion or judgment.

In addition, types of influence other than formal authority are pointed out by some of the authors in this chapter (notably Goldhammer and Shils)—for example, covert manipulation by management. However, our discussion is concerned with formal decision making by management and the motivations for subordinates to obey these decisions when they are overtly communicated.

Why Authority Systems Come to Be

Why do systems of authority arise? What are the forces in society that cause people to form such systems? In our view, there are two basic reasons: the technological-economic attributes of modern organizations; and human nature.

Technological Necessity

In an Industrial Society. There are certain reasons why systems of authority arise which have to do with the *technological* characteristics of modern society. These characteristics are revealed in the arguments that have been put forth on the question of how authority systems come into being: whether laws (rules and decisions) originate with a people and their customs, or with their leaders.

A theoretical controversy on this question has existed for two hundred years. Great scholars like Savigny, Saint-Simon, and Jeremy Bentham addressed themselves to it. (This controversy appears also in the history of sociology, with the "natural organization" school on one side and the "rational school" on the other). On the one hand, Savigny and Saint-Simon held that law should follow the customs of society, that legislatures or courts should discover these customs and codify them. This, essentially, is the position of many group theorists, who hold that groups should develop their own distribution of authority, operating customs, and the like.

On the other hand, Bentham argued that legislatures should be creative in deciding what a society needs or *should* be; that they should prescribe laws, communicate them, and enforce them. This was the position of Auguste Comte, one of Saint-Simon's students, who felt that, with the progress of science and learning, men should solve their organizational problems (make decisions) rationally, specifying what dynamic behavior *should* take place on the part of individuals and subgroups and what their *relationships* should be. Max Weber [7], pointing out the advantages of the "ideal bureaucracy," sided with Bentham and Comte in his general argument.

W. Friedmann [3], asserts that the growth of technology, industrialization, and urbanization, coupled with increase in the size of organizations, are bringing about the prescriptive (legislative-rational) approach in our society: prescriptive, or *rational,* law is superseding derived, or *common,* law as a source of social organization:

> A highly urbanised and mechanized society, in which great numbers of peoples live close together and are ever more dependent upon each other's actions and the supply of necessities outside their own sphere of control, has led to an increasingly active and creative role of the conscious law-making instrumentalities of the State.

Friedmann goes on to say that some modern writers oppose rational law. He quotes Hayek's analogy that this type of law "commands people which road to take, whereas the latter only provide signposts," which defends the view that government should follow, not plan or lead society. On this point, Friedmann says:

> Even if we accept this as an adequate parable of the problem of the function of law in modern society, we need only to point to the vast number of one-way streets in modern cities to illustrate the superficiality of this distinction. No sane person would advocate the abolition of one-way streets in cities with heavy motor traffic so as to restore a measure of individual freedom of decision. . . . Such a measure would make sense only if the volume of traffic, in particular the use of motor-cars, were severely restricted. . . .

Before translating the technological necessity for authority systems into terms of the business firm (as contrasted with a total society), let us quote the statements of two other well-known writers to convey the interconnected and complex nature of an industrial system. Charles A. Beard [1], a noted historian, put it this way:

> Every enterprise in the Great Society, as well as the Great Society itself, rests upon administration. Industry on a large scale depends upon organization—upon the management of large numbers of employees of different crafts and arts and the disposition of material goods. In some industries, the administrative organization is national and even international in its range. Thousands, hundreds of thousands, of men and women must be brought together and distributed among various departments of production. They must be graded in a vast economic hierarchy, with skilled engineers and managers at the top and laborers at the bottom. They must be assigned specific and appropriate tasks in the operation of the organization. They must be directed, controlled (p. 148).

Finally, Thorstein Veblen [6], the economist, noted:

> The country's industrial system . . . is a comprehensive and balanced scheme of technological administration. Industry of this sort—mechanical, specialized, standardized, running to quantity production, drawn on a large scale, is highly productive; provided always that the necessary conditions of its working are met in some passable fashion. . . . The mechanical technology is impersonal and dispassionate, and its end is very simply to serve human needs, without fear or favor or respect of persons, prerogatives, or politics. It makes up an industrial system of an unexampled character—a mechanically balanced and interlocking system of work to be done. The foundation and driving force of it all is a massive body of technological knowledge (Ch. 5).

In the Enterprise. If we view the corporation as a system in itself, we see that a great part of the action (behavior) which takes place is dictated by the decision-making process of corporate staff men and general managers, and that this process is largely dictated by technology. Staff men and general managers are usually trained in the technology of business—marketing, finance, manpower planning, research and development planning, and production planning—and are immersed in a vast technological input-output system, in which the principal objective is to maximize the ratio of output to input.

In marketing, the techniques of market research (which now include applications of mathematics and the behavioral sciences) are aimed at rationally and more or less scientifically determining the total volume of a company's flow of output, and the exact amount of output for each sub-area. Advertising media research and motivational research are combined to influence qualitative and quantitative output by area. Quotas for salesmen are used to determine how many men are needed (manpower planning), and both quotas and compensation (a technical field in itself) are used for motivational purposes.

The result of these techniques is to structure a marketing *organization* which has sub-objectives, specified numbers of men, procedures for determining routings, and procedures for suggesting how salesmen can appeal to customers. Product analysis helps determine which products will be emphasized and which de-emphasized, resulting in a particular pattern of company output.

In production planning, the traditional functions of plant layout, routing of goods in process, and scheduling have been revolutionized by linear programming, queueing theory, and other technologies. The PERT network itself is a form of organizational diagram, since each "event" is a goal or sub-objective in time and cost for a lower organizational department. Each "activity" is a job description to be assigned to someone.

In accounting and finance, the entire complex budget of a company, sometimes involving 100 to 200 pages (exhibits) for divisions, lower departments, and sections, is itself a mathematical model, which starts with company output and moves backward through the production process to allocate the right number of men and right amount of materials for each step in the chain of production.

Finally, in the area of long-run planning of fixed assets, there are technologies which determine what kinds of plants or divisions there will be in the organizational chart, and what the job descriptions will be. Methods such as incremental analysis and discounted-cash-flow analysis actually determine what product divisions a company will have and how many people will be working in them.

In summary, there are powerful technologies for determining the output of a company and powerful technologies for determining the inputs of manpower, materials, capital machines and facilities, and money. Given organizational *interest* in planning and allocation, buttressed by the *value* a society places on the production of needed goods and prevention of waste (minimizing inputs), we can see why the establishment of rules and procedures (law and order) are deemed necessary.

The Human Desire for Authority

The impulse to create authority systems imbedded in human nature was explained by John Locke, the English philosopher, writing more than two hundred years ago. Like Garibaldi, the father of modern Italy, he wondered why a free people would favor setting up a state which made laws, communicated them, and enforced them. Locke tells us that men want greater assurance of property protection than is afforded by "the law of Nature." Because men are "biased by their [self] interest, . . . [they] are not apt to allow of [the law of Nature] as a law binding to them in the application of it to their particular cases." Because of this, men need an "established, settled, known law" to be the standard of right and wrong. But, because men are "partial to themselves, passion and revenge is very apt to carry them too far" in their self-interest, making them negligent of the rights of other men. Thus men also desire an "indifferent [impartial] judge" to interpret the law. Finally, because some men will persist in their own self interest, men want "power to back and support" the decisions of the judge who applies the settled laws.

Very much this same argument is presented by Ranyard West [8], a philosopher of the mid-twentieth century (quoted in the selection by Cyril O'Donnell):

> The prime requisite and firm creator of any community life is a law or order maintained by force. For human nature is such that, in all its most necessary social relationships, it is subject to the permanent threat of the self-assertive impulse, which misinterprets facts, misjudges events, and then, through consequent self-justificatory passion, breaks the social bond, unless externally restrained. We claim this as adequately confirmed. Nursery studies and family life confirm it. Social and natural history confirm it. Modern psychology confirms it. And, finally, our common sense tends to confirm it—for all others except ourselves, which is in itself a final confirmation. Individual, group, or nation-state, we cannot [properly] judge our own cause.

Research into the dynamics of group interaction tends to confirm this view. Referring to the reading by Bennis and Shepard following Chapter 3, we note that even small groups, starting out with no authority structure, develop a system of customs or norms, and certain individuals emerge who are leaders in suggesting group action—leaders in the sense that others in the group accept their suggestions.

As a further development in group theory, there is a school of thought which believes that *conflict,* not cooperation, is the most important phenomenon occurring when people get together.

Differing orientations toward authority might be at the root of such conflict. As Bennis and Shepard indicate, there are those who want to be dependent on others, some who have a strong desire to tell others what to do (the type who will engage in a power struggle), and those who wish to be independent. It is the first type who readily submits to authority; the second who promotes anarchy (in O'Donnell's terms): and the third who eventually becomes Locke's "indifferent judge."

What other individual differences contribute to Locke's "bias by [self] interest"? Recalling Leavitt on perception following Chapter 3, we know that different people "see" *different things* "out there," depending on their own needs, motives and attitudes. The same objective fact simply isn't the same when filtered through the psychological processes of individual thinking and perception. Is it any wonder, then, that when men live close together, in interdependent situations, they can do so only with the aid of rules, judges, and the power to back them up?

Finally, Robert Presthus, in a selection following this chapter, presents other reasons for authority systems. He stresses the fact that, in large organizations, deference to authority is economical because it insures internal discipline (preventing behavior which does not coordinate with standard behavior) and because it decreases interpersonal conflict, which takes up valuable time.

Why People Obey

The motivation of people to obey is important in understanding what makes authority systems and events operate. We will outline below some of the phenomena that motivate people to obey.

Leadership Authority

In two of the readings, Presthus and Goldhammer and Shils refer to *charismatic* authority as originally conceived by Max Weber. Weber analyzed organizations in a number of different national cultures to show that people may follow a man, usually a great hero, simply because they believe he might "take care of them" or "save them." Acceptance of this type of leader often occurs when the people are threatened, or in a condition of acute deprivation or chaos. The man who can inspire the population may actually produce results—settle internal conflict or win external conflict—or he may simply catch the imagination and admiration of the people. In Weber's terms, the motivation is often of metaphysical character.

Such leaders exist in modern business corporations. For example, according to many middle managers in the IBM Corporation, both Thomas Watson, Sr., and Thomas Watson, Jr., have been regarded in this light. The modern reasons for the appeal of charismatic leadership are technological. We have described the vast complexity and delicate, interlocking nature of technology and the dependence it develops. It is not unreasonable to assume that, just as Weber's political leader helped warring cities or kingdoms bring order out of chaos, so today's corporation executive, general or staff, may inspire simply because his subordinates want order made out of what would be technological chaos without central coordination and planning.[2]

Chester Barnard gives us another kind of leader. This is the general executive, whose mind must receive information from many specialists, and whose *judgment* or *wisdom* is respected because of his past performance. Subordinates see this man taking into account both the overall good of the organization and the interests of its various *parts* in balancing his judgment. (This is what is meant by Barnard's emphasis on "local perspective.")

Employees and middle managers at each successively higher level of organization recognize that they themselves have neither an overall perspective, nor a local perspective on the parts as they interlock with the larger system. Barnard is careful to point out that it is the executive's ability to absorb communication from both the local situation and the larger system which gives him the knowledge he can put to use in exercising judgment. Subordinates view such an executive as "responsible." Good judgment on the part of a line executive

[2]The concept of *anomie,* put forth by another sociologist, Durkheim, has been applied to industrial organizations by many writers. When so interpreted, this is a feeling of helplessness in large technological organizations because one's own job and perspective represent so small a part of what seems a vast, uncontrollable system. To the extent that a human being has a vague, generalized, and nonspecific feeling of this kind, it could account for dependence on a leader.

"makes the fiction of superior authority a reality" and insures that his decisions will be readily accepted by his subordinates.

Henri Fayol summarized this line of thinking in his doctrine of the "reasonable-minded man." That is, if general executives act wisely, subordinates will be reasonable, and recognize that their superiors are acting on behalf of the whole organization, including the interests of its local parts. As for the staff specialist, it is mentioned in a number of the readings that his expertise and competence in his own area (whether it be financial investment or biochemistry) serve as his authority credentials.

Status Authority

In the Barnard model, subordinates obey a general executive because of his *position* as well as for his personal charisma. This phenomenon is observed in the military, when an enlisted man salutes a lieutenant—it is not the *individual* who causes the behavior but the *status position* represented by the bars on his shoulder, which are his *status symbols.* In a business firm, the status positions of "president" or "vice president" are cues for behavior. This phenomenon in relation to a line or general executive position is called "hierarchical status;" in relation to a staff specialist position, it is called "functional status."

To emphasize the authority of status as opposed to the authority of persons, Barnard tells us that if a *competent* person makes a decision and communicates it to others *without* a position of status and power, it is "personal advice [to be acted upon] at the risk of the taker."

Personal and status authority also tend to reinforce each other. Because communication networks tend to converge at certain positions, subordinates perceive these positions as sources of wise and intelligent instructions. And to the extent that such instructions are issued, these positions will continue to be regarded as authoritative. In the case of staff specialists, as Simon and his colleagues explain, the subordinate may not be able to judge the expertise or competence of the individual, so the alternatives are blind deference to functional status or blind disobedience.

Sociocultural Deference

There is in all cultures a learned ethic developed from early childhood and conditioned throughout life, to the effect that one *ought* to obey laws and legitimate persons of authority. Goldhammer and Shils with their "ethical imperative," Presthus citing studies of national cultures, and Simon-Smithburg-Thompson reminding us that "one of the values with which [people] are indoctrinated is that a person should play according to the rules of the game" call attention to this ethic as an important reason why authority systems arise and why authority events take place.

Not all individuals learn the same degree of deference to authority. In the modern business operation, individuals vary widely in their attitudes toward authority. Presthus postulates that there are three kinds of people in an organization, classifiable by their accommodation to rules and authority: those who accept legitimate and rational authority, those who do their day's work and fight neither for nor against the system, and those who are ambivalent—who find the success available in organizations attractive but cannot play the role necessary to attain it. Some extreme situations also exist, in which the individual cannot tolerate authority, or the system is irresponsible, or both occur together.

Rational Calculation and The Zone of Indifference

When an individual joins an organization, that organization's rule system and *ad hoc* decision system may impose upon him a wide range of "contributions" (Simon-Smithburg-Thompson) or "burdens and sacrifices" (Barnard). On the other hand, the person receives certain inducements. The latter are material (money, pleasant physical facilities) or nonmaterial (social pleasure at work, an inherent feeling of productivity, a sense of belonging, a feeling of security, and so on).

Each policy or *ad hoc* decision can be arranged in the order of its acceptability. Furthermore, the individual has alternatives—to remain in, or leave, the organization. Thus acceptability is calculated on the basis of the net inducements minus burdens (or the ratio of inducements to burdens), coupled with the man's estimate of what he might gain or lose by moving to another organization.

Some orders will be clearly unacceptable (disobeyed), some will be barely acceptable or barely unacceptable (ambivalent), and some will be clearly acceptable. These latter fall within the "zone of indifference" (Barnard) or "area of acceptance" (Simon-Smithburg-Thompson).

Clearly, this is another form of "reasonable minded man" doctrine. It assumes that men know consciously, and can rationally calculate, what needs they have regarding employment, and how the operation of the company affects these needs.

Authority by Sanction

The concept of authority presented earlier recognizes that authority events occur not only when a person carries out a rule or instruction "without thinking," but also when he obeys even though he may disagree with the decision.

We might explain such behavior in terms of sanctions—rewards and penalties. In the business corporation today, there are a variety of rewards which may operate as positive motivations to obey (for instance, for Presthus' "upward mobiles"), or penalties which operate as negative threats in order to force obedience (applied to those who otherwise would not conform to the organizations' requirements—"ambivalents" or outright rebels). These rewards and penalties taken together might also be termed "power."

Almost all writers on authority agree that negative sanctions are necessary. Locke tells us that some members of society will persist in the pursuit of self-interest even after laws are instituted and after judges have ruled. The history of international law and justice is an example of this principle applied to nations. Although the treaty system and the international courts have achieved some success, they cannot enforce peaceful relationships among nations. Both the League of Nations and the United Nations found that they had to provide for some forms of sanction.

Speaking for the business firm, even Barnard, who insists that authority arises from below, says:

> If objective authority is flouted for arbitrary or temperamental reasons, if . . . there is a deliberate attempt to twist an organization requirement to personal advantage . . . then there is a deliberate attack on the organization itself. . . . To fail in an obligation intentionally is an act of hostility. This no organization can permit; and it must respond with punitive action. . . .

Presthus regards acceptance of authority as extending from the top downward, because executives possess sanctions passed down to them from a larger system:

> Big organizations are composed of many subhierarchies, each bound together by authority, interest, and values in a way similar to that in the total organization. Each has its internal power structure headed by a leader who is supreme within his own system, but who is a nonleader when viewed from the perspective of the larger hierarchy. This devolution of power has important consequences. It ensures discipline, since the life chances of those in each subhierarchy are determined largely through representations made on their behalf by such subleaders. As a result, an upward-looking posture characterizes the whole organization. The will of the minority is transmitted downward through the organization by the subleaders, reinforcing their own authority and status vis-à-vis their subhierarchy.

A further distinction made by Goldhammer and Shils seems important, because it highlights a difference between the viewpoints of those who have a total organization, "law-and-order" orientation (Barnard, Locke, Fayol, O'Donnell, etc.) and those who have an individual-psychological or small-group orientation (viz., many of the authors in psychology and small-group sociology). The former assume that the system and its managers will appear reasonable to employes. Barnard explains the kind of behavior on the part of executives which will produce a "reasonable-minded" system. Most rules and directives will therefore fall within the natural "area of acceptance" of employes. Goldhammer and Shils distinguish between the one type of authority (legitimate power acknowledged by subordinates) and "coercion" (power of sanctions, accepted but not recognized as legitimate by subordinates).

Many authors, particularly those with a psychological orientation, do not assume that the system and its leaders integrate the desires of subordinates into its rules and decisions. They cite studies reported elsewhere in this book to show how, for this reason, legitimate authority breaks down. They therefore see coercion as a prime motivational strategy in organizations, and predict that it does not work in the long run.

To the authors' knowledge, neither of these viewpoints has been conclusively proven. Pragmatically, one theory may be true in one company situation and the other true in another. It behooves us to be acquainted with both.

The Reduction of Anxiety

"Anxiety reduction" is cited in the reading by Presthus as an important motivation to obey authority—in fact, Presthus views this as the central motivation to explain organizational behavior. It will be our purpose at this point to clarify the meaning of anxiety reduction, to show that other authors, under different labels, regard this motivation as important, and to distinguish between anxiety caused by the superior-subordinate relationship and that caused by the relationships among peers or equals.

In Superior-Subordinate Relations. When people join large organizations, there is *in fact* a disparity of power (rewards and penalties) possessed by individuals, including middle managers, on the one hand and by higher office holders on the other. In short, the organization is a hierarchical system of status and power. People are placed in a specific job with explicit duties (actions, behavior), guided by policies and procedures which limit individual discretion, and given varying sanctions that they can use for or against others.

Given these characteristics of the job and the impersonality of rule systems, Presthus suggests that human motivations *other than* material benefits and satisfaction from productivity do not derive from the organization, specifically such motivations as the desires for love and self-realization. As a result, most human beings focus at work on the rewards which the organization *can* offer, obtaining satisfaction of other needs away from the job.

But the individual is confronted with the fact that whether or not he achieves job satisfaction is to a great degree determined by the persons who control him. This dependency is a continual source of anxiety or insecurity. The cause-effect relationships are:

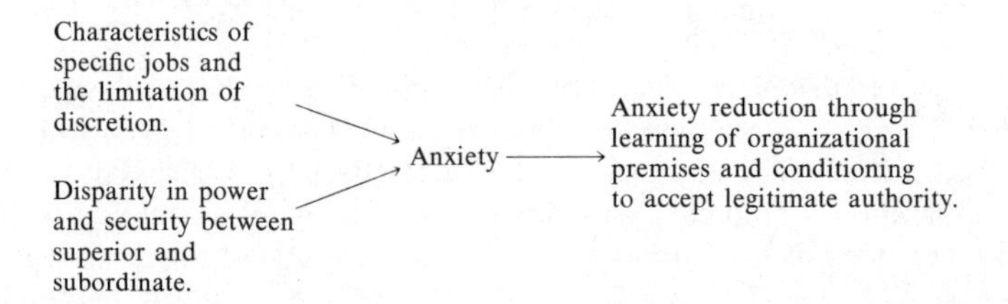

Barnard offers similar reasoning. He says that one reason people obey is that if the individual countermands orders received from above, he runs "the risk of being wrong." There is a process of "delegating upwards" from subordinate to superior, in which the subordinate gives up some freedom, discretion, or self-actualization to his superior in exchange for a lessening of his feeling of such risk. This phenomenon, which the sociologist Robert Merton [5] stressed, is similar to Presthus' anxiety reduction.

Another source of anxiety is the disparity between theory and reality. In our society there are strong egalitarian social values which say that "people are created equal" or that "democratic organizations are best" or that "all actions should be in accord with the goal of brotherly love." If the individual compares these ideals to the disparity of power and discretion that actually occurs in organizations, he experiences anxiety. The tension created by this inconsistency of ideal and action is also called *cognitive dissonance* by psychologists.

The selection by Gouldner proposes a way whereby this conflict can be reconciled by the promulgation of formal rules, policies, job descriptions, departmental objectives, and the like. These standing decisions reduce the number of contacts between superiors and subordinates, preventing a superior from giving too many direct orders. Because it is a "rule of the game," the standing decision or policy protects both the superior and the subordinate:

> [A standing rule] impersonally bolsters a supervisor's claim to authority without compelling him to employ an embarrassing and debatable legitimation in terms of his personal superiority. Conversely, it permits [subordinates] to accept managerial claims to deference without committing them

to a merely personal submission to the supervisor that would betray their self-image as 'any man's equal.'

In Peer Relations. Another form of anxiety is caused, not by managers and executives who control organizational sanctions, but by peers in the organization who exercise informal sanctions.

The basis for this anxiety is explained, at the level of a society, by John Locke. Without legitimate rules, judges to interpret them, and power to back up the rules and judges, man would find himself in power struggles with peers; each individual would seek to attain his own self-interest, sometimes acting with open and conscious hostility, at other times misjudging what is good for the whole and underestimating or ignoring the needs of others.

For example, a city with no traffic regulations, no courts to hear disputes, and no police to apprehend offenders, might experience such property destruction and human strife that eventually people would either be afraid to drive or, more likely, demand a modern equivalent of Locke's system—traffic regulations, traffic courts with disinterested judges, and police who could arrest those who failed to see the "good " in paying the damages they were ordered to pay.

Given the technological dependence of modern man (his need for a place to work or be occupied, and his need for monetary reward in an exchange economy), the same desire for order exists within the modern corporation. If some managers or workers intentionally, or through bias or perceptual error caused by self-interest, exercise judgment so bad that it threatens the survival of the organization, then other workers and managers might well feel what Veblen [6] describes:

> Any defect or hindrance in [the interlocking input-output system's] technical administration, any intrusion of nontechnical considerations, any failure or obstruction at any point, unavoidably results in a disproportionate setback to the balanced whole and brings a disproportionate burden of privation on all these peoples whose productive industry has come within the sweep of the system.

At the small-group level, reaction may take the form of sanctions informally worked out by the group. For example, Gouldner [4] tells of a mining operation in which certain unpleasant operations had to be performed if the whole specialized mining organization were to work. How were men chosen or assigned to this job? Gouldner asked one of the men who had been through the process. "It's simple," he replied. "We all just turn around and *look* at the newest guy in the group and he goes and does it."

Here was a set of informal rules and norms for administering "justice." The procedure was to assign the job to a new man, who would earn a better life later. But note that all the men were interested in getting that part of the mining operation done—they didn't want the mine to close down and throw them out of work, and they did not want endless fighting among themselves. The group could administer "pain, failure, or ego degradation," in the terms used by a psychologist, Norman R. F. Maier. Incidentally, Maier was explaining the mental state—frustration—which produces anxiety.

Barnard puts it this way:

> Since the efficiency of the organization is affected by the degree to which individuals assent to orders, denying the authority of an organizational [decision] is a threat to the interests of all individuals who derive a net advantage from their connection with the organization. . . . Accordingly, at any given time there is among most of the contributors an active personal interest in the maintenance of the authority of all orders which to them are within the zone of indifference. The maintenance of this interest is largely a function of informal organization. Its expression goes under the names of "public opinion," . . . "group attitude," etc.

Why People Command

Throughout most of this chapter, we have been looking at why people obey the decisions and rule systems formulated by others. Authority systems and authority phenomena have been explained in terms of the forces "from the bottom" which bring them into being. This is only one side of the coin. The fact is that authority systems and phenomena could not exist if organizations were made up of all Indians and no chiefs. For every group of people who follow decisions, there must be another group whose motivations cause them to make decisions. Only after we have developed a more detailed understanding of the forces at work "from the top"—in the behavior of executives or oligarchs—will we have presented a complete understanding of political systems in relation to organizations. This latter aspect of organizational behavior is covered in greater detail in Chapter 9, "Influencing Behavior Through Political Action."

References

1. Beard, C. A. *Public Policy and the General Welfare.* Holt, Rinehart & Winston, 1941.
2. Fayol, H. *General and Industrial Management.* London: Pitman, 1949.
3. Friedmann, W. *Law in a Changing Society.* London: Stevens, 1959.
4. Gouldner, A. W. *Patterns of Industrial Bureaucracy.* The Free Press, 1954.
5. Merton, R. "Bureaucratic Structure and Personality." *Social Forces,* No. 18 (1940), 560–568.
6. Veblen, T. *The Engineers and the Price System.* Viking, 1921.
7. Weber, M. *The Theory of Social and Economic Organization,* tr. A. M. Henderson and T. Parsons. The Free Press, 1947.
8. West, R. *Conscience and Society,* 1942.

Readings

Concerning Civil Government

JOHN LOCKE

The great and chief end, therefore, of men uniting into commonwealths, and putting themselves under government, is the preservation of their property; to which in the state of Nature there are many things wanting.

Firstly, there wants an established, settled, known law, received and allowed by common consent to be the standard of right and wrong, and the common measure to decide all controversies between them. For though the law of Nature be plain and intelligible to all rational creatures, yet men, being biased by their interest, as well as ignorant for want of study of it, are not apt to allow of it as a law binding to them in the application of it to their particular cases.

Secondly, in the state of Nature there wants a known and indifferent judge, with authority to determine all differences according to the established law. For every one in that state of being both judge and executioner of the law of Nature, men being partial to themselves, passion and revenge is very apt to carry them too far, and with too much heat in their own cases, as well as negligence and unconcernedness, make them too remiss in other men's.

Thirdly, in the state of Nature there often wants power to back and support the sentence when right, and to give it due execution. They who by any injustice offended will seldom fail where they are able by force to make good their injustice. Such resistance many times makes the punishment dangerous, and frequently destructive to those who attempt it.

Thus mankind, notwithstanding all the privileges of the state of Nature, being but in an ill condition while they remain in it are quickly driven into society. Hence it comes to pass, that we seldom find any number of men live any time together in this state. The inconveniences that they are therein exposed to by the irregular and uncertain exercise of the power every man has of punishing the transgressions of others, make them take sanctuary under the established laws of government, and therein seek the preservation of their property. It is this makes them so willingly give up every one his single power of punishing to be exercised by such alone as shall be appointed to it amongst them, and by such rules as the community, or those authorised by them to that purpose,

The Great Ideas, Vol. 35 (pp. 53–54), Encyclopaedia Britannica, Inc., 1952.

shall agree on. And in this we have the original right and rise of both the legislative and executive power as well as of the governments and societies themselves.

For in the state of Nature to omit the liberty he has of innocent delights, a man has two powers. . . .

The first power—viz., of doing whatsoever he thought fit for the preservation of himself and the rest of mankind, he gives up to be regulated by laws made by the society, so far forth as the preservation of himself and the rest of that society shall require; which laws of the society in many things confine the liberty he had by the law of Nature.

Secondly, the power of punishing he wholly gives up, and engages his natural force, which he might before employ in the execution of the law of Nature, by his own single authority, as he thought fit, to assist the executive power of the society as the law thereof shall require. For being now in a new state, wherein he is to enjoy many conveniencies from the labour, assistance, and society of others in the same community, as well as protection from its whole strength, he is to part also with as much of his natural liberty, in providing for himself, as the good, prosperity, and safety of the society shall require, which is not only necessary but just, since the other members of the society do the like. . . .

. . . And so, whoever has the legislative or supreme power of any commonwealth, is bound to govern by established standing laws, promulgated and known to the people, and not by extemporary decrees by indifferent and upright judges, who are to decide controversies by those laws; and to employ the force of the community at home only in the execution of such laws, or abroad to prevent or redress foreign injuries and secure the community from inroads and invasion. . . .

Law in a Changing Society

W. FRIEDMANN

The controversy between those who believe that law should essentially follow, not lead, and that it should do so slowly, in response to clearly formulated social sentiment—and those who believe that the law should be a determined agent in the creation of new norms, is one of the recurrent themes of the history of legal thought. It is tellingly illustrated by the conflicting approaches of Savingy and Bentham.

For Savingy, a bitter opponent of the rationalizing and law-making tendencies, spurred by the French Revolution, law was "found," not "made." Only when popular custom in part articulated by lawyers, had fully evolved, could

From *Law in a Changing Society,* by W. Friedmann. London: Stevens & Sons, Ltd., 1959, pp. 3–6 and 22–23. Reprinted by permission of Stevens & Sons, Ltd.

and should the legislature take action. Savingy particularly deprecated the trend towards the codification of law, inaugurated by the Napoleonic Codes, and spreading rapidly over the civilized world.

By contrast, Bentham, a fervent believer in the efficacy of rationally constructed reforming laws, devoted a great part of his life to the drafting of codes for a large number of countries, from Czarist Russia to the newly emergent republics of Latin America. While most of these efforts were not immediately successful, notably in his own country, whether in the field of civil law, criminal law, evidence or poor law, his philosophy became increasingly influential as the nineteenth century progressed. It was Bentham's philosophy, and that of his disciples, which turned the British Parliament—and similar institutions in other countries—into active legislative instruments, effecting social reforms, partly in response to, and partly in stimulation of, felt social needs. It is essentially the judge-made law that, in the countries of the common law world, has still in large measure resisted legislative—as distinct from judicial—reform, although even in the traditional fields of the common law, legislative activity is steadily increasing. In most other fields—of which electoral reform, social welfare legislation in the broadest sense, tax law and the reform of the machinery of justice are examples—the Bentham philosophy triumphed in the practice of States, as the urbanisation and industrialisation of nineteenth-century Western society proceeded, and long before political and social cataclysms of the twentieth century posed a series of new challenges. . . .

A highly urbanised and mechanized society, in which great numbers of peoples live close together and are ever more dependent upon each other's actions and the supply of necessities outside their own sphere of control, has led to an increasingly active and creative role of the conscious law-making instrumentalities of the State.

The traditional view is not without its modern defenders, especially among *laissez-faire* economists who oppose the growing role of the State in the planning and regulation of contemporary social life. Thus, Professor Hayek has restated a distinction similar to that drawn by Ehrlich by opposing the planned State to the rule of law and asserting that the former "commands people which road to take, whereas the latter only provides signposts." Even if we accept this as an adequate parable of the problem of the function of law in modern society, we need only to point to the vast number of one-way streets in modern cities to illustrate the superficiality of this distinction. No sane person would advocate the abolition of one-way streets in cities with heavy motor traffic so as to restore a measure of individual freedom of decision, with the inevitable consequence of a vastly increased rate of accidents to life and property. Such a measure would make sense only if the volume of traffic, in particular the use of motor-cars, were severely restricted, in other words, if individual freedom of property and movement were far more drastically curtailed. This might become a necessary and acceptable measure to advocate for those who accept the planning function of the law, but not for the advocates of unrestricted individual freedom.

However, the traffic problem hardly touches the core of the matter, for it may well be accepted even by the most outspoken individualists as a typical police function, and therefore properly within the regulatory function of government. The shift in public opinion and in the legislative policy of all major parties and of contemporary governments has gone much further. Conservatives and

Liberals, Democrats and Republicans, Socialists and individualists, all hold the State responsible for ensuring conditions of stable and full employment through public works and relief schemes, tax policies and other instruments of public policy; it is expected by the community to provide minimum standards of living, housing, labor conditions and social insurance. While there is controversy on the degree of public controls and the socialisation of industries and public utilities, some degree of public operation or control of business is recognized by all major parties as necessary, and practiced in all modern States. In Britain, as in Australia, France, Sweden or India, not to speak of the Soviet Union, a number of important public utilities, such as electricity, forestry and transport, are run by the government or by State-controlled corporations. The Federal Government and other public authorities in the United States control a vast proportion of the generation of electric power, harbour facilities and other public utilities. Public housing programmes and social insurance schemes, farm support and other subsidy schemes have been enacted to an increasing extent.

Technical facts and a gradual change in the public philosophy thus combine to effect a drastic and organic change in the relation between lawmaking and social evolution. . . .

Public opinion on vital social issues constantly expresses itself not only through the elected representatives in the legislative assemblies, but through public discussion in press, radio, public lectures, pressure groups and, on a more sophisticated level, through scientific and professional associations, universities and a multitude of other channels.

Because of this constant interaction between the articulation of public opinion and the legislative process, the tension between the legal and the social norm can seldom be too great. It is not possible in a democratic system to impose a law on an utterly hostile community. But, a strong social ground-swell sooner or later compels legal action. Between these two extremes there is a great variety of the patterns of challenge and response. On the one hand, the law may at length, and tardily, respond to an irresistible tide of social habit or opinion. Such is the case with the gradual enlargement of divorce grounds in the great majority of non-Catholic Western countries—either through the addition of new divorce grounds (cruelty, incompatibility, etc.) or the judicial extension of existing grounds for divorce or annulment (e.g., annulment for fraud in the State of New York). The extension of legitimate divorce is a response to the increasing freedom of the movement of married women in modern Western society, a loosening of religious ties and social taboos, and the development of social habits which lead to the dissolution of a vastly increased number of marriages, with or without the sanction of law. Here the alternative for the legislator is to permit an increasing gap between legal theory and social practice to develop, or to respond to an overwhelming change in the social facts of life. . . .

We have seen that, in a democratic system of State organization, there is a great variety of interactions between social evolution and legal change. The stimulus may come from a variety of sources, some of which have been briefly surveyed. There may be the slowly growing pressure of changed patterns and norms of social life, creating an increasing gap between the facts of life and the law, to which the latter must eventually respond. There may be the sudden imperious demand of a national emergency, for a redistribution of natural resources or a new standard of social justice. There may be a far-sighted initiative of a small group of individuals, slowly moulding official opinion until the time is ripe for action. There may be a technical injustice or inconsistency of the law demanding correction. There may be a new scientific development calling for new forms of legal evidence (such as acceptance of blood-group tests for the negative proof of paternity).

The Law responds in various ways, too. The speed and manner of its response is usually proportionate to the degree of social pressure. It is also influenced by the constitutional structure. But circumstances and personalities may hasten or retard the response. In the sphere of "political law" or where a new status is created, legislative action is required. In other fields, there is a give and take between legislative and judicial remedial action in part determined by the subject-matter but in part by the changing and diverse attitudes of legislators and judges.

The Theory of Authority

CHESTER I. BARNARD

The Source of Authority

If it is true that all complex organizations consist of aggregations of unit organizations and have grown only from unit organizations, we may reasonably postulate that, whatever the nature of authority, it is inherent in the simple organization unit; and that a correct theory of authority must be consistent with what is essentially true of these unit organizations. We shall, therefore, regard the observations which we can make of the actual conditions as at first a source for discovering what is essential in elementary and simple organizations.

Now a most significant fact of general observation relative to authority is the extent to which it is ineffective in specific instances. It is so ineffective that the violation of authority is accepted as a matter of course and its implications are not considered. It is true that we are sometimes appalled at the extent of major criminal activities; but we pass over very lightly the universal violations, particularly of sumptuary laws, which are as "valid" as any others. Even clauses of constitutions and statutes carrying them "into effect," such as the Eighteenth Amendment, are violated in wholesale degrees.

Violation of law is not, however, peculiar to our own country. I observed recently in a totalitarian state under a dictator, where personal liberty is supposed to be at a minimum and arbitrary authority at a maximum, many violations of positive law or edict, some of them open and on a wide scale; and I was reliably informed of others.

Nor is this condition peculiar to the authority of the state. It is likewise true of the authority of churches. The Ten Commandments and the prescriptions

---

and prohibitions of religious authority are repeatedly violated by those who profess to acknowledge their formal authority.

These observations do not mean that all citizens are lawless and defy authority; nor that all Christians are godless or their conduct unaffected by the tenets of their faith. It is obvious that to a large extent citizens are governed; and that the conduct of Christians is substantially qualified by the prescriptions of their churches. What is implied is merely that which specific laws will be obeyed or disobeyed by the individual citizen are decided by him under the specific conditions pertinent. This is what we mean when we refer to individual responsibility. It implies that which prescriptions of the church will be disobeyed by the individual are determined by him at a given time and place. This is what we mean by moral responsibility. . . .

We may leave the secondary stages of this analysis for later consideration. What we derive from it is an approximate definition of authority for our purpose: Authority is the character of a communication (order) in a formal organization by virtue of which it is accepted by a contributor to or "member" of the organization as governing the action he contributes; that is, as governing or determining what he does or is not to do so far as the organization is concerned. According to this definition, authority involves two aspects: first, the subjective, the personal, the *accepting* of a communication as authoritative, the aspects which I shall present in this section; and, second, the objective aspect—the character in the communication by virtue of which it is accepted—which I present in the second section, "The System of Coördination."

If a directive communication is accepted by one to whom it is addressed, its authority for him is confirmed or established. It is admitted as the basis of action. Disobedience of such a communication is a denial of its authority for him. Therefore, under this definition the decision as to whether an order has authority or not lies with the persons to whom it is addressed, and does not reside in "persons of authority" or those who issue these orders. . . .

Our definition of authority no doubt will appear to many, whose eyes are fixed only on enduring organizations, to be a platform of chaos. And so it is—exactly so in the preponderance of attempted organizations. They fail because they can maintain no authority, that is, they cannot secure sufficient contributions of personal efforts to be effective or cannot induce them on terms that are efficient. In the last analysis the authority fails because the individuals in sufficient numbers regard the burden involved in accepting necessary orders as changing the balance of advantage against their interest, and they withdraw or withhold the indispensable contributions.

We must not rest our definition, however, on general opinion. The necessity of the assent of the individual to establish authority *for him* is inescapable. A person can and will accept a communication as authoritative only when four conditions simultaneously obtain: (1) he can and does understand the communication; (2) *at the time of his decision* he believes that it is not inconsistent with the purpose of the organization; (3) *at the time of his decision,* he believes it to be compatible with his personal interest as a whole; and (4) he is able mentally and physically to comply with it.

1. A communication that cannot be understood *can* have no authority. An order issued, for example, in a language not intelligible to the recipient is no order at all—no one would so regard it. Now, many orders are exceedingly

difficult to understand. They are often necessarily stated in general terms, and the persons who issued them could not themselves apply them under many conditions. Until interpreted they have no meaning. The recipient either must disregard them or merely do anything in the hope that this is compliance.

Hence, a considerable part of administrative work consists in the interpretation and reinterpretation of orders in their application to concrete circumstances that were not or could not be taken into account initially.

2. A communication believed by the recipient to be incompatible with the purpose of the organization, as he understands it, could not be accepted. Action would be frustrated by cross purposes. The most common practical example is that involved in conflicts of orders. They are not rare. An intelligent person will deny the authority of that one which contradicts the purpose of the effort as *he* understands it. In extreme cases many individuals would be virtually paralyzed by conflicting orders. They would be literally unable to comply—for example, an employee of a water system ordered to blow up an essential pump, or soldiers ordered to shoot their own comrades. I suppose all experienced executives know that when it is necessary to issue orders that will appear to the recipients to be contrary to the main purpose, especially as exemplified in prior habitual practice, it is usually necessary and always advisable, if practicable, to explain or demonstrate why the appearance of conflict is an illusion. Otherwise the orders are likely not to be executed, or to be executed inadequately.

3. If a communication is believed to involve a burden that destroys the net advantage of connection with the organization, there no longer would remain a net inducement to the individual to contribute to it. The existence of a net inducement is the only reason for accepting *any* order as having authority. Hence, if such an order is received it must be disobeyed (evaded in the more usual cases) as utterly inconsistent with personal motives that are the basis of accepting any orders at all. Cases of voluntary resignation from all sorts of organizations are common for this sole reason. Malingering and intentional lack of dependability are the more usual methods.

4. If a person is unable to comply with an order, obviously it must be disobeyed, or, better, disregarded. To order a man who cannot swim to swim a river is a sufficient case. Such extreme cases are not frequent; but they occur. The more usual case is to order a man to do things only a little beyond his capacity; but a little impossible is still impossible.

Naturally the reader will ask: How is it possible to secure such important and enduring coöperation as we observe if in principle and in fact the determination of authority lies with the subordinate individual? It is possible because the decisions of individuals occur under the following conditions: (1) orders that are deliberately issued in enduring organizations usually comply with the four conditions mentioned above; (2) there exists a "zone of indifference" in each individual within which orders are acceptable without conscious questioning of their authority; (3) the interests of the persons who contribute to an organization as a group result in the exercise of an influence on the subject, or on the attitude of the individual, that maintains a certain stability of this zone of indifference.

1. There is no principle of executive conduct better established in good organizations than that orders will not be issued that cannot or will not be obeyed. Executives and most persons of experience who have thought about it know that to do so destroys authority, discipline, and morale. For reasons to be stated shortly,

this principle cannot ordinarily be formally admitted, or at least cannot be professed. When it appears necessary to issue orders which are initially or apparently unacceptable, either careful preliminary education, or persuasive efforts, or the prior offering of effective inducements will be made, so that the issue will not be raised, the denial of authority will not occur, and orders will be obeyed. It is generally recognized that those who least understand this fact—newly appointed minor or "first line" executives—are often guilty of "disorganizing" their groups for this reason, as do experienced executives who lose self-control or become unbalanced by a delusion of power or for some other reason. Inexperienced persons take literally the current notions of authority and are then said "not to know how to use authority" or "to abuse authority." Their superiors often profess the same beliefs about authority in the abstract, but their successful practice is easily observed to be inconsistent with their professions.

2. The phrase "zone of indifference" may be explained as follows: If all the orders for actions reasonably practicable be arranged in the order of their acceptability to the person affected, it may be conceived that there are a number which are clearly unacceptable, that is, which certainly will not be obeyed; there is another group somewhat more or less on the neutral line, that is, either barely acceptable or barely unacceptable; and a third group unquestionably acceptable. This last group lies within the "zone of indifference." The person affected will accept orders lying within this zone and is relatively indifferent as to what the order is so far as the question of authority is concerned. Such an order lies within the range that in a general way was anticipated at time of undertaking the connection with the organization. For example, if a soldier enlists, whether voluntarily or not, in an army in which the men are ordinarily moved about within a certain broad region, it is a matter of indifference whether the order be to go to A or B, C or D, and so on; and goings to A, B, C, D, etc., are in the zone of indifference.

The zone of indifference will be wider or narrower depending upon the degree to which the inducements exceed the burdens and sacrifices which determine the individual's adhesion to the organization. It follows that the range of orders that will be accepted will be very limited among those who are barely induced to contribute to the system.

3. Since the efficiency of organization is affected by the degree to which individuals assent to orders, denying the authority of an organization communication is a threat to the interests of all individuals who derive a net advantage from their connection with the organization, unless the orders are unacceptable to them also. Accordingly, at any given time there is among most of the contributors an active personal interest in the maintenance of the authority of all orders which to them are within the zone of indifference. The maintenance of this interest is largely a function of informal organization. Its expression goes under the names of "public opinion," "organization opinion," "feeling in the ranks," "group attitude," etc. Thus the common sense of the community informally arrived at affects the attitude of individuals, and makes them, as individuals, loath to question authority that is within or near the zone of indifference. The formal statement of this common sense is the fiction that authority comes down from above, from the general to the particular. This fiction merely establishes a presumption among individuals in favor of the acceptability of orders from

superiors, enabling them to avoid making issues of such orders without incurring a sense of personal subserviency or a loss of personal or individual status with their fellows.

Thus the contributors are willing to maintain the authority of communications because, where care is taken to see that only acceptable communications in general are issued, most of them fall within the zone of personal indifference; and because communal sense influences the motives of most contributors most of the time. The practical instrument of this sense is the fiction of superior authority, which makes it possible normally to treat a personal question impersonally.

The fiction[1] of superior authority is necessary for two main reasons:

1. It is the process by which the individual delegates upward, or to the organization, responsibility for what is an organization decision—an action which is depersonalized by the fact of its coördinate character. This means that if an instruction is disregarded, an executive's risk of being wrong must be accepted, a risk that the individual cannot and usually will not take unless in fact his position is at least as good as that of another with respect to correct appraisal of the relevant situation. Most persons are disposed to grant authority because they dislike the personal responsibility which they otherwise accept, especially when they are not in a good position to accept it. The practical difficulties in the operation of organization seldom lie in the excessive desire of individuals to assume responsibility for the organization action of themselves or others, but rather lie in the reluctance to take responsibility for their own actions in organization.

2. The fiction gives impersonal notice that what is at stake is the good of the organization. If objective authority is flouted for arbitrary or merely temperamental reasons, if, in other words, there is deliberate attempt to twist an organization requirement to personal advantage, rather than properly to safeguard a substantial personal interest, then there is a deliberate attack on the organization itself. To remain outside an organization is not necessarily to be more than not friendly or not interested. To fail in an obligation intentionally is an act of hostility. This no organization can permit; and it must respond with punitive action if it can, even to the point of incarcerating or executing the culprit. This is rather generally the case where a person has agreed in advance in general what he will do. Leaving an organization in the lurch is not often tolerable.

The correctness of what has been said above will perhaps appear most probable from a consideration of the difference between executive action in emergency and that under "normal" conditions. In times of war the disciplinary atmosphere of an army is intensified—it is rather obvious to all that its success and the safety of its members are dependent upon it. In other organizations, abruptness of command is not only tolerated in times of emergency, but expected, and the lack of it often would actually be demoralizing. It is the sense of the justification which lies in the obvious situation which regulates the exercise of the veto by the final authority which lies at the bottom. This is a commonplace

[1] The word "fiction" is used because from the standpoint of logical construction it merely explains overt acts. Either as a superior officer or as a subordinate, however, I know nothing that I actually regard as more "real" than "authority."

of executive experience, though it is not a commonplace of conversation about it.[2]

The System of Coördination

Up to this point we have devoted our attention to the subjective aspect of authority. The executive, however, is predominantly occupied not with this subjective aspect, which is fundamental, but with the objective character of a communication which induces acceptance.

Authority has been defined in part as a "character of a communication in a formal organization." A "superior" is not in our view an authority nor does he have authority strictly speaking; nor is a communication authoritative except when it is an effort or action of organization. This is what we mean when we say that individuals are able to exercise authority only when they are acting "officially," a principle well established in law, and generally in secular and religious practice. Hence the importance ascribed to time, place, dress, ceremony, and authentication of a communication to establish its official character. These practices confirm the statement that authority relates to a communication "in a formal organization." There often occur occasions of compulsive power of individuals and of hostile groups; but authority is always concerned with something *within* a definitely organized system. Current usage conforms to the definition in this respect. The word "authority" is seldom employed except where formal organization connection is stated or implied (unless, of course, the reference is obviously figurative).

These circumstances arise from the fact that the character of authority in organization communications lies in the *potentiality of assent* of those to whom they are sent. Hence, they are only sent to contributors or "members" of the organization. Since all authoritative communications are official and relate only to organization action, they have no meaning to those whose actions are not included within the coöperative system. This is clearly in accord with the common understanding. The laws of one country have no authority for citizens of another, except under special circumstances. Employers do not issue directions to employees of other organizations. Officials would appear incompetent who issued orders to those outside their jurisdiction.

A communication has the presumption of authority when it originates at sources of organization information—a communications center—better than individual sources. It loses this presumption, however, if not within the scope or field of this center. The presumption is also lost if the communication shows an absence of adjustment to the actual situation which confronts the recipient of it.

Thus men impute authority to communications from superior positions, provided they are reasonably consistent with advantages of scope and perspective

---

[2]It will be of interest to quote a statement which has appeared since these lines were written, in a pamphlet entitled "Business—Well on the Firing Line" (No. 9 in the series "What Helps Business Helps You," in *Nation's Business*). It reads in part: "Laws don't create Teamplay. It is not called into play by law. For every written rule there are a thousand unwritten rules by which the course of business is guided, which govern the millions of daily transactions of which business consists. These rules are not applied from the top down, by arbitrary authority. They grow out of actual practice—from the bottom up. They are based upon mutual understanding and compromise, the desire to achieve common ends and further the common good. They are observed *voluntarily,* because they have the backing of experience and common sense."

that are credited to those positions. This authority is to a considerable extent independent of the personal ability of the incumbent of the position. It is often recognized that though the incumbent may be of limited personal ability his advice may be superior solely by reason of the advantage of position. This is the *authority of position.*

But it is obvious that some men have superior ability. Their knowledge and understanding regardless of position command respect. Men impute authority to what they say in an organization for this reason only. This is the *authority of leadership.* When the authority of leadership is combined with the authority of position, men who have an established connection with an organization generally will grant authority, accepting orders far outside the zone of indifference. The confidence engendered may even make compliance an inducement in itself.

Nevertheless, the determination of authority remains with the individual. Let these "positions" of authority in fact show ineptness, ignorance of conditions, failure to communicate what ought to be said, or let leadership fail (chiefly by its concrete action) to recognize implicitly its dependence upon the essential character of the relationship of the individual to the organization, and the authority if tested disappears.

This objective authority is only maintained if the positions or leaders continue to be adequately informed. In very rare cases persons possessing great knowledge, insight, or skill have this adequate information without occupying executive position. What they say ought to be done or ought not to be done will be accepted. But this is usually personal advice at the risk of the taker. Such persons have influence rather than authority. In most cases genuine leaders who give advice concerning organized efforts are required to accept positions of responsibility; for knowledge of the applicability of their special knowledge or judgment to concrete *organization* action, not to abstract problems, is essential to the worth of what they say as a basis of organization authority. In other words, they have an organization personality, as distinguished from their individual personality, commensurate with the influence of their leadership. The common way to state this is that there cannot be authority without corresponding responsibility. A more exact expression would be that objective authority cannot be imputed to persons in organization positions unless subjectively they are dominated by the organization as respects their decisions.

It may be said, then, that the maintenance of objective authority adequate to support the fiction of superior authority and able to make the zone of indifference an actuality depends upon the operation of the system of communication in the organization. The function of this system is to supply adequate information to the positions of authority and adequate facilities for the issuance of orders. To do so it requires commensurate capacities in those able to be leaders. High positions that are not so supported have weak authority, as do strong men in minor positions.

Thus authority depends upon a coöperative personal attitude of individuals on the one hand; and the system of communication in the organization on the other. Without the latter, the former cannot be maintained. The most devoted adherents of an organization will quit it, if its system results in inadequate, contradictory, inept orders, so that they cannot know who is who, what is what, or have the sense of effective coördination.

This system of communication, or its maintenance, is a primary or essential continuing problem of a formal organization. Every other practical question of effectiveness or efficiency—that is, of the factors of survival—depends upon it. In technical language the system of communication of which we are now speaking is often known as the "lines of authority."

It has already been shown [elsewhere] that the requirements of communication determine the size of unit organizations, the grouping of units, the grouping of groups of unit organizations. We may now consider the controlling factors in the character of the communication system as a system of objective authority.

1. The first is that *channels of communication should be definitely known.* The language in which this principle is ordinarily stated is, "The lines of authority must be definitely established." The method of doing so is by making official appointments known; by assigning each individual to his position; by general announcements; by organization charts; by educational effort, and most of all by habituation, that is, by securing as much permanence of system as is practicable. Emphasis is laid either upon the position, or upon the persons; but usually the fixing of authority is made both to positions and, less emphatically, to persons.

2. Next, we may say that *objective authority requires a definite formal channel of communication to every member of an organization.* In ordinary language this means "everyone must report to someone" (communication in one direction) and "everyone must be subordinate to someone" (communication in the other direction). In other words, in formal organizations everyone must have definite formal relationship to the organization.[3]

3. Another factor is that *the line of communication must be as direct or short as possible.* This may be explained as follows: Substantially all formal communication is verbal (written or oral). Language as a vehicle of communication is limited and susceptible of misunderstanding. Much communication is necessarily without preparation. Even communications that are carefully prepared require interpretation. Moreover, communications are likely to be in more general terms the more general—that is, the higher—the position. It follows that something may be lost or added by transmission at each stage of the process, especially when communication is oral, or when at each stage there is combination of several communications. Moreover, when communications go from high positions down they often must be made more specific as they proceed; and when in the reverse direction, usually more general. In addition, the speed of communication, other things equal, will be less the greater the number of centers through which it passes. Accordingly, the shorter the line the greater the speed and the less the error.

How important this factor is may be indicated by the remarkable fact that in great complex organizations the number of levels of communication is not much larger than in smaller organizations. In most organizations consisting of the services of one or two hundred men the levels of communication will be from three to five. In the Army the levels are: President, (Secretary of War),

---

[3]In some types of organizations it is not unusual, however, for one person to report to and to be subordinate to two or three "superiors," in which case the functions of the superiors are defined and are mutually exclusive in principle.

General, Major-General, Brigadier-General, Colonel, Major, Captain, Lieutenant, Sergeant, men—that is, nine or ten. In the Bell Telephone System, with over 300,000 working members, the number is eight to ten.[4] A similar shortness of the line of communication is noteworthy in the Catholic Church viewed from the administrative standpoint.

Many organization practices or inventions are used to accomplish this end, depending upon the purpose and technical conditions. Briefly, these methods are: The use of expanded executive organizations at each stage; the use of the staff department (technical, expert, advisory); the division of executive work into functional bureaus; and processes of delegating responsibility with automatic coördination through regular conference procedures, committees for special temporary functions, etc.

4. Another factor is that, in principle, *the complete line of communication should usually be used.* By this is meant that a communication from the head of an organization to the bottom should pass through every stage of the line of authority. This is due to the necessity of avoiding conflicting communications (in either direction) which might (and would) occur if there were any "jumping of the line" of organization. It is also necessary because of the need of interpretation, and to maintain responsibility.[5]

5. Again, the *competence of the persons serving as communication centers, that is, officers, supervisory heads, must be adequate.* The competence required is that of more and more *general* ability with reference to the work of the entire organization the more central the office of communication and the larger the organization. For the function of the center of communication in an organization is to translate incoming communications concerning external conditions, the progress of activity, successes, failures, difficulties, dangers, into outgoing communications in terms of new activities, preparatory steps, etc., all shaped according to the ultimate as well as the immediate purposes to be served. There is accordingly required more or less mastery of the technologies involved, of the capabilities of the personnel, of the informal organization situation, of the character and status of the subsidiary organizations, of the principles of action relative to purpose, of the interpretation of environmental factors, and a power of discrimination between communications that can possess authority because they are recognizably compatible with *all* the pertinent conditions and those which will not possess authority because they will not or cannot be accepted.

It is a fact, I think, that we hardly nowadays expect individual personal ability adequate to positional requirements of communication in modern large-scale organization. The limitations of individuals as respects time and energy alone preclude such personal ability, and the complexity of the technologies or other special knowledge involved make it impossible. For these reasons each major center of communication is itself organized, sometimes quite elaborately. The immediate staff of the executive (commanding officer), consisting of deputies, or chief clerks, or adjutants, or auxiliaries with their assistants, constitute an executive unit of organization only one member of which is perhaps an "executive," that is, occupies the *position* of an authority; and the technical matters

[4] Disregarding the corporate aspects of the organization, and not including board of directors.

[5] These by no means exhaust the considerations. The necessity of maintaining personal prestige of executives as an *inducement to them* to function is on the whole an important additional reason.

are assigned to staff departments or organizations of experts. Such staff departments often are partly "field" departments in the sense that they directly investigate or secure information on facts or conditions external to the organizations; but in major part in most cases they digest and translate information from the field, and prepare the plans, orders, etc., for transmission. In this capacity they are advisory or adjutant to the executives. In practice, however, these assistants have the function of semi-formal advice under regulated conditions to the organizations as a whole. In this way, both the formal channels and the informal organization are supplemented by intermediate processes.

In some cases the executive (either chief or some subordinate executive) may be not a person but a board, a legislature, a committee. I know of no important organizations, except some churches and some absolute governments in which the highest objective authority is not lodged in an *organized* executive group, that is, a "highest" unit of organization.

6. Again, *the line of communication should not be interrupted during the time when the organization is to function.* Many organizations (factories, stores) function intermittently, being closed or substantially so during the night, Sundays, etc. Others, such as army, police, railroad systems, telephone systems, never cease to operate. During the times when organizations are at work, in principle the line of authority must never be broken; and practically this is almost, if not quite, literally true in many cases. This is one of the reasons which may be given for the great importance attached to hereditary succession in states, and for the elaborate provision that is made in most organizations (except possibly small "personal" organizations) for the temporary filling of offices automatically during incapacity or absence of incumbents. These provisions emphasize the non-personal and communication character of organization authority, as does the persistent emphasis upon the *office* rather than the *man* that is a matter of indoctrination of many organizations, especially those in which "discipline" is an important feature.

The necessity for this is not merely that specific communications cannot otherwise be attended to. It is at least equally that the *informal* organization disintegrates very quickly if the formal "line of authority" is broken. In organization parlance, "politics" runs riot. Thus, if an office were vacant, but the fact were not known, an organization might function for a considerable time without serious disturbance, except in emergency. But if known, it would quickly become disorganized.

7. The final factor I shall mention is that *every communication should be authenticated.* This means that the person communicating must be known actually to occupy the "position of authority" concerned; that the position includes the type of communication concerned—that is, it is "within its authority"; and that it actually is an authorized communication from this office. The process of authentication in all three respects varies in different organizations under different conditions and for different positions. The practice is undergoing rapid changes in the modern technique, but the principles remain the same. Ceremonials of investiture, inaugurations, swearing-in, general orders of appointment, induction, and introduction, are all essentially appropriate methods of making known who actually fills a position and what the position includes as authority. In order that these *positions* may function it is often necessary that the filling of them should be dramatized, an essential process to the creation

of authority *at the bottom,* where only it can be fundamentally—that is, it is essential to inculcate the "sense of organization." This is merely stating that it is essential to "organization loyalty and solidarity" as it may be otherwise expressed. Dignifying the superior position is an important method of dignifying *all* connection with organization, a fact which has been well learned in both religious and political organizations where great attention to the subjective aspects of the "membership" is the rule.

This statement of the principles of communication systems of organizations from the viewpoint of the maintenance of objective authority has necessarily been in terms of complex organizations, since in a simple unit organization the concrete applications of these principles are fused. The principles are with difficulty isolated under simple conditions. Thus, as a matter of course, in unit organizations the channels of communication are known, indeed usually obvious; they are definite; they are the shortest possible; the only lines of authority are complete lines; there is little question of authentication. The doubtful points in unit organization are the competence of the leader, never to be taken for granted even in simple organizations; and whether he is functioning when the organization is in operation. Yet as a whole the adequately balanced maintenance of these aspects of simple leadership is the basis of objective authority in the unit organization, as the maintenance of the more formal and observable manifestations of the same aspects is the basis of authority in the complex organizations.

Authority: Its Nature and Motives

HERBERT A. SIMON
DONALD W. SMITHBURG
VICTOR A. THOMPSON

From a psychological standpoint the exercise of authority involves a relationship between two or more persons. On the one side we have a person who makes proposals for the action of others. On the other side we have a person who accepts the proposals—who "obeys" them. Now a person may accept another's proposals under three different sets of circumstances:

1. He may examine the merits of the proposal, and, on the basis of its merits become convinced that he should carry it out. We shall exclude such instances of acceptance from our notion of authority, although some writers on administration have called this the "authority of ideas."
2. He may carry out the proposals without being fully, or even partially, convinced of its merits. In fact he may not examine the merits of the proposal at all.

3. He may carry out the proposal even though he is convinced it is wrong—wrong either in terms of personal values or of organizational values or both.

We will treat both the second and third cases as instances of the acceptance of authority. Of course in any actual instance all three of the "pure types" of acceptance listed above may be combined in various proportions. In actual practice authority is almost always liberally admixed with persuasion. . . .

Because the person who accepts proposals may do so for a variety of motives, there will be seen in any organization a number of different types of authority relationship, corresponding to these different motives for acceptance. . . .

People accept the proposals of persons in whom they have great confidence. In any organization there are some individuals who, because of past performance, general reputation, or other factors, have great influence or authority. Their proposals will often be accepted without analysis as to their wisdom. Even when the suggestions of such a person are not accepted, they will be rejected reluctantly and only because a stronger authority contradicts them.

The authority of confidence may be limited to a special area of competence in which a person has acquired a reputation.

. . . The willingness to accept authority on the basis of confidence, both within and outside organizations, goes even one step further. Not only is the layman generally unable to judge the quality of the advice he is getting from the specialist, but he often is in no position to judge the competence of the specialist, except on the basis of certain superficial and formal criteria that give the specialist his *status.*

. . . [T]here are at least two kinds of status, which may be called *functional status* and *hierarchical status.* It is with functional status that we are concerned at the moment. A person has functional status in a particular area of knowledge when his decisions and recommendations in that area are accepted as more or less authoritative.

In the established professions, status is generally conferred on the basis of standards developed by the profession itself. The M.D. degree is conferred on the young doctor by the medical profession (acting through an "accredited" medical school). Law and engineering degrees and the certificate of the public accountant are awarded in much the same way. In other cases, job experience in a particular field confers functional status in that field. A person with long experience in a professional position in the Interstate Commerce Commission may acquire status as a transportation economist.

. . . Confidence can be a powerful support for hierarchical as well as for nonhierarchical authority. A subordinate will much more readily obey a command of a superior if he has confidence in the intelligence and judgment of that superior or if he believes that the superior has knowledge of the situation not available to himself.

In particular, where a problem requiring decision affects the work of several units in an organization, the superior who has hierarchical authority in the formal organization plan over all the units involved is often accepted as the person best located—because he has the "whole picture"—to make the decision. Hence, the coordinating functions that are commonly performed by those in hierarchical authority are based, in part at least, upon the authority of confidence—upon the belief of subordinates that the superior is the best informed about the situation as a whole. . . .

The most generally recognized weapon of the superior is the sanction—the ability of the superior to attach pleasant or unpleasant consequences to the actions of the subordinate.

. . . The relationship of the authority of sanctions with the organizational hierarchy can be viewed from a more general standpoint. When a person joins an organization he is accepting a system of relationships that restricts his individuality or his freedom of action. He is willing to do so because he feels that, in spite of the organizational restraints, being a member of the organization is preferable to other alternatives available to him. To continue as a member of the organization, he must continue, to some extent, to abide by the complex of procedures which constitutes the organization. Although, increasingly, the power to discharge an employee is not lodged in any specific superior (because of merit systems, central personnel offices, labor unions, etc.), nevertheless, this power resides somewhere in the organization, being, in fact, one of its working procedures. The sanctions discussed in this section are increasingly *organization* sanctions, brought into play through the working procedures of the organization, and not the special prerogatives or powers of *individual superiors*. . . .

For the most part the authority of sanction rests on the behavior responses that are induced by the *possibility* that a sanction may be applied. An organization member is seldom presented with an ultimatum "to do so and so or suffer the consequences." Rather, he anticipates the consequences of continual insubordination or failure to please the person or persons who have the ability to apply sanctions to him, and this anticipation acts as a constant motivation without expressed threats from any person. . . .

There is another reason why employees accept the proposals of other organization members—a reason less rationalistic but probably more important than the desire to avoid the organization sanctions discussed above. People accept "legitimate" authority because they feel that they *ought* to go along with the "rules of the game."

. . . [T]hroughout their development to maturity and after, people are educated in the beliefs, values, or mores of society. They learn what they ought to do and what they ought not to do. One of the values with which they are indoctrinated is that a person should play according to the rules of the game. This ethic is acquired very early. When a child enters a ball game in the sand lot he does not expect the game to be altered at various points to suit his convenience. Rather he expects to adjust his behavior to the rules of the game. Although there may be disputes as to what the rule is on some point, once this is established, the proposition that he should abide by the rule is unquestioned.

Likewise, when people enter organizations most of them feel that they ought to abide by the rules of the game—the working procedures of the organization. These working procedures define how the work will be done; how working problems will be solved when they arise; how conflicts will be settled. They prescribe that on such and such matters the individual will accept the suggestions of this or that person or organization; secure the advice of such and such unit; clear his work with so and so; work on matters that come to him in such and such a way; etc.

The working procedures of an organization prescribe that the individual member will accept the proposals of other members in matters assigned to them. This acceptance is one of the rules of the game which he feels he should abide by. Thus, individuals in organizations also accept the authority of other persons because they think they *ought* to accept it.

. . . The working relationships in an organization designated by the term "hierarchy" constitute a particular organization procedure for handling the authority of legitimacy. Acceptance of the working procedures of an organization by a member includes acceptance of the obligation to go along with the proposals of an hierarchical superior, at least within a limit of toleration—the "area of acceptance." Thus, whether the other reasons for obedience are operating or not (confidence, identification, or sanctions), organization members will feel that they ought to obey their superiors. Legitimacy is one of the most important sources of the authority of the hierarchical superior.

The feeling that hierarchical authority is legitimate is immensely strengthened by previous social conditioning. Hierarchical behavior is an institutionalized behavior that all organization members bring to the organization with them. Like the players in the Oberammergau Passion Play who begin to learn their roles in early childhood, "inferiors" obey "superiors" because they have been taught to do so from infancy, beginning with the parent-child relationship and running through almost constant experience with social and organizational hierarchies until death brings graduation from this particular social schooling. Hierarchical behavior involves an inferior-superior role-taking of persons well versed in their roles. "Inferiors" feel that they ought to obey "superiors"; "superiors" feel that they ought to be obeyed.

Our society is extremely hierarchical. Success is generally interpreted in terms of hierarchical preferment. Social position and financial rewards are closely related to hierarchical preferment, as also are education and even perhaps romantic attainment. Advancement up a hierarchy is generally considered a sign of moral worth, of good character, of good stewardship, of social responsibility, and of the possession of superior intellectual qualities.

Hierarchy receives a tremendous emphasis in nearly all organizations. This is so because hierarchy is a procedure that requires no training, no indoctrination, no special inducements. It rests almost entirely on "pre-entry" training—a training so thorough that few other organization procedures can ever compete with it. Furthermore, hierarchy is a great simplification. . . .

The Source of Managerial Authority

CYRIL J. O'DONNELL

For four decades none of the writers in the management field inquired into the nature of authority, not even into its source. This is not strange, of course, when one considers that their main interest was in the specialization of enterprise tasks. But it is significant that none seemed to think that the right of managers to give orders would be questioned. Seeing all about them that business men, in fact, did give orders and that they were generally obeyed, that the state promulgated laws and that these were generally obeyed also—seeing these things, the facts seemed to point to acceptance of the idea that the right to issue orders must certainly rest with the business managers. Indeed, if the question had been put to them they probably would have agreed with Petersen and Plowman, who state that:

> Under our democratic form of government the right upon which managerial authority is based has its source in the Constitution of the United States through the guaranty of private property. Since the Constitution is the creature of the people, subject to amendment and modification by the will of the people, it follows that society, through government, is the source from which authority flows to ownership and thence to management. . . .[1]

First among the writers in the field of management theory to question this accepted doctrine was Chester I. Barnard, Harvard graduate, successful top manager of large-scale enterprises, and the author of *The Functions of the Executive.*[2] Apparently reading widely in the fields of philosophy and psychology, and being much impressed by the political theory of Harold Laski, Barnard postulates that a correct theory of authority must be consistent with the facts and then proceeds to enumerate several instances wherein the members of an organization have refused to obey persons in authority. On the basis of these "facts" he states that ". . . the decision as to whether an order has authority or not lies with the persons to whom it is addressed, and does not reside in 'persons of authority' or those who issue these orders." This concept means, if anything, that the source of authority lies in the members of an organization, that they confer authority upon their superior by deigning to accept and act upon commands, that they may, if they wish, decide to accept orders seriatim, and that they may withdraw conferred authority at any time by refusing to obey the commands of their superiors.

Reprinted by permission from the *Political Science Quarterly,* Vol. 67, No. 4 (December 1952), pp. 573–88.

[1] Elmore Petersen and E. Grosvenor Plowman, *Business Organization and Management* (Chicago, 1949), p. 62. This is a very restricted view of the source of authority.

[2] Cambridge, 1950. Succeeding quotations from Barnard are from his chapter xii.

. . . Robert Tannenbaum[3] dubs as "formal" the authority of a manager when it is viewed as "originating at the top of an organization hierarchy and flowing downward therein through the process of delegation." He thinks of "informal" authority as a right conferred upon a manager by his subordinates. Thus, informal authority is equated with Barnard's complete concept. But Tannenbaum, as a practical matter, does not actually differ from Barnard because he says:

> The real source of the authority possessed by an individual lies in the acceptance of its exercise by those who are subject to it. It is the subordinates of an individual who determine the authority which he may wield. Formal authority is, in effect, nominal authority. It becomes real only when it is accepted.

In order to substantiate this conception of authority, Tannenbaum quotes approvingly from Barnard, Kardiner, Benne, and Simon. . . . And I may add that Selekman[4] simply cannot make up his mind on the subject so he says:

> It is true enough that the management executive must, directly or indirectly, obtain consent to his decisions from the men under him; the importance of such consent now receives ever-increasing recognition. Nonetheless, the manager still wields authority over his workers as of right—a right delegated to him by the owners of the business. . . .

Authority is the right to command or to act. It implies the possession of the power to coerce, for obviously if there were no way to enforce an order the enterprise would become disorganized and unable to achieve its purpose. To realize how clear this is, the reader should imagine what would happen in a business if workers failed to adhere to the opening and closing hours of work; if individual players on a football team decided to engage their opposites in competition at any time. . . .

Now, the *order* in organized behavior implies authority—the right to command coupled with the right to coerce. Malinowski is emphatic in saying that "submission to laws as well as the power to enforce laws and rules are indispensable in human behavior."[5] Otherwise, there will only be anarchy. West is of the opinion that

> *The prime requisite and firm creator of any community life is a law or order maintained by force.* For human nature is such that, in all its most necessary social relationships, it is subject to the permanent threat of the self-assertive impulse, which misinterprets facts, misjudges events, and then, through consequent self-justificatory passion, breaks the social bond, unless it be externally restrained. We may claim this as adequately confirmed. Nursery studies and family life confirm it. Social and natural history confirm it. Modern psychology confirms it. And finally, our common sense tends to

---

[3]Robert Tannenbaum, "Managerial Decision-Making," *The Journal of Business,* XXIII, 1 (January 1950).

[4]Benjamin M. Selekman, *Labor Relations and Human Relations* (New York, 1947), pp. 175–76.

[5]Bronislaw Malinowski, *Freedom and Civilization* (New York, 1944), p. 27.

> confirm it—for all others except ourselves, which is in itself a final confirmation. Individual, group or nation-state, we cannot judge our own cause. And if we try to do so, we shall be reduced again and again to fighting for a supposed 'right' against a supposed 'wrong,' for one set of illusions against another. . . .[6]

In the case of private business enterprise the authority relationships operate in much the same way. Americans have not deprived themselves of their common-law freedom to engage in business activity. It is true that elaborate safeguards for the rights of others have been spelled out in ordinance, rule, law and constitution, but within this framework anyone can engage in business as an individual proprietorship or on a partnership basis without special permission. Since corporations are legal persons created by law, their managers exercise authority which has reached them through the chain of delegation from the people to their constitution and thence through government to its creature. But whether a manager is operating an incorporated enterprise or not, his subordinates are obliged to obey his lawful orders, as long as the employer-employee relationship exists, because the right to command issues ultimately from the collective will of the people. Neither the individual subordinate nor the trade union to which he may belong is in a position to disobey those commands. . . .

[6] Ranyard West, *Conscience and Society* (London, 1942), p. 240.

Toward a Theory of Organizational Behavior

ROBERT PRESTHUS

During the recent past the analysis of organization has shifted from a preoccupation with structured rationality to an emphasis upon individual behavior. Much of this emphasis has been sociological, that is, it is concerned mainly with small groups and with the ways in which such groups shape the alignment and use of power in the organization. The following analysis attempts to add another dimension to this main drift by pulling together the insights of several social sciences into a general theory of organizational behavior. Such efforts seem required, however crude and abstract they may be at this early stage in the development of administrative science.

In line with Merton's plea for more attention to the interplay between bureaucratic structure and personality,[1] some psychological formulations are brought to bear upon two major variables, the total organizational situation and

Abridged from Robert Prestus, "Toward a Theory of Organizational Behavior," *Administrative Science Quarterly,* Vol. 3, No. 1 (June 1958), pp. 48–72. Reprinted by permission of the author and the *Administrative Science Quarterly.*

[1] Robert K. Merton, Bureaucratic Structure and Personality, *Social Forces,* 17 (1940), 560–568.

the individual. Such a framework seems well suited to the complexity of organizational behavior, which is the product of interaction among the whole culture, a given organization, and an individual personality which itself is the result of the genetic composition and unique experience of any given individual. In this context an organization may be viewed as a miniature society in which traditional social controls over the individual appear in sharp focus. The organization draws upon the accumulated learning and experience of the individual, who brings to it certain socially inculcated attitudes that encourage a satisfactory accommodation to the organization's major values and expectations. Obviously not all individuals achieve this kind of accommodation, but the vast majority do so at varying levels of identification and self-realization.

Without denying the influence of informal, small-group liaisons, we assume that individuals have several reference points other than their immediate work group, including the organization as a whole. This concept of differentiated reference foci is suggested by the dichotomy between "cosmopolitans" and "locals," between those whose loyalty is bound up with their own organization (locals) and those whose referential context is profession-wide and national (cosmopolitans).[2] Here we are concerned mainly with "locals" who tend to accommodate successfully. While our theory necessarily includes an "ambivalent" type who tends to reconcile inapposite adjustment by resignation, aggression, and withdrawal, this inquiry is directed toward those "upward-mobiles" and "indifferents" to whom the organizational bargain is either satisfactory or at least insufficiently unsatisfactory to provoke disengagement. The question thus becomes, What aspects of the dynamic interplay between the total organizational situation and the individual encourage these different kinds of accommodation? Part of the answer seems to lie in the individual's perception of the organization as a social instrument and in the ways that the organization engages the deep-seated attitudes of the individual toward authority.

In this general framework, organization is defined as a system of structured interpersonal relations, that is, individuals are differentiated in terms of authority, status, and role with the result that personal interaction is prescribed or "structured." Anticipated reactions tend to occur, while ambiguity and spontaneity are decreased. It is hypothesized that the resultant psychological field has exceptional influence upon learning and accommodation to the organization.[3] A related hypothesis is that behavior will tend to be more predictable in complex, structured organizations than in so-called voluntary associations. These assumptions reflect Harry Stack Sullivan's interpersonal theory of psychiatry and particularly his view that "the human organism is so extraordinarily adaptive that not only could the most fantastic social rules and regulations be lived up to, if they were properly inculcated in the young, but they would seem very natural and proper

---

[2]Cf. Alvin W. Gouldner, Cosmopolitans and Locals: Toward an Analysis of Latent Social Roles, *Administrative Science Quarterly,* 2 (Dec. 1957–March 1958), 281–306, 440–480.

[3]By "organization" I mean the ideal-typical bureaucratic model, characterized by large size, hierarchy, specialization, centralized formal power, and an orientation toward written rules and tradition as the main guides to behavior. Examples include a government bureau, a large university, an industrial concern with something over one thousand employees, an army command at the regimental level or above. Members of these organizations are usually selected on the basis of technical skill; typically, they view their vocation as a career, with clearly defined avenues. This model is highly idealized, of course, but perhaps no more so than the economist's "law" of supply and demand, which has proved quite useful for analytical purposes.

ways of life."[4] It would seem that the rational character and demands of the typical big organization will surely appear less than "fantastic" to its members.

According to Sullivan, personality is the result of a "self-system" worked out through successful (anxiety-reducing) accommodations to the wishes of successive authority figures, such as parents, teachers, supervisors, and so on. The theory of anxiety is central, since anxiety is the principal medium by which the individual is exposed to the values of those in authority. Sullivan's conclusions as to the significance of the anxiety-conformity-approval syndrome can be summed up as follows: "I believe it fairly safe to say that anybody and everybody devotes much of his lifetime and a great deal of his energy. . . . to avoiding more anxiety than he already has, and if possible, to getting rid of some of this anxiety."[5]

It is assumed here that anxiety is probably the most critical variable in organizational behavior, when such behavior is defined as an interpersonal process occurring in a highly structured environment. Such behavior is always associated with individual reactions to authority, which in turn are mediated by anxiety and the structure of the immediate interpersonal situation. It is important to add that anxiety occurs along a continuum, ranging from extreme, disorganizing fear to the natural uneasiness felt by most people in a strange situation. For our purposes, anxiety is defined as an unpleasant tension that, in Sullivan's terms, guides the development of the self-system, is present in some measure in all interpersonal relations, and is the main influence determining how such relations develop. This degree of tension may be called "adaptive anxiety" because in most cases it facilitates personal accommodation. In terms of organizational needs, such anxiety and the "security operations" that seek to overcome it are usually functional.

This is not to say that anxiety reduction is the *only* motive for accommodation. Individuals seek opportunities for joy, love, self-realization, and power, which are not necessarily tied to anxiety, although they may be. Certainly, because power in our society can usually be equated with the control of organized resources, organizations provide unusual opportunities to satisfy this drive. But for the majority such expansive states as deep emotional satisfaction, love, and self-realization are not usually obtainable within the organization, which instead tends to stifle the spontaneous, idiosyncratic satisfactions that individuals seek. The "professional mask," the pleasant detachment, the rivalry, and the anxiety that characterize interpersonal relations in big organizations are germane. For most of us, impersonality, limited discretion, built-in power inequities, and the fact that work often becomes a means of buying more meaningful off-the-job satisfactions suggest that less positive motives such as anxiety reduction warrant closer analysis.

Something may now be said about the relation of anxiety to learning. Anxiety is apparently a kind of free-floating dread that affects most interpersonal relations to some degree. Unlike fear which has objective referents, anxiety is often vague. Moreover, whereas fear usually relates to physical injury, anxiety relates to threats against personal esteem. But anxiety also has a positive role:

---

[4] H. S. Sullivan, *The Interpersonal Theory of Psychiatry* (New York, 1953), p. 6.

[5] H. S. Sullivan, "Tensions, Interpersonal and International," in H. Cantril, ed., *Tensions That Cause Wars* (Urbana, Ill., 1950), p. 95.

it facilitates learning by sharpening both motivation and perception. As Sullivan concludes, "The first of all learning is called out to avoid recurrence of the extremely unpleasant tension of anxiety, which is, and always continues to be, the very antithesis of everything good and desirable. . . . the child soon learns to discriminate *increasing* from *decreasing* anxiety and to alter activity in the direction of the latter. The child learns to chart a course by the anxiety gradient." . . .[6]

These several formulations underlie the present assumption that the patent status and power apparatus of organizations sharpens anxiety and thus increases the probability that behavior will reflect organizational premises. Complex organizations have an exceptional influence upon individual behavior because they are organized systems of expectation. Their status and authority symbols function as patterns of manifest stimuli that reinforce the human tendency to honor majority values. The probability of compliance is increased by the fact that organizational behavior is group behavior of an exceptionally structured kind.

All human behavior occurs within some normative framework, consciously articulated or (more frequently) tacitly assumed. In big organizations there is a fairly consistent hierarchy of values, culminating in a final ideal, the "good of the organization." Among the advantages of such a criterion is its flexibility and ambiguity—it can be manipulated to meet most exigencies. Because the organization must always compete for popular approval, consumer loyalty, and legislative protection and because its power must be constantly nourished, its major values become important tactical instruments. They are personified by the leaders of the organization and explicit in its traditions, and they provide behavioral cues for its rank and file. The assumed best interest of the organization thus provides a standard for determining policy, evaluating individual performance, defining loyalty, and rationalizing injustice if injustice becomes necessary. Obviously this standard may be misapplied in any given instance, but this possibility is not significant here because the decision makers always try to apply it rationally.

Imperatives such as these are reflected in the psychology of the organization. They result in a conscious effort to increase its predictability and internal discipline. The organization tends to become a routine of skill, energy, and opinion. The structured interpersonal relations with which this analysis is concerned are part of this rational climate. They increase the probability that individual behavior will reflect organizational necessity. The individual is conditioned to accept the legitimacy of obedience, for example, by the very fact that he has been hired to do a specific job with explicit obligations, by the provision of rules and regulations that limit his discretion, and by the definition of his place in a hierarchy of authoritative relationships. But such situational factors become most meaningful in terms of the psychological impact they have upon members of the organization. The resultant attitudes, it must be said, obviously help the organization achieve its objectives, but they also have certain unanticipated consequences that are dysfunctional in terms of such goals and of personal adjustment.[7]

---

[6] *Ibid.;* also see John Dollard and N. E. Miller, *Personality and Psychotherapy* (New York, 1950), p. 190; O. H. Mowrer, Anxiety Reduction and Learning, *Journal of Experimental Psychology* 27 (1940), 497–516.

[7] Merton, *op. cit.;* C. Argyris, The Individual and Organization: Some Problems of Mutual Adjustment, *Administrative Science Quarterly,* 2 (June 1957), 1–24.

We turn first to learning theory, because individual accommodation to the organization is essentially a matter of learning. Learning may be defined as a modification of behavior resulting from repeated exposures to a certain kind of stimuli. Learning proceeds according to a stimulus-response mechanism; its effectiveness depends upon various factors, including the number and strength of existing habits, perception, and the strength of the drive evoked by the stimulus. Perception is the process of becoming acquainted with the environment. Its motives include anxiety and what seems to be an instinctive tendency to use our sense organs functionally.[8] Random observation suggests that we appraise new social situations in order to orient ourselves, to decide what role is required. Our perception of a situation defines our behavioral limits in the sense that its speed and accuracy determine the appropriateness of the role we choose.

Obviously differences in intelligence, emotional maturity, and motivation influence perception and behavior. Some individuals have a limited social sensitivity, that is, their reactions are inappropriate to the "normal" expectations of a given situation. Such behaviors reflect, in part, inadequate or distorted perception. Among higher animals, whose perceptual organization is acquired (learned), the sensitivity toward, range of, and discrimination among stimuli are greater than in lower animals, who depend largely upon inherent perceptual facility. Man is highly susceptible to learning because he is more aware of stimuli and more selective than other animals. It is also clear that perception is bound up with environment, since the latter provides the potential stimulus field. This leads to a basic assumption: *In the structured milieu of a big organization, we can assume that both perception and conditioning are facilitated by the manifest, authoritative nature of the stimuli. . . .*

To say that authority is defined by consent suggests that the subordinate has a real choice between acceptance and refusal, that his response to an authoritative order is an "either-or" proposition.[9] But this view not only neglects the disparities in power and security between the organization and the individual and between different individuals in the same organization; it also posits too great a degree of free will and too simple a social situation. Here again psychology and anthropology are helpful.[10] As we have seen, from infancy on the individual is trained to defer to authority. He develops over time a generalized deference to the authority of parenthood, experience, knowledge, power, and status. Moreover, in any given dependency situation, many factors operate to negate the "either-or" notion. There are so many degrees of compliance, ranging all the way from enthusiasm to resignation, that outright rejection of an order becomes a gross and unlikely alternative, particularly among highly socialized (aggression-repressing) members of the organization. (We assume that most middle- and upper-level members will tend to be highly socialized owing to the technical demands of organization and the extended education required to gain the necessary skills.) We assume that consent will be normal. In a structured situation, when consent is withheld it is expressed in socially acceptable terms: orders are evaded, misunderstood, forgotten, or projected upon someone "better qualified," and so on. In any event, so long as subordinates know that a superior

---

[8] S. S. Stevens, *Handbook of Experimental Psychology* (New York, 1951), pp. 357–358.
[9] Cf. Chester I. Barnard, *Functions of the Executive* (Cambridge, Mass., 1938), pp. 163–169.
[10] Among others, see A. Inkeles and D. J. Levinson, "National Character: The Study of Modal Personality and Sociocultural Systems," in Gardner Lindzey, ed., *Handbook of Social Psychology* (Cambridge, Mass., 1954), pp. 990–993; M. Mead, *Soviet Attitudes Toward Authority* (New York, 1951).

controls ultimate sanctions to compel obedience if his orders are resisted, how can authority validly be defined as a matter of consent?

When authority and the symbols that define it are organized and patent and there are known sanctions to encourage desired reactions, we seem to have left the permissive level of influence for the authoritative level of power. In terms of a continuum of sanctions, we can say that authority is a condition that is subject to being reinforced by sanctions, while influence usually secures compliance without reference to sanctions. This difference accounts in part for our assumption that interpersonal relations in big organizations tend to rest upon authoritative premises rather than upon influential ones. This is not to say that organizations do not use influence. With the possible exception of those in military organizations, interpersonal relations are usually articulated in permissive terms, but there is little reason to suppose that those concerned are unaware of the relative power disequilibrium. Moreover, aside from other motives for consent such as personal ambition, anxiety reduction, and the desire for group approval, the very fact that an order emanates from someone with higher status and more power tends to induce consent based upon an assumed legitimacy of his role. This is only another way of saying that the very fact of hierarchy in complex organizations encourages compliance.

Obviously authority in organizations does not always function hierarchically. In addition to informal loci of power, there is the fact that technical skill demands recognition. Thus a superior must often defer where technical considerations are decisive. Yet as the experience of the atomic physicists suggests, the control of technical personnel in terms of recruitment, promotions, security, and the ends to which the product will be put is usually determined by authority according to the formal hierarchy. The conflicts between administrators and scientists and researchers on this score are well documented.[11]

An appraisal of authority must also include the fact that big organizations are composed of many subhierarchies, each bound together by authority, interest, and values in a way similar to that in the total organization. Each has its internal power structure headed by a leader who is supreme within his own system, but who is a nonleader when viewed from the perspective of the larger hierarchy. This devolution of power has important consequences. It ensures discipline, since the life chances of those in each subhierarchy are determined largely through representations made on their behalf by such subleaders. As a result, an upward-looking posture characterizes the whole organization. The will of the minority is transmitted downward through the organization by the subleaders, reinforcing their own authority and status vis-à-vis their subhierarchy.

Here the ambiguity of personal and organizational goals may be seen. To retain his position and preserve the hope of future rewards, each subleader must simultaneously promote organization-wide values and yet retain the loyalty of his immediate associates by defending their interests against both competing subhierarchies and neglect by the elite. Although ambivalence may result, his career is in the hands of the elite, and we can assume that he will give priority to its will, as he must if he is to fulfill his role as an agent for carrying out its policy. He will be measured by the loyalty and affirmation with which organiza-

[11] Among others, see *Administrative Science Quarterly* vol. 1, Special Issue on the Administration of Research (Dec. 1956).

tion policies are effected. Thus the tribute that the upward mobile subleader pays for marginal power and localized status is upward-directed anxiety and ambiguous interpersonal relations.

In sum, authority includes legal, psychological, moral, and technical factors. Their relative weights vary with the particular situation, mainly in terms of how manifest and compelling the authoritative stimuli are. Thus the hypothesis: *The more obvious and powerful (structured) the stimuli in a given interpersonal situation are, the more predictable and constant the response.*

Despite the complexity resulting from the interplay of these situational and psychological factors, we can assume that bureaucratic structure produces exceptional probabilities that individuals will defer. We know that the recognition that one occupies a hierarchical position clearly subordinate to others encourages deference. We also know that a positive assumption of authority on whatever grounds enhances compliance. Haythorn found that "when one member of a group was aggressive, self-confident, interested in an individual solution to a task, and showed initiative, the other members of the group showed less of such behavior than they normally did."[12] This tendency reflected the group's desire to avoid conflict. The way that group values are imposed will be considered presently, after we have seen how the organization encourages the loyalty and obedience of its members.

As Donald Calhoun has suggested, this is done by convincing the followers of the legitimacy and rationality of the organization, mainly by equating authority with ethical and ideological principles.[13] Of course, all institutions strive to find some basis other than sheer power for their authority. Evocative symbols and rituals are enlisted to inspire loyalty to the organization. If loyalty is to be thought merited, the values and motives, as well as the routine behaviors, of the organization must be seen as selfless; if possible the organization must appear to be the embodiment of certain universal ideals that are beyond individual criticism. This process may be called legitimation.

Max Weber posited three kinds of legitimacy: legal, traditional, and charismatic. The first is based upon the assumption that the organization seeks the good of everyone and merits support accordingly. Traditional legitimacy is the belief that the organization and its values are hallowed by age and experience and ought not be challenged by any time-blinded individual. Charismatic legitimacy is based upon an irrational faith in the values and goals of the organization and its leaders. The charismatic personality is able to inspire among his followers a desire for sacrifice and devotion.

Most organizations enlist all of these legitimations in justifying their claims to loyalty, and the appeals are usually articulated in terms of the general welfare. It is necessary, however, for organizations to simplify what is really happening, since their objectives are actually more complex and less disinterested than this. While they do in part seek to advance the common good, they are also concerned with perpetuating the organization and its individual prerogatives and with mediating conflicting demands within the organization. As Calhoun says, however, if mass loyalty is to be maintained, all three activities must be rationalized

[12] Cited in L. F. Carter, "Leadership and Small-Group Behavior," in M. Sherif and M. O. Wilson, eds., *Group Relations at the Crossroads* (Norman, Okla., 1953), p. 273.
[13] I am indebted here and elsewhere to his insightful paper, "The Illusion of Rationality," in R. Taylor, ed., *Life, Language, Law: Essays in Honor of Arthur Bentley* (Yellow Springs, O., 1957).

in terms of the first objective. Since it is impossible to define the general welfare, much less achieve it, the organization is obliged to draw upon another ideological resource, the myth that it is founded upon unquestionable, unchanging principles.

Once these principles are accepted, it becomes possible to attribute any patent shortcomings, blunders, and injustice of the organization to its members, leaving its ideals intact. This sacrificial behavior is seen in the dramatic "confessions" that occur periodically in the Communist party, but mechanisms that differ mainly in degree are employed by most big organizations. Necessity demands that failure be personalized and projected in a way which shows that human error was involved rather than organizational legitimacy. Certain highly self-conscious organizations, among which one can safely include the Marine Corps, the medical profession, and the Foreign Service, exhibit this collective idealization, often evoking exceptional loyalty from enchanted members. By contrast the individual may appear to himself to be ineffectual. The ritual, continuity, and power of the organization reinforce this self-perception.

Another psychological aspect of big organization is the illusion of unanimity among its members. Differences of interest and opinion are ignored in an effort to present a public image of discipline and unity that will enhance the organization's competitive chances. Dissent is confined within the organization. Once a decision has been hammered out, everyone must accept it, since further discussion would impair the desired solidarity. In part, the tendency of organizations to limit participation reflects a desire to avoid the appearance of internal disharmony that active participation entails. The common organizational requirement that communications be cleared through a "public information" agency is germane. The remarks of uninstructed members can thus be dismissed more easily as unauthorized. It follows that only certain individuals are actually responsible spokesmen. These are its priests, who explain the organization to the outside world, interpret its catechism, and rationalize any disparity between its ideals of service and its daily behavior.

To increase the probability that individual behavior will reflect the unanimity principle, various appeals are invoked. Affirmative stimuli include inspirational calls for loyalty, sacrifice, perpetuation of the organization's ideals, and so forth. Negative stimuli are latent but powerful. The organization depends mainly upon the sensitivity, the learned deference behaviors, the anxiety-reduction needs, and the ambition of the individual. Such psychological mechanisms reduce the need for sanctions. This climate permits us to view the complex organization as an institution of learning which calls upon deep-seated individual needs and experiences to support ends that in point of time and significance are often prior to those of any given individual. In effect the individual's "self-system" of successful accommodation to authority is coopted by the organization, and the stimuli that initially induced its development are systematically reinforced in ways described below.

Some of the implications of learning theory for organized behavior can now be specified. We suggested earlier that organizations elicited an exceptionally strong tendency to defer and, generally speaking, that it seemed reasonable to assume that the consistency of individual responses was correlated with the power and ease of recognition of stimuli. Psychologically speaking, the very definition of a "structured field" is that stimuli are stable, obvious, and compelling, in the sense that they define appropriate behavior. Learning is a function of perception and motivation, and both depend upon the quality and the number of stimuli, as well as upon individual sensitivity and receptivity. We have also defined bureaucratic structure as a system of manifest, authoritative stimuli, reinforced by known sanctions and a high reward potential. A related hypothesis follows: *Individual responses will be more certain and constant in bureaucratic structure than in so-called "voluntary associations."* To put it another way, big organizations have decided influence on individual behavior patterns, which are defined as a consistent way of reacting to interpersonal situations.

Perhaps the most common kind of manifest and authoritative stimuli are status and prestige indexes. In organizations status and authority are designated by appropriate symbols including title, size of office, accessibility, and income. In this sense the organization presents a "structured field." Such indexes, which differentiate members on the bases of authority, prestige, skill, and seniority, enhance the structured character of organizations by providing a network of signals that curtail spontaneity, limit alternatives, and generally define interpersonal relations. For this reason status consciousness tends to become a built-in part of bureaucratic psychology, as well as a necessary personal skill.

The present importance of status symbols seems to reflect a change from an economy of scarcity to one of conspicuous consumption. But conspicuous consumption is difficult to achieve today because mass production and productivity have made the symbols of material success available on so large a scale. The resulting disenchantment of once-favored classes is interestingly seen in the Middle East, where the periphery of material benefits is slowly being expanded through industrialization and inflation. There the elite feels deprived, owing to the loss of indexes that once set it apart. In the United States the diminution of this psychic income suggests that subtle, nonmaterial distinctions will become more highly valued, since they will be more difficult to establish.

The social framework of status also includes the fact that its symbols tend to become a substitute for values no longer attainable. The declining opportunity for individual autonomy through self-employment, which reflects the trend toward size, concentration, and difficulty of entry; the employment of the "independent" professions on a salary basis; the devaluation of professional training and increased status anxiety—all seem related.[14] The effort to achieve status through word magic is suggested in the attempts to borrow prestige by assigning status-laden titles to socially devalued jobs: news analyst for reporter, mortician for undertaker, executive for salesman, engineer for all sorts of routine jobs, and the widespread cooptation of the honored symbol "professional."

The American assumption of upward mobility, generation by generation, is thus related to status idealization. A cross-cultural comparison with class-bound European and Middle East societies suggests that in time sheer age, the maturing of the economy, and declining occupational mobility in the United States will

[14] This interpretation of master occupational trends is based mainly upon the emergence of an "employee" society and the implications of this for the conditions of individual participation. The most objective index for this interpretation is the sharp increase in the number of salaried employees that has accompanied industrialization during this century. In the United States the total gainfully employed population increased by 49 per cent from 1910 to 1940. During this time the number of individual proprietors increased by 17 per cent, manual workers by 49 per cent, and salaried employees by *127 per cent* (R. Bendix, *Work and Authority* [New York, 1956], pp. 211, 211–226 *passim*). See also *Statistical Abstracts of the United States* for these years.

tend to aggravate status consciousness, resulting in greater reliance upon inherited distinctions as objective means to status become more difficult to achieve. A free and easy democracy requires a social and economic situation in which there is relatively free access to abundant natural resources. A mature society checkmates this competitive situation as the lessons of power are learned by previously disadvantaged groups, and an uneasy equilibrium between major interests tends to follow. In this milieu big organizations turn to subtle status rewards as compensation for personal dependence and limited mobility. The honoring of seniority is an obvious example, as is the small gap between initial and upper-level incomes in the bureaucratized occupations.[15]

As a rule those who have organizational power possess exceptional status and prestige reinforcements, such as size and *décor* of office, expense accounts, and staff and secretarial assistance (ideally including a handsome private secretary whose loyalty and maternal protectiveness may achieve Freudian intensity), that formalize access and encourage attitudes of deference. Such stimuli are patent and compelling, and we can assume that the responses to them will be more predictable than in less structured situations. Their effectiveness is increased by the fact that status anxiety is common in big organizations.

In addition to being obvious and authoritative, organizational stimuli are relatively constant. Authority and its symbols are structured so that the individuals who personify it may change, but the *system* of authority relationships remains. Indeed, bureaucratic structure may be defined as a relatively permanent system of authority relationships. As a result there is little ambiguity or uncertainty about rights and obligations which attach to the "position" rather than to its incumbent. In comparison with social and political power, which is often vague and transitory, organizational power is obvious and definable. Moreover, insofar as organized behavior is group behavior, the authority of legitimated stimuli is increased by sheer numbers. The acceptance of organization values by the majority fosters a consensus that makes dissent seem quixotic.

As was discussed earlier in this paper, such conformity responses have a basis in individual learning and experience, namely, in the successive authority relationships that begin in childhood. It may be assumed that the individual develops considerable sensitivity to authority in all interpersonal situations. An example of the resulting pattern of anticipated reactions is the effect of rank insignia in the military. The mere sight of a high-rank symbol, identifiable at twenty paces, evokes a whole battery of conditioned responses from those affected. The relationship is reciprocal; all concerned know what their proper roles are. Deference, degree of familiarity, tone of voice—indeed the whole character of the interpersonal situation is mediated with ease and dispatch by this single evocative cue. For most organizations the operational consequence of such signals seems clear: the more patent and authoritative the stimulus, the more prompt and certain the response. Related functional aspects of status systems include the recognition of individual achievement and the legitimation of formal authority.

An interesting latent consequence of status-directed behavior is an exaggerated picture of conformity demands, which is often dysfunctional because

---

[15] For a careful study of the bureaucratization of work conditions, see T. Caplow, *The Sociology of Work* (Minneapolis, 1957).

it aggravates the fear of action and responsibility often seen in big organizations. As A. K. Davis shows, the military situation encourages an "affirm and conform" pattern of accommodation, reflecting the overemphasis on authority and status anxiety.[16] This distorted perception reflects the anxiety of the individual to please his superiors. Since the elite is remote and its will in specific instances cannot be known definitely, the individual seeks to anticipate its expectations. As a result such expectations may seem more compelling than they really are. The individual is not inclined to underestimate them for fear of alienating those upon whom his career chances rest, and he thereby increases the burden of his anxiety. This rule of exaggerated response seems to be a common dysfunctional consequence of big organization.

Despite such consequences, the over-all psychological situation is generally economical, ensuring internal discipline, dispatch, and a minimum of overt interpersonal conflict. Bureaucracy's task is simplified because the reactions it evokes are already deep-seated, having been inculcated by a succession of social institutions. Since birth the individual has been conditioned to operate in a structured environment. Noncoercive sanctions including custom, mobility expectations, and potential rewards practically eliminate the use of gross instruments of control. Because obedience becomes almost automatic, its significance is easily overlooked, or it may be repressed as an uncomfortable reality in a society where individualism is a pervasive theme. This notwithstanding, authority relations in any society become institutionalized between parent and child, teacher and student, leader and follower, officer and man, boss and worker, and so on. Although the resulting power situation may be activated by imperative cues, usually the mere presence of an authority figure, his spoken name, or an appropriate stimulus such as a title or military rank is sufficient to provoke desired responses. We have seen that organisms become conditioned to whole classes of stimuli. The patterns of obedience initiated by parents become generalized to accommodate a whole range of such authoritative stimuli.

We can assume that the anxiety evoked by authority sharpens the individual's perception of organization cues. Pavlov was among the first to argue (on the basis of empirical observation in mental institutions) that anxious people acquire conditioned responses with exceptional rapidity and stability. More recent evidence supports this view. Eysenck cites a study in which normal individuals required twenty-five repetitions of a nonsense syllable accompanied by a buzzer stimulus before a conditioned response was established, whereas anxiety neurotics required only eight repetitions.[17] Similarly, a study by Franks comparing neurotics, normals, and hysterics found that conditioning was much faster and more efficient among neurotics.[18] If, as Sullivan insists, most of us spend much of our time trying to reduce the anxiety we already have and to avoid getting more, we can assume that anxiety reduction by deferring to authoritative others will be a common behavior in complex organizations. Because the range of potential responses is thus limited, behavior becomes more predictable. . . .

Compliance in organizations is thus encouraged by a variety of sanctions, most of which invoke the anxiety-conformity-approval syndrome but vary con-

[16] A. K. Davis, Bureaucratic Patterns in the Navy Officer Corps, *Social Forces,* 27 (Dec. 1948), 143–153.
[17] E. Eysenck, *The Psychology of Politics* (London, 1954), pp. 260–261.
[18] Franks, cited in *ibid.*

siderably according to the situation and the personalities concerned. Given dominant values of success and security, middle-class child training and education seem to foster a high degree of adaptive anxiety, discipline, and repression of aggression in outside-the-home interpersonal relations, whereas a lower-class milieu is somewhat more tolerant of aggression.[19] In industrial work situations ridicule, censure, and even blows are used to discipline nonconformants. On the other hand, in organizations engaged in highly technical work requiring considerable education and training (correlated in turn with middle-class social expectations), we find that sanctions are apt to be rather more Machiavellian and that rewards meet status needs to a greater extent than they do economic ones.

Any useful theory must account for such differences, and research in the framework outlined above would have to differentiate among organization members according to class, motivation, educational background, and attitudes toward authority, since these factors play a significant role in accommodation. I would propose three general patterns of accommodation to the bureaucratic situation: the upward-mobiles, the indifferents, and the ambivalents. (There is some evidence that items in the Adorno "F" scale are helpful in identifying each type.[20]) A preliminary sketch of each ideal type follows. Type one is characterized by an ability to identify with the long-range, abstract goals of the total organization and to make these a meaningful basis for participation, in other words, to accept the legitimacy and rationality of the organization. Allied with this attitude is a capacity for action despite conflicting alternatives and contradictory aims; the organization's values are accepted as decisive. An acceptance of the demands and operational necessity of the organization's authority and status systems seems another functional attitude. For example, it is well known that the successful executive tends to regard his superiors as friendly and sympathetic.[21] These formulations permit us to suggest a third major research hypothesis: *Individual patterns of accommodation to the organization are associated with attitudes toward authority and with socioeconomic status.*

Type two, the indifferents, seem to comprise the most common pattern of accommodation. Rejecting majority values of success and power, the indifferent's orientation is essentially *extravocational.* His work is separated from the assumed-to-be more meaningful aspects of life. His references lie outside the organization, which merely provides the income necessary to indulge off-the-job satisfactions; and unlike the upward-mobiles, these activities rarely reinforce his organizational role. His relationship with the organization is essentially an economic bargain in which he sells his time and energy for a certain number of hours per week but jealously guards the remaining time as his own.

The third type of adjustment pattern is to be seen in the ambivalents, who comprise that small minority who can neither resist the appeals of power and

[19] A. Davis, "Socialization and Adolescent Personality," in G. E. Swanson, T. M. Newcomb, and E. L. Hartley, eds., *Readings in Social Psychology* (New York, 1952), pp. 520–531; A. Davis and R. Havighurst, *Father of the Man* (Boston, 1947); A. Davis, *Social-Class Influences upon Learning* (Cambridge, Mass., 1948); A. Davis and R. Havighurst, Social Class and Color Differences in Child Rearing, *American Sociological Review,* 11 (1946), 494–501; A. C. Kinsey *et al., Sexual Behavior in the Human Male* (Philadelphia, 1948). More recent studies, however, raise questions about the extent of class differences in socialization; among others, see R. A. Littman, R. C. A. Moore, and John Pierce-Jones, Social Class Differences in Child Rearing, *American Sociological Review,* 22 (1957), 694–703.

[20] See T. W. Adorno *et al., The Authoritarian Personality* (New York, 1950).

[21] Among others, see Burleigh Gardner, Successful and Unsuccessful Executives, *Advanced Management,* 13 (Sept. 1948), 116–125.

success available through the organization nor play the role required to attain them. The ambivalent seems to need security, which the organization's structure and power could provide, but he is temperamentally unable to make the accommodation necessary to obtain it. This conflict seems to reflect inapposite views toward authority and an aggressive sense of individuality which will not permit him to accept the organization as a collective instrument seeking ends that are beyond those of any individual in point of time and significance. He is thus unable to make decisions in terms of organizational premises, exhibiting instead a particularistic point of view which places friendship and similar subjective values above the objective universalistic values that ensure success in the upward-mobiles' case. As E. G. Mishler has shown, "particularism," or the preference for individual over against collective (organizational) values, is "associated with the rejection of authority, a permissive view of dissent, an acceptance of one's own impulses, and an objective appraisal of one's parents."[22] On this basis it seems appropriate to suggest a relationship between particularism, which is organizationally dysfunctional and characteristic of the ambivalent type, and universalism, which is organizationally functional and characteristic of the upward-mobile type. . . .

[22] E. B. Mishler, Personality Characteristics and the Resolution of Role Conflicts, *Public Opinion Quarterly,* vol. 17 (Spring 1953); see also S. A. Stouffer and J. Toby, "Role Conflict and Personality," in T. Parsons and E. Shils, eds., *Toward a General Theory of Action* (Cambridge, Mass., 1951). Burleigh Gardner's research findings that successful executives tend to idealize their parents, and particularly their fathers, while maintaining somewhat less identification with their mothers, is also germane (*op. cit.*).

Types of Power and Status

HERBERT GOLDHAMMER
EDWARD A. SHILS

A person may be said to have *power* to the extent that he influences the behavior[1] of others in accordance with his own intentions. Three major forms of power may be distinguished in terms of the type of influence brought to bear upon the subordinated individual. The power-holder exercises *force* when he influences behavior by a physical manipulation of the subordinated individual (assault, confinement, etc.); *domination* when he influences behavior by making explicit to others what he wants them to do (command, request, etc.);[2] and *manipulation* when he influences the behavior of others without making explicit the behavior which he thereby wants them to perform.[3] Manipulation may be exercised by utilizing symbols or performing acts. Propaganda is a major form of manipulation by symbols. The undermining of confidence in an enterprise by sabotaging its activities may be taken as an example of manipulation by acts.

Most power-holders claim legitimacy for their acts, i.e., they claim the "right to rule" as they do. If the legitimacy of the exercise of power is acknowledged by the subordinated individuals we speak of *legitimate power;* if it is not recognized we call it *coercion* (provided, of course, that the intention of the power-holder is realized). There are three major forms of legitimate power. Legitimate power is regarded as *legal* when the recognition of legitimacy rests on a belief by the subordinated individuals in the legality of the laws, decrees, and directives promulgated by the power-holder; *traditional* when the recognition of legitimacy rests on a belief in the sanctity of traditions by virtue of which the power-holder exercises his power and in the traditional sanctity of the orders which he issues; and *charismatic* when the recognition of legitimacy rests on a devotion to personal

Reprinted from *Journal of Sociology* (September 1939), pp. 171–182, by permission of The University of Chicago Press.

[1]Behavior is here to be understood as both covert and overt behavior. Influence is to be understood as both an alteration of behavior and a maintenance of behavior as it was, but other than what it would have been without the intervention of the power-holder.

[2]"Shoulder arms!" and "Please close the door" are both cases of domination, provided, of course, that these utterances succeed in realizing the intention of the speaker. It may be that everyday associations render "Please close the door" as an example of domination somewhat surprising. A polite request, however, is as much a way of getting people to do what one wants them to do as is the most brutally uttered command. Polite requests often enable a person to exercise power over another where a command containing no elements of deference may fail. The relation between the exercise of power over, and the granting of deference to, subordinated individuals is not treated here.

[3]Since the distinction between domination and manipulation rests on the degree to which the power-holder makes his intention explicit to the person whose behavior he wants to influence, the two frequently shade off into each other. It often happens, of course, that the context in which the power-holder's behavior takes place is such as to enable him to assume that his intention is quite clear to the person whom he is attempting to influence. It is desirable to include such cases under domination.

It is clear that manipulation excludes modifications of behavior following the communication of factual representations in discussion. In the case of discussion the intentions of the discussants are evident to each other. This, of course, does not preclude the possibility of manipulatory elements entering into a discussion. As in the cases discussed in the first paragraph, the line between discussion and manipulation may (in certain concrete cases) be difficult to draw.

qualities of the power-holder. Usually, of course, these personal qualities are, or appear to the followers to be, extraordinary qualities such as sanctity and heroism.[4]

A person whose general position as a power-holder is recognized as legitimate may exercise force, domination, or manipulation. But, as far as the recognition of the legitimacy of individual acts of power is concerned, it is clear that manipulation cannot be legitimate power, since in the case of manipulation there is no recognition by the subordinated individual that an act of power has been effected. Persons who are subject to force (especially as an initial form of influencing behavior and not as a sanction) frequently do not recognize the legitimacy of such acts of power. Generally, therefore, the recognition of a power-holder as a legitimate exerciser of power rests on the recognition of the legitimacy of his acts of domination. However, this need not mean that he may not also exercise force or manipulation.

Attempted domination may meet with obedience or disobedience. The motivation for obedience and disobedience is *instrumental* to the extent that it is based on an anticipation of losses and gains, and *noninstrumental* to the extent that it is based on ethical or affective imperatives of conduct dictating obedience or disobedience to the command. In the case of obedience these imperatives may derive either (a) from a belief that the recognition of power as legitimate, i.e., as legal, traditional, or charismatic, imposes obedience as a norm of conduct or (b) from norms of conduct (e.g., the mores) which dictate, not obedience to the power-holder but the performance of the particular acts commanded. In the case of disobedience the imperatives will likewise derive either (a) from a belief that the recognition of power as nonlegitimate, i.e., coercive, imposes disobedience as a norm of conduct or (b) from norms of conduct which dictate not disobedience to the power-holder but the nonperformance of the particular acts commanded.[5] Although one may recognize the legitimacy of power, yet one may also obey or disobey out of instrumental considerations. This signifies in the case of disobedience that the instrumental considerations outweigh the motivation toward conformity arising from the recognition of legitimacy.

If the attempt of a person to exercise power fails, the power act may be followed either by a substitute power act or by a sanction. A *substitute power act* is intended primarily to attain the original aim of the first act. Substitution may take place both within or between types of power. Thus a command may be substituted for a polite request (both forms of attempted domination), or unsuccessful propaganda may be succeeded by an outright command (manipulation and domination). A *sanction* is a power act initiated primarily as a reprisal for nonconformity with a prior act of power; its intent is punitive and not primarily directed toward achieving the goal of the prior unsuccessful power act. Since persons who are subjected to attempted exercise of force or manipulation do not—unlike persons subjected to commands—either obey or disobey, sanctions may most prop-

[4]The classification of types of legitimate power is that of Max Weber (cf. *Wirtschaft und Gesellschaft* [Tübingen, 1925], I, 124).

[5]Motivation for conformity with, or rejection of, the expressed wish or demand of the power-holder is here considered only in terms of perceptions by the subordinated person of certain selected characteristics of the power-holder and the commanded act. Clearly a number of other factors would be relevant in a complete analysis of why one individual obeys or disobeys another, e.g., the personality of the obeying person. Such factors are not considered here since the above classification is not being used as a basis for a complete causal explanation of obedience or disobedience.

erly be spoken of as a reprisal for disobedience to a command (domination) rather than as nonconformity to other types of power. However, it may be true that an unsuccessful propagandist or unsuccessful exerciser of force may (irrationally) take actions with punitive intent against persons who fail to succumb to his propaganda or to his attempt to exercise force.

A sanction may be either a deprivation of values already possessed or an obstruction to the attainment of values which would have been realized were it not for the punitive intervention of the power-holder. A sanction may be either a physical loss (beating, confinement, etc.) or a nonphysical loss (fining, confiscation, removal from office, ridicule, etc.).

Disobedience to the command of a power-holder may result not only in consciously intended sanctions but also in unintended penalizations (such as guilt feelings, loss of prestige, etc.), the anticipation of which may motivate the individual to conform. Market operations afford an important case of unintended penalizations. The demands of buyers and sellers upon each other produce a collective compromise expressed in the price level. Intransigent buyers and sellers are not necessarily subject to intended losses, but their intransigence is, in fact, likely to squeeze them out of the market. The conformity of the buyers or sellers to the imperatives of market conditions involves, in this case, conformity not only to the immediate demands of those with whom they have direct relations but through them, indirectly, with all other persons in the market. Unintended consequences may also be derivative penalizations, i.e., they may be unintended results from the infliction of an intended sanction. Thus imprisonment may (even after release) result in the loss of job, prestige, and associations.

Sanctions may be exercised either directly by the power-holder himself or indirectly through others in official or nonofficial positions. Most power-holders of any consequence possess a staff of officials to whom the exercise of sanctions is delegated. Although power-holders may instigate persons without official position (mobs, the public, "the consumer," etc.) to take reprisals against nonconformists, the exercise of sanctions by nonofficials is perhaps most important in the case of unintended and derivative penalizations and in the case of intended sanctions without instigation from official power-holders.

A power relation is *unilateral* if only one party to the relationship exercises power over the other and *bilateral* if both parties exercise power over each other. The power relationships between officers and privates in an army are typically unilateral. A major form of bilateral power relation is the case of bargaining power, to the extent that each party influences the behavior of the other in the intended direction. In bargaining each party attempts to influence the behavior of the other either by depriving him of values already possessed or by obstructing the attainment of values not yet possessed but desired. Bilateral power relations exist not only in the case of domination (as when each party is able to make demands on the other) but also in the case of manipulation. That is, each party may influence the behavior of the other party without making explicit what behavior is desired. Thus parties may mutually influence each other's behavior in a desired direction by propaganda or by acts. The outcome of attempted bilateral domination or manipulation may be complete fulfillment of the intentions of both parties (provided they are not incompatible) or a compromise, i.e., a partial success by both parties or the fulfilment (partially or fully) of the intention of only one party or, finally, modes of behavior completely different from the intention of either party.[6]

The exercise of power is *direct* when the power-holder alters the behavior of others without utilizing an intermediary and *indirect* when a chain of direct power acts is initiated by a power-holder who utilizes one or more subordinate power-holders. The control of an army by a general or of factory workers by a large-scale entrepreneur is largely by means of indirect power. The chain of direct power acts constituting the exercise of indirect power may be composed of different types of direct power acts. Thus the initial act may be a command (domination) to a subordinate power-holder who may alter the behavior of others by propaganda (manipulation) in order to instigate mob violence (force) against certain groups, thus attaining the intention of the initiating power-holder. The personnel utilized in the sequence of direct power acts composing indirect power may be both official and nonofficial. . . .

[6] The last case is only an *attempted* bilateral power relation since neither party accomplished his intention. The case in which only one party accomplishes his intention is marginal to the definition of bilateral power and may be characterized as being a case of attempted bilateral power with culmination in unilateral power.

Some Functions of Bureaucratic Rules

A. W. GOULDNER

The Explicational Functions of Bureaucratic Rules

In this context, some of the functions performed by bureaucratic rules can perhaps be more readily discerned. First, it can be noted that the rules comprise a functional equivalent for direct, personally given orders. Like direct orders, rules specify the obligations of the worker, enjoining him to do particular things in definite ways. Usually, however, rules are given, or are believed to be given, more deliberation than orders, and thus the statement of obligations they explicate can be taken to be definitive. Since the rules are also more carefully expressed, the obligations they impose may be less ambiguous than a hastily worded personal command. Looked at in this light, rules are a form of *communication* to those who are seen as desirous of evading responsibilities, of avoiding commitments, and of withholding proper and full performance of obligations. Comprising in one facet an explicit body of obligations, the rules serve to draw a worker's *attention* to managerial expectations and to dissolve the residues of diffuseness which may allow the worker to "hedge." Thus, on the one hand, the rules explicate the worker's task while on the other, they shape and specify his relationships to his superior. Stated in the language of the political scientist, the rules serve to narrow the subordinate's "area of discretion." The subordinates

Reprinted with permission of The Macmillan Company from *Patterns of Industrial Bureaucracy* by A. W. Gouldner. Copyright 1954 by The Free Press.

now have fewer options concerning what they *may* or *may not* do, and the area of "privilege" is crowded out by the growing area of "obligation." . . .

The Screening Functions of Rules

A second, less obvious, function of bureaucratic rules can be observed if we notice that, in part, they provide a substitute for the personal repetition of orders by a supervisor. Once an obligation was incorporated into a rule, the worker could not excuse himself by claiming that the supervisor had failed to tell him to do a specific thing. To take one example: The worker who operated a machine without using the safety guard could not "pass the buck" by saying that the supervisor neglected to mention this when he gave him a task. Since there existed a standing rule that "safety guards should always be used," the supervisor need not warn the worker of this every time he instructed him to use a machine.

Once standing rules have been installed, there are fewer things that a supervisor has to direct a worker to do; thus the frequency and duration of worker-foreman interaction in their *official* capacities is somewhat lessened. Moreover, even if the super does intervene in his capacity as a superior, he need not appear to be doing so on his own account; he is not so apt to be seen as "throwing his weight around." He can say, as one foreman said about the no-absenteeism rule: "I can't help laying them off if they're absent. *It's not my idea.* I've got to go along with the rules *like everyone else.* What *I* want has nothing to do with it." In other words, the rules provide the foreman with an impersonal crutch for his authority, screening the superiority of his power which might otherwise violate the norm of equality. Instead, equality presumably prevails because, "like everyone else," he, too, is bound by the rules which the plant manager has sanctioned.

Differences in power which are not justifiable in terms of the group's norms, or which violate them, seem to establish a situation requiring the utilization of impersonal control techniques. Impersonal and general rules serve in part to obscure the existence of power disparities which are not legitimate in terms of the group's norms.[1] The screening function of the rules would seem, therefore, to work in two directions at once. First, it impersonally bolsters a supervisor's claim to authority without compelling him to employ an embarrassing and debatable legitimation in terms of his personal superiority. Conversely, it permits

---

[1] William F. Whyte has made an observation in his restaurant studies which, if reconceptualized, in effect constitutes an interesting example of this pattern. Whyte points out that tension arises between the waitresses and the pantry help who fill their orders, under several conditions: when the waitresses are *younger* than the pantry people—even though both groups are women; or when those in the pantry are *men.* It would seem that these tensions emerge because *traditional* criteria of authority in our society are being violated. That is, younger people are initiating action for older people, while our cultural prescriptions prefer that power be vested in older folk. Again, women are initiating action for men, while the culture prescribes that men should wield the power. In an acute analysis, Whyte makes the following interpretation of the "insignificant-looking spindle" on which the waitresses place their orders, and from which the pantry people take them. "Wherever the people on the receiving end of the orders are related to the order givers as males vs. females, or older vs. younger, then it is important for the pantry help to have some *impersonal* barrier to block the pressure from themselves." (Ibid., p. 75.) In other words, instead of having the waitresses orally inform the pantry help of what they want, the waitresses can now write it out and place their order on the spindle. The pantry personnel can pick the order off the spindle without coming into direct interaction with the waitresses and without seeming to take orders from those culturally prescribed as inferiors. The spindle thus masks the existence of a relationship which violates internalized cultural prescriptions.

workers to accept managerial claims to deference without committing them to a merely personal submission to the supervisor that would betray their self-image as "any man's equal."

The "Remote Control" Function of Rules

It would be a mistake, however, to continue assuming that management instituted rules only when it perceived workers as unmotivated. For top management was often as much concerned with the low motivation of those in the lower echelons of its own ranks, i.e., middle management, as it was with workers'. This was quite evident in Peele's feeling that foreman and supervisors were "shirking." It was also a pattern that was more generally evident. Thus, for example, if all supervisors could be "counted on" to enforce safety regulations there would have been no need for the main office to employ a "safety engineer" to check upon safety conditions in the local plants.

The problem of handling the "enemy within" was sometimes more difficult than that of coping with those in the "out-group." For at least on the factory level, in-group and out-group could stand face to face and might sniff watchfully at each other, and could place their confidence for a while in "close supervision." But what could the safety engineer, for example, do to control some twenty-five plants? How could he control the supervision of safety work throughout the entire Company by means of "close supervision" alone? (Notice that the safety engineer's problem was only an extreme case of a common problem; it was not qualitatively different from that experienced by many of the plant's middle managers).

In some way the safety engineer had to utilize a "spot check" system. That is, he made occasional visits to a plant, spending a little while there, and then moved on to another factory. If, however, each plant was to operate on a unique basis, each having its own distinctive techniques for handling safety, it would be difficult for the safety engineer to make his *own* judgment about plant conditions. He would be forced to place greater reliance on local management, which was precisely what he wanted to avoid. Insofar as he had established certain general rules applying to all plants, he could go to each one and "see for himself." He could "tell at a glance" whether the rules concerning machine guards or debris on the floor were being followed. In part, then, the existence of general rules was a necessary adjunct to a "spot check" system; they facilitated "control from a distance" by those in the higher and more remote reaches of the organization.

There was another aspect of the rules which was also helpful to control from a distance. This was their *public* character. Because the rules were publicly known, an "enemy" could be used to control an "ally." For example, when the safety engineer inspected a plant he was not averse to speaking to workers whom he himself characterized as "troublemakers." The safety engineer told of a plant tour which he had made while in the company of a "troublemaker." This worker showed the engineer that there was a pile of debris in front of the blacksmith's bench, and took him to another spot and showed him how a machine had had its guard removed. He could only do this because the rules were public knowledge, and like everyone else, the "troublemaker" knew what they were. On the basis of these observations the safety engineer could then apply pressure to the supervisors. In sum, the *public* character of the rules enabled deviance to be detected by the *out-group*. This enlarged the information channels open to the heads of the in-group, in turn enabling them to keep their own junior officers in line.

These considerations lead us to expect that bureaucratic rules flourish, other things being equal, when the senior officers of a group are impressed with the recalcitrance of those to whom they have delegated a measure of command. In other words, bureaucratic patterns are particularly useful to the degree that distrust and suspicion concerning role performance has become diffuse and directed to members of the "in-group," as well as to those on the outside; and when, as the Old Testament puts it, "A man's enemies are the men of his own house."

The Punishment Legitimating Functions of Rules

Faced with subordinates who were only reluctantly performing their roles, or at least, who were seen in this way, management was experiencing a status-threatening and hence aggression-provoking situation. The supervisor wanted to eliminate these threats when they arose and to prevent their recurrence. These were the supervisor's needs which emerged from his relations with workers when the latter began to behave apathetically ("goldbricking") or disobediently ("talking back"). On another level, the personality plane, the supervisor was beginning to "burn-up" and was getting set to "blow his top." He was, in brief, accumulating a cargo of aggression with which he had to do something.

Why didn't the supervisor express his aggression and "tell the worker off"? Why didn't he *punish* the worker, thereby killing two birds with one stone; namely, unburdening himself of hostile feelings and compelling the worker to conform to his expectations? After all, punishment, or the infliction of "pain, failure, or ego-degradation"[2] upon the worker might help to bolster the supervisor's threatened status and salve his wounded ego.

There was one important drawback. Among surface workers in particular, and for the Company as a whole, supervisors were expressly forbidden, formally, to express aggression. As seen when contrasting miners with the more bureaucratized surface workers, the overt expression of aggression was taboo among the latter. Moreover the Company "labor relations manual" asserted that "A *friendly* attitude toward . . . all employees will provide the basis for sound Company-employee relations in each plant." The manual also insisted that one of the characteristics of every good employee was an "ability to *control emotion.*" In the face of these proscriptions, it was difficult to express aggression openly.

In our society, moreover, it is not permissible to inflict a punishment under any and all conditions. There seems to be a deep-grooved inscription in our culture which asserts that punishment is permissible only on the condition that the offender could know *in advance* that certain of his behaviors are forbidden.[3] This is one of the sentiments which underlies the rejection of *ex post facto* laws

[2] Norman F. Maier, *Frustration.* McGraw-Hill Book Co., 1949, p. 194.

[3] Here, again, there is evidence suggesting that we are dealing with a culturally induced sentiment rather than one peculiar to this factory or to industrial phenomena alone. On the basis of their wartime studies of the U.S. Armed Forces, the authors of *The American Soldier* suggest that punishment is more likely to be effective if "the men are given specific *advance* warning about the consequences of an occurrence of the offense, since *most men consider fair warning as a condition for fair punishment.*" Ibid., p. 425. (My emphasis—A. W. G.)

in our legal structure. If it has become a formally announced legal principle that "ignorance of the law is no excuse," this has, in part, been necessary because traditional folkways informally insist that ignorance of the law constitutes an extenuating circumstance.

Within the plant, orientation to this traditional norm was expressed in several ways. First, the frequent claim that so-and-so was a good foreman because he gave his workers a "second chance," a factor in the "indulgency pattern," implied that such a foreman did *not* take the first opportunity that presented itself to inflict a punishment. Instead he used this first deviation as an occasion to *warn* the worker that future infractions would meet with punishment.

That punishments which were not preceded by warnings were only doubtfully legitimate, in the eyes of plant personnel, can be inferred from the introduction of the formal warning notice. One of the functions of the *worker's signature* on the warning notice was to forestall a claim that he had not been warned and could not, therefore, be punished. Day, the old personnel manager, complained precisely of this point after he had been demoted, saying, "Why didn't Peele tell me about it long before now, instead of just replacing me?"

Bureaucratic rules, then, serve to legitimate the utilization of punishments. They do so because the rules constitute statements in advance of expectations. As such, they comprise explicit or implicit *warnings* concerning the kind of behavior which will provoke punishment.

In actuality, the establishment of a rule explicating an obligation is frequently accompanied by a specific statement of the punishment, i.e., another rule specifying the punishment which will result if the first rule is violated. Two things, rather than one, have thus been clarified: (1) what is expected of the man and (2) what will happen to him if he does *not* fulfill these expectations. For example, the no-absenteeism rule did not merely state that the worker must not be absent without cause; it also specifically provided that he was to be layed off a like number of days for those which he took.

In brief, when rules explicate obligations, they are producing consequences recognized and intended by most participants in the situation. When rules explicate a punishment, however, they are legitimating the use of punishments, a consequence sometimes not at the center of the group's intention or awareness. The relationship between the explication and the punishment functions of rules is like the relation between the locomotive and the trains which it pulls. Attention can all too readily be diverted to the noisy, smoking locomotive in the vanguard, while the attached trains carrying the pay load are easily neglected.

An example of the punishment function of the rules occurred in the dehydrating section of the mill: There were a number of large vats, used to heat and dehydrate the gypsum into powder, which occasionally needed to be cleaned out. A rule specified that the man who went down into one of these vats must wear a harness with a rope leading up to the top; there was also supposed to be someone at the top holding onto the rope and watching the man inside. These precautions stemmed from the fear that a man at the bottom of a vat could be killed by fumes or smothered by a cave-in of the "cake" covering the inside of the vat.

One day a main office executive passed through the plant on an inspection tour and noticed a rope leading down into a vat. He looked over the side and saw a worker cleaning it out, but there was no one around at the top watching the man and guarding the rope. Immediately the executive looked for the man's foreman, who was not to be seen. After a search, however, he discovered the foreman doing exactly the same thing, cleaning out a vat without having someone watch him. The executive then "raised hell" with the foreman and took it to higher plant authorities.

In short, the first thing the executive did when he discovered the infraction of vat-cleaning rules, was to look for someone to punish and blame. Instead of calling the man up from the vat, he left him down there. Instead of doing something to forestall an accident, the manifest function of this rule, he exploited the situation as an opportunity to inflict a punishment.

The rules thus channel aggression, providing permissible avenues for its expression and legitimating the utilization of punishments. To the extent that possible objects of punishment and aggression are members of the "in-group," as suggested in our discussion of the "remote control" function of rules, it becomes all the more necessary to legitimate meticulously the use of these control measures. For, by and large, aggression and punishments directed toward in-group members are not preferred patterns of behavior in our culture and require especially unambiguous justification. Bureaucratic rules are thereby particularly functional in a context in which reliance upon the in-group has been shaken.

The "Leeway" Function of Rules

Another commonplace pattern observable in management's application of bureaucratic rules, which is related to their punishment function, was the curious rhythmic quality with which rules were *enforced.* Sometimes demands for rigorous conformance to a rule would be made, but would later lapse into periods of disinterest when the rules were ignored or only fitfully observed. For example, occasionally the plant guard would carefully examine packages which workers brought out of the plant, while at other times these would be given only cursory inspection. Sometimes punctual "punching in" would be rigorously enforced; at other times lateness would be given only casual comment. What was the significance of these periodic alternations? A clue to part of their meaning may be found in the *contexts* in which enforcement or relaxation of rules occurred.

Usually, it was noted that a fever of enforcement occurred when small tensions between workers and their supervisors began to coalesce into more definite rifts. A case in point was the "no-floating around" rule which specified that workers must stay at their work-place, except to go to the washroom or to eat. When foremen felt that things were going smoothly in their group, that their men were "doing a day's work" and were friendly and "cooperative," they would allow their workers to "sneak off" for a smoke, and they would make no caustic comments if they wandered over to talk to a friend. If, however, a man or the group as a whole was felt to be "goofing off," or was becoming "snotty," foremen were then more likely to invoke the "no-floating" rule.

By a strange paradox, *formal* rules gave supervisors something with which they could "bargain" in order to secure *informal* cooperation from workers. The rules were the "chips" to which the Company staked the supervisors and which they could use to play the game; they carved out a "right" which, should supervisors wish to, they could "stand upon." In effect, then, formal bureaucratic rules served as a control device not merely because they provided a legitimating framework for the *allocation* of punishments, but also because they established a punishment which could be *withheld.* By installing a rule, management provided itself with an instrument which was valuable even if it was not used; the rules were serviceable because they created something which could be *given up* as well as *given use.*

The Apathy-Preserving Function of Bureaucratic Rules

Nor is this the last of paradoxes. For though bureaucratic rules were fostered by situations involving worker apathy, or its semblance, the rules actually contributed to the preservation of work apathy. Just as the rules facilitated punishment, so, too, did they define the behavior which could permit punishment to be *escaped.* The discussion of the "leeway" function of rules has considered the importance of this from the supervisor's standpoint, but it was also significant for the worker as well. The rules served as a specification of a *minimum* level of acceptable performance. It was therefore possible for the worker to *remain* apathetic, for he now knew just how *little* he could do and still remain secure.

For example, after Peele had ruled that workers could not "punch in early" and accumulate a little overtime in that way, one mill worker said acidly.

> "Well, if that's the way he wants it, that's the way he wants it. But I'll be damned if I put in any overtime when things get rough and they'd like us to."

Said another worker:

> "O.K. I'll punch in just so, and I'll punch out on the nose. But you know you can lead a horse to water and you can lead him away, but it's awful hard to tell just how much water he drinks while he's at it."

This, of course, is the stuff of which "bureaucratic sabotage" is made. "Bureaucratic sabotage" is deliberate apathy fused with resentment, in which, by the very act of conforming to the letter of the rule, its intention is "conscientiously" violated. The worker's feeling and attitudes toward his work were thus essentially left untouched by the bureaucratic rules. The worker could, as it were, take any attitude toward his work that he wished, so long as he conformed to the rules. The rules did little to modify *attitudes* toward work, but were significant primarily as guidelines for *behavior.* In the last analysis, it would seem that proliferation of bureaucratic rules signify that management has, in effect if not intention, surrendered in the battle for the worker's motivation. In his study of *Social Organization,* Charles Horton Cooley came to much the same conclusion:

> "Underlying all formalism, indeed, is the fact that it is psychically cheap; it substitutes the outer for the inner as more tangible, more capable of being held before the mind *without fresh expense of thought and feeling.*"[4]

And again:

> ". . . the merely formal institution does not enlist and discipline the soul of the individual, but takes him by the outside, his soul being left to torpor or to irreverent and riotous activity."[5]

---

[4] C. H. Cooley, *Social Organization,* Chas. Scribner's Sons, 1919, p. 349. (My emphasis—A. W. G.)
[5] Ibid., p. 343.

Thus bureaucratic rules may be functional for subordinates, as well as for superiors; they permit "activity" without "participation;" they enable an employee to work without being emotionally committed to it.

This function of bureaucratic rules is of peculiar importance since it suggests one of the inherent sources of bureaucratic rules' instability; for the rules do not seem to *resolve* the very problem, worker apathy, from which they most directly spring. Insofar as formal rules merely "wall in," rather than resolve, worker apathy, it may be expected that other mechanisms more competent to muster motivations will challenge and compete with them.[6]

Bureaucratic Rules and Close Supervision

What does this mean in terms of the problem of "close supervision?" It implies that bureaucratic rules do not eliminate the need for "close supervision" but, instead, primarily function to reduce the tensions created by it. Insofar as close supervision springs from management's perception of workers as failing to perform their role-obligations and as being unmotivated, the institution of rules in no way suffices to resolve this problem. The rules do not recharge the worker's motivation, but merely enable him to know what management's expectations are and to give them minimal conformance. Thus the tensions originally spurring supervisors to use "close supervision" remain untouched.

It is, instead, the secondary problems created by close supervision that are somewhat mitigated by bureaucratic rules: With the rules, the supervisor is now enabled to show that he is not using close supervision on his own behalf, but is merely transmitting demands that apply equally to all (the screening function); the supervisor is now more able to use a "spot-check" system to control workers with whom he cannot have frequent interaction (the remote control function); he now has a clear-cut basis for deciding, and demonstrating to his superiors if need be, that workers are delinquent in their role-performances (the explicational function); he now has firm grounds for punishing a worker if he finds him withholding obligation-performance (the punishment-legitimating function); or he can relax the rules, thereby rewarding workers, if they do perform their role obligations as he wants them to (the leeway function). In general, then, the rules reduce certain role tensions.

To repeat: These various functions of the rules largely serve to mitigate tensions *derivative* of "close supervision," rather than to remove all the major tensions which *create* it. Indeed, the rules now make close supervision feasible. The rules thus actually perpetuate one of the very things, i.e., close supervision, that bring them into being. . . .

---

[6]It may well be that this is one of the organic contradictions of bureaucratic organization that make it susceptible to infiltration and displacement by "charismatic" elements, which involves loyalty to leadership based on belief in the leader's unusual *personal* qualities. Weber vaguely explained the vulnerability of bureaucracy as a breakdown of its efficiency in the face of new problems and accumulating tensions. He did little to analyze the specific nature of these tensions and tended to focus on their origins in the environment, neglecting their inner-organizational sources. We are suggesting, in effect, that bureaucratic authority is supplanted by charismatic when it is no longer possible to bypass the question of motivation. Charismatic leadership, it has been widely noted, has an ability to arouse new enthusiasms and to ignite irrational sources of motivation inaccessible to the bureaucrat. Indeed, some observers have insisted that this is one of the distinctive characteristics of modern totalitarianism. Thus George Orwell, in his *1984,* brings this novel to its climax when his hero is being tortured not merely to confess, nor to conform—but to *believe.*

Questions for Discussion

1. Recall the reasons postulated by John Locke for why political systems arise or come into being, and then analyze what is happening in the following incident (the facts are abstracted from an actual case history):

   The National Electronics company once manufactured complete computers in one plant, located in Newark, N.J. When the company's sales increased greatly, a plant was opened in Boston to produce circuits for the computer and ship them to Newark—the Boston plant would therefore supply semi-finished parts (output) to become parts (input) of the Newark plant. After the Boston plant had been in operation about a year, the manager of the Newark plant complained that the finished circuits were not arriving from Boston on schedule, and that the output of his own plant (to customers) was therefore delayed. He explained that his own purchasing department took the customer-demand schedule and ordered parts from Boston in advance, but that the Boston plant often fell behind schedule. He wrote a letter to company headquarters in New York City, recommending that industrial engineers from the headquarters staff be sent to look at (1) Newark operations, (2) Boston operations, and (3) the time and logistic links between the two plants. He also recommended that production time standards at both places (particularly in Boston) be formulated more precisely, and placed in operating manuals.

   His recommendation was accepted by New York management, the standards were worked out, using conventional and operations research techniques, and local managers at both plants were brought to New York for a one-week training program to learn the new system.

   After eight months of operation under the new system, the Newark manager noticed that shipments from Boston were again falling behind. He intends to ask New York management to call this to the Boston manager's attention. When asked why he did not call the Boston manager directly, he stated: "I've mentioned this to him, but I'd rather not call him again. I've learned from experience that it's better to do it the other way."

2. Recall the reasons for organizational obedience postulated by Presthus, derived from psychology, and then again analyze the above case history.

3. From the standpoint of *individual motivation* (of both leaders and followers), why do political structures come into being? In your answer, be sure to include the causal forces as presented in political philosophy, psychology (perception, anxiety reduction) and small-group theory. It may be helpful to refer to the Leavitt and Bennis and Shepard articles following Chapter 3, as well as to the text and readings following Chapter 7.

4. Considering the nature of the technological system which exists in society and in most companies, why do political structures come into being? In your

answer, make use of the readings (and text) relating to jurisprudence, history, and the conventional tools of management.

5. What difference is there in the two following motivations on the part of subordinates to obey the authority of their leaders?
   a) Charismatic leadership (Weber).
   b) Executive wisdom (Barnard).

6. From your own experience of living in an organization (family, fraternity, sports team, the military, a job situation, etc.) cite some case history or event which took place which illustrates the following theories. Divide your paper into two parts: (1) a case history which describes the situation in narrative (usually chronological) form, and (2) an analysis which interprets the chronological series of events in terms of the theory.
   a) Someone issues an "authoritative" instruction to someone else, and the second person obeys, because the instruction falls within his "zone of indifference" or "zone of acceptance."
   b) A similar situation occurs, but the person obeys because he is motivated by charismatic leadership.
   c) A similar situation occurs, but the person obeys to reduce anxiety in peer relations.

   Note: The narrative part of your presentation might be like the narrative in Question 1. However, because that statement is short and abstract, it is expected that your paper will be more concrete and detailed.

III

Managing and Changing Organizations

Chapter Eight

Managing and Changing Organizations by Direct Influence

This chapter has three purposes: (1) It will introduce the "applied" section of the book, which concentrates on the *managing* and *changing* of the organizations, as contrasted with the *understanding* or *analyzing* of organizations. (2) It will present management processes which are direct (face-to-face) actions intended to influence the basic needs and attitudes of people. This contrasts with indirect methods of changing the environment, or organizational structure, *around* the individual. (3) It will summarize seven processes of direct influence used in business corporations.

In addition, the latter part of the chapter will take up some unanswered questions related to training for leadership: What about technical training, as opposed to training which helps managers to be more effective in dealing with subordinates' needs and attitudes? What about the daily "direction" of people through the dissemination of policies, procedures, and programs? How does this behavior fit in with direct-influence leadership? Finally, we will raise the question of the ethics of manipulating individuals in organizations.

Management as Applied Behavioral Science

In Part II we examined various viewpoints, theories, and models, each of which helps us to "see" certain behavioral events that occur in an organization. It is true that different authors "see" different things—and their theories reflect these differences in the organizational variables which they abstract. For example, some authors may see conflict, others may see cooperation, and still others may see bargaining as the central phenomenon in human relationships. Some focus on human needs for self-actualization (freedom); others focus on human needs for law and order (limitations of individual freedom).

It is possible that all of these theories may be useful, because scholars have not found a way to make sense of the world in all its buzzing confusion except by studying it in parts. They do so by studying isolated systems of phenomena—either in logical terms, using the familiar *ceteris paribus* from economics, or in experimental terms, using controls to keep out upsetting factors and maintain in the experiment only those variables they have under study. Thus, if an investigator is studying trust, confidence, or conflict in group behavior, his experimental group will be insulated against any power or authority outside the group.

Beginning with this chapter, we will be studying *professional* processes—processes for use in the world of action rather than scientific concepts for use in analyzing and understanding the world. The change in approach will be like applying electrical engineering techniques for building television sets, instead of explaining models from the science of physics to understanding electrical phenomena. Thus the body of knowledge in Part III is a form of technology rather than science. Two terms, synonymous in Chapters 8, 9, and 10, will be used to describe this "technology": *managing,* or *changing,* organizational behavior.

We have no exact name for the *people* who learn this technology and its related science. From the readings in Part III it will be seen that the people practicing the technology (managing or changing organizational behavior) are sometimes employees of the company, either staff or line. In these cases, common parlance calls both "managers." In other cases, the persons doing the work are outside specialists in applying the behavioral sciences. These have been called "consultants" in lay terminology and either "practitioners" or "change agents" in the scholarly literature.

While the following categories are of little value intellectually, they may help toward understanding the purpose of the three chapters in Part III. This chapter is closer to the science of psychology or social psychology than to any other discipline; hence, it can be thought of as "psychological" managing. Chapter 9 is closer to political science than to any other discipline. It could be called "political" managing. Finally, Chapter 10 is closer to the science of sociology than to any other discipline: hence, "sociological" managing.

Changing Organizational Behavior

Psychologists have suggested managing or changing organizations by changing the *people* in them. They have pointed out that, although new roles or job structures may be designed in a company, unless the workers are changed in their attitudes and beliefs the new system will not work any better than the old. On the other hand, sociologists have pointed out the opposite: people in an organization may be changed in their attitudes and beliefs, but on their jobs they face other people who haven't changed or a structure of authority which hasn't changed. The new self will not work in the old structure.

There is truth in both of these points of view—that is, both theories are respectable academically. When we ask which view is pragmatic, we get a similar answer. The executive can approach organizational change by either method, but his chances of success are considerably better if he uses direct individual influence *and* adjustments in organizational structure.

Indirect means of changing organizational behavior by changing organizational structure, work patterns, or the power-authority system are covered in Chapters 9 and 10. The present chapter is addressed to the *direct* influencing of individuals. By direct, we mean need satisfactions and attitudes influenced by face-to-face contacts, actions, and reactions between two or more people.

Leadership: The Key to Direct Influence

The sum total of the behavior of an executive in his direct relations with subordinates could be termed "leadership." All of the selections following this chapter imply a type of leadership behavior called "employee-oriented leadership" or "participative leadership."[1] Although these terms carry little meaning in themselves, the behavior pattern they signify is clarified in the Tannenbaum and Schmidt, McGregor, and Kolb articles. For example, Tannenbaum and Schmidt argue that research supports the theory that a fairly high degree of subordinate-centered leadership is called for if managers want to raise the level of employee motivation and increase the readiness of employees to accept change.

The object of direct influence is the behavior of subordinates, and the levers of this influence are the two personality factors discussed in Chapter 3—the provision of means for satisfying certain higher-order needs and the development over time of certain attitudes toward the self and toward the organization.

To influence the behavior of his subordinates, the kind of leader identified above puts a subordinate to *thinking* about the problems of his job, his leader's job, and acquiring general knowledge of company operations. As the subordinate lives through these kinds of experiences day in and day out, he increases his knowledge of the company and his skill in problem solving. He becomes more *competent.* In this process of self-actualization and growth, he derives satisfaction and confidence from attaining competence and mastery.

Satisfaction of the higher-order needs, achieved continually over time, thus create important feelings about the self—confidence and self-esteem. At the same time, the subordinate who is in fact helping to solve organizational and managerial problems is seen as being a more mature man, growing in ability and achievement. Thus prestige, status, and the *respect of others* are achieved along with self-respect.

Since the leader encourages this development and since he and his position are perceived as part of the organization, the subordinate tends to develop positive attitudes about the *organization*—"this is a good place to work" or "the organization (the boss) is reasonable and fair." These attitudes in turn affect his perception. The subordinate hears communications or interprets the actions of others in the company on the basis of these positive attitudes rather than their opposites.

The foregoing model of behavioral change is summarized in the following diagram. Note that the arrows indicate causation.

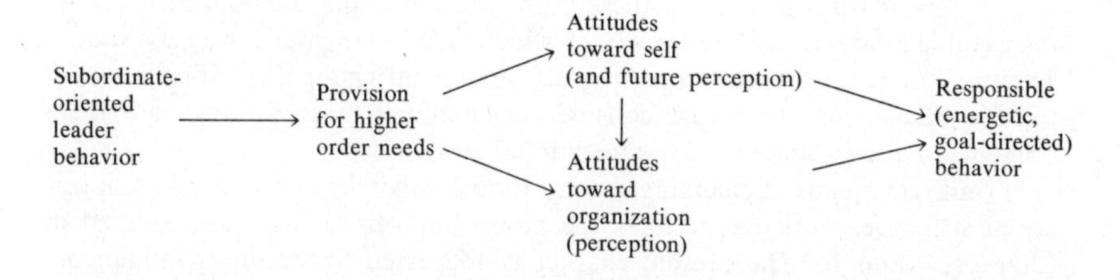

Technology, efficiency, and profits may make it necessary to deviate from this long-run strategy at certain times, depending on the company situation; but

[1] Other types of leadership, such as "authority-centered leadership," "personal-competence leadership," "technology-centered leadership," or "status-centered leadership," are discussed in Chapters 7 and 9.

if the situation calls for temporary leadership patterns that ignore employee growth and needs, managers are more likely to be perceived as acting reasonably by employees who have been treated over the long run by an employee-centered strategy.

Other Management Influence Processes

The subordinate-oriented leadership discussed above is the primary type of direct-influence management process for changing organizational behavior. A second type of management process useful for increasing employee motivation and making better managerial decisions is the combination of a formal procedure and an informal behavior pattern to match. As McGregor presents it, the formal procedure involves four steps in performance planning and appraisal; the informal behavior pattern of the manager involves certain attitudes that "cause" him to act out his relationship with his subordinates in a way that satisfies their higher-order needs and generates responsible attitudes in them.

Formal performance planning and appraisal sessions are only one of the situations that Tannenbaum and Schmidt are talking about in the process of leadership. That is, the executive behavior described in McGregor's piece is applicable to all leadership actions—not just to those times of the year when formal performance appraisals are made.

A third management process for changing organizational behavior involves the formal designation of staff men as *consultants* to line managers, coupled with an informal behavior pattern for staff men which has much in common with that already described. This behavior pattern has one special feature, however. The staff man has two relationships of importance—one in his contacts with lower line managers in the organization and quite another in his contacts with the headquarters line executive who employs him. Kolb discusses the delicate way in which the staff man relates to both parties, helping them solve their problems and becoming privy to much information which he must hold in confidence. Only in this way can the staff man achieve the real trust and confidence of those whom he advises at a lower level. Several major corporations—IBM and General Electric, for example—have experimented with the consulting role for staff men, in which the staff man becomes much less a planner and overseer and more of an advisor to line divisions in their day-to-day problem solving.

A fourth management process can be called *planned mobility*. This process involves removing a man from his customary routine and job duties, either on a permanent basis (job rotation) or on a part-time basis (assignment to a special task force, temporary assignment as an assistant to another executive, assignment to committee work, to a junior board of directors, shop council, etc.). Such programs and assignments are not covered in detail in this book, but important reference is made to them in the article by Schein. Depending on the individual, these programs can be extremely important in helping an individual get rid of some of his stereotyped beliefs, learn to be more open-minded about the views of others, and develop a feeling of competence. To the extent that the individual is receiving benefits in terms of his own development and growth, his life in the organization will generate attitudes of both self-confidence and responsibility for company affairs. Formal plans for mobility have a higher probability of success if they are coupled with leadership behavior by superiors similar to that previously described.

Training for Leadership

Tannenbaum and Schmidt recognize that many managers may not be able to engage in subordinate-centered behavior because of certain attitudes they themselves hold. The authors imply that in these cases, starting with an intellectual or speaking acquaintance with the problem as outlined, the manager should undertake to develop himself to the point where he can *act* as well as talk a good game: where he can be flexible in leadership behavior in the short run and move toward subordinate-centered patterns over the longer period. This type of development is helped by understanding the logic of participation, as presented in the Tannenbaum and Schmidt article, but the real acquisition of this attitude must come through formal executive training. The objective of such training is similar to that envisioned by McGregor, Floyd Mann (in the Katz and Kahn reading), and Kolb: that is, the acquisition of certain attitudes and insights which will help executives behave in a way that will in turn help subordinates to achieve *their* development and growth needs. A review of the Bennis and Shepard article (Chapter 3), the Bethel approach in the piece by Katz and Kahn, and the article by Tannenbaum, Weschler, and Massarik will give some understanding of the techniques for this training.

In order to avoid having some managers trained in participative methods and others whose attitudes are not compatible with such methods, training probably ought to be carried out with the whole of a management group. This can be done by sending the various levels of managers to an outside school or by having training done within the company. In addition to the Tannenbaum, Weschler, and Massarik article, the reading by Katz and Kahn deals with this latter approach in its summaries of Elliot Jacques' work in England and the work of Floyd Mann in the United States.

Management Training Processes

The processes of management previously discussed are carried out within the company by full-time executives. For training processes, company management hires outside temporary help, skilled in training and development. Thus the fifth management process entails enrolling executives in development programs operated by universities or other organizations. In a sense, the faculties of such programs are part-time workers for the company. The sixth and seventh processes involve bringing in a training and development consultant to work for a period of time in the organization itself.

It is difficult to get a realistic understanding of group or sensitivity training by reading about it, as opposed to attending training sessions. This is because many of the insights and attitudes which are developed cannot be "told." Nevertheless, some understanding is possible by recalling the article by Bennis and Shepard from Chapter 3 and by reading Katz and Kahn's short comment on the Bethel approach. Both of these readings refer to training sessions—held by universities, the National Training Laboratories, or other organizations—in which individual executives participate.

The Tannenbaum, Weschler, and Massarik narrative deals with a different approach. In this reading, the whole executive team is developed together, with the aid of an outside training specialist. This piece describes the technological problem faced by a manufacturing plant manager in switching production, and the human problems involved (those of the manager, his subordinates, and therefore in the relationships between them). It describes what takes place in the training sessions, how the plant manager's attitudes toward his subordinates are affected, and how training affects his subordinates' ability to deal with their boss. If the reader pays close attention, he can see how managerial decisions and company operations might be made and carried out more effectively if both parties ceased behaving defensively and concentrated openly and truthfully on the real problems of production.

The last management process to be discussed involves bringing in consultants who not only conduct training sessions but remain in the company over an extended period of time—months or years—and focus on actual company problems rather than on group training problems. The work done by Elliot Jaques, merged with the work done by employees and executives in the Glacier Company of England, is one such example.[2] The work done by Floyd Mann in a company in the United States is a second example. Both of these change processes are summarized in the selection by Katz and Kahn.

Some Unanswered Questions

In this chapter, nothing has been said about technical training in the various operating aspects of a business by lecture or reading. For example, shouldn't managers know something about finance, marketing, production planning, and other matters? They certainly should; such training is necessary for effectiveness. However, it is our contention in this chapter that men will be able to make use of such knowledge in a more effective way if they can remove some of the human roadblocks. They will then be able to talk freely about technical problems, getting more from others in the process and teaching others without encountering defensive barriers. Equally important, company decisions will be improved, since no technical problem is exactly like any other—the formulas have to be worked out by teamwork to fit the situation.

A second question which might be asked about the present chapter is why the managerial process of "direction"—the writing of instructions, conveying policies to subordinates, handing down of decisions, and the like—has not been discussed. This, too, is a vital management process, since there are times when direction and even command are necessary, as will be evident in the chapter on political action. But unless managers in today's corporation maintain a balance toward subordinate-centered leadership over the long period of time, using some of the processes discussed above, the system of rules and procedures in the organization may deteriorate and fail to work in an emergency.

Finally, we must ask about the ethics of individual influence. Here we face two questions. First, *should* managers in organizations attempt to influence attitudes and fulfill needs? This question is really an irrelevant one, often asked by those who are unwilling to face reality. The truth is, managers have no choice as to whether or not they influence attitudes and affect (either fulfill or block) needs. Whenever one person confronts another, talks to him, or acts toward him, he will have an effect on the other person. The effect may be positive or negative, minor or profound, but it *is* there.

The second question is, "Suppose mastery of the processes of influence

---

[2] Reported fully in Elliot Jaques, *The Changing Culture of a Factory* (London: Tavistock Publications, 1951).

is acquired by men who are consciously and deliberately selfish, and who manipulate others for their own ends?" A corollary question is, "Suppose influence processes are used by men of 'good will' who unconsciously 'play God,' thinking that *they* know what is best for others, but who go merrily on acting out their own needs and desires without a responsible understanding of their own behavior or that of others?"

We must face the fact that the risks posed by the foregoing questions are inherent in the application of any technique or device that is effective in gaining power over others—as witness the moral dilemma posed by man's eternal quest for the "ultimate" weapon. Should the awesome destructive power of atomic energy have been unleashed after all? The comparison may seem overblown, but the basic problem is the same.

There is hope, of course. The checks on the foregoing risks rest in the countervailing power of those people who surround the selfish or thoughtless person. If they are trained in an understanding of influence processes, they can more quickly detect the significance of his behavior. Their response to the consciously selfish person may be necessarily emotional, employing the defense mechanisms mentioned in Chapter 3. In relation to the merely thoughtless person, they may be able to use the insights and the skill at frank and open discussion gained from training in the behavioral sciences to bring him to see the true effects of his behavior.

power. People are placed in a specific job with explicit duties (actions, behavior), guided by policies and procedures which limit individual discretion, and given varying sanctions that they can use for or against others.

Given these characteristics of the job and the impersonality of rule systems, Presthus suggests that human motivations *other than* material benefits and satisfaction from productivity do not derive from the organization, specifically such motivations as the desires for love and self-realization. As a result, most human beings focus at work on the rewards which the organization *can* offer, obtaining satisfaction of other needs away from the job.

But the individual is confronted with the fact that whether or not he achieves job satisfaction is to a great degree determined by the persons who control him. This dependency is a continual source of anxiety or insecurity. The cause-effect relationships are:

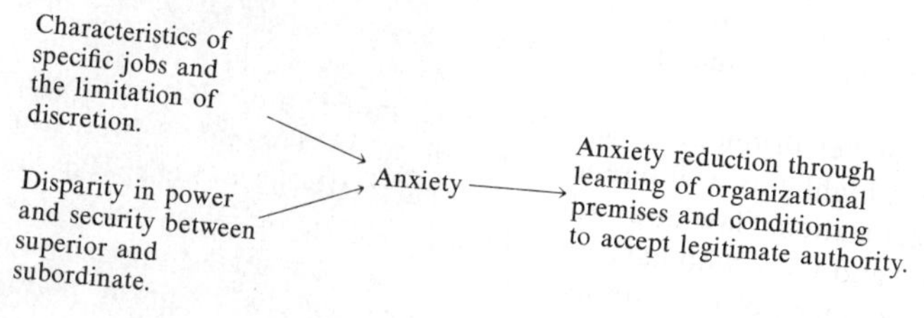

Barnard offers similar reasoning. He says that one reason people obey is that if the individual countermands orders received from above, he runs "the risk of being wrong." There is a process of "delegating upwards" from subordinate to superior, in which the subordinate gives up some freedom, discretion, or self-actualization to his superior in exchange for a lessening of his feeling of such risk. This phenomenon, which the sociologist Robert Merton [5] stressed, is similar to Presthus' anxiety reduction.

Another source of anxiety is the disparity between theory and reality. In our society there are strong egalitarian social values which say that "people are created equal" or that "democratic organizations are best" or that "all actions should be in accord with the goal of brotherly love." If the individual compares these ideals to the disparity of power and discretion that actually occurs in organizations, he experiences anxiety. The tension created by this inconsistency of ideal and action is also called *cognitive dissonance* by psychologists.

The selection by Gouldner proposes a way whereby this conflict can be reconciled by the promulgation of formal rules, policies, job descriptions, departmental objectives, and the like. These standing decisions reduce the number of contacts between superiors and subordinates, preventing a superior from giving too many direct orders. Because it is a "rule of the game," the standing decision or policy protects both the superior and the subordinate:

> [A standing rule] impersonally bolsters a supervisor's claim to authority without compelling him to employ an embarrassing and debatable legitimation in terms of his personal superiority. Conversely, it permits [subordinates] to accept managerial claims to deference without committing them

Readings

How to Choose A Leadership Pattern

ROBERT TANNENBAUM
WARREN H. SCHMIDT

er can be "democratic" in his relations
: maintain the necessary authority and
he is responsible has come into focus

n was not so acutely felt. The successful
ssing intelligence, imagination, initiative,
rally wise) decisions, and the ability to
think of the world as being divided into

ial sciences emerged the concept of "group
the group rather than solely on the leader.
nderscored the importance of employee
sion making. Evidence began to challenge
lership, and increasing attention was paid
n relations.
n group development that sprang up across
ons of leadership began to exert an impact.
efully designed to give people a first-hand
decision making. The designated "leaders"
ir own power and to make group members
g their own goals and methods within the

some of the people who attended the training
leadership as being truly "democratic" and
to build fully participative decision making
n ever their bosses made a decision without
ded to perceive this as authoritarian behavior.

The true symbol of democratic leadership to some was the meeting—and the less directed from the top, the more democratic it was.

Some of the more enthusiastic alumni of these training laboratories began to get the habit of categorizing leader behavior as "democratic" *or* "authoritarian." The boss who made too many decisions himself was thought of as an authoritarian, and his directive behavior was often attributed solely to his personality.

The net result of the research findings and of the human relations training based upon them has been to call into question the stereotype of an effective leader. Consequently, the modern manager often finds himself in an uncomfortable state of mind.

Often he is not quite sure how to behave; there are times when he is torn between exerting "strong" leadership and "permissive" leadership. Sometimes new knowledge pushes him in one direction ("I should really get the group to help make this decision"), but at the same time his experience pushes him in another direction ("I really understand the problem better than the group and therefore I should make the decision"). He is not sure when a group decision is really appropriate or when holding a staff meeting serves merely as a device for avoiding his own decision-making responsibility.

The purpose of our article is to suggest a framework which managers may find useful in grappling with this dilemma. First we shall look at the different patterns of leadership behavior that the manager can choose from in relating himself to his subordinates. Then we shall turn to some of the questions suggested by this range of patterns. For instance, how important is it for a manager's subordinates to know what type of leadership he is using in a situation? What factors should he consider in deciding on a leadership pattern? What difference do his long-run objectives make as compared to his immediate objectives?

Possible Leadership Behavior

Exhibit 1 presents the continuum or range of possible leadership behavior available to a manager. Each type of action is related to the degree of authority used by the boss and to the amount of freedom available to his subordinates in reaching decisions. The actions seen on the extreme left characterize the manager who maintains a high degree of control; those seen on the extreme right characterize the manager who releases a high degree of control. Neither extreme is absolute; authority and freedom are never without their limitations.

Now let us look more closely at each of the behavior points occurring along this continuum:

The manager makes the decision and announces it. In this case the boss identifies a problem, considers alternative solutions, chooses one of them, and then reports this decision to his subordinates for implementation. He may or may not give consideration to what he believes his subordinates will think or feel about his decision; in any case, he provides no opportunity for them to participate directly in the decision-making process. Coercion may or may not be used or implied.

The manager "sells" his decision. Here the manager, as before, takes responsibility for identifying the problem and arriving at a decision. However, rather than simply announcing it, he takes the additional step of persuading his subordinates to accept it. In doing so, he recognizes the possibility of some

y as extending from the top down-
assed down to them from a larger

many subhierarchies, each bound
lues in a way similar to that in the
l power structure headed by a leader
but who is a nonleader when viewed
rarchy. This devolution of power has
cipline, since the life chances of those
largely through representations made
s a result, an upward-looking posture
The will of the minority is transmitted
by the subleaders, reinforcing their
heir subhierarchy.

dhammer and Shils seems important,
n the viewpoints of those who have a
tation (Barnard, Locke, Fayol, O'Don-
ual-psychological or small-group orien-
iology and small-group sociology). The
s managers will appear reasonable to
behavior on the part of executives which
system. Most rules and directives will
acceptance" of employes. Goldhammer
type of authority (legitimate power ac-
rcion" (power of sanctions, accepted but
dinates).
with a psychological orientation, do not
integrate the desires of subordinates into
es reported elsewhere in this book to show
hority breaks down. They therefore see
ategy in organizations, and predict that it

ther of these viewpoints has been conclu-
ory may be true in one company situation
hooves us to be acquainted with both.

n the reading by Presthus as an important
act, Presthus views this as the central moti-
havior. It will be our purpose at this point
eduction, to show that other authors, under
ion as important, and to distinguish between
ordinate relationship and that caused by the
als.
ations. When people join large organizations,
(rewards and penalties) possessed by individ-
on the one hand and by higher office holders
ization is a hierarchical system of status and

Exhibit 1. Continuum of Leadership Behavior.

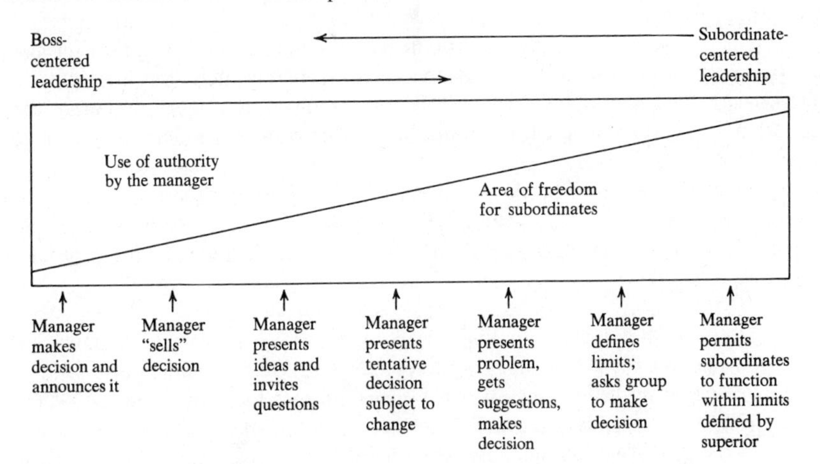

resistance among those who will be faced with the decision, and seeks to reduce this resistance by indicating, for example, what the employees have to gain from his decision.

The manager presents his ideas, invites questions. Here the boss who has arrived at a decision and who seeks acceptance of his ideas provides an opportunity for his subordinates to get a fuller explanation of his thinking and his intentions. After presenting the ideas, he invites questions so that his associates can better understand what he is trying to accomplish. This "give and take" also enables the manager and the subordinates to explore more fully the implications of the decision.

The manager presents a tentative decision subject to change. This kind of behavior permits the subordinates to exert some influence on the decision. The initiative for identifying and diagnosing the problem remains with the boss. Before meeting with his staff, he has thought the problem through and arrived at a decision—but only a tentative one. Before finalizing it, he presents his proposed solution for the reaction of those who will be affected by it. He says in effect, "I'd like to hear what you have to say about this plan that I have developed. I'll appreciate your frank reactions, but will reserve for myself the final decision."

The manager presents the problem, gets suggestions, and then makes his decision. Up to this point the boss has come before the group with a solution of his own. Not so in this case. The subordinates now get the first chance to suggest solutions. The manager's initial role involves identifying the problem. He might, for example, say something of this sort: "We are faced with a number of complaints from newspapers and the general public on our service policy. What is wrong here? What ideas do you have for coming to grips with this problem?"

The function of the group becomes one of increasing the manager's repertory of possible solutions to the problem. The purpose is to capitalize on the knowledge and experience of those who are on the "firing line." From the expanded list of alternatives developed by the manager and his subordinates, the manager then selects the solution that he regards as most promising.[1]

The manager defines the limits and requests the group to make a decision. At this point the manager passes to the group (possibly including himself as a member) the right to make decisions. Before doing so, however, he defines the problem to be solved and the boundaries within which the decision must be made.

An example might be the handling of a parking problem at a plant. The boss decides that this is something that should be worked on by the people involved, so he calls them together and points up the existence of the problem. Then he tells them:

> There is the open field just north of the main plant which has been designated for additional employee parking. We can build underground or surface multilevel facilities as long as the cost does not exceed $100,000. Within these limits we are free to work out whatever solution makes sense to us. After we decide on a specific plan, the company will spend the available money in whatever way we indicate.

The manager permits the group to make decisions within prescribed limits. This represents an extreme degree of group freedom only occasionally encountered in formal organizations, as, for instance, in many research groups. Here the team of managers or engineers undertakes the identification and diagnosis of the problem, develops alternative procedures for solving it, and decides on one or more of these alternative solutions. The only limits directly imposed on the group by the organization are those specified by the superior of the team's boss. If the boss participates in the decision-making process, he attempts to do so with no more authority than any other member of the group. He commits himself in advance to assist in implementing whatever decision the group makes.

As the continuum in Exhibit 1 demonstrates, there are a number of alternative ways in which a manager can relate himself to the group or individuals he is supervising. At the extreme left of the range, the emphasis is on the manager—on what *he* is interested in, how *he* sees things, how *he* feels about them. As we move toward the subordinate-centered end of the continuum, however, the focus is increasingly on the subordinates—on what *they* are interested in, how *they* look at things, how *they* feel about them.

When business leadership is regarded in this way, a number of questions arise. Let us take four of especial importance:

Can a boss ever relinquish his responsibility by delegating it to someone else? Our view is that the manager must expect to be held responsible by his superior for the quality of the decisions made, even though operationally these decisions may have been made on a group basis. He should, therefore, be ready to accept whatever risk is involved whenever he delegates decision-making power to his subordinates. Delegation is not a way of "passing the buck." Also, it should be emphasized that the amount of freedom the boss gives to his subordinates cannot

---

[1]For a fuller explanation of this approach, see Leo Moore, "Too Much Management, Too Little Change," *HBR,* January–February 1956, p. 41.

be greater than the freedom which he himself has been given by his own superior.

Should the manager participate with his subordinates once he has delegated responsibility to them? The manager should carefully think over this question and decide on his role prior to involving the subordinate group. He should ask if his presence will inhibit or facilitate the problem-solving process. There may be some instances when he should leave the group to let it solve the problem for itself. Typically, however, the boss has useful ideas to contribute, and should function as an additional member of the group. In the latter instance, it is important that he indicate clearly to the group that he sees himself in a *member* role rather than in an authority role.

How important is it for the group to recognize what kind of leadership behavior the boss is using? It makes a great deal of difference. Many relationship problems between boss and subordinate occur because the boss fails to make clear how he plans to use his authority. If, for example, he actually intends to make a certain decision himself, but the subordinate group gets the impression that he has delegated this authority, considerable confusion and resentment are likely to follow. Problems may also occur when the boss uses a "democratic" facade to conceal the fact that he has already made a decision which he hopes the group will accept as its own. The attempt to "make them think it was their idea in the first place" is a risky one. We believe that it is highly important for the manager to be honest and clear in describing what authority he is keeping and what role he is asking his subordinates to assume in solving a particular problem.

Can you tell how "democratic" a manager is by the number of decisions his subordinates make? The sheer *number* of decisions is not an accurate index of the amount of freedom that a subordinate group enjoys. More important is the *significance* of the decisions which the boss entrusts to his subordinates. Obviously a decision on how to arrange desks is of an entirely different order from a decision involving the introduction of new electronic data-processing equipment. Even though the widest possible limits are given in dealing with the first issue, the group will sense no particular degree of responsibility. For a boss to permit the group to decide equipment policy, even within rather narrow limits, would reflect a greater degree of confidence in them on his part.

Practical Leadership Behavior

Now let us turn from the types of leadership that are possible in a company situation to the question of what types are *practical* and *desirable.* What factors or forces should a manager consider in deciding how to manage? Three are of particular importance: forces in the manager; forces in the subordinates; forces in the situation.

We should like briefly to describe these elements and indicate how they might influence a manager's action in a decision-making situation.[2] The strength of each of them will, of course, vary from instance to instance, but the manager who is sensitive to them can better assess the problems which face him and determine which mode of leadership behavior is most appropriate for him.

[2] See also Robert Tannenbaum and Fred Massarik, "Participation by Subordinates in the Managerial Decision-Making Process," *Canadian Journal of Economics and Political Science,* August 1950, pp. 413–418.

Forces in the Manager

The manager's behavior in any given instance will be influenced greatly by the many forces operating within his own personality. He will, of course, perceive his leadership problems in a unique way on the basis of his background, knowledge, and experience. Among the important internal forces affecting him will be the following:

1. *His value system.* How strongly does he feel that individuals should have a share in making the decisions which affect them? Or, how convinced is he that the official who is paid to assume responsibility should personally carry the burden of decision making? The strength of his convictions on questions like these will tend to move the manager to one end or the other of the continuum shown in Exhibit 1. His behavior will also be influenced by the relative importance that he attaches to organizational efficiency, personal growth of subordinates, and company profits.[3]
2. *His confidence in his subordinates.* Managers differ greatly in the amount of trust they have in other people generally, and this carries over to the particular employees they supervise at a given time. In viewing his particular group of subordinates, the manager is likely to consider their knowledge and competence with respect to the problem. A central question he might ask himself is: "Who is best qualified to deal with this problem?" Often he may, justifiably or not, have more confidence in his own capabilities than in those of his subordinates.
3. *His own leadership inclinations.* There are some managers who seem to function more comfortably and naturally as highly directive leaders. Resolving problems and issuing orders come easily to them. Other managers seem to operate more comfortably in a team role, where they are continually sharing many of their functions with their subordinates.
4. *His feelings of security in an uncertain situation.* The manager who releases control over the decision-making process thereby reduces the predictability of the outcome. Some managers have a greater need than others for predictability and stability in their environment. This "tolerance for ambiguity" is being viewed increasingly by psychologists as a key variable in a person's manner of dealing with problems.

The manager brings these and other highly personal variables to each situation he faces. If he can see them as forces which, consciously or unconsciously, influence his behavior, he can better understand what makes him prefer to act in a given way. And understanding this, he can often make himself more effective.

Forces in the Subordinate

Before deciding how to lead a certain group, the manager will also want to consider a number of forces affecting his subordinates' behavior. He will want to remember that each employee, like himself, is influenced by many personality variables. In addition, each subordinate has a set of expectations about how the boss should act in relation to him (the phrase "expected behavior" is one we hear more and more often these days at discussions of leadership and teaching).

---

[3]See Chris Argyris, "Top Management Dilemma: Company Needs vs. Individual Development," *Personnel,* September 1955, pp. 123–134.

The better the manager understands these factors, the more accurately he can determine what kind of behavior on his part will enable his subordinates to act most effectively.

Generally speaking, the manager can permit his subordinates greater freedom if the following essential conditions exist:

1. If the subordinates have relatively high needs for independence. (As we all know, people differ greatly in the amount of direction that they desire.)
2. If the subordinates have a readiness to assume responsibility for decision making. (Some see additional responsibility as a tribute to their ability; others see it as "passing the buck.")
3. If they have a relatively high tolerance for ambiguity. (Some employees prefer to have clear-cut directives given to them; others prefer a wider area of freedom.)
4. If they are interested in the problem and feel that it is important.
5. If they understand and identify with the goals of the organization.
6. If they have the necessary knowledge and experience to deal with the problem.
7. If they have learned to expect to share in decision making. (Persons who have come to expect strong leadership and are then suddenly confronted with the request to share more fully in decision making are often upset by this new experience. On the other hand, persons who have enjoyed a considerable amount of freedom resent the boss who begins to make all the decisions himself.)

The manager will probably tend to make fuller use of his own authority if the above conditions do *not* exist; at times there may be no realistic alternative to running a "one-man show."

The restrictive effect of many of the forces will, of course, be greatly modified by the general feeling of confidence which subordinates have in the boss. Where they have learned to respect and trust him, he is free to vary his behavior. He will feel certain that he will not be perceived as an authoritarian boss on those occasions when he makes decisions by himself. Similarly, he will not be seen as using staff meetings to avoid his decision-making responsibility. In a climate of mutual confidence and respect, people tend to feel less threatened by deviations from normal practice, which in turn makes possible a higher degree of flexibility in the whole relationship.

Forces in the Situation

In addition to the forces which exist in the manager himself and in his subordinates, certain characteristics of the general situation will also affect the manager's behavior. Among the more critical environmental pressures that surround him are those which stem from the organization, the work group, the nature of the problem, and the pressures of time. Let us look briefly at each of these:

Type of Organization. Like individuals, organizations have values and traditions which inevitably influence the behavior of the people who work in them. The manager who is a newcomer to a company quickly discovers that certain kinds of behavior are approved while others are not. He also discovers that to deviate radically from what is generally accepted is likely to create problems for him.

These values and traditions are communicated in many ways—through job descriptions, policy pronouncements, and public statements by top executives. Some organizations, for example, hold to the notion that the desirable executive is one who is dynamic, imaginative, decisive, and persuasive. Other organizations put more emphasis upon the importance of the executive's ability to work effectively with people—his human relations skills. The fact that his superiors have a defined concept of what the good executive should be will very likely push the manager toward one end or the other of the behavioral range.

In addition to the above, the amount of employee participation is influenced by such variables as the size of the working units, their geographical distribution, and the degree of inter- and intra-organizational security required to attain company goals. For example, the wide geographical dispersion of an organization may preclude a practical system of participative decision making, even though this would otherwise be desirable. Similarly, the size of the working units or the need for keeping plans confidential may make it necessary for the boss to exercise more control than would otherwise be the case. Factors like these may limit considerably the manager's ability to function flexibly on the continuum.

Group effectiveness. Before turning decision-making responsibility over to a subordinate group, the boss should consider how effectively its members work together as a unit.

One of the relevant factors here is the experience the group has had in working together. It can generally be expected that a group which has functioned for some time will have developed habits of cooperation and thus be able to tackle a problem more effectively than a new group. It can also be expected that a group of people with similar backgrounds and interests will work more quickly and easily than people with dissimilar backgrounds, because the communication problems are likely to be less complex.

The degree of confidence that the members have in their ability to solve problems as a group is also a key consideration. Finally, such group variables as cohesiveness, permissiveness, mutual acceptance, and commonality of purpose will exert subtle but powerful influence on the group's functioning.

The Problem Itself. The nature of the problem may determine what degree of authority should be delegated by the manager to his subordinates. Obviously he will ask himself whether they have the kind of knowledge which is needed. It is possible to do them a real disservice by assigning a problem that their experience does not equip them to handle.

Since the problems faced in large or growing industries increasingly require knowledge of specialists from many different fields, it might be inferred that the more complex a problem, the more anxious a manager will be to get some assistance in solving it. However, this is not always the case. There will be times when the very complexity of the problem calls for one person to work it out. For example, if the manager has most of the background and factual data relevant to a given issue, it may be easier for him to think it through himself than to take the time to fill in his staff on all the pertinent background information.

The key question to ask, of course, is: "Have I heard the ideas of everyone who has the necessary knowledge to make a significant contribution to the solution of this problem?"

The Pressure of Time. This is perhaps the most clearly felt pressure on the manager (in spite of the fact that it may sometimes be imagined). The more that he feels the need for an immediate decision, the more difficult it is to involve other people. In organizations which are in a constant state of "crisis" and "crash programing" one is likely to find managers personally using a high degree of authority with relatively little delegation to subordinates. When the time pressure is less intense, however, it becomes much more possible to bring subordinates in on the decision-making process.

These, then, are the principal forces that impinge on the manager in any given instance and that tend to determine his tactical behavior in relation to his subordinates. In each case his behavior ideally will be that which makes possible the most effective attainment of his immediate goal within the limits facing him.

Long-Run Strategy

As the manager works with his organization on the problems that come up day by day, his choice of a leadership pattern is usually limited. He must take account of the forces just described and, within the restrictions they impose on him, do the best that he can. But as he looks ahead months or even years, he can shift his thinking from tactics to large-scale strategy. No longer need he be fettered by all of the forces mentioned, for he can view many of them as variables over which he has some control. He can, for example, gain new insights or skills for himself, supply training for individual subordinates, and provide participative experiences for his employee group.

In trying to bring about a change in these variables, however, he is faced with a challenging question: At which point along the continuum *should* he act?

The answer depends largely on what he wants to accomplish. Let us suppose that he is interested in the same objectives that most modern managers seek to attain when they can shift their attention from the pressure of immediate assignments:

1. To raise the level of employee motivation.
2. To increase the readiness of subordinates to accept change.
3. To improve the quality of all managerial decisions.
4. To develop teamwork and morale.
5. To further the individual development of employees.

In recent years the manager has been deluged with a flow of advice on how best to achieve these longer-run objectives. It is little wonder that he is often both bewildered and annoyed. However, there are some guidelines which he can usefully follow in making a decision.

Most research and much of the experience of recent years give a strong factual basis to the theory that a fairly high degree of subordinate-centered behavior is associated with the accomplishment of the five purposes mentioned.[4] This does not mean that a manager should always leave all decisions to his assistants. To provide the individual or the group with greater freedom than they are ready for at any given time may very well tend to generate anxieties and therefore inhibit rather than facilitate the attainment of desired objectives. But

---

[4]For example, see Warren H. Schmidt and Paul C. Buchanan, *Techniques that Produce Teamwork* (New London, Arthur C. Croft Publications, 1954); and Morris S. Viteles, *Motivation and Morale in Industry* (New York, W. W. Norton & Company, Inc., 1953).

this should not keep the manager from making a continuing effort to confront his subordinates with the challenge of freedom.

Conclusions

In summary, there are two implications in the basic thesis that we have been developing. The first is that the successful leader is one who is keenly aware of those forces which are most relevant to his behavior at any given time. He accurately understands himself, the individuals and group he is dealing with, and the company and broader social environment in which he operates. And certainly he is able to assess the present readiness for growth of his subordinates.

But this sensitivity or understanding is not enough, which brings us to the second implication. The successful leader is one who is able to behave appropriately in the light of these perceptions. If direction is in order, he is able to direct; if considerable participative freedom is called for, he is able to provide such freedom.

Thus, the successful manager of men can be primarily characterized neither as a strong leader nor as a permissive one. Rather, he is one who maintains a high batting average in accurately assessing the forces that determine what his most appropriate behavior at any given time should be and in actually being able to behave accordingly. Being both insightful and flexible, he is less likely to see the problems of leadership as a dilemma.

Management by Integration and Self-control

DOUGLAS McGREGOR

Let us consider in some detail a specific illustration of the operation of a managerial strategy based on Theory Y. The concept of "management by objectives" has received considerable attention in recent years, in part due to the writings of Peter Drucker. However, management by objectives has often been interpreted in a way which leads to no more than a new set of tactics within a strategy of management by direction and control.

The strategy to be illustrated in the following pages is an application of Theory Y. Its purpose is to encourage integration, to create a situation in which a subordinate can achieve his own goals *best* by directing his efforts toward the objectives of the enterprise. It is a deliberate attempt to link improvement in managerial competence with the satisfaction of higher-level ego and self-actualization needs. It is thus a special and not at all a typical case of the conventional conception of management by objectives.

This strategy includes four steps or phases:

1. The clarification of the broad requirements of the job
2. The establishment of specific "targets" for a limited time period

---

3. The management process during the target period
4. Appraisal of the results

Harry Evans is Vice President, Staff Services, for a manufacturing company with twenty plants throughout the Middle West and the South. The company is aggressively managed and financially successful; it is growing fairly rapidly through acquisition of smaller companies and the development of new markets for its products.

Evans was brought into the company three years ago by the President, who felt that the staff functions of the organization needed strengthening. One of the President's concerns was the personnel department, which had been something of a stepchild since it was established in the early forties. He felt that the management needed a lot of help and guidance in order to fulfill its responsibilities in this field.

Tom Harrison has been Director of Personnel Administration for a little less than a year. Evans selected him from among a number of candidates. Although he is not as well trained professionally as some of his colleagues, he appeared to have good promise as an administrator. He is in his young forties, intelligent, ambitious, personable, a hard worker with ten years of practical experience in personnel administration.

After Harrison had been on the job a few months, Evans had formed the following impressions about him:

1. He is overly anxious to make a good impression on top management, and this interferes with his performance. He watches too carefully to see which way the wind is blowing and trims his sails accordingly. He accepts even the most trivial assignments from any of the top management group, which makes a good impression but does little to strengthen the personnel function. He has done nothing to change the rather naïve top management expectation that personnel administration can be delegated to a staff department ("You take care of the personnel problems and we'll run the business.").
2. Harrison is a poor manager, somewhat to Evan's surprise, since he appeared to function well with more limited supervisory responsibilities. He uses his subordinates as errand boys rather than as resources, and he is much too ready to impose upon them his own practical and common-sense views of what should be done, brushing aside their specialized professional knowledge. He is anxious to reorganize the department, giving key responsibilities to men like himself who have practical experience but limited professional training.

These things added up, in Evans's eyes, to an inadequate conception of the nature of the personnel job and the proper role of the Department within the company. He recognized the value of management's acceptance of Harrison's practical orientation, but he felt that the real needs of the company would not be met unless management acquired a quite different point of view with respect to the function. He was not at all inclined to replace Harrison, since he believed he had the capacity to perform effectively, but he recognized that Harrison was not going to grow into the job without help. His strategy involved the four steps listed below.

Step 1: Determining the Major Requirements of the Job

Evans suggested to Harrison that he would like him to give some intensive thought to the nature of his job in the light of his experience so far. He asked him to list what he felt to be his major responsibilities, using the formal position description in his possession if he wished, but not limiting himself to it. He said, "I'd like to discuss with you at some length *your* view of your job after being on it for the past eight months."

The list of requirements which Harrison subsequently brought in for discussion with Evans was as follows:

1. Organization of the Department
2. Services to top management
   a. Awareness of company problems and provision of programs and policies for solving them
3. Productivity of the Department
   a. Efficient administration of personnel programs and services
   b. Definite assignments of projects to staff with completion dates and follow-up
   c. Periodic appraisals of the performance of department members, with appropriate action
4. Field relations
   a. Providing the field units with advice, adequate programs, information
   b. Periodic visits to assure the adequacy of field personnel units

Harrison and Evans had several lengthy discussions of this list of responsibilities. Evans began by saying, "Tom, I asked you to bring to this meeting a written statement of the major requirements of your job as you see them. Perhaps you expected me to define your job for you, to tell you what I want you to do. If I were to do so, it would not be your job. Of course, I don't expect that I will necessarily see eye to eye with you on everything you have written down. I do take it for granted that we have a common purpose: We both want yours to be the best damned personnel department anywhere.

"The difficulty we are likely to have in discussing your ideas is that if I disagree with you, you'll feel you have to accept what I say because I'm your boss. I want to help you end up with a list that we are both completely satisfied with, but I can't help if you simply defer to my ideas or if I don't express them for fear of dominating you. So try to think of me as a colleague whose experience and knowledge are at your disposal—not as your boss. I'm certain we can resolve any differences that may come up."

In the course of the discussion Evans did bring up his concerns, but he put major emphasis on encouraging Harrison to examine his own ideas critically. Evans talked quite frankly about the realities of the company situation as he saw them, and he discussed his conception of the proper role for a personnel department. He tried to persuade Harrison that his conception of the personnel function was too limited, and that his own subordinates, because of their training and experience, could help him arrive at a more adequate conception. Harrison held a couple of meetings with his own department staff to discuss this whole question, and after each of them he had further conversations with Evans.

The critically significant factor in these discussions was not their content, but the redefinition of roles which took place. Evans succeeded, by his manner more than by his specific words, in conveying to Harrison the essential point that he did not want to occupy the conventional role of boss, but rather, to the fullest extent possible, the role of a consultant who was putting all of his knowledge and experience at Harrison's disposal in the conviction that they had a genuine common interest in Harrison's doing an outstanding job.

As he began to sense this, and to believe it, Harrison's whole perception of his own role changed. Instead of seeking to find out, as would be natural under conventional circumstances, how Evans wanted him to define his job, what Evans wanted him to do, what Evans would approve or disapprove, Harrison began to think for himself. Moreover, with this greater sense of freedom about his own role (and with Evans's open encouragement) he began to perceive his own subordinates not as "hands," but as resources, and to use them thus.

The result, unrealistic as it may seem at first glance, was a dramatic change in Harrison's perception of himself and of his job. The true nature of the change that took place during these discussions with Evans and with his subordinates was revealed in his final statement of his responsibilities as he now perceived them:

1. Organization of the Department
2. Continuous assessment of both short- and long-run company needs through:
   a. Exploration in the field
   b. General awareness of management's problems
   c. Exploration of the views of members of the Department
   d. Knowledge of external trends
3. Professional help to all levels of management
   a. Problem solving
   b. Strategy planning
   c. Research studies
   d. Effective personnel programs and policies
   e. Efficient administration of services
4. Development of staff members
5. Personal development

This first step in Evans's managerial strategy with Harrison is thus consistent with his commitment to Theory Y. He believes that Harrison must take the major responsibility for his own development, but he believes he can help. He conceives of integration as an active process which inevitably involves differences of opinion and argument. He recognizes the likelihood that Harrison may accede too readily to his views without real conviction, and he does not want this to happen. Consequently he attempts to establish a relationship in which Harrison can perceive him as a genuine source of help rather than as a boss in the conventional sense. He knows that the establishment of this relationship will take time, but it is the long-term results which he considers important. Since he does not expect that Harrison will grow into his job overnight, he is prepared to accept a definition of Harrison's job which is considerably short of perfection. He is confident that it will be improved six months hence when they discuss it again.

If Harrison is going to learn and grow in competence, and if he is going to find opportunities to satisfy his higher-level needs in the process, it is essential that he find a genuine challenge in his job. This is unlikely if the job is defined for him by a formal position description or by a superior who simply tells him what he wants done. Thus, the principle of integration is important right at the start. It is not necessary in applying it to ignore the work of the organization planning staff. The necessity for a logical division of responsibilities within any organization is obvious. However, a position description is likely to become a strait jacket unless it is recognized to be a broad set of guidelines within which the individual literally makes his own job. The conception of an organization plan as a series of predetermined "slots" into which individuals are selectively placed denies the whole idea of integration.

The process involved at this step is similar, although more limited in scope, to the one so aptly described by Drucker as discovering "what business we are in." In the case of top management looking at the organization as a whole, this frequently is a highly instructive experience. The same thing can be true even in a limited setting such as this, especially if the superior can, by doing something like Evans is doing, encourage the subordinate to think creatively about his job.

Step 2: Setting Targets

When Evans and Harrison finished their discussion of the major requirements of Harrison's job, Evans suggested that Harrison think about some specific objectives or targets which he might set for himself and his department during the following six months. Evans suggested that he think both about improving the over-all performance of his unit and about his own personal goals. He asked him further to consider in broad terms what steps he proposed to take to achieve these targets. Evans said, "I don't want to tell you how to do your job, but I would like you to do some careful thinking about how you are going to proceed. Perhaps I can be helpful when we discuss your ideas." Finally, Evans asked Harrison to consider what information he would require, and how he might obtain it, in order to know at the end of the period how well he had succeeded in reaching his targets. He suggested that they get together to talk further when Harrison had completed his thinking and planning along these lines.

This is the planning phase, but again the process is one in which the subordinate is encouraged to take responsibility for his own performance. The conventional process is one in which objectives are conceived by higher levels and imposed on lower levels of the organization. The rationale is that only the higher levels have available the broader knowledge necessary for planning. To some extent this is true, but there is an important difference between the kind of planning in which a central group determines in detail what each division or department will do, and that in which the central group communicates what are believed to be the desirable over-all objectives and *asks* each unit to determine what it can contribute.

Even when general objectives are predetermined, they can usually be limited to certain aspects of performance such as production goals, costs, and profit margin. There are other aspects which are subject to local determination, as is, of course, the planning with respect to personal objectives.

The important theoretical consideration, derived from Theory Y, is that the acceptance of responsibility (for self-direction and self-control) is correlated with commitment to objectives. Genuine commitment is seldom achieved when objectives are externally imposed. Passive acceptance is the most that can be expected; indifference or resistance are the more likely consequences. Some degree of *mutual* involvement in the determination of objectives is a necessary aspect of managerial planning based on Theory Y. This is embodied in Evans's suggestions to Harrison.

In the discussion of targets, the superior again attempts a helping role rather than an authoritative one. His primary interest is in helping the subordinate plan his own job in such a fashion that both personal and organizational goals will be achieved. While the superior has a veto power by virtue of his position, he will exercise it only if it becomes absolutely necessary.

To be sure, subordinates will sometimes set unrealistic goals, particularly the first time they approach a task like this. Experience has indicated that the usual problem is that the goals are set too high, not too low. While the superior can, through judicious advice, help the subordinate adjust unrealistic goals, there may often be greater long-run advantages in permitting the subordinate to learn by experience than in simply telling him where his planning is unrealistic or inadequate.

The list of targets which Harrison brought for discussion with Evans was this:

1. Determination of major company needs, long and short range, by:
   a. Field visits and discussions with local management
   b. Intensive discussions with top management
   c. Exploration of the views of the personnel department staff
   A plan, with assignments of responsibility, and a time schedule will be worked out for this. I expect we can complete the study within six months, but a report and subsequent plans will probably not be completed by September.
2. Joint determination with department staff of current projects
   This will involve planning such as you and I are doing.
3. Development of departmental staff members
   Items 1 and 2 can be a vehicle for this. I need help in learning how to work better with my subordinates, and particularly on how to eliminate the friction between the old-timers and the college-trained youngsters.
4. Self-development
   a. I'd like to do some reading to improve my own thinking about personnel administration—or maybe take a university course. I'd like your advice.
   b. I guess I haven't gained as much skill as a manager as I need. I hear rumblings that some of my staff are not happy with me as a boss. I'd like to do something about this, but I'm not sure what is the best way to proceed.
5. Development of a good plan of organization for the department
   In working through some of the above projects, I think I'll get some good ideas about how we ought to be set up as a department.

Since the working relationship between the two men had been quite well established during their earlier discussions, there was a comfortable give and take at this stage. Evans saw the first target as a crucial one which could become the basis for an entirely new conception of the department's role. He felt also that it could be extremely educational for Harrison provided he tackled it with sensitivity and an open mind. Accordingly he spent several hours helping Harrison to think through his strategy for determining the needs of the company with respect to personnel administration. Harrison began to see that this project was a means by which he could work toward all the other targets on his list.

Evans had little difficulty after Harrison's earlier experiences in persuading him to involve his subordinates in developing plans for the project. He suggested that Harrison continue to meet with him to discuss and evaluate this process for a couple of months. He felt—and said—that this might be the best method for Harrison to begin improving his own managerial skills.

They agreed that Harrison would explore possible university programs during the next few months to see if some one of these might meet his needs a little later. Meanwhile, they worked out a reading list and a plan for an occasional session when Harrison could discuss his reading.

In view of the nature of the personnel function, and the particular problems facing Harrison, the targets did not lend themselves to quantitative measurement such as might have been possible in a production operation. Nevertheless, Harrison, under Evans's tutelage, worked out a fairly detailed plan with specific steps to be accomplished by the end of six months. Evans's interest was that Harrison would have a basis for evaluating his own accomplishments at the end of the period.

Evans brought into the discussion the question of their relationship during the ensuing period. He said, "I don't want to be in a position of checking up on you from week to week. These are your plans, and I have full confidence that you will make every effort to reach your targets. On the other hand, I want you to feel free to seek help if you want it. There are ways in which I believe my experience can be useful to you. Suppose we leave it that we'll get together on your initiative as often as you wish—not for you to report how you are doing, but to discuss any problems which you would like my help on, or any major revisions in your plans." Thus Evans helped Harrison still further to perceive the role that he wanted to occupy as a superior, and thus also to clarify his own responsibilities as a subordinate.

Step 3: The Ensuing Period

Since this is a managerial strategy rather than a personnel technique, the period between the establishment of targets and the evaluation of accomplishment is just as important as the first two steps. What happens during this period will depend upon the unique circumstances. The aim is to further the growth of the subordinate: his increased competence, his full acceptance of responsibility (self-direction and self-control), his ability to achieve integration between organizational requirements and his own personal goals.

In this particular situation Evans's primary interests were two: (1) the emergence throughout the company of a more adequate conception of the personnel function, and (2) the development of a competent department which would provide leadership and professional help to all levels of management with respect to this function. He felt that, as a result of steps 1 and 2 of his strategy, Harrison too was committed to these objectives. Moreover, he was persuaded that Harrison's project for assessing company needs in the field of personnel administration—as now conceived—was a highly promising means to these ends. He warned himself that he must be careful on two counts. First he must not expect too much too fast. The company situation was in no sense critical and there was no need for a crash program. Harrison's project was certain to be a valuable learning experience for him and his staff.

Second, Evans recognized that if the best learning was to occur, he must curb his natural tendency to step in and guide the project. Harrison would make mistakes; at his present level of sophistication he would quite possibly fail to appreciate the full scope of the task. Nevertheless, Evans decided more would be gained if he limited his influence to those occasions when Harrison sought his help.

This is what he did. His confidence in Harrison proved to have been justified. He and his staff tackled the project with more ingenuity and sensitivity than Evans would have imagined possible and began rather quickly to understand the true dimensions of the problem. Harrison came in one day to tell him that they had decided to extend their explorations to include visits to several university centers in order to take advantage of the point of view of some top-flight academic people. Also, they planned to test some of their emerging ideas against the experience of several other companies.

After this discussion, and the evidence it provided concerning the expansion of Harrison's intellectual horizons and the use he was making of the resources represented by his subordinates, Evans stopped worrying. He would bail them out if they got into trouble, but he anticipated no such necessity.

Step 4: Self-Appraisal

At the end of August, Harrison reminded Evans (not vice versa!) that the six months was up. "When do you want a report?" was his question. Evans responded that a report was not what he wanted, but Harrison's own evaluation of what he had accomplished with respect to the targets he had set six months earlier. Said Evans, "This can give you a basis for planning for the next six months."

A week later Harrison brought the following notes to a discussion with Evans.

Appraisal, September 1

1. Determination of major company needs:
   a. The field work is completed.
   b. My staff and I are working on a proposal that will involve a new conception of personnel administration in this company. We will have a draft for discussion with you within thirty days, and we want you to take a full day to let us present our findings and proposals to you.
   c. The results of our work make it clear that we have an educational job to do with top management, and I want to include a plan along these lines in my next set of targets.
2. Joint determination with staff of current projects. I am now conducting a set of target-setting meetings with my department staff as a whole in which we are laying our plans for the next year. All major projects—individual or group—are being discussed out in detail there. These department meetings will be followed by individual planning sessions.
3. Development of department staff members
   a. The major project we have been carrying out has changed my ideas about several of my subordinates. I'm learning how to work with them, and it's clear they are growing. Our presentation to you next month will show you what I mean.
   b. I've appreciated how much your target-setting approach has helped my development, and I'm attempting to use it with each of my subordinates. Also, I think the departmental planning mentioned under 2 above is a developmental tool. I've been talking with some people in the B——— Company who do this and I'm excited about its possibilities in our own company.
4. Self-development
   All I can say is I've learned more in the past six months than in the previous five years.
5. Departmental organization

I haven't done a thing about it. It doesn't seem very important right now. We seem to be able to plan our work as a department pretty well without developing a new setup. Perhaps we'll need to come back to this during the next six months, but there are more important things to be done first.

6. General comment

I would rate myself considerably lower than I would have six months ago in terms of how well I'm filling the responsibilities of my job. It's going to take me a couple of years to measure up to what you have a right to expect of the man in this spot, but I think I can do it.

The discussion of this self-appraisal went into considerable detail. Evans felt that Harrison had acquired quite a little insight into his own strengths and weaknesses, and they were able to discuss objectively where he needed to give thought to improving his competence further. Harrison, for example, opened up the whole problem of his "yes-man" attitude in dealing with top management and pointed out that his exploratory interviews with some of these men had resulted in increased self-confidence. He said, "I think maybe I can learn to stand up for my ideas better in the future. You have helped me to realize that I can think for myself, and that I can defend myself in an argument."

They agreed to postpone Harrison's discussion of plans for the next six months until after the one-day session at which Evans would meet with the whole department. "Then," said Harrison, "I want to talk over with you a new statement of my responsibilities which I'm working on."

The Headquarters Staff Man in the Role of a Consultant

HARRY D. KOLB

Theories of organization underlying the American business corporation are not static. Fortunately, continuing process of change is at work. Thus, we find new concepts evolving while old, established ones are challenged and sometimes must give way.

Such is the nature of the subject of this paper. It deals with a changing idea as to what type of relationship should prevail between the staff man in a corporate headquarters and the various key managers he serves. It includes a change in role with respect to the corporate headquarters managers, but even more specifically a change in role with respect to the field organizations. It is in this arena that the internal (or "captive") consultant represents an emerging concept.

An example may illustrate the need. Consider a group of managers from

Harry D. Kolb, *Organizational Theory in Industrial Practice* (New York: John Wiley & Sons, Inc., 1962), pp. 143–152. Reprinted by permission of the publisher.

a variety of field units meeting under the auspices of a headquarters staff department. If given an assignment to discuss what types of help they want from the headquarters staff group, the resulting discussion tends to be cautious and unenthusiastic. It is not difficult to imagine why. The headquarters staff man is normally seen as being in a controlling role rather than a consulting one. He sits in judgment. He has an inherent power of recommendation and communication to the headquarters line management. He has often failed to measure up to the expectations of those in the field who may have looked to him for help.

Even if the headquarters staff man should seek to operate in a new role, he still must deal with the experiences of the past. There have been a variety of roles taken by staff men. These include:

1. The auditor or inspector, who is concerned with enforcement, procedural compliance, faultfinding, and data collection for communication back to the headquarters.
2. The advisor or "helper" who offers unnecessary help and is less than fully responsible for the consequences of his advice.
3. The promoter or experimenter, whose interests are self-centered rather than designed for real problems in the field unit.
4. The technician who, though competent, is too rigid to be adaptable.

And now, the concept of "consultant" is being added as a new type of staff man from headquarters. In the past, field-unit managers have learned to recognize these various types of staff men and have built up their own procedures for dealing with them. The intent here is not to belittle the fundamental usefulness of all these activities; rather, it is to point out that when a new role is created, some light needs to be shed on what is intended and how this new type of staff man should be dealt with.

Field organizations have held certain stereotypes regarding the headquarters staff man. These are inherited and must be examined if a different type of relationship is intended. One of these stereotypes is that headquarters line managers rely on their staff men to provide information to them in order that the line managers can exercise their function of control. This type of staff behavior has to be changed under the consulting relationship that is intended. But, in order to accept this change, headquarters managers must first reexamine their own philosophy which says they need information from their staff people in order to exercise control. Fortunately, the newer consultant concept is an outgrowth of central managers relinquishing control to their field units. Thus, an implementation of true decentralization of control has both permitted and promoted the growth of the concept of the headquarters consultant. It is believed that the use of consultants will grow in proportion to the amount of progress a multi-plant corporation makes in this type of decentralization.

By decentralization is meant the transfer of latitude to the local field unit, particularly in terms of the methods, procedures, and emphasis it uses in how it tackles its job. This also includes the processes used to motivate and communicate and strengthen its own internal organization. It includes the way in which the organization develops its people, the philosophies that underlie its training efforts for its organization and, in general, its latitude in deciding how to utilize resources in order to accomplish its assigned mission.

When headquarters grants real latitude in these directions, it then faces a dilemma as to the amount and kind of staff help and direction which it should furnish, in order to avoid overcontrolling the activities of field managers. Some staff help is still intended, since the philosophy of decentralization does not mean abandonment. In addition, headquarters should provide staff help, first because of its responsibility for the business and, second, because of the inherent potential here for profit improvement.

Let us separate here certain types of staff service essential for financial procedures, for quality control, and for research and technical support. These are not usually areas in which there is as much doubt regarding appropriate staff behavior. More frequently, the question of the staff consulting role comes up in connection with headquarters departments in the fields of employee relations, public relations, organization planning, management development, and various advisory services. The following comments refer to staff work of these latter types of groups in which the focus is on human behavior.

The tradition of using a consulting role for such a staff man is not yet well developed. As a result, the staff man frequently falls into the pitfall of using inappropriate means in order to enhance his status and influence. This may constitute telling the local managers what they may or should not do. It involves utilizing the influence of headquarters management in order to constitute pressure on field units to get them to do what the staff man feels they should do.

The many types of inappropriate behavior are fairly clearly known. Although they may be regarded as inappropriate, even by those who indulge in them, what is not too clear is what alternative behavior is necessary first to be effective and, second, to be acceptable, both in the field and at headquarters.

The headquarters manager has his own concerns about what he should expect of the staff man. On the one hand, he feels the need for furnishing only such central services as can be really justified. On the other hand, he wants to rely on his staff to keep him informed wherever problem areas exist in the field, so that he can then be in a position of protecting the company's interests. This presupposes, therefore, that the staff group renders frequent and critical reports to the headquarters management. Yet doing so prevents growth of the type of consultant who is welcome in the field on the basis of being able to provide professional help, while at the same time maintaining a confidential relationship with his client. It is on this paradox of help to the headquarters manager and a confidential client relationship in the field that the problem is centered.

Herbert Shepard of Case Institute has commented in this direction as follows:

> Staff groups often try to enhance their influence by identifying themselves with groups that have formal authority in the organization. Thus some staff groups may be regarded as spies serving higher levels, as agents of headquarters authority, or as mechanisms for the prevention of decentralization.
>
> Sometimes this reputation is gained through indiscreet use of privileged communication, sometimes by the explicit operating principles of the staff man, as when he identifies himself as being responsible to a higher level.
>
> The temptation may be strong to use privileged communication or observations made in the field to build the staff's influence and reputation

> in the home office. Related to this is the tendency of the staff man, if he is unable to influence lower levels in the direction he thinks best, to try to get someone at higher level to lend his authority. This procedure may be momentarily effective, but turns the staff man into a threat rather than a resource for the future.

Professor Shepard goes on to point out that any indiscretion on the part of the consultant can very quickly render him of little further use. Therefore he concludes that:

> If the staff man thinks certain kinds of information should be shared between groups or levels, his job is to help the parties communicate, rather than to communicate for them.

Headquarters management has to make up its mind whether or not it can rely on its field managers as the source of upward communication regarding problems, needs, and developments. The use of the staff system as a substitute for reliance upon direct upward communication has in the past subverted this more logical and appropriate direct upward channel.

Therefore, one of the essential conditions for an effective consultant role is this confidential relationship between the headquarters staff man and the field unit. The information which he gains regarding the operation of the field unit is not to be communicated by him within the headquarters. When he is in the field unit, he is serving the local manager in the same manner that an outside consultant would; he has a status of independence and, yet, he is working for the local manager.

Until the local unit accepts the fact that the consultant is not going to relay punitive information back to the headquarters, the consultant will not really gain access to reliable sources of information. If, however, this type of trust can be developed, then the staff man can be immensely more valuable to the local manager because he will be in a position to facilitate communication within the organization he is serving. His independence and freedom from immersion in the local organization's channels makes him a powerful mechanism for aiding the organization to surmount blockages that have been built up in its communication network.

If a headquarters management can accept the idea that its specialized consulting staffs do not make reports in the home office, how can it determine that such centralized services are justified or properly being used? The consultant has to rely upon the field management to communicate upward its own evaluation of his worth. This is, of course, risky and perhaps uncomfortable for the staff man. He is frequently by nature one who feels the lack of power in his position and, therefore, tends to want to draw attention to the usefulness of his work in order to enhance his own reputation. To the extent to which he develops a true consultant role, however, he will find less appropriate opportunity for doing this. Yet this can benefit the organization. If line management has to rely on appraisal of the effectiveness of staff work as judged by the clients (rather than as reported by the consultant), there can well be a lifting of standards of performance. Certain kinds of staff support which have been covered up, despite inadequacies in their quality, might by this system be revealed for what they are.

Thus far, we have dealt with the three-party relationship between the staff man, the local manager, and the headquarters manager. Considerably more is to be learned regarding the two-party relationship of the consultant with the local manager. Here is a man free from the bonds of organization channels and, therefore, free to approach the local manager directly. Does this mean that he concentrates his efforts at this spot in the organization, rather than working with lower echelons and rather than working with some counterpart local staff? The answer is not simple or clear-cut since all three types of concentration may be appropriate at different times.

There is no doubt that many an outside consultant has come to the conclusion that his effectiveness depends upon being able to communicate directly with the top man. However, this may be merely a question of strategy in order to get some initial commitment to a study or an undertaking. If the internal consultant is going to be useful, he needs to be able to bridge the gap between local staff and the local manager and to be a communication catalyst and link. Also, if the kinds of activities he is to engage in are those which rightly involve the total organization, he would be ill-advised to confine his contracts to just the top manager. A potential competitiveness exists between the consultant and any counterpart local staff. The effective consultant can recognize this, not be channel-bound because of it, and yet be supportive rather than destructive in order to enhance the position of the local staff man.

Another difficulty can arise when the consultant finds a local situation which is alarming, and yet sees his recommendations for improvement being ignored. What can he do? We have already seen that it would be inappropriate for him to communicate this to headquarters, and yet he is hardly so disinterested as to be able to ignore the situation. Few men are in the position that a famous outside consultant was in once when he rendered a report to a prominent American corporation regarding their labor-relations problems. With his report went his invoice for a substantial fee. Subsequently the president of the corporation called him in and said: "Here's the check for your fee, but we don't plan to do a damn thing about any of the recommendations in your report." Whereupon the consultant said, "If that's the way you feel, we don't need your check." Whereupon he tore up the check in front of the man and left.

This independence is commendable—and rare. Subsequent events proved the consultant right, and the firm recalled him and started to rely on his advice. Perhaps this does suggest that the internal consultant can only rely upon patience, while at the same time trying to maintain his independence and the integrity of his ideas. One of the continual worries is that the internal consultant will tend to sacrifice his own values as a result of pressure to conform, or to fit the requirements of a local situation. If this were to happen, in time the consultant's values would become synonymous with those of his client—frequently with the result that they would have become less valid and less useful to the company.

Another area of considerable interest is the extent to which the consultant should assume the role of an expert. If we are talking about a technician who is brought in to solve a problem of design, methods, or materials, it is normal to expect this staff man to come up with an expert's answer. But the problem changes with problems or changes affecting relationships, motivation, or organization behavior.

What happens if the consultant assumes the role of an expert in these situations? He may prescribe well, and yet accomplish little. The reason for this is clear. The matters we are dealing with here require more than clarity and accuracy of analysis in order for them to be accomplished. Any change affecting these organizational relationships, systems, climate, and standards of behavior will come about only when certain conditions prevail. Not just one person but all the participants themselves need to accept both the need for change and the desirability of a certain type of remedial action. The effectiveness of the change intended is dependent upon involvement of the total group affected. Thus, the consultant's job is more to accomplish this recognition and involvement than to prescribe the solution to the problem. One description of how the consultant should perform has been offered by Chris Argyris of Yale University in a privately published report on the consultant role. Professor Argyris offers the following thoughts:

> The aim of the consultant is to help the participants become more aware of the blocks and barriers that prevent them from achieving their objectives. He also attempts to help the participants develop new diagnostic skills and take concrete actions to resolve their problems.
>
> The consultant strives hard to facilitate effective problem-solving without becoming the center of attention or the control mechanism for change. He attempts to help people by encouraging them to verbalize and clarify their views, to express their feelings, to become more open about their attitudes and beliefs.
>
> The consultant resists making the diagnosis, making alternate recommendations or taking the lead to plan further action. His objective is not to solve a particular problem for the managers. He realizes that the more problems he solves, the more dependent the organization can become upon him. . . . The more the consultant analyzes, recommends and suggests, the more he behaves in ways which are not consonant with self-diagnosis, self-growth, self-responsibility for action.

It is a rather disturbing thought to extend this idea to its logical conclusion. It states that the field unit which invites the consultant of this type in in order to get his help, finds that he is spending his efforts on getting them to solve their own problem rather than offering them a professional opinion or expert solution. Immediately, this creates some confusion. The consultant is brought in because of his superior knowledge, and yet submerges his own opinion in order to concentrate on a developmental job within the group. Obviously, this suggests the real difference here is that the consultant is looked upon as a trainer (or should be) rather than as a man who has a ready prescription.

It is difficult to know how consistently one could follow Argyris' definition. Field managers are in need of help. They are busy. They seek expert advice. They might well become annoyed or disinterested if instead of advice they get suggestions for involvement of their people in self-analysis work. No doubt frequently some compromise will have to occur. The consultant may find that, to stimulate action, he must take some initiative and provide a direction. At the same time, so long as he is concerned with human-behavior problems, he cannot escape the fact that solution to these problems requires a constructive process rather than a prescription. To this extent, as Argyris points out, "A consultant who is interested in helping the organization must give attention to the processes by which plans are developed, introduced, and made a part of the organization." This differs from many consulting relationships, where the ends are considered more important than the means.

Argyris believes that the effective consultant will tend to invite a greater degree of participation on the part of the members of the organization he is working with. He states:

> At the core of his relationships are such factors as openness, authenticity, the capacity to create minimal defensiveness, listening with minimum distortion, etc. Thus we find that even a consultant who provides help on such "hardware" tasks as incentive systems, cost reduction, and production problems may have to concern himself with authenticity and other interpersonal and group issues. Obviously the consultant whose objective is to provide help in the human factors area has no choice but to focus on creating authentic client-consultant relationships. In order to succeed in their work such consultants must be interested in the processes or means, as well as the ends.

What can be set forth as the objective of the consultant on problems involving human relationships? He must be a capable expert in his field, yet his expertness in this sense should also be related to his being able to develop the organization in its capacity to solve its own problems. Thus, the consultant could be said to have achieved his ultimate objective only when the following conditions prevail:

1. The organization has found an appropriate way to handle the problems which were of initial concern.
2. The organization has developed good procedures for identifying future problems.
3. The organization has recognized the benefits from periodic evaluation of its own effectiveness.
4. The organization has learned procedures which will help it maintain a healthy state of adaptability.

The development of internal consultants who meet this description represents a worthwhile objective for management. There is a potential here for effective help and service from a headquarters organization, in contrast with many of the presently acknowledged shortcomings of today's systems for central staff support. More specifically, there is potential for real development of field organizations toward greater self-sufficiency. Therefore, this represents a new and useful form of management development.

Certain specific steps by top management will be essential to its growth. There needs to be, for example, a clear understanding of the latitude available to field managers to use or not to use consultants on their own initiative. Likewise, local managers need to have full latitude with regard to the routes they pick for study, diagnosis, and involvement of their organization in activities of a developmental nature. Likewise, local units clearly need to have the latitude to collect data and yet not be forced to use it in ways amounting to self-incrimination. In place of this, there should be a clear understanding that the organization is judged on the basis of performance criteria rather than symptomatic data collected in its own work in problem diagnosis.

Management should anticipate paying a high premium for real skill and competence in the consultant function—and yet not settle for less in staffing this type of service. In view of apparent shortage of competent men at the present time, attention should be given to the selection and training of candidates with the range of skills needed.

An additional point to bear in mind deals with the importance of keeping the consultant group intact as a centralized staff. One might ask why, in view of a policy of decentralization, a consultant staff should not also be scattered and spotted in the various field units where it might be of help. One reason, of course, is the fact that there is an intermittent need for such help in the field, and therefore economy dictates some centralization. In addition, the highly skilled type of person that is needed further suggests that he be placed so that he can be utilized fully in a variety of locations.

But there are additional important reasons for not having the consultant located full-time and on a continuing basis in the field unit he is serving. To do so is running the risk that he will be absorbed into the unit, bound by organization channels and unable to exercise the independence of comment and judgment essential to a high-quality job. In fact, even when located in the headquarters, it takes special attention to maintain an attitude of true independence. There are the countervening influences of concern about status, reward, promotion into other lines of work, and pressure toward conformity. Is it really possible to accomplish true independence with internal consultants in a modern industrial organization? It is still too early to know. Meanwhile, hope is bright because the bits of experience to date have been encouraging—and the potential benefits are great.

Management Development as a Process of Influence

EDGAR H. SCHEIN

In the present paper I would like to cast management development as the problem of how an organization can influence the beliefs, attitudes, and values (hereafter simply called attitudes) of an individual for the purpose of "developing" him, i.e. changing him in a direction which the organization regards to be in his own and the organization's best interests. Most of the existing conceptions of the development of human resources are built upon assumptions of how people learn and grow, and some of the more strikingly contrasting theories of management development derive from disagreements about such assumptions.[1] I will attempt to build on a different base: instead of starting with assumptions

Edgar M. Schein, "Management Development as a Process of Influence," *Industrial Management Review* (May 1961), pp. 59–77. A publication of the Alfred P. Sloan School of Management, M.I.T., Cambridge, Mass., 02139. Reprinted by permission of the publisher.

[1]An excellent discussion of two contrasting approaches—the engineering vs. the agricultural—deriving from contrasting assumptions about human behavior can be found in McGregor, 1960, Chapter 14.

about learning and growth, I will start with some assumptions from the social psychology of influence and attitude change.

Building on this base can be justified quite readily if we consider that adequate managerial performance at the higher levels is at least as much a matter of attitudes as it is a matter of knowledge and specific skills, and that the acquisition of such knowledge and skills is itself in part a function of attitudes. Yet we have given far more attention to the psychology which underlies change in the area of knowledge and abilities than we have to the psychology which underlies change in attitudes. We have surprisingly few studies of how a person develops loyalty to a company, commitment to a job, or a professional attitude toward the managerial role; how he comes to have the motives and attitudes which make possible the rendering of decisions concerning large quantities of money, materials, and human resources; how he develops attitudes toward himself, his co-workers, his employees, his customers, and society in general which give us confidence that he has a sense of responsibility and a set of ethics consistent with his responsible position, or at least which permit us to understand his behavior. . . .

A Model of Influence and Change

Most theories of influence or change accept the premise that change does not occur unless the individual is *motivated* and *ready* to change. This statement implies that the individual must perceive some need for change in himself, must be able to change, and must perceive the influencing agent as one who can facilitate such change in a direction acceptable to the individual. A model of the influence process, then, must account for the development of the motivation to change as well as the actual mechanisms by which the change occurs.

It is usually assumed that pointing out to a person some of his areas of deficiency, or some failure on his part in these areas, is sufficient to induce in him a readiness to change and to accept the influencing agent's guidance or recommendations. This assumption may be tenable if one is dealing with deficiencies in intellectual skills or technical knowledge. The young manager can see, with some help from his superiors, that he needs a greater knowledge of economics, or marketing, or production methods, and can accept the suggestion that spending a year in another department or six weeks at an advanced management course will give him the missing knowledge and/or skills.

However, when we are dealing with attitudes, the suggestion of deficiency or the need for change is much more likely to be perceived as a basic threat to the individual's sense of identity and to his status position vis-a-vis others in the organization. Attitudes are generally organized and integrated around the person's image of himself, and they result in stabilized, characteristic ways of dealing with others. The suggestion of the need for change not only implies some criticism of the person's image of himself, but also threatens the stability of his working relationships because change at this level implies that the expectations which others have about him will be upset, thus requiring the development of new relationships. It is not at all uncommon for training programs in human relations to arouse resistance or to produce, at best, temporary change because the expectations of co-workers operate to keep the individual in his "normal" mold. Management development programs which ignore these psychological resistances to change are likely to be self-defeating, no matter how much attention is given to the actual presentation of the new desired attitudes.

Given these general assumptions about the integration of attitudes in the person, it is appropriate to consider influence as a process which occurs over time and which includes three phases:

1. *Unfreezing:*[2] an alteration of the forces acting on the individual, such that his stable equilibrium is disturbed sufficiently to motivate him and to make him ready to change; this can be accomplished either by increasing the pressure to change or by reducing some of the threats or resistances to change.
2. *Changing:* the presentation of a direction of change and the actual process of learning new attitudes. This process occurs basically by one of two mechanisms: (a) *identification*[3]—the person learns new attitudes by identifying with and emulating some other person who holds those attitudes; or (b) *internalization*—the person learns new attitudes by being placed in a situation where new attitudes are demanded of him as a way of solving problems which confront him and which he cannot avoid; he discovers the new attitudes essentially for himself, though the situation may guide him or make it probable that he will discover only those attitudes which the influencing agent wishes him to discover.
3. *Refreezing:* the integration of the changed attitudes into the rest of the personality and/or into ongoing significant emotional relationships.

In proposing this kind of model of influence we are leaving out two important cases—the individual who changes because he is *forced* to change by the agent's direct manipulation of rewards and punishments (what Kelman calls "compliance") and the individual whose strong motivation to rise in the organizational hierarchy makes him eager to accept the attitudes and acquire the skills which he perceives to be necessary for advancement. I will ignore both of these cases for the same reason—they usually do not involve genuine, stable change, but merely involve the adoption of overt behaviors which imply to others that attitudes have changed, even if they have not. In the case of compliance, the individual drops the overt behavior as soon as surveillance by the influence agent is removed. Among the upwardly mobile individuals, there are those who are willing to be unfrozen and to undergo genuine attitude change (whose case fits the model to be presented below) and those whose overt behavior change is dictated by their changing perception of what the environment will reward, but whose underlying attitudes are never really changed or refrozen.

I do not wish to imply that a general reward-punishment model is incorrect or inappropriate for the analysis of attitude change. My purpose, rather, is to provide a more refined model in terms of which it becomes possible to specify the differential effects of various kinds of rewards and punishments, some of which have far more significance and impact than others. For example, as I will try to show, the rewarding effect of approval from an admired person is very different in its ultimate consequences from the rewarding effect of developing a personal solution to a difficult situation.

The processes of unfreezing, changing, and refreezing can be identified in a variety of different institutions in which they are manifested in varying degrees of intensity. The content of what may be taught in the influence process may vary widely from the values of Communism to the religious doctrines of a nun, and the process of influence may vary drastically in its intensity. Nevertheless

---

[2]These phases of influence are a derivation of the change model developed by Lewin (1947).
[3]These mechanisms of attitude change are taken from Kelman (1958).

there is value in taking as our frame of reference a model like that proposed and testing its utility in a variety of different organizational contexts, ranging from Communist "thought reform" centers to business enterprises' management development programs. Because the value system of the business enterprise and its role conception of the manager are not as clear-cut as the values and role prescriptions in various other institutions, one may expect the processes of unfreezing, changing, and refreezing to occur with less intensity and to be less consciously rationalized in the business enterprise. But they are structurally the same as in other organizations. One of the main purposes of this paper, then, will be to try to make salient some features of the influence of the organization on the attitudes of the individual manager by attempting to compare institutions in which the influence process is more drastic and explicit with the more implicit and less drastic methods of the business enterprise.

Illustrations of Organizational Influence

Unfreezing

The concept of unfreezing and the variety of methods by which influence targets can be unfrozen can best be illustrated by considering examples drawn from a broad range of situations. The Chinese Communists in their attempt to inculcate Communist attitudes into their youth or into their prisoners serve as a good prototype of one extreme. First and most important was the removal of the target person from those situations and social relationships which tended to confirm and reinforce the validity of the old attitudes. Thus the targets, be they political prisoners, prisoners of war, university professors, or young students, were isolated from their friends, families, and accustomed work groups and cut off from all media of communication to which they were accustomed. In addition, they were subjected to continuous exhortations (backed by threats of severe punishment) to confess their crimes and adopt new attitudes, and were constantly humiliated in order to discredit their old sense of identity.

The isolation of the target from his normal social and ideological supports reached its height in the case of Western civilians who were placed into group cells with a number of Chinese prisoners who had already confessed and were committed to reforming themselves and their lone Western cell mate. In the prisoner of war camps such extreme social isolation could not be produced, but its counterpart was created by the fomenting of mutual mistrust among the prisoners, by cutting off any supportive mail from home, and by systematically disorganizing the formal and informal social structure of the POW camp (by segregation of officers and noncommissioned officers from the remainder of the group, by the systematic removal of informal leaders or key personalities, and by the prohibition of any group activity not in line with the indoctrination program) (Schein, 1960, 1961).

The Chinese did not hesitate to use physical brutality and threats of death and/or permanent non-repatriation to enforce the view that only by collaboration and attitude change could the prisoner hope to survive physically and psychologically. In the case of the civilians in group cells, an additional and greater stress was represented by the social pressure of the cell mates who would harangue, insult, revile, humiliate, and plead with the resistant Westerner twenty-four hours a day for weeks or months on end, exhorting him to admit his guilt, confess his crimes, reform, and adopt Communist values. This combination of physical and social pressures is perhaps a prototype of the use of coercion in the service of unfreezing a target individual in attitude areas to which he is strongly committed.

A somewhat milder, though structurally similar, process can be observed in the training of a nun (Hulme, 1956). The novice enters the convent voluntarily and is presumably ready to change, but the kind of change which must be accomplished encounters strong psychological resistance because, again, it involves deeply held attitudes and habits. Thus the novice must learn to be completely unselfish and, in fact, selfless; she must adapt to a completely communal life; she must give up any source of authority except the absolute authority of God and of those senior to her in the convent; and she must learn to curb her sexual and aggressive impulses. How does the routine of the convent facilitate unfreezing? Again a key element is the removal of the novice from her accustomed routines, sources of confirmation, social supports, and old relationships. She is physically isolated from the outside world, surrounded by others who are undergoing the same training as she, subjected to a highly demanding and fatiguing physical regimen, constantly exhorted toward her new role and punished for any evidence of old behaviors and attitudes, and subjected to a whole range of social pressures ranging from mild disapproval to total humiliation for any failure.

Not only is the novice cut off from her old social identity, but her entry into the convent separates her from many aspects of her physical identity. She is deprived of all means of being beautiful or even feminine; her hair is cut off and she is given institutional garb which emphasizes formlessness and sameness; she loses her old name and chronological age in favor of a new name and age corresponding to length of time in the convent; her living quarters and daily routine emphasize an absolute minimum of physical comfort and signify a total devaluation of anything related to the body. At the same time the threat associated with change is minimized by the tremendous support which the convent offers for change and by the fact that everyone else either already exhibits the appropriate attitudes or is in the process of learning them.

If we look at the process by which a pledge comes to be a full-fledged member of a fraternity, we find in this situation also a set of pressures to give up old associations and habits, a devaluation of the old self by humiliations ranging from menial, senseless jobs to paddling and hazing, a removal of threat through sharing of training, and support for good performance in the pledge role. The evangelist seeking to convert those who come to hear him attempts to unfreeze his audience by stimulating guilt and by devaluating their former selves as sinful and unworthy. The teacher wishing to induce motivation to learn sometimes points out the deficiencies in the student's knowledge and hopes at the same time to induce some guilt for having those deficiencies.

Some of the elements which all unfreezing situations have in common are the following: (1) the physical removal of the influence target from his accustomed routines, sources of information, and social relationships; (2) the undermining and destruction of all social supports; (3) demeaning and humiliating experience to help the target see his old self as unworthy and thus to become motivated to change; (4) the consistent linking of reward with willingness to change and of punishment with unwillingness to change.

Changing

Once the target has become motivated to change, the actual influence is most likely to occur by one of two processes. The target finds one or more models in his social environment and learns new attitudes by identifying with them and trying to become like them; or the target confronts new situations with an experimental attitude and develops for himself attitudes which are appropriate to the situation and which remove whatever problem he faces. These two processes—*identification* and *internalization*—probably tend to occur together in most concrete situations, but it is worth-while, for analytical purposes, to keep them separate.[4]

The student or prisoner of the Chinese Communists took his basic step toward acquiring Communist attitudes when he began to identify with his more advanced fellow student or prisoner. In the group cell it was the discovery by the Western prisoner that his Chinese cell mates were humans like himself, were rational, and yet completely believed in their own and his guilt, which forced him to re-examine his own premises and bases of judgment and led him the first step down the path of acquiring the Communist point of view. In other words, he began to identify with his cell mates and to acquire their point of view as the only solution to getting out of prison and reducing the pressure on him. The environment was, of course, saturated with the Communist point of view, but it is significant that such saturation by itself was not sufficient to induce genuine attitude change. The prisoner kept in isolation and bombarded with propaganda was less likely to acquire Communist attitudes than the one placed into a group cell with more reformed prisoners. Having a personal model was apparently crucial.

In the convent the situation is essentially comparable except that the novice is initially much more disposed toward identifying with older nuns and has a model of appropriate behavior around her all the time in the actions of the others. It is interesting to note also that some nuns are singled out as particularly qualified models and given the appropriate name of "the living rule." It is also a common institution in initiation or indoctrination procedures to attach to the target individual someone who is labelled a "buddy" or "big brother," whose responsibility it is to teach the novice "the ropes" and to communicate the kinds of attitudes expected of him.

In most kinds of training and teaching situations, and even in the sales relationship, it is an acknowledged fact that the process is facilitated greatly if the target can identify with the influence agent. Such identification is facilitated if the social distance and rank difference between agent and target are not too great. The influence agent has to be close enough to the target to be seen as similar to the target, yet must be himself committed to the attitudes he is trying to inculcate. Thus, in the case of the Chinese Communist group cell, the cell mates could be perceived as sharing a common situation with the Western prisoner and this perception facilitated his identification with them. In most buddy systems, the buddy is someone who has himself gone through the training program in the recent past. If the target is likely to mistrust the influence attempts of the organization, as might be the case in a management-sponsored training

[4]Both are facilitated greatly if the influence agent saturates the environment with the new message or attitude to be learned.

program for labor or in a therapy program for delinquents in a reformatory, it is even more important that the influence agent be perceived as similar to the target. Otherwise he is dismissed as a "company man" or one who has already sold out, and hence is seen as someone whose message or example is not to be taken seriously.

Internalization, the discovery of attitudes which are the target's own solutions to his perceived dilemmas, can occur at the same time as identification. The individual can use the example of others to guide him in solving his own problems without necessarily identifying with them to the point of complete imitation. His choice of attitude remains ultimately his own in terms of what works for him, given the situation in which he finds himself. Internalization is only possible in an organizational context in which, from the organization's point of view, a number of different kinds of attitudes will be tolerated. If there is a "party line," a company philosophy, or a given way in which people have to feel about things in order to get along, it is hardly an efficient procedure to let trainees discover their own solutions. Manipulating the situation in such a way as to make the official solution the only one which is acceptable can, of course, be attempted, but the hazards of creating real resentment and alienation on the part of the individual when he discovers he really had no choice may outweigh the presumed advantages of letting him think he had a choice.

In the case of the Chinese Communists, the convent, the revival meeting, the fraternity, or the institutional training program, we are dealing with situations where the attitudes to be learned are clearly specified. In this kind of situation, internalization will not occur unless the attitudes to be learned happen to fit uniquely the kind of personal problem the individual has in the situation. For example, a few prisoners of the Communists reacted to the tremendous unfreezing pressures with genuine guilt when they discovered they held certain prejudices and attitudes (e.g. when they realized that they had looked down on lower class Chinese in spite of their manifest acceptance of them). These prisoners were then able to internalize certain portions of the total complex of Communist attitudes, particularly those dealing with unselfishness and working for the greater good of others. The attitudes which the institution demanded of them also solved a personal problem of long standing for them. In the case of the nun, one might hypothesize that internalization of the convent's attitudes will occur to the extent that asceticism offers a genuine solution to the incumbent's personal conflicts.

Internalization is a more common outcome in those influence settings where the direction of change is left more to the individual. The influence which occurs in programs like Alcoholics Anonymous, in psychotherapy or counseling for hospitalized or incarcerated populations, in religious retreats, in human relations training of the kind pursued by the National Training Laboratories (1953), and in certain kinds of progressive education programs is more likely to occur through internalization or, at least, to lead ultimately to more internalization.

Refreezing

Refreezing refers to the process by which the newly acquired attitude comes to be integrated into the target's personality and ongoing relationships. If the new attitude has been internalized while being learned, this has automatically facilitated refreezing because it has been fitted naturally into the individual's personality. If it has been learned through identification, it will persist only so long as the target's relationship with the original influence model persists unless new surrogate models are found or social support and reinforcement is obtained for expressions of the new attitude.[5]

In the case of the convent such support comes from a whole set of expectations which others have of how the nun should behave, from clearly specified role prescriptions, and from rituals. In the case of individuals influenced by the Chinese Communists, if they remained in Communist China they received constant support for their new attitudes from superiors and peers; if they returned to the West, the permanence of their attitude change depended on the degree of support they actually received from friends and relations back home, or from groups which they sought out in an attempt to get support. If their friends and relatives did not support Communist attitudes, the repatriates were influenced once again toward their original attitudes or toward some new integration of both sets.

The importance of social support for new attitudes was demonstrated dramatically in the recent Billy Graham crusade in New York City. An informal survey of individuals who came forward when Graham called for converts indicated that only those individuals who were subsequently integrated into local churches maintained their faith. Similar kinds of findings have been repeatedly noted with respect to human relations training in industry. Changes which may occur during the training program do not last unless there is some social support for the new attitudes in the "back home" situation.

The kind of model which has been discussed above might best be described by the term "coercive persuasion." The influence of an organization on an individual is coercive in the sense that he is usually forced into situations which are likely to unfreeze him, in which there are many overt and covert pressures to recognize in himself a need for change, and in which the supports for his old attitudes are in varying degrees coercively removed. It is coercive also to the degree that the new attitudes to be learned are relatively rigidly prescribed. The individual either learns them or leaves the organization (if he can). At the same time, the actual process by which new attitudes are learned can best be described as persuasion. In effect, the individual is forced into a situation in which he is likely to be influenced. The organization can be highly coercive in unfreezing its potential influence targets, yet be quite open about the direction of attitude change it will tolerate. In those cases where the direction of change is itself coerced (as contrasted with letting it occur through identification or internalization), it is highly unlikely that anything is accomplished other than surface behavioral change in the target. And such surface change will be abandoned the moment the coercive force of the change agent is lessened. If behavioral changes are coerced at the same time as other unfreezing operations are undertaken, actual influence can be facilitated if the individual finds himself having to learn attitudes to justify the kinds of behavior he has been forced to exhibit. The salesman may not have an attitude of cynicism toward his customers initially. If, however, he is forced by his boss to behave as if he felt cynical, he might develop real cynicism as a way of justifying his actual behavior.

[5]In either case the change may be essentially permanent, in that a relationship to a model or surrogate can last indefinitely. It is important to distinguish the two processes, however, because if one were to try to change the attitude, different strategies would be used depending upon how the attitude had been learned.

Management Development: Is It Coercive Persuasion?

Do the notions of coercive persuasion developed above fit the management development situation? Does the extent to which they do or do not fit such a model illuminate for us some of the implications of specific management development practices?

Unfreezing

It is reasonable to assume that the majority of managers who are being "developed" are not ready or able to change in the manner in which their organization might desire and therefore must be unfrozen before they can be influenced. They may be eager to change at a conscious motivation level, yet still be psychologically unprepared to give up certain attitudes and values in favor of untried, threatening new ones. I cannot support this assumption empirically, but the likelihood of its being valid is high because of a related fact which is empirically supportable. Most managers do not participate heavily in decisions which affect their careers, nor do they have a large voice in the kind of self-development in which they wish to participate. Rather, it is the man's superior or a staff specialist in career development who makes the key decisions concerning his career (Alfred, 1960). If the individual manager is not trained from the outset to take responsibility for his own career and given a heavy voice in diagnosing his own needs for a change, it is unlikely that he will readily be able to appreciate someone else's diagnosis. It may be unclear to him what basically is wanted of him or, worse, the ambiguity of the demands put upon him combined with his own inability to control his career development is likely to arouse anxiety and insecurity which would cause even greater resistance to genuine self-assessment and attitude change.[6] He becomes preoccupied with promotion in the abstract and attempts to acquire at a surface level the traits which he thinks are necessary for advancement.

If the decisions made by the organization do not seem valid to the manager, or if the unfreezing process turns out to be quite painful to him, to what extent can he leave the situation? His future career, his financial security, and his social status within the business community all stand to suffer if he resists the decisions made for him. Perhaps the most coercive feature is simply the psychological pressure that what he is being asked to do is "for his own ultimate welfare." Elementary loyalty to his organization and to his managerial role demands that he accept with good grace whatever happens to him in the name of his own career development. In this sense, then, I believe that the business organization has coercive forces at its disposal which are used by it in a manner comparable to the uses made by other organizations.

Given the assumption that the manager who is to be developed needs to be unfrozen, and given that the organization has available coercive power to accomplish such unfreezing, what mechanisms does it actually use to unfreeze potential influence targets?

The essential elements to unfreezing are the removal of supports for the old attitudes, the saturation of the environment with the new attitudes to be

---

[6]An even greater hazard, of course, is that the organization communicates to the manager that he is not expected to take responsibility for his own career at the same time that it is trying to teach him how to be able to take responsibility for important decisions!

acquired, a minimizing of threat, and a maximizing of support for any change in the right direction. In terms of this model it becomes immediately apparent that training programs or other activities which are conducted in the organization at the place of work for a certain number of hours per day or week are far less likely to unfreeze and subsequently influence the participant than those programs which remove him for varying lengths of time from his regular work situation and normal social relationships.

Are appraisal interviews, used periodically to communicate to the manager his strengths, weaknesses and areas for improvement, likely to unfreeze him? Probably not, because as long as the individual is caught up in his regular routine and is responding, probably quite unconsciously, to a whole set of expectations which others have about his behavior and attitudes, it is virtually impossible for him to hear, at a psychological level, what his deficiencies or areas needing change are. Even if he can appreciate what is being communicated to him at an intellectual level, it is unlikely that he can emotionally accept the need for change, and even if he can accept it emotionally, it is unlikely that he can produce change in himself in an environment which supports all of his old ways of functioning. This statement does not mean that the man's co-workers necessarily approve of the way he is operating or like the attitudes which he is exhibiting. They may want to see him change, but their very expectations concerning how he normally behaves operate as a constraint on him which makes attitude change difficult in that setting.

On the other hand, there are a variety of training activities which are used in management development which approximate more closely the conditions necessary for effective unfreezing. These would include programs offered at special training centers such as those maintained by IBM on Long Island and General Electric at Crotonville, N.Y.; university-sponsored courses in management, liberal arts, and/or the social sciences; and especially, workshops or laboratories in human relations such as those conducted at Arden House, N.Y., by the National Training Laboratories. Programs such as these remove the participant for some length of time from his normal routine, his regular job, and his social relationships (including his family in most cases), thus providing a kind of moratorium during which he can take stock of himself and determine where he is going and where he wants to go.

The almost total isolation from the pressures of daily life in the business world which a mountain chateau such as Arden House provides for a two-week period is supplemented by other unfreezing forces. The de-emphasis on the kind of job or title the participant holds in his company and the informal dress remove some of the symbolic or status supports upon which we all rely. Sharing a room and bath facilities with a roommate requires more than the accustomed exposure of private spheres of life to others. The total involvement of the participant in the laboratory program leaves little room for reflection about the back-home situation. The climate of the laboratory communicates tremendous support for any efforts at self-examination and attempts as much as possible to reduce the threats inherent in change by emphasizing the value of experimentation, the low cost and risk of trying a new response in the protected environment of the lab, and the high gains to be derived from finding new behavior patterns and attitudes which might improve back home performance. The content of the material presented in lectures and the kind of learning model which is used in the workshop facilitates self-examination, self-diagnosis based on usable feedback from other participants, and rational planning for change.[7]

The practice of rotating a manager from one kind of assignment to another over a period of years can have some of the same unfreezing effects and thus facilitate attitude change. Certainly his physical move from one setting to another removes many of the supports to his old attitudes, and in his new job the manager will have an opportunity to try new behaviors and become exposed to new attitudes. The practice of providing a moratorium in the form of a training program prior to assuming a new job would appear to maximize the gains from each approach, in that unfreezing would be maximally facilitated and change would most probably be lasting if the person did not go back to a situation in which his co-workers, superiors, and subordinates had stable expectations of how he should behave.

Another example of how unfreezing can be facilitated in the organizational context is the practice of temporarily reducing the formal rank and responsibilities of the manager by making him a trainee in a special program, or an apprentice on a special project, or an assistant to a high ranking member of the company. Such temporary lowering of formal rank can reduce the anxiety associated with changing and at the same time serves officially to destroy the old status and identity of the individual because he could not ordinarily return to his old position once he had accepted the path offered by the training program. He would have to move either up or out of the organization to maintain his sense of self-esteem. Of course, if such a training program is perceived by the trainee as an indication of his failing rather than a step toward a higher position, his anxiety about himself would be too high to facilitate effective change on his part. In all of the illustrations of organizational influence we have presented above, change was defined as being a means of gaining status—acceptance into Communist society, status as a nun or a fraternity brother, salvation, etc. If participants come to training programs believing they are being punished, they typically do not learn much.

The above discussion is intended to highlight the fact that some management development practices do facilitate the unfreezing of the influence target, but that such unfreezing is by no means automatic. Where programs fail, therefore, one of the first questions we must ask is whether they failed because they did not provide adequate conditions for unfreezing.

Changing

Turning now to the problem of the mechanisms by which changes actually occur, we must confront the question of whether the organization has relatively rigid prescribed goals concerning the direction of attitude change it expects of the young manager, or whether it is concerned with growth in the sense of providing increasing opportunities for the young manager to learn the attitudes appropriate to ever more challenging situations. It is undoubtedly true that most programs would claim growth as their goal, but the degree to which they accomplish it can only be assessed from an examination of their actual practice.

Basically the question is whether the organization influences attitudes

[7]Although, as I will point out later, such effective unfreezing may lead to change which is not supported or considered desirable by the "back home" organization.

primarily through the mechanism of identification or the mechanism of internalization. If the development programs stimulate psychological relationships between the influence target and a member of the organization who has the desired attitudes, they are thereby facilitating influence by identification but, at the same time, are limiting the alternatives available to the target and possibly the permanence of the change achieved. If they emphasize that the target must develop his own solutions to ever more demanding problems, they are risking that the attitudes learned will be incompatible with other parts of the organization's value system but are producing more permanent change because the solutions found are internalized. From the organization's point of view, therefore, it is crucial to know what kind of influence it is exerting and to assess the results of such influence in terms of the basic goals which the organization may have. If new approaches and new attitudes toward management problems are desired, for example, it is crucial that the conditions for internalization be created. If rapid learning of a given set of attitudes is desired, it is equally crucial that the conditions for identification with the right kind of models be created.

One obvious implication of this distinction is that programs conducted within the organization's orbit by its own influence agents are much more likely to facilitate identification and thereby the transmission of the "party line" or organization philosophy. On the other hand, programs like those conducted at universities or by the National Training Laboratories place much more emphasis on the finding of solutions by participants which fit their own particular needs and problems. The emphasis in the human relations courses is on "learning how to learn" from the participant's own interpersonal experiences and how to harness his emotional life and intellectual capacities to the accomplishment of his goals, rather than on specific principles of human relations. The nearest thing to an attitude which the laboratory staff, acting as influence agents, does care to communicate is an attitude of inquiry and experimentation, and to this end the learning of skills of observation, analysis, and diagnosis of interpersonal situations is given strong emphasis. The training group, which is the acknowledged core of the laboratory approach, provides its own unfreezing forces by being unstructured as to the content of discussion. But it is strongly committed to a method of learning by analysis of the member's own experiences in the group, which facilitates the discovery of the value of an attitude of inquiry and experimentation.

Mutual identification of the members of the group with each other and member identifications with the staff play some role in the acquisition of this attitude, but the basic power of the method is that the attitude of inquiry and experimentation *works* in the sense of providing for people valuable new insights about themselves, groups, and organizations. To the extent that it works and solves key problems for the participants, it is internalized and carried back into the home situation. To the extent that it is learned because participants wish to emulate a respected fellow member or staff member, it lasts only so long as the relationship with the model itself, or a surrogate of it, lasts (which may, of course, be a very long time).

The university program in management or liberal arts is more difficult to categorize in terms of an influence model, because within the program there are usually opportunities both for identification (e.g. with inspiring teachers) and internalization. It is a safe guess in either case, however, that the attitudes learned are likely to be in varying degrees out of phase with any given company's philosophy unless the company has learned from previous experience with a given course that the students are taught a point of view consistent with its own philosophy. Of course, universities, as much as laboratories, emphasize the value of a spirit of inquiry and, to the extent that they are successful in teaching this attitude, will be creating potential dissidents or innovators, depending on how the home company views the result.

Apprenticeships, special jobs in the role of "assistant to" somebody, job rotation, junior management boards, and so on stand in sharp contrast to the above methods in the degree to which they facilitate, indeed almost demand, that the young manager learn by watching those who are senior or more competent. It is probably not prescribed that in the process of acquiring knowledge and skills through the example of others he should also acquire their attitudes, but the probability that this will happen is very high if the trainee develops any degree of respect and liking for his teacher and/or supervisor. It makes little difference whether the teacher, coach, or supervisor intends to influence the attitudes of his trainee or not. If a good emotional relationship develops between them, it will facilitate the learning of knowledge and skills, and will, at the same time, result in some degree of attitude change. Consequently, such methods do not maximize the probability of new approaches being invented to management problems, nor do they really by themselves facilitate the growth of the manager in the sense of providing opportunities for him to develop solutions which fit his own needs best.

Job rotation, on the other hand, can facilitate growth and innovation provided it is managed in such a way as to insure the exposure of the trainee to a broad range of points of view as he moves from assignment to assignment. The practice of shifting the developing manager geographically as well as functionally both facilitates unfreezing and increases the likelihood of his being exposed to new attitudes. This same practice can, of course, be merely a convenient way of indoctrinating the individual by sending him on an assignment, for example, "in order to acquire the sales point of view from Jim down in New York," where higher management knows perfectly well what sort of a view Jim will communicate to his subordinates.

Refreezing

Finally, a few words are in order about the problem of refreezing. Under what conditions will changed attitudes remain stable, and how do existing practices aid or hinder such stabilization? Our illustrations from the non-industrial setting highlighted the importance of social support for any attitudes which were learned through identification. Even the kind of training emphasized in the National Training Laboratories programs, which tends to be more internalized, does not produce stable attitude change unless others in the organization, especially superiors, peers, and subordinates, have undergone similar changes and give each other stimulation and support, because lack of support acts as a new unfreezing force producing new influence (possibly in the direction of the original attitudes).

If the young manager has been influenced primarily in the direction of what is already the company philosophy, he will, of course, obtain strong support and will have little difficulty maintaining his new attitudes. If, on the other hand, management development is supposed to lead to personal growth and organizational innovation, the organization must recognize the reality that new attitudes cannot be carried by isolated individuals. The lament that we no longer have strong individualists who are willing to try something new is a fallacy based on an incorrect diagnosis. Strong individuals have always gained a certain amount of their strength from the support of others, hence the organizational problem is how to create conditions which make possible the nurturing of new ideas, attitudes, and approaches. If organizations seem to lack innovators, it may be that the climate of the organization and its methods of management development do not foster innovation, not that its human resources are inadequate.

An organizational climate in which new attitudes which differ from company philosophy can nevertheless be maintained cannot be achieved merely by an intellectual or even emotional commitment on the part of higher-ranking managers to tolerance of new ideas and attitudes. Genuine support can come only from others who have themselves been influenced, which argues strongly that at least several members of a given department must be given the same training before such training can be expected to have effect. If the superior of the people involved can participate in it as well, this strengthens the group that much more, but it would not follow from my line of reasoning that this is a necessary condition. Only some support is needed, and this support can come as well from peers and subordinates.

From this point of view, the practice of sending more than one manager to any given program at a university or human relations workshop is very sound. The National Training Laboratories have emphasized from the beginning the desirability of having organizations send teams. Some organizations like Esso Standard have created their own laboratories for the training of the entire management complement of a given refinery, and all indications are that such a practice maximizes the possibility not only of the personal growth of the managers, but of the creative growth of the organization as a whole.

Conclusion

In the above discussion I have deliberately focused on a model of influence which emphasizes procedure rather than content, interpersonal relations rather than mass media, and attitudes and values rather than knowledge and skills. By placing management development into a context of institutional influence procedures which also include Chinese Communist thought reform, the training of a nun, and other more drastic forms of coercive persuasion, I have tried to highlight aspects of management development which have remained implicit yet which need to be understood. I believe that some aspects of management development are a mild form of coercive persuasion, but I do not believe that coercive persuasion is either morally bad in any *a priori* sense nor inefficient. If we are to develop a sound theory of career development which is capable of including not only many of the formal procedures discussed in this paper, but the multitudes of informal practices, some of which are more and some of which are less coercive than those discussed, we need to suspend moral judgments for the time being and evaluate influence models solely in terms of their capacity to make sense of the data and to make meaningful predictions.

References

Alfred, T. M. [Personal communication], 1960.

Hulme, K. *The Nun's Story.* Boston, Little, Brown, 1957.

Kelman, H. C. "Compliance, identification, and internalization: three processes of attitude change." *J. Conflict Resolution,* 1958, Vol. 2, 51–60.

Lewin, K. "Frontiers in Group Dynamics: Concept, Method and Reality in Social Science." *Human Relations,* 1947, Vol. 1, 5–42.

McGregor, D. *The Human Side of Enterprise.* New York, McGraw-Hill, 1960.

Merton, R. K., Reader, G. G., and Kendall, Patricia L. *The Student-Physician.* Cambridge, Mass.: Harvard University Press, 1957.

National Training Laboratory in Group Development: *Explorations in Human Relations Training: An Assessment of Experience, 1947–1953.* Washington, D.C.: National Education Association, 1953.

Schein, E. H. *Brainwashing.* Cambridge, Mass.: Center for International Studies, M.I.T., 1961.

Schein, E. H. "Interpersonal Communication, Group Solidarity, and Social Influence." *Sociometry,* 1960, Vol. 23, 148–161.

Sensitivity Training for the Management Team

ROBERT TANNENBAUM
IRVING WESCHLER
FRED MASSARIK

Getting the management team to work together smoothly and effectively is sometimes a more complex and difficult problem than setting up production procedures or a control structure. One way to tackle the job is to institute a sensitivity training program for a management hierarchy within the organization.

The development of vertically structured, sensitivity-oriented leadership training groups reflects a growing recognition that interpersonal problems which arise on the job cannot be ignored. Even though these problems are frequently due to factors which are below the level of acute awareness, they should be tackled if an organization is to function at the highest level of effectiveness.

A large majority of on-the-job interpersonal problems stem from misunderstandings, from attributing one's faults to others, and from distortions due to lack of a free flow of interpersonal communication. These can be suitably handled by this kind of training and often resolved with a minimum of serious tension or conflict.

The Nature of Training Programs

Conventional Training Programs

Conventional training programs often have some serious limitations:

1. The trainee is removed from the social setting in which he customarily performs. With relatively few exceptions, each manager in performing his job must get on well with his subordinates, equals, and superiors. Training him in human relations apart from the humans to whom he must relate is like training an albacore fisherman in a trout stream.
2. Programs designed merely to impart human relations information may have little or no effect in inducing desirable changes in behavior. A prerequisite for the successful outcome of leadership training is the motivation to learn about oneself, others, and group process. Unless the trainee feels a need for human relations information, he is not going to "hear" it. Even if he is able to "hear" it—i.e., to accept the information—he will not necessarily be able to apply it on the job. If the new information conflicts with other of his needs, attitudes, and feelings, it will be difficult—if not impossible—for him to behave appropriately.
3. There may be little transfer of learning from the training situation to the work situation. We are not at all sure that insights and skills which are gained in the conventional training session can readily be utilized in the actual work situation. There, the social pressures on the individual to maintain his customary modes of behavior are often so strong that any attempt on his part to change is likely to fail; such change may very well conflict with the larger organizational "ways of doing things," so that he may be forced either to maintain his old behaviors or to resign.

Training vertically structured groups in sensitivity, on the other hand, is likely to yield several desirable outcomes:

1. Changes in interpersonal behavior developed through the training sessions can be carried over to work relations. As new ideas and feelings are discussed, understood, and accepted by the group in the training sessions, there is a good possibility that their impact will be reflected in the daily work contacts of the trainees.
2. The emphasis of this kind of training program is primarily oriented toward awareness of self, of others, and of interpersonal relations rather than toward the acquisition of book knowledge. When awareness occurs at the "gut level" (emotional) as well as the "head level" (intellectual), changes in behavior are more likely to occur.
3. Experience indicates that working together on mutual problems of interpersonal relations produces a more cohesive work team. In the long run, the values and techniques introduced in training may become an important part of day-to-day working procedures, so the point is reached where the group can function at a new level of efficiency. Thus, at regular staff meetings and in other work contacts where serious interpersonal problems may well arise, the members themselves are in a position to deal adequately with these problems which previously remained unrecognized or ignored.

In the vertically structured training group, it may soon become clear that the "executive neurosis" works all the way up and down the line in such a way that each individual in the group protects his status, power, and security.[1] Until the participants learn how to accept and deal with the reality of status, not much progress can be expected. Since the adverse effects of status are largely fostered by the behavior of the "top wheel," it may be necessary for the trainer to deal privately, in advance of the training, with the top individual's own relevant fears. He must be made to realize, for example, that unless he is able to accept criticism, little interchange of opinion is possible. Other private interviews with individuals who are threatened by the training process might also be necessary, before the training program can progress. In some cases, it has been found useful to have the trainer or some other professional act as a personal counselor to those individuals who feel the need to work through, outside the group sessions, personal anxieties which may be generated by the training.

As the participants with the support of the trainer and other members of the group learn to discuss and to understand such problems, they attempt to develop greater skill in dealing with them. As issues become clarified and understood, each trainee is helped to appraise his own behavior with respect to them. In time the training group becomes more secure in its ability to deal with material of this nature, and more complex problems are raised for discussion. This serves to further understanding and acceptance among members and to promote a more cohesive management team.

Sensitivity Training Programs

The training meetings of the group are likely to differ from other work-oriented meetings (such as staff meetings) in several important ways:

The Relative Lack of a Planned Agenda. Though considerable planning on the part of the trainer is involved in setting up and carrying through the training program, the actual content of the program is highly flexible. External time pressures ("to get things done") are kept to a minimum.

Participation in Leadership. Work-oriented meetings are usually chaired by the high-status person in the group; in the training sessions the leadership may pass to the group trainer, to any other person in the group, or they may be conducted as "leaderless" discussions.

Motivation of the Participants. In the training sessions, the participants are prepared to deal with problems which are rarely, if ever, introduced in conventional work-oriented meetings. Discussion tends to focus on the clarification of interpersonal perceptions, as contrasted with technical job issues which often dominate conventional meetings.

The description of sensitivity training in conventional ways sometimes loses much of the flavor of the training process. Therefore, what such a program involves and how it progresses can at times be best described and made meaningful through the device of a narrative.

In this fictional account of "managers in transition" based on a composite of our consulting experiences with many organizations, we learn what happens at Comet Television in Central City when Marv Ingham, management training consultant, is called in to survey the relationships among the members of the

---

[1]The "executive neurosis" has been described by Robert N. McMurry in a stimulating article which appeared in the *Harvard Business Review,* vol. 30, no. 6, pp. 33–47, November–December, 1952.

plant management team and to make his recommendations for improving life in the "executive suite."

Managers in Transition

Michael J. Hunter, plant superintendent of the Comet Television Company, hung his hat in the closet and tossed his brief case onto his desk with a gesture of annoyance. He always felt a little worn after conferences at the home office; besides he hadn't slept very well on the plane. He pressed the button on the intercom, and said, "Betty, get hold of Bill Simpson and Art West and ask them to come in for a few minutes. And send in some coffee, will you?"

Leaning back in his chair, he lit a cigarette. He'd been handed a tough problem, but he was sure he'd made the right decision. It was an opportunity, really, if everybody pitched right in, Mike told himself.

After all, things had gone pretty well since he'd been transferred to Comet's Central City plant a year ago to "put new life into the organization." The president had shown a lot of faith in him, and he had worked hard to do a good job. He thought he *had* done pretty well, too. He liked the spot and, generally speaking, was feeling better than he had for years. Also, he was able to spend more time with his family, and he'd started playing golf again. Certainly he had every right to feel confident of his own abilities. He'd already demonstrated that he had the courage to make decisions and the drive to carry these decisions through.

The Problem

He took a final drag on the cigarette and crushed it out in the ash tray as his secretary opened the door to admit his two division chiefs, Bill Simpson, head of design and engineering, and Art West, head of production. When they were settled with their coffee, Mike told them, "Well, we're off again. The 14-inch color set hasn't been moving as well as they hoped it would. The old man has bought the rights on the new Bergstrom process for the 21-inch color tube. He told me he'd give this plant the first crack at it if we wanted to convert from the 14-inchers. I told him we could handle it. I was counting on you, of course, but . . . do you think we can do it?"

"We'll sure try," said Art amiably. "Of course, it's going to cost something to switch from the 14-inch lines, but we should be able to change over without too much trouble."

Bill couldn't keep a little tone of exasperation out of his voice. "Mike, I don't mean to say I told you so, but remember last February I told you I'd seen Bergstrom's first reports in the journals? That they looked so good I didn't see how we were going to avoid winding up with a multiple prism system? After all, you get a much better balance in color values, and there's a lot less halo, and besides you can handle a larger screen. I even made up a little abstract of his paper for you, remember? But when I didn't hear anything more about it from you, well, I didn't go into it any further. Now we'll have to start absolutely from scratch. It'll take us at least a month, and . . . ."

"O.K., O.K.," Mike cut in, "That's all water over the dam, now, and there's no point in fretting about it. We're just going to have to buckle down and get going on it. Put your boys on overtime if you need to. Couldn't you have something for Art to start on in three weeks?"

When his division heads had left the office, Mike fished another cigarette out of the pack and studied it intently. What was eating Bill, anyhow? A brilliant guy, but sometimes so touchy. Certainly not much like Art, who was really *too* easygoing, especially when it came to handling subordinates. Soft, almost. Sometimes he wondered why people worked as well for Art as they did. Still, Art was easy to talk to, except when he came up with one of those bumbling compliments of his, which embarrassed you so much that you had to change the subject.

Outside Viewpoint

Everyone, Mike reflected, had his peculiarities, and that didn't keep both Bill and Art from turning out good work when the chips were down. At the same time, he was rather glad he'd decided to call in that consultant earlier, even though he wasn't quite sure why he had. To his wife, to the home office, and to his staff members, Mike had said that Marv Ingham, the consultant, was just interviewing the managerial personnel to see if anything could be done to improve plant operation, good as it was. Might be something to it, too. Mike remembered his own days as a cog in a big machine, and he knew a stranger could find out more in a few days than the boss could discover in years through the usual channels.

Mike reached for his brief case and pulled out the report that Marv had submitted. Marv had been interviewing for five days; he had seen everyone in the plant down through the first level of supervision; he also had talked to a few employees on the line and in the shops—not many, but enough to get a feel of things.

The tone of the report was different from any Mike had ever read. Not much about production problems, working conditions, or general plant operation. Instead, there was a lot about seeing things differently, failures in communication, some disturbing "interpersonal problems" among the management group. There was also a suggestion that Mike should look into these problems in the not-too-distant future. Mike believed in action; if a thing was worth looking into, it was worth looking into now. He decided to ask Marv for more details.

New Ideas. Two hours later, Marv sat down with him to explain what he had in mind. Actually, he wasn't much more specific than the report; and Mike, at first, was not too pleased with what he was getting. Marv said something about not being able to violate confidences, and besides he had few facts, only feelings and often contradictory perceptions on which to base his judgments. No statistics, no specific findings—just something about the atmosphere being charged—just some tenuous impressions about people not working well together.

Marv remembered his interview with Bill in engineering. Bill had talked a lot, but said little. He seemed cautious—perhaps too cautious; when asked about Mike, he parried, "Mike is all right—I guess. We get along fine." Marv got the impression that Bill had hostile feelings about Mike that embarrassed him.

Marv hadn't got much further with Art in production. Art seemed more spontaneous than Bill, especially when talking about his own division, but became noncommittal when asked about his relationship to people in the management group.

Some of the others Marv had talked to tried hard to make everything look good, while a few sounded like prophets of impending doom. Some seemed jumpy and talked about trivial issues with more emotion than seemed warranted.

Also, there was a definite lack of communication between management levels. Most of the first-line supervisors often described a common gripe, while the next higher level of management didn't seem to be aware that the complaint existed. Altogether, Marv's impressions of his forty interviews added up to a definite pattern—"all was not well at Comet Television in Central City!"

Mike Resists. Mike felt a certain resistance to these ideas. "I just don't think we have any particular personnel problems," he said. "Don't these things happen in every plant?"

"Yes, they do, but sooner or later they backfire in one way or another. Trouble develops in ways that are hard to deal with—like increased turnover, breakage, delays, breakdowns in communication, secretiveness, and lowered morale and productivity."

Mike frowned. "Are you sure you aren't just oversensitive to these so-called interpersonal relationships?"

"Maybe so. That's my job. But I think the possibility is worth exploring. Do you mind if I ask *you* a few questions?"

Mike leaned back in his chair. "Not at all. Fire away."

Marv's few questions seemed more like a hundred:

"How about your staff meetings? Who talks?"

"How are decisions made? Who makes them?"

"What effect do you think you have on your subordinates? What do you do that they like? What do you do that they don't like? Why not?"

"What kind of a person is Bill? Art? What kind of a relationship do they have to each other?"

"Do you do anything special to help communication between members of the divisions?"

And so on and on.

Mike felt a bit resentful of the questions—they were disturbing, and he didn't have really good answers to them. What finally set him off, though, was Marv's looking squarely at him and asking, "Are you concerned about how your people feel?" Mike barely suppressed a surge of violent anger. He knew it showed in his face. He didn't know why he was so mad; but he was. Obviously Marv didn't understand the cold realities of the business world—he wanted to make a tea party out of a well-ordered business.

"I want to think about these things a little more," he told Marv. "Right now we've had a big production problem tossed in our lap, and it may tie us up for days. I'll get in touch with you later."

Mike discovered that he couldn't put Marv's questions out of his mind. One thing that returned to disturb him was his own angry reaction to Marv's probing. He wondered if there was some connection between his own feelings and the reactions of his men after he had bombarded them with penetrating questions.

At lunch, as he looked across the table at Art and Bill, he wondered if he had more than a superficial understanding of the key men with whom he worked. Maybe he didn't, and maybe that was why he was always so concerned about them. Still, he told himself, there was no use in attempting a curbstone psychoanalysis of everybody in the plant and then trying to adjust himself to their idiosyncrasies. It wasn't his fault if some people couldn't adjust themselves to his way of doing business. He had enough to do without worrying about how other people felt about him. After all, they were paid to do a job.

The Men under Mike

Marv, for his part, welcomed the opportunity of a day or two away from the plant. He wanted time to rearrange the enormous jigsaw puzzle with which he had been struggling, especially now that the talk with Mike had provided some of the missing pieces. He went back to his office and revised his notes. If Mike wanted to go ahead, he would be ready with some suggestions.

Marv was primarily concerned with seven key people. Mike stood at the top of the management pyramid. Directly under him were Bill and Art, each of whom had two branch heads. Bill, in design and engineering, was assisted by Rod Reiner, his chief of design and development, and Joe Beckwith, his chief of inspection. Over in production, Art's top aides were Sid Adams, in charge of cabinet production, and Paul Turner, in charge of chassis production.

What was it that made it difficult for these people to work together effectively? And which courses of action were most likely to bring about improvements? From the copious notes he had made after each interview, Marv had gathered together the material necessary to understand better each of these six men under Mike and their relationships to each other and to the boss.

What about Bill?

First, there was Bill. He had an engineering degree from a leading university. He was brilliant and able, and he knew his job. He also was competitive, and he liked power. Bill wanted recognition from the boss and worked hard to get it. Often, when Mike had a suggestion, Bill went to great lengths to indicate that he had thought about the possibility before. These little lectures were always tinged with overtones of annoyance and aggression.

In the face of them, Mike was emotionally immobilized. He worked so hard to suppress any aggressive feelings of his own that he found it difficult to deal with aggression in Bill. Moreover, it never occurred to Mike that Bill was eager for him to show some approval and support of his efforts. And even if this had occurred to Mike, he wouldn't have known what to do about it. Mike appeared to regard Bill as a self-contained machine.

It would be a waste of time, Marv reflected, to suggest to Bill that he represented a constant threat to his boss. Bill was so concerned with himself that he was not very observant of the inner feelings of others. If he had spoken frankly about Mike, Bill would probably have said that Mike was always stubborn. Yet, he would have sensed no connection between Mike's stubbornness and his own behavior.

Bill's Assistants. Turning to Bill's assistants, Marv noted that their situation was colored by Bill's relationship to Mike. Since Mike was incapable of dealing with Bill's drives, these drives were turned toward Rod and Joe.

During the war, Rod had been in the Navy and had learned some engineering tricks which left Bill baffled. Rod had no degree, but he had ingenuity and initiative. His designs were clean, his ideas good. His work was always out on time, and he liked to work on several projects at once. To say that Bill was jealous would be doing Bill an injustice; he knew that Rod was capable. But Bill just wasn't able to accept the contributions of other people easily. Although it would have been impossible to isolate any single clear-cut instance to support his conclusion, Rod felt that his efforts were minimized and resented. He was puzzled, but he didn't question. He had too much regard for Bill's competence.

On the page headed by Joe's name, Marv had little to write. Joe had refused to talk with him. Obviously, Joe was scared. He was also plenty mad. Marv knew this much, but he didn't know why. If he had been in Joe's office a few days earlier, he'd have understood. Joe's wife had called him on the phone again complaining about the kids, the house, Joe's working late. Joe was also in financial trouble. He was mad at somebody, and he didn't know who. Working for Bill made Joe's troubles twice as unbearable. Joe was a tough, unreasonable inspector, and when Bill got tough, Joe got tougher. When Bill manipulated Joe, Joe manipulated twenty people. If Bill set Rod up for a little ridicule, Joe would dish out twice as much. And so it went, in an endless, cumulative circle.

Art Was Different

In the production division, things were different because Art was different. Art had been with the plant a long time. He had started out making jigs and fixtures; later he had set up production lines. After long years of experience, he'd finally been promoted to head of production. Art was slow, tolerant, patient. He was liked by most of his own people, who depended on him heavily.

Art solved his personal problems by himself. He never got mad. He always gave the appearance of a man who took things easy. He said frankly that he knew when to keep his mouth shut. Art performed best when he was comfortable and secure. In staff meetings with Bill, he said little. He harbored his annoyances. When Bill interfered with his production schedule, he would consider it carefully —and then do nothing. When Mike made decisions that Art should have made, he didn't say a word.

From Bill's point of view, Art was something like Mike. But since Art was an equal, Bill considered him weak and ineffective. At times Bill would become so exasperated with him that he wouldn't talk to him for days except on the most urgent plant business.

Strangely enough, Mike had somewhat the same feeling about Art. He considered Art soft and couldn't understand why he appeared to have such good morale in his unit. When Art talked somewhat affectionately about his people in the plant, Mike and Bill often united in annoyance. At times, Mike would admit to himself a bit of jealousy at Art's way with people. Art was a man in whom people confided easily; Mike himself would be more likely to talk over a fishing trip with him than with anyone else.

For Art's part, he liked Mike. He admired his abilities and education, something he never had or would have. He also learned from Mike. Art found it difficult to express his appreciation; whenever he tried, something strange happened to Mike. Instead of accepting Art's feelings, Mike felt compelled to go into a long discussion on some unrelated topic. In spite of Mike's front of adequacy, he appeared to feel uncomfortable when reminded of his achievements.

Art's Assistants. With Sid, his cabinet man, and Paul, his chassis man, Art had an unspoken understanding: if one was loyal to Art, and Art alone, nothing outside the division could interfere with the work. Art ran interference on everything, and Sid and Paul answered only to him.

Sid didn't make a move without consulting Art. Marv smiled as he recalled Sid saying that Art gave a lecture at least once a week about everyone's having the responsibility of his own unit—adding that Art would be hurt if decisions were made without his prior approval. Sid liked this relationship because it relieved him of all responsibility, but Art spent a considerable portion of his time doing the work of his branch head.

In some respects, Paul seemed a misfit in this group. Paul was middle-aged, a self-taught man who knew his limitations. In the process of growing up, Paul had learned to respect himself. He liked people and was well liked in the plant. He got along well with his superiors. If Art wanted to take over an operation, Paul didn't complain. In a sense, Paul complemented Art as Rod complemented Bill. While Bill needed someone meek and vulnerable, Art needed someone understanding who was personally secure. Art felt comfortable with Paul, and sometimes he'd have long talks with him. These talks left Art feeling better than he had in days, and Paul would sense some inner satisfaction that he'd have found difficult to put into words.

Looking for Improvement

Considering the alignments and the tensions among these seven top men, some observers might have thought it surprising that anything came out right at Comet at all. It didn't surprise Marv, though. He'd seen business teams function even when every issue became a sparring ground for status. He'd seen staffs in which "sheer logic" became an intellectual exercise by which each person attempted to outsmart the other, bringing up facts which were irrelevant and withholding really pertinent information. No, it was not surprising that considerable work was getting done at Comet in the midst of certain conflicts. But that didn't mean that there wasn't plenty of room for improvement.

As to how that improvement could be accomplished, Marv considered the possibilities. He could suggest that he and Mike have a series of talks. There was the possibility of sending individuals to management-training seminars. That procedure had the advantage of putting the minimum strain on the organization. But sometimes, when the individuals returned to the job, they were caught up in the same patterns of activity as before. In the seminars they found out what they should do; however, circumstances on the job just didn't seem to permit change, and some people found it difficult to apply the new skills which they had learned. Sure, if the boss had got this training, it might be different, but after all—he hadn't!

Training the management team right in the plant itself was another possibility. In a way, Marv found this idea the most acceptable. Certainly such a program had many risks, but it also had the greatest potential. *The key person was Mike.* If Mike proved willing to embark on such a program, in full awareness of all the implications, it had a good chance of success. He decided to recommend it if the opportunity arose.

Developing a Program

Later that week he received a call from Mike, asking him to come in. When he entered the office, Marv found that Mike's coolness of the last meeting had vanished. Mike was affable and ready to listen to suggestions. Marv outlined a program in which the key men of the plant would meet together once a week for a two-hour session.

"You mean there'd be lectures?" asked Mike.

"No, very few lectures, plenty of discussion. The meetings would be very informal; there would be no specified objective except to explore problems of common interest."

Mike seemed a bit doubtful. "Sounds like an awfully indirect approach. You really think anything would be accomplished?"

"I think there's a good chance. The real objective, of course, would be to develop better understanding between the members of your group and to work on skills which will improve their effectiveness."

Mike's mind was busy with silent questions:

Would people talk about him?

Were there some problems between Bill and Art which might get into the open?

Would Marv be able to straighten things out?

What if Bill and his outfit opposed it?

Isn't this playing with fire? What if somebody blew up?

What would people at the home office say once they heard about the program?

Wouldn't they think he'd gone off the deep end?

He had some spoken questions, too. Wouldn't some other alternative be better? Mightn't things get worse instead of better? Had Marv ever tried this before? How did it work out?

Marv answered as accurately as he could. He wasn't trying to oversell the idea—the program could never be any better than Mike's willingness to make it work. "If you like, think about it for a few days and let me know," he told Mike. "You know where to reach me."

Mike Decides

At noon, Mike had his lunch sent in and ate alone, as he often did when he was threshing out some problem. Afterwards, he leaned back in his chair, put his feet up on the low window ledge, and smoked his cigarette. This thing reminded him of the time he set up a profit-sharing committee. They all said he was radical, undermining the spirit of free enterprise. He grinned at the thought that many of his critics had since followed the pattern he'd helped develop. Still, pioneering had its risks, and he had considerable misgivings about Marv's proposal.

He wondered what other Comet people would think. All you really needed to be a good supervisor was a firm grasp of the business and a little common sense. Still, if there were hidden difficulties. . . . But no one would wonder about calling in an accountant or an engineer to straighten out a particularly tough problem. Was this essentially any different?

One other thought caused a little frown on Mike's forehead. How would the sessions affect his own relationship with the other men? He'd once read that people who go out of their way to be nice to everyone are merely trying to cover up other feelings of hate and anger. Seemed a bit farfetched, but sometimes he wondered about his own ability to tolerate people who didn't work at the same pace or in the same spirit that he did. There were a lot of other angles, too. When he found himself thinking about time and cost, he knew that he had made up his mind.

The following morning he called in his group, outlined the program as he saw it, and asked what they thought about it. All the men had already met Marv in individual interviews, and that helped. There were no serious objections. Bill was the only one who had much to say, and he was not too critical. Partly to avoid open disagreement with Mike, partly because they saw an opportunity to get some things off their mind, and partly because there was something about the idea that awakened some sparks of real hope, the group acquiesced. A few days later it embarked on its initial training venture.

First Meetings

The first meeting was stiff, perhaps somewhat tense. Marv carried the ball during most of the session. Toward the end of the meeting he asked the group what problems they'd like to take up at subsequent sessions. Rod suggested a discussion on office memos. "Why do we have to put everything in writing; besides, whatever happens to all the suggestions in those memos?" Sid and Paul seemed more concerned with techniques for getting people to tackle a job they were supposed to be doing.

Bill thought they ought to talk about lines of authority in the plant and in relation to the home office. "Why does so much stuff have to be referred to New York? By the time I get permission to hire a hot engineer, somebody else has him." Art suggested they consider methods of improving staff meetings. Joe had nothing to say at all.

Even though nearly everyone had made a suggestion, there was little comment on the ideas from anyone else in the group. When the meeting was over, there was a general feeling of apathy. Most of the men seemed to feel they'd gotten nowhere. There was considerable antagonism toward Marv, who was expected to offer sound advice on each problem raised.

During the second meeting, the group became concerned about getting started. Marv suggested that they appoint an observer each time to help keep track of what happened in the meeting and, as a result, he became the object of some ill-disguised anger.

Afterwards, Marv listened to the recordings of the first two sessions to check his general hunches about how the group was going. Mike and Bill dominated most of the discussion. Very few ideas were picked up by anyone besides the man who offered them; once in a while Rod and Joe followed Bill's suggestions, while Paul and Sid supported Art. Every decision was made by Mike. Marv sensed some strong mixed feelings toward himself. It was apparent that the group was not yet ready to look at the real problems.

By the end of the third meeting almost everyone agreed that the discussion of theoretical topics was impossible. At the end of the fourth meeting, Bill said he didn't think that the meetings were getting anywhere. No one dissented. Marv suggested that it might be worth-while to look at some of the reasons why this was true. The suggestion was passed by—unnoticed.

Change of Pattern

At the fifth meeting the pattern began to change. A few cautious remarks were made to Mike about his attitude in the meetings. Mike expressed surprise and asked for clarification. The talk was a little more open, and a few seemed to want to talk at the same time. Bill's cynical smile disappeared occasionally as he became immersed in the discussion. Joe was still quiet, but several times he'd have spoken if he'd been given a chance. The fifth meeting ran twenty minutes over the usual two hours.

Marv, always sensitive to any change in atmosphere, began to feel that the group was getting on its way. To check his impressions, he spent an afternoon in the plant. Mike told him, "I can't understand why anybody should feel he can't talk freely to me. People shouldn't be so sensitive!"

"If you can't understand it, why not ask a few questions about it in the next meeting?" Marv hoped his suggestion would take root.

When he dropped in on Bill, Marv found him friendly but, as usual, vaguely superior. Bill said he thought the sessions were wasting two hours a week for nothing. "Not that I'm not getting *something* out of them. Undoubtedly I've learned a few things, but nothing that you couldn't read in a book. Tell you what, though. We'd probably get along a lot faster if you could keep people like Paul from talking so much."

Art welcomed Marv into his office. Something was happening to Art, Marv reflected. Each person takes something different away from each session, and Art apparently was on the verge of certain insights. Art recounted an incident in his office in which he had used the listening technique they'd discussed in training; he was obviously pleased at the way it had worked out.

Incidents like this had long ago convinced Marv that what he said in a group was frequently lost, but what he *did* left strong impressions. Long after a training session, people would draw on these techniques for handling similar situations. Talking later with Paul and Sid, Marv was convinced that Art was getting the point.

The Turning Point

There was nothing unusual about the beginning of the sixth meeting. Marv opened the session by asking the members of the group to bring up whatever they felt like discussing. Mike announced that Joe had told him he'd have to miss this session—a rush order was in the process of being inspected.

During the first fifteen minutes there was the usual sparring as to what to talk about. Bill pointed out that they still hadn't come to grips with problems of overlapping authority. Paul thought that plant operations might be improved by a better system of communication. Both of these ideas were allowed to curl up and die.

First Open Discussion

Throughout the preliminary discussion, Mike seemed a bit preoccupied and slightly on edge. At last, during a slight pause, he took the plunge. "You know, after the last meeting I was rather concerned about the feeling you fellows had that you couldn't say what you wanted to me. I've been thinking about it. . . . I can't help it, but it seems to me you're all wet. What I'd like to have are some good, concrete examples. How about it?"

There was a long and slightly uncomfortable silence. Rod picked up a pencil and began drawing fancy doodles on a scratch pad. Paul knocked the ashes out of his pipe and began searching his pockets for his tobacco pouch. "Well, Mike," he said, "I've sometimes had the feeling that you cut Bill and Art off before they'd really finished what they had to say. It's sort of difficult to put your finger on any particular incident; I don't know if I could think of one right now or not."

"I'll give you an example, Mike," said Bill. "Remember a few weeks ago when we were discussing the Bergstrom tube? You cut me off just when I was telling you that we could have got the jump on most of the industry if we'd only followed my hunch that Bergstrom was on the right track. You know, the top engineers in most of these outfits don't really follow the scientific journals closely; they take a look at a couple of the engineering trades and figure they've covered the field. When I saw Bergstrom's report in *Science* a year ago, I knew he had the answer to color. If we'd moved then. . . ."

"Bill, I know all that," Mike interjected, "but, as I told you when we were talking about it, it's water over the dam now. I'd just like to hear some concrete examples of any time that I haven't been willing to listen to any ideas you fellows have. Don't I ask for a report from each of you at staff meetings?"

Art nodded his head. "Yes. Yes, that's right," he said. I don't think I'd say that you reject what other people have to say. In fact, I can think of times when I've made suggestions and you've shown me how to change them around a little bit so that they worked out even better than I thought they would."

Growing Awareness

Mike stared down at the table and squirmed a bit in his chair. "Uh . . . well, I don't know," he said. Frowning a bit, he turned to Marv. "I'd like to get your ideas on this, Marv. Do you think from what you've seen around here that I make it hard for people to talk to me?"

Marv thought for a moment and said, "Well, that's hard to say, Mike. You may want to look more closely at what has been going on here in this last interchange between you and Bill or between you and Art. After all, this is a problem in communication, and you may want to ask Art or Bill how they felt. Do you think there is anything to this?"

Mike looked surprised. "No, I don't see how. They both had a chance to speak, didn't they?" A long silence followed.

Later, while reviewing the recorded tapes of this meeting in the privacy of his office, Marv became convinced that things were beginning to happen. As he saw it, Mike was gradually becoming aware that he was having a negative impact on his staff, and that some people felt that he did not give them a chance to express their feelings.

But while intellectually willing to look at this, Mike wasn't really prepared to accept it emotionally. His opening question immediately forestalled the kind of response which might have been helpful to him. By challenging the group to provide specific instances of his behavior, he tried to defend his own position that his "door was always open."

The interchange with Bill showed he was quite insensitive to Bill's need for recognition and his own role in not letting Bill express himself fully.

In his interchange with Art, Mike handled his embarrassment at receiving praise from Art by ignoring his comments. As a result, he reinforced Art's basic belief that Mike made it difficult for him to express some of his real feelings to him.

Mike's response to Marv's suggestion rather clearly indicated that he was not yet prepared to lower his defenses and look at the impact he was having on others. This incident seemed to Marv to have inherent in it some key to the interpersonal relationship between Mike, Bill, and Art. Similar instances, Marv knew, would inevitably occur in subsequent sessions, but a time might be reached when Mike and the others would be able to look back on these exchanges, and accept fully the implications of their behavior.

The discussion next ranged briefly over a number of topics mostly related to communication problems in the management team. Then Art again expressed dissatisfaction with recent staff meetings. Sid said he had a feeling that the meetings never really came to grips with his own particular problems in coordinating cabinet manufacture with the rest of the plant. Rod suggested that the meetings were too cut and dried—just a series of reports without much discussion on anything except the set agenda. Bill said he didn't see anything wrong with that—you had to have some kind of set program for the meetings or you'd just wind up chasing your tail. Paul thought Rod had a point, though; sometimes things came up at the last minute that ought to be discussed even if unscheduled.

"Well, of course, our meetings may not be perfect," Mike admitted, "but I've always felt they were letting everyone know what the others are doing. You haven't said anything, Art; what do you think?"

"Oh, sometimes the meetings seem helpful, and then again some of them don't seem to be getting anywhere. I think it's sort of a matter of your point of view."

The Flare-up

Rod looked as if he were about to explode. "Art, you really get me sometimes! What *is* your point of view? I'd like to know for once—how you *do* feel about our staff meetings."

Art's bland expression underwent no change. "I think I feel a lot like you guys do. You've just about covered the water front; there isn't much more that I could add."

"Damn it, Art, that's just what I mean! Right here is one of the key difficulties in our meetings—we never know where you stand on anything! When an issue comes up, we have to guess what your position is. I never know whether you think your guys can handle a new set of designs or not."

Art's eyebrows went up. "Gosh, Rod, I didn't mean to get you upset. What I just said is how I really *do* feel about our staff meetings."

"I'm not talking just about staff meetings, Art," Rod persisted. "It seems as if you always keep us in the dark. I'll bet some of the other guys have had similar experiences."

"I don't mind saying that *I* have!" said Bill. "I can think of half a dozen times, Art, when you've clammed up and left me stranded up the river. Remember a couple of weeks ago, when we were talking about a new suppressor circuit for 6218A? You complained that the first designs had a bug in them, but when I suggested that maybe your boys hadn't quite followed specifications, you were noncommittal. I couldn't decide whether the thing ought to be reworked or not!"

"Well, Bill, you'll have to admit that's a heck of a thing to say about the production side unless you really had something to go on," Paul said. "What Art probably wanted to tell you was to take your specifications and go jump in the lake. But he's a peace-loving guy, so he bit his tongue instead."

"O.K., so he bit his tongue. Where did that leave me?" asked Bill.

"Up the creek, probably. I'll admit, Art, there are times when you do a pretty good imitation of the Sphinx," said Paul. "I suppose you could lay it on the line and let the chips fall where they may."

Art looked just the least bit hurt. "Well, a lot of these questions have two sides to them, and some have even more. I think I do the best I can to tell you what I think."

"Only it doesn't work that way in practice," said Bill, resuming his complaint. "I'll give you another example. Remember when Rod came up with an idea for a cove-type picture frame? You didn't want to put an off-white finish on it; you said it might pick up too much light. I told you I thought you were crazy and asked you to talk it over with Rod. After that I never could get you to say much about it, and neither could Rod."

"That's the kind of thing I mean, Art," Rod added; "usually you're easy to work with, but sometimes it just seems as if you won't take a firm position on anything."

"I think you guys are being a little bit unfair," said Sid. "You make it sound as if Art didn't have the courage of his convictions, and you know that isn't true. Sure . . . sometimes he puts off saying just what he thinks. But Bill, if Art takes a position you don't like, you jump all over him. He's just trying to do his job."

"Well, it would be a lot easier for everybody if we knew just where he stood," said Bill.

The thoughtful look on Mike's face had darkened into the suggestion of a frown. Glancing at him, Marv sensed that it made him uneasy to have Art on the hot seat. "Now, wait a minute, fellows," Mike broke in. "I wonder if we're really accomplishing anything all piling on one man. What do you think, Marv?"

Developing Insight

Marv was pleased. He saw real progress in the making—feelings stirred up, important insights developing. Mike wouldn't understand about that—certainly not after what happened before. "I guess it all depends. Art, how do you feel about it? Do you understand what the others are saying to you?"

Art's smile was wry. "I guess so, more or less. It looks as if most of you wish I'd be a little more outspoken. Bill thinks I clam up if I don't agree with him, and even Paul and Sid seem to feel that I don't let them know how I feel."

"And do you think these comments are justified?" asked Marv.

"Well, I suppose they are if everybody feels the same way about it—though to tell you the honest truth, I never noticed it myself. In some cases I figured that, once I'd had my say, I wasn't going to keep belaboring the point; and other times I just couldn't see any advantage in getting into a big hassle which wasn't going to solve anything anyhow. I just don't know."

Marv turned to Mike. "Just a moment ago you asked me what I thought, Mike. Since you haven't made any comment, how do you look at all of this?"

"I don't think Art has much to worry about, myself," Mike replied. "I've always found him easy to talk to. The only question I've had in my mind, Art, is that I only seem to be able to get the good news from you. . . . When things aren't going well in your division, I don't hear a peep out of you. And, well, one other thing. I'm sure that you must not approve of every decision I make, and yet if you don't approve, you never say so. In a way that's very complimentary, and in another way it isn't."

Rod leaned forward and caught Art's eye. "Art, there's just one other thing I'd like to say. I certainly didn't mean to imply that *I* think you're hard to work with, because I don't. What I meant was that when you sort of put me off, I don't know how to proceed. I couldn't decide whether to go ahead on that cove framing or throw it on the junk heap."

"Well, I see what you mean," said Art. "Maybe I just naturally avoid saying so if I think something you do is not so hot. I've always figured that a lot of these things will just work themselves out if you give them enough time. But I can see it makes it hard not to know where you stand."

Marv was pleased with the insight that Art seemed to be gaining. The progress of the group was slow, but undeniable. The recorded tape showed it. Though Paul and Sid had supported Art in the discussion, as they usually did, even they had indicated that Art's failure to communicate had bothered them at times. Bill, characteristically, had used the occasion to become aggressive toward Art, and Art had given him his typical reply—which was none at all. Mike had been disturbed at so much criticism of Art, and yet he too was able to voice some of his real feelings about Art.

Art in turn was able to achieve some intellectual and perhaps even some emotional understanding of what had been said. Perhaps he hadn't found a way of dealing with this problem, but the chances were that he would be much more alert to similar actions on his part in the future. Altogether, it seemed to Marv that Art was making considerable progress. Undoubtedly the others would, too, as the sessions continued.

As the meeting drew to a close, Marv noticed that the atmosphere was more relaxed than it had been before. After a lengthy and not very conclusive discussion of how staff meetings might be improved, Mike glanced at his watch and said, "Well, I guess that's about all for today, fellows—we had to cut the session because of the holiday tomorrow. I'm sure we all have a lot to think about from this meeting—I know that I have some real thinking to do."

Taking Stock

Marv wondered if Mike really had learned something from Art's experience, or, perhaps, even from his own. Did these experiences have direct relevance to him as a person? Could he be searching his own behavior for things that antagonized others? Some of the others may also have taken a new look at themselves. Certainly Art had. These things take time. Time—and again more time. Sometimes it seems like rambling—not getting any place, not showing any concrete accomplishments. But, then, some people do see the light; they do change, and everyone seems the better for it.

Marv again thought of the sixth meeting as a whole. It may well have been the turning point. The barriers were falling. The men were learning to listen and talk to each other—not about things out in space, but about themselves, their aspirations, and their fears of and feelings for each other. They were learning to be sensitive—to their own needs, and to those of others. They were seeing each other differently. They were working on their own blind spots—getting a better perspective on what life in the "executive suite" at Central City was really like. They were beginning to accept each other, not for what they would have liked each other to be, but for what they in fact were—with all their strengths and shortcomings.

What was the future to be like? Marv wondered about that too—and so did all the rest. There was a different spirit emerging—nothing radically different, but perhaps embracing just a little bit more cooperation, a little less competition. Some problems would still be dealt with for what they were—technical difficulties, breakdowns in scheduling, and the like. Others, however, would be recognized as stemming from the men themselves, their likes and dislikes for each other, their frustrations and ambitions. These would be recognized and dealt with—not as before by hidden aggressions or displacements, but by handling them openly and in a mature and forthright manner.

Managers in transition. That's one way of describing what was happening at Central City. Transition takes time. Marv knew this. But at least time was on his side. The top management of Comet was on its way to becoming a team.

Organizational Change

DANIEL KATZ
ROBERT L. KAHN

The major error in dealing with problems of organizational change, both at the practical and theoretical level, is to disregard the systemic properties of the organization and to confuse individual change with modifications in organizational variables. It is common practice to pull foremen or officials out of their organizational roles and give them training in human relations. Then they return to their customary positions with the same role expectations from their subordinates, the same pressures from their superiors, and the same functions to perform as before their special training. Even if the training program has begun to produce a different orientation toward other people on the part of the trainees, they are likely to find little opportunity to express their new orientation in the ongoing structured situation to which they return. . . .

The confusion between individual and organizational change is due in part to the lack of precise terminology for distinguishing between behavior determined largely by structured roles within a system and behavior determined more directly by personality needs and values. The behavior of people in organizations is still the behavior of individuals, but it has a different set of determinants than behavior outside organizational roles. Modifications in organizational behavior must be brought about in a different manner.

Let us examine the individual approach in more detail. Its essential weakness is the psychological fallacy of concentrating upon individuals without regard to the role relationships that constitute the social system of which they are a

---

From Daniel Katz and Robert L. Kahn, *Social Psychology of Organization* (New York: John Wiley & Sons, Inc. 1966), pp. 390–391, 406–425. Reprinted by permission of the publisher.

part. The assumption has been that, since the organization is made up of individuals, we can change the organization by changing its members. This is not so much an illogical proposition as it is an oversimplification which neglects the interrelationships of people in an organizational structure and *fails to point to the aspects of individual behavior which need to be changed.*

Some psychoanalysts, for example, assume that wars are caused by the aggressive impulses of man and that if we can lessen frustrations and redirect aggressive impulses, we can change the belligerent character of the state and eliminate war. Reasonable as this sounds, it has very little to do with the case. The finger that presses the button unleashing a nuclear warhead may be that of a person with very little repressed hostility, and the cabinet or state directorate behind the action may be made up of people who are kind to their families, considerate of their friends, and completely lacking in the psychopathology of aggression. They are merely carrying out their roles in a social system, and unless these roles and the social structure which gives them definition are changed, we will still have wars. Yet we persist in attempting to change organizations by working on individuals without redefining their roles in the system, without changing the sanctions of the system, and without changing the expectations of other role incumbents in the organization about appropriate role behavior.

In short, to approach institutional change solely in individual terms involves an impressive and discouraging series of assumptions—assumptions which are too often left implicit. They include, at the very least: the assumption that the individual can be provided with new insight and knowledge; that these will produce some significant alteration in his motivational pattern; that these insights and motivations will be retained even when the individual leaves the protected situation in which they were learned and returns to his accustomed role in the organization; that he will be able to adapt his new knowledge to that real-life situation; that he will be able to persuade his coworkers to accept the changes in his behavior which he now desires; and that he will also be able to persuade them to make complementary changes in their own expectations and behavior. . . .

Sensitivity Training: The Bethel Approach

The group process of Lewin for achieving agreement among peers on their own problems has been extended by his students to the technique of sensitivity training. Just as the individual has to be isolated from ongoing influences to learn about himself, so too must the group be separated from its usual environment. As the therapist leads the individual to express his own emotional conflicts, to become aware of them, to explore and to attain insight into his own motivations, so too is the group encouraged to express its emotions, to examine its activities, and to become aware of group process.

Since 1947 the National Training Laboratories has held sessions every summer at Bethel, Maine for leaders from industry, government, universities, and other institutions. On this cultural island people leave behind their organizational roles and enter as peers, unrepresentative of their group memberships, into an exploration of group process and leadership. The frustrations in dropping their usual role supports and ingrained organizational techniques lead to a reexamination of methods of participating in groups and influencing other people.

The major device for such learning is the T-group (training group). Each such group consists of approximately ten to sixteen people, including one or two trainers. The group is scheduled for one or two meetings each day over a period of two or three weeks. The meetings typically last for an hour and a half or two hours.

Each group begins without agenda, structure, division of labor, or rules of procedure. The people in each group are strangers to each other, brought together only by the common goal of learning more about themselves, the impact which they have on others, and the ways in which groups can become effective instruments for meeting the needs of their members. The absence of the usual props of officers, agenda, and Robert's Rules of Order creates an initial vacuum which is often quite uncomfortable. As the members struggle to fill this vacuum with meaningful activity and relationships, the trainer attempts to observe problems of communication, attempted seizures of power, misunderstandings, and other phenomena of interpersonal life. He communicates these observations to the group, whose members gradually begin to attend to such matters themselves and to check the accuracy of their own observations by describing them and asking for corroboration or correction from others. By this method (which is difficult to describe but most exciting and rewarding to experience) the members of the group attain increased sensitivity to their own behavior, the actions of others, and the nature of group development. Group members often emerge with a restructuring of their values about people and about their operations in group settings.

Powerful as this method is, its target is essentially the individual and not the organization. When the individuals return to their old structures, they step back into the same definitions of their roles. What is more basic, these roles are intimately related with a number of other organizational roles; the converted returnees may want to redefine their own way of functioning, but the expectations of superiors, subordinates, and colleagues have not changed, nor has there been a change in organizational sanctions and rewards.

If the person who has undergone change happens to be the head of an organization or a major unit of an organization, then organizational change may ensue. But there is no guarantee of significant organizational change even in such an instance. The old methods of operation have forces behind them other than the personal style of the leader, and these too must change to insure system change. Sometimes such changes are beyond the power of the organizational head. Sometimes they are possible but require skills and methods beyond those the chief learned in the laboratory training experience.

In recent years the activities of the National Training Laboratories have greatly expanded, and the methods pioneered by Bradford and his colleagues have been adopted by many organizations and individuals. Laboratory or sensitivity training sessions are conducted under various auspices on a continuing basis in many different locations throughout the country. In addition, many innovations have been introduced and given some research evaluation (Bradford, Benne, and Gibb, 1964). The most important of these, for our present purpose, is the closer linking of the T-group to the realities of specific organizations. This is achieved in part by dealing specifically with problems of organizational change as adjunct curriculum. A more dramatic innovation has been the use of the T-group procedure with people who are members of the same organization, whether company, school, or labor union. Such a group may consist entirely of peers, or of people at different levels in the organizational family, such as a superior and his immediate subordinates.

It is perhaps too early to attempt an evaluation of these variations on the T-group theme. Certainly they offer increased power with respect to generating organizational change, and to the maintenance of changes begun within the group. On the other hand, the role relationships which members bring into the T-group setting add to the initial difficulties of launching the training process, and may continue to impede it. The organizational T-group, in short, is a promising development, but its properties and potentialities require continuing exploration and research evaluation.

The relationship of sensitivity training to group therapy has often been discussed (and as often left unresolved). There is sufficient variation among practitioners of the laboratory method of training and among group therapists to make difficult any estimation of the degree of relationship or separation between the two.

Our own view is that laboratory training is not basically therapeutic in theory or in practice. Laboratory training does not aim at the resolution of unconscious conflicts within the individual but at a fuller perception of his behavior and the behavior of others. The content of the discussion in the T-group, and especially of the comments of the trainer, is consistent with these aims. The comments are strongly oriented toward interpersonal processes as they are directly observable in the group; inferences about the motives and internal conflicts of others are not encouraged. Each member comes to understand that he is expert and can talk well about how he feels or what he sees, but that he is on questionable ground when he attempts to make inferences about the motives of others.

As we have noted, the differences among trainers are great and the distinction between cognitive learning and therapy is not absolute. The distinction is easy to observe, however, if we contrast the training procedures of the National Training Laboratories with those of Elliott Jaques and his former colleagues at the Tavistock Institute. Jaques emphasized the analogy between individual therapy and organizational change. His underlying hypothesis is that many organizational problems are rooted in unconscious motives and their solution opposed by unconscious resistances. The excavation and working through of such material becomes the major means to organizational change, in his view. The basic assumption of the laboratory training method, on the other hand, is that the major problems of human organization are not unconscious and irrational, or at least that they can be successfully attacked at the conscious level and in terms of behavior observable and understandable by the members of the group themselves.

Group Therapy Within Organizations

An interesting attempt to produce organizational change through group therapy introduced into the organization itself has been utilized by the Tavistock Institute in England and is reported by Elliott Jaques (1951). The factory in question is an engineering and metals concern, the Glacier Company. The essence of the procedure is to have the organization change itself by means of group processes occurring at every level in the organization. The immediate target in this approach is the improvement of people's understanding of their organizational interrelationships and their own personal motives. The remote target is organizational restructuring by responsible organizational members themselves. The basic philosophy flows from individual therapy. The research team of outsiders is only one change agent; the major agents of change are the organizational members themselves. To quote Jaques, the research team is "to act only in advisory or interpretive capacity. The team is not here to solve problems for Glacier. They may, however, be able to help with the continuing development of methods of getting a smoother organization."

In accordance with this philosophy the research team began its program only after gaining acceptance from the Director, the Works Council (a body composed of management and elected union representatives), and the factory-wide committee of shop stewards. Instead of applying the therapeutic approach in literal fashion, the Tavistock researchers focused upon organizational problems. Their preliminary move was a historical investigation of the plant, followed by an organizational study to establish the role structure of the system. This latter study included "an examination . . . of how far the social structure of the factory had proved effective in coping with the forces which affected production and group relations."

After the presentation of these background reports to the Works Council, various sections of the organization began to ask the research team for cooperation on specific problems. The procedure of the research team was to direct the groups with which they worked toward the discovery of underlying causes and the expression of partly unconscious motives. Resistances emerging in group sessions were sometimes interpreted by the research teams; in other instances the group was left to make its own discoveries. To use Jaques' words:

> The method used was to draw attention to the nature of the resistance on the basis of the facts known to those concerned. Opportunities were taken to illuminate in the specific situation the meaning of the feelings (whether of fear, guilt, or suspicion) that constituted the unpalatable background to anxieties that were present about undergoing changes that were necessary. When successful, interpretations of this kind allowed group members to express feelings which they had been suppressing sometimes, for years, and then to develop an altered attitude to the problem under consideration. Even awkward or over-blunt comments often came as a relief. (p. 306)

And in the same context Jaques observes:

> The process of helping a group to unearth and identify some of the less obvious influences affecting its behavior is one borrowed from medical psychotherapy, from which is borrowed also the technical term *working-through.* It presupposes access by a consultant trained in group methods to a group accepting the task of examining its own behavior as and while it occurs, and a group able to learn, with the aid of interpretive comment, to recognize an increasing number of forces, both internal and external, that are influencing its behavior. The expectation, then, is that the group will acquire a better capacity to tolerate initially independent insights into phenomena such as scapegoating, rivalry, dependency, jealousy, futility

> and despair and thence a greater ability to deal effectively with difficult reality problems. When we speak of a group working through a problem we mean considerably more than is ordinarily meant by saying that a full discussion of a problem has taken place. We mean that a serious attempt has been made to voice the unrecognized difficulties, often socially taboo, which have been preventing it from going ahead with whatever task it may have had. (p. 307)

The Tavistock researchers regard two factors as necessary for successful working-through, and a third is desirable though not always essential. The first factor is similar to Dewey's initial condition for problem-solving, the existence of a felt difficulty. The group must be hurting; its members must recognize a severe and painful problem. The second factor is group solidarity or cohesiveness. Members must have commitment to the group and its objectives. Otherwise they will not have the motivation to overcome the additional anxieties involved in problem solution. The third condition is a state of frustration created by the failure of denial and other mechanisms of defense to function in their accustomed manner. Groups tend to avoid facing up to the basic causes of their problems through various devices of avoidance and denial. When group members, through the help of a consultant or by other means, find that running away from the problem gives them no relief, they are ready for more realistic exploration.

The group-therapy procedure had an interesting outcome in the Glacier Company, an outcome illustrative of the strengths and weaknesses of the approach. No fundamental restructuring of the organization took place, but inconsistencies and ambiguities were resolved and the pseudo-democratic stance of management was replaced by a clearer authority structure. The Works Council was reorganized to include representatives of various levels of management in addition to top management and union stewards, and its function as an advisory rather than a decision-making body was explicitly formulated. The executive system was clearly separated from the functions of the Works Council so that the line of authority was not interfered with in everyday operations.

The target of change and the nature of the changes attempted and achieved in the Glacier project deserve careful consideration. The group therapy was nondirective in the sense that the research team did not propose specific answers to problems in organizational functioning. Instead, they emphasized a method by which organizational members could discover their own solutions. The focus was upon procedures for enabling groups to gain better understanding of themselves and others. Essentially the approach was aimed at the removal of unrecognized and unconscious forces which impede the rational functioning of people in group relationships.

To the extent that there is a commonality of interests and goals among all subsystems and groupings within an organization, much can be accomplished by aiding people to make full use of their rational faculties in problem solution. The result should be more efficient organizational functioning and improved morale and interpersonal relations. Many of the anxieties of people, whether about their personal lives or about their roles in a social system, are crippling in their effects and often groundless in relation to objective facts. These irrational worries and emotional difficulties can gain group reinforcement and so be more potent in their undesirable consequences. The insecurities of one group can lead to scapegoating and uncooperative behavior toward another group in the same organization and so make the task of the second group unusually difficult.

The great limitation in the use of group therapy is that all conflicts and problems in organizational functioning are not irrational in nature. Many difficulties are based upon genuine conflicts of interest, and the more the irrational anxieties are stripped away, the more clearly these interest conflicts come into focus. In the early history of American industrialism some employers exploited the antagonism of one nationality group against another. To have the Irish at odds with the Poles obscured their common interests and made unionization more difficult. Group therapy in this situation could have reduced the tensions between the different nationality groups, but it would not have solved the basic conflicts between workers and management.

In the Glacier Company, then, the organizational changes should not be construed as a basic restructuring of the organization and a democratic resolution of competing interests within the organization. It is true that the Works Council was to some extent revitalized as a policy-making body, but the broadening of its representative character revitalized the management representatives on the Council more than the workers. Previously management had appointed all its representatives to the Council; now the various echelons of supervisory and management personnel elected their own representatives. In his own account of the later functioning of the company, the Director, Brown (1960), is honest and straightforward in describing the changes which took place. The changes essentially clarified and made consistent the basic philosophy of management and its operational procedures. Some degree of employee representation does not mean that the organization is a democratic political system. In such a system the constituent members elect their officers and legislators, who in turn appoint executive officers; policy on all matters is determined by the constituents or their duly chosen representatives.

The Glacier Company, according to its stated policy as an industrial enterprise concerned with profits, is not governed basically by its Works Council. The Company recognizes three other influential systems: the executive system, the shareholders and their board of directors, and the customers. The representative system comprising both managerial and nonsupervisory employees is only one system, and very limited in the decisions it can make. Neither the written policies of the Company nor its philosophy as described by its Director define an area of discretionary judgment for the Works Council, except to assert that its decisions should not interfere with what the stockholders think desirable in terms of costs and profits, what the customers want in terms of services and products, or what the executive system should handle as the implementation of policy. Moreover, the Director, who is chairman of the Works Council, speaks with several voices in the deliberations of that body. He is the chief representative of the executive system, he speaks for the stockholders and their interests, and he also is the self-admitted spokesman for the customers or clientele of the organization. If the discussion should enter an area which he regards as belonging within the province of the stockholders, or of executive management, or of the customers, he can merely say, "Gentlemen, that is not the legitimate concern of this group" or "Gentlemen, the *given* in this situation by which we must abide is the following wish of our stockholders." Small wonder that few crucial decisions are made by the Works Council.

The Company formula frankly states that the area of discretion or contribution to policy by the employees is defined by their willingness to mobilize whatever power they possess to oppose or support a proposal. If management proposes changes which are likely to lead to rebellion among the employees, this can be tested out in the Works Council. If the representatives of the employees rise up in their wrath and predict that a given change will lead to a strike, management may then back down. The wise use of Council meetings by management can avoid widespread discontent in the company, since management will be guided by what they gauge the opposition forces to be. On the more positive side, management has an opportunity to gain the assent and sanctioning power of the Works Council for those proposals accepted by the Council after discussion.

Fundamentally the representation of employees on one of the policy-making boards of the Company gives the workers a feeling that they will not be pushed too far or too fast by management. Precedents will be followed, people will be heard if drastic changes are contemplated, and management probably will accept a veto which the employees are ready to implement by a strike or a slowdown. Employees are confident that they will have some voice in any change that would fundamentally alter their way of life in the organization, and they have a means of getting a hearing for proposals of their own.

Though the representative system must rely on the power it can mobilize to affect decisions, the full power of the employees is not lodged in it. The trade union and the shop stewards constitute the organized power with which management negotiates, and the union is outside the representative system, though there are relations between the two. In fact, the Works Council includes union men, though they are not elected as such, who can informally represent the point of view of the union and in turn carry back to the union the views of management. This division keeps clear the struggle between management and union over contracts and does not involve the employees in negotiations with the company as representatives in the Works Council. By the same token it reduces the power of the representative system in the overall legislative process.

The group therapy process at Glacier thus helped management clarify its policies and procedures with respect to management responsibility, make unambiguous the character of the executive structure as an order-giving system, and stipulate the part to be played by the representative system and by the union. In the past management had suffered from confusion about the use of consultative democratic procedures, the pretense of democratic participation, and the abdication of management from some of its responsibilities. The Director was reluctant to assert his authority among the divisional managers. At times he refused to take the chair and lead the group, and wanted to appear merely as one of the group members. The role of middle management was weakened because it saw itself as being bypassed. The workers' representatives sat in council with top management and were in fact closer to top management than managers down the line. The very concept of role with its clear demarcation of duties was avoided. The assumption was made that if management and workers could get along amiably, all problems would be solved. The group processes instituted by the Tavistock research team enabled members of management to see clearly what they had been doing and what was necessary for effective operation as the sort of organization they wanted to be.

As leaders of a marginal operation in a competitive industry, top management probably made a correct assessment of the situation with respect to survival. It was not, however, the only possible course of action. They could have attempted to clear up the contradictions of democratic and authoritarian philosophy and practice by moving toward a cooperative enterprise, with employees sharing in the profits and policy decisions and electing the company officials. One difficulty with this solution is that the workers themselves may not have wanted it. To have become true partners in production with management would have meant breaking with the trade union structure and losing the security of long-standing membership in the union, for the sake of becoming members of an unusual partnership which the next turn of the market might wipe out. Moreover, the investment of the stockholders and their legal control of the company also represented a limiting factor in organizational change. Finally, top management was not willing to turn over the direction of the company to employees and perhaps to throw away its years of experience and its special competence in running the company. Management saw itself as dependent upon stockholders and the consuming public, no less than upon employees. As a marginal enterprise the company was very much an open system, and management had been trying to reconcile the demands from outside the organization with the internal needs of the employees.

For all these reasons, the Glacier management rejected a democratic political model as inappropriate for the organization. They did not, however, want to move toward the other logical extreme of machine theory, in which the organization is seen solely as a mechanism for task accomplishment and the people in it as objects to be molded to their job assignments. Management, though giving priority to the nature of the task as determined by the customer system and the stockholder system, also recognized the needs of employees. They hit upon the Glacier formula as an excellent means of preserving the best in machine theory with a clear enough concession to the democratic trend of the times to avoid serious discontent in the plant. This formula swept democratic consultative practices in everyday task decisions out of the door. The executive system was given full and complete authority for getting the job done within the scope of policy decisions made by the Board of Directors and the Works Council. The employees could be heard in the Works Council and when they felt very strongly about a given policy, could get it modified. Moreover, they had their own union to fall back upon for the protection of their interests. Management's recognition of the veto power of employees and its willingness to listen in advance to their wishes helped to sanction the workings of the executive system and to give psychological security to the members of the organization. Clarity of responsibility and authority in the executive system enabled the organization to get the most out of hierarchical authority.

The solution achieved in the Glacier Company is thus a viable compromise, probably well suited both to its immediate situation and to the larger context of British industrial society, with its well established trade union movement and its value emphasis upon gradualism and precedent. The compromise arrangement, however, does not permit the full use of the democratic process with all its potentialities for problem solution, for the development of people, and for motivating them to use their full abilities. Two of the traditional difficulties of machine theory remain unsolved at Glacier: (1) The conflicts of group interest still persist. The deep-seated problems of restriction of production, of worker reliance upon the seniority principle, and of resistance to mechanization and automation have not been touched by the Glacier formula. Such problems do not yield to the use of group therapy. They can be solved only through the internalization of organizational goals by employees, which in turn requires accepting them as real partners in production. (2) The clear change of authority and responsibility in the executive system makes for precise allocation of duties but in so doing loses the advantages of group responsibility and of innovative and cooperative behavior beyond the line of duty.

The use of group therapy in the Glacier Company was, however, a landmark in the theory and practice of organizational change. The Mayo tradition with its emphasis upon informal groups, the Lewinian approach with its use of group process for organizational reform, and the extension of that approach to the sensitivity training of individuals apart from the organizational context had neglected the facts of organizational structure and the properties of organizations as social systems. Individual change was equated with organizational change and small groups were equated with large organizations. It was the genius of the Tavistock workers to combine a knowledge of therapy with a knowledge of the social psychology and sociology of organizations. Their theoretical approach took account of the systemic character of the situation with which they were dealing, even though the method for modifying social structure was that of group therapy. Their first step to gain access to the company was to gain acceptance from the component subsystems of the organization. Their next step was a background study of the system as a whole and its functioning. In working through problems for various sections of the enterprise they were guided by their awareness of the relations of one subsystem to the other subsystems of the organization. Finally, they were perceptive of the high degree of the openness of the company to related systems in the environment which helped to determine its input and the market for its output.

Recently there have been promising attempts to adapt small-group approaches, especially sensitivity training and its variants, to account of the organizational context. The work of Schein and Bennis (1965), Argyris (1964), and Blake and Mouton (1964) are outstanding examples. The final pages of the work by Bradford, Gibb, and Benne (1964) speak of the "extended use of T-groups and laboratory methods in nonlaboratory (i.e., organizational) settings." The Tavistock work deserves to be recognized, however, as the first purposeful and successful fusion of the therapeutic and organizational approaches.

The Systematic Use of Feedback and Group Discussion: The Approach of Floyd Mann

Most organizations have at least one kind of feedback from the environment to guide their operations and indicate the need for organizational change. This feedback is from the reception of their product accorded by the clientele or market. When an automobile company cannot sell its cars it must make changes in the nature of its product. But there is another kind of feedback to the organization which derives from its own internal functioning. Two types of such internally generated information are frequently used by organizations. One concerns the technical side of internal functioning and implies an accounting for each production job in the organization. Some factories still follow the Taylor system in this respect, and at the close of every day report forms are passed up the line from each level of the organization describing the number of pieces produced, the utilization of materials, the amount of scrap and waste material, and the number of hours each employee spent on the various aspects of his job.

The second type of internal information concerns the human side of the productive and production-supportive processes of the organization. Typically such feedback reaches the upper echelons only when some problem has become acute. Top management learns that there has been a disastrous slowdown in the foundry and that castings are not reaching the assembly line on schedule, or that some key engineers and research people have resigned to take jobs with competing companies.

Suggestion systems are sometimes employed both to get ideas about technical improvement and to get feedback on the human problems of organization. Surveys of morale and of employee feelings, attitudes, and beliefs are also conducted by companies to give the latter type of feedback. If there were full and accurate communication up the line such surveys would not be needed, but the barriers to such upward communication are too numerous and too strong to ignore. Nor are these barriers only to peripheral data about employee attitudes. A sharp distinction between information about technical and human processes is false. The concept of the socio-technical system of Emery and Trist (1960) rightly gives emphasis to the complex interrelationships of social and technical processes. An adequate morale survey will furnish information both about the feelings of people and the actual operations of the technical or work system.

The great weakness in the use of surveys of employees' ideas and feelings is the inability of management to utilize this type of feedback about the internal functioning of the organization. Sometimes top management feels that it has done the proper thing just by conducting a survey, and proceeds to file the reports in the personnel office; at other times it will pass the findings along to lower echelons with no specific directives about their use. If the results of the survey are read by these subordinates, the natural tendency is to select the items that reinforce their present biases and to discount findings that run contrary to their own ideas.

Employees have two reactions to such unutilized surveys. The first and perhaps the dominant one is satisfaction in having been asked to express their views and in actually ventilating their feelings. The other reaction, which arises particularly when they have been led to expect positive action, is one of frustration in that nothing happens after all their efforts to tell the company what was wrong and what should be done.

To make the survey an effective form of feedback for organizational change Floyd Mann and his colleagues at the Survey Research Center developed a plan for group discussion of survey results by appropriate "organizational families." Mann's approach was first used in a fairly large company in which there had been a thorough survey by questionnaire and interview of all officers and workers. The concept of the organizational family refers to a supervisor at any hierarchical level and the employees reporting directly to him. Any supervisor thus would have membership in two organizational families. He would be involved in the group he supervises and he would also be a member with his coordinate supervisors of the family reporting to the officer above him. Thus the concept of organizational family takes account of the linking of subgroups in an organizational structure through the dual membership of their top men.

Mann's use of group discussion by such organizational families is like the

Tavistock approach in taking into account the realities of organizational structure. Moreover, the hierarchical character of an enterprise is recognized by starting the feedback process with the top organizational family, for example the president and the vice-presidents reporting to him. The next series of feedback discussions might include each vice-president and the department heads who report to him. Starting at the top of the structure means that the serious examination of survey results is sanctioned or legitimized by the executive system. Every supervisory officer who calls a meeting of his subordinates has already been through a comparable discussion session with his coordinate officers and their chief.

The feedback material prepared for each session by the research team is, moreover, of special relevance for the particular organizational family into which it is introduced. The branch chief meeting with his department heads will be given companywide totals of employee ideas and feelings about all issues as well as branch totals, but, in addition, the branch totals will be broken down for the departments represented at the meeting. Thus, at the meeting the participants can see how their branch compares with the company as a whole as well as the strong and weak points of the departments within the branch. In turn, when the department head meets with his supervisors, they will have before them data to show how their department compares with the branch of which it is a part and how the sections within the department, manned by the supervisors present, compare with one another. In general then each organizational family is presented feedback about its own problems in detail and comparative information about the company as a whole or the larger part of the company to which it belongs.

For example, in one company studied by Mann, the top echelons of one department could immediately see that they compared very unfavorably with the company as a whole on certain aspects of employee morale. A much higher percentage of workers in that department than in the rest of the company had thought about quitting their jobs during the past year and were apparently waiting for the first good opportunity to leave; identification with the company was much lower in that department and dissatisfaction with supervision was higher. These findings brought home forcibly to the departmental officers and to their superiors what they had long been aware of to some degree, namely that top management had at times considered the department as expendable, its services always replaceable by contractual arrangements with outside firms. That company policy had affected rank-and-file employees so deeply was, however, something of a surprise.

The presentation of survey findings to the various organizational families sometimes brought new problems to light. More often it gave an objective and factual basis to problems that had either been brushed aside or dealt with by some opinionated gesture. Not only had vague reports about the perceptions and feelings of employees been reduced to facts and figures, but comparisons could be made among similar groups and the findings could be related to possible causal factors. In this objective atmosphere questions could be raised about the data, many of which could be answered by further analysis of the same data. And this was the emphasis of the Mann feedback procedure—group discussion of facts and figures in a task-oriented atmosphere where people were seeking to analyse the problem, identify possible causes as objectively as possible, and agree upon possible solutions. The reason for utilizing organizational families and presenting to them the relevant data about their operations thus becomes clear. The members of a specific organizational family have been involved in these very problems, already know a good deal about them, and know what questions should be asked to dig deeper into the available data for answers. Moreover, the group members are the immediate agents for implementing any policy changes with respect to problems at their own level. If they understand the causes, have been involved in a discussion of solutions, and perhaps have proposed the new policy, they will be more effective agents for achieving change.

The feedback technique, utilizing group discussion and group involvement, must be used under certain conditions if it is to realize its potential strength. Mention has already been made of the need for a factual, task-oriented atmosphere. A second necessity is the discretion of each organizational family to consider the implications of findings at its own level. Again, an area of freedom is required to utilize group process. General problem areas may be designated at higher echelons, but the detailed answers must be worked out by people closer to the problem.

For example, when the top management family looks at departmental comparisons they may become immediately aware of the low morale in a given branch. They may also note that there is more dissatisfaction with supervision in this branch and may want to attribute its morale problems to the practices of its first-line supervisors. This, however, is something the branch head can look into more definitively when he meets with his own department chiefs. At this meeting they will have a more complete breakdown of survey findings by sections and type of work, and it may become apparent that discontent with supervision is concentrated among the unskilled laborers.

Suppose problems of supervision are revealed to be specific to certain sections and independent of the general disaffection in the department. It becomes apparent that supervisors of unskilled laborers were not helped by the supervisory training program as much as other supervisors. The men under them are more accustomed to authoritarian methods than were other workers. Supervisory training in human relations had confused rather than helped these foremen, in that they were not really enabled to use more consultative methods and yet were made insecure in their use of older authoritarian approaches. They are also of lesser education and ability than the other groups of foremen, and feel the double insecurity of being men in the middle in a marginal department. It is difficult to imagine the revelation and discussion of such material except in the organizational family of its greatest relevance, acting according to its own discretion.

A third requirement for the effective use of the feedback procedure is a reporting back up the line of the outcome of meetings at the lower organizational level. When a department was satisfied that it had some answers to its problems and some recommendations about them, its head could present these findings at a subsequent branch meeting. He could report to the branch meeting to what extent various difficulties could be met at the departmental level and to what extent they seemed to arise from branch and company policies which would have to be changed at higher levels in the organization. The branch then could discuss all departmental reports and could attempt a summary report to go to the sessions of top management. At any point in the procedure the research team might be asked to bring back further breakdowns of relevant data.

One great advantage in this type of feedback with group discussion is its utilization of existing organizational structure. The executive line is not bypassed in securing information and implementing policy. Effective working relationships between supervisory levels are improved and two-way communication facilitated. Management policy is better understood and more fully put into practice, and the special knowledge and competence of all levels is more fully utilized. Mann (1957) recognizes that improving organizational functioning means dealing with the systemic properties of organizational structure:

> Organizations, as systems of hierarchically ordered, interlocking roles with rights and privileges, reciprocal expectations, and shared frames of reference, contain tremendous forces for stability or change in the behavior of individuals or subgroups. Change processes need to be designed to harness these forces for creating and supporting change. (p. 162)

Mann also points out five other related sets of facts which make for the efficacy of systematic feedback of survey data through organizational families.

Participation in the interpretation and analysis of research findings leads to the internalization of information and beliefs. When ideas are a person's own, they are much more likely to be translated into meaningful practices than when they are the suggestions of an outside expert.

The feedback of information and its discussion by the appropriate organizational family makes it highly relevant to the functioning of the subgroup and its members. Principles taught at a general level of abstraction are more difficult to apply than the discovery of principles from a person's own immediate experience.

Knowledge of results can in itself motivate people toward improving their performance. Level-of-aspiration studies indicate that individuals tend to raise their sights when they see the outcome of their efforts. If there is continuous feedback on the basis of some objective criterion of behavior, people will be motivated to attain better scores.

Group support is especially effective where there is continuing membership in a particular group. The members of an industrial organization during most of their waking hours are part of one or two organizational families. If the other members of these permanent groupings also change, there is a continuing reinforcement for individual change. More remote and fleeting group memberships are occasionally significant but one cannot escape the constant pressures of the here and now.

Finally a hierarchical ordering of roles with respect to authority is characteristic of most organizations, or at least of their executive systems. Hence the introduction of feedback starting at the top of the structure not only gives organizational legitimacy to the process but insures that for every individual in the organization there will be expectations from his immediate superior about his behavior. The changes will have been worked out in part by lower levels in the organization but in their final implementation will have the authority of the organizational line of command.

The effectiveness of this type of feedback program was demonstrated in the accounting branch of an industrial enterprise. All employees of the company had been included in a companywide study in 1948, and the results had been fed back to all branches of the organization. In 1950 a similar questionnaire was filled out by all employees of the accounting branch and these returns furnished the basis for the feedback experiment. Four accounting departments participated in the feedback process, which was initiated with a meeting of the accounting executive and his eight department heads. Two of the eight departments were eliminated from the research design because of changes in their key personnel since the 1948 survey was conducted. Two other departments were held out of the feedback process to serve as controls. In the four experimental departments the feedback activities varied somewhat, especially in the extent to which the nonsupervisory employees were involved. The basic pattern was essentially as described above, however, with meetings of organizational families down the line at which were also present a member of the research team and a member of the personnel department of the company. These latter two individuals were not active participants in the discussions except when called upon as resource people for certain types of information.

After an 18-month period in which the natural variations of the feedback programs in the four departments had run their course, a new survey was conducted in the accounting branch. The before and after measures indicated that more significant changes had occurred in the four experimental than in the two control departments. As Mann (1957) states:

> Two measures of change were employed: a comparison of answers to sixty-one identical questions which had been asked in the previous surveys and a comparison of answers to seventeen questions dealing with changes perceived by the workers since the 1950 survey. In the experimental group (comprising four departments), a fourth of the sixty-one items showed relative mean positive changes, significant at the .05 level or better; the change for another 57 per cent of the items was also positive in direction, but not statistically significant. Major positive changes occurred in the experimental groups in how employees felt about (1) the kind of work they do (job interest, importance, and level of responsibility); (2) their supervisor (his ability to handle people, give recognition, direct their work, and represent them in handling complaints); (3) their progress in the company; and (4) their group's ability to get the job done. The seventeen perceived-change items were designed specifically to measure changes in the areas where we expect the greatest shift in perceptions. Fifteen of these showed that a significantly higher proportion of employees in the experimental than in the control departments felt that change had occurred. More employees in the experimental departments saw changes in: (1) how well the supervisors in their department got along together; (2) how often supervisors held meetings; (3) how effective these meetings were; (4) how much their supervisor understood the way employees looked at and felt about things, etc. These findings indicate the extent to which the feedback's effectiveness lay in increasing understanding and communication as well as changing supervisory behavior.
>
> Comparisons of the changes among the four experimental departments showed that the three departments which had two feedback sessions with their employees all showed positive change relative to the control departments. The change which occured in the fourth was directionally positive, but it was not significantly different from the control departments. In

> general, the greatest change occurred where the survey results were discussed in both the departmental units and the first-line organizational units. The greater the involvement of all members of the organization through their organizational families—the department heads, the first-line supervisors, and the employees—the greater the change. (pp. 161–162)

The procedure of feedback to organizational families as developed by Floyd Mann is similar in many ways to the group therapy approach of the Tavistock Institute. It has the same objective of clarification and improvement of organizational functioning through an objective assessment of problems by the organizational members themselves. It differs in four respects:

Mann had the considerable advantage of providing objective feedback on organizational functioning through detailed data furnished by his comprehensive survey. This made possible a task-oriented atmosphere where facts and figures were the guiding criteria. It also made possible the setting of performance norms, and insured a representation of the views of all employees in the consideration of problems by the various levels of management.

Mann's technique covered the entire organizational structure in systematic fashion. The Tavistock research team entered only those sections and groups of the organization to which they were specifically invited, and tended to spend more time with top management than with the lower echelons.

The Tavistock investigators were more active participants in the change process than were Mann and his colleagues. Though the Glacier people were not presented with solutions, they were led persistently to reexamine their thinking and to become aware of unrecognized and unconscious forces in the situation.

This meant that the focus in the Glacier study was more upon irrational sources of difficulty and in the Detroit Edison Company more upon reducing areas of ignorance through the acquisition of facts and modifying vague opinions with documented beliefs. It would be interesting to have a research comparison of the amount of personal and organizational change produced by the two methods and of the mediating processes responsible for whatever changes did occur.

Both methods by choice avoid identifying in advance desired changes in organizational structure and functioning. The objective is to induce the organization to change itself. This has a tremendous advantage in removing from the researcher the onus of deciding what needs to be changed. It has the possible disadvantage of making an organization more vigorous in its present mode of operation even when there may be basic defects in its operating philosophy. For example, a non-union factory, if subjected to the Tavistock group therapy, might emerge with a management clearer in its conception and more ingenious in its pursuit of ways to prevent union organization. In general, the organizational change attained by either the therapy or the feedback technique is likely to be in the direction of more efficient functioning but not in the direction of basic structural change. The oligarchy will still remain an oligarchy, the autocracy still an autocracy. These methods represent the philosophy of mild and bland reform, not radical change.

To state it more precisely, the primary target of the feedback technique employed by Mann is improvement of both personal and role relationships within the organizational family. The objective is not to introduce a systemic change but to improve the relationships among the members of each organizational family and between organizational families, through their discussion of their common problems. The specific changes which occur may vary from one sector of organizational space to another and they may all add up to better understanding and clearer communication in the organization as a whole. But the target has not been to change the system as a system.

This approach thus raises the question of the effective limits of change which is not systemwide in its character. Lippitt, Watson, and Westley (1958), in their incisive analysis of planned change, point out the problems raised by interdependence among the subparts of a system with respect to change processes. Change in one subpart can generate forces in other parts to produce related modifications, but interdependence can also mean that more sources of resistance are mobilized against any alteration of established procedures. Hence these authors emphasize the need for defining the unit in the organization appropriate to the change attempted. They write:

> If the subpart is too small to cope with a given problem, it will be unable to change because of resistance originating outside the subpart, coming either from the larger systems in which it is embedded or from parallel systems to which it is related. If the unit is too large and includes semiautonomous subsystems which are not directly involved in the change process, it may be unable to change because of resistance originating within the system. On the other hand, if the size of the unit selected as a client system is appropriate for a particular change objective and if several subparts of this system all become committed to achieving the same objective, the motivation and energy available to the system for working on change will be intensified by the interdependence and interaction among the subparts. (p. 77)

References

Argyris, C. *Integrating The Individual and the Organization.* Wiley, 1964.

Bradford, L., J. Gibb, and K. Benne (eds.). *T-Group Theory and Laboratory Method: Innovation in Re-Education.* Wiley, 1964. Brown, W. *Exploration in Management.* London: Heinemann, 1960.

Emery, F. E., and E. L. Trist. "Socio-Technical Systems." *Management Sciences Models and Techniques,* Vol. 2. London: Pergamon, 1960.

Jaques, E. *The Changing Culture of a Factory.* London: Tavistock, 1951.

Lippitt, R., J. Watson, and B. Westley. *The Dynamics of Planned Change.* Harcourt, 1958.

Mann, F. C. "Studying and Creating Change: A Means to Understanding Social Organization." *Research in Industrial Human Relations,* No. 17. Industrial Relations Research Association (1957), 146–147.

Schein, E. H., and W. G. Bennis. *Personal and Organizational Change Through Group Methods.* Wiley, 1965.

Questions for Discussion

1. Explain why, from the viewpoint of psychology, employe-centered leadership patterns are good for a department or corporation. In doing this, it might be helpful to draw on the theoretical model in this chapter, as well as on the theory of human needs in Chapter 3. View your answer to this question as a statement of the advantages of employe-oriented leadership.

2. Although there are additional reasons in Chapters 7 and 9 why employe-centered leadership might not, under certain conditions, be appropriate for a given situation, use only the materials in Chapter 8 to explain those forces in a situation which might work against the successful use of such a leadership pattern.

3. Suppose that an executive wishes to develop the ability to behave in an employe-oriented leadership fashion. Does it do any good to read about this type of leadership? What other methods are available, and how do they affect a leader's attitudes and beliefs?

4. Companies often employ headquarters staff specialists in accounting, law, industrial relations, scientific research, industrial engineering, operations research, and the like. These men are traditionally regarded as fact finders and recommenders to a president, to aid him in his decision making. Why might a company like General Electric change this *role?* What new role was expected of staff men in GE? Describe the advantages of this new role.

5. A number of selections in this book, both in Chapter 3 and in Chapter 8, suggest that employe-oriented leadership often requires a change in the *attitudes* of executives. Using the Schein article as an illustration, show why this approach is necessary; that is, why a "knowledge" or "textbook" type of training won't always work.

6. What principal objections have been raised against developing in managers a deeper understanding of the psychology that can be used by them in positions of power? What do *you* think about these objections? (Draw upon text material, but apply your own reasoning and draw your own conclusions.)

Chapter Nine

Influencing Behavior Through Political Action

In this chapter we will analyze the "political" means by which executives influence the behavior of lower-level managers and employes in an organization. More specifically, we will examine such executive behavior from the standpoint of (1) the design of technological systems, (2) the conversion of technological systems into systems of authority, and/or (3) deliberate strategic behavior intended to influence subordinates to conform to technological designs.

However, before taking up our analysis of political behavior, we will first explore the reasons why executives engage in it. In previous chapters we have dealt with the behavior of subordinates in relation to authority systems: in Chapters 3 and 4, their reactions to authority and rule systems, and why they disobey; in Chapter 7, why they tend to obey. But there can be no political system with all followers and no leaders. Therefore, to have a complete understanding of the political systems of behavior in organizations, we need to understand why executives want to command.

The Motivation of Executives to Political Action

The motivation of executives to engage in political action can be divided into (1) the attitude of technological necessity, (2) the desire to head an organization, (3) the competitive urge and the will to conquer, (4) the urge to creative action, (5) the desire for system as a means to feel secure, and (6) pragmatism—"it works."

The Attitude of Technological Necessity

In discussing technological necessity,[1] we begin with the fact that, in industrially developed societies, specialization has progressed to a profound degree. Man and his family are dependent on the production process for almost all material needs. The days of the self-sufficient farm are gone forever, and one of the facts of modern life is what Galbraith has called "the paramount position of production." Thus society provides both "ethical" and "monetary"

[1] The description of the technological system in Chapter 7, including the statements of Veblen, Friedmann, and Beard, gives added emphasis to the necessity for both technological planning and political action.

institutions which reward the executive when his organizational system is efficient and which punish him when it is inefficient. Granted that there are sometimes other motivations which operate to prevent him from striving for *maximum* organizational efficiency, there are nevertheless powerful material and non-material pressures which cause him to put a high value on organizational efficiency.

This means, among other things, that the internal technological system of a firm or department—the rational division of this system into areas of specialization and the rational relating of these areas (planning the input-output system)—must be (1) designed (an act of rule formulation) and (2) cloaked with the symbols of authority and legitimacy.

In addition to the social belief in production and prevention of waste, together with the rewards and penalties which cause executives to *learn* this value, there is the factor of training and education. The student in business or engineering learns finance, operations research, marketing, or any of the sub-fields of administration, and this stored knowledge with its symbolic representation is a form of "invested capital" in his life and career. It represents his functional importance in society—his repertoire of actions that help him cope with life in an industrial and economic world. This commitment no doubt reinforces the original social value attached to planning and implementing an efficient, "well-run," "high-quality" organization.

The Desire to Head an Organization

Some people, particularly those who have risen to high positions in organizations, have found that the way to get—and continue to get—what they want is to gain positions of status and power. Running throughout much management literature is the implication that the successful executive has this motivation to a degree. Joseph Schumpeter, the celebrated sociologist-economist, characterized the entrepreneur this way:

> In the breast of one who wishes to do something new . . . there is the dream and the will to found a private kingdom. . . . The modern world really does not know any such positions, but what may be attained by industrial or commercial success is still the nearest approach to medieval lordship possible to modern man. Its fascination is specially strong for people who have no other way of achieving social distinction. The sensation of power and independence loses nothing by the fact that both are largely illusions.[2]

In moderation, the motivation to power is functional for the executive and for the organization. When Chester Barnard presents the principles of cooperative action (Chapter 7), we see his confidence in his ability to create a system to guide the behavior of large numbers of people. The same might be said of Fayol's explanation of discipline and unity of command; of the casual way in which Newman lays out the purposes of standing policies and procedures; and of the tone in which Cordiner presents General Electric's philosophy for governing the behavior of 281,000 employees. Even Wilfred Brown, head of Glacier Metal

---

[2] Joseph A. Schumpeter, *Theory of Economic Development* (Cambridge: Harvard University Press, 1934), pp. 84–94.

Company in England, who brought industrial psychologists from Tavistock into his company, shows a high degree of confidence in himself as the most important person responsible for instituting a specific "new order" for governing behavior within the firm.

In extreme cases, however, the desire for status and power can be dysfunctional for the executive and for the organization. For example, Shakespeare's King Lear had so strong a desire to retain his kingly status and prerogatives after dividing his kingdom that his plans were unworkable, his daughters rebelled, and his own personality finally disintegrated. Or we need only look at Adolf Hitler, whose obsession with personal power resulted in historic catastrophe.

A number of modern sociologists have cited cases where executives so focused on the rule system and the prerogatives of office that they ignored the changing needs of customers, the problems of technology, and other *facts* which must be considered for effective decision making. The reading by Victor Thompson following Chapter 4 illustrates this phenomenon.

The Competitive Urge and the Will to Conquer

Schumpeter gives us another set of motivations to executive success, which have some verification in subsequent studies in clinical psychology:

> Then there is the will to conquer: the impulse to fight, to prove oneself superior to others, to succeed for the sake, not of the fruits of success, but of success itself. From this aspect, economic action becomes akin to sport—there are financial races, or rather boxing matches. . . .

We recall from Saul Gellerman's summary of the power motive as conceptualized by Alfred Adler (Chapter 3) that all men may have some of this type of motivation. In economics, the very essence of "free enterprise" is the competitive instinct. Experienced to a degree that does not interfere with rational behavior, this motivation can be functional for the organization and for the executive. Too little may result in one's being a follower, not a leader, and too much may result in pathological or dysfunctional behavior.

The Bennis and Shepard reading in Chapter 3 clearly shows that, in their orientations toward authority, people tend to form habitual behavior patterns of dependency, counterdependency, or independency. In extreme cases, we should not discount the possibility that the *executive* may be the one who plays Berne's deadly game, "Now I've Got You, You Son of a Bitch" (Chapter 6), playing for the rules *per se*, without regard for the reality of decisions, and whose primary motivational repertoire consists of the one strategy of checking up on people, of placing the blame.

The Urge to Creative Action

A third executive motivation often cited in the literature is aptly put by Schumpeter:

> [In addition to the dream of a private kingdom, and the will to conquer] there is the joy of creating, of getting things done, or simply of exercising one's energy and ingenuity. . . . Our [executive] type seeks out difficulties, changes in order to change, delights in ventures.

Schumpeter goes on to explain that there *would be no leaders* if there were not some people who possess certain mental characteristics which enable them to get outside their routine in the organization. For most people, this is difficult to do. First, there is great risk—mental risk—in doing something for which the outcome is unknown. Action must be taken without working out all of the details, and success depends partly upon intuition. Secondly, there is subjective insecurity inherent in pioneering. As Schumpeter says:

> In the breast of one who wishes to do something new, the forces of habit rise up to bear witness against the embryonic project. A new and *another kind* of effort of will is necessary. This mental freedom presupposes a great surplus force over the everyday demand and is something peculiar and by nature rare.

Thirdly, the social environment usually reacts against one who wishes to do something new.

In view of the foregoing inhibitions, we can see that the men who actually engage in political action—who actively make rules, and who engage in dynamic action to get them instituted—are motivated in part by the creative urge—Schumpeter's "surplus force." Remembering Maslow's theory of human motivation in Chapter 3, we can also see that such men are engaging in self-fulfillment—and that they have found a way to do this, that of political action.

At a number of points in this book, we have seen that there is another kind of executive who relies on the existing rules to achieve security and status, who "goes by the book," who is satisfied by the feeling of importance of office and title, and who does not want to rock the boat. That there are such executives cannot be denied. They are motivated by the desires to rule and to compete described by Schumpeter, but not to any significant degree by the urge for creative action.

The Desire for System

Mental security—"peace of mind"—results in part when a person lives in an orderly world, in which everything is in its place, and in which the unexpected does not usually appear. This kind of motivation operates for both general (line) executives and specialist (staff) executives. Sociologists have pointed out that many general executives have "a demand for control," and that this causes them to make rules for uniformity and set up standards for measuring results. Given the necessity for technological coordination, the executive is much more secure if he can predict what people will do in the organization and if he has uniform standards and policies so that not all parts and people need be viewed individually. Throughout the readings by Barnard (Chapter 7), Newman, Cordiner, and Brown, we see this need expressed in orderly procedures, policies, and standards.

In the case of specialist executives, this need is expressed in the desire to formulate business operations on the basis of certain established bodies of knowledge. The finance specialist is much more secure in his thinking if he has tools of marginal analysis or discounted cash flow to apply to investment decisions or pricing problems. The marketing specialist's mind is much more at ease if there are known ways of predicting consumer motivation or of choosing advertising media. And the operations research specialist can do his work much more securely through the use of formulas for inventory control than if he had to face entirely new projects without models for approaching them. The desire-for-system motivation is made clear in the Koontz and O'Donnell reading, discussing why staff men are sometimes given "functional authority."

Thus both general executives and specialist executives have good reason for formulating standing plans and rules and for instituting them in organizations. Such rules enable them to pursue their careers, and use their minds, with less mental strain and frustration than if there were no systems, rules, and order.

Pragmatism

A final reason why executives engage in political action is that all human beings need law and order in an interdependent organization, and the executive recognizes that he *can* take such action. This has already been explained in Chapter 7 on more than one level of analysis. Locke's philosophical explanation of human passion, Presthus' emphasis on reduction of anxiety among peers, and Gouldner's explanation of how rule systems reduce anxiety between superiors and subordinates all confirm that the executive can govern human behavior through the formulation of systems of rules and procedure—if he does so wisely.

The many other studies in this book which show that people react to authority systems in dysfunctional ways should, however, serve as a warning. The phrase "if he does so wisely" is an important one. Later in this chapter, we will examine how the technological system is converted to legitimate rules and procedures.

Designing a Technological System

It may seem odd for a chapter on political action to include a section called "Designing a Technological System." Does this not sound like engineering or economics, instead of politics? The answer lies in the fact that the technological system—the organizational output goals, the system of working parts, and the input-output relationships between them—is at one and the same time the technical work operations to be performed by each part of the organization and the rules of human conduct which the part (person or department) should follow.

It is impossible to convey in complete detail how the problems of technological design are solved, since the entire field of microeconomics, much of the fields of accounting and finance, and a great number of current applications of operations research are devoted to the "allocation of resources." Even when these precise quantitative techniques are not applied, detailed qualitative estimates are used (in the form of departmental charters, subsection descriptions of objectives, and job descriptions) for conventional "position" or "departmental" analyses, particularly at the higher levels of planning in large organizations.

To illustrate, then, only the nature of the problem of technological design, we will look at the two patterns of organization which are most often discussed in management literature: functional organization and sub-unitary organization. Because their division of technological work at the operating level gives rise to different forms of work at the management level, they are sometimes called "centralization" and "decentralization."

Certain key concepts have been formulated in management literature to help understand technological planning in these systems:

- Departmentation of primary operations and auxiliary services
- Standing plans: policies, procedures, and methods
- Line and staff departmentation of managerial work
- Decentralized departmentation of managerial work

Functional Departmentation of Primary Operations

As a vehicle of description, we will take a small company producing mimeographed booklets. It receives orders for 600 booklets (quantity objective), on blue paper (quality standard) to be delivered to the customer (spatial objective) by 4 p.m. the following day (timing objective).

Figure 9-1. Functional Pattern of Technology (Form I). Dashed arrows (stencils or pages) represent sub-objectives in the input-output system.

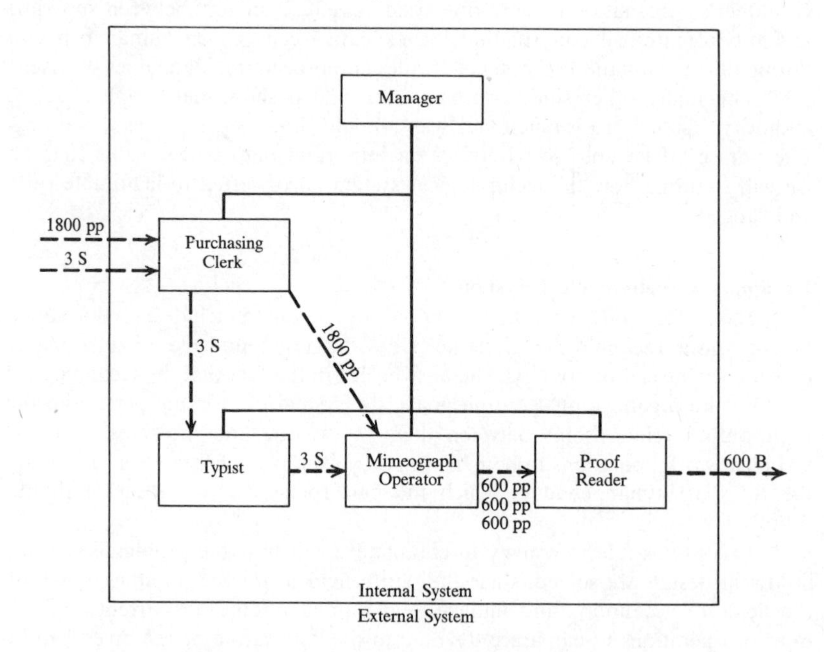

Notice in Figure 9-1 that it is essential for the proof reader to have qualitative, quantitative, spatial, and timing objectives related to the external system, and that each man-machine station has a definite *but different* relationship to the *next* station on these four dimensions.

From the viewpoint of each station, each person has a standing job description, which in most general qualitative terms would read "Operate mimeograph machine," "Purchase all supplies," etc. In quantitative terms, this can be worked out by time and motion study, job analysis, or a variety of techniques. With more recent techniques, such as PERT, objectives (events) correspond to output targets, and activities are pictured by arrows on the diagram.

Even though we have used only one order for one booklet to be processed in one day as our operating example, the same essential technique is used for planning the permanent or fixed resources on the chart. Here are the steps:

1. Estimate the output goals for the total organization (quantities, qualities) for a fixed longer-term time period—say a month, year, or in some cases five to ten years.
2. Analyze the total work to be done and divide it into stations.
3. Estimate the capacity of one station (person, department).
4. Divide the output *for each station* in the series by the capacity of the station, thus computing how many units of resources are needed for that station. That is, how many mimeograph operators are necessary for a given output, how many purchasing clerks, and so on.

In classical management theory, two functional principles have long been firmly enunciated: the *principle of the objective* and the *principle of balance.* Each of these is illustrated in our small print shop: there is an overall organizational objective, there are sub-objectives for each *unit within* the organization, and each unit's output synchronizes in timing, quality, quantity, and space with that of each succeeding unit.

Sub-Unitary Departmentation of Primary Operations

Sub-unitary organization is sometimes called "job enlargement" at the lower levels of organization, and "decentralization" at the upper levels. Here is what would be done to reorganize our printing shop into sub-unitary form (see Figure 9-2):

Figure 9-2. Sub-Unitary Pattern of Technology (Form II). Dashed arrows (stencils or pages) represent sub-objectives of the input-output system.

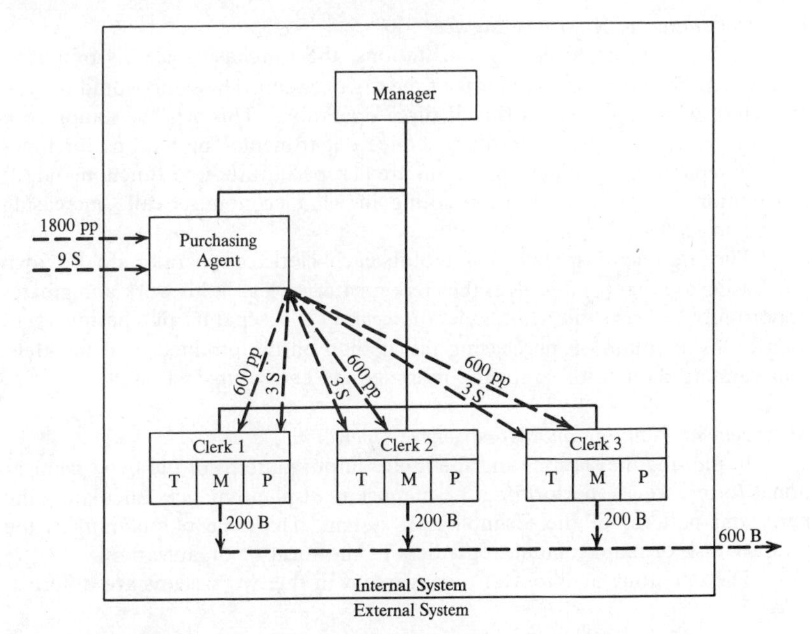

1. One third of the typing, one third of the mimeographing, and one third of the proof reading are assigned to clerk 1, who is to perform all three operations.
2. The same is done for the other two clerks.
3. The flow of work—the objectives of each position, which, taken together, form the input-output system—is rearranged. The objective of each clerk now becomes 200 booklets; it was formerly three stencils for the typist; three stacks of page materials with 600 copies per stack for the mimeograph operator; and three proofread stencils, plus 600 finished booklets, for the proofreader (see Figure 9-1). In addition, the spatial objective connects each clerk with the customer, rather than to other people within the organization.

Note that nine stencils are required in Form II (Figure 9-2) where only three are needed in Form I (Figure 9-1), and that if each clerk is to have the equipment he needs without being dependent on the other two operators, three typewriters instead of one are required. Also, the clerk is more expensive to hire or train than the typist, because he must have skills in all three operations. Thus, in terms of overhead cost, Form I is less expensive.

From the standpoint of worker motivation, we have a different situation altogether. Each operator is given an overall objective—200 booklets. He can also solve in his own way problems of coordination. For example, when typewriter keys are dirty, the periods and commas may come out blurred on final copy. Under Form I, the proof reader might discover this deviation from quality standard and report it to the manager, who would then involve *both* the typist and mimeo operator in getting the quality balance of the system straightened out. Under Form II, however, this situation would involve only one person. Thus, in terms of morale and learning opportunity, the clerk is more strongly motivated than the typist or the proof reader because he has greater responsibility and autonomy. (This is Peter Drucker's "management by objective.")

Departmentation of Auxiliary Services

In both of the foregoing illustrations, the purchasing clerk's output is "consumed" by other *internal* parts of the organization. The same would be true of a clerk who kept records for all three operations. This type of station in a technological design is an auxiliary service department. The reasons for functionally separating auxiliary operations are (1) specialization of function and (2) distribution of overhead costs, resulting in what economists call "increasing returns to scale."

The arguments in favor of letting each clerk or operator do his own purchasing are that (1) this gives the clerk greater variety in his work and greater opportunity to learn the whole operation, and (2) a separate purchasing agent focuses his attention on purchasing rather than on the production of booklets, thus running the risk of confusing intermediate ends with final ends.

Management Planning and Management Operation

In plotting the stations and the input-output patterns of the two organizational forms, we are performing the management planning act: calculating the parts and patterns of the technological system. This type of planning is the primary task of management, regardless of the form of organization.

The operating activities of management in the two systems are different, however—and also different from each other. An examination of Figures 9-1 and 9-2 shows that there are more operational computations to be made for the functional form, even though the physical flows seem simpler, because the operating manager must compute different input and output objectives for each person, and also the relationships among the three functions.

Within a sub-unitary form of organization, the operating manager need only compute one output and two input objectives for all three people. This fact—which also means fewer downward communications in a sub-unitary organization—is a significant point in Cordiner's explanation of General Electric's decentralization philosophy.

Standing Plans

Policies and procedures, as explained in the reading by Newman following this chapter, are enduring rules which relate one job or department to other jobs or departments. In the functional form of organization, these must be much more detailed because the timing, spatial, and quantity specifications must be worked out. On the other hand, the sub-unitary form allows management to formulate broader objectives and policies for each worker.

The Two Forms of Organization at the Large Corporation Level

At the large corporation level, the stations or parts of our small printing firm become major functional departments, or sub-unitary divisions by product or territory. Figure 9-3 is a simplification of what the General Motors organization would look like arranged functionally, and Figure 9-4 is a simplification of what it looks like in sub-unitary form.

In a reading accompanying this chapter, Ralph Cordiner tells us that General Electric has *110* product divisions in its sub-unitary system, corresponding to the trade-name divisions of General Motors. At the time of Cordiner's writing, there were 281,000 employees at GE, and input flowing in from 40,000 suppliers. On the output side, there were 350 distinct product lines, and over *three million* catalog items flowing to 400,000 distributors and customers. As can

Figure 9-3. Functional System of Technology (Form II), Company Level.

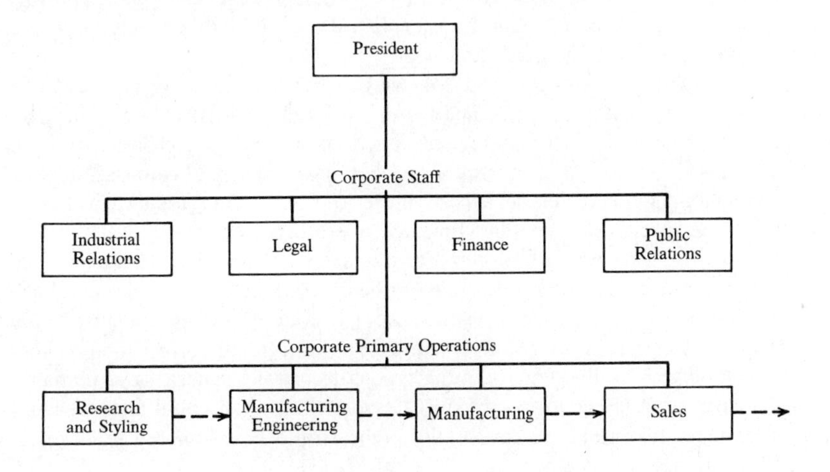

Figure 9-4. Sub-Unitary System of Technology (Form II), Company Level.

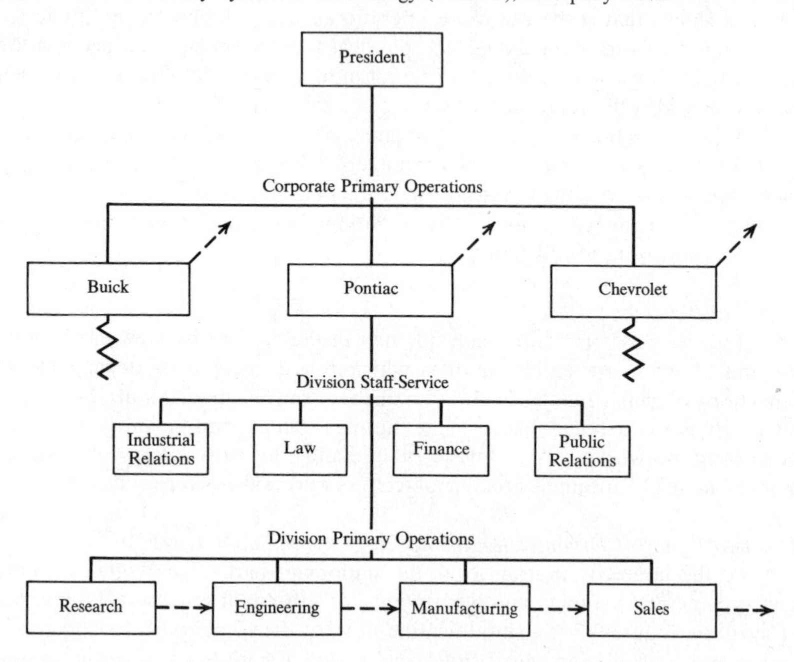

be easily surmised from these figures, when organizations are *very* large, the principles of objective and balance become tremendously complex for both forms—and the timing, quality, quantity, and spacial complexities of functional organization are staggering even to contemplate.

The most immediate difference between the pattern of a large corporation and our small printing firm is the division of labor among management personnel. We see that one manager is no longer able to encompass the vast problems of planning, and that there must be specialists—staff managers—to carry out this planning. In a sub-unitary organization, planning is divided between corporate staff and division management.

By studying Figures 9-3 and 9-4, we can see that the same pro and con principles are involved as in the small company. Form I involves less overhead cost, because there is a duplication of functions within each product division in Form II—duplicate line departments such as sales, and duplicate staff departments such as law. And just as it costs more to hire or train a clerk, so it costs more to hire a separate president for each operating division.

However, since each division in Form II is self-contained, it is a much better training ground for executives. Moreover, the decision and cybernetic (feedback information) systems are smaller—and response is more immediate. Just as the printer's clerk in our initial example can quickly detect and correct the problem of filled type keys on his stencil-cutting typewriter, so the general sales manager for Chevrolet can keep closer tabs on Chevrolet sales than could a single chief sales manager for the entire corporation, who would have to keep track of all the other divisions as well.

Converting Technological Systems to Political Systems: Authoritative Behavior

Executives engage in a number of different "political" actions to ensure that the behavior of the organization conforms to the requirements of the technological system. These political actions fall into two broad classes:

1. *Authoritative* behavior, or actions in support of law and order. These are actions designed to make participants *believe in* the wisdom and logic of following established law and order. They are intended to foster behavior patterns in the organization described in the philosophy of law as the "reasonable man" doctrine.
2. *Strategic* behavior, or actions of intellectual or emotional influence. These are sometimes called "playing politics" and sometimes "strategic planning." They use motivations of participants other than legal reason.

There are six principal kinds of authoritative behavior which stand out in management literature:

1. The codification of internal law (codification of departmental charters and individual job descriptions; codification of objectives, policies, and procedures; codification of authority attached to charters and job descriptions).
2. The appeal to philosophy: the power of ideas.
3. The appeal to science: the authority of fact.
4. The appeal to executive wisdom.
5. The codification of due process.
6. Executive development: a further appeal to wisdom.

The Codification of Internal Law

When delegation is discussed, as in the Newman-Summer-Warren reading following this chapter, a distinction is often made between delegation of *duties* and delegation of *authority.* The purpose of this distinction is to highlight the political nature of designing a technological system. Notice the meaning of the word "duty" in reference to the behavior of a janitor in an office building: "It is his *duty* to sweep the floors." We have described a technological function (sweeping) in political terms.

The term "responsibilities" is used by Cordiner to denote both a technological and a political phenomenon. The reading by Henri Fayol following this chapter stresses the place of agreements in the motivation of employes, and tells us that these legal expectations should be made as clear as possible, so that participants know in advance what technological function and what behavior (duties) are expected of them.

Not only are job descriptions and charters spelled out in organizational manuals, but the *relationships* between stations or parts of the organization are also frequently codified. The Newman reading, which deals with policies, procedures, and methods, provides an example. In one sense, a policy is to a firm as a law is to society. More precisely, a policy might be defined as a *non-sequential rule for the repetitive and interrelated actions of two or more people at their work places.* Thus, the policy "all people shall accrue four weeks vacation per year" does not connect managers' actions in two widely separated places *sequentially*—it says "if and when you grant vacations, here is the behavior to engage in." It does, however, connect the actions of two widely separated managers in *substance.*

Procedures, on the other hand, are *sequential rules for the repetitive and interrelated actions of two or more people at their workplaces.* These may be procedures for passing on physical parts of the work flow, or they may be procedures for passing on bits of information in the decision process. An example of the former would be a production system (stations plus input-output sequences) designed by a linear program; an example of the latter would be Barnard's specification that the transmittal of official communications must follow each position in the management hierarchy in sequence; in other words, go through "channels."

Management writers have devoted more attention to the codification of *authority* than to technological duties or policies and procedures. There has been much attention devoted to the principle of unity of command. In our readings, Fayol and Newman-Summer-Warren take the position that there should be one, and only one, legal authority (and authority position) over each position in the organization. Barnard, though he stresses the need for codification ("every communication should be authenticated"), takes the position that one individual might have two or three superiors, each with formal authority in a special sphere. This corresponds to the legal notion that, for example, both police and sanitation departments of a city have authority over a citizen, but in different spheres.

Of special importance in a survey of management principles is the authority of staff specialists. There seem to be two broad positions on this question. The first is exemplified in the reading by Koontz and O'Donnell following this chapter, which clearly recognizes the possibility of functional authority for staff specialists. The second is represented by the Cordiner selection, in which *services* (G.E. abolished the use of the term "staff," to eliminate especially the symbolic notion of authority) are viewed as performing the following functions: (1) research—that is, technological policy formulation—and (2) advising and educating line executives and other personnel.

In writing organizational and procedural manuals, management attempts to apply the principles of objective and balance to the task of reducing the technology of an enterprise to a system, and then to codify and dignify this system with the language of law and order—"duties," "obligations," "rights of authority"—in short, to create a system based on the "reasonable man" doctrine.

The Appeal to Philosophy: The Power of Ideas

In the history of the world, there are many empirical instances of the *power of ideas* governing human behavior. In the Constitution of the United States, for example, we find a theory of the division of powers, phrased in general language, which has influenced the decisions and behavior of generations of ordinary citizens, judges, governors, and Presidents.

At the corporate level, we need only look at the Cordiner reading to see how top management might use a similar philosophical construct to influence human behavior, in the form of a rationale (the autonomy of divisions, the improvement in decisions, the growth and freedom of executives in sub-units) and an institution (operating and service divisions, the corporate staff), together with the codified rights and duties of each.

The Appeal to Science: The Authority of Fact

For many years, executives have appealed to the power of ideas for influencing behavior, but only recently have we had an appeal to science at the level of the corporation. In the early twentieth century, Frederick Taylor formulated an elaborate system of technology linked to human motivation, which he called "scientific management." At least half of each of Taylor's three most important works is devoted, not to technology, but to human motivation and to human conflict, their causes, and proposed solutions. He theorized that the reason for conflict was an unjust and uninformed management, which did not know the fair statement of duties of employees and therefore assigned duties unjustly and divided company revenues unfairly. Through science and engineering, he hoped to show workers *and* management what the law of technological justice is, and let the facts show, to both parties, the reasonableness of rules.

Taylor failed to convert the U.S. industrial system to his science, primarily because his scientific model did not take into account the growth and development (self-actualization) of workers. But today we have a new movement toward the authority of science. For example, the staff in one corporation does research on both technological problems and human problems. Its projects cost vast amounts of money, but the staff has no power to impose its ideas on lower divisions. Instead, the staff advertises within the company that they have done this research, that they have spent $150,000 on it, and that they know as much about the subject (say, executive compensation methods) as any other group of people in the world. It is then up to the line managers to call in the staff as consultants *if they wish,* to hear more about the research and perhaps to adopt the new methods.

Other examples of the new scientific approach may be found in the area of operations research and computer installation. There are case histories which show clearly that people in positions of corporate "political" power have accepted the recommendations of specialist managers because of a belief in the power of science.

Whether today's "management science" will, over the long run, succeed any better than the "scientific management" of fifty years ago is still to be verified. But the "appeal to science" does work in some cases and executives do use this as a political method of reinforcing their authority.

The Appeal to Executive Wisdom: Actions Speak Louder than Words

One of the most controversial areas in all organizational theory is the question of executive responsibility. Here we are using the term "responsibility" in an ethical and a psychological sense, rather than a legal sense. The test of responsibility can be phrased in these terms: "Does, or can, each executive know enough about the technological and human factors that should be considered in system design decisions, to make decisions which balance these factors so that those around him will see the reason in the resulting system?" This concept of executive responsibility is important, because an employe's feelings (attitudes and beliefs) are influenced more by the parade of decisions made by executives over a period of time—and the total technological-political system which results from these decisions—than they are by codified rules, status, title, office, or even power.

Traditional management literature has answered both parts of the above test question in the affirmative. Running throughout the writings of Henri Fayol, for example, are frequent passages which intimate that the executive both *can* (a descriptive statement) and *should* (a normative or ethical statement) have both facts and values which guide his stream of decisions according to a norm of responsibility. Fayol tells us that the main reason why discipline and *esprit de corps* break down among subordinate personnel is "the ineptitude of leaders." He repeatedly uses phrases like "integrity," "judgement," and "high moral character" to describe the behavior of the executive, and he places moral principle equal to, or higher than, his principles of unity of command and chain of command. He also stresses how important it is for the executive to have frequent meetings with participants in the organization, in order to *know* all of the effects of his decisions.

Referring back to Barnard's reading following Chapter 7, we find an even stronger position taken on the question of executive responsibility. The legitimacy of authority hinges on both how well the organizational communication system keeps the executive informed in "scope" and in "knowledge of local conditions," and with what wisdom and values the executive uses this knowledge. Reading between the lines—although it is important to note that Barnard does not expressly mention it—the other side of the coin has to do with how much the executive is *willing to listen* to the communication system—will he be a King Lear? Or will he have a tin ear?

This brings us to the schools of thought which seem to assume that executives will *not,* in fact, act responsibly (in terms of our definition of responsibility). In the readings by McGregor (Theory X), Thompson, and Argyris following Chapters 3 and 4, executives are *not* seen as wise men, making judgments on the basis of facts at hand and viewing the realities of both technology and human motivation. Rather, they are seen as having various flaws in their ability to make decisions—flaws which would endanger a "reasonable" technological and rule system. In fact, the executive described by McGregor, Thompson, and Argyris is clearly an *unreasonable* man:

1. He is motivated by stereotyped attitudes about human nature. McGregor's description of Theory X includes the managerial assumption that "the average human being prefers to be directed, wishes to avoid responsibility, has relatively little ambition" . . . and "most people must be coerced, controlled, directed."
2. He is motivated by security seeking himself, and puts more value on rules than on technological and human realities. In this view, the executive must have rules to isolate him from the frustration caused by a desire to make decisions for others conflicting with a desire to be "democratic," in a society where both the larger political system (the Declaration of Independence) and the moral system (all men are equal in a world of brotherly love) stress a less active decision-making role for him.[3]
3. In the Argyris model, he is motivated by hostility toward subordinates, who, finding their needs blocked, react with apathy, withdrawal, or hostility themselves. The reactions of subordinates cause the executive to react with more rules and directive control. Pursued to the extreme, this vicious circle leads to the kind of behavior described in Eric Berne's game, "Now I've Got You, You Son of a Bitch." (See Berne's reading following Chapter 6.)

Out of this controversy over the motivations of executives, we can conclude

[3] Alvin W. Gouldner, *Patterns of Industrial Bureaucracy* (New York: Macmillan, 1954).

that some executives do act wisely, with knowledge (scope) and wisdom (balance), and others do act in dysfunctional (stereotypic, status conscious, or hostile) ways. It seems reasonable to conclude further that those executives who act in the former pattern will reinforce the authority system, and those who act according to the latter pattern will eventually destroy the authority system.

Formal Dynamics: The Appeal to Due Process

One approach which seems to accept both of the foregoing views of executive motivation is that advocated by Wilfred Brown in his reading following this chapter. Brown recognizes that, viewed in one way, the rule system may be perceived as legitimate by subordinate personnel; viewed in another, it may be perceived as illegitimate. Furthermore, the decisions of executives in interpreting the rules may be perceived in either way. One test of both the rules and the executives interpreting them is to provide a system of *appeals*—a due process under which decisions by management may be reviewed.

Based on the postulate that differences in opinion (based on both knowledge of facts and judgments, the values attached to facts) are inevitable in a rule system, Brown outlines a formal appeal procedure designed for the Glacier Metals Company. Every member of the company can appeal to the next higher officer, all the way to a point beyond the board of directors: a tribunal composed of the appellant's representative, the management's representative, and an outside representative appointed by the Works Council.

Admitting that such appeals are time-consuming and that they add to the overhead cost of the business, Brown nevertheless cites four advantages of such a formal system:

1. For a middle manager, such a procedure is "comforting." For example, he can say to a complaining subordinate, "I'm sorry, but you have a quite simple means of redress if it is justified. If your problem is not felt by you to be sufficiently important for you to appeal, then I suggest you forget it. If, on the other hand, you are really troubled, then no doubt you will take the steps necessary to put the matter to test."
2. For the higher executive, it is an assurance that middle managers will behave with a degree of responsibility. "Anybody in a senior managerial position in industry is *worried* by the thought that the policy he has set for his subordinate managers may at times be interpreted harshly or erroneously by them."
3. For the employe, it means better decisions. "The existence of an appeals procedure influences all managers to make decisions with much greater care. It is an essential means of attempting to promote natural justice." And it makes a vital contribution to the sense of security of personnel.
4. For the organization, it makes change easier. "I have no doubt that the appeals procedure assists vitally to get people's cooperation in accepting change."

Executive Development: A Further Appeal to Wisdom

In order to develop executives who are open-minded, willing to listen to gain information, and therefore more effective in their authority behavior, many companies maintain executive training programs, either within the company or at a university. If the learning experience is well planned and executed, it is entirely possible to develop or activate certain useful attitudes in the executive:

1. An eagerness to probe deeply into problems and understand them thoroughly before making a decision, to avoid jumping to conclusions.
2. An understanding of his own competence in dealing with others. Such an understanding aids him in obtaining facts and advice for making decisions.
3. An open-minded attitude, a willingness to entertain new thoughts about a subject.

Executive development can also strengthen the sources of authority, if such attitudes are influential in the formulation of codified policies and procedures.

Converting Technological Systems to Political Systems: Strategic Behavior

Strategic behavior in organizations takes the form of "playing politics," propaganda activities, withholding information, the display of power (or the concealing of it), and other such actions. However, there is almost no scholarly literature on the subject. Most of what we have is in the form of novels, such as Cameron Hawley's *Executive Suite,* and the works of J. P. Marquand and Louis Auchincloss.

One reason that we do not have scholarly literature on this aspect of organizational behavior is that whoever writes on this subject does so at his own peril. That is, the author may be depicting the truth about what goes on in the world, but his readers will be so uncomfortable at seeing this reality that they may turn on the author. Like the messenger in ancient Greek drama, he may be condemned for the bad news he brings.

One of the few academic articles on the subject is included in the readings following this chapter—"Strategic Considerations in Planning," by William Newman. In suggesting behavior that might at times intimidate people, confuse them (by concealing the truth of a decision), or lead them to act on emotion rather than reason, Newman clearly takes the so-called "Machiavellian" position that the end (effecting managerial decisions) justifies the means (strategic behavior). We take the position that this is political behavior but not authority behavior, because the latter concept in our view involves overt decisions viewed as legitimate and reasonable. A subordinate has no opportunity to be reasonable if he is being denied information or being frightened by a show of force.

There is clear evidence that executives do, in fact, engage in strategic behavior. When the goals of the organization as perceived by the executive warrant such action, executives not only engage in deceptive behavior but at times in outright coercion. There is evidence, too, that such political action works in certain instances (organization members *do* follow the intended behavior change) and that it does not work at certain times (organization members lose their belief in, and respect for, the authority of rules and leaders).

What determines whether strategic behavior will work or not? And what determines whether it is ethical or not? If we define ethics as rules of behavior that accord with the norms of society, the same factor determines both. To illustrate: In a war, men are engaged in fighting and killing. Generals make plans on how to kill, and soldiers kill, in spite of the usual religious, ethical, and social norms against taking human life. Why? Because national or ideological interests are at stake. The end (national or ideological interest) is seen as justifying the means (killing). There is usually no effective dissent, because the plans, decisions, and orders of leaders reflect the prevailing norms of a society.

Inside the corporation, the same phenomenon can be observed. Subordinates will respond to the strategic behavior of executives in the ways desired if that strategic behavior is attuned to the subordinates' organizational values. This phenomenon is corroborated in small-group research, which shows that a group will follow those members who propose actions which satisfy the needs and wishes of the group.

It is also corroborated by Barnard's concept of the "zone of indifference" (Chapter 7). In the short run, strategic behavior may deviate to a significant degree from what the group wants and knows—since many members will accept decisions within their zone of indifference. However, if executives persist in using strategic behavior as their primary mode over the long run, or if they pursue goals which differ significantly from the wants, needs, and beliefs of members, there will be rebellion, sabotage, or the other types of destructive behavior described by Argyris (Chapter 3).

Readings

Delegation

WILLIAM H. NEWMAN
CHARLES E. SUMMER
E. KIRBY WARREN

It is surprising that such a familiar and fundamental aspect of organization [as delegation] continues to be misunderstood and to be inefficiently handled. Delegation is a perennial topic at management meetings; it is a likely source of difficulty for both a newly appointed supervisor and a senior executive. Judging from the experience of sophisticated managers, we must conclude that delegating is a little more tricky than it appears on the surface. Consequently, we shall find that a clear understanding of its essential features will be a valuable asset to both executives and their subordinates.

Three Inescapable Features of Delegating

Every time a manager delegates work to a subordinate—say, a president to a sales manager, or a foreman to an operator—we can identify three actions that are either expressed or implied:

1. He assigns *duties,* that is, the man who is delegating indicates what work the subordinate must do.
2. He grants *authority.* Along with permission to proceed with the assigned work, he will probably transfer to the subordinate certain rights, such as the right to spend money, to direct the work of other people, to use raw materials, to represent the company to outsiders, or to take other steps necessary to fulfill the new duties.
3. He creates an *obligation.* In accepting an assignment, a subordinate takes on an obligation to his boss to complete the job.

By recognizing that no delegation is complete without a clear understanding of duties, authority, and obligation, an administrator can often save himself a good deal of trouble. These attributes of delegation are like a three-legged stool; each depends on the others to support the whole, and no two can stand alone.

Duties

Duties can be described in two ways. First, we can think of them in terms of function. For instance, we may say that Tom Turner's duties are either to

From *The Process of Management: Concepts, Behavior, and Practice,* 2nd ed., © 1967, pp. 84–95. Reprinted by permission of Prentice-Hall, Inc., Englewood Cliffs, New Jersey.

run a turret lathe, to sell in Oshkosh, to direct a machine shop, to discover and analyze facts about the money market and trends in interest rates, or to measure distribution costs. According to this view, delegating is the process by which we assign to individuals bundles of activities.

Second, we can describe duties in terms of the results we want to achieve. Following this approach, we would say that, in the first two examples given above, Tom Turner's duties are to turn on his lathe a certain number of pieces per day according to engineering specifications, or to build customer good will and secure a prescribed number of orders in the Oshkosh territory. Here we are talking about objectives. We define the duties not just in terms of "going through certain motions," but in terms of accomplishment. To express duties in terms of purpose adds vitality to otherwise neutral statements. Take the description above, "to measure distribution costs." It may be adequate for departmentation, but if we want to avoid aimless activity, we should elaborate our statement and indicate specific purpose—for instance, "to measure distribution costs in order to provide useful information for pricing, controlling costs, and locating warehouses."

Because of differences in jobs, we may state such goals in terms of long-run or short-run results. Our declarations may be general and intangible or specific and readily put into effect. They may represent over-optimism or realistic expectation. Nevertheless, if we phrase delegation of duties in terms of goals, a subordinate is likely to get psychological satisfaction from his work, and he will have advance notice of the criteria on which his performance will be judged. A man's duties are clear to him only when he knows what activities he must undertake *and* what missions he must fulfill.

Authority

If we assign a man duties to perform, is it not obvious that we must give him all necessary authority to carry them out? Tom Turner cannot turn out 20 swivel pins without authority to obtain materials, use a lathe, and, if necessary, call on a helper. An advertising manager needs authority to buy space, hire a copywriter, and take other necessary steps if he is to gain his assigned objective of building customer demand for company products.

Unfortunately, assigning authority is not simple. In fact, a principal source of the difficulty many executives experience in delegating is their inclination to oversimplify this matter of authority. We should understand exactly what kind of authority is within the power of an administrator to grant; in addition, we should recognize the substantial number of restrictions that typically fence in the authority an administrator has at his disposal.

Administrative authority consists of certain permissions or rights: the right to act for the company in specified areas—buy raw material, accept orders from customers, issue press releases, admit people into a plant, for example; the right as spokesman for the company to request other employees to perform activities of various kinds; and the right to impose sanctions and discipline if a subordinate disregards his instructions. These rights are vested in the head of an enterprise by law and custom, and they are supported by the moral approval of society. They stem partly from concepts of private-property rights, partly from acknowledged authority of the political state, and particularly from the long-established human habit of looking to hierarchical leadership in cooperative undertakings. Because of this background, employees and, in fact, our whole society accept the idea that the head of an enterprise—whoever he may be—has certain rights of authority and that he may reassign these rights.

When an employee takes a job, he expects also to take orders from someone designated by the company; he looks to management for permission to use company property or to act as an official representative of the enterprise; and he expects a superior to review his work and bring pressure on him to improve if it is unsatisfactory. Such socially accepted rights constitute formal authority, and management can pass them about when it erects a formal organization.

Throughout history, men have challenged formal authority from time to time. The drawing-up of the Magna Charta, the Boston Tea Party, the mutiny on the Bounty, and sit-down strikes of the 1930's, all represent challenges to constituted authority prevailing at the time. But these events are notable as exceptions to the usual willingness of men to recognize formal authority. By and large, people expect and rely on authority. But we can note two significant changes between the times of the medieval serfs and the unionized workers of the mid-twentieth century: (a) There has been a marked decline in the degree of authority an employer may exercise over an employee, and (b) as a consequence, other techniques of motivation have increased in importance.

Authority is an essential element in any modern enterprise, but we must not confuse it with unlimited power. No company president or plant manager can grant someone of lower rank the power to change the physical laws of the universe, the power to compel customers to sign orders or suppliers to sell raw materials, or the power to compel the *enthusiastic* corporation of associates and subordinates. The rights that an administrator may transfer are more akin to authorization than they are to power.

In addition to inherent limitations on the authority that an executive can delegate, virtually every company imposes limitations of its own. Typically, an executive is permitted to act strictly "within company policy" and "in accordance with established procedures." A manager may in theory have formal authority to hire and fire people in his division, whereas in fact he must adhere to a myriad of restrictive procedures that require him, for example, to refer job descriptions to the planning department before he can fill a new position, to satisfy the personnel department that no capable person is available within the company before he can hire an outsider, to insure that all prospective candidates meet company standards of health and financial dependability, to set salaries within an established range for each job classification, and to refrain from discharging anyone without two prior warnings, at least a month apart. Another department head may have to endure comparable restrictions surrounding purchases of raw materials and, especially, of new equipment. Besides company-wide policies and procedures, it is normal practice for businessmen to place substantive limitations on the authority they grant to an individual. As we explained in the preceding chapter, a manager may reserve to himself decisions on certain matters; in these areas, a subordinate must operate within the boundaries established at higher echelons within the organization.

Because of these various qualifications on authority, we must be clear when we delegate a task to specify what rights are associated with it.

Obligation

By obligation, the third inevitable feature of delegation, we mean the moral compulsion felt by a subordinate to accomplish his assigned duties. When duties are delegated to him, a subordinate is not free either to do the work or leave it, as may happen to suit his convenience. Let us take two examples. During the vacation of a plant superintendent, a young man had the job of unlocking the sales office in a branch warehouse. When he showed up two hours late one morning, casually explaining that his brother had unexpectedly stopped by overnight for a visit, the branch manager had a few choice words to offer about fulfilling obligations to the company.

A similar case concerns a man who had the job of making a final review of all bids sent to customers by a manufacturer of printing machinery. It was his duty to check the bids for completeness, misstatements, and mathematical errors; to make sure that the right number of copies were distributed to the right people; and to maintain a master file. One day, however, in reviewing new business the sales manager noticed one order that appeared to be underpriced. On investigation, he discovered in the bid his firm had submitted a mathematical error that amounted to several thousand dollars. Confronted with this mistake, the man who checked the bids explained, "They sometimes come through in batches, and you know how anxious the salesmen always are to get the bids to the customers. So I just do the best I can and when Friday evening comes if there is a batch of work still on hand, I give it a quick look and send it out. Otherwise, we might have a big backlog and the salesmen would be on my neck for missing orders because the bids did not get out on time." This individual responded more to social pressure than to his obligation to the company to perform his particular job carefully.

Although agreement is usually implied rather than discussed, by accepting an assignment a subordinate in effect gives his promise to do his best in carrying out his duties. Having taken a job, he is morally bound to complete it. He can be held accountable for results. Obligation, then, is primarily an attitude of the person to whom duties are delegated. Dependability rests on the sense of obligation, and without personal dependability our cooperative business enterprises would collapse.

In delineating the chief features of delegating, we have avoided using the word "responsibility" because it means different things to different people. Some use it as a synonym for "duty," whereas others think its meaning is identical with "obligation"; all too often, speakers switch back and forth between meanings without indicating to the listener which sense he intends. To avoid this confusion, we will shy away from the word "responsibility." From time to time, however, we shall use "accountability" as a synonym for "obligation."

Applying Delegation Concepts

Should Duties and Obligations Extend Beyond Authority?

A common saying in popular management literature declares that "authority and responsibility should always be equal." The thought behind this statement is the conviction that if we assign a man duties, we ought to furnish him with enough authority—no more and no less—to carry them out, and if we give him authority, we certainly expect from him a corresponding obligation to use it wisely. Although there are elements of truth in this contention, it is unfortunately an oversimplification. Let us see why.

The first difficulty is the word "equal." Duties are concerned with objectives and activities, authority with rights, and obligation with attitudes. These three things are of different orders, and it is hard for an executive to find a common denominator for measuring equality among them. They are indeed related—as related as, but no more equal than, a small boy's apples, spoon, and fondness for applesauce. Perhaps we should say they are co-extensive. Unhappily, this word, too, gets us into difficulty. Many a man has got himself into hot water by assuming that an assigned duty automatically carried with it all necessary authority. Obviously, we must give a man some authority—the right to try to convince others, if nothing more. But, as we have seen in our discussion of formal authority, there are only certain kinds of rights that an enterprise can pass along to its managers, and there are usually very substantial restrictions on how even these rights may be used. To permit every man to act like a bull in a china closet would lead to chaos. Frequently a man must try to achieve objectives with authority far short of his desires. Especially when duties include dealing with customers or suppliers, or when objectives are stated in long-run terms, the assigned result may depend on forces far beyond any authority that can practically be granted.

Furthermore, to say that obligation is equal to authority may lead to trouble. Many a manager has used as an excuse for a failure to live up to an obligation his lack of necessary authority. We depend on moral compulsion to assure that subordinates fulfill their duties as well as possible under given circumstances. Unfortunately, employees sometimes fall back on the "equal" concept to avoid giving full measure.

A broad statement that duties, authority, and obligation should all be "equal" is likely to bring us more mischief than good. It is more nearly accurate, though not so pat, to say:

1. To the boss, the man doing the delegating, "Duties, authority, and obligation depend on each other and you should therefore correlate them thoughtfully."
2. To the subordinate, the man receiving the delegation, "You are obligated to fulfill your duties to the maximum extent that one can reasonably expect in the light of your authority and the conditions under which you have to work."

An Obligation Cannot Be Delegated

What happens when duties and authority are redelegated? Does this redelegation relieve the executive who makes it of *his* obligation? Suppose the treasurer of the Omaha Chemical Company, for example, delegates to the chief accountant the task of maintaining an accounts-payable ledger. With this assignment, he gives enough authority to set up procedures governing entries in the ledger and to employ and direct a staff to do the actual clerical work. The assignment entails an obligation to maintain records accurately and to inform the cashier's office when various amounts fall due. The chief accountant, being too busy to maintain the records himself, assigns the job to a clerk who is authorized to maintain the records in accordance with established procedure. The clerk also has an obligation to maintain the records accurately and to keep the cashier's office informed.

The redelegation of the job by the chief accountant to the clerk does not change a bit the initial relationship between the treasurer and the chief accountant. The chief accountant still has the same duties and as much authority, and even though he has turned over the major parts of these to the clerk, he can reclaim them if he wishes. More importantly, the chief accountant still has the same obligations to the treasurer. The additional obligation between the clerk and the chief accountant in no way relieves the chief accountant of his obligation. It is as though the treasurer lent ten dollars to the chief accountant and the chief accountant, in turn, lent the money to the clerk; the chief accountant cannot satisfy his obligation to the controller by passing along the clerk's I.O.U.

To abandon this principle that a man cannot delegate obligation would mean that executives in the higher echelons of an organization would have much influence and yet not be accountable for results. Moreover, to allow an executive to evade his obligation—simply by getting someone else to assume the duty—would break the single chain of command; there would be no way of knowing who was accountable for what.

Dual Subordination

An issue we face over and over in delegating is whether each man should have only one boss. On this point, formal organization theory is clear. A worker—operator or manager—may have relations with many people; he may even accept their advice on certain matters. But he needs one supervisor whose guidance can be regarded as final. What are the reasons supporting this single chain of command concept?

Two or More Bosses. Consider the plight of an individual who works, say, a third of his time, for each of three different bosses. In very small companies or in small sections, this arrangement may be the only practical way to handle a small volume of work. As volume increases, however, demand for the man's time will increase and he will find himself in the unenviable position of deciding whose work to do first. He will be unable to fulfill his obligations to all his supervisors, and will eventually be criticized by one or more of them. Dissatisfaction on the part of the bosses and poor morale on the part of the man are likely results.

To resolve the difficulties, management will have to designate one of the supervisors as the line boss and specify that the disputed employee can work for the others only as a service, if at all. Thus, one person can set up work priorities and have the last say in any differences of opinion. Clearly, then, we should use the two-or-more-boss arrangement only when the total work is so light a subordinate can easily apportion his time.

Bypassing Line Supervisors. A related problem arises when an executive gives an order to someone two or more levels below him in the hierarchy. The man who receives the order is in an awkward position. He can scarcely refuse the request of, say, a vice president; in fact, he is probably flattered to work directly for a top-level executive and is tempted to cultivate the relationship. But whose work should he do first? If either executive criticizes him for not doing a first-class job, he finds himself in a tight spot. Also, the executive who has been bypassed is distressed. His status and influence over his subordinate have been undermined. The lower executive probably doesn't dare countermand orders from the vice president, and yet he is not in a position to supervise the work because he knows less about what the vice president wants than his subordinate.

Because of the confusion that results from bypassing, managers now widely recognize that executives should pass orders only along the formal chain of command. Such regulation by no means bars direct conversations and visits of higher executives in a shop or office; indeed, there is much to recommend such face-to-face communication. During these contacts, however, top executives must be very careful to preserve the positions of their deputies who must carry the major load of immediate supervision. . . .

Some Difficulties in Practice

Viewed objectively, delegating is a simple and natural process, an everyday experience for anyone working in a joint enterprise. Nevertheless, difficulties do arise in practice. We have already indicated some of these difficulties, but there are a few others that occur with sufficient frequency to warrant our mentioning them specifically.

Legal Authority that Exceeds Administrative or Operating Authority

We court confusion when we assume that legal authority is always equal to administrative or operating authority. Legal authority is principally a matter of the relationship of outsiders to an enterprise; what we have been discussing is the supervisor-subordinate relationship of people within the enterprise. A company always has a number of people who can represent it to the outside world, that is, to customers, suppliers, prospective employees, bankers, and government officials. These agents can make contracts and otherwise act as legal representatives of the company.

A firm may give a salesman, explicitly or by implication, legal authority to sell to any customer who places an order. His operating authority, however, may be much more restricted, confining him to certain types of customer, and requiring him to secure internal approval from, say, the credit department, before he takes a specific order. Similarly, a company may legally authorize a purchasing agent to buy large quantities of raw material, although operationally he must stay within budget limits and purchase only the kinds of material that other departments requisition. The legal authority of a treasurer to write checks on a company's bank account normally far exceeds his actual rights to spend the company's money. We could give other illustrations of our point that, for practical purposes, an enterprise must often transfer to a member of its staff legal authority far in excess of the permission it grants him to exercise that authority.

Legal authority need cause us no trouble if we recognize that it is different from the administrative rights we have been talking about. In a business enterprise, at least, we can establish a sound management organization and then let lawyers provide for legal authority wherever we need it.

Failure to Make Limits of Authority Clear

Effective delegation requires, among other things, that we make clear the limits of authority to each subordinate. A worker, his boss, and any other people who may be affected, should have a mutual understanding of (a) the worker's rights—to act, to request others to act, to discipline—and (b) any restrictions on how or when action may be taken. Such mutual understanding is not always easy to achieve.

Written job descriptions, policies, and procedures should give some indication of the authority of each member of an organization. Many companies, however, have not felt it worthwhile to prepare such documents; in other companies whatever documents exist give an incomplete picture. In the normal course of business, variations in operating conditions arise that call for shades of meaning to the authorizations that have been granted. Moreover, as men work together over extended periods of time, their relationships will change. An administrator will grant more freedom to an experienced man, particularly as the man demonstrates sound judgment, than he would to the same man when he is first employed. It is obviously impractical to attempt to spell out explicitly and formally all the details and subtle qualifications of each supervisor-subordinate relationship.

In practice, the full meaning of a delegation depends largely on tradition and habit. For example, a foreman may customarily requisition expensive raw materials and supplies according to his own judgment whereas to purchase new equipment, even though a much smaller sum is involved, he must "always clear with Mr. Jones, the treasurer." A subordinate learns how far he is expected to go—partly through training on the job, partly through occasional consultations with his boss, and partly through trial and error. Many of the limits of authority are only implied, and each subordinate must learn to sense them.

A subordinate gets into trouble when the limits of authority are so vague that he either goes far beyond his appropriate sphere of action or fails to exercise the initiative he should. The superintendent of a textile mill, for instance, knew he could lay off a few men when they were not needed, but found himself in a row with the unions and with other mill superintendents in the same company when he cut his entire plant back to a four-day week. To avoid such problems, a wise manager—from president to first-line supervisor—is continually aware of the need to clarify and interpret delegations to each of his subordinates. In dealing with day-to-day problems and in reviewing past performance, he must consciously consider how his subordinates will interpret his attitudes as well as his actions. To cite a simple case, a sales manager puts meaning into the degree of a salesman's authority to phone out-of-town customers by endorsing, or by frowning on, frequent and lengthy long-distance calls. By labeling a particular action—perhaps warranted in an emergency—as an exception to the normal standard of behavior, or by calling attention to failures to make aggressive use of authority, a manager can put substance into broadly stated job descriptions.

Occasionally, people will argue that management should leave the boundaries of authority fuzzy in order to encourage cooperation. This contention is based on a false premise. Clear-cut duties and authorities do not imply that each man should work in his own isolated corner. Instead, in most delegations, managers make it very clear that a subordinate should consult with others and keep them informed as he proceeds with his own duties. Furthermore, a few assignments are specifically joint undertakings. Some companies emphasize their concern with cooperation by saying that a man is accountable for both *work and teamwork,* and they are dissatisfied with a man's performance unless he measures up well on both counts. Cooperation is simply a part of a job and should be as clear as other duties.

Inconsistent Behavior of Managers

A delegation of duties and authorities can work no better than a manager allows. His plans and controls should be consistent with the assignments he gives to his subordinates. The merchandising manager of a department store, for example, told all his buyers that they would be responsible for preparing spring programs for their respective divisions. Several buyers exerted a great deal of effort to compile detailed tables of what to buy and when to have goods delivered, only to have the merchandising manager make substantial changes because he "didn't think that stuff would sell." Here, after the merchandising manager had clearly delegated a planning task, he went ahead with his own spring program regardless of the disappointment and frustration of his buyers.

Control actions are especially apt to be inconsistent with previous assignments. One of the large hotel chains in this country, for instance, is presumably operated on a profit-decentralization basis. Nevertheless, the president requires detailed expense figures and ratios each month, and he is likely to call to task any of his hotel managers for insignificant expenses that he thinks are out of line. Some of the managers are able to keep this needling from interfering with their main tasks, but others spend an unwarranted amount of time preparing for a possible call from "the old man."

Another company, which was decentralizing its operations, had spent a lot of effort convincing its district managers that they were in the best position to determine how much additional equipment they needed to develop their respective territories profitably. The company did not modify control procedures, however, to conform to the new delegation of authority, and a central engineering staff continued to approve or disapprove all new equipment that cost more than ten thousand dollars. Theoretically, the central staff was to be available to advise the district managers at the time they formulated their plans; in fact, the staff exercised a control that was inconsistent with the new set-up.

Obstacles to Actual Delegation

Still another practical difficulty in delegating occurs when, although both boss and subordinate agree on the desirability of transferring certain duties and authority, for some reason the transfer does not actually take place. To understand the reasons behind such mere lip-service to the desirability of delegating, we must examine the attitudes and behavior of both a boss and a subordinate.

Possible Reasons Why a Boss May Fail to Delegate. Many a manager wishes to transfer his heavy load to his subordinates and yet fails to let loose of the work he is doing. What causes this paradox?

1. Some executives get trapped in the *"I can do it better myself"* fallacy. Even if an executive can do a job better than anyone else (which is not true quite so often as he thinks it is), he must nevertheless reconcile himself to turning the job over to someone else whose performance will be "good enough." The choice the executive must make is not between the quality of his work and that of his assistant; rather, he should weigh the advantages of higher-level performance if he does the work himself against the benefit to the total operation if he devotes his attention to the planning and supervision that only he can undertake.
2. An executive's *lack of ability to direct* is another barrier to successful delegation. One of the authors remembers well one of his first bosses, a very friendly individual who had keen business judgment, but who simply could not tell a man working for him what to do more than a few hours ahead. Life for the subordinates was a bit precarious because their success depended on guessing how the boss's mind would work before the boss himself had formulated his ideas. Here was a man who wanted desperately to delegate. But he

could do so only in repetitive situations, because he was unable to identify and communicate the essential features of his long-range plans.

3. A third possible block to effective delegation is *lack of confidence in subordinates.* When we recognize this cause for withholding authority, the remedy is clear: Either we should start a training program immediately, or, if this is impractical, we should find a new subordinate. Often, however, the situation is by no means so clear-cut. An executive may not be fully aware of his lack of confidence; his reaction is subjective and he simply feels uneasy about how someone else will do the work. When this is so, the executive is likely to pay lip-service to the principle of delegation, but be reluctant in an actual working relationship to let go of authority or duties.
4. A related obstacle to delegation is an *absence of sensitive controls that warn of impending difficulties.* Since a good executive is sensitive to his continuing obligation even though work is delegated, he obviously needs some "feedback" about what is going on. He wants to be sure he will know of serious trouble in advance so he can help overcome it. If the control set-up fails to keep him informed as he feels he should be—at least on major matters—he will probably be cautious about delegating.
5. Finally, a manager may be handicapped *by a temperamental aversion to taking a chance.* Any manager who delegates must take a calculated risk. Even with clear instructions, dependable subordinates, and selective control, the possibility remains that something will go wrong. Unless the executive adjusts emotionally, as well as intellectually, to this element of risk, he is likely to be reluctant to delegate anything to anyone.

Possible Obstacles to a Subordinate's Accepting Delegation. Even when a boss is ready and able to turn over authority, a subordinate may shrink from accepting it.

1. Often a subordinate finds it *easier to ask the boss* than to decide for himself how to deal with a problem. Making a wise decision is usually hard mental work. If a man finds that he can take any troublesome problem—with at best only tentative suggestions—to his boss for an answer, it is natural for him to do so. In addition to being easier, this course has the advantage that if the boss does make the decision, the employee is less liable to suffer severe criticism for consequences later.

   An executive can break a subordinate's habit of bringing all tough problems to him by insisting that the subordinate either take action or at least recommend a fully thought-through solution on which he is prepared to stake his reputation. The boss will probably want to continue to give advice in his role as coach. He must, however, be constantly on his guard lest his advice undercut the initiative and sense of obligation he is striving to build.
2. A second factor that may deter a man from embracing greater duties is *fear of criticism* for mistakes. He will usually welcome constructive review, but will resent negative and unreasonable criticism. A subordinate will naturally be inclined to be cautious and play it safe if he has learned from experience that when he takes on more duties, he risks an embarrassing and unwarranted bawling-out. His feeling is, "Why should I stick my neck out for this guy?"
3. Most men hesitate to accept a new assignment when they believe they *lack the necessary information and resources* to do a good job. A person accustomed to a restraining web of budgetary and personal limitations may accept new

duties, knowing full well that he will have to battle at each step. In general, however, because of the frustrations of trying to work handicapped by inadequate information and resources, a man will reject assignments with such a drawback.

4. *Lack of self-confidence* stands in the way of some men in accepting a delegation. Ordering a man to be self-confident will have little effect. In many cases, however, he can develop self-confidence if, by carefully providing experience with increasingly difficult problems, we help him to sense his own potentialities.
5. *Positive incentives may be inadequate.* Accepting additional duties usually involves mental effort and emotional pressure. If we expect a man to take on an additional load enthusiastically, we should offer positive inducements. The inducements may be pay increases, improved opportunity for promotion, a fancy title, acknowledged status in the organization, personal recognition and approval by the boss, and other rewards, both tangible and intangible. We shall explore the whole matter of incentives in a later chapter of this book. The important point here is that a subordinate is more likely to accept new duties when they are sweetened by an incentive that is important to him. . . .

Authority, Discipline, and Unity of Command

HENRI FAYOL

Authority and Responsibility

Authority is the right to give orders and the power to exact obedience. Distinction must be made between a manager's official authority, deriving from office, and personal authority, compounded of intelligence, experience, moral worth, ability to lead, past services, etc. In the makeup of a good head, personal authority is the indispensable complement of official authority. Authority is not to be conceived of apart from responsibility, that is, apart from sanction—reward or penalty—which goes with the exercise of power. Responsibility is a corollary of authority; it is its natural consequence and essential counterpart, and wheresoever authority is exercised, responsibility arises.

The need for sanction, which has its origin in a sense of justice, is strengthened and increased by this consideration, that in the general interest, useful actions have to be encouraged and their opposite discouraged. Application of sanction to acts of authority forms part of the conditions essential for good management, but it is generally difficult to effect, especially in large concerns. First, the degree of responsibility must be established and then the weight of

---

From *General and Industrial Management* (London: Sir Isaac Pitman & Sons Limited, 1949), pp. 21–26. Reprinted by permission of the publisher.

the sanction. Now it is relatively easy to establish a workman's responsibility for his acts and a scale of corresponding sanctions; in the case of a foreman it is somewhat difficult; and [it is] proportionately [more difficult] as one goes up the scalar chain of businesses. As work grows more complex, as the number of workers involved increases, [and] as the final result is more remote, it is increasingly difficult to isolate the share of the initial act of authority in the ultimate result, and to establish the degree of responsibility of the manager. The measurement of this responsibility and its equivalent in material terms elude all calculation.

Sanction, then, is a question of kind, custom, convention, and [in] judging it one must take into account the action itself, the attendant circumstances, and potential repercussions. Judgment demands high moral character, impartiality and firmness. If all these conditions are not fulfilled, there is a danger that the sense of responsibility may disappear from the concern.

Responsibility valiantly undertaken and borne merits some consideration; it is a kind of courage everywhere much appreciated. Tangible proof of this exists in the salary level of some industrial leaders, which is much higher than that of civil servants of comparable rank but carrying no responsibility. Nevertheless, generally speaking, responsibility is feared as much as authority is sought after, and fear of responsibility paralyses much initiative and destroys many good qualities. A good leader should possess and infuse into those around him courage to accept responsibility.

The best safeguard against abuse of authority and against weakness on the part of a higher manager is personal integrity and particularly [the] high moral character of such a manager, and this integrity, it is well known, is conferred neither by election nor ownership.

Discipline

Discipline is in essence obedience, application, energy, behaviour, and outward marks of respect observed in accordance with the standing agreements between the firm and its employees, whether these agreements have been freely debated or accepted without prior discussion, whether they be written or implicit, whether they derive from the wish of the parties to them or from rules and customs, it is these agreements which determine the formalities of discipline.

Discipline, being the outcome of different varying agreements, naturally appears under the most diverse forms; obligations of obedience, application, energy, behaviour, vary, in effect, from one firm to another, from one group of employees to another, from one time to another. Nevertheless, general opinion is deeply convinced that discipline is absolutely essential for the smooth running of business and that without discipline no enterprise could prosper.

This sentiment is very forcibly expressed in military handbooks, where it runs that "Discipline constitutes the chief strength of armies." I would approve unreservedly of this aphorism were it followed by this other, "Discipline is what leaders make it." The first one inspires respect for discipline, which is a good thing, but it tends to eclipse from view the responsibility of leaders, which is undesirable, for the state of discipline of any group of people depends essentially on the worthiness of its leaders.

When a defect in discipline is apparent or when relations between superiors and subordinates leave much to be desired, responsibility for this must not be cast heedlessly, and without going further afield, on the poor state of the team, because the ill mostly results from the ineptitude of the leaders. That, at all events, is what I have noted in various parts of France, for I have always found French workmen obedient and loyal provided they are ably led.

In the matter of influence upon discipline, agreements must be set side by side with command. It is important that they be clear and, as far as is possible, afford satisfaction to both sides. This is not easy. Proof of that exists in the great strikes of miners, railwaymen, and civil servants which, in these latter years, have jeopardized national life at home and elsewhere and which arose out of agreements in dispute or inadequate legislation.

For half a century a considerable change has been effected in the mode of agreements between a concern and its employees. The agreements of former days fixed by the employer alone are being replaced, in ever increasing measure, by understandings arrived at by discussion between an owner or group of owners and workers' associations. Thus each individual owner's responsibility has been reduced and is further diminished by increasingly frequent State intervention in labour problems. Nevertheless, the setting up of agreements binding a firm and its employees from which disciplinary formalities emanate, should remain one of the chief preoccupations of industrial heads.

The well-being of the concern does not permit, in cases of offence against discipline, of the neglect of certain sanctions capable of preventing or minimizing their recurrence. Experience and tact on the part of a manager are put to the proof in the choice and degree of sanctions to be used, such as remonstrances, warnings, fines, suspensions, demotion, dismissal. Individual people and attendant circumstances must be taken into account. In fine, discipline is respect for agreements which are directed at achieving obedience, application, energy, and the outward marks of respect. It is incumbent upon managers at high levels as much as upon humble employees, and the best means of establishing and maintaining it are—

1. Good superiors at all levels.
2. Agreements as clear and fair as possible.
3. Sanctions (penalties) judiciously applied.

Unity of Command

For any action whatsoever, an employee should receive orders from one superior only. Such is the rule of unity of command, arising from general and ever-present necessity and wielding an influence on the conduct of affairs, which to my way of thinking, is at least equal to any other principle whatsoever. Should it be violated, authority is undermined, discipline is in jeopardy, order disturbed and stability threatened. This rule seems fundamental to me and so I have given it the rank of principle. As soon as two superiors wield their authority over the same person or department, uneasiness makes itself felt and should the cause persist, the disorder increases, the malady takes on the appearance of an animal organism troubled by a foreign body, and the following consequences are to be observed: either the dual command ends in disappearance or elimination of one of the superiors and organic well-being is restored, or else the organism continues to wither away. In no case is there adaptation of the social organism to dual command.

Now dual command is extremely common and wreaks havoc in all concerns, large or small, in home and in State. The evil is all the more to be feared in that it worms its way into the social organism on the most plausible pretexts. For instance—

1. In the hope of being better understood or gaining time or to put a stop forthwith to an undesirable practice, a superior S^2 may give orders directly to an employee E without going via the superior S^1. If this mistake is repeated there is dual command with its consequences, viz., hesitation on the part of the subordinate, irritation and dissatisfaction on the part of the superior set aside, and disorder in the work. It will be seen later that it is possible to by-pass the scalar chain when necessary, whilst avoiding the drawbacks of dual command.
2. The desire to get away from the immediate necessity of dividing up authority as between two colleagues, two friends, two members of one family, results at times in dual command reigning at the top of a concern right from the outset. Exercising the same powers and having the same authority over the same men, the two colleagues end up inevitably with dual command and its consequences. Despite harsh lessons, instances of this sort are still numerous. New colleagues count on their mutual regard, common interest, and good sense to save them from every conflict, every serious disagreement and, save for rare exceptions, the illusion is short-lived. First an awkwardness makes itself felt, then a certain irritation and, in time, if dual command exists, even hatred. Men cannot bear dual command. A judicious assignment of duties would have reduced the danger without entirely banishing it, for between two superiors on the same footing there must always be some question ill-defined. But it is riding for a fall to set up a business organization with two superiors on equal footing without assigning duties and demarcating authority.
3. Imperfect demarcation of departments also leads to dual command: two superiors issuing orders in a sphere which each thinks his own, constitutes dual command.
4. Constant linking up as between different departments, natural intermeshing of functions, duties often badly defined, create an ever-present danger of dual command. If a knowledgeable superior does not put it in order, footholds are established which later upset and compromise the conduct of affairs.

In all human associations, in industry, commerce, army, home, State, dual command is a perpetual source of conflicts, very grave sometimes, which have special claim on the attention of superiors of all ranks. . . .

Subordination of Individual Interest to General Interest

This principle calls to mind the fact that in a business the interest of one employee or group of employees should not prevail over that of the concern, that the interest of the home should come before that of its members and that the interest of the State should have pride of place over that of one citizen or group of citizens.

It seems that such an admonition should not need calling to mind. But ignorance, ambition, selfishness, laziness, weakness, and all human passions tend to cause the general interest to be lost sight of in favour of individual interest

and a perpetual struggle has to be waged against them. Two interests of a different order, but claiming equal respect, confront each other and means must be found to reconcile them. That represents one of the great difficulties of management. Means of effecting it are—
1. Firmness and good example on the part of superiors.
2. Agreements as fair as is possible.
3. Constant supervision. . . .

Decentralization: A Managerial Philosophy

RALPH J. CORDINER

Every company should be managed in accordance with some workable, ethically responsible philosophy of management. That is, the managers of the company should be in general agreement on a set of underlying principles that will guide their work in providing leadership for the company.

For some companies, the set of principles that guide the managers may be tacitly understood, without ever being presented systematically. They may be part of the company's tradition or may even reflect the personal philosophy of the chief executive.

While General Electric's present philosophy of management has had a long evolution in Company tradition and reflects the personalities of its great leaders in years gone by, considerable effort has been devoted in the past ten years to "thinking through" and presenting this managerial philosophy in a systematic way.

I should like to discuss the results of these studies: the philosophy of decentralization, and how it has been applied by General Electric in building an organization structure to meet the challenges of an expanding economy. . . .

Explosive Growth Raises Organizational Questions

Up until 1939, the Company was able to operate efficiently under a highly centralized form of management. During World War II, however, General Electric began a period of almost explosive growth which caused its managers to question whether it might not be necessary to evolve new techniques of organizing and managing the Company.

From 1920 to 1939, the Company's sales volume had risen slowly from $200 million to $342 million a year. By 1943, under the pressure of war production, it rose suddenly to $1,370,000,000 a year—over a four-fold increase in four years. Postwar experience and forecasts indicated that this was only the beginning of an opportunity for continuing, rapid growth in serving the nation's demands

From *New Frontiers for Professional Managers* by R. J. Cordiner, pp. 40–69.

for electrical and related products. The Company produced over $3 billion worth of goods and services last year; and if we do the job we should do of satisfying customers, this figure may well rise—as the Company has publicly stated many times—to $6 billion early in the 1960's.

It is obvious that a company with such growth characteristics, and operating on such a scale, requires a different managerial approach than the company of the 1920's and '30's. . . .

From the beginning of the study, it was apparent that the Company was going to require increasingly better planning, greater flexibility, and faster, more informed decisions than was possible under the highly centralized organization structure, which was suited for earlier and different conditions. Unless we could put the responsibility and authority for decision making closer in each case to the scene of the problem, where complete understanding and prompt action are possible, the Company would not be able to compete with the hundreds of nimble competitors who were, as they say, able to turn on a dime.

In addition, General Electric faced the need to develop capable leaders for the future; the need for more friendly and cooperative relationships between managers and other employees; the need to stay ahead of competition in serving the customers; and the very human need to make the work of a manager at all echelons of the organization more manageable. The work had to be made more manageable so that it could be understood and carried out by people of normally available energy and intelligence, thus leaving no requirement for the so-called indispensable man.

The Solution: Decentralization

. . . In General Electric, decentralization is a way of preserving and enhancing these contributions of the large enterprise, and at the same time achieving the flexibility and the "human touch" that are popularly associated with—though not always attained by—small organizations.

Under this concept, we have undertaken decentralization not only according to products, geography, and functional types of work. The most important aspect of the Company's philosophy is thorough decentralization of the responsibility and authority for making business decisions.

Here is the underlying logic. The share owners, through their Board of Directors, delegate to the President responsibility for the conduct of the whole business. The responsibility carries with it all the authority required to get the work done, except such authorities as are specifically withheld by the Board and the share owners. The total responsibility also carries with it full accountability for results. General Electric may be unique in that the Board of Directors has issued a position guide for the President, stating in detail his responsibility, authority, and accountability.

Now, the President is of course unable to do all the work himself, and so he delegates the responsibility for portions of the total work through organization channels to individuals who have the talents and knowledge required to do it. This is done by planning and building the work of the Company into an organization structure which consists of all the necessary positions and components required to do all the work in the most effective and efficient manner.

Each employee thus takes on responsibility for some part of the over-all Company work. Along with this responsibility, each position naturally carries with it full accountability for measured results, and all the necessary authority required for the position except those authorities that are specifically stated as withheld. Therefore each employee of the Company has, in his position, full responsibility, authority, and accountability for a certain defined body of work and teamwork. Through teamwork he recognizes his relationships to the other employees who perform a share of the total work of the Company.

With this philosophy, General Electric achieves a community of purpose between leaders and their associates, and is able to attain that voluntary integration which is the hallmark of a free and decentralized enterprise.

In such compressed statement, this management philosophy may sound somewhat obscure, but its practical result is to put the responsibility for making business decisions not with a few top executives, but with the individual managerial and functional employees who have the most immediately applicable information required to make sound decisions and take prompt action. When such responsibility—along with commensurate authority and accountability—has been delegated according to a carefully planned organization of work, then each individual in the Company has a challenging and dignified position which will bring out his full resources and enthusiastic cooperation.

Ten Guiding Principles

Since philosophy is, by definition, a system of first principles, I should like to list for you ten principles which express General Electric's philosophy of decentralization.

1. Decentralization places authority to make decisions at points as near as possible to where actions take place.
2. Decentralization is likely to get best over-all results by getting greatest and most directly applicable knowledge and most timely understanding actually into play on the greatest number of decisions.
3. Decentralization will work if real authority is delegated; and not if details then have to be reported, or, worse yet, if they have to be "checked" first.
4. Decentralization requires confidence that associates in decentralized positions will have the capacity to make sound decisions in the majority of cases; and such confidence starts at the executive level. Unless the President and all the other Officers have a deep personal conviction and an active desire to decentralize full decision-making responsibility and authority, actual decentralization will never take place. The Officers must set an example in the art of full delegation.
5. Decentralization requires understanding that the main role of staff or services is the rendering of assistance and advice to line operators through a relatively few experienced people, so that those making decisions can themselves make them correctly.
6. Decentralization requires realization that the natural aggregate of many individually sound decisions will be better for the business and for the public than centrally planned and controlled decisions.
7. Decentralization rests on the need to have general business objectives, organization structure, relationships, policies, and measurements known, understood, and followed; but realizing that definition of policies does not necessarily mean uniformity of methods of executing such policies in decentralized operations.
8. Decentralization can be achieved only when higher executives realize that

authority genuinely delegated to lower echelons cannot, in fact, also be retained by them. We have, today, Officers and Managers who still believe in decentralization down to themselves and no further. By paying lip-service to decentralization, but actually reviewing detailed work and decisions and continually "second-guessing" their associates, such Officers keep their organization in confusion and prevent the growth of self-reliant men.

9. Decentralization will work only if responsibility commensurate with decision-making authority is truly accepted and exercised at all levels.
10. Decentralization requires personnel policies based on measured performance, enforced standards, rewards for good performance, and removal for incapacity or poor performance.

Designing Organizational Structure

Now, given this philosophy, how can it be expressed in an organization structure suitable to the General Electric Company? In our experience, the following work must be done to attain a sound, flexible, and dynamic organization structure:

1. Determine the objectives, and the policies, programs, plans, and schedules that will best achieve those objectives; for the Company as a whole and in turn, for each component of the business.
2. Determine the work to be done to achieve these objectives, under such guiding policies.
3. Divide and classify or group related work into a simple, logical, understandable, and comprehensive organization structure.
4. Assign essential work clearly and definitely to the various components and positions in the organization structure.
5. Determine the requirements and qualifications of personnel to occupy such positions.
6. Staff the organization with persons who meet these qualifications.
7. Establish methods and procedures which will help to achieve the objectives of the organization. . . .

General Electric's Organization Structure

In order to achieve these objectives on a continuing and profitable basis, an improved organization structure was devised in accordance with the principles of decentralization. . . .

The organization of General Electric is essentially a three-part structure which carefully distinguishes between Operating work, Services work, and Executive work.

The Operating Components

First let us consider the Operating work. Today, General Electric's products are engineered, manufactured, and marketed by nearly a hundred decentralized Operating Departments, each of them bearing full operating responsibility and authority for the Company's success and profitability in a particular product or service field. The special skills and knowledge required for each operating business are thus brought to bear by a local business managerial team which can concentrate on the opportunities of a specific product or marketing area. Through these integrated managerial teams, each with a specific profit-and-loss responsibility for the operation of a defined business, we achieve the flexibility, drive, and the "human touch" that comes from direct participation in the daily problems of a business.

To demonstrate that the responsibility, authority, and accountability of these Operating Departments is real, not window dressing, consider their pricing authority. The price of a product can be raised or lowered by the managers of the Department producing it, with only voluntary responsibility on their part to give sensible consideration to the impact of such price changes on other Company products. In one area of General Electric products, the major appliances such as refrigerators, ranges, and home laundry equipment, there are two Divisions competing directly with each other. The Hotpoint Division in Chicago and the Major Appliance and Television Receiver Division in Louisville have different facilities, different product designs, different distribution, and different prices. They compete at the market place very aggressively, and, incidentally, very profitably. Other Departments compete with each other by presenting different types of products that perform essentially the same function. For example, there is the competition between electronic tubes and transistors, or between room air conditioners and central air conditioning.

As further evidence of the freedom provided by decentralization to the Operating Departments, consider the fact that the operating budget of the General Electric Company is not a document prepared by the Executive Offices in New York. It is an addition of the budgets prepared by the Operating Department General Managers, with the concurrence of the Division General Managers and Group Executives. These budgets include planned sales volume, product development plans, expenditures for plant and equipment, market targets, turnover of investment, net earnings, projected organization structure, and other related items.

In the days when the Company had a centralized organization, it was the custom for Operating components to submit budgets which were promptly blue-penciled, modified, expanded or contracted, and "second-guessed" by the headquarters Executives. As a result, Operating people did not usually take their budgeting too seriously.

Now they are taking it seriously because they know they will be measured on their ability to achieve the budgeted results which they, themselves, have established as proper goals for their organizations.

We are frequently asked how these Operating Departments can do accurate forecasting and budgeting, and how the Executives can delegate this difficult function to persons less broadly experienced than themselves. The Operating Departments can do better forecasting and budgeting because they are intimately informed as to the conditions which prevail and will prevail in their line of business.

Since they are better informed, they are authorized to make whatever prudent commitments they should on materials, and we have recently increased the approval authority of the Operating Department General Managers over capital expenditures so that they can, by their own decision, make commitments up to $500,000.*

---

*I believe that too much of a fetish has been made in the past of capital expenditures. A manager can lose a lot more money on inventory, foolish pricing policy, careless personnel staffing, or poor production scheduling. Let me illustrate. In General Electric, capital expenditures in 1955 amounted to $153 millions, but we bought $1,400 millions of materials and had a payroll of $1,200 millions.

In such a diversified company as General Electric, it is impossible for the Executives in New York to have detailed knowledge of such a variety of businesses and markets. Executives can help by supplying some general aiming areas for the Company as a whole, and information as to the probable general trends of business. But this information is to be factored in, and not to dominate the budgeting of the Operating Departments, nor does it do so.

The fact is that the Operating Departments are now doing better budgeting than was done by headquarters in years gone by. Last year the Company as a whole was within 1% of its budgeted sales results, although some individual Departments were off by substantially greater percentages one way or another. . . .

It is important to emphasize the voluntary nature of a position in General Electric. For every position in the Company, including these Operating General Managers, a man has the personal right to accept or refuse the position—along with accountability for the results expected, and the risks involved in accepting such responsibilities. If for personal or other reasons he decides not to accept a particular position, there is no prejudice against him. He will receive other offers for which he is qualified as such positions become available. Voluntary and wholehearted acceptance is of course a necessary condition if a man is to be held accountable for results in risk-taking ventures. . . .

To assure that the Operating Departments and their customers will receive the full benefit of the Company's broad resources in knowledge and risktaking capacity, two other types of work are provided for in the Company's over-all organization structure: Services work and Executive work.

The Services

The functional services are components at the corporate level, staffed with the Company's most experienced personnel in the major business functions: accounting, engineering, legal and corporate, management consultation, manufacturing, marketing, public and employee relations, treasury, and research. It is important to note that, in contrast with the powerful Operating authority wielded by headquarters functional Executives under the earlier centralized structure, these Services people have no authority whatsoever over the Operating Departments and Divisions, except the authority of knowledge. They have, instead, two Company-wide responsibilities: to do research, teaching, and long-range guidance in personnel development in their functional field; and to do such functional operating work for the Company as a whole as can best be done at the corporate level.

First, let us consider the research and teaching—what we call "Services functional work." In each business function, such as accounting or marketing, General Electric is trying to apply the same principles of fundamental research and creative study that have long kept it ahead in the area of science and technology. The Services have been deliberately freed of Operating responsibility so that they can think ahead, developing through research the most advanced knowledge, principles, and techniques in their functional field, as well as keeping abreast of current knowledge developed elsewhere.

Services also have the responsibility to convert this new knowledge into usable forms and patterns, and to make it available through advice and teaching, to the Operating Departments and Divisions. Services also help to formulate Company policies appropriate to their function, and maintain a "clearinghouse" of current practices and standards within the Company to help facilitate a free flow of functional knowledge across the entire organization.

Of course, communications should never bog down in channels. If a Section Manager in steam turbine engineering at Schenectady, for example, wants some information pertaining to the engineering of aircraft gas turbines in another section, in Evendale, he does not have to go all the way up through channels to a Group Executive and down the other channel. He is expected to get the information straight across the Company just by picking up the telephone and talking to the fellow in Evendale who has the information.

The duties of Services also include long-range personnel development planning, to assure a continuing supply of outstanding people with the required changing functional skills.

Thus the emphasis in Service functional work is on the future: anticipating future opportunities and future problems, so that when they arrive General Electric will have the personnel and knowledge ready to meet them unsurprised.

The other important duty of the Services is to perform such operating work as can best be done at the corporate level, for the Company as a whole.

This includes, for example, the work of Treasury Services in handling corporate financing and investment activities on an efficient basis. There would be great confusion if the 21 Operating Divisions or 100 Operating Departments were to deal with the banks entirely separately. It should be remembered, however, that the authority to deny the use of capital from the Company's treasury to Operating General Managers who wish prudently to invest is not part of the Treasurer's responsibilities.

Another example of Operating work in the Services is the conduct of public relations programs such as institutional advertising and television, preparation of the annual report, and similar informational activities that deal with the Company as a whole. It is important that Services perform such corporate operating work with great distinction, to serve as a high standard for functional work throughout the Company.

The Executives

Leadership and long-range planning for the Company as a whole constitute the Executive classification of work in the Company structure. To understand this Executive aspect of the General Electric organization, it is important to understand two unusual organizational devices: The President's Office and the Executive Office.

The President's Office is a group of Executives who share the work of the President. In addition to the President, it includes the Chairman of the Board, and five Executive Vice Presidents. The Chairman of the Board, in addition to the duties assigned him directly by the Board, represents the President in such areas as financial affairs, public and governmental liaison, and international matters, and each of the Executive Vice Presidents represents the President in relationships with a specific group of Operating Divisions. This unique organizational device was created in recognition of the fact that no one man would have the time and knowledge required to provide effective Executive leadership for the variety of businesses in a Company as large and as diversified as General Electric. Thus each Executive Vice President serves as the President in a defined Operating area, without in any sense relieving the President of the ultimate responsibility placed upon him by the Board of Directors for the success of the enterprise as a whole.

The Executive Vice Presidents, in General Electric, are true Executives. That is, they have been freed of Operating responsibility and administrative details so that they can devote their time to long-range planning, appraisal of current performance, bringing divisional objectives and plans into a working pattern with over-all Company needs, and making sure of the needed continuity of competent managerial and other personnel in the decentralized businesses.

These seven members of the President's Office, together with the nine Company Officers in charge of the Services, form what is known as the Executive Office. These Senior Officers deliberately set aside about 20% of their time to serve, not as Executives for their particular area of Operations or Services, but as a well-balanced group of general Executives who advise the President on matters that concern all functions and all operations—in other words, the Company as a whole. In this way the Executive Office provides a melding of extensive business judgment and advanced functional knowledge to help the President plan the Company's management, growth, and course ten or more years ahead.

There you have the organizational structure of the General Electric Company: a three-part structure consisting of the Executives, who provide leadership and long-range planning for the Company as a whole; the Services, which provide leadership and advanced research in each functional field; and the Operating components, which have decentralized responsibility for the success, growth, and competitive profitability of the Company's diverse Operating businesses. . . .

Functional Authority

HAROLD KOONTZ
CYRIL O'DONNELL

Functional authority gives a manager power over specified processes, practices, policies, or other matters relating to activities undertaken by personnel in departments other than his own. If the principle of unity of command were followed without exception, authority over these activities would be exercised by line managers, but numerous reasons—including lack of special knowledge, lack of ability to supervise processes, and danger of diverse interpretations of policies—explain why they occasionally cannot exercise this authority. In such cases, the line manager may be deprived of limited authority, and a manager in another department may be delegated specialized, that is, "functional" authority to carry out the activities properly.

Functional authority is not restricted to managers of a particular type of department. It may be exercised by line, service,* or staff department heads, more

---

* Some so-called staff departments are service departments. Since the latter reflect a special grouping of activities and since this discussion is concerned with line and staff authority relationships, the analysis of service departments as a special organizational form is [not treated in this article].

often the latter two, because they are usually comprised of specialists whose knowledge becomes the basis for functional controls.

Development of Functional Authority

The successive steps by which a line manager gradually gives up his authority over particular activities make an interesting study. As has already been emphasized, the pure staff specialist offers advice or recommendations to his line superior, who may issue them as instructions to be filtered down the organization hierarchy. The first modification of this relationship ordinarily occurs when the superior delegates authority to the staff man to transmit information, proposals, and advice directly to the former's subordinates. For example, a personnel assistant might be permitted to transmit directly to the operating department heads information and advice on the handling of labor grievances, instead of transmitting them first to the president for his transmission to the line organization. Obviously, this saves the president time and trouble and expedites the spread of the information.

A second modification might be to allow the staff specialist not only to transmit information and advice to the line managers but to consult with them and show them how the information should be used or how the recommendations should be put into effect. For instance, the personnel assistant might be asked to advise line personnel on procedures to eliminate mishandling of grievances. It will clearly be advantageous to all concerned if the staff man can instruct the persons responsible for this activity. Here, there is no question of his ordering them; the agreement of the line executive concerned is needed; should this not be forthcoming, he can only appeal to his superior to issue the requisite instructions.

The final transition to functional authority is accomplished when the assistant is delegated specific authority to *prescribe* processes, methods, or even policy to be followed in all subdivisions of either staff or operating departments. The personnel assistant, for example, who once could only advise, now may be given limited authority to supervise a special function or process of the line organization. He no longer merely advises his superior or the line organization concerning handling grievances. Now, he may issue orders prescribing procedures. Or, to use another example, a corporation controller may be given authority, not to recommend, but to prescribe the kind of accounting records to be kept by the sales department, the sales division, or the sales district, as well as by the manufacturing departments.

By limiting this authority to function, the factory manager—handling his labor grievances in accordance with procedures prescribed by the personnel manager—and the district sales manager—keeping his records according to instructions of the controller—are still primarily subject to the orders, supervision, and control of their line superiors. The extent of their control by the staff officer is governed by the functional procedure or policy being employed.

Functional Authority Delegation

Functional authority can perhaps be better understood if it is regarded as a small slice of the authority of the line superior. A corporation president, for example, has complete authority to manage the corporation, subject only to limitations placed upon him by such superior authority as the board of directors, the corporate charter and bylaws, and government regulations. In the pure staff situation, his advisers on personnel, accounting, purchasing, or public relations have no part of this authority, their duty being merely to offer counsel. But when functional authority relationships exist, the president delegates some of his authority to issue instructions directly to the line organization to these advisers, as shown in Figure 1.

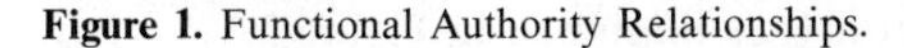

Figure 1. Functional Authority Relationships.

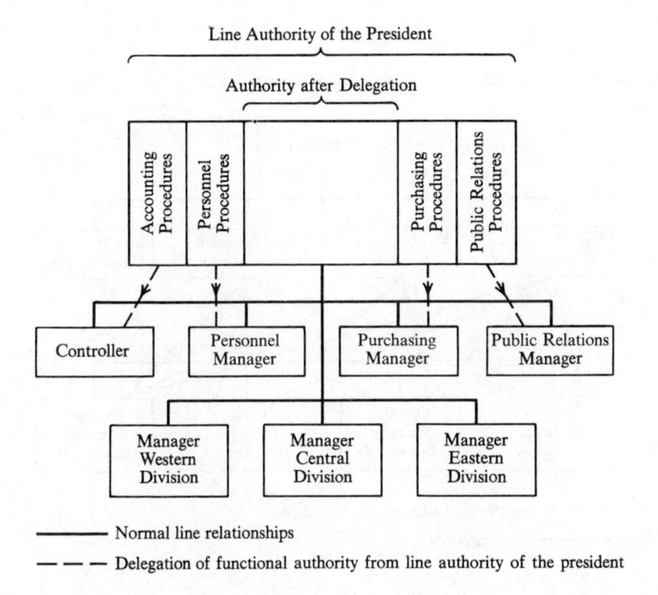

As illustrated, the four staff executives have functional authority over the line organization with respect to procedures in the fields of accounting, personnel, purchasing, and public relations. What has happened is that the president, feeling it unnecessary that such specialized matters be cleared through him, has delegated functional authority to staff assistants to issue their own instructions to the operating departments. Likewise, of course, the various operating managers and their line subordinate managers could themselves set up staff assistants with functional authority, as when a factory superintendent sets up cost, production-control, and quality-control supervisors with functional authority to prescribe procedures for the foremen.

Functional Authority as Exercised by Line Managers

Line department heads sometimes have good reason to control some method or process of another line department. For example, the vice-president in charge of sales may be given functional authority over the manufacturing executives in such matters as scheduling customer orders, packaging, or making available service parts.

Where a company is organized along product lines, the exercise of functional authority over the product division managers by other executives is rather commonplace. For purposes of administrative convenience, particularly coordination at a point in the organization structure, all functions of sales, production, finance, or other so-called line functions (that is, "line" to the enterprise) may be placed under a division or product manager reporting directly to the president, or, as is sometimes the case, to the vice-president in charge of operations. In either case, certain top line officials in charge of a major function of the business might not have a direct line of authority over the product managers. But, to make sure that sales or financial policy is properly followed in the divisions, these officers may be given functional authority, as illustrated in Figure 2.

Figure 2. Functional Authority of Line Departments.

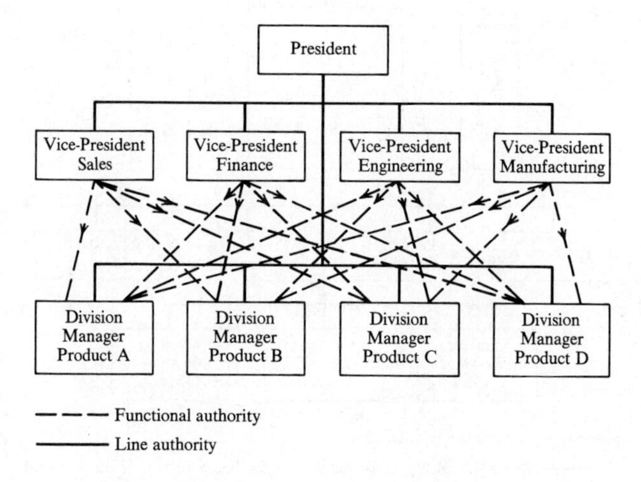

The Area of Functional Authority

Functional authority should be restricted authority. The functional authority of the purchasing manager, for example, is generally limited to the procedures to be used in divisional or departmental purchasing. Although he may *conduct* certain purchasing activities of an over-all company nature, he is thereby acting either as a direct line officer over a portion of purchasing or as head of a service department. The functional authority of the personnel manager over the general line organization is likewise ordinarily limited to the prescription of procedures for handling grievances, for sharing in the administering of wage and salary programs, and for handling vacation procedures and similar matters.

Functional authority is usually limited to the area of "how" and sometimes "when" and seldom applies to "where," "what," or "who." The reason for this limitation is not found in any logical demarcation between normal line authority and functional authority, since the latter *can* be made to apply to any aspect of operations. It is rather that the functionalization of management, if carried to extremes, would destroy the manager's job. As will be recalled from an earlier discussion, whenever a manager loses his authority to plan, organize, staff, direct, and control the activities within his department, he can no longer manage.

To some extent, this occurs when a staff or line executive has functional authority over some part of another manager's job. Even when the personnel manager requires the factory manager to follow seniority in layoffs or to grant employees definite pay and vacation allowances, he is interfering with some of the factory manager's prerogatives. When the accounting department requires district sales managers to file their expense accounts in a certain form, it is, to some extent, interfering with the authority of the general sales manager over his subordinates.

Therefore, well-managed concerns recognize that functional authority should be used sparingly and only where a real necessity exists. This necessity comes often from both outside and inside influences. On the outside are the requirements of such institutions as government and labor unions that must be interpreted and administered by specialists. On the inside are matters of such importance or complexity that the best possible grade of uniform action is required, necessitating in turn that the expert be given sufficient authority to carry out desired procedures. A rather thin line sometimes divides what should be controlled by the expert and what should be under the jurisdiction of the line manager. Where there is doubt, good practice would seem to favor limiting the area of functional authority so that the line manager's position is not weakened.

Unity of Command and the Flow of Functional Authority

Limiting the area of functional authority is, then, important in preserving the integrity of the managerial position. If a company had, as some do, executives with functional authority over procedures in the fields of personnel, purchasing, accounting, traffic, budgets, engineering, public relations, law, sales policy, and real estate, the complications of authority relationships could be great indeed. A factory manager or a sales manager might have, in addition to his immediate line superior, five, ten, or even fifteen bosses, a situation sometimes unavoidable if the advantages of specialization, obtained by the use of functional authority arrangements, are to be gained.

Preservation of some semblance of unity of command can be maintained by requiring that the line of functional authority shall not extend beyond the first organization level below that of the manager's own superior. Thus, in Figure 3 the functional authority of the personnel or public relations director should not extend beyond the level of the vice-presidents in charge of finance, sales, and manufacturing. In other words, functional authority should be concentrated at the nearest possible point in the organization structure, to preserve the unity of command of the line executives.

The manner in which this concentration of functional authority can be effected in large companies with a number of levels of organization is apparent from Figure 4. The manager in charge at each level has concentrated in him the functional authority lines of the principals at each level above him. While these lines of functional authority may seem complicated—and, as any regional manager knows, this intricacy is as real as it is apparent—the complications would be increased many times if the functional authority were not concentrated at each level.

Nevertheless, the actual lines of authority do not operate in this manner, even though they were intended to. From Figure 4, one would expect that the general manager of the eastern division would pass on all instructions from the vice-president of sales to the division sales manager, and that the manager of the New York region would relay instructions of the division sales manager to the regional sales manager. In practice, these instructions would often be relayed without the divisional general manager's or the regional manager's ever having looked at them. But the fact that they are transmitted *through* these managers gives a basis for unity of command that could not be retained if the general line managers at each level were bypassed.

This principle is often violated. Top managers with functional authority sometimes issue instructions directly to personnel throughout the organization. Where the policy or procedure determination is so important that there must be no deviation, both the prestige of the top manager and the necessity of accurate communication may make it necessary and wise to issue such instructions. Issuing them to the responsible line subordinate, as well as to the functional counterpart at the lower level, does not seem seriously to increase the multiplicity of command. As will be noted later, there are forces of centralization of authority that may make this kind of exercise of functional authority unavoidable.

Line and Staff in Practice

The essential character of line and staff relationships becomes readily apparent in the study of well-managed enterprises. Although the semantics of management occasionally mislead the student (and, more often, those managing and being managed), a clear statement of authority relationships will identify the kind of authority—whether line, staff, or functional.

For example, in an organization analysis prepared by one of the nation's leading industrial management firms for a fast-growing enterprise, territorial divisions for major line operations and a staff of top executives to control over-all policy were established. In the organization manual, the treasurer's scope of authority was spelled out as follows:

> The Treasurer has line authority over and is responsible for directing activities of such staff personnel as he requires to establish system policies and procedures for the functions under his jurisdiction and to administer

Figure 3. Line and Functional Authority.

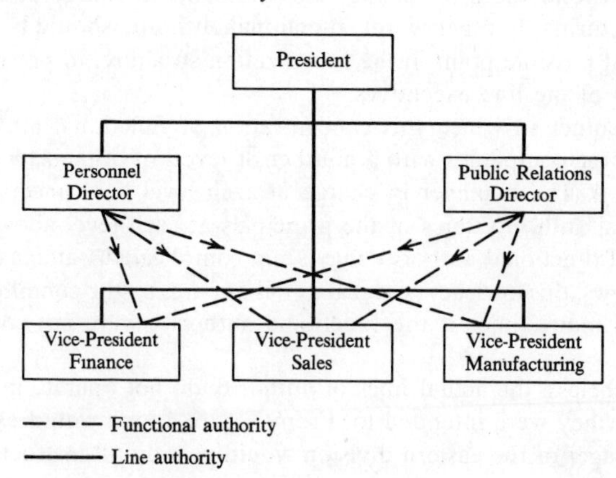

Figure 4. Conception of Functional Authority of the Various Levels of an Organization.

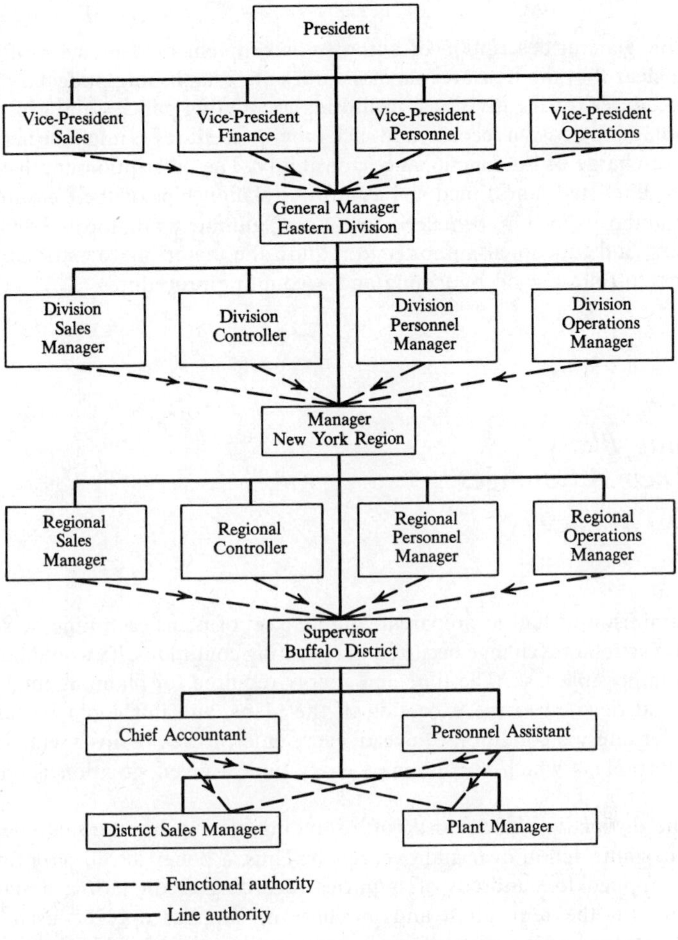

system treasury and accounting functions which are reserved for his staff. He has no direct line authority over the day-to-day activities of accounting personnel in the divisions and regions except as specifically delegated by division or region managements. He is responsible for developing and interpreting budgeting, accounting, and financial policies, for assisting the division organizations in carrying out such policies, and for satisfying himself that such policies are correctly and ably administered in the field.

At the request of division managements, or voluntarily when system welfare is materially concerned, the Treasurer and his staff shall make recommendations concerning the employment, promotion, dismissal, or change in compensation of supervisory personnel engaged in activities within his functional responsibility. Final action on such matters shall be taken by division managements when mutual agreement has been reached with system staff department heads concerned.

This general description of authority is supplemented by a list of duties making clear that the treasurer's major duties are establishing budgetary policy and procedures for the divisions; instituting accounting policies and procedures for maintaining division records, and such other procedures as might be necessary for the discharge of his functional responsibility. The description and list make clear the line, staff, and functional authority relationships of the treasurer: He has line authority over his own department, staff authority with top and divisional managers, and functional authority to require the major line departments, the divisions, to follow good budgeting and accounting procedures.

Standing Plans and Their Advantages

WILLIAM H. NEWMAN

If an administrator had to prepare a complete set of plans each time he wished to initiate action or a change occurred in operating conditions, he would be faced with an impossible task. The time and energy required for planning might well exceed that devoted to the execution of the plans, and this could be justified only under unusual conditions. Instead, every enterprise develops a wide variety of standing plans which are followed every time a given situation is encountered.

The distinctive characteristic of a standing plan is that the same decision is used to guide action over and over again. Thus, a policy to sell only for cash may be applied to hundreds of inquiries regarding credit terms; a standard procedure for the requisition and purchase of supplies may be used in all departments for a wide variety of needs; a standard method for shipping products may be followed by a whole group of packers almost every day in the year.[1]

Such standing plans greatly simplify the task of the administrator. They establish a pattern of action that the planner assumes as normal, and he can then concentrate his attention on the changes he wishes to make in this customary pattern for abnormal circumstances.

Of course, many work habits or business customs just grow without any deliberate planning on the part of executives. Sometimes these behavior patterns simply reflect the way the first employee found it convenient to work, and this

From *Administrative Action: The Techniques of Organization and Management,* 2nd ed., © 1963, pp. 39–47, 48–49, 51–52, 86–98. Reprinted by permission of Prentice-Hall, Inc., Englewood Cliffs, New Jersey.

[1]Some standing plans may not, in fact, be used over and over again. For example, plans for meeting a disaster such as a fire may rarely be put into action. Nevertheless, such stand-by plans are designed so that they can be used time and again if occasion warrants.

method was copied with minor modifications by subsequent employees. In other cases an executive may have been confronted with a specific problem on which he made a decision, and then when the problem came up again he remembered that his original decision worked satisfactorily and so he decided in the second instance to follow the same behavior. After four or five decisions applying to the same situation, this solution becomes, perhaps unconsciously, the standard answer to that kind of a question. If such policies and methods are accepted by the management to the extent that new employees are deliberately trained to follow them and all employees are subject to censure if they deviate from them without good reason or permission, they then become part of the standing plans of the enterprise.

Experience has demonstrated, however, that the administrator can profitably give careful attention to the standing plans he expects to be followed by those under his direction. Gilbreth, Taylor, and other pioneers in the scientific management movement found that even skilled craftsmen following customary methods frequently are not very efficient. Many progressive companies now recognize the value of having good standing plans and make special provision in their organization for the careful study of policies and of methods and procedures.

In considering standing plans it is often helpful for the administrator to give separate attention to: (1) policies, (2) procedures, (3) methods. Each of these will be examined briefly in this section to see how they may be used and what benefits result. Organization structure can also be thought of as a standing plan, inasmuch as the assignment of duties and the relationships established provide a continuing frame of reference to guide employees in their daily activities.

Policies

A *policy* is a general plan of action that guides members of the enterprise in the conduct of its operation.

An illustration of the need for policy is found in the recurring question faced by every executive responsible for machinery of when and how much money should be spent for maintenance. Where repairs are easily made and delays caused by breakdowns are not costly, it may be wise to postpone activity until something goes wrong. In many other situations a policy of preventive maintenance is the wiser course. The commercial airlines, for example, overhaul an airplane motor after a certain number of hours of service, even though it may be running satisfactorily at the time. Sales divisions typically require that salesmen's automobiles be serviced regularly and may, in fact, provide for complete replacement before the need for expensive maintenance arises.

In production operations preventive maintenance provides for the periodic replacement of parts that may break or wear out, regular inspection to detect weaknesses or poor adjustment that may cause trouble at a later time if not taken care of immediately, and similar efforts to anticipate trouble. Once a company has a clear-cut policy as to the extent to which it will engage in preventive maintenance, then the operating executive and the maintenance division itself have a guide that may be used time and again in deciding what action should be taken with respect to a given piece of equipment. This results in considerable economy of the executive's time.

Policies are also helpful in securing consistency of action. For instance, the day is past when layoffs could be made according to the personal inclinations of several different foremen. Union or no union, having one foreman lay off on the basis of seniority, another on the basis of quality of work during the last week, still another on the basis of nationality, with perhaps a fourth using a "good guy" standard is well recognized as a bad practice. Instead, most companies now have a clear-cut policy stipulating the basis for selection of men to lay off when a reduction in staff is necessary. Such a policy can be explained to employees in advance, and when applied throughout the enterprise, it goes a long way toward establishing a sense of fair play in the entire group.

Some policies deal with the fundamental nature of a company's operations. A large New York store, for example, had followed a policy for years of catering to well-to-do women of mature years who wish to buy high-quality, conservatively styled, and, frequently, custom-made apparel. This policy on customers affected the type of salespeople who were employed, the type of training that they received, the pricing policies of the company, the services it rendered, the collection of bills, and many other aspects of the operation. After a decline in sales volume, a new general manager was employed whose background had been in the selling of popular-priced apparel to women of all ages and tastes. A period of confusion followed during which it was not clear whether the store was going to maintain its former customer policy or shift over to a policy similar to that of stores in which the general manager had had his previous experience. During this interval the older customers were sometimes annoyed at the styles and the lower-quality merchandise they found in some departments, new customers attracted by the more flashy advertising found themselves getting personal service that could not be justified in terms of their potential purchases, and considerable difference of opinion arose as to the selection and training of new salespeople. This difficulty was not eliminated until the board of directors made a clear-cut decision as to the type of customer the store was going to try to serve.

Virtually every enterprise should establish a wide range of policies covering its more important operations. A suggestive outline[2] of the subjects that might well be considered in this connection by almost any business establishment is given below.

The administrator of a given enterprise will have to decide which activities should be closely governed by specific policies and which can be better managed on a more flexible basis. He will have to weigh the benefits of clear-cut and detailed policies against the disadvantages of such planning.

Policy Outline for a Typical Business Enterprise

I. Sales Policies
   A. Products or services to be sold
      1. Type of products
      2. Number and variety of products
      3. Quality of products
   B. Customers to whom products will be sold
      1. Channels of distribution
      2. Type of customers

[2] For a discussion of each topic in this outline, see W. H. Newman and J. P. Logan, *Business Policies and Management,* 4th ed., South-Western Publishing Co., 1959.

        3. Size of customers
        4. Location of customers
    C. Prices at which products will be sold
        1. Relation to prices of competing products
        2. Relation to costs of production and distribution
        3. Relation to prices of individual items
        4. Quantity and trade discounts
        5. Frequency of price changes
        6. Resale price maintenance
    D. Sales promotion
        1. Sales appeals emphasized
        2. Types and media of advertising
        3. Use of personal solicitation
II. Procurement Policies
    A. Producing versus buying goods needed
        1. Buying goods for resale
        2. Producing main items, buying others
        3. Producing own raw materials
        4. Producing own services
    B. When and in what quantities to procure goods
        1. Procurement for stock, budgeted needs, or customer's order
        2. Minimum inventories required
        3. Size of production run or purchase order
        4. Stabilization of production
        5. Anticipation of price changes
    C. Selection of vendors
        1. Number of vendors
        2. Type of vendors
    D. Production processes
        1. Basic process to be used
        2. Extent of specialization
        3. Extent of automation
III. Personnel Policies
    A. Selection
        1. Hiring new employees
        2. Promotion of present employees
        3. Discharge of present employees
    B. Training
        1. Purposes of training
        2. Use of on-the-job training
        3. Use of organized training
    C. Compensation
        1. Relation to market rates
        2. Internal alignment
        3. Use of financial incentives
    D. Arrangements for work
        1. Hours of work
        2. Vacations
        3. Working conditions

E. Employee services
 1. Social and recreational activities
 2. Safety and health
 3. Pensions
 4. Group insurance
F. Industrial relations
 1. Companywide and industrywide bargaining
 2. Grievances and arbitration
 3. Union-management cooperation
 4. Other means of communication

IV. Financial Policies
A. Uses of capital
 1. Extent of investment in fixed assets
 2. Restrictions on inventories
 3. Extension of credit to customers
 4. Use of capital not needed immediately for operations
B. Sources of capital
 1. Owners
 2. Long-term creditors
 3. Short-term creditors
C. Protection of capital
 1. Reduction of risks
 2. Insurance
 3. Hedging
 4. Accounting reserves
D. Distribution of earnings
 1. Plowing back earnings
 2. Stable dividend rate
 3. Adequacy of retained earnings

Standard Procedures

The distinction between policies and methods or procedures is useful although it is not clear cut. A *policy* typically covers a broad area or a basic issue, whereas *method* normally deals with the way a policy is carried out. This distinction between the broader aspects of an operating situation and the more detailed and specific considerations is useful in planning because it emphasizes a different viewpoint. Some executives have a tendency to become involved in methods and procedures to the exclusion of policies, whereas others have just the opposite tendency; effective administration gives ample consideration to both policies and methods. Also, the distinction between policies and methods is sometimes helpful in the process of delegation.

This distinction is useful but not fundamental since what is policy and what is method depends upon the position from which the operation is viewed. For instance, the board of directors may regard the choice of advertising media as method of sales promotion, but to the sales manager the use of daily newspapers is a basic policy; similarly, the choice of type font is method to the sales manager, but it may be policy to the layout man. From any given point of view, however, policy is clearly much broader in scope than either method or procedure.

While in common usage *methods* and *procedures* are frequently used interchangeably, in the present study *procedure* will imply a series of steps, often taken by different individuals, whereas *method* is concerned only with a single operation or work place.

In many types of business activity it is highly important to be sure that certain steps are taken and that the work is done accurately. Consequently, a detailed standing plan—in army parlance standing operating procedure, or just S.O.P.—is established. One bank, for example, has established the following standard procedure for the cutting of coupons on bonds that it holds for its own account or for customers' accounts:

> A list, called "Withdrawal of Securities" is prepared from the Cross Index record of bonds. The customers' names, quantity, and title of bonds that have coupons attached, falling due in the next period, are listed. Coupon envelopes are prepared, as well as ownership certificates (see Coupon Dept.). The coupon envelopes are prepared from the Collateral Loan cards and Safekeeping Book, thus acting as a check against the Cross Index record. The securities are then withdrawn from the Vault and Collateral Truck by an officer and clerk, counted and checked to the list, the list signed by both representatives of the bank. The officer retains this list of securities. After the coupons are detached, counted, and placed in the envelopes, the securities are again returned to their respective compartments in the Vault and the customers' accounts, in which case, duplicate credit slips are executed. One copy represents the credit to the account, and the other serves as a mailed notice to the customer.

A standard procedure should make sure that pertinent information flows to the people needing such data and that each person involved in the process understands just what he is to do. By making such steps established routine, the task of administration is significantly simplified.

Many procedures call for the transfer of information in written form. When this is so, the preparation of standard forms to be used is an essential aspect of the procedure. No end of confusion would result from the practice of recording information on sheets of paper of different sizes, to say nothing of the organization of the information on the paper. A well-designed form with lines for all of the essential information facilitates accuracy and completeness of information, permits rapid use, and also standardizes the record storage facilities.

Standard Methods

Standard methods have received considerable attention, especially in manufacturing enterprises, ever since Frederick Taylor and his associates insisted that there was "one best way" to perform any operation. Much study may be necessary to ascertain just what the best method is, and management has a responsibility for maintaining standard operating conditions and for training the workers. Once these conditions are met, however, each worker performing the operation is expected to do it in accordance with the approved method. The net result usually is a substantial improvement in efficiency. There are also collateral benefits in making planning and control significantly easier.

The use of a standard method contributes not only to the efficiency but often to the quality of work and the uniformity of the products produced. For instance, the larger commercial laundries do not permit the girls ironing shirts to follow any method they choose. The order in which the parts of a shirt are pressed, the machine on which each operation is performed, and the portions of the shirt that are to be hand-ironed are carefully specified. Likewise, the folding and the wrapping of the shirt is standardized. If each presser were permitted to follow her own inclinations in handling the work, some shirts would be done with meticulous care while others would come through with wrinkled collars and buttons off; the customer would be particularly aware of the variations in quality because some shirts would be folded one way and others another way. Obviously, the laundry attempts to establish a standard method that will give quality of product consistent with its pricing and customer policies.

Although standard methods have been developed in the most detail and applied most extensively in production operations, the general concept is applicable to some degree in every field of purposeful activity. Thus, the retail store that accepts telephone orders for its merchandise may well standardize (1) the conversation of the order-taker, at least to the extent of the expressions used in answering the phone, closing the conversation, quoting prices, suggesting substitutions, and the like, (2) order writing, including the way the pad is held, the type of pencil used, the inserting of carbons, the tearing out of completed orders, and the order form itself, (3) checking prices and inventory on hand, often through the use of stock lists fully indexed for ready reference. When such methods are carefully developed and a salesperson is properly selected and trained, the time required to handle a call often can be cut in half; moreover, the customers receive more satisfactory service and the amount of sales per call is increased. Contrast this with the results when the salespersons are permitted to take telephone orders on a "catch as catch can" basis.

Flexibility of Plans

Both single-use and standing plans, by their very nature, restrict freedom of action. Men carrying out the plans may object to such restriction, partly because they dislike restrictions of any sort, but more significantly because they believe that the plans are not well suited to the specific problems they face. So exceptions are made; that is, the plan is not carried out in all respects.

If plans are simply disregarded, they obviously fail to serve the purposes we have been discussing in this chapter. On the other hand, some provision for flexibility may be warranted. Fortunately, several ways exist to achieve flexibility without, at the same time, sacrificing the benefits of planning. Three possible ways of securing flexibility are:

1. *Provide for prompt exceptions.* For instance, a company may have standing policies and procedures covering the extension of credit to customers. Most shipments will fit within these plans, but if a special case arises when an exception seems warranted, the credit manager or assistant treasurer is empowered to grant credit beyond the established limits. This kind of arrangement for avoiding rigid application of rules is often called *the exception principle.* It is used most often with standing plans.

To provide real flexibility, the executive who can make an exception to established plans should be available to say "yes" or "no" quickly enough to secure the full benefit of the special concession. Sometimes a pattern develops among the exceptions, and when this occurs, the plans may be elaborated to include the treatment of unusual cases within the regular structure. However, if an executive makes exceptions so often and with no clear and consistent reason for doing so, the stability plans are designed to provide will be dissipated.

2. *Consider possible revisions regularly.* Flexibility is often needed to deal with new conditions that were not anticipated when the plans were formulated. Consequently, many companies provide for periodic review of progress to date and of new information; plans are then revised to the extent that seems strategic.

This revision technique is well suited to single-use plans. It should be used with restraint on standing plans, however, because policies, procedures, and the like serve as a basis for habitual behavior and social structure. Frequent changes in the "rules of the game" are often disconcerting to employees. In fact, in times of rapid change the behavior patterns may become so unstable that little work gets done. Occasional review of standing plans is, indeed, wise; but if changes are to be made, the need for full understanding by the people affected (preferably through their participation in the revision process) and for a retraining period should be recognized.

3. *Distinguish between rules and guides.* Close examination of the actual operation of many companies, including highly successful ones, reveals that plans are often not strictly observed. Local executives or operators make their own exceptions, especially when goals have been clearly established and decentralization is favored. In effect, the policies, methods, programs, and other plans are treated as *guides*—recommended practice—but not as rules which must be obeyed. Obviously, such behavior introduces considerable flexibility into company activities.

In all companies certain plans are strictly enforced. For example, pricing and services to customers may have to be uniform, deviations from quality standards will not be tolerated, accounting classifications must be kept uniform. On such matters the need for consistency and/or the reliance one department places on another requires close adherence to plans. In other matters such as public relations, production methods, or purely internal operations of a department, occasional local variations may give better results.

Flexibility can be enhanced by publicly recognizing this distinction between rules and guides. Instead of letting each employee discover for himself where exceptions will be tolerated, the administrator should be explicit about the matter. By removing uncertainty about when and how much deviation, if any, will be permitted two ends are served: flexibility is introduced where practical, and close observance of the remaining plans is more likely to occur. . . .

Advantages of Using Standing Plans

Most administrators recognize that policies and standard methods and procedures have a place in management planning, but the practical questions are: When should they be used? How specific and detailed should they be? The answers to these questions rest on a careful consideration of the advantages and disadvantages of standing plans as they apply to the specific situation. Among the benefits that an administrator may expect to obtain from the use of standing plans are the following:

1. Executive effort is economized. Once the standing plan is established it is unnecessary for the executive to redecide the same issue. The plan is applicable, of course, only under a given set of conditions. Someone must ascertain

that these conditions prevail in the case at hand, but if this is true, no further decision by the executive is required. Moreover, less time is needed for instructions and explanations of what is to be done.

2. Delegation of authority to act is greatly facilitated. Often the exception principle is utilized, under which subordinates are expected to proceed with action so long as the situation is covered by standing plans, but when exceptional problems arise to bring these to the attention of the supervisor. If this arrangement is carefully observed, an administrator can maintain close control over a large volume of operations with relative ease. He knows that consistent action is being taken on similar cases; he can predict what the action will be; and he knows that the action is in accordance with his best judgment.
3. Widespread use of "the one best way" is possible. If an operation is to be repeated a large number of times, considerable effort to ascertain the most efficient way of performing it is warranted. And, having discovered this method, it is made standard practice for all those who perform that activity. Of course, standing plans may be far from the most efficient; this is likely to happen when plans are not currently adjusted to changing conditions or when traditional behavior is adopted as the standard without critical examination. In such cases, the other advantages of standing plans are still obtainable, but a significant source of economy is being overlooked.
4. Significant personnel economies are possible. The establishment of standing plans for a large part of the duties of a given position allow such positions to be filled with persons of less experience and all-round ability than would be needed if the incumbent made the plans himself. The training of persons to fill such positions is made easier by the existence of recognized policies and procedures, and the transfer of employees from one position to another in the same organization is likewise eased.
5. Control is made easier. Standing plans, especially standard methods and procedures, lead to uniformity of action, and relatively definite performance standards can be established for such activities.
6. Coordination of activities is greatly aided by a preliminary coordination of plans. The clear statement of both single-use and standing plans permits a check of one with another, and opens the way for greater consistency and synchronization.

The Appeals Procedure

WILFRED BROWN

Differences of opinion between people, and particularly between managers and subordinates, are inevitable in an executive system. Means of ventilating these differences, and of seeking redress from a higher level of authority, come into being willy-nilly. If these means are allowed to grow haphazardly, they take on forms which are inefficient and damaging to the company. The chief danger of an unrecognized and, therefore, unformulated appeals mechanism is that it may informally institute by-passing of managerial levels. Decisions are then made without data on the full situation being available. The hearing of a grievance by a high-level manager, without the presence of the manager whose decision is being questioned, or of the intervening managers, undermines the whole managerial-subordinate relationship. . . .

General Features of Our Appeals Mechanism

Our appeals mechanism, in general terms, has the following features (I state them briefly at this point, and will go into them in detail later):

1. Every member of the company has the right of appeal against any decision of his manager to the next level of management, and successively to higher levels of management until he reaches the Managing Director. At most, this can normally involve three levels of appeal only in our company.
2. That, subject to special provisions, he has final right of appeal to an appeal tribunal consisting of a representative, a management member and a tribunal chairman, appointed from outside the company by the chairman of the relevant Works Council.
3. At each appeal hearing, the person appealing is entitled to the assistance of his chosen representative, and the relevant managers must be present.
4. The task of the manager hearing the appeal is to come to a decision in the light of existing policy, standing orders and precedent. His job is to set aside his personal opinion on the matter, and endeavour to arrive at a decision that is in accordance with our internal policies.
5. Either party to an appeal may refer it to a personnel officer for counseling. The personnel officer may make recommendations to both parties. But these are not binding and, if not accepted, the appeal continues to be heard in the normal way.

Subject-Matter of Appeals

All appeals are, in the first place, always against the decision of some manager. The subject-matter appears to fall into two categories. One type of appeal is to the effect that the manager is not entitled to make the decision which is the subject of dispute, because his decision is not consistent with standing orders,

From *Explorations in Management* (New York: John Wiley & Sons, Inc., 1960), pp. 250, 253, 254–259, 266–268. Reprinted by permission.

established policy or precedent. Here are some examples illustrating alleged infringement by managers of their *prescribed* terms of reference under existing policy.

1. A member, having absented himself from work on the day after a holiday, has been refused holiday pay by his manager in accordance with the National Agreement on the subject. The member contends that his manager has not interpreted the National Agreement correctly.
2. A member, being refused an increase of wages, contends that a manager is not entitled to withhold the increase, because his work falls within a category the minimum wage of which is above his existing wage.
3. A member informed by his manager that his performance is not adequate, and that he will not be retained in that command, contends that he has not been given any previous notice of his manager's dissatisfaction; therefore, in accordance with policy, his manager is not entitled to discharge him from his existing role until he has warned him in this way, and given him an opportunity of meeting those criticisms.

Shortening the Procedure

It happens, not infrequently, with this type of appeal that circumstances are new, and the policy which applies is, for example, company rather than factory policy. In such cases, it is often better for a general manager to decide not to hear the appeal, but instead take it to the top of the executive system. If he hears it himself, he may be called upon to give an interpretation in a situation where there is no clear guidance in written policy, and it is likely that his decision will again be the subject of appeal. By deciding to take it to the top without delay, he saves a complete hearing and all the time that it takes. Representatives have recently, in discussion, stressed their own embarrassment about the inefficiency and loss of time taken up by intermediary hearings of an appeal, when they themselves already feel quite certain—because the issue is of a company nature—that it will in the end inevitably have to go to the Chief Executive for decision.

Cases occur when the decision on the appeal is debated not on the grounds of written policy, but by reference to custom or precedent. In these cases also, there are strong grounds for considering whether they should not go to the top at once, in order to save time.

It has always been possible for a manager to agree that cases should be handled in this manner, but up to now it has happened infrequently. It is clear to me, from the experience of hearing appeals, that there are many instances where time would have been saved by applying such a contraction of the appeal mechanism. Indeed, if it were possible, without actually hearing an appeal, to determine fairly precisely its content, then that content would pre-determine the appropriate level at which it should be heard. Decisions about policy appropriate to a unit should be heard by the unit manager, decisions arising out of factory policy by a general manager, etc. Unfortunately, it is very often necessary to hear an appeal in order to determine its content, and at times an individual appeal can involve several levels of policy.

Appeals About Unfair Decisions

A second type of appeal seeks to show that a manager, in using his discretion as to which course to pursue, has made a choice that is unfair to a particular individual. In such a case, the argument is not that policy forbids the manager a particular choice, but that his choice is unfair to his subordinate. Here are three examples:

1. A member, while agreeing that his pay is within the agreed bracket for the job, feels that he should be paid higher within that bracket. He claims that his manager is wrong in rating him the same as A and B, and lower than C and D, with whom he considers himself equal in every way.
2. A manager does not give a member certain types of work to do, because he does not rank the member as being sufficiently skilled and careful to keep the risk of "scrapping" the job within reasonable bounds. The offended member contends that the estimate of his capacity is unfair.
3. A manager, having had many discussions with a member about his shortcomings and having tried to help him by training, decides that the member is not good enough to be retained in his role. The member challenges the soundness of his manager's assessment.

These latter examples are difficult types of appeal cases to deal with. They seem to be the kind of cases which should be referred, if possible, to a personnel officer for counseling. There is a reasonable chance that, as a result of the part played by the personnel officer as an advice-giver, the conflict may be resolved in a manner that is less likely to arise in the atmosphere of the appeal setting, where normally there are only two courses open: either to dismiss the appeal or to uphold it. In most cases it is clearly not realistic for the higher manager to say, in effect, to the lower manager: "I will uphold this man's appeal for a higher wage, for I think your decision about his worth is wrong, and I (after half an hour's acquaintanceship during this hearing) believe that I can decide his proper wage more accurately than you can."

My personal practice in hearing appeals, once it has been made quite clear that the appeal is against the way a manager has used his discretionary authority, is to say to the appellant: "You have a difficult task on your hands. Unless you can show that your manager has come to this decision against you by allowing non-executive matters to influence his judgement, or has in some other way infringed prescribed policy, you cannot hope to win your appeal. My task is to ascertain whether your manager is entitled to make decisions such as the one you feel aggrieved about (and it is clear to me that he is), and to satisfy myself that he had come to his decision, whatever it may be, in an executively realistic manner within prescribed policy." I cannot say "You are a good worker" on the basis of personal observation; but I can assess the consistency of the comments of the immediate manager and those of other managers between me and the member appealing. If they are not consistent, then I may feel that personal bias is entering into the manager's decisions and that his decision may need scrutiny and amendment.

It may be asked if there is any real value in hearing these appeals at all in cases where the way in which a manager has used his discretion is the main content. I have no doubt of the value myself—for the following reasons:

1. The appeal has to be heard in order to ascertain what the difference of opinion is about.
2. The member may not be satisfied when, after two or three hearings at different levels, he must face the fact that, in the absence of real evidence of a manager's personal bias, that manager's assessment of him is the accepted basis of the decision and not his own assessment of himself. There is, however, a very

large volume of evidence to show that people who contest these "unfair to me" decisions of their managers, and who fail to get the decision altered, nevertheless do get a much broader perspective as a result of appealing, and are less aggrieved at the end of the procedure than when they started.

3. The higher manager may learn of the difficulty which surrounds the implementation of some of his own policy, and this may cause him to arrange that it be changed.
4. The higher manager learns a good deal about his subordinates on such occasions. This may cause him to feel satisfied or unsatisfied with the manner in which the managerial task is being carried out in that sector of his total command which is concerned with an appeal. If he is not satisfied, he can later take appropriate steps.

Appeals by Representatives

The third type of appeal is that made by a group or representative body. The subject-matter may be similar to that of individual appeals; but the appeal made by a group tends to be concerned not so much with the effect of a decision that has been made upon some particular individual, but with the future effect on everybody, if a manager's particular interpretation of our policy is permitted to go unchallenged. I will quote one example of this type of appeal.

A shop committee of representatives appealed against the rate of pay which a man, who had just finished his apprenticeship, was offered to take up a skilled job. The man involved was not present, and the committee explained that the fact they were seeking to get established was that the *grounds* given by the manager for offering a lower rate of pay than was customary in similar circumstances were inappropriate. They sought to prove, for instance, that it was outside company policy for the manager to base his decision to offer a lower rate on the fact that the individual had indicated *lack of enthusiasm* for the job, by saying that he wished, as soon as opportunity arose, to apply for a post in another part of the factory at what he considered to be a higher level. The shop committee were upheld on this, and on two other similar points which they made. They did not, however, win the original appeal, which was for a revision of the individual's rate to the customary level. The individual's rate was marginally adjusted by the judgement and instructions given that, unless within two months it was clear that he was working at a lower level than his colleagues, he was to get the customary rate offered in the department for those joining it at the close of serving an apprenticeship. This was primarily a case of people seeking to prevent what they regarded as a bad precedent being set up by a manager's decision.

We thus have three types of appeal against managerial decisions:

1. where it is contended that the manager's decision is wrong, because it is based on an incorrect interpretation of some existing policy, precedent, custom or agreement (wrong interpretation);
2. where it is contended that the manner in which a manager has used his discretion is unfair to the individual (unfair decision);
3. where the subject-matter is either an alleged wrong interpretation or unfair decision, but the appeal is made by a group rather than an individual (representatives' appeals). . . .

Responsibilities of a Manager When Hearing an Appeal

To base his judgement on the provisions and intentions of policy, whether or not these are in accord with his own views or those of his superiors or subordinates (H.2.1).

To adopt an encouraging and friendly attitude towards an appellant who might wish to take his case to a higher level (H.2.2).

To deal with appeals with the minimum possible delay (H.2.3).

To encourage the appellant to have present an officially elected representative as his adviser (H.2.4).

I have these provisos to add for further guidance of managers:

1. Open the appeal by making a statement about anything factual which you know of already, and by asking if, in the opinion of the parties to the appeal, your knowledge is accurate. If this is disputed make it clear that you will let your "facts" be argued.
2. Discover just what the grievance is by letting the appellant talk first.
3. Sometimes the appellant's statement is not clear. Proceed no further until the position has been clarified. I have sometimes failed to do this, with most unfortunate results and a great waste of time. In my experience, every appeal is against the decision of some manager. I am very nearly certain that no other type of appeal is possible. Unless, therefore, the managerial decision against which the appeal is made is clear, the manager hearing the appeal must "dig" for it. If it cannot be discovered, it will be found that the appeal is not an appeal, but a challenge to some existing policy or a dispute with a colleague, in which case it can be dismissed as an appeal, and steered into some other appropriate channel.
4. Insist that all concerned in the case talk to you, and not to each other. Their job is to convince *you* of their point of view. If you do this, you will prevent the development of wordy arguments that do not help you to come to a decision.
5. The integrity of the whole executive system is at stake in an appeal. Uphold its status and dignity in every possible way: e.g., avoid, as far as possible, all interruptions to the procedure; if an appellant or a lower manager casts a slur on, or challenges the integrity of the procedure, insist that such remarks are withdrawn before proceeding; if the appellant refuses, terminate the proceedings; if the defendant refuses, take disciplinary action after the proceedings.
6. Two appeals in my recollection have given rise, during the proceedings, to statements by the appellant that, if he did not succeed in his appeal, he proposed to seek the support of others afterwards, to raise the matter with his union or committee, etc. In other words, there was a threat of subsequent action, unless the verdict was in his favor. It is the responsibility of the responsible manager in any such situation to point out that under no circumstances can the appeal be proceeded with under duress, and to insist on an unqualified withdrawal of such remarks in a manner that will satisfy him that it has been made with sincerity. Failing that, he should dismiss the appeal immediately and report the matter to his superior manager.
7. In the law courts, people are allowed to make statements which outside the court would be actionable. It is quite otherwise in a factory.

In the light of this, the responsible manager must refrain from defamatory comment, and must prevent others present making damaging personal remarks about each other or, especially, about persons not present.

I do not wish to leave the impression that people frequently indulge in such comment at appeals. But sometimes in the heat of the moment, somebody may be approaching such comment, and it is important that the responsible manager should be quick to "nip it in the bud," or immediately insist on a withdrawal if it is in fact uttered.

8. There is a strong tendency at appeals to quote hearsay in support of statements: e.g., one of the parties will say: "Mr. Y, who was this man's manager a year ago, had cause to criticize his work extensively." The responsible manager must be careful not to accept such statements. They must be supported by the person alleged to have made them, if they are to be made use of.
9. The extent to which evidence from witnesses can be obtained is limited by the fact that it is an executive not a legal procedure. Unsupported statements of what can reasonably be assumed to be the facts should be accepted; if the other party agrees to them.
10. Both parties must be given time to state their case in their own way. But it is the duty of the responsible manager to limit expenditure of time by disallowing argument and comment on aspects of the matter which do not assist him to reach a decision.
11. Try and determine if there are any written standing orders or policy bearing on the matter, or policy arising out of established practice and custom, or precedents arising out of management's interpretation of policy, etc. If there is, the application of such policy to the appeal may immediately indicate the proper decision. If it does not, then the task of the responsible manager is to interpret what was the real intention of the policy in such a case. If a manager cannot decide the correct interpretation to place upon such existing policy or standing order, he must send the appeal to his immediate superior.
12. If there is clearly no existing policy on the matter, the manager should exercise the greatest care, remembering that he is making policy by his decision. If the policy he thus has to make covers more than his own extended command, then he must send the case to a higher managerial level.

Strategic Considerations in Planning

WILLIAM H. NEWMAN

Logistics deals largely with numerical matters—time, quantities, places, and the like. Subjective judgments regarding risks and values are also involved, to be sure, but hopefully the final plan will be quite specific, perhaps neatly expressed in a Gantt chart. Strategy, by contrast, deals primarily with the interactions of people. It is much more tenuous and responsive than logistics.

Strategy is used here to mean the adjustment of a plan to the anticipated reactions of those who will be affected by the plans. Many a plan will run into difficulty if attention is not given to the responses of competitors, customers, material suppliers, fellow executives, and others associated within the enterprise. Whom to advise first, whom to notify, how to say it, when and in what setting to act—these are what Henry Dennison calls "political" questions.

Although strategy has been recognized for centuries as a vital aspect of administration in business, government, and military operations, it has received little systematic attention except in connection with military operations. And the military meaning of strategy has serious limitations for our purposes because there are numerous strategies of cooperation where the idea of "my gain is your loss" has no place.

Many executives rely on intuition and habit in picking a strategy. But strategy is too important to be left entirely to unconscious choice. At a minimum the skillful executive should: (a) be aware of alternative strategies he might use (or be subjected to); (b) recognize key factors in choosing a particular strategy for a specific situation.

The strategies described below are not necessarily recommended, nor is any moral judgment intended. They may be good or bad, depending upon the situation and the purpose for which they are used, just like any other phase of administration. The list is in no sense complete. Nevertheless, it does suggest possibilities, and it also serves to show the nature and importance of strategy.

Strategies for Initiating Change

Mass Concentrated Offensive

When Marshall Field & Company decided to liquidate most of its $35,000,000 wholesale business, action was taken in all departments at once, inventories liquidated rapidly, and employees discharged promptly with liberal termination pay. The liquidation was costly, but was virtually completed within a year's time. Mr. McKinsey, chairman of the board, recognized that higher prices for some of the inventory might have been secured if it had been worked off over a period of two or three years, but he believed that these higher prices

From *Administrative Action: The Techniques of Organization and Management,* 2nd ed., © 1963, pp. 86–98. Reprinted by permission of Prentice-Hall, Inc., Englewood Cliffs, New Jersey.

would have been more than offset by the uncertainty and poor morale that would have been inevitable during that period, and by the delay in starting a positive program for the manufacturing activities that were to be retained. Other examples of this strategy include the major reorganization of both General Electric Company and IBM; in each instance, action was fast, uncompromising, and backed by vigorous support of the senior executives.

Fabianism—Avoid Decisive Engagement

This strategy, which recommends gradual rather than revolutionary changes, is in sharp contrast to the one just discussed. It was well illustrated by an executive who was brought into a company that manufactured several distinct lines of products and had been coasting along without many new ideas for well over a decade. The new man was slated to become general manager and might well have insisted that the heads of each of the product departments follow his ideas immediately. Instead, he took a newly created position called Sales Promotion Manager which provided him an opportunity to learn the business and to make suggestions to the experienced men for improvement within their departments. If his ideas were not immediately accepted, he did not try to force them through; he waited until they could be put into effect without a sharp clash with the "old guard." Progress on specific projects was slowed down as a result of this strategy, but internal dissension and lack of cooperation were avoided, and the services of men who had important product knowledge were retained.

Make a Quick Showing

When there is skepticism, though not necessarily opposition, to a change, a prompt and favorable showing on a minor problem may open the way for more extended study of a knotty problem. For instance, proponents of electronic computers often are able to justify an initial installation on the basis of economies in handling payroll or accounts receivable records. Then having demonstrated merit on such routine operations, they can gain acceptance of more elaborate programming tactics, which may take two years of preparatory work.

Industrial engineers, both consultant and company-employed, have long recognized this strategy: "First find some savings that will cover your salary (or fee), then go to work on the tough problems." In fact, Frederick W. Taylor probably would not have been permitted to continue his years of study on "the art of cutting metals" if he had not also developed patents and other changes which provided more immediate benefits.

Camel's Head in the Tent

Sometimes a small beginning can be made when a total program would be unacceptable. For example, when the central purchasing office at the New York headquarters of a shoe company made virtually all purchases for the company, the manager of a new southern plant asked for permission to buy miscellaneous supplies locally. The request was granted, to reduce paper work and to speed up procurement. This arrangement worked well, and a few months later, on the manager's request, repair parts for machinery were added to the items bought locally. The next year new equipment was being obtained for the plant, and the manager pointed out that since engineers at the plant knew most about what was needed and a local purchasing unit was already operating strongly, orders for the equipment could best be handled by his organization. This, too, was done.

At a later date when pressure was being put on the plant manager to lower his costs, he proposed that he be permitted to purchase his raw materials (except for a few items where quantity purchases were clearly advantageous). Reasons advanced for this change were that raw material inventory could be more closely tied to production schedules, responsibility for quality would rest in one place, contact between suppliers and the plants would be simplified, and the ability of the plant to purchase efficiently had been demonstrated. The request was granted—over the protest of the central purchasing office. Had the plant manager asked for the right to buy all his requirements in the first instance, he would undoubtedly have been turned down; whereas the step-by-step approach finally achieved the result.

Boring from Within

This strategy, perhaps best known in the operation of a Communist cell, may be used when some executive has an emotional antagonism toward a project or program. The production manager of one company, for instance, had no use for these "new-fangled personnel ideas." The personnel director, however, did borrow one of the outstanding young executives in the production department for a special project, and during the period when the young man was on loan thoroughly indoctrinated him and enthused him regarding modern personnel practice. Some time after the junior executive returned to his former job, a bad situation developed because a man clearly unqualified had been placed in a foreman position. The junior executive took the opportunity to suggest that they might study the foremen who were successful and those who were not in order to determine what to look for when a new man was to be appointed, and thus he began laying the basis for the use of personnel specifications.

At another time considerable argument arose regarding the rate of pay for the maintenance man in one division because he was receiving substantially less than the maintenance man in another division. This provided an opportunity for the junior executive to point out to several different members in the department that a job evaluation program might be helpful. By the end of two years the groundwork had been prepared for the beginning of a really sound personnel program.

These strategies, ranging from mass-concentrated-offensive to boring-from-within, are suggestive of approaches to get something done. Others of the same category might be the Trojan horse, Achilles' heel, sowing seed on fertile ground.

Joint-Action Strategies

Strength in Unity

Some executives make a practice of seeking allies to work with them in promoting a change. Thus, if a department head wishes to get salary increases for his employees, he will try to get other department heads to join with him in a general request for higher wages; or if a company wishes to oppose or support legislation pending in Congress, it will seek to get other members of the industry to join together so that their representation may be more effective. The rugged individualist, on the other hand, prefers to play a lone hand.

Unwilling Ally

Often an individual who is far from enthusiastic about some plan can be made an active ally by assigning him some important role in connection with its execution. Unless he wants to oppose the whole program, he then finds himself a member of the team promoting it. For example, when some consultants recommended basic changes in the organization of a company, a procedures' analyst within the company was asked to work out the detail and assist in the installation of the change. Although he was lukewarm to the basic proposals, he soon found that he was regarded by other employees as a major proponent and that the effectiveness of his work was going to be judged in a large measure by how well the changes worked out. The power-behind-the-throne strategy is sometimes associated with this unwilling-ally technique.

You Scratch My Back, I'll Scratch Yours

This strategy is well known in the form of *reciprocity* in purchasing and as *log-rolling* in legislative bodies. Actually, the reciprocal exchange of favors is a natural human relationship found in pioneer societies and in political alliances over the ages. Such coalitions usually involve commitments that restrict one's actions to some degree, as well as benefits. Obviously, the question always arises whether the benefits outweigh the restrictions. In reciprocal purchasing, for instance, if the quality, delivery, price, and service of several suppliers is equal, then buying from a firm that is also a good customer imposes no serious sacrifice; but if, say, inferior materials must be accepted, then the restriction imposed by reciprocity may be a great burden. Reciprocal alliances are likely to be stable when each part of the total arrangement is mutually advantageous. If a company or a person finds himself subjected to an onerous restriction, he is apt to press for a better bargain at every opportunity and be open to proposals for new coalitions with different members.

Defensive Strategies

Keep on Sawing Wood or *By Their Works Ye Shall Know Them*

This technique is used by an administrator who wishes to disregard criticism coming his direction. While dramatically illustrated by Galileo and Pasteur who persisted in their experiments despite the criticism of their associates, the technique has been used by countless other people who have faith in what they are doing and put their efforts into doing it well.

Red Herring Across the Trail

This strategy consists of a deliberate attempt to divert attention and confuse the issue. It is commonly used in politics; for example, the injection of the race question into discussions where it has no bearing. A salesman who, when being questioned about his expense account, tries to shift the conversation to the danger that competitors may steal a large account is following a similar tack. Here, again, the strategy is not often desirable for operations within an enterprise where it is usually better to lay the cards on the table and deal with issues frankly. However, at times, such as when evading the questions of a man who is being considered for a transfer, deliberately confusing the issue may be appropriate.

Counter-Invasion

This strategy is seen almost daily in competitive sales promotion. If one company offers a rose bush for a jar top and a five-cent stamp, its competitor is likely to respond by selling his peanut butter in a cocktail glass. Essentially the same thing happened in a company that was having difficulty getting its shipments made promptly and correctly. The manufacturing department, after emphasizing the difficulty, suggested that the shipping department be transferred to it from the sales department, thus giving the manufacturing department control over the physical handling of goods up to receipt by the customer. The sales department, agreeing fully as to the present confusion, countered with the request that warehousing be transferred from the manufacturing department to the sales department so that the sales department would have full control over all activities after the goods were in finished form.

Divide and Rule

This well-known political strategy has been applied in government situations ranging from city council control fights to England's balance of power in Europe. It has also been used within business enterprises, though usually with serious loss of teamwork and coordination. The chief engineer of one company, for example, hoping to strengthen his position by being the person with the balance of power among the senior executives, deliberately stirred up rivalry between the manufacturing and the sales departments. Obviously, if such a strategy were widely used within an enterprise, it could quickly injure cooperation.

Cautious Strategies

Passing the Buck

Rightly or wrongly, this technique of transferring blame to someone else is reported to be common practice among army officers. The alacrity with which the Army agreed that the War Production Board should handle the delicate matter of approving the locations and firms to be affected by cutbacks in military programs after World War II suggests that at least someone in that regime recognizes a disagreeable job when it comes along. As collective bargaining between the unions and the large corporations becomes an increasingly public issue, frequent attempts are made to maneuver the negotiations so that the public will believe that the other side is responsible for disagreement and strikes.

Let Someone Else Pull Your Chestnuts Out of the Fire

While at first glance this strategy suggests cowardice, occasionally its use is quite legitimate. For example, a sales manager may have strong suspicion that the difficulty in quality of a certain product is due to the faulty procedures in the manufacturing department. If he presses the matter with the production manager or the president, he may well be accused of interfering with the other man's affairs. However, if the company has an organization analysis or industrial engineering department, the sales manager may urge this division to look into the matter. In other words, at times a desirable action can be more appropriately taken by someone other than the individual who will benefit from the action.

Conserve Your Gunpowder

In applying incentives, general recognition is given to the wisdom of exercising no more motivation than necessary to accomplish a result and conserving the stronger pressures and tactics until the desired action can be secured only through their use. The same thing is true in other areas. Overselling may not only be wasteful, but it may make later promotions more difficult. The top executive of a company may be deliberately kept out of negotiations with labor unions or material suppliers until a critical point is reached; if he enters at that point, his presence will carry greater prestige and weight.

Negotiating Strategies

Haggling

In several Middle Eastern countries prices are normally set by haggling. The seller asks for more than he expects to get, and the buyer offers less than he expects to pay; then the dickering starts. In the United States, despite a one-price tradition, real estate, automobiles, and even household appliances are often sold in the same way. Some people enjoy the process of haggling; perhaps each party feels that he has made a good bargain when the deal is finally closed.

Haggling is widely practiced in many other kinds of negotiations. It is so traditional in union collective bargaining, for instance, that each party commonly thinks up extra "demands" so that he will have something to concede. While often very real differences of opinion have to be resolved before action can be taken, haggling does invite insincerity and prolonged negotiations.

Lay All Cards on the Table

This strategy is the opposite of haggling. It is based on a frank disclosure of strengths, needs, and what the company or individual is prepared to do. The General Electric Company, for example, has been trying to follow this strategy in its union negotiations, incidentally making its position widely known to all employees in advance of bargaining sessions. (The General Electric unions contend that the practice eliminates not only minor haggling but also opportunity to find creative solutions to genuine differences.)

Within companies, or whenever substantial agreement exists on objectives to be sought, the full disclosure strategy is more widely used than when negotiating parties have sharply different goals. Typical plans for supervisory counseling with subordinates, for instance, rest on the assumption that both boss and subordinate are prepared to be completely frank with each other *because* they share the same objectives. When these conditions do not hold, the counseling techniques tend to break down.

Surprise

A cardinal feature of military strategy is surprise—catching the enemy off-guard by an unexpected maneuver and by bluffing. If the battle analogy is valid, then surprise may be a good strategy in business. But most relationships within a company and between companies are quite the opposite of a battle. Instead, mutual dependence is essential, and this requires predictable behavior. Under these conditions a strategy of *stability and consistency*—not surprise—is needed. Negotiations about one problem lay a foundation for later negotiations on other problems. If a change in objective occurs, this is explained in advance so as to avoid surprise. As illustrations, consider the difference in the U.S.S.R. and the British approach to negotiating with the U.S.A.

Timing Strategies

Strike While the Iron is Hot

This strategy calls for prompt action while the situation is propitious. Thus, a manufacturer of products depending upon a style or fad, such as hula hoops or beehive wigs, must get his goods on the market before public fancy changes. To cite another example in quite a different area, one wise executive who was being promoted to a vice-presidency because of the inefficiency of his predecessor immediately asked for and got more clear-cut authority than probably would have been granted to him after the current difficulties had been corrected. Similarly, a company wishing to change its channel of distribution from wholesalers to direct sales to retailers made the change promptly when demand was on the upswing so there would be a minimum of sales loss during the transition.

Things Must Get Worse Before They Get Better

If the need for a change is not generally recognized, delay is sometimes wise even though the executive is convinced of the need for the action. A controller followed this strategy when he delayed institution of budgets even though he strongly believed they would benefit his company. Other executives disliked new controls, and they would have considered budgets merely as more nuisance with accounting. So the controller waited until the company got into a very tight squeeze with high expenses and low sales; then the idea of budgetary control was welcomed as a device for maintaining a balance between expenses and sales volume. Likewise, the sales manager of a nationally known hosiery company recognized the need of decentralizing to his district manager authority to change prices, but delayed making the change until the desirability of such a move was clearly recognized by the president and other executives of the firm.

Time is a Great Healer

Some actions may be wisely delayed until there is a cooling-off period. In fact, one executive observed after returning from his vacation that he was surprised how many of the things that had been sent to his desk had taken care of themselves apparently quite satisfactorily before he returned. Another executive reports that he postpones, if at all possible, important personnel action for at least a month. During that period it may develop that a man who was scheduled for discharge can be advantageously transferred to another position, or that a clash in personalities which appeared to call for reassignment of duties has been mitigated to the point where no change is necessary.

Keep One Jump Ahead

Attempts to follow this strategy are clearly apparent in the annual change in models of automobiles; for example, in the introduction of economy models, power brakes, air-conditioning, and various body designs. From time to time some of the large industrial companies have attempted to secure favor with their employees by taking the lead in granting wage increases, union-shop provisions, company-financed pensions, or other benefits.

Of course, attempting to lead the parade involves a risk because sometimes the would-be leader finds himself alone on Grand Avenue when the rest of the parade has turned up Broad Street. For example, in the scramble of oil refineries to control their crude oil supply in the years immediately following World War II, the companies that first advanced their buying price usually obtained an advantage while the other companies were making up their minds to follow suit. One autumn, however, a company seeking this advantage was jolted when other companies did not follow it; the supply situation had adjusted itself, so instead of having an advantage, the company found that it was paying well above the market price for its principal raw material.

Selecting a Strategy

The variety of possible strategies an administrator might adopt has been indicated, though by no means completely, in the illustrations given in the preceding pages. Clearly, no single strategy is always the right one to follow. Instead, an administrator should choose one, or some combination, that is well suited to the immediate situation. This choice can be made intuitively, but usually strategy is too important to the success of a plan to be left to hunch. How, then, does an executive select an appropriate strategy?

Timing is one of the most important elements in strategy. It is a factor not only in situations such as those just illustrated, but also in several of the examples to be discussed under other headings.

No magic formula or moral code dictates the choice of strategy. We can, however, identify factors that are often important in making a wise choice. The following list is at least suggestive. Not all these factors in this list will be significant in any specific situation, and others may have to be added. But conscious review of these considerations will stimulate the kind of thinking an administrator should do about the strategies he selects.

Nature of Objectives

Urgency. The need for prompt results often precludes the use of, say, a Fabian or camel's-head-in-the-tent strategy, and suggests mass-concentrated-offensive. Contrariwise, when immediate results are not so vital, an executive may decide to let-someone-else-pull-his-chestnuts-out-of-the-fire.

Agreement on Objectives. When the persons affected by a proposed plan agree on desired results, it is feasible to lay-all-cards-on-the-table; any differences of opinion arise from judgment regarding probable results of the proposed action. Quite another situation exists when the persons affected want different results. Then boring-from-within to change objectives, or some strategy that focuses on the particular action, such as haggling or you-scratch-my-back-and-I'll-scratch-yours, is more appropriate.

Desire for Continuing Cooperation. In most business relationships we expect to deal with the same people over and over again. Consequently, today's strategy becomes part of tomorrow's experience. Thus, counter-invasion or passing the buck may haunt us, whereas stability and consistency may facilitate the subsequent actions. Clearly, the time span that needs to be considered affects the choice of strategy.

Present Situation

Resources Available. A firm with a relatively strong reserve of manpower and capital can give serious attention to a mass-concentrated-offensive, whereas a weaker firm may find strategies such as in-union-there-is-strength or conserve-your-gunpowder more suitable. Even the strong firm—or individual—may not wish to engage in a counter-invasion or to try to keep-one-step-ahead if it is committed to other, more attractive use of its resources.

Temperament of Executives. Any executive can carry out better a strategy suited to his temperament. Some men, for example, are short on patience and find a Fabian or things-must-get-worse-before-they-get-better strategy hard to live with. Other executives are impressed with facts and try to be entirely logical in their conscious behavior; for them haggling and red-herring-across-the-trail are difficult strategies. Of course, each of us does many things that do not exactly fit our temperament, but the chances of success are better if the action comes naturally.

Accepted Mores. The acceptance of the resentment to a particular strategy depends partly upon the prevailing mores of the company, industry, and country where it is used. As already noted, haggling is expected in some situations and frowned upon in others. Marked differences will also be found in responses to divide-and-rule, passing-the-buck, and many other strategies. Typically, an executive should operate within the accepted mores; at least any decision to break with tradition should be a conscious choice.

Chances of Success

Future Environment. An administrator's prediction of future conditions may indicate that a plan will become easier—or more difficult—to put into effect as time passes. This prediction affects strategy. When events are running in our favor, we may adopt such strategies as time-is-a-great-healer or keep-on-sawing-wood. But when we face a now-or-never situation, strike-while-the-iron-is-hot or mass-concentrated-offensive are more appropriate.

Expected Responses. The administrator must also predict how specific people will respond to a given strategy. All the factors in this list can be considered from the viewpoint of each key person affected by a contemplated action, and then *his* counter-strategy predicted. His objectives, his present situation, his expectations, and his costs will all bear on the way he is likely to respond. Such an analysis may indicate that strategy *A* will have clear sailing, whereas strategy *B* will foment considerable resistance. Or, the analysis may indicate that all strategies will encounter some resistance by at least some people; in this case, the chances of overcoming the resistances have to be compared.

Costs

Disruption. Strategies vary in the amount of disruption they cause to established routines of the company, to informal social relationships, and to personal habits and self-concepts. Perhaps industry and other external behavior may be upset. Some disruption is inevitable, but generally one is wise to keep disruption low.

Incentives dissipated. Some strategies may call for large expenditures of energy, out-of-pocket expenses, or even loyalty and good-will. These are scarce resources useful for many purposes. So one consideration in selecting a particular strategy is dissipating incentives only to the degree necessary to achieve the desired result.

Blocking Other Strategies. A particular course of action may require such a commitment of resources or create so much antagonism that it leaves no good alternatives and no easy retreat. Since outcomes are never certain, such a blocking of alternatives creates a risk—or cost. For example, to keep-on-sawing-wood normally leaves more alternatives open than does counter-invasion; a Fabian approach retains greater flexibility than a mass-concentrated-offensive. The more aggressive strategy may be justified for other reasons, but in the total balance should be weighed the sacrificing of opportunity to resort to alternative strategies.

Side Effects. Sometimes a strategy will achieve its main objective but have undesirable side effects. For example, a textile company—acting with surprise and at a propitious moment—closed down its New England mill over the protests of both workers and community. The immediate object was accomplished, but part of the cost was union trouble in other plants and reluctance of several financial institutions to extend long-term credit because of the way the action was taken.

Most of the considerations in choosing a strategy in the preceding list cannot be measured accurately; subjective judgment is the main source of data. Nevertheless, analytical, perceptive thinking about the suitability of alternative strategies can pay high dividends in results achieved.

Questions for Discussion

1. The following quotation is taken from a case history involving the Harrogate Asphalt Products Company, located in Yorkshire, England. This company is a subsidiary of British Commercial Investments, Ltd., a large conglomerate holding company in London. In the case, Mr. Horace V. Lampton, Managing Director (President) of BCI Ltd., describes his philosophy (beliefs, attitudes, principles) for managing subsidiary companies. Drawing upon the discussion of executive motivation in Chapter 9, analyze and explain the reasons behind Mr. Lampton's philosophy.

   Mr. Lampton says:

> We have been trying recently to add services to our subsidiary companies. In today's world, a subsidiary cannot expand and remain a healthy company, to its full potential, without some help from central services provided by BCI and BCI Industries' central staffs. For many years the BCI banking subsidiary management has provided a ready service on financial matters. Until very recently, however, we have been diffident in making other central services available to give specialized advice in particular fields. Recently, the success of our operations research group, the welcome accorded to our chief economist, and the demand for the services of our BCI marketing advisor, all attest to such a need on the part of subsidiary managers. Only in the last three weeks, Mr. J. F. Roberts has joined our staff as computer adviser and has begun to familiarize himself with existing EDP installations and projects. We have been too slow in recognizing the part which EDP techniques will play in the future. We hope to provide companies, individually too small to justify their own EDP units, with access to facilities, and to reduce costs for all by organizing a coordinated network available on a BCI-wide basis.
>
> Finally, I would like to say something about the services rendered to subsidiary operating companies by the BCI Industries director. We like to think that the personalities, experience, and sometimes wider contacts which our directors have, are an important source of help to managements of BCI subsidiary companies.

In an interview with Mr. E. M. Jackson, another official of BCI Investments, the casewriter was told that

> BCI Industries maintains a director (non-executive) on the board of each of its subsidiaries, usually as Chairman. Although non-executive, the BCI nominee usually visits each of his three or four subsidiaries perhaps about once a week, or twice every three weeks. The BCI nominee typically has had considerable industrial experience and educational experience, as an engineer, management consultant, executive of Aluminum Ltd., or other managerial position. Many of them have university education, or have attended advanced management programs such as the Administrative Staff

College at Henley, Harvard Business School, Stanford Business School, or IMEDE in Lausanne.

Mr. Lampton continued:

The position of a BCI Industries director involves a rather heavy responsibility. We are not bankers, interested only in the financial aspects of the business. We are not there to take a normal dividend and let it go at that. In some financial holding companies, the local managements have the idea that they are entirely self sufficient, except for dividends. At the same time, the directors in those companies create the impression that they are banker types—somewhat superior to getting into real operating problems. I personally believe that, in some such holding companies, the subsidiary directors are being supine—they sit there with talent which could add to operations, but which they abdicate from using. Specifically, I am certain that in this day of complex technology and society, the director has a moral responsibility to help his managers—to encourage them to do planning for the future, to aid them in selecting and staffing their operations, and to give evidence in areas where the director has talent or knowledge.

2. In Chapter 9, it is postulated that one of the characteristics of executive personality is the desire for creative, innovative action—the desire to change things. At the same time, we explain certain "blocks" to such action. That is, when a person has such motivation, and tries to act it out, there are certain blocks to his doing so. From your own experience, describe a situation you have faced at some time in your life, explaining your urge to innovative action. Were you successful, or not? Why?

3. Explain Henri Fayol's concept of "discipline." Do you agree or disagree with this concept? Why?

4. What is the nature of the "staff" function in an organization? Under what conditions does functional authority for staff men seem wise?

5. Why *can* an executive in a sub-unitary organization delegate more activities to a subordinate than in a functional organization? Why *must* there be centralization of decision-making in a functional organization? Why *might* there be centralization of power and authority in a sub-unitary organization. [Note: if time permits, illustrate your answer from (1) a small organization such as the printing operation described in Chapter 9, and/or (2) a large organization.]

6. What effects, pro and con, might the "desire to be head of an organization" have on company efficiency? On the executive himself?

Chapter Ten

Managing and Changing Organizations by Modifying Structure

With his two faces, Janus, the Roman god of beginnings and endings, looked backwards and forwards. Similarly, because a manager stands at the interface between internal and external worlds, he must look inward to his organization and outward to his environment. One of his most difficult responsibilities is to mediate between the demands of organization and environment—which means internal adaptation and goal modification in response to changed external conditions.

In this chapter, we shall continue the discussion of how managers attempt to change organization behavior—but with different emphasis. At various points in this volume we have looked at the organization as a system relating sentiments (or attitudes), action (or job duties), and interactions (or communications). Because these factors are mutually dependent, to change organizational behavior the manager should be able to operate through any one of them. In Chapter 8, we described managerial efforts to change behavior and communication by direct influence; in Chapter 9, we described efforts to effect such change through authority and strategy. In this chapter, we shall discuss organizational change resulting from modification of structure—changes in authority assignments, job duties, formal communication flow, and physical conditions. Four topics will be considered: (1) the traditional view of the manager's role in organizational change, (2) a behavioral view of organizational change, (3) the manager's role in maintaining equilibrium, and (4) modifying structure to change behavior.

Organizational Change: The Traditional View of the Manager's Role

Traditional management theory has emphasized the rational decision-making functions of the manager. As an organization develops special functions for its various units and positions, the formulation of plans and decisions becomes a function lodged in positions whose occupants have these specialized roles; such persons are called managers. Since changes are continually taking place both inside the organization and outside in the environment, traditional thinking emphasizes control and adaptation to ensure continuity and necessary adjustments. In this outward-looking approach, the job of the manager is to achieve the common objectives (external) with the resources available (internal).

Just as traditional theory has recognized a unique role for the manager on the interface between internal and external, so has it recognized a need for management to be a change agent in adapting the internal situation to external pressures—or thrusting the whole organization on the environment in a different way. Management spokesmen in the traditional vein have seen this process of adjustment and change as essentially a rational process, vital to continued life for the organization. "The swiftness and ingenuity of adaptation to new or changed forces," wrote Mary Niles [7], "has much to do with the continuance or success of the enterprise. This applies not only to major adjustments, but also to ordinary viscissitudes. . . . The capacity for vital and successful adjustment and sound growth of the organization demands organs for observation, research, planning, control and decision making" (pp. 21–22). These decision-making functions fall on the executive whose job it is to assess the outside world, look at his internal organization, and decide what must be done about internal organization and management goals. Any organizational activity may proceed unchanged until something in the internal or external environment requires adaptation by an action or withholding of action. The decision for adaptation takes place at a specific location in time and space. Making plans and executive decisions, in this view, is the unique function of managers.

In addition, there are apparently continuous forces which make change a vital necessity. "The top executives of any large company," wrote Edmund Learned [5], "are under continued pressure to get things done. The feeling seems to be universal that a competitive business can never stand still; it either gets better or starts to slide back. Since security depends on success, the only way one can achieve security is to keep moving" (p. 46).

A further assumption of the traditional approach is that all information about the relationship between the organization and the external world flows through the top managers. It is one of their functions to feed this information into the firm. Of course, the manager can delegate actual duties to subordinates, but the top manager is "a man who can catch, collect, and check the pressures from above, and tone them down enough so that subordinates can take them without shock and act on them effectively [5, p. 94]." This hierarchical organization, with its monistic influence and man-to-man responsibility, assumes that the top man is the only one responsive to the outside environment. Everyone below is responsive to him. "The chief executive seeks to visualize the entire function of the company, past, present and future, in relation to factors outside the company, in such a way that he can detect the existence of new areas that will need attention [5, p. 203]." Figure 10-1 illustrates this traditional view of organizational change.

Figure 10-1. Traditional View of Organizational Change.

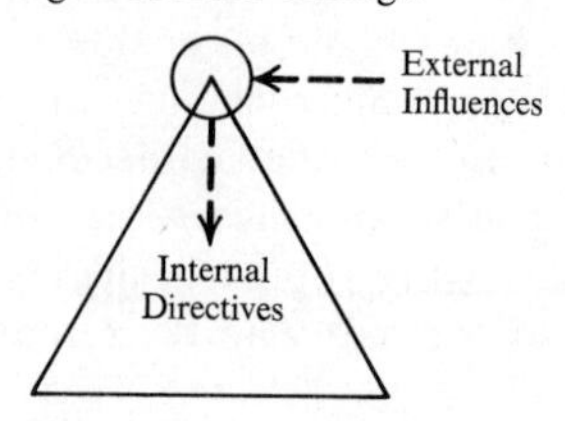

Organizational Change: A Behavioral View of the Manager's Role

Technology is blurring the simple distinction between internal and external just described—and the top executive's role is more ambiguous. Where does an organization confront the outside world? Only at the top supervisory level? Or also at the level of people who actually deal with outsiders? If the structure of an organization should be derived from its relation to environment, should design proceed from the top down or the bottom up? Who really stands at the interface?

As his business expanded and as knowledge and techniques accumulated, the early owner-manager found he could not perform his functions well enough to meet competition, even operating at the peak of his capacity. New business functions and specialties, which seem to be subdivisions of the original owner-manager function, appeared. These new functions did not represent only a parceling out of the activities performed by the former manager; they included new activities developed from a growing body of knowledge and techniques [6]. "More and more," as Victor Thompson [10] observes, "the intellectual or decision-making functions of the organization are shifted to these new specialists, reducing the manager's function more and more to the pure exercise of authority" (p. 85). The boss is still supposed to make decisions, but he has less and less ability to do so because of the advance of science and technology.

In short, power and the ability to mediate between external and internal worlds are no longer so conveniently concentrated in decision-making executive positions. As we saw in Chapter 6, there is a growing dichotomy between knowledge and authority. Knowledge increasingly gravitates to technical and professional specialists; authority remains where it has always been in the old hierarchy. The function of redefining goals and internal structure is therefore fragmented. Thompson continues:

> The right to approve new organization goals, as well as programs, is a superordinate right. However, what new goals an organization is able to undertake is a technical or specialist question, as is the question of whether specific alternatives will achieve certain goals. . . . One suspects that redefinition of organization goals is non-hierarchical; that it is generated internally, or that it results from severe external pressures on various power structures. . . . It is theoretically incorrect to say that the function of the executive is to set the goals or determine the ends of the organization. It is correct to say that he has the right to do so as part of his superordinate role (p. 85).

In traditional theory, the top man is at the center of information flow; he responds to external forces and adjusts internal processes. Actually, most information flow bypasses top management; specialized subordinates respond directly to outside forces. This has implications for organizational control. The ultimate measurement of internal activities by their impact on external environment (or vice versa) provides the rationale and philosophy for management control. Historically, budgets and control systems have rested on a view of information as flowing through the hierarchical levels in a planned manner. As Chris Argyris [1] points out, budgets and control systems assume that external forces impinge at the top and are delegated or parceled downward, and that if plans are met and control maintained, the organization will function as desired.

In fact, external forces may bypass the top; when this happens, subordinate groups are hampered and may surreptitiously circumvent the control system.

Because external pressures actually enter through multiple channels, change therefore occurs at multiple points in the organization. It is not an easy job for the manager to maintain control over this complex process. Obviously, it is not as simple as earlier assumptions about the primacy of the chief executive suggested. A more realistic view of management analyzes the manager's structuring of technology, groups, interaction flows, bargaining, and functions so that appropriate change decisions are made within the organization—not solely by the man at the top. Functional analysis may be helpful. In Part I of this volume we saw that functional analysis views all organizational factors as a systemic whole with mutually dependent elements. The main emphasis is on the totality or unity of organization and its internal and external goals. A central concern is the relationship between the "inside" and "outside" of any organism—between internal *process* and external environment.

Functional analysis looks at an organization of people as though it were a living organism, characterized by the interrelated cyclical functions of maintenance and development. Underlying these characteristics is the general direction of its activity—that is, all activity of a living organization is related to certain objectives. From this perspective, Argyris [2] has defined an organization as

> (1) a multitude of parts, (2) maintaining themselves through their interrelatedness, (3) achieving specific objectives, (4) while accomplishing (2) and (3), adapting to the external environment, thereby (5) maintaining the interrelated state of the parts (pp. 29–30).

Analysis must deal with the process of the parts and the whole adapting to an external environment, thereby maintaining the interrelated state of the parts. There must be a tolerance for balance within each part and among the parts that constitute the whole—that is, among the individuals or the groups within the organization. Research has been directed towards finding the tolerance for balance within each, and among, the parts, and the actual behavioral mechanisms that perform and maintain the tolerance within the whole. Thus, functional analysis is concerned with three major problems: (1) How does the organization maintain itself? How does it encourage contribution from the various parts so that they remain a part of the functioning whole? (2) How does the total organization accomplish its objectives in relation to the external environment? (3) How does the organization modify itself internally in order to respond to environmental changes?

Now we have certainly come to the major problems of any manager. He must mediate between the internal maintenance of the organization and the achievement of external goals. He is the person most concerned with structuring the system of rewards and motivations that attract people to the organization, and he is heavily involved in the interactions and the bargaining activities within that organization. Perhaps even more important, he is intimately concerned with the bargains and interactions that take place between the organization and various consumers, customers, competitors, government and union officials, etc., who form the rest of the world to the firm. Figure 10-2 illustrates this behavioral view of the manager's role in organizational change.

Figure 10-2. Behavioral View of Organizational Change.

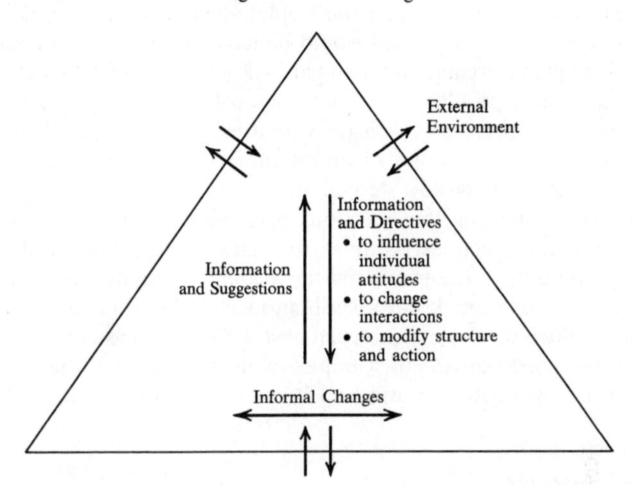

Absorbing and Preventing Stress: The Maintenance of Equilibrium

Our discussion of functional analysis indicates that a manager is concerned with the maintenance of internal equilibrium as well as change. Indeed, the two are intimately related. In our consideration of hierarchy and formal organization in Chapter 4, we described how relative stability, repetition, predictability, and conformity are essential. More effective change results when management limits extraneous factors upsetting organizational equilibrium; management's modification of structure, duties, or authority will then have greater impact. Therefore, before discussing change, let us see how management can control the individual and organizational stress described in Chapter 6.

We have seen that stress is manifested by erratic interactional patterns, in which people become overly aggressive or avoid one another unduly, and which can spread throughout the organization. In addition, we have seen that many of these disturbances spring from the structural aspects of the organization. It is a function of the manager to design and adjust the work relations of individuals so that these disturbances do not interfere with effective performance.

To control such stress, the manager must break into the cycle of cause, effect, and proliferation. There are three ways by which he may be able to do this: personnel transfer; appropriate personal behavior; or modifying organizational structure.

Personnel Transfers

When confronted with organizational problems, managers commonly ascribe them to the personal limitations of supervisors. F. L. W. Richardson [9] reports a managerial tendency to deal with production problems by replacing supervisors: "Of the twelve changes introduced by upper plant management during the ten-month period, eight were attempts to deal with situations diagnosed largely as problems of supervision. Of these eight, seven involved changes in supervisory personnel" (p. 10). To take another example: In a small steel mill the work and work process were modified. Interaction patterns were upset, stress resulted, and productivity suffered. The general manager was infuriated by the lag in output and by the fact that the welders had refused to work overtime for a few weeks, even though they would be handsomely paid. "Replace them all," he told the plant foreman. But to regard all problems as personnel problems is too limited—many problems are simply not solved by "getting a new man." Furthermore, personnel shifts may aggravate stress. We have seen that too many transfers are both an indication of and a cause of stress. Personnel transfers cannot correct faulty work-flow design.

There is no question that judicious personnel selection and transfer are essential managerial functions. At times, the manager may successfully alleviate stressful conditions by shifting and replacing people. Primarily, however, he must redesign organizational work flow. Resilient mechanisms and routines must be developed by which the organization can absorb the compensatory interactional patterns of disturbed individuals. Coupled with this, however, he must take a hard look at his own behavior and how it can be used or modified to alleviate stress.

Managerial Behavior

A former Communications Officer on the U.S.S. "Star" illustrates personal behavior as a means of alleviating and preventing the spread of stress:

> I could tell when the Operations Officer was upset simply by the [stressful] behavior of my own men. . . . I also discovered, however, that if I were the first one he came in contact with after he became upset, he could regain his equilibrium by just talking with me. I usually could make time to sit and listen to him while he cussed, complained, and told me his side of the story. . . . After realizing I was an efficient buffer, I tried to make it a point to be the first one to encounter him after one of his go-rounds with the Executive Officer. In this way, I found I could aid in maintaining the equilibrium of the whole department.

After a frustrating experience, the availability of a colleague to whom one can express pent-up feelings may facilitate a quick readjustment to stress.

Under the demands of stress situations, managers often reduce their contacts with others. This may be because they want to avoid the problem entirely or because they are concentrating on the problem area exclusively. In either case, stress is propagated. As much as possible, a manager should maintain his various communication links. Otherwise, reactivation will be difficult when the stress has passed.

Just as the manager must keep contacts in various directions, he should encourage communication laterally among his subordinates and upward to him. Richardson [9] reports that poor managers are characterized by either very high or very low interaction levels relative to the usual level for that particular position and organization. In addition, poorer supervisors have far less diagonal and upward initiations than more effective supervisors. Research among fifty managers in all kinds of positions [11] indicates only one significant difference in behavior between effective and ineffective managers—effective managers spend more time responding to their subordinates and associates. They are more readily available and receive more contact.

It is clear that the effective manager keeps lines of communication working in many directions. He tries to be consistent and stable in his behavior—especially under stress. Only in this way can the spread of trouble be blocked. Such a manager is described with admiration by a former garment factory employe:

> I enjoyed working there, although I worked very hard. Arthur (the manager) was responsible for my pleasant work experience because he treated me fairly. Evidently, this policy has paid off for him because he has been able to maintain productivity at a high level.
>
> The man obviously had certain leadership qualities because his attitude and manner made you want to work harder. He encouraged everyone to make more money, treated everyone like a human being, and never browbeat an employee. I spoke to him long and often, and I came to the conclusion that he knew precisely what he was doing and why. But his secret always eluded me: how, as he was in the midst of fixing a garment and two girls screamed at him that their machines were jammed, while Ricco complained that he was not getting enough work, and Joe told him that his wife was on the phone in the office, while the machines were roaring, the weather 90 degrees in the shade, and the girls chattering away, *how* in all this, he could remain calm, patient, and composed, I was never able to understand. But whatever his secret, it was this that enabled him to make [it] a successful operation.

Organizational Structure

Morale depends upon the successful adjustment of human beings to one another within the framework of the technical processes in which they have to work. If individuals are to contribute maximum effort, the organization must be constructed so that the kinds of situations that emotionally disturb people are rare.

We have seen that every organization consists of interacting individuals, each of whom attempts to achieve and maintain a state of equilibrium. An important part of the manager's job is to plan and modify structure and work flow in order to minimize the stress-causing patterns that hinder effective performance. That is, if cumulative stress effects are to be avoided, organizational work flow must not involve stressful patterns, and in addition, the effects of disturbances must be "damped out" as they spread from their original sources. Therefore, if an organization is to operate satisfactorily, provision must be made to safeguard against the accumulation of disturbances in the routine relations of individuals.

For example, certain groups may perform buffer roles similar to the individuals described in the preceding section. In one company, a technical staff of product engineers serves as a buffer between field sales and production. All communications are funneled through this product group. Therefore, upsets in production areas are minimized, and sales has technical liaison which responds to their initiation. The flow is essentially uni-directional from sales, which could be stressful to the buffer group. However, these product engineers are specialists with high status and luxurious offices. In addition, their advice is essential to the sales people. Finally, the product men have discretion over the content and time dimension of their replies—consequently, relations between sales and product engineers are good.

The manager must see to it that his subordinate supervisors occupy a position in the work flow where they can play dual roles in representing their subordinates upwards and their superior downwards. Formal assignment of this function is not sufficient. A former laborer on a road repair crew reports that the foreman, because he had to travel about, was separated from his men and thus found it impossible to actually represent them. The truck driver, because of his presence and control over certain rewards (i.e., coffee breaks, rest periods, transportation) was the informal leader, and the only one who could perform the dual role of upward and downward representation. The leader must have an opportunity to stick up for his men, preferably in their presence, to their common superior.

Once the work flow is structured, management must maintain its rhythm. On a simple level, this is expressed by our former road repair laborer:

> The driver's job was to coordinate the pilers and shovelers to finish work just before lunch and quitting time so a car wouldn't hit the piles. We couldn't leave the piles and we didn't want to work overtime without pay. He also directed traffic around the truck while we were loading.
>
> There was mutual dependence between pilers and shovelers. Depending on the particular job, the pilers could make more work than the shovelers could handle, or the shovelers could keep steady pressure on the pilers. The driver could interfere when their work got out of synchronization—the optimum rhythm for both groups. The natural dominance of the truck driver arose automatically out of the situation; it was not delegated to him by the foreman. The continuance of a smooth work flow aided in maintaining the men's satisfaction and the performance.

In other words, from time to time, a man outside the direct work flow must restore an equilibrium or rhythm which has become upset. This man is a manager.

Any organization involves the simultaneous coordination of people who must pass paper, materials, or ideas among themselves in some controlled sequence: giving orders, soliciting suggestions, responding to technological breakdowns, planning, etc. All of these activities and functions must be carried out through interactions with others. Thus, organizational structure is most fundamentally a design of human relationships and patterns of interaction.

We have seen that certain patterns are experienced as distressing—such as uni-directional, unpredictable, and intermittent or inadequate interactions. In responding to such unsettling conditions, participants demonstrate their stress by disturbed or erratic behavior, including changes in the volume, direction, and content of their interactions. In turn, these disturbed interactions upset other people and propagate the structure-based stress throughout the organization. Thus we see that the most basic functions of the manager include designing, maintaining, and stabilizing interrelated work loads so as to prevent organizational stress where possible and absorb it where necessary.

In order to minimize the adverse impact of stress on organizational effectiveness, managers must design and modify organizational structure to prevent upsetting work patterns. Chapple and Sayles describe an approach to organizational structure intended to limit such stress, in a selected reading following this chapter.

Modifying Structure to Change Organizational Behavior

We have defined the function of the manager: to initiate, facilitate, control, and mediate change. The process of change is effectively described by interaction theory. As an example, a participant[1] in a food store reorganization describes the interrelationship of attitudes, interactions, and actions that take place in the change process:

Case 1: Organizational Change in a Food Market

In 1960, the management of the Franklin Food Company realized that demand for food products was increasing in their area. Expansion of existing facilities and a wider diversity of products was necessary if this demand were to be met and the market position of the firm maintained. As a result the company began to expand, and constructed warehouses and retail store facilities.

One of the retail outlets affected by this expansion plan was located in the medium-sized town of Towbridge, New York. Having served the community for more than 27 years, it was still the kind of store where clerks waited on each individual customer. The location was above average in sales potential, and customers were on friendly terms with the employes of the store.

In addition to the store manager, there were three clerks working in the grocery department, one clerk in the produce department, and three butchers. All the employes were unusually friendly with one another and they often stopped to chat or joke with each other. Mr. Russell, the store manager, was a very efficient and cordial person. He insisted on certain work standards, but seldom interfered with his subordinates. All the employes, including Mr. Russell, had been working for the company for at least ten years. Consequently, it was understood and evident that each man knew his particular job.

The congenial relations which existed among the employes may be exemplified further. Certain informal expectations existed. Wilson, Grieves and Mannion—the grocery clerks—were equally capable workers. When they had nothing to do, they often helped the meat department fill orders, or unload deliveries. Coombs, the produce clerk, generally had enough to keep him busy, and when he couldn't handle all the work, Mannion gave him a hand. Besides helping each other with their jobs, various other arrangements existed. Vacations were mutually scheduled so that no more than one employe was absent at a time; a fund had been established to help any employe who suffered loss from sickness; all belonged to the same club, and five played on the same bowling team.

This was the situation in 1961 when the division manager came to the Towbridge store to acquaint Mr. Russell with the plan for Franklin expansion. He stated that the company directors had decided to open a new supermarket in Towbridge to replace the old store because of the increase in sales in the area. Mr. Russell was told that the new store would be ready within eight months and that all employes, except himself, would become part of the staff of the new store. Mr. Russell was to report to the main office in New York City as part of the division staff. The employes received the news optimistically, realiz-

[1] T. O'Keefe, at one time a student in the Graduate School of Business, Columbia University. We are indebted to him for this case, the description, analysis, and writing of which are mostly his.

ing the advantages of the new store and feeling that their experience and seniority would provide them with opportunity for better jobs.

Eight months later, the new Franklin Food Market was completed, and the seven employes of the old store reported to the supermarket for their assignments. Mannion, Wilson and Grieves were assigned as grocery clerks, with no pay raise; Reynolds, the meat manager in the old store, was made assistant meat manager in the new store at $12 per week more; the two other butchers from the old store were given meat-cutting jobs with no raise; Coombs, the produce clerk, was transferred to the dairy department with no raise.

During the next few months the old employes found that routines in the new supermarket were quite different from the old. Within a short time they found that work assignments were received from the various department managers at the beginning of each day, and there was little time for fraternizing. In addition, they found that the new store manager, Mr. Tierney, had little to do with employes directly. Once, when Wilson asked for a day off, he was told by Mr. Tierney to "request such privileges through the proper channels."

The butchers from the old store had even greater problems. Reynolds, the assistant meat manager, had 23 years of experience with the company but reported to a meat manager with only nine years of experience. The latter, a Mr. John Myers, placed most of the work load on Reynolds and gave him great freedom in running the department. However, when supervisors were present, Myers became very bossy and took most of the credit for the meat department's good showing. Of course, Reynolds resented this.

Even worse, the other two butchers found that they now had to cater to a group of women who packaged the meat as it was cut, and distributed it to self-service freezer boxes. Often the girls blamed the butcher for any shortage in supply, even if he had nothing to do with the situation. The girls used abusive language. Sometimes they shouted at the butchers when a customer was in the "meat box," talking with one of the butchers who used to serve her at the old store.

As time passed, tremendous pressure was put on all employes because the ratio of sales to labor was declining. Contact between employes was almost nonexistent. When Wilson, Grieves, and Mannion learned that two better jobs in the store had been filled by new employes, they all quit. Within two months after this, Reynolds asked for a transfer, and the other two butchers quit.

When the report of the resignations reached the division office, an investigation was ordered. Each employe was contacted to determine why he had left after so many years. This is what some of them had to say:

> *Coombs:* "When I went to work in the new store, I felt as if I was working for a different company. They gave me my old job and did not even consider that I had 18 years with the company."
>
> *Reynolds:* "This company doesn't think a hell of a lot of me when they pay me as an assistant manager and know damn well that I'll be doing the work of a manager anyway."
>
> *Wilson:* "I've been working for Franklin for 21 years and enjoyed every minute of it until I came to the new store. When you can't even talk to a fellow worker without getting bawled out, it's time to punch out."

Mannion: "I wasn't a person in the new store anymore. I was a machine. It was getting so that I would go home and take it out on my wife."

After the investigation, the Franklin board of directors decided to initiate a plan for the transfer and promotion of its employes. However, in this case it is certain that harm had already been done and that a loss had been suffered by the company.

The foregoing case illustrates some unfortunate effects of change, but they are not inevitable. More important, implicit in this narrative is a hypothesis about the relationship between organizational variables and sequence in a change process:

Changes in Organizational Environment. The organizational environment includes persons, technology, policies, and procedures. In the Franklin Food Company the most immediate change was in the technology and management structure of the new store. In addition, the manager and several department heads were changed.

Changes in Interaction Flow. Because of the change in structure and technology, interaction flow—who contacts whom, how often, and why—was modified drastically for the veterans of the old store. In terms of interpersonal relations, the new store was a new job. The statements of Wilson and Mannion comment on the decreased interactions with fellow employes and the public.

Changes in Sentiments. The new interaction patterns modified sentiments or attitudes toward the job and toward people in the organization. Wilson liked everything until the change.

Changes in Organizational Effectiveness. Production and productivity suffered. Substantial time and effort were needed to correct the situation.

In this case, Franklin initiated an investigation and issued modified policies, all at some cost to the company, to say nothing of the loss in alienated customers. Arthur Kover describes similar effects of change in a selected reading following this chapter.

Thus we see a movement from technical and personnel changes to activity and interactional changes to changed sentiments, resulting in further unplanned activity and interactional changes—and expenses. An externally imposed technological and organizational change becomes primarily a change in human interactions, which in turn affect and are affected by feelings and actions. Technological change is not new hardware; it consists of new behavior in a social system. A selected article by Leonard Sayles following this chapter, accompanied by a discussion of it, analyzes the intimate relationships among structure, behavior, and attitudes in the change process.

Case 2: Organizational Change in a Retail Chain

An example of structural modification to change behavior is provided by the case of a large department store chain. Historically, there had been substantial centralization of control in an area supervisor who had three to four stores under his jurisdiction. The store managers were relatively weak, with control exercised directly over the department managers by the area supervisor. Since his stores were located in a limited territory, the area manager could exercise fairly close supervision over 15 to 20 subordinates. Most purchasing decisions, however, were even more centralized in a regional purchasing office, and since purchasing is so critical in the retail business, many long-term product decisions were actually made at corporate headquarters.

As the company expanded in the boom period after World War II, corporate management became concerned about inadequate flexibility and initiative at the local store level. They were afraid that the local stores were not sensitive to taste and product opportunities—giving independent competitors an advantage. Even if the local department managers had ideas for creative merchandising, corporate managers feared that the area supervisor, more separated from the local situation, might resist.

In order to promote local autonomy and flexibility, corporate management might have tried to exhort the personnel involved to change their behavior—the area supervisors to exercise less close control and the local managers to exercise initiative. In fact, this was done, but not alone. Given an unchanged structure, people tend to fall back into old habits of initiation and response, and the relations between the area supervisors and local managers might have returned to their old close pattern—if indeed they ever departed.

Accordingly, corporate management instituted a comprehensive reorganization to reinforce and promote (and even force) the desired behavioral change. First, the store manager was strengthened by giving him more authority over department managers (for evaluation, hiring, firing, etc.) and more discretion over expenditures. He received greater authority to purchase local products and vary his total product line. Second, the position of area supervisor was virtually eliminated by converting him to a regional supervisor with a vastly expanded span of control—perhaps 100 stores!

This enormous span of control made it impossible for the former area supervisor to exercise close control over store managers, which allowed the local managers to have greater discretion in their own operations. By setting up a competitive evaluation system, combined with individual bonuses, the local managers were thus encouraged to demonstrate flexibility and initiative.

Such a drastic organizational change is not necessarily desirable in itself. In the retail store chain it works because it is relatively easy to evaluate the performance of individual stores. Monthly sales and profit figures indicate clearly to the regional supervisor what stores are in trouble and where his attention should be directed. Among managers whose performance is more difficult to measure, closer supervision and narrower spans of control would probably be desired.

In a selected reading following this chapter Paul Lawrence describes a similar reorganization in a food store chain.

Case 3: Organizational Change in an Insurance Company

In the foregoing example, organizational structure was modified to change the behavior of store managers and area supervisors—to loosen up control and encourage independence. In a large insurance company,[2] structural changes were instituted for the opposite reason—to facilitate closer and more personal managerial direction of sales agents. Corporate management had for years maintained

---

[2] We are indebted to a colleague, Professor J. J. O'Connell [8] of the Wharton School of Finance and Commerce, the University of Pennsylvania, for this case.

Figure 10-3. Preconversion Personal Insurance Sales Division.

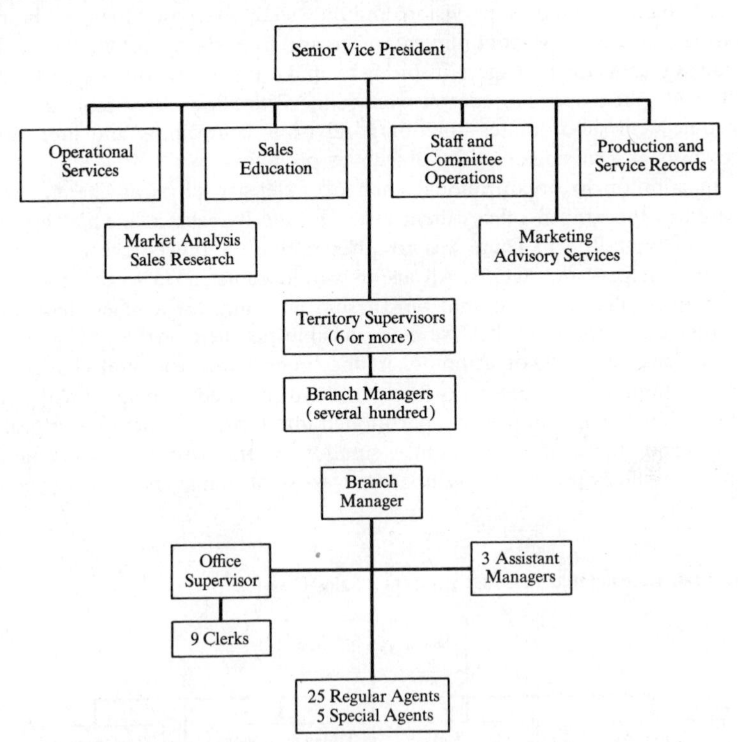

a centralized structure and a system of procedural controls, in spite of the growth of the organization and shifts in the life insurance market.

Figure 10-3 shows the relevant portion of the former organizational chart. As is obvious, spans of control were large. Certainly, at the territorial level, there was little possibility of close supervision or communication between the vice-president and individual branch managers. Even at the level of branch manager, however, close supervision was difficult. The assistant managers were not really managers at all. They acted as super salesmen, handling some accounts personally and assisting agents on others. Branch managers in a typical office thus had control spans of about 35 people.

More recently, corporate management came to feel that the organization had not been aggressive enough in obtaining the right volume and mix of insurance policies. In fact, the company decided that there was a necessity for closer and more personal supervision, especially at the agent level, if it were to halt the decline in its asset size and net cost positions in the industry. As in the retail chain example, the problem could have been handled by exhorting the agents to try harder. Again, this was done, but it was combined with structural change.

In effect, two more supervisory levels were added. As Figure 10-4 shows, a managerial position was created between the territorial vice-presidents and branch managers. This facilitated greater communications between branch managers and higher management. In addition, the assistant manager's duties were redefined to include supervision, and they were interposed between branch managers and agents. All communications to and from the agents were funneled through the assistant managers in order to make them part of the work flow. At all levels, then, spans of control were reduced to allow supervisors to spend more time with subordinates—planning, advising, controlling, and motivating in the spirit of a management-by-objectives program.

In addition to organizational changes, extensive physical changes were instituted in the branch offices themselves. Formerly, each agent had his own desk in a large bull pen. There was no differentiation in office facilities between assistant managers and agents. All agents would come in on Friday mornings for a branch office meeting, and on Tuesday morning for a scheduled report time; the rest of the time they were responsible for their own movements—in the office, making calls, or at home. At the time of the structural change, the company eliminated private desks for agents and supplied each agent with space in a file cabinet. The bull pen was partitioned into three new facilities: a professionally-appointed conference room, a small work area with large work tables, and private offices for the newly upgraded assistant managers.

Figure 10-4. Restructured Personal Insurance Sales Division.

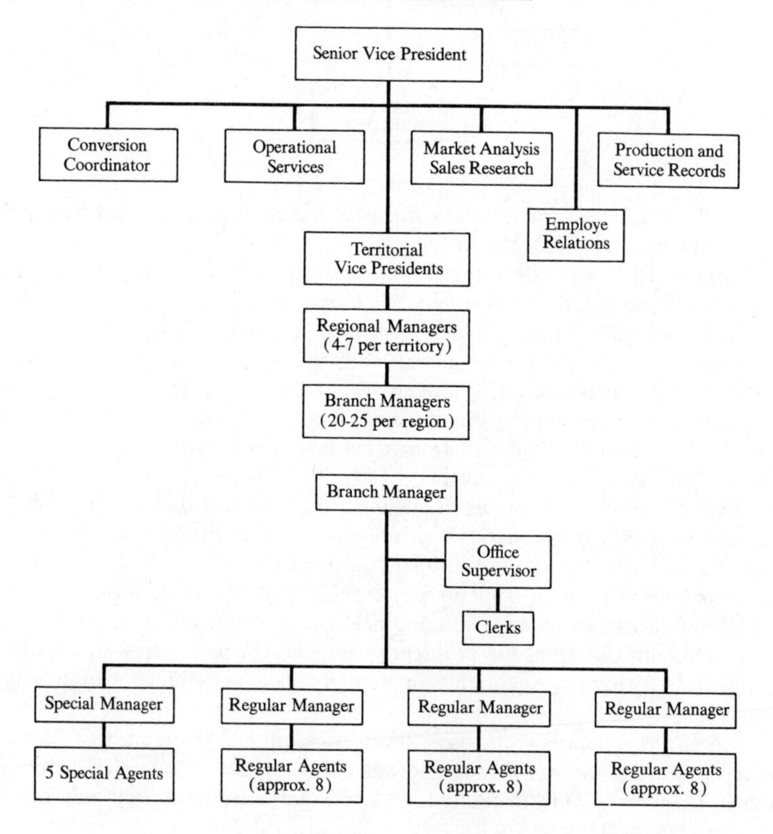

The effort to facilitate closer and more personal supervision included rescheduling the agents' in-office activities. Each agent spent about an hour each week with the assistant manager in his new office. In addition, each assistant manager conferred weekly with his group of agents in the new conference room. Large, general office meetings—which would be virtually impossible in the rearranged office—were no longer scheduled.

The dramatic changes in organizational structure, physical facilities, and scheduling were instituted to facilitate and encourage the type of close superior-subordinate relationship implied in a management-by-objectives program. The changes produced some strong reactions in the agents. A dramatic, though not typical, response to the physical changes was the complaint of one agent: "After twenty-five years I've been reduced to one file drawer." To some, the loss of the desk was a physical symbol of status demotion. More importantly, the agents felt disruption in the former social system. The assignment to four separate units, meeting at different times, broke up many long-standing cliques. Friends might not see one another unless they explicitly arranged meetings outside the office. Thus the changes risked a negative impact on the informal social structure and morale within branch offices. The predictable upheaval came, and produced a (hopefully) temporary reduction in productivity.

Conclusion

An organization is a socio-technical system; both social and technical aspects of the organization must be considered in the change process. As Robert Guest [4] points out:

> On his part the social scientist often makes the error of concentrating on human motivation and group behavior without fully accounting for the technical environment which circumscribes, even determines, the roles which the actors play. Motivation, group structure, interaction processes, authority—none of these abstractions of behavior takes place in a technological vacuum.

In short: "Work flow and the administrative processes by which it is controlled," write Chapple and Sayles [3], "are fundamental in shaping the realities of the organization as a system of relationships." Organization *is* technology in the broader sense—layout, techniques, processes, procedures, policies, controls, formal structural authority, etc.

A number of researchers have commented on the emphasis on engineering planning which precedes technological change, while psychological and social factors are ignored. Some of the financial and human costs of technological changes could be avoided if managers and engineers grasped the social implications of change; in short, if they thought of the organization as a social and technical system. The introduction of technological change forces readjustments in the social system; individuals find that they have to deal with other individuals who are either new to them or stand in a new relationship to them. These changes in relationships are the major variables in the introduction of change. In a fascinating study of the impact of a new plant manager on an automobile assembly plant, Robert Guest [4] has described how the patterns of interaction and social relationship in the organization were improved. Selected passages from his book are included in a reading following this chapter. Another selection, by F. L. W. Richardson and Stephen Zimmerman, elaborates upon this theme.

As means of facilitating organizational change, we place greater emphasis in this chapter on technology, structure, and management policies than on influencing attitudes directly. Many writers place too great an importance on morale as an independent entity. Some managers and even more scholars feel that all problems would be solved if management could improve organizational morale. But morale is not easily subject to direct manipulation. Attitudes that grow out of work situations and interaction patterns tend to become institutionalized; i.e., a given organization takes on a characteristic pattern of attitudes as part of its cultural system. These attitudes are taught to newcomers even before they become aware of the realities of the technology. Richardson [9] points out that, among groups of sub-organizations, it is unusual for sentiment changes to precede action or interactional change. That is, technology and structure must be changed first.

References

1. Argyris, C. *Personality and Organization.* Harper & Row, 1957.
2. ———. *Understanding Organization Behavior.* Dorsey (Irwin), 1960.
3. Chapple, E. D., and L. R. Sayles. *The Measure of Management.* Macmillan, 1962.
4. Guest, R. *Organizational Change: The Effect of Successful Leadership.* Dorsey (Irwin), 1962.
5. Learned, E., D. N. Ulrich, and D. R. Booz. *Executive Action.* Graduate School of Business, Harvard University, 1951.
6. Moore, W. "The Use and Misuse of Creative People and Ideas." In *Individualism and Big Business,* by L. R. Sayles. McGraw-Hill, 1963.
7. Niles, M. C. *The Essence of Management.* Harper & Row, 1958.
8. O'Connell, J. J. *Managing Organizational Innovation.* Dorsey (Irwin), 1967.
9. Richardson, F. L. W. *Talk, Work, and Action.* Monograph No. 3, Society for Applied Anthropology, 1961.
10. Thompson, V. *Modern Organization.* Knopf, 1963.
11. Webber, R. A. "Managerial Behavior, Personality and Organizational Structure." Unpub. Ph.D. dissertation, Columbia University, 1966.

Readings

Work Flow as the Basis of Organizational Design

ELIOT D. CHAPPLE
LEONARD R. SAYLES

In a business of any size, decisions that affect its organizational design are made almost daily. Constant changes in technology, markets, and financial conditions impel management to make decisions to keep the company on its course. The personalities of top management also shape the design; as its members come and go, changes are made to suit their private philosophies and their attitudes toward "proper" organization, although such changes are usually rationalized as fitting the demands of internal conflict or external forces.

For guides to decisions on organizational design, a manager has available the writings of experts in the "management movement" or he can call on a present-day consultant. Taken as generalizations from experience, the rules, doctrines, and principles of organization are thought-provoking. They represent the accumulated experience and wisdom of clinicians. Interpreted in the light of a specific problem, they often can help find the way to a solution. Yet, as in the comparable case of clinical medicine, they do not, in fact cannot, provide the precise criteria for diagnosis and therapy.

The medical axiom "Nature is the great healer" applies to organizations as well as to human beings. Far too many triumphs of clinicians stem from the persistence or inertia of the system. Thus, organizations often show extraordinary resistance to poorly considered attempts to change them. Surveys are made, often costing many hundreds of thousands of dollars; new charts and new manuals of procedure are prepared; and orders are issued to put the recommendations into action. Then, frequently within a few months, the enterprise sloughs off its new organizational skin, and only a few of the new titles remain. The expensive reports and manuals are put in an unused file, and the rest is abandoned.

Many organizations, both private and governmental, are reorganized almost yearly and usually by a different set of experts, each with their personal remedies for presumed organizational illness. The human damage is often great. People

---

are fired, resign, or are moved from one end of the country to the other and back again. Yet, the organization holds together. The old habits are soon reestablished if they were ever put aside even temporarily. Employees with such ill-starred companies, which are often in a financially successful market position, soon develop the uneasy caution of the inhabitants of the Great Plains in the tornado season. At the barest tremor of the barometer or the first trace of blackness in the sky, they dive headfirst into the inactive safety of whatever organizational storm cellar they can find.

Toward a Science of Organization

Certainly there is no lack of clinical experience, but what is needed is a science of organization. To do the job, the criteria for decision on which the practitioner can call, as the physician relies on the laboratory to substantiate or overrule his clinical judgment, must be developed. Fortunately, most of the essentials are already at hand, the tools of measurement and accurate observation.

In the approach to be taken to organizational structure, two elements will appear. The technology or flow of work is the major criterion for designing the structure. This contrasts sharply with a well-established tradition of planning the organization from the top down. Secondly, any tendency to group people and activities together simply because they have or involve similar or purportedly similar functional responsibilities is avoided.

Traditionally, the scientific approach in studying any human group considers the environment and the technology developed to adapt to the environment. Each individual operation involves an implement or machine using some sort of power, a sequence of actions to accomplish the task, and possibly the interaction of several people in some kind of team activity. In this sense, the term "implement" can be applied to any object, a sheet of paper, a loom, an accounting machine, or a bulldozer. The products of business, or of any organization for that matter, result from interrelated techniques, some of which are essential and others secondary.

If an entire technique or series of techniques can be performed by a single individual, such as a silver craftsman who sells his wares himself, no organization results. But, if a division of labor occurs, some interaction between technicians must take place, and organization on the work level results. On the production level, a relatively large number of techniques may be linked together to make up the work flow through the plant, with a single owner-manager providing the entire management. If there is only a small number of employees and few demands on his time for other activities (for example, if he subcontracts for a larger corporation on a regular basis), the owner may have a foreman in the shop even though the operation does not require one. The ensuing growth of such enterprises usually comes about rather simply with the owner taking a partner who is often a relative. Then, the management begins to specialize, typically with one man selling and the other overseeing production.

Regardless of the type of business organization—a small retail shop, the trader or merchant acting as intermediary between buyers and sellers, or a bank—a similar elaboration of organization takes place. The division of labor on the work level may involve sales people, clerks recording transactions, or cashiers; as the division of labor proliferates, so does management. The development of specialized managers or of a management division of labor is clearly secondary in the evolution of business to the growth of specialization on the work-flow level. This sequence is of critical importance in designing the organization.

Yet, in many writings about modern business organizations, the prime and determining influence of technological process is lost sight of. In their writings, the designers of the organization, who are perhaps under the spell of a two-dimensional chart, start at the top. Beginning with the directors and the president, they work down, level by level, discussing the functions of the various divisions, considering the relationships of "staff" or "service" departments to the "line," weighing the importance of the "span of control," and defining their graphic representations by referring to the nature of executive authority and responsibility. They may casually mention the first-line supervisor, but what he supervises is usually incidental to their recommendations. . . .

Clearly, a different approach to the problem of organizational design is needed. The structure built for members of management can be ignored for the moment to go back to the bottom where the work is done.

This requires looking at the way the technology separates out a series of jobs that must be accomplished if the product is to result. We may manufacture something, buy it for resale, or hire it, as in the case of money, but whatever the business—manufacturing, retailing, banking, or service—we follow certain techniques. There is a beginning, when the process starts, something is done, and the process ends. Put another way, something comes in the door, something is done to it, and it moves on its way out another door to the customer.

In the cases to follow, which are drawn from the authors' field studies, the problems created when the work-flow sequence is not used as a criterion of organizational design, as well as the techniques of analyzing the work process and identifying the work-flow sequences will be examined. By using a comparative point of view, we shall describe a method to isolate some general principles of organization.

The Sales-Credit Controversy

In this case, the general sales manager of a manufacturing company was engaged in a major battle with both the credit manager and the treasurer, who was the credit manager's boss. Such conflicts are not rare. Salesmen usually believe the credit department tries to prevent them from making sales, and credit personnel often think the salesmen will sell to anyone, no matter how bad the risk, to get their commissions. This case illustrates the nature of the problem and why management structure and work flow are too often incongruous.

Although interpreted by management as a clash of personalities, the argument between the sales manager and the credit manager stemmed from much more mundane sources. To understand it, it is necessary to look at the actual work flow through their departments and observe the way the work was organizationally split up. The key implement was the salesman's order, which he mailed in to the home office after filling out what the customer required and extending the dollar figures. Figure 1 illustrates what happened to the order and how the people who handled it were divided between the various functional divisions.

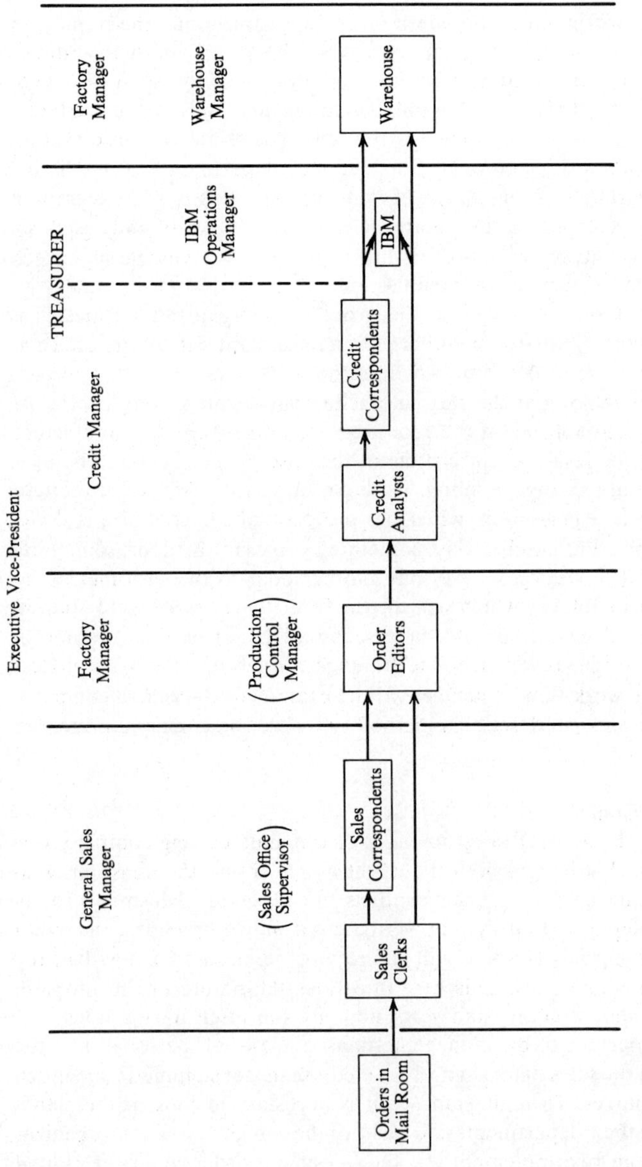
Executive Vice-President
General Sales Manager
(Sales Office Supervisor)
Factory Manager
(Production Control Manager)
Credit Manager
TREASURER
IBM Operations Manager
Factory Manager
Warehouse Manager
Orders in Mail Room
Sales Clerks
Sales Correspondents
Order Editors
Credit Analysts
Credit Correspondents
IBM
Warehouse

Figure 1

When the office opened in the morning, the mail was sorted in the mail room. Orders were separated and taken immediately by a mail boy to the sales office which occupied one section of the large, open general office of the company, a one-floor layout. There, the clerks checked over the orders to see if there were any special problems of handling shipments or questions raised by the salesmen that might require correspondence. Any order presenting a problem was given to a sales correspondent who wrote to the customer or the salesman, if necessary.

When the sales department completed its work, the order was sent to what was called an order-editing department. This was under the jurisdiction of the factory manager because he superintended warehousing. The orders were checked to see that they were correct, the prices up-to-date, the arithmetic accurate, and the goods in stock at the warehouse nearest to the customer. A copy of the order was sent to another warehouse if the closest one did not have stock. If inventory records showed no stock available, the order editor made out a back-order form to be mailed to the customer.

Then one of the editors would take a batch of orders to the credit department, where credit analysts (clerks) checked the credit ratings to be sure each customer's credit was within the limits set by management. They ascertained whether it was permissible to sell on any other terms than C.O.D. and whether the volume of the order was within the limits of his credit rating. If there was a credit problem, i.e., a deviation, the order was given to a credit correspondent who wrote the customer, with a copy for the salesman, telling him his order could not be accepted and stating the terms, if any, on which he could still buy from the company. If the customer was a big-volume account whose credit rating had dropped, the credit manager would make a final decision before the correspondent wrote a letter. It should be mentioned that each salesman had a reference book of the credit ratings for all accounts in his territory and was not supposed to call on any account whose line of credit was below a specified level.

After this processing, the orders were assembled, one copy of each order was sent to the warehouses to be filled and another to be tabulated for accounting purposes. The IBM accounting processing was supervised by the treasurer, and the warehouses were, as mentioned above, under the manager of the factory. Work was organized so that, in theory at least, all of the orders were processed through this office work flow in one day. Thereafter, there was a definite break in timing because accounting did not receive the orders until a batch was completed at the end of each day. The same was true for the warehouses where goods were pulled for shipment and billed.

There was tension between the credit manager and the general sales manager because the credit department, following its procedure faithfully, occasionally canceled an order that a salesman had made, sometimes a large one. Because credit ratings fluctuate, this had happened recently to two large accounts, and the general sales manager was understandably furious. Both customers threatened not to buy from the company again. The situation was more embarrassing because the general sales manager had written each customer a personal letter to thank him for his confidence in their product after the sales correspondent handling the accounts called the orders to his attention.

Now let us look at a series of improvements in the organization. The first and most obvious change in the work flow of handling orders was to reverse the position of the sales and the credit departments. If credit could not be extended, there was no point in checking the accuracy of an order or carrying out the "sales" functions involved. Moreover, this change would prevent recurrences of the kind of embarrassment the general sales manager had undergone. The rearrangement was also more efficient because it eliminated the processing of orders that ultimately would be thrown out. However, it did not deal with more basic issues.[1]

As the organization chart (Figure 1) indicates, three separate divisional heads, reporting to the executive vice-president, were involved in the movement of a piece of paper and its carbons from one clerical position to another in the general office. Not only were three separate divisions writing to the customer (sales, credit, and the order editor if he issued a back order) but also there was no assurance that there would be any coordination in what each said. Credit correspondents were accused by sales of being too brusque with customers and they, in turn, accused sales of promising too much.

Many other practical problems of management arose. The policy of the company was to clear the orders in a single day. Tight scheduling was sometimes necessary to get the work completed because volume fluctuates. Absenteeism, inadequate performance, or the assignment of other work to the people in a department would upset the even flow of work. If there was disagreement because one department was holding up another, the only recourse when the immediate supervisors could not agree was to settle the dispute on the level of the executive vice-president. Thus, in heated disagreements between the general sales manager and the credit manager, the executive vice-president had to listen not only to complaints about customer relations, but also to all the petty grievances each had about the performance or management of the other.

The difficulty was created when the work flow was divided into separate pieces on the basis of functional similarities. The solution was to put it back together as a single flow under a single supervisor. He would control the entire flow of an order from the time the paper arrived in the mail room until it left the general office to go to the tabulating department or the warehouse as well as credits, payments, and invoices after the billing was completed. He was responsible for individual performance and could move people around to fit the needs of fluctuating volume. He did not have to argue with other divisions on the management of the process. See Figure 2.

There was still the problem of functional responsibilities. Sales wanted and deserved some voice in the quality of letters sent to customers. Credit, too, had some legitimate concerns, primarily that company policies regarding credit be followed and any cases not under these policies be referred to higher authority. Both departments outlined standards and procedures that could be carried out by the new department. In this way, representatives of sales or credit would only

---

[1] The reader may consider the illogical arrangement of having the credit checked after sales correspondents and order editors worked on an order as an obvious mistake that anyone should have recognized. However, because it was not recognized for many years in a relatively alert company, it reflects the strong attraction of organizing by functional specialty. All the sales activities were put together and handled first, with salesmen contacting their own departments. Then, and only then, was it time for the next function to begin, in this case, that of the credit department. Unfortunately, the logic of functional organization is rarely challenged in practice.

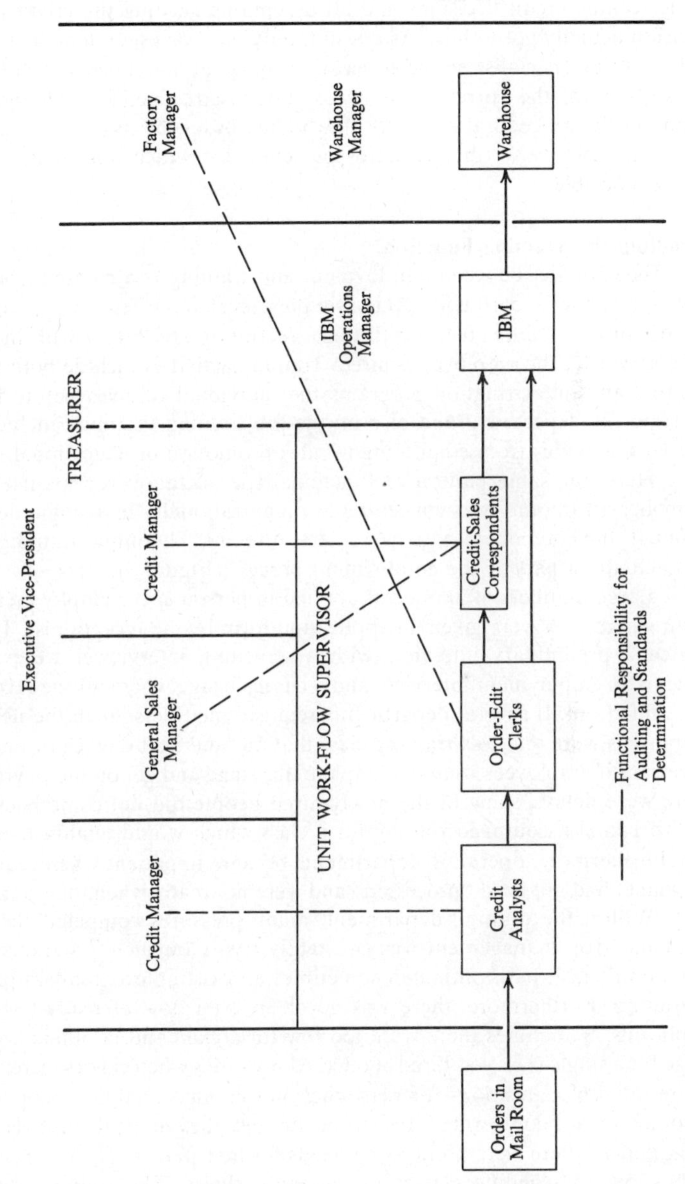
Executive Vice-President
TREASURER
Credit Manager
General Sales Manager
Credit Manager
Factory Manager
UNIT WORK-FLOW SUPERVISOR
IBM Operations Manager
Warehouse Manager
Orders in Mail Room
Credit Analysts
Order-Edit Clerks
Credit-Sales Correspondents
IBM
Warehouse
Functional Responsibility for Auditing and Standards Determination

Figure 2

come into the picture when an exceptional situation required higher-level attention. These procedures also included a periodic auditing program so the sales department could satisfy itself that the correspondents' letters to customers were not antagonistic. The credit department checked that this new work unit only made routine credit decisions and all exceptions needing the credit manager's decision actually got to him. As a result, only one correspondent, a credit-sales-order editing specialist, wrote to each customer although several did identical work. In turn, the correspondent was supervised, together with the clericals handling the proceduralized work flow of the order, by one individual. Credit, sales, and factory set the standards of action for which this single supervisor was responsible. . . .

Handling the Training Function

The conflict between employment and training is a common problem in many personnel departments. At the simplest level, it is often a matter of scheduling because it is difficult to synchronize recruiting and hiring with the training necessary after the employee is hired. Training activities include both the initial training and indoctrination programs the individual receives before he is sent to a specific department and also on-the-job training that may include a wide range of activities from counseling to sales promotion or educational programs.

Here, the same pattern of functional specialization repeats itself. In this company all training was concentrated organizationally in a single department although the component parts were very different. The initial training program was actually a part of the employment process (Figure 3).

Large numbers of applicants applied in person at the employment department where they were given an application form by the receptionist. Those who passed a preliminary interview with a screening interviewer were sent to a systematic employment interview and a clerical stage where all the record forms were filled out. If several departments requisitioned personnel, the newly hired employees were sent to a training class that met the next day. Coordination was necessary if employees were to complete this stage and get on the payroll. When there were delays, some of the newly hired people did not come back because they became discouraged waiting for a class which would qualify them for the job. Furthermore, operating departments became impatient when requisitioned personnel had not been "processed" and were not ready when they were needed.

Within the training department, many pressures competed for the time available. Top management was constantly trying out new programs, some of them on a crash basis, although sometimes an existing program simply needed bolstering. Furthermore, there was never an even flow of ready-to-be-trained applicants. Sometimes there were too few for a class and at others a group too large for a single class was hired at once. Many times when classes were scheduled to tie in with requisitions for personnel, not enough qualified people applied. At other times, people were hired simply because they made themselves available even though there were no pressing needs for new personnel. As a result, it was impossible to schedule classes on a regular basis. The training department complained they could not plan their work efficiently because they had no advance notice, and when they did plan, employment let them down. On the other hand, the employment people thought the training group was uncooperative and unwilling to be flexible in view of the difficulties inherent in the hiring

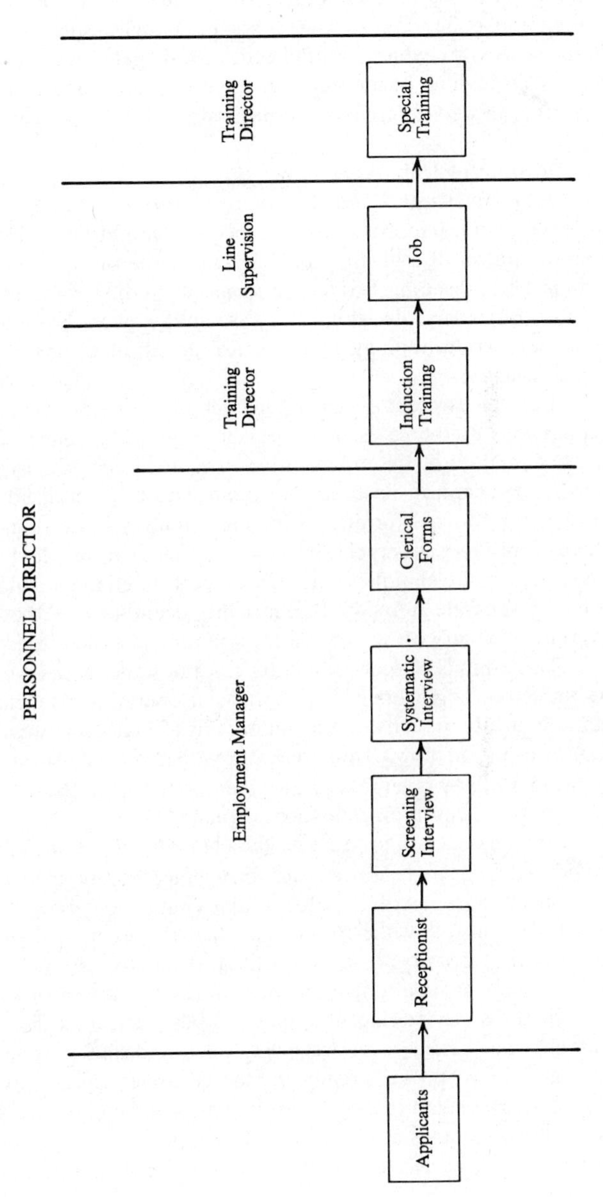
PERSONNEL DIRECTOR
Employment Manager
Training Director
Line Supervision
Training Director
Applicants
Receptionist
Screening Interview
Systematic Interview
Clerical Forms
Induction Training
Job
Special Training

Figure 3

operation. This pattern is typical of functional specialization that divides single work processes into organizational compartments.

The solution was to separate the initial induction training from the other training functions and combine it with the other employment operations described above. See Figure 4. As a result, a single supervisor now controlled the entire process by which an applicant at the "gate" was moved from the initial inquiry through all of the stages of the hiring procedure, largely eliminating the bickering between employment and training.

Identification of Unit Work Flow

Any organization that has more than one supervisor must decide which employees and, therefore, which processes should be under the jurisdiction or span of control of a given manager. This is the old question of who reports to whom. The preceding text was directed to finding some criterion upon which to base this crucial decision. The case studies were presented to illustrate the significance of technology as the critical determinant of this aspect of organizational structure.

But, this concept of technology needs a more careful explanation than the implications of the cases. It should be clear at the outset that the technology or work method of the organization does not refer primarily to the equipment or to the mechanical, electrical, or chemical processes utilized. Every organization has a method of performing work that involves some sequence of operations. These work flows, so crucial in the cases cited, can be identified wherever there is a sequence of techniques that must be performed in a regular or predetermined order by separate individuals. Thus the technology of the organization is the "who does what with whom, when, where, and how often."

These kinds of work flows are not the same as the work-flow analyses of the industrial engineer, which chart each operation in the production process chronologically. In constructing an organizational structure, the interest is in the person-to-person flow. Thus, one individual may perform what the engineer would identify as several separate operations before the work or paper goes to the next person in the production sequence.[2]

The next step is to separate the elements of the work flow that should be considered as a single supervisory unit, which will be called "unit work flows." The concern here is with the quantitative characteristics of the work flow regardless of whether that which "flows" is a person, paper, or material. These characteristics are necessary to set up criteria to identify the unitary work flows and to understand their implications behaviorally in organization design.

In broad terms, the flow of materials, in a manufacturing company for example, that begins at the receiving dock and finally appears at the shipping door as finished product ready for the customer could be considered a single work flow. However, the time coordinates of the complete process are generally too wide; sometimes a matter of weeks or months are needed to complete the manufacturing cycle. Besides the question of physical contiguity is relevant.

---

[2] It is necessary, of course, to know the total time required by each person to complete his activities to determine the duration of that particular stage in the production sequence. This helps establish the rate at which the paper, material, or a person moves through the line. This rate is set by the time required to complete the slowest or longest step in the sequence.

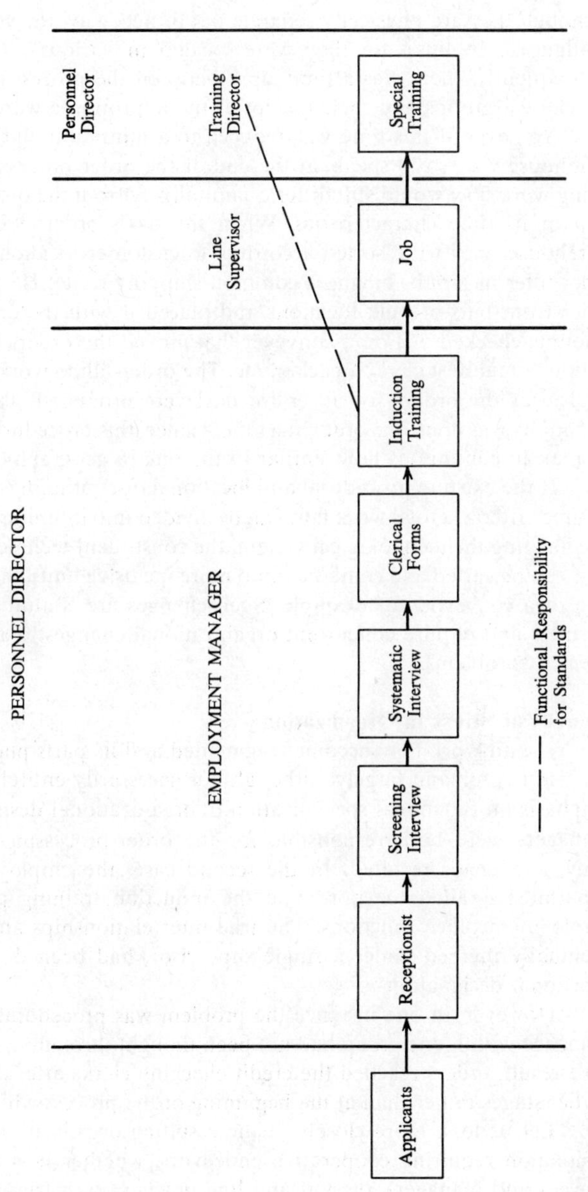
PERSONNEL DIRECTOR
EMPLOYMENT MANAGER
Applicants
Receptionist
Screening Interview
Systematic Interview
Clerical Forms
Induction Training
Line Supervisor
Job
Training Director
Personnel Director
Special Training
Functional Responsibility for Standards

Figure 4

Physical location or layout is an important factor in identifying the unit flows that make up an organizational design.

In the example of processing the salesman's order, a controlling factor in the separation of warehousing work flow from the office work flow was location. Although they are physically separate out of necessity, the warehouses could be contiguous. In this case they were located in various parts of the country. Consequently, there was a time lapse between the processing of the orders by the clerical groups and their receipt at the appropriate warehouses.

Yet, even if this time was reduced to a minimum and the location of the warehouse was, so to speak, at the end of the order processing line, the order-filling work flow would still differ quantitatively from the order-processing work flow in its time characteristics. When the day's orders were received in the warehouse, they were sorted according to customer location and given to each order filler in groups having a common shipping route. He then assembled the order from bins or bulk locations and placed it with the order copy (with the amounts checked off) on a conveyer that moved the orders through a checking station, a manifest clerk, a packer, etc. The order-filling work flow did not begin until after the orders for an entire day were processed; the office work flow essentially was done one order at a time. Hence, this procedural difference caused a break in continuous flow similar to the one in geographical location.

If the existing procedural and locational discontinuities can be determined by time criteria, a total work flow can be divided into its unitary parts.[3] Obviously, by changing the technological system, the constituent techniques in a single unit flow can be varied and combined into more inclusive units, through the introduction of a conveyor, for example. Such changes are continually being made in business and require concurrent organizational changes to avoid creating management problems.

Sources of Stress in Organization

A unit work flow becomes segmented and its parts placed under different chains of command largely, although not necessarily entirely, as a result of the emphasis on functional specialization in organizational design. Sales and credit managers were both responsible for the order-processing flow in one company, and chaos resulted. In the second case, the employment and training departments failed to coordinate the induction training procedure with the employment office functions. The true interrelationships among the processes, eventually merged under a single supervisor, had been disguised by artificial functional designations.

However, in one instance the problem was procedural not structural: the sequence within one group had not been thought through in terms of work flow. As a result, orders reached the credit checking clerks after they passed through earlier stages rather than at the beginning of the process which is more efficient.

Let us look more closely at the resulting organizational disturbances. In a situation requiring cooperative endeavors, whether it is a work group, employees and managers, or staff and line officials, each tries to develop a stable pattern of work, of interaction. When these stable patterns are disturbed, individ-

[3] With the use of statistical techniques, it is possible to determine the homogeneity of the measurements within any unitary flow and to develop accurate criteria to test for discontinuities.

uals experience stress or an uncomfortable feeling of pressure and dissatisfaction. A breakdown in the flow creates opposition as the individuals struggle to restore it. The expected responses from the individuals in the sequence prove inadequate, and new coordination problems arise.

The regularities of actions and interactions disappear when this stress occurs, and erratic variation takes over. The difference is obvious between a smoothly running operation and one with a problem. Under stress, people react emotionally, and, because more than one individual is involved, the reactions usually conflict with each other.

Thus, a vicious circle is established. Something happens in the work situation that causes the relationship of individuals to change or to depart from the normal pattern. This creates a stress, either of opposition or nonresponse, that is further complicated by higher levels of supervision and staff specialists whose unexpected interactions, i.e., outside the usual organization pattern, irritate the disturbed work-flow relations. People get upset; they become angry with each other and, depending on their individual characteristics, react temperamentally. These personality conflicts have direct ramifications in the work process because the emotional reactions change the pattern of contact and interaction. Joe is angry with Bill, so he does not check with him before starting a new experimental run. Consequently, a special test that should have been included in the run is left out, and the whole thing has to be done over. To complete the circle, these emotional disturbances damage the work-flow sequence, which causes additional personality stresses.

Robert Guest of the Yale Technology Project described this accurately when he said:

> Foremen are always getting caught in this familiar vicious circle. Material inspection, say, has failed to spot some faulty pieces. Something goes wrong at a welding operation. The general foreman is on the foreman's neck to "get it straightened out, or else!" The foreman drops everything to spend time on this one item. He cannot pay attention to the man he was breaking in on a new job. He cannot check on the stock bin which the stock man forgot to replenish. He meant to warn an operator about a safety condition. He knew another man was down in the dumps about a personal problem. By the time he has cleared up the original trouble and satisfied the boss, something else has blown up and the general foreman is roaring down the aisle again.[4]

What produced these stresses and where do these changes come from? They are not directly interactional on the worker level. With rare exceptions, the work flow does not require a direct interactional contact between two contiguous persons as team operations do. That is, the upsets and bickerings are not caused by people who occupy adjacent positions in the flow process and place pressures on one another. In fact, orders could be put on the next desk or on a conveyer without any real contact. Material or parts in an assembly operation usually move from one operator to the next on a conveyer. But, they may also be brought and taken away by service personnel, just as a mail boy may move orders from one group to the next in the office. In these examples, the flow of work does

[4] Robert H. Guest, "Of Time and the Foreman," *Personnel,* May, 1956, pp. 478–486.

not cause any direct interpersonal problems,[5] except that the action of one person depends on the action of his predecessor, causing him not to act and thus breaking the sequence. As Guest indicates, however, the initiating sources of stress are primarily fluctuations in the rate at which work flows through the supervisory unit. The critical variable is time. Production schedules require tight coordination; holdups must be avoided. If they occur, production suffers and the relationships of the supervisor to his workers and of the workers among themselves change as a consequence.

The objective of any organizational structure is to minimize the incidence of deviations from the established interaction patterns of the work process. The realistic administrator knows complete stability is a never-to-be-achieved utopia. Equipment will always break down; employees will always be absent; and changes in procedures will be introduced continuously. Work will not always come through on time, or when it does, the quality may be so poor the normal process time must be increased significantly. Rush orders or a flood of work may press upon his unit. Whatever the type of fluctuation, his interaction patterns have to change. He may have to spend more time with individual workers, supervisors in other departments, engineers, mechanics, maintenance men, or various persons in control positions, such as production planners or factory cost controllers, who occupy a place in the paper-work flow of which the line supervisor also is a part. And, as a result, less time is available to maintain other vital contacts.

Even if his unit flow is not complicated by other supervisors who directly affect him, the supervisor will still have coordination and timing problems in his own unit and in his relations with those who give him work and to whom he transmits it. The possibility of stress is much greater if he does not have control over the key individuals who work directly with his segment of the flow and cannot get a response from them when he needs it, as in the case of the maintenance mechanics, or if he must constantly gear his segment to the next one, as in the examples of the material handling and inspection.

This is the major point of the discussion. Although the dynamic organization will always experience changes that cause variations in the work-flow system, most of these can be dealt with effectively by the supervisor affected. But, his job becomes almost impossibly difficult if there is no semblance of stability.[6] If the parts of a unit work flow are distributed among several supervisors, the individual manager cannot hope to maintain any stability in internal relationships because erratic changes are introduced by individuals whose behavior he cannot control. Because these other supervisors are meeting different organizational needs, they do not and cannot adjust to the requirements of any single manager. Significant irregularities in the rate of flow and significant changes in the interaction of the individuals concerned indicate the existence of a point of organization stress.

---

[5] This contrasts with the usual conception of work-flow stress. Among the best known studies in this area is William F. Whyte's work in the restaurant industry. Whyte found stress was caused by the direct pressure emanating from interworker contacts. "Lower-status" runners placed pressure and thus disturbed "higher-status" kitchen personnel, and demanding customers upset the waitress who could not tolerate a high frequency of demands. (William F. Whyte, *Human Relations in the Restaurant Industry,* McGraw-Hill Book Company, Inc., New York, 1948, pp. 49–59, 104–128.)

[6] The degree to which the use of functional organization introduces stress and instability is cogently analyzed by James Worthy, Sears Roebuck and Co., in his paper, "Some Aspects of Organization Structure in Relation to Pressures on Company Decision-Making," in *Proceedings of Fifth Annual Meeting of the Industrial Relations Research Association* (ed. L. Reed Tripp), IRRA Publ. 10, 1953, pp. 69–79.

In companies where such problems are common, informal working arrangements usually develop over the course of time. Assuming the individual supervisors get along, i.e., the frequency or intensity of stress is not too great or their personalities are not obviously incompatible, they frequently get together to plan the work and discuss their mutual problems. The objective is for each supervisor to create the least upset to the next group in the line. Unfortunately, it is almost impossible because the segmentation of the work flow makes informal arrangements vulnerable to unexpected changes emanating from higher up.

Higher Level Management Problems

Because people, not lines on a chart, are the major concern, the elimination of points of stress within the work flow should be the first consideration of organization design. This means, the traditional functional classification must be abandoned and each job analyzed as a part of one or perhaps, as in the case of an executive, many work flows. Merely recognizing that "informal" organization exists and hoping that management will grant it equal importance to the "formal" structure will not solve the problems.

Studies of the informal organization discuss how people actually relate themselves to each other in the process of getting the work done. Thus, the pattern of relationships that evolve in completing the job is what some observers consider the uncontrolled or spontaneous aspect of the organization. The authors believe this aspect must be the objective of the consciously contrived organizational structure. The organization must be designed for people—not in the hope that people will somehow fit into it.

Accordingly, the first step is to identify the unit work flows and set their boundaries, placing each one under a single supervisor. As stated previously, these work flows consist not only of the people through whom the material, paper, or person flows, but also all the individuals who help maintain the flow, the mechanics, service people, etc. All the factors required to get the work done should be concentrated under a single person with responsibility centered at the lowest managerial point, not at the highest, as in the examples where top management officials were constantly arbitrating interdepartmental disputes.

Span of Second-level Supervision

So far, a series of unit flows, each with its own supervisor, has been constructed. However, each still depends upon the other. Although the stress points within the unit work flows are eliminated by effective organizational design, areas of interdependence between these units necessarily remain. As noted above, the pace of the work generally shifts between unit work flows, there are different rhythms and sequences, and, as a result, the coordination problems are not as great, but there is still an obvious need to coordinate relationships. In the example, the application of quantitative criteria revealed that orders went to the warehouse or tabulating or material from a fabricating unit to assembly with a definable discontinuity. This indicates the need for at least one further level of supervision, a manager over the unit work-flow managers whose responsibility is to see that they are coordinated into a larger system.

Controls

Combining unit work flows into a work-flow system does not depend upon arbitrary assumptions as to the number of individuals such a manager can supervise. These factors are determined by analysis of the controls the manager has available to maintain the system, not by abstract formulas. Worthy pointed out that in the Sears organization a store manager may have thirty to forty department heads reporting to him.[7] This works not merely because the company does not want a manager spending too much time with any single department head but, more fundamentally, because the department store manager receives daily and weekly reports which are sufficient to tell him whether significant deviations are occurring in the ratio of stock (inventory) to sales, in markdowns, markups, etc. Consequently, he spends time with subordinates only in cases where managers are in trouble or where the reports suggest difficulties. As the theory of administrative controls is developed, similar control procedures can be adopted for any business operation.

Many companies find it difficult to organize for effective operation because their reporting systems do not adequately pinpoint responsibility. Most administrative controls are by-products of accounting controls. They were developed for financial record keeping, not management control. Consequently, they are issued by the controller as financial documents and, although completely accurate, they are usually so late as to be matters of ancient history and too general because costs are both prorated and arbitrarily assigned. As such, these reports have little use as operating tools.[8] Thus the number of unit work-flow supervisors reporting to the second management level is a function of the state of development of the organization's controls: the measures which assess how things are going in the production process. Primarily, controls signal troubles at the points where two unit work flows come into contact. These juncture points are the potential stress areas that the second level manager oversees. Improvements in management reporting technology, particularly by the computer, will substantially increase the span of control at this management level.

The use of controls is based on the same criterion utilized in defining each of the unit work flows, the time coordinates of the system. The controls should indicate when the individual unit flows are intermeshing with one another. If they show homogeneity, in the statistical sense, in the interrelationships of the component units, the system is operating as planned. If the sequential movement of goods, paper, or people between units is stabilized, as reported through appropriate controls, the manager can relax. He must go into action when his controls show stressful situations are developing that require attention and action to avoid complete breakdowns in the system.

Assuming some ingenuity is shown in the development of controls, the number of unit supervisors within the flow is of little significance, because each unit is self-sufficient.

Handling the Staff-Line Relationships

What is to be done with specialists such as the chief mechanic, the chief inspector, the production planning manager, the training director, and the credit

---

[7] William F. Whyte, *Modern Methods in Social Research,* prepared for the Office of Naval Research under Contract Nonr-401 (2), pp. 25–28.

[8] There is an increasing concern with what is called "management accounting." However, present practice indicates it has by no means reached its declared goal of defining organizational responsibility within an accounting framework. Too many costs are still allocated and prorated. True managerial accounting cannot be achieved without loosening the bonds placed in the way of organizational change by poor accounting logic.

manager? As pointed out previously, the specialists are responsible for developing standards, the procedures to implement these standards, and auditing results. Although this was mentioned explicitly only in the case of the credit manager, each specialist also plays a part in one or more work flows. The significance of the specialists' development and auditing is that they have been removed from direct work-flow decision. The chief mechanic, for example, does not directly or through the foremen decide on what machine the mechanic is to work. He is responsible for the standards of mechanical repair, the program of preventive maintenance, and the evaluation of the mechanic's performance.

Thus, the unit work-flow supervisor and the chief mechanic have a dual responsibility for performance: the first, for the mechanic's contribution in maintaining the production flow, and the latter for the quality of his work. Both factors must be considered in evaluation and control. Otherwise, it is easy to overemphasize short-term gains in production at the cost of the long-run impact on the mechanical equipment.

Moreover, this shift in responsibility gives the specialist time to develop programs and to carry out his auditing responsibility. Otherwise, he is too busy with the day-to-day operating decisions to determine the source of the problems. Under the pressure of the immediate situation, his only interest would be to put the fire out; he would have little time to see what caused the problem in the first place.

However, the specialists need to be fitted into the organizational system. Because they are concerned with developing programs to expedite the work flow and eliminate stresses both within and between unit work flows that affect the total work-flow system, the specialists inevitably become the specialized assistants of the work-flow system manager. Their responsibility then is to act for him in their respective areas to improve the operation on the unit work-flow level. It is important to note the word "responsibility." In the usual sense of the word, specialists do not have staff responsibility with advisory or consultative relations to the line, nor do they have the responsibility of line supervisors, one step removed. They are actually *of* the staff of the manager and accountable to him for developing, installing, and auditing the results of programs in terms of the major objective of removing stress.

Conclusion: Work Flow and Organization Design

The type of organization design just described, based on the actual work flow within a technological and procedural framework, requires the complete use of time measurements as its basis. Not only is the delimitation of unit work flows dependent on the possession of quantitative criteria, but improvements of the technological process, in its broadest sense, require the examination of how each individual, whether worker, specialist, or supervisor, spends his time. The effective use of the method by any company depends also upon layout and location, the techniques by which paper, materials, or people are handled, and the controls used to signal real or impending deviations.

For example, if the record system is not or cannot be tied to individual responsibility, it is that much more difficult to locate points of stress and, in the absurd but common case, the supervisor may have to spend his time continually "on the floor" looking and listening because he does not routinely receive adequate information about his operation. The exception principle, one of the oldest in management, is useful in organizational planning only if the systems and procedures make its use possible.

The work-flow theory requires the specification of what each person does, when, where, with whom, how long, and how often. Therefore a type of job analysis or job description, to use a somewhat discredited term, is needed to outline the flows for each individual and to specify in quantitative measurements the duration of the action and interaction required to carry them out. These administrative patterns will be discussed in the next chapter, with the executive in mind, but similar, although much simpler, descriptions are necessary for the workers themselves. Any contact, whether it is a mechanic repairing a machine, a service boy bringing parts, or a set-up man making adjustments for a new run, involves some interaction, and the time involved is not simply a matter of the actual physical action. . . .

The purpose here has been to suggest criteria upon which to base the design of an organization: the structure must be built from the bottom up and it must be superimposed upon a known technology. In fact, technology, as defined earlier, should be the basis for the distribution and assignment of supervision. Supervisory jobs are largely products of the time coordinates of the production process, regardless of the kind of work the organization does.

Reorganizing in an Advertising Agency: A Case Study of a Decrease in Integration

ARTHUR J. KOVER

A few years ago, the Paragon Advertising Agency was subjected to a profound reorganization which caused a marked decrease in internal communication among the staff and a concurrent increase in the degree of control and coordination over it. One of the results of these changes was increasing alienation from the organization among some of its members. This paper explores the nature of the Paragon Agency, the reorganization and its effects. It concludes by suggesting, on the basis of the data offered by this case, that integration has two necessary components: interpersonal integration and work integration.

The Paragon Advertising Agency—An Aggregation of Professionals

Advertising agencies offer two major professional services to their clients: they offer plans for the contents of an advertising campaign (slogans, layouts, basic selling points) and they offer plans for the media (radio, television, newspapers, magazines, billboards) required to reach the best audience most effi-

From *Human Organization,* Vol. 22, No. 4 (Winter 1963–1964), pp. 252–259. Reprinted by permission of the author and The Society for Applied Anthropology.

ciently.[1] In addition, agencies can offer other services such as aid in marketing and distribution of products and marketing research to test advertising effectiveness. Agency income is derived from a fifteen percent rebate on charges made by the various media or from fees paid directly by the client, usually a large production or commercial enterprise.[2] In order to provide these services, the Paragon Agency employed several hundred persons. The formal organization was as shown in Figure 1.[3] The agency was formed into a number of departments each concerned with professional specialty, the members of each department having a certain professional training in common. Individuals within each department were assigned work on the accounts of one or more clients.

Figure 1. Organization Chart, Paragon Advertising Agency (before Reorganization).

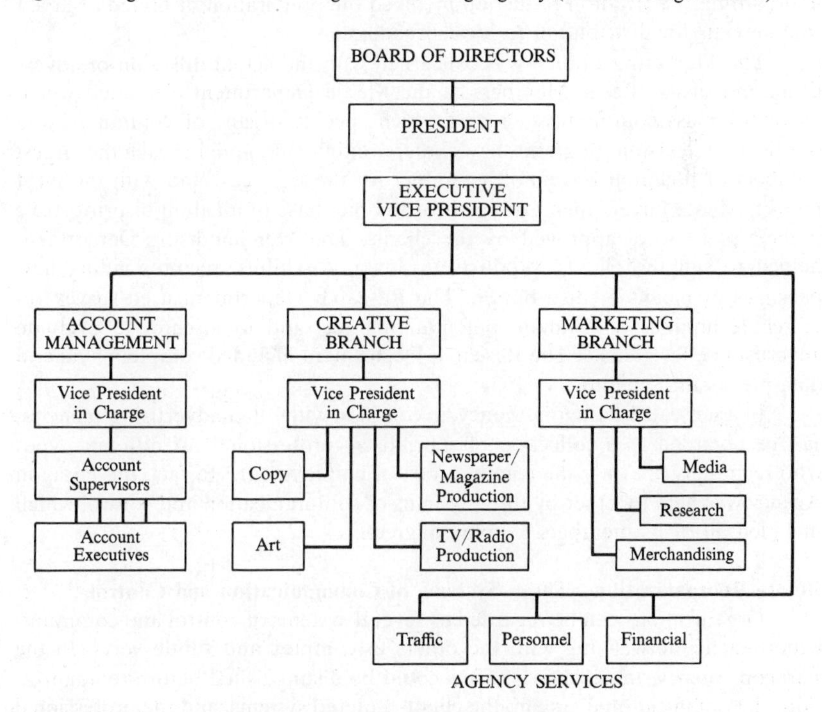

Work on each client's account was coordinated by account management consisting of account executives and account supervisors (senior account executives). Account executives were each attached to one account. They acted as liaison between client and agency and as coordinator of specialists within the

---

[1] Roger Barton, *Advertising Agency Operation and Management,* McGraw-Hill Book Co., Inc., New York, 1955, gives a general picture of advertising agency responsibilities and practice. This source has been used extensively for the first part of this paper.

[2] Irvin Graham, *Advertising Agency Practice,* Harper and Brothers, New York, 1952, pp. 16–19. Also see the news article, "Shell, Ogilvy Sound Paeans Over Fee Setup," *Advertising Age,* XXXI (November 21, 1960), 125–126.

[3] In this diagram as throughout this paper, the names of some organizational positions and departments of the Paragon Agency have been changed slightly.

agency who worked on the clients' accounts. Account supervisors controlled the work of a number of account executives.

The Creative Branch was concerned with the actual creation and production of advertisements and commercials. Members of the Copy Department wrote the scripts for radio or television commercials or wrote the copy (written parts) of printed advertisements. Members of the Art Department planned layouts of printed advertisements and arranged for the provision of appropriate illustrations if required. The Newspaper/Magazine Production and TV/Radio Production Departments took the rough advertisements produced by Copy and Art, put them in finished form, and arranged for their appearance in the mass media. For Newspaper/Magazine Production this meant arranging for reproductions of mats of advertisements to be made and forwarded to newspapers or magazines at the desired time. TV/Radio Production involved the preparation of filmed or taped commercials for distribution to local broadcasters.

The Marketing Branch was concerned with the actual diffusion of advertising and of its effects. Members of the Media Department estimated which means of mass communication and which specific organs of communication (particular television programs, newspapers, and the like) might reach the largest numbers of potential buyers of a product for the least cost and with the most impact. Media buyers then arranged for the purchase of air time or print space if their plans were approved by the clients. The Merchandising Department helped to sell the clients' products by making exhibits, recommending new packages or means of distribution. The Research Department used survey research techniques to estimate potential markets and to attempt to evaluate advertising effectiveness. The Research Department included complete field and data-processing sections.

In a sense, the Paragon Agency, in common with other advertising agencies, can be regarded as a collection of specialists—professionals of different types who seemingly are only the common fact of employment.[4] In fact, the Paragon Agency was held together by three systems of communication and control which included all of its members to some degree.

Before Reorganization—Three Systems of Communication and Control

Organizations can be regarded as several systems of control and communication each interweaving with the others in complex and subtle ways. In the Paragon Agency, three main systems could be distinguished before reorganization: the organizational system, the client-centered systems, and the professional systems.

The *organizational system* roughly reflects the chain of command as shown in the Agency's organization chart (Figure 1). Through these channels flow messages of company maintenance, internal policy, personnel changes, and information about general organizational attitude in regard to clients. There is little in their contents to distinguish these messages from organizational communications in any other bureaucracy of similar size.

Most messages funnelled through the organizational system flowed verti-

[4] See Martin Mayer, *Madison Avenue, U.S.A.*, Harper and Brothers, New York, 1958, for a description of the diversity—both of types of people and types of professions—to be found in an advertising agency.

cally. However, at the higher levels of the organization, horizontal communication tended to be more frequent as top management consulted with each other on matters of general agency interest.

Client-centered systems were each concerned with contacts with and services for a given client. Account supervisors and account executives were the persons designated to act as the agency's liaison with clients. In reality, a large amount of direct communication was also maintained by others in the agency with their opposite numbers in the client organizations. For instance, agency research personnel had frequent contact with the market research departments of clients; copywriters often were called directly by the advertising managers of the client for whom advertisements were being written. In addition to such relatively unstructured contact, creative workers and research personnel often presented their work directly to clients at meetings and had to defend agency policy at these meetings. (See Figure 2.)

With such short cuts to client communication, the coordinating account executive often had a difficult time in keeping track of the people assigned to the account. As one irate but self-knowing account executive put it:

> Control, control? How the hell can I keep track of five or six prima donnas? Each of them [agency professionals in different specialties] tries to play up *his* big idea to the client and half the time I don't know about it until a couple of hours later. If I were stronger I would make the whole pack of them come to me first and get approval first. Yes, before they did *anything.*

Figure 2. Client-Centered Organization (for Company X) Paragon Advertising Agency (before Reorganization). Width of connecting lines roughly indicates amount of contact.

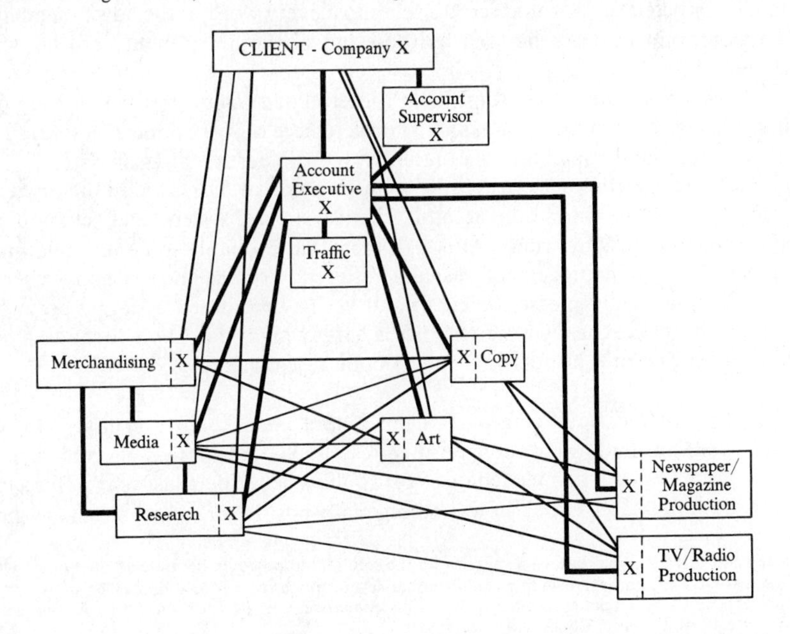

This man was actually faced with an unusual group, but the openness of the client-centered system meant that coordination and control were difficult for all account executives much of the time.[5]

In addition to tying many agency members to clients, client-centered systems tended to knit the Paragon Agency internally. As Figure 2 indicates, a few members were drawn from each specialty department in order to cooperate on work for a given client. Thus, beside the relatively stable departmental organization, the client-centered systems served to tie the whole organization together through communication across departmental lines. A relatively large amount of personnel transfer from one account group to another also tended to increase the number of possible communications within the agency—friendships and contacts were formed which continued for a while when the client-centered nexus was changed.

The *professional systems* were each located within one of the professional departments—Copy, Research, Art and so on. Each department was organized hierarchically with a director, perhaps an assistant director, and one to three other levels of responsibility. Professional communications were mainly concerned with questions of shared knowledge and technique; communications of a professional nature were widespread and pervasive within each department. Many friendships were based on similar professional backgrounds; additionally, aid and advice were shared and matters of professional interest were disseminated through departmental meetings and seminars.

Control in each professional system was exercised in two main ways—through control of professional promotions within the department and through supervision of work done by subordinates. For instance, in the preparation of a major advertising campaign for an important client, the head of the Copy Department would oversee the copywriters producing the advertisements. Using for legitimation a combination of organizational authority and claimed professional competence, he would scrutinize almost every word of the advertisements and would not let them be seen by those out of the department until he was satisfied.

Because of the different (although interrelated) characteristics of each of these systems of communication and control, a piece of work done by a specialist had a value—and sometimes a different value—in regard to each system. For instance, an advertisement written by a copywriter had one value in the organizational system another in the account [client-centered] system, and yet another among his fellow copywriters. Although there was probably some interrelation, the bases of these judgements usually differed. For instance, a copywriter's advertisement might please the client and yet be considered a sloppy piece of work by his colleagues. Or the result of a survey might horrify a client and yet could be a first-rate professional job. As one research supervisor said:

> The most discouraging part of this is that the account executives always want our findings to show positive results. You know, that our advertising is the best and that it's selling soap. That it's better than last year's. But a lot of our research either shows nothing really positive or sometimes shows that

[5] Roby and Lanzetta would probably agree with the solution proposed by the irate account executive. Their tentative experimental findings indicate that several pieces of information can be transmitted more effectively by a smaller number of sources. Reported in George Karlsson, *Social Mechanisms,* The Free Press, Glencoe, Illinois, 1958, p. 116.

> our advertising is worst. There's a lot of pressure to fudge around. I think my biggest job is to show people the truth, not to tell them what they want to hear.
>
> Remember, nobody cares how good our research is except us—the client and the agency only want results. We're in business to sell soap and not to do sophisticated research; that is, as far as they're concerned.

If the agency's organization were to be described in more conventional managerial terms, it was set up as a combination of a functional and a product type of company organization. It was functionally organized in the sense that activities were grouped "on the basis of similarity of function alone" into professional departments.[6] Usually, functional organization is found when one major product is made and in which there is rather little diversity in the sub-types of that product.[7] Obviously, advertising agencies produce many different "products" each tailored to the demands of a hypercritical client. Therefore, the functional groupings of professional departments were made more flexible by the rather ephemeral client-centered systems of control and communications, each of which was a product organization. Product organization is defined as existing when "all . . . activities incident to a given product are grouped under one head."[8] That is, the client-centered groupings, each coordinated by an account executive, provided the flexibility necessary for the proper functioning of the agency.

Reorganization

One of the distinguishing characteristics of the advertising business is the extreme rapidity with which an individual agency's business situation can change. Agencies may gain or lose business quickly, often with no advance warning.

Such changes happened to the Paragon Agency a few years ago—within a short period of time there was a rapid turnover in the major accounts handled by the agency. An agency reorganization was one of the solutions advanced by top management to increase flexibility in this subtle and unpredictable environment. It was hoped that this organizational change would result in increased cooperation and communications between specialists of different types.

The Creative Branch was reorganized as the first step toward this goal. The various creative departments (Art, Copy, the Production Departments) were dissolved; in their stead were formed several composite creative groups, each group being assigned the work of one or more specific clients. The memorandum noting this change stated that:

> This reorganization will allow our creative people to concentrate on and be responsible for all the creative work of the clients to which they will be assigned. We are certain that this change will allow us to give our clients more effective service.[9]

---

[6] E. H. Anderson, "The Functional Concept in Organization," *Advanced Management,* XXV (October, 1960), 17–18. Also see Harold Stieglitz, *Corporate Management Structures* (*Studies in Personnel Policy, No. 183*), The National Industrial Conference Board, New York, 1961, pp. 9–13. George A. Smith, *Managing Geographically Decentralized Companies,* Harvard Business School, Boston, Mass., 1958, pp. 25–33.

[7] Stieglitz, *op. cit.,* p. 9.

[8] *Ibid.,* p. 9.

[9] Paraphrase of a staff memorandum, Paragon Advertising Agency.

Shortly after the change in the Creative Branch, a similar reorganization of the Marketing Branch was undertaken. The stated purpose of this further change was to

> form marketing groups composed of small numbers of different marketing specialists who will work together on the problems of a few clients. These marketing groups will be similar to the groups recently formed by our creative brethren. . . . they will allow the different specialists in the Marketing Branch to be more closely coordinated and thus give clients better and quicker service . . . This reorganization will improve communications not only within the Marketing Branch but also with the Creative Branch and Account Management.[10]

In brief, the existing service departments were disbanded and their personnel were formed into heterogeneous marketing or creative groups to help fulfill the goal of more tightly integrated client service. Service was now provided by formal, permanent client-oriented groups in place of less structured, shifting client assignments.

Each group was assigned to a Group Supervisor who was to be responsible both for internal coordination of work in his group and external coordination of contacts and communication. Note that "external communication" is used here both in the sense of external to the agency (clients), and external to the specific group (communication with other service groups). (See Figure 3.)

To use the language of management again, the Paragon Agency was changed from a functional-product type of organization to a more directly product-oriented company.

Usually, productive enterprises take the option of changing from functional to product organizations under one or more of three types of conditions:

1. Differing production processes; i.e., the technology involved in the products differs.
2. Differing markets; i.e., the customers for each of the products are different.
3. Sufficient demand for the product to maintain a full-time operation.[11]

The Paragon Agency's situation met each of these criteria to some extent. The major positive effects predicted for a change to a product organization are greater flexibility, greater concentration on each "product line," and more efficient control over the production of each product line.[12] In addition, some problems are to be expected, such as segmentation of the internal organization, and possible competition among each of the semi-autonomous units for control of total company resources.

The option of changing organizational patterns is taken fairly frequently by managements, both in large enterprises and in smaller companies such as advertising agencies. Thus, this organizational change at Paragon was not a unique occurrence. Nor were most of the interpersonal effects of this change unique, although of course specific individuals may have reacted to their private fears and hopes in their own unpredictable ways.

---

[10] Paraphrase of a staff memorandum, Paragon Advertising Agency.
[11] Stieglitz, *op. cit.*, p. 9.
[12] *Ibid.*, p. 13.

Figure 3. Client-Centered Organization (for Company X) Paragon Advertising Agency (after Reorganization). Width of lines roughly indicates amount of contact.

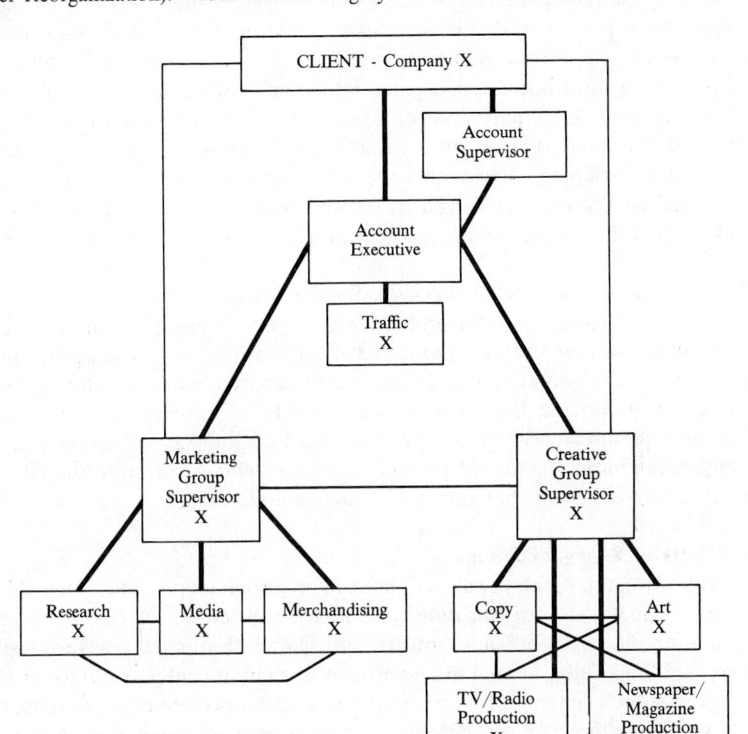

Reorganization and Patterns of Communication and Control

Several important changes in the communication and control systems of the Paragon Agency occurred after reorganization. Among these changes were: 1) Control increased over direct contact between agency personnel and clients, 2) Professional communication decreased sharply, and 3) Communications between members of different service groups both decreased and were more closely controlled as compared with communications between members of former specialty departments.

1. Control of Agency-Client Contact

With a Group Supervisor coordinating the activities of each service group, the problem of control of client communications has been greatly simplified. Now, a Group Supervisor performs primary coordination on account work within the agency; he serves as an organization censor who will not let any client communication out until it satisfies him. This means that client contact can now be limited to account personnel and to Group Supervisors. Although this control is not as complete as had been planned, the amount of direct contact between agency personnel below the level of Group Supervisor and client personnel has diminished considerably. (See Figure 3.) Relationships between client and agency are now restricted to fewer people whose efforts are more tightly coordinated.

2. Decrease in Professional Communication

One of the physical changes made in the Paragon Agency was the moving together of the personnel of the several service groups into contiguous offices. This act which symbolized the breakup of the old specialized departments, also served to make intra-professional communication more difficult.

In addition to actual physical dispersion, reorganization signified that displays of particular skill or virtuosity not connected with satisfying a client's needs would no longer meet with any institutional approval. In other words, professional competence as judged by non-professionals, rather than virtuosity as judged by other professionals, was rewarded.

3. Decrease in Communication Between Service Groups

As is the case for intra-professional communications, communication between client-centered service groups has decreased sharply since agency reorganization. Partly because of physical distance and partly because of the increased emphasis on the client, the tendency has been for communications to cluster within each client-centered group. In effect, the Paragon Agency is now a group of semi-autonomous small advertising agencies which are coordinated and connected only at the higher levels of management.

The Effects of Reorganization

The Paragon Agency was reorganized in order to provide more client-centered service. The reorganization was to have effected this by channeling and coordinating all work for and contacts with clients through a few responsible officers and, hopefully, by making heterogeneous client-centered service groups the organizational centers for all work. In fact, the immediate effect of reorganization was that efficiency of operation did increase if efficiency is expressed as coordinated manipulation and transmission of work and information. More-or-less routine matters were handled with fewer delays, mistakes, or omissions than before. In addition, clients now know that, whenever one of the agency contact people states fact or policy, that this is an official and relatively final agency opinion. Thus, there seems to be an immediate increase in the possibilities for rapport between each client and the agency which did not exist before. This effect has continued in the year since the beginning of the reorganization and, in organizational terms, seems to be a useful innovation.

However, when the personal and interpersonal effects of the reorganization on agency members is examined, the results are somewhat different. One of the most immediate effects of reorganization was a feeling of loss and separation among many of the personnel. Old friendship patterns reinforced by close location and shared training and experiences were suddenly threatened. As one researcher said shortly after the formation of marketing service groups:

> I feel lonely since we have moved offices. There's nobody to talk to except about business. You know, before this happened we used to have other research people look over our work and we used to talk about all sorts of other things. I don't know why it is but I can't seem to warm up to other people in this group.
>
> And another thing, what do these people know about research? I can't talk to them about what I do. So what *do* I talk about—sales figures?

Besides the physical dispersion of the members of former professional (functional) departments, there were other disturbing factors which took longer to make themselves apparent.

One such factor was the imposition of an informal but rather effective system of censorship. With each of the service groups separated both in space and in function, news and gossip flowed slowly among groups. As interest gradually became focussed on the service groups, this partial stoppage of information became even more complete. Official organizational channels of communication began to assume more importance as bearers of information about the condition of the agency. These channels were selective, however. Good news—approved and optimistic news—was emitted by management and circulated through organizational channels. Unpleasant news, such as firings of personnel as a result of temporarily poor business conditions, tended to be suppressed.

In order to allow for passage of gossip and professional information, several informal and semi-covert channels of communication developed in the months following reorganization. The opening of such communicational channels in itself is certainly not a unique occurrence in any organization. However, at Paragon these "new" channels had existed before as part of the organization; now they were superfluous. The semi-secrecy of such communications at first was occasion for somewhat shocked jokes. Later, the very fact of their being not sanctioned meant that each person who participated in such communications subverted organizational goals. To this extent, the need for opening of such gossip and information channels marked an alienation from the organization and a movement toward "divided loyalties, doubts, and guilts."[13]

Another situation which perturbed some agency members soon after reorganization was that, within each of the heterogeneous service groups, there was often no meaningful basis of comparison of performance from one individual to the next. In the former professional groupings, work could be judged by comparison with the similar work of other professionals. But, it is difficult to assess the competence of a copywriter as compared with an artist, or a survey researcher with a person who buys television time. To judge competence or usefulness of an individual in a client-centered service group it became necessary either to judge on personal factors—enthusiasm, friendliness, glibness, or their appearances—or else to compare the individual with his opposite number in another group (a practice not encouraged organizationally). Many of the client's criteria of worth—for instance, how well a client responds to an individual—could no longer be used because of the limitation of client contact to relatively few members of service groups.[14]

Finally, the change in organization marked a shift from dual evaluations of work (both professional and client-centered) toward the single criterion of client satisfaction. This shift was organizationally useful in view of the relationship of the agency to its environment; an advertising agency must depend on clients' satisfaction for its existence. However, this shift meant that judgments of individual output were now usually made by those who did not share an

[13] Victor A. Thompson, "Hierarchy, Specialization, and Organizational Conflict," *Administrative Science Quarterly*, V (1961), 317.

[14] R. Carter Wellford, "Developing Managers in a Product-Type Organization," *Management Record*, XXII (April, 1960), 21.

outlook with professionals. This tended to make such valuations seem somewhat impersonal and strange. Further, because non-professionals are often unable to appreciate specialized skills, the feeling grew that expediency rather than the intricacies of craft was the deciding factor in judgment (which was so in many cases).

At first, most of the personnel below top management levels tended to be worried and confused about themselves and their positions when reorganization was announced. This searching for some sort of anchor point was particularly acute during the time when offices were rearranged into service-group clusters. After this initial period, reactions among members of the agency varied in two ways which were associated with two major types of personal orientation to work and the company.

One group (which we shall call "careerists") tended to think of their work in terms of organizational status and of work and friendship patterns as means to achieve material and social status. Most friendships of this sort are so-called business friendships, that is, contacts and luncheon friendships which are the foundations of possible personal and business advantages.

The other group (called "craftsmen" here) were concerned with their careers as well but viewed them in a somewhat different light. Craftsmen tend to think of careers in terms of the actual work and the satisfactions derived from creative production. And although some friendships are cultivated for the purpose of promotion, craftsmen generally tend to choose as acquaintances those who are also interested in the work done and its content.

In brief, craftsmen and careerists are differentiated by the things which characterize their commitments to their work life. Careerists are committed to organizational status and power and to the use of institutional and personal means to achieve this. Craftsmen are committed to their work and the direct satisfactions derived from it and to the sharing of intra-professional friendships.[15]

For the careerists, reorganization meant that the objects and contents of their business relationships changed somewhat but the essential course of their actions changed little. That is, different people's decisions became binding and their work passed through new channels before it was finally approved. Immediately after reorganization most careerists spent a few anxious weeks assessing the effects of the changes on their chances for advancement within the agency. A few careerists left the agency a month or two after reorganization, mainly because they had been removed from protectors or because of budding conflicts with new superiors. Most of those who remained seemed to adjust to the organizational changes with little apparent thought or bother—new communications with important people were soon arranged and new contacts were found and cemented.

Initial reactions of the craftsmen to reorganization were essentially the same as those of the careerists. Most of them were concerned about the safety of their jobs and about the compatibility of their new bosses. Added to these fears,

---

[15] The differentiation between craftsmen and careerists was suggested by Herman M. Case, "Two Kinds of Crystallized Occupational Choice Behavior: A Problem in Delineation and Relationship," *American Sociological Review,* XIX (1954), 85–87, and to some extent by Alvin W. Gouldner, "Cosmopolitans and Locals: Toward an Analysis of Latent Social Roles—I," *Administrative Science Quarterly,* II (1957), 281–306. Note that the craftsman/careerist distinction is a heuristic device and needs some quantification.

however, were additional ones about losing the friendship and support of their professional friends and colleagues. In a sense, the craftsmen had clothed themselves with a sort of institutional mystique of craft. Many of them feared that they would not be respected for their professional skills as much as in their previous departments and that they might not do as well in the more general types of duties to be demanded in client centered service groups.

These immediate fears were to some extent groundless. Most professionals continued to do the same sort of work and there were few cases in which they needed to fear for their jobs. Group Supervisors proved incompatible with their new subordinates in only a few cases.

However, after several months many craftsmen found that they were becoming increasingly dissatisfied with their work. Mainly, the changes outlined previously affected these craftsmen to a much greater extent than they did careerists, the changes being alienation from professional colleagues and from the professional meaning of the work. This feeling of separation was summarized by a copywriter who left about five months after he had been assigned to a creative group:

> I left because of the nitpicking of my copy. I left because nobody there who could get to the client stood up to him for anything. And I left because once I wrote something it was out of my hands more than at any other place I had ever been.

A year after reorganization was completed, a fair number of the craftsmen in the Paragon Agency had moved on to other jobs, mainly because of dissatisfaction with their jobs at the agency. Those who stayed often did so with grumbling and complaint. Many seem to be less closely tied to the agency—they are more critical; they seem to take less interest in their work and in Paragon's fate.

These changes which occurred in the Paragon Agency after reorganization are rather complex. In general, there has been a lessening of integration within the organization. This decrease in integration has taken place mainly among the craftsmen who began to grow away from the agency within a few months after reorganization and have continued in this state of mind up to the time of writing (about a year after the beginning of reorganization). Careerists, however, seem to have been affected relatively little.

At this time, the Paragon Agency is still in a state of flux. To some extent, the direction it will now take rests on those who have been brought into the agency recently—many of these people have expectations different from those who left or those who stayed on but remain disaffected. And, of course, the future life of the agency depends also on the higher management which determines not only the agency's internal form and organization but also its connections with the supporting external world.

Discussion

Data obtained by participant observation are usually partial and subjective; conclusions drawn from them should be suggestions rather than definitive statements. With this caveat in mind, we can proceed to discuss the contents of this report.

In his important article, "Organizational Structure and Employee Morale," Worthy noted that, even though an organization may look efficient on a chart, interpersonal human factors have great importance in determining how well the organization really works. These factors are referred to as "integration," which is usually taken to mean the warmth and closeness of interpersonal relationships among organization members.[16]

In general, the findings here agree with many other studies which state that integration is an important facet of organizational functioning. However, the complexities of the Paragon Agency case can offer some modifications and enlargements of Worthy's statement.

The first major point is that this case makes it clear that organizational integration has two major aspects: interpersonal integration and work integration. Interpersonal integration is what Worthy meant when he talked about "integration," that is some degree of closeness of interpersonal ties among organization members. The events in the Paragon Agency show that there can be a minimum stage of interpersonal integration which involves rather little in the way of close personal ties. The very existence of channels of interpersonal communication which *allow* interpersonal ties seems to be the minimal criterion for interpersonal integration. For instance, in some of the functional departments of Paragon before reorganization there seemed to be relatively few enduring primary groups; the advertising business is often too competitive to allow really lasting or deep friendships to form. However, in these same departments the opportunity for meaningful communication existed for most members. One young researcher summed his feelings about the Research Department as follows:

> I don't feel bad here. There's no one here I feel close to; no one I would have home for dinner. Yet, at the same time, I feel that I can talk to anyone here in the Research Department and he will listen. I can ask advice and it will be given. I can tell my hates and peeves and they will listen. They share the same likes and troubles and they want to be heard too. And your own troubles aren't so bad if somebody comes to you with the same thing.

In this sense, interpersonal integration could exist without enduring ties.[17]

The other aspect of integration is work integration. It must include some feeling that the work done is important both to the individual and to the organization. This feeling can exist with little external support but this is rare; more often it is buttressed by the judgments and support of other persons who are socially meaningful. In other words, the necessary criterion for work integration is usually the sharing of the work experience with others whose perceptions give some consensual validation whether the work is important or not, well done or not.[18] It is likely that, as work becomes even more specialized and fragmented

---

[16] James C. Worthy, "Organizational Structure and Employee Morale," *American Sociological Review,* XIV (1950), especially 172–173.

[17] This concept of a non-interactive interpersonal community is similar to the community of shared belief of psychotherapists and their patients described by Charles Kadushin, "Social Distance Between Client and Professional," *The American Journal of Sociology,* LXVII (1962), 530.

[18] Harry Stack Sullivan used the term *consensual validation* to refer to the means by which a child learns the social validity of his personal perceptions. The term serves equally well in the context of legitimation of one's activities through responses of meaningful others. See Sullivan's *The Interpersonal Theory of Psychiatry,* W. W. Norton & Co., Inc., New York, 1953.

in larger organizations, the need for validation of work by meaningful others becomes of considerable importance since the individual is less and less able to judge his part in the whole.

The second major point is that those people who mediate integration for individuals have different characteristics according to the person's orientation. In this paper, two types of orientation have been distinguished: that of careerists and craftsmen. The paper also noted that careerists were affected relatively little by the reorganization while craftsmen generally were more alienated from the organization after the change. The reason for this difference lies with each type's group of reference. Careerists' integration was mediated by superiors in the organization with whom quasi-personal contacts were made, and whose judgments fixed the worth of work. Reorganization provided different superiors but did not greatly change the type of relationship. On the other hand, craftsmen depend to a large extent upon fellow professionals at the same level both for personal integration and also for evaluations of work. When the organizational change removed the ties with these meaningful people, integration decreased. Undoubtedly many other meaningful classifications of organization membership have been made and can be made. Any study of organizational integration among groups must include a description of the types of persons who mediate this integration and the content of the relationships between them.

In summary, this paper suggests that organizational integration has two major aspects—work integration and interpersonal integration. The necessary criterion for work integration is some meaningful judgment of the work done by significant others in the organization. The minimal criterion of interpersonal integration is the existence of open channels of communications to make personal contact possible. It was further noted that different types of organizational needs among individuals are met by different reference groups through which integrational ties are made.

The Change Process in Organizations: An Applied Anthropology Approach

LEONARD R. SAYLES

Unfortunately, the subject of change in organizations (or of community or culture) is typically dealt with as a distinct, separate process, apart from the normal functioning of the system. Change is apparently viewed as something that is imposed on an unwilling, unresponsive audience or consumer. The problem of change, therefore, is usually one of gaining consent or acceptance through cajoling, force, participation, spotting the most likely sources of resistance and, occasionally, identifying gate-keepers or possible allies.

From *Human Organization,* Vol. 21, No. 2 (1962), pp. 62–67; 82–85. Reprinted by permission of the author and The Society for Applied Anthropology.

In other words, it is the difficulty of *introducing change* into a resistant system which has captured the attention of most students of the subject. However, if one observes the behavior of managers or leaders it will be noted that this aspect of the problem does not account for a significant amount of the total amount of time and energy expended on administration. Our purpose here, then, is to broaden the analysis to include the total process of change. This means viewing change as an intimate, integral part of the administrator's task of managing—really *stabilizing*—a system of human relations. Change, then, is not a special, for holidays only, activity. It is part and parcel of the normal administrative process of assessing how the system is operating, determining where *significant* deviations are occurring, identifying the source of the disturbances, taking administrative actions to eliminate the source of the instability (what we will call short-run change) and, finally, where the disturbance or deviation is recurring—the introduction of "long-run" change and its implementation and control.

What follows is an exposition of the stages in this process and their interrelationship. This analysis also represents our view of the job of the administrator in operational or interactional terms. It is an effort to depart from subjective, unquantifiable variables that have usually been associated with the analysis of all management processes (not just change) often quasi-psychological variables like the degree of personal security or sensitivity of the leader, the degree of "consideration" he generates and his ability to give assignments which equate authority and responsibility (parenthetically, a most unrealistic and unlikely possibility).

One last point to the introduction and approach. It is naive to assume that the administrator-leader suddenly commits himself to the accomplishment of change and then devotes all his efforts to this objective. Change must be accomplished simultaneously with the continued operations of an organization or system of work relationships. There is no "breathing spell," typically, where the organization can go all-out in the effort to pull itself up by its boot straps. This, of course, is another reason for considering change as part of the total organizational process.

The Paradox: Change and Stability

Paradoxically, the manager's job is to accomplish both stability and change. In order to maximize both the productivity of the processes under his jurisdiction and maintain high motivation among subordinates (which in turn facilitates productive efforts), he must endeavor to minimize the frequency with which the patterns of work flow and coordination are disturbed. In fact, the frequency with which such actual or potential interruptions to the work patterns occur, as we have described in a recent book,[1] are the prime determinants of the work load of the manager. It is the development and maintenance of work flow routines which is his major objective, and these "predictable and repeated patterns of interaction" are the source of morale or the absence of debilitating stress and its concomitant: destructive emotional reaction (what we have called compensatory behavior).[2]

---

[1] Eliot D. Chapple and Leonard R. Sayles, *The Measure of Management,* Macmillan, New York, 1961, pp. 46–68.

[2] *Ibid.,* pp. 114–141.

> In a situation requiring cooperative endeavors, whether it is a work group, employees and managers, or staff and line officials, each tries to develop a stable pattern of work, of interaction. When these stable patterns are disturbed, individuals experience stress or an uncomfortable feeling of pressure and dissatisfaction. A breakdown in the flow creates opposition as the individuals struggle to restore it. The expected responses from the individuals in the sequence prove inadequate, and new coordination problems arise.
>
> The regularities of actions and interactions disappear when this stress occurs, and erratic variation takes over. The difference is obvious between a smoothly running operation and one with a problem. Under stress, people react emotionally, and, because more than one individual is involved, the reactions usually conflict with each other.
>
> Thus, a vicious circle is established. Something happens in the work situation that causes the relationship of individuals to change or to depart from the normal pattern. This creates a stress, either of opposition or nonresponse, that is further complicated by higher levels of supervision and staff specialists whose unexpected interactions, i. e., outside the usual organization pattern, irritate the disturbed work-flow relations. People get upset; they become angry with each other and, depending on their individual characteristics, react temperamentally. These personality conflicts have direct ramifications in the work process because the emotional reactions change the pattern of contact and interaction. Joe is angry with Bill, so he does not check with him before starting a new experimental run. Consequently, a special test that should have been included in the run is left out, and the whole thing has to be done over. To complete the circle, these emotional disturbances damage the work-flow sequence, which causes additional personality stresses.[3]

But, of course, as we "sophisticated" observers know, the achievement of this stability—which is the manager's objective—is a never-to-be-attained ideal. He is like a symphony orchestra conductor—endeavoring to maintain a melodious performance in which the contributions of the various instruments are coordinated and sequenced, patterned and paced—while the orchestra members are having various personal difficulties, stage hands are moving music stands, alternating excessive heat and cold is creating audience and instrument problems, and the sponsor of the concert is insisting on irregular changes in the music to be played.

In other words, the manager faces constant internal and external interruptions. As we shall see, some of these require mere palliatives—readjustments—in order to bring the system of relationships back to stability, for example, a disciplinary action (which is one type of change). Other disturbances require more drastic action if the system is to be stabilized, for example, the introduction of new methods or personnel as a result of a change in market conditions or the demands of some other part of the organization.

Presumably we might call this a moving equilibrium. External pressures and internal problems require constant "change," but the manager endeavors to accomplish this as he returns the system to equilibrium.

---

[3] *Ibid.*, pp. 37–38.

Detecting Disturbances or Deviations

Thus, an important element in the manager's job is the detection of disturbances or deviations in the system of human relationships which comprise his work flows. This is the control function of the manager: developing methods of detection whereby he can assess and appraise how and where he should devote his managerial efforts, perhaps supplemented by the assistance of other specialists.

We need to be aware that a manager's scarcest resource is (or ought to be) his own time and energy, and that of other members of management. Therefore, he needs to devote his attention to what are indeed problems and avoid spending time in areas which are functioning well.

How does the manager "check" or control? He looks at statistical reports of quality, quantity, turnover, and what have you. He "inquires around" as to how people are doing and he endeavors to "sense" when people are acting differently. Unfortunately, some of this is usually done intuitively and there is little systematic attention to an integrated control system.[4] In a well-developed theory of organization change, we would expect to set forth the actual pattern of control: how frequently and with whom or what the manager checks. We would also expect to see an integrated series of controls involving technical measures of performance (e.g. quality, quantity, etc.) embodied in relatively automatic data processing systems combined with measures of organizational relationships.

Among others, F. L. W. Richardson, Jr., has shown that one can interrelate variations in the technical performance of a system with variations in the human relations dimensions.[5] In other words, there are correlations between such things as output and changes in internal work group interactions, manager-subordinate interactions and subordinate-outside group interactions. These provide the new materials of an effective and objective monitoring system. The manager need not be able to "smell trouble."

Assessing the Significance of the Deviation

The next step in the process is the manager's assessment of the significance of the deviations he is observing. It is likely that Parkinson's Law could be stated more realistically in terms of managers making work for themselves and others by going into action to deal with a problem that is not a problem—in other words, to introduce a change in a system which is operating within *expected limits of variation.*

The mathematical statisticians have begun to work on just this problem—noting that management can introduce serious instabilities into inventory maintenance systems, that is, can really amplify variations—by endeavoring to over-correct for variation. We see the same thing in human relations terms—where the supervisor contacts his own subordinates and others to discuss "mutual problems," where the contact itself creates the problem, and none existed before. The foolishness is never detected, of course, because the endeavor to over-correct

---

[4] There has been inadequate attention paid to the development of a theory of systems control outside of some of the recent efforts of the mathematical statisticians. Eliot Chapple is also concerned with this problem, and his remarks may concentrate on this area.

[5] F. L. W. Richardson, *Talk, Work,* and *Action,* Monograph No. 3, Society for Applied Anthropology, 1961.

the system *does create a problem* which in turn justifies the supervisor's attention and energy expenditure.

Of course, the opposite is the more traditionally identified difficulty: the failure to detect quickly enough or to move quickly enough to quench a real fire. Thus the manager requires as part of his control apparatus a theory of significant differences which will enable him to place certain "limits" on the occurrence or amplitude of the phenomenon he is observing. This requires a knowledge of the limits on normal or expected variation, given the nature of the system. He then hoards his managerial actions for the significant deviations in the system—and avoids becoming himself a source of upset where none existed before.

It may be well to repeat here that this theory of change encompasses deviations or disturbances in the system that are imposed by superior fiat or environmental change as well as internal malfunctioning. We would expect that instabilities from the "outside" would be transmitted through his contacts with his own superior and other managers as well as through the flows of relationship in which his subordinates participate with "outsiders" in their job activities.

From the point of view of organization design and the specification of managerial actions, it thus becomes possible to set forth explicitly (and thus control and check the performance of) managerial surveillance actions. These would include operationally definable patterns for what to check, how and how often, as well as techniques of data analysis to ascertain significant differences. This becomes another step in the process of making managerial actions less art and intuition and more science, but within the realm of human relationships. For example, we can distinguish those checks that require the manager to initiate, those initiated to him, and those that come from reports. All, however, require organizational analyses, that is, a knowledge of the time dimensions of the work-flow system which are to be controlled, prior to the elaboration of the "checking" and "evaluation" procedures.

Corrective or Stabilizing Action

In moving toward a science of administration we would view the next task of the manager in the control-change sequence as taking corrective actions where significant deviations have been revealed. Here, too, we can be explicit about the interaction pattern required. These are the "short-run" changes. This area is the one usually encompassed by the human relations literature when it deals with getting a behavior change. This means the traditional techniques of order-giving, criticism, discipline, training, communication and persuasion (of course, we would insist that these can all be described in operational, interaction terms[6]).

We can, in fact, write sequences of remedial action which the supervisor takes (or should take) in endeavoring to bring the work flow system back to a stable state. Some of these patterns involve outside contacts as well which may serve to bring the system back to normal. For example, the unsatisfactory pacing of the activities of a service department may be creating internal problems. The manager may move through his superior or other channels in seeking to bring the tempo of these activities more in alignment with his needs. Or additional personnel may have to be secured through recruitment channels or permission

---

[6] Cf. Chapple and Sayles, *op. cit.*, pp. 48–64.

to work overtime secured from higher management in order to adjust to pressures for increased output. From the point of view of the organization as a whole, the manager operating these controls also must be required to alert his manager and others who may be affected by the departures from equilibrium of his system. This enables them to take complementary actions to avoid having the disturbance spread from the jurisdiction of this manager through the entire organization. All of these actions can be prescribed and quantified interactionally.

Analyzing Recurring or Continuing Sources of Deviation and Stress

Some of the problems with which the supervisor must cope will not be solved by the administrative actions to which we have referred. These are the ones we distinguish as recurring problems. They are the cause of comments like this:

> I am always having to go down to engineering and have a battle over specifications—hardly a week goes by in which there isn't an argument here and probably a big meeting as well.

Some are not recurring, they are just never solved. We have referred to these in our recent book as "spiralling" or cumulating deviations.[7] Figuratively an initial source of infection in the organizational system "spreads" to other flows and these, in turn, may react back on the original source, thus adding to the disturbance at that point. These are the so-called major crises or explosions. In either case the detection by the supervisor that such a problem exists should bring into action additional remedial measures.

The first of these may well be an investigatory pattern. After all, these are the problems which consume inordinate amounts of supervisory time and create major losses to the organization. Their occurrence suggests that some more significant and far reaching change is required than an adjustment in the attention or the immediate activity pattern of the supervisor. So-called staff groups, or consultant-specialists, unfortunately even task force committees, may be used to assess the situation. They come into action, or should be mobilized *only* when the controls maintained by the manager identify this type of problem or when the auditing mechanisms of the staff group themselves so indicate. It is well to note at this point that large, complex organizations frequently assign to staff groups the responsibility for accumulating some of the data that the manager uses for control purposes.[8]

As part of the investigatory process, the manager needs to be intellectually aware of the likely structural sources of stubborn instability. At some future time control mechanisms may be developed which will identify the source as well as the problem. The applied anthropologist has contributed a great number of "classic cases" for such an analysis:

1. Heavily "unbalanced" interaction patterns such as some of the jobs in Whyte's

---

[7] *Ibid.*, p. 161.

[8] The so-called staff-line problem is usually the result of a failure to organize on this basis. Staff groups go into action and initiate to the supervisor in areas and at times when the supervisor has not agreed there is a significant deviation. Then his dealing with the staff itself becomes a stressful relationship and a time-consuming one. In turn, this is partially the result of the failures of traditional administrative management theory in conceptualizing the staff "role." Apart from its audit functions the staff ought to be measured on its success in bringing deviating systems back to equilibrium—which, in turn, would minimize their conflicts with line managers. For a fuller discussion of this problem see G. Strauss and L. Sayles, *Personnel*, Prentice-Hall, New York, 1960, pp. 399–417.

restaurants,[9] and as exhibited by poor supervisors and conflict-laden union-management relations.[10]
2. Unstable or irregular patterns (e.g. Whyte's time-study-man analysis[11]), also other staff positions.
3. Contacts where there is an inadequate frequency of contact (e.g. see Sayles discussion of "Erratic Groups"[12] and Tavistock studies of the Longwall coal-getting method[13] and the Indian Weaving Shed.[14])

The applied anthropologist has identified these as typical sources:

1. Locations where the manager's jurisdiction has been poorly conceived such that "unit work flows" are broken by the organization. These are interrelated work positions between which a constant "rhythm" needs to be maintained, that is the parameters of the flow are identical.
2. Service groups outside of these flows which become "scarce resources."
3. Work positions where the requirements of the job are incompatible with personality of the incumbent.
4. Employees in positions which have undergone transformations to which they have not yet adjusted (e.g. the "succession" problem, the change in "status" and power of the nurse or the first line supervisor, and see also the many examples in H. O. Ronken and P. R. Lawrence, *Administering Changes*).[15]
5. "Men in the middle."
6. The impact of organizational innovations such as staff groups or incentives.

This then is an interim requirement for the change process—technical diagnoses of potential organizational trouble spots which can drain managerial time and energy. Beyond the diagnosis the manager has a great deal of work to do. This is the implementation process.

Usually we find that the manager must spend a great deal of time convincing superiors in the organization that a structural or "long-run" change is necessary, even before he gets an opportunity to engage in the difficult job of establishing the change in the organization. Many managers—or leaders—are kept so busy "putting out fires" that they never take on the job of seeking to find the source of recurring blazes. In a sense a rather great capital investment, in terms of time and energy, is necessary to provide a more permanent solution. The manager must take time away from his regular activities to undertake lengthy "selling" contacts with superiors and others plus the major problems of coping with affected subordinates. Many lack the energy and the ability to do this, and this is the major reason why "change" is not introduced at an appropriate rate in the organization, *not* the recalcitrance of subordinates, unions and habits!

Implementing the Change

The traditional human relations literature has also concentrated on the problem of gaining acceptance for structural changes. Here is where one reads

---

[9] William F. Whyte, *Human Relations in the Restaurant Industry* McGraw-Hill, New York, 1948.
[10] William F. Whyte, *Pattern for Industrial Peace* Harper & Bros., New York, 1951.
[11] William F. Whyte, *Money and Motivation,* Harper & Bros., New York, 1955.
[12] Leonard R. Sayles, *Behavior of Industrial Work Groups* Wiley, New York, 1958, pp. 78–79.
[13] E. L. Trist and E. W. Bamforth, "Social and Psychological Consequences of the Longwall Method of Coal-getting", *Human Relations,* IV (1951), 8.
[14] A. K. Rice, "Productivity and Social Organization in an Indian Weaving Shed," *Human Relations,* VI (1953), 297–329.
[15] Harvard University, Division of Research, Graduate School of Business Administration, Boston, 1952.

about participation and timing, the use of informal leaders, etc. Arensberg, however, again from the point of view of the applied anthropologist, has provided the only clearly operational description of the implementing process.[16]

1. First an increase in managerial initiative to subordinates.
2. Opportunity for increased inter-worker contacts (presumably informal group activity).
3. Followed by an increase in redressive contacts or initiations to the manager (and in turn the manager must be prepared time-wise to accept these).
4. Rewarding managerial responses to these subordinate initiations (often the change period is such a hectic one that time is not available for this step).

In our terminology both (2) and (3) represent compensatory behavior—reactions of the individuals to the stress of changed jobs, managerial contact patterns, etc.

Again these are time consuming patterns of administration and detract from the other commitments of the supervisor. In addition, the organization typically may neglect the more formalized accommodation patterns identified by the anthropologist as easing major dislocations in human patterns of interaction. We have in mind the *rites de passage* and symbolic ceremonies which the community has evolved for such crises.

Validating the Change

The manager cannot afford to assume that a change he has introduced has actually become part of the operating system. We know that human relations systems tend to return to previous equilibria when pressures are removed which have shifted them away from that position. However, it would be a mistake to assume that all changes are imposed on "comfortable" equilibria, although these are the ones which are grist for the case writers. There are many situations in which people are under substantial stress and tension; the organization is not providing them with personal satisfactions, and they welcome change. Whether initially welcomed or not, the manager must utilize methods of appraisal to validate that the change has become stabilized. Essentially this means checking to see that the flow, sequence and coordinating patterns are as planned.

Organization Change vs. Conversion

It should now be evident that the applied anthropologist's theory of change and administration encompasses both traditional methods of persuasion and influence, usually emphasized in social psychological terms but operationally definable in behavioral, interaction terms, and more long-run or permanent alterations in the organizational constraints. In another work we have chosen to call the former "conversion" by which we meant simply that the manager seeks to convince or persuade a subordinate to shift his behavior in some way and thus eliminate a source of disturbance.[17]

Obviously, this type of administrative activity is important and constantly used. It is involved in the giving of brief orders and lengthy disciplinarian sessions. But the administrator who relies solely on this type of change is ignoring one of the most important parts of his job: seeking out and remedying the

[16] Cf. Conrad Arensberg and Geoffrey Tootell, "Plant Sociology: Real Discoveries and New Problems," in Mirra Komarovsky, (ed.), *Common Frontier of the Social Sciences,* The Free Press, Glencoe, Illinois, 1957.

[17] Chapple and Sayles, *op. cit.*

persisting and compounding problems. These require, as we have endeavored to illustrate, the introduction of changes in the organizational constraints: the flow of work, the components of jobs, the incumbents on jobs, the structure of authority, the incentives and even the controls themselves that are used.

Conclusion

We have endeavored to write an operational description of the change process as an integral part of the manager-leader's day-to-day administrative activities. This analysis lends itself to behavioral quantification and objective validation so that the organization can provide for change within its structure and appraise the success of its members in carrying forth these patterns. Rather than a "last straw", when all else has failed, change, in the applied anthropologist's view can precede serious crises. Further, administrators can be trained in terms of unambiguous behavioral skills to carry forth such programs.

In our view, the process of change has consisted of these interrelated sequences of managerial action:

1. Specific organizational and technical checks (of prescribed characteristics and frequency) on the stability of the system under the jurisdiction of the manager.
2. Established criteria for evaluating significant deviations from the desired stable state.
3. Prescribed administrative patterns of corrective action to bring the system back to equilibrium. (Short-run change)
4. Appraisals of recurring or continuing instabilities in the system with provision for staff (or specialist) assistance in investigating potential structural sources of organization stress and remedial measures.
5. Administrative patterns for implementing "long-run" organizational structural change.
6. Administrative action to validate the change.

We have purposely ignored the usual shibboleths about starting at the top of the organization and getting "grass roots" support, etc., etc. In our view of change as part of every manager's operational job requirement, this pattern is repeated at each level with adjustments in controls to view the processes below. There is no starting or ending point as such—change is an integral and essential part of all organizational behavior.

What is the implication for this description of the change process in organizations for the growing social concern with the impact of large hierarchical structures or initiative and creativity? It would seem to me that this type of analysis presents a far different prognosis for the role of the individual than the usual political science view of delegated and strictly delimited authority or the psychologists' emphasis on palliatives to reduce the sting of hierarchical power.

In our recent research we have viewed the actual behavior of managers in a very large organization and we find that their organizational positions give them much "leeway" in utilizing their personality skills and energies in meeting the challenges of constant restabilization requirements and the need to initiate to introduce change. The notion that the lower level manager deals passively as a transmitter of orders from higher ups and a feedback mechanism, reporting what is going on below, is just not reality, except where the manager's personality is inadequate to taking the initiative. We would not want, however, to minimize the number in the latter category.

When the organization is viewed as a complex series of interlocking patterns of human relationships, work flow patterns and control patterns, the opportunity for the individual to innovate and shape his own environment becomes apparent. Creativity and innovation are a product of the individual's ability to extract the time and energy from the "fire fighting" preoccupations of the moment, in order to modify the pressures and stresses which are being showered on himself and on his subordinates. The hierarchy is no barrier to this—it is, as it has been in every culture—the challenge to the able.

Discussion[18]

Leonard Sayles

What I am saying is that, in an organization, the need for change is actually brought home to the administrator at any level or in any position if the organization is using adequate controls and if it has a reasonably decent structure. The need for change is imposed on him by requiring that he spend his time on and worry about and deal with certain kinds of deviations that are the result of internal malfunctioning of one sort or another or the failure of his particular unit to coordinate appropriately with other parts of the organization. If the administrator can be given knowledge and an appropriate analytical method, he can relate the ways he is spending his time and energy to the deviations he is observing and attempting to damp out.

If he can be given the method of relating his control system to organizational processes, you then have an administrative technique for relating the two. He knows that these kinds of controls are indicating that there are problems in these particular parts of his organization or other people's sub-organizations that are impinging on his. If the controls are well designed they will identify the nature of the human relations problem at least in part. He can then begin to utilize the specialized services that many modern organizations provide; what I call in my paper long-run solutions or structural changes.

A typical difficulty in implementing change is that the administrator wants to stand pat and feels that various people with good ideas are trying to push him into change, because the system is not designed so that the need for change is a pressure on the administrator. He can be shown ways to relate these needs, pressures, and disturbances to the source of the problem. When he can do this, he is then more than anxious to ask for help from the staff people, consultants, and other people in the organization who are willing to make studies and do analyses which will serve to identify what changes need to be made to eliminate these pressing and disturbing problems.

Robert Guest

I would like to make a few comments about assumptions that we are making as to the effectiveness of the behavioral scientist alone or the skilled administrator in effecting change in organizations and go on to something that I think is basic and obvious to anyone who has spent much time in production organizations.

[18] This discussion followed the presentation of the foregoing paper.

Herbert Shepard discussed the intervention of the behavioral scientist in creating interpersonal openness and a problem-solving climate. He talked about the steps that one uses in bringing about this kind of openness which allows people to solve problems. I know that Chapple and Sayles are aware of some of the comments I want to make, but I would like to remind us of some obvious things which have to do with the interventions of persons other than those interested in the behavior of groups and the relationship of people in an hierarchical organization. I refer to the intervention of the technical man himself, the engineer. When we really get close to a situation in a shop and find expressions of dissatisfaction, antipathy, and conflict and look at these expressions and their environment, we find very often that there are some basic technical factors in the workflow system, such as the operations of machines, assembly lines, or paper-work systems that are, in fact, creating these conflicts. Quite often we have talked with foremen, foremen and workers, and different supervisors. As they talk about their relationships with other people, one could say superficially that there are personality conflicts, strains due to authoritarian relationships. If you look at it, however, it may be that these people are in a built-in conflict situation. To be concrete about it, if a foreman is charged with the operation of his section, and the materials that are coming into his section on which his workers are working are damaged or imperfect, this immediately places him, regardless of what kind of a person he is, in a conflict situation with the man in charge of material controls. In order to carry out his responsibilities, what kind of interaction must he have with this other person? It is one of conflict, of course. We have often seen situations which, on superficial analysis, indicate that there are stresses and strains that are built into the organization due to different perceptions that people in different positions have toward one another. However, when the technical system itself is improved, when, for example, production schedules are evened out, where you have improvements in the product mix, a more efficient system for the distribution and replacement of tools in an organization, a better system of preventive maintenance, paper-work systems made clearer—all this reduces the need for the persons in the organization to be in conflict.

This is an obvious point (and as a behavioral scientist myself) I am just suggesting that, in the reality of our research, we ought to look into the workflow systems themselves. We must also work with those persons responsible for making technical changes and not simply assume that some of the most important changes can be made in the field of organizational behavior itself. One of the things that we have noticed has been put quite well by Arthur Turner. It is the circular effect that takes place in the attitudes that people have toward one another and their interactions. We have all conceived situations in which groups of people, foremen and other persons in the organization have had the opportunity and the kind of climate that leads to interpersonal openness, Sayles would put it, able to zero in on a technical problem and, once having done that, being able to solve the technical problem which, in turn, eliminates further technical problems and this, in turn, makes it possible for them to take time to get together and to continue to solve further technical problems.

Chris Argyris

I want to ask you a question and make one comment, Leonard Sayles, I would like you to take a hypothetical example and show what precisely are some of the differences between what you are talking about and the conversion approach.

In his paper, Chapple suggested to me a way of trying to put both these approaches together. It is not a way that I am sure he would prefer, but it is a way that I would like to offer for consideration. He gave the model of a quality-control system. Now a quality-control system usually has some limits which you cannot go beyond unless you want trouble. A quality-control system points to the trouble beautifully, but does not tell you what to do about it. For example, if you have a chemical system or a mechanical system, the control system will tell you things are going wrong, but then you go to chemistry or whatever product you are dealing with to make changes. I should like to suggest that the way of putting these two things together would be that the interaction pattern can be used as precise indicators of trouble and that when you ask what to do about it, you need then to utilize the conversionist approach.

Leonard Sayles

Argyris has asked for an example. Let us take an organization that was having financial difficulty at the production level, which also had an incentive plan that never worked. There were very serious conflicts between first- and second-line supervisors. The foremen felt that middle management never supported them. They did not understand how difficult these workers were to supervise or how ethnic problems entered into the situation. The foremen were stuck with responsibility for a process which they could not control.

It seems to me that Argyris and Shepard would have urged that these people get together and learn more about how each saw the other and how all saw the problem in the belief that greater recognition of these conflicting perceptions would have led first to better understanding and then some integration or rationalization of the various positions. Then, on the basis of this better feeling and better understanding, the parties might develop a solution to their more serious problems.

It seems to me that one should first look at the sort of thing Guest discussed; that is, the level of operating work in the department. Similarly, in the organization to which I refer, management discovered that human relations disturbances frequently occurred because of various problems in the division of labor, in the way people had to come together to get a rather complex job done. Once these were solved, on the basis of interaction, this intra-management dispute became very minimal. I am sure that they still did not understand each other well yet and it would have paid them to get together more because there were still many points of friction between the two levels of management but the number of disturbances emanating from the workflow decreased markedly. As a result, the first-level supervisor had many less pressures on him from middle management to meet production quotas. He had to go many fewer times to the second level and say, in effect:

> Why don't you support us on these union grievances where the union claims were pushing them too hard, and why don't you do things in terms of the contract that will not permit the union to engage in wildcat strikes and all the rest?

The reorganization of the workflow system minimized the frequency of disturbance and minimized the need for extra organizational mechanisms such as group meetings, conferences and what have you. The whole point we are making is perhaps too simple to merit additional emphasis. It is merely that an analysis of how people come together in organized situations, observed either by those in this situation or by an outsider, permits one to identify where the organization is malfunctioning. Through this kind of analysis, change can be introduced through regular organizational procedures which obviates the need for rather time-consuming extra organizational meetings and what have you.

Chris Argyris

Why would a foreman not be able to do this without interaction theory? Why could not any four or five people do this without any of this theory that you have brought up here?

Leonard Sayles

Maybe the word interaction theory is the red herring. What we are proposing is something that anthropologists have always done. They have watched people in their relationships with one another—the way they come together, under what circumstances they come together, what happens when they come together in getting their respective jobs done. Whether this is a division of labor in the family, in a community or in a business firm, one is able to observe where personality or structural defects are causing people to come together in ways that are stressful for them. One can then prescribe changes in process or structure procedure which will minimize the frequency of these stressful occurrences. Want to call it interaction theory? Okay.

Eliot Chapple

I would just like to comment on Chris Argyris' remark about quality control. Sophisticated quality control procedures are not simply a matter of a measurement and of determining that you are having trouble. It is, rather, to isolate the variables which are responsible and to run quality control on those essential variables. Now then, we can argue whether the variables we are describing are sufficient to make the predictions.

F. L. W. Richardson, Jr.

This is really a spurious dichotomy—the conversionist and the interactionist. There is a very interesting historical change taking place which explains a lot about this so-called conversionist point of view being effective and why the argument is somewhat spurious. We began, historically, with the proverbial old-fashioned line organization where orders came from the top. Technology was relatively simple and there was a structure inherited from the past—the aristocratic, elite structure of educated people above and uneducated workers below. We have moved from that to a period now where there is a largely educated population. We have moved from a simple technology to a complex one which has been reproduced organizationally in the so-called staff-line organization. The terminology and description I deplore, but the point is you have a much more complex organization with many specialists and the supervisor has on his staff a large number of specialists who handle various aspects of his job. Now this has required a great deal of lateral communication and, incidentally, interaction between the individuals concerned in order to coordinate the activities. A manager now who has a personnel department, machine maintenance, quality control, manufacturing, engineering, marketing and production control, has a lot to coordinate. He cannot encompass all the specialized knowledge easily. The hospital has been going through a comparable evolution in the last few decades. Now, many people have been brought up in a tradition that makes them want to be big shots, and they want to give orders and go places. They go places by giving orders and hobnobbing with the brass and playing politics and manipulating those below them. They usually do not know that this is going to end in their defeat and discredit if they do it too openly and too unskillfully. Now come the conversionists and what they do is to demonstrate that aggressive dominant behavior is not as rewarding as these people have been consciously schooled or conditioned to assume.

If you are an interactionist, you would analyze for, e.g., the vertical interaction patterns between boss and subordinate from the top to the bottom of the hierarchy. You would, for example, show 1) that eighty percent of all vertical contacts are initiated from boss to subordinate and 2) that bosses consume ninety percent of all this conversational time. You would further show that, in the few departments where (1) was sixty-five percent and (2) seventy percent, morale and productivity were highest. Now, having analyzed this and presented it to management, nothing happens until one day they hire a Chris Argyris who converts them.

These conversionists are much more skillful than interactionists usually in bringing about change although their diagnostic skills are usually far inferior. While the interactionists are pioneering in research, the conversionists, as clinicians, are, at the moment, fulfilling a very important, vital historical need.

Leonard Sayles

Richardson has identified an important historical point but I think it has some ramifications that he did not state. I recall speaking to a manager the other day who said that he is responsible for six or seven million dollars of expenditures. He has only eighteen immediate subordinates but he deals with 200 to 300 other people in the organization, over whom he has no superordinate relationship. This is one of our reasons for uneasiness about getting people to be less "authoritarian." Organizations are changing into structures where lateral relations predominate, where there are tremendous numbers of overlapping networks of servicing, staff, and specialized interest groups. In order to get your job done, you, as the manager, must influence large numbers of people, over most of whom you have zero authority.

One of the things that has disturbed me is that in some of the writing of the conversionists (perhaps we should drop that term at this point) there is an over-emphasis on the authority relationship and its debilitating effects. In the modern organization, whether it is a hospital or a corporation, these are becoming quite secondary in terms of the frequency in importance in that most people are not suffering from pressure from the boss. They are suffering from an inability to meet the enormous interaction requirements of these 200-odd relationships, if it happens to be the kind of company I referred to a moment ago. Where

I disagree with Richardson is that I think people can understand, analyze, and cope with overlapping networks of service, staff, customer, and audit relationships in the organization by interaction. The administrator can be provided with a framework to identify where these networks are not working out well, where they are stressful for their people and precipitate one organizational crisis after another, and where the network is working out rather well. People do not necessarily have to understand one another or agree with one another in order to make those kinds of organizational changes (which, in turn, will improve their showing on the various controls the organization is using to evaluate the performance of managers.)

Vincenzo Petrullo

I should like to ask a question. It seems to me that the discussion has revolved around two assumptions. One is that all organizations are very large organizations and the other is that the top executive is quite willing to go along with any change the anthropologist proposes. Now, I have dealt with rather small organizations, ranging from 300 to about 1,000 employees. In nearly every case, the chief executive has been the owner or his family has been the owner. I find that there is something in those organizations which has been avoided in our discussions. There is a tradition of how to get things done. Very often the executive is the son of the person who ran the organization his own way and there are many older employees around and a great deal of intimacy. The distance that has been implied is not always present between production control and quality control. There is a great deal of interaction and a great deal of intimacy and there are problems in the organization. I would like to ask about the middle-sized organization, with four or five hundred people in it, where the fundamental problem is inducing the owner and the chief executive to change. The reaction I get all of the time is, "Well, now, will you please change: everybody else but me?" How do you go about coping with that kind of situation, because, unless he changes, there is nothing that can be done with the organization.

Leonard Sayles

The executive may be in the position of the chief of the tribe being imposed upon by the missionary or the anthropologist. The organization might be fine as far as he is concerned and no one is suggesting that just because certain people have been rewarded for thinking up changes (and I am thinking now of consultants as well as staff people) that change is always viewed as a good thing. That perhaps is the other side of what I was saying earlier, that many times the staff group or the consultant or someone else in the organization has a reward system whereby he gets paid off for changes (regardless of their necessity) but those in key positions are not in any way rewarded for change and therefore resist it. Insofar as the introduction of change is not tied into the normal organizational controls or processes, there is no reason to believe that people will want to change. First, I would want to know whether the top man has pressures on him to change. If he is not experiencing this, if everything is functioning well, it may well be that the new conveyor or the new computer, or the fancier paper handling system and so on may not be worthwhile.

The Changing of Organizational Behavior Patterns: A Case Study in Decentralization

PAUL E. LAWRENCE

Introduction

The executives [of "Food World"] were planning a concerted effort to "decentralize" their chain of supermarket stores. (The term "decentralization" inadequately describes their organizational plans but it must serve for the moment.) Their motivation for this change came from two principal sources. First, they believed that the company needed to move in this direction to compete more effectively in its industry. Secondly, they believed that such a move would make their organization a better place to live and work. This dual motivation added to the attractiveness of the project. Furthermore, the planning for the changes was nearly complete and the researcher could be present at their inception. The company was big enough to provide an example of the reorganizational problems of a large-scale enterprise and small enough so that the researcher would not get lost. The top management group was highly articulate and highly cooperative. The researcher was intrigued, and the project was undertaken.

Upon undertaking the study, the researcher's first problem was to state and clarify the research questions that were to be answered and the research methods to be used in securing these answers. The researcher finally settled on two major sets of questions which in turn required the use of two quite different types of research methods. The early part of the research effort was concerned with the questions: What is the nature of the basic behavior patterns in this organization? What are the key factors involved in changing these patterns? These questions called for the use of the dual research methods of direct observation of behavior and interviews. The researcher spent many days talking to people at all levels in many parts of the organization and observing them going about their work. He kept voluminous field notes on what they said and did. His research interviews were open-ended—he was interested in what the individual thought was important to describe about his job and his work relationships. He observed what people did, with whom they dealt, and the way they handled themselves in these relationships. . . .

The top management executives, in their roles as leaders of the Food World social system, wished to change some of the critical behavior patterns of the system. They were motivated to do this as a result of their observation of

From Paul E. Lawrence, *The Changing of Organizational Behavior Patterns: A Case Study of Decentralization* (Boston: Division of Research, Harvard Business School, 1958), pp. 1–4, 62–68, 130–140. Reprinted by permission of the publisher.

anticipated external pressures on the system and as a result of their perception of certain malfunctioning in the system itself that threatened its health and survival. They wanted their plans to have a significant effect on behavior throughout the entire organization. The researcher, however, could not hope to observe and measure all the effects of the reorganization. He chose, therefore, to concentrate his observations on two strategically critical positions; the store manager and the district manager. This choice was made on the assumption that the men in these positions would have to make the most changes in their behavior, and the desired results further down the line would be dependent upon their making these changes. We shall therefore be focusing our intensive study on the behavior of the people in these two strategic positions.

Members of top management stated their ideas about the desired behavior changes in terms of "decentralization" and "clear-cut administrative framework." They were not completely happy with these terms because they knew that they were subject to differing definitions, but regardless of the words they had a pretty clear idea of what they wanted. For our research purposes, however, we need to define these desired behavioral changes in more concrete and measurable terms. To do this we shall take the two key positions, the store manager and the district manager, and see in what specific ways management desired them to change their behavior. In other words, what were management's new requirements for the roles of these positions?

New Required Role—Store Manager

For convenience and clarity we shall subdivide the role requirements into the three elements of behavior—the kind of *activities* the store manager was to engage in, the kind of *interaction* he was to have with others, and the kind of *sentiments* he was to hold.

Activities: Management expected the new store manager to spend considerable time in all departments of the store observing what was going on (in contrast to doing physical work). It expected him to analyze past performance and work out future plans and objectives.

Interactions: Management expected the new store manager to interact down the line primarily with his three department heads (in contrast to working directly with clerks). These interactions were to be two-way, problem-solving conversations in which the subordinate participated in choosing departmental objectives and merchandising methods, and in making personnel decisions. It expected the store manager to initiate interactions with the staff merchandisers to seek their technical assistance in the perishable department but not to let themselves or their department managers be dominated by these merchandisers. As regards his superior, the district manager, he was expected not only to receive and interpret instructions from above but also to pass on ideas and problems.

Sentiments: Management expected the store manager to conceive of himself as a businessman concerned with the over-all well-being of his store for the future as well as the present. He was to be loyal to the organization but feel more self-sufficient rather than dependent on his superiors. He was to have an enthusiasm for the possibilities of the store that would be reflected in his subordinates' attitudes. He was to think of himself as a leader and developer of his subordinates rather than as a dominator of them.

In considering the required role described above, we need to remember that the organization plans called for recruiting most of the new store managers from positions as grocery managers or other departmental managers in stores. The new store manager role requirements are by no means the same thing as the existing pattern of activities, interactions, and sentiments practiced by departmental managers. In fact, it might be predicted that these changes are so great that they could not be successfully made without the intelligent and active support of his immediate supervisor, the district manager.

New Required Role—District Manager

The district managers had traditionally been a strong link between top management and the store organization. They were traditionally giving their store personnel frequent and detailed supervision on the way top management wanted the work of the stores conducted. These were the men who were accustomed to making hundreds of detailed decisions about how the stores were to operate. They were giving instructions on how they wanted merchandise displayed, how they wanted work schedules handled, how they wanted the store plant maintained, and the hundreds of other detailed items involved in good store operation. The whole system worked so that the store people had been trained to be loyal and hard-working order takers, and, so far as they were concerned, these orders were emanating from the district manager who to them had always been their personal "big boss," who would have the dominant voice in determining their own personal future with the organization. Under the new organizational plan, these district managers were being asked to change drastically their traditional role. Top management's new role requirements for the district managers are spelled out below in terms of concrete behavior.

Activities: The district manager was still expected to spend most of his time going from store to store in his territory observing and talking with his subordinates. He was, however, expected to spend more time looking over the perishable departments because of his loss of the assistant district managers. He was also expected to spend more time on planning functions and less on "fire fighting" current problems.

Interactions: The district managers were expected to provide opportunities for their subordinate store managers to assume more decision-making functions. They would have to converse with their fledgling store managers so that these men would assume greater responsibilities and discharge them adequately. This meant that in their interactions with their subordinates they were expected to make a fundamental change toward adopting a more problem-solving, two-way type of communication. They would have to strike a relatively even balance between the amount of time they spent talking to their subordinates and the time their subordinates spent doing the talking to them. It was expected that the district managers would still be in frequent contact with the staff merchandisers (their former assistant district managers), but instead of the traditional boss-subordinate pattern it was to be a relationship of a line-staff nature with the district manager calling on the merchandiser for advice and staff assistance and, in turn, teaching the store manager to use this staff assistance intelligently. The district manager was also to be expected to adopt different interaction practices with his superiors in the organization. This was most apparent in the way the plan called for conducting different types of headquarters meetings with the district manager group. These meetings were no longer to be primarily briefings where the district managers were told what top management orders they were to carry out, but rather they were now expected to do a more systematic job of keeping top management informed on the problems arising in the field and on the suggestions for improvement that were coming from the field. What is more, they were expected to participate more in making the plans and decisions that affected operations.

Sentiments: Like the store managers, the district managers were expected to conceive of themselves as more independent, self-sufficient businessmen who were concerned with the long-range well-being of their districts. They were even to think of their role as superiors, as being more that of teachers and developers of the capacities of their store managers.

These new role requirements were in considerable contrast to the customary ways of thinking and behaving that prevailed among these men. The district managers were, then, expected to change their role in the organization drastically—to change their behavior in every one of their key relationships, up, down, and sideways, that made up their daily work existence. These changes were strategically critical to the success of the entire reorganization plans since they were an essential prerequisite to changing the daily working practices of the people in the stores. It is for this reason that we shall be focusing in the succeeding chapters on the problems of change in the behavior of district managers in their relations with the new store managers, and certainly not because the individual district managers "ought" (in a moral sense) to change their behavior any more than anyone else.

Management Change Methods

The top management of Food World adopted a number of specific methods to clarify the new role requirements for store managers and district managers. The executives worked out new job definitions with the people concerned, gave speeches on what they expected of the new setup, wrote up various descriptions of what they wanted in the company's house organ, and redrew the company's official organization chart. They knew, however, that these customary steps to establish the new required roles had to be supplemented by other change methods—new work procedures and new incentives.

The new control procedures that required sales and expense goals to be agreed on at the store manager and district manager level were designed to foster the required interaction pattern. The same was true of the new procedure for having these supervisors participate in the systematic evaluation of their employees. Likewise the new type of management meetings were designed to give these supervisors a chance to practice filling the required roles.

Finally top executives gave their supervisors some explicit and implied incentives for behaving in terms of the new roles. They offered store departmental managers the incentive of a higher status title, "store manager," and increased pay for demonstrating that they could adequately meet the role requirements for store manager. With the district manager they implied that the larger, more desirable districts or even higher management jobs would go to those who could meet the new role requirements, while there was an implicit threat that failure to meet the requirements could result in demotion.

These, then, were the formal steps that management could and did make to translate the new required roles from the planning stage into the actual day-to-day behavior of the key supervisors. It remained to be seen if these formal steps were successful in making the plans a reality.

In early 1955 the observer heard a newly appointed store manager ask a kidding question of another store manager:

> Have you heard the new definition of a store manager? It's a grocery manager with a raise in pay.

This comment epitomized the question that was on the minds of many in the organization. Could management's plan get beyond the overt changes they could effect directly—the changes in title, in pay, and in job descriptions? Could it be transformed from a paper change into a basic change in the daily work habits of many people? Could it be a change of substance as well as of form? . . .

Interaction Patterns—Three District Managers

The principal organizational changes that the top management group wished to make were in the overt behavior between superiors and subordinates at certain key spots in the organization. To succeed in effecting these changes, they had to get the members of their supervisory forces to actually change their interaction patterns—their customary conversational practices with their subordinates. Top management could not be content with gaining a mere intellectual understanding of what they wanted, nor would it be enough to secure merely verbal agreement with their plans. And, since all the district managers spent most of their time talking to subordinates in the stores, the important question was not who the district managers talked to, but rather how they talked to their subordinates. The on-the-job, moment-to-moment, verbal behavior of people had to change or the new organizational model would not become a reality. Because this overt behavior was the true test of the success of the change, it also had to be the researcher's way of measuring the change. This fact ruled out the use of many research methods for checking the degree to which the change was actually implemented. It ruled out the use of questionnaires or various pencil and paper tests. It forced the researcher to search for ways to observe and record the overt interactions of the key individuals in the change.

In the last three chapters we have presented one way of reporting research on the behavior of people in an organization, the reporting of a sample of episodes of their behavior. This method has the advantage of helping us get a "feel" for these people and of seeing some of the dynamics of their behavior. However, this method used by itself leaves us with some doubts and shortcomings. Was the sample biased? Can we be sure that a change has occurred between one point of time and another? To overcome these doubts and problems, the researcher decided to supplement his direct recording of behavior episodes with a way of quantifying the overt interaction pattern between a superior and a subordinate. This chapter will briefly describe this research method and then give the results of using it with our three key district managers.

The Research Method

On a somewhat trial-and-error basis and by borrowing ideas from Bales' interaction analysis methods,[1] the researcher evolved a research method that was

[1]See Robert Bales, *Interaction Process Analysis* (Cambridge, Addison-Wesley Publishing Co., 1950).

simple enough to be practical in making direct on-the-job observations and that provided a quantified measure of the interaction pattern between a superior and a subordinate. In practice the method worked as follows. The researcher entered a store with the supervising district manager. Every time the district manager and the store manager engaged in conversation with each other, the researcher noted: who talked; the length of each separate speech; the category of speech involved (that is, was it (1) asking a question, (2) supplying information, (3) giving an opinion, or (4) giving directions or suggestions); the type of topic involved; and finally who initiated new topics. The topic classifications that were used were, (1) discussion of people, (2) merchandise, (3) record systems, (4) physical plant, and (5) small talk.

These observational categories follow closely the required changes in the interaction aspects of the new supervisory role. It follows, then, that if we can get reliable quantitative data on these items, we can measure the degree to which the behavior of our three district managers is meeting the new role requirements for interactions. The data will also serve as a check on the validity of the descriptive analysis of the district managers' behavior presented in the preceding three chapters.

The interaction patterns of our three key district managers were systematically observed over a period of five months in the summer and fall of 1955. This was roughly the same time period in which the episodes occurred that are reported in the three preceding chapters. At this time each of these men was supervising the work of several newly appointed store managers. The theory behind the store manager program had been fully explained to them. They had had enough exposure to the new arrangements so that the first novelty of the system had worn off. All the formal steps to implement the program had been made, but it was still a very new thing. Our data should give us a measure, then, of the degree to which the behavior of our three district managers coincides with the new model at an early date, but after all the formal and direct organizational steps had been taken to implement the new system.

The researcher was anxious to get a representative sample of the interactions of each key district manager so that the resulting data would reflect accurately the supervisory characteristics of the district manager and not other extraneous factors. To do this, the district managers were observed working with several different store managers to minimize the effect of the personality of a particular store manager on the interaction pattern. The district managers were also observed calling on stores on different days of the week, and for considerable amounts of time. This was done to minimize the possibility of seeing a district manager handling only a few types of problems in a store. Because of the need to suit the job convenience of the district managers, it was not possible to get a perfect distribution of observing time in all these factors, but, as is indicated by Table 1, interactions were observed under a variety of circumstances to reduce

TABLE 1. Prevailing Conditions During Observation of DM Interaction Patterns

District Manager	Total Interaction Time Observed	Time Early in Week	Time Late in Week	No. of Separate Comments Recorded	No. of SMs Involved	No. of Separate Store Visits
DM1	227 min.	157 min.	70 min.	1,115	3	9
DM2	277 min.	134 min.	143 min.	1,173	3	5
DM3	466 min.	293 min.	173 min.	2,092	3	4

the possibility that the differences between the three men could be ascribed to factors other than the habitual interaction pattern of the men themselves.

Results

The systematic observation of the interaction patterns of the three district managers turned up some striking differences between them. The most important differences are indicated by Figure 1. This figure presents a profile of each district manager's interaction pattern with three of his subordinate store managers and each district manager's average profile. The figure shows the percentage of total talking time that was used by each party to the conversation and the category of speech used. There are three observations that can be made from these data that are of special importance.

Figure 1. Percentage of DM and SM Talking Time by Categories.

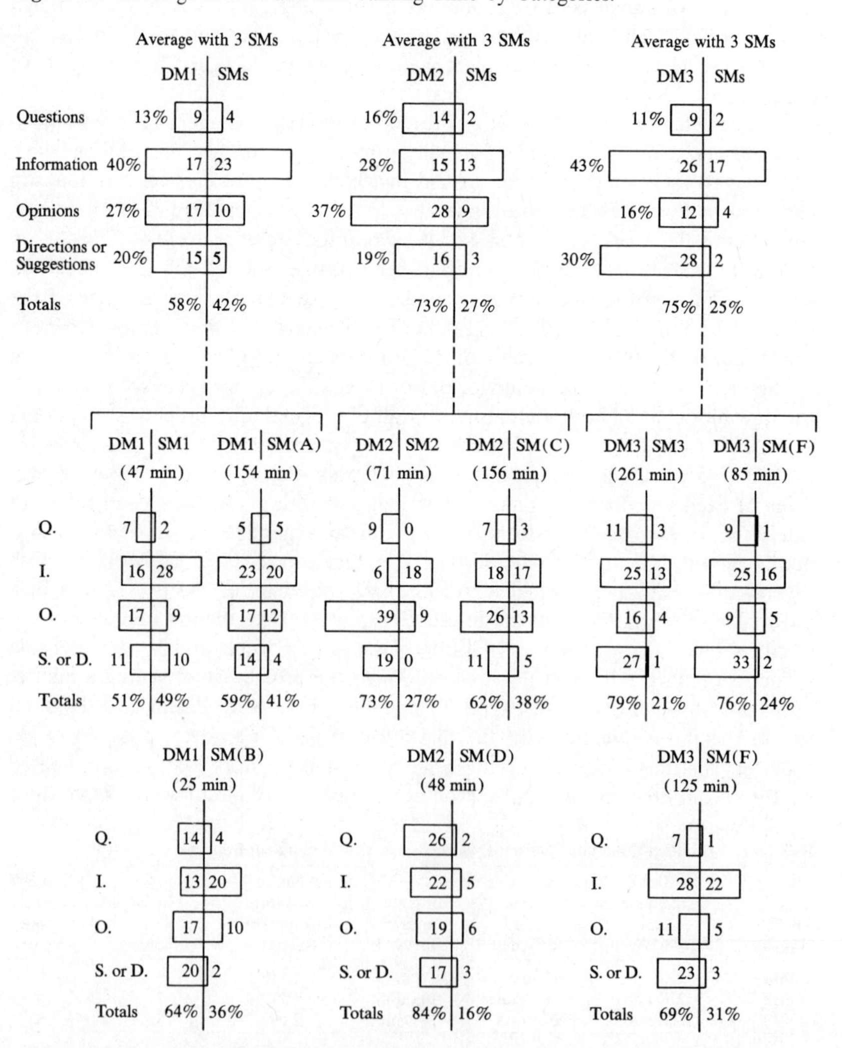

First, the total talking time used by each district manager relative to his subordinates indicates the degree of dominance of the district managers in these conversations. The relatively balanced talking time between DM1 and his store managers indicates that DM1's behavior most nearly coincides with the model requirement of two-way communication in this relationship. The figures indicate that DM3 deviates the most from the new organizational model. For DM3 the words going down the line are three times as much as those coming up the line.

Secondly, the breakdown of talking time into categories of speech gives us another check on the degree of balance in each district manager's interaction pattern. The breakdown indicates that DM1's interaction behavior was not only balanced over-all, but also relatively well balanced within each category of speech. This is especially evident in comparing DM1's record with the others in the categories of *questions, opinions,* and *suggestions or directions.* DM3's behavior is again the furthest from coinciding with the organizational model, going to an extreme of imbalance in the *suggestions or directions* category. For DM3 giving suggestions or directions was distinctly a one-way street.

Thirdly, the figure indicates the relative amount of time spent in each category of speech. This indicates the type of conversation that predominated in these exchanges and provides some clues to the problem-solving values of the conversations. When DM1 was talking with his store managers, most of the time was spent in exchanging *information,* with *opinions, suggestions or directions,* and *questions* following down in that sequence. This is the same sequence of time distribution followed by his average store manager and, in fact, by the averages of the store managers working for DM2 and DM3. This suggests that this particular sequence of time distribution among categories reflects a useful problem-solving type of discussion. This hypothesis, of course, could only be established by much more research.[2] This sequence contrasts with DM2's which is very heavy on *opinions* and of DM3's which is heaviest on *suggestions or directions.* In summary, Figure 1 indicates that DM1's interaction pattern most nearly coincides with the organizational requirement of a two-way, problem-solving interaction pattern in this critical relationship. DM3's behavior coincides the least with this model.

Figure 2 presents the breakdown of the amount of DM-SM talking time that was devoted to the major topical headings. Again some clear differences emerge between the three district managers. These figures indicate the principal topical orientation that each district manager brought to his work. DM1 clearly put his emphasis on the handling and development of people. DM2 puts his chief stress on handling the merchandise, while DM3 was heavily oriented toward the record systems with a secondary emphasis on merchandise. All three gave about the same amount of time to the topic of the physical plant of the store. In the small talk category it is interesting how little time DM3 spent on this in relation to the other two men—DM3 stuck consistently to business in his conversations with subordinates.

It is not too easy to say which topical pattern most nearly coincides with the new organizational requirements since the model itself is hard to define in terms of topics. However, the emphasis of DM2 and DM3 on merchandise and record systems indicates their concern with the activities that had traditionally

[2]The research studies of Robert Bales on problem-solving patterns in discussion groups tend to support this hypothesis.

Figure 2. Percentage of DM and SM Talking Time by Topics.

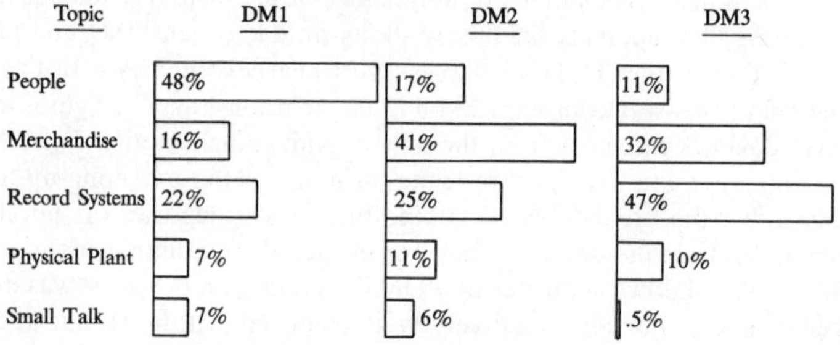

Topic	DM1	DM2	DM3
People	48%	17%	11%
Merchandise	16%	41%	32%
Record Systems	22%	25%	47%
Physical Plant	7%	11%	10%
Small Talk	7%	6%	.5%

been the focus of management attention. While it is not quite so clear, DM1's emphasis on the topic of people would seem to indicate that he was giving conscious and explicit attention to discussing the interaction patterns (delegation, coaching, coordination procedures) and sentiments (morale, discipline, feelings about promotions, demotions, and transfers), all of which more directly involve the people in the business. In this sense DM1 seems to be most nearly following top management's model for changing organizational behavior.

Figure 3 shows the ratio between the number of new conversational topics initiated by the district managers and those initiated by their subordinate store managers. While each of the district managers initiated many more topics than their subordinates, DM1 was slightly more balanced on this score than his two colleagues. This provides another test for two-way communication.

Figure 3. Percentage of New Topics Initiated by DMs and SMs.

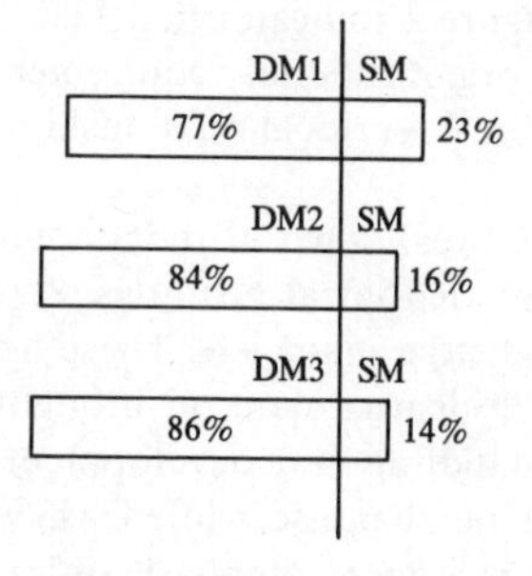

Figure 4 gives the average length in minutes of a single speech (or comment) by the district managers and their store managers. The figure indicates what the earlier data would lead us to expect, namely that DM1 again shows the best balance in the average length of his single speech in relation to his subordinates and DM3 shows the least balance. DM1 gave the shortest single speeches of the three men and his subordinates gave the longest speeches. This would seem to indicate a relative lack of a sense of restraint on the part of DM1's subordinates in conversation with him and again indicates two-way communication.

Figure 4. Average Duration of a Single Comment in Minutes.

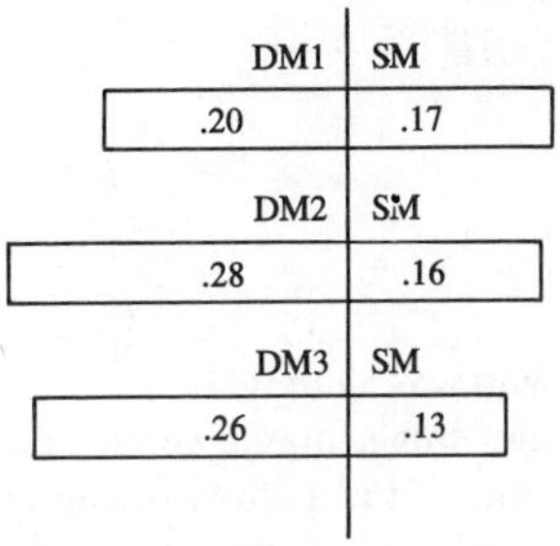

DM1	SM
.20	.17

DM2	SM
.28	.16

DM3	SM
.26	.13

The quantitative data given above consistently confirm [our] tentative conclusions. Without exception, every measure of the interaction pattern of all three district managers shows that DM1's behavior was most nearly coinciding with the desired model while DM3's was furthest from the new model.

The data in this article allow us to make some additional observations about the nature of the organizational behavior changes that were being attempted at Food World. First of all, the data help clarify an essential characteristic of the change that needs emphasis. The interaction pattern of our three district managers has been quantified by observing them making hundreds of discreet acts of speech at a rate of several per minute. It was this overt behavior pattern that top management wanted them to change. Changing this pattern is a far cry from the more customary changes, such as introducing new forms or work procedures, changing the allocation of job time, transferring to a new district, and so on. Such changes, by comparison, would be easy to effect. The desired changes involve a man's intuitive, instantaneous responses to the entire range of supervisory issues. They involve some of a man's most intimate and persistent assumptions about himself and others. Of course, top management did not define in such concrete operational terms the changes they desired but, nevertheless, this is what their expectations meant in terms of actual behavior. The point is that the desired changes constituted severe demands on the key individuals involved.

One of the district managers used an analogy to explain to the researcher how difficult it was to make this transition.

> This organizational switch-over that we are going through now is really tough. I can only make a rather earthy kind of comparison to give you an idea of how difficult it is. I think it is about like a woman who has lived with one man for thirty years suddenly becoming a widow and marrying a second husband. I think her adjustment in trying to live with that second husband and the difficulties that it must put her through is comparable to what we are going through.

Organizational Change: The Effect of Successful Leadership

ROBERT H. GUEST

This is a study of a patient who was acutely ill and who became extemely healthy. The "patient" was not a man but a management, the management of a large, complex industrial organization. It is a study of the process of change, not only in attitudes but also in the pattern of actions and relationships, which, in the span of three years, measurably altered the performance of the entire organization. . . .

Using everyday language to describe what took place in this industrial plant, we have placed considerable reliance on events and relations as perceived and described by the participants themselves. It remains to stand a bit farther back from the running story and to gain some perspective on the essential differences between the Plant Y of 1953 and the "same" organization of 1956. Obviously the relationships among those managing the system changed substantially, but can we see any pattern to the change? Can we introduce any quantitative evidence, even if only crudely derived, showing how interactions between individuals and groups differed from one period to the next? What meaningful contrasts can be made in the expressed attitudes and feelings which the members held toward one another? And most important, what is the *proof* that the organization did in fact change when measured by performance results?

To answer these questions the material will be organized around three categories of description: "interaction," "sentiment," and "performance."[1] Other word symbols might have been used, but these appeared to be general enough to include all dimensions of behavior and specific enough to highlight the differences between two "system states," Plant Y in 1953 and Plant Y in 1956. Our concern here is with the "before" and "after," not with the process of moving from one state to another. This follows later.

Interaction

The survival of any living organism depends upon the ongoing interactions of its component parts. In a human group the elementary parts are people. The relationship between the members of the group may be described in many ways and at different levels of abstraction, the simplest and least abstract involving direction, frequency, and duration of interpersonal contacts. As used here the term "interaction" describes an occurence involving two or more people in which the actions of one person stimulate a reaction by another (or others). By definition interaction involves *direction* from one person, the originator, to another, the responder. A distinction is made between initiation of interaction with no

---

From Robert H. Guest, *Organizational Change: The Effect of Successful Leadership* (Homewood, Ill.: Richard D. Irwin, Inc., 1962), pp. 82–105. Reprinted by permission of the author and the publisher.

[1] These terms are borrowed from George C. Homans, *The Human Group*, p. 34, except that Homans calls performance the "results of activity."

response and initiation which causes the responder to take some kind of action. All contacts between one person and another cannot be considered as completed interactions; there must be some kind of action following a contact. If the response of A to a contact by B (or to a situation) is to do nothing, then the interaction is not complete; something has blocked the response. Interactions usually take place in paired events (one person originating for another). They also take place in set events (one person originating for two or more persons). *Frequency,* the number of times events take place between two or more people, is also implied. And in any given event there is a time element—the *duration* of the interpersonal contact.

Direction, frequency, and duration of interaction are capable of being observed and given mathematical symbols of measurement. Arensberg,[2] Chapple and Coon,[3] Homans,[4] Whyte,[5] Richardson[6] and others have done just this. In the present study direct and constant observation was not possible,[7] and interactional data have been derived from statements by those interviewed. The most that can be expected are generalized statements about what appeared to be typical differences in the interaction patterns of the two time periods. Further, the presentation is not wholly free of comments about the content of interactions and the circumstances under which they occurred. The inclusion of content might not be acceptable to a "pure" interactionist. Yet the use of interaction as an analytical device, however crudely applied, was found to be one among several useful ways of describing this social system in two time periods.

The General Pattern

As one views interpersonal events in 1953 from the division level to the plant manager and down through the hierarchy to the lowest levels of supervision, it is apparent that members of the organization acted primarily in response to actions initiated by their superiors; the *direction* was predominantly downward. In 1953 there were approximately five superior-originated interactions for every one subordinate-originated interaction (based on possible analysis of 36 of the 48 respondents). In 1956 the ratio was approximately two to one (based on possible analysis of 31 out of 43 respondents). It is difficult to say precisely whether the total number of interactions—that is, *frequency,* regardless of direction—increased or decreased by 1956. Certain types of interactions decreased, while others increased. Here one must consider the conditions and content. A

---

[2]Conrad M. Arensberg, "Behavior and Organization: Industrial Studies," in John H. Rohrer and Muzafer Sherif (eds.), *Social Psychology at the Crossroads.*

[3]Eliot D. Chapple and Carleton Coon, *Principles of Anthropology.*

[4]Homans, *op. cit.*

[5]William F. Whyte, "Framework for the Analysis of Industrial Relations," *Industrial and Labor Relations Review,* Vol. 3, No. 3 (April, 1950).

[6]Frederick L. W. Richardson and Charles R. Walker, *Human Relations in an Expanding Company;* and F. L. W. Richardson, *Talk, Work, and Action.*

[7]The magnitude of the task of direct observation of interactions may be illustrated by one study conducted under the author's direction. Each of fifty-six production foremen in an assembly plant was observed for an eight-hour day. Every incident which lasted fifteen seconds or more was recorded and coded. In all, 32,652 behavioral incidents were recorded. Approximately 20,000 of these events involved interpersonal interactions which were coded according to origination (direction), duration, and frequency, plus four other categories (topic, activity, place, and person). To have done the same thing in the present study involving several levels and departments would have made it virtually impossible to have acquired the detailed interview material upon which this study is based. See R. H. Guest, "Of Time and the Foreman," *Personnel,* Vol. 32, No. 6 (May, 1956), p. 478.

reduction in technical difficulties substantially reduced the need to interact in emergencies. The number of orders and directives from the division, the plant manager, and each level of supervision decreased. On the other hand, there was an increase in the number of interactional events involving planning and the transmission of technical and administrative information vertically (up and down) and horizontally (among sections and departments). This was reported by all but two of the 43 respondents in 1956. On balance, and considering the state of "chronic emergency" existing in 1953, there is reason to believe that the gross volume of interaction was *less* in 1956.

As to the average duration of face-to-face interactions, there appears to have been a much greater number of longer two-way discussions in 1956. A reduction in work-flow problems increased the availability of time for such exchanges of information.

A final general comment: The *number* of individuals with whom a given person interacted appears to have increased by 1956.[8] Several members said they had gotten to know more people in the "front office" and in other staff departments. Interdepartmental meetings brought them together. Long-range planning, a key factor in Plant Y's success, required the exchange of information among many persons and groups. A high rate of transfers meant that the individuals involved came to know more people.

Vertical Interactions

The Two Managers Compared. As agent of the division and corporation and as head of the subordinate organization each manager held a key position in the system of communications. From what each reported and from comments by those at higher and lower levels, the pattern of interaction linking them to superiors and to subordinates showed marked differences. Plant Y in 1953, and especially the manager, was subject to constant inquiries or directives from above. Stewart, the manager in the early period, rarely initiated requests for action from the division, whereas Cooley often sought and received support from headquarters. That the frequency of all contacts between division and plant appears to have been reduced is suggested by observations of division staff members such as, "Plant Y (1953) is our biggest headache and we have to keep in touch all the time." Later in 1956, he said, "Our contacts with Plant Y are routine. The critical spot now is Plant D." What does seem clear is that, whatever the frequency rate, the proportion of interactions originated *from* division *to* plant manager was higher in 1953 than in 1956. The way it was often expressed by the manager and his staff in 1956 was, "They're letting us run our own show."

The patterns of interaction between the two managers and those in the upper levels of supervision were different from each other. Five production department heads and seven nonproduction heads in 1953, and the incumbents of the same positions in 1956, reported approximately the same number of contacts with the manager in an average week (ranging between three and fourteen). However, only one of the twelve in 1953 indicated that contacts to and from the manager were "fifty-fifty." In 1956 most of the higher supervisors indicated a balance in the direction (initiation) of interactions with the manager.

The new manager and his subordinates interacted in set events (groups)

[8] Reported in 1956 by nineteen of the twenty-five who were foremen in 1953.

much more frequently than had the former manager. It is true that the former manager had often summoned two or more members for emergency meetings, but no individual had met with the manager as often and as regularly over an extended period of time as was the case with the new manager's regularly scheduled meetings. To the members of the organization the function of the meetings not only increased the frequency of interaction within the group and between the staff members and the manager, but also the fact of *regularity* was seen as having a stabilizing effect on the group and on the entire organization. Agendas could be planned. Recommendations leading to decisions could be considered in advance. A sense of order without constraint developed.

These meetings provided a new interaction mechanism which had not been present earlier and which reinforced the pattern existing between the manager and others in day-to-day administrative activities. That is, they were a means by which subordinates could "originate" to the manager, as well as the reverse. Reports from those attending the meetings contrasted them with the former *ad hoc* meetings which had been used in 1953 by the manager primarily to issue orders for action.

To compare the two managers and their relationship to subordinates simply in interaction terms is, of course, a sterile comparison unless the pattern is linked to the action preceding and following a particular interaction event. Under Stewart, lack of co-ordination in the technical organization brought about certain actions leading to "crisis" interactions. Cooley started at the other end. He first "reorganized" the interaction pattern, which led to better control of technical problems. To be sure, he made significant concrete changes on the technical side, but these were not made until changes in the interaction pattern had begun to evolve. In effect, he instituted a new way of developing, processing, and implementing technical ideas.[9]

Below the Plant Manager. The interaction patterns of manager to the division and manager to subordinates were not unlike the patterns found at lower levels. In 1953 when foremen talked about the general foremen (and general foremen about superintendents) most of the incidents centered on actions originating from the superior. Such a pattern is understandable in the light of the emphasis placed on discipline and order giving. In 1956, with the marked reduction in production holdups, there was less need for superiors to "prod" their subordinates constantly. Twenty-one out of twenty-five foremen in 1956 indicated that general foremen were giving fewer orders to the foremen and that the foremen were freer to seek action from the general foremen.

This observation is supported by what we already know about the way decisions were made under the new administration. That is, with a greater exchange of technical and administrative information at lower levels, a given problem could be solved at these levels without interference from those in higher positions. On major problems affecting many sections and large numbers of people, problems that ultimately required a decision and an order from someone at higher levels, there was less need for those at higher levels to apply "close supervision" in implementing the decision. The over-all plan of action was well understood by those at lower levels before the final decision was reached. Section meetings of foremen and general foremen, or of general foremen and super-

[9]The author is grateful to William F. Whyte for pointing out this distinction.

intendents, preceded the final discussions of department heads and the plant manager. When a top-level decision was made, it often took but a single general order to put the agreed-upon decision into effect. Each incumbent knew what he was to do and when it was to be done.

The reduction in technical breakdowns in time not only reduced the frequency of orders from a general foreman to a foreman, but it allowed the foremen and general foremen to discuss problems which, left unsolved, might become critical in the future. This in turn tended to prevent further technical difficulties and to require less interference (interactions originating from superiors) from above.

Much of what has been said about superior/subordinate interaction applies also to peer interactions within the production department, especially at the foreman level. The number of complaints among foremen was considerably reduced, but the incidence of information sharing was greatly increased. Foremen had more time to discuss problems and the discussions followed a more "give-and-take" pattern; the responder was more compliant to a request. There were fewer interruptions.

General foremen and superintendents also reported fewer "complaint" contacts and more information-sharing contacts with their counterparts in other areas and departments. Formerly, upper management had stressed interdepartmental competition; peers had been looked upon as competitors. Competitors could, as one member commented, "scream at each other like a bunch of washerwomen," but it was the norm to "play your cards close to the chest" about sharing information. By 1956, it was generally recognized that highly integrated continuous-flow operations required the lateral exchange of information.

Interaction Patterns of Production to Nonproduction Groups

With respect to interactions between production and nonproduction groups, among those groups whose primary function was direct *service* to production, such as the material or maintenance groups, there was a reduction by 1956 in the total volume of interactions.[10] Improved material flow, better layout of equipment, and a sustained program of "preventive maintenance" had sharply reduced the number of breakdowns and delays. There was less need for production foremen and general foremen to make frequent emergency calls (i.e., originate interaction) to representatives of the material or maintenance departments. Any given interactional event was not likely to be dominated by one party or the other, as had been the case earlier; discussions were more reciprocal. Also, there was less tendency for those in production and those in the service groups to respond to differences of opinion by taking the problem through their formally separate channels for resolution at the top.

Individual and group interactions involving production supervision and those in departments with *control* functions, such as inspection and work standards, were distinctly altered by 1956. By the nature of its function, inspection was and continued to be the originator of many interactions directed at production supervision, but by 1956 inspection's function was no longer exclusively that of telling production supervision when the quality of work was unsatisfactory. Production foremen and general foremen observed in 1956 that "they got together

[10]All fifteen foremen who made specific comments about their contacts with these service groups reported this to be true.

much more often" with inspection supervision to clarify and to agree upon the meaning of inspection specifications. Knowing clearly what would "pass" or "not pass," foremen were able to halt "bad" jobs before they were passed on to later sections of the line, where "repair" would be much more difficult. Eliminating later repairs, and especially at points of "final" inspection, also reduced the necessity for those at later check points to initiate complaints back through earlier sections of the line. With less absenteeism and turnover of hourly workers and with more thorough training of new workers (foremen and their utility men had more time to work with the new men), the quality of output improved. This, in turn, reduced the necessity of inspection to interact with production.

As to another control group, the work standards department, in 1953 the determination of how much work a worker was to perform or how the several operations were to be distributed among a group of men under a foreman was often dictated by a representative of the work standards department. As it was often expressed, "They went strictly by the book." Interactions were originated primarily by work standards; the response was compliance or evasion by the foreman. By 1956 management altered work standards' role so that it came to accept a service as well as a control function. Foremen more frequently determined who was to do how much with respect to what job on the assembly line. In terms of interaction this meant fewer contacts were originated by work standards and directed at production supervision, and the proportion of contacts (not necessarily the total volume) made by the foreman to the work standards representative for technical advice was higher in 1956. As in many other events involving production and nonproduction groups, discussions between operating supervision and work standards were oriented more toward the future, that is, toward planning in advance for readjustments of work loads in light of a known schedule change to come.

Interactions between operating supervisors and the comptroller's office took on a completely different pattern by 1956. Previously there had been virtually no contact between the two. The accounting function had been primarily that of gathering cost data and of distributing standard reports to the internal organization and to the division. This primary reporting and controlling function had not changed by 1956, but the information was geared more closely to the requirements of the technical work flow and to the needs of supervision. Seen in interaction terms, what happened was that members of the comptroller's department, on the initiative of the plant manager, began to interact frequently with operating supervision. These interactions took place in paired events—between a representative of the comptroller's department and a line supervisor—as well as in set events at weekly cost meetings and group conferences. It became common practice for foremen and general foremen to go *to* the comptroller's department for information and for members of the comptroller's group to "go out on the floor." This was the pattern during 1954 and 1955. By 1956 detailed systems and procedures on cost data had become thoroughly routinized and accepted by production. The pattern of reciprocity continued when schedule changes were being discussed, but the gross rate of interaction was lower.

Summary of Interaction Patterns

An attempt has been made in this section to organize the qualitative material of the study in terms of a quantitative descriptive device, interaction. A general observation was made to the effect that, whereas no basic changes were made in the formal organization, there were substantial changes in the pattern of interactions among its members. In the former period a far greater proportion of interactions had been originated by superiors and directed to subordinates than was the case in the later period. In 1953 a superior's stimulus to act was most often based on *his* superior's action toward *him* and not on the advice or suggestions of his subordinate, as was more often the case in 1956. In events involving production supervisors and their peers in production and nonproduction departments the origin of interactions took on a more reciprocal pattern.

So much for *direction:* What about *frequency?* What can be said about gross differences in the total volume of interactions in 1956 when compared with 1953? We frankly cannot state as a fact that in one period it was greater or less than in the other period. Yet, the persistent and recurring theme in the interviews to the effect that members of Plant Y had "fewer emergencies and more time to plan" suggests that the total volume of interpersonal contacts *may have been considerably less* in 1956. For those who tend to correlate frequency of interaction and "group cohesiveness" the above observation raises some questions. The answers may be found when we consider more fully the technical as well as the social aspects of the total system.

For the balance of the present section we shall look at Plant Y in 1953 and in 1956 in terms of contrasting patterns of "sentiment" and, finally, in terms of measurable "performance" results.

Sentiments

The shift in the pattern of interactions among members of Plant Y from one period in time to another was accompanied by a change in the feelings that its members expressed toward one another. These expressed feelings will be labeled "sentiments," as defined and used by Homans.[11] The term represents something considerably less specialized than that found in the lexicon of psychology. Our purpose here is simply to look at the qualitative data presented earlier and to put forward what appear to be the major points of differences in sentiments.

Sentiments were expressed about interpersonal relationships in general and about the behavior of one person to another in specific events. The earlier period had been marked by expressions of intense dissatisfaction at all levels. In the relationships of subordinates to superiors certain themes recurred. These were expressed as "fear," "confusion," "suspicion," and "pressure": for example, "This plant operates in a constant atmosphere of suspicion and pressure." Almost without exception the respondents deplored these conditions. Even the former manager, who was bitterly criticized by subordinates, admitted that he disliked having to deal autocratically with subordinates: "I can't treat my superintendents the way I get treated." But both he and his subordinates felt they had to conform to the pattern or lose their jobs even though "the system" was completely contrary to their basic feelings of "fair play." One of the general foremen, it is recalled, put it this way: "I began to believe that my whole thinking was wrong and that I should pattern myself after the way the people on top operated." Others frankly admitted that there was no alternative but to conform.

[11]Homans, *op. cit.*, p. 37.

Subordinates repeatedly expressed to this observer ideas and suggestions as to what superiors should do to improve interpersonal relationships and technical operations. They said that their ability to communicate upward was blocked for many reasons, principal among them being emphasis on formal status and on the use of power inherent in each office.

> Those higher up never listen to us.
> The foremen are scared to make decisions.
> There is too much superiority in rank.
> This plant runs on fear alone.
> They just issue orders but don't understand the effects.
> They don't know how to get down to our level.

By 1956, expressions such as these were rare. All members accepted the same basic goals of production that they had before, but now they felt they were being motivated and were motivating others within an entirely different set of relationships.

> We still have pressure, but the pressure comes from us. It isn't based on fear.
>
> My boss listens to my ideas.
>
> Management expects me to run my section, but I get help when I ask for it.
>
> The boss treats me right because that's the way he is treated.
>
> It isn't perfect yet, but we're moving in the right direction.

There seemed to be little question in the minds of members of supervision that the behavior of the manager set the pattern from the day he took over. Nevertheless, it was only after subordinates saw action in the form of physical and organizational changes that their sentiments changed. The initial announcement by the manager that he did not believe in motivating people by threats and firings brought an immediate favorable response, but it was many months later (when the incumbents saw that there *were* no firings) before they came to believe what they had heard at first. "Action, not words, is what counts," is the way it was expressed.

In 1953 the source of expressed dissatisfaction had been as much "technical" as it was "personal." Most activity during the workday had centered on emergencies which stopped or threatened to stop the movement of the lines. "This place is just one damned emergency after another." Supervisors at all levels had complained (to this observer, but usually not to superiors) that they had no means of predicting possible breakdowns. They had attributed this condition to lack of information as to how their own individual operation fitted into the total picture. "We have to operate with departmental blinders on."

The favorable feelings expressed in 1956 may be attributed in part to the fact that *the members now saw much more of the total picture; their opinions were asked; they made suggestions.* They still had to obey orders in response to changing conditions brought about by outside forces, but since they now had a say in planning for change, they were much more willing to accept orders.

This shift in sentiments, they believed, came about not only through individual contacts, but by means of group meetings which increased in number and changed in content. The meetings in the early period had been looked upon as punishing, not rewarding experiences. "The manager just tries to put us on the spot." They reinforced what the participants had experienced with their own superiors in individual contacts on the shop floor. Meetings after 1953 were regarded as having a different kind of function. All present joined in attacking a technical problem. *The focus was on the problem, not on people.* That is, *individuals* were no longer singled out as scapegoats. Each member came to understand better the interrelationship of his own technical and social roles with those of others. "We came to look at the other guy's problems from *his* point of view." The manifest purpose of group meetings was to solve "business" problems, yet the experience of meeting as a group was meaningful in and of itself to the members.

The sentiments of those in production toward those responsible for service, control, and reporting functions changed rather remarkably. In both time periods members of operating supervision were held accountable for the efficiency of operations and for the quality of the product. In 1953, however, foremen had regarded the presence and actions of staff members with suspicion and resentment. The comptroller's efficiency figures had been used as a threat, not as an aid. The work standards representatives were believed to be "dictating" how the foremen should establish work loads. Foremen had come to feel that inspection's role was solely to "put us on the spot."

By 1956, with virtually no change in the functions of nonoperating groups as prescribed "in the manual," the roles of these groups were perceived quite differently and favorably. Those in the supporting groups were looked upon as agents for supplying information which was useful and helpful to the foremen for predictive purposes. Foremen felt that greater control was being given rather than being taken away from them.

The change in sentiments was not limited to a few people but, with only two exceptions, was generalized among all the members of the managerial staff from top to bottom. Some interviews were held with a superior and subordinate both of whom occupied the same positions in relation to one another in both periods. To hear what each said about the other in 1953 one would assume that the expressed antagonisms were functions of some basic "personality" differences. That such was not the case is revealed in the positive and favorable comments made in 1956. As one general foreman put it: "There are some people around here who I used to think were real bastards but they have changed a lot." *What seems to have happened is that conditions and relationship patterns had changed to such an extent that the members of the organization believed that the "personality" of a superior or subordinate had in fact changed.*

Here is an interesting and perhaps significant finding. This observer is not in a position to interpret these personality changes from the point of view of the clinical psychologist, but if they were as substantial as they appear to have been, the finding casts some doubt about the "constancy" of personality traits. Furthermore, one cannot avoid questioning the usefulness of many psychological tests as predictive devices when, as this study would indicate, prediction is so crucially dependent upon knowledge of the social and technical forces impinging on the individual at the time of the test.

The finding also has relevance to training. There is a basic assumption behind many "human relations" training programs throughout industry that it is possible to teach human relations "skills" apart from the socio-technical matrix in which such skills are to be exercised. The observation made here strongly suggests that "getting people to co-operate with one another" is not something that can be taught. A willingness to co-operate evolves from a change in the total system of relationships. It cannot be generated in the training classroom alone but must start at the top and permeate down through the entire organization in day-to-day relationships.[12]

Is it possible, one might ask, that new kinds of negative sentiments emerged in the later period to replace the old? As far as could be determined none could be discerned. What dissatisfactions were expressed revolved around the theme of goal achievement. "We're going in the right direction but not fast enough."

If one were to make the most general kind of observation about the shift from one pattern of sentiments (negative) to another (positive), it would be this. Members of Plant Y adopted a mode of social behavior toward one another which more closely approximated the norms of behavior expected among friends and neighbors in the culture beyond the factory gates. At the same time this behavior, when it concerned the business at hand, was highly rational; it was as much problem oriented as it was person oriented.

With the present discussion of a marked shift in *sentiments* and an earlier description of an underlying shift in *interaction* patterns, it remains to discover whether the change in these two behavior elements bore any relationship to actual performance.

Performance Results

Interpersonal contacts (interactions) and expressions of attitudes and feelings (sentiments) were related to the thousands of physical acts (activities) performed by members of Plant Y every day. The cumulative effect of these activities brought about certain *results* which could be measured according to indices of performance. The purpose of this summary section is to indicate the changes in performance that took place from 1953 to 1956. The data on performance include:

General efficiency (direct labor costs measured against standards)
Efficiency loss and recovery in periods of schedule change
Efficiency loss and recovery in periods of annual model change
Indirect labor costs
Quality performance
Safety record
Labor grievances
Absenteeism
Turnover

These measures, especially those of efficiency and quality, were generally regarded by all members of management at plant and corporate levels as the most

[12] Further support for this assertion may be found in The Ohio State University studies. See especially E. A. Fleishman, W. E. Burtt, and E. F. Harris, *Leadership and Supervision in Industry: An Evaluation of a Supervisory Training Program.*

important indices of performance. The first five are direct measures of organization performance. The last four are not measures of output as such, but the fact of a good or poor record in these categories can influence output substantially.

General Efficiency

It was observed earlier that in 1953 Plant Y required 16 per cent more direct labor to run the plant than was needed according to the standard of 100 per cent set by the division for all of its plants.[13] The next "poorest" performer measured 110 per cent: that is, it used 10 per cent more labor than was required by standards. (No plant among the six operated below 102 per cent.)

By 1956 Plant Y's direct labor costs had gone down 14 per cent. Its position was superior to that of any other plant in the division. Although no specific figures were available, a rough computation of average wages and total man hours indicates that a 14 per cent improvement represented a savings of more than $2 million in one year.

Graph 1 compares Plant Y with the other plants in both time periods.

Graph 1. General Efficiency—Changes in Direct Labor Costs for Six Plants, 1953 and 1956 (in Per Cent above 100% Labor Standards).

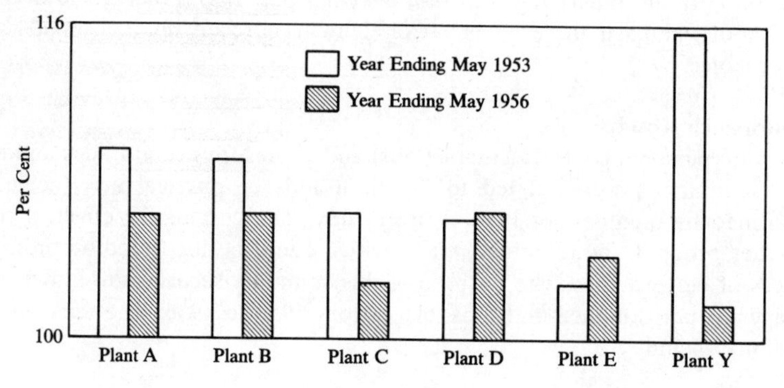

Efficiency Loss and Recovery in Periods of Schedule Change

It is characteristic of every schedule change that labor costs rise precipitously for the first week after substantial increases or decreases in production are ordered. This is principally due to the fact that the work load of each of hundreds of line operations must be altered. The work of each operator must be rearranged to synchronize it with the speed of the conveyor. The ability of a plant to make a "quick recovery to normal" within three or four weeks can mean substantial savings, literally in hundreds of thousands of dollars. Recovery is generally regarded as a measure of administrative effectiveness.

In the 1953 period there had been a number of changes in production schedules which each plant had to face. The precise figures for this period were not available, but a senior staff member of the division reported that Plant Y's

[13]In 1953 there were six plants in the division. Later another plant was built. Some of the figures used in this section do not include the new plant.

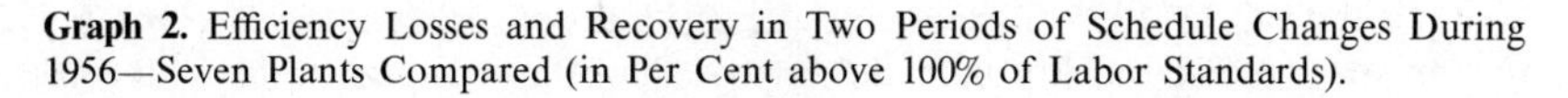
Graph 2. Efficiency Losses and Recovery in Two Periods of Schedule Changes During 1956—Seven Plants Compared (in Per Cent above 100% of Labor Standards).

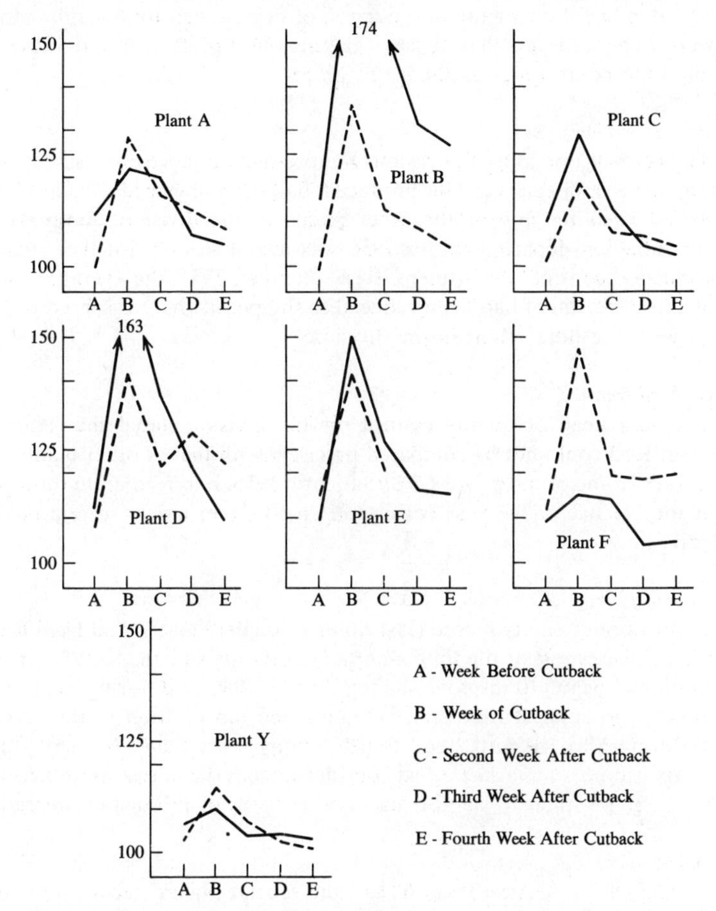

costs had risen higher than those of any other plant during major schedule changes and that its recovery had been slower.

In 1956 there were at least two major schedule changes affecting all plants. Both changes involved drastic cutbacks in production due to market conditions. Not only did Plant Y's costs rise *less* than did those of the other six plants, but it "recovered" more quickly than any of the others.

Graph 2 plots the losses for each plant for each of two schedule changes beginning with the week before the production cutback and continuing to the fourth week after the cutback.

Efficiency Loss and Recovery in Periods of Model Change

The introduction of new models is the industry's "annual headache" from a production standpoint. As in the case of schedule changes, each plant tries to reach the required line speed as quickly as possible and at the least possible cost.

In the fall of 1956 (introducing the 1957 car models), Plant Y came up to line speed more quickly than did any of the other six plants. Also, during the three months following the introduction of new models total manufacturing costs were *15 per cent less* than those of the next best performer and *50 per cent lower* than the poorest among the seven plants.

Indirect Labor Costs

The costs of operating the various nonproduction departments, relative to the estimated cost of each car unit produced, had been higher in 1953 at Plant Y than it had been for any of the other plants in the division. A breakdown for nonproduction departments for 1956 was available only for the "material and production control" department. By September, 1956, the average cost per unit for this department had been reduced to the point where it shared the best position with one other plant in the division.

Quality Performance

The staff head of quality control for the division stated that Plant Y's position in 1953 could not be compared precisely with that of other plants, "but it was certainly one of the poorest." By January, 1956, it moved up to third place and for the balance of the year consistently held either top or second position in the division.

Safety Performance

In its monthly safety record (lost-time accidents) Plant Y had been fourth, fifth, or last place most of the time among the division's plants in 1953. In 1955 its position had begun to improve slightly, but by 1956, and during each month from January to June of that year, it maintained top position in the division. In fact, during May, 1956, it stood fourth among more than 126 plants in the entire corporation, a remarkable feat considering that the potential for accidents was clearly higher than it was for many other types of production operations.

Labor Grievances

As Graph 3 indicates, Plant Y had the second highest record number of formal labor grievances per month per 100 employees in 1953. In the twelve months prior to June, 1956, not only had the average number of grievances per month been reduced, but its record, as shown in Graph 3, was substantially better than that of any of the other six plants in the division.

Absenteeism

Plant Y's absentee rate (short-term personal absenteeism measured as a percentage of scheduled work) dropped from 4.1 per cent in 1953 to 2.5 per cent in 1956.

Turnover

Plant Y's average monthly rate of turnover among hourly workers dropped from 6.1 per cent in 1953 to 4.9 per cent in 1956.

Summary of Performance

Considering the basic purpose of Plant Y as a production organization the evidence is overwhelming that a sharp, dramatic change took place when one compares the two time periods. Not only was there a substantial improvement noticeable when Plant Y's performance was measured against itself, but its performance, when compared with five (later six) other similar assembly plants, went from bottom to top position in most indices of performance. These comparative data are important as proof that the improvement was something generated internally inasmuch as *all* plants were subject to the same external market conditions. All were similar in product, technology, and formal structure of organization. All managers reported to the same divisional manager. In short, the performance change which took place in this organization over the span of three years can hardly be explained on the basis of chance.

Conclusions

The purpose of this article has been to compare the organization in two periods of time using three elements of behavior as a descriptive framework. Two distinct patterns were observed. Plant Y as a "system state" in Time I when contrasted with Time II was characterized by a communications system in which a high proportion of interactions were originated by superiors to subordinates. Expressed sentiments about one's relationship to others and about conditions in general were extremely negative. Performance was inferior both when compared with Plant Y's later performance and when contrasted with the perform-

Graph 3. Average Number of Grievances Per 100 Workers, 1953 and 1956 (based on monthly averages for seven plants).

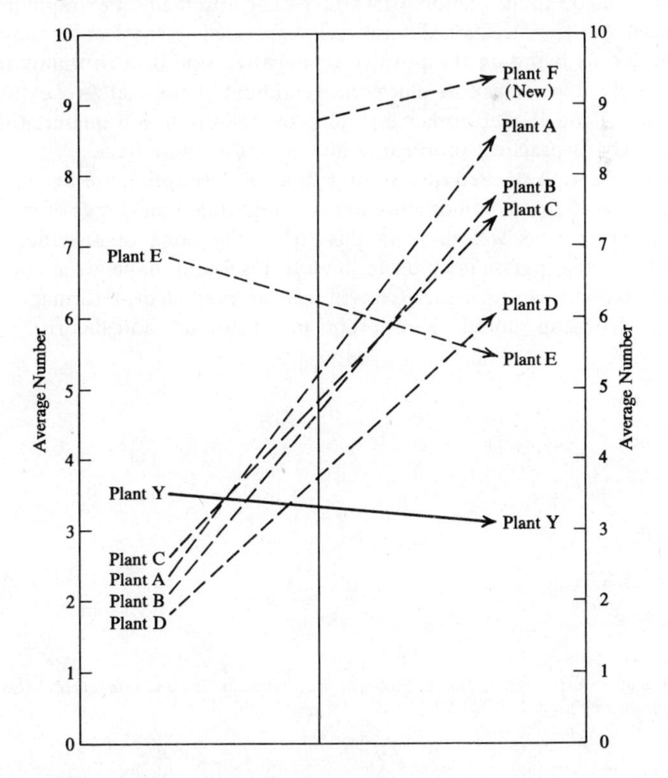

ance of other similar plants. Time II was marked by a greater "balance" in interactions between levels and functions, highly favorable sentiments, and superior performance.

This observation supports in part Homans' hypotheses about small group behavior, except that it can now be stated so as to include the "product" of a given interaction-sentiment pattern. Thus, to the extent that interactions between persons at various levels of a complex hierarchical group are originated by superiors or by members of one specialized group to others, sentiments of tension and hostility will be high and performance will be low.

Stated in this way this hypothesis oversimplifies an extremely complex set of conditions and relationships. Nevertheless, it may be regarded as a first step—a way of handling qualitative data in a more quantitative manner. For example, Gouldner describes "punishment-centered" versus "representative" behavior in bureaucratic organizations and in a general way links this behavior to expressed feelings of the members and by inference, to performance. In many other studies (mostly in small groups) patterns of communication are linked to attitudes and feelings but only occasionally, to performance.[14]

When it comes to understanding behavior in complex organizations, the "evidence" linking a pattern of communications to "morale" is frequently stated in qualitative form. Subordinates express *hostility* to a *directive* or *authoritarian* pattern of communications. The assumption is then made that such conditions must lead to poor performance results.

What is being suggested here is that qualitative labels need to be and can be made more precise; they can be quantified. Interactions can be counted. The pattern of who originates action for whom can be observed (or extrapolated from interviews) and the direction determined. Expressed feelings or sentiments can be identified as being on the positive or negative side of a continuum. In the present study it was easy to place the sentiment pattern at two extremes in Time I and Time II. Performance results, by definition, are quantitative data. The researcher's practical problem is how to get at these data.

As more sophisticated quantitative tools of description are devised, it will become easier to find common ground for comparing many types of production organizations. Or, as was done in this study, the same organization can be described at two separate intervals in time. If it is found that a given interaction-sentiment pattern can be associated with certain predicted performance results, this kind of finding should be important to practitioner and theorist.

---

[14] L. Coch and J. R. P. French, Jr., "Overcoming Resistance to Change," *Human Relations,* Vol. 1, No. 4 (August, 1948), pp. 512–32.

Comprehending the Process of Organizational Improvement

F. L. W. RICHARDSON
STEPHEN ZIMMERMAN

Throughout every organization, there exist individuals skilled in solving organizational behavioral problems, but practically no one knows how they do it. Moreover, such persons often are not at all entirely sure themselves. Are people and organizations really so complicated that they defy analysis? Many no longer think so, but what is it that such persons do? One of the authors has spent a professional lifetime examining skilled and unskilled managers to learn just the answer. And much of this time he himself has entered the fray as an *organizational diplomat-catalyst*[1] to facilitate fundamental changes necessary to all concerned. The following article includes such insight, methods and understanding as he has gained that apply to the successful resolution of familiar organizational problems such as centralizing a decentralized function, coordinating a new activity, or otherwise managing people.

Technical Systems and Social Systems

A point of view likening organizations to technical systems has been gaining momentum since World War II. Material flow, information and mathematical methods have been the focus. Organizations are thus conceived as extensions of modern, complex electro-mechanical systems, controlled by carefully contrived feedback mechanisms. Moreover, some of the results, methods of inventory and material flow for example, have even been dramatic. This point of view is in seeming opposition to that prevailing in the social sciences—that organizations represent social systems.

It is well recognized, for example, that focussing on engineering concepts and methods to repair a malfunctioning organization does not always work and sometimes even worsens matters. The concept that for every action there is a reaction certainly applies both to persons and things. Whether, however, human reactions are "equal and opposite" (Newton's Third Law), they certainly appear not to be.

The first premise of this paper, therefore, is that at this point in time, concepts and methods appropriate for technical systems are sometimes inappropriate for social systems. Perhaps this is so because of current differences in complexity and in our understanding. Organizational systems not only are more complex than current models of man-made electromechanical systems, but each individual within an organization is vastly more complex. Man, after all, represents the most advanced "current model" yet evolved out of hundreds of millions

---

From *Management of Personnel Quarterly,* Vol. 4, No. 4 (Spring 1965), pp. 3–15. Reprinted by permission.

[1] Floyd Christopher Mann and Franklin W. Neff, *Managing Major Change in Organizations,* Ann Arbor: Foundation for Research on Human Behavior, 1961, 92 pages (especially pp. 53–59).

of years of biological evolution. Compared to such subtle, complex feed-back processes in mammals and men as body repair, temperature control, immunization and sizing up a rival, the feedback mechanisms in manufactured machines are still relatively simple and crude.

To comprehend the functioning of a system, mathematical precision is no substitute for recognizing and appraising only the relevant factors. One of the authors has written a paper[2] suggesting that far more miscalculations are made in human affairs because of the failure even to consider important factors than from miscalculating those identified. Scientific advance often proceeds from subjective to objective recognition and then from rough to precise quantitative description. Effective, deductive, mathematical theorizing in physics and engineering, after all, is a relatively recent development evolving out of 400 years of concerted effort. Thousands of years of struggle, identifying and isolating significant and relevant variables, preceded this refinement. It seems a reasonable induction from experience, therefore, that during the emergence of a body of knowledge from the stage of all art to part science, quantitative rigor may represent a lower priority than recognizing the relevant.

It is the second premise and central, if not obvious, thesis of this paper that a business organization can more appropriately be conceived as a joint, interdependent technical and social system. Whereas the methods and concepts of physics and chemistry apply largely to the former, those of biology are more relevant for the latter.

In the past several decades, few natural or social scientists have focussed their investigations and writing on the close interdependence between the technical and social systems of business organizations. Among the exceptions are three small groups of investigators—a group of applied anthropologists.[3] British psychologists and others belonging to the Tavistock Institute in London,[4] and those associated with the Technology Project, Yale University, who concentrated exclusively on this subject.[5]

Relevant Organizational Processes

In an attempt to systematize for business organizations the interdependence of technical and social systems, one of the writers, who has been associated with two of these groups, has identified and discussed in a number of publications[6]

---

[2]F. L. W. Richardson, Jr., "Crucial Problems in Applying Anthropology," *Transactions of the New York Academy of Sciences,* Series II, Vol. 12, No. 3, January 1950, pages 98–105.

[3]Eliot D. Chapple and Leonard R. Sayles, *The Measure of Management,* New York: MacMillan Company, 1961, 218 pages.

F. L. W. Richardson and Charles R. Walker, *Human Relations in an Expanding Company,* New Haven: Yale Labor and Management Center, 1948, 24 pages.

F. L. W. Richardson, Jr., *Talk, Work, and Action,* Monograph Number 3, Society for Applied Anthropology, 1961, 96 pages.

William F. Whyte, *Men at Work,* Dorsey Irwin, 1961, pages 123–235.

[4]A. K. Rice, *Productivity and Social Organization: The Ahmedabad Experiment,* London: Tavistock Publications, 1958, 298 pages.

[5]Charles R. Walker and Robert H. Guest, *The Man on the Assembly Line,* Cambridge, Mass.: Harvard University Press, 1952, 180 pages.

Charles R. Walker, Robert H. Guest and Arthur N. Turner, *The Foreman on the Assembly Line,* Cambridge, Mass.: Harvard University Press, 1956, 197 pages.

Charles R. Walker, *Modern Technology and Civilization,* New York: McGraw-Hill Book Co., 1962, 469 pages.

[6]F. L. W. Richardson and C. R. Walker, 1961, op. cit.

F. L. W. Richardson, 1961, op. cit.

four interconnected processes. It is the third premise of this paper that the malfunctioning of a business organization can usually be attributed to one or more of these four organizational processes.

Every manager knows that it takes many different actions to develop and maintain a high level of productivity in any group, be the output sales, products, services or reports. We identify four key functions. The word 'function' is not used here in its traditional sense of referring to the major areas of business such as sales, engineering, manufacturing, accounting or personnel. Instead, it refers to four other categories of process or action sequence which determine the output of any group.

These four functions with associated sub-functions are:

1. Work processing and flow
   a. downstream
   b. reject backflow
2. Work progress complaints[7]
3. Supervisory and grievance
4. Flow regulating
   a. job progress reporting
   b. scheduling
   c. expediting

All four are so closely interdependent that as one varies, the others vary also. This article makes the claim that in order to raise or maintain a high level of productivity, these four functions are crucial. Management should recognize, audit, measure and control each of them.

The Case Studied

This paper focuses on the problems which a manufacturing organization in the defense industry experienced with its proposal-cost preparation procedures in quoting its custom-made new business. After several years of chaos, the system finally became effectively regularized and ordered. In analyzing this situation, the above list of functions was examined, but, as we shall discover, in this particular instance, supervisory communication and the human relations aspects of scheduling and expediting practices proved to be the most crucial for restoring order.

As a method of obtaining new business, proposal-cost preparation, long standard in the construction business, has since World War II become standard in the defense industries, in particular those producing relatively small quantities of complex equipment requiring new designs. As the processing of the proposals and cost estimates necessitated new procedures, inevitably new problems arose. This is the account of one company's successful experience in meeting them.

The organization studied, one division of a large industrial firm, specialized in high precision manufacturing toward which the engineering contribution constituted about one-third the total value of the product. The proposal-cost preparation was the sole method of obtaining new contracts. The task entailed receiving a customer's inquiry, determining the suitability of the job for the division, gathering relevant information on cost and returning the information to the customer in the form of a proposal or quote.

---

[7]Complaints refer to failure to meet schedules, which usually have come from peers, organizational supervisors or customers, whereas grievance refers to dissatisfaction among subordinates. As this study was primarily concerned with horizontal relationships, grievances are here ignored.

The history of this effort can be separated into three phases. Phase 1 lasted nine years, at the beginning of which the preparation of cost-proposals was accomplished with little difficulty. Gradually, toward the end of the nine years, the number of cost-proposals increased, as did competition from other firms, therefore, requiring greater detail and accuracy to be accomplished in shorter time. The division, with its then current practices, was unsuccessful in adapting itself to the new situation. As a first major corrective step, the activity was centralized under one proposal planning manager, thus ushering in Phase 2. But for one year thereafter, major processing difficulties continued. A second major change, therefore, became unavoidable. A second manager replaced the first, thus ushering in Phase 3. His endeavors brought dramatic results in only a matter of months, and improvement continued at least for a year thereafter, up to the date of this writing. What was it that occurred in those first few months of Phase 3 to transform years of malfunctioning into successful operation?

Decentralized Chaos—Phase 1

Phase 1 was not an organized effort at all. It is surprising to find that a division doing virtually all of its business on the basis of negotiation, and more than half of it with an agency of the federal government, had for the first nine years of its existence, neither a formal nor a centralized procedure for systematically gathering data for proposals.

Instead, each of 12 salesmen was responsible for following his particular inquiry through the relevant departments in the organizations. But the department heads had not designated individuals to supply needed information; the need was recognized but was given very low priority.

The salesmen were competing not only against the regular work assignments of the estimators, who had other duties, but also against each other. The shortcomings in Phase 1 became evident as a direct result of two crises occurring at about the same time.

One crisis occurred at a meeting between the division and a division of a rival company which acted as a buying office for a government agency. This rival division requested quotes and imposed standards and specifications on the division. The situation provided a constant source of irritation between the purchaser and supplier. To alleviate this stress, periodic meetings were held between the top managements of the organizations.

At one such meeting, the division of the rival company displayed a chart showing "date inquiry sent," "date reply requested," and "date reply received" on all inquiries submitted to the rival supplying division for the previous year. After agreeing that most of the "requested" dates were quite reasonable (since another division of the rival firm in the same business was able to meet them), the division of the company here studied was made to see that its "time-to-quote" was excessively long. Not only was the division forced to endure the embarrassment of this confrontation, but it had to accept the data of the other firm as correct since it did not file such information itself and had no way of even attempting to refute it.

The second crisis was precipitated by the federal government. Congress passed, and the President signed, Public Law 87-653, which provided for a $10,000 fine and/or 10 years in prison for falsifying, either deliberately or through ignorance, cost information provided the government for contracts. As some of the estimates had been more casually than carefully derived, this law caused the management some anxiety.

Centralization—Phases 2 and 3

The need for a central effort and for responsibility concerning the submitting of bids was now clear. The division reacted by creating the proposal planning section whose manager reported directly to the marketing manager. The formal responsibilities of the proposal planning section as stated in a letter from the general manager to the division include "*. . . administering, coordinating and compiling all division's pre-bid cost estimates,* maintaining accurate and complete cost estimate files, pre-planning forecasted orders on the division's work load *and scheduling all proposals.*" (The italics are the authors' to draw attention to functions discussed in this paper.) The section had two members in Phase 2 and three in Phase 3, but only one person performed the tasks of interest here. His title was "proposal planner."

Despite centralization in Phase 2, chaos still reigned for about a year. It was only following a second reorganization, Phase 3, that the crises ceased and the essential secondary task of cost proposal preparation began to be performed in an effective routine fashion.

Dramatic Improvement

The difference in the number of overdue and completed proposals provides crucial evidence of marked improvement in Phase 3 as against Phase 2. In the last five weeks of Phase 2, about four proposals a week were late; a negligible number were late from the eighth to the seventeenth week of Phase 3 (allowing for an initial seven weeks changeover period). The startling change brought about in Phase 3 is readily apparent in Table 1 and Chart 1.

TABLE 1

	Phase 2 Final 6 Weeks	Phase 3 Final 6 Weeks Data Available
Average number of new inquiries received per week	11.8	13.2
Average time required to complete a proposal (in working days)	20.5	11.5
Average number of proposals completed per week	11.8	13.7
Average weekly backlog	48.2	31.0

Convincing as the statistical evidence of improvement may be, it fails to convey the impression of Phase 2 as a prolonged crisis in contrast to Phase 3, a time of routinized fulfillment. (See Charts 2 and 3.) Note for example the striking contrast in the change from widespread to negligible complaining and the marked improvement in work and reject flow. The next section presents some of the detailed evidence.

A general note of caution must be pointed out.[8] The complexities of organizations are such that it is difficult to know and account for all changes simultaneously. There is always the danger of identifying the wrong factors as

[8]This paragraph was suggested by my colleague, Trevor Sainsbury.

Chart 1. Proposals Completed and Proposals Overdue for a 24-Week Period.

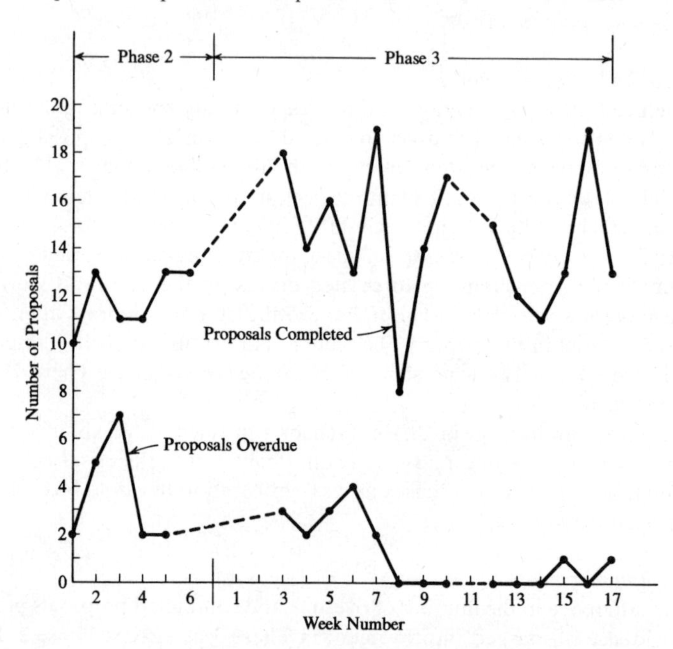

being mainly responsible for inducing change. In comparing the changes occurring between Phases 2 and 3, we have assumed that as the technical work flow system was essentially similar for both periods, it was not in this instance a significant factor. In contrast, *changes* in the supervisory and flow regulating functions of the social system were *major.* As our investigation leads us to believe that this is no coincidence, we attribute the marked improvement mainly to these functions. However, Phases 2 and 3 were dissimilar in other respects also. Take, for example, the number of organizational changes in the division. During Phase 2, it appears that there were in fact more changes in managerial positions in the top three levels than in Phase 3, but in neither were they numerous. However, prior and subsequent to Phases 2 and 3, more extensive reorganizations did occur. Our judgment therefore is that the managerial reorganizations (other than the change in proposal planning managers) were not a major factor explaining the marked improvement between Phases 2 and 3.

Work Flow and Complaint Functions

During Phase 2, complaining usually commenced after repeated and unsuccessful attempts by the proposal planning manager to persuade an estimator to complete his work on time. (Roman numerals refer to arrows on Chart 2.)

He first complained to the estimator himself (I) whose overt behavior might have been quite agreeable but whose covert reaction was quite different. Getting no results from the estimator, the proposal planning manager then complained to the estimator's boss, the section head (II). The section head agreed to inquire into the delay. He discussed it with the estimator and, customarily, favored his subordinate's side of the story. The proposal planning manager got only excuses.

By now, the lateness of the information was getting serious. The proposal planning manager went to see the department manager (III). The tone of his visit was critical. His unspoken comments were "What kind of outfit are you running around here?" and "I want action!" This, of course, shifted all of the department manager's defense mechanisms into high gear and erected a mental barrier between them.

Getting no results here, the proposal planning manager went to his supervisor, the marketing manager, to complain (IV). But the marketing manager could do little except offer suggestions as to how to get cooperation, and it was by then too late for that.

By this time, the delays were reaching a crisis: some proposals were over a month overdue. Throughout this period, salesmen were hounding the proposal planning manager to provide the proposals. As a last resort, he wrote a letter to the general manager (V) that the departmental estimators refused to give him cooperation and that he could not get the department managers to do anything about it. He then added the fact that some proposals were over thirty days overdue.

Since a number of complaints had already been received from customers, this got results. The general manager ordered all departments to drop everything and clean up overdue proposals immediately, with the resulting disruption of

Chart 2 (Phase 2). Crisis Work Flow and Complaints (for simplicity only one department is shown at left).

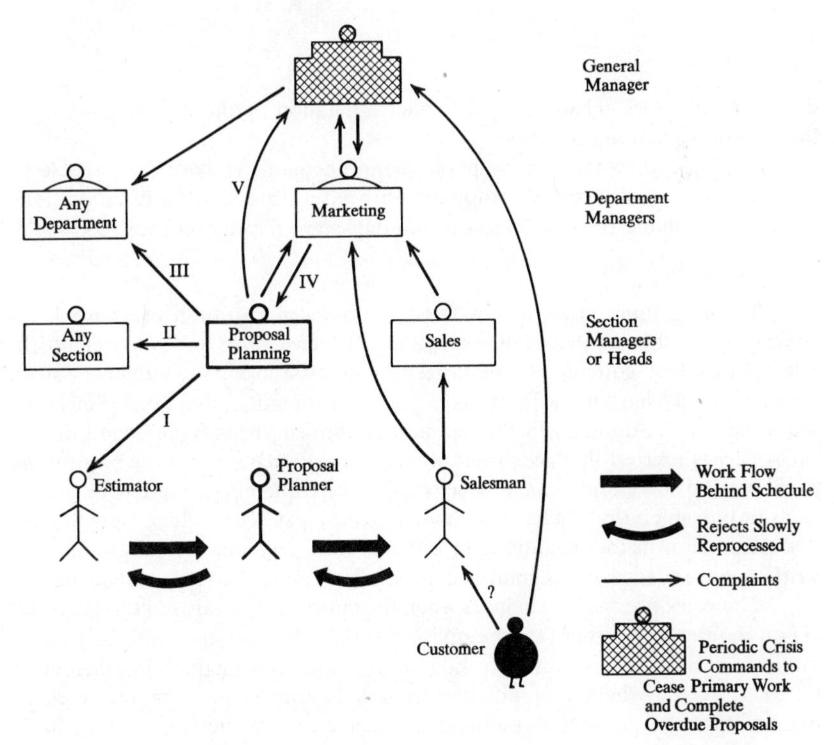

Chart 3 (Phase 3). Routine Work Flow Replacing Crisis Flow.

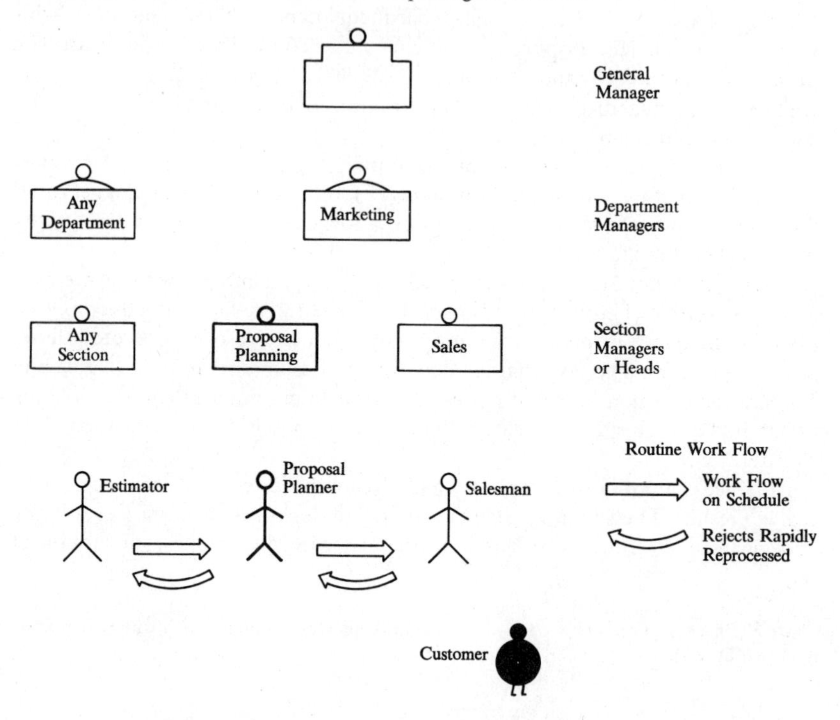

departmental work schedules and further alienation of the departments from the proposal planning manager.

In Phase 3, when the proposal planning manager had been replaced, complaining virtually ceased, proposals were rarely late, and on rare occasions those unacceptable for one reason or another were rapidly reprocessed.

Formal Work Flow

To bring some order out of the chaotic decentralization of Phase 1, an orderly work flow sequence for preparing the cost proposals was set up. In Chart 4 this flow sequence is summarized by superimposing the sequences on an organizational chart to facilitate comparison with other diagrams. Since the sequence was set up early in Phase 2 and continued virtually unaltered during Phase 3, we inferred that *the formal work flow sequence was not the basis of the problem.* The successful change is believed to be explained primarily by alterations in the supervisory, scheduling and expediting systems, which we will later discuss in turn. In the meantime, to provide a more complete background, the work flow sequence is diagrammed in Chart 4 and briefly described below.

The work process commences when the customer forwards to the salesman (1) an inquiry requesting that the division supply the customer with cost information on the work contained in the inquiry. Sales and Engineering then meet (2, 3) to decide whether or not the division is able to perform the work or manufacture the product as outlined in the inquiry. If the Engineering/Sales review agrees that the project outlined in the inquiry is within the capabilities of the division, Engineering forwards a completion date to Proposal Planning and begins work on estimating the design portion of the proposal.

When Proposal Planning receives the completed Engineering estimate (4), it has sufficient copies made for the various departments. Proposal Planning then has each department agree to a date when it will complete its portion of the estimate. These dates then become the proposal schedule. The Engineering estimate is then distributed to the departments (5).

It should now be pointed out that while the various departments are shown as one block, a considerable amount of coordination within that block is required. Some departments can work in parallel (Purchasing can price out the bill of materials at the same time Production and Manufacturing Planning are preparing their estimates), while others depend on previous inputs (Quality Assurance usually cannot provide an estimate until it sees how Production will perform its task).

Each department returns its completed estimate to Proposal Planning (6). Proposal Planning collects the completed estimates, expediting the ones that are late. When all of the estimates are in, Proposal Planning forwards the estimate package to Sales (7).

Sales analyzes the package to determine whether or not the customer's requirements have been fully met. If they have, a management review and cost

Chart 4. Stages in Proposal-Cost Flow. Arrows indicate direction of flow. Numbers indicate process (see text).

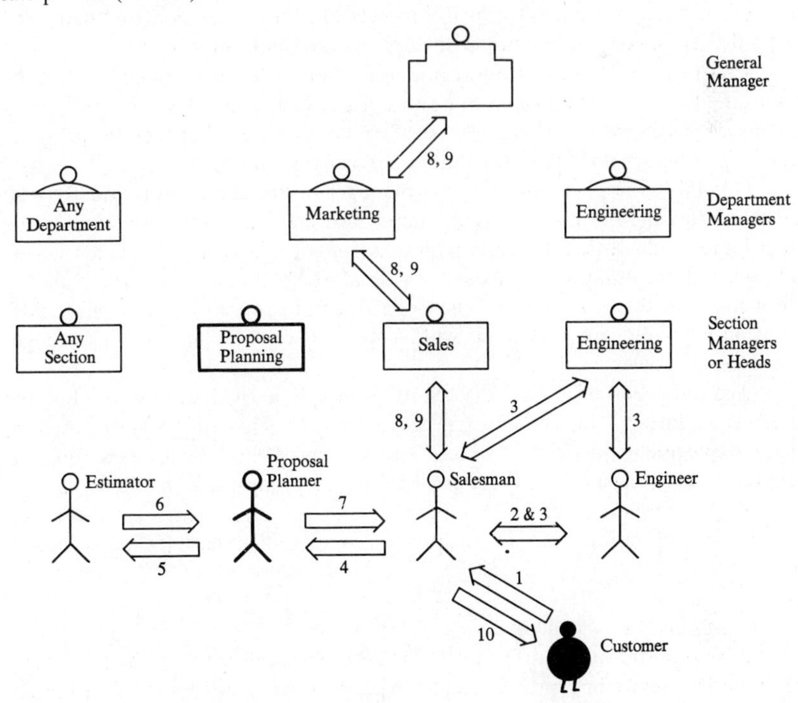

certification (8) is the next step. Then the package is returned to the cognizant salesman (9) who forwards it to the customer for his consideration (10).

Some technical improvements in record-keeping came about gradually, beginning in Phase 2, such as estimating for all constituent items rather than presenting bulk estimates for numbers of items. In this fashion, the record system was refined by placing, for example, the costs of all unit items on IBM cards. This speeded up considerably the process of proposal-cost preparation and insured greater uniformity and accuracy, but the full benefits of it were not fully realized until Phase 3. Technical considerations facilitating the flow of work were thus not entirely absent; however, our informants generally agreed that these were of minor importance in explaining the sudden improvement that took place during Phase 3. That these technical improvements were apparently gradual rather than sudden strengthens their claim.

Supervisory Functions

Perhaps the most fundamental difference between the phases was that in one the work was done by existing supervisors; in the other a rival supervisory function was set up.

In Phase 2, the proposal planning manager dealt directly with all the departmental estimators. Initially, he set about practicing modern permissive management. He held weekly conferences, for example, with all his estimators so that all could become involved together in establishing their own schedules. Thus no one committed any estimator to a date for completion as all estimators directly committed themselves. By allowing "his estimators" this degree of participative management, the proposal planning manager and his proposal planner developed frequent expediting relationships directly with them and ensured their speedy adherence with their work commitments.

Frequently, however, the estimators failed to meet their own self-determined schedules. The commonest excuse was that their section supervisors had assigned other work. This gave rise, of course, to conflict between the proposal planning manager and departmental supervisory personnel.

Officially, the proposal planning manager in Phase 3 dealt indirectly with the estimators though his proposal planner sent them schedules weekly. On the other hand he dealt directly daily with department managers who, when necessary, passed information on to section heads who directly, in turn, handled problems with their estimators. The departmental supervisors, after all, could, for example, reallocate work loads among their personnel. The proposal manager had no such power.

The manager in Phase 2 set himself up as a rival supervisor, but the manager in Phase 3 worked through the already existing supervisory functions of the departments, a strategy which not only caused less disturbance, but was simpler and required less effort. Personnel people, long-range planners, and all staff persons who do otherwise commonly create more problems and dissension than those they relieve and, in the process, wear out themselves and those all around them.

Interpreting an Authorization

It is important to realize that both these practices, opposed as they were, represent legitimate interpretations of the general manager's letter of authorization. In Phase 2 the proposal planning manager considered the departmental estimators assigned as "his men," as primarily working directly for him, a view for which the wording of the general manager's letter of authorization gave him ample grounds, for the letter states: Each "department head shall assign individuals . . . who are cognizant of the task involved and designate such assignment as *their first order of work.*" But for many, if not most, of these individuals, their proposal work constituted less than ten per cent of their total assignments. Thus, they naturally looked first to their own section supervisor. Moreover, the proposal planning manager, more and more frustrated by the excuses of his estimators and their tardy proposals, became increasingly aggressive toward their section and department managers; and as one informant put it, he came to take on the characteristics of a "good drill sergeant."

At the start of his incumbency, the manager in Phase 3, confronted with a virtually complete breakdown of rational communication between the proposal section and the departments, personally visited each department manager to assure him of his desire to assist. In sessions which averaged three-quarters of an hour, he asked for their help and cooperation and for suggestions to improve the system. Later, when making changes, he made an effort to incorporate even marginal suggestions to show the departmental managers and personnel that he had, in fact, listened to them. From these sessions with departmental managers, he learned that they seldom received notice of difficulties in advance and before they had become too serious for simple remedial action. It was this complaint, and his own grasp of the situation, that convinced him to work through the existing departmental supervisory organization. His own function he conceived as that of nothing more than the coordinator and organizer of this essential secondary task: providing a service, particularly of information, to assist departmental personnel themselves to accomplish their task satisfactorily and on time.

No one can ever spell out in full detail the entire content of any job. There are too many subtleties, alternate paths and contingencies. Job descriptions are no more than the grossest of approximations, and sometimes they are misleading. Once a formal technical work system has become established, cooperative success in any organization usually depends far more on interpersonal subtleties than on any rationally conceived procedure. To emphasize that managing is largely a cognitive skill is to misrepresent the reality; it is even more a behavioral and interactional art.

Personality and Experience

What might explain the two men's contrasting interpretations? It is our guess that this not only reflected their personalities but to a large extent was also a function of their age and experience. The manager in Phase 2 was a graduate engineer in his early thirties, promoted from a sales engineer. He had had no previous managerial experience.

The proposal planning manager who replaced him in Phase 3 was older, more experienced and more knowledgeable in matters of managerial rivalry and interdepartmental conflict. He not only benefitted from the mistakes of his predecessor but from far longer corporate and managerial experience, as well as from more advanced education; he lacked only the thesis to achieve a Ph.D. in economics. Thus, he *did not use* the general manager's letter of authorization as a *mandate* for asserting direct authority over the departmental estimators—they were not *his* men. Instead, he had the determination to accomplish this essential secondary function with the least possible disturbance of either the primary engineering and manufacturing function or the existing supervisory order.

It is pertinent also that the manager in Phase 2 suffered the misfortune of having a proposal planner who failed to carry his full weight, particularly when his superior was out of the room. It appears that, whatever his shortcomings as a supervisor, he was in any case insufficiently aware of appropriate managerial functions. A more experienced manager not only would never allow himself to be burdened with clerical functions but would take more positive steps to lead—for example, such steps as his successor took when he actively encouraged and rewarded his men for useful suggestions.

Flow Regulating Functions

In this example of proposal-cost, the *scheduling* and *expediting* sub-functions were *crucial,* whereas *job progress reporting* had *minor* or even negligible significance. However, it should be pointed out that as regards the proposal planning group, the scheduling sub-function automatically included reports of job progress; thus, the two remained undifferentiated. Only when summary reports of job progress were submitted to those not concerned with scheduling details were the two sub-functions differentiated.

Reporting Job Progress

Summary reports of job progress activity were regularly distributed to department managers and the general manager, beginning in the latter part of Phase 2. (The routing of them in Phases 2 and 3 is indicated on Charts 5 and 6.) The only difference of any significance between the two periods is the fact that in Phase 2 the proposal planning manager personally prepared the summary progress reports himself, whereas in Phase 3 they were prepared by the proposal planner, who is one level lower. Thus in keeping with his general tactics, the manager in Phase 3 freed himself from as much detail as possible.

Scheduling and Expediting

Management folklore defines expediting as a necessary evil, a device to be used in an emergency when work is falling behind and when normal routine scheduling fails. It usually amounts to one individual contacting another, often by phone, and pleading, begging and cajoling him to complete his task immediately.

Expediting is usually done across departmental and company lines with the result that the individuals involved do not stand in a supervisory-subordinate relationship to each other. This means that the success of the expediting function is directly a function of the goodwill existing between them. But crises are not conducive to goodwill. In this instance, the scheduling and expediting functions were second in importance only to the supervisory function, with which they were closely linked.

The contrasts between the scheduling and expediting functions in Phases 2 and 3 were equally as striking as the contrasts in the supervisory function just described. Whereas scheduling and expediting were conducted in Phase 2 as part of the new rival supervisory function set up by the proposal planning manager, in Phase 3 the new manager assisted departmental supervisors so that they could more effectively take responsibility themselves for expediting their own departmental cost-proposals. The former has been labeled *direct expediting* and the latter *indirect expediting.*

Direct Expediting

In the direct expediting of Phase 2 (diagrammed on Chart 5), the departmental estimators became the principal expediting and the only scheduling target of the proposal planning manager. No departmental supervisor received a schedule. When expeditors failed to fulfill their commitment, the proposal manager directed his expediting activities to the section supervisors. If the latter failed him, the department managers then became the target. Whereas the proposal manager personally expedited any single estimator on an average of three times weekly, for any one department manager the average was monthly.

When he failed to achieve the desired result despite democratic measures, the practice of direct expediting inevitably left the assertive, ambitious and conscientious manager more than a little frustrated. Not unnaturally, his business-like approach to expediting gave way to a more emotional relationship

Chart 5 (Phase 2). Direct Expediting (note radial pattern emanating from proposal manager).

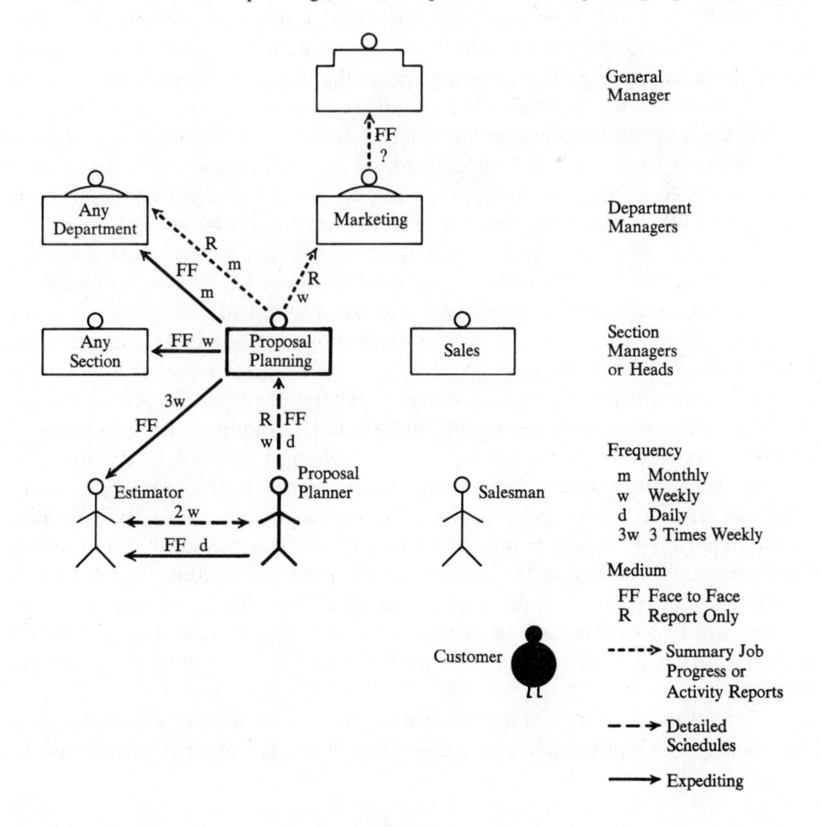

manifested in his tone of voice, more aggressive mannerisms and more threatening language. His tactics thus changed from rational expediting (Chart 5) to what we have already labeled as *complaining* (Chart 2).

In Phase 2, to reemphasize his attempts to proceed in a rational businesslike way, the proposal manager forewarned "his estimators" not only by personally visiting them but by having his proposal planner forward pink slips as well—one pink slip for each late proposal. Annoyed when the estimators universally blamed their departmental supervisors for demanding a higher priority for other jobs, the proposal manager had, he felt, no recourse but to assert his authority, as laid down in the general manager's letter of authorization. But as the estimators looked more to their own departmental supervisors than to the proposal planning manager, their natural disposition was to ignore the requests of the latter and more and more to resent his increasingly insistent demands. This, in turn, naturally further incited the proposal manager in Phase 2 to more aggressive behavior. In such a situation, it takes little imagination to sense how expediting could easily become complaining. To the unhappy manager, his situation was like a dream in which the more he tried to escape some danger, the less he was able to move: he confessed to one of the authors that he was at wit's end. At the end of a year of mounting frustration, he was finally replaced by the new and more experienced manager who ushered in Phase 3.

Indirect Expediting

In Phase 3, the new manager introduced indirect expediting (Chart 6). Instead of making the departmental estimator the initial expediting target, he directed his expediting two levels higher, to the department manager.

Considering some of the details of indirect expediting, we note the proposal planner drew up a schedule each Monday for the week on which the departments were listed across the top of the page, and the days of the week were listed down the side. The sheet then listed the proposal numbers due out of each department each day. Also on the page was a place for overdue proposals left over from the previous week. The schedule was then reproduced so that each estimator and department head received one copy on Monday. (In Phase 2 copies were not sent to departmental supervisors.) A total of about fifty copies were made up, including those to be used later for expediting as follows (Roman numerals refer to arrows on Chart 6).

Each morning, the proposal planner and the proposal planning manager scrutinized the schedule for overdue proposals (I). Finding one, the proposal planning manager then circled the overdue proposal number or numbers for a given department with a red pencil on one of the additional copies of the schedule reproduced for this purpose. He also scribbled a friendly little note to the department manager informing him of the late proposal(s) and asking his cooperation in cleaning the matter up. The proposal planning manager then carried the notice to the department head (II). Thus the department manager became informed of the situation with sufficient time to talk it over with the section supervisor (III) who in turn worked out a solution with his estimator (IV).

One of the authors of this paper was constantly amazed at how successfully the manager in Phase 3 elicited cooperation from the other departments. By

Chart 6 (Phase 3). Indirect Expediting by Proposal Manager (note circular pattern).

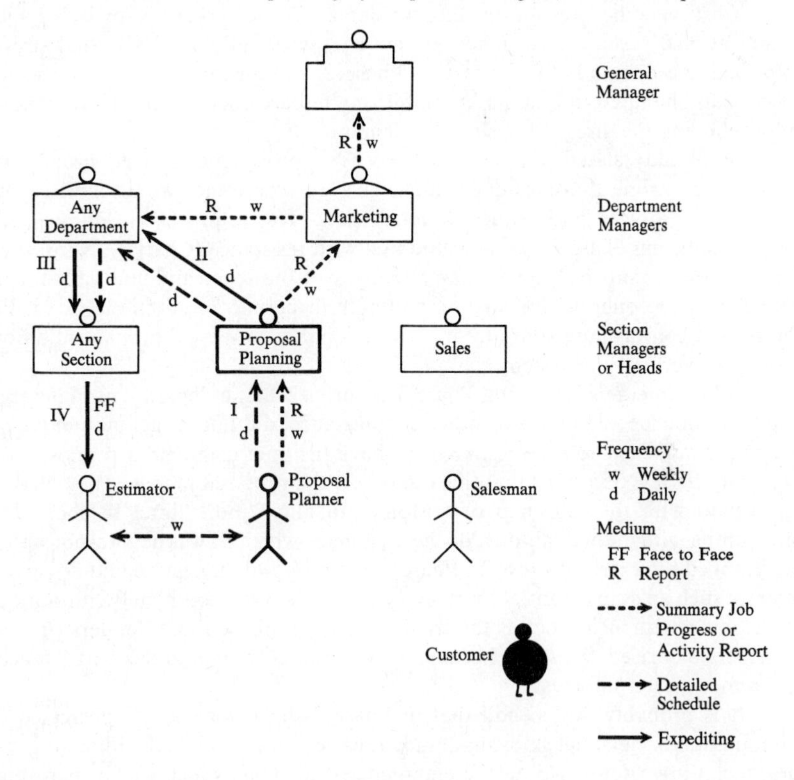

delivering the report in person, he maintained a continuing personal relationship with the department heads which was a great asset in times of stress. His expediting notes were always friendly and courteous, never sarcastic or demanding. Sometimes, to the amusement of the recipient, he would use long strings of big words such as "your continued conscientious consideration will be an invaluable asset in the elimination of these paltry encircled proposals from the schedule." When, on one occasion, a department head had no proposals overdue, he presented him with a blank routine expediting sheet and a short note, thanking him for his efforts and congratulating him for his department's promptness. The department head posted the sheet along with a note thanking his people for their efforts. Certainly positive reinforcement was useful here.

To summarize, direct expediting (Chart 5) resulted in the three-pronged radial pattern emanating from the proposal manager, in contrast to the circular or inverted U pattern of indirect expediting (Chart 6). The proposal manager initiated the latter sequence by informing the department manager who informed the section supervisor who in turn prodded his estimator. These contrasting radial and circular patterns represent marked contrasts in routine expediting systems. Other practices adopted by each proposal manager to meet special emergencies further served to differentiate Phase 3 from Phase 2.

Skill in Meeting Emergencies

To survive the stress of meeting the demands of emergency, any living and organizational system must generate new energy or relieve the external stress imposing the demand. In contrast to Phase 2, the emergency demands were successfully handled in Phase 3 by mobilizing reserve energies and by resourcefully relieving the stress imposing the demand.

As already stated, one emergency was re-processing rejected proposals. From time to time the sales department or even a customer would have cause to reject a proposal and request a re-estimate. The re-processing of rejected proposals during Phase 2 was slow and met with resistance (Chart 2). Naturally, the added stress superimposed on an already over-burdened and malfunctioning system was too onerous for anyone willingly to permit an additional load. In Phase 3, in contrast, the addition of an occasional re-processed proposal did not seriously overload the system.

Other emergencies during Phase 3 occurred when a department manager, due to an unexpected illness or other circumstance, did not in fact momentarily command sufficient reserve resources to have his men complete a proposal on time. On the few occasions that this did occur, the proposal manager personally intervened with the salesman or customer to allow more time. In short, by intervening with individuals outside the system for which he was held responsible, he removed the external stress. In Phase 2, the proposal manager could not even attempt such an adjustment, for not only were his energies completely committed to chronic emergencies, but as the friction between himself and the department managers increased, the strain became too emotional for him to recognize, much less remove external stress.

It is probably fair to add that in Phase 3 the manager also possessed a combination of personal skills that made it easier for him to deal with emergencies, including a sensitivity to the emergencies of others which was in part due to his ability to listen and establish effective rapport with them. Another quality was his particularly persistent and convincing persuasiveness, used appropriately, as already mentioned in the instance of inducing salesmen and customers to extend due dates.

Recommendations

As the behavior of persons often proves too difficult not only to analyze but to change, a common expedient is the shuffling or replacing of individuals. An inescapable by-product is change in behavior. To reduce the uncertainty in reshuffling, executives learn by rule of thumb to gamble on those who have already demonstrated success in handling difficulties.

What other simple rules of thumb emerge from the foregoing description? We make these seven recommendations as important and deserving of wider consideration:

Recommendation 1

Beware of assigning a man to set up a new managerial job who himself has had no managerial experience. Since setting up a new job usually requires far more behavioral skill and experience than the later routine running of the job, it is sound tactics to get a more experienced man on temporary loan to set it up and meanwhile to set about training a replacement. An experienced man is less liable to be deluded by the verbal willingness of another to change and to be more resourceful in heading off later difficulties unforeseen in pre-change discussions.

Recommendation 2

Consider applying to organizations the widely accepted principle of economy in design, i.e., using the fewest parts to perform a given function. The zealous setting up of a new department to take over a secondary task completely may risk the unnecessary disrupting of the primary task. For example, do not introduce a new operating department if the work load is no more than from 10 to 15 per cent of that of an already existing department and can be dispatched by the existing personnel. Consider appointing, instead, a coordinator with the behavioral skills necessary to work through or in close cooperation with the supervisors of the existing departments.

Recommendation 3

Any function is sure to suffer if the persons involved are continually disinterested or bored or, worse, annoyed with one another. Enjoying one another's company, showing a little respect or introducing a little fun may not be wasteful but in fact prove to be a vital investment that pays off when the chips are down.

Recommendation 4

Until better methods are developed for analyzing jobs, do not bother writing detailed job descriptions, as the behavioral subtleties are too little understood. Encourage individuals, instead, to probe discreetly to discover the limits of their capabilities and authority rather than to assume rigidly defined and enforceable limits. Following a job description literally may actually do more damage than going counter to it.

Recommendation 5

Carefully and confidentially discuss any early signs of malfunctioning with relevant persons, e.g., a supervisor bogged down in detail. Identifying and correcting behavioral problems in the early stages is usually less disruptive and costly than the usual shuffling of people after the problem has assumed crisis proportions.

Recommendation 6

For operating purposes, conceive of the productive output of an organization as being mainly dependent on the four functions listed at the beginning of this paper, and consider the behavioral as well as the technical aspects of each. Of these four, two—supervising and flow regulation—are often, if not usually, the most critical.

Recommendation 7

If behavioral interaction comprises the crucial process of a social system, then management must develop systematic ways of thinking about, auditing and measuring it. A method whereby managers record their own contacts was developed and usefully applied by one of the authors in three organizations over a five-year period.[9] Two other methods lie waiting to be applied.[10] Potentially, this makes available to management as important and revolutionary a set of tools for use in social systems as operations research is now providing for technical systems.

Conclusions

From the specific recommendations, we now turn to the general purpose of this paper which is to comprehend the process of organizational improvement. It is obvious that the process usually is both technical and social. It is our contention, moreover, that the social process can better be conceived of as essentially *behavioral.*

The desire of a person to do something does not always result in the doing thereof. The manager in Phase 2 could not easily translate decisions into appropriate actions. Human behavior is, after all, part of a highly complex neurophysiological process, and we are all aware of difficulties in carrying out the organizational practices we think we want.

From the perspective of evolution, cognitive control represents only a superimposition over unthinking, primordial responses that have been evolving through hundreds of millions of years. With predators and rivals omnipresent, survival has depended on instantaneous, automatic responses too critical for deliberation. Thus, much of our behavior represents unthinking response; this is true particularly in our relationships with others.

It seems that some persons possess a native skill in stimulating and responding to others, altering their behavior in such ways as to transform a malfunctioning social system into a highly productive one. It is the thesis of this paper that the elements of such skill can be identified, analyzed and in part learned. The following four points are suggested as providing a general interpretation of the behavioral process leading to organizational improvement.

1. The processing and flow of things is usually and correctly conceived of as a technical matter, but many overlook the obvious fact that *people* often participate in processing these things. After all, technical systems are owned, designed, run, regulated and repaired by people. The first clear general conclusion, therefore, is that technical and social systems not only are inextricably intermixed but *technical systems depend on social systems.* Technical adjustments to speed up the flow of work and minimize rejects depend, in the first instance, on the social system of workers, engineers and others directly involved in the work process. Thus, in the example here cited, the work did

---

[9] A more detailed form of "Technical Supplement—Correlation between Manager Contact Patterns and Group Productivity" (13 pages) has been deposited as Document number 8425 with the American Documentation Institute Auxiliary Publications Project, Photoduplication Service, Library of Congress, Washington 25, D.C. A copy may be secured by citing the Document number and by remitting $2.50 for photoprints, or $1.75 for 35 mm. microfilm. A more detailed form of "Executive Action Stimulating others to Greater Performance" has been deposited as Document number 8426 with the ADI, and a copy may be secured by citing the Document number and by remitting $3.75 for photoprints, or $2.00 for 35mm. microfilm. Advance payment is required. Make checks or money orders payable to: Chief, Photoduplication Service, Library of Congress.

[10] E. D. Chapple and L. R. Sayles, op. cit.

E. D. Chapple, "Quantitative Analysis of Complex Organization Systems," *Human Organization,* Vol. 21, No. 2, 1962, pages 67–80.

not flow on schedule until adequate supervisory and expediting relationships had become established.

2. The processing and flow of things is also usually and correctly conceived of as dependent on information, and that information is transmitted by words. But it is customary to overlook the entire process of communicating information. The spoken word is always accompanied, for example, by associated postures and gesturing as well as volume, rhythm and tone of voice. Communication is, thus, also as much, if not more, a highly complex audio-behavioral-interactional process, as it is a mere matter of transmitting verbal content. From the foregoing example, in Phases 2 and 3 the managers provided a striking contrast in their manner of communicating. The second clear general conclusion, therefore, is that often the functioning of a technical system *depends more on subtle aspects of communication than on the verbal content of information.*

   The flow of papers provides a case in point. The processing and flow of papers is sometimes conceived of as a technical, informational matter. Indeed it is, to the extent that filling out forms with, for example, x's and numbers may sometimes be a merely routine matter, so little affected by feelings and emotions as to approximate technical processing. But written words, phrases and numbers are part of the highly complex process of human communication. In addition, it must be recognized that the mere act of passing a paper or thing to another may itself transmit a vital message. Along an assembly line, for example, a standard practice to annoy one's fellow workers is to withhold units for a time and then dump them all at once on a moving belt so that they then descend as an avalanche on those further down the line. Another occurs commonly when, unannounced, management speeds up the assembly line. To such a communication, organized workers commonly respond by transmitting such unambiguous messages as a flood of defective units off the end of the line. Reactions in such instances do, in fact, speak louder than words.[11]

3. The processing and flow of things, in addition, is usually and correctly conceived of as depending ultimately on critical decisions. Many, therefore, naturally concern themselves with the process of decision-making, some focussing on the rational processes involved—let us say rational technically in the sense of improving, in some definable way, the total functioning of the technical system. But too often human emotions intervene, as occurred in Phase 2 between the proposal planning manager and the estimators and supervisory personnel in other departments. Then, the curt, aggressive, if not belligerent behavior of the manager induced retaliatory reactions in these others, damaging the technical system and inhibiting rationality. Once a state of feuding begins within an organization, company-wide rational cooperation ceases.

   Human emotions, those primordial, neuro-glandular, gut responses of the autonomic nervous system, intervene daily with most of us to divert for a

---

[11] Edward Hall, *Silent Language,* New York: Doubleday, 1959, 240 pages.
Edward Hall, "The Silent Language in Overseas Business," *Harvard Business Review,* Vol. 38, No. 3, May–June, 1960, pages 87–96.
Edward Hall and W. F. Whyte, "Intercultural Communications: A Guide to Men of Action," *Human Organization,* Vol. 19, No. 1, 1960, pp. 5-12.

time our rational preoccupation with technical matters to more self-gratifying, if not retaliatory, preoccupations. Obviously, decisions may range from rational to emotional, from cognitive to neuroglandular. Hence, the third general conclusion, the hypothesis that *behavioral-interactional stimuli activate emotional reactions that in turn inhibit rational considerations* (i.e., rational technically, as defined above). Physiologically, this process presumably takes place through the mediation of the autonomic nervous systems.

4. Thus, the processing and flow of things is also commonly and correctly conceived of as dependent on the emotions, feelings or attitudes of the persons at work. But emotions, feelings and attitudes are sometimes seen just as internal psychological states whose genesis remains vague. Rarely are they consciously and clearly seen as part of the process of persons stimulating and responding to one another.

   Our own internal, physiological responses are so profoundly meaningful to us, so personal, so deeply felt, that we become obsessed with the light of their flame, ignoring the source. As flames respond to fuel, so among interacting persons, attitudes, feelings and emotions respond to behavioral stimuli. Interaction involves, on the one hand, visible behavior and audible sound, but, on the other, internal, unseen, physiological responses. It is through the former that we can more easily control the latter.

   For management it is obviously important to control behavioral stimuli that repress rational behavior by provoking emotional reactions. It is unrealistic to expect individuals to further the goals of an enterprise if they find themselves part of a behavioral system that overstimulates emotion. This leads to a final general conclusion, an applied version of the third, and in part presented previously as Recommendation 7, namely: one of management's most important functions is to *develop and control an audio-behavioral-interactional system out of which rational behavior can emerge.*

   An organization is not just a collection of individuals. It is, rather, an association of interacting individuals, stimulating and responding to one another. The central point of the conclusions here is that behavioral-interactional realities represent the core of any social system, the vital process of social living. Such commonplace abstractions as authority, goals and values, without the addition of significant behavioral content, provide but an illusion of the core.

   If behavioral interaction represents the core of a social system, it is appropriate that biological as well as social considerations be made central in any analysis of it. As physics and chemistry provide the basic sciences for technical systems, so the emerging social sciences as well as biology provide the foundation for social systems.

Questions for Discussion

1. Why is balance between stability and change essential in any organization?

2. How can a manager maintain stability and equilibrium?

3. What is the difference between a "structural" or "systemic" approach to change, as compared with a "conversionalist" approach?

4. An old-fashioned, hard-nosed manager might maintain that our discussion of change is ridiculous. The boss is the boss. His job is to decide what change is desirable and to tell subordinates to do it. It they don't respond, he should replace them with people who will. Discuss the pros and cons of such an attitude.

5. A new college president desires to improve the caliber of teaching at his institution. He can exhort his faculty members to pay more attention to preparing for class and making themselves available to students. Perhaps he could hire some new professors. But what structural or organizational changes can he initiate to improve teaching?

6. Some companies have made organizational changes to merge purchasing, warehousing, and production under a materials-planning and production group. Similarly, others have merged traffic, distribution, and marketing functions. Why?

7. Since 1945, and particularly since 1961, there has apparently been a trend in the U.S. Department of Defense toward centralization of decision making. What might be the reasons for such organizational change? And what might be some of the problems incurred?

8. The management of a large chemical company wants to change its industrial engineering division. Historically, the division had performed a service function, with young engineers remaining an average of three years before transferring to other departments. In effect, industrial engineering was something of a training area for production management. Management wants to convert the industrial engineering division into an innovative organization where people will remain for longer periods—even for entire careers. How might management make this change?

Index

4 5 6 7 8 9 10 11 12 13 14 15 16 17 18 19 20 21 22 23 24 25 PI 74 73 72 71 70